Handbook of Reading Disability Research

Bringing together a wide range of research on reading disabilities, this comprehensive *Handbook* extends current discussion and thinking beyond a narrowly defined psychometric perspective. Examining reading disabilities from sociopolitical and historical perspectives, as cultural and psychological constructs, from the point of view of an interventionist, and emphasizing that learning to read proficiently is a long-term developmental process involving many interventions of various kinds, all keyed to individual developmental needs, it addresses traditional questions (What is the nature or causes of reading disabilities? How are reading disabilities assessed? How should reading disabilities be remediated? To what extent is remediation possible?), but from multiple or alternative perspectives.

Taking incursions into the broader research literature represented by linguistic and anthropological paradigms, as well as psychological and educational research, the volume is on the front line in exploring the relation of reading disability to learning and language, to poverty and prejudice, and to instruction and schooling.

The editors and authors are distinguished scholars with extensive research experience and publication records and numerous honors and awards from professional organizations representing the range of disciplines in the field of reading disabilities. Throughout, their contributions are contextualized within the framework of educators struggling to develop concrete instructional practices that meet the learning needs of the lowest achieving readers.

Anne McGill-Franzen is Professor and Director of the Reading Center at the University of Tennessee. She was recipient of the International Reading Association Nila Banton Smith Award, co-recipient (with Dr. Richard L. Allington) of the IRA Albert J. Harris Award for research published in the field of reading disabilities, and the 2004 recipient of the IRA Dina Feitelson Award honoring an empirical study of language and literacy acquisition with clear implications for instruction. Dr. McGill-Franzen was a member of the Board of Directors of the National Reading Conference, serves on the editorial advisory boards of several major journals, and was Technical Consultant for the UNESCO funded project on diagnostic teaching of reading in Kenya, Ghana, and Tanzania.

Richard L. Allington is Professor of Education at the University of Tennessee. He has served or serves on the editorial advisory boards of *Reading Research Quarterly*, *Review of Educational Research*, *Journal of Educational Psychology*, *Reading Teacher*, *Elementary School Journal*, *Journal of Literacy Research*, and *Remedial and Special Education*. A past president of the National Reading Conference and the International Reading Association, he was co-recipient (with Dr. Anne McGill-Franzen) of the IRA Albert J. Harris Award for contributions to improving professional understanding of reading/learning disabilities, and was elected to the Reading Hall of Fame.

Handbook of Reading Disability Research

Edited By

Anne McGill-Franzen
University of Tennessee

Richard L. Allington
University of Tennessee

Part Editors

George Hruby

John Elkins

Peter Johnston

S. Jay Samuels

Susan Hupp

Victoria Risko

Patricia Anders

William Rupley

Victor L. Willson

Routledge
Taylor & Francis Group

NEW YORK AND LONDON

Acknowledgments

When undertaking a project like this handbook, there are always a lot of folks to thank. We'd like to begin by acknowledging all the work Dr. Maria Cahill did on this project as a graduate research assistant and prior to beginning her career at Texas Womens University. Maria was gentle with us, even when it was our fault we could not find something we needed (and knew we had seen).

We would also like to thank our Part Editors for all the work they did reviewing these manuscripts, and often providing chapter authors with just the sort of useful information they needed to revise and complete a better chapter. While we read all the chapters and offered editorial comments on many, we didn't have the necessary expertise across all of the domains the chapters cover to offer advice to everyone.

We would also like to thank the chapter authors, even those whose manuscripts arrived a bit beyond our original deadline. This book has been several years in the making and yet every author stayed with us, even those who sent us manuscripts before the original deadline! We appreciate the effort involved in writing each chapter and the generous sharing of knowledge by so many of our colleagues in service of a better understanding of reading disabilities. So, again, thank you authors.

We gratefully acknowledge the contributions of Patti Fagg, our departmental secretary, who made more copies for us than any one person should ever have to, and Naomi Silverman, our editor at Routledge, who has graciously accepted the fact that we have missed deadline after deadline. We hope she will agree that it was worth the wait.

Finally, our appreciation to Lane Akers whose good humor and charm convinced us we should edit this volume.

Thank you one and all.

1

The Political Contexts of Reading Disabilities

Patrick Shannon and Jacqueline Edmondson
Pennsylvania State University

The study of politics is the investigation of power within particular contexts. Power circulates through discourses among various groups who make use of and are used by values and language to participate in on-going events (e.g., Foucault, 1980; Gonick, 2003; Peet, 2007). These discourses and uses of discourse set parameters, influence actions, and position participants within events. Those who wield power in some contexts are powerless in others as negotiations push and pull participants in ways of their own making, but not entirely within their control. The discourses surrounding DIBELS (Dynamic Indicators of Basic Early Literacy Skills) can serve as a short introduction to the political contexts of reading disabilities, demonstrating how power works.

Each summer our campus supports a reading program for children and youth who are experiencing difficulty in learning to read at school. The program serves as a practicum for masters degree students seeking reading specialist certification. Working from a 3-to-1 students/teacher ratio, we enroll between 20 and 30 children each year. Traditionally, the enrollment process begins in late spring after teachers and parents have conferred about a student's progress throughout the academic year and their projections for success in the next grade. In the past, parent phone calls would trickle in during late May and early June with discussions about "summer regress" and "a boost going into next year." Over the last 3 years, however, our program is full with a waiting list by the end of January. Parents call with panic in their voices, reporting that their kindergarten and first grade children are "reading disabled" because they have not "passed the DIBELS tests."

The Dynamic Indicators of Basic Early Literacy Skills are a set of six fluency tests (letter names, initial sounds, phoneme segmentation, nonsense words, oral reading, and retelling) designed to enable regular monitoring of "pre-reading and early reading skills" (www.dibels.org). The purpose, content, and format of DIBELS are built upon the evidence-based conclusions of the National Reading Panel

(2000) and Snow, Burns, and Griffin (1998) and are pronounced valid and reliable based on their correlations with other established tests. In these ways, DIBELS performs the discourse of experimental science—its language, logic, appearance, and values—constructing reading abilities and disabilities in its wake.

At the same time, DIBELS is a product that competes in a market created when the need for regular monitoring of these skills became generally accepted within the reading field. Although the basic materials of DIBELS can be downloaded from a website, and students' scores can be processed and packaged into reports for $1 per student, the tests are also available commercially in several forms along with test preparation materials and technical and human support as well. These products and services are advertised through professional journals and the Internet. In these ways, DIBELS incorporates the discourse of business, working for a market share and to maximize profits, complicating what it means to determine reading ability and disability.

The market for the regular measurement of early reading was officially sanctioned when the Bush administration implemented its Reading First Initiative of the No Child Left Behind education law of 2002. In order to insure that all students would test "proficient in reading" by 2014, the Department of Education connected federal funding to state and school district compliance with testing systems that could track schools' progress toward that goal. With the discourses of science and business firmly underlying modern policy making, federal officials searched for a valid and reliable technology to standardize the practices and outcomes of reading education across the country. According to a Department of Education Inspector General's Report (September, 2006), Reading First officials pressured states and school districts to adopt DIBELS as the appropriate technology in order to comply with federal policy and qualify for funding. In these ways, DIBELS projects a government discourse, framing the use of its tests as lawful to be the solution to individual variation, leading from accurate measurement to classroom instruction to individual remediation. The discourse established a normal range in the process of reading, the ways in which it is learned, and the speeds with which it is acquired. Students within this range become able readers, and those outside this normal range are disabled. Presuming all student capacities being equal, only teacher error kept these disabled readers from the normal able process, approach, and speed. At the same time, the discourse of science positioned psychologists as experts within this field of reading and reading education, applying scientific methods to new issues of concern. Philosophers, theologians, historians, literary scholars, or even other social scientists became less important, less powerful in the discussions and actions surrounding reading ability and disability.

The rise of the scientific discourse in reading education has been neither straight nor smooth, but to the extent that evidence-based or scientifically based policy and practice are currently considered the norm, it has been successful. Across the 20th century, its increasing influence can be mapped in professional organizations (e.g., National Society for the Study of Education, American Educational Research Association, National Council of Teachers of English, International Reading Association, National Reading Conference, and Society for the Scientific Study of Reading), their journals and meetings, and state-of-the-field reports (NSSE Yearbooks Horn, 1919; Gray, 1925; Gray, 1937: Gates, 1949; Austin & Morrison, 1963; Barton & Wilder, 1964; Durkin, 1978; Anderson, Heibert, Scott, & Wilkinson, 1985; Adams, 1990; Snow et al., 1998; National Reading Panel, 2000). Throughout, there has been a tone of certainty—now coming full circle back to physiology.

> Reading reflects language, and reading disability reflects a deficit within the language system....Using functional brain imaging, scientists around the world have discovered not only the brain basis of reading but also a glitch in the neural circuitry for reading in children and adults who struggle to read. (Shaywitz & Shaywitz, 2004, pp. 7, 8)

Discourses of Business

The rhetoric of *A Nation at Risk* (1983), and that of the reports of crisis that followed, described reading ability and disability in economic terms (Shannon, 1998). Such crisis-based analyses suggest that those who are able to meet the literacy demands of a global economy are those who will prosper and help the United States prosper. Those who are unable to meet those demands are those who will face difficult times, becoming social and economic liabilities. The ability to read in socially acceptable ways, then, becomes capital—something that can be accounted for and spent personally and socially. In this way, the financial well-being of the individual and society are embedded within the framing, infrastructure, and practices that surround reading ability and disability. Literacy skills required within particular economies set the parameters of who is consid-

ered able or disabled. As demands or perceived demands shift, the numbers in each group change accordingly. The technology and organization required to ensure ability and prevent disability move as well, creating markets and new areas of expertise in their wake. Teachers' and students' daily classroom practices are altered by these expectations, organizations, and technologies—even their relationships with one another and society transform.

Of course, the economic rationale for reading instruction is not new. Northern colonies in the New World were taught reading in order to save individual souls, but used the metaphor of home economies to describe the responsibilities and practices of early public reading instruction (Smith, 2002). Thomas Jefferson and Horace Mann, nearly 50 years apart, argued that public schooling would create active citizens and able workers in order to develop democracy and build an economy one citizen at a time. In the 1800s, even the content of the school readers encouraged Americans to be industrious, entrepreneurial, and efficient (Mosier, 1965). In this way, students became consumers of values as well as literacy skills through reading instruction. As the economy turned more and more from agriculture to industry, the organizational schemes of business and industry were considered to be the primary solutions to consequent social challenges—industrialization, urbanization, and immigration.

The first sustained effort to bring business and industrial principles to public education is found in the work of the Committee on the Economy of Time in Education. Members of that committee sought to rationalize school curricula and instruction according to Frederick Winslow Taylor's scientific management (Taylor, 1912), replacing personal judgment and rule of thumb with scientifically developed technology and standard practices. Their logic was that importing these business principles would increase both efficiency and the quality of the teachers' work and product, running more smoothly, cheaply, and productively. Toward that end, the practices of the most productive teachers were analyzed in terms of tested results, useless movements discarded, and divided into elemental parts that could be described completely on instructional cards. These cards would enable any literate person to follow the one best system of teaching reading. Within these moves, students became more than metaphorical products of teachers' labor. Their learning was subject to quality control of tests, and teachers' efforts were standardized in order to increase their continuous fidelity to that system.

The four reports of the committee demonstrate the incomplete application of this business model to schooling in general and reading in particular. The first report presented a national survey in order to establish standards of expectations for teachers in each grade. Issues such as subjects within the curriculum, time devoted to reading instruction, rates of reading, vocabulary loads in textbooks, and the tests available to determine student progress were listed to establish norms of expectations (Wilson, 1915). In the second and third reports, William S. Gray delved deeper into daily practices of reading instruction, advocating that silent reading instruction was preferable to oral because of its utility and efficiency in everyday tasks and provided a first glimpse of his tests—Standardized Oral Reading Paragraphs and Silent Reading (Wilson, 1917). The fourth report was to be the equivalent of the instructional card for scientific management.

> The effort throughout has been to put its recommendations in simple, direct language, that its report may constitute a handbook and guide for the use of teachers and supervisors who are interested in planning classroom procedures with due regard for both economy and efficiency in teaching and learning. (Wilson, 1918, pp. 7–8)

Gray deduced 48 principles for reading instruction from 35 studies, covering norms for student progress across grade levels, suggestions for oral and silent reading, and specifications for printed materials. He emphasized that the experiments demonstrated that no single textbook method of teaching reading was necessarily superior to all others in terms of test results. Rather he argued that instructional efficiency and productivity varied according to how well teachers used the materials available to them. Just as Taylor had found in the steel mills, master teachers of reading were working in classrooms beside teachers who demonstrated little talent. Even before the publication of the fourth report, the NSSE formed the Committee on Materials in Education, combining the Committee on the Measurement of Educational Products and the Committee on the Economy of Time in Education. "At this point, the Society assigned to the present Committee the task of embodying, in concrete materials to be used in classrooms, the principles arrived at by the earlier committees" (Bagley, 1920, p. 11). In short, the new committee was to develop a technology that would raise the methods of struggling teachers to the same productivity of the master teachers. In this way, teachers became consumers and subjects of tests and materials in order to promote reading ability and prevent reading disability.

The need for more effective technologies of quality monitoring of student learning and teacher instruction created new markets within the reading community (Shannon, 2001). Tests within reading lessons, tests of reading progress over short and long periods, and diagnostic tests became ubiquitous in classrooms and schools across the next decades. Experts took pains to explain the benefits and limits of informal sampling of students' reading that teachers could implement and analyze themselves, and standardized reading tests which required outside monitoring to be used effectively in order to identify specific areas of weaknesses among students. As early as 1906, existing textbook companies (e.g., World Book, Lippincott, and Public School) and companies created to publish tests (e.g., Courtis and Thorndike published their own tests before selling them to companies) entered this market. As with the textbook market, many of the tests were modest variations of a few popular products. The authors' intended purpose of these tests was (as it is to this day) to sort students into categories of able and disabled readers (typically with scales within each category) in order to direct teachers' attention and instruction to the areas designated as the causes of individual reading disability. The publishers' purpose, however, was (as it is to this day) to insure that every reader was tested in every way necessary in order to maximize the companies' profits. Increased economic demands for literate workers fueled, as it continues to fuel, the need for more and better tests, keeping the test publishing market lucrative. Currently it is a multi-billion of dollars per year industry (PBS, 2008).

The prevention and remediation of reading disability also created markets for publishers. The need for standardized instruction across classrooms led to the production of teachers' manuals, which set the path for able development (Shannon, 1989). Although most teachers used textbooks during reading instruction prior to 1920, those books printed only brief directions for teachers within the students' books. During the 1920s, psychologists' calls for explicit directions to standardize teaching practices created a market for textbooks enhanced by lengthy teachers' guidebooks. Reminiscent of Taylor's instructional cards, the tone and content of directions set the scope, sequence, and expected outcomes of each lesson.

Across the decades to the present, advances in reading psychology led publishers to identify new markets for better and better materials—manuals, anthologies, practice books and sheets, and informal and standardized tests—to monitor students' flow through its system. Most reading experts proclaimed the scientific basis of each new set of materials and accessories, increasing the power of businesses in schools. Many of the more prominent experts worked for basal (later core) reading program publishers. Although periodically some experts have criticized the conservative influence of publishers on classroom practices and conceptions of ability and disability (e.g., Durkin, 1978; Goodman, Shannon, Freeman, & Murphy, 1988), most continued and continue to support the use of basal or core reading programs during reading instruction, citing the quality control over teaching (e.g., Anderson, Osborn, & Tierney, 1984).

Adjusting quickly to changes in the professional rhetoric surrounding reading education to supply new supplementary products, basal publishers, however, have not changed the basic structure of these materials since the 1920s. New information is added, and the nomenclature changes in order to gain new customers, but the structures and formats remain remarkably the same to maintain the old market (Chall & Squires, 1991). Early in the century, publishers maintained their influence through direct involvement in NSSE committee work in order to provide recommendations on reading education and instruction. In the 1950s, publishers contributed to the start-up capital of the International Reading Association, and continue to fund the professional meetings of that and other organizations concerned with reading and reading instruction (Jerrolds, 1977; Sears, 2007). For the educational materials publishing industry, all these efforts and expenses are simply marketing.

A recent successful marketing venture concerns the consequences of testing of reading ability. As described by Garan (2005), readers who fail to reach the able range require more and perhaps different attention because standardized technological solutions have been unsuccessful. Prior to taking the tests, readers designated as "at risk" of failure can be served by extra preparation. Test publishers, basal publishers, and independent entrepreneurs have moved rapidly into this market, supplying goods and services to improve the odds of passing. Those who still fail provide a market for more materials and services as well. Since public schools are responsible for students becoming able readers, the tutoring market provides a new conduit for public education funds to flow toward private companies and businesses. The continued flow has apparently been lucrative (PBS, 2008). Although there were scores of basal programs at the beginning of the 20th century, there are only five major programs and three publishers that control the reading materials market today. The news media designated some publishing companies as "Bush stocks" when the No Child Left Behind legislations passed (Metcalf, 2004).

Government Discourses

In North America, government discourse entered reading education in 1642 when the Massachusetts legislature passed a law requiring towns to make certain that "all youth under family Government be taught to read perfectly the English Tongue, have knowledge in capital laws, and be taught some orthodox catechisms, and that they be brought up to some honest employment, profitable to themselves and to the Commonwealth" (quoted in Cubberley, 1933, p. 18). In this statement, the colonial legislature presaged six values to be found in later U.S. government discourse: (a) the United States is a republic and not a democracy (legislators made the decision), (b) rule of law (all youth—knowledge of capital laws), (c) equal protection of those considered citizens (under family government), (d) building infrastructure to develop the economy (taught to read—some honest employment), (d) accountability (perfectly), and (e) ideology of party in power rules (English—orthodox catechisms). In 1789, with the ratification of the U.S. Constitution and its first 10 amendments, education was secured as a state's right, continuing what had been the uneven commitment to public education and reading education across the various colonies. By necessity, each state legislature has had to address a series of questions:

What type of education should the state sponsor?
Who should pay for that education?
Who should determine what is taught and how it is taught in a state sponsored school?
Who should have the opportunity to study? For how long? Toward what end?
Who should decide and how should they decide when students are sufficiently educated?
Who should decide who is qualified to teach?

Variability in state legislature's answers to these questions resulted in beautifully idiosyncratic consequences yet also standardized outcomes (On the one hand, think of the wonderful classroom libraries that developed in California schools when the state legislature argued that students should read more in the 1980s, but would not fund school libraries. On the other hand, consider the effects of large state textbook adoptions on the production of basal or core reading programs from which smaller states must also choose). Currently, definitions of reading ability and disability by state vary greatly because, under No Child Left Behind (P.L. 107-100), states have the right to determine these categories according to state standards and examinations. Students can change their classification simply by crossing a state boundary. Arguments for district, municipal, or other local control to address these questions would only increase such differences. However, as Coffey (1933) made clear, it is state governments that have the right to regulate local school districts. Local control is a courtesy, not a right.

> The maintenance of public schools is a matter of state, rather than of local concern. School districts exist because the state finds this is a convenient way to carry out its educational program. It may require these districts to do any act, which it might perform directly. It may place restrictions upon them as it seems essential. It has full authority, unless its constitution provides otherwise, to prescribe the subject matter that may or shall be taught in its schools. (Coffey, 1931, p. 386)

Although the states have the authority to enforce their educational decisions through sovereign power, economic sanctions have been the primary incentive since the end of World War II. When local communities' tax bases decline, school districts become more dependent on state funding, and thereby are compelled to comply with state regulations and demands.

The federal government may lack a constitutional mandate to manage public education, but its direct involvement began after the Soviet launch of *Sputnik* in 1957 when it appeared that the United States was losing the technological advantage that it had demonstrated during the World War II (Kaestle & Smith, 1983). The National Defense Education Act (P.L. 85-864) provided substantial funding for research on, and development of, school curricula deemed vital to the national defense and security—science, second language and mathematics curriculum—and asserted for the first time that general curriculum could be improved as well. With this legislation, two new values were added to the government discourses. First, public schools were recognized as a national security concern, and therefore, the federal government had a direct interest in schooling and curriculum. Second, funding would be the primary federal incentive to gain state compliance with its education initiatives. The federal government would fund research as well as direct payments to schools to enable programs. Subsequent federal legislation (e.g., Elementary and Secondary Education Act of 1965, P.L. 89-10, and the Education of All Handicapped Children Act of 1975, P. L/ 94-142) reinforced these and the original government values and practices.

The role of ideology within government discourses becomes most apparent in the shift of the hierarchy of values over the last half century. All administrations demonstrated governmental values by their choice of rhetoric, legislation, and research funding, but each positioned those values according to its underlying political ideology (Shannon, 2007). Contrast the emphasis in the rhetoric surrounding Project Head Start (Economic Opportunity Act of 1964, P.L. 88-452), a program designed to promote equal opportunity for disadvantaged children through federal funding, during the Johnson as compared to the Reagan administrations. Consider the following two quotes from each in turn.

> Archimedes told us many centuries ago: give me a lever long enough and a fulcrum strong enough and I can move the world. Today, at last, we have a prospect of a lever long enough and support strong enough to do something about our children of poverty. The lever is education, and the fulcrum is federal assistance. (Commissioner of Education Francis Keppel, 1965, p. 6)

> First the President wanted to reduce substantially federal spending for education. Second, he wanted to strengthen local and state control of education and to reduce dramatically the federal responsibility in this area....Fourth, the President wanted to encourage the establishment of laws and rules that would offer greatly expanded parental choice and that would increase the competition for students among schools in newly created public and private structures patterned after the free market system that motivates and disciplines U. S. business and industry. (Secretary of Education Terrell Bell, 1986, p. 482)

Although both the liberal and conservative official expressed his commitment to schooling, the difference in values is explicit expressed in their statements. Ideology is also evident in the rhetoric employed by the neoliberal Clinton administration (Edmondson, 2000) and the neoconservative G. W. Bush administration (Goodman, Shannon, Goodman, & Rappaport, 2004). Regardless of the ideology, Head Start was never sufficiently funded under any administration to enroll all eligible children.

Furthermore, consider two federal attempts to protect minorities' rights in public schools. In 1965, the Elementary and Secondary Education Act (P.L. 89-10, which has passed through several iterations to its current form No Child Left Behind) was originally the educational weapon in the War on Poverty, supporting other federal programs for food, health care, and housing. Gaps in achievement between the poor and the not poor were attributed to social inequalities that were to be addressed with a comprehensive and national plan. In schools, this required compensatory supplemental instruction for demonstrably poor, including racial minority, students. Lack of progress in reading was defined as a social disadvantage. In 1975, the Education for All Handicapped Children Act (later renamed Individuals with Disabilities Education Act, P.L. 108-446) sought services for a non-visible or demographically recognizable minority—children with physical and cognitive handicaps. This legislation marked the official entry of the language of disability into federal law (McGill-Franzen, 1987). To qualify for special educational services, students had to be tested and score outside the normal range, and gaps in scores were attributed to individual traits and not social conditions. Clearly, the testing since the beginning of the standards movement in the 1990s to the testing of NCLB follow this latter definition of reading disability as a personal deficit with a simple instructional solution. To overcome those gaps, the federal government began to fund research on best methods to assure success in reading before and during school.

Such federal funding of research is a third way in which ideology influences government discourses on reading education. The influence has not been singular or linear. Contrast the eclectic approaches of the First Grade Studies (Bond & Dykstra, 1967) and Project Head Start (1960s), the information processing of The Center for the Study of Reading (1970s), the disciplined agenda of the National Institute for Child Health and Development (1970s–90s), and the "contextual" work of the Center for the Improvement of Early Reading Achievement (1997–2002). Federal and state administrations spent tens of millions of dollars to discover which methods would teach all American children to read. In order to translate those results for school personnel, the federal government funded a series of state-of-the-field reports: *Becoming a Nation of Readers* (Anderson et al., 1985), *Beginning to Read* (Adams, 1990), *Preventing Reading Difficulties in Young Children* (Snow et al., 1998), and the National Reading Report (2000). In each, the definitions of reading ability and disability are contingent on who was at the table as the content of the reports were decided.

> The areas of focus and the methods of analyses were decided by who was selected to the panel. The five areas of the [National Reading Panel] Report do not capture all there is to reading. Rather they are the specialties of the panel members. Tom Trabasso in comprehension, Linnea Ehri in phonics, me for fluency. I fought for my topic as did the others. The outcome could not have been otherwise. That does not compromise the report. It simply demonstrates its limits. (Samuels, 2006)

Connections, Contradictions, Constants

As demonstrated by the foregoing review, the political contexts of reading disabilities are mediated by the discourses of science, business, and government. The power of these discourses circulate through and among participants near and far in ways that establish opportunities and limits, impact actions, and position participants within their immediate circumstances. It is circumstance, not position, that determines participants' power (Fraatz, 1987). In order to understand the political contexts of reading disabilities, researchers must locate these discourses and map the landscape of the situation accordingly. Note that the discourses do not always work in conjunction with one another, because the values of one discourse can trump those in another.

McGill-Franzen, A. (1987). Failure to learn to read: Formulating a policy problem. *Reading Research Quarterly, 22,* 475–490.

Metcalf, S. (2004). Reading between the lines. In A. Kohn & P. Shannon (Eds.), *Education inc.: Turning learning into a business* (pp. 49–75). Portsmouth, NH: Heinemann.

Mosier, R. (1965). *Making the American mind: Social and moral ideas in the McGuffey readers.* New York: Russell and Russell.

National Commission on Excellence in Education. (1983). *A nation at risk: The imperatives of educational reform.* Washington, DC: Government Printing Office.

National Reading Panel. (2000). *Report of the National Reading Panel: Teaching children to read: An evidence-based assessment of the scientific research literature and its implications for reading instruction.* Washington, DC: National Institute of Child Health and Human Development.

PBS. (2008, February 18). http://www.pbs.org/nbr/site/onair/transcripts/080218i

Pearson, K. (1896). *The grammar of science.* New York: MacMillan.

Peet, R. (2007). *Geographies of power.* New York: Zed Books.

Samuels, S. J. (2006, May 3). Statement made during the question and answer session of the Reading Hall of Fame presentation at International Reading Association Convention, Chicago, IL.

Sears, L. (2007). *Reaction, initiation, and promise: A historical study of the International Reading Association.* Unpublished doctoral dissertation, University of Pittsburgh.

Shannon, P. (1989). *Broken promises: Reading instruction in 20th century America.* Westport, CT: Bergin & Garvey.

Shannon, P. (1998). *Reading poverty.* Portsmouth, NH: Heinemann.

Shannon, P. (2001). *iSHOP/you shop: Raising questions about reading commodities.* Portsmouth, NH: Heinemann.

Shannon, P. (2007). *Reading against democracy: The broken promises of reading instruction.* Portsmouth, NH: Heinemann.

Shaywitz, S., & Shaywitz, B. (2004). Reading disability and the brain. *Educational Leadership, 6*(6), 6–11.

Shore, M. (2001). Psychology and memory in the midst of change: The social concerns of late 19th century North American psychologists. In C. Green, M. Shore, & T. Tao (Eds.), *The transformation of psychology: Influences of 19th century philosophy, technology, and natural science* (pp. 63–86). Washington, DC: American Psychological Association.

Smith, N. B. (2002). *American reading instruction* (5th ed.). Newark, DE: International Reading Association.

Snow, C., Burns, S., & Griffin, P. (1998). *Preventing reading difficulties in young children.* Washington, DC: National Academy Press.

Taylor, B., Anderson, R., Au, K., & Raphael, T. (2000). Discretion in the translation of research to policy: A case from beginning reading. *Educational Researcher, 29,* 16–26.

Taylor, F. W. (1912). The present state of the art of industrial management. The *American Magazine, 71,* 1–9.

Thorndike, E. L. (1906). *The principles of teaching based on psychology.* New York: A. G. Seler.

Thorndike, E. L. (1914). The measurement of ability in reading. *Teachers College Record, 15,* 1–17.

Tolman, C. (2001). Philosophical doubts about psychology as a natural science. In C. Green, M. Shore, & T. Tao (Eds.), *The transformation of psychology: Influences of 19th century philosophy, technology, and natural science* (pp. 175–194). Washington, DC: American Psychological Association.

Toulmin, S., & Leary, D. (1992). The cult of empiricism in psychology and beyond. In S. Koch & D. Leary (Eds.), *A century of psychology as science* (pp. 594–617). Washington, DC: American Psychological Association.

U.S. Department of Education's Inspector General. (2006, September 22). *The Reading First Program's Grant Application Process: Final Inspection Report.* Washington, DC: Government Printing Office.

Venezky, R. (1984). The history of reading research. In P. D. Pearson, R. Barr, M. Kamil, & P. Mosenthal (Eds.), *Handbook of reading research* (pp. 3–38). New York: Longman.

Ward, S. (2002). *Modernizing the mind: Psychological knowledge and the remaking of society.* Westport, CT: Praeger.

Wilson, H. (Ed.). (1915). *Minimum essentials in elementary school subjects — Standards and current practices.* 14th Yearbook of the National Society for the Study of Education. Bloomington, IL: Public School Publishing.

Wilson, H. (Ed.). (1917). *Second report of the committee on minimum essentials in elementary school subjects.* 16th Yearbook of the National Society for the Study of Education. Bloomington, IL: Public School Publishing.

Wilson, H. (Ed.). (1918). *Third report of the committee on economy of time in education.* 17th Yearbook of the National Society for the Study of Education. Bloomington, IL: Public School Publishing.

2

Second Language Reading Disability

International Themes

LEE GUNDERSON, REGINALD D'SILVA
University of British Columbia

LOUIS CHEN
University of Toronto

Introduction

There appears to be the belief around the world that learning to read is foundational to becoming a contributing, participating member of global society. Many view reading as the prerequisite that allows individuals' participation in school, socialization into society, ability to learn, and academic and professional success. In reality millions of human beings lead healthy productive lives without ever learning to read; however those who do read appear to have better access to the world economy, to technology, and to the rapidly expanding knowledge base. Different jurisdictions proudly proclaim their institutional success in achieving high literacy levels in their populations (see, for instance, Kerala.gov.in/education/status.htm). Organizations such as the International Association for the Evaluation of Education Achievement (see http://nces.ed.gov/surveys/pirls/) measure reading achievement and use these data to compare or rank countries. Reading, often referred to as literacy, is widely considered to be important.

In 1955 the eminent American reading expert William S. Gray noted that literacy problems affected countries around the world:

> Reports from abroad show that every country, language, and culture faces many such problems, which are in urgent need of intensive study. This situation is due in large measure to two closely related facts: first, a clear recognition by all nations of the tremendous role that world literacy might play in promoting individual welfare, group progress, international understanding, and world peace; and, second, the many challenging problems faced everywhere in efforts to help both children and adults to acquire sufficient competence in reading to use it effectively in promoting personal development and group progress. (p. 11)

Gray's comments concerned learners involved in the teaching and learning of their First Language (L1). Times have changed since 1955. For various reasons learners around the world are often involved in learning to read languages that are different from their home or first languages.

In this chapter we address issues related to reading disability in the case of learners attempting to learn to read a language that is different from the language they speak at home. In the process, we will attempt to identity salient themes in the international literature base—a daunting task. The chapter begins with a description of the millions of human beings who attempt to learn to read a language other than their L1. The terms *reading disability* and *dyslexia* are described and defined, and research findings are discussed, including notions related to orthographic depth. Reading disability related to three major languages—English, Hindi, and Chinese—is reviewed. The chapter concludes with a number of overall themes related to the international view of reading disability.

Second Language Reading

Millions of human beings are enrolled in programs to learn to read a language that is different from the one they speak at home; sometimes this is called the mother tongue. In many cases they learn a second (L2), a third (L3), a fourth (L4), or more languages. The focus of the discussion in this chapter is disability related to the learning of reading in an additional language. As it turns out, the number of individuals attempting to learn to read in an additional language is huge and the reasons they do so are interestingly complex.

Individuals learn to read an additional language for political, economic, social, and personal reasons. However, these categories are not exclusive. Migration from one country to another as immigrants or refugees often requires the learning of a new language. Migrants arrive in their new countries with complex language backgrounds including those who are literate or illiterate in their home languages, those who have a variety of motivations to learn to read, and those who may have different levels of ability in the languages of their new countries. Around the world there are those involved in learning, for example, such additional languages as Danish, German, Spanish, English, Greek, French, Russian, Turkish, Swahili, Arabic, Mandarin, and Cantonese.

Another major reason for people needing to learn a language other than their first language exists in countries where the language of instruction is chosen for pragmatic or political reasons. The language of instruction in China and Taiwan is Mandarin, while many learners come from different dialect or language groups. The language of instruction in the Ukraine was Russian, although that has changed. It is now Ukrainian. In India most students learn to read Hindi, although rough estimates are that about 350 million Indians out of about 1 billion speak it as a first language, often in a form known as *Hinglish* (Baldauf, 2004). Hinglish is Hindi interspersed with English words or phrases and sometimes even whole sentences in English. For instance, a news headline in Hinglish might read as follows:

> *Aaj ke* news *mein Mumbai ke* municipal elections *per ek* special report (In today's news: A special report on Bombay's municipal elections).

It is not unusual for Hinglish to be written in Roman script. It is used mainly in urban India. In many parts of Africa the language of instruction is Swahili, French, or English.

Finally, learners often attempt to read English as an additional language because it is important for them in studying and learning in their academic fields, success in their professional endeavors, or to enhance their ability to access information. The issue involved in second language learning are wonderfully complex. Consider, for instance,

the graffiti in Figure 2.1 photographed just outside a school in Canada in which a fairly large portion of the population included students from such countries as Russia, the Ukraine, Georgia, Croatia, and Moldova.

In Figure 2.1, the graffiti is written in Russian (translated by Daria Semenov of the University of British Columbia). It is an adaptation of an old Soviet slogan that reads "Let's (we will) demolish (destroy) damned (cursed) capitalism." The Russian is filled with errors that suggest the author was not an L1 Russian speaker. There are also a number of primary-like English letters. It may be that the author was an immigrant from the Ukraine where he or she studied in Russian as a second language or possibly a Croatian speaker. Russian was the second language, the one used in schools for these two groups of immigrants. Sometimes second language writing appears to be very primitive or under-developed because learners are just beginners.

It is sometimes difficult to distinguish between a developmental feature of learning a second language and a disability feature in the second language. Indeed, developmental features and features that suggest a student has a learning disability are often similar. Is the Russian slogan noted above filled with errors as a result of the author being a beginning Russian learner or because she/he had a Russian learning disability? It is extremely difficult to identify a second language reading disability (Gunderson & Siegel, 2001) for a variety of reasons. One reason is that the identification of first language reading disabilities is not always straightforward or simple.

Reading Disability Defined

The concept of reading disability is subsumed within the broader term *learning disability*, except in a number of jurisdictions that classify reading disability as dyslexia. In the United States the U.S. National Joint Committee on Learning Disabilities revised and expanded on a definition of learning disabilities:

> Learning disabilities...[refer] to a heterogeneous group of disorders manifested by significant difficulties in the acquisition and use of listening, speaking, reading, writing, reasoning, or mathematical abilities. These disorders are intrinsic to the individual, presumed to be due to central nervous system dysfunction, and may occur across the life span. Problems in self-regulatory behaviors, social perception, and social interaction may exist...but do not by themselves constitute a learning disability. Although learning disabilities may occur...with other handicapping conditions (for example, sensory impairment, mental retardation, serious emotional disturbance), or with extrinsic influences (such as cultural differences, inappropriate or insufficient instruction), they are not the result of them. (National Center for Learning Disabilities, 1990)

There appears to be a general view concerning the definition of learning disability around the world. The definition can be stated succinctly: an individual is learning disabled if the individual's intelligence is normal, but achievement is

Figure 2.1 Graffiti.

two or more years below grade level. A review of definitions reveals that formal school-based or governmental-based definitions almost always include three features: (a) the notion of discrepancy, (b) the notion that the discrepancy is not wholly a result of intellectual, physical, emotional, or environmental features, and (c) the notion that the causal variables are likely genetic, neurological, or biochemical, or some combination of these factors. In India, for instance, the National Center for Learning Disabilities notes:

LD is a neurological disorder that affects the brain's ability to receive, process, store and respond to information. The term *learning disability* is used to describe the seeming unexplained difficulty a person of at least average intelligence has in acquiring basic academic skills. These skills are essential for success at school and at workplace, and for coping with life in general. LD is not a single disorder. It is a term that refers to a group of disorders in listening, speaking, reading, writing, and mathematics. The other features of LD are: (a) a distinct gap between the level of achievement that is expected and what is actually being achieved (b) difficulties that can become apparent in different ways with different people (c) difficulties with socio-emotional skills and behavior. (Sakhuja, 2004, paragraph 3)

The Learning Disabilities Association of Canada notes:

The general category is often broken down into specific areas such as reading disability and math disability. Learning disabilities range in severity and may interfere with the acquisition and use of one or more of the following:

- oral language (e.g., listening, speaking, understanding);
- reading (e.g., decoding, phonetic knowledge, word recognition, comprehension);
- written language (e.g., spelling and written expression); and
- mathematics (e.g., computation, problem solving; The Learning Disabilities Association of Canada, n.d., paragraph 3).

These are often referred to as *specific learning disabilities*. This term is used to identify the individual who has significant difficulty learning to read, while others use the term *dyslexia*.

Reading Disability and Dyslexia

The generally preferred term in education in North America appears to be *reading disability*, while the term *dyslexia* seems to be preferred in most jurisdictions outside of North America, although the term appears to have originated in the United States and seems to be a feature of the language of those who are involved in exploring the neurological correlates of reading disability and those who explore the neurological roots of reading disability (see, for instance, Pugh et al., 2000). The term *dyslexia* was developed by ophthalmologists, physicians, and neurologists (Critchley, 1964).

The International Dyslexia Association (formerly the Orton Dyslexia Society) currently defines the term as:

Dyslexia is a specific learning disability that is neurological in origin. It is characterized by difficulties with accurate and/or fluent word recognition and by poor spelling and decoding abilities. These difficulties typically result from a deficit in the phonological component of language that is often unexpected in relation to other cognitive abilities and the provision of effective classroom instruction. Secondary consequences may include problems in reading comprehension and reduced reading experience that can impede the growth of vocabulary and background knowledge. (The International Dyslexia Association, n. d., paragraph 1)

Problems with the Discrepancy Definition in L2

There are a number of ways to measure discrepancies (Gunderson & Siegel, 2001). The basic approach is to administer an intelligence test and to observe whether there is a significant discrepancy between intelligence (apparent capacity) and actual level of functioning (reading achievement). The difficulty is that the measurement of intelligence or IQ is neither reliable nor valid, especially for those who are tested in a language that is not their home or first language. Gunderson and Siegel have noted:

The concept of "intelligence" should signify skills in reasoning, problem solving, critical thinking, and adaptation to the environment. Although this notion appears logical, it breaks down when one carefully examines the content of IQ tests. Typically they consist of factual knowledge, definitions of words, memory recall, fine-motor control and fluency of expressive language: they probably do not measure reasoning or problem-solving skills. They assess what a person has learned, not what he or she is capable of doing. (p. 49)

From this perspective, intelligence tests are not culture- or language-free measures. In addition, learners are often given extra points for quick responses. Such an approach does not take into consideration different cultural norms relative to such features as reflectiveness. Gunderson and Siegel also have made the point that translating an IQ test from one language to another is not appropriate because these cultural norms cannot be translated. Unfortunately, the identification of discrepancy is typically through the use of such a measurement. These authors argue that students with reading disabilities can be identified by teachers using reading measures. The notion of "Response to Intervention" in the United States promotes a different view related to identifying individuals with reading disability.

Response to Intervention (RTI)

The concept of Reading Recovery was developed on the premise that early intervention could help students overcome early reading problems (Clay, 1985, 1987). It has been suggested that intervention can also serve as a kind of assessment tool to identify students who have specific reading disabilities (Vellutino et al., 1996). Response to Intervention (RTI) was approved by the US Congress in 2004 as part of the Individual with Disabilities Education Improvement Act of 2004 (IDEA) (PL:108-446). In essence, students who are identified as those with possible learning disabilities are included in intense intervention and their progress is monitored carefully. Students' response to instruction is used to judge whether or not they have specific learning disabilities. This is a fairly new development in defining reading disability that does have some difficulties related to reliability (see, for example, Fuchs & Fuchs, 2006). The reliability problem is related to the variety of different measures of reading used by different researchers.

A potential contribution of RTI is that it may reveal that students will respond positively to expert, intensive, appropriate reading instruction. As a result, with beginning readers, reading difficulties may be overcome by appropriate instruction and that most LD students will no longer be learning disabled. RTI has the potential for demonstrating that most learning disabled students actually suffer from a lack of appropriate instruction (see chapter 13 of this volume).

RTI's application to second language students has not been explored, but it seems like a promising area of research. The difficulty is determining which behaviors are related to reading disability and which are features of learning an additional language.

Alderson (1985) questioned whether learning a second language was a reading problem or a language problem. He suggested that: poor reading in a foreign language is due to poor reading ability in the first language and that good L1 readers should develop into good L2 readers. Alternatively, he suggested poor reading in a second language results from "an inadequate knowledge of the target language" (p. 4). This raises several related and important issues to discuss: interdependence, Common Underlying Proficiency (CUP), L1 transfer, and L2 threshold.

First- vs. Second-Language

Cummins (1983, 1984) and Cummins and Swain (1986) proposed a Common Underlying Proficiency (CUP) model based on the notion that "literacy-related aspects of a bilingual's proficiency in L1 and L2 are seen as common or interdependent across languages" (p. 82). In essence, this supports Alderson's notion that good (or poor) L1 readers become good (or poor) L2 readers. There is evidence to support CUP (Baker & deKanter, 1981; Cummins, 1983, 2000). Hakuta, Butler, and Witt (2000) have shown more recent evidence that transfer does occur. Common underlying proficiency has also been referred to as the interdependence principle. Cummins (2000) defines interdependence as:

> To the extent that instruction in Lx is effective in promoting proficiency in Lx, transfer of this proficiency to Ly will occur provided there is adequate exposure to Ly (either in school or environment) and adequate motivation to learn Ly. (p. 29)

Cummins (2000) reviewed considerable evidence to support the notion of common underlying proficiency or interdependence demonstrating that ESL students take longer to acquire academic language than social language (Collier, 1987, 1994; Cummins, 1981a; Saville-Troike, 1984).

Cummins (1979, 1980, 1981a, 1981b) proposed that there were two kinds of language proficiencies to be learned, "basic interpersonal communicative skill" (BICS), the language of ordinary conversation or "the manifestation of language proficiency in everyday communicative contexts" (1984, p. 137), and cognitive academic language proficiency (CALP), the language of instruction and academic texts, which has come to be known as academic language proficiency. However, it has been suggested these labels might lead to a misinterpretation of the complexities they seek to describe (Edelsky et al, 1983; Rivera, 1984) and imply a deficit model of language. Edelsky (1990) likens CALP to "test-wiseness" and develops an additional acronym; SIN, "skill in instructional nonsense" (p. 65).

Threshold

Threshold is another concept discussed by Cummins (2000). Threshold is related to the notion by Alderson noted above: one has to acquire a certain level of L2 proficiency to learn to read in the L2 (Cummins, 1979, 2001; Skutnabb-Kangas & Toukamaa, 1977). Cummins (1979) notes, "… a cognitively and academically beneficial form of bilingualism can be achieved only on the basis of adequately developed first language (L1) skills" (p. 222). He adds that "The threshold hypothesis assumes that those aspects of bilingualism which might positively influence cognitive growth are unlikely to come into effect until the child has attained a certain minimum or threshold level of competence in a second language" (p. 229). Cummins also spoke of a lower and an upper threshold. In essence, the lower threshold allows the learner to develop interpersonal competence, while the upper threshold allows students to be involved in learning that involves complex cognitively difficult language. However, Edelsky et al. (1983) disagreed strongly with Cummins:

> The definition of cognitive academic language proficiency is the ability to do what many schools unfortunately define as achievement of various kinds. The definition of school achievement is cognitive academic language proficiency, which often amounts to scores on standardized reading tests. What explains scores on reading tests is cognitive academic language proficiency. This circularity is hardly illuminating. (p. 8)

Despite this early criticism, the two terms continue to be used (see Cummins, 2000; Gunderson, 2007). These issues and concepts are important to the discussion of second language disabilities that follow. Students who have difficulties learning to read a first language are likely to have difficulties learning a second. This is the prediction one makes on the basis of the common underlying proficiency theory and the notion of threshold.

problem with English—a deep orthography—which is not what is predicted. Indeed, the Wydell and Butterworth (1999) findings seem more predictable than the Miller-Guron and Lundberg findings. Human beings are complex and their disabilities concerning languages are, indeed, extremely complex.

Summary, Themes, and Implications

The purpose of this chapter was to explore international themes related to second language reading disabilities. Considering the number of languages in the world and the number of human beings involved in learning to read second languages, the task is extremely challenging. However, there are some themes that seem to occur across countries, academic disciplines, and educational and governmental institutions. The reader is advised to consider these themes as interesting, but not necessarily definitive.

Themes There is a disability/dyslexia dichotomy: authors refer to the great difficulty some have in learning to read as *reading disability* or *specific reading disability*; while others refer to it as *dyslexia*. The term *disability* is used most often in the United States by educators and *dyslexia* appears used most often in Europe and other parts of the world and by cognitive neuroscience researchers in the United States. The existence and recognition of reading disability is not standard in many countries, and many languages have no equivalent for the term (see, for instance, Stevenson et al., 1982). Educators in many countries have just begun to recognize that there are students who have trouble learning to read. The notion of reading disability appears to develop in stages around the world:

1. denial or non-awareness;
2. initial awareness often developing in urban areas;
3. developed awareness in which individuals, educational groups, and governmental agencies recognize the term.

Unfortunately, in countries where the notion is developing, researchers and educators often adopt the model used to describe disability in English (see below).

Students learning to read a second language often display behaviors similar to those associated with disabled readers in the L2. The problem is that these behaviors may represent perfectly normal reading development. The difficulty is to determine when the behaviors are, in fact, signs of a second language learning disability. When a learning disability is overlooked because the teacher believes it is simply a feature of normal development, a serious life-long problem may be unrecognized or identified. Gunderson (2007) spoke of fuzzy benchmarks and suggests that second language learners, particularly those learning to read English, should begin to learn basic reading skills after no longer than three to four years of instruction depending upon their first language literacy backgrounds (Gunderson, 2009).

English plays a significant role around the world relative to second language learners. The evidence noted above suggests that English is one of the most difficult languages to learn to read. There is a fairly standard view concerning the definition of the term. Around the world the term is defined as a discrepancy between potential and actual performance. The theme is that the reading disability definition includes three features:

1. the notion of discrepancy;
2. the notion that the discrepancy is not wholly a result of intellectual, physical, emotional, or environmental features;
3. the notion that the causal variables are likely genetic, neurological, or biochemical, or some combination of these factors.

This definition is based on research related to disabilities in English that has been expanded to speakers of other languages around the world even though some researchers have cautioned that a model based on English is not appropriate because of differences in processing related to orthography. Reading processes differ according to their orthographies. Unfortunately, while it is not appropriate to use IQ tests to measure disability in second language learners, it is the most widely used procedure.

Orthographies represent languages in different ways and have been classified according to their reliability in representing the relationships between their graphemes and language. English is a deep orthography, while Spanish is shallow. Students learning to read shallow orthographies learn quickly. Students learning to read shallow orthographies rely on grapheme-phoneme decoding, while English learners rely on rhyme and whole word strategies.

Reading disability in English appears to be related to phonological awareness and decoding, while disability in shallow languages in more likely associated with slower reading speed. The deficit and double-deficit theories propose that disabled readers in English have trouble processing phonological information, while those in shallow orthographies have trouble in naming speed. Second language students can have a deficit in one or the other or both of these processes.

A final theme that appears in our review is that students who have trouble learning to read a first language will probably have trouble learning a second language. This appears to be generally true, although there are exceptions. One theme that appears to be changing is that reading disability does not exist. Instead, a student having difficulty learning to read is characterized as not having the intelligence or the commitment to learn to read. What seems missing is that other jurisdiction around the world are using the older child-centered model for reading/learning disabilities that holds that the problem is related to the child rather than to insufficiencies in instruction. This suggests that students with second language problems may actually be involved in poor or deficient second language instruction.

English and Reading Disability

English is a language associated with the most powerful country in the world and it is also a major feature associated with access to knowledge, technology, and the internet. English reading disability is one of the most studied and analyzed research areas in education. Indeed, "Much of what we know about the nature and the origin of developmental dyslexia comes from studies that were conducted in English-speaking countries" (Ziegler, Perry, Ma-Wyatt, Ladner, & Schulte-Körne, 2003, p. 170). Second language reading problems appear to be often related to the learning of English as an additional language. Ziegler et al. (2003) note that "The slower rate of learning to read in English does not seem to occur because of variations in teaching methods across different countries, rather it seems due to the relatively low orthographic consistency of English" (p. 13). English is the most difficult language to learn to read, and there appears to be more individuals who have trouble learning to read it. "The empirical evidence that is presented … clearly suggests that reading acquisition in the English writing system proceeds slowly than any other orthography that has been looked at so far" (Landerl, 2006, p. 514). Hispanic students who are born in the United States and immigrants who have Spanish as their first language are over-represented in remedial reading and special education classes (Klingner, Artilles, & Barletta, 2006; Rueda & Windmueller, 2006). Clearly, the learning of reading in English as an additional language is not easy.

Some have suggested that the processes underlying reading are universal (e.g., Goodman & Goodman, 1979). It has become evident, however, that this may not be true. The processes underlying reading, and especially their distinctions in reading disability, may not be the same in other languages as they are in English. There is evidence that the processes underlying reading (Akamatsu, 2006; Aro, 2006; Escribano, 2007; Goswami, 2006; Joshi, Høien, Feng, Chengappa, & Boulware-Gooden, 2006; Landerl, 2006; Seymour, 2006) and reading disability (Frith, Wimmer, & Landerl, 1998; Katzir, Shaul, Breznitz, & Wolfe, 2004; Milles, 2000; Spencer & Hanley, 2003) vary relative to orthography.

Orthographic Depth

Differences in reading processes among languages are often attributed to orthographic depth. Spanish, for instance, is considered a shallow orthography, while English is a deep orthography. The degree to which an orthography represents the phonemes of a language has been referred to as orthographic depth (see various authors in Joshi & Aaron, 2006). An orthography that has a one-to-one relationship between its orthography and the phonemes in its language is said to be shallow, while those that are less reliable are said to be deep. Languages such as Italian, Spanish, and Turkish have shallow orthographies, while Danish and German are deeper and less consistent. English is a deep orthography, perhaps the deepest.

Ziegler and Goswami (2005) developed a theory they referred to as the "grain size" or "granularity" model. Their view is that there are differences both within and between orthographies in the size of the units represented; whole words, syllables, onset-rimes, and letters. These authors posited that smaller grain sizes were less consistent than larger grain sizes and that some languages such as English have a wider variety of grain sizes in their orthographies than other languages such as Spanish.

One of the key findings of cross-language research is that children learning to read a regular orthography rely to a greater extent on grapheme-phoneme decoding whereas children in English-speaking countries supplement grapheme-phoneme decoding by rhyme and whole word strategies (Goswami, Ziegler, Dalton, & Schneider, 2003; Ziegler & Goswami, 2005; Ziegler et al., 2003). Kiswahili, for instance, is a non-European language that is "perfectly regular from grapheme to phoneme; each grapheme maps onto only one phoneme" (Alcock, 2006, p. 405). Learners very quickly learn to decode written Kiswahili. This is the case with many languages. Interestingly, Korkeamäki and Dreher (1993) found that beginning readers in Finland learned to decode successfully in primary grades, but when instruction began to be focused on comprehension they did not do as well. In essence, they learned quickly to decode the shallow Finnish orthography, but did not appear to comprehend well what they were reading.

Danish and English are considered deep orthographies and some learners have difficulty learning them. English appears to be one of the most difficult languages for second language learners to learn to read. Typically researchers find that "The most striking outcome was the evidence of profound delays in the development of simple decoding skills in English" (Seymour, Aro, & Erskine, 2003, p. 160). They add, "Quantification of this effect, using the regression method, suggested that a reading age of 7.5 years or above was necessary before accuracy and fluency matched the European levels" (p. 160). Their sobering conclusion is, "Five-year-old children may lack the maturity necessary for mastery of an alphabetic orthography" (p. 165). However, the strongest conclusion is "... the researchers and teachers working within consistent orthographies are well advised not to base their theories and instructional choices solely on English findings" (Aro, 2006, p. 544). In deeper orthographies more whole-word teaching may be required because explicit teaching of grapheme-phoneme correspondences is unreliable.

Öney and Goldman (1984) showed that Turkish students were more accurate at recognizing pseudowords than were American students. German students have superior phonological recoding skills than English-speaking students (Frith et al., 1998; Goswami, Ziegler, Dalton, & Schneider, 2001; Näslund, 1999; Wimmer & Goswami, 1994). German dyslexic learners were better than English learners at recognizing pseudowords (Landerl, Wimmer, & Frith, 1997). Interestingly, reading problems in more transparent orthographies appear to be associated with small but growing body of research in reading disabilities in India (Ramaa, 2000).

It appears that the normal course of events is that students in India learn to read in two languages; English-Hindi (in urban schools), English-local language, Punjabi-Hindi, and in pre-university and university level courses instruction is almost entirely in English. The situation is complex. However, India becomes even more complex when one considers the number of orthographies, e.g., Brahmi, Kharishthi, Devanagari, Gujarati, Gurmuki, Bengali, Oriya, Sinhala, Kannada, Telugu, Malayalam, Tamil, Tibetan, and a number of other derivatives as discussed by various authors (Daniels & Bright, 1996). In these cases the orthographies are syllabaries or semi-syllabaries. Generally, they are shallow orthographies.

Karanth (1992) reports on two case studies; one of an English-Kannada-Hindi learner and the other of an English-Kannada learner. In both cases, the learners were disabled in all of the languages they attempted to learn to read. Mishra and Stainthorp (2007) reported on a study of Oriya-English learners in Oriya-medium or English-medium schools in Orissa, India. The authors noted "Awareness of the large phonological units of Oriya contributed significantly to Oriya reading when children were learning it as their first literacy language, but not when they were learning it as their second literacy language" (p. 33). They concluded that "These data support the view that phonological awareness is an important contributor to word reading ..." (p. 35).

Karanth (2006) noted that in studies involving Kannada about 10% have difficulty learning to read "because of factors such as deficits in auditory sequential memory, visual-verbal association, and poor word analysis and synthesis skills" (p. 401). The general conclusion of a number of different studies conducted in India is that phonological awareness is a factor in learning to read both local semi-syllabaries and English.

The Overall Incidence of Reading Disabilities

The notion of reading disability appears to have been development in the United States. For years it was assumed that reading disability was a feature of English. Makita (1974), for instance, in speaking of reading disability argued that "its incidence in Japan is so rare that specialists in Japan do not get any referrals" (p. 250). As reported in Stevenson, Stigler, Lucker, Hsu, and Kitamura (1982), Kuo, a psychologist who conducted a survey in Taiwan, concluded that "Chinese children seldom have a problem of reading disabilities" (p. 1165). Stevenson and colleagues also reported that they had similar comments from experts in the People's Republic of China and Hong Kong. Such conclusions were based, in part, on the notion that Japanese and Chinese orthographies better represented the languages. Stevenson and colleagues (1982) conducted a study that showed that Japanese and Chinese reading problems were "not less severe than those found for English-speaking children in the United States" (p. 1174). In general, it seems

from studies, such as the Progress in International Literacy Study (PIRLS), that about 10% to 20% of students appear to have trouble learning to read in their first languages (see http://nces.ed.gov/Surveys/PIRLS/index.asp).

It is not clear, how many have trouble learning to read a second language, although there is some general information. Elley (1992) looked at the reading achievement scores of students in thirty-two countries who spoke a language at home that was different from the language of school. He found there were major discrepancies. Nine-year-old students in New Zealand, for instance, were on the average 70 points below their native English-speaking classmates, a difference that increased to 81 points for 14-year-olds. Students in the United States were 61 points below their native English-speaking classmates. Students in Botswana, Cyprus, Indonesia, Nigeria, Germany, Spain, and Thailand did not show the same pattern; non-native speakers were reading about as well as their native-speaking classmates. Second-language students in many countries are not learning to read L2 at their appropriate grade-levels, while some appear to have no difficulty achieving at or above grade-level norms, even though the programs they are enrolled in are second language programs.

Students in some countries appear to learn to read more successfully in a second language than do students in other countries. Gunderson (2007) concluded that there were many factors such as socio-economic status that might account for these second language differences.

L1 and L2 Anomalies

There appears to be a degree of consensus that human beings who have difficulty learning to read in a first language will have difficulty learning to read a second language, although there are a number of mitigating factors, e.g., L1 vs. L2 orthographic depth; L1 vs. L2 ability; L1 vs. L2 instruction. The research literature contains a number of reports on what appear to be anomalies. Gunderson (2007), in a retrospective case study, described an immigrant student who learned to read successfully in his first language (Cantonese), but appeared to be reading disabled in English. Indeed, after 5 years of instruction he was unable to consistently recognize any words in English, while his Chinese character reading appeared to be quite good. Learning to read Chinese successfully should have predicted success in learning to read a second language, but it did not, because the language was English, a deep orthography. In a widely cited article, Wydell and Butterworth (1999) described a 16-year-old English/Japanese bilingual "whose reading/writing difficulties are confined to English only" (p. 273). The authors concluded that their learner's achievement was predictable on the basis of the transparency of the orthographies.

Miller-Guron and Lundberg (2000) note that the common assumption is that "our reading skills are most proficient in the language with which we are most familiar" (p. 41). Findings showed that L1 dyslexic students (Swedish)—a shallow orthography—did not necessarily have the same

Implications   Educators need to be aware that English is a difficult second language to learn to read. They should be aware that the development of English reading skills is different than the development of reading in other languages. Teachers should be aware that English is a deep orthography and that phonics instruction alone is not as sufficient as it may be in shallow languages.

Teachers and other educators should understand that normally developing human beings should not have persistent difficulties in learning to read a first or second language. Those who do have persistent problems that continue for more than two or three years should be evaluated by someone who knows about first- and second-language reading development. Indeed, Gunderson and Siegel (2001) argued that the trained teacher can accurately identify students who have disabilities by a careful analysis of their spelling behavior, oral reading behavior, and writing behavior. The administration of standardized tests of letter recognition, word recognition, and comprehension can help to identify students with disabilities. The difficulty, of course, is that they also need the time and training to perform such analyses and to provide the appropriate instruction.

References

Adams, J., & Hirsch, M. (2007). *English for everyone*. Retrieved August 3, 2008, from http://www.newsweek.com/id/32295

Akamatsu, N. (2006). Literacy acquisition in Japanese-English bilinguals. In R. M. Joshi & P. G. Aaron (Eds.), *Handbook of orthography and literacy* (pp. 481–496). Mahwah, NJ: Erlbaum.

Alcock, K. J. (2006). Literacy in Kiswahili. In R. M. Joshi & P. G. Aaron (Eds.), *Handbook of orthography and literacy* (pp. 405–419). Mahwah, NJ: Erlbaum.

Alderson, J. C. (1985). Reading in a foreign language: A reading problem or a language problem? *RELC Journal, 16*(2), 1–24.

Aro, M. (2006). Learning to read: The effect of orthography. In R. M. Joshi & P. G. Aaron (Eds.), *Handbook of orthography and literacy* (pp. 531–550). Mahwah, NJ: Erlbaum.

Badian, N. A. (1997). Dyslexia and the double deficit hypothesis. *Annals of dyslexia, 47*, 69–87.

Baker, K. A., & deKanter, A. A. (1981). *Effectiveness of bilingual education: A review of the literature*. Washington, DC: Office of Planning and Budget, U.S. Department of Education.

Baldauf, S. (2004). *A Hindi-English jumble, spoken by 350 million*. Retrieved January 13, 2008, from http://www.csmonitor.com/2004/1123/p01s03-wosc.html

Bowers, P. G., & Wolf, M. (1993). Theoretical links among naming speed, precise timing mechanisms and orthographic skill in dyslexia. *Reading and writing, 5*, 69–85.

Clay, M. M. (1985). *The early detection of reading difficulties* (3rd. ed.). Aukland, New Zealand: Heinemann.

Clay, M. M. (1987). Learning to be disabled. *New Zealand Journal of Educational Studies, 22*, 155–173.

Collier, V. P. (1987). Age and rate of acquisition of second language for academic purposes. *TESOL Quarterly, 21*, 617–641.

Collier, V. P. (1994). *Sociocultural processes in academic, cognitive, and language development*. Plenary Address, TESOL International, Baltimore, MD.

Critchley, M. (1964). *Developmental dyslexia*. London: William Heinemann.

Cummins, J. (1979). Linguistic interdependence and the educational development of bilingual children. *Review of Educational Research, 49*, 222–251.

Cummins, J. (1980). The entry and exit fallacy in bilingual education. *NABE Journal, 4*, 25–59.

Cummins, J. (1981a). Age on arrival and immigrant second language learning in Canada: A reassessment. *Applied Linguistics, 2*, 132–149.

Cummins, J. (Ed.). (1981b). The role of primary language development in promoting educational success for language minority students. *Schooling and Language minority students* (pp. 3–49). Los Angeles: California State University.

Cummins, J. (1983). Language proficiency and academic achievement. In J. W. Oller (Ed.), *Issues in language testing research* (pp. 108–129). Rowley, MA: Newbury House.

Cummins, J. (1984). *Bilingualism and special education: Issues in assessment and pedagogy*. Clevedon, England: Multilingual Matters.

Cummins, J. (2000). *Language, power and pedagogy* Toronto, ON: Multilingual Matters.

Cummins, J. (2001). Instructional conditions for trilingual development. *International journal of bilingual education and bilingualism, 4*, 61–75.

Cummins, J., & Swain, M. (1986). Linguistic interdependence: A central principle of bilingual education. In J. Cummins & M. Swain (Eds.), *Bilingualism in education* (pp. 80–95). New York: Longman.

Daniels, P. T., & Bright, W. (Eds.). (1996). *The world's writing systems*. New York: Oxford University Press.

Edelsky, C. (1990). *With literacy and justice for all: Rethinking the social in language and education*. London: The Falmer Press.

Edelsky, C., Hudelson, S., Flores, B., Barkin, F., Altwerger, J., & Jilbert, K. (1983). Semilingualism and language deficit. *Applied Linguistics, 4*, 1–22.

Elley, W. B. (1992). *How in the world do students read?* Grindledruck, Germany: The International Association for the Evaluation of Educational Achievement.

Escribano, C. L. (2007). Evaluation of the double-deficit hypothesis subtype classification of readers in Spanish. *Journal of Learning Disabilities, 40*, 319–330.

Frith, U., Wimmer, H., & Landerl, K. (1998). Differences in phonological recoding in German- and English-speaking children. *Scientific Studies of Reading, 2*, 31–54.

Fuchs, D., & Fuchs, L. S. (2006). Introduction to response to intervention: What, why, and how valid is it? *Reading Research Quarterly, 41*, 93–99.

Goodman, K. S., & Goodman, Y. M. (1979). Learning to read is natural. In L. B. Resnick & P. A. Weaver (Eds.), *Theory and practice of early reading* (Vol. 1, pp. 137–154). Hillsdale, NJ: Erlbaum.

Goswami, U. (2006). Orthography, phonology, and reading development: A cross-linguistic perspective. In R. Malatesha & P. G. Aaron (Eds.), *Handbook of orthography and literacy* (pp. 463–480). Mahwah, NJ: Erlbaum.

Goswami, U., Ziegler, J. C., Dalton, L., & Schneider, W. (2001). Pseudohomophone effects and phonological recoding procedures in reading development in English and German. *Journal of Memory and Language, 45*, 648–664.

Goswami, U., Ziegler, J. C., Dalton, L., & Schneider, W. (2003). Nonword reading across orthographies: How flexible is the choice of reading units? *Applied Psycholinguistics, 24*, 235–247.

Gray, W. S. (1955). Current reading problems: A world view. *The Elementary School Journal, 56*, 11–17.

Gunderson, L. (2007). *English-only instruction and immigrant students in secondary school: A critical examination*. Mahwah, NJ: Erlbaum.

Gunderson, L. (2009). *ESL (ELL) literacy instruction: A guidebook to theory and practice*. New York: Routledge.

Gunderson, L., & Siegel, L. S. (2001). The evils of the use of IQ tests to define learning disabilities in first- and second-language learners. *The Reading Teacher, 55*, 48–55.

Hakuta, K., Butler, Y. G., & Witt, D. (2000). *How long does it take English learners to attain proficiency?* Santa Barbara: Univeristy of California, Linguistic Minority Research Institute.

Ho, C. S.-H. (1997). The importance of phonological awareness and verbal short-term memory to children's success in learning to read Chinese. *Psychologia, 40*, 211–219.

Ho, C. S.-H., & Bryant, P. (1997). Phonological skills are important in learning to read Chinese. *Developmental psychology, 33*, 946–951.

Ho, C. S.-H., Chan, D. W.-O., Tsang, S.-M., Chan, S.-H., & Lee, S.-H. (2002). The cognitive profile and multiple-deficit hypothesis in Chinese developmental dyslexia. *Developmental Psychology, 38*, 543–553.

Ho, C. S. H., & Fong, K.-M. (2005). Do Chinese dyslexic children have difficulties learning English as a second language? *Journal of Psycholinguistic Research, 34*, 603–618.

Hu, C.-F., & Catts, H. W. (1998). The role of phonological processing in early reading ability: What we can learn from Chinese. *Scientific Studies of Reading, 2*, 55–79.

Huang, H. S., & Hanley, J. R. (1995). Phonological awareness and visual skills in learning to read Chinese and English. *Cognition, 54*, 73–98.

Hudson-Ross, S., & Dong, Y. R. (1990). Literacy learning as a reflection of language and culture: Chinese elementary echool education. *The Reading Teacher, 44*, 110–123.

Joshi, R. M., & Aaron, P. G. (Eds.). (2006). *Handbook of orthography and literacy*. Mahwah, NJ: Erlbaum.

Joshi, R. M., Høien, T., Feng, X., Chengappa, R., & Boulware-Gooden, R. (2006). Learning to spell by ear and by eye: A cross-linguistic comparison. In R. M. Joshi & P. G. Aaron (Eds.), *Handbook of orthography and literacy* (pp. 569–577). Mahwah, NJ: Erlbaum.

Karanth, P. (1992). Developmental dyslexia in bilingual-biliteractes. *Reading and Writing: An Interdisciplinary Journal, 4*, 297–306.

Karanth, P. (2006). The Kagunita of Kannada-Learning to read and write an Indian alphasyllabary. In R. M. Joshi & P. G. Aaron (Eds.), *Handbook of orthography and literacy* (pp. 389–404). Mahwah, NJ: Erlbaum.

Katzir, T., Shaul, S., Breznitz, Z., & Wolfe, M. (2004). The universal and the unique in dyslexia: A cross-linguistic investigation of English-speaking children with reading disorders. *Reading and Writing: An Interdisciplinary Journal, 17*, 239–768.

Khan, A. (Director). (2007). *Taare zameen par*. In A. Khan (Producer). India: PVR Pictures.

Klingner, J. K., Artilles, A. J., & Barletta, L. M. (2006). English language learners who struggle with reading? Language acquisition or LD? *Journal of Learning Disabilities, 39*, 108–128.

Korkeamäki, R., & Dreher, M. J. (1993). Finland, phonics, and whole language Beginning reading in a regular letter-sound correspondence language. *Language Arts, 70*, 475–482.

Kulkarni, M., Karande, S., Thadani, A., Maru, H., & Sholapurwala, R. (2006). Educational provisions and learning disability. *Indian Journal of Pediatrics, 73*, 789–793.

Landerl, K. (2006). Reading acquisition in different orthographies: Evidence from direct comparisons. In R. M. Joshi & P. G. Aaron (Eds.), *Handbook of orthography and literacy* (pp. 513–530). Mahwah, NJ: Erlbaum.

Landerl, K., Wimmer, H., & Frith, U. (1997). The impact of orthographic consistency on dyslexia: A German-English comparison. *Cognition, 63*, 315–334.

Learning Disabilities Association of Canada. (n.d.). *Official definition of learning disabilities*. Retrieved January 13, 2008, from http://www.ldac-taac.ca/Defined/defined_new-e.asp

Lundberg, I., & Høien, T. (1990). Patterns of information processing skills and word recognition strategies in developmental dyslexia. *Scandinavian Journal of Educational Research, 34*, 231–240.

Makita, K. (1974). Reading disability and the writing system. In J. E. Merritt (Ed.), *New horizons in reading* (pp. 246–262). Newark, DE: International Reading Association.

Malaviya, R. (2002). *Thinking differently*. Retrieved February 10, 2008, from http://www.hinduonnet.com/thehindu/quest/200204/stories/2002041300070100.htm

McBride-Chang, C., & Chang, L. (1995). Memory, print exposure, and metacognition. *International Journal of Psychology, 30*, 607–616.

McBride-Chang, C., & Ho, C. S.-H. (2000). Developmental issues in Chinese children's character acquisition. *Journal of Educational Psychology, 92*, 50–55.

Miller-Guron, L., & Lundberg, I. (2000). Dyslexia and second language reading: A second bite at the apple? *Reading and Writing: An Interdisciplinary Journal, 12*, 41–61.

Milles, E. (2000). Dyslexia may show a different face in different languages. *Dyslexia, 6*, 193–201.

Mishra, R., & Stainthorp, R. (2007). The relationship between phonological awareness and word reading accuracy in Oriya and English: A study of Oriya-speaking fifth-graders. *Journal of Research in Reading, 30*, 23–37.

Näslund, J. C. (1999). Phonemic and graphemic consistency: Effects on decoding for German and American children. *Reading and Writing: An Interdisciplinary Journal, 11*, 129–152.

National Center for Learning Disabilities. (1990). *Learning disabilities: Issues on definition*. Retrieved January 3, 2008, from http://www.ncld.org/content/view/458/

Öney, B., & Goldman, S. R. (1984). Decoding and comprehension skills in Turkish and English: Effects of the regularity of grapheme-phoneme correspondences. *Journal of Educational Psychology, 76*, 447–568.

Porpodas, C. D. (1999). Patterns of phonological and memory processing in beginning readers and spellers of Greek. *Journal of Learning Disabilities, 32*(406–416).

Pugh, K. R., Mencl, W. E., Jenner, A. R., Katz, L., Frost, S. J., Lee, J. R., et al. (2000). Functional neuroimaging studies of reading disability (developmental dyslexia). *Mental Retardation and Developmental Disabilities Research Review, 6*, 207–213.

Ramaa, S. (2000). Two decades of research on learning disabilities in India. *Dyslexia, 6*, 268–283.

Rivera, C. (Ed.). (1984). *Language proficiency and academic achievement*. Clevedon, England: Multilingual Matters.

Rodrigo, M., & Jiménez, J. E. (1999). An analysis of the word naming errors of normal readers and reading disabled children in Spanish. *Journal of Research in Reading, 22*, 180–197.

Rueda, R., & Windmueller, M. P. (2006). English language learners, LD, and overrepresentation: A multiple-level analysis. *Journal of Learning Disabilities, 39*, 99–107.

Sakhuja, S. (2004). *Education for all and learning disabilities in India*. Retrieved January 13, 2008, from http://www.sspconline.org/article_details.asp?artid=art10

Saville-Troike, M. (1984). What really matters in second language learning for academic achievement? *TESOL quarterly, 18*, 199–219.

Seymour, P. H. K. (2006). Theoretical framework for beginning reading in different orthographies. In R. Malatesha & P. G. Aaron (Eds.), *Handbook of orthography and literacy* (pp. 441–462). Mahwah, NJ: Erlbaum.

Seymour, P. H. K., Aro, M., & Erskine, H. J. M. (2003). Foundation literacy acquisition in European orthographies. *British Journal of Psychology, 94*, 143–174.

Sharma, G. (2004). A comparative study of the personality characteristics of primary-school students with learning disabilities and their nonlearning disabled peers. *Learning Disabilities Quarterly, 27*, 127–140.

Shu, H. (2003). Chinese writing system and learning to read. *International Journal of Psychology, 38*, 274–285.

Shu, H., Chen, X., Anderson, R. C., Wu, N., & Yuan, Y. (2003). Properties of school Chinese: Implications for learning to read. *Child Development, 74*, 22–47.

Skutnabb-Kangas, T., & Toukamaa, T. (1977). *The colonial legacy and language-planning in Sub-Saharan Africa*. Cambridge: Multilingual Matters.

Spencer, L. H., & Hanley, R. J. (2003). Effects of orthographic transparency on reading and phonemic awareness in children learning to read in Wales. *The British Journal of Psychology, 94*, 1–28.

Stevenson, H. W., Stigler, J. W., Lucker, G. W., Hsu, C., & Kitamura, S. (1982). Reading disabilities: The case of Chinese, Japanese, and English. *Child development, 53*, 1164–1181.

The International Dyslexia Association. (n.d.). *Definition of Dyslexia*. Retrieved August 3, 2008, from http://www.interdys.org/ewebeditpro5/upload/Definition_Fact_Sheet_3-10-08.pdf

The Learning Disabilities Association of Canada. (n.d.). *Official definition of learning disabilities*. Retrieved January 13, 2008, from http://www.ldac-taac.ca/Defined/defined_new-e.asp

Times of India. (2006). *HC boost for dyslexic students*. Retrieved

for the most part, these have not been addressed in studies that profile within-reader differences (see the conclusion for a discussion of this issue). Studies that examined profiles for the purpose of classifying students as learning disabled or comparing approaches to classification (e.g., Fletcher et al., 1994) or those that primarily included more general measures of cognition and perception such as attention, serial memory, cross-modal transfer, knowledge, modality, visual perception, and memory were not included although they may be of interest to some readers (cf. Swanson, Howard, & Saez, 2006; Vellutino & Denckla, 1991; Vellutino et al., 2004).

I take a conceptual approach to this review, rather than an exhaustive one, examining a number of different ways researchers have investigated and thought about reader profiles and various reader subgroups or subtypes. This is motivated, in part, by the fact that "reader profiles" is not a specific area of research such as individual differences, neurological processes, assessment, phonological awareness, and intervention. Therefore, this chapter draws from studies across a range of research priorities and topics with an eye toward those that consider multiple contributors to understanding the reading patterns of individual students. Across these studies, profiles are sometimes referred to as reader subtypes, cognitive profiles, component analysis, or reader types. All are used interchangeably in this review.

The focus for this volume is children with reading difficulties. Nevertheless, it is important to understand that most researchers take a dimensional perspective toward reading understanding—that reading ability is normally distributed across populations (Snow et al., 1998). The same skills, strategies, and factors influence reading competence at all points along the continuum with the lower end of the distribution representing reading disability. What this suggests is that there is no predetermined cut point for categorizing students as reading disabled or abled. As a result, the research reviewed here uses a variety of definitions and approaches to identify and examine profiles of struggling readers, thus making it difficult to compare specific findings. However, by examining the conceptual questions and general findings across studies, we begin to get a sense of how reader profiles might be considered and how they might help inform instruction.

The first section of this chapter provides background for this view of reader profiles, beginning with a brief history of early efforts to understand the complex nature of reading difficulty. The next section, reviews the research related to reader profiles by organizing the studies reviewed into three groups corresponding to general approaches used to study within-reader variability. The first group of studies draws from the work of educational psychologists who have examined multiple cognitive processes, often with an eye toward those underlying skilled and unskilled reading. The second group of studies examines interactions between specific types of instruction and particular reader abilities; these studies examine the differential efficacy of instruction for students with various patterns of reading

strengths and needs. The third group of studies originates from educational policy and related concerns about instructional interventions that are assigned to students based on their scores on high-stakes assessment. In the final section of the chapter, I raise several issues that I believe should be considered as educators interpret research on reader profiles, consider implications for practice, and chart the course for future research.

Background on Reader Profiles

Perhaps one of the earliest efforts to examine variability of reading skills and strategies within an individual student can be traced to the work of William S. Gray and individual tests of oral reading (for excellent historical reviews see Pelosi, 1977b; Lipson & Wixson, 1986; Wixson & Lipson, 1991). Following the scientific movement in education at the turn of the century and the development of educational tests, including Thorndike's first norm-referenced test of silent reading in 1914, there was a sense that objective evidence proved that many students across the country were failing to learn to read. This gave impetus into investigations of the problems students were experiencing and the causes of reading difficulty. Thorndike had called for more objective, accurate, and convenient measures of a student's ability in four areas: pronounce words and sentences; understand the meaning of words and sentences read; appreciate "good literature" (Pelosi, 1977a, p. 39); and read orally clearly and effectively. For the most part, psychologists and educators of the time tried to isolate and evaluate these and other specific factors associated with good and poor reading. William Gray, a student of Thorndike, published the first oral reading test in 1916 with an eye toward examining various components of skilled reading.

Gray saw oral reading as a window on an individual's reading abilities rather than an artful performance as others had. In addition to measuring the student's rate of oral reading and ability to pronounce words and sentences, Gray also analyzed and categorized oral reading errors using a series of increasingly difficult reading passages much like informal reading inventories used today. Gray pointed out common types of errors and explained how they affected oral reading, and he noted that reading ability was influenced by the interaction of various factors. For example, he pointed out that purpose, text difficulty, and interest determined if the material would be understood (Lipson & Wixson, 1986) and brought attention to overreliance on rate as the sole criterion for judging good or poor reading (Pelosi, 1977a). Gray and his colleagues at the University of Chicago continued to conduct studies using the oral reading test as a window on the causes of reading disability, concluding in 1946 that reading problems were not typically caused by any one factor but by a combination of factors (Lipson & Wixson, 1986). So, the concept of individual and varying reader profiles was present as far back as the early 1900s.

In the 1970s and 1980s two groups of researchers took an

interest in subgroups of students with reading difficulties. In the field of learning disabilities, interest was spurred by efforts to improve the classification system and reduce heterogeneity of children identified as learning disabled (Kavale & Forness, 1987). This led to studies aimed at more precisely identifying homogeneous subtypes of learning disabled students based on their abilities across multiple factors or multiple levels within a single factor (e.g., IQ scores). Most often researchers in this field focused on neuropsychological, psychoeducational, and linguistic processing and skills to help them identify learning disabled students (Kavale & Forness, 1987). At about the same time, according to Wixson and Lipson (1991), information-processing research in the reading field was similarly exploring characteristics associated with reading disabilities, often focusing on cognitive processes underlying successful and unsuccessful reading and trying to simplify the problem by focusing on a single etiology. A good deal of the good-poor reader research led to efforts to link performance differences between the groups to reading disability. However, these good-poor reader studies often masked variability within the groups by averaging scores to compare groups. For example, if on average, poor readers were found to lack phonological skills it could not be assumed that all students in that group had poor phonological skills or that, by extension, all poor readers needed instruction in phonological skills. In fact, research is fairly clear that there is substantial variability within groups of poor readers as well as good readers; there is a good deal of heterogeneity within groups as well as between groups.

This brief review highlights the early interest in within-reader variability associated with the development of the first diagnostic reading assessments. In the 1970s and 1980s, however, with increased attention to students who were failing to learn to read, efforts turned to finding a simpler indicator or predictor of learning and reading disabilities. Nevertheless, research continued to suggest substantial variability within both good and poor readers and interest has turned, once again, to trying to understand the complex patterns of reading processes and strategies that underlie the reading difficulties of individual students.

Review of Research

Reading Processes

Foundational studies on reading profiles.   Most studies related to reader profiles have been conducted by educational psychologists who examine the reading and learning to read processes and subprocesses. A major influence on these studies has been the so-called simple view of reading proposed by Gough and Tunmer (1986) and Hoover and Gough (1990) which suggests that reading comprehension is composed of two basic, independent components: word recognition and listening comprehension. Reading comprehension is assumed to be predicted from the product of the two. This model suggests that poor readers possess three different profiles: difficulties in word identification only,

difficulties in listening comprehension only, and difficulties in both word identification and listening comprehension.

Catts, Hogan, and Fey (2003) investigated these three profiles. They confirmed the presence of the profiles as well as the overall independence of word identification and comprehension in a group of second-grade poor readers. Using composite scores from multiple measures of listening comprehension, phonological processing, word recognition, and reading comprehension, they reported that approximately one-third of the students had good or adequate listening comprehension but poor word recognition, approximately one-sixth had poor listening comprehension and good or adequate word identification, and approximately one-third had both poor listening comprehension and word identification skills. However, although poor readers differed in their strengths and weaknesses in word identification and comprehension, they didn't cluster into homogenous subgroups. In other words, poor readers demonstrated a wide range of abilities in both word recognition and comprehension, a finding that is in line with the dimensional perspective suggested by Snow et al. (1998) described above. Surprisingly, approximately 13% of the students didn't fall into any of the three categories. They scored above cutoff levels in both word recognition and listening comprehension, yet they had poor reading comprehension—a pattern that could not be explained by the model. Catts et al. (2003) hypothesized that this inability to account for children with what they termed *nonspecific reading disorders* might be attributed to measurement error or to variables other than word recognition and listening comprehension that contribute to reading comprehension. These basic findings ground much of the work related to reader profiles.

Detailed models of reading profiles.   Spear-Swerling (2004) took a somewhat different approach to differentiating reading profiles by proposing a developmental model of the various cognitive processes involved in skilled reading. Based on the work of Spear-Swerling and Sternberg (1994) and influenced by cognitive psychologists such as Adams (1990), Hoover and Gough (1990), and LaBerge and Samuels (1974), Spear-Swerling described six phases of reading development. Virtually all students pass through these phases, although at different rates, as they progress from preschool to high school or college: (a) visual cue word recognition, (b) phonetic-cue word recognition, (c) controlled word recognition, (d) automatic word recognition, (e) strategic reading, and (f) proficient reading. Although the first three stages are fairly linear, once readers reach the third phase, controlled word recognition, the phases overlap, and students continue to develop word recognition and automaticity as well as strategic knowledge through the final three phases. Spear-Swerling conceptualized reading disabilities as deviations from this developmental path. She categorized students into three general performance profiles corresponding to Catts et al.'s (2003) three groups, and she added a layer of specificity to the subprofiles within each (see Figure 3.1). Thus, Spear-Swerling draws our attention

Sheila W. Valencia

TABLE 3.1
Cognitive Patterns of Reading Disability

Profile	Phase → Pattern	Word Recognition	Oral Language Comprehension	Reading Comprehension
SWRD	Visual cue → Nonalphabetic	No phonological decoding skills; uses visual skills	Average or better	Weak due to limited word recognition
	Phonetic cue → Inaccurate	Some inaccurate phonological decoding; uses context cues to supplement	Average or better	Adequate with undemanding text; difficulty with more demanding text
	Controlled word → Nonautomatic	Accurate, effortful word recognition; uses sentence context to supplement	Average or better	Adequate with undemanding text; difficulty with more demanding text
	Automatic → Delayed	Accurate and automatic word recognition but lags behind peers	Average or better	Weak, impaired use of comprehension strategies
SCD	Strategic reading → Nonstrategic	Fairly accurate, automatic word recognition; acquired at normal rate	Sometimes below average	Weak, impaired use of comprehension strategies and weak comprehension
	Strategic reading → Suboptimal	Fairly accurate, automatic word recognition; acquired at normal rate	Sometimes below average	Basic comprehension strategies but lacks higher-order strategies and comprehension
GVPR		Word recognition difficulties in any of the four subcategories	Below average	Usually weak due to below average word recognition and comprehension

Source: Spear-Swerling (2004)

to both a developmental element and differentiation within the broad categories associated with the simple view.

According to Spear-Swerling's (2004) model, difficulty in the first four phases of reading development results in a specific word-recognition deficit (SWRD), which is characterized by four subprofiles. Each is associated with one of the first four developmental stages, increasing in skill from non-alphabetic to delayed (see Table 3.1). Students in each of these four profiles do not have underlying general language problems or intellectual impairments, yet all of them demonstrate difficulty with reading comprehension as a result of deficient word recognition skills.

Students falling in the second major category, specific comprehension deficit (SCD), are characterized by adequate word recognition in the early grades yet difficulty with comprehension that may be related to limited prior knowledge, comprehension strategies, motivation, or general language abilities. Thus, reading comprehension difficulties may, but do not always, align with listening comprehension difficulties. The two SCD subcategories, Nonstrategic and Suboptimal, represent similar profiles of comprehension difficulty that differ in degree of severity and ability in higher-levels of reading comprehension.

The last major category in this model, garden-variety poor reading (GVPR), is comprised of students who experience difficulty with both word identification and listening comprehension. Their word identification problems are often obvious in the primary grades but their comprehension difficulties are often overlooked initially because the texts are not demanding and reading comprehension cannot take place without a basic level of word reading. However, even after their word recognition difficulties have been addressed, comprehension continues to present difficulties for

these students, in part, because of their general language comprehension problems.

Spear-Swerling (2004) argued that cognitive profiles such as these can be exceedingly useful in early identification and instructional planning for students with reading difficulties. For example, a child with poor reading comprehension that is related to word identification difficulties requires a different instructional approach than a child who has low performance in both word recognition and overall language skills. Furthermore, the developmental descriptions of subcategories within each broad area are likely to provide needed specificity to help with diagnosis and instruction. Spear-Swerling cautioned, however, that both intrinsic factors (e.g., motivation, temperament) and extrinsic factors (e.g., experience, instruction, home environment) play a role in good and poor reading and are likely to influence how students engage their skills while reading. Consequently, this developmental model must be considered together with other influences on reading performance.

A question that arises from Spear-Swerling's (2004) developmental model is whether children exhibit different patterns of reading abilities or disabilities at different points in their development. On the one hand, students' instructional experiences, language development, and cognitive maturation over time are likely to influence their skill and strategy development. On the other hand, they are also progressing through stages of reading development in which the focus shifts from learning to read to reading to learn—from a primary emphasis on phonological and word recognition skills to a primary focus on comprehension and deep understanding of text. Both are likely to influence definitions of reading competence, primacy of different reading components, and, ultimately, the profiles of struggling readers (Chall, 1983). This concept was investigated in the study described next.

Leach, Scarborough, and Rescorla (2003) examined the reading profiles of fourth- and fifth-grade students, some of whom had been identified in third grade as reading disabled (early identified) and others who had not been identified as reading disabled until fourth or fifth grade (late identified). They were interested in the nature of reader profiles of low-performing students at different stages in their reading development. Using eight separate measures of literacy skills, the authors categorized students as having a reading comprehension deficit (reading and listening comprehension) and/or a word-level deficit (speed and accuracy of pseudoword and real word reading, spelling). This resulted in four groups, similar to the basic groups identified in studies reviewed above by Catts et al. (2003) and Spear-Swerling (2004): comprehension deficit but no word level deficit; word deficit but no comprehension deficit; deficits in both word identification and comprehension; no deficits (no reading disability).

Four findings from this study contribute to a growing understanding of reader profiles. First, late-identified students in fourth and fifth grade were not a homogeneous group, a finding that mirrors that of Catts et al.'s (2003) with second-grade poor readers. Approximately one-third had word-level deficits without comprehension deficits, one-third had weak comprehension skills with good word-level skills, and one-third demonstrated deficits in both areas. As in the other studies, this evidence supports the concept of within-student variability. Second, reader profiles for early- and late-identified students differed substantially. Very few (6%) early-identified third-grade students had a deficit only in comprehension as compared to 33% of the late-identified students in fourth or fifth grade. These results are consistent with others that find reading comprehension problems prevalent among older students (RAND, 2002). However, Leach et al. (2003) also note that comprehension difficulties may be difficult to detect in the early grades because primary texts and tests of comprehension are generally not conceptually challenging. This finding holds implications for the types of measures that are used in determining reader profiles. In the example of this study, alternative measures of comprehension at third grade may have produced different reader profiles and may have identified some children who were later identified at fourth or fifth grade.

A third finding from Leach and colleagues (2003) that illuminates issues related to reader profiles is that late-identified students did not simply demonstrate more severe forms of the difficulties experienced by children in early grades, nor were they inadvertently overlooked in earlier grades. They displayed profiles of reading difficulty that were not present for them in earlier grades; their difficulties were not just late identified, they were also late emerging (see also Badian, 1999). This suggests that using reading profiles in the early grades to identify students in need of early intervention is insufficient. Students' reading profiles need to be reexamined at later grades using measures that align with increasing comprehension demands so that newly emerging reading difficulties can be identified. Finally, data from multiple assessments administered in this study indicated that reading comprehension difficulties in late-identified students did not stem solely from poor word recognition skills but were likely influenced by multiple factors including oral language, vocabulary, background knowledge, and inferential abilities. Conversely, students with poor word-level skills but strong reading comprehension, vocabulary, and listening abilities were likely able to comprehend by using their strong linguistic abilities and context clues to compensate for low phonological awareness and speed and accuracy of word reading. These findings are a reminder of the interactive and compensatory nature of reading (Stanovich, 1980), even in models that purport to have independent components, and of the added specificity provided by multiple measures that might productively inform instruction.

In sum, each of the studies in this section addressed somewhat different aspects of reader profiles, ranging from three basic reader subgroups to more detailed developmental descriptions of profiles. The heterogeneous nature of reading disabilities and developmental changes in students' profiles suggest further study is needed of reading components, assessments, and the frequency of profile construction. All the studies reviewed share a common model of reading ability and disability—the simple view of reading—in which reading comprehension is predicted to result from word identification and listening comprehension. This seems to be the general case for most studies related to reader profiles that flow from the research of educational psychologists and special educators who study reading disability at the elementary level. As a result, the components that have received most attention are word recognition (and related phonological and decoding skills) and comprehension (listening and reading). Although several researchers in this field have acknowledged the role of psychological, contextual, and cultural factors on reading ability (Aaron, Joshi, Gooden, & Bentum, 2008; Spear-Swerling, 2004), few have systematically addressed them.

Student-Instruction Interactions

A second area of study that has touched on the concept of reader profiles is instruction. The studies most relevant to a focus on within-reader variability are those that examine interactions between individual students' skills and the nature of the instruction they receive—often referred to as student-instruction interactions. Some studies investigate general classroom instruction to examine its effectiveness for students who have a range of reading needs; others are beginning to target specific instructional interventions for students with particular needs. This concept of differential responses and differential instruction has been highlighted by the National Reading Panel Report (NICHD, 2000) in its call for additional research on instructional strategies

Adams, M. J. (1990). *Beginning to read: Thinking and learning about print*. Cambridge, MA: MIT Press.

Allington, R. L. (2006). *What really matters for struggling readers: Designing research-based programs* (2nd ed). Boston: Pearson Education.

Allington, R. L., & Wamsley, S. A. (Eds.). (2007). *No quick fix: Rethinking literacy programs in America's elementary schools*. New York: Teachers College.

Anderson, R. C., Hiebert, E. H., Scott, J. A., & Wilkinson, I. G. (1985). *Becoming a nation of readers: The report of the Commission on Reading*. Washington DC: The National Institute of Education.

Badian, N. A. (1999). Reading disability defined as a discrepancy between listening and reading comprehension: A longitudinal study of stability, gender, and prevalence. *Journal of Learning Disabilities, 32*, 138–148.

Carr, T. H., Brown, T. L., Vavrus, L. G., & Evans, M. A. (1990). Cognitive skill maps and cognitive skill profiles: Componential analysis of individual differences in children's reading efficiency. In T. H. Carr & B. A. Levy (Eds.), *Reading and its development: Component skills approaches*. San Diego, CA: Academic Press.

Catts, H. W., Hogan, T., & Fey, M. E. (2003). Subgrouping poor readers on the basis of individual differences in reading-related abilities. *Journal of Learning Disabilities, 36*(2), 151–164.

Chall, J. S. (1983). *Stages of reading development*. New York: McGraw-Hill.

Clay, M. M. (2001). *Change over time in children's literacy development*. Portsmouth, NH: Heinemann.

Connor, C. M., Morrison, F. J., Fishman, B. J., Schatschneider, C., & Underwood, P. (2007). Algorithm-guided individualized reading instruction [Electronic Version]. *Science, 315*, 464–465. Retrieved December 15, 2008, from http://www.sciencemag.org/cgi/content/full/315/5811/464/DC1

Connor, C. M., Morrison, F. J., & Katch, E. L. (2004a). Beyond the reading wars: Exploring the effect of child-instruction interactions on growth in early reading. *Scientific Studies of Reading, 8*, 305–336.

Connor, C. M., Morrison, F. J., & Petrella, J. N. (2004b). Effective reading comprehension instruction: Examining child x instruction interactions. *Journal of Educational Psychology, 96*(4), 682–698.

Cronbach, L. J., & Snow, R. (1977). *Aptitudes and instructional methods: A handbook for research on interactions*. New York: Irvington.

Daneman, M. (1991). Individual differences in reading skills. In R. Barr, M. L. Kamil, P. Mosenthal, & P. D. Pearson (Eds.), *Handbook of reading research* (Vol. II, pp. 512–538). New York: Longman.

Fletcher, J. M., Shaywitz, S. E., Shankweiler, D. P., Katz, L., Liberman, I. Y., Stuebing, K. K., et al. (1994). Cognitive profiles of reading disability: Comparisons of discrepancy and low achievement definitions. *Journal of Educational Psychology, 86*(1), 6–23.

Gough, P. B., & Tunmer, W. E. (1986). Decoding, reading, and reading disability. *Remedial and Special Education, 7*, 16–10.

Heubert, J. P., & Hauser, R. M. (1999). *High stakes testing for tracking, promotion, and graduation*. Washington, DC: National Academy Press.

Hoff, D. J. (2008). Schools struggling to meet key goal on accountability [Electronic Version]. *Education Week, 28*(1), 14–15. Retrieved January 2, 2009, from http://www.edweek.org/ew/articles/2008/12/18/16ayp.h28.html

Hoover, W. A., & Gough, P. B. (1990). The simple view of reading. *Reading and Writing: An Interdisciplinary Journal, 2*, 127–160.

Johnston, P. H. (2002). Commentary on "The interactive strategies approach to reading intervention." *Contemporary Educational Psychology, 27*, 636–647.

Juel, C., & Minden-Cupp, C. (2000). Learning to read words: Linguistic units and instructional strategies. *Reading Research Quarterly, 35*, 458–492.

Kavale, K. A., & Forness, S. R. (1987). The far side of heterogeneity: A critical analysis of empirical subtyping research in learning disabilities. *Journal of Learning Disabilities, 20*(6), 374–382.

LaBerge, D., & Samuels, S. J. (1974). Toward a theory of automatic information processing in reading. *Cognitive Psychology, 6*, 293–323.

Langer, J. A. (2001). Beating the odds: Teaching middle and high school students to read and write well. *American Educational Research Journal, 38*(4), 837–880.

Leach, J. M., Scarborough, H. S., & Rescorla, L. (2003). Late-emerging reading disabilities. *Journal of Educational Psychology, 95*(2), 211–224.

Lee, J., Grigg, W. S., & Donahue, P. L. (2008). The nation's report card: Reading 2007 [Electronic Version]. Retrieved November 20, 2008, from http://nces.ed.gov/nationsreportcard/pubs/main2007/2007496.asp

Lipson, M. Y., & Wixson, K. K. (1986). Reading disability research: An interactionist perspective. *Review of Educational Research, 56*(1), 111–136.

National Institute of Child Health and Development (2000). *Report of the National Read Panel. Teaching children to read: An evidence-based assessment of scientific research literature on reading and its implication for reading instruction. (NIH Publication No. 00-4769)*. Washington, DC: U.S. Government Printing Office.

Pelosi, P. L. (1977a). *The origins and development of reading diagnosis in the United States: 1896–1946*. New York: State University of New York at Buffalo.

Pelosi, P. L. (1977b). The roots of reading diagnosis. In H. A. Robinson (Ed.), *Reading and writing instruction in the United States: Historical trends*. Newark, DE: International Reading Association.

Pressley, M., Duke, N. K., Gaskins, I. W., Fingeret, L., Halladay, J., Hilden, K., et al. (2009). Working with struggling readers: Why we must get beyond the Simple View of Reading and visions of how it might be done. In T. Gutkin & C. R. Reynolds (Eds.), *The handbook of school psychology* (4th ed.) (pp. 522–554). Hoboken, NJ: Wiley.

Price, J., & Koretz, D. (2005). Building assessment literacy. In K. Boudett, E. City, & R. Murnane (Eds.), *Data wise: A step-by-step guide to using assessment results to improve teaching and learning* (pp. 29–55). Cambridge, MA: Harvard Educational Press.

RAND Reading Study Group (2002). *Reading for understanding. Toward an R & D Program in reading comprehension*. Santa Monica, CA: RAND.

Riddle Buly, M., & Valencia, S. W. (2002). Below the bar: Profiles of students who fail state assessments. *Educational Evaluation and Policy Analysis, 24*(3), 219–239.

Rupp, A. A., & Lesaux, N. (2006). Meeting expectations? An empirical investigation of a standards-based assessment of reading comprehension. *Educational Evaluation and Policy Analysis, 28*(4), 315–333.

Snow, C. E., Burns, M. S., & Griffin, P. (Eds.). (1998). *Preventing reading difficulties in young children*. Washington, DC: National Academy Press.

Spear-Swerling, L. (2004). A road map for understanding reading disability and other reading problems: Origins, prevention, and intervention. In R. B. Ruddell & N. Unrau, J. (Eds.), *Theoretical models and processes of reading* (5th ed., pp. 517–573). Newark, DE: International Reading Association.

Spear-Swerling, L., & Sternberg, R. J. (1994). The road not taken: An integrative theoretical model of reading disability. *Journal of Learning Disabilities, 27*(2), 91–103, 122.

Speece, D. L. (1990). Aptitude-treatment interactions: Bad rap or bad idea? *Journal of Special Education, 24*, 139–150.

Stanovich, K. E. (1980). Toward an interactive-compensatory model of individual differences in the development of reading fluency. *Reading Research Quarterly, 16*(1), 32–71.

Swanson, H., L., Howard, C. B., & Saez, L. (2006). Do different components of working memory underlie different subgroups of reading disabilities? *Journal of Learning Disabilities, 39*(3), 252–269.

Taboada, A., Tonks, S. M., Wigfield, A., & Guthrie, J. T. (2009). Effects of motivational and cognitive variables on reading comprehension. *Reading and Writing: An Interdisciplinary Journal, 22*, 85–106.

Taylor, B. M., & Pearson, P. D. (Eds.). (2002). *Teaching reading: Effective schools, accomplished teachers*. Mahwah, NJ: Lawrence Erlbaum.

Valencia, S. W., & Riddle Buly, M. (2004). Behind test scores: What struggling readers really need. *The Reading Teacher, 57*(6), 520–533.

Vellutino, F. R., & Denckla, M. B. (1991). Cognitive and neuropsychological foundation of word identification in poor and normally developing readers. In R. Barr, M. L. Kamil, P. Mosenthal, & P. D. Pearson (Eds.), *Handbook of reading research* (Vol. II, pp. 571–608). New York: Longman.

Vellutino, F. R., Fletcher, J. M., Snowling, M. J., & Scanlon, D. M. (2004). Specific reading disability (dyslexia): What have we learned in the past four decades. *Journal of Child Psychology and Psychiatry, 45*(1), 2–40.

Vellutino, F. R., & Scanlon, D. M. (2002). The interactive strategies approach to reading intervention. *Contemporary Educational Psychology, 27*, 573–635.

Vellutino, F. R., Scanlon, D. M., Sipay, E., R., Small, S. G., Pratt, A., Chen, R., et al. (1996). Cognitive profiles of difficult-to-remediate and readily-remediated poor readers: Early intervention as a vehicle for distinguishing between cognitive and experiential deficits as basic causes of specific reading disability. *Journal of Educational Psychology, 88*(4), 601–638.

Wixson, K. K., & Lipson, M. Y. (1991). Perspectives on reading disability research. In R. Barr, M. L. Kamil, P. Mosenthal, & P. D. Pearson (Eds.), *Handbook of reading research* (Vol. II, pp. 539–570). New York: Longman.

4

Language Development and Reading Disabilities

LUDO VERHOEVEN
Behavioural Science Institute, Radboud University

This chapter deals with the relationship between language development and reading disabilities. When describing the language development in children, we assume that there is continuity between the development of speech and writing skills. In the first years of life, the emphasis is on the development of spoken language skills in the context of the here-and-now. Gradually, children learn to use language not only in interactive situations in which the context is given, but also in situations in which this context is lacking, as is the case in storybook reading. Moreover, children spontaneously learn to pay attention to the formal aspects of language. They gradually develop a metalinguistic awareness in which implicit knowledge of both the functions and structure of language is made explicit. Objectification of language enables children to discover written language as a new modality. In the present chapter, we will start out with a focus on the continuities between language and literacy. In addition, we go into the processes of early language and literacy development, and the linguistic precursors of word decoding, on the one hand, and reading comprehension, on the other hand. Individual differences in language an literacy will also be discussed. Finally, a perspective on educational practice is given.

Continuities Between Language and Literacy

Literacy has come to be viewed as a complex of skills which is defined in terms of the print demands of occupational, educational, civic, community, and personal functioning. The question is what psycholinguistic abilities underlie a functional literacy level in the individual. According to Verhoeven (1994, 1997), a distinction can be made between the following types of competences: grammatical competence, discourse competence, (de)coding competence, strategic competence, and sociolinguistic competence. Grammatical competence covers the mastery of phonological rules, lexical items, morphosyntactic rules, and rules of sentence formation. Discourse competence refers to the knowledge of conventions regarding the cohesion and coherence of various types of discourse. Grammatical and discourse competence refer to those abilities involved in controlling the formal organization of written discourse. The competence to code and decode written text comprises the technical abilities of writing and reading. Strategic competence refers to the ability to perform planning, execution and evaluative functions to implement the communicative goal of language. Sociolinguistic competence comprises the literacy conventions which are appropriate in a given culture and in varying social situations, and the mass body of cultural background knowledge.

Given the continuities between oral and written language, the abilities involved in grammatical and discourse competence constitute basic components of functional literacy. Though the linguistic devices used to comprehend or produce written language are not completely identical to those involved in oral discourse, a close relationship can still be expected. Decoding and coding abilities relate to the mastery of the essentials of the written language code itself. It has been claimed by many educators that orthographies differ in degree of learnability. From comparative studies of writing systems (see Perfetti, 1998), it can be concluded that all systems represent spoken language at one level or another and that readers activate speech codes during the decoding process—even in morphemic writing systems such as the Chinese. Alphabetic codes have the advantage of a small number number of symbols (letters) needed to map the phoneme inventory of a language. However, from an extensive body of research (see Seymour, Aro, & Erskine, 2003), it has been shown that alphabetical codes are difficult in the sense that phonemes as the constituent units can hardly be perceived. The acquisition of alphabetic systems appears to be affected by the 'goodness of it' between oral and written language units which is relatively high for Finnish and relatively low for English.

With respect to the continuities between langauge and literacy, the particular sociolinguistic position of ethnic minorities should be recognized (e.g., Geva & Verhoeven, 2000). Grammatical and discourse abilities become very critical for people from ethnic minorities who have to learn to read and write in an unfamiliar (second) language. Children who acquire literacy in a second language are faced with a dual task: learning the written code learning grammatical and discourse competency In many cases children learning to read in a second language (L2) are less proficient in the target language than their native language speaking peers are. Thus, it can be hypothesized that L2 learners have difficulty in using (meta)linguistic cues while reading. Limited oral proficiency in a second language may influence the various subprocesses of reading (see Droop & Verhoeven, 2003). With respect to word recognition and word spelling, there can be difficulties in phonic mediation, resulting in a slow rate of acquisition of graphemephoneme correspondency rules. There can also be difficulties in the use of orthographic constraints, due to a restricted awareness of phoneme distribution rules in the second language. Furthermore, there may be differences between first and second language readers as to higher order processes which follow the identification of words. Due to restricted lexical and syntactic knowledge, or limited background knowledge, L2 learners may have difficulty in parsing sentences into their constituents and in finding their underlying propositions.

Early Language and Literacy Development

It is interesting to note how the development of language and literacy interact in the course of primary school. In the first years of life, the emphasis is on the development of speech skills in the context of the here-and-now. Gradually, a number of major shifts take place in the language acquisition process. To begin with, children make considerable progress in their conceptual development. As a result, their vocabulary grows rapidly. To increase their stock of content words, children need to link the correct meanings to word forms (cf. Clark, 2002). In the first stage, children use words to refer to a much larger class of objects, acts, or events than adults do. Step by step, children learn to demarcate the meaning of each word. With regard to the attempt to increase the stock of content words, it should be noted that children do not learn by making simple associations between specific sound patterns and meanings. Research into the vocabulary development has actually shown that children continuously use information from the context to make assumptions as to the possible semantic boundaries that characterize the underlying concept of a certain word form. It is therefore generally assumed that vocabulary acquisition proves particularly successful when words are being offered in a context-rich environment.

In the course of elementary education, children also show an increasing ability to apply language functionally in a wide variety of language-use situations. They learn to use various language functions such as explaining, requesting, reasoning, and providing arguments (cf. Ninio & Snow,

1996). Further development of communicative skills first of all presupposes that children are willing to cooperate in terms of speech and listening. In conversations, this cooperation becomes apparent in the appreciation of each other and their open attitude towards each other's points of view. Development of *speech skills* means that children become increasingly better at putting their thoughts and feelings into words. Progress is made in at least four areas. First of all, children become increasingly better at taking into account what their conversation partners already know about a certain topic. Second, children learn to provide correct information in a conversation and also to provide not much more information than required. They begin to realize that making up information can lead to all kinds of misunderstandings. Third, they learn to provide only information that is relevant at the moment of speaking. They become increasingly better at keeping their minds focused on a certain topic of conversation, and they express themselves in less ambiguous terms.

Development of listening skills presupposes that children are able to focus their attention and keep it focused over a certain period of time. While listening, children need to structure the message conveyed by the speaker. This entails that, at decisive moments, conclusions are drawn on the basis of the knowledge of the world that the children possess already. They also need to learn how to distinguish between central and peripheral information and to determine and follow the main line of reasoning in a conversation. Simultaneously, their knowledge of reference words is put to the test. Speakers often use pronouns that point back to something mentioned previously. Furthermore, children learn to use language not only in interactive situations in which the context is given, but also in situations in which this context is lacking. This is the case when they process monologues such as stories and informative texts. Monologues are marked by hierarchically structured representations of ideas and logical relations between these ideas, while dialogues possess much more informal characteristics. In a dialogue, the listener has access to a wide range of contextual cues, which are almost entirely lacking in monologues. Research has shown that text structures confront children with different degrees of complexity (cf. Karmiloff-Smith, 1997). Relatively easy are descriptions of the here-and-now in a given context. This is the case, for example, when they are asked to describe a concrete situation. Somewhat more complex are narrative texts that refer to a concrete experience, which is not or only partially shared by the child and the other participant. Taking into account the listener's prior knowledge, the child needs to separate main issues from side-issues, and to explicitate information on persons, time and space as well as cause-effect relations. Even more complex are narrative and informative texts that do not refer to the child's personal experience.

Children spontaneously learn to pay attention to the formal aspects of language. They gradually develop a metalinguistic awareness in which implicit knowledge of both the functions and structure of language is made explicit.

They learn to make language the object of their thinking. Objectification of language enables children to explicitate their implicit knowledge of the functions and structure of language. In this type of knowledge, the emphasis shifts from the communicative content of language to the grammatical design of language. Metalinguistic awareness includes in any case behaviors that presuppose a certain degree of abstraction of language use aspects, and, ideally, it is reflected in the explicit formulation of linguistic knowledge. In view of becoming literate, the development of word awareness and phonological awareness are particularly important. Word awareness involves the insight that words are not concrete things, but labels referring to abstract concepts (objectification) and that words constitute the building blocks of sentences. Phonological awareness refers to reflection on the distinguishable word components. This finds expression in the ability to divide words up into syllables or phonemes, to recognize rhyme (end rhyme and alliteration), to use syllables and phonemes to form words, and to omit, add, or replace phonemes in words. Children find it particularly hard to make phonological judgments. What makes phonological judgments so complex is primarily the problematic character of our alphabetic writing system. The speech sounds to which our letters refer, prove to be very abstract and hardly perceivable in spoken language (Adams, 1990). Research has shown that children develop word awareness before they develop phonological awareness. Particularly reflection on phonemes as the smallest units of speech proves to be very difficult for children.

Notwithstanding the complexity of written language, many children know a great deal about reading before formal reading instruction starts. Through interactions with their parents, they discover the uses and functions of print, know something about orthography, and know something about the different forms of discourse. This process of emergent literacy mainly develops in rich literate contexts and through meaningful interactions with adults. Research on emergent literacy has indeed shown that interactive activities, such as storybook reading, communicative writing and language games, have some impact on children's oral and written language development (see Yaden, Rowe, & MacGillivray, 2000; Scarborough, 2005). The interaction with symbols in their environment with literate others helps children to learn that print carries meaning, that written texts may have various forms and functions, and that ideas can be expressed with (non)conventional writing. Moreover, from interactive storybook reading children learn new vocabulary and gain insight into the structure of narrative text. Conditions that strengthen the relevance and purpose of literacy turned out to be quite important for the development of pre-school literacy. Empirical studies have made clear that the attainment of literacy can be stimulated aand extended by offering children a school environment where valid understandings about literacy can continue to emerge (cf. Snow, Burns, & Griffin, 1998). In such an environment, children have the opportunity to enhance the positive literacy experiences they have had prior to school. However encouraging,

these findings should not overshadow the crucial role of direct instruction in the alphabeic code (National Reading Panel (NRP), 2000). It is one of the most well documented facts in educational psychology that direct instruction in the orthographic code is more helpful for children than indirect instruction where children are left to infer the grapheme-phoneme mappings on their own. This is true especially for children with relatively poor language abilities while other children appear to be able to learn to read with practicaly any method of teaching.

Language Precursors of Word Decoding

Word decoding, or the accurate and fast retrieval of the phonological code for written word forms, is commonly assumed to play a central role in children's reading development. More specifically, the automatization of word decoding skills and attainment of fluent reading levels is considered essential for the development of reading comprehension (Perfetti, 1992; Stanovich, 2000). In learning to read, children acquire elementary decoding skills and gradually apply these skills with greater speed and accuracy. The word recognition process becomes increasingly automated with the *direct* recognition of such multiletter units as consonant clusters, morphemes, syllables, and entire words as the result (Ziegler & Goswami, 2005). From first grade on, individual differences in the word decoding abilities of children have also been shown to clearly predict their later word decoding abilities (Foorman, Francis, Shaywitz, Shaywitz, & Fletcher, 1997). Automated word recognition frees mental resources for closer consideration of the meaning of a text and thereby allows readers to employ reading as a tool for the acquisition of new information and knowledge (NRP, 2000; Perfetti, 1998).

There is general agreement that in the case of alphabetic writing systems the acquisition of literacy involves the rediscovering of the principles of phonological recoding (Jorm & Share, 1983; Ehri, 1994, 1999). In the process of understanding written language, children begin with a rough approach of a limited collection of words that have personal meaning to them. Subsequently, they discover the alphabetic principle on the basis of an analysis of familiar words involving their constituent sounds and letters. Phonological recoding can be seen as an inductive learning mechanism on the basis of which children learn to crack the code by mapping letters to sounds (see Share, 1995), while phonological mediation remains an obligatory component of lexical access which is routinely activated in advanced reading (see Perfetti, 1992). Given the fact that visual word identification consists in making a familiar phonological form connected to an orthographic form, it can be assumed that the quality of phonological processing plays an essential role in children's early understanding of the alphabetic principle (Anthony & Francis, 2005).

In the literature, word decoding problems turn out to be highly associated with problems in phonological awareness. Phonological awareness refers to the understanding of and access to the sound structure of spoken language, that is the consciousness that oral language can be broken down into individual words, and words into phonemes (cf. Wagner et al., 1997). A large body of research has been conducted on the relation between phonological awareness and learning to read. Numerous correlation studies in primarily English speaking countries have shown a substantial relation between measures of phonemic awareness administered to 5-year-olds and tests of word recognition and word spelling among the same children in primary school (cf. Blachman, 2000; Swanson, Trainin, Necoechea, & Hammill, 2003). There is also research evidence from training studies that phonemic awareness can be seen as a critical component in understanding the alphabetic principle (Bus & IJzendoorn, 1999; Troia, 1999).

Strong support has also been provided to show that the lack of phonological awareness can cause difficulties with the acquisition of reading and writing skills (de Jong & van der Leij, 2003). Being able to distinguish and identify the different phonemes in a word is part of this awareness. Research in the past decades has provided ample evidence that dyslexic children have problems with phonological awareness and certain other aspects of phonological processing. There is a general agreement that this initial processing deficit has to do with problems in phonological encoding (Snowling, 2000). Poor readers are less precise in phonemic discrimination; they have problems on a variety of phoneme segmentation and awareness tasks (Vellutino, Fletcher, Snowling, & Scanlon, 2004), and they are slower in rapid naming of objects, digits, and letters (Wolf & O'Brien, 2001), as well as in producing rhyming words (Lundberg & Høien, 2001). It can be hypothesized that dyslexia is fundamentally a linguistic problem that involves a deficit in phonological encoding. A lack of full auditory discrimination of speech sounds may hamper the assignment of a full range of correct pronunciations to individual letters. A limited perception of the categorical distribution of phonemes may hamper the onset of the inductive learning mechanism which is able to acquire new letter names and to form words with them. It was indeed found that particular difficulties with the discrimination of synthetic speech stimuli containing a fast formant transition, such as /ba/ and /da/, may indeed lead to subsequent literacy problems (Stackhouse, 2000). It can also be assumed that phonemic awareness and alphabetic understanding are at least partially dependent on the distinctness of representation of lexical items. Elbro, Borstrøm, and Petersen (1998) found indeed that the quality of phonological representations in young children is a determinant of phonemic awareness and of the development of phonological recoding skills in later reading.

Linguistic Predictors of Reading Comprehension

It is well known that the understanding of written text calls upon both bottom-up word recognition processes and top-down comprehension processes (e.g., Verhoeven & Perfetti,

2008). Interactive models of reading comprehension therefore provide the best framework for the study of individual variation in the development of reading comprehension. Interactive models of reading state that the reader uses both graphic and contextual information to grasp the meaning of a text (see Rayner & Pollatsek, 1989). In other words, the processing of text involves the flexible use of different sources of information. Information from higher levels of processing can influence the processing of information at lower levels and vice versa. And the development of reading comprehension presumably reflects the development of all these underlying processes (cf. Hoover & Tunmer, 1993; Perfetti, Landi, & Oakhill, 2005).

To be able to comprehend a text, children must also learn to make inferences, integrate information, utilize the text structure, and monitor their comprehension. Research showed younger and poorer readers to have more problems with these processes than older and better readers (e.g., Oakhill & Cain, 2003; Yuill & Oakhill, 1991). In a longitudinal study, Vauras, Kinnunen, and Kuusela (1994) examined the development of text processing skills in third to fifth-grade children. They found that young children tend to process text in a linear, element by element fashion and that higher level processing skills are increasingly utilized with age. The most critical development took place for use of local and global processing skills (i.e., making inferences, integrating the information from different text parts, and forming a general representation of the text). The specific developmental patterns were dependent on the initial reading and achievement level of a child. Average and high achievers made clear progress, while low achieving children showed little or only slow progression.

In Perfetti's verbal efficiency model (1992), the possible interaction between decoding and comprehension processes is elaborated. In the "bottleneck hypothesis" both speed and automaticity of decoding and semantic access are viewed as central to the explanation of comprehension failure. It is assumed that the processes of decoding and comprehension compete for a limited amount of space in short term memory. If decoding is slow, then less short-term processing room is available for comprehension processes, and comprehension will consequently be hampered. Following this train of thought, knowledge of word meanings or, in other words, vocabulary skill can be seen as critical for reading comprehension. Both the reading comprehension of children and adults are supported by knowledge of words, which may include the precision of the reader's orthographic, phonological, and semantic representations. Skilled readers are better able than less skilled readers to take advantage of word training events by remembering a new association between an orthographic form and a meaning.

According to the so-called lexical quality hypothesis (Perfetti & Hart, 2001), moreover, not only the quality of the reader's lexical representations but also the sheer number of available words may directly affect reading comprehension. In fact, there is strong evidence of an association between vocabulary size and reading comprehension (cf.

teacher or by skilled peers in order to become fluent readers (Adams, 1990; Perfetti, 1998; Snow et al., 1998). Our endorsement of formal and structured reading instruction does not conflict, though, with our conviction that children are active learners who need to participate meaningfully in literacy to progress optimally. Children with low abilities especially benefit if they believe they can control their academic progress through effort. Instruction must thus teach students to use strategies to accomplish literacy tasks, and, at the same time, to persuade them that their successes and failures on literacy tasks are due to their efforts to use appropriate strategies (cf. Pressley, 2006).

With respect to more advanced reading processes, previous research makes it clear that as children develop better word-decoding skills, their reading comprehension becomes more constrained by their vocabulary and listening comprehension skills. Nevertheless, for even children in the highest elementary grades, the association between word decoding and reading comprehension prevails. It can thus be concluded that continued attention to the speed and automaticity of word decoding and lexical access throughout the elementary school years is essential to avoid comprehension problems or delays. Furthermore, it is shown that the levels of vocabulary and listening comprehension characteristic of a child at the onset of reading instruction highly predict his or her later reading development. Children with limited vocabularies or other linguistic skills at the preschool level should therefore be given abundant opportunities to strengthen these skills prior to the initiation of formal reading instruction. Given the reciprocal relations between vocabulary skills, listening comprehension, and reading comprehension, all of these abilities should be emphasized during children's reading instruction.

Teachers should recognize that the content of most textbooks is not equally familiar to all children. Such pre-reading activities as preparatory discussion of the content of a story, the provision of background information, the establishment of shared experiences, and the explanation of difficult words are therefore recommended. Children's vocabulary knowledge appears to be an extremely important factor for effective reading comprehension. Intense vocabulary training should therefore be provided throughout the elementary school years. Children should be encouraged to build a large sight vocabulary in order to automatically access word meanings. Low frequency words should be made particularly relevant. And, in order to encourage children to not avoid difficult words, lessons should be specifically devoted to the issue of how to tackle less frequent or tricky words in addition to high frequency but otherwise unfamiliar words (Snow et al., 1998). Reading instruction should be explicitly devoted to promotion of deeper levels of processing. Numerous encounters with a word in a variety of contexts should also occur in order to foster the elaborate encoding of a word and deeper semantic processing of a word (Cunningham & Allington, 2007).

Finally, for the child to develop a sustained motivation and interest in literacy, it is important to focus on meaningful experiences and to stimulate critical thinking in reading and creative expression in writing. Advanced reading and writing demands the development of vocabulary, insight into the structure of sentences and larger textual structures, such as episodes and paragraphs, and knowledge of rules for punctuation. Comparisons between expert and novice learners have also called attention to the importance of control processes, such as planning and monitoring reading and writing processes. Literacy in advanced classes is fostered by teachers who plan lessons that have a clear conceptual focus. Students should be given time to reflect, to practice relevant strategies, and to achieve depth of meaning and understanding. Instruction should focus on principles and ideas that help children make connections between prior knowledge and the new information in the text. However, from observation studies we know that very little time is devoted to explicit or direct instruction of reading and writing strategies. Strategies, such as comprehension monitoring, using graphic organizers and activating prior knowledge must be taught not just as recipes for learning but as flexible learning devices (see Pressley, 2000). Students should come to realize that they can use written language as a foundation for building new concepts and new structures of meaning. By doing so, they will gain more and more inner control and become less dependent on others and more confident in using their own strategies for reading and writing.

References

Adams, B. C., Bell, L. C., & Perfetti, C. A. (1995). A trading relationship between reading skill and domain knowledge in children's text comprehension. *Discourse Processes, 20*, 307–323.

Adams, M. J. (1990). *Beginning to read: Thinking and learning about print.* Cambridge, MA: MIT Press.

Anthony, J. L., & Francis, D. (2005). Development of phonological awareness. *Current Directions in Psychological Science, 14*, 255–259.

Balota, D. A., Flores d'Arcais, G. B., & Rayner, K. (Eds.). (1990). *Comprehension processes in reading.* Hillsdale, NJ: Erlbaum.

Barton, D., & Hamilton, M. E. (1990). *Researching literacy in industrialised countries: Trends and prospects.* UIE Reports 2. Hamburg, Germany: Unesco Institute for Education.

Bast, J., & Reitsma, P. (1998). Analyzing the development of individual differences in terms of Matthew effects in reading: Results from a Dutch longitudinal study. *Developmental Psychology, 34*, 1373–1399.

Bishop, D. V. M., & Snowling, M. J. (2004). Developmental dyslexia and specific language impairment: Same or different? *Psychological Bulletin, 130*, 858–886.

Blachman, B. (2000). Phonological awareness. In M. Kamil, P. Mosenthal, P. Pearson, & R. Barr (Eds.), *Handbook of reading research, vol. III* (pp. 483–501). Mahwah, NJ: Erlbaum.

Bus, A. G., & Van IJzendoorn, M. H. (1999). Phonological awareness and early reading: A meta-analysis of experimental training studies. *Journal of Educational Psychology, 91*, 403–414.

Cain, K., & Oakhill, J. (2006). Profiles of children with specific reading comprehension difficulties. *British Journal of Educational Psychology, 76*, 683–696.

Carver, R.P. (1994). Percentage of unknown vocabulary words in text as a function of the relative difficulty of the text. *Journal of Reading Behavior, 26* (4), 413–437.

Chen, R. S., & Vellutino, F. R. (1997). Prediction of reading ability: A cross-validation study of the simple view of reading. *Journal of Literacy Research, 29*, 1–24

Clark, E. V. (2002). Making use of pragmatic inferences in the acquisition of meaning. In D. Beaver, S. Kaufmann, B. Clark, & L. Casillas (Eds.), *The construction of meaning* (pp. 45–58). Stanford, CA: CSLI.

Cunningham, P., & Allington, R. (2007). *Classrooms that work: They can all read and write.* Boston: Allyn & Bacon

de Jong, P., & van der Leij, A. (2003). Effects of phonological abilities and linguistic comprehension on the development of reading. *Scientific Studies of Reading, 6,* 51–77.

Droop, M., & Verhoeven, L. (2003). Language proficiency and reading ability in first- and second-language learners. *Reading Research Quarterly, 38,* 78–103.

Ehri, L. C. (1994). Development of the ability to read words: Update. In R. B. Ruddell, M. R. Ruddell, & H. Singer (Eds.), *Theoretical models and processes of reading* (pp. 323–358). Newark, DE: International Reading Association.

Ehri, L. C. (1999). Phases of development in learning to read words. In J. Oakhill & R. Beard (Eds.), *Reading development and the teaching of reading* (pp. 79–108). Oxford, UK: Blackwell.

Elbro, C., Borstrøm, I., & Petersen, D. K. (1998). Predicting dyslexia from kindergarten. The importance of distinctness of phonological representations of lexical items. *Reading Research Quarterly, 33,* 36–60.

Foorman, B. R., Francis, D. J., Shaywitz, S. E., Shaywitz, B., & Fletcher, J.M. (1997). The case for early reading intervention. In B. Blachman (Ed.), *Foundations of reading acquisition: Implications for intervention and dyslexia* (pp. 243–264). Hillsdale, NJ: Erlbaum.

Geva, E., & Verhoeven, L. (2000). Basic processes in early second language reading. *Scientific Studies of reading, 4*[Special issue], 261–353.

Goff, D., Pratt, C., & Ong, B. (2005). The relations between childrens reading comprehension, working memory, language skills and components of reading decoding in a normal sample. *Reading and Writing, 18,* 583–616.

Hoover, W. A., & Tunmer, W. E. (1993). The components of reading. In G. B. Thompson, W. E. Tunmer, & T. Nicholson (Eds.), *Reading acquisition processes* (pp. 1–19). Clevedon, PA: Multilingual Matters.

Hoover, W. A., & Gough, P. B. (1990). The simple view of reading. *Reading and Writing: An Interdisciplinary Journal, 2,* 127–160.

Jorm, A. F., & Share, D. L. (1983). Phonological recoding and reading acquisition. *Applied Psycholinguistics, 4,* 103–147.

Karmiloff-Smith, A. (1997) Promissory notes, genetic clocks or epigenetic outcomes? *Behavioral and Brain Sciences, 20,* 359–377.

Lundberg, I., & Høien, T. (2001). Reading disabilities in Scandinavia. In D. P. Hallahan & B. K. Keogh (Eds.), *Research and global perspectives in learning disabilities: Essays in honor of William M. Criuckshank* (pp. 109–123). Mahwah NJ: Erlbaum.

Muter, V., Hulme, C., Snowling, M. J., & Stevenson, J. (2004). Phonemes, rimes and language skills as foundations of early reading development: Evidence from a longitudinal study. *Developmental Psychology, 40,* 663–681.

Nation, K. (2005). Children's reading comprehension difficulties. In M. F. Snolwing & C. Hulme (Eds.), *The science of reading* (pp. 248–265). Oxford, UK: Basil Blackwell.

National Reading Panel. (2000). *Teaching children to read: An evidence-based assessment of the scientific research literature on reading and its implications for reading instruction.* Washington, DC: The National Institute of Child Health and Human Development.

Ninio, A., & Snow, C. E. (1996). *Pragmatic development: Essays in developmental science.* Boulder, CO: Westview Press.

Oakhill, J., Cain, K., & Bryant, P. E. (2003). The dissociation of word reading and text comprehension: Evidence from component skills. *Language and Cognitive Processes, 18,* 443–468.

Perfetti, C. A. (1992). The representation problem in reading acquisition. In P. B. Gough, L. C. Ehri, & R. Treiman (Eds.), *Reading acquisition* (pp. 145–174). Hillsdale, NJ: Erlbaum.

Perfetti, C. A. (1998). Learning to read. In P. Reitsma & L. Verhoeven (Eds.), *Literacy problems and interventions* (pp. 15–48). Dordrecht, The Netherlands: Kluwer.

Perfetti, C. A., & Hart, L. (2001). The lexical quality hypothesis. In L. Verhoeven, C. Elbro, & P. Reitsma (Eds.), *Precursors of functional literacy* (pp. 189–214). Amsterdam: John Benjamins.

Perfetti, C. A., Landi, N., & Oakhill, J (2005). The acquisition of reading comprehension skill. In M. J. Snowling & C. Hulme (Eds.), *The science of reading: A handbook* (pp. 227–247). Oxford, UK: Blackwell.

Pressley, M. (2000). What should comprehension instruction be the instruction of? In M. L. Kamil, P. B. Mosenthal, P. D. Pearson, & R. Barr (Eds.), *Handbook of reading research, Vol III* (pp. 311–336). Mahwah, NJ: Erlbaum.

Pressley, M. (2006). *Reading instruction that works: The case for balanced teaching.* New York: Guilford.

Rayner, K., & Pollatsek, A. (1989). *The psychology of reading.* New York: Prentice Hall.

Scarborough, H. S. (2005). Developmental relationships between language and reading: Reconciling a beautiful hypothese with some ugly facts. In H. W. Catts & A. G. Kamhi (Eds.), *The connections between language and reading disabilities* (pp. 3–24). Mahwah, NJ: Erlbaum.

Sears, S., & Keogh, B. (1993). Predicting reading performance using the Slingerland procedures. *Annals of Dyslexia, 43,* 78–89.

Seymour, P. H., Aro, M., & Erskine, J. M. (2003). Foundation literacy in European orthographies. *British Journal of Psychology, 94,* 143–174.

Share, D. L. (1995). Phonological recoding and self-teaching: sine qua non of reading and spelling acquisition. *Cognition, 55,* 151–218.

Snow, C. E., Burns, M. S., & Griffin, P. (1998). *Preventing reading difficulties in young children.* Washington, DC: National Academy Press.

Snowling, M. J. (2000). Language and literacy skills: Who is at risk and why? In D. V. M. Bishop & L. B. Leonard (Eds.), *Speech and language impairment in children: Causes, characteristics, interventions and outcome* (pp. 245–260). Hove, UK: Psychology Press.

Stackhouse, J. (2000). Barriers to literacy development in children with speech and language disabilities In D V. M. Bishop & L. B. Leonard (Eds.), *Speech and language impairment in children: Causes, characteristics, interventions and outcome* (pp. 245–260). Hove, UK: Psychology Press.

Stanovich, K. E. (2000). *Progress in understanding reading: Scientific foundations and new frontiers.* New York: Guilford.

Swanson, H. L., Trainin, G., Necoechea, D. M., & Hammill, D. D. (2003). Rapid naming, phonological awareness, and reading: A meta-analysis of the correlation evidence. *Review of Educational Research, 73,* 407–440.

Troia, G. A. (1999). Phonological awareness intervention research: A critical review of the experimental methodology. *Reading Research Quarterly, 34,* 28–52.

Tunmer, W., & Hoover, W. (1993). Components of variance models of language-related factors in reading disability: A conceptual overview. In R. J. Joshi & C. K. Leong (Eds.), *Reading disabilities: Diagnosis and component processes* (pp. 135–173). Dordrecht, The Netherlands: Kluwer.

Vauras, M., Kinnunen, R., & Kuusela, L. (1994). Development of learning strategies in high-, average- and low-achieving primary school children. *Journal of Reading Behavior, 26,* 361–389.

Vellutino, F. R., Fletcher, J. M., Snowling, M. J., & Scanlon, D. M. (2004). Specific reading disability (dyslexia): What we have learned in the past four decades? *Journal of Child Psychology and Psychiatry, 45,* 2–40.

Verhoeven, L. (1994). Modeling and promoting functional literacy. In L. Verhoeven (Ed.), *Functional literacy. Theoretical issues and educational implications* (pp. 3–34). Amsterdam: John Benjamins.

Verhoeven, L. (1997). Functional literacy. In V. Edwards & D. Corson (Eds.), *Encyclopedia of language and education (Vol. 2): Literacy* (pp. 127–132). Dordrecht, The Netherlands: Kluwer

Verhoeven, L. (2000). Components in early second language reading and spelling. *Scientific Studies of Reading, 4,* 313–330.

Verhoeven, L., & Perfetti, C. (2008). Advances in text comprehension: Model, process and development. *Applied Cognitive Psychology, 22,* 293–301.

Verhoeven, L., & van Leeuwe, J. (2008). Predictors of text comprehension development. *Applied Cognitive Psychology, 22,* 407–423.

Vermeer, A. (2001). Breadth and depth of vocabulary in relation to L1/

L2 acquisition and frequency of input. *Applied Psycholinguistics, 22,* 217–234.

Voss, J. F., & Bisanz, G. L. (1985). Knowledge and the processing of narrative and expository texts. In B. K. Britton & J. B. Black (Eds.), *Understanding expository text* (pp. 173–198). Hillsdale, NJ: Erlbaum.

Wagner, R. K., Torgesen, J. K., Rashotte, C. A., Hecht, S. A., Barker, T. A., Burgess, et al. (1997). Changing relations between phonological processing abilities and word-level reading as children develop from beginning to skilled readers: A 5-year longitudinal study. *Developmental Psychology, 33,* 468–479.

Wells, G. (1985). *Language development in the preschool years.* Cambridge, UK: University Press.

Wells, G. (1990). Talk about text: Where literacy is learned and taught. *Curriculum Inquiry, 20*(4), 369–405.

Wilson, P. T., & Anderson, R. C. (1986). What they don't know will hurt them: The role of prior knowledge in comprehension. In J. Orasanu (Ed.), *Reading comprehension: From research to practice* (pp. 31–48). Hillsdale, NJ: Erlbaum.

Wolf, M., & O'Brien, B. (2001). On issues of time, fluency, and intervention. In A. Fawcett & R. Nicolson (Eds.), *Dyslexia: Theory and best practice* (pp. 124–140). London: Whur Publishers.

Yaden, D. B., Rowe, D. W., & MacGillivray, L. (2000). Emergent literacy: A matter of perspectives. In M. L. Kamil, P. B. Mosenthal, P. D. Pearson, & R. Barr (Eds.), *Handbook of reading research, Vol III* (pp. 425–454). Mahwah, NJ: Erlbaum.

Yuill, N., & Oakhill, J. (1991). *Children's problems in text comprehension: An experimental investigation.* Cambridge, UK: Cambridge University Press.

Ziegler, J. C., & Goswami, U. (2005). Reading acquisition, developmental dyslexia and skilled reading across languages: A psycholinguistic grain size theory. *Psychological Bulletin, 131,* 3–29.

5

Sociocultural Perspectives on Children with Reading Difficulties

ELLEN MCINTYRE
North Carolina State University

Why do some children struggle with reading? From a sociocultural perspective, a child's success or failure at learning depends on the child's environment; in particular, it depends on the child's interactions with others in the context of her cultural and historical background, the history of which is indicated in the learner's cognitive functioning. Indeed, the environment interacts with the child's cognition during learning and development.

This chapter focuses on reading and reading difficulties from a sociocultural perspective. The word disabilities is purposely avoided because the prefix *dis*, indicating *not*, seems to have little place within a theoretical and research paradigm that rarely examines what is lacking in the learner. Instead, studies of culture and learning have consistently illustrated what learners can do, often displaying knowledge and abilities not previously recognized. Of course, sociocultural theory does not eliminate the concept of reading failure but instead argues that failure is a perception contextualized and constructed within a learner's history, culture, institutions, and interactions. How the perception of failure is constructed by schools and other institutions is essential to understanding why viewing reading from a sociocultural lens is so critically important today.

In this chapter I will describe the shift in reading theory and research toward a socicocultural view of literacy, illustrating the key dimensions of the perspective with respect to reading and reading development. I will then review recent studies that examine sociocultural variables on academic achievement, especially reading, and conclude with a section on implications for teaching, especially in schools.

Dimensions of Sociocultural Theory

For much of its history, the field of reading research has defined reading primarily as a perceptual and/or cognitive process, and research on reading focused on the individual and what happens inside his head as he reads. This simple view of reading (Pearson & Stevens, 1994) led to the

general belief that a breakdown in the ability to read in a conventional sense resulted from something within the brain or mind of the reader. In the wake of the cognitive revolution, however, a new view of reading began to emerge. The work of linguists, anthropologists, social psychologists, and educators widened their view to include factors outside the heads of readers. In particular, the social interactions embedded in the readers' multiple contexts were seen as essential to understanding the learner and learning. Reading began to be viewed as a social process, and reading development was studied through a social lens. Researchers focused on readers across school and out-of school contexts and examined both how reading structured social interactions, and how social relationships affected reading (Bloome & Green, 1984; Gee, 2000). These studies contributed to new understandings of the role of reading in cultural transmission as well as how culture affects the reading process.

This sociocultural view of reading has underscored several dimensions that are vital to understanding why some children struggle with reading. These dimensions have profound implications and include the following assertions: (a) Old assumptions that cast learners, their families, and their backgrounds as deficient are mistaken; (b) the study of any phenomenon without an examination of its broader context will result in an incomplete explanation of that phenomenon; (c) all actions, including reading, are mediated by tools, of which language is the primary tool; and (d) a learner's development occurs through assisted performance. These dimensions of sociocultural theory will be addressed in more detail.

Deficit Perspective Interrupted The simple view of reading and the focus on the individual in isolation failed to explain why many ordinary children did not learn to read or read well in the conventional sense (Labov, 2003). Many of these children did not have health, neurological, or language difficulties, and yet they did not perform as others did on tests of reading. Many happened to come from poor or minority communities, and common explanations for their achievement differences suggested that these populations in the United States were inherently intellectually deficient (e.g., Herrnstein & Murray, 1994). Other explanations suggested that children from poor and minority groups lacked the proper experiences necessary to learn, that particular dialects were barriers to learning to read, and that families of learners in these populations were themselves deficient parents and caretakers and perhaps could not assist their children in learning. This deficit view of learners prevailed and has only recently been interrupted by some educators.

Today, sociocultural theory and the research disputes these deficit perspectives by describing and critiquing the misevaluation of learners (Heath, 1983, 1994; Michaels, 1981; Moll, 1994) and arguing for alternative ways of viewing what counts as knowing (Stone, 2004; Rogoff, 2003; Moll, 1994). Studies have shown that classroom practices can often constrain—and educators often underestimate—what children from poor and minority groups are able to display intelligently (Heath, 1994; Moll, 1994). At the same time, linguistic studies have illustrated that non-standard forms of dialects are not sloppily half-formed variations of English, but instead are well developed and rule governed language forms. Moll (1994) suggests that the rejection of deficit views, in particular the view that poor and minority children are devoid of proper experiences necessary for learning, is perhaps the most important construct that has governed a sociocultural view of learning.

The Primacy of Context   The emergence of sociocultural theory and research was especially marked by the discovery by Americans and Europeans of the work conducted in the 1930s by Russian psychologist Lev Vygotsky. Vygotsky's work (1978, 1987) emphasized both history and culture as influential in how and what is learned. Because culture is not a static construct, it is impractical to study it without an historical view. A study of a person or a phenomenon cannot be captured in one moment in time, but must include the background and history of the person or phenomenon. Much has been written about how major historical movements or events worldwide affected literacy practices of particular groups and individuals (Brandt, 2001; Heath, 1991, 1994; Miller, 1995; Street, 1985). In the United States, the civil rights movement affected literacy practices of minority populations (Heath, 1994) and later educational policies (e.g., separate schools for African Americans) and has been shown to affect achievement patterns across generations of populations (Miller, 1995). Studies also illuminated the power of community institutions, such as the black church, in raising literacy levels of its members. Heath (1994) illustrated how desegregation affected the literacy practices of two young African American mothers in the mid-1980s during a time when they witnessed little overt political action as they struggled to keep their jobs, feed their children, and provide better living conditions for their families. Thus, a study of the reading practices or development of an individual without an examination of the historical and cultural influences will result in an incomplete understanding of that learner.

During this time, the concept of the reading context changed (Pearson & Stevens, 1994). Reading researchers moved from viewing context as the larger text surrounding a point in the text to viewing the context of the reading process as everything outside the mind of the reader—the teacher's words, the text read, the broader classroom setting, the school and district policies, the learner's prior experiences with text, her home and community environment, the larger national political movements, and more. Many researchers from the fields of anthropology, psychology, sociology, language, ecology, and education have contributed to this view and have shown how learners affected their context even as their context affected them. Rogoff's (e.g., 2003) work in particular illustrated how multiple fields or planes intersect and transform the child as the child, in turn, affects his world. James Wertsch, a Vygotskian scholar who has written extensively on the primacy of context, suggests, "the ideal unit of analysis preserves in a microcosm as many dimensions of the general phenomenon under consideration as possible, thereby allowing one to move from one dimension to another without losing sight of how they fit together into a more complex whole" (Wertsch, 1991, p. 121).

From a sociocultural view, reading success or failure is grounded in analyses of each child's history, culture, and environment, including her schooling and instructional interactions within her school. Thus, the questions about why some children struggle and why whole populations of children perform less well than others led researchers to look both deep and wide for contextual answers to this serious, perplexing problem.

Mediation and Tools   As reading began to be viewed as a social process, the study of social interactions and what mediates the interactions became prominent. Vygotsky had been interested in the use of signs and tools in mediating learning, including and especially the role of speech. He conducted a series of small scale studies (although not designed in the manner in which many psychologists design them today) that examined learning, remembering, and generalizing words/concepts. Vygotsky referred to his own method as "experimental-developmental" (1978, p. 61) in that the experiments he conducted with learners provoked their development and thus illustrated it for analysis. His studies involved both qualitative and quantitative observations and measures of small numbers of learners, and he based his theoretical explanations on these experiments.

These studies illustrated that when a child learns something, she uses signs and tools to accomplish tasks, such as reading a passage. Wertsch (1991, 1998) explained that a learner's cultural tools are his mediators of action, and one cannot truly understand the learner or development without attention to the tools. Wertsch used the example of the pole for the pole vaulter to illustrate this relationship. For instance, there is a dynamic tension between a learner and an appropriate tool, in that certain tools necessarily affect the learner; the tool might "do some of the thinking" (1998, p. 29) involved in the activity. Vygotsky would refer to mnemonics or a teacher's interactions as psychological tools or signs, and a pole or book as a technical tool.

The use of tools in learning to read at school often occurs on the interpersonal plane when the teacher is scaffolding the learner in the learner's zone of proximal development (ZPD), one of Vygotsky's (1978) most celebrated concepts. He defines ZPD as "The distance between the actual developmental level as determined by independent problem solving and the level of potential development as determined through problem solving under adult guidance or in collaboration with more capable peers" (p. 86). Vygotsky claimed that what children can do with the assistance of others might be more indicative of their mental development that what they can do alone (p. 85). He theorized development from the interpersonal to the personal plane through the use of tools such as self-talk. He used the term fossilized to indicate that the learning is permanent. Later, when the learner is just able to complete the task alone, the behaviors becomes internal. Vygotsky (1978) explained: "The entire operation of mediated activity (for example, memorizing) begins to take place as a purely internal process" (pp. 55–56). "We call the internal reconstruction of an external operation internalization" (p. 56). Vygotsky further explains that "What was initially done externally, is then done internally.... An interpersonal process is transformed into an intrapersonal process" (p. 57). Later, he refers to the internalization process in relation to the zone of proximal development as he states, "What is in the ZPD today will be the actual developmental level tomorrow" (p. 87).

These concepts of mediation, tools, and the zone of proximal development affected multiple studies on the reading process and how educational researchers conceptualize reading development and instruction that assists the performance of the reader. The following section theorizes reading development through the concept of assisted performance, a fourth key dimension of sociocultural theory.

Assisted Performance and Reading Development   The process of learning to read, or learning a sub-skill of reading such as decoding or predicting the end of a story, occurs when the learner works as an apprentice alongside the teacher (Lave & Wenger, 1991; Rogoff, 2003; Tharp & Gallimore, 1993). Assisted performance occurs naturally in all cultures as children grow and learn in their early years; novices learn from experts as they work together on meaningful, purposeful tasks. Tharp and Gallimore (1993) lamented that learning as assisted performance is easily identified in homes and communities but less so in classrooms. They explicate assisted performance by theorizing Vygotsky's ZPD as occurring in stages representing a change from social regulation (provided by the teacher) to self-regulation. In the first stage of the zone, assistance is given with the teacher doing the work of reading (social control) while the child participates as an apprentice and

gradually takes on more of the responsibility (self-control). For example, the teacher might first read a book aloud to a child; then, the teacher reads it again, and this time has the child join in reading some passages in choral fashion; then, the teacher models how to read by decoding, phrasing, and visualizing certain parts of the text; and then, the teacher assists the child in using those strategies while the teacher provides coaching, questioning, and feedback for support. In the second stage of the ZPD, the child self-assists; the teacher provides time for independent practice, monitoring the reading by observing the student carefully while the reader uses self-speech to take herself through the task. If the child does not remain engaged, the teacher intervenes with strategies from Stage 1. Finally, the child moves into Stage 3, when reading becomes fossilized. In this stage, the teacher primarily encourages reading and provides more and different texts.

On any given day, the teacher knows the text, strategy, and verbal assistance it might take to engage the learner in his ZPD. She knows when she must explicitly demonstrate or explain a concept or strategy and which subskills need daily systematic attention for a particular child. The teacher knows the student and something about his background, interests, attitudes, and ways of communicating and participating. She uses this knowledge about the learner in planning the sequence of instruction and in her interactions during the teaching episodes. This social/cultural/historical knowledge of the learner helps the teacher determine the child's developmental level and how best to assist him. This theoretical developmental instructional sequence is complex because it takes knowing what is going on inside the heads of the readers. It requires knowing where beginning readers are in their development, and thus which kind of support is needed. From a sociocultural perspective, of course, it also requires knowing something about the child's history and culture, such as whether the child has observed reading in the home, how reading is perceived there, and who reads. It requires knowing something about the child's cultural language use, including speech patterns and participation structures. Unfortunately, this is a lot for any teacher to know about all her students. Hence, there may be more ordinary students who struggle with reading.

Sociolinguistic Variables and Reading Success

While historical shifts in literacy practices have been documented, it has not always clear why or how certain events affected literacy. Many studies have been conducted worldwide that examined the specific variables that affect reading or general academic development. These variables fall into three broad categories: (a) historical and political variables affecting the community; (b) family variables such as race/ethnicity, language, family, income, and literacy practices; and (c) school variables, including curriculum, instruction, dispositions of teachers, identity and agency of the students in the school context, the cultural compatibility of home and school discourses, expectations teachers have for students' reading success, and the level of expertise in scaffolding provided by the teacher. These categories overlap, intersect and affect one another. They are addressed separately for convenience.

Community Variables   The social and cultural history of any community affects literacy practices, development, and achievement. Although an historical examination of literacy trends is beyond the scope of this chapter, it is essential from a sociocultural perspective to mention that the broad historical and cultural context of literacy is essential to understanding reading development and why some children struggle with reading. Indeed, throughout the history of the United States, societal movements and laws have affected literacy practice in qualitative and quantitative ways. For example, removal of children from the work force into schools raised literacy levels (Heath, 1994), and people's interest in their own civil rights increased reading and writing for social purposes (Brandt, 2001). Any sizable increase in literacy levels for a population depended upon changes in community organizations such as churches, or changes in economic patterns that provide more leisure time, which, at least until the last few decades, meant more time for literacy (Brandt, 2001; Heath, 1994).

As more students were tested on standardized measures, achievement patterns by demographic groups emerged, and reading skill varied widely by group. In general, students from middle class families performed better on these measures than those from poor or working class backgrounds; majority populations performed better than minority populations (i.e., in the U.S., whites performed better than non-whites, but this is confounded by variables suggested below); and native-born students performed better than immigrants. Group achievement differences led researchers to examine *why* these differences exist. Many researchers sought to understand what was happening within these populations to explain differences.

Family Variables   With the emergence of sociocultural theory, educators have moved away from genetic, neurological, or perceptual explanations of reading success and failure and, to some extent, away from explanations of whole demographic groups because those explanations tended to stereotype or blame groups. Yet, group achievement patterns do exist, and researchers from multiple paradigms continue to attempt to unpack the factors that might explain these differences (Arzubiaga, Rueda, & Monzo, 2002; Grissmer, Flanagan, & Williamson, 1998; Linnakyla, Malin, & Taube, 2004; Marks, Cresswell, & Ainley, 2006; McGill-Franzen, 1987; Miller, 1995; Portes, 1999; Golden, Rueda, & August, 2006; van Steensel, 2006; Wasik & Hendrickson, 2004). Most studies conclude that explanations lie primarily with factors related or embedded within families' socioeconmic status (SES), such as cultural practices, literacy access, or race/ethnicity and immigration status. A family's SES appears to be the best predictor of academic achievement and failure for a student (Lareau, 2000; Hart & Risley, 1995;

Miller, 1995; Rothstein, 2002; Wells, 1987), although poverty is in no way a causal factor for lack of literacy achievement. Further, even though cultural differences among ethnic groups of similar income exist (Miller, 1995; Ogbu, 2003; Rothstein, 2002), and children's everyday experiences related to print differ despite income (Hart & Risley, 1995; Purcell-Gates, 1996; Taylor & Dorsey-Gaines, 1988; Teale, 1986), the pattern of SES and achievement is most resilient. Indeed, the differences in resources among families are much greater than the differences among schools (Linnakyla et al., 2004; Miller, 1995).

Combinations of home literacy variables are more highly correlated with literacy achievement than any one specific factor, even when individual factors are disaggregated (Aram & Levin, 2001; Lee and Bowen, 2006; Leseman & de Jong, 1998; Weinberger, 1996). Importantly, Leseman and de Jong (1998) found that SES differences across families were less important than the parents' literacy practices in correlating with achievement. Aram and Levin (2001) found that the factors closest to the child—literacy tools and activities and maternal mediation—were those that most directly affected achievement. Lee and Bowen (2006) illustrated the educated middle class parents' school involvement practices correlated with school learning processes more than the practices of poor or working class families. In these studies, the contributions of individual factors were calculated after controlling for other sociocultural factors. It was the inter-correlations among the sociocultural factors that resulted in failure or achievement.

Studies of home literacy variables are not confined to young children. Several recent studies of adolescents (Arzubiaga et al., 2002; Hall, in press; Lee & Bowen, 2006; Levinson, 2007; Linnakyla et al., 2004; Love & Hamston, 2003; Lewis, Enciso, & Moje, 2007; Ogbu, 2003) illustrate the complexity of factors that interact to result in ordinary students of low socioeconomic status failing in school. Attitudes, identities, personalities, dispositions, and agency contribute to how students see themselves as readers. Hall (in press) illustrated a pattern of students who did not want to be publicly identified as struggling readers. In Levinson's study (2007) of teens living in a gypsy culture, highly capable students saw little value in school-related reading and thus participated in literate activity only when necessary. Linnakyla et al. (2004) illustrated that readers' personal characteristics and attitudes, such as low self esteem, has also been shown to affect achievement. Love and Hamston (2003) studied putatively reluctant readers who rejected parents' school-based forms of literacy for their own practices (mainly digital), illustrating the role agency has in affecting literacy practices and the sociocultural contexts in which those practices occur.

John Ogbu, a leading linguist of the latter 20th century, studied affective and cultural factors of low-achieving students in the United States, and his 2003 study shed light on the role of families on school achievement, stirring some controversy among educators. He asked the question, What is it about African Americans and other "involuntary minorities" (1992) that determine their relative lack of success in public schools in this country? Ogbu studied middle- and upper-middle-class students in the Shaker Heights school district in Ohio, which historically has had an excellent reputation and overall high test scores. The African American students in the district were not performing as well as their white peers or as well as the immigrant minorities in the school, thus illustrating that a class-based or race-based analysis of the problem is not sufficient. His study delineated several influences that went beyond race or SES to cultural practices and identity. For instance, some of the students refused to become engaged with school for fear of acting white; doing so implied the renouncing of black identity, which was greatly affected by peer pressure. Further, Ogbu showed that while the parents of these students had high expectations for their children's school success, these parents were less involved in schools because they worked more hours than white parents (in order to live in the neighborhood) and they monitored their children's homework and leisure practices less than the white parents.

Ogbu's explanation is not meant to exonerate schools and certainly not to blame minority parents, nor does his study neglect school factors as contributing to the students' disengagement. But, Ogbu argues, the role of family and community forces should be incorporated into the discussion of academic achievement by researchers, theoreticians, policy makers, educators, and minorities themselves who genuinely want to improve academic achievement of their children. Other studies of the role of parent involvement in school are equally complex (Epstein, Coates, Salinas, Sanders, & Simon, 1997; Lareau, 2000) but will not be addressed in detail here. However, it is evident that the types and amount of school involvement, as well as when it occurs in a child's development, appear to relate to academic achievement in school.

Some studies that examined sociocultural variables neglected to assess literacy in homes and families over time, thus eliminating the crucial cultural/historical element. When studies are conducted from a sociocultural perspective methodologically, they often focus on what is there and what happens as opposed to what is not there, what does not happen, and how the lack of something may correlate with achievement levels. Moll and González (2003), their colleagues, and many researchers since (McIntyre, Kyle, & Rightmyer, 2005; McIntyre, Rosebery, & González, 2001) sought to document literacy and understandings in homes and families, referring to the knowledge that families hold in order to function successfully as "funds of knowledge" (Moll & Greenburg,1992, p. 322). They documented what the families knew and were able to do in order for teachers to build on these skills and understandings. They found that literacy was embedded within the acquisition and development of funds of knowledge; people used reading and writing to mobilize relationships and to teach one another valuable concepts and skills for survival and prosperity. Moll and González (2003) theorize that the social networks outside of school function to aid the exchange of resources and transmission of knowledge, cultural values, and norms. Moll (1994) illustrated that the application of cultural resources in classroom instruction is one way of inviting change in students' performance. The instructional implications of this will be addressed elsewhere in the chapter.

School Variables   The sociocultural turn in education research led to studies of how school and classroom contexts affect reading and reading development. Because reading was viewed as a social process, the teacher-student interactions provided the context for when, why, and how much students learned. Studies began to show differential treatment of readers such that some students received a very different education than others (Allington, 1977, 1983; Anyon, 1997; McDermott, 1977; Michaels, 1981; Rist, 1970). These differences included differences in teachers' expectations for some children and differences in curriculum and instruction. These studies excited the field and moved it toward a better understanding of why some ordinary children struggle with reading.

Sometimes, the explanations for school interactions came from teachers' perceptions and expectations for learners (Anyon, 1997; Finn, 1999; Rist, 1970; Weinstein, 2004). There is substantial evidence that teachers' expectations of particular students' abilities affect their academic achievement, including reading (Rist, 1970; Rothstein, 2002; Weinstein, 2002) resulting in a self-fulfilling prophecy (Stanovich, 1986; Weinstein, 2004). Some teachers believe that poor students are in dire need of being rescued from their communities, families, and cultures (Finn, 1999; Lee, 2008; Marx, 2006). Many well-meaning teachers believe that students living in poverty and/or minority groups cannot achieve as capably as can middle-class students, largely due to their backgrounds, families, and life circumstances, and that they need to be remediated with basic skills (Delpit, 1986, 1988; Ferguson, 1998; Weinstein, 2004). Expectations can be heard in educators' comments about particular student populations, such as "They need the structure," "They need phonics," "They don't have language," and "They need direct instruction." This problem extends to the families of the groups as well, such as, "They don't care about education," "They don't care about their kids," "They are never home," and "They spend all their extra money on videos" (McIntyre & Hulan, 2008). These "overly deterministic pronouncements" (Lee, 2008, p. 275) reflect stereotypes of poor people and their children.

Beyond teacher expectations, many studies illuminated differential access to literacy based on curricular and instructional practices afforded to some children and not others. One of the most documented patterns in U.S. public schools is that education for students from middle- and upper-middle-class backgrounds generally looks quite different from schools primarily serving poor students (Anyon, 1997; Finn, 1999). Even today, looking into classrooms, we find that, in general, the children in schools serving students of poverty receive rote, scripted, or programmed instruction, even as those in the suburbs receive instruction focused on high-level thinking and creativity.

Anyon's 1997 study was only one of many that illustrated this sort of curricular inequity across SES groups. It is common for educators to recommend programs focused on basic skills for struggling readers. The argument is that struggling readers cannot do high-level thinking because they do not have the requisite basic skills. The other argument is that some of these programs have been shown to work, as described below. Yet, a curriculum focused on basic skills arguably limits what students can learn by limiting access to high quality instruction (Allington & McGill-Franzen, 2003; McGill-Franzen & Allington, 1991; Miller, 1995) and, in fact, may be one of the causes of school failure.

The Problem of Basic Skills for Struggling Readers

There is a widely accepted belief that rudimentary or basic skills in reading, such as the ability to decode words or comprehend sequentially ordered information, is learned prior to being able to search for information, make generalizations from reading, summarize or synthesize information from multiple sources, or other more advanced reading skills. Indeed, the reading test of the National Association of Educational Progress (NAEP) is organized in a way that assesses these skills in this hierarchical manner. Further, most reading researchers have shown some kind of developmental sequence to what children learn as they acquire the ability to read (Ehri, 1991; Ferriero & Teberosky, 1982). However, there seems to be no guarantee that learning rudimentary or basic skills leads to more advanced skills in reading. Miller (1995) illustrated that while reading achievement for 9-year-olds has gone up for minorities in the past few decades, it has only moved from the most rudimentary level to the basic level, suggesting that these students have not learned to relate ideas, analyze, summarize, or synthesize. Thus, most educators agree that basic skills such as phonics are a necessary but not sufficient part of a good reading curriculum.

Discussions about basic skills can become problematic when making curricular decisions for a school serving a large population of students considered at risk for school failure. Because it is widely accepted that phonics and other basics must be learned as part of comprehending, educators sometimes choose carefully sequenced, scripted reading programs for whole classes of children. Although these programs may have some value for some children at some time (McIntyre, Rightmyer, & Petrosko, 2008; McIntyre, Rightmyer, Powell, Powers, & Petrosko, 2006), the practice of adopting the programs for whole classes of schools becomes problematic from a sociocultural perspective. At no time in these programs can teachers attend to the individual needs and cultural/linguistic backgrounds of learners. I return to this point later in this section.

There is evidence that some programs focused on basic skills do succeed in raising student achievement of students considered to be struggling. In one study, Slavin, Madden, Karweit, Livermon, & Nolan (1990) measured the effects of a scripted reading program, Success for All, on pre-schoolers through third graders, 76% of whom were recipients of the federal free lunch program. The researchers found that primary grade children, especially kindergartners and third graders, scored significantly better on individually-scored reading and language assessments than did children in control groups after only 1 year. While the children in this study did not score better on standardized tests, a later study (Ross, Smith, & Casey, 1997) showed that children receiving Success for All instruction scored better than students in a control group on both standardized and individually administered tests through second grade, although not in third grade. This study also showed that minority students improved at a better rate than white students. Similarly, McIntyre et al. (2008) found that first-grade struggling readers who had received scripted instruction achieved more on phonics measures than a matched group of students who had received what teachers called balanced instruction. There were no significant differences found in reading achievement.

Researchers also compared the phonics and reading achievement of struggling readers in classrooms in which the teachers purposefully planned time for reading connected text with students in classrooms in which there was little reading of connected texts (McIntyre et al., 2006). First graders in classrooms with less reading performed better on phonics than first graders who read more connected text, and there were no differences on the reading measure. However, the second-grade children in classrooms who read a lot of connected text for 2 consecutive years gained significantly more on the reading achievement measure than second graders without 2 consecutive years in classrooms with extensive reading.

In a study in Spain, researchers Castells and Solé (2008) came to similar conclusions. They examined the relationship between the level of phonological awareness and letter knowledge and the ability to read different kinds of texts and write conventionally in 5-year-old children taught in Catalan, the primary language of Barcelona. Participants included 69 children from 3 different classrooms. Their teachers held different conceptions about teaching early literacy. These conceptions were related to either an analytical, synthetical, or analytical-synthetical perspective. Students' knowledge was assessed at the beginning and at the end of the school year on a variety of tasks: letter recognition, oral word segmentation, reading words, reading a sentence, and a dictation. The results showed that the ability to segment a word into syllables orally seemed to be a sufficient marker for children to start reading in a conventional way in Catalan. Furthermore, students used phonological knowledge in relatively different ways depending on the students' development and skill with reading and writing. This study indicated that appropriate instruction is relative to what the student is able to do at the time.

Other recent studies that support this contextual and developmental argument raise additional theoretical, practical, and methodological questions about scripted instructional programs. For instance, some studies have illustrated that the discourse of the instructional script is exactly what conflicts with the discourse of home and community of minority groups and some white families (Dudley-Marling & Paugh, 2005; Tharp & Gallimore, 1993), thus raising questions of appropriateness. Some researchers question findings of school districts reporting positive effects for scripted models by suggesting that the students only perform well with the scripted models during the first year or two of implementation (Land & Moustafa, 2005). And some studies suggest that the scripted models adversely affect students' engagement, creating more disengaged or passive learners (Powell, McIntyre, & Rightmyer, 2006). Finally, Edelsky and Bomer (2005) suggest that studies which show positive results for scripted programs do so because some teachers, who do not operate from a deficit model, have supplemented scripted programs with better practices.

Studies such as these shed light on sociocultural theory because they raise questions about the relationship between students' development as readers and the instructional practices that did or did not meet their individual needs. Studies of children's acquisition of reading have shown that many children go through a period when they focus exclusively on words and word parts over meaning (Biemiller, 1970; Hiebert & Taylor, 2000; Mason, 1984; McIntyre & Freppon, 1994; Purcell-Gates, 1995; Sulzby, 1985). There is movement from a great reliance on syntactic and semantic cues when reading to an increased use of graphic information (Barr, 1984; Biemiller, 1970; Clay, 1993; Ferriero & Teberosky, 1982; Mason, 1984). Specifically, children move through an "aspectual" stage (Sulzby, 1985, p. 471) of reading in which they struggle with mastering the code to the exclusion of meaning making. This stage often indicates that children are just becoming readers, a period in which much assistance is critical (Tharp & Gallimore, 1993). As a group, these studies measured readers who may have been developmentally ripe for the phonics teaching they received, as opposed to the other students who were further along in their reading development, and this may account for their achievement.

These studies suggest the possibility that the reading failure of some children may be in part related to the students' reading curriculum over multiple years. Although explicit instruction in phonics is almost indisputable in terms of its success in helping most children learn phonics, a phonics-heavy instructional program may not be beneficial in helping children move from the most rudimentary reading skills toward more advanced levels, which may contribute toward an explanation of achievement differences by population, such as those analyzed by Miller (1995). Our education system, including educational research, often fails to take the long view about what students may need across multiple years. When a program, model, teacher, or intervention appears to be effective for a particular group of children for a short period, it is seen as potentially successful for all and adopted. But a steady diet of a basic skills curriculum may indeed be one of the causes of reading failure.

Instructional Implications for a Sociocultural Approach to Reading

In the last few decades, in concert with the upsurge of research and theory from a sociocultural perspective, classroom practices across the country have changed. Many teachers today cultivate a less competitive and more cooperative classroom environment, build instruction from students' prior understandings, and honor home languages. Especially in elementary classrooms, the physical environment indicates changes in orientation as the space is arranged so that children can interact and learn from one another. Of course, many educators would agree much change is still needed.

Reading instruction from a sociocultural perspective takes the child's contextual world into account. Ideally, educators would learn as much about the reader as possible. Perhaps the teacher might want to know about the reader's cultural and historical background. There are numerous potential questions teachers may ask in this regard, such as: How does the child's race/ethnicity play a role in the child's life? What languages are spoken in the home and community? How does the family identify themselves semantically, culturally, socially, and through everyday routines? What is the family make-up and what characteristics of the family are significant to the child? How much education does the child's family have? Who reads and writes in the family and for what purpose? What does the family do for a living? What does the family do outside of work and school and with whom do they do it? What sorts of material resources does the family have that affect academic development? What other interests does the family have? How does the child spend out-of-school time? These sorts of questions assess the student's history and culture, including variables that have been shown to correlate with school success and failure (e.g., race/ethnicity, language, SES, geography, social capital).

The teacher must also attempt to understand the reader as a person and as a student. Questions for exploration might include: What has the child's school life been like so far? What are the child's interests? Who are his friends? What is the child good at? How does the child deal with emotional stress? What does the child like about school? What sorts of books does he choose? Does he prefer to read alone or with others? Why? These sorts of questions get at identity, agency, and motivation.

The teacher must learn about the child's reading skills and behaviors that allow for the assessment of the learner's zones of proximal development. What texts does the child prefer? What texts can the child read independently? What can she read successfully with help from a peer? What can she read somewhat with help from the teacher? What can't she read at all? What strategies does the child use to tackle text that is challenging? What words can the child encode and decode with scaffolding by a knowledgeable teacher? What can the child write independently? What can she write with expert scaffolding?

Based on a sociocultural approach, understanding the learner is the primary tool for teaching. This tool encompasses all else and is used in making instructional decisions about the learner. Yet, it is imperative that teachers do not use information gained from assessment of the learner to form lower expectations of the child based on the family's history or education. Indeed, it may be necessary for teachers to have an avenue to explore their own assumptions about families before undertaking the goal of visiting homes or interviewing parents (McIntyre et al., 2005). Further, Heath (1994) emphasized that the goal is not to use cultural knowledge about minorities' ways of using language and habits of learning to tailor classrooms to fit the daily habits of the each minority group, but to learn about the various ways people use language in order to accept and support the language learning of all students. Moll (1994) claimed that when students are encouraged to participate in ways that respect their language and cultural patterns (such as collaboration or overlapping speech), students perform in ways unexpected by their teachers, resulting is less misevaluation of the learner. The following sections elaborate on further instructional implications, each of which extends from knowledge about the learner.

Culturally Responsive Instruction   Culturally responsive instruction or culturally relevant pedagogy (Gay, 2000, 2002; Irvine, 2006; Ladson-Billings, 1994; Nieto, 1999; Tharp, Estrada, Dalton, & Yamauchi, 2000; Williams, 1996) is based on the idea that teachers can tailor curriculum and instruction to make students' school experiences more compatible with their natal culture (Tharp, 1989). In the funds of knowledge work discussed earlier, teachers respect what the learner comes to school with and extends that learning (Moll & González, 2003; McIntyre et al., 2001). Teachers attend to students' language and participation practices by taking into account differential practices around competition or cooperation (Tharp, 1993) or interactional speech styles (Michaels, 1981; Adger, Wolfram, & Christian, 2007) that can affect classroom interactions to support or constrain learning. For instance, some children grow up in homes in which family members speak and react directly, with gestures and body language that communicate in ways that others may view as blunt. Other children are raised in homes in which overlapping speech is expected; still others would be taught that overlapping speech is rude. Most educators recommend that teachers attend closely to students' interaction styles, and at a minimum ask themselves whether styles in which they are unfamiliar might be cultural.

Teachers can learn to modify their own discourse to build on the students' styles to reflect, for example, "call and response" (Foster & Peele, 2001, p. 33), or "signifying" (Lee, 1998, p. 193) language patterns of African Americans. Signifying is a discourse style often called "playin' the dozens," "rappin'," "soundin'," or "talkin' shit," and it is characterized by using innuendo and double meanings to communicate. When students participate in signifying, their teacher can honor their capacities and build on them to

help students learn school concepts such as metaphor, irony, and symbolism. Boykin, Wade, and Others (1986, cited in Ferguson, 1998, p. 347) found that African American elementary students do better when their teachers allowed "verve," or mixing or switching back and forth between tasks, rather than focusing on one task at a time for longer periods. In her study, all the students improved when tasks were mixed, but the African American students improved more. Further, Boykin showed in other studies that physical movement, music in the background, and working in teams with group rewards were all highly correlated with higher achievement of African American children.

Additional pedagogical strategies that have been advocated by minority scholars and scholars of minorities include group work and dialogic instruction. Students must have opportunities to practice academic talk in safe environments and with expert scaffolding by the teacher to clarify misconceptions or nudge students' thinking. Students learn from one another, should have opportunities for frequent movement and use of manipulatives along with high levels of support in the name of direct and explicit teaching of skills, small group instruction, tutoring programs, and heavy monitoring of individual progress. Hale (2003) also suggested the curriculum be heavily tied to the arts, while Williams (1996) promoted developing resilience-promoting strategies in students, teachers, and schools where the burden of adversity is reduced and opportunities for learning advanced.

Finally, culturally responsive instruction does not communicate low standards or an unconstrained approach. Irvine (2006) emphasized student achievement as the ultimate goal. The curriculum ought to be rigorous and focused on high expectations, problem solving, an unwillingness to give up on any student, an advanced curriculum with regular feedback and celebration of progress, and uplifting curricular materials grounded in students' experiences. Marva Collins, of Chicago, is an often-cited example of a teacher whose rigorous teaching is of something worth being rigorous about (although most would not describe her approach as sociocultural): She aims to nurture in students the belief that they are destined to become important people.

In summary, culturally responsive instruction can be characterized by teaching that is meaningful, challenging, collaborative, dialogic, and connected to the students' home and community experiences. Yet, due in part to the many confounding factors in a child's sociocultural world, there have been few well-designed studies illustrating achievement effects through culturally responsive instruction.

Research-Based, Culturally Responsive Reading Instruction   Culturally responsive instruction makes intuitive sense. If educators link instruction to what students know from their cultural backgrounds and attend to students' linguistic communication patterns, students should learn more. Yet, it is clear from decades of research on what works in reading instruction that culturally responsive instruction may not be a sufficient paradigm for raising student achievement. In the 1990s, when many studies and commentary revealed that many children still were not learning how to read (Snow, Burns, & Griffin, 1998; Torgesen, 2002), some reports suggested that students who struggle with reading may need much more explicit instruction than was currently in vogue (Delpit, 1995; McIntyre, Kyle, & Moore, 2006; McIntyre & Pressley, 1996). As stated earlier, the National Reading Panel (NRP) reviewed studies on reading instruction, teacher education in reading, and on technology and reading. In terms of instruction, the studies focused on alphabetics (phonemic awareness and phonics), reading fluency, and reading comprehension, which included text comprehension and vocabulary (NICHD, 2000). The NRP delineated the importance of each of these instructional areas and reported that findings were significant enough to recommend the inclusion of a variety of techniques in any reading program, but were not quite fully committed to endorsing even these unconditionally. The panel's report and subsequent publications (e.g., Farstrup & Samuel's, 2002) emphasized instructional strategies, largely from a cognitive strategy paradigm, that had been examined in experimental studies. Although these strategies have been shown to be effective with some populations in some contexts, a question remains: Can research-based reading instruction be culturally responsive? The answer seems to be affirmative if teachers learn enough about their students to adapt instruction to individual needs.

In a recent study (McIntyre & Hulan, 2008), researchers used a design-based approach to study whether and how four teachers implemented research-based reading instruction while adhering to premises and practices of culturally responsive instruction. The four teachers were participants in a graduate class that theorized and illustrated the potential of this model of instruction, and then the four participated in a post-course study that lasted eight months. The teachers' goal was to teach the content of research-based instruction, largely defined by the NRP report, using strategies shown to increase student achievement while also attending to students' backgrounds, linguistic patterns, text interests, participation patterns, and more. These four teachers were all successful in hybridizing (Gutiérrez, Baquedano-Lopez, & Alvarez, 2001) their practices in these ways, illustrating the potential for this kind of teaching. Yet, they spoke of the struggles they had in maintaining the balance of this sort of teaching day in and day out. At times, teachers felt they diluted good reading instruction when they focused on students' interests and texts; or, they became inattentive to cultural relevance when teaching phonics because they did not know how to adapt the instruction culturally. Sometimes it was simply the materials at hand that dictated the reading instruction. What they all focused on, though, was attention to the individual child and being flexible enough to adapt any lesson to the needs of their students.

There are many other studies of teachers who have implemented varied, flexible approaches that focus on individuals, even though they may not have been explicitly designed to attend to both culture and achievement. In one group of studies of teachers of high achieving first graders, teams of researchers (Pressley, Allington, Wharton-McDonald, Collins-Block, & Morrow, 2001; Wharton-McDonald, Pressley, & Hampton, 1998) found that the teachers of the high achieving students often designed their own curricula, borrowing from many different resources to address the needs of the students. They balanced skills instruction with complex literacy tasks. The teachers knew how to adjust and amend group instruction toward the needs of individual students, and they adopted ways to regularly monitor the students' varied progress. They were educated decision makers and superb motivators of children, handling the overlapping events of the classroom with finesse and focus. This body of work on teachers' attention to individual students and their contexts has been a major contribution of the sociocultural perspective in reading. Future research is needed to develop tools and procedures for documenting literacy instructional that is both research-based and culturally responsive, such as the protocol developed by Rightmyer and her colleagues (2008).

Intensive Intervention with Opportunity and Access   The research-based, Vygotskian-based, culturally responsive instruction described above is what most scholars advocate for all learners, yet, extra support for struggling learners is only implied. Some may argue that in classrooms with expert teaching, children do not slip through the cracks. But, in reality, they do. The conditions for teaching in today's schools, with 25 or sometimes many more students assigned to elementary teachers and over 100 or more to middle and high school teachers, weekly monitoring of progress and immediate intervention for the struggling students may be necessary. The intervention could come in the form of additional teaching in the needed area. This often means intensive, daily instruction in small groups (or one-on-one, if that is affordable) for the lagging students before, after, or even during school.

One example of how this approach works in elementary classrooms is described in a book of studies of effective early literacy interventions by Hiebert and Taylor (2000). In one intervention, students who are perceived as lagging behind the rest of the class are targeted early in the school year for an extra reading lesson each day. The teacher begins her day with this group when she is freshest, and while the other students are engaged in meaningful, independent work (reading, research, problem solving). The teacher has students read and re-read, discuss, read more, work on decoding skills, and read more during an intensive 30-minute period. Then, her regular day begins with her usual grouping practices with all her students, again including those students in the intervention group. The intervention group students may graduate from the group after a few weeks or months, depending on what is needed. Other children may be drawn into the group as needed. The key is that the teacher works with the bottom 20% of her class in the morning when she is freshest and during the time when the other students are also freshest and therefore

of sociohistorical psychology (pp. 319–348). New York: Cambridge University Press.

Nieto, S. (1999). *The light in their eyes: Creating multicultural learning communities.* New York: Teachers College Press.

Ogbu, J.U. (2003). *Black American students in an affluent suburb: A study of academic disengagement.* Mahwah, NJ: Erlbaum.

Pearson, P. D., & Stevens, D. (1994). Learning about literacy: A 30-year journey. In R. B. Rudell, M. R. Rudell, & H. Singer (Eds.), *Theoretical models and processes of reading* (pp. 22–43). Newark, DE: International Reading Association.

Portes, P. R. (1999). Social and psychological factors in the academic achievement of children of immigrants: A cultural history puzzle. *American Educational Research Journal, 36,* 489–507.

Powell, R., McIntyre E., & Rightmyer, E.C. (2006). Johnny won't read, and Susie won't either: Reading instruction and student resistance. *Journal of Early Childhood Literacy, 6,* 5–31.

Pressley, M., Allington, R. L., Wharton-McDonald, R., Collins-Block, C., & Morrow, L. (2001). *Learning to read: Lessons from exemplary first-grade classrooms.* New York: Guilford.

Purcell-Gates, V. (1995). *Other people's words: The cycle of low literacy.* Cambridge, MA: Harvard University Press.

Purcell-Gates, V. (1996). Stories, coupons, and the "TV Guide": Relationships between home literacy experiences and emergent literacy knowledge. *Reading Research Quarterly, 31,* 406–428.

Rist, R. C. (1970). Student social class and teacher expectations: The self-fulfilling prophecy in ghetto education. *Harvard Educational Review, 40,* 411–451.

Rogoff, B. (2003). *The cultural nature of human development.* New York: Oxford University Press.

Ross, S. M., Smith, L. J., & Casey, L. P. (1997). Preventing early school failure: Impacts of Success for All on standardized test outcomes, minority group performance, and school effectiveness. *Journal for Education for Students Placed at Risk, 2,* 29–53.

Rothstein, R. (2002). *Class and schools using social, economic, and educational reform to close the black-white achievement gap.* New York: Teachers College Press.

Shanahan, T. (2000). Research synthesis: Making sense of the accumulation of knowledge in reading. In M. L. Kamil, P. B. Mosenthal, P. D. Pearson, & R. Barr (Eds.), *Handbook of reading research* (vol. 3, pp. 209–228). Mahwah, NJ: Erlbaum.

Slavin, R E., Madden, R. A., Karweit, N. L., Livermon, B. J., & Nolan, L. (1990). Success for All: First year outcomes of a comprehensive plan for reforming urban education. *American Educational Research Journal, 27,* 255–278.

Snow, C. E., Burns, M. S., & Griffith, P. (Eds.). (1998). *Preventing reading difficulties in young children.* Washington, DC: National Academy Press.

Stanovich, K. E. (1986). Matthew effects in reading: Some consequences of individual differences in the acquisition of literacy. *Reading Research Quarterly, 21,* 360–406.

Stone, C. (2004). Contemporary approaches to the study of language and literacy development: A call for the integration of perspectives. In C. A. Stone, E. Silliman, B. J. Ehren, & K. Apel (Eds.), *Handbook of*

language and literacy: Development and disorders (pp. 3–24). New York: Guilford.

Street, B. (1985). *Literacy in theory and practice.* New York: Cambridge University Press.

Sulzby, E. (1985). Children's emergent abilities to read favorite storybooks: A developmental study. *Reading Research Quarterly, 20,* 458–481.

Taylor, D., & Dorsey-Gaines, C. (1988). *Growing up literate: Learning from inner-city families.* Portsmouth, NH: Heinemann.

Teale, W. H. (1986). Home background and young children's literacy development. In W. H. Teale & E. Sulzby (Eds.), *Emergent literacy: Writing and reading* (pp. 173–206).Norwood, NJ: Ablex.

Tharp, R. G. (1989). Psychocultural variables and constants: Effects on teaching and learning in schools. *American Psychologist, 44,* 349–359.

Tharp, R. G. (1993). Institutional and social context of educational practices and reform. In E. A. Forman, N. Minick, & C. A. Stone (Eds.), *Contexts for learning: Sociocultural dynamics in children's development* (pp. 269–282). New York: Cambridge University Press.

Tharp, R. G., Estrada, P., Dalton, S. S., & Yamauchi, L. (2000). *Teaching transformed: Achieving excellence, fairness, inclusion, and harmony.* Boulder, CO: Westview Press.

Tharp, R. G., & Gallimore, R. (1993). *Rousing minds to life: Teaching, learning, and schooling in social context.* Cambridge, UK: Cambridge University Press.

Torgesen, J. K. (2002). The prevention of reading difficulties. *Journal of School Psychology, 40,* 22–42.

van Steensel, R. (2006). Relations between socio-cultural factors, the home literacy environment and children's literacy development in the first years of primary education. *Journal of Research in Reading* 29(4), 367–382.

Vygotsky, L. S. (1978). *Mind in society: The development of higher psychological processes.* Cambridge, MA: Harvard University Press.

Vygotsky, L. S. (1987). *Thought and language* (Ed. Alex Kozulin). Cambridge, MA: MIT Press.

Wasik, B. H., & Hendrickson, J. S. (2004). Family literacy practices. In C. A. Stone, E. R. Silliman, B. J. Ehren, & K. Apel (Eds.), *Handbook of language and literacy: Development and disorders* (pp. 154–174). New York: Guilford.

Weinberger, J. (1996). A longitudinal study of children's early literacy experiences at home and later literacy development at home and school. *Journal of Research in Reading, 19,* 14–24.

Weinstein, R. (2004). *Reaching higher: The power of expectations in schooling.* Cambridge, MA: Harvard University Press.

Wells, G. (1987). *The meaning makers: Children learning language and using language to learn.* Portsmouth, NH: Heinemann.

Wertsch, J. V. (1991). *Voices of the mind: A sociocultural approach to mediated action.* Cambridge, MA: Harvard University Press.

Wertsch, J. (1998). *Mind as action.* New York: Oxford University Press.

Wharton-McDonald, R., Pressley, M., & Hampton, J. M. (1998). Literacy instruction in nine first grade classrooms: Teacher characteristics and student achievement. *Elementary School Journal, 99,* 101–128.

Williams, B. (1996). *Closing the achievement gap: A vision for changing beliefs and practices.* Alexandria, VA: Association for Supervision and Curriculum Development.

6

Instructional Texts and the Fluency of Learning Disabled Readers

Shailaja Menon
TextProject

Elfrieda H. Hiebert
University of California, Berkeley

In this chapter, we explore the role played by texts in supporting fluent reading in students, especially those with learning disabilities (LD). Our basic premise is that texts have an important role to play in the acquisition of this knowledge and that, until this role is better understood and recognized, interventions will limp along, working hard to make a difference and often failing to do so. The texts of reading instruction, especially for beginning readers, have increased substantially in difficulty over the past two decades. These shifts, we will demonstrate, particularly have consequences for students with LD. The discrepancy between the proficiency of students with LD and the demands of the text are great, setting students up for continued failure. Further, current textbooks are not based upon an empirical understanding of the kinds of scaffolds needed by beginning or struggling readers to acquire the orthographic proficiency needed for becoming proficient and fluent readers. We describe the empirical basis for a model of text that can be supportive of fluent reading in readers with LD.

Fluency and Students with LD

We begin by reviewing the basic research on reading processes that underlie our hypothesis that carefully constructed texts are important for learning to read fluently, especially for readers with LD. We build our argument by developing a working definition of fluency and its link to proficient reading. Next, we describe difficulties with remediating fluency in older or struggling readers and hypothesize that lack of word recognition automaticity might be a powerful explanation for this pattern. Finally, we draw upon the double deficit hypothesis to suggest that core deficits in acquiring automaticity with word recognition skills might be an important characteristic that distinguishes dysfluent readers from readers with phonological deficits and from their normally achieving peers. Well-designed texts might provide critical scaffolds in helping such students learn to read fluently.

Fluency as a Critical Characteristic of Proficient Reading

Fluency has been defined in various ways (see Wolf & Katzir-Cohen, 2001). For this review, we have chosen Meyer and Felton's (1999) definition of fluency as "the ability to read connected text rapidly, smoothly, effortlessly, and automatically with little conscious attention to the mechanics of reading such as decoding" (p. 284). We selected this definition of reading fluency over others that emphasize comprehension (e.g., Hudson, Lane, & Mercer, 2005) to maintain a distinction between fluent and proficient reading. If proficient reading is accurate reading at an appropriate rate with prosody and deep understanding, then fluent reading is automaticity with the lower level skills that permits reading with deep understanding. Fluency, then, is a critical characteristic of proficient reading and a desired outcome of reading instruction.

While fluency is a multi-dimensional and developmental rather than a unitary construct (Wolf & Katzir-Cohen, 2001), accurate recognition of the visual stimuli presented during reading and the rate of recognizing these stimuli are critical features of fluent reading (Torgesen & Hudson, 2006). These two characteristics of accuracy and rate have been combined into an index of oral reading rate—the number of words accurately identified per minute. Oral reading rate is a significant predictor of comprehension and proficient reading (Chard, Vaughn, & Tyler, 2002; Jenkins, Fuchs, van den Broek, Espin, & Deno, 2003; Schatschneider et al., 2004). Schatschneider and colleagues (2004) reported that oral reading rate accounted for 56% of the variance on the Florida Comprehensive Achievement Test (FCAT). The students in the lowest of five reading levels on the FCAT read at half the rate of students who read on an average level. Among Florida's third-grade students, 22% fell into this group. It is this bottom quartile of students whose needs we speak to in this chapter

Remediating Fluency: The Link to Word Recognition Skills

While critical to proficient reading, fluency appears difficult to remediate. Over an 8-week intervention, Torgesen et al. (2001) reported that third- to fifth-grade students made large gains in phonemic decoding accuracy (2nd to 39th percentile), text reading accuracy (4th to 23rd percentile), and reading comprehension (13th to 27th percentile). Reading fluency scores, however, scarcely changed (3rd to 5th percentile). At a 2-year follow-up, the group was at the 4th percentile in reading fluency. Similarly, in a series of interventions that emphasized increased modeling and practicing of fluent reading, students who had moderate reading disabilities (10th percentile) showed only limited growth in age-based percentile ranking for fluency (Torgesen, Rashotte, Alexander, Alexander, & MacPhee, 2003).

Such results beg the question: Why is fluency so hard to remediate in struggling readers? Torgesen and Hudson (2006) argue that inefficiencies in identifying single sight words account for individual differences in text reading fluency in students with LD. Jenkins et al. (2003) reported that individual differences in students' ability to read isolated words was the most important factor accounting for differences in reading fluency at low levels of fluency. In contrast, differences among students in their performance on a reading comprehension measure accounted for the largest share of variance in reading fluency among the more fluent readers in the sample. In other words, sight word recognition is a critical factor contributing to overall fluency levels of struggling readers.

There are two components to the limitation of sight word vocabularies in dysfluent readers: the range of words that can be recognized by sight (size of sight word lexicon available to the student), and the rate of accurately recognizing these words. The size of sight word lexicon is directly influenced by the amount of accurate reading practice in which students engage. Students who have difficulties with acquiring reading skills spend less overall time reading, such that skilled readers read three times as many words weekly as less-skilled readers (Allington, 1984). These differences begin early and are exacerbated over time, such that students with poor reading skills spend only a fraction of the time reading as students with normally developing reading skills (Cunningham & Stanovich, 1998). This lack of reading practice results in severe limitations in the number of words that students with reading disabilities can recognize automatically (Ehri, 2002) and of which they know the meaning (Stanovich & West, 1989). Further, the amount of *accurate* reading practice is also less for students with LD (Anderson, Evertson, & Brophy, 1979; Sindelar, Monda, & O'Shea, 1990). We will elaborate upon this theme later when describing a model of text as fluency intervention.

As well as having smaller sight word vocabularies, dysfluent readers recognize words more slowly than normally achieving peers. While sight word efficiency has been found to account for 67% of the variance in fluency of students of all reading levels, sight word efficiency and non-word efficiency together accounted for between 68% and 80% of the variance in samples of students in intensive or preventive interventions (Torgesen, Rashotte, & Alexander, 2001). Torgesen, Rashotte, et al. (2001) also reported that the gap between reading fluency and reading accuracy was not as large in the prevention as compared to the remediation samples. This pattern—the more severe the reading disability, the more significant the *rate* of accurately recognizing words in fluent reading—has been confirmed by Cramer and Rosenfield (2008) in a study of fourth-grade readers. Results such as these suggest that it is inefficiency rather than accuracy in word identification that is resistant to remediation. Students with such deficits spiral into a negative feedback loop. They do little reading and end up having a smaller repertoire of sight words, contributing to a further decrease in their overall rate of accurate reading as compared to their more normally achieving peers.

Word Recognition and LD Readers: The Double Deficit Hypothesis

Having established that automaticity with word recognition skills is impaired in many readers with LD, we now briefly examine research on developmental dyslexia to gain insight into the role that texts might play in the remediation of fluency-based problems. Failure to acquire automaticity in lower-level reading processes has long been known to be a significant contributor to dyslexia (Denckla & Rudel, 1976), a finding that spawned a long line of research on rapid automatized naming (RAN) tasks. Naming speed differentiates dyslexic students from average readers and from "garden variety" poor readers (Denckla & Rudel, 1976; Meyer, Wood, Hart, & Felton, 1998). These differences are apparent as early as the beginning of kindergarten and are the most pronounced for letter naming tasks (Wolf, Bally, & Morris, 1986). Further, naming speed is a powerful predictor of reading success and impairments in languages such as German, Dutch, Finnish, and Spanish with more transparent orthographies than English (e.g., Korhonen, 1995). These findings suggest that, when phonological skills play a less important role, naming speed becomes an even stronger predictor of reading performance and is relatively independent of phonological processing skills.

Empirical work and theoretical speculation have raised the possibility that the ability to form, store, and access orthographic representations may account for some of the residual variance in word recognition skills not explained by phonological factors (Cunningham & Stanovich, 1990; Stanovich & West, 1989). This "double deficit" model of reading disabilities (Wolf & Bowers, 1999; Wolf & Katzir-Cohen, 2001) postulates that efficient phonological processing is a necessary, but not sufficient condition for orthographic learning. Phonological awareness and naming speed appear to contribute relatively separately to successful reading, such that the former contributes significantly to word attack skills in reading, while the latter contributes more to the orthographic aspects of word identification (Bowers & Swanson, 1991).

Wolf and Bowers (1999) describe four discrete groups of children based on this classification system: the first group has no deficits; the second and third groups have single deficits in either phonological processing or in naming speed; and the last group has deficits in both phonological processing and naming speed. The latter double deficit group consists of the most impaired readers. Students with phonological deficits will almost certainly end up as dysfluent readers but they might be responsive to interventions that focus on word attack skills or decoding. Students who have a rate deficit or double deficits likely require multi-pronged efforts to compensate for their dysfluent reading skills.

It is probable that neuronal aberrations in visual processing in the brains of dyslexic students lead to a slowing down of lower-level processes that ultimately contribute to a disruption of fluency, particularly in the reading and understanding of connected text. Wolf (1999) hypothesizes that this delayed processing speed could manifest in a number of related ways during reading as "...(1) slower letter-pattern identification; (2) slower naming speed for visual stimuli; (3) delayed induction of common orthographic patterns in written language; and (4) the need for multiple exposures before a letter pattern is adequately represented in the child's repertoire" (p. 17). Ehri and Saltmarsh's (1995) work confirms that sight word learning is significantly different in normal and dyslexic readers, with the latter group being similar to beginning readers in that they process only partial alphabetic information in words. Disabled readers require more trials—approximately nine—to learn words by sight than average or garden variety poor readers who needed between six to seven trials to acquire words by sight.

Additional insight into the pivotal role played by sight word recognition in dyslexics is provided by recent studies using functional brain imaging techniques (fMRI) (e.g., Shaywitz & Shaywitz, 2007). Some adults who were dyslexic as children have compensated by learning to recognize the most familiar words. These compensating readers have more pronounced activity in the occipito-temporal region of their brains—an area of the brain responsible for recognizing words as wholes, rather than by sounding out—as compared to adult dyslexics who do not recognize familiar words. Normal readers, on the other hand, have stronger connections between the part of the brain responsible for the repeated sounding out of words and that responsible for recognizing words as wholes. Normal readers likely first sound out whole words and, over repeated encounters, come to recognize words by sight (Share, 1995), while compensating dyslexics may learn whole words without engaging in analyzing the smaller orthographic patterns within the words (Lovett, 1991).

Contesting the validity of orthographic processing deficits as a separate category of dyslexia, Ziegler and Goswami (2005) suggest that the key difficulty for all readers who have dyslexia lies in the establishment of efficient processing at a small grain size (i.e., at the phoneme-level). Based on an extensive review of the literature on developmental dyslexia across languages, Ziegler and Goswami suggest that children with phonological difficulties may never attain automaticity at the smallest grain sizes, regardless of the orthography being learned. However, when small grain-size correspondences are inconsistent (e.g., English), beginning readers have to learn additional correspondences for larger orthographic units, such as syllables, rimes, or whole words. There are many more orthographic units to learn when consistency is achieved at larger grain sizes, than at smaller grain sizes. For instance, to decode the most frequent 3,000 monosyllabic English words at the level of the rime, a child needs to learn mappings between approximately 600 different orthographic patterns and 400 phonological rimes (Ziegler & Goswami, 2005, p. 19).

Regardless of whether dyslexia is attributed to a single (phonological) deficit or to a double deficit, the findings reviewed in this section lend themselves to suggestions for the texts used in fluency interventions for dysfluent readers. From the vantage point of the double-deficit hypothesis, students with a single phonological deficit who need to develop word attack skills would benefit most from highly decodable texts, students with rate deficits an approach emphasizing automaticity and fluency, and those with double-deficits texts that incorporate both approaches. The results of brain imaging and cross-linguistic studies would lead to the hypothesis that most, if not all, dyslexic readers lack the ability to gain automaticity with smaller grain-sizes (i.e., phonemes), making difficulties with fluent reading more pronounced in orthographies such as English where the units of smaller grain sizes are inconsistent. Texts that aid in compensating for this deficit would need to provide opportunities to acquire automaticity with units of larger grain sizes (i.e., rimes, whole words) that appear more amenable to compensation than individual phonemes. We will develop these ideas in a later section on texts as fluency interventions. Prior to doing that, we examine what is known about the features of current texts and how these texts match with proficiencies of struggling readers.

The Task of Current Texts

In the previous section, we established that students with LD have critical needs with developing fluency and that gaining automaticity with larger orthographic grain sizes is key to achieving fluency for such readers. In this section, we ask: How do these understandings match with the texts currently available in American classrooms? Analyses of the features of texts for beginning readers have a fairly long history (see Chall, 1967/1983). We are not going to review the historical nature of these changes from texts controlled by high-frequency words, to texts selected for their literary quality, to (most recently) texts controlled by phonemes, since these patterns have been described elsewhere (Hiebert, 2005). What we focus on here is the match between text features and the needs of readers with LD—that is, how well do these texts support automaticity with word identification for these readers?

Features of Current Texts Literature-based anthologies and texts based on predictable sentence patterns were the mainstays of American reading instruction in the 1990s (Hoffman et al., 1994). Hoffman, Roser, Patterson, Salas, and Pennington (2001) investigated first-graders' ability to read texts selected for their literary engagingness and found that a full 40% of the students were not highly accurate with any of the texts, including those at the earliest levels. Cunningham et al. (2005) analyzed the supports provided for word recognition learning in a set of the texts that Hoffman et al. described as prototypical of literary engagingness. Cunningham et al. concluded that these texts provided only moderate support for word recognition instruction and almost none for decoding instruction in the use of onsets and rimes. Johnston's (2000) analyses of student performances with predictable texts confirm that, even after at least 10 readings of a text, most beginning readers learned only 4%–5% of unfamiliar words.

As the shortcomings of predictable texts for beginning readers were recognized, state-wide adoptions mandated decodable texts—texts that present only words with grapheme-phoneme correspondences that have been introduced in lessons in the accompanying teachers' guides of a reading program. Following the Texas mandates for such texts, Foorman, Francis, Davidson, Harm, & Griffin (2004) divided first-grade textbooks from six programs into six instructional blocks and analyzed phonics patterns, high-frequency word status, and the number of repetitions within and across these blocks. They reported that as much as 70%–84% of the words appeared only a single time across the instructional blocks of the six different programs. Foorman et al. concluded their analyses with the question of how first graders can be expected to acquire letter-sound correspondence knowledge when only 20% of the words in texts are repeated two or three times.

Hiebert (2005) analyzed the texts of a prominent basal program (one of two that Chall (1967/1983) identified as a prototypical mainstream basal reading program) over a 40-year period from 1962 to 2000. From 1983 to 1993, the rate of new, unique words increased substantially in both first- and second-grade texts and it stayed at that rate even with the move to decodable texts in 2000. The percentage of words falling within the 1000 most highly frequent words fell from 60% at the end of first grade in the 1962 copyright, to 37% in the 2000 copyright of the program. Exposure to this set of highly frequent words would presumably improve the rate of word recognition of dysfluent readers. Subsequently, Hiebert (2008) analyzed the 2007/2008 copyright of the same prominent basal reading program that she had previously examined for shifts across time. The profile of linguistic information, at least with regard to high frequency words, flattened out by the middle of first grade—that is, these texts paid no more attention to the presentation of

highly frequent words than the texts of later grades. The decodability of rare words at first grade was somewhat lower than that in the higher grades, indicating that more of the rare words in the grade-six texts were multisyllabic than in the first-grade text. Even in the first-grade texts, however, many monosyllabic words with complex and variant vowel patterns were present.

Features of Current Texts and Reading Proficiencies of Students with LD As well as analyzing features of current texts, Hiebert (2008) compared the word-level features of current texts with students' performances on the sight word efficiency sub-test of the Test of Word Reading Efficiency (TOWRE) (Torgesen, Wagner, & Rashotte, 1999). The sight word efficiency sub-test of the TOWRE assesses students' recognition of a particular set of words within a 45-second period. Hiebert established that the recognition of approximately 30 words served as a benchmark in terms of content. Up to this point, words came exclusively from the 1,000 most-frequent words; after this point, less common, multisyllabic words became prominent. Hiebert reported that students at the 90th percentile attained that benchmark in Grade 1, students at the 50th percentile in Grade 3, and those at the 10th percentile had yet to attain this level by Grade 6. Next, Hiebert compared the tasks of the texts of a basal reading program to the performance patterns on the TOWRE. Already at Grade 1, approximately 20 of every 100 running words were moderately frequent or rare words, falling beyond the 1,000 most-frequent words.

Foorman et al.'s (2004) and Hiebert's (2005) analyses of the decodable text-based programs reveal that they have several problematic aspects, especially in light of the proficiencies and needs of learners with LD. First, these texts are based on the assumption that the systematic presentation of individual phonemes will aid with word recognition efforts by beginning and struggling readers. Yet, we have been unable to locate any large-scale interventions that attest to the efficacy of this text type over others. Jenkins, Peyton, Sanders, and Vadasy (2004) assigned at-risk first graders to tutoring in more or less decodable texts, and failed to find any post-test differences between the two groups on an array of decoding, word reading, passage reading, and comprehension measures.

Second, the rapid pace of introduction of new linguistic information in such programs is alarming. A textbook's accessibility is decided solely on the basis of the match between phonemes in the student texts and their appearance in the teacher's manuals. As a result, even the kindergarten components of basal reading programs are considerably more ramped up than the programs of the late 1980s (Hiebert, 2008). Whereas the kindergarten component of the late 1980s copyright of a basal reading program had no student texts, the current copyright requires students to apply at least 30 different grapheme-phoneme correspondences without any seeming mandate on the number of repetitions of these phonemes within or across texts (Hiebert, 2008). Third, there is no developmental progression in the presentation of linguistic information that is discernible in these programs. That is, the demands of second-grade texts are not substantially different than the demands of fourth-grade texts, and so on. Finally, even in "decodable" textbook programs, the texts of the anthologies shift to authentic children's literature after the first semester of first grade. Literature-based programs have high vocabulary loads, low repetition of words and word patterns, and no clear progression in the word-level curriculum across individual grade levels or across grade levels (Hiebert, Martin, & Menon, 2005).

Current textbook programs appear to be based on the assumption that the speed with which phonemes are presented doesn't have to be controlled or developmentally sensitive. If a high percentage of phonemes can be covered in kindergarten, then more interesting texts can be presented in the anthologies (and decodable texts) at an earlier point. The evidence that has been reviewed suggests that this assumption may be contributing to a considerable gap between the tasks of the texts and students' reading proficiencies, especially those of students with LD. Irrespective of whether literature-based anthologies or decodable texts are the focus of the analysis, approximately 40% of the students are unsuccessful on these texts—the percentage of students who fail to reach the basic reading benchmark on the National Assessment of Educational Progress (Perie, Grigg, & Donahue, 2005). How can texts be designed to be more considerate of the instructional needs of these students (and of their teachers), especially as related to acquiring automaticity with word recognition? What role have texts traditionally played in fluency interventions and what role could they play in future efforts to develop fluency? Answers to these questions are considered in the following section.

Texts as Fluency Interventions

In this section, we take a closer look at the role of texts within the repeated reading approach that has been identified as facilitating fluency (NICHD, 2000). We focus in particular on the recommendation that difficult, even frustration level, texts be used for repeated reading (Kuhn & Stahl, 2003). Drawing upon insights from our review and knowledge of dyslexic readers, we ask: How can texts be used to create generalizable fluency gains for such students?

Repeated Reading Revisited   While a number of reviews are available that consider the efficacy of fluency interventions (Chard et al., 2002; Kuhn & Stahl, 2003; Meyer & Felton, 1999; Yang, 2006), the role of texts is rarely examined systematically either in reviews or the interventions themselves. In this section, we examine the repeated reading research with an eye on two dimensions of this research: (a) its effectiveness in developing fluency for struggling readers, and (b) insights into the role played by texts in instruction.

The repeated reading approach has its roots in the LaBerge and Samuels (1974) model of information process-

ing that suggests that readers must simultaneously recognize the words in text while constructing meaning. As readers have a limited amount of attention available for any given task, the amount of attention spent on a single process means that less attention is available for the other process. Similarly, Perfetti's (1977) verbal efficiency model theorizes that a slow rate of word recognition obstructs ability to hold large units of text in working memory. Aiding students to achieve automaticity with word recognition processes will free up resources for comprehension. Automaticity can be best achieved through successive exposures to print.

The repeated reading approach is the instructional instantiation of this line of thinking (Samuels, 1979). The basic repeated reading approach calls for the reading of text at a student's instructional level repeatedly, until a desired rate of reading (measured in words per minute) is achieved. This is followed by reading another passage at the same level repeatedly, and so on. Variations of this method include repeated reading with a model versus without. Moderate effect sizes have been reported in meta-analyses of repeated reading studies (e.g., Chard et al., 2002; Meyer & Felton, 1999; NICHD, 2000; Yang, 2006).

Repeated Reading and Readers with LD   Most of the repeated reading studies have been with populations of average readers (second grade and above) or older, struggling readers (Kuhn & Stahl, 2003). Two recent reviews have focused specifically on the efficacy of the repeated reading technique with readers with LD. Based on 24 published and unpublished studies conducted with students with LD, Chard et al. (2002) concluded that repeated reading was effective with this population of readers. The effective interventions that they reviewed included explicit modeling of fluent reading, multiple opportunities to repeatedly read familiar text independently and with corrective feedback, and performance criteria for increasing the difficulty of texts. Yang (2006), in a meta-analysis of repeated reading studies, concluded that interventions involving remedial readers and students with disabilities produced larger effects than interventions involving normal readers. Yang observed that these larger effects could reflect longer training periods and/or easier texts and assessments in interventions for students with LD than for average students.

While repeated reading appears to have potential as an intervention technique for readers with LD, much remains to be understood about whether it may need to be adjusted to optimally address the unique needs of these children. In their review of fluency interventions, Kuhn and Stahl (2003) note an irony in that repeated reading was developed as a technique to aid the automatic recognition of words, yet, while effective in improving a number of reading related skills including accuracy, rate, and comprehension at the passage level, it has *not* been effective in improving the rapid recognition of isolated words. It is possible that average and poor readers who are non-dyslexic (such as those included in many of the studies reviewed by Kuhn & Stahl, 2003) are able to use higher-order semantic and syntactic connections to achieve better rate and accuracy through the repeated reading of passages in spite of not being able to recognize isolated words faster. This leaves open the question of whether dyslexic readers, who struggle with word analysis at a small grain size and compensate by acquiring whole sight words (as described in an earlier section), are at a disadvantage with the repeated reading method, if it is currently not effective in facilitating isolated word recognition. We would hope that the fluency gains achieved on one set of passages will hold for both near and far transfer tasks. This premise has yet to be demonstrated with dyslexic readers through the repeated reading method.

Repeated Reading: Does Text Difficulty Matter? Kuhn and Stahl (2003) concluded their review on fluency interventions with the statement: "Some have argued that having children read easy text improves fluency...but it seems that the most successful approaches involved children reading instructional-level text or even text at the frustration level with strong support..." (pp. 17–18). This conclusion has been cited frequently, including in documents aimed at practitioners and policy makers (e.g., Snow, Griffin, & Burns, 2007). Consequently, we examined the studies reviewed by Kuhn and Stahl to examine the basis for their conclusion.

Only two studies in their review focused on the efficacy of repeated readings over control or baseline conditions and attended to text features or difficulty. The first was Mathes and Fuchs's (1993) comparison of the use of easy and difficult texts. Neither text difficulty nor repeated reading made significant differences. In the second study, Rashotte and Torgesen (1985) compared the use of texts with a high overlap of words with texts with a low overlap of words, and found that texts with a high overlap of words facilitated the development of fluency more than did texts with a low overlap of words.

An examination of the remaining studies showed that approximately half (55%) employed texts that were at the students' instructional levels (i.e., "easier" text); 32% of studies used texts that were at grade level or above students' instructional levels (i.e., "difficult" text); and information on text level was missing from the remainder of the studies. Of the studies that used easier texts, approximately two thirds reported significant gains over time for the treatment group. Approximately 70% of the studies using difficult texts reported gains over time for the treatment group. In other words, gains for treatment group over the control group was the predominant trend, irrespective of the difficulty level of the texts used. It should be noted that many of the studies that reported significant gains did not compare gains to a criterion. Using gains as a measure of success, independent of set criteria, is problematic and can be misleading. We are left with less than conclusive evidence on the role of text difficulty from this review.

Kuhn and Stahl (2003) also cited a study from their own line of research on fluency—Fluency-Oriented Reading Instruction (FORI)—as support for the argument that difficult texts work better than easier texts (later published as Stahl and Heubach, 2005). In FORI, students read grade-level texts repeatedly with assistance (i.e., teachers, peers, aides, parents). Overall, students in the FORI intervention made a 2-year gain on an informal reading inventory over a school year. Even with this instructional support, students who were reading below primer level did not make much progress. It is likely that these students are the ones who are the focus of this chapter—students with LD. Further, a closer examination of the texts in the Stahl and Heubach implementation indicates that students who made gains rarely read texts on which they had less than 85% accuracy and very often read texts in the 90%–92% accuracy range— that is, texts within or close to their instructional levels. This begs the question: would larger gaps in accuracy levels be bridgeable by the considerable instructional support described in the FORI intervention? It is conceivable that students with LD will have accuracy levels of far less than the average of 85% accuracy on grade-level texts reported in the FORI studies.

Even more pertinently, is it realistic to expect that the considerable instructional support that was available to poor readers in the FORI intervention would be available to poor readers in typical American classrooms? Swanson, Wexler, and Vaughn (2009), in a syntheses of instructional research, report that students with LD are engaged in oral reading from between 1.1 minutes and 7.47 minutes in regular classrooms. The range is only a little higher in the resource room: 4.4 minutes to 13.4 minutes. Clearly, this is a far cry from the levels of text reading and instructional support described in the FORI intervention. Such findings suggest that the reality of text reading conditions in American classrooms require consideration when it is recommended that poor readers be given difficult texts (Kuhn & Stahl, 2003).

Further, it is a fairly well-established pedagogical principle that task completion, on-task behavior, and task comprehension are related to the difficulty level of the task (Gickling & Armstrong, 1978). Vygotsky (1978) proposed that learners are best able to learn when working in their zones of proximal development (ZPD) with the help of an adult or a more capable peer. It is possible that this ZPD (or, instructional level) extends to as low as 85% accuracy on certain texts for certain students with the right kinds of instructional support. Yet, to dismiss the existence of such a zone would be foolhardy. The difficulty level of the text read by students may be reciprocally linked to the amount and kinds of instructional support available—within certain limits set by the ZPDs of students. We would argue that current evidence that instructional support alone can compensate for text difficulty is sparse. Further validation is needed before such a conclusion becomes the accepted wisdom of the field.

We located several studies that were not included in the Kuhn and Stahl (2003) review. Young and Bowers (1995) evaluated the impact of text difficulty on oral reading fluency in fifth-grade average and poor readers. Poor readers were significantly slower than average readers on even the easiest stories, even when accuracy was not a factor. Further, significant declines in reading rate, accuracy, and prosody occurred with each increase in text difficulty. Similar findings were reported by O'Connor, Bell, Harty, Larkin, Sackor, and Zigmond (2002), who studied the effects of texts that were matched for reading- or grade-level on the growth of poor readers' reading ability over 18 weeks of one-to-one tutoring. Forty-six third to fifth graders, including 25 with disabilities, were assigned randomly to one of two tutoring approaches or a control condition. Between approaches, the only significant difference was oral reading fluency, which favored students who read material at their reading level. Students who began with lower fluency made stronger gains in text matched to reading level; students with higher fluency profited from both treatments. Cramer and Rosenfield (2008) reached a similar conclusion in studying fourth graders' reading of texts at their independent, instructional, and frustrational levels, finding a positive, significant correlation between word recognition accuracy and rate. Further, students with LD have a faster rate of word identification on mastery-level as compared to instructional-level texts (Sindelar et al., 1990). The findings of this handful of studies lend support to the recommendation that poor readers should be given texts for fluency training with which they are fairly accurate.

Creating Generalizable Gains　　Fluency interventions will ultimately be as successful as the transfer they facilitate—is the automaticity acquired on one set of texts transferable to other texts and other contexts? Multiple studies attest to the effectiveness of repeated reading as a fluency intervention (typically over business-as-usual reading instruction) (NICHD, 2000). But not only have the effect sizes rarely been higher than moderate (NICHD, 2000; Yang, 2006), it is not entirely clear what these effect sizes represent. Automaticity with word recognition processes was the originally hypothesized mechanism (Samuels, 1979), but as Kuhn and Stahl (2003) noted, the irony is that word recognition in isolation does not become faster or more automatic with repeated reading as it is practiced today. An alternative hypothesis is that repeated reading increases the total amount of text read and that increases to print exposure alone contribute to fluency development. We examine the evidence for this idea in the following section.

Increasing the total amount of text read: Repeated Reading and the self-teaching hypothesis.　　Robust evidence indicates that print exposure alone contributes to the acquisition of reading-specific knowledge. An early elaboration of this view was Jorm and Share's (1983) self-teaching hypothesis that suggested that beginning readers learn (in part) to read by successful decoding encounters with novel words (Share, 1995). As the reader encounters and successfully decodes familiar orthographic patterns and then whole words, these orthographic patterns and whole words are added to the sight lexicon of the reader, such that the reader eventually responds automatically to these familiar orthographic configurations. This happens through a process of phonological recoding of the information present in the orthographic representations encountered in text. Share (2004) suggests that the first encounter with a novel word results in the most learning, giving as evidence the letter-by-letter strategy of third graders on the first encounter with a novel word and their more fluent recognition on subsequent encounters.

Drawing upon connectionist models (e.g., Ehri, 2002), Hiebert and Martin (2008) have theorized that the initial encounter with a novel word or orthographic pattern may form partial representations in the reader's memory, while subsequent encounters with the same word or pattern may enable a refinement of that representation. While in shallower orthographies, such as Hebrew, increasing the number of repetitions of the target word did not result in greater accuracy of word identification on the orthographic measure, in deeper orthographies, such as English, more exposures to target words may be needed to form detailed orthographic representations within memory (Sindelar et al., 1990).

The question of whether orthographic processing skills are entirely parasitic upon phonological processing abilities or is a relatively independent ability is an open one. Evidence from a long line of research led by Stanovich and Cunningham (e.g., Cunningham & Stanovich, 1998) provides support for the dual processing model underlying the double deficit hypothesis of dyslexia. Stanovich and West (1989) demonstrated that exposure to print alone was a significant predictor of variance in the orthographic processing ability of adults, after factoring out the variance contributed by phonological processing abilities. Given that print exposure is an environmentally mediated variable, the authors concluded that differences in orthographic processing skills were not simply indirect products of differences in phonological processing ability. This result has since been validated with children (Cunningham & Stanovich, 1990). Based on an extensive review, Cunningham and Stanovich (1998) concluded that the primary contribution of print exposure to word recognition is via the build up of the orthographic lexicon and is only insignificantly correlated to phonological processing skills. It is highly possible that a certain level of phonemic awareness is necessary before print exposure can foster the growth of orthographic knowledge. Once this critical milestone of phonemic awareness is achieved, however, exposure to print can contribute relatively independently to the growth of orthographic processing skills. What these findings imply for fluency development is that orthographic deficits in dyslexic readers cannot be remediated via phonological training alone. Many dysfluent readers may need specific help to acquire the orthographic representations of English.

Attention to orthographic features of text.　　If students learn (in part) to read by successful encounters with print, it stands to reason that what they encounter—the linguistic content of the texts—will matter in what they learn and how well they learn it. Only a handful of studies speak to this issue, and all of them establish that this is, indeed, the case.

As already described, Rashotte and Torgesen (1985) compared repeated readings of a sample of dysfluent readers under different text conditions. When texts had few shared words, repeated reading was not more effective for improving speed than an equivalent amount of nonrepetitive reading. Rashotte and Torgesen's study raises the possibility that Kuhn and Stahl's (2003) conclusions are true of repeated reading *as it is currently practiced* where little, or no attention is paid to the linguistic content in the selection of texts. Indeed, in a comparison of wide reading (comparable amount of reading but with different texts) and repeated reading of the same texts, Kuhn et al. (2006) reported that wide reading was as effective as repeated reading.

Hiebert et al. (2005) found that only approximately 28% of the words were shared across the first-grade texts of two mainstream basal reading programs, a majority of which belonged to the 300 most highly frequent words. Such low word overlap across texts likely encourages highly localized word recognition skills (restricted to the text on which repeated readings was performed), such that the rate of word recognition beyond a given text is not enhanced significantly. This could be especially true of disabled readers, who have core deficits with establishing efficient word recognition skills.

To address the need for designing texts supportive of word recognition for beginning and struggling readers, Hiebert (2002) created the *Text Elements by Task* (TExT) model. The model attends to two aspects of text, the first of which is cognitive load—the number of different words that need to be recognized within a text. The logic of attending to the repetition of words within texts is similar to that of repeated readings of texts: when fewer words are repeated more often, chances for developing automaticity with these words becomes greater. Summarizing results on fluency interventions conducted with readers with LD, Lovett (1991) concluded that "...when the attention and practice allocated individual words is increased by including a large number of consolidation and practice opportunities in training, the learning of disabled readers appears to be facilitated" (p. 302). The second component is linguistic content which refers to knowledge about words and word components. The frequency of a word's appearance in written English is one aspect of linguistic content. A second consists of common, consistent vowel patterns such as the orthographic representations with larger grain sizes (such as rimes) (Ziegler & Goswami, 2005).

Menon and Hiebert (2005) conducted a 15-week intervention for first graders with books that had been reordered to conform approximately to the guidelines of the TExT model. Intervention students at all levels—struggling, average, and high—performed significantly higher than comparison students on reading of texts and of isolated words in word lists.

Extending Menon and Hiebert's model of text, Compton, Appleton, and Hosp (2004) conducted a 15-week study with 204 average achieving and 44 low achieving second graders. The readability, decodability, percentage of high frequency words and of multisyllabic words, and average words per sentence were established for each text. Accuracy of text reading was uniquely predicted by the percentage of high frequency words in the text, whereas both the percentage of high frequency words and text decodability made unique contributions to variance in text-reading fluency. The relationship between text-leveling variables and reading performance was similar for both average and low groups.

In a subsequent study, Hiebert and Fisher (2006) assigned first-grade English Language Learners to one of three groups: Decodable texts created on a phoneme model, texts that systematically introduced phonetically regular, high-frequency, and high-imagery words, or typical classroom decodable texts based on a phoneme model. Students who received the "multiple-criteria" texts had a gain of 2.8 words correct per minute for every week of instruction as compared to 2.4 words gained by students who read the experimental decodable texts and 2.0 words per week by classroom decodable texts.

These findings represent an emerging line of research that considers whether text features can be carefully selected to optimize generalizable fluency gains, especially for beginning and struggling readers. It is not our intent to suggest that text selection alone can succeed in creating significant fluency gains for struggling readers. However, we believe that there is sufficient evidence to argue that text is one of several critical variables that contribute to fluency. There is additional evidence that transfer effects during repeated reading with predictable texts can be facilitated by explicit word study (Johnston, 2000). Further, even when using texts with a high percentage of shared words, assisted reading conditions may produce stronger gains than unassisted conditions (Young, Bowers, & MacKinnon, 1996), pointing to the importance of high quality instruction along with well designed texts.

Implications for a model of text. The evidence presented in this section has multiple implications for a model of text for beginning and/or struggling readers. Since the self-teaching hypothesis suggests that successful decoding encounters with novel words leads to the formation of stable orthographic representations, both adequate exposure to print and successful encounters with print are critical. It also suggests that multiple exposures to novel words are needed to form stable orthographic representations in deep orthographies (e.g., English). We are challenged to think about how this process would differ for students with LD who possibly have core deficits in acquiring extensive, automatic sight word lexicons, and may, additionally, have difficulties with phonologically recoding the subsyllabic linguistic features of words. For such students, the self teaching mechanism may not work as it does in normal readers. Repetition of words and larger word chunks in texts may be even more critical than for their average achieving peers. The current instructional solution—decodable texts that are based on the introduction of individual phonemic elements—may not be a good match for the abilities of these readers, given their difficulties with fine-grained phonological analysis. At the same time, the typical version of repeated reading may not be optimally adjusted to the needs of dysfluent readers, given the lack of attention to text features that may facilitate transfer and automaticity.

Conclusions

Torgesen (1998) noted that work on teaching decoding skills has been accomplished; now attention needs to turn to whether fluency can be amenable to intervention. A decade later, the question of how to move beyond effective decoding interventions to effective fluency interventions for struggling readers remains perplexing. This question has been the focus of this chapter, particularly as it pertains to the role of instructional texts in supporting fluency development in readers with LDs. We have delved into the empirical and theoretical literature to construct an argument that links several key ideas: (a) English is a language with low orthographic consistency; (b) many readers with LD have specific orthographic processing deficits linked to inefficiencies in the rate of word identification, suggesting that remediation should go beyond teaching word attack skills to facilitating automaticity and fluency with word recognition processes; (c) current American instructional textbooks fail to provide supportive practice with connected text to beginning and struggling readers; and (d) fluency interventions, such as those involving the repeated reading of text, also pay scant attention to the features of the texts. Taken together, these ideas point to a critical gap in current attempts at supporting and remediating fluency acquisition.

While some have argued that the focus should be on the nature of high-quality instruction and not on curricular materials, Ziegler and Goswami (2005) argue that "The slower average rate of learning to read in English does not seem to occur because of variations in teaching method.... Rather, it seems due to the relatively low orthographic consistency of English" (p. 13). This low orthographic consistency makes it critical that teachers are not asked to compensate for poorly constructed texts. If print exposure significantly contributes to reading skills (Cunningham & Stanovich, 1998), then it stands to reason that closer attention needs to be paid to *what* students are reading, particularly the orthographic features of texts. Yet, as described in this chapter, there have been large and dramatic shifts in the textbooks of reading instruction—shifts that have gone largely unexamined, and with particular consequences for students with LD.

Policy makers view decodable texts as the key to providing struggling readers with texts that scaffold the acquisition of word recognition skills. Yet two aspects of decodable texts may be problematic for dysfluent readers: the unit of emphasis (the individual phoneme) and the pace of introduction of new linguistic information. The research reviewed here suggests that orthographic units with larger grain sizes

might be more accessible to readers with LD than individual phonemes. Considering the features of the instructional texts read by beginning and struggling readers is especially critical in light of the difficulties investigators have had in remediating fluency. Torgesen and Hudson (2006) have argued compellingly that attempts at remediating fluency must aim at closing the gap in the sight word vocabularies between struggling readers and their peers. Repeated reading is moderately successful at remediating fluency but it has proved to be ineffective thus far in remediating the rate of isolated word recognition skills (Kuhn & Stahl, 2003)—an area of particular need for readers with LD, many of whom struggle with automaticity in word recognition.

The question remains: How can repeated reading be modified so that the primary locus of its effect shifts to aiding automaticity in word reading efficiency? Supporting the development of sight word lexicons seems to be the critical missing link at present in classrooms and in fluency intervention efforts involving repeated readings of text. We have attempted to demonstrate in this chapter that attending to the orthographic features of the texts used in fluency interventions (and in the regular classroom) is crucial to this effort. Along with Torgesen and Hudson (2006), we believe that "...effective interventions for students struggling with reading fluency must substantially increase the number of opportunities these students have to accurately practice reading previously unknown words" (p. 137).

References

Allington, R. L. (1984). The reading instruction provided readers of different reading abilities. *Elementary School Journal, 83,* 549–559.

Anderson, L. M., Evertson, C. M., & Brophy, J. E. (1979). An experimental study of effective teaching in first-grade reading group. *The Elementary School Journal, 79*(4), 193–223.

Bowers, P. G., & Swanson, L. B. (1991). Naming speed deficits in reading disability: Multiple measures of a singular process. *Journal of Experimental Child Psychology, 51,* 195–219.

Chall, J. S. (1967/1983). *Learning to read: The great debate* (3rd ed.). Fort Worth, TX: Harcourt Brace.

Chard, D., Vaughn, S., & Tyler, B. J. (2002). A synthesis of research on effective interventions for building reading fluency with elementary students with learning disabilities. *Journal of Learning Disabilities, 35,* 386–406.

Compton, D. L., Appleton, A. C., & Hosp, M. K. (2004). Exploring the relationship between text-leveling systems and reading accuracy and fluency in second-grade students who are average and poor decoders. *Learning Disabilities Research & Practice, 19*(3), 176–184.

Cramer, K., & Rosenfield, S. (2008). Effect of degree of challenge on reading performance. *Reading & Writing Quarterly, 24,* 119–137.

Cunningham, A. E., & Stanovich, K. E. (1990). Assessing print exposure and orthographic processing skill in children: A quick measure of reading experience. *Journal of Educational Psychology, 82,* 733–740.

Cunningham, A. E., & Stanovich, K. E. (1998). What reading does for the mind. *American Educator, 22*(1-2), 8–15.

Cunningham, J. W., Spadorcia, S. A., Erickson, K. A., Koppenhaver, D. A., Sturm, J. M., & Yoder, D. E. (2005). Investigating the instructional supportiveness of leveled texts. *Reading Research Quarterly, 40,* 410–427.

Denckla, M. B., & Rudel, R. G. (1976). Rapid automatized naming (R.A.N.): Dyslexia differentiated from other learning disabilities. *Neuropsychologia, 14,* 471–479.

Ehri, L. C. (2002). Sight word learning. In B. Blachman (Ed.), *Foundations of reading acquisition and dyslexia: Implications for early Intervention* (pp. 163–190). Mahwah, NJ: Erlbaum.

Ehri, L. C., & Saltmarsh, J. (1995). Beginning readers outperform older disabled readers in learning to read words by sight. *Reading and Writing: An Interdisciplinary Journal, 7*, 295–326.

Foorman, B. R., Francis, D. J., Davidson, K. C., Harm, M. W., & Griffin, J. (2004). Variability in text features in six grade 1 basal reading programs. *Scientific Studies of Reading, 8*, 167–197.

Gickling, E. E., & Armstrong, D. L. (1978). Levels of instructional difficulty as related to on-task behavior, task completion, and comprehension. *Journal of Learning Disabilities, 11*(9), 32–39.

Hiebert, E. H. (2002). Standards, assessment, and text difficulty. In A. E. Farstrup & S. J. Samuels (Eds.), *What research has to say about reading instruction* (3rd ed., pp. 337–369). Newark, DE: International Reading Association.

Hiebert, E. H. (2005). State reform policies and the reading task for first graders. *Elementary School Journal, 105*, 245–266.

Hiebert, E. H. (2008). The (mis)match between texts and students who depend on schools to become literate. In E. H. Hiebert & M. Sailors (Eds.), *Finding the right texts for beginning and struggling readers: Research-based solutions* (pp. 1–20). New York: Guilford.

Hiebert, E. H., & Fisher, C. W. (2006, July 7). *A comparison of two types of text on the fluency of first-grade English language learners.* Paper presented at the annual meeting of the Society for the Scientific Study of Reading, Vancouver, BC.

Hiebert, E. H., & Martin, L. A. (2008). Repetition of words: The forgotten variable in texts for beginning and struggling readers. In E. H. Hiebert & M. Sailors (Eds.), *Finding the right texts for beginning and struggling readers: Research-based solutions* (pp. 1–21). New York: Guilford.

Hiebert, E. H., Martin, L. A., & Menon, S. (2005). Are there alternatives in reading textbooks? An examination of three beginning reading programs. *Reading and Writing Quarterly, 21*, 7–32.

Hoffman, J. V., McCarthey, S. J., Abbott, J., Christian, C., Corman, L., Curry, C., et al. (1994). So what's new in the new basals? A focus on first grade. *Journal of Reading Behavior, 26*, 47–73.

Hoffman, J., Roser, N., Patterson, E., Salas, R., & Pennington, J. (2001). Text leveling and little books in first-grade reading. *Journal of Literacy Research, 33*, 507–528.

Hudson, R. F., Lane, H. B., & Mercer, C. D. (2005). Writing prompts: The role of various priming conditions in the compositional fluency of developing writers. *Reading and Writing: An Interdisciplinary Journal, 18*, 473–495.

Jenkins, J. R., Fuchs, L. S., van den Broek, P., Espin, C., & Deno, S. L. (2003). Sources of individual differences in reading comprehension and reading fluency. *Journal of Educational Psychology, 95*, 719–729.

Jenkins, J. R., Peyton, J. A., Sanders, E. A., & Vadasy, P. F. (2004). Effects of reading decodable texts in supplemental first-grade tutoring. *Scientific Studies of Reading, 8*, 53–85.

Johnston, F. R. (2000). Word learning in predictable text. *Journal of Educational Psychology, 92*(2), 248–255.

Jorm, A., & Share, D. (1983). Phonological recoding and reading acquisition. *Applied Psycholinguistics, 4*, 103–147.

Korhonen, T. T. (1995). The persistence of rapid naming problems in children with reading disablties: A nine-year follow-up. *Journal of Learning Disabilities, 28*(4), 232–239.

Kuhn, M. R., & Stahl, S. A. (2003). Fluency: A review of developmental and remedial practices. *Journal of Educational Psychology, 95*, 3–21.

Kuhn, M. R., Schwanenflugel, P. J., Morris, R. D., Morrow, L. M., Woo, D., Meisinger, B., et al. (2006). Teaching children to become fluent and automatic readers. *Journal of Literacy Research 38,* 357–387.

LaBerge, D., & Samuels, S. J. (1974). Toward a theory of automatic information processing in reading. *Cognitive Psychology, 6,* 293–323.

Lovett, M. W. (1991). Reading, writing, and remediation: perspectives on the dyslexic learning disability from remedial outcome data. *Learning and Individual Differences, 3*(4), 295–305.

Mathes, P. G., & Fuchs, L. S. (1993). Peer-mediated reading instruction in special education resource rooms. *Learning Disabilities Research and Practice, 8,* 233–243.

Menon, S., & Hiebert, E. H. (2005). A comparison of first graders' reading with little books or literature-based basal anthologies. *Reading Research Quarterly, 40*(1), 12–38.

Meyer, M. S., & Felton, R. H. (1999). Repeated reading to enhance fluency: Old approaches and new directions. *Annals of Dyslexia, 49,* 283–306.

Meyer, M. S., Wood, F. B., Hart, L. A., & Felton, R. H. (1998). The selective predictive values in rapid automatized naming within poor readers. *Journal of Learning Disabilities, 3,* 106–117.

National Institute of Child Health and Human Development (NICHD). (2000). *Report of the National Reading Panel. Teaching children to read: An evidence-based assessment of the scientific research literature on reading and its implications for reading instruction* (NIH Publication No. 00-4769). Washington, DC: U.S. Government Printing Office.

O'Connor, R. E., Bell, K. M., Harty, K. R., Larkin, L. K., Sackor, S. M., & Zigmond, N. (2002). Teaching reading to poor readers in the intermediate grades: A comparison of text difficulty. *Journal of Educational Psychology, 94*(3), 474–485.

Perfetti, C. A. (1977). Language comprehension and fast decoding: Some psycholinguistic prerequisites for skilled reading comprehension. In J. T. Guthrie (Ed.), *Cognition, curriculum, and comprehension* (pp. 20–41). Newark, DE: International Reading Association.

Perie, M., Grigg, W. S., & Donahue, P. L. (2005). *The nation's report card: Fourth-grade reading 2005.* Washington, DC: U.S. Department of Education, Institute of Education Sciences.

Rashotte, C. A., & Torgesen, J. K. (1985). Repeated reading and reading fluency in learning-disabled children. *Reading Research Quarterly, 20,* 180–188.

Samuels, S. J. (1979). The method of repeated readings. *The Reading Teacher, 32,* 403–408.

Schatschneider, C., Buck, J., Torgesen, J. K., Wagner, R. K., Hassler, L., Hecht, S., et al. (2004). *A multivariate study of factors that contribute to individual differences in performance on the Florida Comprehensive Reading Assessment Test.* Technical Report # 5, Florida Center for Reading Research, Tallahassee, FL.

Share, D. L. (1995). Phonological recoding and self-teaching: sine qua non of reading acquisition. *Cognition, 55,* 151–218.

Share, D. L. (2004). Orthographic learning at a glance: On the time course and developmental onset of self-teaching. *Journal of Experimental Child Psychology, 87,* 267–298.

Shaywitz, S. E., & Shaywitz, B. A. (2007). What neuroscience really tells us about reading instruction. *Educational Leadership, 64*(5), 74–76.

Sindelar, P. T., Monda, L. E., & O'Shea, L. J. (1990). Effects of repeated readings on instructional-and mastery-level readers. *Journal of Educational Research, 83,* 220–226.

Snow, C., Griffin, P., & Burns, M. S. (2007). *Knowledge to support the teaching of reading: Preparing teachers for a changing world.* San Francisco: Jossey-Bass.

Stahl, S. A., & Heubach, K. (2005). Fluency-oriented reading instruction. *Journal of Literacy Research, 37,* 25–60.

Stanovich, K. E., & West, R. F. (1989). Exposure to print and orthographic processing. *Reading Research Quarterly, 24,* 402–433.

Swanson, E., Wexler, J., & Vaughn, S. (2009). Text reading and students with learning disabilities. In E. H.Hiebert (Ed.), *Reading more, reading better* (pp. 210–230). New York: Guilford.

Torgesen, J. K., Alexander, A. W., Wagner, R. K., Rashotte, C. A., Voeller, K., Conway, T., & Rose, E. (2001). Intensive remedial instruction for children with severe reading disabilities: Immediate and long-term outcomes from two instructional approaches. *Journal of Learning Disabilities, 34,* 33–58.

Torgesen, J. K., & Hudson, R. F. (2006). Reading fluency: Critical issues for struggling readers. In S. J. Samuels & A. Farstrup (Eds.). *What research has to say about fluency instruction* (pp. 130–158). Newark, DE: International Reading Association.

Torgesen, J. K., Rashotte, C. A., & Alexander, A. (2001). Principles of fluency instruction in reading: Relationships with established empirical outcomes. In M. Wolf (Ed.), *Dyslexia, fluency, and the brain* (pp. 333–356). Parkton, MD: York Press.

Torgesen, J. K., Rashotte, C., Alexander, A., Alexander, J., & MacPhee, K. (2003). Progress towards understanding the instructional conditions necessary for remediating reading difficulties in older children. In B. Foorman (Ed.), *Preventing and remediating reading difficulties: Bringing science to scale* (pp. 275–298). Baltimore, MD: York Press.

Torgesen, J. K., Wagner, R. K., & Rashotte, C. A. (1999). *Test of word reading efficiency.* Austin, TX: PRO-ED.

Vygotsky, L. S. (1978). *Mind in society: The development of higher psychological processes.* Cambridge, MA: Harvard University Press.

Wolf, M. (1999). What time may tell: Towards a new conceptualization of developmental dyslexia. *Annals of Dyslexia, 49,* 3–28.

Wolf, M., Bally, H., & Morris, R. (1986). Automaticity, retrieval processes, and reading: A longitudinal study in average and impaired readers. *Child Development, 57,* 988–1000.

Wolf, M., & Bowers, P. (1999). The "Double-Deficit Hypothesis" for the developmental dyslexias. *Journal of Educational Psychology, 91*(3), 1–24.

Wolf, M., & Katzir-Cohen, T. (2001). Reading fluency and its intervention. *Scientific Studies of Reading, 5,* 211–239.

Yang, J. (2006). *A meta-analysis of the effects of interventions to increase reading fluency among elementary school students.* Unpublished doctoral dissertation, Vanderbilt University, Nashville, TN.

Young, A., & Bowers, P. (1995). Individual differences and text difficulty determinants of reading fluency and expressiveness. *Journal of Experimental Child Psychology, 60,* 428–454.

Young, A., Bowers, P., & MacKinnon, G. (1996). Effects of prosodic modeling and repeated reading on poor readers' fluency and comprehension. *Applied Psycholinguistics, 17,* 59–84.

Ziegler, J. C., & Goswami, U. (2005). Reading acquisition, developmental dyslexia, and skilled reading across languages: A psycholinguistic grain size theory. *Psychological Bulletin, 131*(1), 3–29.

7

Teacher Education and Reading Disabilities

Susan M. Benner, Sherry Mee Bell, and Amy D. Broemmel
University of Tennessee

Introduction

Many types of teachers and specialists have instructional responsibilities for students with reading disabilities. The standards set for the preparation of different types of teachers have distinctions separating them from one another. Teacher preparation paths may even conflict with one another for those preparing to work with students who have reading disabilities. Nonetheless, the preparation of all teachers should be centered on three primary concerns: what kinds of knowledge, what skills, and what professional commitments are needed to be effective (Bransford, Darling-Hammond, & LePage, 2005). For preparation of teachers who instruct children with reading disabilities, these three concerns vary depending upon who is doing the preparation and his or her understanding of the needs of children experiencing difficulty in learning to read.

In classrooms today inclusion of students with disabilities is a common practice. Teachers from general education, reading education, and special education find themselves working beside one another with the same children. In the past, classroom teachers have reported that their education prepared them to teach the average student, not those with special needs (Lewis et al., 1999). There has been an increasing push to advance the achievement level of poorly performing students to a minimally acceptable level, so greater attention is now being given to working with students at the lower end of the achievement scale. Multitiered models of reading intervention mandated in Reading First, a federal reading initiative launched in the early 2000s, are gaining prominence in the form of Response to Intervention (RTI) as a result of the Individuals with Disabilities Education Improvement Act of 2004 (IDEA 2004). Although teacher preparation for RTI is too new to have a depth of research related specifically to its efficacy, we do explore collaborative models of teacher preparation, which have been in place much longer.

Beliefs Underlying Common Instructional Approaches

What is the source of a reading disability? Do reading disabilities really exist, or do some children just need more time and attention than others while learning to read? Does a child who is struggling to learn to read need better instruction, more instruction, or different instruction? Does a child's struggle to read ever become severe enough to be considered a disability? These questions set the stage for the differing beliefs held and interpretations of research findings by educators.

While there is not an extensive line of research regarding how teacher education programs influence teacher beliefs about reading disabilities, what is available is informative. Mallette, Kile, Smith, McKinney, and Readence (2000) conducted case studies of six elementary education preservice teachers and found that stances each took toward reading difficulties predisposed them to construct reading difficulties in different ways even though these preservice teachers were initially unaware of their stances.

Bondy (1990) reported that children's responses when asked why people read matched the instructional approaches used by their teacher for reading instruction. Children identified as having low reading ability indicated that reading was about word calling and associated reading with school work. For these children, reading was not related to pleasure. Children considered high ability readers indicated that reading was about making meaning from what is read. Reading could be social, something one could enjoy with a friend. Preservice teachers hold beliefs about reading based upon their own life experiences with reading. Such beliefs then influence their behaviors in the classroom. However, as McMahon (1996) found, given support, preservice teachers can deepen their understanding of the meaning of reading difficulties.

The reading research is characterized by a belief that, in general, teachers can be successful with the vast majority of students if they simply pay attention to student needs (Allington & Walmsley, 1995). Snow, Burns, and Griffin (1998) indicated that it is commonly accepted that most students who struggle with reading do not need significantly different instruction. In fact, Spear-Swerling and Sternberg (1996) went so far as to state that, "there is currently little educational basis for differentiating school-labeled students with Reading Disability (RD) from other kinds of poor readers" (p. 4). As such, it is understandable that the standards set forth by the International Reading Association (IRA) focus on teachers' knowledge and understanding of a wide range of teaching strategies rather than specialized instructional techniques.

Students in the lower grades spend considerable time learning to read. Students in the middle grades are expected to be able to read to learn (Chall, 1996). English, a phonetically and orthographically complex language, is challenging and takes most students several years to master sufficiently to read independently for meaning. Students with reading disabilities tend to struggle learning to read after they are expected to be able to read to learn (Mastropieri, Scruggs, & Graetz, 2003; McCray, Vaughn, & Neal, 2001).

Teacher preparation for middle and secondary grades has a much stronger emphasis on content and content teaching than elementary preparation (Floden & Meniketti, 2005; Vacca, 2002). Struggling readers at this level might receive additional reading instruction though a remedial reading class or from a special education resource teacher, but the bulk of their academic content instruction comes from content-prepared teachers who have typically taken one course in teaching reading in the content fields and one introductory special education course (Bean, 2000; Blanton & Pugach, 2007).

The role of reading specialists as teacher leaders seems to be taking hold as many report doing more than just teaching. In one survey, over 90% of reading specialists indicated that they were involved with both instructing students and serving as a resource to teachers (Bean, Cassidy, Grumet, Shelton, & Wallis, 2002). There appears to be agreement that they must be both expert classroom teachers who can identify and implement the instruction needed by individual children and effectively communicate with classroom teachers (Dole, 2004).

Though the field of special education has generally embraced efforts toward collaboration with general education, teacher preparation remains grounded in a within-the-child orientation. Of the 13 disability categories identified in IDEA, the learning disability (LD) category is arguably the most controversial. Some critics contend that LD is a social construct (Dudley-Marling, 2004; Skrtic, 2005). Nonetheless, the Learning Disabilities Roundtable, convened in 2002 and 2004, comprised of representatives from 14 professional associations including IRA, International Dyslexia Association (IDA), and several divisions of Council for Exceptional Children (CEC), concluded that there is strong converging evidence that LD is a valid construct, characterized by intra-individual variability in cognitive abilities and academic skills. Further, Shaywitz (2003) asserted that dyslexia, a reading disability characterized by differences in brain functioning related to phonological and rapid naming deficits, is the most common of all learning disabilities.

Despite special education's adherence to a within-the-child model, increasingly, inclusive education is the preferred approach for teaching students with mild disabilities. Research that questions the efficacy of pull-out programs (e.g., McGill-Franzen, 1987; Vaughn, Moody, & Schumm, 1998; Walmsley & Allington, 1995), poor performance of students with disabilities on group achievement tests, and rising costs of special education services, have combined to create an impetus toward inclusion.

Standards, Content, and Courses

What does effective teacher preparation look like for teachers of students with reading disabilities? What content is the right content to prepare such teachers? What should be the nature of preservice clinical experiences? What should be the relationship between local models of intervention and program adoptions and teacher preparation?

The work of the Teacher Education Subgroup of the National Reading Panel as reported by the National Institute for Child Health and Human Development (NICHD) (2000), indicated that there has been little systematic research to determine the most effective methods and content to prepare teachers for reading, much less interventions for struggling readers. However, they did note that we are beginning to have research that can document efficacy of teacher education.

In her review of research on pedagogical approaches used in teacher education, Grossman (2005) emphasized the strong connection between the field of teacher education and the approaches used to prepare future teachers. She reviewed a wide array of research on pedagogical approaches ranging from case-based instruction, action research, portfolios, to inquiry. Clift and Brady (2005) identified 24 research studies focused on methods courses and field experiences related to English, which included reading education. Of these, five studies were related to reading education; two particularly focused on reading education for struggling readers. Bowman and McCormick (2000) compared the effects of peer coaching to a traditional model of supervision for reading education. Under the peer coaching model, preservice teachers were placed together in the same classrooms for a field experience. They observed and provided feedback to one another. They found the peer coaching approach to supervision resulted in significantly increased use of clarity skills (e.g., stating objectives, using examples, repeating items, and practice time), improved pedagogical reasoning and action, and expression of more positive attitudes about the field experience.

Effective reading instruction depends upon the content knowledge held by teachers and the opportunities they have to work in the field, making decisions about instruction, interacting with others and reflecting on the efficacy of instruction (Swalord, Chapman, Rhodes, & Kullis, 1996). Through the combination of content knowledge and reflective practice, preservice teachers actively participate in building their knowledge and the skills needed to work effectively with children learning to read (Roehler, Duffy, Herrmann, Conley & Johnson, 1988). The importance of having interactions with children to build teacher self-confidence in their ability to teach a child to read was evident in the research on preservice elementary education students' attitudes after completion of a reading education course (Commeyras, Reinking, Heubach, & Pagnucco, 1993). With a balance of instruction, tutoring opportunities, and interactive activities, preservice teachers in a diagnosis of a reading problems course grew from relying primarily on subjective knowledge to procedural knowledge that required integration and application of their learning (Roskos & Walker, 1994). Without guidance from a strong master teacher, well-intentioned preservice teachers who express a commitment to using a rich variety of teaching materials and instructional strategies grew more and more dependent upon the basal reading program that was available to them during a student teaching experience. Their limited confidence level played a key role in their behavior.

The Holmes Group (1995) reported that evidence was clear that good teachers were at the heart of good schools. The members of this group understood the close link between teacher preparation and the schooling of PreK–12 students, emphasizing the futility of attempting to make isolated reforms. They argued the importance of teaching being "regarded as intellectually challenging work and that prospective and practicing teachers should be people capable of making informed professional judgments" (p. 21). It is the combination of a teacher's knowledge of her subject and her students that she then integrates into the act of teaching.

Early Childhood and Elementary   The Association for Childhood Education International (ACEI) has established standards developed in conjunction with the National Council for Accreditation of Teacher Education (NCATE) to identify what elementary teachers should know upon completion of their initial licensure program. Of the seven curriculum-related standards, one is dedicated to reading, writing, and oral language, and contains seven elements, one of which relates specifically to supporting language development and reading acquisition in diverse populations. Under the category of instruction, the ACEI (2006) standards specifically address adapting to meet the needs of diverse learners. Supporting materials detail expectations associated with understanding varied learning styles, seeking assistance from specialists, and planning appropriate instructional tasks.

In 1998, IRA and the National Association for the Education of Young Children (NAEYC) issued a position statement on developmentally appropriate teaching practices for young children, which was endorsed by other organizations including the Division for Early Childhood/Council for Exceptional Children (DEC/CEC). It included research and recommended practices for use in classrooms, as well as suggested policies to shape programs and schools. Shortly thereafter, NAEYC's (2001) revised standards for initial licensure programs included changes in general standards for teacher education with an impetus for enhanced emphasis on subject matter with specific expectations regarding language and literacy. NAEYC again reached across professional organization borders by supporting a DEC/CEC (2007) position paper incorporating preparation for work with special needs children for early childhood teacher preparation.

IRA (2004), too, has created performance-based *Standards for Reading Professionals*, which is organized into five categories. IRA recommends that classroom teachers in grades PreK-5 have a minimum of 12 hours of coursework in reading and reading instruction. Through research supported by IRA, Harmon et al. (2001) identified eight features shared by excellent reading teacher preparation programs. From those eight, IRA developed six standards and associated rubrics for evaluating teacher education programs. One standard focuses on diversity, indicating the importance of preparing teachers to work effectively with students from diverse backgrounds; however, the only mention of preparation for working with students of varied ability levels falls under the standard related to field experiences (IRA, n.d.).

Authors of the IRA (2000) position statement, *Excellent Reading Teachers* specify six qualities of excellent classroom reading teachers: (a) they understand reading and writing development and believe all children can read and write; (b) they continually assess children's individual progress and relate reading instruction to children's previous experiences; (c) they know a variety of ways to teach reading, when to use each method, and how to combine the methods into an effective instructional program; (d) they offer a variety of materials and texts for children to read; (e) they use flexible grouping strategies to tailor instruction to individual students; and (f) they are good reading coaches.

Austin and Morrison (1961) offered the first systematic documentation of preservice preparation for the teaching of reading in the United States; 15 years later, their follow up research indicated that most of their 22 original recommendations had been implemented (Morrison & Austin, 1977). Three hours of coursework in reading appeared to be standard at that point. Almost 10 years later, Flippo and Hayes (1985–86) found that 24 states required two reading-related courses for elementary certification. Not until nearly 20 years later, when Hoffman & Roller (2001) surveyed over 900 reading teacher educators from across the United States, did any other researchers attempt to characterize the practices in reading teacher preparation. Hoffman's and Roller's results indicated that the mean number of required semester hours of reading courses was 6.36, a substantial increase. Sixty-one percent of respondents indicated that reading courses had an accompanying field experience. Over 40% reported offering reading specializations requiring an average of 16 undergraduate hours of reading coursework.

Hoffman and Roller (2001) found that approximately three-quarters of respondents who taught introductory reading methods courses used a basic methods textbook for the course. Respondents also indicated that their programs were meeting or exceeding standards for all content areas but one: the structure of the English language. That area was also the only one not rated in the "very important" or "essential" range. However, Spear-Swerling and Brucker (2006) argued that it is important for teacher preparation programs to provide future teachers with knowledge of word structure. Harmon et al. (2001) further examined eight excellent reading teacher preparation programs and found eight common features, one of which identified specific content-related features including: foundation in research and theory, word-level instructional strategies, text-level comprehension strategies, reading-writing connections, instructional approaches and materials, and assessment.

Middle and Secondary Grades   Though secondary teachers have a long tradition of content area specialization, middle grades education has evolved more recently and is defined differently in different states (National Middle School Association, 1996). Further, many states historically granted licenses for grades K–8 or 1–8. Consequently, the additional requirement of content area competence for seventh- and eighth-grade teachers has presented challenges to middle school teachers and administrators.

Professional organizations develop standards appropriate to their specific content area. In the case of reading, English, and language arts, the National Council for Teachers of English (NCTE) and IRA (NCTE and IRA, n.d.) developed joint standards to guide curriculum development. The IRA also has standards that include teachers at the middle and high school levels. IRA's standards target five areas (foundations, instruction, assessment, environment, and professional development). A minimum of 6 credit-hours in reading and reading instruction is recommended (IRA, 1996–2008).

Although many adolescents have difficulty reading grade level materials (Hargis, 2006), most middle and secondary teachers' preparation focuses on skills and knowledge in their particular content area(s) and pedagogy. If a reading course is included in the curriculum, it tends to focus on teaching students to read in the content areas (Dynak & Smith, 1994). Preservice teachers assume that their students have already obtained basic reading skills (Ratekin, Simpson, Alvermann, & Dishner, 1985; Stewart & O'Brien, 1989). Bintz (1998) described the "reading nightmares" of 131 middle and secondary teachers who found themselves unprepared to assist struggling readers in their content area classes. Despite recognition by experts that reading instruction is critical into the upper grades for students with reading disabilities (Manset-Williamson & Nelson, 2005), most teacher education programs do not emphasize reading instruction at this level.

Reading Specialists   In the 1960s many reading specialists were hired as "remedial reading teachers" to work with struggling students (Bean, Swan, & Knaub, 2003). The call for such specialists was renewed with the publication of *Preventing Reading Difficulties in Young Children* (Snow et al., 1998). The role of the reading specialist has grown from one in which the focus was working with struggling students, supplementing or supplanting the work of the classroom teacher to a multifaceted one in which the specialist works collaboratively to support and extend the work of the classroom teacher in a variety of ways (Jaeger, 1996; Bean et al., 2003; Dole, 2004).

Requirements for obtaining a reading specialist credential are set at the state level then translated into practice by individual institutions offering the coursework, resulting in little consistency from state to state. The influence of NCLB, particularly the pressures associated with increasing test scores, has affected the goal of literacy coaches; the associated Reading First grants often provided states with money to pay reading coaches to train teachers to prepare students for testing (Shaw, 2007). However, IRA and NCATE have collaborated to establish expectations for graduate programs preparing students for specialized roles in reading education that go beyond basic test-preparation training. In order to be identified as a recognized program it must include a minimum of 24 graduate credit hours in reading, language arts, and related areas, plus a 6-hour supervised practicum, for a total of no less than 30 credit hours. The program must meet all five IRA standards, and at least 15 of 19 of the reading specialist elements.

Special Education   The CEC developed standards for teachers of students with learning disabilities, early childhood students, and other specific disability categories. In addition to instructional planning, strategies, and assessment, CEC standards address historical, legal, and philosophical foundations, development and characteristics of learners with disabilities, individual learning differences, learning environments and social interactions, language, professional and ethical practice, and collaboration.

There is scant research on special education teacher preparation (Brownell, Ross, Colón, & McCallum, 2005). Sands, Duffield, and Parsons (2006) noted that some universities are approaching the need to prepare future teachers to meet a diverse range of needs through curriculum infusion. That is, special education content is infused into the entire teacher preparation program as opposed to stand-alone courses (e.g., Lesar, Benner, Habel, & Coleman, 1997).

Blanton and Pugach (2007) described three teacher education approaches: (a) *discrete*, in which there is little or no coordination between special and general education preparation; no expectation for faculty collaboration; disparate assessments of candidates; dichotomous training that does not prepare them to collaborate as teachers; licensure in both areas essentially requires meeting requirements of two separate programs; (b) *integrated*, in which there is intentional curriculum overlap; faculty participate in ongoing collaboration to deliver an integrated curriculum; assessments are coordinated and aligned; candidates are prepared to collaborate; and licensure in special education license builds on the base of the general education license; and (c) *merged*, in which an integrated curriculum is the same for general and special education. In merged programs, all faculty contribute to the curriculum; program faculty collaborate on routinely and intensively; assessment reflects shared goals, graduates are prepared to share roles as teachers; and candidates typically earn licenses in both general and special education. According to Blanton and Pugach (2007), merged programs are not necessarily superior to integrated programs but discrete programs are not considered adequate.

Collaborative Teacher Education Models

The increased attention on the performance of students with disabilities on high-stakes tests as well as their graduation rates, combined with the philosophical preference for inclusion models prevalent in the field of special education has increased the availability of collaborative service delivery models in PreK–12 schools. Concurrently, teacher preparation programs have put an emphasis on preparing teachers to collaborate. In this section we present material in three sections: teacher education for multitiered instruction and RTI, teacher education for co-teaching, and curriculum and instructional development in pull-out programs.

Teacher Education for Multitiered Instruction and RTI   What criteria should determine when a child receives additional reading instruction and what should the nature of such instruction be? Who should provide reading instruction for these students?

General education.   There is some confusion surrounding how teachers feel about their preparation for teaching students with special needs. Citing Taylor and Sobel, Blanton and Pugach (2007) noted that general education preservice students anticipate working with children who have disabilities and are concerned about their depth of preparation. Citing Cook, they noted that preservice teachers feel more prepared to work with students with learning disabilities than with other disabilities. However, Lewis, Parsad, Carey, Bartfai, Farris, and Smerdon (1999) indicated that while 71% of teachers teach students with disabilities, only 21% report feeling well-prepared to do so. Snow, Griffin, and Burns (2005) supported this concern in acknowledging that some developmental challenges do exceed the knowledge base of the average classroom teacher, including those with experience. Like others (e.g., Allington & Baker, 1999; Allington & Johnston, 1989; Allington & Walmsley, 1995; Banks, et al., 2005) Snow and colleagues emphasized the importance of collaboration with other specialized school personnel; however, they added all teachers need a basic knowledge base about special needs of some students related to reading instruction.

The need to prepare future educators to teach students of varying levels of reading achievement appears quite often in the literature (Allington, 1997; Allington & McGill-Franzen, 1989; O'Sullivan, Ysseldyke, Christenson, & Thurlow, 1990). However, instructional needs cannot be determined based solely on categories or labels, such as "learning disabled," "dyslexic," or "struggling reader" (Allington, 2002b; Allington & McGill-Franzen, 1989; McGill-Franzen 1987; Spear-Swerling & Sternberg, 1996). Consequently, it is generally accepted that well-prepared teachers need to learn how to identify students' reading problems and generate possible solutions to them based on individual child characteristics. The consistent focus on meeting the needs of individual students espoused by reading researchers, then, fits well within the renewed emphasis on multitiered instruction as a result of RTI. Exemplary classroom teachers can reduce the number of children with reading difficulties in their classes (Allington & Baker, 1999), but such instruction requires a solid understanding of varied assessment and instructional strategies. The IRA (2007) identified six content-related elements of effective reading teacher education programs and suggested that packaging the pieces of knowledge together in broad principles, like assessment-driven instruction and responsive and adaptive teaching, principles that are revisited in multiple courses and contexts, will solidify the connections between such knowledge and classroom practice.

Some have suggested more should be done to prepare teachers specifically for meeting the needs of struggling readers. Duffy and Atkinson (2001) found that despite a course focused explicitly on effective practices and principles of reading instruction, most preservice teachers did not feel prepared to teach struggling readers. In a study of primary level preservice and inservice teachers, Bos, Mather, Dickson, Podhajski, and Chard (2001) found that these educators did not demonstrate deep knowledge of phonological awareness or the terminology associated with language structure and phonics. Moats (1999), too, argued that teachers have been consistently unprepared to teach the complex process of reading.

Banks et al. (2005) indicated that all teachers need to establish classroom environments that are not only accepting of differences, but are also supportive of children. They questioned the deficit orientation toward diagnosis of disabilities and stressed educational experiences that allow students to build on strengths to expand learning, indicating that strategic instruction does impact student achievement. While there is agreement in what effective elementary teachers should be able to do in terms of meeting the needs of diverse learners, controversy lingers about how to accomplish this task most effectively within preservice teacher education.

Special education.   Since the passage of IDEA 2004, special education textbooks, both introductory texts designed for all educators (e.g., Turnbull, Turnbull, & Wehmeyer, 2007; Vaughn, Bos, & Schumm, 2007) and texts designed for special education majors (e.g., Bos & Vaughn, 2006; Lerner, 2006) explicitly address RTI as both a model of instruction and a means of identifying LD. In addition, books solely focused on RTI are now in publication (e.g., Bender & Shores, 2007; Haager, Klingner, & Vaughn, 2007). Multitiered instruction typically includes three or four levels, with the first tier delivered by the classroom teacher and the second one delivered either by the classroom teacher or others, ranging from reading specialists to paraprofessionals. Most models do not suggest that the second tier be delivered by special educators. In many models, the third tier is special education and may be delivered either via inclusion or pull-out services.

Teacher Preparation for Co-Teaching The increased impetus for including students with disabilities in general education classrooms heightens the need for effective collaboration among professionals responsible for educating these students. Blanton and Pugach (2007) note that the need for collaboration is a critical component of educational services to insure full educational opportunities for students with disabilities. Though current texts on special education invariably contain material on models of service delivery, including collaborative, co-teaching and pull-out approaches, these topics are less likely to be addressed in reading/literacy texts. Following is a brief description of the most common instructional models for meeting needs of students with reading and other disabilities.

Collaboration-consultation. According to Bryant, Smith, and Bryant (2008), in the collaboration-consultation model, the general education teacher delivers instruction with ongoing support from the special educator. Both are involved in development of lessons and assessments. Schloss, Smith, and Schloss (2001) identified several advantages of this approach for secondary teachers, including reduced stigma for special education students, mutual professional growth opportunities, and benefits for students who are not eligible for special education. Schloss and colleagues noted that true collaboration requires willing participants and that may be a challenge for general and special educators who have previously taught in separate settings. Idol, Nevin, and Paolucci-Whitcomb (1994) identified six stages of the collaboration-consultation process: (a) establishing team goals; (b) problem identification, based on assessment data; (c) intervention recommendations; (d) implementation of recommendations; (e) monitoring progress; and (e) follow up. Though these recommendations predate RTI's inclusion in special education law, they are consistent with the progress monitoring component of the RTI and multitiered instructional models.

Co-teaching. Co-teaching involves two teachers directly engaged in delivering instruction to a group of students. Successful inclusion is predicated on successful co-teaching by the general educator and the special educator. Several researchers have defined and evaluated different models of co-teaching. For example, Vaughn, Schumm, and Arguelles (1997) identified four models: (a) one group—one lead teacher in which one teacher provides whole group instruction while a second teacher provides short, targeted lessons to one or more students during or after the whole group lesson; (b) two mixed-ability groups—two teachers teaching the same content, which allows teachers to gauge student understanding and engagement and may be used as a follow up to a; (c) two same-ability groups—teachers teach different content, which allows teachers to differentiate instruction based on skill levels of the students; and (d) whole class—two teachers teach together in which both teachers cooperate to deliver instruction. The general educator may focus on content while the special educator focuses on strategies.

Positive benefits of co-teaching may include improved social skills and academic gains of students with disabilities and, for teachers, professional growth, satisfaction, and support (Walther-Thomas, 1997). However, Murawski and Swanson (2001), based on a review of research on co-teaching, concluded that there were strong positive effects on language arts skills, moderate positive effects for mathematics, and no significant effects on social skills. In some studies, special educators have indicated they feel subordinate to the general educator in the co-teaching model (Salend, Gordon, & Lopez-Vona, 2002; Trent, 1998). Salend and colleagues (2002) reported that time for planning is essential to effective co-teaching. To further increase the chance for success, roles and approaches should be mutually defined by the general and special educator, instructional philosophies compared, expectations discussed, and students told how instruction and discipline will be addressed (Salend, Gordon, & Lopez-Vona, 2002).

Curriculum and Instructional Development in Pull-Out Programs For over three decades, the resource room has been the most common site for special education service delivery for students with LD (Schloss et al., 2001). Though criticized for failure to deliver on the promise to raise student achievement (Moody, Vaughn, Hughes, & Fischer, 2000; Vaughn et al., 1998; Walmsley & Allington, 1995), service delivery in the resource room is still widespread. Some advantages of resource room placement were noted by Schloss et al. (2001). Resource services allow for students with identified disabilities to receive more intensive services than in the general education classroom while allowing these same students to remain in classes with nondisabled peers for most of the school day. Further, the special education teacher can provide collaborative support for the general educators with whom these students do have classes. However, several researchers have concluded that the amount and quality of reading instruction in resource rooms is inadequate for many of the students they serve (Moody et al., 2000; Vaughn et al., 1998; Walmsley & Allington, 1995). Large heterogeneous classes, lack of coordination with general education class instruction, massive amounts of paperwork, and limited professional development contribute to the lack of effectiveness of some pull-out programs. Moody and colleagues concluded that students in the resource room were not receiving intensive instruction but also questioned the effectiveness of instruction solely through inclusion. They called for a restructuring of the resource room to allow more individualized, intensive instruction. The current popularity of RTI is a response in part to perceived lack of effectiveness of traditional special education and presents a unique opportunity for collaboration of general educators, special educators, reading specialists, and other school professionals.

Controversies and Critique of Teacher Education for Reading Disabilities   The "ownership" of reading disabilities has been contentious at times, as reading educators historically placed an emphasis on working with students struggling to read largely due to economic factors while special educators developed services for students with learning disabilities, which conceptually excludes children whose problems in reading are due to environmental factors associated with poverty (Allington, 2002b; Klenk & Kibby, 2000; McGill-Franzen, 1987). The LD category, which is predominately comprised of students with difficulties in reading, expanded exponentially immediately after its creation in the 1970s through the 1980s. Many federal dollars followed students away from remedial reading programs into special education. Teacher preparation, likewise, splintered between the two fields. Terms, such as *remedial reading*, *dyslexia*, *reading disabilities*, and *learning disabilities*, take on so many different meanings that they can inhibit communication rather than advancing it.

Federal policy drove and followed the reconceptualization of difficulties in reading as being derived from external forces (e.g., poverty) to internal differences within the child, who was then labeled as disabled. Although Title I programs continued to receive substantial funding, much of the funding for remedial reading programs shifted away from Title I to special education. Since remedial reading programs were an option and special education services became mandatory for all students who met eligibility criteria (McGill-Franzen & Goatley, 2001), educational administrators had to channel funds to serve any student identified with a learning disability, but could maintain waiting lists for those considered in need of remedial reading.

Education and teacher education have become highly political fields, with many arguing on behalf of teacher preparation directly matched to programs that qualify as grounded in scientifically-based reading research (SBRR) per federal policy. For a reading program to be designated SBRR, it has to be proven effective through clinical or empirical trials (U. S. Department of Education, 2002). Some in teacher education have been supportive of the concept of SBRR and aligned their programs to be consistent with the federally funded Reading First initiative (e.g., Hawkins, 2006; Hougen, 2006). The National Reading First Higher Education Consortium, based at the Vaughan Gross Center for Reading and Language Arts at the University of Texas,

has served as a formal network for such programs. Prior to enactment of SBRR-infused legislation, restrictive views of reading research attached to SBRR were being questioned (Taylor, 1998). After passage of the Reading Education Act, others critiqued the SBRR movement and its potential encroachment into higher education (e.g., Allington, 2002a; Coles, 2003).

While university-based teacher education programs contend with debates about SBRR and an array of accreditation requirements, federal policy has expanded alternative routes for persons to become credentialed teachers without passage through traditional programs (U. S. Department of Education, 2004). In particular, three alternative programs have been supported: Troops to Teachers, Transition to Teaching, and Teach for America. Concurrently, states have been given increasing flexibility over approval of alternative programs. Prospective teachers may bypass teacher education, receiving much of their instruction from publishing companies hired by school districts that have purchased their products and other for-profit professional development agencies.

As critics of existing teacher education programs, Lyon and Fletcher (2001) pronounced that teacher education has often been the cause of reading failure. One of their primary recommendations to prevent reading disabilities was to rest no hope in the reformation of existing teacher education programs. Rather, they considered the answer to the prevention of reading failure to lie in the development of alternative licensure and specialized professional development of teachers in the area of reading as delivered in concert with Reading First programs funded through the federal Reading Excellence Act.

The efficacy of such independent training is subject to great variability and well beyond the scope of this chapter. However, quality, efficacy, and content of teacher preparation programs have been and continue to be challenged (e.g., Kanstoroom & Finn, 1999; Walsh, Glaser, & Wilcox, 2006; Levine, 2006). The quality of the critics' work has, in turn, been the target of critique (e.g., Allington, 2007).

As a part of their work, the National Reading Panel (NRP) formed a subgroup charged with review of scientifically based research on teacher education and reading. (NICHD, 2000). In their work analyzing and synthesizing teacher education reading research, they focused exclusively on experimental research in which teacher behavior or knowledge was the focus of the study. While the database upon which they drew their conclusions was sparse, the NRP subgroup reached the conclusion that well-designed teacher education does result in higher student outcomes (NICHD, 2000). They found a consistent trend, where data were available, that when teacher change (as a result of preservice or in-service professional development) was significant so was student achievement. When there were no changes in teacher behavior, there were no gains in student outcomes. The nature and duration of the inservice training varied so widely across studies that no meaningful conclusions should be drawn from them.

Conclusions

Klenk and Kibby (2000), speaking from the orientation of reading education, characterized the differences in beliefs between the various factions who prepare teachers to work with struggling readers. They noted that reading educators generally adhere to the belief that there is no clearly defined etiology for reading difficulties and identify print-based reading instruction as the only viable means of correcting reading problems. In contrast, they note that special educators view LD and associated reading difficulties as deriving from perceptual or neurological dysfunction that requires different types of instruction, including perceptual development.

Though most special educators would likely endorse the view that learning disabilities are physiologically based (e.g., dyslexia), it is doubtful that most would endorse the practice of perceptual instruction. Although there are differences of opinion regarding the place of perceptual difficulties in the identification of a learning disability, the mainstream research and recommended interventions prominent in the field of learning disabilities today focus on text-based instruction for reading disabilities rather than perceptual activities. While sensorimotor integration therapy, auditory perception training, and other similar interventions *may* be part of the comprehensive related services that children with various types of disabilities receive, such therapies are not typically used by the special educator working in a classroom setting with struggling readers. According to Zigmond and Baker (1995), the purpose of special education is to provide "specific, directed, individualized, intensive, remedial instruction" (p. 178). It is apparent that the perceptions held by general, reading and special educators about one another are inconsistent with the beliefs each hold about themselves and others.

The research literature available on effective teacher preparation recounted throughout this chapter offers a challenge to the concept of a one-size-fits-all SBRR model of teacher preparation. The emphasis found in the research and professional standards has been on preparing intelligent thoughtful teachers who are capable of collaborating with one another, reflecting upon their beliefs and integrating knowledge and skills for individual children. Effective education for struggling readers does not come via a program that teachers are asked to implement without deviation or thoughtful consideration of the context and students. Effective education comes through the development of teachers who have content knowledge, pedagogical skills, on-the-spot decision-making capacity, and high standards for themselves and their students. Teacher education programs that are effective are based on the premise that graduates become increasingly knowledgeable and skilled over time as their own contextualized expertise develops (Bransford, Darling-Hammond, & LePage, 2005). Effective teachers, especially those working with struggling readers, do not simply follow the rules set by a publishing company that has added the "scientifically-based" label to its marketing materials.

Instruction of students identified with reading disabilities is the responsibility of classroom teachers, special educators, reading specialists, and other professionals (e.g., speech-language pathologists). Nonetheless, because of differing standards, professional organizations, theoretical and political beliefs, and separate preparation paths, these professionals may not be primed to collaborate effectively. It is the challenge of teacher education programs to prepare future educators from various fields to communicate and collaborate effectively.

References

Allington, R. L. (1997). Why does literacy research so often ignore what really matters? In C. K. Kinzer, K. A. Hinchman, & D. J. Leu (Eds.), *Inquiries in literacy theory and practice* (46th yearbook of the National Reading Conference) (pp 1–12). Chicago: National Reading Conference.

Allington, R. L. (2002a). *Big brother and the national reading curriculum: How ideology trumped evidence.* Portsmouth, NH: Heinemann.

Allington, R. L. (2002b). Research on reading/learning disability interventions. In A. S. Farstrup & S. J. Samuels (Eds.), *What research has to say about reading instruction* (3rd ed., pp 261–290). Newark, DE: International Reading Association.

Allington, R. L. (2007). What education schools, maybe, aren't teaching about reading…: Or maybe not. *Journal of Reading Education, 32,* 5–9.

Allington, R. L., & Baker, K. (1999). Best practices in literacy instruction for children with special needs. In L. B. Gambrell, L. M. Morrow, S. B. Neuman, & M. Pressley (Eds.), *Best practices in literacy instruction* (pp. 292–310). New York: Guilford.

Allington, R. L., & Johnston, P. (1989). Coordination, collaboration, and consistency: The redesign of compensatory and special education interventions. In R. E. Slavin, N. L. Karweit, & N. A. Madden (Eds.), *Effective programs for students at risk* (pp. 320–354). Needham Heights, MA: Allyn & Bacon.

Allington, R. L., & McGill-Franzen, A. (1989). School response to reading failure: Instruction for chapter 1 and special education students in grades 2, 4, and 8. *The Elementary School Journal, 89*(5), 529–542.

Allington, R. L., & Walmsley, S. A. (Eds.). (1995). *No quick fix: Rethinking literacy programs in America's elementary schools.* Newark, DE: International Reading Association.

Association for Childhood Education International. (2006). *ACEI Standards.* Retrieved April 16, 2008, from http://www.acei.org/2006StandardsRevision_final.doc.

Austin, M. C., & Morrison, C. (1961). *The torch lighters: Tomorrows teachers of reading.* Cambridge, MA: Harvard University Press.

Banks, J., Cochran-Smith, M., Moll, L., Richert, A., Zeichner, K., LePage, P., et al. (2005).Teaching diverse learners. In L. Darling-Hammond &J. Bransford (Eds.) *Preparing teachers for a changing world: What teachers should learn and be able to do* (pp. 232–274). San Francisco: Jossey-Bass.

Bean, R. (2000). Discourse and sociocultural studies in reading. In M. L. Kamil, P. B. Mosenthal, P. D. Pearson, & R. Barr (Eds.), *Handbook of reading research, vol. III* (pp. 195–208). Mahwah, NJ: Erlbaum.

Bean, R. M., Cassidy, J., Grumet, J. V., Shelton, D., & Wallis, S. R. (2002). What do reading specialists do? Results from a national survey. *The Reading Teacher, 55,* 736–744.

Bean, R. M., Swan, A. L., & Knaub, R. (2003). Reading specialists in schools with exemplary reading programs: Functional, versatile, and prepared. *The Reading Teacher, 56,* 446–455.

Bender, W. N., & Shores, C. (2007). *Response to intervention: A practical guide for every teacher.* Thousand Oaks, CA: Corwin Press and Council for Exceptional Children.

Bintz, W. P. (1998). Exploring reading nightmares of middle and secondary school teachers. *Journal of Adolescent and Adult Literacy, 41*, 12–24.

Blanton, L. P., & Pugach, M. C. (2007). *Collaborative programs in general and special teacher education: Action guide for higher education and state policy makers.* Washington, D C: Council of Chief State School Officers in partnership with the American Association of Colleges for Teacher Education

Bondy, E. (1990). Seeing it their way: What children's definitions of reading tell us about improving teacher education. *Journal of Teacher Education, 41*(5), 33–45.

Bos, C., Mather, N., Dickson, S., Podhajski, B., & Chard, D. (2001). Perceptions and knowledge o f preservice and inservice educators about early reading instruction. *Annals of Dyslexia, 51*, 97–120.

Bos, C., & Vaughn, S. (2006). *Strategies for teaching students with learning and behavior problems* (6th ed.). Boston: Allyn & Bacon.

Bowman, C., & McCormick, S. (2000). Comparison of peer coaching versus traditional supervision effects. *The Journal of Educational Research, 93*, 256–261.

Bransford, J., Darling-Hammond, L., & LePage, P. (2005). Introduction. In L. Darling-Hammond & J. Bransford (Eds.), *Preparing teachers for a changing world: What teachers should learn and be able to do* (pp. 1- 39). San Francisco: Jossey-Bass.

Brownell, M. T., Ross, D. D., Colón, E. P., & McCallum, C. L. (2005). Critical features of special education teacher preparation: A comparison with general teacher education. *The Journal of Special Education, 38*(4), 242–252.

Bryant, D. P., Smith, D. D., & Bryant, B. R. (2008). *Teaching students with special needs in inclusive classrooms.* Boston: Pearson.

Chall, J. S. (1996). *Stages of reading development* (2nd ed.). Fort Worth, TX: Harcourt Brace.

Clift, R., & Brady, P. (2005). Research on methods courses and field experiences. In M. Cochran-Smith & K. Zeichner (Eds.), *Studying teacher education: The report of the AERA Panel on Research and Teacher Education* (pp. 309–424). Mahwah, NJ: Erlbaum.

Coles, G. (2003). *Reading the naked truth: Literacy, legislation, and lies.* Portsmouth, NH: Heinemann.

Commeyras, M., Reinking, D., Heubach, K. M., & Pagnucco, J. (1993). Looking within: A study of an undergraduate reading methods course. In D. J. Leu & C. K. Kinzer, *Examining central issues in literacy research, theory, and practice. Forty-second yearbook of the National Reading Conference* (pp. 297–304). Chicago: National Reading Conference.

Division for Early Childhood of the Council for Exceptional Children. (2007). *Promoting positive outcomes for children with disabilities: Recommendations for curriculum, assessment, and program evaluation.* Missoula, MT: Division for Early Childhood.

Dole, J. A. (2004). The changing role of the reading specialist in school reform. *The Reading Teacher, 57*, 462–471.

Dudley-Marling, C. (2004). The social construction of learning disabilities. *Journal of Learning Disabilities, 37*, 482–489.

Duffy. A. M., & Atkinson, T. S. (2001). Learning to teach struggling (and non-struggling) elementary school readers: An analysis of preservice teachers' knowledges. *Reading Research and Instruction, 41*, 83–102.

Dynak, J., & Smith, M. J. (1994). Summarization: Preservice teachers' abilities and instructional views. In C. K. Kinzer & D. J. Leu (Eds.), *Multidimensional aspects of literacy research, theory, and practice. Forty-third yearbook of the National Reading Conference* (pp. 387–393). Chicago: National Reading Conference.

Flippo, R., & Hayes, D. (1985–1986, Winter). Graduate preparation and licensure examination for reading specialists. *Journal of Reading Education, 11*(2), 18–28.

Floden, R., & Meniketti, M. (2005). Research on the effects of coursework in the arts and sciences and in the foundations of education. In M. Cochran-Smith & K. Zeichner (Eds.), *Studying teacher education: The report of the AERA Panel on Research and Teacher Education* (pp. 261–308). Mahwah, NJ: Erlbaum.

Grossman, P. (2005). Research on pedagogical approaches in teacher education. In M. Cochran-Smith & K. Zeichner (Eds.), *Studying teacher*

education: The report of the AERA Panel on Research and Teacher Education (pp. 425–476). Mahwah, NJ: Erlbaum.

Haager, D., Klingner, J., & Vaughn, S. (Eds.). (2007). *Evidence-based practices for response to intervention.* Baltimore, MD: Paul H. Brookes.

Hargis, C. H. (2006). Setting standards: An exercise in futility? *Phi Delta Kappan, 87*(5), 393–395.

Harmon, J., Hedrick, W., Martinez, M., Perez, B., Keehn, S., Fine, J. C., et al. (2001). Features of excellence of reading teacher preparation programs. In J. V. Hoffman, D. L. Schallert, C. M. Fairbanks, J. Worthy, & B. Maloch (Eds.), *Fiftieth yearbook of the National Reading Conference* (pp. 262–274). Chicago: National Reading Conference.

Hawkins, B. (2006). The impact of the Reading First Teacher Education Network on increasing the reading proficiency of American Indian children—How a summer reading institute brought together educators, parents, and a community. *Journal of American Indian Education, 45*, 72–76.

Hoffman, J. V., & Roller, C. M. (2001). The IRA excellence in reading teacher preparation commission's report: Current practices in reading teacher education at the undergraduate level in the United States. In C. M. Roller (Ed.), *Learning to teach reading: Setting the research agenda* (pp. 32–79). Newark, DE: International Reading Association.

Holmes Group. (1995). *Tomorrow's schools of education.* East Lansing, MI: The Holmes Group.

Hougen, M. (2006, January 26). *The Texas Reading First Higher Education Collaborative: Integrating scientifically based reading research into preservice courses.* Paper presented at the annual meeting of the American Association of Colleges for Teacher Education. Retrieved May 26, 2008, from http://www.allacademic.com/meta/p36132_index.html

Idol, L., Nevin, A., & Paolucci-Whitcomb, P. (1994). *Collaborative consultation* (2nd ed.). Rockville, MD: Aspen Systems.

Individuals with Disabilities Education Improvement Act of 2004, 20 U. S. C. §§ 1400-1485 (2004 supp. IV), Pub. L. No. 108-446 (2004), 108th Congress, Second Session. Individuals with Disabilities Education Act of 2004 Regulations, 34 C. F. R. § 300.1-.818.

International Reading Association. (n.d.). *Certificate of distinction for the reading preparation of elementary and secondary teachers: Standards and rubrics.* Retrieved April 16, 2008, from http://www.reading.org/downloads/resources/quester_application_process.pdf

International Reading Association. (1996–2008). *IRA Style Guide. Standards for reading professionals.* Retrieved April 16, 2008, from http://www.reading.org/styleguide/standards_reading_profs.html

International Reading Association. (2000). *Excellent reading teachers: A position statement of the International Reading Association.* Retrieved May 27, 2008, from http://reading.org/downloads/positions/ps1041_excellent.pdf

International Reading Association. (2004). *Standards for reading professionals-revised 2003.* Newark, DE: International Reading Association.

International Reading Association. (2007). *Teaching reading well: A synthesis of the International Reading Association's research on teacher preparation for reading instruction.* Newark, DE: International Reading Association.

Jaeger, E. L. (1996). The reading specialist as collaborative consultant. *The Reading Teacher, 49*, 622–629.

Kanstoroom, M., & Finn, C. (Eds.). (1999). *Better teachers, better schools.* Washington, DC: Fordham Foundation.

Klenk, L., & Kibby, M. W. (2000). Re-Mediating reading difficulties: Appraising the past, reconciling the present, constructing the future. In M. L. Kamil, P. B. Mosenthal, P. D. Pearson, & R. Barr (Eds.), *Handbook of reading research, vol. III* (pp. 667–690). Mahwah, NJ: Erlbaum.

Learning Disabilities Roundtable. (2005). *2004 Learning disabilities roundtable: Comments and recommendations on regulatory issues under the Individuals with Disabilities Education Improvement Act of 2004 Public Law 108-466.* Retrieved December 18, 2006, from http://www.ncld.org/index.php?option=content&task=view&id=278

Lerner, J. (2006). *Learning disabilities and related disorders. Characteristics and teaching strategies.* Boston: Houghton Mifflin.

Lesar, S., Benner, S. M., Habel, J., & Coleman, L. (1997). Preparing general education teachers for inclusive settings: A constructivist teacher education program. *Teacher Education and Special Education, 20,* 203–220.

Levine, A. (2006). *Educating school teachers.* Retrieved May 31, 2007, from http://www.edschools.org/pdf/Educating_Teachers_Report.pdf

Lewis, L., Parsad, N., Carey, N., Bartfai, N., Farris, E., & Smerdon, B. (1999). *Teacher quality: A report on the preparation and qualifications of public school teachers.* Washington, DC: U.S. Department of Education, National Center for Education Statistics.

Lyon, G. R., & Fletcher J. M. (2001). Early warning system: How to prevent reading disabilities. *Education Matters, 1*(2), 23–29. Retrieved May 11, 2008, from http://www.hoover.org/publications/ednext/3389276.html

Mallette, M., Kile, R., Smith, M., McKinney, M., & Readence, J. (2000). Constructing meaning about literacy difficulties: Preservice teachers beginning to think about pedagogy. *Teaching and Teacher Education, 16,* 593–612.

Manset-Williamson, G., & Nelson, J. M. (2005). Balanced strategic reading instruction for upper-elementary and middle school students with reading disabilities: A comparative study of two approaches. *Learning Disability Quarterly, 28*(1), 59–74.

Mastropieri, M. A., Scruggs, T. E., & Graetz, J. E. (2003). Reading comprehension instruction for secondary students: Challenges for struggling students and teachers. *Learning Disability Quarterly, 26,* 103–116.

McCray, A. D., Vaughn, S., & Neal, L. I. (2001). Not all students learn to ready by third grade: Middle school students speak out about their reading disabilities. *The Journal of Special Education, 35*(1), 17–30.

McGill-Franzen, A. (1987). Failure to learn to read. Formulating a policy problem. *Reading Research Quarterly, 22,* 475–490.

McGill-Franzen, A., & Goatley, V. (2001). Title I and special education: Support for children who struggle to learn to read. In S. Neuman & D. Dickinson (Eds.), *Handbook of early literacy research* (pp. 471–483). New York: Guilford.

McMahon, S. I. (1996). Book club: The influence of a Vygotskian perspective on a literature-based reading program. In L. Dixon-Krauss (Ed.), *Vygotsky in the classroom: Mediated literacy assessment and instruction* (pp. 59–75). White Plains, NY: Longman.

Moats, L. C. (1999). *Teaching reading IS rocket science: What expert teachers of reading should know and be able to do.* Washington, DC: American Federation of Teachers. (Item No. 372).

Moody, S. W., Vaughn, S., Hughes, M. T., & Fischer, M. (2000). Reading instruction in the resource room. Set up for failure. *Exceptional Children, 66,* 305–316.

Morrison, C., & Austin, M. C. (1977). *The torch lighters revisited.* Newark, DE: International Reading Association.

Murawski, W. W., & Swanson, H. L., (2001). A meta-analysis of co-teaching research: Where are the data? *Remedial and Special Education, 22*(5), 258–267.

National Association for the Education of Young Children. (2001). NAEYC standards for early childhood professional preparation: Initial licensure programs. Retrieved April 16, 2008 from http://naeyc.org/faculty/pdf/2001.pdf

National Council for Teachers of English and International Reading Association. (n.d.). *Standards for the English Language Arts.* Retrieved April 16, 2008, from http://www.ncte.org/print.asp?id=110846&node=204

National Institute of Child Health and Human Development. (2000). *Report of the National Reading Panel. Teaching children to read: An evidence-based assessment of the scientific research literature on reading and its implications for reading instruction.* (NIH Publication No. 00-4754). Washington, DC: U.S. Government Printing Office.

National Middle School Association. (1996). *NMSA research summary: Middle level licensure.* Retrieved April 16, 2008, from http://www.nmsa.org/Research/ResearchSummaries/Summary7/tabid/259/Default.aspx

No Child Left Behind Act of 2001, 20 U. S. C. A. §§ 6301 *et. seq., Pub.* L. No. 107–110, 115 Stat. 1425 (2002).

O'Sullivan, P. J., Ysseldyke, J. E., Christenson, S. L., & Thurlow, M. L. (1990). Mildly handicapped elementary students' opportunity to learn during reading instruction in mainstream and special education settings. *Reading Research Quarterly, 25,* 131–146.

Ratekin, N., Simpson, M., Alvermann, D., & Dishner, E. (1985). Why teachers resist content reading instruction. *Journal of Reading, 28,* 432–437.

Roehler, L. R., Duffy, G. D., Herrmann, B. A., Conley, M., & Johnson, J. (1988). Knowledge structures as evidence of the &personal': Bridging the gap from thought to practice. *Journal of Curriculum Studies, 20,* 159–165.

Roskos, K., & Walker, B. (1994). Preservice teachers' epistemology in the teaching of problem readers. In C. K. Kinzer & D. J. Leu (Eds.), *Multidimensional aspects of literacy research, theory, and practice. Forty-third yearbook of the National Reading Conference* (pp. 418–428). Chicago: National Reading Conference.

Salend, S. J., Gordon, J., & Lopez-Vona, K. (2002). Evaluating cooperative teaching teams. *Teaching Exceptional Children, 37,* 195–200.

Sands, D. I., Duffield, J. A., & Parsons, B. A. (2006). Evaluating fused content in a merged special education and general education teacher preparation program. *Action in Teacher Education, 28,* 92–103.

Schloss, P. J., Smith, M. A., & Schloss, C. N. (2001). *Instructional methods for secondary students with learning and behavior problems* (3rd ed). Boston: Allyn.

Shaw, M. (2007). Preparing reading specialists to be literacy coaches: Principles, practices, possibilities. *Journal of Language and Literacy Education* [Online], *3*(1), 6–17. Retrieved from http://coe.uga.edu/jolle/2007_1/preparing.pdf

Shaywitz, S. E. (2003). *Overcoming dyslexia. A new and complete science-based program for reading problems at any level.* New York: Alfred A. Knopf.

Skrtic, T. (2005). A political economy of learning disabilities. *Learning Disabilities Quarterly, 28,* 149–155.

Snow, C. E., Burns, M. S., & Griffin, P. (Eds.). (1998). *Preventing reading difficulties in young children.* Washington, DC: National Academy Press.

Snow, C. E., Griffin, P., & Burns, M. S. (Eds.). (2005). *Knowledge to support the teaching of reading: Preparing teacher for a changing world.* San Francisco: Jossey-Bass.

Spear-Swerling, L., & Brucker, P. (2006). Teacher-education students' reading abilities and their knowledge about word structure. *Teacher Education and Special Education, 29,* 116–126.

Spear-Swerling, L., & Sternberg, R. (1996). *Off track: When poor readers become "learning disabled."* New York: Westview.

Stewart, R., & O'Brien, D. (1989). Resistance to content area reading: A focus on preservice teachers. *Journal of Reading, 32,* 396–401.

Swalord, J., Chapman, V., Rhodes, R., & Kullis, M. (1996). A literate analysis of trends in literacy education. In D. J. Leu, C. K. Kinzer, & K. A. Hinchman (Eds.), *Literacies for the 21st century: Research and practice. Forty-fifth yearbook of the National Reading Conference* (pp. 437–446). Chicago: National Reading Conference.

Taylor, D. T. (1998). *Beginning to read and the spin doctors of science: The political campaign to change America's mind about how children learn to read.* Urbana, IL: National Council of Teachers of English.

Trent, S. C. (1998). False starts and other dilemmas of a secondary general education collaborative teacher: A case study. *Journal of Learning Disabilities, 31*(5), 503–513.

Turnbull, A., Turnbull, R., & Wehmeyer, M. L. (2007). *Exceptional lives: Special education in today's schools.* Upper Saddle River, NJ: Pearson.

U.S. Department of Education. (2002). *Scientifically-based research.* Retrieved May 8, 2008, from http://www.ed.gov/nclb/methods/whatworks/research/index.html

U.S. Department of Education. (2004). The facts about…good teachers. Retrieved May 8, 2008, from http://www.ed.gov/nclb/methods/teachers/teachers.html

Vacca, R. T. (2002). Making a difference in adolescents' school lives: Visible and invisible aspects of content area reading. In A. E. Farstrup & S. J. Samuels (Eds.), *What research has to say about reading instruction, 3rd ed.* (pp 184–204). Newark, DE: International Reading Association.

Vaughn, S., Bos, C. S., & Schumm, J. S. (2007). *Teaching students who are exceptional, diverse, and at risk in the general education classroom* (4th ed.). Upper Saddle River, NJ: Prentice Hall.

Vaughn, S., Moody, S. W., & Schumm, J. S. (1998). Broken promises: Reading instruction in the resource room. *Exceptional Children, 64,* 211–225.

Vaughn, S., Schumm, J. S., & Arguelles, M. E. (1997). The ABCDEs of co-teaching. *Teaching Exceptional Children, 39*(2), 4–10.

Walmsley, S. A., & Allington, R. L. (1995). Redefining and reforming instructional support programs for at-risk students. In R. L. Allington, & S. A. Walmsley (Eds.), *No quick fix: Rethinking literacy programs in America's schools* (pp. 19–44). New York: Teachers College Press.

Walsh, K., Glaser, D., & Wilcox, D., (2006). *What education schools aren't teaching about reading and what elementary teachers aren't learning.* Retrieved May 30, 2006, from http://www.nctq.org/nctq/

Walther-Thomas, C. (1997). Co-teaching experiences: The benefits and problems that teachers report. *Journal of Learning Disabilities, 30*(4), 395–407.

Zigmond, N., & Baker, J. M. (1995). Concluding comments: Current and future practices in inclusive schooling. *Journal of Special Education, 29,* 245–250.

8

Neuroscience and Dyslexia

STEVEN L. STRAUSS
Franklin Square Hospital, Baltimore

Reading disabilities are demonstrated by atypical reading behaviors and presumed cognitive irregularities. These effects could be attributed to a range of factors or conditions, and necessary conditions could likely include multiple factors. But in the disabilities literature the cause of reading disabilities as indicated by these behaviors and cognitive efforts is often localized in the brain. Neuroscience is the field of study concerned with the structure and function of the human brain, the most complex example of any known neurological system. The brain's tens of billions of nerve cells, or neurons, enable its possessor to think, plan, listen—and read. When the brain develops improperly, or is traumatized or stricken of its oxygen supply, its capacity to think, plan, listen, and read may be adversely affected. Thus, a fuller understanding of what enables normal reading, and how the reading disability literature describes the ways this can break down, should include a review of some fundamental concepts from neuroscience.

Models of Process

The complexity and variety of theoretical paradigms about reading in neuroscience, psychology, and reading research, including research on reading disorders, is surprisingly similar. A fundamental dichotomy in all three fields presents a theoretical tension between bottom-up and top-down processing. Bottom-up models assume a succession of processes that begin with the smallest elements of signification (i.e., images, letters, etc.) and work towards their accrual and construction into coherent and meaningful wholes (comprehension of situations, texts, etc.). Top-down models, conversely, presume the importance of prior knowledge structures about coherent wholes (schemas, scripts, gestalts, etc.) for identifying pertinent smaller elements and matching them to, and possibly adding to, the existing knowledge base.

In reading, bottom-up models emphasize the need to begin with the orthographic display in order to eventually arrive at meaning. Top-down models emphasize the meanings readers already bring with them to the task of reading—their world knowledge and beliefs, their syntactic and semantic competence, even the meanings partially developed from having read preceding text—and how these meanings function as contextual resources to help analyze the incoming visual orthography. Similarly, in psychology, bottom-up models emphasize how increasingly abstract concepts are derived from component elements. Top-down psychologies, by contrast, begin with an impetus for purposeful behavior as an intentional context for making sense of sensory and perceptual patterns, and the elements they comprise. Both behaviorism and information-processing cognitive psychology have a bottom-up thrust, with the former attempting to explain how stimuli are responded to and the latter how information is processed. Gestalt psychology and situated cognition are examples of top-down psychology.

In neuroscience, theories of bottom-up processing have prevailed historically, but top-down theories are becoming more widely accepted and studied. Bottom-up models see the organism as first collecting sensory information through its sense receptors, then relaying this information to the thalamus, a collection of neurons deep in the brain, then finally to the higher-level outer cortex for more global analysis. The notion that the cortex is divided into increasingly abstract primary, secondary, and tertiary regions reflects this bottom-up view (Luria, 1973; Mesulam, 1998). Top-down approaches, on the other hand, draw support from the notion that neural connections begin in the cortex and track towards deeper brain regions, far outnumbering connections originating at the bottom (Hawkins, 2004; Gilbert & Sigman, 2007; Strauss, Goodman, & Paulson, 2009). These top-down neural tracts may be part of an intentional feed-forward system, rather than a feedback system, as has been traditionally assumed.

Although more sophisticated interactive models have been posited of reading, psychological process, and neurological process, the bottom-up/top-down dichotomy is of longer provenance and seems to continue to inform debate regarding policy, as indicated by the requirements of the Reading First provision of the No Child Left Behind Act of 2002. Therefore, in this chapter I will review neuroscience research related to dyslexia with a basic overview of brain structure and function as portrayed by these two paradigmatic models. I will begin with a review of bottom-up models of dyslexia, the more widely discussed of the two among neuroscientists. This will allow me to tease out the neurobiological principles underlying bottom-up models of dyslexia. I will then review more recent top-down models from neurobiology with an eye towards understanding their relation to top-down views of reading and reading disorders.

The Role of Psychological Models in Neuroscience Research

Psychology is the point of contact between neuroscience and dyslexia research. Psychological processes are one of the chief functions of the brain. And reading itself is a psychological event. This means that an understanding of the connection between neuroscience and reading cannot proceed without considering implicitly, or explicitly, stated psychological models. This also means that points of disagreement are bound to exist in how to understand the neuroscience of reading and dyslexia. A new psychological understanding of how a reader interprets a certain category of words does not have to wait for confirmation from neuroscientists, for example. Thus, the fields advance in parallel, but at uneven tempos and combine unevenly. There is always the possibility that some current conceptualization of the reading process may be tied to an older, and discredited, psychological paradigm. Or there may be advances in our understanding of the brain's structure and function that would be more compatible with an alternative conception of psychological reading processes.

The behaviorist linguist Leonard Bloomfield argued in the 1940s that a proficient reader of English was someone who "has an overpracticed and ingrained habit of uttering one phoneme of the English language when he sees the letter *p*, another when he sees the letter *i*, another when he sees the letter *n*, still another when he sees the letter *m*, still another when he sees the letter *d*, and so on" (1942, p. 26). This behaviorist view was greatly modified in the wake of the cognitive revolution, with an information processing approach retaining the primacy of such letter-sound conversion, even as more constructivist models of cognition suggested that such graphophonemic processing was largely subordinate to the mental construction of meaning.

As another example of paradigmatic contrast, consider the widely accepted view of reading articulated by Marilyn Adams according to which "unless the processes involved in individual word recognition operate properly, nothing else in the system can either" (1990, p. 6). This position relates to an associated theory of dyslexia, wherein the inability to read is tied to the breakdown of the processes involved in individual word recognition. But Adams' view might need serious revision if advances in neuroscience clearly demonstrated that proficient readers do not fixate on a substantial number of words in the written text display. Indeed, eye movement research has already suggested this (Paulson & Goodman, 2008).

In reviewing the field of neuroscience and dyslexia, therefore, it must be kept in mind that every position in the field of reading research, including reading disability research, has an associated model within psychology, and that every claim about the structure and functioning of the human brain also entails a position on how mental life is generated. Although it would be scientifically pleasing for models of reading, psychology, and neuroscience to all cohere, it is precisely in their contradictions that questions are posed and challenges for further research are raised.

Overview of Brain Structure and Function

From the standpoint of both theory and methodology, scientific studies of the structure and psychological function of the human brain fall into two broad, mutually supportive categories. One set of studies entails the *localizationist* approach, wherein the goal is to identify the specific locations in the brain where discrete psychological operations occur. The other set of studies seek to identify the anatomic and physiologic basis of more global cerebral processes such as that which might coordinate localized activity.

The psychological processes studied by the localizationists cross the entire spectrum, from perception of sensory stimuli to abstract conceptualization. Visual information is analyzed and processed in the occipital lobes of the brain, auditory information in the posterior temporal lobes, and touch and temperature sensation in the parietal lobes (see Figure 8.1). For most people, expressive language is found in the left frontal lobe (Broca's area) and receptive language in the left temporoparietal lobe (Wernicke's area). Recognizing faces and experiencing music, on the other hand, are generally felt to draw largely on the right hemisphere.

By contrast, global processes act on specific areas, but are similar from one area to another. For example, all the sensory receptors, including the eyes, ears, and skin, convert physical stimuli into neurological signals. Most early, rudimentary signals are sent first to the thalamus, then to their respective homes in primary occipital, temporal, or parietal cortices of the brain. The cortical neurons carrying the rudimentary signals connect to adjacent secondary neurons that represent more abstract properties of the signal— recognizable objects from lines, colors, and orientations; melodies from sounds and timing, and so on.

The distinct sensory modalities can connect across the cortical surface of the brain, into so-called tertiary regions, so that multimodal mental representations can be constructed—a visual scene with background traffic noise, an opera singer with a background stage design. Indeed, one prominent neuroscientist has commented on the philosophical significance of this arrangement:

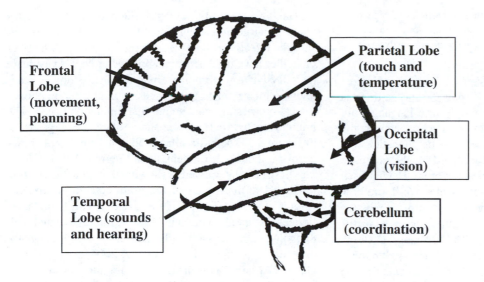

Figure 8.1 Lobes and their basic functions (left hemisphere).

Sensory information undergoes extensive associative elaboration and attentional modulation as it becomes incorporated into the texture of cognition.... The resultant synaptic organization ... allows each sensory event to initiate multiple cognitive and behavioural outcomes. Upstream sectors of unimodal association areas encode basic features of sensation such as colour, motion, form and pitch. More complex contents of sensory experience such as objects, faces, word-forms, spatial locations and sound sequences become encoded... by groups of coarsely tuned neurons. (Mesulam, 1998, p. 1013)

Mesulam further notes,

The highest synaptic levels... bind multiple unimodal and other transmodal areas into distributed but integrated multimodal representations. Transmodal areas in the midtemporal cortex, Wernicke's area, the hippocampal–entorhinal complex and the posterior parietal cortex provide critical gateways for transforming perception into recognition, word-forms into meaning, scenes and events into experiences, and spatial locations into targets for exploration. All cognitive processes arise from analogous associative transformations of similar sets of sensory inputs. (1998, p. 1013)

Mesulam's conception of brain organization suggests that cognition is derived from sensation. In regard to making sense of print, one might say that linguistic meaning derives from visual processing and its transformations across unimodal and transmodal cortex. Mesulam's account combines the localizationist perspective of distinct pathways for the special senses with a global perspective of parallel transformations along unimodal routes to more complex and abstract levels of mental representation. But it is even more than that. It also expresses, in a very clear manner, the bottom-up model of brain organization.

According to this model, "[a]ll cognitive processes arise from ... sensory inputs" (Mesulam, 1998, p. 1013). This is so even when it is recognized, as Mesulam does, that nerve tracts not only travel from the bottom up, that is to say, from raw sensory neurons to more abstract conceptual neurons,

but from the top down as well. "Connections from one zone to another are reciprocal and allow higher synaptic levels to exert a feedback (top-down) influence upon earlier levels of processing" (Mesulam, 1998, p. 1013).

Within a bottom-up conception of brain organization and functioning, top-down pathways are believed to play a subordinate role. This explains the use of the term *feedback*, as if to say that it cannot even operate unless feed-forward electrical activity occurs first. The physiologic function of feedback connections is, presumably, to act as a kind of brake on the feed-forward pathways. When adequate impulses from sensory sources arrive to trigger the next impulse, the feedback mechanism kicks in.

Bottom-up Localization and Dyslexia   Models of dyslexia have been developed within Mesulam's conceptual framework. Such models seek to identify the localizations in the brain where the normal transformation of visual print into meaning occurs, that is, of sensation into cognition, as well as those sites of breakdown that lead to reading problems. One important proposal within this framework is due to Shaywitz and colleagues (Shaywitz, 2004; Shaywitz et al., 1996). They maintain that, for alphabetic languages, reading begins with the transformation of visual letters into auditory phonemes. Phonemes, in turn, are sequenced together to form words. At this point, having identified the spoken form of the word, the reader can enter the language system of the brain, where the ordinary synaptic transformations of spoken language can operate to ultimately generate meanings.

Referring to this model in their chapter on dyslexia in a leading pediatrics textbook, Shaywitz, Lyon, and Shaywitz (2006) write that "among investigators in the field, a strong consensus now supports the phonological theory" (p. 1244). This theory

... recognizes that speech is natural and inherent, whereas reading is acquired and must be taught. To read, the beginning reader must recognize that the letters and letter strings (the orthography) represent the sounds of spoken language. To read, a child has to develop the insight that spoken words can be pulled apart into the elemental particles of speech (phonemes) and that the letters in a written word represent these sounds. Such awareness is largely missing in dyslexic children and adults. (p. 1244)

Thus, the reason reading must proceed via phonological processing of the orthographic display is that the brain is said to be hard-wired to process only oral language, not written language: "The reader must somehow convert the print on a page into a linguistic code—the phonetic code, the only code recognized and accepted by the language system" (Shaywitz, 2004, p. 50) of the brain. Having been "translated into the phonetic code, printed words are now accepted by the neural circuitry already in place for processing spoken language. Decoded into phonemes, words are processed automatically by the language system" (Shaywitz, 2004, p. 51). With this view, Shaywitz's phonological processing model offers a fairly narrow definition of reading and dyslexia. Reading is the conversion of print to speech and dyslexia is fundamentally an impairment of phonological processing. Following either accurate or impaired phonological conversion, what now technically occurs is just spoken language processing.

Neuroscientific technology has been used to support this theory. Functional magnetic resonance imaging (fMRI) is the machine of choice in most studies, but others are available as well, including positron emission tomography (PET) and magnetoencephalography (MEG). All are capable of identifying the sites in the brain where the neurological correlates to phonological processing occur.

Three sites in particular have been identified, all in the left hemisphere (see Figure 8.2). According to this schema, visual word information is initially sent to the word form area in the posterior part of the brain. It next travels anteriorly for further linguistic analysis. It finally arrives in the frontal region for oral articulation. Thus, this model combines both localizationist and bottom-up notions. Studies of phonological processing have revealed that subjects identified as dyslexic underutilize the posterior processing sites and overutilize the anterior site.

The obvious utility in identifying dedicated brain sites that play a role in reading is that they can be used to measure the effectiveness of various interventions. A number of studies have used neuroimaging technology to evaluate the effectiveness of intensive phonics instruction or other interventions claimed to be necessary for accurate phonological processing (e.g., sound discrimination tasks). The brain image before treatment shows attenuated regions, as in Figure 8.3. The brain image following treatment shows normal regional recruitment, as in Figure 8.2. These findings have been interpreted as showing that such intervention leads to "normalization of the brain activation profiles" (Simos et al., 2002, p. 1210) in dyslexic children, "ameliorates disrupted function in brain regions associated with phonological processing" (Temple et al., 2003, p. 2860), or leads to "brain repair" (Shaywitz, 2004, p. 86; see also Gaab, Gabrieli, Deutsch, Tallal, & Temple, 2007).

The final neuroscientific piece of the phonological processing puzzle comes from research on the biological basis of failed phonological processing. A variety of studies claim to have identified an anatomic risk factor for dyslexia, with additional studies arguing even more forcefully for a mechanism that ties the risk factor to the impairment of phonological processing. One relatively early anatomic discrepancy claimed to exist between normal and dyslexic readers is in the size of the planum temporale, a region of the temporal lobe that includes the auditory processing region. Normal readers tend to have a larger left planum temporale, with this asymmetry reversed in dyslexics.

A number of studies, however, have challenged this alleged asymmetry, but have argued for other anatomic distinctions. Eckert and colleagues (2003) measured the size of various brain regions in normal reading and dyslexic fourth through sixth graders. They found a significantly smaller right anterior cerebellar lobe in dyslexic subjects, along with discrepancies in some other areas as well. They did not find an alleged reversal of planum temporale asymmetry. Some studies suggest that the source of these anatomic discrepancies lies in genetics. Several candidate

Figure 8.2 The three activated sites in the left hemisphere of a proficient, nonimpaired reader.

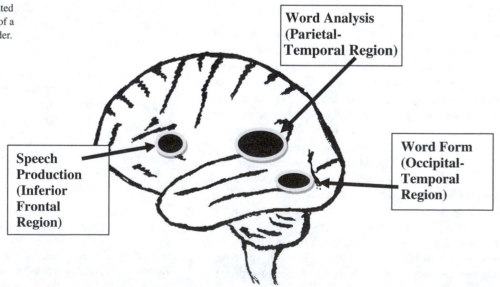

Word Analysis (Parietal-Temporal Region)

Speech Production (Inferior Frontal Region)

Word Form (Occipital-Temporal Region)

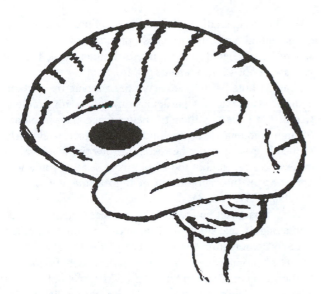

Figure 8.3 Dyslexics underutilize the posterior regions and overutilize the anterior region.

genes for dyslexia have been proposed. These include *DCDC2* (Schumacher et al., 2006), and *Dyx1c1* (Rosen et al., 2007). For reviews, see Gibson and Gruen (2008) and Wood and Grigorenko (2001).

The genetics research itself is motivated by a variety of epidemiologic observations, such as that "50% of children of dyslexic parents, 50% of siblings of dyslexics, and 50% of parents of dyslexic children are affected," with "estimates of heritability [that] range from 44% to 75%" (Meng et al., 2005, p. 17053). Suspected dyslexia genes have been identified on at least 8 of the 23 pairs of human chromosomes, thus supporting the view that reading disability "is a complex phenotype and several, if not many, genes are involved" (Meng et al., 2005, p. 17053). Similarly, developmental dyslexia has been claimed to be a "complex genetic disorder in which multiple genes play a role" (Cope et al., 2005, p. 581).

A leading candidate for the mechanism by which suscep-tibility genes generate their effect is via impaired migration of neurons to the brain's specific reading sites (Meng et al., 2005; Chang et al., 2005). Indeed, Meng et al. have claimed that *DCDC2* "localizes to the regions of the brain where fluent reading occurs" (p. 17053). Of crucial significance is the fact that subjects for these genetics studies are typically identified on the basis of screening tests that reveal impaired phonological processing. Since such subjects generate neuroimaging pictures with the usual signal impairments, researchers have concluded that genetics studies of reading disability "are consistent with the latest clinical imaging data" (Meng et al., 2005, p. 17053).

Neurobiological Principles of the Phonological Processing Model

Implicit in the discussion above are five neurobiological principles that together constitute the phonological process-ing model. These are summarized as follows:

Principle 1. The brain is hard-wired to process oral language, not written language.

Principle 2. Neuroimaging technology has revealed specific brain sites recruited for reading, that is, phonological processing.

Principle 3. Neuroimaging technology has demonstrated that intensive phonics instruction can repair a patho-logic brain.

Principle 4. The biological basis of dyslexia is evidenced by the anatomic size discrepancies of certain regions of the brain between dyslexic and normal readers.

Principle 5. The biological cause of dyslexia lies in a genetic abnormality that places the gene carrier at risk.

None of these principles has gone unchallenged. A discussion of the most serious challenges follows, treat-ing, in order: (a) The problematic concept of hard-wiring in the brain, (b) the limits of neuroimaging technology, (c) issues related to physiology, and (d) issues related to genetics.

Hard-Wiring of the Brain The principle that oral lan-guage is natural and written language is artificial is crucial for the phonological processing model, since otherwise there would be no theoretical compulsion to turn visual lan-guage into oral language. But the principle actually predates the phonological processing model, having been advanced in other scientific contexts. For instance, behaviorists main-tained that alphabetic letters of writing "conventionally represent" (Bloomfield, 1942, p. 26) the phonemes of the spoken language. And some early cognitivists argued that writing is a cultural phenomenon, whereas spoken language is rooted in biology, that is, in the human brain (Lenneberg, 1967). A clear contemporary exposition of this viewpoint can be found in Caplan (1987):

> Reading and writing have often been considered 'second-ary' forms of language representation. Though all normal humans exposed to spoken language learn to speak and comprehend auditory language, many people do not learn to write or read, and many languages have never devel-oped a written form. Normal children learn to use spoken language before they learn to use written language. For all these reasons, spoken language is undoubtedly the basic form of language, and written language a secondary means of expression. (p. 233)

Despite its initial plausibility, the principle is not without certain significant problems. For example, even Lenneberg (1967) observed that deaf children develop a fluency with sign language as effortlessly as do normal hearing children with oral language. And contemporary linguistic science has argued quite cogently that sign language conforms to all the expected syntactic and semantic laws of human language. It is real human language, not merely a collection of gestures. If the phonetic code were truly the only code recognized and accepted by the language system, then even sign language would have be considered a representation of speech. But it most certainly is not.

Like sign language, written language can be viewed as another form of language that retains a rich syntactic and semantic structural topography beneath its outer surface. Arguably, a system that adheres to universal linguistic laws of syntax and semantics, no matter what its outer form, will be accepted by the language system of the brain, without first having to be translated into a neurologically privileged oral form.

A similar line of argument can be applied to a phenomenon like fine motor control in humans. As with spoken language, all normal humans possess this capability. And all children go through a documented developmental sequence in the course of its biological maturation. Interestingly, there is generally no problem for children with polydactyly, that is, more than five fingers on a hand. Their extra fingers adapt to the system of fine motor control as seamlessly as do children with five-fingered hands. To some neurologists, this shows that "the brain develops according to what it is given" (al-Chalabi, Turner, & Delamont, 2006, p. 221). That is, it takes the available form and adapts it to the functional requirements.

The notion that written language is real language, and not a secondary notation for it, is also implicitly suggested even by advocates of the phonological processing model. In arguing for early intervention in pre- and elementary school, many have observed that learning to read appears to become more difficult past the age of 9 years. But in raising this as an argument for early intensive instruction in letter-sound decoding, the question is begged as to why such a cut-off should even exist. If a child learning to read is regarded as a type of language learning, then, as with oral language, the brain will impose its critical period constraints (Lenneberg, 1967), after which the learning process changes.

Not all advocates of bottom-up, that is to say, orthography-driven, word identification agree that the phonetic code is the only passport to the brain's language system. Caplan (1987) summarized the view of many that the numerous exceptions to English letter-sound patterns means that there must be another route from orthography to word identification besides the phonological one. He noted that the secondary nature of written language is what gives the strictly phonological processing route its considerable intuitive appeal. But he also observed "the existence of exception words, which simply cannot be read in their entirety through a phonologically mediated route at all" (Caplan, 1987, p. 237).

He also pointed out that the various observed types of acquired dyslexia cannot be fully explained on the basis of a single, phonologically mediated route from spelling to pronunciation. In *phonological dyslexia*, an individual is typically unable to read aloud phonologically regular nonsense words. In *surface dyslexia*, an individual typically produces pronunciations that are "phonologically and visually similar to the presented written stimulus word" (Caplan, 1987, p.

248), such as in reading *island* as /izland/. In *deep dyslexia*, an individual typically produces a pronounced word that is semantically related to the printed stimulus word, such as *play* for *act* or *shut* for *close* (p. 248).

Caplan noted that cases have been reported in which a surface dyslexic has particular difficulty with irregular words, but does significantly better when the words are of high frequency. He concluded that "since irregularly spelled words can only be recognized by the whole-word route, this suggest that the whole-word reading route was operating in the recognition of high-frequency words" (Caplan, 1987, p. 258).

The debate can be found in the area of functional neuroimaging. In one study, for example, functional MRI was used to demonstrate the existence of dual routes in the brain for recognition of written words. Fiebach, Friederici, Müller, and von Cramon (2002) used MRI technology and a lexical decision task to study the processing differences among high frequency words, low frequency words, and phonologically regular nonwords. Words, but not pseudo-words, activated bilateral occipito-temporal brain regions as well as the left middle temporal gyrus. Low-frequency words (typically more phonologically regular than high-frequency words) and pseudowords showed significantly greater activation than high-frequency words of the superior pars opercularis of the left inferior frontal gyrus. The authors concluded that a dual route to the mental lexicon, one relying on grapheme-phoneme correspondences and the other on direct lexical access from the visual word form, is supported by neuroimaging data.

Though the strict phonological processing model is used to support an instructional emphasis on intensive, direct phonics instruction, not all advocates of phonics have supported a strictly bottom-up approach. Richard Venezky (1999), for example, wrote:

> Phonics is a means to an end, not an end itself. Its functions are somewhat speculative, but most scholars agree that at least three are crucial to the acquisition of competent reading habits. One is to provide a process for approximating the sound of a word known from listening but not recognized quickly by sight. For this to work, decoding patterns need not generate perfect representations of speech. Instead they need to get the reader close enough that, with context, the correct identification can be made. (p. 231)

This view is based, in part, on Venezky's extensive study of English orthographic patterns, and his conclusion that the system is simply too complex to be the sole practical route to word identification. It must be supplemented with use of contextual information.

A rigid bottom-up approach eschews all sources of information useful for word identification that do not pertain to the orthographic display. Thus, Shaywitz, possibly among the most ardent of the bottom-up advocates, writes:

> The ability to read nonsense words is the best measure of phonological decoding skill in children.... The reader literally has to penetrate the sound structure of the word

and sound it out, phoneme by phoneme; there is no other way. Most children generally reach their full capacity to sound out nonsense words by adolescence. (2004, pp. 133–134)

Her methodology sees contextual information as muddying the attempt to identify a child with dyslexia:

In the schoolage child, the most important element of the psychometric evaluation is how accurately the child can decode words — that is, read single words in isolation. Reading passages allows bright children with dyslexia to use the context to guess the meaning of a word they might otherwise have trouble decoding. As a result, readers with dyslexia often perform better on measures of comprehension and worse on measures of the ability to decode isolated single words. In practice, the reliance on context makes such tests as multiple-choice examinations, which typically provide scanty context, especially burdensome for readers with dyslexia. (Shaywitz, 1998, p. 308)

Reid Lyon, former director of the reading research division of the National Institute of Child Health and Human Development, echoes this view, stating that "in contrast to what conventional wisdom has suggested in the past, expert readers do not use the surrounding context to figure out a word they've never seen before. The strategy of choice for expert readers is to actually fixate on that word and decode it to sound using phonics" (Lyon, 1997, cited in Clowes, 1999, p. 7). Apparently, this kind of phonological processing model is, in fact, an extreme version of Marilyn Adams' word identification approach to reading. It would seem to permit no top-down processing whatsoever. And all the bottom-up processing must be tied to the alphabetic letters and their alleged phonemic values.

Limits of Neuroimaging   Claims from neuroimaging research that the brain's reading sites have been discovered must be weighed against the full spectrum of neuroimaging studies. It goes without saying that if a subject is asked to read a non-word, the only way this can be done is by recruiting one's knowledge of letter-sound patterns. Then, if a special brain site is implicated through neuroimaging research, all that can be said about this site is that it is where letter-sound processing occurs. The further claim that this is where *reading* occurs is in no way demonstrated by the research, unless the experiments already *assume* that reading is phonological processing.

The claim that reading is phonological processing derives entirely from considerations outside neuroimaging. Neuroimaging studies have identified a number of brain sites that are relevant to an understanding of the phenomenon of reading. These include sites of visual orthographic processing, phonological processing, and semantic processing (see Demb, Poldrack, & Gabrieli, 1999).

But imaging studies can be applied to locate correlates to behaviors or tasks that may have little to do with neural processes typically employed in processing texts in a typical fashion. Brain imaging studies have been carried out

that show the brain sites recruited when a subject is asked to list words beginning with a particular letter (reported in al-Chalabi et al., 2006). Indeed, neuroimaging is such a powerful technology it can identify sites of cognitive processing that are of questionable functional utility in any act of ordinary language use. For example Posner and Raichle (1997) provide PET scan images of subjects performing the task of identifying false fonts. However beautiful these pictures are, and however powerful the technology is, such studies merely reinforce the notion that, until phonological processing can be independently demonstrated to play a crucial role in reading, any neuroimaging study that identifies its special brain location has merely demonstrated that the technology is a powerful enough tool to show us where yet another meaningless cognitive task occurs in the brain of subjects asked to carry out that task.

The claim that intensive phonics instruction can repair a dyslexic brain is based on neuroimaging studies before and after the intervention. Before intensive exposure to letter-sound drills, a dyslexic brain can be imaged to show impaired recruitment of the usual sites of phonological processing. After treatment, the images take on a normal appearance, in which the now treated dyslexic reader demonstrates neurological activity correlating to phonological processing in the same way that a normal reader does (see earlier discussion). The results of these studies have appeared in the popular media.

Yet Rosenberger and Rottenberg (2002), responding to Simos and colleagues (2002), raised serious objections to these assertions.

What, then, should we conclude from the findings of Simos et al.? They suggest that a "deficit in functional brain organization" has been "reversed" by remedial training. Some reservations may be in order regarding this conclusion. First, of the eight children studied, six suffered from attention deficit disorder and were placed on stimulant medication throughout the 2-month study period. Second, investigators using other neuroimaging techniques (MRS and functional MRI) and different stimulus paradigms have reported conflicting results of instructional intervention. (p. 1139)

Rosenberger and Rottenberg (2002) further noted:

Finally, it is often difficult to know how "increased activity" in a particular brain region relates to a subject's proficiency at a given task, or indeed whether it merely reflects that the subject is doing something different (or differently). In the study by Simos et al., it appears that as a result of remedial training the dyslexic children are doing what normal readers do naturally, and presumably what they themselves "should have been doing" all along. Why don't the dyslexic children do it naturally? It is not clear that the study of Simos et al. brings us any closer to the answer. (p. 1139)

These arguments apply generically to all neuroimaging claims about alleged brain repair from intensive phonics instruction, or from any other instructional technique, for that matter.

Anatomic Discrepancies   Authors of morphometric studies have claimed notable differences between the brains of normal and dyslexic readers, although these claims may not be fully justified by the data. For example, a smaller left planum temporale in dyslexics does not automatically imply that the genesis of dyslexia somehow lies in that abnormal piece of brain tissue. Nothing more than known principles of brain anatomy are needed to explain the findings. It is well known, for example, that brain tissue can grow in response to persistent activity in a certain area. This is known as *plasticity*. The plasticity of the human brain is responsible for continued growth, even into adulthood, of areas of the brain that are utilized for special purposes.

An interesting study of London taxi drivers showed that the volume of gray matter in the posterior hippocampus was significantly greater than in age-matched controls and that this increased even further with the amount of experience driving a taxi (Maguire et al., 2003). The authors also demonstrated that their findings did not represent an "innate navigational expertise" (p. 208). They concluded that their study demonstrated the plasticity of a part of the brain that plays a crucial role in acquiring spatial representations.

What morphometric and imaging studies consistently omit from discussion is that dyslexic readers not only cannot read, but, precisely because of that impairment, they *do not read*. One would therefore expect dyslexics to have some smaller brain regions, on the basis of the plasticity principle, and that they recruit different areas of the brain, on the basis of the undeveloped nature of their reading. These notions could certainly be tested by studying individuals who have grown up in a totally pre-literate environment.

Genetic Markers for Dyslexia   The finding of genes linked to dyslexia exposes an interesting problem of definition and principle. It is fair to ask why one should even expect a genetic basis for reading problems given the phonological processing paradigm's other neurobiological principles. Within this paradigm there can be no reading-specific gene or gene complex precisely because reading is, by hypothesis, not hard-wired in the brain. Therefore, there can be no abnormality of such a gene, that is, there can be no dyslexia gene. This means that any abnormal gene that leads to dyslexia must be nonspecific and should therefore manifest itself in other irregularities of psychological processing (cf. Hruby & Hynd, 2006). Unfortunately, this is not possible, because dyslexia, by the phonological processing paradigm's own definition, is a disorder of reading in the setting of otherwise normal mental functioning. According to Shaywitz (1998):

> Developmental dyslexia is characterized by an unexpected difficulty in reading in children and adults who otherwise possess the intelligence, motivation, and schooling considered necessary for accurate and fluent reading. (p. 307)

Indeed, she also called dyslexia a "specific reading disability" (p. 307) conveying the notion that it is unconnected to other cognitive disabilities. If dyslexia were associated with other cognitive or attentional disorders, then impairment of phonological processing could not be the only scientifically plausible mechanism for its existence.

Top-Down Neuroscience and Top-Down Reading

There is, strictly speaking, no purely top-down approach to understanding mechanisms of brain function in general, nor any of its various manifestations, including reading. Even among those researchers who advocate a top-down psychology of reading, it is clearly recognized that reading depends on the visual, orthographic display (Goodman, 1964). The distinguishing characteristic of top-down models in both neuroscience and psychology is that higher processes drive, direct, or at least mediate, the lower ones, in the sense that lower-level inputs are subordinate to higher-level purposeful behavior. In reading, the higher-level purposeful behavior is making sense of print. Of course, this is not really behavior, especially in silent reading. It is cognitive activity.

Meaning making is arguably a pre-theoretical phenomenon; it will occur and need explanation no matter what theory of reading is ultimately developed by researchers to explain it. In top-down approaches, researchers have maintained that readers construct meaning using a variety of cognitive resources which they employ as they interact with the visual language display. They use their knowledge of letter-sound relationships, but also use their knowledge of syntax and semantics. They use their knowledge and beliefs about the social and physical world.

For example, if a proficient reader reads a sentence that begins "The big, jolly man married the skinny, shy ___", only to find that the sentence continues on the next page, a proficient reader already anticipates the last word even before the page has been turned. Oral reading studies clearly demonstrate that proficient readers make good guesses, using a variety of contextual cuing systems. In this case, knowledge of syntax, semantics, and social customs allows the proficient reader to predict that the next, as yet unseen, word is "woman." No knowledge of letter-sound connection is needed in this case. But if the reader has any doubt, scanning the visual representation of the next word, whether "woman" or "wife," can provide additional information from the graphophonic cuing system that now functions, not to identify the word, but to confirm or discomfirm the prediction. For this reason, the constructivist approach to reading has been called a "psycholinguistic guessing game" (Goodman, 1967, p. 127). The purpose of reading—to make sense of print—is the top-down component of the model. The dependence on visual input provides the subordinate, bottom-up component. Reading is said to be a constant cycling back and forth between the two sets of processes.

Within the constructivist model, reading problems are multifactorial, and mainly revolve around identifying whether and how the reader utilizes the various cuing systems to construct meaning. The term *dyslexia* is generally avoided, since it tends to obscure the fact that many reading problems may be due to factors other than an inability to carry out low-level processing of the visual display. In fact, the constructivist model emphasizes that an over-reliance on the graphophonic cuing system may create reading problems, because it can divert the reader's attention away from the primary goal—the construction of meaning.

In recent years, the constructivist model of reading has utilized eye movement research to test its claims. Traditional behavioral studies of eye movement have focused on the neural circuits involved in automatic eye movements. These are saccades and fixations. Saccades are very fast glances from one fixation point to another. They are so fast that no visual information can be collected between fixations. The speed is greater than that which can be achieved by a conscious decision to change fixations, and for that reason it is assumed that saccades must be automatic.

More recent analyses of eye movements, however, are leading to a quite different perspective. Krauzlis (2005), for example, noted that the traditional understanding of pursuit and saccades is that they "are driven automatically by low-level visual inputs" (p. 124). However, based on more current studies, he concludes that "pursuit and saccades are not automatic responses to retinal inputs but are regulated by a process of target selection that involves a basic form of decision making. The selection process itself is guided by a variety of complex processes, including attention, perception, memory, and expectation" (p. 208). Thus, eye movements are achieved via automatic neural mechanisms under the direction of higher-level, purposeful brain activity.

Eye movement studies in reading are consistent with Krauzlis's view. Readers do not fixate on each and every word in the textual display. They typically omit about 20% to 30% of the words (Rayner, 1997), or more (Hogaboam, 1983; Just & Carpenter, 1987; Paulson, 2002). Furthermore, the words most commonly resistant to fixation are function words (e.g., "of"). These are the most predictable in the text, as long as a reader is reading for meaning and using the syntactic cuing system. Even predictable content words are less frequently fixated. According to Ehrlich and Rayner (1981), "contextual information does allow a reduction in readers' reliance on visual information" (p. 653). See Paulson and Freeman (2003) for further discussion.

Further neuroscientific support for the constructivist model actually comes from some of the phonological processing model's own neuroimaging studies. This is because both models recognize that readers use letter-sound connections in the reading process. What the phonological processing proponents call the brain site for letter-sound conversion the constructivists would call the brain site for the graphophonic cuing system. Neuroimaging, however, cannot be used to study the more global processes of reading described by the constructivists. The employment of background knowledge and beliefs, which certainly cover wide cerebral territory, is beyond the capacity of neuroimaging technology, which, by its very nature, can only study processes of extremely short duration and very narrow localization.

But other developments in neuroscience are clarifying the brain mechanisms involved in non-automatic cognitive activities, including the brain's projection of predictions and its devices for confirming and disconfirming the predictions. In this sense, these developments provide significant biological plausibility to the constructivist view (for a review of the neurological studies on processes related to reading comprehension, see Hruby, 2009).

Traditionally, the thalamus has been thought of as a sensory gatekeeper. Sensory inputs collected by the peripheral sense organs—the eyes, ears, and touch receptors in the skin—travel as electrically coded information along axons to neural terminals in the thalamus. They arrive at very specific assemblies of thalamic cell bodies, called nuclei. There the sensory nerve axons synapse onto nerve cells that will next travel to very specific parts of the cortex. These relay cells connect the lateral geniculate nucleus to the occipital lobe, the medial geniculate nucleus to the temporal lobe, and the dorsolateral nucleus to the parietal lobe. From these primary sensory areas, information of more and more abstract form is relayed to secondary sensory areas, then eventually to mixed, or heteromodal, regions of the cortex.

As the gatekeeper to the cortex, the thalamus is regarded as controlling which external and internal sensory inputs can pass to the cortex for further processing. This is a powerful role to play, since, on Mesulam's account, the cortex utilizes the auditory, visual, and other sensory raw material it receives to piece together the mental representations of experience. However, more recent assessments are turning this relationship on its head. Instead of the thalamus controlling which inputs reach the cortex for further processing, the cortex can instead first formulate its plans and goals, entirely independent of sensory stimuli, and then direct the thalamus, along with a host of other subcortical structures, to seek out sensory confirmation or disconfirmation.

When the cortex is conceived of as acting on the sensory stimuli it has received from the thalamus, it is natural to conceive of it as an information processing machine. But when the cortex acts in advance of any sensory input, so that the thalamic sensory nuclei subordinate their role to the needs of the cortex, then the cortex is no mere information processor. It is, as Hawkins (2004) has stated, "an organ of prediction" (p. 89). By implication, the thalamocortical neurons then constitute the organ of confirmation and disconfirmation.

There are a number of facts about the cortex and thalamus that are driving this shift in interpretation. Thalamus experts Sherman and Guillery (2006) observed that in addition to the existence of relay neurons running from the thalamus to the cortex, there are also neurons that begin in the cortex and synapse in the thalamus. Indeed, as Destexhe (2000) has remarked, "thalamic circuits ... in addition to providing a relay of afferent inputs to cerebral cortex ... are massively innervated by fibres arising from the cortex itself.... This corticothalamic projection provides the major source of excitatory synapses on thalamic neurones and in particular, corticothalamic synapses largely outnumber afferent synapses" (p. 391).

That the corticothalamic neurons far outnumber the thalamocortical neurons suggests not only that the bottom-up view is untenable, but that even a simple bidirectional view is not entirely accurate. There are two directions of neuronal transmission, with one direction, the corticothalamic one, dominant over the other, the thalamocortical one.

As a consequence of these developments in neuroscience, Sherman and Guillery observed that the classical view is "beginning to be less useful than it was in the past" (2006, p. 4). The cortical influence on "thalamic circuitry allows transmission to be modified in relation to current behavioral needs or constraints" (p. 6). The thalamus functions as a relay station not just from the periphery to the cortex, but "from one cortical area to another" (p. 6). Sherman and Guillery noted that the "importance of this pathway, which allows one cortical area to receive inputs from another cortical area through a thalamic relay that can be modulated in accordance with behavioral constraints, is not widely appreciated and has been but poorly explored" (p. 6).

Destexhe (2000) noted other facts besides the numerical superiority of corticothalamic pathways over thalamocortical pathways in support of revising the classical model. First, neurons originating in the cortex and destined to synapse in the thalamus land on parts of the thalamic neurons that seem to physically complement the landing sites of sensory neurons also headed towards the thalamus. Furthermore, the corticothalamic synapses can both excite and inhibit the action of the thalamic relay neurons. Overall, the effect of excitatory and inhibitory cortical action on the thalamus is to synchronize the electrical activity of distinct thalamic cell groupings, which, as experimental preparations have demonstrated, are desynchronized when disconnected from the cortex.

On the basis of these empirical observations, Destexhe was led to several important conclusions. First, since "corticothalamic synapses largely outnumber afferent synapses … the notion of the thalamus as a relay station, linking the periphery to the cerebral cortex, should clearly be revised" (Destexhe, 2000, p. 391). Second, whereas "early studies have most often considered the cortex as passively driven by a 'thalamic pacemaker'," the cortically-driven synchronized electrical activity of the thalamus demonstrates that "rather than providing an autonomous, independent drive, the thalamic pacemakers are controlled and co-ordinated by the cortex" (p. 391). And third, because "corticothalamic inputs seem capable of complementing the sensory information at the level of relay cells," this "corticothalamic information could therefore be a 'prediction' of the sensory input" (p. 405).

Hawkins (2004) described the matter similarly, noting that, from a biological perspective, prediction and confirmation is a process whereby "the neurons involved in sensing … become active in advance of them actually receiving sensory input. When the sensory input does arrive, it is compared with what was expected" (p. 89). That is to say, cortical neurons inform the thalamus about what sensory information to look out for. The thalamic sensory inputs do not merely proceed unmodified to the cortex. Rather, they are compared to the cortically based expected inputs, and further transmission is adjusted accordingly.

Just as the information processing model of brain function accommodates the phonological processing paradigm of reading and dyslexia, so too does the cortically-based prediction paradigm accommodate meaning-centered models of reading. Such models emphasize the role of the reader in constructing meaning not only by means of raw interpretations of the author's words and phrases, but by supplying its own idiosyncratic background knowledge and belief systems to aid in meaning construction. The fundamental psychological event in this model is not the processing of externally supplied information, but rather the prediction that such information will be found, supplemented with the search for confirmatory or disconfirmatory evidence.

And just as the phonological processing paradigm confers its own design on the definition of dyslexia, so too does the prediction paradigm. Each can be described in both biological and psychological terms. The phonological processing paradigm defines dyslexia as an impairment of phonological processing not otherwise explained by impairments elsewhere. The biological correlate is that there is impairment in the utilization of the special brain site devoted to turning letters into sounds. The prediction model has been much looser in its definition of reading problems and dyslexia. It assesses the capacity of readers to utilize the full complement of meaning-laden cuing systems, such as syntax, semantics, background knowledge, and background beliefs. Clearly, lacking knowledge of an idiomatic expression, a genre, or a topic will limit the reader's capacity to make appropriate predictions about such language patterns or information.

Summary and Conclusions

Although it is interesting to compare distinct approaches to neuroscience, reading, and dyslexia, it is equally instructive to consider how one approach is viewed by the other. What does the phonological processing model say about the constructivist model? What does the constructivist model say about the phonological processing model?

From the standpoint of neuroscience, phonological processing advocates have maintained that constructivists do not sufficiently acknowledge what biological research indicates about graphophonemic processing in reading. It is easy to understand where this assertion comes from. It is based, in part, on the fact that the constructivist model emphasizes those aspects of the reading process that are not easy to study biologically. There is no one site in the brain where predicting an upcoming word or phrase based on background knowledge occurs. This is a global operation that likely varies in its particulars from one reading situation to another. But this is certainly a biological phenomenon, whose global properties are being studied by neuroscientists, and to which the constructivists are contributing through their research on eye movements in reading.

On the other hand, from the constructivist standpoint, the phonological processing model emphasizes biological aspects of reading to the exclusion of social, cultural, and certain psycholinguistic aspects. More problematically, the constructivists would argue that the biological emphasis in the phonological processing model is artificially narrow. It emphasizes specific brain localizations where certain processes occur, but not the global brain organization that explains why or how these processes occur.

Furthermore, this narrow emphasis is reinforced by a powerful set of technologies—brain imaging—that produces magnificent statistical charts of the neural correlates to cognitive activity, but which comes with a very severe limitation in terms of their temporal and spatial capabilities. The longer the event occurs and the larger the brain region where that event occurs, the less reliable is the data generated by the machine. Functional MRI, for instance, favors events that span a period of milliseconds in very small, circumscribed regions.

In the end, the neuroimaging technology must be understood as subordinate to the psycholinguistics of reading. This is true for a very simple reason: the most theoretically useless cognitive events can be found to take place in very specific regions of the brain by the neuroimaging technology. Neuroimaging cannot by itself decide the question of which cognitive functions play a role in reading and which do not. Only an independent theory of reading based on studies of reading behaviors and their patterns of development can adjudicate that.

References

Adams, M. J. (1990). *Beginning to read: Thinking and learning about print*. Cambridge, MA: MIT Press.

al-Chalabi, A., Turner, M., & Delamont, R. S. (2006). *The brain: A beginners guide*. Oxford, UK: Oneworld Publications.

Bloomfield, L. (1942). Teaching children to read. In L. Bloomfield & C. L. Barnhart (Eds.), *Let's read: A linguistic approach* (pp. 19–42). Detroit, MI: Wayne State University Press.

Caplan, D. (1987). *Neurolinguistics and linguistic aphasiology: An introduction*. Cambridge, UK: Cambridge University Press.

Chang, B. S., Ly, J., Appignani, B., Bodell, A., Apse, K. A., Ravenscroft, R. S., et al. (2005). Reading impairment in the neuronal migration disorder of periventricular nodular heterotopias. *Neurology, 64,* 799–803.

Clowes, G. A. (1999). Reading is anything but natural: An interview with G. Reid Lyon. *School Reform News*. Retrieved from http://www.heartland.org

Cope, N., Harold, D., Hill, G., Moskvina, V., Stevenson, J., Holmans, P., et al. (2005). Strong evidence that KIAA0319 on chromosome 6p is a susceptibility gene for developmental dyslexia. *American Journal of Human Genetics, 76,* 581–591.

Demb, J. B., Poldrack, R. A., & Gabrieli, J. D. E. (1999). Functional neuroimaging of word processing. In R. Klein. & P. McMullen (Eds.), *Converging methods for understanding reading and dyslexia* (pp. 245–304). Cambridge, MA: MIT Press.

Destexhe, A. (2000). Modeling corticothalamic feedback and the gating of the thalamus by the cerebral cortex. *Journal of Physiology, 94,* 394–410.

Eckert, M. A., Leonard, C. M., Richards, T. L., Aylward, E. H., Thomson, J., & Berninger, V. W. (2003). Anatomical correlates of dyslexia: Frontal and cerebellar findings. *Brain, 126,* 482–494.

Ehrlich, S. F., & Rayner, K. (1981). Contextual effects on word perception and eye movements during reading. *Journal of Verbal Learning & Verbal Behavior, 20,* 641–655.

Fiebach, C. F., Friederici, A. D., Müller, K., & von Cramon, D. Y. (2002). fMRI evidence for dual routes to the mental lexicon in visual word recognition. *Journal of Cognitive Neuroscience, 14,* 11–23.

Gaab, N., Gabrieli, J. D. E., Deutsch, G. K., Tallal, P., & Temple, E. (2007). Neural correlates of rapid auditory processing are disrupted in children with developmental dyslexia and ameliorated with training: An fMRI study. *Restorative Neurology and Neuroscience, 25,* 295–310.

Gibson, C. J., & Gruen, J. R. (2008). The human lexinome: Genes of language and reading. *Journal of Communication disorders, 41,* 409–420.

Gilbert, C. D., & Sigman, M. (2007, June 7). Brain states: Top-down influences in sensory processing. *Neuron, 54,* 677–696.

Goodman, K. S. (1964). The linguistics of reading. *The Elementary School Journal, 64,* 355–361.

Goodman, K. S. (1967). Reading: A psycholinguistic guessing game. *Journal of the Reading Specialist, 4,* 126–135.

Hawkins, J. (2004). *On intelligence.* New York: Henry Holt.

Hogaboam, T. W. (1983). Reading patterns in eye movement data. In K. Rayner (Ed.), *Eye movements in reading: Perceptual and language processes* (pp. 309–332). New York: Academic Press.

Hruby, G. G. (2009). Grounding reading comprehension theory in the neuroscience literatures. In S. Israel & G. Duffy (Eds.), *Handbook of research on reading comprehension* (pp. 189–223). New York: Routledge Taylor and Francis Group.

Hruby, G. G., & Hynd, G. W. (2006). Decoding Shaywitz: The modular brain and its discontents [book review essay on "Overcoming dyslexia"]. *Reading Research Quarterly, 41,* 544–556.

Just, M. A., & Carpenter, P. A. (1987). *The psychology of reading and language comprehension.* Newton, MA: Allyn and Bacon.

Krauzlis, R. J. (2005). The control of voluntary eye movements: New perspectives. *Neuroscientist, 11,* 124–137.

Lenneberg, E. (1967). *Biological foundations of language.* New York: Wiley.

Luria, A. R. (1973). *The working brain: An introduction to neuropsychology.* New York: Basis Books.

Lyon, G. R. (1997, July 10). Testimony before the Committee on Education and the Workforce, U.S. House of Representatives. Retrieved June, 2000, from http://edworkforce.house.gov

Maguire, E. A., Spiers, H. J., Good, C. D., Hartley, T., Frackowiak, R. S. J., Burgess, N. (2003). Navigation expertise and the human hippocampus: A structural brain imaging analysis. *Hippocampus, 13,* 208–217.

Meng, H., Smith, S. D., Hager, K., Held, M., Liu, J., Olson, R. K., et al. (2005). DCDC2 is associated with reading disability and modulates neuronal development in the brain. *Proceedings of the National Academy of Sciences USA, 102,* 17053–17058.

Mesulam, M.-K. (1998). From sensation to cognition. *Brain, 121,* 1013–1052.

Paulson, E. J. (2002). Are oral reading word omissions and substitutions caused by careless eye movements? *Reading Psychology, 23,* 45–66.

Paulson, E. J., & Freeman, A. E. (2003). *Insight from the eyes: The science of effective reading instruction.* Portsmouth, NH: Heinemann.

Paulson, E. J., & Goodman, K. S. (2008). Re-reading eye-movement research: Support for transactional models of reading. In A. D. Flurkey, E. J. Paulson, & K. S. Goodman (Eds.), *Scientific realism in studies of reading* (pp. 25–47). Mahwah, NJ: Erlbaum.

Posner, M. J., & Raichle, M. E. (1997). *Images of mind.* New York: W. H. Freeman.

Rayner, K. (1997). Understanding eye movements in reading. *Scientific Studies of Reading, 1,* 317–339.

Rosen, G. D., Bai, J., Wang, Y., Fiondella, C. G., Threlkeld, S. W., Lo-Turco, J. J., et al. (2007). Disruption of neuronal migration by RNAi of Dyx1c1 results in neocortical and hippocampal malformations. *Cerebral Cortex, 17,* 2562–2572.

Rosenberger, P. B., & Rottenberg, D. A. (2002). Does training change the brain? *Neurology, 58,* 1139–1140.

Schumacher, J., Anthoni, H., Dahdouh, F., Konig, I. R., Hillmer, A. M., Kluck, N., et al. (2006). Strong genetic evidence of DCDC2 as a susceptibility gene for dyslexia. *American Journal of Human Genetics, 78,* 52–62.

Shaywitz, S. E. (1998, January 29). Dyslexia. *New England Journal of Medicine, 338,* 307–312.

Shaywitz, S. E. (2004). *Overcoming dyslexia: A new and complete science-based program for reading problems at any level.* New York: Alfred A. Knopf.

Shaywitz, S., Lyon, G. R., & Shaywitz, B. A. (2006). Dyslexia (specific reading disability). In F. Burg, J. Ingelfinger, R. Polin, & A. Gershon (Eds.), *Current pediatric therapy* (pp. 1244–1247). Philadelphia: W.B. Saunders.

Shaywitz, S. E., Shaywitz, B. A., Pugh, K., Skudlarski, P., Fulbright, R. K., Constable, R. T., et al. (1996). The neurobiology of developmental dyslexia as viewed through the lens of functional magnetic resonance imaging technology. In G. R. Lyon & J. M. Rumsey (Eds.), *Neuroimaging: A window to the neurological foundations of learning and behavior in children* (pp. 79–94). Baltimore, MD: Paul H. Brookes.

Sherman, S. M., & Guillery, R.W. (2006). *Exploring the thalamus and its role in cortical function* (2nd ed). Cambridge, MA: The MIT Press.

Simos, P. G., Fletcher, J. M., Bergman, E., Breier, J. I., Foorman, B. R., Castillo, E. M., et al. (2002). Dyslexia-specific brain activation profile becomes normal following successful remedial training. *Neurology, 58,* 1203–1213.

Strauss, L. S., Goodman, K. S., & Paulson, E. J. (2009). Brain research and reading: How emerging concepts of neuroscience support a meaning construction view of the reading process. *Educational Research and Review, 4*(2), 21–033.

Temple, E., Deutsch, G. K., Poldrack, R. A., Miller, S. L., Tallal, P., Merzenich, M. M., et al. (2003). Neural deficits in children with dyslexia ameliorated by behavioral remediation: Evidence from functional MRI. *Proceedings of the National Academy of Sciences, 100,* 2860–2865.

Venezky, R. L. (1999). *The American way of spelling.* New York: Guilford.

Wood, F. B., & Grigorenko, E. L. (2001). Emerging issues in the genetics of dyslexia: A methodological preview. *Journal of Learning Disabilities, 34,* 503–511.

Part II

Causes and Consequences of Reading Disability

EDITOR: JOHN ELKINS

9

Home Differences and Reading Difficulty

Jeanne R. Paratore and Susan Dougherty
Boston University

This chapter is built on two major tenets: first, that there is substantial evidence that home and family characteristics (including poverty, language, and educational experiences) have important effects on children's early and later reading success; and second, that knowledgeable, thoughtful, and responsive teachers working with parents and with a rich and worthy curriculum can mediate these differences. We develop these central ideas within three sections. In the first section, we distinguish between reading disability and reading difficulty (arguing that the children who are the focus of this chapter are more appropriately described as children with reading difficulty rather than reading disability), and we situate our discussion within the context of sociocultural and sociocognitive learning theories. In the second section, we consider the external factors that make children's reading success more or less probable. In the third section, we focus on studies of instructional practices that reflect a view of parents as a learning resource. Finally, we summarize what is known and we use existing studies to speculate about the types of instruction and collaborative actions that could change the learning trajectory of children whose home experiences and resources set them apart from their higher-achieving (and, typically, more economically advantaged) peers.

Learning to Read and Write as a Sociocultural and Sociocognitive Process

We begin our discussion with a definition of reading disability (RD). According to Spear-Swerling (2004), reading disability is:

> Intrinsic, presumably biologically based, learning difficulties (as opposed to reading failure associated with poverty, for example, as well as a specific cognitive deficit or set of deficits (as opposed to generalized learning problems). Thus, genuine cases of RD have been viewed as involving "unexpected" reading failure that cannot be accounted for by other disabilities, generalized cognitive-linguistic weaknesses, or obvious environmental causes, including a lack of appropriate instruction. (p. 518)

With this as a definition, the children who are our focus in this chapter are not "reading disabled"; rather, our concern is children whose reading difficulty stems largely from factors external to them: poverty (Bourdieu, 1986; Compton-Lilly, 2007; Hart & Risley, 1995; Lareau, 1989, 2003; Neuman & Celano, 2001), language (Davidson & Snow, 1995; DeTemple & Beals, 1991; Dieterich, Assel, & Swank, 2006; Heath, 1983; Leseman & de Jong, 1998; Purcell-Gates, 1995; Tabors, Beals, & Weizman, 2001; Tabors, Roach, & Snow, 2001; Weizman & Snow, 2001), and educational experiences at home (Aulls & Sollars, 2003; Baker, Fernandez-Fein, Scher, & Williams, 1998; Baker, Scher, & Mackler, 1997; Dearing, Kreider, & Simpkins, 2006; de Jong & Leseman, 2001; DeTemple, 2001; Leseman & de Jong, 1998; Morrow, 1983; Purcell-Gates, 1994; Rashid, Morris, & Sevcik, 2005; Sénéchal, LeFevre, & Thomas, 1998; Snow, Barnes, Chandler, Goodman, & Hemphill, 1991; Sonnenschein & Munsterman, 2002; Swalander & Taube, 2007; Teale, 1986).

The difficulty that confronts children who differ in socioeconomic status and social class, language knowledge and use, and educational experiences can be understood through the lens of a sociocognitive perspective on learning. In Gee's (2004) words,

> A broad perspective on reading is essential if we are to speak to issues of access and equity in schools and workplaces … reading and writing cannot be separated from speaking, listening, and interacting, on the one hand, or using language to think about and act on the world, on the other. (p. 116)

Moreover, as Heath (1991) explained, becoming literate is a complex and dynamic enterprise:

The literateness of any individual is also only somewhat stable; it is dynamic, iterative, and sometimes erratic and daring in its representations. On some occasions, those who think of themselves as literate can read a poem and see through it to both personal and universal meanings; at other times, the poet's words fall like dry chips with no connection to life. A word spelled or even identified and pronounced correctly at one point slips away into uncertainty on other occasions. Literates do not trust with certainty that the right words will come to sum up the essence of a meeting or to launch a charity campaign. Those who assume a sense of being literate in modern postindustrial nations know that they depend on far more than separate and individual skills for their literate identities. Being literate depends on the essential harmony of core language behaviors and certain critical supporting social relations and cultural practices. (pp. 5–6)

Heath argued that children who are learning to read and write must not only learn to understand and confront the fluid nature of what it means to be literate, but they must also acquire ways of thinking that allow them to act in contexts that are uncertain and unstable. Some children—those who arrive at school from "mainstream, school-oriented, upwardly mobile aspiring groups" (Heath, 1991, p. 12)—have the particular advantage of having experienced "redundant, repetitive, and multiply reinforced ways of socializing… [that] provide the bedrock discourse forms that sustain what schools define as critical thinking" (p. 13). But there is substantial evidence (Delgado-Gaitan, 1992; Delpit, 1995; González, Moll, & Amanti, 2005; Heath, 1983; Purcell-Gates, 1995; Schieffelin & Cochran-Smith, 1984; Taylor & Dorsey-Gaines, 1988; Valdés, 1996) that children who are raised in non-mainstream families hear and learn discourses that are different from those that commonly characterize schools and classrooms. Although as Gee (2004) noted, almost all children, even poor children, enter school with substantial and complex vocabulary, syntax, and experiential knowledge, some lack "specific verbal abilities tied to specific school-based practices, and school-based genres of oral and written language" (p. 131).

Many argue that the complexity of becoming literate is obscured by a simplistic view of what it takes to be a successful reader. Paris (2005), for example, argued that flaws in traditional research designs have caused researchers and policymakers to misinterpret (or ignore) "fundamental differences in the developmental trajectories of reading skills" (p. 184). Space does not permit a full discussion of this important issue, but, in a nutshell, Paris and others (Chall, Jacobs, & Baldwin, 1990; Gee, 2004; Snow, 1991) argue that evidence of the early effects of phonemic awareness, phonological development, and phonics abilities on reading achievement has obscured the equally significant effects of language and concept knowledge. As a result, at the present time, in many classrooms, instruction (for both capable and struggling readers) privileges code knowledge at the expense of vocabulary and language knowledge. For children who are socialized at home into the vocabulary, language, and discourse of the school curriculum, these instructional

practices typically have few negative consequences; but for those from non-mainstream families and communities whose home language practices differ from the academic discourse that is fundamental to reading and writing success, these instructional emphases in the early years can make the difference between reading success and reading difficulty in the later years. The importance of addressing the differences in literacy, language, and conceptual knowledge early on is well-established (Juel, 1988, 2006; Stanovich, 1986; Whitehurst & Lonigan, 2002). However, the types of instructional practices known to be effective in supporting the reading success of children whose home environments differ from those of mainstream children are far from universally available to children (Biemiller, 2006; Dickinson, McCabe, & Essex, 2006; Dickinson & Smith, 1994; Dickinson & Sprague, 2002; Juel, 2006; McCarthey, 1999; McCarthey, 1997; McGill-Franzen, Lanford, & Adams, 2002). Thus, our purpose in the remainder of this chapter is twofold: to explain in greater detail the home differences that contribute to reading difficulty that some children experience in both early and later years of school; and to describe the types of instructional practices that effectively engage parents in supporting children's reading and writing success.

Home Differences and Reading Difficulty

The role families play in children's literacy learning has been widely studied, and these investigations have led to some widely-held conclusions about the types of experiences children have prior to school that are influential in their reading and writing success. In an apt summary, Leseman and van Tuijl (2006) identified three categories of early literacy experiences that distinguish "optimal from less optimal literacy-supporting environments" (p. 212). The first type includes literacy events and interactions that occur as part of the conduct of daily life. This category includes the reading or "leafing through" of print materials that are commonly found at home—advertising circulars, food market coupons, religious texts, and so forth. It also includes shared storybook reading, a parent-child activity that has been identified as having special significance in preparing young children to read (Bus, van Ijzendoorn, & Pellegrini, 1995; Heath, 1986; Heath & Branscombe, 1986; Purcell-Gates, 1996, 2001; Sénéchal & LeFevre, 2002; Whitehurst & Lonigan, 2002).

The second category relates to the informal or incidental instruction that is often embedded within cognitive, linguistic, and social interactions, such as reciting nursery rhymes and songs or playing with letters, letter sounds, and words. These types of interactions are thought to be especially important because they contribute to the development of a particular subset of skills that have been found to be of critical importance to early reading: phonological skills and alphabetic knowledge (de Jong & Leseman, 2001; Dodici, Draper, & Peterson, 2003; Muter, Hulme, & Snowling, 2004; Sénéchal et al., 1998; Sonnenschein & Munsterman, 2002; Whitehurst & Lonigan, 2002).

The third category is affective: the development of a favorable disposition toward reading and writing that emerges from satisfying and comforting social interactions with parents, siblings, or caregivers around literacy events or activities (Baker et al., 1997; Bus, 2003; Durkin, 1966; Landry, Miller-Loncar, Smith, & Swank, 2002; Landry & Smith, 2006; Morrow, 1983; Sonnenschein & Munster-man, 2002; Wigfield & Asher, 1984). It seems important to note that these studies are limited to the examination of children's disposition toward the types of reading and writing activities that are common to schools and classrooms. It is unknown, therefore, whether developing a favorable dispositions towards literacy experiences that are valued at home, but not at school, has any relationship to reading and writing success.

We begin by asking how each of the categories of literacy experiences and events play out in the home and community lives of families who are culturally, linguistically, or socially different from mainstream families.

Virtually All Families Practice Literacy Evidence of a relationship between reading and writing as daily occurrences and success in learning to read is both voluminous and long-held. Huey (1908) is often cited as one of the earliest to place parents at the heart of children's early reading success: "The secret of it all lies in parents reading aloud to and with the child" (p. 332). In subsequent years, studies by Durkin (1966) and Clark (1976) were fundamental to understanding that parents of children who experienced early success in reading engaged them often in a variety of reading and writing tasks and events, including reading to and with them, encouraging them to notice, name, and write letters and sounds, and providing models of engaged and interested readers and writers. These characterizations led many researchers and practitioners to assume that homes that lacked these particular types of literacy events and interactions were low literate or even non-literate. However, studies of language, literacy, and social interactions in families that were characterized as linguistically, culturally, or economically different from those studied by Durkin and Clark led to very different understandings.

In her landmark, 10-year ethnography of the ways families in three communities (Trackton, a low-income Black community; Roadville, a low-income White community, and Maintown, a middle-income White community) used language and literacy in the course of their daily lives, Heath (1983) found that virtually all of the Trackton and Roadville families engaged children in rich and literate discourse, but they did so in ways that were substantially different from mainstream Maintown families. Children in Trackton had few experiences asking or answering "school-like" questions (i.e., the types of questions for which the adult knows the answer) or otherwise displaying their knowledge through labeling and describing; they rarely recounted or retold shared experiences; and they had few experiences with storybook reading. They did, however, answer many questions related to genuine queries; they learned names of objects and events

as they were encountered during daily events or interactions; and they learned to tell stories in collaboration with others, usually co-constructing a narrative within a process sprinkled with frequent interruptions and embellishments, both true and false. These differences were consequential, preventing children from readily mapping their experiences and resulting predispositions toward language and literacy use neatly onto the expectations of the classroom.

In Roadville, parents engaged children in some book reading (most books of the labeling type rather than narrative, fictional texts), and, like the children of Maintown, they were often asked school-like questions, but their literacy interactions largely ended here. Unlike Maintown parents, Roadville parents did not link book reading with other events in their children's lives, and for the most part, parent participation in book reading ended when the children entered school. At the start, Roadville children do reasonably well in school; they learn to write letters and decode basic words. But as learning expectations move beyond reading and writing simple texts, they, like the children of Trackton, begin to fall behind.

In their study of 6 inner-city, African American families, Taylor and Dorsey-Gaines (1988) observed purposeful, complex uses of reading and writing woven into the fabric of the everyday lives of adults and children. However, like the families studied by Heath (1983), Taylor and Dorsey-Gaines found that the ways these families used literacy did not map onto the ways children were expected to use literacy in school. Perhaps the most striking differences between home and school literacies were in connectedness and purposefulness. At home, literacy uses by both adults and children were initiated for the purposes of achieving a particular goal or completing an important task, effectively characterized as "situated action" (Gee, 2004, p. 117). In contrast, in school, the underlying purposes were not social or problem-solving in nature. Rather, they were most often decontextualized actions initiated to complete a learning task, unrelated to any purposeful or meaningful social act. Both in the classroom and as homework, children practiced writing their names, writing lists of words, completing fill-in-the-blank worksheets. These were unfamiliar tasks for the children observed by Taylor and Dorsey-Gaines and presupposed knowledge about print that they had not acquired at home. Like the children of Trackton and Roadville, most of these children found school difficult.

Over a period of 3 to 18 months, Teale (1986) observed 24 preschool children (8 Anglo, 8 Black, 8 Mexican American) residing in low-income families. He recorded any instance during which a person "produced, comprehended, or attempted to produce or comprehend written language" (p. 177). The total number of visits ranged from 5 to 47 per household and totaled over 1,400 hours of observations. Like Heath and Taylor and Dorsey-Gaines, Teale reported that the uses of reading and writing varied widely across families both in quantity and type, and as well, he found that the "most striking" (p. 184) feature of the literacy events and interactions he observed was their social nature. Children and parents engaged in literate activity to accomplish meaningful and purposeful tasks, rather than to "practice" reading or writing for the purposes of advancing literacy knowledge.

Similar accounts can be found in the work of many others and these accounts stretch across nearly three decades and document literacy events and actions in the homes of families representing many cultures, languages, and social classes (Anderson & Stokes, 1984; Compton-Lilly, 2003, 2007; Leichter, 1984; Madigan, 1992; Purcell-Gates, 1995, 1996; Taylor, 1997; Valdés, 1996; Vasquez, Pease-Alvarez, & Shannon, 1994; Volk & Long, 2005; Voss, 1996). Nonetheless, as explained in the next section, when it comes to preparation for school-based literacy, the presence of some types of literacy practices seems to be outweighed by the absence of others.

Differences in How Literacy is Practiced Matter   Notwithstanding the evidence that "virtually all children in a literate society like ours have numerous experiences with written language before they ever get to school" (Teale, p. 192), some types of early literacy experiences more readily map onto the demands of the school curriculum.

Engaging in print at more complex levels.   Studies tell us that the type of print and the ways children engage in print are important to the development of their concepts about print (Baker et al., 1998; Goodman, 1986; Purcell-Gates, 1996, 2001, 2004; Sulzby, 1985; Sulzby & Edwards, 1993; Yaden, Smolkin, & Conlon, 1989). For example, Purcell-Gates (1996) measured the literacy knowledge of 24 children, ages 4 to 6, residing in 20 low-socioeconomic status homes. With a team of research assistants, she collected data on each of the 7 days of the week, spreading out observations during the hours of the day when both adults and children were awake and at home. Researchers observed and recorded parent or child literacy events; noted the participant structure of the event; noted materials in the home related to literacy; and collected children's samples of drawing, writing, or scribbling. Children also completed a set of written language assessments. Like Teale, Purcell-Gates reported that all families engaged in literacy events, but the range was wide, varying from .17 events per hour to 5.07 events per hour. Hypothesizing that the complexity of the texts being read and written might be as important as the frequency of engagement in literacy events, Purcell-Gates also rated the text level of materials used in each event by "placing them on a continuum of size of the linguistic unit, and the features commonly associated with written, as composed to oral, language" (p. 416). Across literacy events, texts composed of words and phrases, for example, coupons, ads, food or container labels were most numerous. While not as numerous as word and phrase level texts, significant quantities of children's storybooks and adult reading materials and written products were identified within the literacy events. Overall numbers only offer a partial picture, however; as might be expected, it was the variability in the use of texts of different levels and for different purposes that mapped on to the

literacy development of the children in these families. She concluded that the role of print experiences in the home is far more complex than is commonly thought, noting that children who experienced early reading success had certain types of home literacy experiences. Most children in the study—but not all—acquired an understanding of the purposes of print and its uses in daily living routines. Children who had grasped the "big picture" (p. 422) engaged more frequently in literacy events that involved print (an average of 1.2 literacy events per hour observed) and had many print-related interactions with their mothers (an average of .71 interactions per all observed literacy events). In addition to grasping the "big picture," some children acquired knowledge about how language works—"the nature and forms of written language as well as its alphabetic nature" (p. 423); these children had many opportunities to experience "print-embedded activities that were either directed to them or were engaged in by literate others involving text at the more complex levels of written discourse found in storybooks, novels, magazine articles, and newspapers" (p. 426). Purcell-Gates argued that simply seeing a lot of print did not, by itself, lead children to an understanding of critical concepts about print, i.e., that children's recognition of environmental print may be less important than many assume. Instead, "children are better served by observing and experiencing the reading and writing of connected discourse decontextualized from physical (such as signs and containers) and pictorial contexts" (p. 426). Based on a comprehensive review of the features of written language in the home environment and of children's opportunities to interact with various written language registers, Purcell-Gates (2004) argued that the importance of the written language register has been underestimated in discussions of early literacy development. In particular, she questioned the widely-held assumption that sophisticated oral language knowledge (e.g., rare words and complex grammatical structures) is foundational for early reading development. Instead, she claimed that the evidence supports a direction reversal—that is, that "exposure to print and to print use" (p. 112) paves the way for development of complex lexical and syntactical knowledge; this knowledge, in turn, prepares children for success in both early and later stages of reading development. Moreover, she claims that neglecting this understanding is consequential, leading classroom teachers and family literacy program providers to over-emphasize the facilitative effects of the ways parents talk to children and under-emphasize the importance of print resources that support the development of the written language register.

What seems important to us as we think about the "research to practice" connections is less the direction of the effect, and more the nature of the interaction in the oral and written language registrars. It seems clear that certain types of print (e.g., extended text that in some way introduces children to academic talk and concepts) help children build fundamental literacy concepts, and certain types of adult interactions (e.g., prompting children to notice and manipulate text and elaborating and discussing ideas in text) help children to development concepts about print that facilitate reading and writing success.

Engaging in storybook reading. Related to Purcell-Gates's argument for the importance of the written language register as a staple of home literacy environments is the widely-held belief that storybook reading is an important family literacy event (Anderson, Hiebert, Scott, & Wilkinson, 1985). However, studies have led to some disagreement about the significance of the relationship between this particular literacy event and success in early reading (Bus, van Ijzendoorn, & Pellegrini, 1995; Dunning, Mason, & Stewart, 1994; Lonigan, 1994; Scarborough & Dobrich, 1994). Most prominently, although Bus et al. (1995) and Scarborough and Dobrich (1994) agreed that the relationship between parent-child reading and literacy achievement accounted for about 8% of the variance in overall achievement, they interpreted the outcome differently. Scarborough and Dobrich concluded that the findings "do not provide much support for the hypothesis that parent-preschooler reading experiences…are more predictive of literacy development than conventional demographic indices of family background" (p. 290). However, Bus et al. noted that the overall effect size of $d = 0.59$ yielded by their meta-analysis of all available studies fell within Cohen's (1977) criteria for a medium ($d = 0.50$) to strong ($d = 0.80$) effect size. They concluded that the differences in findings between their study and that of Scarborough and Dobrich are explained by the methodological advantages of meta-analysis.

Subsequent studies have provided insight into the particular conditions that lead to beneficial outcomes of parent-child reading. For the most part, studies indicate that repeated readings lead to greater vocabulary gains and more active child engagement than do single readings (Roser & Martinez, 1985; Sénéchal, 1997; Snow & Goldfield, 1983). Interactional styles during book reading also have differential effects on children's language learning from books. Asking and answering questions, focusing on novel words, and engaging children in conversations that help them go beyond the text and make connections between events, objects, or ideas in the text and their own lives relate to later reading achievement (e.g., DeTemple & Snow, 2003; Haden, Reese, & Fivush, 1996; Reese, Cox, Harte, & McAnally, 2003; Sénéchal, 1997; Sonnenschein & Munsterman, 2002). However, the effects of particular actions may vary according to children's vocabulary knowledge and the assessed outcome. Reese, Cox, Harte, and McAnally (2003) found that when children's vocabulary knowledge was the focus, children with lower initial vocabulary scores showed the greatest gains when mothers labeled and described objects and ideas, while children with higher initial vocabulary scores benefited most when mothers focused on overall story comprehension. When print knowledge was the focus, children with lower initial comprehension did better with a read-aloud style that favored story comprehension, while children with higher comprehension did better when the read-aloud style favored describing and labeling.

Other studies of interactional styles indicate the ways parents and children interact with texts varies in relation to text genres. ABC and concept books seem to prompt mothers to talk more about print and also prompt children to engage in more print-related activities, including attempts to identify letters and spell words (Baker et al., 1998; Bus & van Ijzendoorn, 1988; Cornell, Sénéchal, & Broda, 1988; Yaden et al., 1989). As well, expository texts may elicit more interaction from mothers and children than do narrative texts (Pellegrini, Perlmutter, Galda, & Brody, 1990). Some studies (e.g., Manyak, 1998) indicate that when content of books is related to families' experiences, parent-child interactions are more elaborated and interpretive.

A group of studies has also focused on the particular reading skills that children acquire through parent-child reading. There is general agreement that there is a relationship between shared reading and vocabulary and language development (Arnold & Whitehurst, 1994; Baker, Fernandez-Fein, Scher, & Williams, 1998; Crain-Thoreson & Dale, 1999; DeTemple & Snow, 2003; Jordan, Snow, & Porche, 2000; Sénéchal, 1997; Sénéchal & LeFevre, 2002; Valdez-Menchaca & Whitehurst, 1992; van Kleeck, 2003; Weizman & Snow, 2001; Whitehurst et al., 1994; Yaden, Tam, & Madrigal, 2000) and little evidence of a relationship between shared reading and phonological awareness or alphabet knowledge (Baker et al., 1998; Landry & Smith, 2006; Stahl, 2003). However, there is also solid evidence that the outcomes related to storybook reading are more complex when viewed over time. Two longitudinal studies are especially noteworthy in clarifying the relationship. Sénéchal and LeFevre (2002) found that storybook reading had effects at different stages of reading development. That is, in the beginning stage of reading, when children are focused primarily on unlocking the code, there is little evidence that parent-child reading has any influence. However, in the later years, when the texts that children read in school become more linguistically and conceptually complex, the language knowledge associated with early storybook reading becomes important. Similar outcomes are evident in a study by de Jong and Leseman (2001). For word decoding, they reported an "overall decline in the size of the relationships with the home education facets from the end of first grade to the end of third grade" (p. 11). Conversely, they found that the relationship between home education rated as high in the facets of instructional quality and socioemotional quality and reading comprehension increased from grade one to grade three. De Jong and Leseman argued that it is not likely that home literacy directly affected third-grade reading outcomes, but rather, as suggested by Snow (1991), home literacy experiences that are rich in opportunities for language learning not only lead to immediate learning of new vocabulary and concepts, but also mediate the acquisition and development of language over time.

Finally, access to books and other print resources is uneven. Based on their analysis of resources available to families in four neighborhoods (2 low-income and 2 middle-income), Neuman (2006) reported "stark and triangulated differences in resources" (p. 31), with fewer bookstores, fewer libraries—with shorter hours of operation—and fewer print resources in preschools and school libraries in the low-income neighborhoods. Among the many statistics that reveal the details of the disparity between the low- and middle-income communities is the fact that print resources available for purchase in stores in the community ranged from 13 titles for every child in one of the middle-income neighborhoods to 1 book per 300 children in one of the low-income neighborhoods. Data from day care centers and libraries are equally disparate.

Engaging in nursery rhymes and other sorts of language play. Phonological awareness and alphabet knowledge are well-established as predictors of early reading achievement (see, for example, Snow, Burns, & Griffin, 1998). With regard to the contribution of home and community experiences to the acquisition of these abilities, there is a general finding of a relationship between children's knowledge of nursery rhymes and higher levels of phonological awareness and alphabet knowledge (Baker et al., 1998; Bryant, Bradley, MacLean, & Crossland, 1989; Maclean, Bryant, & Bradley, 1987; Sonnenschein, Brody, & Munsterman, 1996). Moreover, there is evidence (Baker, et al., 1998; Sénéchal & LeFevre, 2002; Sonnenschein et al., 1996) of a direct relationship between parents' self-report of engaging children in various types of formal and informal word-learning activities (e.g., hand-clap games, singing, interactions with educational books, writing letters and words) and higher levels of skills directly related to word recognition. Important to this discussion of home differences are studies that indicate that children's exposure to rhyme differs by social class, with middle-income children more often engaged in rhyming activities than are low-income children (Baker et al., 1998).

Hearing lots of talk and talk that is lexically and syntactically complex. The relationship between children's early language development and success in reading and writing also has been widely studied, and many have studied the particular contribution of parent talk to children's language knowledge. There is clear evidence of a relationship between the quantity (Hart & Risley, 1995), lexical complexity (Beals, 2001; Beals, DeTemple, & Dickinson, 1994; Dickinson & Beals, 1994; Hoff, 2006; Tabors, Beals, & Weizman, 2001; Tabors, Roach, & Snow, 2001; Weizman & Snow, 2001), and syntactic complexity (Hoff, 2006; Huttenlocher, Vasilyeva, Cymerman, & Levine, 2002) of parent talk and children's language learning. Greater incidences of pretend talk (during play); greater use of narrative and explanatory talk that require extended conversations (during mealtime, play, and book reading); and greater exposure to and explanation of sophisticated or rare words relate to higher rates of vocabulary learning among children in low-income groups. Moreover, vocabulary knowledge in the early years is thought to be important not only because of its connection to children's development of deep stores of

conceptual knowledge, but also because of its contribution to the development of phonological awareness (Metsala & Walley, 1998; Sénéchal, Ouellette, & Rodney, 2006). As explained by Metsala and Walley (1998), "words with many similar sounding neighbors reside in 'dense' neighborhoods" (p. 101), and the sound similarities (e.g., bag, bib, bit) prompt children to notice "fine-grained" (p. 101) differences in words, thus sharpening their awareness of sounds in words.

Engaging in experiences that motivate children toward print-engagement. A few investigations provide evidence of a relationship between children's interest in and motivation to engage in school-based reading activities and the frequency and nature of reading and other activities at home. Lomax (1976) and Morrow (1983), for example, found that kindergarten children with high interest in reading were read to more often than children with low interest in reading. Morrow (1983) also found that children with high interest watched less television, visited the library more often, and had greater access to books in their homes than did children with low interest in reading. Sonnenschein et al. (1996) and Sonnenschein and Munsterman (2002) found that the affective quality of the interaction during parent-child storybook reading, defined as the extent to which the parent used the text to engage and focus the child, was significantly related to children's reading motivation. This outcome is consistent with a series of studies by Bus and her colleagues (Baker et al., 1997; Bus, 2003; Bus & van Ijzendoorn, 1988; Bus & van Ijzendoorn, 1992, 1995; Bus, Leseman, & Keultjes, 2000) in which they observed that the ways mothers responded to children's disengagement correlated with child's interest in reading. That is, children were more likely to maintain engagement or interest in books when mothers responded to lack of focus by skipping a page, allowing the child to comment on an object or event, or connecting events and objects in texts to familiar experiences in the child's life.

Making Sense of the Evidence of Home Differences and Reading Difficulty

Our review of literature related to understanding the ways parents and children of diverse economic, linguistic, and cultural groups use reading and writing in their home and community settings leads us to a definitive (and long-held) understanding: literacy uses and events of various types are embedded within the daily routines of virtually all families. Equally definitive is the evidence that particular types of home literacy experiences make school success more probable. Literacy uses and events that are highly congruent with the school reading and writing curriculum that occur in children's preschool years give children a head start; conversely, experiences that are not a good match for the school curriculum are largely invisible (McCarthey, 1997) and thus are unrecognized as potential building blocks for school success. Studies of interventions at home and at school convince us that it need not be this way—that effective teachers who are knowledgeable about how to work collaboratively with parents can take advantage of what children already know, and with parents, extend what children need to know to experience reading and writing success. In the next section, we address this area of research.

Instructional Practices that Mediate Home Differences In a review of research that examined the effectiveness of various interventions used to improve the reading performance of struggling readers, Torgesen (2004) stated, "Preventive and remedial instruction must be substantially more intense than regular classroom instruction if it is to accomplish its purposes" (p. 364). He suggested two ways to increase intensity of reading instruction: by increasing instructional time or by decreasing group size, thereby increasing amount of time the teacher can dedicate to each child. We argue that there is a third way to increase intensity for children who struggle or who are at risk for reading difficulties—even as a result of differences in home literacy environments—and that is to view parents as an instructional resource. This argument is grounded in a review of studies that fall into two general categories. The first category includes studies in which parents effectively serve as learning partners with their children. These shared literacy interactions are accomplished in different ways. In some cases, parents are simply provided with materials and basic instructions for providing support to their children at home. In other cases, such as when a child seems to be struggling to a substantial degree or when parents are less familiar with a particular technique, informational and instructional sessions may be provided. At times, when parents themselves lack the English literacy skills necessary to assist their children—or when their own school experiences were negative and have left them suspicious of schools or doubtful that their children will fare any better—full-scale family literacy projects provide support to them and their children. The second category includes studies in which parents are learning partners with teachers; in these interactions, teachers share information with parents about family literacy routines that would support children in school; in addition, teachers seek to learn from parents about family and community routines and events and about children's interests and experiences outside of school, and to use what is learned as a foundation for and connection to the classroom curriculum. Our intent in this section is not to present an exhaustive review of related studies, but rather to present trustworthy examples that are useful in considering present and future directions.

Parents as Learning Partners with Their Children When teachers ask parents to participate with their children as learning partners, the types of activities they assign to them typically fall within three types: reading to children, listening to children read, or engaging children in activities intended to develop specific reading skills or abilities (Sénéchal, 2006).

Reading to children. Perhaps the most widespread attempt by teachers to initiate home-school connections is sending home books with children, with the expectation that parents will read these books to the children. Because parents vary in the ways that they engage in storybook reading, such efforts have been found to vary widely in effectiveness (Edwards, 1994; Goldenberg, Reese, & Gallimore, 1992). Some studies help us to understand the types of actions we might take as teachers to increase the likelihood of success of such collaborations.

Edwards (1991) implemented a parent-child shared reading program with 25 lower-socioeconomic-status mothers and their children. The program included three phases: coaching, peer modeling, and parent-child interaction, with each phase lasting approximately 6–7 weeks and each session lasting 2 hours. Parents viewed videotape of effective storybook reading sessions, and they were provided a progression of steps to follow. At first, as parents practiced the strategies, the university-leader-coach intervened and scaffolded the dialogue. Over the course of the three phases, responsibility for the shared reading was gradually released from the coach, to peers, and eventually entirely to the parent. Observational data indicated that children engaged more often in book-related conversations and asked and answered more questions about the text. Although school achievement data were not collected, teachers reported that children increased their knowledge of written language, concepts about print, and story comprehension. Edwards concluded that with explicit and extended coaching, parents with low levels of literacy and with negative experiences during their own years of schooling could be enlisted as effective storybook readers with their children.

Krol-Sinclair (1996) trained parents who were immigrants with limited English proficiency and limited reading ability in read-aloud strategies for the purpose of reading aloud in elementary classrooms and also reading with their children at home. Like Edwards, she offered parents extended instruction (between 4 and 7 sessions) in read-aloud strategies, and she also provided opportunities to rehearse selected books in front of an audience of peers. She observed all classroom read-aloud sessions, and parents audiotaped at-home read-aloud sessions. She found that parents learned to incorporate effective discourse practices into their read-alouds both at home and in the classrooms they visited. Moreover, she found that parents brought personal strategies to the classroom reading sessions. That is, they incorporated read-aloud strategies that were not directly addressed in training. She also found that parents' limited literacy skills (in English or in their first language) did not prevent them from successfully engaging in read-alouds of carefully selected and rehearsed books. Further, because of the classroom reading component of this intervention, teachers had an opportunity to observe parents as they read and interacted with children, and they noted and acknowledged (sometimes with surprise) the parents' capacity to serve as learning resources for their children. Most of the teachers commented that they acquired an increased awareness of parents' commitment to reading.

Whitehurst and colleagues (Arnold & Whitehurst, 1994; Valdez-Menchaca & Whitehurst, 1992; Whitehurst et al., 1994; Zevenbergen & Whitehurst, 2006) conducted several studies of the effects of a technique they termed dialogic reading. As described by Zevenbergen and Whitehurst (2006), in dialogic reading, "the child is encouraged to become the teller of the story over time; the adult's role is to prompt the child with questions, expand the child's verbalizations, and praise the child's efforts to tell the story and label objects within the book" (p. 178). In most of these studies (Arnold & Whitehurst, 1994; Valdez-Menchaca & Whitehurst, 1992; Whitehurst et al., 1994), researchers studied effects of training both preschool teachers and parents in dialogic reading, and the designs did not allow researchers to study the effects of a home-only intervention. However, noting this, Lonigan and Whitehurst (1998) conducted a study that allowed them to contrast the effects of three conditions: a home-only condition, a school-only condition, and a school-plus-home condition with a no-treatment group. Children in the study were 3- and 4-year-olds from low-income, English-speaking households. All but two of the parents of children in the home-reading condition attended two training sessions on dialogic reading; two parents attended only the first training. Parents were asked to engage in dialogic reading daily over a 6-week period, and to complete a daily log sheet of when dialogic reading occurred and to record the titles of the books shared. Children in all treatment conditions did significantly better on post-test measures than did children in the control group, and effects were largest for children engaged in home reading, particularly when the outcome measure was expressive language. The researchers suggest that this finding may be accounted for by the opportunity for elaborative and extended talk that parent-child (one-to-one) reading provided (as opposed to the group-based reading of the classroom).

To this point, each of the interventions described included some sort of training program. Teachers often acknowledge such initiatives as worthy and important, but argue that they simply do not have the resources to implement them. We wondered if it was possible to obtain results with no instructional or informational training in read-aloud strategies. To answer that question, we turned to a study by Robinson, Larsen, and Haupt (1996). These researchers observed the effects of sending high-quality picture books home with kindergarten children on at-home reading behaviors. Children in four kindergarten classes participated in the study. Two of the classrooms, comprising 35 children, served as the treatment group, while the two other classrooms, comprising 40 children, served as the control group. In both groups, one classroom was drawn from a school in a middle-class neighborhood and the other was drawn from a Chapter I school (designated as low-SES by the researchers). At the beginning of the study, all four classrooms were provided with 40 picture books. In the treatment classrooms, children were given time daily to select books to be taken home and returned the next day. Children in the non-treatment classrooms had access to the books at school, but were not given the opportunity to take them home. Data were collected through telephone interviews conducted with parents (treatment and non-treatment) once a week over the course of the 12-week intervention. During each phone call, which took place in the evenings, the parent was asked to think about the current day and recall any literacy events that occurred. Results indicated that children who were given the opportunity to take books home from their classroom each day were read to more often at home than children who were not afforded the same opportunity. This was true for children from both middle-class and low-SES homes. Although number of books shared did not emerge as a factor in the comparison of middle-class and low-SES families, the amount of time spent reading to the children did vary by social group, with middle-class parents reading more than the low-SES parents in the same treatment group. There was also a gender difference in the findings. The difference in the number of books read was significant for both boys and girls, but more pronounced among boys. The boys in the treatment group read 14.6 more books on the days sampled than boys in the non-treatment group. Because child achievement data were not gathered, it is not possible to know if the take-home book intervention accelerated the literacy development of these kindergartners.

In these examples, initiatives focused on supporting parent-child storybook reading, with and without a parent-training component, resulted, in most cases, in more time reading and in learning gains for children, especially in the area of vocabulary knowledge. As well, studies indicate that parent-child reading provides children an opportunity to learn to talk about books, and as we think about how to bridge home and school differences, this is an important outcome. That is, from shared book reading, children acquire the discourse of "book talk" that is so important to the classroom: learning to think about words and language, to consider characters and events and relationships between and among parts of a story, and to ask and answer questions (Pellegrini & Galda, 2003).

Nonetheless, the conclusion that increasing the frequency of parent-child shared reading has generally positive outcomes for literacy learning is not uncontested. Examining studies of storybook reading interventions with parents and children in multicultural contexts, Anderson, Anderson, Lynch, and Shapiro (2003) concluded that the studies yielded "a much more modest effect on literacy development of non-mainstream children than is commonly believed" (p. 209). This review is problematic, however, because the focal studies were both few in number and of many types: in some, children read to parents, in others, parents read to children. In most of the studies cited, shared texts were not high-quality children's literature, but rather, school textbooks.

These researchers also challenged the assumption that storybook reading is a "natural" family literacy event.

Citing their own work (Anderson & Morrison, 2000) and that of others (e.g., Janes & Kermani, 2001) as evidence, they argued that, in families in which joint reading is not a familiar routine, shared storybook reading can be an unwelcome intrusion sometimes perceived by parents as a "tension-filled chore" (p. 213) that "can be problematic when families feel pressured to share books in highly pre-scribed ways" (p. 214). Results such as these underscore the importance of developing a full understanding of existing family beliefs, routines, and practices and considering the potential consequences of introducing an unfamiliar literacy event into family contexts.

Listening to children read. This group of studies fits into Sénéchal's (2006) "parents listen to children" read category and is based on the simple premise that the more children read, the better they get at reading (Taylor, Frye, Maruyama, 1990; Stanovich, 1986). We have selected two examples of this type of mediation—one that included a parent-training component and one that did not.

Rasinski and Stevenson (2005) studied the effects of a fluency-based family literacy intervention called Fast Start, an approach that combined reading to and listening to children read. Parents of first graders attending a sub-urban school participated in a 60-minute training program on engaging children in supported and repeated readings of simple texts. The modeling portion of the session was followed by parents practicing a lesson with their children. Over the course of the next 11 weeks, parents worked with their children daily for approximately 10 to 15 minutes using the same text for a week. As an additional support, the 15 parents were called weekly and asked to report the amount of time they spent on the program and given the opportunity to ask questions about the program. Surveys that solicited parents' opinions about the program were sent home at the conclusion of the intervention. Children in both the experimental and control groups were categorized as high, medium, and low readers on the basis of pretest results, and the effect of the intervention on each of these groups was evaluated. Although as a whole the perfor-mance of children participating in Fast Start did not differ significantly from that of children in the control group, the initially lower-achieving children in the experimental group showed growth that was significantly greater than that of the lower-achieving children in the control group, suggesting that the intervention was of greatest benefit to the children who entered first grade with lower than expected literacy skills.

Hindin and Paratore (2007) also examined effects of a home-repeated-reading intervention, but unlike Rasinski and Stevenson (2005), they did not include a parent-training component. Working with struggling second-grade read-ers from a low-income urban community, the intervention engaged children in repeated readings of each week's classroom instructional text. On Thursday of each week, the participants met individually with a researcher and read aloud the grade-level, shared reading text that had been used

in the child's classroom throughout the week. After reading the text once with the researcher, the child was given a copy of the text and four audio tapes and asked to take the text home and read it with a parent four times over the course of the week. On the subsequent Thursday, the researcher met again with each child, and the take home text was read once more. Then the child read aloud the new take-home text and the cycle began again. Eight children (all reading at least 1 year below grade level at the start) participated in the intervention for at least 9 weeks and completed at least four story cycles. Using single-subject across-subjects design and a pre-post design, the researchers found that all participants made substantially fewer errors during the intervention than they had in baseline and all students experienced decreased error rates from the first to the last reading of stories. All children also increased fluency from the beginning to the end of the intervention, with two chil-dren achieving grade-level norms for fluency by the end of the intervention. An independent measure was used as a pre- and post-test measure of change over the course of the study. By the end of the intervention, 5 of the 8 participants performed at grade level on an isolated word reading task and 6 of the 8 participants performed at grade level on an oral reading and on a comprehension assessment.

These results were achieved without a parent-training component, suggesting that it may be possible for schools to establish rather simple (and inexpensive) intervention programs that some parents can deliver at home that will change the achievement trajectory for children who show signs of struggle in the lower elementary grades. However, the results also offer some evidence that parent training might be necessary in some circumstances. The children who made the greatest gains were those whose parents of-fered higher levels of word-level support when the children made oral reading errors. Hindin and Paratore (2007) noted that three of the four parents who offered the least amount of word-level support were acquiring English as a second language. They speculated: "Although they were moderately proficient in conversational English, they might not have had the ability or confidence to provide word-level support. These parents might have benefited from further training and encouragement to advance their word-level support of their children's reading" (p. 328).

Parents trained to instruct at home. A third category of home-school interventions includes those that focus on training parents to teach particular literacy skills (Sénéchal, 2006). Reutzel, Fawson, and Smith (2006) designed and implemented a parent involvement program that focused on developing the word reading and word writing abilities of first graders. The program, called *Words to Go!*, was implemented with first-grade parents from two, high poverty schools (one a treatment school and the other serving as a control group). Both schools offered the same school-based comprehensive family literacy program and both used the same instructional phonics program (Cunningham, 2000) as part of classroom reading instruction. Parents with children attending the four first-grade classrooms in the treatment school were invited to attend a workshop at which parents were provided training and materials necessary to implement at home "making and breaking" word lessons. Sixty-five percent of the parents of first graders attended one of the three training sessions; detailed instructions for implementing the program were sent home to the remaining parents. Once per week, a new program lesson, which included the necessary materials and a script, were sent home. Parents were asked to work with the words daily, and were asked to fill out a report recording what had been completed over the course of a week. Students who participated in the *Words to Go!* program scored significantly higher on post-tests measuring word reading and word-writing abilities than did students from the control group (effect sizes of $\eta^2 = .2$ and .23, respectively). *Words to Go!* children also out-performed control group children on a state-administered "end-of-level" test, suggesting that they were able to apply the word-level skills learned through the program to the reading of connected texts (effect size of $\eta^2 = .19$). The researchers speculated that the high rates of participation and strong fidelity of implementation may be explained by the high degree of congruence between the focal tasks and parents' expectations and beliefs about how children learn to read and write. Because the research report did not separate data collected from parents who did and those who did not attend the training session, the facilitative effects of the training session are unknown.

Jordan and colleagues (2000) studied the impact of a year-long project conducted with the parents of 177 midwestern kindergarteners; another 71 kindergarteners served as the control group for the intervention. Project EASE took place over a 5-month period during which parents of kindergarteners were invited to monthly training sessions and provided with children's books and scripted activities to use at home. During the parent training meetings, information about the importance of various types of language interactions (e.g., building and extending vocabulary knowledge) was presented. Next, the month's activities were modeled by the presenters followed by an opportunity for parents to engage in the activities with their children. Parents took home 3 weeks worth of materials after each training session and returned 1 month later for another session. The five training sessions addressed vocabulary learning, telling personal narratives, discussing storybook narratives, discussing informational texts, and learning about letters and sounds. In addition to a parent survey, which was used to gather information about home literacy behaviors and the home literacy environment, pre- and post-intervention testing was done to evaluate child outcomes. The gains made by children whose parents participated were statistically greater than those made by children in the control group. Of the three literacy-related categories addressed during the study, the greatest advantage for treatment group participants was in the Language skills composite, with the project having an effect size of $d = .64$. Moreover, children who entered kindergarten with the lowest levels of language skill experienced the greatest language gains. By the end of the project, the children in the experimental group who began with the lowest language skills were performing at a level equivalent to the children in the control group who had begun the school year with high language skills.

Also notable within the Project EASE data was the finding that those parents whose survey responses earned higher scores initially tended to participate more fully in the project, as measured both by attendance at training sessions and completion of the Scripted At-Home Book activities. This finding may have important implications for similar projects undertaken in other schools. Project EASE was conducted in a suburban school district that was perceived as offering solid literacy instruction and the results of the initial parent surveys suggested that "these were not families that were extremely limited in their literacy support" (p. 538). Undertaking such an endeavor in an environment in which the initial support for literacy at home is lower might require more attention to participation and consideration of how to encourage parents to become more fully involved.

Parents and children learn to read together. Some projects are intended to advance the literacy knowledge of both children and their parents. These are typically multifaceted and long-term, and they vary widely in design, purpose, and instructional approaches. Because comprehensive reviews of programs of this type are both recent and widely available (e.g., DeBruin-Parecki & Krol-Sinclair, 2003; Purcell-Gates, 2000; Wasik, 2004; Yaden & Paratore, 2002), we offer only a summary of the evidence here. Programs of this type can lead to improved literacy knowledge of children (concepts about print, alphabet knowledge, phonemic awareness (Brooks, 1998; Brooks et al., 1997; Brooks, Gorman, Harman, Hutchison, & Wilkin, 1996; Paratore, Melzi, & Krol-Sinclair, 1999; Rodriguez-Brown, 2001; Shanahan, Mulhern, & Rodriguez-Brown, 1995); improved parent literacy (e.g., Paratore, 1993, 1994, 2001); improved English language proficiency for parents (Rodriguez-Brown, 2001; Shanahan, Mulhern, & Rodriguez-Brown, 1995); and improved relationships between parents and teachers (Paratore et al., 1999; Rodriguez-Brown, 2001).

Parents and Teachers as Learning Partners   This category includes programs in which parents and teachers understand and value the knowledge each holds and are positioned to learn from each other. Among the most influential work in this approach to bridging home-school differences is that of Moll and his colleagues (González et al., 2005; Moll & Greenberg, 1991; Moll, Amanti, Neff, & González, 1992). Their work with families typically viewed as "deficient" due to their status as English Language learners or working class provides compelling evidence that such households "[contain] ample cultural and cognitive resources with great, *potential* utility for classroom instruction" (p. 134). They termed these resources *funds of knowledge*, and critical to the success of uncovering and building on these resources is the education of the teachers, themselves. As part of visiting homes, teachers were trained in "conversational" interviewing, observing, and taking field notes. They also engaged in after-school study groups to discuss what they observed and learned and to consider ways they could incorporate the household resources into their classroom curriculum. They found that parents and other community members had rich backgrounds and much that they could share with teachers and students about topics related to science (e.g., plants, herbs, music and sound); and social studies (e.g., immigration, community relationships), and they used the information to enrich content area units. Moll et al. (1992) described the "symmetrical relationship" (p. 139) that developed between parents and teachers when teachers visited their students' homes with the goal of identifying funds of knowledge and they concluded, "This relationship can become the basis for the exchange of knowledge about family or school matters, reducing the insularity of classrooms, and contributing to the academic content and lessons" (p. 139).

The work of McCarthey (1997, 1999) also has been instructive in understanding and implementing ways to exchange information with parents. Working with elementary teachers, McCarthey encouraged teachers to review school records and initiate conversations with parents and children to learn more about children's lives outside of school. McCarthey (1999) reported that

> If teachers believed that students came from impoverished backgrounds, they did not build on their backgrounds nor provide experiences that would promote home-school connections. When teachers were informed about and valued students' individual backgrounds, they were more inclined to adjust the curriculum to build upon students' out-of-school experiences and to address important issues such as racial tension. (p. 103)

Nistler and Maiers (1999) offer another example of what can happen when a teacher endeavors to "provide an exchange between home and school to support students' literacy growth" (p. 110). Maiers, a first-grade teacher, invited the parents of her students to join their children in her classroom 15 times over the course of the school year. On these mornings, parents participated with their children in the regular classroom literacy activities and in activities that allowed them to support their children's literacy learning during the sessions. Parents engaged in whole-class, teacher-led activities, such as reading the morning message, and in small group, cooperative activities, such as literacy stations and word work with a familiar poem. Maiers also met with individual parents during these visits, which allowed for the sharing of information or concerns about each child's literacy development. Data collected during the 2 years of program implementation included a personal journal kept by Maiers, observers' field notes, and audio-taped interviews conducted with each family three times during the school year. The extent of the partnership is evident in the number of parents who participated: in year 1, 96.5% of the students in Maiers' class were

represented at the Friday sessions, and in year 2, 94.5% were represented.

During interviews, parents said that they became more aware of what their children could do with support and that they had begun to provide similar support at home as "they engaged in activities introduced, modeled, and practiced during the biweekly Friday sessions" (p. 672) or as they modified home literacy practices to reflect what they saw in the school visits. Nistler and Maiers (1999) concluded,

> Friendships were built as parents and teacher learned from one another. The formal and informal parent/teacher interactions gave parents the opportunity to talk about community issues and personal experiences and to express their thoughts and opinions in a nonthreatening and caring environment. (p. 675)

While the study by Nistler and Maier was initiated by a teacher who was already cognizant of the importance of recruiting parents as partners in their children's education, Steiner (2008) offers an example of how teachers can be encouraged to shift their views about parents and children through professional development. In a study of two teachers in urban, low-income, first-grade classrooms (one a treatment classroom and one a control) and six families from each classroom, Steiner implemented two intervention strands. In one, she worked directly with parents to introduce them to storybook reading strategies and gave them appropriate texts to share with their children. In addition, over the course of the 8 workshops, she and the parents discussed the children's classroom "lives" and ways parents might support their children in school-related tasks and activities. In the second intervention strand, Steiner worked directly with the teacher in the treatment classroom. In a series of 8 meetings, they read research related to home-school partnerships and discussed implications of the findings for work in this particular school setting. They co-planned events for involving parents in their children's classroom, and they also discussed ways for the classroom teacher to work with parents to learn more about the children's lives outside of school, and ways to incorporate what she learned into her classroom lessons. Steiner examined intervention effects on three groups of children: those whose parent and teacher participated in the intervention, those whose teacher participated in the intervention, and those for whom neither the teacher nor the parent participated in the intervention. She measured effects on children's literacy knowledge (concepts about print, alphabet knowledge, phonemic awareness, and reading connected text), on teachers' and parents' attitudes about parents' roles in children's academic learning, on parents' use of reading strategies, and on teachers' actions to bridge home and school resources. She found statistically significant differences in treatment group parents' initiation of effective storybook strategies from pre- to post-intervention joint book reading. She also found that the classroom teacher planned substantially more events and meeting designed to exchange information with parents, and she incorporated newly acquired knowledge about children's lives outside of school in both individual and group interactions with children (and the control teacher made no changes in her parent-involvement activities). Results also indicated changes in the beliefs of parents and teachers about the role of parents in their children's literacy learning. Parents who participated in the intervention reported that they developed a stronger understanding of their children's literacy development and strengthened their relationships with the teacher as a result of their increased time spent in school. Finally, a combination of teacher and parent participation in the intervention led to statistically significant differences in students' scores on the Concepts About Print assessment when compared to students in the control classroom. No differences were found in children's alphabet knowledge or phonemic awareness (findings consistent with earlier evidence that storybook reading has few effects on word-level skills, e.g., Baker et al., 1998; Landry & Smith, 2006; Stahl, 2003). She also found no effects on in-context reading, an outcome that might suggest that an 8-week intervention is too brief to affect overall literacy proficiency.

In a final example, Paratore and her colleagues suggested that parent-teacher conferences provide a "ready-made" context for parent-teacher interface since, in many schools, they serve as the "primary vehicle for parent-teacher communication" (Paratore, Hindin, Krol-Sinclair, & Durán, 1999, p. 58). Paratore et al. examined the discourse of parent-teacher conferences when parents came to the conference with a portfolio that held evidence of their children's home literacy activity. Each of the four conferences analyzed was held between a Latino, immigrant mother and her child's teacher, who in each case was a Spanish-English bilingual. To prepare for the conference, parents were asked to collect evidence of the ways their children used literacy at home, and to be prepared to describe each portfolio artifact with teachers. The researchers found obvious differences between the discourse of the conferences when the literacy portfolios were being discussed and other topics of discussion:

> It was clearly evident in all cases that during discussions either about home literacy or initiated in response to a home portfolio artifact, teachers and parents engaged in collaborative and connected conversations about children's learning. During these conversations, parents shared, and in one case, even dominated the floor much of the time. We found parents and teachers in extended, and at times, seamless discussions about children's learning at home and at school, as they used portfolio samples to shift the focus quickly and easily from home to school and from school to home....The conversations that centered on home literacy stood in stark contrast to the teacher-controlled, monologic conversations that characterized the discourse when virtually any other topic was on the table. (p. 79)

As a result of the balanced participation in discussions about home literacy, several of the parents reported feeling more confident and better able to communicate with the teacher. Each of the 4 teachers suggested that they became more aware of the potential of these parents as a valuable

resource for their children. Paratore et al. concluded, "The [teachers'] affirmation may serve as encouragement to the parent to continue the interactions; the awareness may serve as encouragement to the teacher to draw upon the parents' enthusiasm and expertise in helping children succeed in school" (p. 80). While in this particular case the parents arrived at the conference with the portfolios in hand, it seems quite plausible these results could be reproduced—at least to some degree—if parents were invited to bring artifacts from home to the conference or to simply talk about experiences related to literacy development that they have observed at home.

The research reviewed in this section demonstrates that if parents are to be recruited as a resource for intensifying children's literacy experiences, teachers must communicate both explicitly (through invitations and opportunities to become involved) and implicitly (through their behaviors as they interact with parents) that they truly believe that the home environment is a vital, and valued, resource.

Summary and Conclusions

We began this chapter with two claims: that there is substantial evidence that home and family characteristics (including poverty, language, and educational experiences) have important effects on children's early and later reading success; and that knowledgeable, thoughtful, and responsive teachers working with parents and with a rich and worthy curriculum can mediate these differences. Evidence of the first claim is strong and definitive—it is fair to say that we *know* that home and family experiences and resources have important consequences for children's literacy learning; children's whose family experiences differ from those typical of mainstream children are more likely to experience reading difficulty. With regard to the second claim, although the evidence is less voluminous, there is certainly substantial promise in the data: teachers who treat children's families and communities as both partners and resources in learning to read and write create for their students better odds for success.

Nonetheless, a survey reported by the National Comprehensive Center for Teacher Quality and Public Agenda (2008) indicates that, as a profession, we remain largely reactive in our work with parents. Only 51% of new teachers reported that they received preparation that addressed how to work with parents and community members. When we toss into the mix issues of diversity, the likelihood that new teachers receive adequate preparation for working with parents is even less likely: only 4 in 10 teachers reported that instruction related to addressing issues of ethnic and racial diversity helped them in the classroom. We need to do better. Our failure to acknowledge and bridge home differences as a critical component in children's literacy success is pushing children who have the capacity for success into deep pockets of failure, and once they are there, their chances for success diminish substantially (Juel, 1988; Stanovich, 1986).

As the studies we presented indicate, we know enough to get started. We know that, with prompting and support, parents with both high and low levels of education and parents with high and low levels of English language proficiency can effectively implement various types of reading interventions at home, including storybook reading, fluency practice, and specific skill practice. We also know that, with prompting and support, teachers can learn to implement approaches and practices that help them to uncover family and community resources and connect these to classroom curricula.

As we reflect on the theory and research we reviewed and on our experiences in schools and classrooms of all types, four areas of need emerge. First, at present, we seem to treat home-school partnerships as a topic that is "good to know about," but not as a topic that is essential to preventing reading failure for some children. We need to shift this perception to one in which understanding the importance of home and community partnerships is viewed as a critical domain for effective teaching and a central element of both pre-service and in-service education.

Second, in conceptualizing courses or professional development efforts, we must heed the evidence that virtually all families have funds of knowledge (Moll & Greenburg, 1991) that, if recognized, will provide a bridge to academic skills and content. Such acknowledgement requires an approach to engaging parents and communities that is characterized by collaboration rather than compliance.

Third, we need more research that helps us to understand precisely how to uncover home and community resources, and how to integrate what we learn into the academic curriculum. Existing studies provide some promising directions, but investigations are limited in number, in scope, and in the diversity of the families.

Fourth, we need more and better studies that help us to know and understand the precise relationship between the home-school partnerships we implement and advances in children's reading and writing. There are so many factors that, at present, we largely guess at: is there a "timing" issue of some sort (i.e., does engaging parents at a particular time in the school year or at a particular age of child) that leads to better or more sustained partnerships? Are there more or less advantageous contexts, that is, do parents and teachers work better together as dyads, as small groups, or as large groups; are home and community settings more effective than school settings? Do contextual effects vary for different groups (i.e., mothers or fathers, different cultural or social groups)? When parents are themselves learning to read or speak English, what particular types of actions and interactions that are more likely to be beneficial for both parents and children?

We close with a quote from Allen (2007) who straightforwardly summarized the pathways to meaningful home-school collaborations:

> Parents teaching parents. Parents teaching teachers. Teachers teaching parents what they want to know. Dialogue that is based on mutual respect. These are powerful settings for the kind of parent involvement that makes a genuine difference in a child's life as a learner. (p. 105)

This sounds so simple, but of course, it is not. There is much for us to learn if we are to create such settings in all schools so that children who most need everyone in their learning lives to work together can count on it to happen.

References

Allen, J. (2007). *Creating welcoming schools.* New York: Teachers College Press.

Anderson, A., & Stokes, S. (1984). Social and institutional influences on the development and practice of literacy. In H. Goelman, A. Oberg, & F. Smith (Eds.), *Awakening to literacy* (pp. 24–37). Exeter, NH: Heinemann.

Anderson, J., Anderson, A., Lynch, J., & Shapiro, H. (2003). Storybook reading in a multicultural society: Critical perspectives. In A. van Kleeck, S. A. Stahl, & E. B. Bauer (Eds.), *On reading books to children: Parents and teachers* (pp. 203–230). Mahwah, NJ: Erlbaum.

Anderson, J., & Morrison, F. (2000). *Parents as literacy supporters (PALS): A culturally responsive family literacy program.* Langley, British Columbia, Canada: Langley School District.

Anderson, R. C., Hiebert, E. H., Scott, J., & Wilkinson, I. (1985). *Becoming a nation of readers.* Washington, DC: U. S. Department of Education, National Institute of Education.

Arnold, D. S., & Whitehurst, G. J. (1994). Accelerating language development through picture book reading: A summary of dialogic reading and its effects. In D. K. Dickinson (Ed.), *Bridges to literacy: Children, families, and schools* (pp. 103–128). Cambridge, MA: Blackwell.

Aulls, M. W., & Sollars, V. (2003). The differential influence of the home environment on the reading ability of children entering grade one. *Reading Improvement, 40*(4), 164–178.

Baker, L., Fernandez-Fein, S., Scher, D., & Williams, H. (1998). Home experiences related to the development of word recognition. In J. L. Metsala & L. C. Ehri (Eds.), *Word Recognition in Beginning Literacy* (pp. 263–288). Mahwah, NJ: Erlbaum.

Baker, L., Scher, D., & Mackler, K. (1997). Home and family influences on motivation for reading. *Education Psychologist, 32,* 69–82.

Beals, D. E. (2001). Eating and reading. In D. K. Dickinson & P. O. Tabors (Eds.), *Beginning literacy with language: Young children learning at home and at school* (pp. 75–92). Baltimore, MD: Brookes.

Beals, D. E., DeTemple, J. H., & Dickinson, D. K. (1994). Talking and listening that support early literacy development of children from low-income families. In D. K. Dickinson (Ed.), *Bridges to literacy: Children, families, and schools* (pp. 19–42). Cambridge, MA: Blackwell.

Biemiller, A. (2006). Vocabulary development and instruction: A prerequisite for school learning. In D. K. Dickinson & S. B. Neuman (Eds.), *Handbook of Early Literacy Research* (Vol. 2, pp. 41–43). New York: Guilford.

Bourdieu, P. (1986). The forms of capital. In J. G. Richardson (Ed.), *Handbook of theory and research for the sociology of education* (pp. 241–258). New York: Greenwood.

Brooks, G. (1998). The effectiveness of family literacy programmes in England and Wales for parents. *Journal of Adolescent and Adult Literacy, 42,* 130–132.

Brooks, G., Gorman, T., Harman, J., Hutchison, D., Kinder, K., Moor, H., et al. (1997). *Family literacy lasts.* London: The Basic Skills Agency.

Brooks, G., Gorman, T., Harman, J., Hutchison, D., & Wilkin, A. (1996). *Family literacy works.* London: The Basic Skills Agency.

Bryant, P., Bradley, L., MacLean, M., & Crossland, J. (1989). Nursery rhymes, phonological skills and reading. *Journal of Child Language, 16,* 407–428.

Bus, A. G. (2003). Social-emotional requisites for learning to read. In A. van Kleeck, S. A. Stahl, & E. B. Bauer (Eds.), *On reading books to children: Parents and teachers* (pp. 3–15). Mahwah, NJ: Erlbaum.

Bus, A. G., Leseman, P. P. M., & Keultjes, P. (2000). Joint book reading across cultures: a comparison of Surinamese-Dutch, Turkish-Dutch, and Dutch parent-child dyads. *Journal of Literacy Research, 32*(1), 53–76.

Bus, A. G., & van Ijzendoorn, M. H. (1988). Mother-child interactions, attachment, and emergent literacy: A cross sectional study. *Child Development, 59*, 1262–1272.

Bus, A. G., & van Ijzendoorn, M. H. (1992). Patterns of attachment in frequently and infrequently reading dyads. *Journal of Genetic Psychology, 153*, 394–403.

Bus, A. G., & van Ijzendoorn, M. H. (1995). Mothers reading to their three year olds: The role of mother-child attachment security in becoming literate. *Reading Research Quarterly, 40*, 998–1015.

Bus, A. G., van Ijzendoorn, M. H., & Pellegrini, A. D. (1995). Joint book reading makes for success in learning to read: A meta-analysis in intergenerational transmission of literacy. *Review of Educational Research, 65*, 1–21.

Clark, M. (1976). *Young fluent readers: What they can teach us.* London: Heinemann.

Chall, J. S., Jacobs, V. A., & Baldwin, L. E. (1990). *The reading crisis: Why poor children fall behind.* Cambridge, MA: Harvard University Press.

Cohen, J. (1977). *Statistical power analysis for the behavioral sciences.* New York: Academic Press.

Compton-Lilly, C. (2003). *Reading families: The literate lives of urban children.* New York: Teachers College Press.

Compton-Lilly, C. (2007). The complexities of reading capital in two Puerto Rican families. *Reading Research Quarterly, 42*(1), 72–98.

Cornell, E., Sénéchal, M., & Broda, L. (1988). Recall of picture books by 3-year-old children: Testing and repetition effects in joint reading activities. *Journal of Educational Psychology, 80*, 537–542.

Crain-Thoreson, C., & Dale, P. S. (1999). Enhancing linguistic performance: Parents and teachers as book reading partners for children with language delays. *Topics in Early Childhood Special Education, 19*(1), 28–39.

Cunningham, P. M. (2000). *Systematic sequential phonics they use: For beginning readers of all ages.* Greensboro, NC: Carson-Dellosa.

Davidson, R. G., & Snow, C. E. (1995). The linguistic environment of early readers. *Journal of Research in Childhood Education, 10*, 5–21.

Dearing, E., Kreider, H., & Simpkins, S. (2006). Family involvement in school and low-income children's literacy: Longitudinal associations between and within families. *Journal of Educational Psychology, 98*(4), 653–664.

DeBruin-Parecki, A., & Krol-Sinclair, B. (2003). *Family literacy: From theory to practice.* Newark, DE: International Reading Association.

de Jong, P. F., & Leseman, P. M. (2001). Lasting effects of home literacy on reading achievement in school. *Journal of School Psychology, 39*(5), 389–414.

Delgado-Gaitan, C. (1992). School matters in the Mexican-American home: Socializing children to education. *American Educational Research Journal, 29*(3), 495–513.

Delpit, L. (1995). *Other people's children: Cultural conflict in the classroom.* New York: The New Press.

DeTemple, J. M. (2001). Parents and children reading books together. In D. K. Dickinson & P. O. Tabors (Eds.), *Beginning literacy with language: Young children learning at home and at school* (pp. 31–52). Baltimore, MD: Brookes.

DeTemple, J. M., & Beals, D. E. (1991). Family talk: Sources of support for the development of decontextualized skills. *Journal of Research in Childhood Education, 6*, 11–19.

DeTemple, J., & Snow, C. E. (2003). Learning words from books. In A. van Kleeck, S. A. Stahl, & E. B. Bauer (Eds.), *On reading books to children: Parents and teachers* (pp. 16–36). Mahwah, NJ: Erlbaum.

Dickinson, D. K., & Beals, D. E. (1994). Not by print alone: Oral language supports for early literacy. In D. Lancy (Ed.), *Children's emergent literacy: From research to practice* (pp. 29–40). Westport, CT: Preager.

Dickinson, D. K., McCabe, A., & Essex, M. J. (2006). A window of opportunity we must open to all: The case for preschool with high-quality support for language and literacy. In D. K. Dickinson & S. B. Neuman (Eds.), *Handbook of early literacy research* (Vol. 2, pp. 11–28). New York: Guilford.

Dickinson, D. K., & Smith, M. M. (1994). Long-term effects of preschool teachers' book readings on low-income children's vocabulary and story comprehension. *Reading Research Quarterly, 29*, 105–122.

Dickinson, D. K., & Sprague, K. E. (2002). The nature and impact of early childhood care environments on the language and early literacy development of children from low-income families. In S. B. Neuman & D. K. Dickinson (Eds.), *Handbook of early literacy research* (pp. 263–280). New York: Guilford.

Dieterich, S. E., Assel, M. A., & Swank, P. (2006). The impact of early maternal verbal scaffolding and child language abilities on later decoding and reading comprehension skills. *Journal of School Psychology, 43*(6), 481–494.

Dodici, B. J., Draper, D. C., & Peterson, C. A. (2003). Early parent-child interactions and early literacy development. *Topics in Early Childhood Special Education, 23*(3), 124–136.

Dunning, D. B., Mason, J. M., & Stewart, J. P. (1994). Reading to preschoolers: A response to Scarborough and Dobrich (1994) and recommendations for future research. *Developmental Review, 14*, 324–339.

Durkin, D. (1966). *Children who read early.* New York: Teachers College Press.

Edwards, P. A. (1991). Fostering early literacy through parent coaching. In E. Hiebert (Ed.), *Literacy for a diverse society* (pp. 199–213). New York: Teachers College Press.

Edwards, P. A. (1994). Responses of teachers and African-American mothers to a book-reading intervention program. In D. K. Dickinson (Ed.), *Bridges to literacy: Children, families, and schools* (pp. 175–210).

Gee, J. P. (2004). Reading as situated language: A sociocognitive perspective. In R. B. Ruddell & N. J. Unrau (Eds.), *Theoretical models and processes of reading* (5th ed., pp. 116–132). Newark, DE: International Reading Association.

Goldenberg, C., Reese, L., & Gallimore, R. (1992). Effects of literacy materials from school on Latino children's home experiences and early reading achievement. *American Journal of Education, 100*(4), 297–536.

González, N., Moll, L. C., & Amanti, C. (2005). *Funds of knowledge: Theorizing pracices in households, communities, and classrooms.* Mahwah, NJ: Erlbaum.

Goodman, Y. (1986). Children coming to know literacy. In W. Teale & E. Sulzby (Eds.), *Emergent literacy: Writing and reading* (pp. 1–14). Norwood, NJ: Ablex.

Haden, C. A., Reese, E., & Fivush, R. (1996). Mother's extratextual comments during storybook reading: Stylistic differences over time and across texts. *Discourse Processes, 21*, 135–169.

Hart, B., & Risley, T. R. (1995). *Meaningful differences in the everyday experiences of young American children.* Baltimore, MD: Brookes.

Heath, S. B. (1983). *Ways with words.* Cambridge, UK: Cambridge University Press.

Heath, S. B. (1986). What no bedtime story means: Narrative skills at home and at school. In B. B. Schieffelin & E. Ochs (Eds.), *Language socialization across cultures* (pp. 97–126). Cambridge, UK: Cambridge University Press.

Heath, S. B. (1991). The sense of being literate: Historical and cross-cultural features. In R. Barr, M. L. Kamil, P. Mosenthal, & P. D. Pearson (Eds.), *Handbook of Reading Research* (Vol. II, pp. 3–25). New York: Longman.

Heath, S. B., & Branscombe, S. (1986). The book as narrative prop in language acquisition. In B. B. Schieffelin & P. Gilmore (Eds.), *The acquisition of literacy: Ethnographic perspectives* (pp. 16–34). Norwood, NJ: Ablex.

Hindin, A., & Paratore, J. R. (2007). Supporting young children's literacy learning through home-school partnerships: The effectiveness of a home repeated-reading intervention. *Journal of Literacy Research, 39*(3), 307–333.

Hoff, E. (2006). Environmental supports for language acquisition. In D. K. Dickinson & S. B. Neuman (Eds.), *Handbook of early litercy research* (Vol. 2, pp. 163–172). New York: Guilford.

Huey, E. B. (1908). *The psychology and pedagogy of reading.* Cambridge, MA: MIT Press.

Huttenlocher, J., Vasilyeva, M., Cymerman, E., & Levine, S. (2002). Language input and child syntax. *Cognitive Psychology, 45,* 337–375.

Janes, H., & Kermani, H. (2001). Caregivers storyreading to young children in family literacy programs: Pleasure or punishment? *Journal of Adolescent and Adult Literacy, 44,* 458–446.

Jordan, G. E., Snow, C. E., & Porche, M. V. (2000). Project EASE: The effect of a family literacy project on kindergarten students' early literacy skills. *Reading Research Quarterly, 35,* 524–546.

Juel, C. (1988). Learning to read and write: A longitudinal study of 54 children from first through fourth grades. *Journal of Educational Psychology, 80,* 437–447.

Juel, C. (2006). The impact of early school experiences on initial reading. In D. K. Dickinson & S. B. Neuman (Eds.), *Handbook of early literacy research* (Vol. 2, pp. 410–426). New York: Guilford.

Krol-Sinclair, B. (1996). Connecting home and school literacies: Immigrant parents with limited formal education as classroom storybook readers. In D. J. Leu, C. K. Kinzer, & K. A. Hinchman (Eds.), *Literacies for the 21st Century: Research and practice* (pp. 270–283). Chicago: National Reading Conference.

Landry, S. H., Miller-Loncar, C. L., Smith, K. E., & Swank, P. R. (2002). The role of early parenting in children's development of executive processes. *Developmental Neuropsychology, 21*(1), 15–41.

Landry, S. H., & Smith, K. E. (2006). The influence of parenting on emerging literacy skills. In D. K. Dickinson & S. B. Neuman (Eds.), *Handbook of early literacy resarch* (Vol. 2, pp. 135–148). New York: Guilford.

Lareau, A. (1989). *Home advantage: Social class and parental intervention.* New York: Falmer Press.

Lareau, A. (2003). *Unequal childhoods: Class, race, and family life.* Berkeley: University of California Press.

Leichter, H. J. (1984). Families as environments for literacy. In H. Goelman, A. Oberg, & F. Smith (Eds.), *Awakening to literacy* (Vol. 38–50). Portsmouth, NH: Heinemann.

Leseman, P. M., & de Jong, P. F. (1998). Home literacy: Opportunity, instruction, cooperation and social-emotional quality predicting early reading achievement. *Reading Research Quarterly, 33*(3), 294–318.

Leseman, P. M., & van Tuijl, C. (2006). Cultural diversity in early literacy: Findings in Dutch studies. In D. K. Dickinson & S. B. Neuman (Eds.), *Handbook of early literacy research* (Vol. 2, pp. 211–229). New York: Guilford.

Lomax, C. M. (1976). Interest in books and stories at nursery school. *Educational Research, 19,* 100–112.

Lonigan, C. J. (1994). Reading to preschoolers exposed: Is the emperor really naked? *Developmental Review, 14,* 303–323.

Lonigan, C. J., & Whitehurst, G. J. (1998). Relative efficacy of parent and teacher involvement in a shared-reading intervention for preschool children from low-income backgrounds. *Early Childhood Research Quarterly, 13,* 263–290.

Maclean, M., Bryant, P., & Bradley, L. (1987). Rhymes, nursery rhymes, and reading in early childhood. *Merrill-Palmer Quarterly, 33,* 255–281.

Madigan, D. (1992). Family uses of literacy: A critical voice. In C. K. Kinzer & D. J. Leu (Eds.), *Literacy research, theory, and practice: Views from many perspectives* (pp. 87–100). Chicago: National Reading Conference.

Manyak, P. (1998). *"Este Libro Es Mi Historia": Mother-child interactions during storybook reading in a Mexican-American household* (No. ED 418 383). Los Angeles: University of Southern California.

McCarthey, S. (1999). Identifying teacher practices that connect home and school. *Education and Urban Society, 32,* 83–107.

McCarthey, S. (1997). Connecting home and school literacy practices in classrooms with diverse populations. *Journal of Literacy Research, 29,* 145–182.

McGill-Franzen, A., Lanford, C., & Adams, E. (2002). Learning to be literate: A comparison of five urban early childhood programs. *Journal of Educational Psychology, 94*(3), 443–464.

Metsala, J. L., & Walley, A. C. (1998). Spoken vocabulary growth and the segmental restructuring of lexical representations: Precursors to phonemic awareness and early reading ability. In J. L. Metsala & L. C. Ehri (Eds.), *Word recognition in beginning literacy* (pp. 89–120). Hillsdale, NJ: Erlbaum.

Moll, L., & Greenberg, J. B. (1991). Creating zones of possibilities: Combining social contexts for instruction. In L. C. Moll (Ed.), *Vygotsky in Education* (pp. 319–348) New York: Cambridge University Press.

Moll, L. C., Amanti, C., Neff, D., & González, N. (1992). Funds of knowledge for teaching: Using a qualitative approach to connect homes and classrooms. *Theory into Practice, 31,* 132–141.

Morrow, L. M. (1983). Home and school correlates of early interest in literature. *Journal of Educational Research, 76,* 221–230.

Muter, V., Hulme, C., & Snowling, M. J. (2004). Phonemes, rimes, vocabulary, and grammatical skills as foundations of early reading development: Evidence from a longitudinal study. *Developmental Psychology, 40*(5), 665–681.

National Comprehensive Center for Teacher Quality and Public Agenda. (2008). Lessons learned: New teachers talk about their jobs, challenges, and long-range plans. Retrieved June 20, 2008, from http://www.publicagenda.org/lessonslearned/

Neuman, S., & Celano, D. (2001). Access to print in low-income and middle-income communities: An ecological study of four neighborhoods. *Reading Research Quarterly, 36*(1), 8–26.

Neuman, S. B. (2006). The knowledge gap: Implications for early education. In D. K. Dickinson & S. B. Neuman (Eds.), *Handbook of early Literacy* (Vol. 2, pp. 29–40). New York: Guilford.

Nistler, R. J., & Maiers, A. (1999). Changing parents roles in school: Effects of a 2-year study of a family literacy program in an urban first-grade classroom. *Education and Urban Society, 32,* 108–126.

Paratore, J. R. (1993). Influence of an intergenerational approach to literacy on the practice of literacy of parents and their children. In C. Kinzer & D. Leu (Eds.), *Examining central issues in literacy, research, theory, and practice* (pp. 83–91). Chicago: National Reading Conference.

Paratore, J. R. (1994). Parents and children sharing literacy. In D. Lancy (Ed.), *Children's emergent literacy* (pp. 193–216). Westport, CT: Preager.

Paratore, J. R. (2001). *Opening doors, opening opportunities: Family literacy in an urban community.* Needham Heights, MA: Allyn and Bacon.

Paratore, J. R., Hindin, A., Krol-Sinclair, B., & Durán, P. (1999). Discourse between teachers and Latino parents during conferences based on home literacy portfolios. *Education and Urban Society, 32,* 58–82.

Paratore, J. R., Melzi, G., & Krol-Sinclair, B. (1999). *What should we expect of family literacy? Experiences of Latino children whose parents participate in an intergenerational literacy program.* Newark, DE: International Reading Association.

Paris, S. G. (2005). Reinterpreting the development of reading skills. *Reading Research Quarterly, 40*(2), 184–202.

Pellegrini, A., & Galda, L. (2003). Joint reading as a context: Explicating the ways context is created by participants. In A. van Kleeck, S. A. Stahl, & E. B. Bauer (Eds.), *On reading books to children: Parents and Teachers* (pp. 321–335). Mahwah, NJ: Erlbaum.

Pellegrini, A., Perlmutter, J. C., Galda, L., & Brody, G. (1990). Joint reading between Black Head Start children and their mothers. *Child Development, 61,* 443–453.

Purcell-Gates, V. (1994). Nonliterate homes and emergent literacy. In D. Lancy (Ed.), *Children's emergent literacy* (pp. 41–52). Westport, CT: Preager.

Purcell-Gates, V. (1995). *Other people's words: The cycle of illiteracy.* Cambridge, MA: Harvard University Press.

Purcell-Gates, V. (1996). Stories, coupons, and the TV Guide: Relationships between home literacy experiences and emergent literacy knowledge. *Reading Research Quarterly, 31,* 406–428.

Purcell-Gates, V. (2000). Family literacy. In M. L. Kamil, P. B. Mosenthal, P. D. Pearson, & R. Barr (Eds.), *Handbook of reading research* (Vol. III, pp. 853–870). Mahwah, NJ: Erlbaum.

Purcell-Gates, V. (2001). Emergent literacy is emerging knowledge of written, not oral, language. *New directions for child and adolescent development, 92,* 7–22.

Purcell-Gates, V. (2004). Family literacy as the site for emerging knowlege of written language. In B. Wasik (Ed.), *Handbook of family literacy* (pp. 101–116). Mahwah, NJ: Erlbaum.

Rashid, F. L., Morris, R. D., & Sevcik, R. A. (2005). Relationship between home literacy environment and reading achievement in children with reading disabilities. *Journal of Learning Disabilities, 38*(1), 2–11.

Rasinski, T., & Stevenson, B. (2005). The effects of Fast Start Reading: A fluency-based home involvement reading program, on the reading achievement of beginning readers. *Reading Psychology, 26,* 109–125.

Reese, E., Cox, A., Harte, D., & McAnally, H. (2003). Diversity in adults' styles of reading books to children. In A. van Kleeck, S. A. Stahl, & E. B. Bauer (Eds.), *On reading books to children: Parents and teachers* (pp. 37–57). Mahwah, NJ: Erlbaum.

Reutzel, D. R., Fawson, P. C., & Smith, J. A. (2006). *Words to Go!*: Evaluating a first-grade parent involvement program for "making" words at home. *Reading Research and Instruction, 45*(2), 119–159.

Robinson, C. C., Larsen, J. M., & Haupt, J. H. (1996). The influence of selecting and taking picture books home on the at-home reading behaviors of kindergarten children. *Reading Research and Instruction, 35,* 249–259.

Rodriguez-Brown, F. V. (2001). Home-school collaboration: Successful models in the Hispanic community. In P. R. Schmidt & P. B. Mosenthal (Eds.), *Reconceptualizing literacy in the new age of multiculturalism and pluralism* (pp. 273–288). Greenwich, CT: Information Age.

Roser, N., & Martinez, M. (1985). Roles adults play in preschoolers' response to literature. *Language Arts, 62,* 485–490.

Scarborough, H. S., & Dobrich, W. (1994). On the efficacy of reading to preschoolers. *Developmental Review, 14,* 245–302.

Schieffelin, B., & Cochran-Smith, M. (1984). Learning to read culturally: Literacy before schooling. In H. Goelman, A. Oberg, & F. Smith (Eds.), *Awakening to literacy* (pp. 3–23). Exeter, NH: Heinemann.

Sénéchal, M. (1997). The differential effect of storybook reading on preschoolers' acquisition of expressive and receptive vocabulary. *Journal of Child Language, 24,* 123–138.

Sénéchal, M. (2006). *The effect of family literacy interventions of children's acquisition of reading from kindergarten to grade 3: A meta-analytic review.* Louisville, KY: National Center for Family Literacy.

Sénéchal, M., LeFevre, J.A., & Thomas, E. M. (1998). Differential effects of home literacy experiences on the development of oral and written language. *Reading Research Quarterly, 33,* 96–116.

Sénéchal, M., & LeFevre, J. (2002). Parental involvement in the development of children's readingskill: A five-year longitudinal study. *Child Development, 73*(2), 445–460.

Sénéchal, M., Ouellette, G., & Rodney, D. (2006). The misunderstood giant: On the predictive role of early vocabulary to future reading. In D. K. Dickinson & S. B. Neuman (Eds.), *Handbook of early literacy research* (Vol. 2, pp. 173–182). New York: Guilford.

Shanahan, T., Mulhern, M., & Rodriguez-Brown, F. (1995). Project FLAME: Lessons learned from a family literacy program for minority families. *Reading Teacher, 48,* 586.

Snow, C. E. (1991). The theoretical basis for relationships between language and literacy development. *Journal of Childhood Education, 6*(1), 5–10.

Snow, C., & Goldfield, B. (1983). Turn the page please: Situation-specific language acquisition. *Journal of Child Language, 10,* 551–569.

Snow, C. E., Barnes, W. S., Chandler, J., Goodman, I. F., & Hemphill, L. (1991). *Unfulfilled expectations: Home and school influences on literacy.* Cambridge, MA: Harvard University Press.

Snow, C.E., Burns, M. S., & Griffin, P. (1998). *Preventing reading difficulties in young children.* Washington, DC: National Academy Press.

Sonnenschein, S., Brody, G., & Munsterman, K. (1996). The influence of family beliefs and practices on children's early reading development. In L. Baker, P. Afflerbach, & D. Reinking (Eds.), *Developing engaged readers in school and home communities* (pp. 3–20). Mahwah, NJ: Erlbaum.

Sonnenschein, S., & Munsterman, K. (2002). The influence of home-based reading interactions on 5-year-olds' reading motivations and early literacy development. *Early Childhood Research Quarterly, 17*(3), 318–337.

Spear-Swerling, L. (2004). A road map for understanding readng disability and other reading problems: Origins, prevention, and intervention. In R. B. Ruddel & N. J. Unrau (Eds.), *Theoretical models and processes of reading, 5th edition* (pp. 517–573). Newark, DE: International Reading Association.

Stahl, S. A. (2003). What do we expect storybook reading to do? How storybook reading impacts word recognition. In A. van Kleeck, S. A. Stahl, & E. B. Bauer (Eds.), *On reading books to children: Parents and teachers* (pp. 363–384). Mahwah, NJ: Erlbaum.

Stanovich, K. E. (1986). Matthew effects in reading: Some consequences of individual differences in the acquisition of literacy. *Reading Research Quarterly, 21,* 360–407.

Steiner, L. M. (2008). Effects of a school-based parent and teacher intervention to promote first-grade students' literacy achievement. Unpublished doctoral dissertation, Boston University.

Sulzby, E. (1985). Children's emergent abilities to read favorite storybooks: A developmental study. *Reading Research Quarterly, 20,* 458–481.

Sulzby, E., & Edwards, P. (1993). The role of parents in supporting the literacy development of young children. In B. Spodek & O. N. Saracgi (Eds.), *Yearbook in early childhood education: Volume 4. Early childhood language and literacy.* New York: Teachers College Press.

Swalander, L., & Taube, K. (2007). Influences of family based prerequisites, reading attitude, and self-regulation on reading ability. *Contemporary Educational Psychology, 32*(2), 206–230.

Tabors, P. O., Beals, D. E., & Weizman, Z. O. (2001). You know what oxygen is: Learning new words at home. In D. K. Dickinson & P. O. Tabors (Eds.), *Beginning literacy with language: Young children learning at home and at school* (pp. 93–110). Baltimore, MD: Brookes.

Tabors, P. O., Roach, K. A., & Snow, C. (2001). Home language and literacy environment. In D. K. Dickinson & P. O. Tabors (Eds.), *Beginning literacy with language: Young children learning at home and school* (pp. 111–138). Baltimore, MD: Brookes.

Taylor, D. (1997). *Many families, many literacies.* Portsmouth, NH: Heinemann.

Taylor, D., & Dorsey-Gaines, C. (1988). *Growing up literate: Learning from inner-city families.* Portsmouth, NH: Heinemann.

Taylor, B. M., Frye, B. J., & Maruyama, G. M. (1990). Time spent reading and reading growth. *American Educational Research Journal, 27*(2), 351–362.

Teale, W. H. (1986). Home background and young children's literacy development. In W. H. Teale & E. Sulzby (Eds.), *Emergent literacy: Writing and reading* (pp. 173–206). Norwood, NJ: Ablex.

Torgesen, J. K. (2004). Lessons learned from the last 20 years of research on interventions for students who experience difficulty learning to read. In P. McCardle & V. Chhabra (Eds.), *The voice of evidence in reading research* (pp. 355–382). Baltimore, MD: Brookes.

Valdés, G. (1996). *Con respeto: Bridging the differences between culturally diverse families and schools.* New York: Teachers College Press.

Valdez-Menchaca, M. C., & Whitehurst, G. J. (1992). Accelerating language development through picture book reading: A systematic extension to Mexican day care. *Developmental Psychology, 28,* 1106–1114.

van Kleeck, A. (2003). Research on book sharing: Another critical look. In A. van Kleeck, S. L. Stahl, & E. Bauer (Eds.), *On reading books to children: Parents and teachers* (pp. 271–320). Mahwah, NJ: Erlbaum.

Vasquez, O., Pease-Alvarez, L., & Shannon, S. M. (1994). *Pushing boundaries: Language and culture in a Mexicano community.* New York: Cambridge University Press.

Volk, D., & Long, S. (2005). Challenging myths of the deficit perspective: Honoring children's literacy resources. *YC Young Children, 60*(6), 12–19.

Voss, M. M. (1996). *Hidden literacies: Children learning at home and at school.* Portsmouth, NH: Heineman.

Wasik, B. H. (2004). *Handbook of family literacy.* Mahwah, NJ: Erlbaum.

Weizman, Z. O., & Snow, C. E. (2001). Lexical input as related to children's vocabulary acquisition: Effects of sophisticated exposure and support for meaning. *Developmental Psychology, 37*(2), 265–279.

Whitehurst, G. J., Arnold, D. S., Epstein, J. N., Angell, A. L., Smith, M., & Fischel, J. F. (1994). A picture book reading intervention in day care and home for children from low-income families. *Developmental Psychology, 30*(5), 679–689.

Whitehurst, G. J., & Lonigan, C. J. (2002). Emergent literacy: Development from prereaders to readers. In S. B. Neuman & D. K. Dickinson (Eds.), *Handbook of early literacy research* (Vol. 1, pp. 11–29). New York: Guilford.

Wigfield, A., & Asher, S. R. (1984). Social and motivational influences on reading. In P. D. Pearson, R. Barr, M. L. Kamil, & P. Mosenthal (Eds.), *Handbook of reading research* (pp. 423–452). New York: Longman.

Yaden, D., & Paratore, J. R. (2002). Family literacy at the turn of the millenium: The costly future of maintaining the status quo. In J. E. Flood, D. Lapp, J. Jensen, & J. Squire (Eds.), *Research in English and the language arts* (Vol. II, pp. 532–545). Mahwah, NJ: Erlbaum.

Yaden, D. B., Smolkin, L. B., & Conlon, A. (1989). Preschoolers' questions about pictures, print conventions, and story text during reading aloud at home. *Reading Research Quarterly, 24*, 188–214.

Yaden, D. B., Jr., Tam, A., & Madrigal, P. (2000). Early literacy for inner-city children: the effects of reading and writing interventions in English and Spanish during the preschool years. *The Reading Teacher, 54*(2), 186–189.

Zevenbergen, A. A., & Whitehurst, G. J. (2006). Dialogic reading: A shared picture book intervention for preschoolers. In A. van Kleeck, S. A. Stahl, & E. B. Bauer (Eds.), *On reading books to children* (pp. 107–202). Mahwah, NJ: Erlbaum.

10

Persistent Reading Disabilities

Challenging Six Erroneous Beliefs

LINDA M. PHILLIPS, DENYSE V. HAYWARD, AND STEPHEN P. NORRIS
University of Alberta

Persistent reading disabilities is an explanatory term because of its reference to an underlying psychological trait. Confusion on this matter abounds, such as in a definition of reading disabilities as "reading achievement that is significantly below expectancy for both individual reading potential and for chronological age or grade level" (Harris & Hodges, 1995, p. 210). Here the ability is defined in terms of the performance, whereas the performance might be due to other factors. Among those identified as having persistent reading disabilities, there are those who have profound learning difficulties and have little prospect of learning to read. Included among this group are those with severe language impairment, deviant language acquisition patterns including serious neurobiological and perceptual abnormalities (Paul, 2007), congenital word blindness (Hinshelwood, 1917), and irremediable severe cerebral defects (Fletcher, Lyon, Fuchs, & Barnes, 2007). Students with profound learning difficulties are not the focus of this chapter. Rather, our focus is on students deemed to have persistent reading difficulties as a consequence of factors such as limited exposure to reading, instructional materials that are too difficult, and learned dependence.

Among those identified as having persistent reading disabilities are those whom we contend are more properly described as having persistent reading *difficulties*, a term that has more descriptive than explanatory connotations. This is a much larger group than the former whose members can readily benefit from appropriate language and reading assessments and interventions. The persistence of their reading difficulties is an artifact of their environments rather than an outgrowth of their psychologies or physiologies. We shall concentrate on this group and illustrate our point through the examination of six erroneous beliefs: (a) that relative reading achievement is immutable, (b) that poverty and gender create ceilings on reading expectations and ability, (c) that waiting to be sure a child has reading problems is good practice, (d) that simply reading to children can prevent most reading difficulties, (e) that conventional tests serve all groups equitably, and (f) that intervening in reading instruction is always better than doing nothing over and above the normal. We have chosen to challenge these six erroneous beliefs because they are prevalent, conflict with research findings, complicate the experience of reading for those who least need matters made worse, overplay the credibility of risk factors such as poverty and gender, encourage the misuse of tests, and promote evangelical support for unidimensional and misguided programs.

Relative Reading Achievement Is Mutable

Regrettably, a single study of 54 children from first to fourth grades by Juel in 1988 is cited frequently as evidence that if a child is a poor reader in the first grade, then the child will be a poor reader in the fourth grade. The 54 children lived in an area designated as low socioeconomic and all attended the same elementary school. Consider the following conditional probabilities reported by Juel (a) .88 that a child would be a poor reader at the end of fourth grade, if the child was a poor reader at the end of the first grade; (b) .12 that a child would be a poor reader at the end of fourth grade, if the child was at least average at the end of first grade; (c) .87 that a child would be an average reader at the end of fourth grade, if the child was an average reader at the end of first grade; and (d) .13 that a child would be an average reader at the end of fourth grade, if the child was a poor reader at the end of first grade. That is, poor reading begets poor reading and average reading begets average reading in a rather immutable fashion. Further evidence to support the constancy of relative reading achievement was provided by Smith (1997) who identified 64 children in preschool and found 57 of them in third grade 5 years later. Unlike Juel's study, these children had scattered across 32 elementary schools. She found that 71% of the children with the lowest preschool reading assessment were reading below grade level in Grade 3; and 93% of the children reading in the top quartile in preschool were reading at or above grade level in grade three. Yet others maintain that if a child fails to learn to read adequately in first grade, there is a 90% probability that that child will remain a poor reader by grade 4 and a 75% probability that he or she will be a poor reader in high school (Francis, Fletcher, Shaywitz, Shaywitz, & Rourke 1996; Torgesen & Burgess, 1998).

By way of contrast, Phillips, Norris, Osmond, and Maynard (2002) reported on the relative reading achievement of 187 children as they progressed from grades 1 through 6. They were interested in the general question addressed as follows: "What is the relative reading achievement of boys and girls from first through sixth grades, and to what extent is that relative reading achievement immutable?" (p. 4). The results of this much larger and more extensive study challenged the stability of reading categorization reported in the previous studies. In comparison with the previous studies by Juel (1988) and Smith (1997), the Phillips et al. study was three times larger, tracked reading achievement over a longer period and on a yearly basis, attended assiduously to gender differences, and was "unconfounded by reading interventions, pullouts of children from regular classroom instruction, or language, racial, and ethnic differences" (p. 4). They found reading categories to be more porous than previously reported in other research. In particular, they found a much higher probability for children below average in first grade to be average in subsequent grades (.53); a significant probability for average students to achieve above average performance (.11), where none were documented previously; and an almost equal probability of above-average readers becoming average (.48) as remaining above average (.52). The Phillips et al. results also showed that, whereas until the end of third grade reading categorization and gender were dependent with boys populating the lowest category to a higher degree, at the end of fourth grade this dependency disappeared.

According to these data, relative reading achievement is quite mutable indeed. The significance of this result is that it challenges the presumption of inevitability connected to reading achievement epitomized in belief in the Matthew Effect. Enormous changes in relative reading achievement were witnessed even without special interventions. This result suggests that with appropriate assessment and intervention, children might make even greater progress. This is the most basic and fundamental of our points because if one believes that reading achievement cannot change, then the situation is hopeless.

Similar results have been documented. Many children who are poor readers in the early school years catch up later, whereas other children are average readers early on but under achieve later (Badian, 1999; Cox, 1987; McGee, Williams, & Silva, 1988; Wright, Fields, & Newman, 1996). Denton, Fletcher, Anthony, and Francis (2006) concluded that converging evidence from two decades of research suggests that with appropriate instruction, nearly all students can become competent readers. Thus, there is ample evidence to challenge the view that reading disabilities need be persistent.

Positive Expectations for Reading Can Offset Negative Influences

Children start school with expectations—including that they are going to learn to read. Unfortunately, that expectation goes unfulfilled for too many children (Snow, Barnes, Chandler, Goodman, & Hemphill, 1991). In an extensive study of ethnically diverse and low-income children, Snow et al. (1991) noted that, even though children from middle-income families tend to have higher reading achievement than children from low-income families, within low-income class children there are those who perform very well. Thus, low-income families cannot be considered monolithically, and the question of what contributes to the differences among children *within this class* is important. What Snow et al. found is that within the low-income class there were many families in which literacy was valued, whose parents communicated with the schools and held high expectations for their children's school performance. In such families, children tended to perform as well as middle-income children. Despite the prevalent school and societal expectations that children from low-income families will perform poorly, contrary expectations from the home can have an even more powerful effect in the opposite direction.

Canada's national longitudinal survey of 22,831 children and youth (NLSCY) (Willms, 2002) further corroborated the findings of Snow et al. (1991) and challenged the "culture of poverty" (p.165) thesis and "the widespread belief that the children of poor families do not fare well because of the way they are raised" (p. 165). Within this very large dataset, parenting practices were neither strongly related to SES nor to family structure. Furthermore, children of parents who provided a warm and caring environment and who valued an education demonstrated positive childhood outcomes regardless of SES, and such environments were as likely to be found within one class as another.

The NLSCY further identified early signs of vulnerability. Frempong and Willms (2002) reporting on the same NLSCY data asked whether school quality can compensate for socioeconomic disadvantage. They reported large and statistically significant differences among schools and classrooms in children's levels of achievement. They told a poignant story. Imagine two families both of equal SES and with kindergarten children of the same level of ability. One of the children attends a school with above-average performance and expectations and the other with below-average performance and expectations. By the time both children start high school, the child in the below-average school will be a full grade level below the other child. They further found that the most successful schools and classrooms were those that did not practice grouping and enforce policies that segregate students on the basis of ability or SES, thus holding the same expectation for all groups of students.

Spear-Swerling and Sternberg (1996) "think that most children with reading disabilities begin school with vulnerability for reading failure. However, what happens very early in schooling—in kindergarten and first grade—may be pivotal in deciding whether or not an individual child's vulnerability to RD is realized as poor reading" (p. 250). According to their analyses, children identified as reading disabled frequently are highly similar to those known to be garden-variety poor readers. The difference between them is that those identified as disabled fall below the IQ cutoff essential for a reading disability classification, and perhaps possess some additional characteristic such as being male, coming from a low SES, and being disruptive in school. Many researchers in language and reading (Bishop, 1997; Lahey, 1990; Paul, 2007; Rack, Snowling, & Olson, 1992; Rice, Warren, & Betz, 2005; Siegel 1992; Stanovich, 1991; Vellutino, 1979) challenged such use of IQ scores and have expressed dismay at the use of such a criterion for classificatory purposes rather the use of specific assessment information for the purposes of improving programs and interventions for children.

As Spear-Swerling and Sternberg (1996) point out, being labeled as reading disabled is a serious matter, because the label may alter teachers' and parents' expectations. The child may be seen as hopeless by teachers and parents. Children thus classified can be seen to have an immutable "defect" (Spear-Swerling & Sternberg, 1996, p. 308) and consequently are not provided strategic and informed assessment and intervention. However, rather than having immutable defects, such children might not have been introduced to print concepts, the letters of the alphabet, their printed names, and the structure of narrative prior to schooling. Such children can have difficulties not because they cannot learn but because they have not had the opportunity to learn the essential print concepts expected by schools. Despite these important distinctions, they are all too often categorized the same as children with serious learning problems (Elkins, 2007). Thus, the reasons for their difficulties are not considered for purposes of intervention.

Furthermore, the media (Fine, 2001) and some research literature (Francis, 2005; Jha & Kelleher, 2006; PISA, 2005) claim that girls outperform boys and those boys therefore need alternative programs and instruction. However, even though dyslexia is frequently reported to be more prevalent in boys than girls, the evidence does not support the reports and shows that boys are victims of a referral bias for behavioral reasons (Fletcher et al., 2007; Flynn & Rahbar, 1994; Phillips et al., 2002).

The reading disabled label is known to lead to regression in most children's performance and to lowered expectations (Fletcher et al., 2007). They are expected to read with difficulty, to have less motivation to read, and to read less, and they fall naturally to these expectations. Consequently, the effects generalize to poorer vocabulary, knowledge of story structure, and memory.

Early and Focused Intervention Is Beneficial

At the outset of schooling, approximately 25% of all children are at risk of school failure (Lee & Burkham, 2002).

Such risk is identifiable at 3 years of age with proper testing. Nevertheless, most children are not tested even by kindergarten unless they have specific needs such as speech or language difficulties. If tested in Grade 1 for reading difficulties, it is likely not to take place until mid-year. It is often the case in many parts of Canada, for example, that children will not be given formal tests to qualify for literacy-specific intervention programs until grade four. These delays of up to 6 years make it next to impossible for these children to ever catch up to their peers because reading problems become "intractable as children age" (Mathes & Denton, 2002, p. 186). Furthermore, one-half to three-quarters of children exhibiting reading difficulties also have underlying impairments in language abilities (Catts, Fey, Zhang, & Tomblin, 2001; McArthur, Hogben, Edwards, Heath, & Mengler, 2000). Yet, even when tested, children frequently do not receive assessments of both language and reading skills, resulting in incomplete knowledge of their abilities and incomplete and fragmented interventions. We know that the vast majority of low SES children starting as young as 3 years can benefit dramatically from a family intervention program (Phillips, Hayden, & Norris, 2006). Even with later interventions in Grade 3, particularly disadvantaged children, such as those in First Nations, can benefit from a specific and well-targeted classroom administered language-based program (Hayward, Das, & Janzen, 2007).

In order to maximize the benefits of early intervention, parents need to know and understand that their literacy behavior can have immediate effects on their children's lives. For instance, emergent literacy skills are known to provide the foundation to children's success in school. Knowledge of the alphabet at entry into school is one of the strongest single predictors of literacy success in the short and long-term (Adams, 1990; Lonigan et al., 1999). Early literacy concepts (Phillips, Norris, & Mason, 1996) and phonological awareness are key precursors to the acquisition of early reading skills (Wagner & Torgesen, 1987). It should come as no surprise, then, that there is a strong relation among emergent literacy skills and social and linguistic competence.

Other sources of disadvantage can be lessened by the ways in which parents interact with their children and through early and specifically focused intervention programs (Phillips & Sample, 2005). For instance, Lonigan et al. found that problems of inattention were substantially, consistently, and often uniquely associated with less well-developed emergent literacy skills in preschool children (1999, p. 8). Their research and that of others (e.g., Hinshaw, 1992; Shaywitz, Fletcher, & Shaywitz, 1994) has shown that problems with both inattention and emergent literacy skills place the child at an even greater disadvantage for success in schooling. Parents can help direct their children's attention during literacy activities to great effect as discussed in the following section.

To receive focused literacy intervention early and fast requires that target populations of children are reached and that limited resources are used efficiently. A comprehensive review of the adequacy of tools for assessing reading competence found them highly variable and wanting (Kame'enui et al., 2006), although assessment of performance is critical for effective instructional policy and programming responsive to individual students' needs (p. 3). Dozens and dozens of early reading tests are available. However, they are validated based upon correlations with other instruments, which themselves rely upon the same sort of highly indirect support; include too few subjects; are typically aimed at school-age children; do not measure what they claim to measure; have low reliability coefficients; do not assess the correlates of reading; are aspect-specific rather than comprehensive measures; are not normed on contemporary populations; and are not designed to serve as a precursor for specifically developed intervention programs (Hayward, Stewart, Phillips, Norris, & Lovell, 2008).

Unfortunately, the situation with currently available language tests is not much better. Several studies show that many of these tests have poor diagnostic accuracy (Gray, Plante, Vance, & Henrichsen 1999; Peña, Spaulding, & Plante, 2006; Plante & Vance, 1995); disproportionate representation of mainstream groups in normative samples; measure only discrete skills and do not take into account comprehension and use of language in context; use errors made on language tests to generate intervention objectives, resulting in an inaccurate conceptualization of a child's abilities or impairments because the testing situations bear little or no resemblance to the contexts in which a skill or behavior is used in everyday contexts; and use the same tests both for the identification of impairment and the measurement of progress (Brown, 1991; Hayward et al., 2008; McCauley & Swisher, 1984), which risks either an underestimation or overestimation of progress. Thus, although effective assessments are crucial in the implementation of early interventions, the current state of affairs could do with considerable improvement.

Reading to Children Works Under the Right Conditions

Reading to children can have a positive and lasting impact on emergent reading development. The specific nature of that impact and the conditions required for its occurrence are, however, less well known. A review of some key studies (Phillips, Norris, & Anderson, 2008) showed that children do not learn print concepts simply by having a parent or other adult read to them, but that there are shared-reading practices that can enhance children's emergent literacy development. Unfortunately, reading to children is sometimes compared to a miracle drug. Consider the eloquent excerpt from Hoffman, Roser, and Battle (1991), who were critiquing this mindset: "Reading to children is to literacy education what two aspirins and a little bed rest was to the family doctor in years gone by. Students have an impoverished vocabulary? Read to them. Students struggling with comprehension? Read to them. Students beset with

negative attitudes or lack of motivation? Read to them. Students have second language acquisition problems? Read to them" (p. 1).

Is the "Read to Them" mantra fair to families looking for advice and guidance on how best to help their children to read? We think not. It implies a simplistic and magical answer to a complex and long-term process. Families in the Phillips and Sample (2005) study astutely recognized the lack of magic in mere reading to their children. However, they directed the problem at themselves: "I must not know how to read to my children"; "I must not be doing it right"; "My boys want to learn their ABCs, but they're not and I read to them everyday"; and "I am depressed, 'cause I read to Suzie all the time, but she's not learning to read, if she is, I don't see it". Nevertheless, they implied in their expressions of concern a belief that the answers to their children's reading problems lay in reading to them.

We are confident that those promoting mere reading to children did not anticipate that it would disadvantage and undermine the very people they were trying to enlist by confusing them and diminishing their self-confidence. The field is rife with the simple view of promoting passive reading to children by adults as one of the best-kept secrets of parenting, as the way to ensure success at school, and as the answer to all reading and learning problems (e.g., Meyer, Stahl, Wardrop, & Linn, 1992). Yet, the evidence does not support the claims (Phillips et al., 2008).

Much is known about the specific reading skill outcomes of parent-child shared reading. The research repeatedly confirms that parents do not direct children's attention to print. Parents do not use their shared story time to teach their children letter names, letter sounds, numbers, color words, similarities in words, word reading, repeated readings of literary sentences, discussion of word meanings during reading, elaboration of possible points, questioning of key incidents, and reading strategies. However, we know that the situation does not have to be so. In a longitudinal study of family literacy (Phillips et al., 2006), specific expectations were placed on parents related to the development of reading skills and strategies: Drawing children's attention to the print around them; matching letters with other letters, identifying letters, and making letter-sound matches; expecting children to engage in writing; encouraging children to spell and to listen to the sounds they hear; teaching children to count, to identify colours, and colour words; teaching child to write and spell their names; analyzing word meanings; teaching parents the difference between a book to be read to children and one that children can be expected to read; and helping children make explicit connections between their background knowledge and the story being read.

The program worked for children regardless of gender and no matter their beginning reading age between 36 and 60 months. This study showed that when taught specific skills and strategies to read and write, children learn. These children and their families demonstrated that letter knowledge, phoneme awareness, word recognition, and story comprehension can be learned with direct instruction, explicit expectations, and active engagement in print that matters.

Current Tests Are Biased but Need not Be So

Conventional testing rests heavily on the assumption that test takers have had comparable backgrounds and opportunities to acquire information. However, these assumptions are suspect with children from non-mainstream backgrounds (Campione & Brown, 1987; Hayward, 2002). Consider a developmental screening test used to assess children's emergent literacy. One item on that test has had a profound effect on the amount of attention and caution we have since exercised toward all forms of assessment. Mickey was a chubby, bright-eyed 5-year-old. Along with other children his age, he was doing a developmental test designed as an aid in identifying delays in development and behaviour (Phillips, 1997). The item was designed to assess young children's understanding of language through an examination of the following concepts: *on top of, below, to the side of*, and *behind*. Children were given a large colourful pencil and asked to demonstrate each of these positions by placing the pencil where they thought it should go in relation to a pile of books on the table. Mickey whizzed through the first three (*on top of, below, to the side of*), but stopped to think about the fourth one (*behind*). He stood up from his chair, leaned over, and reviewed the first three by pointing and subvocalizing. Then he said subvocally, "There's only one place left—'in back of'." He placed the pencil "in back of" the books and sat down. According to the test specifications, Mickey could not be given credit for the item because he did not use the word "behind." It was clear, that Mickey certainly did understand the concept of behind, though the word "behind" was not part of his vocabulary in the limited context of the test. Mickey's linguistic environment included a number of vocabulary differences that were held against him in his kindergarten screening even though he was bright, interested, and highly engaged. Mickey's language was different from that of the language on the test and used by the teachers and for that he was maligned.

The existence of content, linguistic and experiential biases in conventional standardized measures have potentially serious consequences. According to Sternberg and Grigorenko (2002), dynamic assessment models (DA) have shown promise in addressing a number of the concerns raised about conventional tests. DA is distinguished from conventional assessment formats by involving *test-teach-retest* phases that occur over a short time period. The *test* phase parallels conventional methods and involves administration of tests without feedback. During the brief *teach* phase, normally one to two short sessions (20–40 minutes each), examiners teach skills or strategies that a child needs to perform a particular task and provide feedback to the child regarding task performance. In the *retest* phase, tests are re-administered giving the child the opportunity to apply the strategies that were evoked or acquired during the teach phase.

Unlike conventional measures, DA may be helpful in differentiating children with actual difficulties from those with cultural or experiential differences and for estimating responsiveness to intervention (e.g., Gutierrez-Clellen, Brown, Conboy, & Robinson-Zanartu, 1998; Kramer, Mallett, Schneider, & Hayward, 2007; Ukrainetz, Harpell, Walsh, & Coyle, 2000). If such proves to be the case, there are significant implications for both service delivery and resource allocation (Hasson & Joffe, 2007). Take for example, two children both of whom receive low scores on conventional tests of word reading. The children then participate in two short sessions in which the examiner teaches reading strategies. Observations of the children during the teach sessions reveals that following four to five strategy exemplars the first child applies the strategies independently while the second child needs continual examiner support to apply the strategies. The children are retested with the conventional word reading test and the first child shows a significant improvement while the second child once again obtains a low score. Had only conventional testing been conducted, both children would have been considered poor readers and reading intervention programming recommended. Following the DA not only would different diagnostic decisions be reached for these children, but the observations made during the teach sessions would guide decisions regarding the specific amount, intensity, and type of support each child needs.

Although there is a dearth of research evidence applying DA to the reading domain, examination of available studies demonstrates findings similar to those reported for language learning. For example, Spector (1992) showed that a DA of phonemic awareness skills at the beginning of kindergarten better predicted end of year phonemic awareness and word reading skills than conventional measures. Day and Zajakowski (1991) used DA to examine reading comprehension in grade five children with good and poor reading ability. The children were required to locate the main idea in a series of short expository texts. There was no difference between groups on conventional reading measures but poor readers had much greater difficulty learning to find the main ideas in texts in the teach sessions. Thus, these researchers showed that DA measures revealed subtle differences between good and poor reader groups that conventional measures did not.

Of interest to us is the word reading skills of beginning readers for two reasons. First, beginning readers, particularly boys, from non-mainstream backgrounds are more likely to be diagnosed as poor readers using conventional testing methods. Some of these children may not have acquired word reading strategies but nonetheless may be able to do so quite readily if given the opportunity. Second, word reading and reading comprehension abilities are inextricably linked at the beginning reader stage. Children need to be able to read words in isolation quickly and accurately to support text level reading (Catts, Hogan, & Fey, 2003; Leach, Scarborough, & Rescorla, 2003; Stanovich, 1993). So, if boys and girls with word reading difficulties are correctly identified, not only can interventions begin early to preempt long term reading failure; such intervention should result in improvements to both word and text level reading. Thus, it is essential to use measures that can help to tease apart actual from contrived deficits so that children who genuinely need additional support receive it in a timely manner and children who do not need support are not mislabeled and placed in interventions unnecessarily (Hayward & Schneider, 2000). The importance of this line of our current research goes beyond these direct benefits to individual children but has implications regarding policy decisions at a school and district level for resource allocation and service delivery. Given that school administrators generally operate with a limited set of resources, information furnished from DA has the potential to support efficient and effective use of this resource pool.

Not All Intervention Programs Are Beneficial

Effective reading instruction is a topic of abiding interest and debate. Many children who should be capable of reading well cannot do so, which suggests that the instructional methods available to them are not appropriate (Pressley, 1998). There is no shortage of programs and methods dedicated to improving early reading instruction. The specific strengths and weaknesses of many programs and methods are largely unmeasured. Indeed, very few studies have explored the efficacy of early literacy programs and methods within highly defensible parameters. John Pikulski (1994) reviewed and identified the critical features of five claimed to be successful programs for at-risk first grade children. His main conclusions corroborate the need for excellent and coordinated intervention and classroom instruction; some children may require more instruction time and one-on-one tutoring than others even though all are identified to be at-risk; first grade is a crucial time to prevent further development of reading difficulties, and support beyond Grade 1 is likely necessary; texts should be simple enough to ensure success and to entice rereading and to develop word identification skills; attention to letters and words coupled with writing is critically important in early intervention programs; ongoing assessment should inform instruction; inclusion of the home is necessary in daily reading with the child; and teachers who provide consistently effective instruction anchor successful programs (p. 38).

In addition to the above indicators of successful programs, numerous studies of phonological awareness (PA) conducted over the past three decades indicate that it has a strong positive and powerful effect on subsequent reading achievement (Bradley & Bryant, 1983; Byrne & Fielding-Barnsley, 1995; Lundberg, Frost, & Petersen, 1988; Lundberg, Olofsson, & Wall, 1980; Perfetti, Beck, Bell, & Hughes, 1987; Stanovich, 1986; Torgesen, Wagner, & Rashotte, 1994; Vellutino & Scanlon, 1987). Not only is there a clear indication that PA is related to reading success, but it also appears that learning to read helps develop children's PA (Blachman, 2000; Bus & van Ijzendoorn, 1999;

Byrne & Fielding-Barnsley, 1989; Ehri et al., 2001; Perfetti et al., 1987; Wagner, Torgesen, & Rashotte, 1994).

Research studies on PA and the meta-analyses of these studies have implications for instruction. Bus and van Ijzendoorn (1999) concluded that preschoolers tend to profit most from PA training. The National Reading Panel (NRP) of experts named by the Director of the National Institute of Child Health and Human Development (NICHHD, 2000) argue that the reason kindergartners and preschoolers gain the most from such training is that these groups start out with the least phonological awareness. The NRP included a length-of-instruction variable in its meta-analysis and found that 5 to 18 hours of PA instruction were more effective than longer or shorter periods. Ehri et al. (2001) stated, "These findings suggest that phonological awareness instruction does not need to be lengthy to exert its strongest effect on reading and spelling" (p. 269). Bus and van Ijzendoorn (1999) stress that although "phonological awareness affects learning-to-read processes in a positive and substantial way" (p. 405), PA is not sufficient for learning to read. They estimate that PA explains approximately 12% of the variance in reading skills. Ehri et al. (2001) calculate the overall variance in reading outcomes explained by PA instruction to be 6.5%, rising to 10% when letters were added and to 28% for preschoolers. Thus, although PA has been shown to be important in reading words, it is but one component among a complex array of literacy experiences that help children learn to read (Cunningham 2001; Pressley, Allington, Wharton-McDonald, Block, & Morrow, 2001; Snow, Burns, & Griffin, 1998). In sum, it must be remembered that phonics instruction is a means to an end, that being the ability not just to decode but to comprehend and interpret written text.

Notwithstanding the knowledge of PA cited above, research to date does not provide definitive answers regarding the amount of emphasis that should be placed on phonics or the best way to teach phonics (Cunningham, 2003; NICHHD, 2000; Stahl, Duffy-Hester, & Stahl, 1998).

Into this mix, a large western Canadian city adopted a phonics-based reading program for some of its schools in low SES areas. Phillips, Norris, and Steffler (2007) conducted a 3-year longitudinal study of the program, which was a prescriptive, linear, and intensive reading program in seven schools all in low SES areas. *Literacy M.A.P. Meaningful applied phonics: Explicit phonics through direct instruction* (Hunter & Robinson, 2002) was a prescriptive, linear, and intensive reading program.

The treatment group was taught using the program. The same group of students was followed for 3 years, starting at the outset of Grade 1. The general features of M.A.P., as presented by Hunter and Robinson (2002) include: (a) M.A.P. is an explicit, teacher-directed approach; (b) M.A.P. is a logical, sequential program that organizes and paces the lessons, moves from graphemes to spelling words, and to reading and writing activities; (c) M.A.P. segments and blends words into syllables when reading and writing unfamiliar words; (d) M.A.P. teaches the 70 graphemes for the first 26 single letter sounds of the alphabet as well as vowel and consonant digraphs; and (e) M.A.P. focuses on phonics, spelling, and grammar for approximately 30 minutes each day combined with 60 minutes of reading and writing.

There are also more specific features of M.A.P advocated by Hunter and Robinson (2002). The program involves teacher-directed whole-class instruction and a sequential development of skills for approximately 90 minutes each day. This sequence starts with students learning to print correctly the letters of the alphabet following a detailed set of instructions. As they practice writing each letter, they also learn the sounds of that letter. After students have learned to print and say the sounds of the alphabet (referred to as "graphemes" in the manual), they follow the same routine to learn 28 multiple-letter "graphemes" (sometimes also referred to as "phonemes" in the manual) (p. 105).

Students are also given a spelling rule for each word and orally repeat each rule. After students have learned nine spelling words, the teacher incorporates dictated sentences using the mastered words into their phonics lessons. Dictated paragraphs and stories are added when children can spell enough words to proceed to this level of writing (see Hunter & Robinson, 2002, p. 23). The foregoing is consistent with the recommendation in the M.A.P. program that material be presented to students in small sequential steps so as "to provide students with a safe and secure environment from which they can concentrate on the mechanics of writing" (Hunter & Robinson, 2002, p. 25).

The reading process outlined in the M.A.P. model proceeds from the writing process described above. The reading process begins with graphemes taught in isolation. Graphemes are followed by spelling words, dictated sentences, dictated paragraphs and stories, reproducible stories, and, finally, children's literature. The M.A.P. program also incorporates instructions and strategies for teaching fluency, comprehension, and vocabulary. For example, in the section entitled "Comprehension Activities," pre-reading discussions, predictions, corrective reading strategies, paraphrasing, mental imagery, and graphic organizers are listed and briefly described (see Phillips et al., 2005 and 2007 for further discussion). The bulk of the manual contains organizing charts (for kindergarten to Grade 6), instructions on how to print and pronounce graphemes, and spelling word lists. These provide the means "to ensure that teachers and children have the knowledge, skills, and background to succeed on their journey toward literacy" (Hunter & Robinson, 2002, p. 4). Thus, the program manual, like the teaching program, provides explicit directions intended to help teachers to lead children to reading success. The M.A.P. resource is 311 pages and includes program explanations, approximately 200 pages of graphemes, spelling word lists, 115 pages of grapheme sequence lists, and thematic word lists.

The control group was taught according to a balanced literacy approach modeled after Cunningham and Hall's *Four-Blocks Literacy Model* (2001). The model is described as incorporating "four different approaches each day to teach children how to become better readers, writers, and

spellers" (see www.four-blocks.com, Overview, p.1) and was developed with the needs of a diverse range of students (different literacy levels, interests, and ways of learning) in mind. The control students were taught a balanced program with approximately equal amounts of time given to the four sections, namely: guided reading, self-selected reading, writing, and working with words. Guided reading, which includes learning about story elements and about how to learn from informational texts, "is always focused on comprehension" (Cunningham & Hall, 2001, p. 1, under the Guided Reading block, see www.four-blocks.com). Teachers and students read together big books and the initial reading texts, and other books and formats are introduced as the year progresses. At various points, teachers work with the whole class, but students also read together in small groups, with partners, individually, and with the teacher. During the self-selected reading block, children read what they themselves have chosen. Students are asked to respond to what they have been reading, to share their reading and responses with others and to conference with the teacher.

The writing block includes mini-lessons on the fundamentals of writing, such as how to get started, revise, and edit their writing. Children are also invited to share their writing and respond to the writing of their peers. The fourth block, working with words, is intended to "ensure that children read, spell, and use high frequency words correctly, and that they learn the patterns necessary for decoding and spelling" (Cunningham & Hall, 2001, p. 1, under the Working with Words block, see www.four-blocks.com). Strategies include making words and a word wall, with suggestions for grouping such activities into a five-lesson cycle. This approach is intended to help teachers meet mandates for including systematic, sequential phonics in reading instruction. The school board staff indicated that the four blocks are collapsed into three large blocks: working with words, reading, and writing for a total of 90 minutes each day.

We showed that, although the treatment children's reading, writing, and spelling appeared to show some gains in the first year, achievement over the 3 years deteriorated for children in the lowest- and highest-performing schools (even though the schools maintained their relative ranking as the lowest and highest). Children in the middle performing schools had become more alike in their performance but had also fallen compared to the norming populations. Gender was not found to be related to achievement. This result is consistent with other longitudinal studies we have conducted (Phillips et al., 1996, 2002, 2006), as well as those of other researchers including Biemiller and Siegel (1997), Halpern (2004), and Hyde (2005). Seven schools participated in the study. Schools 3, 4, and 5 maintained their relative ranking through the study. Schools 1 and 7, the worst and best performing, respectively, showed the least improvement and the greatest diminution. These results suggest that the middle group fared the best. One interpretation of these findings is that the students of School 1 were not ready for the heavy emphasis on phonics offered through the M.A.P. program and that the students of

School 7 were sufficiently advanced that the program was of little or no merit.

There was a significant *negative* effect of treatment on achievement when compared to the control group. The control group comparison provides strong evidence that early literacy achievement experienced by the children in the treatment schools was *less* than would be expected had the children been taught the same program as the control children. The differences were such that the control children, who underperformed the treatment children at the end of Grade 1, outperformed them at the end of both Grades 2 and 3. Clearly, the M.A.P. program did not have as beneficial an effect on students' literacy achievement as the programs used in the control schools (Phillips et al., 2005, 2007). The M.A.P. program provided a high dose of phonics and is unidimensional. It is known that a unidimensional focus is likely to be less effective for emergent readers (Foorman, Francis, Fletcher, Schatschneider, & Mehta, 1998; IRA, 1997; Pressley, 2002; Torgesen, 1998) than a balanced and multi-dimensional program such as the four-blocks literacy model. Our study demonstrates that all potential innovations, even those based to a degree upon sound research, need to face critical appraisal of their effectiveness.

Concluding Comments

In this chapter we discussed six erroneous beliefs surrounding persistent reading disabilities. First, is the belief that relative reading achievement is immutable. Not only is this belief false in the light of effective interventions, relative reading achievement is porous even under typical classroom settings. For this reason, the belief is particularly pernicious in nullifying any hope of improvement for many children. Second, there is the belief that poverty and gender create ceilings on reading ability. This belief creates expectations for a poor performance from certain groups. The evidence shows that within any group there are enormous spreads in quality of performance so that identifying individuals on the basis of the mean performance of the individual's group can be both grossly inaccurate and unfair. Third, it is a common practice to wait to be sure a child has reading problems before acting. In contrast, the evidence suggests that early and focused interventions are the most effective ones and that waiting can result in intractable problems. Fourth, simply reading to children is a practice promoted to prevent most reading difficulties. Although seductive, the practice is only partly correct. Reading to children is beneficial, but only when time is taken to draw children's attention to print and to engage them directly in learning print concepts. Fifth, it is widely believed that conventional tests serve all groups equitably. We know, however, that this is not the case. Worse, the groups most in need of help are the ones most poorly served. In addition, there are approaches to testing that show promise of correcting this failure. Finally, there is a belief among some that intervening in reading instruction is always better than doing nothing over and above the normal—an anything is better than noth-

ing view. Yet, interventions need to be well-planned and well-executed based upon available and specific research because it has been shown that some interventions make bad situations worse.

In the context of the six erroneous beliefs we have refuted, we conclude that the term, *persistent reading disabilities* is much over-used and applied to too many children.

References

Adams, M. (1990). *Beginning to read: Thinking and learning about print.* Cambridge, MA: MIT Press.

Badian, N. A. (1999). Persistent arithmetic, reading, or arithmetic and reading disability. *Annals of Dyslexia, 49,* 45–70.

Biemiller, A., & Siegel, L. (1997). A longitudinal study of the effects of the *Bridge Reading Program* for children at risk for reading failure. *Learning Disability Quarterly, 20*(2), 83–92.

Bishop, D. (1997). *Uncommon understanding: Development and disorders of language comprehension in children.* Sussex, UK: Psychology Press.

Blachman, B. A. (2000). Phonological awareness. In M. L. Kamil, P. B. Mosenthal, P. D. Pearson, & P. Barr (Eds.), *Handbook of reading research: Vol. III* (pp. 484–502). Mahwah, NJ: Erlbaum.

Bradley, L., & Bryant, P. E. (1983). Categorizing sounds and learning to read — a causal connection. *Nature, 301*(5899), 419–421.

Brown, J. R. (1991). The retrograde motion of planets and children: Interpreting percentile rank. *Psychology in the Schools, 28*(4), 345–353.

Bus, A. G., & van Ijzendoorn, M. H. (1999). Phonological awareness and early reading: A meta-analysis of experimental training studies. *Journal of Educational Psychology, 91*(3), 403–414.

Byrne, B., & Fielding-Barnsley, R. (1989). Phonemic awareness and letter knowledge in the child's acquisition of the alphabetic principle. *Journal of Educational Psychology, 81*(3), 313–321.

Byrne, B., & Fielding-Barnsley, R. (1995). Evaluation of a program to teach phonemic awareness to young children: A 2- and 3-year follow-up and a new preschool trial. *Journal of Educational Psychology, 87*(3), 488–503.

Campione, J., & Brown, A. (1987). Linking dynamic assessment with school achievement. In C. S. Lidz (Ed.), *Dynamic assessment: An interactional approach to evaluating learning potential* (pp. 82–115). New York: Guilford.

Catts, H., Fey, M., Zhang, X., & Tomblin, J. B. (2001). Estimating the risk of future reading difficulties in kindergarten children: A research-based model and its clinical implications. *Language, Speech, and Hearing Services in Schools, 32*(1), 38–50.

Catts, H., Hogan, T., & Fey, M. (2003). Subgrouping poor readers on the basis of reading-related abilities. *Journal of Learning Disabilities, 36*(2), 151–164.

Cox, T. (1987). Slow starters versus long term backwards readers. *British Journal of Educational Psychology, 57*(1), 73–86.

Cunningham, J. W. (2001). The National Reading Panel Report. *Reading Research Quarterly, 36,* 326–335.

Cunningham, P. M. (2003). What research says about teaching phonics. In L. M. Morrow, L. B. Gambrell, & M. Pressley (Eds.), *Best practices in literacy instruction* (pp. 65–86). New York: Guilford.

Cunningham, P.M., & Hall, D. (2001). *Four-blocks literacy model.* Greensboro, NC: Carson-Dellosa Publishing.

Day J. D., & Zajakowski, A. (1991). Comparisons of learning ease and transfer propensity in poor and average readers. *Journal of Learning Disabilities, 24*(7), 421–433.

Denton, C. A., Fletcher, J. M., Anthony, J. L., & Francis, D. J. (2006). An evaluation of intensive intervention for students with persistent reading difficulties. *Journal of Learning Disabilities, 39*(5), 447–466.

Ehri, L. C., Nunes, S. R., Willows, D. M., Schuster, B. V., Yaghoub-Zadeh, Z., & Shanahan, T. (2001). Phonemic awareness instruction helps children learn to read: Evidence from the National Reading Panel's meta-analysis. *Reading Research Quarterly, 36*(3), 250–287.

Elkins, J. (2007). Learning Disabilities: Bringing fields and nations together. *Journal of Learning Disabilities, 40*(5), 392–399.

Fine, S. (2001, August 27). Schools told to fix boys' low grades. *Globe and Mail*, p. A1.

Fletcher, J. M., Lyon, G. R., Fuchs, L. S., & Barnes, M. A. (2007). *Learning disabilities*. New York: Guilford.

Flynn, J .M., & Rahbar, M. H. (1994). Prevalence of reading failure in boys compared with girls. *Psychology in the Schools, 31*(1), 66–71.

Foorman, B. R., Francis, D. J., Fletcher, J. M., Schatschneider, C., & Mehta, P. (1998). The role of instruction in learning to read; Preventing reading failure in at-risk children. *Journal of Educational Psychology, 90*(1), 37–55.

Francis, B. (2005). *Reassessing gender and achievement: Questioning contemporary key debates*. New York: Routledge.

Francis, D. J., Fletcher, J. M., Shaywitz, B. A., Shaywitz, S. E., & Rourke, B. P. (1996). Defining learning and language and disabilities: Conceptual and psychometric issues with the use of IQ test. *Language, Speech, and Hearing Services in Schools, 27*(2), 132–143.

Frempong, G., & Willms, J. D. (2002). Can school quality compensate for socioeconomic disadvantage? In J. D. Willms (Ed.), *Vulnerable children* (pp. 277–304). Edmonton, AB: University of Alberta Press.

Gray, S., Plante, E., Vance, R., & Henrichsen, M. (1999). The diagnostic accuracy for four vocabulary tests administered to preschool-aged children. *Language Speech and Hearing Services in Schools, 30*(2), 196–206.

Gutierrez-Clellen, V. F., Brown, S., Conboy, B., & Robinson-Zanartu, C. (1998). Modifiability: A Dynamic Approach to assessing immediate language change. *Journal of Children's Communication Development, 19*(2), 31–42.

Halpern, D. (2004). A cognitive-process taxonomy for sex differences in cognitive abilities. *Current Directions in Psychological Science, 13*(4), 135–139.

Harris, T. L., & Hodges, R. E. (Eds.). (1995). *The literacy dictionary*. Newark, DE: International Reading Association.

Hasson, N., & Joffe, V. (2007). The case for Dynamic Assessment in speech and language therapy. *Child Language, Teaching & Therapy, 23*(1), 9–25.

Hayward, D. (2002). Norm-referenced testing: Issues of measurement and application. In S. Warren & W. Janzen (Eds.), *Power in research II. Special issues*. Edmonton, AB: Rehabilitation Research Centre.

Hayward, D., Das, J. P., & Janzen, T. (2007). Innovative programs for improvement in reading through cognitive enhancement: A remediation study of Canadian First Nations children. *Journal of Learning Disabilities, 40*(5), 443–457.

Hayward, D. V., & Schneider, P. (2000). Effectiveness of teaching story grammar knowledge to preschool children with language impairments: An exploratory story. *Child Language, Teaching & Therapy, 16*(3), 255–284.

Hayward, D. V., Stewart, G. E., Phillips, L. M., Norris, S. P., & Lovell, M. A. (2008). *Language, Phonological Awareness, and Reading Test Directory*. London, ON: Canadian Centre for Research on Literacy and Canadian Language and Literacy Research Network.

Hinshaw, S. P. (1992). Externalizing behavior problems and academic underachievement in childhood and adolescence: Causal relationships and underlying mechanisms. *Psychological Bulletin, 111*(1), 127–155.

Hinshelwood, J. (1896). Word-blindness and visual memory. *Lancet, 146*(3773), 1564–1570.

Hunter, C., & Robinson, S. (2002). *Literacy M.A.P. Meaningful applied phonics, explicit phonics through direct instruction*. Edmonton, AB: Edmonton Public Schools.

Hoffman, J.V., Roser, N. L., & Battle, J. (1991). *Storytime in classrooms: What is, what could be, what should be*. Paper presented at the 41st annual meeting of the National Reading Conference, December 4, Palm Springs, California.

Hyde, J. S. (2005). The gender similarities hypothesis. *American Psychologist, 60*(6), 581–592.

International Reading Association. (1997). Summary statement of Role of phonics in reading instruction. A position statement of the International Reading Association. Available from http://www.reading.org/resources/issues/positions_phonics.html

Jha, J., & Kelleher, F. (2006). *Boys underachievement in education*. London: Commonwealth of Learning and the Commonwealth Secretariat.

Juel, C. (1988). Learning to read and write: A Longitudinal study of 54 children from first through fourth grades. *Journal of Educational Psychology, 80*(4), 437–447.

Kame'enui, E. J., Fuchs, L., Francis, D. J., Good III, R., O'Connor, R., Simmons, D., Tindal, G., & Torgesen, J. K. (2006). The adequacy of tools for assessing reading competence: A framework and review. *Educational Researcher, 35*(4), 3–11.

Kramer, K., Mallett, P., Schneider, P., & Hayward, D.V. (2007, May). *Dynamic Assessment of Narratives with Grade 3 Children in a First Nations Community*. Presented at the Symposium on Research in Child Language Disorders, Madison, Wisconsin.

Lahey, M. (1990). Who shall be called language-disordered? Some reflections and one perspective. *Journal of Speech and Hearing Disorders, 55*, 612–620.

Leach, J., Scarborough, H., & Rescorla, L. (2003). Late-emerging reading disabilities. *Journal of Educational Psychology, 95*(2), 211–224.

Lee, V. E., & Burkham, D. T. (2002). *Inequality at the starting gate: Social background differences in achievement as children begin school*. Washington, DC: Economic Policy Institute.

Lonigan, C. J., Bloomfield, B. G., Anthony, J. L., Bacon, K. D., Phillips, B. M., & Samwel, C. S. (1999). Relations among emergent literacy skills, behavior problems, and social competence in preschool children from low- and middle-income backgrounds. *Topics in Early Childhood Special Education, 19*(1), 40–53.

Lundberg, I., Frost, J., & Petersen, O. (1988). Effects of an extensive program for stimulating phonological awareness in preschool children. *Reading Research Quarterly, 23*(3), 263–284.

Lundberg, I., Olofsson, A., & Wall, S. (1980). Reading and spelling skills in the first school years predicted from phonemic awareness skills in kindergarten. *Scandinavian Journal of Psychology, 21*(1), 159–173.

Mathes, P. G., & Denton, C. A. (2002). The prevention and identification of reading disability. *Seminars in Pediatric Neurology, 9*(3), 185–191.

McArthur, G. M., Hogben, J. H., Edwards, V. T., Heath, S. M., & Mengler, E. D. (2000). On the "specifics" of specific reading disability and specific language impairment. *Journal of Child Psychology and Psychiatry, 41*(7), 869–874.

McCauley, R. J., & Swisher, L. (1984). Use and misuse of norm-referenced tests in clinical assessment: A hypothetical case. *Journal of Speech and Hearing Disorders, 49*, 338–348.

McGee, R., Williams, S., & Silva, P. A. (1988). Slow starters versus long-term backwards readers: A replication and extension. *British Journal of Educational Psychology, 58*(3), 330–337.

Meyer, L. A., Stahl, S., Wardrop, J. L., & Linn, R. L. (1992). *The effects of reading storybooks aloud to children*. Paper presented at the 41st annual meeting of the National Reading Conference, December 4, Palm Springs, California.

National Institute of Child Health and Human Development. (2000). *Report of the National Reading Panel: Teaching children to read: An evidence based assessment of the scientific research literature on reading and its implications for reading instruction*. (NIH Publication No. 00-4769). Washington, DC: U.S. Government Printing Office. Available from http://www.nichd.nih.gov/publications/nrp/report.html

Paul, R. (2007). *Language disorders from infancy through adolescence*. St. Louis, MO: Mosby Elsevier.

Peña, E., Spaulding, T., & Plante, E. (2006). The composition of normative groups and diagnostic decision making: Shooting ourselves in the foot. *American Journal of Speech-Language Pathology, 15*(3), 247–254.

Perfetti, C. A., Beck, I., Bell, L. C., & Hughes, C. (1987). Phonemic knowledge and learning to read are reciprocal: A longitudinal study of first grade children. *Merrill-Palmer Quarterly, 33*, 283–319.

Phillips, L. M. (1997). Theoretical Considerations of Assessment and Evaluation. In V. Froese (Ed.), *Language across the curriculum* (pp. 250–271). Toronto, ON: Harcourt Brace Canada.

Phillips, L. M., Hayden, R., & Norris, S. P. (2006). *Family literacy matters: A longitudinal parent-child literacy intervention study.* Calgary, AB: Temeron/Detselig.

Phillips, L. M., Norris, S. P., & Anderson, J. (2008). Unlocking the door: Is parents' reading to children the key to early literacy development? Special issue of *Canadian Psychology* on *Literacy Development in Canada, 49*(2), 82–88.

Phillips, L. M., Norris, S. P., & Mason, J. (1996). Longitudinal effects of early literacy concepts on reading achievement: A kindergarten intervention and five-year follow-up. *JLR: Journal of Literacy Research, 28*(1), 173–195.

Phillips, L. M., Norris, S. P., Osmond, W., & Maynard, A. (2002). Relative reading achievement: A longitudinal study of 187 children from first through sixth grade. *Journal of Educational Psychology, 94*(1), 3–13.

Phillips, L. M., Norris, S. P., & Steffler, D. J. (2005). *Meaningful applied phonics: A longitudinal early literacy study.* Vancouver, B.C.: Society for the Advancement of Excellence in Education.

Phillips, L. M., Norris, S. P., & Steffler, D. J. (2007). Potential risks to reading posed by high-dose phonics. *Journal of Applied Research on Learning, 1*(1), 1–18.

Phillips, L .M., & Sample, H .L. (2005). Family literacy: Listen to what the families have to say. In J. Anderson, M. Kendrick, T. Rogers, & S. Smythe (Eds.), *Portraits of literacy across families, communities and schools: Intersections and tensions* (pp. 91–107). Mahwah, NJ: Erlbaum.

Pikulski, J.J. (1994). Preventing reading failure: A review of five effective programs. *Reading Teacher, 48*(1), 30–39

PISA. (2005). *Program for International Assessment.* Paris: Organization for Economic Co-operation and Development.

Plante, E., & Vance, R. (1995) Diagnostic accuracy of two tests of preschool language. *American Journal of Speech–Language Pathology, 4,* 70–76.

Pressley, M. (1998). *Reading instruction that works.* New York: Guilford.

Pressley, M. (2002). *Reading instruction that works: The case for balanced teaching.* New York: Guilford.

Pressley, M., Allington, R. L., Wharton-McDonald, R., Block, C. C., & Morrow, L. M. (2001). *Learning to read: Lessons from exemplary first-grade classrooms.* New York: Guilford.

Rack, J. P., Snowling, M., & Olson, R. K. (1992). The nonword reading deficit in developmental dyslexia: A review. *Reading Research Quarterly, 27*(1), 28–53.

Rice, M. L., Warren, S. F., & Betz, S. K. (2005). Language symptoms of developmental language disorders: An overview of autism, Down syndrome, fragile X, specific language impairment, and Williams syndrome. *Applied Psycholinguistics, 26*(1), 7–27.

Shaywitz, S. E., Fletcher, J. M., & Shaywitz, B. A. (1994). Issues in the definition and classification of attention deficit disorder. *Topics in Language Disorders, 14*(4), 1–25.

Siegel, L. (1992). An evaluation of the discrepancy definition of dyslexia. *Journal of Learning Disabilities, 25*(10), 618–629.

Smith, S. S. (1997). A longitudinal study: The literacy development of 57 children. In C. Kinzer, K. A. Hinchman, & D. J. Leu (Eds.), *Inquiries in literacy theory and practice* (pp. 250–264). Chicago: National Reading Conference.

Snow, C. E., Barnes, W. S., Chandler, J., Goodman, I. F., & Hemphill, L. (1991). *Unfulfilled expectations: Home and school influences on literacy.* Cambridge, MA: Harvard University Press.

Snow, C. E., Burns, M., & Griffin, P. (Eds.). (1998). *Preventing reading difficulties in young children.* Washington, DC: National Academy Press.

Spear-Swerling, L., & Sternberg, R. J. (1996). *Off track: When poor readers become "learning disabled."* Boulder, CO: Westview.

Spector, J. E. (1992). Predicting progress in beginning reading: Dynamic assessment of phonemic awareness. *Journal of Educational Psychology, 84*(3), 353–363.

Stahl, S. A., Duffy-Hester, A. M., & Stahl, K. A. D. (1998). Everything you wanted to know about phonics (but were afraid to ask). *Reading Research Quarterly, 33*(3), 338–355.

Stanovich, K. E. (1986). Matthew effects in reading: Some consequences of individual differences in the acquisition of literacy. *Reading Research Quarterly, 21*(4), 360–406.

Stanovich, K. E. (1991). Discrepancy definitions of reading disability: Has intelligence led us astray? *Reading Research Quarterly, 26* (1), 7–29.

Stanovich, K. E. (1993). The language code: Issues in word recognition. In S. Yussen & M. C. Smith (Eds.), *Reading across the life span* (pp. 111–135). New York: Springer-Verlag.

Sternberg, R. J. & Grigorenko, E. L. (2002). *Dynamic testing. The nature and measurement of learning potential.* Cambridge, UK: Cambridge University Press.

Torgesen, J. K. (1998). Instructional interventions for children with reading disabilities. In B. K. Shapiro, P. J. Accardo, & A. J. Capute (Eds.), *Specific reading disability: A view of the spectrum* (pp.197–220). Timonium, MD: York Press.

Torgesen, J. K., & Burgess, S. R. (1998). Consistency of reading-related phonological processes throughout early childhood: Evidence from longitudinal-correlational and instructional studies. In J. Metsala & L. Ehri (Eds.), *Word recognition in beginning reading* (pp. 161–188). Hillsdale, NJ: Erlbaum.

Torgesen, J. K., Wagner, R. K., & Rashotte, C. A. (1994). Longitudinal studies of phonological processing and reading. *Journal of Learning Disabilities, 27*(5), 276–286.

Ukrainetz, T. A., Harpell, S., Walsh, C., & Coyle, C. (2000). A preliminary investigation of dynamic assessment with Native American kindergartners. *Language, Speech, and Hearing Services in Schools, 31*(2), 142–154.

Vellutino, F.R. (1979). *Dyslexia: Theory and research.* Cambridge, MA: MIT Press.

Vellutino, F. R., & Scanlon, D. M. (1987). Phonological coding, phonological awareness, and reading ability: Evidence from a longitudinal and experimental study. *Merrill-Palmer Quarterly, 33,* 321–363.

Wagner, R. K., & Torgesen, J. K. (1987). The nature of phonological processing and its casual role in the acquisition of reading skills. *Psychological Bulletin, 101*(2), 192–212.

Wagner, R. K., Torgesen, J. K., & Rashotte, C. A. (1994). Development of reading-related phonological processing abilities: New evidence of bidirectional causality from a latent variable longitudinal study. *Developmental Psychology, 30*(1), 73–87.

Willms, D. (2002). *Vulnerable children.* Edmonton, AB: University of Alberta Press.

Wright, S. F., Fields, H., & Newman, S. P. (1996). Dyslexia: Stability of definition over a five year period. *Journal of Research in Reading, 19*(1), 46–60.

11

Prenatal Drug and Alcohol Exposure and Reading Disabilities

DIANE BARONE
University of Nevada, Reno

In 1995, I wrote about prenatal crack/cocaine exposure and the difficulties of separating truth from fiction (Barone, 1995). I even used a quote from *Maniac Magee* where Spinelli (1991) cautions readers to pretend to "Run your hand under your movie seat and be very careful, very careful not to let the facts get mixed up with the truth." Spinelli's caution is worthwhile today as even with extensive research since 1995, teasing out truth from fiction with respect to prenatal drug and alcohol exposure is still an essential task when making sense of this research base. To facilitate this task, I have organized this chapter around research issues related to this topic, a synthesis of the research, and connections to schools and how best to support such children.

Cautions About the Research

There are numerous issues surrounding research on prenatal drug and alcohol exposure. Some issues center on the rigor of the research while others cross all research endeavors such as the amounts of drugs or alcohol used during pregnancy. When gleaning information from the research base it is important to consider possible flaws and limitations within this research or in particular studies.

Questions About the Published Research and its Rigor

The research surrounding crack/cocaine is particularly interesting in the lessons it can teach about perceptions becoming reality. When the foundational research was conducted on children prenatally exposed to crack/cocaine, the media had identified these children as future sociopaths (Barone, 1999; Griffith, 1995). Simultaneous with these vivid portrayals was the acceptance or rejection of research surrounding prenatal exposure; in this case, journals more often rejected manuscripts that disputed calamitous outcomes for these children (Gonzalez & Campbell, 1994; Greider, 1995; Hutchings, 1993; Lester & Tronick, 1994). Frank and Zuckerman (1993) wrote about this situation:

The early reports of adverse effects of prenatal exposure to cocaine including neurobehavioral dysfunction, a remarkably high rate of SIDS [Sudden Infant Death Syndrome], and birth defects were initial observations that constitute the legitimate first step in the scientific process. However, these unreplicated findings were uncritically accepted by scientists and lay media alike, not as preliminary, and possible unrepresentative case reports, but as "proven" facts. It is not easy to disseminate scientific data contrary to prevailing popular belief. Our own experience, confirmed by others, has been that the popular media is disinterested in negative reports or in statements by researchers indicating uncertainty regarding the impact of prenatal cocaine exposure. (p. 299)

This early work still finds its ways into the belief systems of teachers and the public. They assume that prenatal drug exposure, by itself, results in a whole host of educational issues, all negative, related to these children. Later in this chapter a more realistic view is offered.

In addition to the selectivity of publishers and editors with the early research, Mayes, Granger, Bornstein, and Zuckerman (1992) evaluated the methodological rigor of the early work. They noted serious flaws in much of this research centered on the preferred selection of participants who were poor and the lack of any control or comparison group. A more recent meta-analysis of articles from 1984 to 2000 (Frank, Augustyn, Grant, Knight, Tripler, & Zuckerman, 2001) found that of 74 articles, only 36 met the requirements for methodological rigor. They noted that among the issues related to rigor, few studies controlled for a mother's use of other drugs such as opiates, methamphetamines, or tobacco. From the articles that met their selection criteria, they determined there was no consistent negative association between prenatal cocaine drug exposure and physical growth, developmental test scores, or receptive or expressive language. These results are certainly in contrast to the results of less rigorous earlier studies. However, they are also less likely to be familiar to teachers and the public who without the media reports often pay less attention to the more current research.

Another issue that pertains to early and current studies is centered on women participants. Because it is not possible to track a pregnant mother's use of drugs during pregnancy, all reports of drug use are based on self-report data. Mothers, because of the stigma attached to drinking or using other drugs during pregnancy, underreport their use of such substances (Sokol, Delaney-Black, & Nordstrom, 2003). Most hospitals lack protocols for identifying pregnant women who use alcohol or other drugs (Brady, Posner, Lang, & Rosati, 1994). While alcohol detection is quite difficult in an infant as there is no reliable biological marker available, this is not the case for tobacco or cocaine as a urine assay can detect tobacco and benzoylecgonine levels in meconium can detect cocaine (Frank, Augustyn, Knight, Pell, & Zuckerman, 2001). These tests, however, can result in false positives or fail to reveal other drug use because the substances have metabolized (Mayes et al., 1992). While these tests can detect that a mother used a certain substance late in pregnancy, up to 48 hours before delivery, they do not identify a mother's use throughout a pregnancy (Miller, 1989). Moreover, if a baby is full term and appears healthy, doctors rarely look for subtle signs of drug or alcohol exposure (Soby, 2006). This lack of identification and reliance on self-report data are large limitations regarding research on drug and/or alcohol use during pregnancy and the results to children.

Another criticism of this research is that researchers tried to study children exposed to a single drug. While this might be an ideal for research, the reality is that most pregnant women, who use a drug of choice, also use other drugs when available, smoke, and/or drink alcohol. Researchers are now using the word, *polydrug*, rather than singling out a specific drug for research (Bateman, Ng, Hansen, & Heagarty, 1993; Frank, Augustyn, Knight, Pell, et al., 2001). Future research will need to investigate the synergistic effects of exposure to multiple substances on children's development, rather than the simpler earlier research that attempted to target only a single substance (Coles & Black, 2005; Coles, Platzman, Smith, James, & Falek, 1992).

Finally, as researchers continue to study the effects of prenatal exposure, they must consider other variables that affect these children simultaneously:

1. Most pregnant mothers who use drugs or alcohol seek no or limited prenatal care (Barone, 1999).
2. Often their children are born prematurely. Prematurity can result in language delays, fine motor issues, attention and learning issues, and socioemotional relationship difficulties (Bennett, 1992; Gregorchik, 1992).
3. Poor maternal nutrition during pregnancy (Thomas, 2004).
4. Maternal health and age. Mothers over the age of 30 influence fetal susceptibility to long term effects of intrauterine growth retardation, small-for-gestational-age infants, long term growth impairments, and cognitive difficulties (O'Shea, Klinepeter, Goldstein, Jackson, & Dillard, 1997).
5. Fetal genetic susceptibility. Some fetuses are more or less resilient to their mother's use of drugs or alcohol (O'Shea et al., 1997).
6. Drug factors such as frequency and type of use, the way drugs are used, contaminants used in street drugs, and the characteristics of drugs (McConnell et al., 2002; Soby, 2006).
7. Most identified children come from high poverty families. These families often suffer from disorganization and violence (Singer et al., 2004).

Clearly, research in the area of prenatal alcohol and drug exposure is no easy task. The flaws in earlier research provide a lesson for newer researchers as they try to understand the implications of drug and alcohol exposure. Kronstadt (1991) suggests that because of the difficulties surrounding this research, those interested should expect to see differing results even when studies pose the same questions. The quality of the results is necessarily tied to the rigor of the study's design, and therefore meta-analyses are especially important in understanding this research.

Issue of Which Drug Is Most Damaging Once again, the 1980s and 1990s media helped the public believe that cocaine was the drug that did most damage to children (Frank & Zuckerman, 1993). The reality is that cocaine, like other drugs including alcohol, presents a full continuum of effects from no effects to complex effects that include low birth weight and smaller head circumference (Bennett, 1992; Berlin, 1991; Brodkin & Zuckerman, 1992; Chasnoff, 1991; Cohen & Taharally, 1992; Villarreal, McKinney, & Quackenbush, 1991). The media focus today is more targeted to methamphetamine use and its consequences, so the prediction would be that more research will occur in this area that is under-researched at present (Soby, 2006).

While cocaine has shared extensive media coverage, alcohol and cigarettes result in equal or more detrimental effects to an infant (Brodkin & Zuckerman, 1992). Both of these drugs result in children who have lower birth weight and smaller head circumference. Miller et al. (2006) observed that about 35% to 80% of urban youth are exposed to environmental smoke and this exposure is associated with reduced fetal growth, neuro-developmental problems, and diseases like asthma and cancer. Alcohol exposure results in a myriad of issues as well for children that include mild to severe cognitive deficits such as mental retardation (Charmichael, Morse, & Huffine, 1998). Additionally, these children have been found to have poor social judgment, fail to comprehend consequences, and/or have difficulty understanding social cues (Charmichael, Feldman, Streissguth, Sampson, & Bookstein, 1998). Interestingly, Coles and Black (2005) noted that alcohol and tobacco have not been as much as a health concern to the public as illicit drugs so there have been fewer studies in these areas, although the consequences to children are similar or more damaging than cocaine or other drug exposure.

The National Institute on Drug Abuse (NIDA, 1996) estimated that about 5.5% of pregnant women use illicit drugs. For alcohol, 50% of women of childbearing age drink alcohol, and approximately 20% report that they continue to drink when pregnant. Coupled with this usage report, current research documents that as little as a small amount of alcohol per day (.5 drinks per day) can result in adverse effects for an infant (Coles & Black, 2005; Sokol, Delaney-Black, & Nordstrom, 2003). Fetal Alcohol Syndrome's prevalence in the United States is approximately 1 case per 100 live births with about 2,000 infant deaths per year attributed to alcohol use (Burd, Cotsonas-Hassler, Martsolf, & Kerbeshian, 2003).

Cocaine exposed children range from 1% to 5% (Besharov, 1990) of live births per year. In the 1980s the total estimate was 375,000 drug-exposed infants in the United States, with over 4 million predicted by 2000 (Kusserow, 1990). Marijuana exposed children range from 3% to 20% of children born (MacGregor, 1990) per year. Costs associated with these children included increased placement in foster care (Thomas, 2004) and medical costs. In a Florida study (www.fdhc.state.fl.us/index.shtml), drug-exposed babies more often than non-exposed infants required more expensive medical care.

Prenatal exposure of children to both licit (alcohol and cigarettes) and illicit drugs (cocaine, marijuana, and opiates) is a substantial problem in the United States. Each year approximately 757,000 pregnant women use alcohol and 820,000 smoke cigarettes. About 220,000 pregnant women use illicit drugs at least once during pregnancy. Finally, 32% of women who use one illicit drug also smoke and drink (Wenzel et al., 2001). Using these estimates, about 1 million children each year are prenatally exposed to licit and illicit drugs.

NIDA (2003, www.drugabuse.gov/infofacts/nation-trends.html) provided a fact sheet demonstrating national trends in drug abuse representing 21 major U.S. cities. The following trends were noted:

- Cocaine/crack rates were high and were increasing in many cities.
- Heroin use was stable.
- Misuse of prescription opiates was increasing.
- Marijuana is the most frequently abused drug, and abuse is high among adolescents and young adults.
- Methamphetamine abuse is spreading even to rural areas.

They also estimated the cost of alcohol and drug abuse to be $245.7 billion in 1992. These costs centered on drug-related crime, damage to property, police and legal services, among other items. It did not include the costs related to children prenatally exposed to alcohol or drugs. Today it could be predicted that this amount would be substantially larger in scope.

The data do not show that one drug is more damaging to children, especially since mothers typically use more than one drug during pregnancy. Rather, it demonstrates that there are large numbers of children born each year who have been prenatally exposed to drugs or alcohol, and in most cases a combination of these substances. For some children the effects of their mother's drug or alcohol are significant and for others moderate to insignificant.

Frank, Augustyn, Knight, Pell, et al. (2001) document that much is still unknown about the effects of prenatal drug and alcohol exposure. For instance, even if no effects are found for children from 6 months to 6 years old, the increasing academic complexity in school may identify effects previously not observed (Fried & Watkinson, 2000). Cumulative environmental effects may also exacerbate negative cognitive or behavioral outcomes that were previously not present.

Issue of Who Uses Drugs Prenatally   Often, the perception is that poor women engage in the use of drugs and alcohol during pregnancy more often than other socioeconomic groups. The reason behind this perception is that urine toxicology tests are more common in hospitals that serve poor families. When hospitals participated in studies, they discovered that all social classes were documented to have children prenatally exposed to drugs and alcohol (Villarreal, McKinney, & Quackenbush, 1991).

As with other issues surrounding drug and alcohol exposure, there are policy issues related to the discovery surrounding the use of drugs. A vivid example from cocaine use demonstrates the intersection of policy and drug use (Thomas, 2004). In the early 1980s, cocaine was thought to be a recreational drug used by the middle class. Policy at this time involved rehabilitation, and the morality of mothers was not in question. In the 1980s and early 1990s, cocaine use was connected to low-income families living in urban areas. Mothers were vilified, and many states took a punitive approach to them. If their use was discovered, they could be imprisoned for abuse to their unborn baby. The punitive policies left drug and alcohol abusing women without medical care during pregnancy as they were afraid that doctors would report their use and they would be arrested (Barone, 1999). At the end of the 1990s when cocaine use moved to the background, many of the punitive laws were voted down. More recently, in 2001, the Center for Reproductive Law and Policy challenged the constitutionality of drug tests without consent in hospitals serving low-income families. The result of *Ferguson v City of Charleston* is that this practice is being discontinued as it was deemed unconstitutional as it resulted in poor women being victimized along with their unborn child not benefiting from prenatal care (Thomas, 2004).

Drugs and alcohol are used by people in all socioeconomic levels and in all kinds of communities. There is no typical profile for a pregnant woman who uses drugs or alcohol during pregnancy (Chasnoff, 1989). Because poor women were more easily identified for their drug or alcohol use, this perception came to be. Moreover, as researchers identified participants for their research, poor children were typically easier to identify as they were drug screened in the hospital, confirming their use of drugs (Barone, 1993a, 1993b). When considering the research, high-poverty children and children of color are overrepresented in the research samples. This sampling problem is difficult to change as few middle class women who have private doctors are screened in the hospital or would be willing to participate in research studies. The outcomes are that the public believes that more urban poor children have been prenatally exposed to drugs or alcohol and more poor children are participants in studies. The second outcome results in more variables that cloud the research as these children are most often poor, living in urban centers, and attend schools noted for their less exemplary instruction.

A Synthesis of the Research

Kronstadt (1991) noted that some principles are important to consider when exploring the damage exerted by prenatal substance exposure. These principles include:

1. *A child's development is influenced by genetic predispositions as well as environment.* Children vary in their physical, biological, and temperamental makeup. For instance, there is a reciprocal relationship between a mother's use of substances and a child's resilience (Conners et al., 2003). Some fetuses prenatally exposed to crack/cocaine are miscarried and never reach birth (Barone, 1999). After birth, some children cry and draw away from their mothers resulting in a mother making fewer advances to the child. Such behavior results in a disruption of their relationship.
2. *Each child varies in how he or she responds to multiple insults.* Some children are more resilient in withstanding physical and environmental insults. For instance, a child might experience his or her mother's use of drugs in utero, poor nutrition, no prenatal care, and neglect or abuse during their early years and still be successful in school (Barone, 2004). One child may successfully respond to all of these insults while another may be vulnerable to just one. Just considering drug or alcohol exposure alone does not take into account these numerous, possible responses to physical, emotional, and environmental insults (Watson & Westby, 2003).
3. *Each child experiences numerous events that can influence development.* For instance, prenatal drug exposure may not have long-term influence over a child. And conversely, a child may not show immediate signs of drug or alcohol exposure but later indications of this exposure may be evident.
4. *Infants demonstrate plasticity in development.* For instance, many infants prenatally exposed to drugs are born with smaller head circumference. However, with proper diet their head size approaches or meets normal statistics (Mayes et al., 1992). Additionally, a child might

respond positively with only one impact or risk but with others added on they may become vulnerable.
5. *Infants need to establish an attachment with a caregiver.* Children who cannot form attachments with a caring adult are in jeopardy of behavioral difficulties in later life. Infants who arrive home with a drug or alcohol abusing mother potentially are at greater risk of developing these relationships (Beeghly, Frank, Rose-Jacobs, Cabral, & Tronick, 2003; Minnes, Singer, Arendt, & Satayathum, 2005; Watson & Westby, 2003).

These principles are important to keep in mind as each substance and its effects are explored.

Alcohol The use of alcohol during pregnancy can result in a constellation of characteristics clustered under the term *Fetal Alcohol Spectrum Disorder* (FASD), and alcohol use during pregnancy is noted as the most common cause of mental retardation in the United States (Chiriboga, 2003; Sokol, Delaney-Black, & Nordstrom, 2003). Unlike other drug effects, children can exhibit facial distortions such as an unusual head shape, small head circumference, low set ears, eyelid skin folds protruding over the inner corner of the eye, short upturned nose, thin upper lip, and a face that looks flat (Soby, 2006). The brain is not affected globally as some brain regions are more affected than others such as the limbic system that includes the corpus callosum and cerebellum. These abnormalities do not change as a child gets older and persist into adolescence (Sowell et al., 2002).

Mental retardation is the dominant feature of fetal alcohol syndrome (FAS). Youngsters with FAS typically have IQ scores in the mildly retarded range (68 mean with a range from 58–83) and children with fetal alcohol effects (FAE) score in the borderline range (73 mean) (Soby, 2006). They are also more variable on tasks requiring timing and accuracy (Wass, Simmons, Thomas, & Riley, 2002).

The major diagnostic criteria for Fetal Alcohol Spectrum Disorder include characteristic patterns of facial anomalies, growth retardation, central nervous system neurodevelopmental abnormalities, and a mother's known history of alcohol consumption (Soby, 2006). Similar to other prenatal drug abuse, there is wide variability of these effects presented in children.

Amphetamines and Methamphetamines Some of the research with these drugs shows similarities to cocaine or heroin. In this research, most researchers are concerned with their inability to control for poor prenatal care or foster care placements (Dixon, 1989; Little, Snell, & Gilstrap, 1988). In studies, Eriksson and colleagues (Eriksson, Larsson, & Zetterstrom, 1981; Eriksson, Steneroth, & Zetterstrom, 1986) found no significant differences between mothers who had not used drugs and those that used amphetamines or methamphetamines and physical health, IQ, and performance on psychometric tests of their children. The research has not documented any long-term consequences for these children.

Cocaine and Polydrug Exposure   In a 2001 article by Frank et al. sharing the results of a meta-analysis, the following statements were made:

- There is little impact of prenatal cocaine exposure on children's scores on nationally normed assessments of cognitive development (p. 1615).
- The literature on prenatal exposure to cocaine has not shown consistent effects on cognitive or psychomotor development (p. 1616).
- Among children up to 6 years of age, there is no convincing evidence that prenatal cocaine exposure is associated with any developmental toxicity different in severity, scope, or kind from the sequelae of many other risk factors (pp. 1623–1624).
- Many findings once thought to be specific effects of in utero cocaine exposure can be explained in whole or in part by other factors, including prenatal exposure to tobacco, marijuana, or alcohol, and the quality of the child's environment (p. 1614).

One major study (Chasnoff, 1991, 1992) centered on the long-term effects of cocaine and/or polydrug exposure on children. Chasnoff identified children (approximately 300) with prenatal polydrug exposure and still living with their mother and also identified a control group of similar children. Each year, children came to his center and participated in numerous tests to document physical, emotional, and cognitive development. In 1992 he and his colleagues found that "60 percent of the children show no mental or behavioral deficits. Many of the children in the project test within the normal range cognitively" (p. 2). The remaining 40% of children showed developmental difficulties in the areas of attention, self-regulation, behavior, and language. Chasnoff noted that these children were showing progress, however. The results of this study are impressive as these children lived with their mothers in urban poverty.

Barone (1993a, 1993b, 1994, 1999) studied 26 children prenatally exposed to crack/cocaine over 4 years. She visited their homes and schools to document their experiences with literacy in school. Her results indicated that 5 of the 26 children experienced difficulty in school for a variety of reasons from behavioral issues to classroom learning environments. The remaining children (21) achieved grade level expectations in literacy with 4 children qualifying for gifted and talented programs. Her work is unusual as it targeted preschool and school age children and used systematic observation in homes and schools. Most research in this area is centered on infants and toddlers.

Singer et al. (2004) studied the cognitive effects of cocaine-exposed children living in foster or adoptive situations and those living with their biological mothers. They discovered that cocaine-exposed youngsters living with non-relative adoptive or foster parents had the lowest occurrence of mental retardation and were similar to non-exposed infants. Those children living with their biological mother or in relative care had the highest rate of retardation and

differed from cocaine-exposed children living in foster or adoptive situations or the non-exposed group of children. These researchers attributed these differences to the more stimulating environments provided to children by better educated caregivers. They also cautioned that the biological mothers presented additional risks to their children such as mental health issues that can jeopardize cognitive, emotional, and physical development of youngsters.

Accornero, Anthony, Morrow, Xue, and Bandstra (2006) studied behavioral issues around children prenatally exposed to cocaine. Their participants were all African American children of 7 years, and they found no associated behavioral problems with children prenatally exposed to cocaine.

Summing up this research, children exposed to cocaine or polydrugs are at risk for a variety of physical, cognitive, and/or emotional difficulties. Carta, Atwater, Greenwood, McConnell, McEvoy, and Williams (2001) studied 278 infants, toddlers, and preschool children and noted that prenatal substance exposure and postnatal environmental risk covaried, and both were related to developmental trajectories for children. While each added to the prediction of developmental level and rate of growth, environmental risk accounted for more variance than did prenatal exposure. Clearly, many infants can compensate for these early insults to their well-being by being placed in safer environments or by having their mothers participate in supportive programs to change their current lifestyle choices. Other children, because of their postnatal environments, may be susceptible to developmental delays that result in achievement problems (McConnell et al., 2002).

Marijuana   Most studies centered on marijuana use report lower birth weight for infants, although there is variability in this finding (Zuckerman, 1988). The research centered on marijuana is interesting in that any noted effects disappear when demographic and other confounding factors are controlled (O'Connell & Fried, 1991).

Opiates   Heroin and methadone are opiates with methadone being administered to heroin-addicted women in treatment programs. Newborns who experience heroin prenatally go through withdrawal that may include irritability, poor feeding, poor weight gain, and tremors (Kronstadt, 1991). Similar to other drug effects, these infants are often low in birth weight and have a small head circumference (Zuckerman, 1989).

Long-term studies indicate that children exposed to heroin suffer from below average weight and length, adjustment problems, and language deficits at age 6 (Deren, 1986). Researchers (Chasnoff, 1983; Johnson, Rosen, & Glassman, 1983) have not noted any long-term effects for methadone use and these infants are healthier at birth (Kaltenbach & Finegan, 1989; Maas, 1990).

Related to methadone and heroin use, only 48% children of untreated heroine users lived with their mothers at their first birthday, while 80% of children of methadone users lived with their mothers. As children matured to preschool age, only 9% lived with their mothers who were active heroin users; 50% of children of methadone users stayed at home (Wilson, Desmond, & Wait, 1981). This information is critical when determining long-term effects of either of these drugs as multiple foster placements can result in differences in development (Kronstadt, 1991).

Tobacco   Interestingly, the effects of nicotine use on the developing brain are similar to cocaine in that they involve vasoconstriction and hypoxia (Frank et al., 2001), which can result in moderate impairment of cognitive functioning and behavioral problems. Moreover, low birth weight is associated with tobacco use (Breslau, Paneth, Lucia, & Paneth-Pollak, 2005; Lightwood, Phibbs, & Glantz, 1999). Frank et al. (2001) indicate that prenatal smoking with the result on low birth weight has cost approximately $263 million (1995 dollars) in medical costs for neonatal care.

Summing up this research, there is little evidence that most prenatal exposure is linked with large deficits on standardized developmental tests. Alcohol exposure shows that there can be more significant effects to infants and children. However, all of the research documents the confounding variables of children living in disadvantaged homes where children not exposed to drugs or alcohol in utero also show declining performance on school-related tasks. Researchers need to provide comparison or control groups to document if lower performance can be isolated to prenatal drug or alcohol exposure or if it is muddied by the post birth environment of such children.

Connections to Schools and How Best to Support Prenatally Exposed Children

Educators are concerned with how to support prenatally exposed drug and alcohol children in their classrooms so that they are successful learners. Although all of the research on this topic has not been completed, teachers can provide effective interventions for these students.

For educators, knowledge of prenatal alcohol and/or drug exposure may provide a marker for potential issues related to development (Coles & Black, 2005). However, there is no direct, causal link between exposure and developmental outcomes. Therefore, these children, like others, would be treated as individuals who may or may not require intervention strategies for success in school. Importantly, prenatal exposure does not lead directly to any specific outcome displayed by children (McConnell et al., 2002). Therefore, the intervention must be matched to individual student need and like other interventions be carried out systematically and intensively (Watson, Westby, & Gable, 2007).

Early Childhood and Family Interventions   Early childhood interventions are best when focused on the following:

- providing basic survival needs to disorganized families. These needs would be met through social service agencies and in some cases, schools;

- providing education for parents in parenting which is done with the support of social and school district services;
- providing referrals to appropriate agencies when necessary; and
- intervention efforts need to be coordinated with community and other services (Beckwith, 1990; Seitz & Provence, 1990).

In the hospital, interventions can begin to help the infant regulate his or her responses. Caregivers can protect the newborn with calming voices and the avoidance of bright lights and loud noise. Swaddling the baby and an upward rocking motion have also been shown to calm the newborn (Griffith, 1995).

McConnell et al. (2002) suggest that early intervention should focus on child language and cognitive development. At first these interventions would have parents and children interacting to increase the rates of talk and positive feedback from parents. These early interventions produced changes in the language interaction between parents and children.

Chasnoff (1992) observed that Head Start and speech therapy proved successful for many of the children in his study, even those in the most detrimental home circumstances. In Barone's (1999) study, many of the foster parents worked together to find support for the children in their care. They brought in experts to share with them ways to care for their children. They supported one another so that when one mother needed a break, another mother took care of her children for a brief time. Moreover, they took advantage of state and district programs for their children. Many of the children qualified for language and speech support documented in assessments, and the parents took the children to programs to support these needs.

Elementary School Intervention

Additional Support   When considering that there is no single prediction of the effects of drug or alcohol exposure, it follows that there cannot be one recommendation for intervention. With today's Response to Intervention model (RTI; Allington & Walmsley, 2007) in schools, the framework is provided for additional student support. Certainly, some children will require extensive, systematic interventions while others may qualify for at grade or above grade level intervention. The message to teachers is the same as for other students, to best match the intervention to assessment results.

In Barone's study (1995), many children (10) qualified for special education support when they were only 5 years old because of language delays. However, during the years of the study, 6 children qualified out of special education support, documenting that their needs were transitory rather than permanent. These results demonstrate that special education services may be important to certain students' academic growth, but are not necessarily permanent because of a single cause, drug or alcohol exposure.

In the past there were special programs to support the learning needs of children exposed especially to crack/cocaine. Project Daisy and the Los Angeles Experience were two of these projects (Sautter, 1992). The projects were structured so that children were involved in active learning with multiage groupings for reading and writing experiences. The major discovery of these programs was that prenatally exposed youngsters flourished in active learning communities. The founders of the programs believed that no child who participated would require special education support in elementary school.

Schools do not need to consider special programs for children prenatally exposed to drugs or alcohol. The programs that are in place should support the learning needs of these children. The school, however, may want to create lists of community support to help families in need so that their more basic concerns are handled.

In Classroom Support   At one time, teachers were told to limit all physical stimulation in their classrooms so that they removed mobiles, bright bulletin boards, and learning stations (Odom-Winn & Dunagan, 1991; Waller, 1993). Rather than these more extreme suggestions, teachers are cautioned to provide routines so that children are aware of classroom expectations (Calkins, 1986; Griffith, 1992; Jackson, 1990). These routines allow children, especially those who come from disorganized homes, to understand the expectations of the class. Other than having routines and providing exemplary instruction, there are no specific adjustments that teachers need to make because a child was exposed to drugs or alcohol. Individual children may require adjustments to instruction, but these would be individual, not necessarily for all children within a category.

Other strategies that are common in classrooms, cognitive modeling and coaching, have been suggested as general strategies to support students prenatally exposed to drugs or alcohol (Watson et al., 2007). For instance, with coaching, a teacher may share with a student that he or she is struggling with an assignment and offer the student a plan to offset the difficulty. With cognitive modeling, a teacher might problem-solve with a student as he or she struggles with a math problem for example.

Teachers may be surprised at this finding, but there are no general suggestions for teachers based solely on prenatal drug or alcohol exposure. Each child must be considered as an individual where strengths and needs are used to form instructional decisions.

Final Thoughts

It will be important for teachers to not be biased about children who have been prenatally exposed to drugs or alcohol. Prenatal exposure does not directly lead to out-of-control youngsters with numerous learning difficulties (Cohen & Taharally, 1992; Frank et al., 2001). The complex interactions of a child's prenatal exposure, his or her home environment, and the quality of the school and its instruction all support or hinder a child's academic success (Barone, 2004).

This more complicated way of considering children may be difficult for teachers at first, as preconceived ideas must be put aside and moving beyond a single cause for learning or behavior must be accomplished. If educators make decisions based on myths, then children will be hurt and their full potential never reached. The best instructional recommendation for teachers who work with children prenatally exposed to drugs or alcohol is to provide exemplary instruction to all students and support students with daily intervention blocks.

References

Accornero, V., Anthony, J., Morrow, C., Xue, L., & Bandstra, E. (2006). Prenatal cocaine exposure: An examination of childhood externalizing and internalizing behavior problems at age 7 years. *Epidemiologia E Psichiatria Sociale, 15*(1), 20–29.

Allington, R., & Walmsley, S. (Eds.). (2007). *No quick fix: The RTI edition.* Newark, DE: International Reading Association.

Barone, D. (1993a). Dispelling the myths: Focusing on the literacy development of children prenatally exposed to crack/cocaine. In D. Leu & C. Kinzer (Eds.), *Examining central issues in literacy research, theory, and practice: Forty-second yearbook of the National Reading Conference* (pp. 197–206). Chicago: National Reading Conference.

Barone, D. (1993b). Wednesday's child: Literacy development of children prenatally exposed to crack or cocaine. *Research in the Teaching of English, 27,* 7–45.

Barone, D. (1994). The importance of classroom context: Literacy development of children prenatally exposed to crack/cocaine — year two. *Research in the Teaching of English, 28,* 286–312.

Barone, D. (1995). "Be very careful not to let the facts get mixed up with the truth": Children prenatally exposed to crack/cocaine. *Urban Education, 30,* 40–55.

Barone, D. (1999). *Resilient children: Stories of poverty, drug exposure, and literacy development.* Newark, DE: International Reading Association and National Reading Conference.

Barone, D. (2004). A longitudinal look at the literacy development of children prenatally exposed to crack/cocaine. In H. Waxman, Y. Padrón, & J. Gray (Eds.), *Educational resiliency: Student, teacher, and school perspectives* (pp. 87–112). Greenwich, CT: Information Age.

Bateman, D., Ng, S., Hansen, C., & Heagarty, M. (1993). The effects of intrauterine cocaine exposure in newborns. *American Journal of Public Health, 83,* 190–193.

Beckwith, L. (1990). Adaptive and maladaptive parenting implications for intervention. In S. Meisels & J. Shonkoff (Eds.), *Handbook on early childhood intervention* (pp. 53–77). New York: Cambridge University Press.

Beeghly, M., Frank, D., Rose-Jacobs, R., Cabral, H., & Tronick, E. (2003). Level of prenatal cocaine exposure and infant-caregiver attachment behavior. *Neurotoxicology and Teratology, 25*(1), 23–38.

Bennett, F. (1992). Recent advances in developmental interventions for biologically vulnerable infants. *Infants and Young Children, 3,* 33–40.

Berlin, C. (1991). Effects of drugs on the fetus. *Pediatrics in Review, 12,* 282–287.

Besharov, D. (1990). Crack children in foster care. *Children Today, 19*(4), 21–35.

Brady, J., Posner, M., Lang, C., & Rosati, M. (1994). *Risk and reality: The implications of prenatal exposure to alcohol and other drugs.* Washington, DC: U.S. Department of Health and Human Services and the U.S. Department of Education.

Breslau, N., Paneth, N., Lucia, V., & Paneth-Pollak, R. (2005). Maternal smoking during pregnancy and offspring IQ. *International Journal of Epidemiology, 34,* 1047–1053.

Brodkin, A., & Zuckerman, B. (1992). Are crack babies doomed in school failure? *Instructor, 101*(7), 16–17.

Burd, L., Cotsonas-Hassler, T., Martsolf, J., & Kerbeshian, J. (2003). Fetal alcohol syndrome: Neuropsychiatric phenomics. *Neurotoxicology and Teratology, 25,* 697–705.

Calkins, L. (1986). *The art of teaching writing.* Portsmouth, NH: Heinemann.

Carta, J., Atwater, J., Greenwood, C., McConnell, S., McEvoy, M., & Williams, R. (2001). Effects of cumulative prenatal substance exposure and multiple environmental risks on children's developmental trajectories. *Journal of Clinical and Consulting Psychology, 30,* 327–337.

Charmichael, O., Feldman, J., Streissguth, A., Sampson, P., & Bookstein, F. (1998). Neuropsychological deficits in adolescents with fetal alcohol syndrome: Clinical findings. *Alcoholism Clinical and Experimental Research, 22,* 1998–2012.

Charmichael, O., Morse, B., & Huffine, C. (1998). Development of psychopathology; Fetal alcohol syndrome and related conditions. *Seminars in Clinical Neuropsychiatry, 3,* 262–284.

Chasnoff, I. (1983). Phencyclidine: Effects on the fetus and neonate. *Developmental Pharmacology and Therapeutics, 6,* 291–293.

Chasnoff, I. (1989, December). *The Pinellas County study: Illegal drug use across socioeconomic lines.* Paper presented at the National Association for Perinatal Addiction Research and Education Conference, Miami, Florida.

Chasnoff, I. (1991). Methodological issues studying cocaine use in pregnancy: A problem of definitions In M. Kibey & K. Asghar (Eds.), *Methodological issues in controlled studies of effects of prenatal exposure to drug abuse* (pp. 55–56). Rockville, MD: National Institute on Drug Abuse.

Chasnoff, I. (1992). President's message. *Perinatal Addiction Research and Education Update, 1*(1), 2–3.

Chiriboga, C. (2003). Fetal alcohol and drug effects. *Neurologist, 9,* 267–279.

Cohen, S., & Taharally, C. (1992). Getting ready for young children with prenatal drug exposure. *Childhood Education, 69*(1), 5–9.

Coles, C., & Black, M. (2005). Introduction to the special issues: Impact of prenatal substance exposure on children's health, development, school performance, and risk behavior. *Journal of Pediatric Psychology, 31,* 1–4.

Coles, C., Platzman, K., Smith I., James, M., & Falek, A. (1992). Effects if cocaine and alcohol use in pregnancy on neonatal growth and neurobehavioral status. *Neurotoxicology and Teratology, 14*(1), 23–33.

Connors, N., Bradley, R., Mansell, L., Lia, J., Roberts, T., & Burgdorf, K. (2003). Children of mothers with serious substance abuse problems: An accumulation of risks. *American Journal of Drug and Alcohol Abuse, 29,* 743–758.

Deren, S. (1986, April). Children of substance abusers in New York state. *New York State Journal of Medicine,* 179–184.

Dixon, S. (1989). Effects of transplacental exposure to cocaine and methamphetamine on the neonate. *The Western Journal of Medicine, 150,* 436–442.

Eriksson, M., Larsson, G., & Zetterstrom, R. (1981). Amphetamine addition and pregnancy: Pregnancy, delivery, and the neonatal period: Socio-medical aspects. *Acta Obstetricia et Gynecologica Scandinavica, 60,* 253–259.

Eriksson, M., Steneroth, G., Zetterstrom, R. (1986). Influence of pregnancy and child-rearing on amphetamine-addicted women. *Acta Psychiatrica Scandinavica, 73,* 634–641.

Frank, D., & Zuckerman, B. (1993). Children exposed to cocaine prenatally: Pieces of the puzzle. *Neurotoxicology and Teratology, 15,* 298–300.

Frank, D., Augustyn, M., Grant, W., Knight, W., Pell, T., & Zuckerman, B. (2001). Growth, development, and behavior in early childhood following prenatal cocaine exposure. *Journal of the American Medical Association, 285*(12), 1–33.

Frank, D., Augustyn, M., Grant, W., Knight, W., Tripler, P., & Zuckerman, B. (2001). Growth, development, and behavior in early childhood following prenatal cocaine exposure. *Journal of the American Medical Association, 285*(12), 1–33.

Fried, P., & Watkinson, B. (2000). Visuoperceptual functioning differs in 9- to 12-year-olds prenatally exposed to cigarettes and marijuana. *Neurotoxicology and Teratology, 22,* 11–20.

Gonzalez, N., & Campbell, M. (1994). Cocaine babies: Does prenatal exposure to cocaine affect development? *Journal of the American Academy of Child and Adolescent Psychiatry, 33,* 16–19.

Gregorchik, L. (1992). The cocaine-exposed children are here. *Phi Delta Kappan, 73,* 709–711.

Greider, K. (1995). Crackpot ideas. *Mother Jones, 20,* 52–56.

Griffith, D. (1992). Prenatal exposure to cocaine and other drugs: Development and educational prognoses. *Phi Delta Kappan, 74*(1), 30–34.

Griffith, D. (1995). Prenatal exposure to cocaine and other drugs: Developmental and educational prognoses. *Juvenile and Family Court Journal, 46,* 83–92.

Hutchings, D. (1993). Response to commentaries. *Neurotoxicology and Teratology, 15,* 311–312.

Jackson, S. (1990). "Crack babies" are here! Can you help them learn? *California Teachers Association Action,* 11–13.

Johnson, J., Rosen, T., & Glassman, M. (1983). *Children of methadone-maintained mothers: Three-year follow-up.* Rockville, MD: National Institute on Drug Abuse. (ERIC Document Reproduction Service No. ED 323 726)

Kaltenbach, K., & Finegan, L. (1989). Children exposed to methadone in utero. *Annals of New York Academy of Sciences, 562,* 360–362.

Kronstadt, D. (1991). Complex developmental issues of prenatal drug exposure. *The Future of Children, 1,* 36–49.

Kusserow, R. (1990). *Crack babies, Report of the Office of the Inspector General.* Washington, DC: Department of Health and Human Services.

Lester, B., & Tronick, E. (1994). The effects of prenatal cocaine exposure and child outcome. Special issue: Prenatal drug exposure and child outcome. *Infant Mental Health Journal, 15,* 107–120.

Lightwood, J., Phibbs, C., & Glantz, S. (1999). Short term health and economic benefits of smoking cessation: Low birth weight. *Pediatrics, 104,* 1312–1320.

Little, B., Snell, L., & Gilstrap, L. (1988). Methamphetamine abuse during pregnancy: Outcome and fetal effects. *Obstetrics and Gynecology, 72,* 541–544.

Maas, U. (1990). Infrequent neonatal opiate withdrawal following maternal methadone detoxification during pregnancy. *Journal of Perinatal Medicine, 18,* 111–118.

MacGregor, S. (1990). Prevalence of marijuana use during pregnancy: A pilot study. *The Journal of Reproductive Medicine, 35,* 1147–1149.

Mayes, L., Granger, R., Bornstein, M., & Zuckerman, B. (1992). The problem of prenatal cocaine exposure: A rush to judgment. *Journal of the American Medical Association, 267,* 406–408.

McConnell, S., Rush, K., McEvoy, M., Carta, J., Atwater, J., & Williams, R. (2002). Descriptive and experimental analysis of child-caregiver interactions that promote development of young children exposed prenatally to drugs and alcohol. *Journal of Behavioral Education, 11,* 131–161.

Miller, G. (1989). Addicted infants and their mothers. *Zero to Three Bulletin of the National Center for Clinical Infant Programs, 9*(5), 20–23.

Miller, T., Rauh, V., Glied, S., Hattis, D., Rundle, A., Andrews, H., et al. (2006). The economic impact of early life environmental tobacco smoke exposure: Early intervention for developmental delay. *Environmental Health Perspectives, 114,* 1585–1588.

Minnes, S., Singer, L., Arendt, R., & Satayathum, S. (2005). Effects of prenatal cocaine/polydrug use on maternal-infant feeding interactions during the first year of life. *Journal of Developmental and Behavioral Pediatrics, 26,* 194–200.

National Institute of Drug Abuse. (1996). *National pregnancy and health survey: Drug use among women delivering live births.* Rockville, MD: Substance Abuse and Mental Health Service Administration.

O'Connell, C., & Fried, P. (1991). Prenatal exposure to cannabis: A preliminary report of postnatal consequences in school-age children. *Neruotoxicology and Teratology, 13,* 631–639.

O'Shea, T., Klinepeter, K., Goldstein, D., Jackson, B., & Dillard, R. (1997). Survival and developmental disability in infants with birth weights of 501 to 800 grams, born between 1979 and 1994. *Pediatrics, 100*, 982–986.

Odom-Winn, D., & Dunagan, D. (1991). *Crack kids in school*. Freeport, NY: Educational Activities.

Sautter, R. (1992). Crack: Healing the children. Kappan special report. *Phi Delta Kappan, 74*(3), K1–K12.

Seitz, V., & Provence, S. (1990). Caregiver-focused models of early intervention. In S. Meisels & J. Shonkoff (Eds.), *Handbook on early childhood intervention* (pp. 400–427). New York: Cambridge University Press.

Singer, L., Minner, S., Short, E., Arendt, R., Farkas, K., Lewis, B., et al. (2004). Cognitive outcomes of preschool children with prenatal cocaine exposure. *Journal of the American Medical Association, 291*, 2448–1256.

Soby, J. (2006). *Prenatal exposure to drugs/alcohol* (2nd ed.). Springfield, IL: Charles C. Thomas.

Sokol, R., Delaney-Black, V., & Nordstrom, B. (2003). Fetal alcohol spectrum disorder. *Journal of the American Medical Association, 290*, 2996–2999.

Sowell, E., Thompson, P., Mattson, S., Tessner, K., Jernigan, T., Riley, E., et al. (2002). Regional brain shape abnormalities persist into adolescence after heavy prenatal alcohol exposure. *Cerebral Cortex, 12*, 856–865.

Spinelli, J. (1991). *Maniac Magee*. Boston: Little Brown.

Thomas, J. (2004). *Educating drug-exposed children*. New York: RoutledgeFalmer.

Villarreal, S., McKinney, L., & Quackenbush, M. (1991). *Handle with care: Helping children prenatally exposed to drugs and alcohol*. Santa Cruz, CA: ETR Associates.

Waller, M. (1993). Helping crack-affected children succeed. *Educational Leadership, 50*(4), 57–60.

Wass, T., Simmons, R., Thomas, J., & Riley, E. (2002). Timing accuracy and variability in children with prenatal exposure to alcohol. *Alcoholism Clinical Disorders, 16*, 111–121.

Watson, S., & Westby, C. (2003). Prenatal drug exposure: Implications for personnel preparation. *Remedial and Special Education, 24*, 204–214.

Watson, S., Westby, C., & Gable, R. (2007). A framework for addressing the needs of students prenatally exposed to alcohol and other drugs. *Preventing School Failure, 52*, 25–32.

Wenzel, S., Kosofsky, B., Harvey, J., Iguchi, M., Steinberg, P., Watkins, K., et al. (2001). *Prenatal cocaine exposure: Scientific considerations and policy implications*. New York: RAND Drug Policy Research Center.

Wilson, G., Desmond, M., & Wait, R. (1981). Follow-up of methadone-treated women and their infants: Health, development, and social implications. *Journal of Pediatrics, 98*, 716–722.

Zuckerman, B. (1988). Marijuana and cigarette smoking during pregnancy: Neonatal effects. In I. Chasnoff (Ed.), *Drugs, alcohol, pregnancy, and parenting* (pp. 73–86). London: Kluwer.

Zuckerman, B. (1989). Effects of maternal marijuana and cocaine use on fetal growth. *The New England Journal of Medicine, 320*, 762–768.

12

Aliteracy, Agency, and Identity

STERGIOS BOTZAKIS
The University of Tennessee

LEIGH A. HALL
The University of North Carolina, Chapel Hill

Defining the term struggling reader has been likened to "trying to nail gelatin to a wall" (Alvermann, 2001, p. 679), but defining disabled readers carries a more authoritative tone because of the various measures and assessments associated with determining disability. However, these measures and assessments that focus on reading ability are based on specific activities, such as story recall or identifying main ideas, details, and word or passage meaning, which are themselves discrete skills. These discrete skills have been determined over time to be correlative or indicative of reading ability, and measuring certain of them are the basis of determining reading ability and disability (Mueller, 2001). Statistical analyses of reading disabled people have shown that reading disabilities tend to be correlative with race and social class (Blanchett, 2006; Coutinho, Oswald, & Best, 2002) and that aspect begs the question of how much socio-cultural characteristics define what reading should be and how well people read.

The idea that reading is socially situated is not a new one, and one of the most common ways of conceptualizing it draws from the work of Street (1984/1995) who saw reading research being mainly of two schools, ideological and autonomous. With the ideological model, reading is regarded as a social practice that is dependent on culture and power structures such as race, class, and gender. The ideological model contrasts with the autonomous model, which assumes that reading is a neutral set of skills that people learn in roughly the same manner. Under the autonomous model, reading instruction can occur in a roughly systematic manner where learners develop according to steps of mastery and maturation. While much reading research draws upon or at least acknowledges ideological aspects of reading, much of what has come down from U.S. education entities as de facto policy (e.g., National Institute of Child Health and Human Development, 2000; National Institute for Literacy, 2007) relies heavily on an autonomous model of reading, even though over the past two decades reading has become

more a sub-category of a larger conception of literacy. The purpose of this chapter is to examine more ideological literacy education research, to provide a counterpoint to the view that reading is simply the acquisition of skills or the mastery of a certain "five pillars" without reference to socio-cultural considerations.

Literacy and Identity

Reading is a component of the umbrella term literacy, but literacy has undergone several changes in definition across history and social groups. Literacy has been defined variably as being the ability to speak and sing, to orate publicly, to sign one's name, and to read a sentence (The University of Kansas Students Tutoring for Literacy, n.d.). The latter abilities of writing and reading were especially bound into public practices such as land ownership and voter registration, and those definitions were used to limit access to those practices. Just as culture can determine what counts as literacy, so too can culture "construct what counts as reading and who counts as a reader" (Alvermann, 2001, p. 676). Variously, reading can be used for scanning or comprehending print text, tracking animal footprints, recognizing a person's expressions and gestures, divining a fortune by examining tea leaves or palms, determining the age of geographic formations using rock strata, distinguishing amino acid patterns in DNA, and understanding the world (Freire, 1970; Manguel, 1997).

More recently, reading has been defined by New Literacies researchers as bound up in identity and social practices. Reading is a practice where people use texts and to explore, experience, question, and gain advantages in their social worlds, particularly drawing upon the work of Gee (1991, 1996). Gee (1996) posited that people use D/discourses in creating "identity kits" (p. 3) where language was used to order social worlds and affect people's actions. This conception of identity kits included the functions that social institutions played in constructing what counted as literacy as well as in affecting how people spoke, wrote, and took on social roles.

Discourses were not quickly assumed however; they could not simply be learned. Rather, they came to be formed by the process of acquisition, "a process of acquiring something (usually, subconsciously) by exposure to models, a process of trial and error, and practice within social groups, without formal teaching" (Gee, 1996, p. 138). The acquisition of a primary discourse took place from a very early age and continued over time. One learned about customs, common household items, and the other mundane features of their lives. By extension, "learning to read [was] always learning some aspect of some discourse" (Gee, 1991, p. 6), and literate activity was very much bundled up in identity. Learning to read in one's primary discourse could lead to difficulties if those practices were not consistent with reading practices performed in formal school settings. Acquiring secondary discourses was described as being more difficult, as certain ingrained behaviors, feelings, and thoughts might be at odds with learning and acquisition.

In the field of literacy education, reading and texts typically have been grouped and examined as in- and out-of-school activities. There is a long tradition in education of examining the socio-cultural aspects of reading in- and out-of-school. Included in this tradition is the work of Heath (1983) who studied three communities, a Black working-class community, a White working-class community, and a racially mixed middle-class community, over a decade. What she discovered was that children in these communities were socialized into different language practices but, that in the context of school, middle class students who used language most like their teachers were more likely to be academically successful. Heath's study pointed to the effects of literacy practices in home and community settings, not just schools. Hull and Schultz (2001) note Heath's work, as an instance "when researchers examined literacy in out-of-school contexts ... [and] arrived at new constructs that proved generative for literacy studies" (p. 578).

The tradition of examining what goes on outside of school was carried over more recently into what was called the New Literacy Studies (NLS) which sought "to investigate literacy and discourse and to place a special emphasis on revealing, understanding, and addressing power relations" (Hull & Schultz, 2001, p. 585); this was a specific brand of critical inquiry which was used in addressing social justice issues, using the "notion of Discourse to reframe understandings of literacy, especially in relation to identity" (p. 585). In the context of NLS, the traditionally valued discourse of school was seen in terms of power relations where certain literacy practices are emphasized while others are seen as secondary or inferior. In NLS, there is an element of critical theory in a drive to address disparities between social groups, to ensure that the middle-class practices Heath (1983) saw as dominant are not privileged to the point where other practices are pushed aside as inferior.

The theme of inferiority is not limited to any one identity population in the United States, but has carried over across many social groups in the form of various educational crises, perhaps the most famous of which was perpetuated by the A Nation at Risk report (National Commission on Excellence in Education, 1983). This constant state of inferiority influences the global identities of U.S. students, and New Literacies educators have also taken it upon themselves to defuse continual educational panics. Williams (2007) critiques this constant state of crisis where students are reported as failing or being in danger of falling behind, tracking it back to as early as 1879. Instead of a knee jerk reaction to go back to basics, she puts forth another option where we teach students "to understand how language, identity, and culture work together" to prepare them to "read and write in any context" (p. 181), which is particularly important within our current context where rapid technological and informational change abound. Part of being literate in these times has to do with students being capable to adapt to circumstances, which requires innovative ways of thinking and problem solving, not simply learning basic facts and skills.

Agency and Aliteracy

The autonomous and ideological models Street (1984/1995) put forth are dichotomous, but they speak to the constant interplay of institutions and the individuals that dwell within them. Much New Literacies research draws from the tactical idea of people trying to "make do" in everyday life as de Certeau (1984) stated. This work explores manners in which textual and social practices are intermingled by reference to the behaviors that people engaged in order to exist in their environments. Delineating how identity is created speaks to how texts and reading interact with social actions in people's lives. Within this conception of literacy, power does not simply lie in institutional rule but also in those who take part in the institution as well. For example, struggling readers do not simply get created and are forced to act certain ways in schools, they also find ways to butt up against these rules or at least mitigate circumstances in ways that they find more palatable.

The term most often used to speak about these individualized actions is agency, a term that originated in the work of Holland, Lachicotte, Skinner, and Cain (1998) and that is defined as "a person's capacity to act upon the world" (Heron, 2003, p. 568). Ideally, in academic circumstances, educators would foster a sense of positive agency in their students where they could find success in learning. In the case of reading disabled students however, there are frequently many more negative experiences that inhibit such agency and that push students to exercise a different type of agency to alleviate their negative circumstances. Such actions might include taking more passive roles in class or, at the opposite extreme, engaging in disruptive behaviors in protest of classroom pursuits. Bound up in agency is the notion that individuals have the ability to act back upon their social contexts. Sometimes within this relationship, inactivity is a viable tactic.

In terms of reading, the negative example of agency would be aliteracy, defined by Mikulecky (1978) as capable readers "choosing not to read" (p. 3) because the stultifying activities that often accompany reading for school or work discourage any sense of enjoyment. Mikulecky identified aliteracy as a danger to the ever-rising state of literacy that would be needed in the United States to foster workplace growth and innovation. More recently the term has been expanded to include "slow and frustrated readers ... who chose to read despite feeling enormous stress, confusion, and pressure" (Ramsay, 2002, p. 56), those who will be turned off of reading in the near future because of their struggles and negative experiences with books. In both cases, the outcomes of the task do not match up to the effort put into it, so people simply do not read when it is not required. Aliteracy is a response to the disconnection some people feel between the expectations for reading that they hold from their families or communities and those being perpetuated by the institutional authority of school.

The interplay between institutions and individuals is an important characteristic of literacy studies in general, and in the two sections that follow, we catalog education research that speaks to this relationship. The first section pertains to how family and community institutions help form social and literate identities, while the second details how students exercise their agency and respond to these institutional pressures within the context of schools.

Home Experiences of Struggling Readers

In looking at students who struggle as readers, a number of researchers have looked at how individuals' social identities are formed by their family and community relations and also at how these relations come to bear on students' educational experiences. Heath's landmark work Ways with Words (1983) reports on data collected during a decade spent living in two working-class communities located only a few miles apart in the piedmont Carolinas where agriculture and textiles were important industries. She assigned pseudonyms to these communities, Trackton, a Black community, and Roadville, a White community and examined how children learned to use language and how their uses of language established their identity, roles, and relationships among families and friends. Heath found that Roadville and Trackton residents each had differing expectations from those of their children's teachers concerning uses of language. Additionally, reading was not something typically done at home in either group, and so, ultimately, both groups developed difficulties in school. Roadville and Trackton students who were used to more freedom and to learning "by watching, listening, and trying" (p. 348) were unsettled by the discontinuity of what was expected in terms of reading, speaking, and learning in classrooms.

Heath compared the students of Trackton and Roadville with a group who did find scholastic success, whom she called the townspeople. Most critical to the townspeople's academic successes were certain ritualized uses of language, such as assignment of labels to objects, response to questions whose answers were already known to the questioner, and recitation of discrete points of factual information separated from context. Townspeople, both Black and White, who adopted these practices and accepted them as "normal" saw their schoolwork and extracurricular activities as essential to their children's future success. The townspeople practiced language usage most alike to that done in schools, in ways that were more common to the teachers' expectations, and Heath attributed their relative lack of academic difficulties to this close match. Differences between home and school uses of language and expectations about using language created learning difficulties that inhibited children's ability to do well in school, and in turn limited their options for growth and employment later in life.

Years later, in revisiting some of the children from her original study, Heath (2003) found that "habits of language socialization were likely to change very slowly" (p. 191) and that the children of Trackton's children were learning and engaging in language use in similar ways to their own parents, even in new contexts as the working-class communities of Heath's prior study had disbanded and ceased to exist for almost 20 years. Heath found that these participants were struggling to maintain housing and employment in the new urban contexts in which they found themselves and also that they were engaging in limited language interactions with their children. A cycle of academic and accompanying later-life struggles seems to have been reproduced.

A longitudinal research study of 40 families in Kansas City conducted by Hart and Risley (2003) makes a different point about the significant differences regarding the development of vocabulary in children from different socioeconomic groups. Their analyses of data collected during home visits and recorded interactions between parents and children indicated that the vocabulary used by parents in the upper socioeconomic group exceeded working-class parents by 678 words and parents receiving welfare by 1,202 words. The vocabulary used by children of the upper socioeconomic group exceeded that used by children from working-class families by 376 words and children of families receiving welfare by 591 words. In addition, the researchers extrapolated that by age 3 that there was a gap of 32 million word exchanges between the upper socioeconomic group of children and those from families receiving welfare. The monumental difference in the sheer number of language interactions these children would come to school with was seen as an indicator of how well prepared (or not) they would be for further language learning in classroom contexts.

Classroom Experiences of Struggling Readers

Reading and learning disabled students are typically identified and labeled via a system of educational assessment from an early age, as early as kindergarten, and they often have had to experience education practices that are geared specifically to deal with their disability. This process of labeling students as special education students is not easily halted, even by advocates and parents who are aware of the consequences of their children being put into such classes and who were prepared to protest such an assignment (Rogers, 2002). Mueller (2001), in a series of case studies of at-risk adolescent students, described how Mick, a student who was designated as learning disabled at the end of second grade went through schooling that largely took place in resource rooms where he received extra time and assistance in reading and writing until seventh grade. The emphasis in these classes was placed on decoding and reading comprehension activities, and although well intentioned, these activities did not help Mick form a larger concept of why he should engage in reading or what he could be getting out of it. In resource rooms, Mick was repeatedly confronted with reading as an enterprise he could not master. He did not see himself as a reader nor could he see what reading could contribute to his life.

Students who have reading disabilities are frequently called upon to read on a frustration level in their everyday classroom activities (Morris, Ervin, & Conrad, 2000), or alternatively to take part in remedial reading with an emphasis on decoding and isolated reading comprehension skills (Mueller, 2001). These two situations can confuse, frustrate, and leave students with an impression of reading as either a monumental task or a series of unrelated, arcane processes. Given these social contexts, reading disabled or struggling students have a number of options in dealing with reading, many of which are forms of aliteracy.

Faking It   Some students take part in school lessons and procedures and begin to see what is happening as proof of their inferiority. This can take place in a relatively short span of time, as Lee and Jackson (1991) indicate when they state that the label of "learning disabled" can "cripple children" and place them "in the back of the line" (p. xvii). In a shared account of Lee's learning and Jackson's academic assistance with him, they detail how by fourth grade a student "learned how to keep [his] mouth shut" (p. 11) and avoid difficulty by faking his way through school, misinforming his friends about the special pull-out classes he was required to attend, ignoring notes from girls who liked him rather than admit he could not read them, and cheating off of other students' work so that he could pass. He admitted that he was discovered by teachers but that his status as a reading disabled student largely meant that they would turn a blind eye to his actions. Lee and Jackson recognize these kinds of actions as coping behaviors that point to the brightness and inventiveness of such students to learn "the art of conning" (p. 3) in order to avoid dealing with difficulties that make learning difficult in school environments.

Hiding Out in Classrooms   A number of researchers have detailed how struggling readers orchestrate a number of "hiding out and bluffing behaviors" in order "to avoid ridicule by exposing their 'stupidity' in class" (Brozo, 1991, p. 324). In an observational study of an 11th-grade social studies classroom, Brozo found seven common tactics that struggling readers undertake in classroom contexts in order to mitigate their circumstances: (a) avoiding eye contact, (b) disrupting instruction, (c) listening well, (d) using classmates to get answers, (e) using friends to get answers, (f) forgetting books/materials, and (g) manipulating the teacher. Some of these behaviors are helpful for students to participate in classroom learning, but most are demonstrations of agency which derail learning opportunities in an attempt to escape from academic activity.

Silence is another tool students use to avoid attention in classroom settings. Using Gee's concept of discursive identity as a theoretical lens, Hall (2007) examined three middle school struggling readers who spoke of how they were strategically silent when it came to reading. In part, they were quiet in order to find out information, to see how other classmates handled tasks such as science laboratory work, or where to find answers to an assignment, but more often they did not speak in order to protect themselves from peers or teachers noticing that they were having reading difficulties. Because they did not want to draw attention to themselves or their struggles, lest others think that they were inferior or unintelligent, these students engaged in solitary, detrimental behaviors such as choosing to work by themselves even when given group assignments, not asking questions when they are confused, or not using reading strategies learned in class because they felt that they would be a sign to others that they were poor readers. Projecting an image of "a successful student and a good reader" (Hall, 2007, p. 137) to their teachers, parents, and peers became more important than any classroom activities or learning. The students that Hall worked with were not unmotivated to learn, but their fears of being singled out caused them to neglect situations and strategies that could have helped them develop as readers and learners.

Dropping Out   Perhaps the most drastic action that can be taken would be to exit the educational system entirely. In terms of referring, labeling, and working with learning disabled (LD) students in the United States, there has historically been much variability (Fine, 1991), and some have critiqued this variability as a vehicle to misreport and misrepresent graduation rates and grades on standardized assessments (Snell, 2002). Reading disabled students are numbered among the LD population, and they are not typically identified as a specific population when statistical analyses are done. U.S. Department of Education reports that high school non-completion rates of U.S. students with learning disabilities in the 1999–2000 school year was 27.6%, which is higher than the national average of 10.9% (Office of Special Education Programs, 2002). Another study, the National Longitudinal Transition Study, begun with data from the school year 1988–1989, shows that 41.7% of the students with LD left school without graduating. A 5-year follow up with these students revealed that 30% of those students had returned to some adult education setting, but only 3% of them had attained their General

Equivalency Diploma (Wagner, D'Amico, Marder, Newman, & Blackorby, 1992). Before this study, Bruck (1987) reviewed four other outcome studies and found that drop-out rates highly depended on the population studied, and found a range of 0% (from a private school for LD students) to 62%. Even though specific numbers of high school dropouts who leave because of their reading disabilities is not known, it is clear that students who have learning disabilities in general are significantly more likely to leave school and not graduate than non-LD students.

Instruction that Connects with Struggling Readers

The preceding research studies paint a bleak picture of what happens with struggling readers in school environments, but there are ways of avoiding such situations and drawing such students into productive, positive classroom activities. Mick, a student who was mentioned earlier in this chapter (Mueller, 2001), found academic success with reading outside of the resource room environment when he became involved in readers workshops in his seventh-grade classroom. Given time and space to make his own choices, respond in his own manner, and receive individual attention and feedback helped him to make a more personal connection to reading and the classroom. Replicating such an occurrence, where a struggling student receives appropriate, individualized attention and can make connections with school success has been an ongoing goal of educators and researchers, although via different pathways.

A group of NLS scholars, the New London Group (1996), address the need for educational equity when, instead of focusing on one type of literacy, they espoused a notion of addressing "multiliteracies." This term referred to how different modes of communication interacted with new social relations in an attempt to address the vast diversity in language and literacy which exists in our postmodern present. Instead of hierarchical relations of literacy where certain activities and abilities were privileged above others, they shifted categories of literacy in a more horizontal fashion. The effect of this on education was palpable. Multiliteracies "create a different kind of pedagogy, one in which language and other modes of meaning are dynamic representational resources constantly being remade by their users as they work to achieve their various cultural purposes" (New London Group, 1996, p. 64). Clearly, this conception draws very much on Street's (1984/1995) ideological model of reading.

Traditionally privileged modes of literacy such as the ones Heath (1983) connected to middle-class education are seen as only one avenue of educational practice among many, not the only correct way that students should be taught. Within the New London Group's conception of pedagogy was that schools should be truly democratic entities that "must include a vision of meaningful success for all" (p. 67) and that produce students who can engage the world critically, flexibly, and capably. According to these scholars, the students of the future, regardless of reading or learning disability, must be able to adapt to the demands of a rapidly changing environment where shifts in language, social activity, and technology abound.

Taking up the idea of multiliteracies, some researchers have expanded the definition of literacy to include such disparate social actions that at first glance might not be considered worthwhile or sophisticated. These researchers used the term literacy to apply to what may seem atypical practices, some of which were not very reliant upon print and some of which did not rely on the use of technology. They studied or highlighted activities that were usually thought of as trivial or even detrimental literacy practices, such as passing notes (Finders, 1997), playing video games (Gee, 2003), or engaging in gang activities (Moje, 2000). Even though not always officially recognized as such, these students from these studies led complex lives and were able to navigate through their increasingly complicated worlds using a variety of literacy practices. The aim of a great number of New Literacies researchers is to bridge these various out-of-school activities with in-school learning in ways that create a sense of relevance and worth. In what follows we will present three studies from New Literacies researchers that describe opportunities to accomplish this aim.

Building on Students Interests and Competencies   Working with a number of middle school students in an after-school media club, Alvermann (2001) presents the case of Grady, a ninth grader who is reading at the fifth-grade level. He was not an enthusiastic reader and did not take part in many of the literacy activities with the other students, and preferred to go off by himself to play video games. Over time the researchers discovered that Grady was not avoiding reading altogether but that he was doing it in isolated ways. Over a series of email exchanges, they found that he was studying manuals on the various video games he was playing, learning codes and special moves to help him succeed. He was actually engaged in typically school sanctioned activities, namely studying and taking notes in order to do well on a later assessment, in this case embodied as video game performance.

The point in this observation is not to make the great leap that video games need be part of the school curriculum but rather that this type of behavior is one that should be highlighted and be made aware to his instructors. That Grady is capable of reading, understanding, and gathering pertinent information and linking those actions to what he should be doing in school could be a powerful way to show him that getting a grasp on school tasks may not be as difficult as he has been led to believe. Many students who struggle with reading already have competencies that would assist them in their academic endeavors, only they may lay unrecognized as reading that does not really count. Grady was a reader after all, but neither he nor his teachers recognized that in a way that would help him with his school work. There was no transfer of his study skills to academic work.

Developing Critical Thinking via Alternative Avenues   In his qualitative research on classrooms that use new literacies, Kist (2005) presented a classroom in Deux Montagnes, Quebec, a suburb of Montreal, where an English teacher worked with "at-risk" high school students who had "reached the end of the line" (p. 92) in terms of their positions in school. Recognizing that these students required different kinds of teaching to keep them in school, the teacher provided a different kind of classroom, one where students watched films and critically analyzed and compared them, created Flash animations, and edited video footage to create their own narratives. Surprisingly, these students felt compelled to attend classes on a very regular basis, in contrast to their attendance records throughout their academic careers, and even though they were not to receive a high school diploma from their particular program of study. Kist likened the arrangement to a kind of work-study program where students found their interests met and where they could work in a medium that did not intimidate them the same way that paper and pen assignments did.

What Kist (2005) found was that students in this class could "read and write media texts with considerable sophistication," "were able to identify ideologies in a text and relate them to their own experiences," and "were more willing to undertake the kind of school writing they were expected to do, using media texts as a source for their writing" (p. 93). Students in his class found that they had competencies and abilities they were unaware of, and for some there was some transfer of critical thinking skills from the media of film to that of reading stories and books. These students who typically disregarded what went on in school, who had their share of academic struggles and difficulties were able to focus much more time, attention, and energy into their activities than they had in years. The happenings in this classroom pointed to the potential of developing critical thinking skills with students using different contexts and media as curricula.

Facilitating Reading and Writing with Digital Literacies
Similarly, presenting research on struggling adolescent readers and how they "multimediated," O'Brien (2006) noted how much more capable these students were in digital environments than in typical, paper-and-pen ones. In different media labs and centers, he found that students who were identified as being at least 2 years under grade level were capable of composing digital reports on deer hunting, webpages about specific sports teams and players, reading instructions and clues for video game versions of quests and murder mysteries, and incorporating visuals, movies, and writing in a multimedia presentation about favorite musicians. Certainly these projects all built from student interest, but what O'Brien made particular note of was the ability of these students to delve into the digital environments in ways that they would not approach print ones.

In using computers and other technologies, these students were not helpless but more motivated and engaged. They took chances and used trial and error in some instances, a risk they would not typically take when it came to more traditional reading and writing. O'Brien attributes part of their success to the flexibility of technology and how this flexibility allows students to "transform [their] sense of competence and agency, particularly as it has been defined in relation to print-based activities" (p. 31). These students felt more capable in digital environments, and they engaged more readily in activities they would be loathe doing with paper and pen. O'Brien partly attributed some of this change to the accessibility and user-friendliness of technology, but also somewhat to the familiarity of the students with various media formats. Because they did not carry the weight of past failures with technology the same way they had with print-centered texts, these students underwent a conversion from helplessness to competency.

(In)conclusion

The way that research has been presented in this chapter can be seen as an easy narrative, where students who are labeled as reading disabled can find school success once their specific interests are appealed to and their needs addressed through instruction: What simply needs to be done is to make connections between home and school, so that students can see their identities reflected in academic texts and activities and are more motivated to display positive agency. We do not want to leave with the impression that this task is an easy one, or one that teachers have not been trying to tackle with varying degrees of success. Finding specific reading strategies to address students with reading disabilities may be helpful, but they must be used mindfully lest they become redundant or done simply for the sake of completion (Fisher & Frey, 2008). Focusing on students' skill deficits may lead to the continuation of an achievement gap (Teale, Paciga, & Hoffman, 2007) as well as creating an isolated version of what reading is. Building on students' interests may work but does not guarantee student success without complementary instruction (Kamil, 2008; Krashen, 2001), nor may it be possible to do within the walls of a school building (e.g., MacGillvray & Curwen, 2007). Using computers and other forms of technology does not create a playing field where students become equally capable (Wilder & Dressman, 2006). In other words, there are no easy fixes.

When working toward creating competence in our students with reading disabilities in the 21st century, "research provides limited information about the context-specific variations, [and] teachers need to experiment to determine how to vary their attentions given their subject-area foci and their particular students' needs and expertise" (Hinchman, Alvermann, Boyd, Brozo, & Vacca, 2004, p. 308). Teachers need to be mindful and informed about what they are teaching, how they are teaching it, and to whom they are teaching. This task is not an easy one, but one necessary prerequisite is creating kinds of instruction where students can see the connections between what they learn and what they will learn in school (Smith & Wilhelm, 2002; Sutherland, Botzakis, Moje, & Alvermann, 2008). Without such a connection, academic matters will be divorced from their realities, easily dismissed, forgotten, and a cycle of aliteracy will continue.

References

Alvermann, D. E. (2001). Reading adolescents' reading identities: Looking back to see ahead. *Journal of Adolescent & Adult Literacy, 44*(8), 676–690.

Blanchett, W. J. (2006). Disproportionate representation of African American students in special education: Acknowledging the role of white privilege and racism. *Educational Researcher, 35*(6), 24–28.

Brozo, W. G. (1991). Hiding out in content classrooms: Coping strategies of unsuccessful readers. *Journal of Reading, 33*(5), 324–328.

Bruck, M. (1987). The adult outcomes of children with learning disabilities. *Annals of Dyslexia, 37,* 252–263.

Coutinho, M. J., Oswald, D. P., & Best, A. M. (2002). The influence of socio-demographics and gender on the disproportionate identification of minority students as having learning disabilities. *Remedial and Special Education, 23*(1), 49–59.

De Certeau, M. (1984). *The practice of everyday life* (S. Rendall, Trans.). Berkeley: University of California Press.

Finders, M. J. (1997). *Just girls: Hidden literacies and life in junior high.* New York: Teachers College Press.

Fine, M. (1991). *Framing dropouts.* Albany: State University of New York Press.

Fisher, D., & Frey, N. (2008). What does it take to create skilled readers? Facilitating the transfer and application of literacy strategies. *Voices from the Middle, 15*(4), 16–22.

Freire, P. (1970). *Pedagogy of the oppressed.* New York: Continuum.

Gee, J. P. (1991). What is literacy? In C. Mitchell & K. Weiler (Eds.), *Rewriting literacy: Culture and the discourse of the other* (pp. 3–11). New York: Bergin & Garvey.

Gee, J. P. (1996). *Social linguistics and literacies: Ideology in discourses* (2nd ed.). Philadelphia: Routledge Falmer.

Gee, J. P. (2003). *What video games have to teach us about learning and literacy.* New York: Palgrave Macmillan.

Hall, L. A. (2007). Understanding the silence: Struggling readers discuss decisions about reading expository text. *Journal of Educational Research, 100*(3), 132–141.

Hart, B. & Risley, T. (2003). The early catastrophe. *American Educator, 47*(1), 4–9.

Heath, S. B. (1983). *Ways with words.* New York: Cambridge University Press.

Heath S. B. (2003). The children of Trackton's children: Spoken and written language in social change. In R. Ruddell & N. Unrau (Eds.), *Theoretical models and processes of reading* (5th ed., pp.187–209). Newark, DE: International Reading Association.

Heron, A. H. (2003). A study of agency: Multiple constructions of choice and decision making in an inquiry-based summer school program for struggling readers. *Journal of Adolescent & Adult Literacy, 46*(7), 568–579.

Hinchman, K. A., Alvermann, D. E., Boyd, F. B., Brozo, W. G., & Vacca, R. T. (2004). Supporting older students' in- and out-of-school literacies. *Journal of Adolescent & Adult Literacy, 47*(4), 304–310.

Holland, D., Lachicotte, W., Skinner, D., & Cain, C. (1998). *Identity and agency in cultural worlds.* Cambridge, MA: Harvard University Press.

Hull, G., & Schultz, K. (2001). Literacy and learning out of school: A review of theory and research. *Review of Educational Research, 71*(4), 575–611.

Kamil, M. L. (2008). How to get recreational reading to increase reading ability. In Y. Kim, V. J. Risko, D. L. Compton, D. K. Dickinson, M. K. Hundley, R.T. Jimenez, et al. (Eds.), *57th yearbook of the National Reading Conference.* Oak Creek, WI: National Reading Conference.

Kist, W. (2005). *New literacies in action: Teaching and learning in multiple media.* New York: Teachers College Press.

Krashen, S. (2001). More smoke and mirrors: A critique of the National Reading Panel report on fluency. *Phi Delta Kappan, 83*(2), 119–123.

Lankshear, C., & Knobel, M. (2006). *New literacies: Everyday practices & classroom learning, 2nd Edition.* Philadelphia: Open University Press.

Lee, C., & Jackson, R. (1991). *Faking it.* Portsmouth, NH: Heinemann.

MacGillvray, L., & Curwen, M. S. (2007). Tagging as a social literacy practice. *Journal of Adolescent and Adult Literacy, 50*(5), 354–69.

Manguel, A. (1997). *The history of reading.* New York: Penguin.

Mikulecky, L. (1978). *Aliteracy and a changing view of reading goals.* Paper presented at the Annual Meeting of the International Reading Association, Houston, TX.

Moje, E. (2000). "To be part of the story": The literacy practices of gangsta adolescents. *Teachers College Record, 102,* 651–690.

Morris, D., Ervin, C., & Conrad, K. (2000). A case study of middle school reading disability. In D. W. Moore, D. E. Alvermann, & K. A. Hinchman (Eds.), *Struggling adolescent readers: A collection of teaching strategies* (pp. 8–18). Newark, DE: International Reading Association.

Mueller, P. N. (2001). *Lifers: Learning from at-risk adolescent readers.* Portsmouth, NH: Heinemann.

National Commission on Excellence in Education. (1983). *A nation at risk: The imperative for educational reform.* Washington, DC: U.S. Government Printing Office.

National Institute of Child Health and Human Development. (2000). *Report of the National Reading Panel. Teaching children to read: An evidence-based assessment of the scientific research literature on reading and its implications for reading instruction: Reports of the subgroups* (NIH Publication No. 00-4754). Washington, DC: U.S. Government Printing Office.

National Institute for Literacy. (2007). *What content area teachers should know about adolescent literacy.* Washington, DC: U.S. Government Printing Office.

New London Group. (1996). A pedagogy of multiliteracies: Designing social futures. *Harvard Educational Review, 66*(1), 60–92.

O'Brien, D. G. (2006). "Struggling" adolescents' engagement in multimediating: Countering the institutional construction of incompetence. In D. E. Alvermann, K. A. Hinchman, D. W. Moore, S. F. Phelps, & D. R. Waff (Eds.), *Reconceptualizing the literacies in adolescents' lives* (pp. 29–45). Mahwah, NJ: Erlbaum.

Office of Special Education Programs. (2002). *Twenty-fourth annual report to Congress on the implementation of the Individuals with Disabilities Education Act.* Washington, DC: U.S. Department of Education. Retrieved January 14, 2009, from http://www.ed.gov/about/reports/annual/osep/2002/index.html

Ramsay, J. G. (2002). Hell's bibliophiles: The fifth way of looking at an alliterate. *Change, 54*(1), 50–56.

Rogers, R. (2002). Between contexts: A critical discourse analysis of family literacy, discursive practices, and literate subjectivities. *Reading Research Quarterly, 37*(3), 248–277.

Smith, M.W., & Wilhelm, J.D. (2002). *"Reading don't fix no Chevys": Literacy in the lives of young men.* Portsmouth, NH: Heinemann.

Snell, L. (2002). Special education confidential: How schools use the "learning disability" label to cover up their failures. *Reason, 34*(7), 40–46.

Street, B. V. (1995). *Literacy in theory and practice.* New York: Cambridge University Press. (Original work published 1984)

Sutherland, L. A., Botzakis, S., Moje, E. B., & Alvermann, D. E. (2008). Drawing on youth cultures in content learning and literacy. In D. Lapp, J. Flood, & N. Farnan (Eds.), *Content area reading and learning: Instructional strategies* (2nd ed., pp. 133–156). Englewood Cliffs, NJ: Prentice-Hall.

Teale, W. H., Paciga, K. A., & Hoffman, J. L. (2007). Beginning reading instruction in urban schools: The curriculum gap ensures a continuing achievement gap. *The Reading Teacher, 61*(4), 344–348.

The University of Kansas Students Tutoring for Literacy. (n.d.). *History of Literacy*. Retrieved January 14, 2009, from http://www.ku.edu/~stl/historyofliteracy.htm

Wagner, M., D'Amico, R., Marder, C., Newman, L., & Blackorby, J. (1992). *What happens next? Trends in post-school outcomes of youth with disabilities: The second comprehensive report from the National Longitudinal Transition Study of Special Education Students*. Menlo Park, CA: SRI International.

Wilder, P., & Dressman, M. (2006). New Literacies, enduring challenges? The influence of capital on adolescent readers' internet practices. In D. E. Alvermann, K. A. Hinchman, D. W. Moore, S. F. Phelps, & D. R. Waff (Eds.), *Reconceptualizing the literacies in adolescents' lives* (2nd ed., pp. 205–227). Mahwah, NJ: Erlbaum.

Williams, B. T. (2007). Why Johnny can never, ever read: The perpetual literacy crisis and student identity. *Journal of Adolescent & Adult Literacy, 51*(2), 178–182.

Part III

Assessing Reading Proficiency

EDITOR: PETER JOHNSTON

13

Response to Intervention as an Assessment Approach

Donna M. Scanlon
The University at Albany

Until recently, the determination of whether a child should be considered learning disabled, has involved one basic "test" and multiple exclusionary criteria. The test was whether there was a substantial discrepancy between the child's achievement and intellectual ability, both measured by standardized tests. Exclusionary criteria included perceptual challenges such as uncorrected vision or hearing difficulties and psychological and social circumstances. It addition, students were not to be considered for learning disability designation unless they had had an *adequate* opportunity to learn. Among many problems that have been identified in the traditional definition of LD (see Fletcher, Denton, & Francis, 2005; Gresham, 2002; Vellutino, Scanlon, & Lyon, 2000), perhaps the most critical, was the limited attention to the role of instruction in the evolution of learning difficulties. As the legislation provided no clear criteria for determining whether a child's instruction had been adequate, "adequate instruction" took on many different meanings and often simply meant that the child had attended school regularly. In light of the widely recognized variability in teacher effectiveness and the differences in service delivery models across educational settings (e.g., some schools routinely offered remedial reading services to struggling first graders while others delayed support services until second or third grade), there were growing concerns that many children were being identified as learning disabled because of inadequacies in their instructional experiences. An article by Clay (1987) was perhaps the first clear articulation of the notion that children should not even be considered for learning disability designation until high quality and responsive instruction had been provided and failed to accelerate the child's progress. Since Clay's article, a number of studies have instituted instructional interventions that were successful in preventing and/or remediating early reading difficulties thereby confirming that intensification of instruction can reduce the incidence of reading difficulties (e.g., Brown, Denton, Kelly, Outhred, & McNaught, 1999; Center, Wheldall, Freeman, Outhred, & McNaught, 1995; Mathes et al., 2005; Gomez-Bellenge, Rogers, & Fullerton, 2003; O'Connor, 2000; Scanlon, Vellutino, Small, Fanuele, & Sweeney, 2005; Scanlon, Gelzheiser, Vellutino, Schatschneider, & Sweeney, 2008; Torgesen et al., 2001; Vaughn, Linan-Thompson, & Hickman, 2003; Vellutino et al., 1996). Further, several studies specifically evaluated the relationships between students' response to instruction and the size of the discrepancy between their measured IQ and achievement levels (Fletcher et al., 1994; Stanovich & Siegel, 1994; Vellutino, Scanlon, & Lyon, 2000) and found little relationship.

Together, this body of research made it clear that (a) most early reading difficulties can be prevented through instructional enhancements, and (b) the discrepancy between an individual's intellectual and achievement levels have little relevance to how the student will grow as a reader, at least during the early literacy stage. These understandings had substantial influence on the federal legislation that governs the procedures by which children are identified as learning disabled. With the passage of the Individuals with Disability Educational Improvement Act (IDEIA) in 2004 and in accord with the corresponding regulations issued in 2006 (Yell, Shriner, & Katsiyannis, 2006), states now have the option of using an evaluation of a child's response to intervention (RTI) as a key indicator in determining whether a student should be considered learning disabled. In fact, the legislation allows for the possibility that response to intervention could be the sole "test" of whether a child should be identified as learning disabled.

Overview of RTI

Most RTI models involve a tiered approach to the implementation of instructional modifications. The most widely described model involves three tiers. In this model, low performing students are identified and monitored as they participate in classroom instruction (often referred to as Tier 1 instruction). Those who do not appear to be making sufficient progress to meet grade level expectations by the end of the school year are provided with a second, more intensive tier of instruction in the hope of accelerating their progress. Intensification might be accomplished by providing more time in instruction, smaller instructional groupings, or both. The second tier is intended to be provided in addition to (rather than instead of) classroom instruction and might be provided by a specialist teacher in a small group context. Once again, the students' progress is monitored. Children who do not show accelerated progress with Tier 2 intervention are considered for possible LD classification and such a placement becomes their third tier of intervention.

Despite the popularity of this model in discussions of RTI, there is little to no research in which this specific model has been explicitly evaluated (Allington, 2006). In fact, in the body of research that contributed to the development of RTI processes there are almost as many models of intervention as there are research groups investigating the utility of intervention. All that is known for sure is that many children who struggle at the early stages of learning to read will show accelerated learning when provided with more intensive and/or higher quality instruction. There is very little research demonstrating positive impacts of interventions for older struggling readers (Vaughn et al., 2008; Torgesen, Rashotte, Alexander, Alexander, & MacPhee, 2003) and, in what exists, positive impacts have been identified only in the context of fairly intensive intervention (Lovett et al., 2008; Torgesen et al., 2001) provided beyond the classroom (Tiers 2 or 3). There is no evidence that a period of classroom instruction only (Tier 1) would help older struggling readers to accelerate their progress—the basic goal of providing intervention.

In RTI approaches, students' performance is monitored as they proceed through the tiers and it is the documentation of limited progress over time in spite of multiple attempts to adjust the amount and/or type of instruction that the student receives, that serves as the major criterion in deliberations regarding LD classification. Each of the components (progress, time, and instruction) of this criterion represents a place where opinions about appropriate practice vary, sometimes dramatically. For example, with regard to documenting progress, there are no commonly agreed upon instruments or methods for assessing progress nor is there agreement about how frequently progress should be documented. With regard to the issue of timing, there is debate about when (at what grade level) intervention efforts should begin, about how long children should remain at a given tier, and about how many tiers of intervention should be instituted before discontinuing the process (either because the child no longer needs support or because all intervention efforts have failed to accelerate progress). Instructional issues needing attention include such things as the basic nature of the instruction offered (i.e., what programs or approaches will be used) and the degree of coherence between classroom and intervention settings and across the tiers. Each of these general areas will be discussed below. However, because

RTI efforts are, basically, driven by two underlying purposes it is important to first consider those purposes since one's dominant purpose will influence decision making relating to the components of RTI.

Prevention vs. Classification Accuracy   RTI may be thought of as having two primary and related purposes: (a) the prevention of long-term learning difficulties, and (b) improvement in the accuracy of LD classifications. From the classification accuracy perspective, the focus is on making sure that children are not classified as learning disabled largely as a result of inadequate instructional experience. An underlying assumption of the classification accuracy perspective is that some children are qualitatively distinct from their peers with regard to their ability to learn to read and that they need to be identified as early as possible so that the necessary individualized instructional resources can be brought to bear (Fuchs & Fuchs, 2008). In comparison to the preventative perspective, relatively little instructional intervention might be offered before considering an LD classification. In fact, Caffrey, Fuchs, and Fuchs (2008) recently suggested that responsiveness to instruction might ultimately "be determined in a single assessment session" (p. 256) using a procedure known as dynamic assessment in which the child is tested, offered a limited amount of instruction related to the content/concepts tested, and then tested again on the same content. Such an approach seems extreme, but it highlights the concern with classification accuracy that characterizes much of the research on RTI. While the research focused on classification accuracy uses more protracted periods of intervention than suggested by Caffrey et al., the periods are, nevertheless, relatively brief (6 to 12 weeks). Moreover, the logic that guides these approaches has strongly influenced the literature targeted at educational practitioners. For example, according to Brown-Chidsey and Steege (2005) students could be eligible for LD classification after as little as 12 weeks of intervention effort and as young as first grade and according to Mellard and Johnson (2008) lack of acceleration in Tier 2 during a 9- to 12-week period may warrant referral for disability determination.

From a prevention perspective, on the other hand, children are viewed as much more malleable (Dweck, 1999) and instruction as much more powerful in influencing the students' trajectories. Efforts to intervene on behalf of children who appear to be at risk of experiencing learning difficulties would be initiated as soon as potential difficulties can be identified on the assumption that it is easier to address knowledge gaps when they are relatively small and before children come to view themselves as academically less able than their peers. Consistent with this perspective, most of the early research on intervention for reading difficulties provided intervention in first grade (e.g., Center, Wheldall, Freeman, Outhred, McNaught, 1995; Pinnell, 1989; Torgesen & Wagner, 1999; Vellutino et al., 1996) and some of the more recent studies have initiated intervention efforts in kindergarten (O'Connor, Harty, & Fulmer, 2005;

Scanlon et al., 2005, 2008; Simmons, Kame'enui, Stool-miller, Coyne, & Harn, 2003). Further, the interventions tended to be for longer duration (1 or more years) than those advocated by much of the practitioner literature.

Some of these studies (e.g., O'Connor et al., 2005; Scanlon et al., 2005) have demonstrated that many children who do not accelerate with Tier 2 instruction do meet grade level expectations when provided with more intensive (one-to-one) intervention for a protracted period of time. Whether children who need such intensity should be considered LD is a question that the field will probably debate for years to come. However, for the children, it is fairly clear that more and better instruction can enable most who struggle initially to catch up and to avoid the potentially disabling effects for being identified as disabled.

The Role of Instruction   Even though intervention is a central feature of RTI there has been remarkably little research on the characteristics of instruction that are associated with student progress within and across the tiers. Rather, in many studies, teachers are encouraged to implement a particular intervention program *with fidelity*. If students do not make progress in the context of this instruction, it is often assumed that the problem lies with the child rather than with the program. It could certainly be argued, however, that the push for fidelity limits the teachers' ability to respond to the needs of individual children and that the child is unresponsive *because* the instruction is unresponsive. Indeed, a student's response to intervention could well be construed as a test of the quality and appropriateness of instructional efforts. While many aspects of instruction need consideration, in what follows I focus on a few that seem to be particularly important to schools as they attempt to develop their RTI processes.

Two general models for RTI implementation have gained prominence. The problem solving approach (Marston, Reschly, Lau, Muyskens, & Canter, 2007) entails collaborative efforts on the part of several members of the school community to identify and implement optimal instructional interventions for each child who appears to be at risk for school learning difficulties. Within this approach, decisions about instructional modifications across the tiers of intervention involve a team of professionals. The team assembles and develops an instructional plan designed to be responsive to the needs of the individual. The child's response to such interventions determines future intervention plans in an iterative manner. The alternative approach is referred to as a standard protocol approach which, as the name suggests, involves the implementation of standard interventions for children who appear to be at risk for difficulties in particular areas (Fuchs, Mock, Morgan, & Young, 2003). Either model might entail the utilization of highly prescriptive and manualized instructional programs, however, in the problem solving model, the programs selected would, presumably, be selected because they were more closely matched with the student's particular skills.

The response to children offered by these two approaches

is radically different and would seem likely to have dramatically different effects on their progress. However, with the exception of studies reported by Mathes et al. (2005), and Foorman et al. (2003), which showed little differential effect of more highly prescribed as opposed to more teacher responsive instructional approaches, there is very little research evaluating the relative impact of implementing standard protocol approaches as compared to instructional approaches that depend heavily on teacher planning and decision making.

It should also be noted that there are important gradations between standard protocol and problem solving approaches that are often ignored in the literature. For example, the intervention work that my colleagues and I have done (Scanlon et al., 2005, 2008; Vellutino et al., 1996) is often described as a standard protocol approach. However, our approach is standard only to the extent that children who qualify for intervention are offered intervention provided by a teacher who has been trained in the Interactive Strategies Approach (ISA; Scanlon, Anderson, & Sweeney, 2010; Vellutino & Scanlon, 2002). This approach calls for the teacher to plan and deliver instruction that is responsive to the children by taking account of both what the children know and are able to do and by considering the characteristics and expectations of the classroom curriculum.

Classroom instruction.   Classroom instruction represents the critical first tier in RTI approaches. The effectiveness of classroom level instruction is evaluated by assessing the performance patterns of each class as compared with other classes at the same grade level. It is widely agreed that, in situations where high numbers of students within a class perform below expectations there is a need for intervention for the classroom teacher. However, there is no consensus regarding how to set expectations. For example, national, state, district, or building level norms might be used. Conclusions about instructional adequacy are likely to be very different depending upon the reference point employed. Further, little is known about how to enhance the quality of instruction in situations where many students are found to be underperforming. In fact, Chard (2004) has argued that "the science of teaching reading has outpaced the science of professional development in reading instruction" (p. 176).

The most common recommendation for enhancing the quality of classroom instruction is that a research-based, core curriculum be adopted and implemented *with fidelity* (Brown-Chidsey & Steege, 2005; Fuchs, & Fuchs, 2008; Mellard & Johnson, 2008). There are at least two potential problems with this recommendation. One is that there are virtually no restrictions on the application of the label "research-based." In fact, contrary to the belief of most educators, the effectiveness of most core curricula that carry the research-based label have not actually be scientifically evaluated. Another problem with the recommendation is the issue of implementation *with fidelity* which, to most, implies that instruction should faithfully follow the curriculum and may be taken by many to mean that teachers should not deviate from the curriculum even if their students are not learning or have already learned the content (Achinstein & Ogawa, 2006).

Such recommendations ignore the evidence that student outcomes are more dependent on what teachers do than on the curriculum they use (Bond & Dykstra, 1967; Duffy & Hoffman, 1999; Nye, Konstantopoulos, & Hedges, 2004; Scanlon et al., 2008; Tivnan & Hemphill, 2005). The published research on teacher effectiveness generally demonstrates a substantial impact of classroom instruction on student performance and that impact is generally stronger than the impact of adopted instructional programs or approaches to instruction. Such a recommendation also implies a one-size-fits-all view of classroom instruction and provides little encouragement for differentiation to accommodate the broad range of reading abilities that characterize the typical classroom. Further, this admonition is in direct contrast to results reported by Taylor, Pearson, Clark, and Walpole (2000) who found that whole class, undifferentiated instruction is more common in less effective schools. Scanlon et al. (2008) found a similar pattern in comparing more and less effective kindergarten teachers—the more effective teachers spent substantially more time providing instruction to small skill-based groups. Thus, schools that adhere strictly to the advice to implement the core with fidelity might actually find increasing numbers of students qualifying for Tier 2 and Tier 3 intervention because classroom instruction is not appropriately responsive to students and, as a result, what began as small gaps have the opportunity to grow. Of course, lack of differentiation might well limit the growth of the more advanced readers because they will not be offered texts at an appropriate level of challenge.

A few studies have implemented professional development for classroom teachers in the context of RTI implementations or other efforts to reduce the incidence of early reading difficulties (e.g., Foorman and Moats, 2004; McCutchen et al., 2002; McGill-Franzen, 2006; O'Connor et al., 2005; Scanlon et al., 2008). Most of these have *not* focused on preparing teachers to implement specific core curricula. Rather, the focus has been on the development of more generalized teacher knowledge that can be drawn upon regardless of the curriculum in use. For example, in the Scanlon et al. study (2008), professional development for kindergarten classroom teachers emphasized knowledge related to early literacy development and helping teachers to identify and respond to students' literacy learning difficulties using, for the most part, the curricular materials that were in place before the professional development program began. This professional development yielded substantial reductions in the number of at-risk kindergartners who continued to qualify as at risk at the beginning of first grade and these outcomes were apparent both during the year in which the professional development program was provided and during the following year.

Interventions beyond the classroom. Even though intervention is a central feature of RTI there has been remarkably little research on the characteristics of instruction that are associated with student progress within and across the tiers. Rather, as for classroom instruction, intervention teachers are encouraged to implement particular intervention programs with fidelity. If students do not make progress in the context of this instruction, it is often assumed that the problem lies with the child rather than with the program. It is certainly possible, of course, that the push for fidelity limits the teachers' ability to respond to the needs of individual children and that the child is unresponsive because the instruction is unresponsive.

Yet another concern with the interventions that may be offered in RTI programs is the amount and frequency of switching between and among instructional approaches that is sometimes recommended (e.g., Brown-Chidsey & Steege, 2005; Mellard & Johnson, 2008). These recommendations are made despite the fact that consistency in literacy instruction has been linked to better student outcomes (Mosenthal, Lipson, Torncello, Russ, & Mekkelsen, 2004) and in face of long standing concerns about fragmentation and lack of congruency of instruction across instructional settings (Allington & McGill-Franzen, 1989). In informal interactions with several schools as they attempt to develop RTI programs, I have encountered many where the belief is that, in order to properly implement an RTI program, each struggling learner needs to be offered at least two or three distinct prescriptive programs before concluding that he/she is not responding. Reading involves a complex set of interactive processes. Many prescriptive programs target only a subset of the processes. To provide a child with a program focused on developing phonics skills, for example, find that the program does not help to accelerate the child's growth, and then to place the child in a program that has a very different focus, say fluency, is apt to further confuse the child who is already confused about the reading process.

Given the sheer number of products that are available as potential intervention tools there is reason to be concerned that RTI approaches implemented with a liberal dose of program switching will exacerbate children's early difficulties. Indeed, such children are essentially being asked to learn *more* than their peers. For instance, the classroom and intervention teachers may use different keywords to remind the children of letter-sound correspondences, may use different terminology to refer to the same concepts (e.g., uppercase/capital, silent e/bossy e, period/stop dot) and/or may teach different strategies for word solving or comprehension monitoring.

As, in the age of evidence-based practice, schools sometimes appear to feel pressured to purchase intervention programs that will help to solve their students' learning difficulties, it is important to note that the intervention programs marketed to schools as *evidence-based* or *research-based*, often have not been rigorously evaluated. Rather, many are merely *based* on the extant research. Unfortunately, there are no restrictions on the circumstances under which an instructional product can claim to be research-based. There is nothing to stop someone from reading the research, developing a program based on that research, and publishing a *research-based* program. Further, it should be noted that, among the prescriptive programs that have been evaluated, very few demonstrate efficacy with regard to promoting the development of reading comprehension—the most critical target of reading instruction (see the reports provided by the U.S. Department of Education's What Works Clearinghouse, http://ies.ed.gov/ncee/wwc).

Despite this relative lack of evidence that prescriptive programs have a positive impact on reading comprehension, some have argued that the use of prescriptive programs and a standard protocol approach is preferable because, generally, such programs require less teacher expertise (Fuchs & Fuchs, 2006). However, it could certainly be argued that the children who are making the slowest progress are most in need of expert and responsive instruction. The fact that some children do not demonstrate accelerated growth in the context of instruction that relies on highly prescriptive programs may well be a reflection on the program rather than the child. Thus, the child's lack of progress may be due to faulty instructional decision making rather than to underlying characteristics of the child that would warrant a special designation.

Approaches that utilize a more responsive approach to intervention attempt to avoid such difficulties by having intervention teachers take greater account of what is being covered in the classroom program. For example, in research utilizing the Interactive Strategies Approach (Scanlon et al., 2005, 2008; Vellutino et al., 1996), the intervention teacher incorporates critical classroom concepts into her own instruction. At the very least, the intervention teacher makes every effort to teach about decoding concepts and word identification strategies in ways that complement and reinforce what is being taught in the classroom. Further, the intervention teacher maintains ongoing contact with the classroom teacher so that, as new concepts and skills are addressed in the classroom, the intervention teacher can reinforce them in the intervention setting. We believe that, in doing so, we magnify the effects of intervention by enhancing the child's ability to profit from classroom instruction. Indeed, Borman, Wong, Hedges, and D'Agostino (2001) provided evidence that while such collaboration and coordination is rare (see also Johnston, Allington, & Afflerbach, 1985), a greater degree of curricular congruence across instruction settings was associated with stronger reading outcomes in the early primary grades.

Timing of Intervention Efforts Timing issues related to intervention efforts concern questions about the grade level at which the RTI process should be initiated and how long a student should remain at a given tier of intervention before decisions are made about changes in instructional intensity and/or programming.

When Should the RTI Process Begin? Unlike the IQ-Achievement Discrepancy approach, which has been characterized as a "wait to fail" approach (Fuchs & Fuchs, 2006), RTI approaches generally emphasize early attention to meeting the needs of struggling learners. Thus, the vast majority of research on RTI has focused in the primary grades with most studies initiating intervention attempts in kindergarten or first grade. A motivating factor in this emphasis on very early intervention is that it is easier to address learning gaps when they are small and the students have yet to lose confidence in their learning abilities. While the logic of initiating intervention as soon as children demonstrate difficulty seems transparent, some have raised the concern that beginning efforts to identify children who are at risk for later reading difficulties in kindergarten yields too many false positives, that is, too many children are identified as at risk at kindergarten entry who do not ultimately demonstrate reading difficulties and that, as a result, the schools' instructional resources will be overly taxed. However, my colleagues and I have found that kindergarten classroom instruction has a substantial influence on children's risk status (Scanlon & Vellutino, 1996, 1997; Scanlon et al., 2008), and it seems likely that both the high false positive rates and the high false negative rates reported by Torgesen (2002) and Jenkins and O'Connor (2002) are due, at least partially, to variation in the quality of kindergarten classroom instruction. Particularly striking evidence of the influence of classroom instruction at the kindergarten level emerged in a recent study in which my colleagues and I tracked children's risk status from the beginning of kindergarten to the beginning of first grade as they participated in the baseline cohort of a larger intervention study. For the baseline cohort, there was substantial variation by classroom teacher in the percentage of children identified as at risk at kindergarten entry who continued to qualify as at risk at the end of kindergarten and the beginning of first grade. Some teachers reduced the percentage of children who qualified as at risk by more than half (from 50% to 20% at risk) while, for other teachers, there was virtually no change, or even a slight increase, in the percentage of students who qualified as at risk from the beginning to the end of the kindergarten with approximately 50% of the children qualifying as at risk at both time points (Scanlon et al., 2008). Further, in an earlier study (Scanlon et al., 2005) we found that, when the at-risk kindergartners were provided with intervention services in both kindergarten and first grade as opposed to in first grade only, they were substantially less likely to experience serious reading difficulties by the end of first grade. Such data argue strongly in favor of initiating intervention efforts in kindergarten—if not earlier.

How long should an intervention be tried and how many tiers should be used? The appropriate duration for intervention attempts is another under-researched topic. While the practitioner oriented literature makes recommendations suggesting that rather limited intervention periods will allow for a determination of whether a child should be considered for learning disability designation (Brown-Chidsey & Steege, 2005; Fuchs & Fuchs, 2008; Mellard & Johnson, 2008), there is insufficient evidence to support such a conclusion. For example, Vaughn et al., (2003) studied response to intervention among struggling second graders who were provided with small group intervention instituted in 10 week intervals. At the end of each interval, the students were re-evaluated. Children who met exit criteria were discontinued and those who had not were regrouped and continued. Each successive intervention interval helped additional children meet the exit criteria. Similarly, several other research groups found that more children met grade level expectation when interventions were continued for longer periods of time and/or when the interventions became more intensive (Denton, Fletcher, Anthony, & Francis, 2006; O'Connor et al., 2005; Phillips & Smith, 1997; Scanlon et al., 2005). These results argue for allowing a longer and more intensive period of intervention before classifications are considered. However, there is a need for caution in calling for greater intensity. For example, Wanzek and Vaughn (2008) recently reported that when first graders who did not respond well to Tier 2 intervention were provided with additional, more intensive intervention (2 small group sessions per day) no acceleration occurred. There is, no doubt a limit to how much a young child can handle in terms of instructional intensity. Moreover, Wanzek and Vaughn do not indicate whether the additional instruction simply utilized the same approach to instruction that was ineffective the first time. It seems likely that, for the children who are hardest to accelerate, instruction needs to be individually tailored. For example, there is some suggestive evidence emanating from work with the Reading Recovery model indicating that many children who did not show accelerated growth during their first experience with Reading Recovery did accelerate when given ongoing, intensive, and individually tailored intervention (Phillips & Smith, 1997).

Progress Monitoring   One of the hallmarks of RTI approaches is that the children who are identified as being at risk are frequently assessed to monitor their progress. The monitoring is intended to yield the data needed to guide decisions concerning instructional modifications. Much of the research on RTI models and much of the guidance offered to practitioners involves the use of curriculum based measures (CBMs), typically using CBMs to refer to measures that do not actually sample the curriculum (as the concept was originally construed). Rather, CBMs in today's educational context, often consist of either brief measures of oral reading speed (typically referred to as measures of oral reading fluency or ORF) or maze tests that involve children in selecting the correct responses while reading grade level passages in which every seventh word, or so, has been deleted and replaced by 3 or 4 words, one of which is the original word. Both of these types of measures assess speeded responding and in no way reference the curriculum

to which the children have been exposed. Proponents of these measures suggest that they serve as reasonable proxies for more comprehensive measures of reading ability (Fuchs, Fuchs, Hosp, & Jenkins, 2001; Good, Simmons, & Kame'enui, 2001). However, others would argue that the relationships are due to the relationship between oral reading accuracy (i.e., the ability to read the words) and comprehension rather than to any major influence of speed per se (Paris, 2005).

In addition to the endorsement of these measures by prominent researchers, the popularity of CBMs is also due to the fact that they take little time to administer, are fairly highly correlated with more comprehensive and comprehension-focused measures of reading achievement, and are more sensitive to small increments of change in reading skill than are the more comprehensive measures. Further, multiple alternate forms are available which makes it possible to administer the same assessment frequently without concern for practice effects.

However, there is considerable debate about the use of these measures with the Diagnostic Indicators of Basic Early Literacy Skills (DIBELS; Good, Kaminski, Smith, Laimon, & Dill, 2001), which is widely used in the Reading First program, receiving the greatest amount of attention. Unfortunately for the schools that have invested so much time and energy in instituting this form of progress monitoring, current research is highlighting serious problems with these instruments. One problem is that such assessments assume that the passages utilized at a given grade level are of equivalent difficulty—but they are not. For example, Francis and colleagues (2008) recently pointed out that the Spache readability estimates used to equate the DIBELS passages were quite different than estimates derived using other readability formulas. Further, Ardoin, Suldo, Witt, Aldrich, and McDonald (2005) found that readability indices have limited utility for predicting oral reading fluency. Moreover, of the eight formulas evaluated by Ardoin et al., the Spache estimates were found to be among the worst predictors of the fluency with which passages are read. The implications of these findings for assessment of progress in RTI implementations is clear—depending upon the passage used at a particular measurement point a student's performance level may appear to have changed substantially more or substantially less than it actually has. Thus, efforts to accurately measure progress in literacy acquisition, which is the basic reason for frequent measurement of ORF are seriously undermined.

Beyond the technical inadequacies of such measures there is also serious concern about the way such measures might shape understandings of what constitutes reading competence and, therefore, influence instruction. For example, measures such as the ORF run the clear risk of sending the message, to both students and teachers, that speed is valued more than comprehension (for elaborations on these concerns see Pearson, 2006, and Samuels, 2007). Further, these measures provide teachers with virtually no information about how to respond to and plan for students with difficulties. They simply serve to flag students who may be struggling.

In light of the inadequacies of ORF-type measures, maze measures might seem like a reasonable alternative since they at least focus on comprehension. However, early research on the cloze task, which is the predecessor of the maze task, demonstrated that accurate responses did not generally require comprehension beyond the sentence or phrase level (see Shanahan, Kamil, & Tobin, 1982, for an enlightening illustration in which performance levels were unchanged when passage sentences were presented in normal versus random order). Further, maze-type measurers clearly suffer from the same problems of lack of comparability across alternate forms.[1]

Advocates for monitoring progress using the types of speed-based measures described above might argue that the lack of comparability across forms is compensated for by the frequency with which they are administered. Thus, it is the students' growth rate or slope that is of interest rather than their absolute performance level at any given point in time. RTI processes call for providing students who show little or no growth with more intensified and/or different interventions. However, Schatschneider, Wagner, & Crawford (2008) recently reported that slopes computed on the basis of multiple administrations of the DIBELS ORF measure in first grade did little to improve instructional decision making. Schatschneider et al. used DIBELS data collected in the context of the Reading First implementation by the state of Florida. The sample consisted of over 23,000 first graders. The analyses attempted to predict end of first-grade and end of second-grade reading comprehension performance using either a single measure of DIBELS ORF administered toward the end of first grade or a slope for ORF performance computed on four administrations of the DIBELS ORF given at 2 to 3 month intervals during the first-grade year. Results revealed that the use of DIBELS slopes did nothing to enhance prediction accuracy beyond the accuracy obtained using a single end of year measure. Schatschneider et al. argue that their findings question a core assumption of RTI models—that growth over time should predict ultimate outcomes.

However, it is important to note that, in this study, no account was taken of the amount, type, quality, and timing of instruction or intervention that the children received during their first and second grade. All of these factors are likely to impact student progress and end of year performance. In fact, as argued above, variability in the quality and characteristics of instructional experiences are a major determinant of growth in reading skills.

In contrast to "standardized" speed measures like those described above, some RTI advocates (e.g., Brown-Chidsey & Steege, 2005) propose the use of true curriculum based measures that actually sample the entire curriculum. Teachers are advised to create multiple versions (at least 20) of assessments that sample content that is to be taught across the school year. These assessments would then be administered as often as daily in order to determine whether

sufficient growth toward mastering the curriculum is occurring. While such an approach has the potential to provide more useful information to guide instruction than do ORF or maze-type measures, the approach has serious problems, particularly when used to make important decisions about individual children. Teachers are not equipped to develop alternate forms of assessments that are appropriately reliable and valid. This is a task that challenges even the most experienced and well-funded test developers.

Yet another problem with response to intervention measures (whether measures are based on the curriculum or are of the proxy variety) is that, for many aspects of reading development, children do not grow in a way that can be adequately represented by a straight line. In fact, Paris (2005) makes a cogent argument for the fact that linear growth is only likely for relatively low level skills such as speeded word reading.

The discussion above should make it clear that there is much to be learned about how to guide the decision-making process in RTI models. There is no clear evidence that outcomes for struggling learners are enhanced by the addition of very frequent assessment. Even some of the strongest proponents of frequent progress monitoring acknowledge that little improvement accrues for students unless teachers are simultaneously provided with guidance on how to interpret and respond to students who are making limited progress (Stecker, Fuchs, & Fuchs, 2005). Thus, it may well be that the research that was taken to suggest that frequent progress monitoring using CBM-type measures helped teachers to more effectively meet the needs of their students, was actually indexing the effects of helping teachers to think more carefully about what their students were ready to learn. In support of this suggestion, it is useful to note that in a series of studies on instructional approaches to preventing early reading difficulties my colleagues and I did not collect "formal" assessment data more than 3 or 4 times per year (Scanlon et al., 2005, 2008; Vellutino et al., 1996). Rather, the intervention teachers used checklists of instructional objectives (many of them ordered to highlight the typical course of development) and daily lesson sheets on which they documented students' skills and problem solving approaches. These record keeping devices were intended to keep the teachers focused on planning instruction that was appropriate for their students. The records were based on the teachers' observations of the children as they taught and so did not require interruption in instruction in order to document success (or lack thereof). Of course, in order to effectively use such observation tools, teachers needed a fair amount of engagement in professional development. But the professional development was focused on the direct connection between what the teacher observed the students doing and the implications of those observations for instructional planning. No such connections exist when the progress monitoring data are comprised of speed-based performance levels.

The use of observational approaches to decision making also have their limitations, of course. Chief among them is that it is difficult to determine where to draw the line in terms of deciding whether children are making adequate progress. The periodic use of standardized but more comprehensive measures of literacy development could certainly augment the decision-making process. However, it must be acknowledged that, to a certain extent, any decision about adequate progress, regardless of the tool used to evaluate progress, will ultimately involve a somewhat arbitrary choice about what level of performance and/or what level of growth is sufficient.

Summary

Response to Intervention is, essentially, the latest test for whether a child should be considered learning disabled. While a student's response is, no doubt, partly attributable to factors beyond the control of the instructional setting, in this chapter, the focus has been on factors that the school controls. The argument was made that a student's response to intervention, and instruction more generally, is the result of a fairly complex interplay between and among several instructional and assessment factors: the nature and quality of the instruction provided at each of the tiers, the intensity and duration of instruction, the congruence of instruction across tiers, the tools and timelines used to assess progress, and so on. There are widely divergent views on how each of these aspects of the RTI process should be operationalized, and there is far too little convergent research to support some of the most common recommendations that are being made, particularly in the practitioner-oriented literature. All that we know for sure is that most early reading difficulties can be prevented through enhanced instruction. Rather than withholding the most intensive instructional resources until a child has been identified as disabled, RTI approaches allow schools to muster their instructional resources early in the child's school career and to strive to keep achievement gaps from growing and becoming disabling.

The foregoing discussion of RTI as an alternative approach to identifying children as learning disabled has, more or less, taken as a given the notion that there are learning disabled students. However, there is certainly reason to question the utility of the construct. In light of the fact that prevention/intervention efforts can be very effective in reducing the number of children who experience severe reading difficulties (Denton et al., 2006; Pinnell, 1989; Pinnell, Lyons, Deford, Bryk, & Seltzer, 1999; Scanlon et al. 2005, 2008; Vaughn, et al., 2003; Vellutino et al., 1996) and that most school-based post-classification instructional efforts tend to be largely ineffective in accelerating student achievement (Allington, 1994; Bentrum & Aaron, 2003; Kavale & Forness, 1999; Torgesen et al., 2001), the value of such a classification seems questionable. However, for administrative purposes, it is likely that the concept of learning disabilities will be part of the educational landscape for some time to come, partly because it represents a major source of funds for schools and also because the educational community has yet to prevent reading and other types of learning difficulties on a broad enough scale to convincingly argue that the construct is largely unnecessary.

Notes

1. Those familiar with oral reading fluency and maze-type measures may question the suggestion that the alternate forms are not comparable owing to fairly high alternate form reliability estimates that are provided by the test publishers. It is important to note that these reliabilities reflect the fact that individuals will be similarly ranked by alternate forms. However, their absolute performance levels (e.g., the number of words read correctly in a minute could be very different on the two forms [see Francis et al., 2008]).

References

Achinstein, B., & Ogawa, R. T. (2006). (In)Fidelity: What the resistance of new teachers reveals about professional principles and prescriptive educational policies. *Harvard Educational Review, 76*(1), 30–63.

Allington, R. L. (1994). What's special about special programs for children who find learning to read difficult? *Journal of Reading Behavior, 26*, 95–115.

Allington, R. L. (2006). Research and the three tier model. *Reading Today, 23*(5), 20.

Allington, R. L., & McGill-Franzen, A. (1989). School response to reading failure: Chapter I and special education students in grades 2, 4 and 8. *Elementary School Journal, 89*, 529–542.

Ardoin, S. P., Suldo, S. M., Witt, J., Aldrich, S., & McDonald, E. (2005). Accuracy of readability of estimates' predictions of CBM performance. *School Psychology Quarterly, 20*(1), 1–22.

Bentrum, K. E., & Aaron, P. G. (2003). Does reading instruction in learning disability rooms really work? *Reading Psychology, 24*, 361–382.

Bond, G. L., & Dykstra, R. (1967). The cooperative research program in first-grade reading instruction. *Reading Research Quarterly, 2*, 5–142.

Borman, G. D., Wong, K. K., & D'Agostino, J. V. (2001). Coordinating categorical and regular programs: Effects on Title I students' educational opportunities and outcomes. In G. D. Borman, S. C. Stringfield, & R. E. Slavin (Eds.), *Title I: Compensatory education at the crossroads* (pp. 79–116). Mahwah, NJ: Erlbaum.

Brown, W., Denton, E., Kelly, L., Outhred, L., & McNaught, M. (1999). RRs effectiveness: A five-year success story in San Louis Coastal Unified School District. *ERS Spectrum* (Winter), 3–10.

Brown-Chidsey, R., & Steege, M. W. (2005). *Response to intervention: Principles and strategies for effective practice.* New York: Guilford.

Caffrey, E., Fuchs, D., & Fuchs, L. S. (2008). The predictive validity of dynamic assessment: A review. *Journal of Special Education, 41*(4), 254–270.

Center, Y., Wheldall, K., Freeman, L., Outhred, L., & McNaught, M. (1995). An evaluation of Reading Recovery. *Reading Research Quarterly, 30*, 240–263.

Chard, D. J. (2004). Toward a science of professional development in early reading instruction. *Exceptionality, 12*(3), 175–191.

Clay, M. (1987). Learning to be learning disabled. *New Zealand Journal of Educational Studies, 22*, 155–173.

Denton, C. A., Fletcher, J. M., Anthony, J. L., & Francis, D. J. (2006). An evaluation of intensive intervention for students with persistent reading difficulties. *Journal of Learning Disabilities, 39*, 447–466.

Duffy, G. G., & Hoffman, J. V. (1999). In pursuit of an illusion: The flawed search for a perfect method. *Reading Teacher, 53*(1), 10–16.

Dweck, C. S. (1999). *Self-Theories: Their role in motivation, personality, and development.* Philadelphia: Taylor & Francis.

Fletcher, J. M., Denton, C. A., & Francis, D. J. (2005). Validity of alternative approaches for the identification of learning disabilities: Operationalizing unexpected underachievement. *Journal of Learning Disabilities, 38*(6), 545–552.

Fletcher, J. M., Shaywitz, S. E., Shankweiler, D., Katz, I., Liberman, I.,

Steubing, K. K., et al. (1994). Cognitive profiles of reading disability: Comparisons of discrepancy and low achievement definitions. *Journal of Educational Psychology, 86,* 6–23.

Foorman, B. R., Francis, D. J., Chen, D. T., Carlson, C., Moats, L., & Fletcher, J. (2003). The necessity of the alphabetic principle to phonemic awareness instruction. *Readings and Writing, 16,* 289–324.

Foorman, B. R., & Moats, L. C. (2004). Conditions for sustaining research-based practices in early reading. *Remedial and Special Education, 25*(1), 51–60.

Francis, D. J., Santi, K. L., Barr, C., Fletcher, J. M., Varisco, A., & Foorman, B. R. (2008). Form effects on the estimation of students' oral reading fluency using DIBELS. *Journal of School Psychology, 46,* 315–342.

Fuchs, D., & Fuchs, L. S. (2006). Introduction to response to intervention: What, why, and how valid is it? *Reading Research Quarterly, 41*(1), 93–98.

Fuchs, L. S., & Fuchs, D. (2008). The role of assessment within the RTI framework. In D. Fuchs, L. S. Fuchs, & S. Vaughn (Eds.), *Response to intervention: A framework for educators* (pp. 105–122). Newark, DE: International Reading Association.

Fuchs, L. S., Fuchs, D., Hosp, M. K., & Jenkins, J. R. (2001). Oral reading fluency as an indicator of reading competence: A theoretical, empirical, and historical analysis. *Scientific Studies of Reading, 5,* 239–256.

Fuchs, D., Mock, D., Morgan, P. L., & Young, C. L. (2003). Responsiveness-to-Intervention: Definitions, evidence, and implications for the learning disabilities construct. *Learning Disabilities Research & Practice, 18*(3), 157–171.

Gomez-Bellenge, F. X., Rogers, E., & Fullerton, S. K. (2003). *Reading recovery and descubriendo la lectura national report 2001–2002.* Columbus: Ohio State University, Reading Recovery National Data Evaluation Center.

Good, R. H., Kaminski, R. A., Smith, S., Laimon, D., & Dill, S. (2001). *Dynamic indicators of basic early literacy skills* (5th ed.). Eugene: University of Oregon.

Good, R. H., Simmons D. C, & Kame'enui, E. J. (2001). The importance and decision-making utility of a continuum of fluency-based indicators of foundational reading skills for third-grade high-stakes outcomes. *Scientific Studies of Reading, 5,* 257–288.

Gresham, F. M. (2002). Responsiveness to intervention: An alternative approach to the identification of learning disabilities. In R. Bradley, L. Danielson, & D. Hallahan (Eds.), *Identification of learning disabilities: Research to practice* (pp. 467–564). Mahwah, NJ: Erlbaum.

Jenkins, J. R., & O'Connor, R. E. (2002). Early identification and intervention for young children with reading/learning disabilities. In R. Bradley, L. Danielson, & D. Hallahan (Eds.), *Identificaiton of learning disabilities: Research to practice* (pp. 99–149). Mahwah, NJ: Erlbaum.

Johnston, P. H., Allington, R. L., & Afflerbach, P. (1985). The congruence of classroom and remedial reading instruction. *Elementary School Journal, 85,* 465–478.

Kavale, K. A., & Forness, S. R. (1999). Effectiveness of special education. In C. R. Reynolds & T. B. Gutkin (Eds.), *The handbook of school psychology* (3rd ed., pp. 984–1024). New York: Wiley.

Lovett, M. W., De Palma, M., Frijters, J., Steinbach, K., Temple, M., Benson, N., et al. (2008). Interventions for Reading Difficulties. *Journal of Learning Disabilities, 41*(4), 333–352.

Marston, D., Reschly, A. L., Lau, M. Y., Muyskens, P., & Canter, A. (2007). Historical perspectives and current trends in problem solving: The Minneapolis story. In D. Haager, J. Klingner, & S. Vaughn (Eds.), *Evidence-based reading practices for Response to Intervention* (pp. 265–285). Baltimore, MD: Brookes.

Mathes, P. G., Denton, C. A., Fletcher, J. M., Anthony, J. L., Francis, D. J., & Schatschneider, C. (2005). The effects of theoretically different instruction and student characteristics on the skills of struggling readers. *Reading Research Quarterly, 40*(2), 148–182.

McCutchen, D., Abbott, R. D., Green, L. B., Beretvas, S. N., Cox, S., Potter, N. S., et al. (2002). Beginning literacy: Links among teacher knowledge, teacher practice, and student learning. *Journal of Learning Disabilities, 35*(1), 69–86.

McGill-Franzen, A. (2006). *Kindergarten literacy: Matching assessment and instruction in kindergarten.* New York: Scholastic.

Mellard, D. F., & Johnson, E. (2008). *RTI: A practitioner's guide to implementing response to intervention.* Thousand Oaks, CA: Corwin Press.

Mosenthal, J., Lipson, M., Torncello, S., Russ, B., & Mekkelsen, J. (2004). Contexts and practices of six schools successful in obtaining reading achievement. *Elementary School Journal, 104*(5), 343–367.

Nye, B., Konstantopoulos, S., & Hedges, L. V. (2004). How large are teacher effects? *Educational Evaluation & Policy Analysis, 26*(3), 237–257.

O'Connor, R. E. (2000). Increasing the intensity of intervention in kindergarten and first grade. *Learning Disabilities Research & Practice, 15*(1), 43–54.

O'Connor, R. E., Harty, K. R., & Fulmer, D. (2005). Tiers of intervention in kindergarten through third grade. *Journal of Learning Disabilities, 38*(6), 532–538.

Paris, S. G. (2005). Reinterpreting the development of reading skills. *Reading Research Quarterly, 40*(2), 184–202.

Pearson, P. D. (2006). Foreword. In K. S. Goodman (Ed.), *The truth about DIBELS: What it is, what it does* (pp. v–viii). Portsmouth, NH: Heinemann.

Phillips, G., & Smith, P. (1997). *A third chance to learn: The development and evaluation of specialized interventions for young children experiencing the greatest difficulty in learning to read.* Wellington, NZ: New Zealand Council for Educational Reserach.

Pinnell, G. (1989). Reading Recovery: Helping at risk children to read. *Elementary School Journal, 90*(2), 159–181.

Pinnell, G., Lyons, C., Deford, D. E., Bryk, A., & Seltzer, M. (1994). Comparing instructional models for the literacy education of high-risk first graders. *Reading Research Quarterly, 29,* 8–39.

Samuels, S. J. (2007). The DIBELS tests: Is speed of barking at print what we mean by reading fluency? *Reading Research Quarterly, 42*(4), 563–566.

Scanlon, D. M., Anderson, K., & Sweeney, J. M. (2010). *Early intervention for reading difficulties: The interactive strategies approach.* New York: Guilford.

Scanlon, D. M., Gelzheiser, L. M., Vellutino, F. R., Schatschneider, C., & Sweeney, J. M. (2008). Reducing the incidence of early reading difficulties: Professional development for classroom teachers vs. direct interventions for children. *Learning and Individual Differences, 18,* 346–359.

Scanlon, D. M., & Vellutino, F. R. (1996). Prerequisite skills, early instruction and success in first-grade reading: Selected results from a longitudinal study. *Mental Retardation and Developmental Disabilities Research Reviews, 2,* 54–63.

Scanlon, D. M., & Vellutino, F. R. (1997). A comparison of the instructional backgrounds and cognitive profiles of poor, average and good readers who were initially identified as at risk for reading failure. *Scientific Studies of Reading, 1,* 191–216.

Scanlon, D. M., Vellutino, F. R., Small, S. G., Fanuele, D. P., & Sweeney, J.M. (2005). Severe reading difficulties—Can they be prevented? A comparison of prevention and intervention approaches. *Exceptionality, 13*(4), 209–227.

Schatschneider, C., Wagner, R. K., & Crawford, E. C. (2008). The importance of measuring growth in response to intervention models: Testing a core assumption. *Learning & Individual Differences, 18*(3), 308–315.

Shanahan, T., Kamil, M. L., & Tobin, A. W. (1982). Cloze as a measure of intersentential comprehension. *Reading Research Quarterly, 17,* 229–255.

Simmons, D. C., Kame'enui, E. J., Stoolmiller, M., Coyne, M. D., & Harn, B. (2003). Accelerating growth and maintaining proficiency: A two-year intervention study of kindergarten and first grade children at-risk for reading difficulties. In B. R. Foorman (Ed.), *Preventing and remediating reading difficulties: Bringing science to scale* (pp. 197–228). Baltimore, MD: York Press.

Stanovich, K. E., & Siegel, L. S. (1994). Phenotypic performance profiles of children with reading disabilities: A regression-based test of the phonological-core variable-difference model. *Journal of Educational Psychology, 86*(1), 24–53.

Stecker, P. M., Fuchs, L. S., & Fuchs, D. (2005). Using curriculum based measurement to improve student achievement: Review of research. *Psychology in the Schools, 42*(8), 795–819.

Taylor, B. M., Pearson, P. D., Clark, K. M., & Walpole, S. (2000). Effective schools and accomplished teachers: Lessons about primary-grade reading instruction in low-income schools. *Elementary School Journal, 101*, 121–165.

Tivnan, T., & Hemphill, L. (2005). Comparing four literacy reform models in high-poverty schools: Patterns of first grade achievement. *The Elementary School Journal, 105*(5), 419–441.

Torgesen, J. K. (2002). The prevention of reading difficulties. *Journal of School Psychology, 40*(1), 7–26.

Torgesen, J. K., & Wagner, R. K. (1999). Preventing reading failure in young children with phonological processing disabilities: Group and individual responses to instruction. *Journal of Educational Psychology, 91*(4), 579–593.

Torgesen, J. K., Alexander, A. W., Wagner, R. K., Rashotte, C. A., Voeller, K., & Conway, T. (2001). Intensive remedial instruction for students with severe reading disabilities: Immediate and long-term outcomes from two instructional approaches. *Journal of Learning Disabilities, 34*, 33–58.

Torgesen, J. K., Rashotte, C., Alexander, A. W., Alexander, J., & MacPhee, K. (2003). Progress toward understanding the instructional conditions necessary for remediating reading difficulties in older children. In B. Foorman (Ed.), *Preventing and remediating reading difficulties: Bringing science to scale* (pp. 275–298). Parkton, MD: York Press.

Vaughn, S., Fletcher, J. M., Francis, D. J., Denton, C. A., Wanzek, J., Wexler, J., et al. (2008). Response to intervention with older students with reading difficulties. *Learning and Individual Differences, 18*(3), 338–345.

Vaughn, S., Linan-Thompson, S., & Hickman, P. (2003). Response to treatment as a means of identifying students with reading / learning disabilities. *Exceptional Children, 69*(4), 391–409.

Vellutino, F. R., & Scanlon, D. M. (2002). The interactive strategies approach to reading intervention. *Contemporary Educational Psychology, 27*, 573–635.

Vellutino, F. R., Scanlon, D. M., & Lyon, G. R. (2000). Differentiating between difficult-to-remediate and readily remediated poor readers: More evidence against the IQ—Achievement discrepancy definition of reading disability. *Journal of Learning Disabilities, 33*(3), 223–238.

Vellutino, F. R., Scanlon, D. M., Sipay, E. R., Small, S. G., Pratt, A., Chen, R., et al. (1996). Cognitive profiles of difficult-to-remediate and readily remediated poor readers: Early intervention as a vehicle for distinguishing between cognitive and experiential deficits as basic causes of specific reading disability. *Journal of Educational Psychology, 88*, 601–638.

Wanzek, J., & Vaughn, S. (2008). Response to varying amounts of time in reading intervention for students with low response to intervention. *Journal of Learning Disabilities, 42*(2), 126–142.

Yell, M. L., Shriner, J. G., & Katsiyannis, A. (2006). Individuals With Disabilities Education Improvement Act of 2004 and IDEA Regulations of 2006: Implications for educators, administrators, and teacher trainers. *Focus on Exceptional Children, 39*(1), 1–24.

14

Patterns of Reading Disabilities across Development

Louise Spear-Swerling
Southern Connecticut State University

Jason is a second grader in an affluent school district who has struggled in reading since kindergarten. Although Jason has an extensive oral vocabulary and excellent listening comprehension, his difficulties with decoding printed words have greatly impaired his reading comprehension in grade-appropriate text. William, a third grader in an urban school, has severe decoding difficulties similar to Jason's but also has limited vocabulary knowledge that affects his comprehension adversely, in listening as well as reading activities. Grace, an eighth grader in a suburban junior high, progressed normally in reading in the early grades and has no history of word decoding problems. However, she cannot comprehend many of the complex texts used at upper grade levels and is having particular difficulty understanding textbooks in content areas such as science. None of the children has intellectual, sensory, or emotional disabilities that might account for his or her poor reading.

At one time, of these three youngsters, it is likely that only Jason would have met identification criteria for learning disabilities (LDs), the category under which children with reading disabilities (RDs) are served in public schools. However, landmark changes in federal legislation, the Individuals with Disabilities Education Improvement Act (P.L. 108-446) of 2004 (IDEA 2004), have transformed this situation. It is now quite possible for all three students, and many others like them, to be identified with reading disabilities. Is this event a desirable one? It could be, if being identified with RDs led to some clear advantages for the children, for example, receiving earlier or more effective intervention that helped them overcome their reading difficulties. However, for those benefits to be realized, many problems with school identification of reading disabilities must be addressed. Why IDEA 2004 will likely lead to identification of more varied patterns of reading disabilities, and how knowledge about the patterns can improve educational practice to benefit struggling readers (whether or not they have genuine RDs), are the subjects of this chapter.

The chapter begins by discussing how reading disabilities are generally conceptualized and defined, both in the scientific literature and in educational settings. The second section of the chapter summarizes research findings on problems with school classification of struggling readers as having RDs; the third and fourth sections review research on reading development and different patterns of difficulties in reading and explain why more varied patterns of reading disabilities may be identified in educational settings under IDEA 2004. The fifth section presents five challenges that must be met to avoid perpetuating certain problems involved in classification of students with RDs, which can be informed or addressed by knowledge about patterns of reading difficulties. The chapter concludes with some suggestions for educators with regard to assessment in reading.

Definitions of Reading Disabilities

Three concepts have long been central to definitions of reading disabilities: unexpected low achievement, the intrinsic nature of RDs, and specificity (e.g., Fletcher, Lyon, Fuchs, & Barnes, 2007; Spear-Swerling & Sternberg, 1996; Stanovich, 1986, 1991; Torgesen, 1991). Unexpected low achievement involves the idea that RDs cannot be explained by other known causes of poor reading, such as other disabilities associated with reading failure (e.g., hearing impairment or intellectual disabilities), poverty, poor instruction, or lack of opportunity to learn. Reading disabilities also are viewed as intrinsic, that is, they are assumed to be caused primarily by genuine disorders in learning, not by extrinsic factors such as inadequate teaching. Poor teaching or lack of educational opportunities certainly may exacerbate reading disabilities. However, reading difficulties due mainly to these kinds of extrinsic factors, rather than to intrinsic learning problems, would not be considered true RDs by the vast majority of past or current authorities in the field.

Specificity means that reading disabilities entail difficulties in a subset of academic and cognitive domains rather than generalized cognitive impairments or broad developmental delays. In relation to reading, specificity is a thorny concept, because difficulties in a relatively circumscribed area of reading, such as word recognition, can impact literacy and overall academic functioning quite broadly (Stanovich, 1986). For example, inaccurate word recognition tends to be associated with slow rate of reading and poor reading comprehension, which in turn may affect performance across many academic domains that depend upon good reading skills. Nevertheless, children with RDs usually are viewed as having certain areas of academic strength (e.g., mathematics or vocabulary knowledge), as well as typical development in most or all areas of adaptive functioning (e.g., social skills and self-help skills such as dressing oneself) that contrast with their weaknesses in reading.

In federal and state educational guidelines, reading disabilities are subsumed under the umbrella category of learning disabilities, the largest single category in which K–12 students with disabilities are served in special education in American public schools. Nationwide, approximately half of all students in special education are classified with LDs (Denton, Vaughn, & Fletcher, 2003), with the majority of these students identified due to problems in reading (e.g., Kavale & Reese, 1992). Although educational guidelines vary somewhat from state to state and require several different criteria to be met in order for children to be identified with LDs, the following criteria are prominent.

First, low achievement is necessary. With regard to RDs, children may be identified based on low achievement in basic reading skills, reading comprehension, or reading fluency. Second, exclusionary criteria must be met. Exclusionary criteria require other disabilities, as well as extrinsic factors such as poverty and inadequate teaching, to be ruled out as primary causes of children's learning problems in order for them to be identified with LDs. And third, prior to IDEA 2004, federal and most state guidelines required an ability-achievement discrepancy, usually operationalized as a discrepancy between IQ and reading achievement. IQ-achievement discrepancy criteria involve comparing children's IQ scores to their reading achievement on individually administered standardized tests; to meet the discrepancy requirement, a child's IQ must be high relative to his or her reading achievement. However, IDEA 2004 and its accompanying 2005 federal regulations grant schools the option to drop IQ-achievement discrepancy criteria and instead to employ response-to-intervention (RtI) approaches to identification—the landmark change alluded to above.

Response-to-intervention approaches involve far more systematic attempts to rule out inadequate instruction as the primary cause of a child's reading difficulties than have previous approaches to identification of LDs. In RtI approaches, children with RDs are conceptualized as those who respond insufficiently to research-based reading instruction and interventions that are effective with most students. RtI models emphasize high-quality general education practices as a way to prevent reading problems in many children, as well as the need to screen all children and monitor their reading progress so that problems can be detected and addressed early. Universal screening and progress monitoring also may avoid the potential bias inherent in relying upon teacher referral as a gate to identification and intervention (see, e.g., Shaywitz, Shaywitz, Fletcher, & Escobar, 1990; Speece, Case, & Molloy, 2003). Interventions in RtI approaches involve multiple tiers or levels, with increasing intensity of intervention across tiers. Children who fail to make adequate progress even at the most intensive level of intervention are candidates for special education evaluation and services. Those who meet eligibility criteria for RDs (e.g., children with inadequate progress in basic reading, reading fluency, and/or reading comprehension, who also meet exclusionary criteria) would be assumed to have genuine reading disabilities.

IDEA 2004 and RtI approaches do not abandon the three concepts fundamental to RDs mentioned earlier: unexpectedness, specificity, and their intrinsic nature. However, in RtI models, unexpectedness is defined partially in relation to expected progress in reading: Children with RDs are those who demonstrate unexpectedly poor progress despite appropriate intervention, with poor progress usually measured both in relation to children's level of performance and to their rate of growth (e.g., Speece et al., 2003). Moreover, although IDEA 2004 maintains a clear distinction between reading disabilities and the more generalized problems characteristic of intellectual disabilities, it may lead to a weaker version of the assumption of specificity and result in the identification of a wider range of reading problems in the category of LDs, as discussed further below.

Problems in Classifying Struggling Readers as Having RDS

Two basic premises of this chapter are that genuine reading disabilities do exist, and that identification may benefit children with true RDs by providing them with early, appropriate intervention. However, research on school identification of RDs has yielded many disturbing findings. For example, myriad problems with the IQ-achievement discrepancy requirement have been detailed in the scientific literature (e.g., Fletcher et al., 2007; Siegel, 1988; Spear-Swerling & Sternberg, 1996; Stanovich, 1991, 2000). These problems include the following: discrepancy criteria make early identification of RDs difficult, because it takes time for struggling readers to amass a sufficiently large discrepancy to qualify for services; IQ tests are not valid measures of broad potential for learning and are especially problematic for certain populations such as English language learners and low-socioeconomic status (SES) children; there is little evidence to justify an educational distinction between IQ discrepant and nondiscrepant poor readers (i.e., children whose IQs are not high enough relative to their reading achievement for them to meet discrepancy criteria); and nondiscrepant poor readers may be erroneously viewed as intellectually "limited" and incapable of improvement. In addition, discrepancy criteria provide little instructionally relevant information to teachers and may contribute to inadequate remedial efforts (Aaron, Joshi, Gooden, & Bentum, 2008; Vaughn, Levy, Coleman, & Bos, 2002).

Other research on educational identification of reading disabilities has raised concerns about the role that general education practices play in many children's reading problems. Classroom reading instruction often fails to employ the kinds of instructional approaches found effective with at-risk students (Allington & McGill-Franzen, in press; Juel & Minden-Cupp, 2000; Spear-Swerling & Sternberg, 1996), both with regard to basic word-recognition skills and to comprehension. Children enter kindergarten with substantial individual differences in language and literacy knowledge (e.g., Neuman & Dickinson, 2002), and unfortunately, formal schooling sometimes may exacerbate rather than ameliorate these initial differences. For example, Duke (2000) found pervasive differences in first graders' exposure to and experiences with print based on the socioeconomic status of their schools, with students at very high-SES schools having more library resources, more opportunities to use those resources, and more experience with extended forms of text, than students at very low-SES schools. Consistent with the idea that formal schooling sometimes intensifies initial differences among students, Scarborough (1998) points out that the relationship between SES and reading achievement is more complex than is sometimes recognized, with the SES-reading achievement correlation much stronger at the level of the school than at the level of individual students' families.

Studies involving at-risk primary-grade children suggest that, with well-designed, research-based intervention, most struggling readers can reach grade-level expectations (Al Otaiba, 2001; Vellutino & Scanlon, 2002). Nevertheless, the requirement to rule out inadequate instruction before classifying struggling readers with LDs rarely appears to have been addressed seriously in educational practice; in fact, students classified with LDs frequently do not meet basic eligibility requirements for that category (MacMillan & Speece, 1999; Scruggs & Mastropieri, 2002). Individual teachers' readiness to refer children for learning disabilities evaluations is heavily influenced by contextual factors, including children's gender and behavior, as well as teachers' instructional preferences and available resources. For instance, Shaywitz et al. (1990) found that, although serious reading difficulties occurred roughly as often in girls as in boys, boys were more likely to be identified as having LDs by schools, apparently because boys were more likely to be perceived by their teachers as having behavior problems. Drame (2002) gave teachers descriptions of children with academic or behavioral problems and found that teachers who preferred whole-class groupings for reading instruction were more likely to recommend children for evaluations for LDs than were teachers who used a combination of grouping practices. Once in the special education system, children

classified as having LDs usually show limited progress and rarely catch up to their grade-level peers (Bentum & Aaron, 2003; Moody, Vaughn, Hughes, & Fischer, 2000; Vaughn, Moody, & Schumm, 1998).

These kinds of research findings helped to prompt the changes in federal legislation described at the outset of the chapter, allowing the elimination of IQ-achievement discrepancy criteria and the use of response-to-intervention methods of identification. However, because IDEA 2004 makes the elimination of IQ-achievement discrepancy criteria optional, it appears that many states will retain the use of an IQ-achievement discrepancy in identification of LDs (Zirkel & Krohn, 2008), often in conjunction with RtI approaches. These approaches can only be as effective as the quality, appropriateness, and timeliness of the intervention offered to struggling readers. As will be discussed next, struggling readers vary in their intervention needs, with these needs best understood in relation to typical reading development.

Reading Development across the K–12 Grade Span

Research-based models of reading development in typical children (e.g., Chall, 1983; Ehri, 1991; Gough & Tunmer, 1986; Rupley, Willson, & Nichols, 1998; Spear-Swerling, 2004a; Stanovich, 2000) have emphasized the importance of two broad types of abilities in learning to read: word recognition and oral language comprehension. Each of these two broad types of abilities encompasses many important related skills, abilities, and types of knowledge. For instance, word recognition includes knowledge of letter-sound relationships, an understanding of basic print concepts, the ability to decode unfamiliar words, and automatic as well as accurate recognition of words; oral language comprehension includes vocabulary knowledge, sentence and discourse processing, knowledge of text and discourse structure, background knowledge, inferencing, and the capacity to use a variety of comprehension strategies.

Phonological processes play an important role in word recognition in English and other alphabetic languages. Phonological processes involve the use of phonological codes (abstract mental representations of speech sounds), or of actual speech, in a variety of cognitive and linguistic tasks, including memory and oral language as well as written language (Scarborough & Brady, 2002). For example, phonemic awareness, which involves awareness and manipulation of individual sounds in spoken words (e.g., being able to blend orally the three separate sounds, /w/, /i/, /sh/, into the spoken word wish) greatly assists decoding of printed words. Morphemic knowledge—knowledge about meaning units in words, such as common roots, prefixes, and suffixes—also plays an important role in word recognition, as well as in vocabulary and spelling, especially as children advance beyond the beginning stages of learning to read.

Word recognition and comprehension abilities develop in tandem with each other in reading acquisition. Nevertheless, most models of reading development emphasize the relatively greater importance of children's acquisition of word-recognition skills in the early grades, and the relatively greater importance of higher-order comprehension abilities in the later grades. Without some threshold level of word recognition, children cannot comprehend even the simplest texts, so in the early grades, limitations on reading comprehension often revolve around word recognition. However, as typical readers advance beyond Grade 3, most have already acquired basic word-recognition skills, and the texts used in school become increasingly longer and more challenging in terms of comprehension, so limitations on reading comprehension begin to center more upon language comprehension.

Reading demands continue to escalate throughout middle and high school, especially with regard to volume of reading and the complexity of comprehension tasks (e.g., contrasting two different novels with similar themes, or analyzing and synthesizing information from a variety of sources to write a paper). Moreover, children's reading experiences outside of school influence their subsequent language and literacy development; for example, independent pleasure reading is an important source of vocabulary and background knowledge, especially among older children and adults (Cunningham & Stanovich, 1991). In other words, reading and oral language have an interactive, mutually facilitative relationship. Of course, children's reading development also is heavily influenced by their experiences in school, and in particular, by the nature of instruction (Allington & McGill-Franzen, in press; Duffy, 2004; Juel & Minden-Cupp, 2000; Spear-Swerling, 2004a; Vellutino & Scanlon, 2002). Reading acquisition therefore must be viewed as a lengthy, ongoing process that taps many interacting abilities over time, with certain types of abilities relatively more important at particular stages of development, and with development influenced by experience and instruction as well as children's innate capacities.

Common Patterns of Reading Difficulties across Development

Researchers have identified at least three patterns common in struggling readers: children who have good oral language comprehension but specific word recognition difficulties, usually associated with poor decoding skills (e.g., Jason in the opening anecdote to this chapter); children who have good word recognition and decoding skills but specific reading comprehension difficulties (e.g., Grace); and mixed reading difficulties involving both word recognition and comprehension (e.g., William). Here the term comprehension-based reading difficulties will be used to allude to the latter two patterns collectively.

Although the prevalence of each pattern is nontrivial across many studies (Aaron, Joshi, & Williams, 1999; Badian, 1999; Catts, Fey, Zhang, & Tomblin, 1999; Catts, Hogan, & Adlof, 2005; Catts, Hogan, & Fey, 2003; Leach, Scarborough, & Rescorla, 2003; Nation, 2005; Nation

& Snowling, 1997; Spear-Swerling, 2004b), the relative frequency of the patterns has varied depending on methodology (e.g., the specific measures used to assess reading-related abilities and the specific criteria for defining poor performance), as well as on the age and characteristics of the population studied. For example, Leach et al. (2003) found that specific reading comprehension difficulties involved only about 6% of reading problems identified in third grade or earlier, with most reading difficulties about evenly split between the other two patterns; however, reading problems identified after Grade 3 were highly heterogeneous, with each of the three patterns constituting roughly one-third of poor readers. In a sample of children with a high incidence of early language impairments, Catts et al. (2005) identified approximately 31% of struggling second-grade readers as adequate decoders but poor comprehenders in reading, and even higher percentages of this pattern in fourth and eighth grade (roughly 45% and 54%, respectively, of poor readers).

The focus of the review in this section involves children learning to read English; the cognitive correlates of reading disabilities and developmental patterns associated with poor reading may vary across languages, especially between alphabetic languages like English and nonalphabetic languages such as Chinese (e.g., Ho, Chan, Leung, Lee, & Tsang, 2005). Of course, merely demonstrating a given pattern of reading difficulties does not mean that an individual has reading disabilities. Rather, to be consistent with past and present conceptualizations of RDs, an individual's difficulties must be unexpected with regard to other known causes of poor reading (e.g., sensory disabilities), relatively specific (e.g., distinct from intellectual disabilities), and apparently intrinsic (e.g., not primarily associated with some clear extrinsic cause, such as inadequate instruction).

Specific Word Recognition Difficulties

Children with this pattern have approximately age-appropriate or better oral comprehension of language, including age-appropriate vocabulary knowledge, coupled with problems in word recognition. The problems typically are manifested in reading both real words and pseudowords such as gleck, although sometimes a child with a relatively strong sight vocabulary will have difficulty only with pseudowords (Spear-Swerling, 2004b; Spear-Swerling & Sternberg, 1996). Spelling also is notably impaired. For children with genuine reading disabilities, this is the most extensively researched pattern of RDs (e.g., Blachman, 1997; Fletcher et al., 2007; Stanovich, 1991, 2000; Stanovich & Siegel, 1994; Torgesen et al., 2001), as well as the one with the lengthiest research history (e.g., Hinshelwood, 1896). Although some investigators have attempted to establish different subtypes of specific word recognition disabilities, such as orthographic and phonological dyslexia (e.g., Castles & Coltheart, 1993), evidence suggests a phonological deficit in most children with this pattern of RDs (Rack, Snowling, & Olson, 1992; Shankweiler, Crain, Brady, & Macaruso,

1992; Spear-Swerling, 2004a; Stanovich, 2000; Stanovich & Siegel, 1994), and the term dyslexia has become a synonym for this pattern.

Specific word recognition difficulties frequently involve word recognition that is slow as well as inaccurate, with these difficulties affecting both text reading rate and speed of reading isolated words. Furthermore, it is possible to identify a group of poor readers whose word recognition difficulties involve only rate, not accuracy (Lovett, 1987). Slow reading is common in students with a history of inaccurate word recognition, even after accuracy has been remediated (Bruck, 1992; Torgesen et al., 2001). Practice plays an important role in developing speed of reading, and poor readers tend to have much more limited practice reading than do good readers, both in and out of school (Allington, 1983; Biemiller, 1977-1978; Cunningham & Stanovich, 1998). In children with a history of decoding problems, slow reading may be primarily due to cumulative deficits in exposure to printed words. Once established, these cumulative deficits in experience may extremely difficult to overcome (Torgesen et al., 2001). Whether some cases of slow word recognition constitute a separate subtype of reading disabilities emerging without a prior history of inaccurate decoding, and with distinct cognitive underpinnings such as slow naming speed (e.g., Wolf & Bowers, 1999), is controversial (Fletcher et al., 2007; Vellutino, Fletcher, Scanlon, & Snowling, 2004).

Specific word recognition difficulties appear early in schooling, when basic reading skills are first learned. Poor phonemic awareness—for instance, unusual difficulty blending sounds to form words or difficulty segmenting sounds in spoken words—is commonly associated with this pattern. Assuming a child has had adequate opportunity to learn phonological skills, poor phonemic awareness is generally believed to reflect the core deficit in dyslexia. For children with this pattern of reading disabilities, instruction in phonemic awareness and phonics is very important, and intensive instruction in these areas may be required for some children to achieve grade-level performance (Vellutino & Scanlon, 2002). Early identification and timely remediation of inaccurate word recognition also may help to prevent the problems with slow reading that are often seen in children with specific word recognition difficulties (Torgesen et al., 2001).

Specific Reading Comprehension Difficulties

This pattern of reading difficulties is characterized by roughly age-appropriate word recognition and phonological skills, coupled with reading comprehension difficulties. Often the comprehension problems emerge around fourth grade or later, and there is no history of early decoding difficulties. Many children with this pattern appear to have oral language weaknesses that affect listening as well as reading comprehension. That is, the children have language problems that are nonphonological in nature (Scarborough, 2005), and that usually are not severe enough for the child to meet criteria for speech/language services (Nation, 2005; Nation Clarke, Marshall, & Durand, 2004). Relatively subtle language weaknesses may not impact reading comprehension until the middle grades or later, when the texts used in school become much more challenging in terms of comprehension. However, the risk of developing reading problems at some future date is as great in young children with nonphonological language weaknesses as in those with difficulties in the phonological domain (Scarborough, 2005).

Oral language comprehension and reading comprehension are strongly related and draw upon many identical abilities; vocabulary is one good example. Obviously, if a child does not know the meaning of a word such as dejected, then even if he or she can decode the word, comprehension will suffer, in both listening and reading. Common comprehension difficulties affecting both listening and reading include not only vocabulary, but also problems with working memory, discourse integration skills, inferencing, comprehension monitoring, and many comprehension strategies such as summarization and prediction (Cain, Oakhill, & Bryant, 2000; Francis et al., 2006). However, other abilities underlying reading comprehension may be more specific to reading text. For instance, strategies such as rereading when something in a text does not make sense, and varying one's approach to reading to suit the purpose for reading (e.g., reading a text in preparation for an exam vs. skimming a text to find information for a research paper), are not usually applied in listening, because one does not ordinarily have the same control of the input in listening as in reading. Furthermore, reading comprehension can be influenced by factors beyond cognitive-linguistic abilities, such as engagement and motivation (e.g., Guthrie, Wigfield, Metsala, & Cox, 1999). Hence, one might expect to find that specific reading comprehension difficulties can occur even in children with good listening comprehension. Consistent with this view, the children with specific reading comprehension difficulties studied by Leach et al. (2003) functioned well within average range on a listening comprehension measure and had listening comprehension far above their level of reading comprehension. Likewise, in a longitudinal study, Catts et al. (2005) found that 15% of poor readers in second grade, 14% in fourth grade, and 24% in eighth grade fell into a "nonspecified" group: students who had poor reading comprehension despite having generally adequate skills in both word recognition and listening comprehension.

Research on specific comprehension difficulties is at a much earlier stage of development than is research on specific word recognition difficulties (Fletcher et al., 2007). Given the wide range of abilities that may contribute to reading comprehension across the K–12 grade span, multiple subtypes of RDs involving specific comprehension difficulties may exist—for example, difficulties related primarily to limitations in vocabulary knowledge vs. those related mainly to strategic weaknesses. These subtypes would likely have different intervention needs.

Mixed Reading Difficulties

Children with mixed reading difficulties have problems involving both word recognition and comprehension (Catts et al., 2005; Leach et al., 2003). They share the core phonological difficulties of children with dyslexia (Stanovich, 2000; Stanovich & Siegel, 1994), but their reading comprehension difficulties extend beyond what can be accounted for by inaccurate or slow word reading, to include the kinds of broader comprehension weaknesses mentioned in the previous section, such as weaknesses in vocabulary, listening comprehension, working memory, inferencing, or discourse integration skills. The term garden-variety poor readers has sometimes been used for children with this pattern of difficulty (Gough & Tunmer, 1986). Mixed reading difficulties usually become apparent in the early primary grades due to the child's poor decoding, but persist even after the remediation of word-recognition problems or even when the child is reading material he or she can decode accurately, because there is an additional comprehension component to the child's difficulties. The intervention requirements of children with this pattern of reading disabilities are relatively complex. Most will require intervention that addresses not only phonemic awareness and phonics, but also their particular comprehension needs (e.g., vocabulary development vs. comprehension strategies vs. inferencing).

Possible Shifts in Individual Children's Patterns across Development

It must be emphasized that individual children's patterns of reading difficulties may shift over time. For example, in a longitudinal study, Chall, Jacobs, and Baldwin (1990) followed a group of low-SES children with a pattern of specific reading comprehension difficulties: adequate reading progress in the early grades, but later comprehension difficulties associated with limitations in vocabulary knowledge. Although children's vocabulary weaknesses became apparent around Grade 4, these weaknesses did not significantly impact reading comprehension until about Grade 6 or 7, with a progressive decline in reading comprehension from that point on. Decelerations in vocabulary also were associated with subsequent decelerations in word recognition and spelling, perhaps because of the role of vocabulary and morphemic knowledge in reading more sophisticated words at upper grade levels (Ehri, 1991). For instance, a pure decoding process may yield a rough approximation of the words phenomenon and vociferous, but knowledge of the meaning of the words, and oral familiarity with them, would greatly assist accurately reading them. As another example of a possible pattern shift, children with specific word recognition difficulties in the early grades might show more mixed reading difficulties later if their instruction does not sufficiently address vocabulary and comprehension development.

Despite possible long-term shifts in poor readers' pat-terns of difficulties, information about the patterns is very useful in planning instruction for individual children at particular points in time. This information also can enable preventive educational programming for many at-risk children. For instance, early, effective teaching of phonemic awareness and phonics can help prevent specific word recognition difficulties (Juel & Minden-Cupp, 2000; Vellutino & Scanlon, 2002); greater emphasis on vocabulary development in early reading curricula may prevent the cumulative vocabulary deficits seen in many low-SES children and subsequent reading comprehension declines in the middle grades (Biemiller, 1999).

The Impact of IDEA 2004

Specific word recognition difficulties are the pattern most commonly associated with reading disabilities when an IQ-achievement discrepancy is one of the requirements for identification, as was generally true prior to IDEA 2004. IQ tests used in most school evaluations have a strong verbal component, for example, tasks that require defining word meanings or explaining how two objects are similar. Poor readers with strong verbal skills, and especially those with good vocabularies (Sternberg & Grigorenko, 2002), are more likely to have IQ scores that substantially exceed their reading achievement. Conversely, this IQ-reading gap is less likely for poor readers with broad language and vocabulary weaknesses, which are more characteristic of children with comprehension-based reading disabilities, including both specific comprehension difficulties and mixed reading difficulties.

Currently, children identified with reading disabilities usually have problems with word recognition (Fletcher et al., 2007). However, this situation could change in the future with less frequent use of the discrepancy requirement. With unexpectedness defined in relation to reading progress rather than IQ, many children with comprehension-based reading difficulties could be classified with RDs, assuming they meet exclusionary criteria and have failed to make adequate progress with appropriate research-based interventions. Children with comprehension-based reading disabilities probably will have broader academic problems than do those with dyslexia. As Stanovich (2000) notes, the assumption of specificity central to definitions of dyslexia led most researchers to emphasize word recognition as its locus, "rather than a process which operates across a wide variety of domains" (p. 114). It is difficult to identify a domain of schooling not directly influenced by comprehension processes. Although the word recognition and phonological problems characteristic of dyslexia often indirectly affect many academic areas, as when students' inaccurate or slow reading impairs their reading comprehension, these problems still are likely to be relatively narrow compared to those of students with comprehension-based reading disabilities. For example, in content areas such as social studies or science, a student with dyslexia usually can do well acquiring information presented orally, whereas some students with comprehension-based reading disabilities may have as much difficulty comprehending oral information as with reading.

Challenges and Opportunities

The provisions of IDEA 2004, and RtI approaches in particular, provide opportunities to improve educational practice and benefit struggling readers, including those with genuine reading disabilities. To ensure that these provisions actually help children rather than repeat past mistakes, some key challenges will need to be met. RtI entails many technical problems, such as difficulties involved in bringing RtI to large-scale implementation in schools, as well as the need for additional research in many areas, such as on the use of RtI at the middle and secondary levels (e.g., Denton et al., 2003; Fuchs & Deshler, 2007; Vaughn & Fuchs, 2003). These issues are important and should be addressed. Here, however, the focus will be on challenges that could be met, or at least ameliorated, if what is already known about reading development and patterns of reading difficulties were applied consistently in educational practice.

Challenge #1: Complete Elimination of IQ-Achievement Discrepancy Criteria
Unlike information about patterns of reading difficulties, IQ-achievement discrepancy criteria fail to provide educators with instructionally useful information. As of this writing, however, it appears that many states will continue using an IQ-achievement discrepancy in identification of RDs, often in combination with RtI approaches (Zirkel & Krohn, 2008). Likewise, some professional practitioner groups, such as school psychologists, appear generally to embrace RtI while remaining reluctant to eliminate the use of an IQ-achievement discrepancy (Machek & Nelson, 2007).

Continued use of an IQ-achievement discrepancy will perpetuate many problems mentioned earlier: limited validity of IQ tests as measures of broad capacity for learning, time and resources expended on IQ testing that is not educationally useful and sometimes actually harmful (e.g., in creating low expectations for some children), and the lack of evidence to justify an educational distinction based on IQ-achievement discrepancy. A discrepancy requirement also will tend to impede identification of children with true comprehension-based reading disabilities, who may be viewed as lacking "potential" to learn, and it may serve to maintain existing identification practices with only lip service paid to RtI. The IQ-achievement discrepancy must go. Replacing it with a focus on common patterns of reading difficulties would provide teachers with a much more accurate, educationally relevant way to conceptualize RDs.

Challenge #2: Early Identification of Comprehension-based Reading Disabilities
At present, screening measures for reading problems in the primary grades usually emphasize phonological awareness and decoding skills. These measures are very helpful in early identification of children whose difficulties include word recognition. However, the addition of nonphonological language measures to screening assessments, such as oral vocabulary or listening comprehension, might improve the accuracy of early identification efforts (Gersten & Dimino, 2006; Riedel, 2007; Scarborough, 2005) as well as detect more children with difficulties in the domain of comprehension. In some cases of specific comprehension difficulties, nonphonological language measures might detect risk for reading problems before actual reading difficulties have emerged (e.g., Chall et al., 1990), enabling intervention efforts focused on vocabulary and language comprehension to prevent later reading comprehension problems entirely. This possibility is important because, just as in the domain of word recognition, once children have fallen substantially behind their peers in vocabulary knowledge and language comprehension, catching them up is often very difficult (Biemiller, 1999).

Nevertheless, not all students with comprehension-based difficulties have poor listening comprehension or poor vocabularies; therefore, even the best primary-grade identification efforts will miss some of these children, such as those whose problems emerge only in relation to escalating reading comprehension demands at the middle and secondary levels. This phenomenon requires conceptualizing "early identification" as involving identification at the point when problems first become detectable, not necessarily identification in the primary grades.

Challenge #3: Diagnostic Assessment of Struggling Readers
Although some patterns of reading difficulties are more common at certain grade levels, each pattern occurs across a wide grade range. Distinguishing whether an individual struggling reader has specific word recognition difficulties, specific reading comprehension difficulties, or mixed difficulties in both areas, necessitates diagnostic assessment that measures areas such as phonemic awareness, word recognition, decoding, vocabulary, oral comprehension, and reading comprehension. Furthermore, for children with comprehension-based reading difficulties, diagnostic assessment of different comprehension-related abilities at the sentence and discourse levels (e.g., use of comprehension strategies, inferencing, understanding of text and discourse structure) is important for effective intervention.

Unfortunately, most existing reading comprehension tests are broad measures that do not help teachers pinpoint specific comprehension weaknesses in individual students (see Francis et al., 2006, for a counter-example). They rarely approximate the kinds of complex comprehension tasks required of children in school, especially beyond the early grades, and may sometimes fail to detect children with significant comprehension weaknesses (Allington & McGill-Franzen, in press; RAND Reading Study Group, 2002). Therefore, a thorough diagnostic assessment of comprehension requires multiple measures and procedures—including not only standardized tests but also observations, questionnaires, think-alouds, informal reading inventories, and curriculum-based measures—as well as a consideration of the strengths and limitations of each type of measure (Klingner, Vaughn, & Boardman, 2007). The classroom and instructional context, and how individual students' performance may vary depending on context, also must be taken into account (Johnston & Costello, 2005).

Studies highlighting the heterogeneity of patterns of reading difficulties (Catts et al., 2005; Leach et al., 2003; Spear-Swerling, 2004b) have shown that word recognition difficulties remain relatively common in older struggling readers, either as specific difficulties or as part of the mixed pattern of difficulties involving both word recognition and comprehension; for instance, approximately 46% of eighth-grade struggling readers in Catts et al. (2005) and approximately two-thirds of struggling readers identified beyond Grade 3 in Leach et al. (2003) had difficulties with word recognition. As noted earlier, word-recognition difficulties may sometimes emerge at upper grade levels, even when children do not have a history of early decoding problems, in relation to vocabulary weaknesses and demands for reading more complex, multisyllabic words (Chall et al., 1990). Diagnostic assessment of reading comprehension should routinely include this area as well as the many others important to good reading comprehension mentioned above.

Challenge #4: Effective Interventions Matched to Children's Needs

Evidence about different patterns of reading difficulties demonstrates that struggling readers have different intervention needs. Research-based phonemic awareness and phonics interventions will do little for children with specific comprehension difficulties; research-based comprehension interventions will be insufficient for most children with specific word recognition difficulties unless accompanied by effective teaching of phonemic awareness and phonics. Furthermore, to avoid inadvertently manufacturing additional reading problems simply from lack of opportunity to learn, interventions for various types of reading difficulties must occur in the context of comprehensive reading instruction that develops a range of important reading-related abilities and that provides ample opportunities for all students to read engaging text. If appropriately matched interventions and comprehensive instruction are not employed in RtI models, struggling readers will continue to be labeled with disabilities when the true culprits are inadequate teaching and lack of opportunity to learn.

For children with genuine RDs, differentiating instruction by pattern is essential for children to benefit from special education services. Studies of the reading instruction offered to students in special-education settings (Allington & McGill-Franzen, in press; Bentum & Aaron, 2003; Vaughn et al., 1998, 2002) indicate that children in these settings frequently experience poorly differentiated instruction emphasizing worksheets and seatwork rather than actual reading, in part because of high pupil-teacher ratios and highly heterogeneous groups. These problems may account for the limited progress of many students in spe-

cial education. Encouragingly, Aaron et al. (2008) showed that intervention targeting struggling readers' identified weakness—word recognition vs. comprehension—results in better outcomes than does traditional resource room instruction. This kind of intervention matching will be even more vital as varied patterns of reading disabilities are identified under IDEA 2004. Furthermore, assumptions often made for students with LDs, such as that these students can readily obtain information presented verbally, may not hold as well for students with comprehension-based disabilities as for those with dyslexia. Therefore, classroom modifications and accommodations for students with RDs also must consider individual students' patterns of difficulties. Table 14.1 summarizes information about the performance on reading assessments common to each pattern of reading difficulties and the types of interventions typically needed for each pattern.

Challenge #5: Professional Development about Patterns of Reading Difficulties

Teacher adaptations to specific interventions and programs may be inevitable (Datnow & Castellano, 2000). Moreover, teacher knowledge and skill may well contribute independent variance to student outcomes beyond that accounted for by specific interventions (McGill-Franzen, 2005), and teachers who are knowledgeable about literacy development appear less likely to refer struggling readers to special education (Johnston & Costello, 2005). Although teachers rarely control many important school and district variables that can impact children's reading achievement (e.g., selection of curriculum or availability of resources), teachers remain a key influence on children's learning (Darling-Hammond, 2007).

However, even experienced teachers, including both general and special educators, often lack knowledge about early literacy acquisition and children's word-recognition difficulties (Spear-Swerling, in press; Spear-Swerling, Brucker, & Alfano, 2005); teacher knowledge and skill in the area of comprehension are equally critical and take considerable time and support to develop (Allington & McGill-Franzen, in press; Duffy, 2004). Professional development for general and special educators on literacy and the needs of struggling readers across the K–12 grade range is therefore essential. As part of preservice preparation and ongoing professional development, information about the different patterns of reading difficulties, and opportunities to apply that information in diagnostic assessment and instructional planning, should be routinely included. This information can improve teachers' abilities to identify reading problems early, differentiate classroom instruction, and provide appropriate intervention to struggling students.

Suggestions for Assessment in Reading

The research reviewed in this chapter has a number of implications for teachers, school administrators, and others responsible for assessment of children's reading achievement. Here are some suggestions for educators:

TABLE 14.1
Performance on Assessments and Intervention Needs Typical of Different Patterns of Reading Difficulties*

Pattern	Assessments of Word Recognition and Phonemic Awareness (PA)	Assessments of Reading Speed	Assessments of Oral Language Comprehension and Oral Vocabulary	Assessments of Reading Comprehension (RC)	Typical Intervention Needs**
Specific word recognition difficulties	Below average performance on tests of out-of-context word recognition and decoding skills, often accompanied by poor phonemic awareness (PA).	Speed of reading usually is below average.	Average or better vocabulary and oral language comprehension; performance on verbally presented tasks usually is at least average and may be a notable strength.	Usually below average, due to poor or slow word recognition, but some students may perform at average levels on some RC tests. RC difficulties may be evident in everyday classroom performance.	Explicit, systematic phonics instruction, integrated with PA instruction if PA is low; focused techniques to increase speed, such as repeated readings, if speed is a significant problem.
Specific reading comprehension difficulties	Average or better performance on tests of out-of-context word recognition, decoding skills, and PA.	Speed may or may not be impaired.	Some, but not all, students are below average on tests of oral vocabulary and/or oral language comprehension; these students' difficulties may be evident on verbally presented tasks as well as in reading.	Below average reading comprehension associated with: 1) below average oral vocabulary/language comprehension, and/or 2) factors specific to reading text, such as lack of knowledge about text structure.	Instruction targeting the student's specific reading/oral comprehension weakness(es), such as vocabulary, inferencing, information about text structure, or teaching of specific comprehension strategies. If speed is a significant problem, use focused techniques to build speed.
Mixed reading difficulties	Below average performance on tests of out-of-context word recognition and decoding skills, often accompanied by poor PA.	Speed is almost always below average.	Some, but not all, students are below average on tests of oral vocabulary and/or oral language comprehension; these students' difficulties may be evident on verbally presented tasks as well as in reading.	Below average reading comprehension, due in part to poor or slow word recognition; however, RC difficulties exceed what can be accounted for by poor word recognition. For example, students may have difficulty comprehending even when reading material that they can decode accurately.	Explicit, systematic phonics instruction, integrated with PA instruction if PA is low; instruction that targets the student's specific reading/oral comprehension weaknesses; focused techniques to build speed of reading.

*In an RtI model, genuine reading disabilities are differentiated from other types of reading problems in part by lack of adequate response to appropriate interventions in students with disabilities. Students with genuine reading disabilities usually require more intensive versions of the interventions listed in the table (e.g., more intervention time, a smaller teacher-student ratio, more opportunities for practice) not qualitatively different interventions.
**Interventions should occur in the context of a broad, comprehensive program of literacy instruction (e.g., a program that includes comprehension instruction for students with specific word recognition difficulties; and grade-appropriate basic skills instruction, such as direct teaching of spelling skills, for students with specific comprehension difficulties).

1. *Use technically adequate assessments appropriate to their intended purpose.* Information about the technical adequacy (e.g., reliability and validity) of many published tests can be found in print resources such as textbooks on reading assessment, as well as online resources such as the Buros Institute's Test Reviews Online (see http://buros.unl.edu/buros/jsp/search.jsp) and the web site of the National Center on Student Progress Monitoring (www.studentprogress.org). The intended purpose of a particular assessment also must be considered. For example, summative assessments, such as many state-mandated assessments of reading achievement, are meant to evaluate children's cumulative learning at a particular point in time and usually are time-consuming to administer; progress-monitoring assessments are given more frequently to check growth, such as response to intervention, and often employ brief timed tasks that correlate well with overall reading competence in children of a given age. However, these brief timed tasks are not intended as a substitute for a thorough diagnostic assessment in children whose difficulties require further clarification (as is often the case). Use of an inappropriate type of assessment, such as using a summative assessment for progress-monitoring or only a progress-monitoring assessment when more thorough diagnostic assessment is needed, may not yield the desired information and may waste valuable instructional time.

2. *Assess (and develop) nonphonological language abilities as well as phonological skills in young children.* Phonological measures will detect many reading problems early, including specific word recognition difficulties and mixed reading difficulties, especially when used in conjunction with other important predictors of beginning reading such as knowledge of letters. However, the addition of nonphonological language measures to assessment batteries—for instance, measures of receptive vocabulary, expressive vocabulary, and listening comprehension—could facilitate earlier identification of children with specific comprehension difficulties and help provide more comprehensive interventions for children with mixed reading difficulties (i.e., interventions incorporating both phonics-based and comprehension-based remediation, as shown in Table 14.1). Furthermore, increased attention to developing nonphonological language abilities, in addition to phonological skills, in early reading curricula might prevent reading difficulties in some children (Biemiller, 1999).

3. *Maintain identification and intervention efforts into the middle grades and secondary level.* Because some reading difficulties emerge only at later grade levels and in relation to increasing grade expectations, primary level identification and intervention efforts cannot detect or prevent all reading problems. Continued monitoring of all students' reading progress is therefore vital, as is maintaining the availability of interventions for struggling readers through the secondary level.

4. *Use more than one measure to assess reading comprehension, and consider the nature of the measures when evaluating individual children's performance.* Evaluations of children's reading comprehension should be based on more than one measure because different measures of reading comprehension can yield quite varied results for individual children. Among other possibilities, some children's performance may vary as a function of test format, such as whether the test involves a cloze task or a question-answering task (Spear-Swerling, 2004b), as well as of many other factors, such as whether the child responds to questions orally or in writing (Jenkins, Johnson, & Hileman, 2004). Furthermore, some tests employ questions that children can answer without actually having read the accompanying text (e.g., questions involving vocabulary or background knowledge). On these tests, certain children, especially those with specific word recognition difficulties, may obtain falsely inflated reading comprehension scores (Keenan & Betjemann, 2006).

5. *Take everyday classroom performance into account.* Not only can measures of reading comprehension yield different results for individual children, but these measures also generally fail to tap many complex comprehension abilities required for success in reading, particularly at middle and upper grade levels. For instance, a child with slow speed of reading may perform well on reading comprehension tests with liberal time limits, but may nevertheless have great difficulty meeting middle or upper grade expectations involving a high volume of reading. Test scores should always be interpreted in conjunction with information about everyday classroom performance.

6. *Assess important reading-related abilities in isolation to help pinpoint struggling readers' difficulties and target interventions appropriately.* To locate specific difficulties in individual children and match interventions in the manner illustrated in Table 14.1, diagnostic assessment of important reading-related abilities is critical. Assessment of out-of-context performance is necessary for accurate measurement of many reading-related abilities, including word recognition and oral vocabulary, because these abilities interact when children are reading in context (e.g., in passages) in ways that confound interpretation of specific abilities. For example, children with word recognition difficulties may use semantic and syntactic cues to compensate for weak decoding when reading in context, appearing to have better word-recognition skills than they actually do (Stanovich, 2000); children with specific reading comprehension difficulties may have significant vocabulary weaknesses that are not apparent in passages making few demands on vocabulary knowledge.

7. *For children with comprehension-based reading difficulties, pinpoint specific language and reading comprehension problems as much as possible.* Struggling readers with mixed reading difficulties or

specific reading comprehension difficulties require further pinpointing of weaknesses (and strengths) within the domain of comprehension in order to target interventions correctly. For instance, an intervention focused on vocabulary probably will not be helpful to a poor comprehender whose main difficulty involves inferencing. Diagnostic assessment of comprehension should also consider whether children's difficulties are confined mainly to reading comprehension or extend to listening comprehension; difficulties with listening or oral language should be addressed along with reading in instruction.

8. *Routinely rule out (or rule in) word recognition difficulties in struggling readers, even at upper grade levels.* There is considerable debate about the relative percentages of struggling readers with word recognition vs. comprehension difficulties in the middle and upper grades (see, e.g., Biancarosa & Snow, 2004, and Fletcher et al., 2007, for contrasting viewpoints on this issue). Nevertheless, the research reviewed here demonstrates that the possibility of word recognition difficulties cannot be discounted in struggling readers of any age. Furthermore, administering a test of out-of-context word recognition is reasonably easy and quick, usually taking only about 5 or 10 minutes. These kinds of tests, which should employ both real and pseudo-words, should be used routinely to determine whether word recognition difficulties might be a factor in poor reading comprehension for any struggling reader, so that problems can be addressed appropriately in instruction.

Conclusion: Taking the Leap

A popular saying counsels, "Leap, and the net will appear." Response-to-intervention models for identification of RDs require some major conceptual leaps: among others, the convictions that struggling readers, with and without disabilities, can be successful; that effective curriculum and instruction can make powerful differences in children's learning; and that access to interventions should not depend upon a disability classification. Given these conceptual shifts, as well as the practical challenges of RtI implementation, educators' reluctance to discard the safety net of familiar identification practices (e.g., the IQ-achievement discrepancy) may be understandable. However, it makes little sense to eschew promising, though challenging, approaches to identification and intervention, in favor of practices that lack scientific support and are potentially damaging to children. Although further research on RtI models certainly is necessary, educational practice could be greatly improved by applying what already is known about children's reading development and common patterns of reading difficulties. Doing so could begin to provide a different, better safety net, both for teachers and children, and assist the field of LDs with its leap into the future.

References

Aaron, P. G., Joshi, M., & Williams, K. A. (1999). Not all reading disabilities are alike. *Journal of Learning Disabilities, 32,* 120–137.

Aaron, P. G., Joshi, M., Gooden, R., & Bentum, K. (2008). Diagnosis and treatment of reading disabilities based on the component model of reading: An alternative to the discrepancy model of LD. *Journal of Learning Disabilities, 41,* 67–84.

Allington, R. L. (1983). The reading instruction provided readers of differing abilities. *Elementary School Journal, 83,* 548–559.

Allington, R. L., & McGill-Franzen, A. (in press). Comprehension difficulties among struggling readers. *Handbook of Research on Comprehension.*

Al Otaiba, S. (2001). Children who do not respond to early literacy instruction: A longitudinal study across kindergarten and first grade. *Reading Research Quarterly, 36,* 344–346.

Badian, N. (1999). Reading disability defined as a discrepancy between listening and reading comprehension: A longitudinal study of stability, gender differences, and prevalence. *Journal of Learning Disabilities, 32,* 138–148.

Bentum, K., & Aaron, P. G. (2003). Does reading instruction in learning disability resource rooms really work? A longitudinal study. *Reading Psychology, 24,* 361–382.

Biancarosa, G., & Snow, C. E. (2004). *Reading Next — A vision for action and research in middle and high school literacy: A report to Carnegie Corporation of New York.* Washington, DC: Alliance for Excellent Education.

Biemiller, A. (1977–78). Relationships between oral reading rates for letters, words, and simple text in the development of reading achievement. *Reading Research Quarterly, 13,* 223–253.

Biemiller, A. (1999). *Language and reading success.* Cambridge, MA: Brookline Books.

Blachman, B. (1997). *Foundations of reading acquisition and dyslexia: Implications for early intervention.* Mahwah, NJ: Erlbaum.

Bruck, M. (1992). Persistence of dyslexics' phonological awareness deficits. *Developmental Psychology, 28,* 874–886.

Cain, K., Oakhill, J. V., & Bryant, P. (2000). Phonological skills and comprehension failures: A test of the phonological processing deficits hypothesis. *Reading and Writing, 13,* 31–56.

Castles, A., & Coltheart, M. (1993). Varieties of developmental dyslexia. *Cognition, 47,* 149–180.

Catts, H. W., Fey, M. E., Zhang, X., & Tomblin, J. B. (1999). Language basis of reading and reading disabilities: Evidence from a longitudinal investigation. *Scientific Studies of Reading, 3,* 331–361.

Catts, H. W., Hogan, T. P., & Adlof, S. M. (2005). Developmental changes in reading and reading disabilities. In H. W. Catts & A. Kamhi (Eds.), *The connections between language and reading disabilities* (pp. 25–40). Mahwah, NJ: Erlbaum.

Catts, H. W., Hogan, T. P., & Fey, M. E. (2003). Subtyping poor readers on the basis of individual differences in reading-related abilities. *Journal of Learning Disabilities, 36,* 151–164.

Chall, J. (1983). *Stages of reading development.* New York: McGraw-Hill.

Chall, J., Jacobs, V. A., & Baldwin, L. E. (1990). *The reading crisis: Why poor children fall behind.* Cambridge, MA: Harvard University Press.

Cunningham, A. E., & Stanovich, K. E. (1991) Tracking the unique effects of print exposure in children: Associations with vocabulary, general knowledge, and spelling. *Journal of Educational Psychology, 83,* 264–274.

Cunningham, A. E., & Stanovich, K. E. (1998). What reading does for the mind. *American Educator, 22,* 8–15.

Darling-Hammond, L. (2007). The flat earth and education: How America's commitment to equity will determine our future. *Educational Researcher, 36,* 318–334.

Datnow, A., & Castellano, M. (2000). Teachers' responses to Success for All: How beliefs, experiences, and adaptations shape implementation. *American Educational Research Journal, 37,* 775–799.

Denton, C. A., Vaughn, S., & Fletcher, J. M. (2003). Bringing research-based practice in reading intervention to scale. *Learning Disabilities Research & Practice, 18*, 201–211.

Drame, E. R. (2002). Sociocultural context effects on teachers' readiness to refer for learning disabilities. *Exceptional Children, 69*, 41–53.

Duffy, G. G. (2004). Teachers who improve reading achievement: What research says about what they do and how to develop them. In D. Strickland & M. Kamil (Eds.), *Improving reading achievement through professional development* (pp. 3–22). Norwood, MA: Christopher-Gordon.

Duke, N. K. (2000). Print environments and experiences offered to first-grade students in very low- and very high-SES school districts. *Reading Research Quarterly, 35*, 456–457.

Ehri, L. C. (1991). Learning to read and spell words. In L. Rieben & C. A. Perfetti (Eds.), *Learning to read: Basic research and its implications* (pp. 57–73). Mahwah, NJ: Erlbaum.

Fletcher, J. M., Lyon, G. R., Fuchs, L. S., & Barnes, M. A. (2007). *Learning disabilities: From identification to intervention.* New York: Guilford.

Francis, D. J., Snow, C. E., August, D., Carlson, C. D., Miller, J., & Iglesias, A. (2006). Measures of reading comprehension: A latent variable analysis of the Diagnostic Assessment of Reading Comprehension. *Scientific Studies of Reading, 10*, 301–322.

Fuchs, D., & Deshler, D. (2007). What we need to know about responsiveness to intervention (and shouldn't be afraid to ask). *Learning Disabilities Research & Practice, 22*, 129–136.

Gersten, R., & Dimino, J. (2006). RTI (response to intervention): Rethinking special education for students with reading difficulties (yet again). *Reading Research Quarterly, 41*, 99–108.

Gough, P. B., & Tunmer, W. E. (1986). Decoding, reading, and reading disability. *Remedial and Special Education, 7*, 6–10.

Guthrie, J. T., Wigfield, A., Metsala, J. L., & Cox, K. E. (1999). Motivational and cognitive predictors of text comprehension and reading amount. *Scientific Studies of Reading, 3*, 231–256.

Hinshelwood, J. (1896). A case of dyslexia: A peculiar form of word-blindness. *Lancet, 101*, 1451–1454.

Ho, C., Chan, D., Leung, P., Lee, S., & Tsang, S. (2005). Reading-related cognitive deficits in developmental dyslexia, attention-deficit/hyperactivity disorder, and developmental coordination disorder among Chinese children. *Reading Research Quarterly, 40*, 318–337.

Jenkins, J. R., Johnson, E., & Hileman, J. (2004). When is reading also writing: Sources of individual differences on the new reading performance assessments. *Scientific Studies of Reading, 8*, 125–152.

Johnston, P., & Costello, P. (2005). Principles for literacy assessment. *Reading Research Quarterly, 40*, 256–267.

Juel, C., & Minden-Cupp, C. (2000). Learning to read words: Linguistic units and instructional strategies. *Reading Research Quarterly, 35*, 458–492.

Kavale, K. A., & Reese, L. (1992). The character of learning disabilities: An Iowa profile. *Learning Disability Quarterly, 15*, 74–94.

Keenan, J. M., & Betjemann, R. S. (2006). Comprehending the Gray Oral Reading Test without reading it: Why comprehension tests should not include passage-independent items. *Scientific Studies of Reading, 10*, 363–380.

Klingner, J. K., Vaughn, S., & Boardman, A. (2007). *Teaching reading comprehension to students with learning difficulties.* New York: Guilford.

Leach, J. M., Scarborough, H. S., & Rescorla, L. (2003). Late-emerging reading disabilities. *Journal of Educational Psychology, 95*, 211–224.

Lovett, M. W. (1987). A developmental approach to reading disability: Accuracy and speed criteria of normal and deficient reading skill. *Child Development, 58*, 234–260.

Machek, G. R., & Nelson, J. M. (2007). How should reading disabilities be operationalized? A survey of practicing school psychologists. *Learning Disabilities Research & Practice, 22*, 147–157.

MacMillan, D. L., & Speece, D. L. (1999). Utility of current diagnostic categories for reearch and practice. In R. Gallimore, L. P. Bernheimer, D. L. MacMillan, D. L. Speece, & S. Vaughn (Eds.), *Developmen-tal perspectives on children with high-incidence disabilities* (pp. 111–113). Mahwah, NJ: Erlbaum.

McGill-Franzen, A. (2005). In the press to scale up, what is at risk? *Reading Research Quarterly, 40*, 366–370.

Moody, S W., Vaughn, S., Hughes, M. T., & Fischer, M. (2000). Reading instruction in the resource room: Set up for failure. *Exceptional Children, 66*, 305–316.

Nation, K. (2005). Children's reading comprehension difficulties. In M. J. Snowling & C. Hulme (Eds.), *The science of reading: A handbook* (pp. 248–266). Oxford, UK: Blackwell.

Nation, K., & Snowling, M. (1997). Assessing reading difficulties: The validity and utility of current measures of reading skill. *British Journal of Educational Psychology, 67*, 359–370.

Nation, K., Clarke, P., Marshall, C. M., & Durand, M. (2004). Hidden language impairments in children: Parallels between poor reading comprehension and specific language impairment? *Journal of Speech, Language, and Hearing Research, 47*, 199–211.

Neuman, S. B., & Dickinson, D. K. (2002). *Handbook of early literacy research.* New York: Guilford.

Rack, J. P., Snowling, M. J., & Olson, R. K. (1992). The nonword reading deficit in developmental dyslexia: A review. *Reading Research Quarterly, 27*, 28–53.

RAND Reading Study Group. (2002). *Reading for understanding: Toward an R&D program in reading comprehension.* Arlington, VA: RAND.

Riedel, B. W. (2007). The relation between DIBELS, reading comprehension, and vocabulary in urban first-grade students. *Reading Research Quarterly, 42*, 546–567.

Rupley, W. H., Willson, V. L., & Nichols, W. D. (1998). Exploration of the developmental components contributing to elementary school children's reading comprehension. *Scientific Studies of Reading, 2*, 143–158.

Scarborough, H. S. (1998). Early identification of children at risk for reading disabilities: Phonological awareness and some other promising predictors. In B. K. Shapiro, P. J. Accardo, & A. J. Capute (Eds.), *Specific reading disability: A view of the spectrum* (pp. 75–119). Timonium, MD: York Press.

Scarborough, H. S. (2005). Developmental relationships between language and reading: Reconciling a beautiful hypothesis with some ugly facts. In H. W. Catts & A. Kamhi (Eds.), *The connections between language and reading disabilities* (pp. 3–24). Mahwah, NJ: Erlbaum.

Scarborough, H. S., & Brady, S. A. (2002). Toward a common terminology for talking about speech and reading: A glossary of the *"phon"* words and some related terms. *Journal of Literacy Research, 34*, 299–334.

Scruggs, T. E., & Mastropieri, M. A. (2002). On babies and bathwater: Addressing the problems of identification of learning disabilities. *Learning Disabilities Quarterly, 25*, 155–168.

Shankweiler, D., Crain, S., Brady, S., & Macaruso, P. (1992). Identifying the causes of reading disability. In P. B. Gough, L. C. Ehri, & R. Treiman (Eds.), *Reading acquisition* (pp. 275–305). Hillsdale, NJ: Erlbaum.

Shaywitz, S. E., Shaywitz, B. A., Fletcher, J. M., & Escobar, M. D. (1990). Prevalence of reading disability in boys and girls: Results of the Connecticut Longitudinal Study. *Journal of the American Medical Association, 264*, 998–1002.

Siegel, L. S. (1988). Evidence that IQ scores are irrelevant to the definition and analysis of reading disability. *Canadian Journal of Psychology, 42*, 201–215.

Spear-Swerling, L. (2004a). A road map for understanding reading disability and other reading problems: Origins, intervention, and prevention. In R. Ruddell & N. Unrau (Eds.), *Theoretical models and processes of reading, vol. 5.* Newark, DE: International Reading Association.

Spear-Swerling, L. (2004b). Fourth-graders' performance on a state-mandated assessment involving two different measures of reading comprehension. *Reading Psychology, 25*, 121–148.

Spear-Swerling, L. (in press). Response to intervention and teacher preparation. In E. Grigorenko (Ed.), *Educating individuals with disabilities: IDEA 2004 and beyond.* New York: Springer.

Spear-Swerling, L., Brucker, P., & Alfano, M. (2005). Teachers' literacy-related knowledge and self-perceptions in relation to preparation and experience. *Annals of Dyslexia, 55,* 266–293.

Spear-Swerling, L., & Sternberg, R. J. (1996). *Off track: When poor readers become "learning disabled."* Boulder, CO: Westview Press.

Speece, D. L., Case, L. P., & Molloy, D. W. (2003). Responsiveness to general education instruction as the first gate to learning disabilities identification. *Learning Disabilities Research & Practice, 18,* 147–156.

Stanovich, K. E. (1986). Cognitive processes and the reading problems of learning disabled children: Evaluating the assumption of specificity. In J. K. Torgesen & B. Y. L. Wong (Eds.), *Psychological and educational perspectives on learning disabilities* (pp. 87–131). New York: Academic Press.

Stanovich, K. E. (1991). Discrepancy definitions of reading disability: Has intelligence led us astray? *Reading Research Quarterly, 26,* 7–29.

Stanovich, K. E. (2000). *Progress in understanding reading: Scientific foundations and new frontiers.* New York: Guilford.

Stanovich, K. E., & Siegel, L. S. (1994). Phenotypic performance profile of children with reading disabilities: A regression-based test of the phonological-core variable-difference model. *Journal of Educational Psychology, 86,* 24–53.

Sternberg, R. J., & Grigorenko, E. L. (2002). Difference scores in the identification of children with learning disabilities: It's time to use a different method. *Journal of School Psychology, 40,* 65–84.

Torgesen, J. K. (1991). Learning disabilities: Historical and conceptual issues. In B. Y. L. Wong (Ed.), *Learning about learning disabilities* (pp. 3–37). San Diego, CA: Academic Press.

Torgesen, J. K., Alexander, A., Wagner, R. K., Rashotte, C., Voeller, K., & Conway, T. (2001). Intensive remedial instruction for children with severe reading disabilities: Immediate and long-term outcomes from two instructional approaches. *Journal of Learning Disabilities, 34,* 33–58.

Vaughn, S., & Fuchs, L. S. (2003). Redefining learning disabilities as inadequate response to instruction: The promise and potential problems. *Learning Disabilities Research & Practice, 18,* 137–146.

Vaughn, S., Levy, S., Coleman, M., & Bos, C. (2002). Reading instruction for students with LD and EBD. *Journal of Special Education, 36,* 2–13.

Vaughn, S., Moody, S. W., & Schumm, J. S. (1998). Broken promises: Reading instruction in the resource room. *Exceptional Children, 64,* 211–225.

Vellutino, F. R., Fletcher, J. M., Scanlon, D. M., & Snowling, M. J. (2004). Specific reading disability (dyslexia): What have we learned in the past four decades? *Journal of Child Psychiatry and Psychology, 45,* 2–40.

Vellutino, F. R., & Scanlon, D. M. (2002). Emergent literacy skills, early instruction, and individual differences as determinants of difficulties in learning to read: The case for early intervention. In S. B. Neuman & D. K. Dickinson (Eds.), *Handbook of early literacy research* (pp. 295–321). New York: Guilford.

Wolf, M., & Bowers, P. G. (1999). The double-deficit hypothesis for the developmental dyslexias. *Journal of Educational Psychology, 91,* 415–438.

Zirkel, P. A., & Krohn, N. (2008). RtI after IDEA: A survey of state laws. *Teaching Exceptional Children, 40,* 71–73.

15

Traditions of Diagnosis

Learning from the Past, Moving Past Traditions

KATHLEEN A. GORMLEY AND PETER MCDERMOTT
The Sage Colleges

Introduction and Overview

Assessment is about judgment and it always is interpretive. Summative assessments, which are often the result of legislative initiatives requiring data collection at specified times, examine individuals, schools, and/or programs and facilitate making judgments about past learning. On the other hand, formative assessments, which are assessments for learning, happen during the process of teaching and inform decision-making relative to the instructional process (Chappuis & Chappuis, 2007). Both summative and formative assessments have essential roles to play in literacy education because they provide differing perspectives on learners, but summative assessment is given a wider public platform than formative assessment.

In this chapter reading assessment refers to the broadest category of educational tools and practices for measuring students' reading. Federal and state agencies, school districts, building principals, and classroom teachers all use assessments to fit their measurement needs. Reading assessments range from nationally prepared norm-referenced tests that states use to compare or evaluate school districts to those that are more local such as a teacher's observations and notes of children's oral reading of classroom books.

Reading diagnosis looks at the needs of an individual learner and provides an in-depth and personalized analysis of the student's reading. In this respect a reading diagnosis resembles a full-length movie of a student's strengths and needs in reading and not just a snapshot at a given point in time that is obtained through a group norm-referenced test. The primary purpose of a diagnosis is to understand a student's reading processes so that instruction can be designed and targeted to improve learning. A reading diagnosis uses multiple assessment tools and practices to gather information, including analyses of a student's oral and silent reading with texts at varied levels of difficulty and interest. A norm-referenced test may be part of the array of assessments used by the diagnostician, but the primary goal of a diagnosis is to inform instruction and not to measure a student against a norm group. For the purposes of this chapter, we use the term *diagnostician* to mean any professional with advanced training in assessing individual learners' reading performances.

The chapter discusses major traditions in reading diagnosis occurring throughout the last century in the United States. It examines those traditions and practices that have been widely employed in reading diagnosis as well as theories that have influenced or offer potential for informing diagnosis. Due to the focus of this book on reading, the chapter does not review the diagnosis of writing difficulties, although many of its challenges are similar to reading.

Teaching practices frequently flow from teachers' beliefs about what constitutes desired reading behaviors (e.g., DeFord, 1985; Shaw, Dvorak, & Bates, 2007), and diagnostic practices often originate from their models of reading. The professional literature at the turn to the 20th century, for instance, considered "good" reading to be primarily correct oral pronunciation for engaging elocutions; thus diagnosis focused on accurate oral performance. Now, as well as for many decades, some literacy professionals have believed that good reading consists fundamentally of accurate word pronunciation, and, consequently, their diagnostic practices focus on children's oral reading accuracy. Still other practitioners believe that reading's primary goal is comprehension, and therefore their diagnostic practices investigate children's cognitive strategies for understanding what they read. Consequently, teachers' models and beliefs about reading have influenced our diagnostic traditions, and wide variability about them is found in their classroom practices.

This chapter is organized into three sections. An overview of diagnostic traditions in reading is first presented. Here, special attention is given to the growth of the testing movement, the expansion of psychology as a profession and its influence on education, the practices and policies in teaching reading to students with special learning needs, and the recent and increasing role of the federal government on school accountability in reading. The second section addresses diagnostic traditions in schools, and the final section examines sociocultural research and its contributions to diagnostic theory. The three chapter sections appear as follows:

- Overview of Diagnostic Traditions in Reading
- Reading's Diagnostic Traditions in Schools
- Sociocultural Research and Its Contributions to Diagnostic Theory in Reading

Overview of Diagnostic Traditions in Reading

The 20th century served as a forum for extensive discussions about public education, and foremost among these pertained to the assessment of students' learning. In particular, the scientific movement and the development of norm-referenced testing have had long lasting effects on schools. Norm-referenced testing has become a well-established tradition in reading diagnosis that remains robust today.

Group norm-referenced testing, which is most often used for initial screening of reading problems, remains virtually unchanged in the past 50 years. This long-standing attractiveness of group testing is due to ease of administration, cost effectiveness, and data generated for comparison purposes. These tests commonly identify learners who may need more assistance and often determine eligibility for special programs. Once students are identified as having possible reading problems, they are likely to be diagnosed individually, typically by reading specialists, school psychologists and/or special educators.

Today, a dichotomy exists in current practices for diagnosing reading difficulties in specific learners. Although diagnosticians administer one-on-one assessments, they tend to rely either on authentic assessment strategies that are embedded in the classroom curricula (Afflerbach, 2007a), or they use norm-referenced assessments (Bell & McCallum, 2008) that provide comparable statistics (e.g., stanines and standard scores). Authentic assessment strategies include texts and tasks that constitute real or actual reading that children do in and out of school. Reading and paraphrasing ideas from books, magazines, or websites, for instance, are examples of authentic texts and tasks, whereas selecting answers from a series of multiple choice questions about a single paragraph or pronouncing a list of unrelated words from a norm-referenced test are not. While some diagnosticians use a combination of these approaches (DeVries, 2004), most tend to lean one way or the other. Although much has been written about performance assessments (e.g., portfolios, oral presentations, dramatizations, essay writing, visual arts presentations), such approaches are rarely utilized when diagnosing reading difficulties. Performance assessments could demonstrate students' literacy knowledge in a variety of ways, they are rarely incorporated as part of reading diagnosis (Afflerbach, 2007b).

An examination of our country's history provides insights into why reading diagnosis tends to be bifurcated, relying almost exclusively on either authentic or norm-referenced assessments. There are four major factors that have had direct bearing on reading's diagnostic traditions:

1. The objectification of students' reading performance;
2. The expansion of psychology as a profession;
3. Growth and influence of special education legislation (e.g., PL94-142);
4. Increased involvement of federal government in education.

The first two factors are closely related—the reciprocal links between the perceived value of objective psychometric measures and the niche of psychology in measuring learning (including reading) are clear. Similarly, the latter two factors are enmeshed—the quests for access to public education by all learners and the federal government's pursuit of accountability are entangled.

Objectification of Students' Reading Performance The roots of this first factor rest with intelligence testing that began with screening of millions of World War I army recruits to determine job fit (e.g., identify potential officers). This testing effectively segmented large numbers of military personnel into categories. Using multiple choice questions for assessment purposes eventually expanded and resulted in the sorting of children into particular levels of programs in a tiered educational system (elementary, junior, and high schools).

During the early decades of the 20th century (1900–1930), immigration was at an unprecedented level with the growth of industrialization. Population centers shifted from rural communities to cities, and school districts became more centralized and consequently larger. Concomitantly, compulsory school attendance laws resulted in increasingly diverse and larger numbers of students. All of these challenges pressed schools to make decisions on how best to deal with large numbers of non-English speaking students and to prepare increasing numbers of secondary students to enter the work force. Reading assessment incorporated multiple-choice questions in group, timed tests. Thorndike, a renowned educational psychologist who asserted strong correlations among genetic inheritance, gender, and race, was tremendously influential in developing the tools for designing and interpreting reading tests (Willis, 2008). Trusting of scientific measurement to determine achievement and potential for achievement (intelligence testing), under the guise of objectivity and fairness, gained a lasting foothold in early part of the century (Monahan, 1998).

The scientific movement shaped thinking about reading assessment as well, and norm-referenced testing became one of the foremost traditions in diagnosis. Group norm-referenced testing in reading is widely used today to screen students in need of further assessment, and individual norm-referenced tests are often used to contextualize diagnosticians' analyses of students' reading performance.

Influence of Psychology as a Profession   In the early
decades (1900–1930) assessment of intellectual capabilities
extended its expertise into schools via educational psychology. Formalized instruments assessed students' intellectual
and academic abilities, including the assessment of reading.
Reading was viewed as psychological processing and the
descriptive statistics that quantified performance on reading
assessments were considered reliable and more important
than daily performance (Pearson & Hamm, 2005). Psychometric expertise enabled educational psychology to develop
a niche for assessing learners who were not progressing
suitably. The standardization of students' intelligence and
reading test scores along a normal distribution became
educational psychology's ultimate measure (McCormick
& Braithwaite, 2008). In essence, norm-referenced testing
became customary, conventional, and time-honored with
little questioning of the influence of background or other
factors on reading. Quantitative information was valued
more than teacher judgment or any other qualitative information (Brown, 1992). The quantification of students'
reading performance in terms of reading levels, accuracy
rates, and comprehension scores became a diagnostic tradition largely because of educational psychology's use of
comparative statistics.

Growth and Influence of Special Education   Despite
compulsory school laws, more than 1,000,000 students
with disabilities were not served in public schools in 2007
(USDE, 2007). Frequently these students were placed in
segregated settings (Hunt & Marshall, 2002), and those
with significant disabilities (e.g., blindness or deafness)
often attended schools away from their families. PL 94-142
[titled initially *Education of All Handicapped Children Act*
(1975) and now titled *Individuals with Disabilities Education Act* (IDEA) (1990, 1997, 2004)] was the landmark
legislation that built on the gains made by the civil rights
movement of the 1960s. This legislation mandated free and
appropriate education, non-biased assessment and education in the least restrictive environment. The 1997 IDEA
amendments increased student opportunities to participate
in the general education programs, improved coordination
between regular and special education, and increased the
accountability of schools in meeting the educational needs
of students with disabilities.

One of the key components in IDEA is non-discrim-
inatory testing, including the use of multiple measures.
Although IDEA does not require norm-referenced testing,
the reality is that such instruments are most often selected
for data sources in Individualized Educational Plans (IEPs)
(Hunt & Marshall, 2002). Norm-referenced testing is attractive in special education because such instruments give
the impression of fairness and objectivity. Special educators have used the assumptions pertaining to the validity
and reliability of these tests to determine how discrepant
a student's performance is relative to age and grade level
norms. Although some states are changing to Response to
Intervention (RtI) policies for documenting students with

learning disabilities (IDEA Amendments of 2004), most
still rely on the older measure of disability: a discrepancy
between students' intelligence scores and their classroom
achievements (Hollenbeck, 2007). (See chapter 13 in this
volume for a detailed discussion of this issue.)

Special education's history echoes the exclusion and
segregation experienced by other minority groups (Lipsky
& Gartner, 1996). Prior to IDEA, students with disabilities
were perceived as unable to thrive in general education
and therefore relegated to separate specialized programs.
In addition, it is well documented that there has been an
overrepresentation of students from underrepresented
groups in special education (Artiles, 2003; Dunn, 1968;
Skiba, Poloni-Staudinger, Gallini, Simmons, & Feggins-
Azziz, 2006; Zhang & Katsiyannis, 2002). Some research
(McGill-Franzen, 1987) suggests that funding availability
has influenced the classification of children with reading
difficulties—specifically, as funding increased for special
education services, more schools classified children as
learning disabled rather than remedial readers because of
the monetary incentive to label students as having special
needs.

The expansion of services to students with special needs
and the inclusion movement represented needed reforms
in public education. Yet, there have been adverse effects of
this legislation on reading's diagnostic traditions. Implicit
in special education was the re-conceptualization of the
origin of reading problems from that of disadvantaged
backgrounds to disabilities caused by children's psychological processing of print, and with this new etiology,
teachers often lowered their expectations for students with
disabilities (McGill-Franzen, 1987; Stainback & Stainback,
1984). Although there has been much improvement since
the original legislation, special educators often differ from
classroom and reading teachers in their theoretical views
about children's learning to read, and these differences
became evidenced in a lack of coordination between classroom, remedial and special education services (Allington &
McGill-Franzen, 1989; Ysseldyke, Thurlow, Mecklenburg,
Graden, 1984). Special education's preference for norm-
referenced testing at the expense of more formative assessments of reading, such as close observation and analysis of
children's interactions with print over time, increased the
prominence of standardized testing in schools.

***Increased Involvement of Federal Government in Educa-
tion***   Individual states hold the responsibility for public
education through the Reserve Clause of the United States
Constitution (i.e., Tenth Amendment). Yet, over the course
of the 20th century, the federal government became increasingly more active through various public policy initiatives
for improving student achievement, protecting the civil
rights for all students, establishing special education legislation, and more recently promoting learning standards
and reducing the achievement gaps in our schools (McGill-
Franzen, 2000).

In 1957 the Soviets launched *Sputnik*, and the U.S. government's immediate reaction was to increase funding for science and mathematics education. In 1964, as a result of President Johnson's Great Society, monies poured into the public school systems through ESEA grants and various title monies that targeted underserved or poor performing populations. The government enacted the Education for All Handicapped Children Act in 1975, and it radically changed educational services to children with disabilities. A decade later several reports critical of public education (e.g., National Commission on Excellence in Education, 1983) noted the rising tide of mediocrity and underscored the need for increased expectations or standards for America's failing schools. In 1998 the Educate America Act, commonly called Goals 2000, articulated ambitious expectations that all students would enter school ready to learn, and students' competency in reading (and other areas) would be assessed in grades 4, 8, and 12. Goals 2000 established the National Education Standards and Improvement Council, which had as its task the codification of standards across states and disciplines. Most of the specialty educational associations, including the International Reading Association (IRA), developed standards and expectations for learners (and to a lesser extent teachers) in subject areas. Some states adopted educational standards with associated assessments to determine student success in reaching them. These state assessments, with their psychometric assurances, identified at-risk or low-performing students, and placed expectations on schools to improve all students' performances in reading as well as in other subject areas.

The report of the National Reading Panel (NRP), funded by the National Institute of Child Health and Human Development (2000), provided the basis for what would quickly become the most influential piece of federal legislation to ever impact reading instruction and by extension reading diagnosis—the No Child Left Behind Act (NCLB) addressed the teaching of reading in low-performing, high-poverty schools, through its Reading First grants that required use of federally approved reading programs based on the five NRP elements (i.e., phonemic awareness, phonics, fluency, vocabulary, and comprehension). Despite questions (e.g., Goodman, 2006; IRA, 2006) about the theoretical underpinning of some of the approved programs and associated benchmark measures, such as the Dynamic Indicators of Basic Early Literacy Skills (DIBELS), many Reading First programs instituted the recommended instructional programs and assessment tools (Good, Kaminski, Smith, Laimon, & Dill, 2002; Reidel, 2007). Central among these plans was the use of both norm-referenced testing and the frequent use of Curriculum-Based Measurement (CBM) for documenting learners' progress over time. Reidel (2007) recently concluded that the comprehension measure of the DIBELS (one minute Retell Fluency score) lacks empirical support, but the measure continues to be popular.

The NCLB goal of having all students read at grade level is praiseworthy for its vision of closing the achievement gaps for children from diverse ethnic and economic backgrounds. Yet, unanswered questions concern how student success in reading is measured and how much weight the results from norm-referenced testing and other commercially prepared assessments, such as the DIBELS, should receive. Most importantly, NCLB's emphasis on summative testing has resulted in more adverse than praise-worthy effects on reading's diagnostic traditions. NCLB's emphasis on outcome rather than process has had a negative effect on reading's diagnostic traditions because many teachers are now more concerned about students' progress on the program assessments rather than understanding their reading processes.

Reading Diagnostic Traditions in Schools

An overview of diagnostic traditions in schools throughout the 20th century reveals that there were significant advances in our understanding of the reading process, but diagnostic practices lagged behind. In this section three issues relating to diagnostic traditions in schools are discussed. The first describes major trends and practices in the professional literature during the 20th century. The second discusses the contributions of researchers making a difference in reading's diagnostic practices, and the third examines recent effects of federal education legislation on diagnosis.

Major Trends and Practices in the Professional Literature about Diagnosis At the beginning of the 20th century the primary form of assessment was observing children's oral reading recitations (Gray, 1916). Later the scientific movement introduced norm-referenced testing of children's silent reading comprehension, and these tests became widely used in schools.

In 1946 the informal reading inventory (IRI) was proposed as a new method for diagnosing children with reading difficulties (Betts, 1946), and it became one of most utilized approaches in reading's diagnostic traditions. Reading inventories relied on existing classroom materials as the context for assessing children's reading, and consequently they offered greater content validity than other assessment tools available at the time. Importantly the IRI placed teacher expertise at the center of the diagnostic process because inventories required a high degree of knowledge and skill for their construction and administration, as well as interpretations of student performance. Although most of the inventories today are commercially produced (Afflerbach, 2007b; Nilsson, 2008), the IRI continues to be widely used in schools and clinics for diagnosing reading problems and examining learners' use of cue sources (McKenna & Picard, 2006; Paris & Carpenter, 2003; Walpole & McKenna, 2006).

In the 1950s and 1960s there was great public interest in the best method for teaching reading. A widely popular view at the time was seen in Flesch's (1955) book, *Why Johnny Can't Read*, in which reading was seen as a code-breaking activity. Later, Chall's review of the research literature (1967) concluded that a code-emphasis approach was the most effective way to teach beginning reading, and her work similarly received wide readership. Despite the conclusions from a nationwide longitudinal research project, *The First Grade Studies* (Bond & Dykstra, 1967), that there was no one best method for teaching reading and that teacher knowledge was the most important factor affecting student learning, the popularity of code-emphasis methods greatly influenced the teaching of reading. Many diagnosticians adopted a code-emphasis model by focusing on decoding skills, with some teachers even assessing children's reading with pseudo words rather than real ones, but often comprehension was neglected.

Psycholinguistic research represented a major change in theoretical views about reading and its diagnostic traditions because of its arguments against the use of isolated lists of words and nonsense words for understanding children's reading processes (e.g., Goodman, 1967, 1969, Goodman & Goodman, 1977; Smith, 1978). Psycholinguists demonstrated the value of looking at reading as a meaning-making activity. They argued that the syntactic and semantic quality of readers' oral reading errors were of more importance than children's accuracy at oral reading. Psycholinguistics influenced teachers' views about the interactive nature of the reading process—good reading required the construction of meaning and not simply word recognition accuracy. Diagnosis began to consider whether miscues were significant and disrupted the author's intended meaning.

New understandings about oral reading fluency (Chomsky, 1978; LaBerge & Samuels, 1974) further reinforced the importance of using connected discourse as the measure of good reading, and word recognition accuracy was considered insufficient for understanding students' reading abilities. Research about fluency demonstrated that both accuracy and rate reflected a level of automaticity that allowed readers to attend to the meaning of what was being read and thereby use appropriate expression, intonation and stress (prosody). Most recently, the importance of prosody in early reading as a measure of fluency and an indicator of comprehension has again been confirmed in research (Klauda & Guthrie, 2008; Miller & Schwanenflugel, 2008). Today, many diagnosticians use a measure of fluency when assessing children's oral reading (Fountas & Pinnell, 1996).

The 1980s witnessed the whole language movement and with it some teachers began using portfolios and other classroom-based assessment measures to document and showcase children's reading processes. These portfolios often included children' annotated lists of books that they had read, samples of their running records on texts of varied or increasing levels of difficulty, and response journals based on their independent reading, Although whole language's emphasis on assessing children's reading performance on classroom materials offered much promise, only a few schools moved in this direction and its long-term impact on reading diagnosis was negligible.

Adam's (1990) comprehensive review of research about beginning reading pointed to the importance of phonemic awareness (ability to focus on and manipulate phonemes in spoken words) and phonics (symbol sound associations) as essential understandings for learning to read. Adam's findings resulted in extensive national discussion about early reading and teaching strategies for developing children's phonemic awareness (e.g., Ehri, 1991; Ehri & McCormick, 1998; Yopp & Yopp, 2000). In particular, an emerging diagnostic tradition from this research was that of assessing children's ability to manipulate sounds in oral language such as found in onsets and rimes (Yopp, 1995).

Research during the 1970s and 1980s, a time period often referred to as the "cognitive revolution," focused on the internal processes readers use to understand text. Research from these decades advanced our understanding of the reading process, and its contributions eventually improved diagnostic practices in comprehension. Prior to cognitivism, diagnosticians assessed individual children's comprehension very differently than many do today. Children's responses to comprehension questions were judged as correct or incorrect depending on the textual information that was included in their answers. Teachers used Bloom's taxonomy (1965) and developed higher order questions to help inform their assessment, but comprehension was still viewed as coming primarily from the passage itself. Cognitive theorists demonstrated that prior knowledge (Anderson & Pearson, 1984) and text structure, particularly its propositional organization (Kintsch & van Dijk, 1978; Stein & Glenn, 1979), influenced readers' understanding of what they read. Others explained that comprehension is a strategic process in which readers apply a variety of cognitive processes for understanding what they read (e.g., Brown & Day, 1983; Lipson & Wixson, 1986). Most importantly, cognitivists demonstrated that comprehension is an interactive process between the reader, the text, and the instructional context—it is not a recall of textual information only (Pressley, 2002; Rowe & Rayford, 1987).

Today, findings from the cognitive and constructive nature of reading comprehension are widely incorporated into the diagnosis of students with reading difficulties. It is standard practice for diagnosticians to consider learner's prior knowledge about topics before they read, and published informal reading inventories typically include prior knowledge assessment in their protocols. Many diagnosticians now routinely ask students about their thinking while reading and have them reflect on why they read the way they do (Garner, 1987; Paris & Jacobs, 1984; Schmitt, 1990).

Major Researchers Influencing Reading's Diagnostic Traditions

Although there have been numerous researchers influencing our understanding of reading and by extension reading diagnosis, there have been four who have been particularly influential in reading's diagnostic traditions— Kenneth and Yetta Goodman, Marie Clay, and P. David Pearson. While many other researchers have contributed to our understandings of reading, these persons translated theory into practice and greatly affected reading's diagnostic traditions.

The Goodmans' application of psycholinguistic theories

to reading processes transformed the ways teachers analyzed children's oral reading performance and retellings of what they read (K. Goodman, 1967,1969; Goodman & Goodman, 1977). Among their contributions to reading and diagnostic practices are the value of miscue analyses, retellings, and readers' self-evaluations of their own reading processes. Their work represented a new tradition in reading diagnosis. Prior to the Goodmans' work, children's oral reading was assessed primarily according to word recognition accuracy and frequency of types of errors (e.g., omissions), and comprehension was assessed through teacher questioning rather than first eliciting children's retells of what read. More recently the Retrospective Miscue Analysis has actively involved students in self-evaluation and discussion of their own oral reading miscues (Y. Goodman, 1996). The Goodmans highlighted the importance of looking at the syntactic and semantic quality of children's mispronunciations as miscues and language strategies rather than as random mistakes associated with symbol-to-sound association difficulties.

Clay's (1985, 1987, 1993a, 1993b) contributions to emergent reading and early intervention for children with reading difficulties have been momentous in their effects on how young children are assessed. Prior to her research, schools assessed children's early reading with norm-referenced readiness tests containing question items often having little to do with reading, such as knowledge of numbers, shapes, colors, gross and fine motor skills. In addition, schools typically waited several years before providing intervention services for children encountering difficulty learning to read. Clay's work dramatically changed how early reading was viewed, and her observational assessment battery became a new tradition in the diagnosis of young children having difficulty learning to read.

Instead of looking at prerequisites for learning to read as consisting of certain levels of intelligence and fixed maturational stages, Clay re-conceptualized early reading as an emergent development in which children were always in the process of becoming readers and writers, providing they were in contact with print in meaningful ways. Her promising early intervention research, as seen in *Reading Recovery*, demonstrated the value of intensive early intervention services by highly trained teachers rather than waiting until ineffective reading behaviors were well established. Clay's research has brought about substantive changes in the ways intervention programs have been implemented particularly in regard to the importance of early intervention. Her recommendations for precise observations of children's reading behaviors over time, the specificity and importance of book leveling, the comprehensiveness of rich book introductions, the use of a consistent lesson structure, and the need to focus children's attention to the details of print transformed old and ineffective readiness models of reading. In addition to these many contributions, Clay's work (1987) foreshadowed recent Response to Intervention (RtI) legislation when she argued that children's reading difficulties are often sustained and aggravated by inadequate instruction.

Pearson and his collaborative work with students and colleagues (e.g., Fielding & Pearson, 1994; Hansen & Pearson, 1983; Pearson & Dole, 1987; Pearson, Hiebert, & Kamil, 2007; Pearson & Johnston, 1982; Pearson, 1985; Raphael & Pearson, 1985; Valencia & Pearson, 1988) have significantly influenced reading and its diagnostic practices. His research pertaining to prior knowledge and questioning helped us to better understand the complex nature of comprehension. That is, a learner's poor comprehension may reflect many issues from not understanding what questions are asking (Raphael & Au, 2005) to limited background knowledge. As a result of his work, most published inventories (e.g., Johns, 2008) now include protocols for assessing prior knowledge so that children's performance on both familiar and unfamiliar topics can be assessed. Pearson's research pertaining to questioning helped us see how explicit, implicit and scriptal information represents three different facets of overall comprehension (Pearson & Dole, 1987), and he reminded us that comprehension assessment is a very complex process.

Federal Legislation and Its Effects on Reading's Diagnostic Traditions   Although the federal government has attempted to improve literacy learning throughout the country, the complexity of reading has not been incorporated into its legislation. This is particularly true with NCLB legislation that has brought about an overemphasis on children's performance on norm-referenced testing. Although such testing is seemingly practical and efficient in determining whether schools and their teachers are successful in helping children learn to read, it has produced a narrowing of diagnostic practices; students' performance on a single high-stakes test oversimplifies assessment because multiple measures of students' oral and silent reading of different texts are needed to be informative for teachers (Coyne, Kame'enui, & Simmons, 2001; Snyder, Caccamise & Wise, 2005).

There is great variability in how children read (Lipson & Wixson, 1986), depending on their interest in the topic, the difficulty of the text and task required. Consequently, it is highly unlikely that a norm-referenced test, particularly a group test, provides useful information to teachers about children's underlying reading processes. While there have been admonitions against over-relying on norm-referenced assessments (e.g., Fiene & McMahon, 2007) and warnings against 1 minute assessments (Goodman, 2006), such cautions have largely been ignored in governmental policies. Many of these quick curriculum-based measures, such as assessing children's oral reading accuracy and rates, originated from special education's interest in data-based instruction (e.g., Deno, 1985; Deno & Fuchs, 1987), but these same measures have devalued much of what we have learned about comprehension and the richness and complexity of the reading process (Reidel, 2007). Instead of viewing reading as a constructive activity involving the processing of cognitive, linguistic, and social sources of information, these curriculum-based measures have oversimplified the reading process by having students read benchmark texts to assess word recognition accuracy, rate and simple measures of comprehension.

Response to Intervention is the latest outgrowth of NCLB, and it has already impacted reading's diagnostic traditions and the assumptions about the etiology of children's reading difficulties. In the 1960s public policy, as seen in ESEA legislation, associated reading disability with poverty and cultural disadvantageness. In 1975 the Education of All Handicapped Children Act (1975) shifted the focus from children's sociocultural environments as the associated cause of reading difficulty to children's psychological processing of text (McGill-Franzen, 1987). The significance of RtI is that it represents a change in thoughts about the etiology of reading difficulty because it encourages schools to examine the quality of instruction children receive before identifying them as disabled.

The effect of RtI on reading diagnosis has the potential to be quite profound. Although still relatively new to schools, RtI is influencing reading's diagnostic traditions because of its focus on the quality of instruction children receive and demonstration over time that instruction, which must be scientifically based, is improving student learning (Allington, 2009; Fuchs & Fuchs, 2006; Fuchs & Fuchs, 2008; Mesmer & Mesmer, 2008; Vaughn & Fuchs, 2003; Vaughn, Linan-Thompson, & Hickman, 2003). Our concern is that what is easily measured may not represent the richness of the reading process, particularly that of comprehension. Quick and easy seems to be the guise for most RtI measures (e.g., accuracy and reading rate), and we agree with Mesmer and Mesmer (2008) in questioning whether such measures capture the complexity of learners' reading vocabulary and comprehension.

The politics of education in the beginning of the 21st century has affirmed norm-referenced testing results as the gold standard for elementary schools. This emphasis on norm-referenced testing has lessened our understanding about what children know about reading and how their teachers might help them read better (Lipson & Wixson, 2009). Recent RtI legislation offers potential for the use of more formative and on-going measures of children's reading, but as of yet it is unclear whether such formative measures will be gathered.

Sociocultural Research and Its Contributions to Diagnosis Theory

There is a wealth of research about the sociocultural influences on learning to read (e.g., Delpit, 1995; Heath, 1983; Ladson-Billings, 1994; Willis, 1995). Despite the plethora of literature on the topic diagnosticians have treated all students the same regardless of their sociocultural backgrounds.

Reading diagnosis is generally viewed as free of outside influences. Yet, there are convincing arguments to the contrary. Johnston (1997) and Johnston and Costello (2005) explain that a reading assessment is actually influenced by many of the same factors that occur in everyday interactions.

Social systems—such as rich or poor communities, White or Black neighborhoods, professional or working-class backgrounds—are all factors that influence student reading. Cultural issues—such as relationships that are constructed between teachers and their students, teachers' expectations regarding student learning, students' motivation to succeed, and school-to-home connections—further affect students' reading performances in school.

Many students have been misdiagnosed and mislabeled because diagnosticians have not considered sociocultural issues affecting their reading development (McDermott, 2004). Often, the cognitive and linguistic strengths children bring to school are unrecognized by monolingual diagnosticians who hold middle-class views about language and culture. In particular, assessment, which is based on the experiences and views of the dominant social groups, places low-income African American, Latino, and other minority children at a decided disadvantage in terms of reading. For example, assessment tasks relying on standard English may over-identify dialect speakers as having reading difficulties when the issue actually lies with language differences rather than difficulties in oral reading skills or comprehension strategies (Weber, 1968, 1973). These dialectal mismatches may receive diagnostic/instructional attention when in fact they represent learners' language patterns and not actual reading difficulties. The absence of sociocultural theory in diagnosis has meant that children from minority backgrounds are far more likely to be diagnosed with reading problems, labeled as having learning disabilities, and even retained in school than children from White middle-class backgrounds (Artiles, 2003).

Norm-referenced, standardized testing is a particularly troublesome area in reading diagnosis for children from sociocultural backgrounds that differ from the dominant society. Tests privilege students who have cultural familiarity with the passage topics and vocabulary, and students who lack the same prior knowledge face greater challenge in answering the same test items; these students may answer the test items incorrectly because of a lack of experience with the topic rather than then having a difficulty in their reading skills (Banks, 2006; Freedle, 2003; Moore, 1996). Sometimes children are unable to correctly answer test items because they misconstrue the social assumptions applied in the questions even when they have the knowledge to correctly answer them (Cicourel, 1974; Moore, 1996). Shannon (1998) argues that most standardized, norm-referenced reading tests "…hide the social construction of privilege behind a cloud of scientific objectivity" (p. 75).

Diagnosticians often observe children's interactions during reading instruction. Yet, observations of students' classroom interactions can easily be misinterpreted when there are sociocultural differences between teachers and their students (Cazden, 2001). Language skills and patterns and styles of speaking that are successful at home do not automatically translate to success into school (Au & Mason, 1981; Delpit, 1995; Health, 1983). Everyday school or classroom events can even be interpreted differently depending on students' race and ethnicity (Willis, 1995).

Students' life experiences affect the kinds of information they bring to school and their motivation to read. Yet, schools privilege middle-class knowledge, and teachers are rarely aware of the richness of the life experiences children from minority communities bring to school and how they can be incorporated into their lessons (Moll, Amanti, Neff, & Gonzalez, 1992). Furthermore, students' motivation to read is affected by their cultural backgrounds and ethnicities (Fordham & Ogbu, 1986). Some students may actively decide to under-perform in school so that they do not alienate themselves from peers who do not value academic knowledge (Ogbu, 1995). Other students may see little value in reading because classroom materials do not tie to their life experiences and perceptions of the world (Tatum, 2008). Yet, we do not see any evidence of students' life experiences having bearing on the diagnostic approaches used with pupils.

Sociocultural research pertaining to children's language, funds of knowledge, ways of speaking, and understandings about the relationships between home and school should have informed our diagnostic practices—but they have not. There are no simple answers to how this might be done, but at this point the consideration of sociocultural information has been strikingly absent in the diagnosis of students' reading achievement.

There should be an emphasis in teachers' professional development to recognize that almost all children, regardless of the diversity of their sociocultural backgrounds, possess the cognitive and linguistic abilities for learning to read well. Diagnostic practices need to describe and explain the contexts in which children can and will succeed in reading, rather than only focusing on what they do not know or how their performance contrasts with a standard. The sooner diagnostic practices align with this research the better.

Conclusion

Throughout this chapter we identified and described successive changes in reading diagnostic traditions. Theoretical shifts from oral reading at the beginning of the 20th century, to silent in the 1930s, then to a focus on phonics in the 1960s, and eventually to an understanding of the interactive and constructive nature of reading during the 1980s have affected diagnostic protocols. Clay, the Goodmans, and Pearson have informed our understanding of the reading process and brought about important effects on reading's diagnostic traditions, particularly in the assessment of emergent readers, the analysis of children's oral miscues and the measurement of text comprehension.

Some issues in reading diagnosis, such as the use of norm-referenced testing and the role of phonics, have brought undue influence on how children are diagnosed in schools. The federal government, especially in its NCLB regulations, has been primarily responsible for the current overdependence on testing to assess children's reading performance. Norm-referenced testing, although it may contribute, does not constitute a reading diagnosis because these tests are unlikely to identify students' reading levels, skills, strategies, or motivation to read.

Contextual effects on children's reading are well established in the research literature, but children are typically diagnosed as if reading were context free. Children from low-income minority and multilingual backgrounds, in particular, have been the unfortunate recipients of misdiagnosis; all too often diagnosticians misunderstand the interplay between children's linguistic and cognitive processes in reading with the social and cultural contexts in which they live.

Reading's diagnostic traditions have been slow to change with the growth of the digital technologies. Yet, today many children read on computer screens as much if not more than with conventional printed texts. Diagnostic practices have not yet addressed children's use of the digital literacies, and many reading teachers have less knowledge of them than the children they teach. Reading diagnosis needs to catch-up and develop protocols for assessing children's use of the digital literacies if diagnoses are to be pertinent and education is to be relevant.

The purpose of diagnosis is to inform teaching and improve student learning, but we have lost our way. Schools have gone astray in their over emphasis on and faith in norm-referenced testing. Diagnosticians should be assessing the processes students use for decoding and constructing meaning as well as learning what motivates them to read. Recent attention to what matters in student learning has been misdirected. It is now common for diagnosticians to spend more time analyzing students' performance on isolated elements of reading, such as on phonemic awareness activities and word recognition accuracy, than developing an understanding of children's skills and strategies with connected discourse. Certainly there is hope that schools will move past such recent traditions and improve their diagnosis of students with reading difficulties. The recent recommendations for teachers' on-going professional development, as seen in national teaching standards (NCATE/IRA), are a welcome change for connecting classroom practices with research and diagnosis. The current use of literacy coaches has the potential to positively impact classroom teachers' professional development, and the need for knowledgeable and skilled reading diagnosticians is increasingly important in RtI programs.

Reading diagnosis needs to be more educationally relevant, and it must respond more quickly and thoughtfully to change, particularly at incorporating the digital technologies and connecting students' out-of-school experiences to classroom learning. Diagnosticians, who embrace and synthesize the findings from research into good practice, are critical for preparing all students, including those with difficulties in reading and those from historically underrepresented groups, for full and successful participation in school and society.

References

Adams, M. (1990). *Beginning to read: Thinking and learning about print.* Cambridge, MA: MIT Press.

Afflerbach, P. (2007a). Best practices in literacy assessment. In Gambrell, L. B., Morrow, L. M., & Pressley, M. (Eds.), *Best practices in literacy instruction* (pp. 264–282). New York: Guilford.

Afflerbach, P. (2007b). *Understanding and using reading assessment K-12.* Newark, DE: International Reading Association.

Allington, R. L. (2009). *What really matters in response to intervention: Research-based designs.* Boston: Pearson/Allyn & Bacon.

Allington, R. L., & McGill-Franzen, A. (1989). School response to reading failure: Chapter 1 and special education students in grades 2, 4, and 8. *Elementary School Journal, 89,* 529–542.

Anderson, R. C., & Pearson, P. D. (1984). A schema-theoretic view of basic processes in reading comprehension. In P. D. Pearson (Ed.), *Handbook of reading research* (pp. 255–291). New York: Longman.

Artiles, A. J. (2003). Special education's changing identity: Paradoxes and dilemmas in view of culture and space. *Harvard Educational Review, 73*(2), 164–202.

Au, K., & Mason, J. M. (1981). Social organizational factors in learning to read: The balance of rights hypothesis. *Reading Research Quarterly, 17,* 115–152.

Banks, J. (2006). A comprehensive framework for evaluating hypotheses about cultural bias in educational testing. *Applied Measures in Education, 19*(2), 115–132.

Bell, S. M., & McCallum, R. S. (2008). *Handbook of reading assessment.* Boston: Pearson/Allyn & Bacon.

Betts, E. A. (1946). *Foundations of reading instruction.* New York: American Book.

Bloom, B. (1965). *Taxonomy of educational objectives: The classification of educational goals.* New York: David McKay.

Bond, G. L., & Dykstra, R. (1967). The cooperative research program in first-grade reading instruction. *Reading Research Quarterly, 2,* 5–141.

Brown, A., & Day, J. (1983). Macrorules for summarizing text: The development of expertise. *Journal of Verbal Learning and Verbal Behavior, 22,* 1–14.

Brown, J. (1992). *The definition of a profession: The authority of metaphor in the history of intelligence testing (1890–1930).* Princeton, NJ: Princeton University Press.

Cazden, C. (2001). *Classroom discourse: The language of teaching and learning.* Portsmouth, NH: Heinemann.

Chall, J. (1967). *Learning to read: The great debate.* New York: McGraw-Hill.

Chappuis, S., & Chappuis, J. (2007). The best value in formative assessment. *Educational Leadership, 65*(4), 14–19.

Chomsky, C. C. (1978). When you still can't read in third grade after decoding, what? In S. J. Samuels (Ed.), *What research has to say about reading instruction* (pp. 13–30). Newark, DE: International Reading Association.

Cicourel, A. (1974). *Language use and school performance.* New York: Academic Press.

Clay, M. M. (1985). *The early detection of reading difficulties* (3rd ed.) Portsmouth, NH: Heinemann.

Clay, M. M. (1987). Learning to be learning disabled. *New Zealand Journal of Educational Studies, 22*(2), 155–173.

Clay, M. M. (1993a). *An observational survey of early literacy achievement.* Portsmouth, NH: Heinemann.

Clay, M. M. (1993b). *Reading Recovery: A guidebook for teachers in training.* Portsmouth, NH: Heinemann.

Coyne, M. D., Kame'enui, E. J., & Simmons, D. C. (2001). Prevention and intervention in beginning reading: Two complex systems. *Learning Disabilities Research & Practice, 16*(2), 62–73.

Deford, D. E. (1985). Validating the construct of theoretical orientation in reading instruction. *Reading Research Quarterly, 20*(3), 351–367.

Delpit, L. (1995). *Other people's children: Cultural conflict in the classroom.* New York: New Press.

Deno, S. L. (1985). Curriculum-based measurement: The emerging alternative. *Exceptional Children, 52,* 219–232.

Deno, S. L., & Fuchs, L. S. (1987). Developing curriculum-based measurement systems for data-based special education problem solving. *Focus on Exceptional Children, 19*(8), 1–16.

DeVries, B. A. (2004). *Literacy assessment and intervention in the elementary classroom.* Scottsdale, AZ: Holcomb Hathaway.

Dunn, L. M. (1968). Special education for the mildly retarded: Is much of it justifiable? *Exceptional Children, 13*(2), 5–22.

Education of All Handicapped Children Act. (1975). Public Law 94-142 (S. 6).

Ehri, L. C. (1991). Development of the ability to read words. In R. Barr, M. L. Kamil, P. Mosenthal, & P. D. Pearson (Eds.), *Handbook of reading research* (Vol. 2, pp. 383–417). New York: Longman.

Ehri, L. C., & McCormick, S. (1998). Phases of word learning: Implications for instruction with delayed and disabled readers. *Reading & Writing Quarterly, 14,* 135–164.

Fielding, L., & Pearson, P. D. (1994). Reading comprehension: What works. *Educational Leadership, 51*(5), 62–68.

Fiene, J., & McMahon, S. (2007). Assessing comprehension: A classroom-based process. *The Reading Teacher, 60*(5), 406–416.

Flesch, R. (1955). *Why Johnny can't read.* New York: Harper & Row.

Fordham, C., & Ogbu, J. (1986). Black school success: Coping with the burden of "acting White." *The Urban Review, 28,* 176–208.

Fountas, I. C., & Pinnell, G. S. (1996). *Guided reading: Good first teaching for all children.* Portsmouth, NH: Heinemann.

Freedle, R. O. (2003). Correcting the SAT's ethnic and social-class bias: A method of reestimating SAT scores. *Harvard Educational Review, 73*(1), 1–44.

Fuchs, D., & Fuchs, L. S. (2006). Introduction to response to intervention: What, why, and how valid is it? *Reading Research Quarterly, 41*(1), 93–99.

Fuchs, L. S., & Fuchs, D. (2008). Progress monitoring within a multi-tiered prevention system: Best practices. In J. Grimes & A. Thomas (Eds.), *Best practices in school psychology* (pp. 2147–2164). Bethesda, MD: National Association of School Psychologists.

Garner, R. (1987). *Metacognition and reading comprehension.* Norwood, NJ: Erlbaum.

Good, R. H., Kaminski, R. A., Smith, S. Laimon, D., & Dill, S. (2002). *Dynamic indicators of basic early literacy skills* (6th ed.). Eugene, OR: Institute for the Development of Educational Achievement. Retrieved April 15, 2008, from http://dibels.uoregon.edu

Goodman, K. S. (1967). Reading: A psycholinguistic guessing game. *Journal of the Reading Specialist, 6,* 125–135.

Goodman, K. S. (1969). Analysis of reading miscues: Applied psycholinguistics. *Reading Research Quarterly, 5,* 9–30.

Goodman, K. S. (2006). *The truth about DIBELS: What it is, what it does.* Portsmouth, NH: Heinemann.

Goodman, K. S., & Goodman, Y. M. (1977). Learning about psycholinguistic processes by analyzing oral reading. *Harvard Educational Review, 47,* 313–333.

Goodman, Y. M. (1996). Revaluing readers while readers revalue themselves: Retrospective Miscue Analysis. *The Reading Teacher, 49*(8), 600–609.

Gray, W. S. (1916). *Standardized oral reading paragraphs.* Bloomington, IL: Bloomington Public Schools.

Hansen, J., & Pearson, P.D. (1983). An instructional study: Improving the inferential comprehension of good and poor fourth-grade readers. *Journal of Educational Psychology, 75*(6), 821–829.

Heath, S. B. (1983). *Ways with words: Language, life, and work in communities and classrooms.* Cambridge, UK: Cambridge University Press.

Hollenbeck, A. F. (2007). From IDEA to implementation: A discussion of foundational and future responsiveness-to-intervention research. *Learning Disabilities Research & Practice, 22*(2), 137–146.

Hunt, N., & Marshall, K. (2002). *Exceptional children and youth* (3rd ed.) Boston: Houghton Mifflin.

Individuals with Disabilities Education Improvement Act. (2004) P.L. 108-446

International Reading Association. (2006). *A call to action and a framework for change: IRA's position on NCLB reform.* Retrieved November 1, 2008, from http://www.reading.org/publications/reading_today/samples/RTY-0704-monitoring.html

Johns, J. L. (2008). *Basic reading inventory* (10th ed.). Dubuque, IA: Kendall/Hunt.

Johnston, P. (1997). *Knowing literacy: Constructive literacy assessment.* York, ME: Stenhouse.

Johnston, P., & Costello, P. (2005). Principles of literacy assessment. *Reading Research Quarterly, 40*(2), 256–267.

Kintsch, W., & van Dijk, T.A. (1978). Toward a model of discourse comprehension and production. *Psychological Review, 85,* 363–375.

Klauda, S. L., & Guthrie, J. (2008). Relationship of three components of fluency to reading comprehension. *Journal of Educational Psychology, 100,* 310–321.

LaBerge, D., & Samuels, S. J. (1974). Towards a theory of automatic information processing in reading. *Cognitive Psychology, 6,* 293–323.

Ladson-Billings, G. (1994). *The dreamkeepers: Successful teachers of African American children.* San Francisco: Jossey-Bass.

Lipsky, D. K., & Gartner, A. (1996). Inclusion, school restructuring, and the remaking of American society. *Harvard Educational Review, 66*(4), 762–797.

Lipson, M. Y., & Wixson, K. K. (1986). Reading disability research: An interactionist perspective. *Review of Educational Research, 6*(1), 111–136.

Lipson, M. Y., & Wixson, K. K. (2009). *Assessment and instruction of reading and writing difficulties: An interactive approach* (4th ed.). Boston: Pearson/Allyn & Bacon.

McCormick, S., & Braithwaite, J. (2008). Fifty years of remedial and clinical reading in the United States: A historical overview. In M. J. Fresch (Ed.), *An essential history of current reading practices* (pp. 157–185). Newark, DE: International Reading Association.

McDermott, R. (2004). Putting literacy in its place. *Journal of Education, 184*(1), 11–20.

McGill-Franzen, A. (1987). Failure to learn to read: Formulating a policy problem. *Reading Research Quarterly, 22*(4), 475–490.

McGill-Franzen, A. (2000). *The relationship between reading policy and instruction: A recent history.* Albany, NY: National Center on English Learning and Achievement. (Report 13004). Retrieved April 30, 2008, from http://cela.albany.edu/reports/mcgill/mcgill relationship13004.pdf

McKenna, M. C., & Picard, M. (2006). Revisiting the role of miscue analysis in effective teaching. *The Reading Teacher, 60*(4), 378–380.

Mesmer, E. M., & Mesmer, H. A. (2008). Response to intervention (RTI): What teachers of reading need to know. *The Reading Teacher, 62*(4), 280–290.

Miller, J., & Schwanenflugel, P. (2008). A longitudinal study of the development of reading prosody as a dimension of oral reading fluency in early elementary school children. *Reading Research Quarterly, 43*(4), 336–354.

Moll, L. C., Amanti, C., Neff, D., & Gonzalez, N. (1992). Funds of knowledge in teaching: Using a qualitative approach to connect homes and classrooms. *Theory into Practice, 31*(2), 132–141.

Monahan, T. (1998). *The rise of standardized educational testing in the United States: A bibliographic overview.* Troy, NY: Rensselaer Polytechnic Institute.

Moore, A. (1996). Assessing young readers: Questions of culture and ability. *Language Arts, 73*(5), 306–317.

National Commission on Excellence in Education. (1983). Retrieved May 29, 2008, from http://www.ed.gov/pubs/NatAtRisk/risk/html

National Institute of Child Health and Human Development. (2000). *Report of the National Reading Panel. Teaching children to read: An evidence-based assessment of the scientific research literature on reading and its implications for reading instruction.* (NIH Publication No. 00-4769). Washington, DC: U.S. Government Printing Office.

Nilsson, N. L. (2008). A critical analysis of eight informal reading inventories. *The Reading Teacher, 61*(7), 526–536.

No Child Left Behind Act of 2001. (2002), Pub. L. No.107-110, 115 Stat. 1425

Ogbu, J. (1995). Literacy and black Americans: Comparative perspectives. In V. Gadsden & D. A. Wagner (Eds.), *Literacy among African-American Youth: Issues in learning, teaching, and schooling* (pp. 83–100). Cresskill, NJ: Hampton Press.

Paris, S. G., & Carpenter, R. D. (2003). FAQ's about IRIs. *The Reading Teacher, 56*(6), 578–581.

Paris, S. G., & Jacobs, J. E. (1984). The benefits of informed instruction for children's reading awareness and comprehension skills. *Child Development, 55,* 2083–2093.

Pearson, P. D. (1985) The changing face of reading comprehension instruction. *The Reading Teacher, 38*(8), 724–738.

Pearson, P. D., & Dole, J. (1987). Explicit comprehension instruction: Review of research and a new conceptionalization of comprehension. *Elementary School Journal, 88*(2), 151–165.

Pearson, P. D., & Hamm, D. N. (2005). The history of reading comprehension assessment. In S. G. Paris & S. A. Stahl (Eds.), *Children's reading comprehension and assessment* (pp. 13–70). Mahwah, NJ: Erlbaum.

Pearson, P. D., Hiebert, E. H., & Kamil, M .L. (2007). Vocabulary assessment: What we know and what we need to learn. *Reading Research Quarterly, 42*(2), 282–296.

Pearson, P. D., & Johnston, P. (1982). *Prior knowledge, connectivity, and the assessment of reading comprehension.* Technical Report. No. 245. ERIC Document Reproduction Service ED217402.

Pressley, M. (2002). Metacognition and self-regulated comprehension. In A. E. Farstrup, & S. Samuels (Eds.), *What research has to say about reading instruction* (pp. 291–309). Newark, DE: International Reading Association.

Raphael, T., & Au, K. (2005). QAR: Enhancing comprehension and testing taking across grades and content areas. *The Reading Teacher, 59*(3), 206–221.

Raphael, T., & Pearson, P. D. (1985). Increasing students' awareness of information for answering questions. *American Educational Research Journal, 22*(2), 217–235.

Reidel, B. W. (2007). The relation between DIBELS, reading comprehension, and vocabulary in urban first-grade students. *Reading Research Quarterly, 42*(4), 546–567.

Rowe, D. W., & Rayford, L. (1987). Activating background knowledge in reading comprehension assessment. *Reading Research Quarterly, 22*(2), 160–176.

Schmitt, M. C. (1990). A questionnaire to measure children's awareness of strategic reading processes. *The Reading Teacher, 43*(7), 338–340.

Shannon, P. (1998). A selective social history of the uses of reading texts. In S. Murphy, P. Shannon, P. Johnston, & J. Hansen (Eds.), *Fragile evidence: A critique of reading assessment* (pp. 75–88). Mahwah, NJ: Erlbaum.

Shaw, D., Dvorak, M.J., Bates, K. (2007). Promise and possibility - hope for teacher education: Pre-service literacy instruction can have an impact. *Reading Research and Instruction, 46*(3), 223–254.

Skiba, R. J., Poloni-Staudinger, L., Gallini, S., Simmons, A. B., & Feggins-Azziz, R. (2006). Disparate access: The disproportionality of African American students with disabilities across educational environments. *Exceptional Children, 72*(4), 411–424.

Smith, F. (1978). *Understanding reading: A psycholinguistic analysis of reading and learning to read.* New York: Holt, Rinehart and Winston.

Snyder, L., Caccamise, D., & Wise, B. (2005). Reading comprehension's new look: Influences of theory and technology on practice. *Topics in Language Disorders, 25*(1), 33–50.

Stainback, W., & Stainback, S. (1984). A rationale for the merger of special and regular education. *Exceptional Children, 51,* 102–111.

Stein, N. L., & Glenn, C. G. (1979). An analysis of story comprehension in elementary school children. In R. O. Freedle (Ed.), *New directions in discourse processing: Advances in discourse processing* (Vol. 2, pp. 53–120). Norwood, NJ: Ablex.

Tatum, A. (2008). Toward a more anatomically complete model of literacy instruction: A focus on African American male adolescents and texts. *Harvard Educational Review, 78*(1), 155–180.

USDE. (2007). *Twenty-five years of progress in educating children with disabilities through IDEA.* Retrieved May 21, 2008 from http://www. ed.gov/policy/speced/leg/idea/history.pdf

Valencia, S. W., & Pearson, P. D. (1988). Principles for classroom assessment. *Remedial and Special Education, 9*(1), 26–35.

Vaughn, S., & Fuchs, L. S. (2003). Redefining learning disabilities as inadequate response to instruction: The promise and potential problems. *Learning Disabilities Research & Practice, 18*(3), 137–146.

Vaughn, S., Linan-Thompson, S., & Hickman, P. (2003). Response to instruction as a means of identifying students with reading/learning disabilities. *Exceptional Children, 69*(4), 391–409.

Walpole, S., & McKenna, M. C. (2006). The role of information reading inventories in assessing word recognition. *The Reading Teacher, 59,* 592–594.

Weber, R. (1968). The study of oral reading errors. A survey of the literature. *Reading Research Quarterly, 68*(4), 96–119.

Weber, R. (1973). Dialect differences in oral reading: An analysis of errors. In J. L. Laffey & R. Shuy (Eds.), *Language differences do they interfere?* (pp. 47–62). Newark, DE: International Reading Association.

Willis, I. A. (1995). Reading the world of school literacy: Contextualizing the experience of a young African American male. *Harvard Educational Review, 65*(1), 30–49.

Willis, I. A. (2008). *Reading comprehension research and testing in the US: Undercurrents of race, class, and power in the struggle for meaning.* New York: Erlbaum.

Yopp, H. (1995). A test for assessing phonemic awareness in young children. *The Reading Teacher, 49*(1), 20–30.

Yopp, H., & Yopp, R. (2000). Supporting phonemic awareness development in the classroom. *The Reading Teacher, 54*(2), 130–143.

Ysseldyke, J. E., Thurlow, M. L., Mecklenburg, C., & Graden, J. (1984). Opportunity to learn for regular and special education students during reading instruction. *Remedial and Special Education, 5,* 29–37.

Zhang, D., & Katsiyannis, A. (2002). Minority representation in special education: A persistent challenge. *Remedial and Special Education, 23*(3), 180–187.

16

Reading Fluency

What Is It and How Should It Be Measured?

S. J. ALT AND S. JAY SAMUELS
University of Minnesota

According to *Reading Today* (Cassidy and Cassidy, 2003/2004), reading fluency is a very hot topic. Though reading fluency has experienced fluctuating periods of high and low status over the years, it is currently experiencing a place of prominence in the classroom. This may be attributed to the shocking finding published by the NAEP (Daane, Campbell, Grigg, Goodman, & Oranje, 2005) that nearly half of the fourth-grade students studied were not fluent in reading grade-level materials, and to two other prestigious reports that emphasized the need for reading fluency to be an important goal of reading curriculums (NRC as reported in Snow, Burns, & Griffin, 1998), and the finding that the method of repeated reading is an effective method for improving word recognition, fluency, and comprehension across grade levels (National Reading Panel, 2000). As a result of these reports, reading fluency has gained new recognition as an essential element of reading programs, especially for students who struggle with reading (Allington, 2008; Hudson, Lane, & Pullen, 2005).

As an extension of reading fluency's new found notoriety, both its definition and its measurement have fallen under intense scrutiny. Now that reading fluency has been added to most, if not all, reading programs, a plethora of developmental methods and interventions have flooded the school systems, along with a number of mass marketers of testing products claiming to have assessments measuring reading fluency. At issue here then is the question of whether or not these assessments really assess reading fluency. To answer this question we must first answer the basic question of, what is reading fluency?

To this end, our goal is twofold: (a) to compose a definition of reading fluency based on automaticity theory. This is important because definitions are critical in determining how a construct should be measured; and (b) to explore the question of how fluency should be measured, because even though reading fluency is indeed a hot topic today, due to existing conflicting definitions, it is also a battleground in terms of how best to measure it.

A Bit of History

It could be said that the birth of reading fluency occurred with the 1908 publication of Edmund Huey's book, *The Psychology and Pedagogy of Reading*, a book so instrumental in the study of reading fluency that it was reissued 60 years later and has just been reissued a second time, roughly 100 years after its original publication. There are two possible reasons for the book's popularity first in 1908, again in 1968, and once again in 2009. One reason may be that the original publication occurred before the paradigm of behaviorism and the reissuings have occurred again as the paradigm shifted from behaviorism to cognitivism and a renewed desire to study cognitive aspects of reading (like comprehension) occurred. The second and probably primary reason for the book's stamina may be attributed to Huey's naissance of automaticity theory. A theory instrumental to the findings of Samuels, LaBerge, & Bremer (1978) that beginning readers become fluent readers in stages: first reading by letters, then by groups of letters or syllables, then by whole words, and eventually whole sentences.

With the re-emerging interest in reading fluency, reading curriculums came under attack (Goodman & Goodman, 1979; Smith, 1973), and reading wars between whole language groups, skills based groups, and advocates of a balanced approach. It is during this time period that the University of Minnesota started its research institute, The Human Learning Center, and LaBerge and Samuels developed their theory of reading—a theory focusing on the development of automaticity in word recognition. This theory distinguishes a fluent reader from a non-fluent reader based on automaticity. In other words, if a student is not automatic at word recognition then the important job of reading for meaning has to be done in two stages. During the first stage the student's attention is on the task of decoding the words in the text, and because the word recognition task is not automatic all of the available cognitive resources are being used for this task. During the second stage the student switches his or her attention and cognitive resources to comprehension. This two-step process is slow and places a heavy demand on the memory systems. However, over a period of time and with a lot of practice reading books in the student's zone of reading ability or Zone of Proximal Development (ZPD) (Vygotsky, 1978, 1986), the student becomes automatic at the decoding task. With the decoding task now being automatic, the two tasks of decoding and comprehension can be done together (LaBerge and Samuels, 1974).

While LaBerge and Samuels focused on how the automatic decoding of words facilitated comprehension, Schreiber (1980, 1987) took a linguistic approach. He reasoned that the route to fluency was brought about by students learning to parse a text (automatically) into its linguistic units such as a noun phrase and verb phrase. Accordingly, fluent readers were able to use punctuation to rapidly determine where to place emphasis and separate text into grammatical units. For example, when we see a question mark at the end of a sentence our voices change in tone and emphasis to indicate we are asking a question and not making a statement. When breaking a text into linguistic units occurs effortlessly, it frees up cognitive resources for comprehension. Others (i.e., Thurlow & van den Broek, 1997) have extended the idea to be as reading skills increase, more and more of the sub-skills become automatic. This has lead to the recent reconceptualization of what can be automatic in reading that goes beyond word identification to include components of the comprehension process as well, specifically that the inferential process can become automatic.

Automaticity Theory's Role

Why automaticity—because reading is a complex skill that requires the coordination of many sub-processes within a very short period of time (less than .225 msec.). Therefore, if each sub-process requires attention to get it done, performance of the complex skill will be impossible because the capacity of attention will be exceeded. However, if enough of the processing component sub-skills become automatic, then the load on attention will be within tolerable limits and the skill can be successfully performed. Therefore getting students to decode at an automatic level permits allocation of attention to comprehension so the two processes can occur at the same time.

There are any number of empirical research findings that support the idea that people are capable of doing two things at the same time (Allport, Antonis, & Reynolds, 1972; Spelke, Hirst, & Neisser, 1976). Intuitively we know this to be true as well. How else would we be able to drive a car, talk, and change the radio station all at the same time? How is it that we can walk and talk at the same time? Perhaps the answer for it lies in the fact that these actions require the use of different cognitive sub-skills and therefore, there is no conflict between the resources required to carry them out. Or, you might argue that not everyone can drive

a car, talk, and change the radio station at the same time, and you'd be correct. For example, novice drivers cannot do these things as well as seasoned drivers. So, what is the difference between the novice driver and the seasoned driver? Automaticity. The seasoned driver has developed automaticity in the skills needed to drive and therefore has no interference between the automatic process (driving) and other concurrent activities (talking and changing the radio station).

What does this mean in terms of a definition for reading fluency? It has a great deal to do with definitions that posit decoding is occurring at the automatic level. This is because with little effort or attention being spent on decoding words, the bulk of attention can be focused on comprehension. An example can be seen in a study by Daneman and Carpenter (1983) where children are read stories that contain inconsistencies. The inconsistencies were either explained right away (at the time the inconsistencies occurred in the story) or the explanation was delayed and occurred after a number of intervening sentences. When clarification occurs immediately (at the time of the inconsistency), there was no difference between the poor comprehenders and good comprehenders groups. However, if there are several sentences interposed between the inconsistencies and the clarification, poor comprehenders were much less likely to understand the text. Therefore, Daneman and Carpenter concluded that the crucial difference between the two groups is in their working memory capacity—one group (good comprehenders) had developed to the automatic level freeing up working memory for comprehension and the other group (poor comprehenders) did not.

Regardless of whether the definition incorporates the simultaneous decoding and comprehension of text or simply addresses its secondary characteristics (speed, accuracy, and prosody), both rely on the assumption that attentional capacity is limited. Therefore, quick and effortless word identification is important, and the multi-task functioning of the fluent reader is made possible by the reduced cognitive demands needed for word recognition and other reading processes, thus freeing cognitive resources for other functions, such as drawing inferences (NICHD Pub. No. 00-4769 in National Reading Panel, 2000). Automaticity theory lends credence to the NICHD and the NRP because, according to automaticity theory, a behavior or skill is automatic when two or more complex activities can be done at the same time. In other words, when a given stimulus is repeatedly paired with the same response, it progressively appears to take less and less attentional resources, and to interfere less and less with other concurrent tasks (Baddeley, 1990).

One of the most famous examples of automaticity can be seen in the Stroop task (Stroop, 1935; Cohen, Dunbar, & McClelland, 1990). In this task, words that name colors (e.g., red, green, blue) are printed in different colors. For example, the word red printed in green ink or the word green printed in red ink is shown to a participant, and the task is for the participant to name the color that the word is printed in, while ignoring the actual word. John Ridley

Stroop (1935) found that it took longer for a fluent reader to name the color that the word was printed in, than a non-fluent reader. This was because a fluent reader's automatic reading processes identify the word almost immediately, and this interferes with naming the color in which the word was printed.

Since the mid-1970s when LaBerge and Samuels (1974) presented their general theory of automatic information processing in reading, Shiffrin and Schneider (1977) addressed visual and memory search for letters and words, and Posner (1978) addressed letter recognition. Both coming to the conclusion and positing an expansion of Stroop's interference theory to include a multi-path and/or parallel processing component. A position in agreement with LaBerge and Samuels (1974), whereby they state the visual processing of words could take a variety of routes. Their model of visual memory shows that the following units could be used to recognize a word: distinctive features, letters, letter groups or spelling patterns, and the word itself. For skilled readers, the micro-level sub-skills (e.g., knowing letter-sound rules, letter combinations, and the meanings of words and their connections) became automatic. These units of recognition could be processed either with the services of attention, as the beginning reader might use, or automatically, as a skilled reader might do. Logan (1988, 1991), in discussing the LaBerge and Samuels' model states that in addition to the shift in the size of the unit used in word recognition, there is also a strengthening of the connections between the visual code and the phonological code.

While LaBerge and Samuels (1974) have traced the developmental route from beginning to fluent reading in their model, that is, from letter-by-letter identification leading to word recognition as a holistic process, they never attempted to explain the process whereby a word could be identified automatically. It took other researchers such as Logan (1997) and Stanovich (1990) to explain the mechanism whereby words could be identified with little attention and effort, and bring to the fore a memory phenomenon in which disparate separate actions can be chunked and stored into a single unit, as well as the idea of parallel processing and multiple pathways available for the complex sub-processes of reading. Neurological studies of the phonological loop provide some clues into this phenomenon. Its association with comprehension has been shown by the deficits in comprehension that have occurred when heavy loads have been placed on the phonological store (Baddeley, 1990). For example, the process of overt or covert articulation involves setting up and running speech motor programs. If this sub-process has the function of maintaining items in the phonological store by refreshing (rehearsing) their fading traces, then the faster it can run, the more items will be maintained and the longer the memory span. This is critical to comprehension in reading text. Much of the activity that goes on during comprehension of a written text by a fluent reader depends only minimally on the sound characteristics of the material being read and is much more dependent on its meaning. Therefore, it would appear that students maintain

something approaching a verbatim representation of much of a given sentence, while dumping that representation as they move from one sentence to the next. Since this involves carrying information over from one sentence to the next, there must be some form of representation that is other than a verbatim record. The quality of comprehension that occurs will then heavily depend on the accuracy of these representations and/or inferences.

To further enhance our understanding of multiple pathways available for reading words, we will investigate two possible routes for reading: the first is the grapheme to phoneme conversion route and the second is the visual lexicon through semantic route. The grapheme to phoneme conversion route begins with seeing the written word, processing it in the visual analysis system, sending it directly to the grapheme phoneme conversion system, and then having it go to the phonemic buffer before externalizing it as a spoken word—once seen the written word is processed through three stages before the word is spoken aloud. On the other hand, the visual lexicon through semantic route (also) begins with seeing the written word and then proceeds on to the following five stages; the visual analysis system, the visual input lexicon, the semantic system, (comprehension occurs between these two stages), the phonological output lexicon, and the phonemic level buffer before the word is spoken aloud. The existence of these two routes explains why a students' reading speed and accuracy can surpass their comprehension in reading text. For example, by training students to say words as quickly and accurately as possible (to the level of automaticity) does not necessarily mean the student is going to comprehend what they have said. This is because by focusing on speed and accuracy we may be forcing the use of the grapheme to phoneme conversion route which *bypasses* the semantic system and phonological output lexicon where comprehension takes place. Therefore, definitions of reading fluency that do not include comprehension may be implementing developmental practices and assessments that merely measure the student's ability to "bark at text" (Samuels, 2007). Consequently, though automaticity is a good thing for freeing up working memory capacity so comprehension can occur, caution must be taken not to assume the visual lexicon through semantic route is being taken without actually testing for comprehension.

The theory of automaticity and its relationship to beginning and fluent readers can be further explained by the use of fMRI to map reading sub-process. In the complex mapping of mental sub-processes, the researchers (Pihlajamaki et al., 2000; Shaywitz, Mody, & Shaywitz, 2006) argue for the capacity of parallel processing. In a very complex system comprised of a set of five subsystems (primary visual—where decoding takes place, auditory, somatosensory, gustatory, and olfactory) each of which are connected to the Conceptual/Associative subsystem (where the phonological loop resides and comprehension takes place), which itself is in turn connected to each of the two motor output subsystems (manual and vocal), and where all of these subsystems are further interconnected to four additional subsystems (hippocampal, basal ganglia, cerebellar, and amygdale); it is the *interconnectedness* of these subsystems that permits the possibility of attaining automaticity and the by-passing of some subsystems. In theory, when something is learned to automaticity it could conceivably enter the primary visual subsystem, go directly to the hippocampus or amygdala (by-passing semantic operations in the Conceptual/Associative subsystem altogether) and exit directly to the motor output subsystem. In fact, this pathway has been shown to exist in studies of brain damaged patients. For example, Ellis and Young (1988) found that patients who had damage to the C/A (Conceptual/Associative Subsystems) while having intact VPI (Visual Perceptual Input) and VMO (Vocal Motor Output) were able to read without semantics or showed word meaning deafness. In other words, they were able to read without comprehension.

The further works of cognitive psychologists (Ackerman, 1987; Logan, 1988, 1991; Posner & Snyder, 1975; Shiffrin & Schneider, 1977) describe the characteristics of reading fluency to be highly skilled and complex, and they agree that the seemingly effortless automatic text processing skills required for reading are acquired gradually and as a result of extended practice. This is because automatic processes are fast and effortless (from the standpoint of allocation of cognitive resources), unitized (proceduralized) such that they may not be easily altered by a subject's conscious control, and may allow for parallel operation with other information processing within and between tasks. Note that when a person is automatic at decoding it allows for parallel processing and the person is able to perform several tasks at the same time such as; decode words in a text, break words into proper grammatical units, and comprehend. This concept of parallel processing is essential to the definition of fluency and to its valid measurement.

First Goal—A Definition

Reading fluency is a complex psychological construct comprised of numerous sub-processes, and because it is, it can mean different things to different people. The conundrum is that there are currently three camps, each with a different definition of reading fluency. Two camps fracture reading fluency into its secondary characteristics of speed, accuracy, and prosody. One of these two camps defines reading fluency as the ability to read a passage of text with speed and accuracy (Daane et al., 2005; Armbruster, Lehr, & Osborn, 2001), a process that occurs in two stages with word recognition or decoding occurring at stage one and comprehension occurring at stage two. This two-stage process is what beginning readers do, not what fluent readers do. In another, but similar, camp are those who define reading fluency as the ability to read with speed, accuracy and expression/prosody (Hudson, Lane, & Pullen, 2005; Rasinski, 2007; Denton, Bryan, Wexler, Reed, & Vaughn, 2007). This camp believes that if a student spends most of his effort focused on word recognition or reading one word

at a time without phrasing, then his ability to comprehend is compromised. Further suggesting prosody coupled with speed and accuracy is evidence of comprehension. Therefore, if a person reads with accuracy and prosody, but slowly then no comprehension has taken place. Implicit in their definition is that the articulation or enunciation of a word is directly related to knowing its meaning. For instance, if a person can't pronounce a word, then she doesn't understand it and if a person can pronounce a word she does understand it. A problem with this definition is that it is not always true. For example, there are individuals who know the meaning of words but may not pronounce them correctly (perhaps the individuals have not used the word or heard it used in conversation), and there are individuals who do not know the meaning of words they can pronounce (they have heard it before). The third camp consists of those who define reading fluency as the ability to simultaneously decode and comprehend text (LaBerge & Samuels, 1974; NICHD Pub. No. 00-4769 in NRP, 2000; Samuels, 2002, 2006, 2007; Wolf & Katzir-Cohen, 2001). This approach relies on fluency being a one-step process, something fluent readers do. It relies on automaticity theory and the belief that decoding can occur at an automatic level (fast and accurate), thereby leaving working memory resources available for comprehension to occur at the same time.

Though at first blush the three camp's connotations may appear equivalent in that they contain secondary characteristics of reading fluency (speed, accuracy, and prosody), they are not. The reason they are not the same has to do with how they deal with the issue of comprehension. The definitions offered by the first two camps do not explicitly include a comprehension component. One assumes speed and accuracy provides a bridge to comprehension. For example, if a listener is able to understand what the reader is reading then the reader must be able to comprehend it as well (Armbruster, Lehr, & Osborn, 2001)—comprehension is implicit. The other includes a third characteristic—prosody, believing that if all three characteristics are done well then comprehension is a given—comprehension is explicit in the form of prosody. There are two problems with these two camp's definitions. The first problem is that they misapply automaticity theory's role in reading fluency by assuming if a person exhibits these secondary characteristics well and quickly then the person will automatically use the freed up attentional resources for comprehension. However, these camps do not explicitly check (measure) to see if the person really does comprehend what they've just read. A second problem is the misconception that the complex cognitive processes necessary for comprehension can be measured behaviorally and that all individuals will display the same behavioral affects (expression) for comprehension. This is further confounded by the effect of grammar, dialectical, and idiom rules for expression in reading that can be mimicked without comprehension of the involved text. For example, these definitions do not explain why a person can read a passage of text either in a foreign language (be it an English as a second language student reading a passage in

English or an English-speaking individual reading a passage in French) or in the form of Jabberwocky (Carroll, 1872) with great speed, accuracy, and prosody and yet when tested for comprehension shows none. For example, Alice of *Alice's Adventures in Wonderland* reads the following poem:

'Twas brillig, and the slithy toves
Did gyre and gimble in the wabe:
All mimsy were the borogoves,
And the mome raths outgrabe.
Beware the Jabberwock, my son!
The jaws that bite, the claws that catch!
Beware the Jubjub bird, and shun
The frumious Bandersnatch!…

and then comments, "it seems very pretty, but it's rather hard to understand!" So, though Alice is perfectly capable of reading the poem with speed, accuracy, and prosody, she admits to not understanding it.

Consequently, while the secondary characteristics (speed, accuracy, and prosody) are necessary for reading fluency, they are not sufficient. In view of this fact, the first two camp's definitions of reading are specious because they define the two-stage process of what beginning readers do, decode at time one and then comprehend at time two, not what a fluent reader does, decode and comprehend simultaneously. It is only the third camp's definition that definitively defines the one-stage process fluent readers do, simultaneous decoding and comprehending. Even so, we must be cautious and recognize that fluency is not a dichotomous variable where a person is considered to be either fluent or not fluent, but one that occurs on a continuum (Logan, 1991). For example, a student can be very fluent when reading material is of interest to him and less fluent when he has had no previous exposure to the material or finds it of little interest. For this reason, a fluent reader should not be thought of as a stage of development in which all words can be processed quickly, for even highly skilled readers can encounter uncommon, low frequency words that they are unable to recognize automatically (Shiffrin & Schneider, 1977).

Further support for the third camp's definition comes from the neuropsychological research of Ellis and Young (1988), Pihlajamaki et al. (2000), Miller and Cohen (2001), and Shaywitz et al. (2006) that shows multiple pathways for seeing, processing and saying written words. For example, the Ellis and Young mode depicts two possible routes for the pronunciation of a written word. These routes are the grapheme to phoneme conversion route and the visual lexicon through semantic route. Support for these two routes (Ellis & Young, 1988) has been found from having participants read real words and non-words; non-words take longer to pronounce and cause more error. This error is presumed to occur due to the conflict between the two different routes it could have taken. For example, when studying a patient known as TOB, Ellis and Young found that though TOB had little difficulty reading aloud regular words and non-words, he could not read irregular words, he had strong regularization of exception words, and he was not able to explain the meaning of any word he could not pronounce correctly—he took the path known as the grapheme to phoneme conversion route. Further, studying a patient known as Norman, they found Norman could read most words well but could not read non-words, and he could reliably distinguish between exception words and non-words even though he could not pronounce them—he took the path known as the lexical-semantic route.

The definitive definition of reading fluency is seen written word goes to the visual analysis system and then to the visual input lexicon, once recognized as a word it travels to the semantic system, and then to the phonological output lexicon to the phonemic level buffer, and finally comes out as speech. This route includes the semantic system whereby meaning is attached to the word or sentence, facilitating comprehension. The specious definitions of fluency are the grapheme phoneme conversion route—seen written word, visual analysis system, grapheme phoneme conversion, phonemic level buffer, and speech. This route does not include the semantic system and phonological output lexicon that are necessary for word meaning attachment, and hence no comprehension is taking place. Therefore the only true definition of reading fluency is the one posited by the third camp—the ability to simultaneously decode and comprehend text. This definition sets the ground rules for the next goal of how reading fluency should be measured.

Second Goal—How to Measure Reading Fluency

Automaticity theory provides the foundation necessary for defining the construct of reading fluency (the simultaneous decoding and comprehension of text) and identifies the resulting secondary characteristics (speed, accuracy, and expression). These characteristics further provide concrete areas for the instruction and development of reading fluency, and are, in turn, necessary for the assessment of that fluency. More than ever, in these times of high-stakes testing, valid reading fluency assessments are imperative. To this end, reading fluency assessments must not only measure the secondary characteristics of speed, accuracy, and prosody, but must also *explicitly* assess comprehension. However, not all assessments professing to measure reading fluency actually do (DIBELS), and even some assessments that don't profess to measure reading fluency are being misused (CBM) to falsely report reading fluency scores. For these reasons, reading fluency assessment tools are in need of extensive review.

Snow, Burns, and Griffin (1998) state, "because the ability to obtain meaning from print depends so strongly on the development of word recognition accuracy and reading fluency, both should be regularly assessed in the classroom" (p. 7). However, we must first develop a valid measure, and to do so we must be steadfast in our definition of the construct being measured. In this case, the main characteristic of reading fluency is the ability to do at least two tasks simultaneously, i.e., decoding and comprehension. Therefore, only measurement tasks that include a comprehension component can hope to be valid measures of reading fluency.

Whereas the methods for developing reading fluency seem clear, the methods for measuring reading fluency are not so clear. One method used in the 1990s involved eye movements (saccads) and fixations to measure reading speed and comprehension. Underwood, Hubbard, and Wilkinson (1990) found eye fixation duration was a successful predictor of reading comprehension. Though they did not find a correlation between reading speed and comprehension, they did find a relationship between fixation durations and comprehension. Nevertheless, they caution that decreasing fixations may not lead to better comprehension because it could be that better comprehension leads to shorter fixations. Subsequently, Everatt and Underwood (1994) found increased information seeking behavior is related to reading speed and comprehension, but reading speed had no relationship with comprehension. For instance, shorter initial and gaze fixations are related to better comprehension, but the re-reading of text is not related to comprehension so much as it is to speed. Though these are two excellent examples of using saccads to measure comprehension (they also show no correlation between reading speed and comprehension), they are not amenable to classroom implementation so much as laboratory clinical studies.

When it comes to the implementation of classroom assessment tools for reading fluency, the goal is to find out if students are simultaneously decoding and comprehending. A common method of doing this is to inform the student at the time of testing that they will be asked to first read a passage of text orally and then be tested on comprehension by either retelling as much of the story as they can or answering questions about the text they just read. This method is a good match for measuring reading fluency because it requires the reader to decode and comprehend simultaneously.

Progress Monitors or Measures of Fluency?

Progress Monitors

Curriculum based measurement. Curriculum Based Measurement (CBM) was developed by Dr. Stanley Deno (1985) for the purpose of helping teachers evaluate a student's week-by-week *growth rate* while learning to read. This method required students to read for 1 minute from a text typically used in the student's regular instruction. The number of words read correctly in that 1-minute period of time was the students score. Often the student is tested over three passages, and the median score is the score used for an evaluation. A week later the student would be tested again on a similar passage and scored. If the student is making progress, then the score should increase from week to week. Deno's intent was for CBM to be used as a tool for measuring weekly progress in reading speed, not

as a measure of fluency. CBM was also created in order to provide an alternative to mastery measurement, which measured short-term accomplishments that often did not accumulate into broad competence (Fuchs, 2004). Placement and monitoring decisions require continuous measurement over time of a student's performance of a skill and then comparing results of prior efforts to current performance. Further, according to Deno (1985), any other decisions involved in the determination of program eligibility for a student should also incorporate a peer comparison. In other words any screening or changes in instructional goals and objectives for a student should not rest solely on their CBM scores but should also include a comparison of the student to their peers. CBM norms, words read correctly in 1 minute (WCPM), were established by Hasbrouck and Tindal (1992), and the median scores for various grades were set: Grade 2—53 WCPM, Grade 3—79 WCPM, Grade 4—99 WCPM, and Grade 5—105 WCPM.

Because misuse of the tool has led to the misperception that the development of efficient word recognition skills leads to improved comprehension (Calfee & Piontkowski, 1981), CBM has been widely used around the country to determine if a student is a fluent reader. In fact, McGlinchey and Hixson (2004) assessed the correlation between CBM and standardized reading scores and found supporting evidence for concurrent validity. However, Cramer and Rosenfield (2008) found no correlations between reading speed and reading fluency. What's more, Pressley, Hilden, and Shankland (2005) not only found no correlation, but found reading speed to be a poor predictor of reading fluency.

DIBELS. DIBELS is an acronym for Dynamic Indicators of Basic Early Literacy Skills and is made up of multiple measures, all of which have the term *fluency* attached to them. The measures are initial sound fluency, letter naming fluency, phoneme segmentation fluency, nonsense word fluency, oral reading fluency (ORF), and retell fluency (RF). Typically, the initial sound, letter naming, and phoneme segmentation fluency are given in kindergarten; the nonsense word and oral reading fluency are given in first grade, and the oral reading fluency in the second grade. The definition of reading fluency is "the effortless, automatic ability to read words in connected text—the ability to translate letters to sounds fluently and effortlessly" (Sheehan, 2007).

The developers of DIBELS state that it is designed to assess a student's development of phonological awareness, alphabet understanding, and automaticity and fluency. They also claim that the tests are indicators of a student's early literacy development and predictive of later reading proficiency. They are intended to identify students who are not progressing as expected.

For the ORF part of the test, students are required to read aloud a grade-appropriate passage. During the reading, the instructor/tester listens to the student reading and marks down missed words. These words are then subtracted from the total read, and a score is assigned to the student.

Errors are considered to be words that the student stumbles over, skips over, or does not self-correct within a 3-second time period. The RF part, if it is given at all, is given after the student has read the passage. Once the passage is read, the instructor/tester again records the number of words the student uses to retell the story. The quality of the words, how well they actually retell the story, is of no consequence. It is the number of words used that is important. This is how comprehension is measured.

The test does have a number of strengths. For instance, the test only takes between 5 and 10 minutes per child of the instructor's time. This is key for teachers who are pressed to test upwards of 100 students three times a year. The test can be repeated either in one sitting or throughout the school year, a quality the creators emphasize with their recommendation of at least three times a year. The tests are free to download and are accessible to anyone who wants them. So, not only can teachers download the test, but so can parents. Parents who want their children to get a head start on the test can download them and practice with their children. The tests also provide information on what parents, teachers, and students themselves can do to improve their reading skills. For instance, students who are found to read at an excessively slow rate may need to engage in repeated and assisted readings. Students whose decoding accuracy is poor may need additional word study and phonics instruction, and students who do poorly on the fluency rubric (prosody) may need additional coaching and support in reading with expression and meaning. Therefore, the test not only supposedly identifies specific areas that are giving students trouble; it also provides quick and easy solutions for those problems.

However, the tests also have weaknesses. One of the worst issues is that it reduces reading to discrete skills that have, at best, minimal connection to actual reading. As a consequence of this, students are required to do drilling of nonsense words and focus on narrow slices of what is being read. The creators believe the whole is clearly the sum of the parts and that somehow comprehension emerges from the fragments being tested (Goodman, 2006b). However, the tests have been shown to mis-predict reading performance, measuring reading speed and not comprehension (Pressley et al., 2005). The retell fluency component is said to be a measure of comprehension, yet though this test may be reliable it is not valid. It may be reliable in that it is possible to obtain consistent scores on the retelling; however, these retellings are not valid measures of comprehension. They are not valid because they are measuring the number of words uttered regardless of whether or not those words make senses and actually relate to the story just read.

This issue of validity also occurs in the ORF task. The test lacks validity in that the speed and accuracy of the ORF is expected to be measuring fluency, but how can it measure fluency when there is no comprehension component? Therefore it does not test the construct of reading fluency because it only tests two of the secondary characteristics— speed and accuracy. Unfortunately, students catch on very quickly that this is a test of speed and not comprehension. This has lead to a finding that 15% of the students who took the ORF were misidentified as good readers when they actually have poor comprehension (Riedel, 2007). This is because most of the validation studies use a procedure that mimics what beginning readers do when they read a text, not what fluent readers do. At time one, the research tests oral reading speed, at time two (a later time), comprehension is tested using a completely different test than what was used to test reading speed. This separation of the decoding from comprehension would naturally provide significant correlations with speed and comprehension like those found using the CBM. In fact, Cramer and Rosenfield (2008) found that using a comprehension task coupled with a speed of reading task that there was no correlation between reading speed and comprehension.

With the widespread use of the DIBELS tests (used to assess more than 1,800,000 students from kindergarten to sixth grade), a number of scholars in the field of reading have evaluated them (i.e., Cramer & Rosenfield, 2008; Goodman, 2006a; Pressley et al., 2005; Samuels, 2007). For example, Pearson (2006) stated, "DIBELS is the worst thing to happen to the teaching of reading since the development of flash cards" (p. 5). Goodman (2006) is concerned that despite warnings to the contrary, the tests have become a de-facto curriculum in which the emphasis on speed convinces students that the goal in reading is to be able to read fast and that understanding is of secondary importance. There is certainly enough concern by these leading scholars to warrant further review.

Measures of Fluency   An appropriate measure of reading fluency must include a measure of comprehension. It must mimic reading fluency by measuring the simultaneous decoding and comprehension of text. An appropriate method proposed by Samuels (2002) requires first determining the student's reading ability level and then choosing a one- to two-page passage of text within that level which the student will have to read orally. However, before the student begins reading the text orally, (s)he is given the following instructions, "Read this passage orally and when you are done I will take the passage away. You will then have to recall the content of the passage by either retelling the story to me or by answering some questions about what you have just read." This method mimics reading fluency because it requires the student to do three things at the same time: (a) decode the text, (b) understand the text material while decoding, and (c) hold the material in memory until the text is completed.

This is a process very similar to the one used by the American Guidance Services for measuring reading fluency. Its main strength is that it actually measures reading fluency—whether or not the student is decoding and comprehending at the same time.

American Guidance Services Reading Fuency Indicator.   The Reading Fluency Indicator (RFI) created by

Kathleen Williams (2005) of American Guidance Services is contained in the companion assessment to GRADE (Group Reading Assessment and Diagnostic Evaluation). This program provides a concise, criterion-referenced measure of oral fluency—including rate, accuracy, and comprehension.

This assessment is designed to be given individually, can be taken in 5 to 10 minutes, and provides a systematic approach to rating prosody, the ability to read with proper expression, should you choose to use it. The RFI measures phonological awareness, phoneme-grapheme, word reading, and vocabulary prior to first grade and comprehension beginning in the first grade.

The assessment begins by first estimating a student's reading level by having the student pronounce a list of words in increasing difficulty until the student is no longer able to correctly pronounce at least 9 out of 10 words. Once the reading level is established, passages of text are then selected at that reading level for the student to read out loud. There is then a script/directions told to the student prior to their reading the passage—"You are going to be reading a passage of text out loud, when you are finished I will ask you some questions about what you have read." Words read correctly in 1 minute are recorded and the comprehension questions are presented. Therefore the RFI tests fluency in terms of three components—reading time, miscues, and comprehension. Comprehension is tested on two levels: For sentence comprehension the students must select missing target words (from a list of possible choices) from a sentence based on the context clues or sentence meaning. For passage comprehension the students are given multiple choice questions with varying levels of understanding—questioning and clarifying ability, predicting and summarizing ability, and metacognitive strategies such as questioning, predicting, clarifying, and summarizing.

The test has strengths. It has the flexibility to view the student or the classroom as a whole for strengths and weaknesses in reading skills. It provides information for individual, group, and parents that are easy to read and understand. It provides the software for scoring and reporting the findings, or American Guidance Services will score it for you. It also allows for comparison from year to year in growth scale values (GSV) in readiness skills so that growth can be shown in readiness even though the performance level of the student may still be below average.

A weakness of the test is that it does not give interpretive information of what it means when a student gets three questions wrong out of the four questions given compared to a student who gets two questions wrong out of the four questions given.

Conclusion

Reading fluency has had a wavering group of enthusiasts over the years, mainly due to the discrepancies in defining it as a psychological construct. Part of the problem arose due to the shifting psychological paradigms. It is very dif-

ficult to define a construct in terms of cognition when the prevailing paradigm in place is behaviorism. With advances in technology, such as the fMRI, and the growth of cognitive psychology to neuropsychology, reading fluency has found new support. Maintaining fidelity to one and only one definition of reading fluency is necessary if we hope to create valid developmental strategies and assessments. With the old behavioral ideology that fluency can be measured by observing an increase in reading speed, accuracy and prosody being replaced with the cognitive perspective that we must also test whether or not comprehension is simultaneously occurring with these secondary characteristics in place, we are off to a good start. However, there is much work to be done. For instance, we must remember that reading speed is just a secondary characteristic of fluency and as such we must be sure not to push reading speed to such an extent that we compromise the true goal—comprehension. We must also begin to rigorously ferret out assessments that do not measure fluency from our school systems. By retaining these tests, we are doing our children a great disservice. For though school staff may be doing a good job of implementing and developing reading fluency methods, if the evaluation instruments are less than adequate then the tests will give faulty results that may very well lead to incorrect formative and summative evaluation decisions. It is therefore time for the federal government to support studies that re-evaluate the adequacy and validity claims of these testing instruments claiming to measure the theoretical construct—reading fluency.

References

Ackerman, P. L. (1987). Individual differences in skill reading: An integration of psychometric and information processing perspectives. *Psychological Bulletin, 102,* 3–27.

Allington, R. L. (2008). *What really matters in fluency: From research to practice.* New York: PearsonAllynBacon.

Allport, D. A., Antonis, B., & Reynolds, P. (1972). On the division of attention: A disproof of the single channel hypothesis. *Quarterly Journal of Experimental Psychology, 24,* 225–235.

Armbruster, B. B., Lehr, F., & Osborn, J. (2001). *Put reading first: The research building blocks for teaching children to read.* Washington, DC: National Institute of Child Health and Human Development and U. S. Department of Education. Retrieved from http://www.nifl.gov/nifl/publications.html

Baddeley, A. D. (1990). *Human memory: Theory and practice.* Boston: Allyn and Bacon.

Calfee, R. C., & Piontkowski, D. C. (1981). The reading diary: Acquisition of decoding. *Reading Research Quarterly, 16,* 346–373.

Carroll, L. (1872). *Jabberwocky. Through the looking-Glass and what Alice found there.* Retrieved from http://www.jabberwocky.com/carroll/jabber/

Cassidy, J., & Cassidy, D. (2003, Dec./Jan. 2004). What's hot, what's not for 2004. *Reading Today,* 3.

Cohen, J. D., Dunbar, K., & McClelland, J. L. (1990). On the control of automatic processes: A parallel distributed processing account of the Stroop effect. *Psychological Review, 97,* 332–361.

Cramer, K., & Rosenfield, S. (2008). Effect of degree of challenge on reading performance. *The Reading and Writing Quarterly, 24*(1), 119–137.

Daane, M.C., Campbell, J.R., Grigg, W.S., Goodman, M.J., and Oranje, A. (2005). *Fourth-Grade Students Reading Aloud: NAEP 2002 Special*

Study of Oral Reading (NCES 2006-469). U.S. Department of Education. Institute of Education Sciences, National Center for Education Statistics. Washington, DC: Government Printing Office. http://nces. ed.gov/nationsreportcard/pubs/studies/2006469.asp

Daneman, M., & Carpenter, P. A. (1983). Individual differences in integrating information between and within sentences. *Journal of Experimental Psychology: Learning, Memory and Cognition, 9*, 561–584.

Deno, S. L. (1985). Curriculum-based measurement: The emerging alternative. *Exceptional Children, 52*, 219–232.

Denton, C., Bryan, D., Wexler, J., Reed, D., & Vaughn, S. (2007). Fluency. In *Effective Instruction for Middle School Students with Reading Difficulties: The Reading Teacher's Sourcebook* (pp. 221–232). University of Texas System: Texas Education Agency.

Ellis, A. W., & Young, A. W. (1988). *Human cognitive neuropsychology*. London: Erlbaum.

Everatt, J., & Underwood, G. (1994). Individual differences in reading subprocesses: Relationships between reading ability, lexical access, and eye movement control. *Language and Speech, 37*, 283–297.

Fuchs, L. S. (2004). The past, present, and future of curriculum-based measurement research. *School Psychology Review, 33*(2), 188–192.

Goodman, K. (2006a). *A critical review of DIBELS, What it is, what it does*. Heinemann, NH: Reed Elsevier.

Goodman, K. (2006b). The DIBELing of little children. http://www.districtadministration.com/pulse/commentpost.aspx?news=no&postid=16874

Goodman, K. S., & Goodman, Y. M. (1979). Learning to read is natural. In L. B. Resnick & P. A. Weaver (Eds.), *Theory & practice of early reading, Volume 1* (pp. 137–154). Hillsdale, NJ: Erlbaum.

Hasbrouck, J. E., & Tindal, G. (1992). Curriculum-based oral reading fluency norms for students in grades 2 through 5. *Teaching Exceptional Children, 24*(3), 41–44.

Hudson, R. F., Lane, H. B., & Pullen, P. C. (2005). Reading fluency assessment and instruction: What, why, and how? *The Reading Teacher, 58*(8), 702–714.

Huey, E. B. (1968). *The Psychology and Pedagogy of Reading*. Cambridge, MA: MIT Press. (Original work published 1908)

LaBerge, D., & Samuels, S. J. (1974). Toward a theory of automatic information processing in reading. *Cognitive Psychology, 6*, 293–323.

Logan, G. D. (1988). Automaticity, resources and memory: Theoretical controversies and practical implications. *Human Factors, 30*, 583–598.

Logan, G. D. (1991). Automaticity and memory. In W. Hockley & S. Lewandowsky (Eds.), *Relating theory and data: Essays on human memory in honor of Bennet B. Murdock* (pp. 347–356), Hillsdale, NJ: Erlbaum.

Logan, G. D. (1997). Automaticity and reading: Perspectives from the instance theory of automatization. *Reading and Writing Quarterly, 13*, 123–146.

McGlinchey, M. T., & Hixson, M. D. (2004). Using curriculum-based measurement to predict performance on state assessment in reading. *School Psychology Review, 33*, 193–203.

Miller, E. K., & Cohen, J. D. (2001). An integrative theory. *Annual Review of Neuroscience, 24*, 167–202.

National Reading Panel. (2000). *Teaching children to read: An evidence-based assessment of the scientific research literature on reading and its implications for reading instruction* (NICHD Pub. No. 00-4769). Washington, DC: National Institute of Child Health and Human Development.

Pearson, P. D. (2006). Foreward. In Gloria Pipkin (Ed.), *The truth about DIBELS, what it is, what it does* (pp. v–xix). Heinemann, NH: Reed Elsevier.

Pihlajamaki, M., Tanila, H., Hanninen, T., Kononen, M., Laakso, M., Partanen, K., et al. (2000). Verbal fluency activates the left median temporal lobe: an fMRI study. *Annals of Neurology, 47*, 470–476.

Posner, M. I. (1978). *Chronometric explorations of mind*. Hillsdale, NJ: Erlbaum.

Posner, M. I., & Snyder, R. R. (1975). Attention and cognitive control. In R. L. Solso (Ed.), *Information processing and cognition: The Loyola symposium* (pp. 55–85). Hillsdale, NJ: Erlbaum.

Pressley, M., Hilden, K., & Shankland, R. (2005). *An evaluation of end-grade-3 Dynamic Indicators of Basic Early Literacy Skills (DIBELS): Speed reading without comprehension, predicting little*. East Lansing, MI: Literacy Achievement Research Center.

Rasinski, T. V. (2007). Teaching fluency artfully. In R. Fink & S. J. Samuels (Eds.), *Inspiring reading success, interest, and motivation in an age of high stakes testing* (pp. 117–140). Newark, DE: International Reading Association.

Riedel, B. (2007). The relation between DIBELS, reading comprehension, and vocabulary in urban first-grade students. *Reading Research Quarterly, 42*(4), 546–567.

Samuels, S. J. (2002a). Reading fluency: Its development and assessment. In A. E. Farstrup & S. J. Samuels (Eds.), *What research has to say about reading instruction* (3rd ed., pp. 166–183). Newark, DE: International Reading Association.

Samuels, S. J. (2002b). Reading fluency: What is it? How can I teach it? How can I measure it? *Instructional Leader, 15*(6), 1–12.

Samuels, S. J. (2006). Reading fluency: Its past, present and future. In T. Rasinski, C. Blachowicz, & K. Lems (Eds.), *Fluency instruction research based best practices*.

Samuels, S. J. (2007). The DIBLES Tests: Is Speed of Barking at Print What We Mean by Reading Fluency? *Reading Research Quarterly, 42*(4), 568–570.

Samuels, S. J., LaBerge, D., & Bremer, C. D. (1978). Units of Word Recognition: Evidence for Developmental Changes. *Journal of Verbal Learning and Verbal Behavior, 17*, 715–720.

Schreiber, P. A. (1980). On the acquisition of reading fluency. *Journal of Reading Behavior, 12*, 177–186.

Schreiber, P. A. (1987). Prosody and structure in children's syntactic processing. In R. Horowitz & S. J. Samuels (Eds.), *Comprehending oral and written language* (pp. 243–270). New York: Academic Press.

Shaywitz, S. E., Mody, M., Shaywitz, B. A. (2006). Neural mechanisms in dyslexia. *Current Directions in Psychological Science, 15*, 278–281.

Sheehan, T. (2007). IDEA: Institute for the Development of Educational Achievement (2002–2004). Retrieved from http://reading.uoregon.edu/flu/

Shiffrin, R. M., & Schneider, W. (1977). Controlled and automatic human information processing: II. Perceptual learning, automatic attending, and a general theory. *Psychological Review, 84*, 127–190.

Smith, F. (1973). Twelve easy ways to make learning to read difficult. In F. Smith (Ed.), *Psycholinguistics and reading* (pp. 183–196). New York: Holt, Rinehart & Winston.

Snow, C. E., Burns, M. S., & Griffin, P. (1998). *Preventing reading difficulties in young children*. Washington, DC: National Academy Press.

Spelke, E. S., Hirst, W., & Neisser, U. (1976). Skills of divided attention. *Cognition, 4*, 215–230.

Stanovich, K. E. (1990). Concepts in developmental theories of reading skill: Cognitive resources, automaticity, and modularity. *Developmental Review, 10*, 72–100.

Stroop, J. R. (1935). Studies of interference in serial verbal reactions. *Journal of Experimental Psychology, 18*, 643–662.

Thurlow, R., & van den Broek, P. (1997). Automaticity and inference generation. *Reading and Writing Quarterly, 13*, 165–184.

Underwood, G., Hubbard, A., & Wilkinson, H. (1990). Eye fixations predict reading comprehension: The relationship between reading skill, reading speed and visual inspection. *Language and Speech, 33*, 69–81.

Vygotsky, L. S. (1978). *Mind in society: The development of higher psychological processes* (M. Cole, V. John-Steiner, S. Schribner, & E. Souberman, Eds. & Trans.). Cambridge, MA: Harvard University Press. (Original work published 1934)

Vygotsky, L. (1986). *Thought and language*. MIT Press, Cambridge, MA: MIT Press.

Williams, K. (2005). *American Guidance Services (Pearson Learning) Reading fluency indicator: A quick individualized assessment*. Circle Pines, MN: AGS Publishing.

Wolf, M., & Katzir-Cohen, T., (2001). Reading Fluency and Its Intervention. *Scientific Studies of Reading, 5*(93), 211–239.

Part IV

Developmental Patterns of Reading Proficiency and Reading Difficulties

EDITORS: S. JAY SAMUELS AND SUSAN HUPP

17

Shifting Perspectives in Emergent Literacy Research

Renée M. Casbergue
Louisiana State University

Lea McGee
The Ohio State University

Toward the end of the year, two kindergarten children work side-by-side at the science center in their classroom recording their observations of caterpillars' metamorphoses into butterflies. They then turn to a book about butterflies to help them identify the stage of development they are observing. Cienna's journal entry consists of a drawing comprised of a vertical squiggle below a single horizontal line, underneath which she has written a series of letters—jdpeiknati—which she later reads to her teacher as, "The caterpillar is all wrapped up." Roberto's entry includes a drawing that clearly illustrates a primitive cocoon attached to a leaf. His writing says, "It md a crsls," which he reads as, "The caterpillar made a chrysalis."

The children together carefully examine pictures in a simple leveled text, stopping on the page showing a chrysalis dangling from a leaf on a milkweed plant. Cienna points to the picture and says, "That's what they look like now." Roberto agrees and, running his finger under the line of print below the picture, reads aloud, "The caterpillar from (forms) a chrysalis." He returns to his journal entry and erases "crsls," then copies the correct spelling from the book.

That there are significant differences in the knowledge young children bring to school literacy activities, even as early as kindergarten, is evident. Some children clearly have more conventional understanding of print than others. They are able to write using alphabetic invented spelling, and can locate information in simple leveled books in which they are able to read most of the print. In contrast, some children display more emergent literacy knowledge. Their writing suggests that they have not yet mastered the alphabetic principle, and instead use random strings of letters to represent meaning. They are able to use pictorial information in books, but show no inclination or ability to read the print independently.

Teachers of young children are not at all surprised to see such significant differences in the literacy development of children in their classrooms. They may have questions, however, about what these differences mean. Should the first

child be given more challenging work than his classmates? Of greater concern, is the second child showing early signs of reading disability? Should she spend more of her time receiving explicit instruction to develop her phonological ability? Is there any benefit at all to engaging her in meaning-based reading and writing activities to which she is unable to produce more conventional responses? How these questions are answered may depend on the manner in which individuals have been prepared to regard emergent literacy and on the research literature upon which they rely.

Shifts in Perspectives

The term *emergent literacy* was coined by Marie Clay (1966) to illustrate the distinction between then prevalent readiness views of early literacy and a more constructivist perspective of the process of literacy development in early childhood. Readiness perspectives were based in behaviorist theories (Skinner, 1950, 1989) that proposed most learning could be accounted for by reinforcing and shaping responses to specific stimuli. A behaviorist view held that complex tasks, including learning to read and write, could be reduced to their smallest constituent parts, each of which could be introduced and reinforced until mastery. Alongside the behaviorist view, a prevailing belief of others through the 1960s and into the 1970s was that actual reading was too complex a task to be introduced to children with mental ages younger than six. Thus, literacy instruction prior to first grade was focused on getting children ready for later reading and writing with simple tasks thought to be precursors to actual literacy. Readiness activities such as having children discriminate among shapes and produce rows of circles and lines were believed to be necessary preparation for later instruction in recognizing and writing individual alphabet letters. Auditory and visual discrimination tasks likewise focused on preparing children to eventually discriminate among various sounds and letters. Mastery of the ability to recognize and produce those letters and sounds was widely accepted to be prerequisite to any attempt to elicit meaning from, or create meaning with, connected print.

The work of some of the first early literacy researchers, however, opened the door to entirely new understandings of just how much knowledge about print—its forms, functions, meanings, and links between meaning and form (McGee & Richgels, 1990)—children are capable of constructing for themselves long before they begin formal schooling. Embedded in constructivist theories of learning (Vygotsky, 1978) rather than behaviorist models, researchers over the next three decades and into the early 21st century expanded and honed insights about emergent literacy, examining and celebrating the complexity of children's attempts to make sense of print and use it for their own purposes.

Most recently, however, emphasis seems to have shifted somewhat away from what young children *do* know to a focus on what they lack in their understanding of print. This is especially true regarding children deemed at risk of reading disability. It appears that many educators and policy makers are returning to a view of the preschool and kindergarten years as a time for getting children ready to read and write, albeit with a more sophisticated understanding of the kinds of knowledge children need to develop in order to achieve conventional literacy in the primary grades. For the moment, more behaviorist perspectives seem to be winning out over constructivist views in choices about instructional programs for preschool and kindergarten children, with scripted, skills-based curricula increasingly commonplace.

The review of literature that follows traces trends in early literacy research over the past 40 years. From identifying types of knowledge young children develop about print to investigating which instructional programs are most likely to improve children's knowledge of specific aspects of reading and writing, researchers from the fields of early childhood language and literacy development, psychology, medicine, and special education have provided evidence that supports different approaches to addressing the literacy of children prior to first grade.

Research from an Emergent Literacy Perspective

Young Children's Emergent Conceptualization of Print

Clay's 1966 dissertation study, focused on young children's emergent understanding of print, was completed about the same time as Durkin's longitudinal study of "early readers," defined as those children who entered first grade able to recognize basal reader vocabulary without any prior formal reading instruction (Durkin, 1966a). These researchers were among the first to acknowledge that such achievement was even possible, directly contradicting the widely accepted notion that preschool and kindergarten children did not have the cognitive capacity for literacy learning. Durkin cautioned that her relatively small sample of early readers with significantly higher IQ scores was atypical of the general population of school children, and that her results therefore should not be assumed to imply that literacy instruction could begin earlier than first grade for all students. She did

suggest, however, that the ways those children learned to read at home could have significant implications for beginning reading instruction in schools.

Early studies that attempted to determine how young children learned to read prior to formal instruction entailed identifying early readers once they entered school and interviewing their parents regarding their recollections of how they supported their children's literacy development (Durkin, 1966b; Price, 1976; Read, 1975). Parents typically reported they did not remember doing anything specific beyond reading aloud to their preschoolers. They did note that their children appeared to memorize favorite storybooks and then make connections to the print without assistance, leading to the inaccurate notion that mastery of print was a process of natural development dependent primarily on exposure and maturation.

Other studies that entailed careful documentation of children's early interactions with print, however, revealed that parents might have underestimated the amount of support and direction they provided. Well-documented case studies (Baghban, 1984; Bissex, 1980; Dyson, 1982a, 1984; Ferreiro, 1986; McGee & Richgels, 1989; Schickedanz, 1990; Taylor, 1983) illustrated that parents frequently called children's attention to print in their environments, by pointing out and reading aloud traffic signs, for example, or helping children read boxes in the pantry to find the cereal they want. They also offered information—such as that reading begins on the left side of the page, or that a particular word matches an illustration. Further, they confirmed children's observations, acknowledging for instance a child's recognition that McDonalds printed on a fast food bag starts with the same letter as the child's name. Parents were also observed providing assistance with authentic reading and writing tasks such as deciphering and creating lists, labels, signs, and notes. From these case studies, researchers concluded that parents of early readers did far more than simply read to their children.

Varying Influence of Family and Home Literacy Practices
Many of these case studies examined literacy practices among mainstream, literate, middle-class families. In recognition that the ways parents engage their children with print are inseparable from communities' valuing of literacy and language interaction styles, Feitelson and Goldstein (1986) expressed concern that studies focused exclusively on interactions among well-educated parents and children who appeared to effortlessly master print concepts did not offer information educators need in order to assist children who did not easily achieve literacy upon introduction to print in school.

Investigations of family literacy practices across a variety of communities attempted to address that concern. Clay (1971) examined home influences on aspects of language and reading development among 5- and 6-year-old children with four different language backgrounds in New Zealand. She found that Samoan children, who as a group exhibited "inferior" oral language achievement as compared to Maori children upon school entry, nonetheless outperformed their more "linguistically superior" classmates on reading tasks in school. She concluded that parental attitudes favoring educational achievement and significant modeling of reading and writing at home most likely compensated for language deficits and contributed to Samoan children's higher achievement.

Heath's work (1982, 1983) examined differences in family dynamics, literacy activities like storybook reading, parenting and community interaction patterns, and the ways those patterns affected children's language acquisition between African American and White families in rural and suburban working-class communities. She found that the language patterns in the African American families did not include the kind of simplified talk used by White families to scaffold children's speech, and that the types of questions children were asked to answer during conversations with adults were very dissimilar from the types of questions teachers typically ask in school settings. For example, African American parents were more likely to engage children in conversations about things in the immediate environment, while White, middle-class parents engaged children in more conversations about past or future activities, similar to the types of discussions conducted in many classrooms. Heath hypothesized that these differences contributed to some young children's less frequent use of decontextualized language, less varied vocabularies, and difficulties adjusting to the language and literacy routines and expectations of typical classrooms.

Others, including Ninio and Bruner (1978), Leseman and de Jong (1998), Schieffelin and Cochran-Smith (1984), Snow (1983), and Teale (1986) conducted extensive investigations of the connections between the ways children learn about oral and written language and family communication patterns. They identified a variety of ways that parents provided opportunities for children to develop language and literacy skills, ranging from structured interactions like storybook reading to more casual interactions such as reading environmental print aloud and engaging children in using grocery lists as a natural part of daily living routines. They also noted that some families provided almost no supported interactions with print. As did Heath, many of these researchers suggested that differences between home and school literacy practices might underlie some children's struggles to become literate upon school entry.

Beyond exploring the types and frequency of opportunities for children to engage with print in their homes, other researchers (e.g., Britto, Brooks-Gunn, & Griffin, 2006; Bus & van Ijzendoorn, 1995; Elley 1989; Ezell & Justice, 1998; Hammett, van Kleeck, & Huberty, 2003; Justice, Weber, Ezell, & Bakeman, 2002; Justice, Kaderavek, Bowles, & Grimm, 2005; Justice & Kaderavek, 2003; Leseman & de Jong, 1998; Labbo, 1996; Mason, 1980; Purcell-Gates, 1996; Senechal, LeFevre, Thomas, & Daley, 1988; Yaden, Smolkin, & Conlon, 1989; van Kleeck & Beckley-McCall, 2002) moved toward investigating specific aspects of parents' interactions with children during

storybook reading to help explain differences in children's language and literacy development. This body of research suggested that parents varied the aspects of storybooks upon which they focused their preschoolers' attention as well as the topics they discussed. They also found that children's questions while listening to books read aloud were more often directed toward pictures and stories than to elements of print, suggesting that shared storybook reading alone, while probably supporting early comprehension skill, was not sufficient to explain children's mastery of print concepts. Rather, those children with superior decoding skills likely had their attention drawn to the print itself, with parents supplying and helping children locate high frequency or interesting words in books. Thus, this research suggests that the manner in which parents engage their children while sharing picture books may influence what children learn. The research therefore did not lead to specific conclusions regarding recommended strategies for facilitating language and literacy development.

Beyond exploration of children's understandings of print through shared story reading activities, many studies investigated young children's developing writing ability. As with studies related to shared storybook reading, researchers examined children's interactions with adults or peers outside of formal classroom contexts to determine the influence of those interactions on how children conceptualize writing, the functions their writing serves, and the forms their writing takes (Burns & Casbergue, 1992; DeBaryshe & Buell, 1996; Dyson, 1984; Henderson & Beers, 1980; Read, 1986; Zutell, 1976). Again, these researchers noted that adults varied in the elements of writing to which they called children's attention, with some focusing more heavily on meaning and composition, and others addressing specific aspects of print, especially letter identification, letter formation, and spelling. These findings suggest that children may enter formal schooling with very different understandings of print, differences that may put some children at risk of early literacy difficulty depending on the focus of their classroom literacy program. A program that focuses heavily on mastery of letters and sounds, for example, may disadvantage those children whose prior experience with writing was more focused on function and meaning. Conversely, a program in which children are expected to begin composing from the first day of school, without significant concern at first for correct spelling and letter formation, may disadvantage children whose home experience leads them to define writing as handwriting and copying.

Emergent Writing Attempting to develop more specific understanding of children's writing development, whether in home or school contexts, early literacy researchers examined the nature of children's emerging concepts about writing, especially the manner in which they attempted to map print onto oral language. Read's (1971) groundbreaking work established consistent patterns in children's seemingly random use of letters in their early spelling attempts and laid the ground work for others who identified stages of invented spelling (e.g., Beers & Henderson, 1977; Gentry, 1978; Paul, 1975; Richgels, 1995; Zutell, 1976). Those stages illustrated the manner in which children gradually came to understand the alphabetic principle—that alphabet letters represent sounds in spoken language—and the increasingly sophisticated ways in which sounds can be encoded, from use of letter names to determine sounds to strategies that move beyond phonetic information, as in the use of syllable juncture rules and morphemic consistency to determine spellings.

Other researchers turned their attention to broader aspects of children's writing, recognizing that children's construction of meaning and the ways in which they understand print can be used for both communication and exploration of ideas is not always cleanly related to their encoding efforts (Dyson, 2002). Much of this work investigated how children evolve in their understanding of symbolic language in general, and the manner in which written symbols represent meaning. Investigations of children's drawings and talk while drawing (Dyson, 1982b; 1984) and of the social and cultural contexts within which their communications are situated (Clay, 1998; Dyson, 1997; Purcell-Gates, 1996) illustrate the complexity of knowledge children must orchestrate in order to develop the ability to write with increasing sophistication. This complexity of knowledge about symbol systems, forms, functions, and meanings of writing underscores the importance of approaches to early writing instruction that allow children to explore all of these aspects of writing as opposed to those that focus children's attention more narrowly on learning letters and sounds to the exclusion of more meaning based aspects.

Emergent Literacy During Play   One context for both reading and writing that has been researched extensively is children's dramatic play. Case studies of children's literate behaviors prior to school cited earlier almost universally include descriptions of children experimenting with print as part of their dramatic play. Recognizing that literacy behaviors occur in everyday activities—and that play comprises a large portion of preschoolers' activity—many researchers turned their attention to documenting the types of literate behaviors demonstrated by children during play, both at home and at school. Neuman and Roskos (1992) observed children at play in classroom centers to document the variety of ways they used print in their attempts to read and write, especially during dramatic play. While most of the attempts were pretend reading and writing, they were accompanied by rich language interactions and exploration of print as, for example, when two 4-year-olds discussed how to write phone numbers when taking messages from pretend callers. As they compared their notes, one child pointed out to the other that what was supposed to be a phone number couldn't be correct because it contained letters. He then proceeded to show his friend how to write a phone number by writing a string of nine numerals, explaining that phone numbers couldn't have any "abc's." Thus, research containing detailed analyses of specific knowledge

displayed by children through their play (Christie & Stone, 1999; Kantor, Miller, & Fernie, 1992; Pellegrini & Galda, 1993; Neuman & Roskos, 1992, 1997; Rowe, 1998) suggested the importance of play in the school curriculum for young children.

The body of literature briefly summarized thus far is varied in its focus, including studies of how children begin to develop early concepts about print, the role of adult/child interactions in supporting emergent literacy development, and the broader contexts within which children engage in reading and writing. What the studies all have in common is an attempt to deepen understanding of children's developing conceptualization of print—its forms, functions, and meanings, and the connections among all three.

Emergent Literacy Intervention Research

Understanding of the ways in which children developed concepts about written language offered researchers new hypotheses about how to maximize children's early literacy development. That new knowledge spurred intervention studies, an avenue of research that became increasingly relevant as differences in children's literacy achievement in early primary grades became a focus of concern. Indeed, many researchers have noted that the preschool years are critical to children's language and literacy development, with gaps in achievement between children from low- and middle-income families appearing well before first grade (Chaney, 1992; Dickinson & Snow, 1987; Dickinson & Sprague, 2002; Hart & Risley, 1995; Fernandez-Fein & Baker, 1997; Justice & Ezell, 2001; Laosa, 1983; Walker, Greenwood, Hart, & Carta, 1994).

Family Literacy Interventions   One body of intervention research included studies of programs designed to address disparities noted between the home and community literacy environments of low socioeconomic status and middle-class families. Some federal initiatives such as the Even Start Family Literacy Program and programs sponsored by the National Center for Family Literacy included services to both adults and children from low-income households, attempting to address parents' literacy levels and children's preparation for formal schooling (Brizius & Foster, 1993; Darling & Hayes, 1989). Evaluations of parent and child outcomes from Even Start revealed some increases in the number of parents earning GEDs as compared to control groups, and positive gains in home learning environments. Although control group parents demonstrated similar gains in learning environments even without Even Start services, parents participating in Even Start activities demonstrated a wider range of different kinds of reading materials available to children and, after the second year, stronger gains in cognitive stimulation of children as compared to the control group (St. Pierre et. al, 1995; Tao, Games, & Tarr, 1998). Evaluations of programs following the National Center for Family Literacy model also demonstrated positive outcomes for children, including higher than predicted gains in vocabulary and higher teacher ratings for academic performance, motivation to learn, and classroom behavior (Darling & Hayes, 1989, 1996; Philliber, Spillman, & King, 1996).

In addition to these types of comprehensive programs, researchers have investigated the effects of intervention approaches that entailed coaching parents to effectively implement strategies for engaging their children with print. Most of the suggested strategies were among those that had been demonstrated to be successful for middle-income parents and children, including actively engaging children in read aloud sessions, directly calling their attention to print, and assisting them in writing for a variety of purposes. Studies that focused on assisting parents to engage in these types of rich literacy interactions with their children (e.g., Delgado-Gaitan, 1994; Edwards, 1991, 1994; Ezell & Justice, 2000; Ezell, Justice, & Parsons, 2000; Justice & Ezell, 2000; Neuman & Gallagher, 1994; Neuman, Hagedorn, Delano, & Daly, 1995; Neuman, 1996; Whitehurst, Arnold, et al., 1994; Whitehurst, Epstein, et al., 1994) demonstrated that parents could adapt their book sharing and other literacy routines and in many cases impact children's vocabularies and understanding of print concepts. Collectively, they provided evidence that parents can learn to use research-tested strategies for sharing books with their children. For examples parents have successfully learned to use dialogic reading and draw their children into writing (grocery lists, notes, and so on), resulting in significant positive effects on preschool children's knowledge of concepts about print, writing ability, linguistic awareness, expressive language, and mean length of utterance.

Preschool Classroom Interventions   Another avenue of intervention research focused on improving classrooms as early literacy environments. The variable impact of the quality of preschool experiences on children's social, cognitive, language, and literacy skills has been widely documented (Burchinal et al., 2000; NICHD, 1999; Peisner-Feinbert & Burchinal, 1997). Even within relatively high quality childcare and preschool environments, however, effective attention to language and literacy development is not always a given (Bryant, Buchinal, Lau, & Sparling, 1994; Dickinson, 2002; Dunn, Beach, & Kontos, 1994; High/Scope, 1997; Justice, 2004; Burchinal et al., 2000). The National Research Council, through its report, *Preventing Reading Difficulties in Young Children* (Snow, Burns, & Griffin, 1998), implored early childhood educators to implement research-based approaches to support literacy, particularly those working in programs that serve low-income children.

Recognizing the urgency of improving literacy instruction in early childhood, many researchers had long since developed intervention programs designed to improve preschool classroom environments in support of young children's emergent literacy. As early as 1974, Durkin completed a longitudinal study of reading achievement in primary grades of children who enrolled in a 2-year language arts program that focused on recognizing and writing letters and connecting letters to sounds prior to first grade as compared to classmates who did not participate in such a literacy focused program. She found that reading achievement of children in the experimental group surpassed that of those in the control group at the end of each year in grades 1 through 4, illustrating the power of specific literacy interventions focused on preschool and kindergarten children (Durkin, 1974).

More recent interventions incorporated knowledge gained from studies of children's emergent literacy development. Whether examining the effects of creating library corners with related literacy activities (McGill-Franzen, Allington, Yokoi, & Brooks, 1999; Morrow & Weinstein, 1986), redesigning dramatic play areas to provide opportunities for authentic engagement with print (Hall, 1987; Neuman & Roskos, 1989), or infusing classrooms with clustered print materials to provoke sustained interaction with print (Neuman & Roskos, 1990), classroom environment research demonstrated that enhanced literacy environments increased both the amount and complexity of children's literacy play. Further studies provided evidence that play in literacy enhanced preschool environments positively influenced children's understanding and creation of narratives (Branscombe & Taylor, 2000), production of oral language (McCune, 1995), and emergent writing (Pellegrini, Galda, Dresden, & Cox, 1991).

Most recently, the Early Reading First program (U. S. Dept. of Education, 2001), has spurred a variety of interventions designed to transform adequate preschool classrooms into exemplary early literacy environments. Each federally funded project must address the classroom literacy environment as well as provide research-based instruction to develop emergent literacy for 3- and 4-year-old children. All projects must also have a strong professional development component for preschool teachers. An independent national evaluation of Early Reading First found that the program had positive, statistically significant impacts on several classroom and teacher outcomes, including improvements in language environments, book-reading practices, provision of phonological-awareness activities, teaching practices to support print and letter knowledge and writing, and extensiveness of child-assessment practices. Analysis of effects of these improvements revealed positive impact on children's print and letter knowledge, but not oral language (expressive and receptive language and vocabulary) or phonological awareness, as compared to control groups from similar backgrounds (Jackson, et. al., 2007).

All of the interventions described above have in common a comprehensive approach to improving the literacy development of young children. They entail improvements in physical environments, materials, instructional strategies, and adult-child interactions. The goal of these interventions, and the research that supports them, is overall improvement in children's language and literacy, with particular emphasis on receptive and expressive vocabulary, phonological awareness, print concepts, and comprehension. The interventions typically reflect a constructivist perspective that honors children's ability to construct understanding of print through their own exploration as well as via explicit instruction.

Basic Skills Research

At the same time that the emergent literacy research cited thus far was conducted, a parallel line of research took a more reductionist approach to early literacy. Beginning in the 1990s, a decided emphasis on one aspect of early literacy—phonological skill—emerged. A series of national reports in the 1990s spurred renewed interest in basic skills approaches to literacy. Based in large part on studies of children with severe reading disabilities conducted by the National Institute of Child Health and Human Development (NICHD), these reports encouraged direct, explicit approaches to teaching basic skills deemed to be prerequisite to literacy development. Particular attention was devoted to developing phonemic awareness in preschool and kindergarten children, and phonics skills in first grade and beyond. Reports from the Center for the Future of Teaching and Learning (1996) and the National Reading Panel (2000) shifted attention away from holistic emergent literacy research toward studies investigating "scientifically based" approaches to teaching basic skills.

Both reports, and the studies from which their recommendations were drawn, were guided by models of research that assumed learning problems among struggling readers were due to deficits within the children themselves. Driven by a medical approach to understanding the sources of reading disabilities, researchers from the fields of medicine, psychology, speech and language pathology, and special education worked to identify causes for children's difficulties as a means to develop instructional interventions and therapies to ameliorate disabilities. Beginning in the late 1980s, consensus began to emerge among such researchers that basic cognitive deficits, especially in language domains, including the phonological domain, greatly impact children's ability to master the alphabetic code (Boudreau & Hedberg, 1999; Larrivee & Catts, 1999; Lewis, O'Donnell, Freebairn, & Taylor, 1998; Lombardino, Riccio, Hynd, & Phnheiro., 1997; Vellutino, 1987; Vellutino et al., 1996). Yet these researchers also acknowledged that the cause of those deficits could be ineffective early literacy instruction that failed to help young children make the connection between letters and sounds (Vellutino & Scanlon, 2002).

Interest in instructional approaches to beginning reading certainly preceded release of the national reports. Bond and Dykstra (1967), Chall (1967), and Levin and Williams (1970) each attempted to establish the research base supporting various approaches to teaching young children to read. Whether reporting results of their own studies or synthesizing the work of others, their conclusions were similar, supporting the importance of code-based instruction. All stopped short of recommending any particular approach to teaching the code, however, and eschewed

"phonics first" or "phonics only" approaches, instead highlighting the importance of embedding phonics instruction in meaningful reading.

These basic findings and recommendations have been supported in most meta-analyses and reviews of research on approaches to reading instruction conducted since then (Adams, 1990; Anderson, Hiebert, Wilkinson, & Scott, 1985; Balmuth, 1982; NRP, 2000; Stahl, 2002). Large experimental studies also yielded similar findings that supported the importance of early systematic phonics instruction, with some researchers interpreting their findings to recommend synthetic over analytic approaches (Foorman, Fletcher, Francis, Schatschneider, & Mehta, 1998; Vellutino & Scanlon, 1987; Vellutino et al., 1996; Johnson & Watson, 1997). It is important to note that most of the studies measured reading achievement of children exposed to different approaches by assessing isolated word reading or phonological awareness rather than comprehension of connected text (Taylor, Anderson, Au, & Raphael, 2000; Stahl, 2002). In fact, in an advance report of the findings of the National Early Literacy Panel, Shanahan (2008) noted that the vast majority of studies located by the panel in its meta-analysis of early literacy research were devoted to identifying variables that predict later decoding, with many fewer investigations of variables that predict comprehension.

It is this definition of reading as word identification, or in many cases, the ability to decode nonsense words, that led to such intense interest in phonological awareness as a precursor to literacy, a relatively new focus in contrast to early phonics studies focused on connections between oral and written language. Thus, studies of the effects of phonological awareness instruction, including phonemic awareness training and other code-based activities, on measures of participating children's reading achievement began to dominate the research literature (e.g., Ball & Blachman, 1991; Blachman, 1994; Bradley & Bryant, 1983; Ehri & Wilce, 1985; Foorman, Francis, Novy, & Liberman, 1991; Lundberg, Frost, & Petersen, 1988; Vellutino, 1991). Of 291 intervention studies that met the National Early Literacy Panel's criteria for inclusion in its meta-analysis, 78 of the interventions were categorized as "helping children make sense of the code," with many fewer studies in each of the other four categories of interventions (reading and sharing books with children, parent and home programs focused on improving young children's literacy, preschool and kindergarten programs, and language enhancement studies) (Shanahan, 2008).

Collectively, code-based intervention studies demonstrated that children who received instruction in phonology had fewer instances of reading problems, particularly when reading achievement was assessed with measures emphasizing decoding. The studies did not demonstrate similarly large effects on oral reading, comprehension, word recognition, or spelling, particularly if letters were not included in the training (Hohn & Ehri, 1983; NRP, 2000; Shanahan, 2008). Nonetheless, this body of research formed the basis of many subsequent federal initiatives to shape early literacy instruction nationwide, most notably through mandates included in the No Child Left Behind legislation. The shift in perspective away from constructivist toward reductionist views of early literacy is reflected in the types of assessments and instructional programs those who accept Reading First and Early Reading First funding are required to use.

Discussion

Because many of the studies supporting skills-based, reductionist approaches to research and instruction were conducted on behalf of children with reading disabilities, it is tempting to assume that there is consensus regarding appropriate instruction for both struggling young readers and those at risk for later reading difficulties. That is not the case.

At roughly the same time that the National Reading Council (Snow et al., 1998) and the National Reading Panel (2000) were reviewing decades of experimental research to determine the most effective ways to prevent reading disability, many special educators began to call for a move away from deficit thinking toward social constructivist approaches in the education of children with special needs (Denti & Katz, 1995; Dudley-Marling & Dippo, 1995; Poplin, 1985, 1988; Trent, Artiles, & Englert, 1998). While deficit models of instruction emphasize direct instruction of target literacy skills—often through repetition of predetermined, scripted prompts, social constructivist approaches stress the individualized nature of learning and acknowledge that children construct their own knowledge with varying levels and types of support from those with more skill. Social constructivist researchers and theorists emphasized the importance of embedding skills instruction within meaningful literate activity. Relying on Vygotskian theories, they posited that it is impossible for children with disabilities to become active learners when knowledge is separated from goal-embedded contexts, forcing children with disabilities to amass discrete aspects of print into meaningful wholes (Trent et al., 1998). Rather than relying on reductionist approaches, they used Vygotsky's (1978, 1993) work to suggest that "teachers should mediate performance in ways that enable a child to solve a problem or achieve a goal that would be beyond his or her unassisted efforts. Such scaffolds make it possible for the learner to participate in a complex process from the very beginning" (Trent et al., 1998, p. 286). This includes the complex process of becoming literate.

An examination of leading journals in the fields of special education and speech and language pathology from the 1980s through 2007 reveals that, in keeping with this social constructivist perspective of instruction for children at risk of reading disability, the preponderance of articles related to *early* literacy instruction in particular (as opposed to instruction for children in first grade and beyond) espouse approaches that embed skills instruction in meaningful

contexts. Kouri, Selle, and Riley (2006) investigated the effects on language impaired children's oral reading of both meaning-based and phonemic key word activities prior to reading, and found both to be effective strategies, with the phonemic activity more effective only for facilitating correction of miscues. Many others conducted studies of the effects of storybook reading and other meaning-embedded interventions on children's knowledge of print concepts, phonemic awareness, and word learning (e.g., Englert et al., 1995; Englert, Raphael, & Mariage, 1994; Ezell & Justice, 2000; Justice, 2002; Justice & Ezell, 2002; Justice & Kaderavek, 2002; Justice, Meier, & Walpole, 2005; Klenk, 1994; McFadden, 1998; and van Kleeck, Woude, & Hammett, 2006). All found meaning-based approaches to be effective for increasing the emergent literacy skills of children with language impairments or those otherwise at risk for reading disability.

This suggests that there is more agreement regarding approaches to emergent literacy instruction among early childhood literacy researchers, speech and language pathologists, and special educators than is commonly recognized. Why, then, the continued emphasis on reductionist, medical models of assessment and teaching promoted by policy makers who have been able to significantly influence the direction of federal funding and the mandates that come attached to it?

The answer apparently does not lie simply in which body of research is more convincing. Rather, it appears that political considerations, and a desire on the part of some officials charged with administering programs under No Child Left Behind to privilege the vendors of some favored programs over others (U.S. Dept. of Education, 2006), are at the heart of a continued reliance on narrowly focused research aimed at the 10%–20% of the population affected by specific reading disability (Harris & Sipay, 1990; Shaywitz, Escobar, Shaywitz, Fetcher, & Makuch, 1992) to influence programs for all children. While many of the programs supported by policy makers are worthwhile and effective, it is important that those who influence literacy instruction not lose sight of the value of continued research into the full range of literate behavior that must continue to be investigated by researchers and supported by knowledgeable teachers.

In response to the findings of the National Early Literacy Panel, Shanahan (2008) noted the preponderance of studies that used decoding as the primary measure of reading ability and called for more research designed to identify predictors of comprehension as the ultimate measure of reading achievement. In the limited number of studies that did utilize this broader measure of reading achievement, researchers found that children's concepts about print and print awareness were better predictors of later achievement than were phonological variables that predict later decoding. Thus, it is worth considering that in terms of preventing later reading disabilities, preschool children might best be served by programs that attend to all of the predictors of later reading achievement, not just those that focus on the phonological ability that impacts later decoding.

References

Adams, M. (1990). *Beginning to read: Thinking and learning about print.* Cambridge, MA: MIT Press.

Anderson, R., Hiebert, E., Wilkinson, I., & Scott, J. (1985). *Becoming a nation of readers.* Champaign, IL: Center for the Study of Reading.

Baghban, M. (1984). *Our daughter learns to read and write.* Newark, DE: International Reading Association.

Ball, E., & Blachman, B. (1991). Does phoneme awareness training in kindergarten make a difference in early word recognition and developmental spelling? *Reading Research Quarterly, 26,* 49–66.

Balmuth, M. (1982). *The roots of phonics: A historical introduction.* New York: McGraw-Hill.

Beers, J., & Henderson, E. (1977). A study of developing orthographic concepts among first grade children. *Research in the Teaching of English, 11,* 133–148.

Bissex, G. (1980). *Gnys at wrk: A child learns to write and read.* Cambridge, MA: Harvard University Press.

Blachman, B. (1994). Early literacy acquisition: The role of phonological awareness. In G. Wallach & K. Butler (Eds.), *Language learning and disabilities in school children and adolescents: Some underlying principles and applications* (pp. 253–274). Columbus, OH: Merrill.

Bond, G., & Dykstra, R. (1967). The cooperative research program in first-grade reading instruction. *Reading Research Quarterly, 2,* 5–142.

Boudreau, D., & Hedberg, N., (1999). A comparison of early literacy skills in children with specific language impairment and their typically developing peers. *American Journal of Speech-Language Pathology, 8,* 249–260.

Bradley, L. ,& Bryant, P. (1983). Categorizing sounds and learning to read: A causal connection. *Nature, 303,* 419–421.

Branscombe, N., & Taylor, J. (2000). "It would be good as Snow White": Play and prosody. In K. Roskos & J. Christie (Eds.), *Play and literacy in early childhood: Research from multiple perspectives* (pp.169–188). Mahwah, NJ: Erlbaum.

Britto, P., Brooks-Gunn, J., & Griffin, R. (2006). Maternal reading and teaching patterns: Associations with school readiness in low-income African American families. *Reading Research Quarterly, 41,* 68–89.

Brizius, J., & Foster, S. (1993). *Generation to generation: Realizing the promise of family literacy.* Ypsilanti, MI: High/Scope Press.

Bryant, D., Burchinal, M., Lau, L., & Sparling, J. (1994). Family and classroom correlates of Head Start children's developmental outcomes. *Early Childhood Research Quarterly, 9,* 289–310.

Burchinal, M., Roberts, J., Riggins, R., Zeisel, S., Neebe, E., & Bryant, D. (2000). Relating quality of center-based child care to early cognitive and language development longitudinally. *Child Development, 71,* 339–357.

Burns, M. S., & Casbergue, R. (1992). Parent-child interactions in a writing context. *Journal of Reading Behavior: A Literacy Journal, 20,* 289–312.

Bus, A., & van Ijzendoorn, M. (1995). Mothers reading to their 3 year olds: The role of mother-child attachment security in becoming literate. *Reading Research Quarterly, 30,* 998–1015.

Center for the Future of Teaching and Learning. (1996). Thirty years of NICHD research: What we now know about how children learn to read. *Effective School Practices, 15,* 33–46.

Chall, J. (1967). *Learning to read: The great debate.* New York: McGraw-Hill.

Chaney, C. (1992). Language development, metalinguistic skills, and print awareness in 3-year-old children. *Applied Psycholinguistics, 13,* 485–514.

Christie, J., & Stone, S. (1999). Collaborative literacy activity in print-enriched play centers: Exploring the "zone" in same-age and multi-age groupings. *Journal of Literacy Research, 31,* 109–131.

Clay, M. (1966). *Emergent reading behavior* (Unpublished doctoral dissertation). University of Auckland, Auckland, New Zealand.

Clay, M. (Ed.). (1971). *Research on language and reading in Pakeha and Polynesian groups.* Newark, DE: International Reading Association.

Clay, M. (1998). *By different paths to common outcomes.* Portland, ME: Stenhouse.

Darling, S., & Hayes, A. (1989). *The William R. Kenan Jr. Charitable Trust Family Literacy Project, First Report 1988–1989.* Louisville, KY: National Center for Family Literacy.

Darling, S., & Hayes, A. (1996). *The power of family literacy.* Louisville, KY: National Center for Family Literacy.

DeBaryshe, B. D., & Buell, M. J. (1996). What a parent brings to the table: Young children writing with and without parental assistance. *Journal of Literacy Research, 28*(1), 71–91.

Delgado-Gaitan, C. (1994). Sociocultural change through literacy: Toward empowerment of families. In B. Ferdman, R. Weber, & A. Ramirez (Eds.), *Literacy Across Languages and Cultures* (pp. 143–170). Albany, NY: State University of New York Press.

Denti, L., & Katz, M. (1995). Escaping the cave to dream new dreams: A normative vision for learning disabilities. *Journal of Learning Disabilities, 28,* 415–424.

Dickinson, D., & Snow, C. (1987). Interrelationships among prereading and oral language skills in kindergartners from two social classes. *Early Childhood Research Quarterly, 2,* 1–25.

Dickinson, D., & Sprague, K. (2002). The nature and impact of early childhood care environments on the language and early literacy development of children from low-income families. In S. Neuman & D. Dickinson (Eds.), *Handbook of early literacy research* (pp. 263–280). New York: Guilford.

Dudley-Marling, C., & Dippo, D. (1995). What learning disability does: Sustaining the ideology of schooling. *Journal of Learning Disabilities, 28,* 408–414.

Dunn, L., Beach, S., & Kontos, S. (1994). Quality of literacy environment in day care and children's development. *Journal of Research in Childhood Education, 9,* 23–34.

Durkin, D. (1966a). The achievement of pre-school readers: Two longitudinal studies. *Reading Research Quarterly, 1*(4), 5–36.

Durkin, D. (1966b). *Children who read early.* New York: Teachers College Press.

Durkin, D. (1974). A six year study of children who learned to read in school at the age of four. *Reading Research Quarterly, 10*(1), 9–61.

Dyson, A. H. (1982a). Reading, writing, and language: Young children solving the written language puzzle. *Language Arts, 59,* 829–839.

Dyson, A. (1982b). The emergency of visible language: Interrelationships between drawing and early writing. *Visible Language, 16,* 360–381.

Dyson, A. H. (1984). Learning to write: Learning to do school: Emergent writers' interpretations of school literacy tasks. *Research in the Teaching of English, 18*(3), 233–263.

Dyson, A. (1997). *Writing superheroes: Contemporary childhood, popular culture, and classroom literacy.* New York: Teachers College Press.

Dyson, A. (2002). Writing and children's symbolic repertoires: Development unhinged. In S. Neuman & D. Dickinson (Eds.), *Handbook of early literacy research* (pp. 126–141). New York: Guilford.

Edwards, P. (1991). Fostering literacy through parent coaching. In E. H. Hiebert (Ed.), *Literacy for a diverse society: Perspectives, practices, and policies* (pp. 199–214). New York: Teachers College Press.

Edwards, P. (1994). Responses of teachers and African-American mothers to a book reading intervention program. In D. K. Dickinson (Ed.), *Bridges to literacy: Children, families, and schools* (pp. 175–208). Cambridge, MA: Blackwell.

Ehri, L., & Wilce, L. (1985). Movement into reading: Is the first stage of printed word learning visual or phonetic? *Reading Research Quarterly, 20,* 163–179.

Elley, W. (1989). Vocabulary acquisition from listening to stories. *Reading Research Quarterly, 24,* 174–187.

Englert, C., Garmon, A., Mariage, T., Rozendal, M., Tarrant, K., & Urba, J. (1995). The early literacy project: Connecting across the literacy curriculum. *Learning Disability Quarterly, 18,* 253–275.

Englert, C., Raphael, T., & Mariage, T. (1994). Developing a school-based discourse for literacy learning: a principled search for understanding. *Learning Disability Quarterly, 17,* 2–32.

Ezell, H., & Justice, L. (1998). A pilot investigation of parent questions about print and pictures to preschoolers with language delay. *Child Language Teaching and theory, 13,* 273–278.

Ezell, H., & Justice, L., (2000). Increasing the print focus of adult-child shared book reading through observational learning. *American Journal of Speech-Language Pathology, 9,* 36–47.

Ezell, H., Justice, L., & Parsons, D. (2000). A clinic-based book reading intervention for parents and their preschoolers with communication impairment. *Child Language Teaching and Theory, 16,* 121–140.

Feitelson, D., & Goldstein, Z. (1986). Patterns of book ownership and reading to young children in Israeli school-oriented and non-school-oriented families. *The Reading Teacher, 39,* 924–930.

Fernandez-Fein, S., & Baker, L. (1997). Rhyme and alliteration sensitivity and relevant experiences among preschoolers from diverse backgrounds. *Journal of Literacy Research, 29,* 433–459.

Ferreiro, C. (1986). *The interplay between information and assimilation in beginning literacy.* Norwood, NJ: Ablex.

Foorman, B., Fletcher, J., Francis, D., Schatschneider, C., & Mehta, P. (1998). The role of instruction in learning to read: Preventing reading failure in at-risk children. *Journal of Educational Psychology, 90,* 37–55.

Foorman, B., Francis, D., Novy, D., & Liberman, D. (1991). How letter-sound instruction mediates progress in first-grade reading and spelling. *Journal of Educational Psychology, 83,* 456–469.

Gentry, J. (1978). Early spelling strategies. *Elementary School Journal, 79,* 88–92.

Hall, N. (1987). The literate home corner. In P. Smith (Ed.), *Parents and teachers together* (pp. 134–144). London: Macmillan.

Hammett, L., van Kleeck, A., & Huberty, C. (2003). Patterns of parents' extratextual interactions during book sharing with preschool children: A cluster analysis study. *Reading Research Quarterly, 38,* 442–468.

Harris, A., & Sipay, E. (1990). *How to increase reading ability* (9th ed.). New York: Longman.

Hart, B., & Risley, R. (1995). *Meaningful differences in the everyday experience of young American Children.* Baltimore, MD: Brookes.

Heath, S. B. (1982). What no bedtime story means: Narrative skills at home and school. *Language and Society, 11*(1), 49–76.

Heath, S. B. (1983). *Ways with Words: Language, life and work in communities and classroooms.* New York: Cambridge University Press.

Henderson, E. H., & Beers, J. W. (1980). *Developmental and cognitive aspects of learning to spell: A reflection of word knowledge.* Newark, DE: International Reading Association.

High/Scope Educational Research Foundation. (1997). *Early returns: First year report of the Michigan school-readiness programs evaluation.* Ypsilianti, MI: Author.

Hohn, W., & Ehri, L. (1983). Do alphabet letters help prereaders acquire phonemic segmentation skill? *Journal of Educational Psychology, 75,* 752–762.

Jackson, R., McCoy, A., Pistorino, C., Wilkinson, A., Burghardt, J., Clark, M., et al. (2007). *National evaluation of Early Reading First: Final report.* U.S. Department of Education, Institute of Education Sciences, Washington, DC: U.S. Government Printing Office.

Johnston, R. S., & Watson, J. (1997). Developing reading, spelling and phonemic awareness skills in primary school children. *Reading, 31,* 37–40.

Justice, L. (2004). Creating language-rich preschool classroom environments. *Teaching Exceptional children, 37,* 36–44.

Justice, L., & Ezell, H. (2000). Enhancing children's print and word awareness through home-based parent intervention, *American Journal of Speech-Language Pathology, 9,* 257–269.

Justice, L., & Ezell, H. (2001). Descriptive analysis of written language awareness in children from low income households. *Communication Disorders Quarterly, 22,* 123–134.

Justice, L., & Ezell, H. (2002). Use of storybook reading to increase print awareness in at-risk children. *American Journal of Speech-Language Pathology, 11,* 17–29.

Justice, L. M., & Kaderavek, L. M. (2002). Using shared book reading to promote emergent literacy. *Teaching Exceptional Children, 34,* 8–13.

Justice, L., & Kaderavek, J. (2003). Topic control during shared storybook reading: Mothers and their children with mild to moderate language impairment. *Topics in Early Childhood Special Education, 23,* 137–150.

Justice, L., Kaderavek, J., Bowles, R., & Grimm, K. (2005). Phonological awareness, language impairment, and parent-child shared reading: A feasibility study. *Topics in Early Childhood Special Education, 25,* 143–156.

Justice, L. M., Meier, J., & Walpole, S. (2005) Learning new words from storybooks: Findings from an intervention with at-risk kindergarteners. *Language, Speech, and Hearing Services in Schools, 36,* 17–32.

Justice, L., Weber, S., Ezell, H., & Bakeman, R. (2002). A sequential analysis of children's responsiveness to parental print references during shared book-reading interactions. *American Journal of Speech-Language Pathology, 11,* 30–40.

Kantor, R., Miller, S., & Fernie, D. (1992). Diverse paths to literacy. *Reading Research Quarterly, 27,* 184–201.

Klenk, L. (1994). Case study in reading disability: An emergent literacy perspective. *Learning Disabilities Quarterly, 17,* 36–54.

Kouri, T., Selle, C., & Riley, S. (2006). Comparison of meaning and graphophonemic feedback strategies for guided reading instruction of children with language delays. *American Journal of Speech-Language Pathology, 15,* 236–246.

Labbo, L. D. (1996). Beyond storytime: A sociopsychological perspective on young children's opportunities for literacy development during story extension time. *Journal of Literacy Research, 28*(3), 405–429.

Laosa, L. (1983). Families as facilitators of children's intellectual development at 3 years of age. In L. M. Laosa & I. E. Spiegal (Eds.), *Families as learning environments for children* (pp. 1–45). New York: Plenum.

Leseman, P., & de Jong, P., (1998). Home literacy: Opportunity, instruction, cooperation and social-emotional quality predicting early reading achievement. *Reading Research Quarterly, 33*(3), 294–318.

Levin, H., & Williams, J. (Eds.). (1970). *Basic studies on reading.* New York: Basic Books.

Lewis, B., O'Donnell, B., Freebaim, L., & Taylor, H. (1998). Spoken language and written expression - Interplay of delays. *American Journal of Speech-Language Pathology, 7,* 77–84.

Lombardino, L., Riccio, C., Hynd, G., & Phnheiro, S. (1997). Linguistic deficits in children with reading disabilities. *American Journal of Speech-Language Pathology, 6,* 71–78.

Lundberg, I., Frost, J., & Petersen, O. (1988). Effects of an extensive program for stimulating phonological awareness in preschool children. *Reading Research Quarterly, 23,* 263–285.

Mason, J. M. (1980). When do children begin to read: An exploration of four year old children's letter and word reading competencies. *Reading Research Quarterly, 15*(2), 203–227.

McCune, L. (1995). A normative study of representational play at the transition to language. *Developmental Psychology, 31,* 198–201.

McFadden, T. (1998). Sounds and stories: Teaching phonemic awareness in interactions around text. *American Journal of Speech-Language Pathology,* 5–13.

McGee, L., & Richgels, D. (1989). K is Kristen's: Learning the alphabet from a child's perspective. *The Reading Teacher, 43,* 216–225.

McGee, L., & Richgels, D. (1990). *Literacy's beginnings.* New York: Allyn & Bacon.

McGill-Franzen, A., Allington, R., Yokoi, L., & Brooks, G. (1999). Putting books in the room seems necessary but not sufficient. *Journal of Educational Research, 93,* 67–74.

Morrow, L., & Weinstein, C. (1986). Encouraging voluntary reading: The impact of literature programs on children's use of library corners. *Reading Research Quarterly, 21,* 330–346.

National Reading Panel. (2000). *Report of the National Reading Panel.* Washington, DC: National Institute of Child Health and Development. Retrieved from http://www.nationalreadingpanel.org

Neuman, S. (1996). Children engaging in storybook reading: The influence of access to print resources, opportunity, and parental interaction. *Early Childhood Research Quarterly, 29,* 495–513.

Neuman, S., & Celano, D. (2006). The knowledge gap: Implications of leveling the playing field for low-income and middle-income children. *Reading Research Quarterly, 41,* 176–201.

Neuman, S., & Gallagher, P. (1994). Joining together in literacy learning: Teenage mothers and children. *Reading Research Quarterly, 29,* 382–401.

Neuman, S., Hagedorn, T., Delano, D., & Daly, P. (1995). Toward a collaborative approach to parent involvement in early education: A study of teenage mothers in an African-American community. *American Educational Research Journal, 32,* 801–827.

Neuman, S., & Roskos, K. (1989). Preschoolers' conceptions of literacy as reflected in their spontaneous play. In S. McCormick & J. Zutell (Eds.), *Cognitive and social perspectives for literacy research and instruction* (pp. 87–94). Chicago: National Reading Conference.

Neuman, S., & Roskos, K. (1990). The influence of literacy-enriched play settings on preschoolers' engagement with written language. In J. Zutell & S. McCormick (Eds.), *Literacy theory and research: analyses from multiple perspectives* (pp. 179–187). Chicago: National Reading Conference.

Neuman, S., & Roskos, K. (1992). Literacy objects as cultural tools: Effects on children's literacy behaviors in play. *Reading Research Quarterly, 27,* 202–225.

Neuman, S., & Roskos, K. (1997). Literacy knowledge in practice: Contexts of participation for young writers and readers. *Reading Research Quarterly, 32,* 10–33.

NICHD Early Child Care Research Network. (1999). Child outcomes when child care center classes meet recommended standards for quality. *American Journal of Public Health, 89,* 1072–1077.

Ninio, A., & Bruner, J. (1978). The achievement and antecedents of labelling. *Journal of Child Language, 5,* 5–15.

Paul, R. (1975). Invented spelling in kindergarten. *Young Children, 31,*195–200.

Peisner-Feinberg, E., & Burchinal, M. (1997). Concurrent relations between child care quality and child outcomes: The study of cost, quality, and outcomes in child care centers. *Merrill-Palmer Quarterly, 43,* 451–477.

Pellegrini, A., & Galda, L. (1993). Ten years after: A reexamination of symbolic play and literacy research. *Reading Research Quarterly, 28,* 162–175.

Pellegrini, A., Galda, L., Dresden, J., & Cox, S. (1991). A longitudinal study of the predictive relations among symbolic play, linguistic verbs, and early literacy. *Research in the Teaching of English, 25,* 215–235.

Philliber, W., Spillman, R., & King, R. (1996). Consequences of family literacy for adults and children: Some preliminary finds. *Journal of Adolescent and Adult Literacy, 39,* 558–565.

Poplin, M. (1985). Reductionism from the medical model to the classroom: The past, present and future of learning disabilities. *Research Communications in Psychology, Psychiatry and Behavior, 10,* 37–70.

Poplin, M. (1988). The reductionistic fallacy in learning disabilities: Replicating the past by reducing the present. *Journal of Learning Disabilities, 21,* 389–400.

Price, E. (1976). How thirty-seven gifted children learned to read. *The Reading Teacher, 30*(1), 44–48.

Purcell-Gates, V. (1996). Stories, coupons, and the "TV Guide:" Relationships between home literacy experiences and emergent literacy knowledge. *Reading Research Quarterly, 31*(4), 406–428.

Read, C. (1971). Pre-school children's knowledge of English phonology. *Harvard Educational Review, 41,* 1–34.

Read, C. (1975). *Children's categorization of speech sounds in English.* Urbana, IL: National Council of Teachers of English.

Read, C. (1986). *Children's creative spelling.* London: Routledge & Kegan Paul.

Richgels, D. J. (1995). Invented spelling ability and printed word learning in kindergarten. *Reading Research Quarterly, 30*(1), 96–109.

Richgels, D. (2002). Invented spelling, phonemic awareness, and reading and writing instruction. In S. Neuman & D. Dickinson (Eds.), *Handbook of early literacy research* (pp. 142–158). New York: Guilford.

Rowe, D. (1998). The literate potentials of book-related dramatic play. *Reading Research Quarterly, 33,* 10–35.

Schickedanz, J. (1990). *Adam's righting revolutions.* Portsmouth, NH: Heinemann.

Schieffelin, B., & Cochran-Smith, M. (1984). Learning to read culturally: Literacy before schooling. In H. Goelman, A. Oberg, & F. Smith (Eds.), *Awakening to literacy* (pp. 3–23). Exeter, NH: Heinemann.

Senechal, M., LeFevre, J., Thomas, E., & Daley, K. (1998). Differential effects of home literacy experiences on the development of oral and written language. *Reading Research Quarterly, 32,* 96–116.

Shanahan, T. (2008). *The National Early Literacy Panel: What research does a review of research recommend?* Paper presented at the International Reading Association Annual Conference, Atlanta, GA.

Shaywitz, S., Escobar, M., Shaywitz, B., Fetcher, J., & Makuch, R. (1992). Evidence that dyslexia may represent the lower tail of a normal distribution of reading ability. *New England Journal of Medicine, 326,* 145–150.

Skinner, B. F. (1950). Are theories of learning necessary? *Psychological Review, 57*(4), 193–216.

Skinner, B. F. (1989). *Recent issues in the analysis of behavior.* New York: Merrill.

Snow, C. (1983). Literacy and language: Relationships during the preschool years. *Harvard Educational Review, 53,* 165–189.

Snow, C., Burns, M. S., & Griffin, P. (1998). *Preventing reading difficulties in young children.* Washington, DC: National Research Council.

Stahl, S. (2002). Teaching phonics and phonological awareness. In S. Neuman & D. Dickinson (Eds.), *Handbook of early literacy research* (pp. 333–347). New York: Guilford.

St. Pierre, R., Swartz, J., Gamse, B., Murray, S., Deck, D., & Nickel, P. (1995). *National evaluation of the Even Start Family Literacy Program, final report.* Bethesda, MD: Abt Associates.

Tao, F., Games, B., & Tarr, H. (1998). *National evaluation of the Even Start Family Literacy Program, 1994–1997, final report.* Washington, DC: U.S. Department of Education, Planning, and Evaluation Service.

Taylor, B., Anderson, R., Au, K., & Raphael, T. (2000). Discretion in the transition of reading research to policy. *Educational Researcher, 29,* 16–26.

Taylor, D. (1983). *Family literacy: Young children learning to read and write.* Exeter, NH: Heinemann.

Teale, W. (1986). Home background and young children's literacy development. In W. H. Teale & E. Sulzby (Eds.), *Emergent literacy: Writing and reading* (pp. 173–206). Norwood, NJ: Ablex.

Trent, S., Artiles, A., & Englert, C. (1998). From deficit thinking to social constructivism: A review of theory, research, and practice in special education. *Review of Research in Education, 23,* 277–307.

U.S. Department of Education. (1993). *Life in preschool: Volume one of an observational study of early childhood programs for disadvantaged four-year-olds: Final report, 1993.* Cambridge, MA: Abt Associates.

U.S. Department of Education, (2006). *The Reading First Program's grant application process: Final inspection report.* Washington, DC: Author.

van Kleeck, A., & Beckley-McCall, A. (2002). A comparison of mothers' individual and simultaneous book sharing with preschool siblings. *American Journal of Speech-Language Pathology, 11,* 175–189.

van Kleeck, A., Woude, J., & Hammett, L. (2006). Fostering literal and inferential language skills in head start preschoolers with language impairment using scripted book-sharing discussions. *American Journal of Speech-Language Pathology, 15,* 85–95.

Vellutino, F. (1987). Dyslexia. *Scientific American,* 34–41.

Vellutino, F. (1991. Introduction to three studies on reading acquisition: Convergent findings on theoretical foundations of code-oriented versus whole language approaches to reading instruction. *Journal of Educational Psychology, 83,* 189–264.

Vellutino, F., & Scanlon, D. (1987). Phonological coding, phonological awareness, and reading ability: Evidence from a longitudinal and experimental study. *Merrill-Palmer Quarterly, 33,* 321–363.

Vellutino, F., & Scanlon, D. (2002). The interactive strategies approach to reading intervention. *Contemporary Educational Psychology, 27,* 573–635.

Vellutino, F., Scanlon, D., Sipay, E., Small, S., Pratt, A., Chen, R., et al. (1996). Cognitive profiles of difficult-to-remediate and readily remediated poor readers: Early intervention as a vehicle for distinguishing between cognitive and experiential deficits as basic causes of specific reading disability. *Journal of Educational Psychology, 88,* 601–638.

Vygotsky, L. (1978). *Mind in society.* Cambridge, MA: Harvard University Press.

Vygotsky, L. (1993). The collective as a factor in the development of the abnormal child. In R. W. Rieber & A. S. Carton (Eds.), *The collected works of L. S. Vygotsky: The fundamentals of defectology (abnormal psychology and learning disabilities), Vol. 2* (pp. 191–208). New York: Plenum.

Walker, D., Greenwood, C., Hart, B., & Carta, J. (1994). Prediction of school outcomes based on early language production and socioeconomic factors. *Child Development, 65,* 606–621.

Whitehurst, G., Arnold, D., Epstein, J., Angell, A., Smith, M., & Fischel, J. (1994). A picture book reading intervention to day care and home for children from low-income families. *Developmental Psychology, 3,* 679–689.

Whitehurst, G., Epstein, J., Angell, A., Payne, D., Crone, D., & Fischel, J. (1994). Outcomes of an emergent literacy intervention in Head Start. *Journal of Educational Psychology, 86,* 542–555.

Yaden, D., Smolkin, L., & Conlon, A. (1989). Preschoolers' questions about pictures, print conventions, and story text during reading aloud at home. *Reading Research Quarterly, 24,* 188–214.

Zutell, J. (1976). Spelling strategies of preschool children and their relationships to the Piagetian concept of decentration. *Dissertation Abstracts International, 36,* 5030A.

18

Developmental Patterns of Reading Proficiency and Reading Difficulties

Marcia Invernizzi and Latisha Hayes
University of Virginia

Difficulty with word recognition is by far the most apparent symptom a of reading disability, and its prevalence is so great that consensus exists that word-level reading difficulties are synonymous with the most profound reading difficulty known as dyslexia. Indeed, the very definition of dyslexia offered by the International Dyslexia Association (IDA) focuses on word recognition and describes the disability as being primarily "characterized by difficulties with accurate and/or fluent word recognition and by poor spelling and decoding abilities" (IDA, 2002).

Despite individual differences among the reading disabled, the major problem characterizing children with dyslexia is difficulty with word recognition. This basic problem with word recognition leads to profound interferences with overall reading and writing fluency that pervade all areas of academic achievement. Even definitions of reading fluency and reading comprehension rely on theories of word recognition for their explanatory power. While the construct of reading fluency involves more than word recognition and includes such cognitive processes such as automaticity, rapid naming, and the prosodic rendering of text, most studies specifically addressing fluency problems describe concomitant difficulties with word recognition and theoretical discussions of reading fluency center around accurate and automatic word recognition (Fletcher, Lyon, Fuchs, & Barnes, 2007). For this reason, the major measurement used as a proxy for reading fluency has been the number of words recognized correctly per minute, reflecting the emphasis on accurate and automatic reading of words. Theories of reading comprehension also assume adequate word reading skills and research has repeatedly found that levels of reading comprehension approach levels of listening comprehension as word recognition and decoding skills become accurate and automatic (Perfetti, 1985). As Stanovich (1994) stated:

> Reading for meaning (comprehension) is greatly hindered when children are having too much trouble with word

recognition. When word recognition processes demand too much cognitive capacity, few cognitive resources are left to allocate to higher-level processes of text integration and comprehension. (p. 281)

Thus, there is general consensus that the ability to read and decode words accurately and effortlessly is a prerequisite to reading fluently and with understanding, even though these latter constructs integrate other cognitive and linguistic processes as well. Given this degree of agreement regarding the pivotal role of word recognition in reading, the ability to read words accurately and fluently has been the focus of most research on reading disabilities. Most germane to this volume is the research on the development of word recognition skill, since an understanding of how children learn to read and write words is key to helping them do so more easily.

In this chapter we review the predominant theories of word recognition and focus on their explanatory appeal in reconciling the word recognition behaviors of disabled readers. The chapter will then turn to the more recent developmental models of word recognition that emphasize learning and instruction. Developmental theories of word reading emphasize the interrelatedness of word recognition, decoding, and spelling skill and the interaction among phonology, orthography, and semantics. Children's spelling attempts have long been considered a window through which to view their understanding of how written words work, and the chapter will present studies linking the development of orthographic knowledge to word recognition. The chapter will conclude with a discussion of instructional implications.

Models of Word Recognition

Written word recognition involves the access of a word's pronunciation and meaning from memory. The nature of that access has been the subject of controversy for many years. Some say the access is direct from the visual ortho-graphic display to meaning while others say the access is mediated through phonological processes which themselves are controversial. Still others conceptualize the recognition of written words as a complex interactive process involving networks of weighted connections that are ever changing in relation to experience with print. From a pedagogical point of view, the most important aspect of written word recognition is how it develops. Only by understanding this development can we begin to plan effective instruction for students with word recognition difficulties. This section discusses three models of word recognition: dual route, con-nectionist, and developmental. A discussion of variations of the first two models, such as the dual-route cascaded model and other computational models, may be found elsewhere (cf. Coltheart, 2007).

The Dual Route Theory of Word Recognition   The most predominant theory of word recognition is the dual route theory. According to that theory of word recognition, individuals are able to identify words either by linking the graphemes to phonemes, which, in turn, link to the lexical store of known words in memory, or, conversely, by linking the word's visual, orthographic display directly to the word's meaning without phonological mediation. The former way of identifying words is referred to as the phonological or sub-lexical route, and explains how individuals are able to read pseudowords such as *redoip* or *chasidoolid* that have no meaning at all. The latter route, often termed the *visual* or *orthographic*, route, explains how individuals read irregularly spelled exception words such as *have* or *sugar*. One reason the dual route theory has maintained such longevity is because it provides a possible explanation for these two word reading phenomena that are often associated with subtypes of dyslexia. Individuals who can't read pseudowords like *blait*, but whose reading of ir-regularly spelled exception words is relatively unimpaired, are referred to as "deep" or "phonological" dyslexics. In contrast, individuals who can read pseudowords but have difficulty reading irregularly spelled exception words like *ocean* are often called "surface" or "orthographic" dyslex-ics. Instructional implications of this model have sometimes led to the use of a whole word method for "phonological" dyslexics who cannot access the deeper phonological underpinnings of written words but who can nevertheless capitalize on the visual orthographic display on the surface. Conversely, the logic of this theory has sometimes led to a phonics-based approach for orthographic dyslexics who have difficulty with the surface, orthographic representa-tion despite their ability to access the deeper phonologi-cal elements within a written word. The concept of deep (phonological) versus surface (orthographic) dyslexia has led to metaphorical descriptions differentiating Phoenician (phonological) from Chinese (orthographic) readers (Baron & Strawson, 1976).

There are several limitations to the dual route theory of word recognition. First, the dual route theory evolved from the study of adults who sustained sudden brain injury resulting in an acquired reading disability (alexia), not from the study of children who struggle to learn to read (devel-opmental dyslexia). Second, investigations of children with word reading disabilities reveal difficulty with *both* the phonological and orthographic routes. Standing in contrast to the either-or paradigm of the dual route model, Stanovich, Seigel, and Gottardo (1997) reported that most children with word reading disabilities experienced problems with both phonological *and* orthographic components of word recognition. Manis, Seidenberg, Doi, McBride-Chang, and Peterson (1996) also found that children with dyslexia had difficulties reading both pseudowords and irregularly spelled exception words, and in their research, the so-called surface dyslexics performed no differently than matched reading level controls. Third, Zabell and Everatt (2002) found that even adults who met the description of phonological or sur-face dyslexia were not significantly different on a variety of phonological processing measures. Fourth, many argue that words are read utilizing multiple connections as opposed to only two separate routes of word recognition. Manis et al. argued that their results were more in keeping with a connectionist model of word recognition (Foorman, 1994; Seidenberg & McClelland, 1989) in which reading phoneti-cally regular or irregularly spelled exception words of any kind activates everything that is known about the word's phonological, orthographic, and semantic representations. Fifth, difficulty reading irregularly spelled exception words does not appear to be an indicator of a specific disability but rather an indicator of experience with print. Griffiths and Snowling (2002) argued that while the decoding deficit that characterizes dyslexia stems from poorly specified phonological representations, difficulty reading irregularly spelled exception words is primarily the result of limited print exposure. This argument was based on their finding that while measures of phonological processing contributed unique variance to pseudoword reading the only unique predictor of irregularly spelled exception word reading was a measure of reading experience. Rather than concluding that the accurate recognition of irregularly spelled excep-tion words occurs via a visual or orthographic route, these researchers suggested that orthographic processing is de-pendent on experience with print. Since surface dyslexia is most often reported as a characteristic of younger children, Stanovich (1994) posited that the inability to read exception words could simply be a transient delay in the development of word recognition skills due to inexperience.

These findings, in combination with the prevalence of dyslexic children's struggle with both the phonological and orthographic aspects of words, undermine the dual route theory of word recognition. Moreover, Vellutino, Scanlon, and Chen (1995) have questioned the very no-tion of orthographic coding as a separate construct in the dual route theory of word recognition, on the grounds that phonological knowledge and orthographic knowledge are inseparable and must work together to help young readers crack the alphabetic code.

Connectionist Models of Word Recognition An alternative model that considers the interplay of phonological, orthographic, and semantic information are connectionist models of word recognition. These models seek to explain developmental dyslexia by configuring a computational model of the reading impairment and seeing if it simulates the dyslexic behavior (Seidenberg, 2005). Connectionist models of word recognition provide a way to test causal hypotheses about various reading impairments and can also test the learning potential of different simulated instructional practices. Though the technical aspects of these computational models are challenging, they offer an interesting check on the many theoretical assumptions underlying theories of word recognition and consider different types of information (phonological, orthographic, semantic) as they interact rather than different types of processing that are separated into two different routes. Growing from parallel processing models (e.g., Just & Carpenter, 1987; Rayner & Pollatsek, 1998) that avoid the serial requirements of the earlier models, connectionist models challenge two critical assumptions of the dual-route theory: (a) recognizing words involves either learning rules for pronouncing regularly spelled words like *gave* and *save*, or memorizing irregularly spelled exception words like *have*, and (b) rule and memory systems are acquired and governed by two different mechanisms or routes.

Following the logic of Venezky and Massaro (1979) and Glusko (1979), connectionist models of word recognition question the categorical labeling of written words as "regular" or "irregular," and argue that words can have orthographically regular patterns even if individual letter sounds are irregular, as in *eigh* words like *eighth, freight*, or *neigh*. Instead of describing written words categorically as either regular or irregular, connectionists consider the consistency of spelling-to-sound relationships on a continuum. Many of the so-called "exception" words share commonalities with regularly spelled words. For example, the word *pint* shares three fourths of the letter—sound consistencies found in regularly spelled words like *pant* and *pine* (Seidenberg, 2005). Additionally, when pattern is taken into account, *pint* follows the i-consonant-consonant pattern in *kind, find, mind, blind*, and *grind*. By forcing exception words like *pint* into one of only two possible categories (or routes), the spelling-sound regularities that do exist are ignored. In this view, rather than two different routes for word recognition and two different corresponding instructional approaches (whole words vs. phonics) connectionist models theorize a "learning device" that can discover whatever phonological, orthographic, and semantic correspondences occur across many different words. Just like beginning readers who struggle to read a new word, the connectionist model learns to compute an accurate pronunciation from a given spelling pattern by finding an appropriate set of weights across orthographic and other linguistic systems such as phonology, syntax, and semantics. Rather than two separate routes of word recognition, reading pseudowords and irregularly spelled exception words

simply involves differential weighting of the connections. In this light, performance on any given word is influenced by knowledge of other words.

Connectionist models have been successful in "learning" to pronounce thousands of words of all degrees of spelling-to-sound consistency and suggest that the most optimal learning algorithms involve multiple layers of information about the visual and linguistic identities of written words that are simultaneously distributed across many connections. Some connectionist models are also known as neural network models and involve both "cooperative and competitive" interactions among inputs (Plaut, 2007). Cooperative input is processed through a linear integration function while competitive input is processed through a nonlinear activation function. The linear integration function explains how readers deal with words with cooperating (or similar) properties. Through a linear integration function, readers can generalize properties of known words to unknown words. For example, the nonword *zill* would be pronounced correctly given positive connections to words like *hill, pill, fill* that have the same sound and spelling pattern. However, since some words are only partially regular, these models use a nonlinear activation function to explain how readers approach irregular exception or words that may have features that compete with features that are phonetically regular. The nonlinear activation function allows the reader to pronounce *have* with a "short a" rather than with a "long a" like *gave* by weighting connections to other words that share similar features such as *had* or *salve*.

Unlike the dual route theory of word recognition, connectionist models consider the process of learning, which could provide important information not only about developmental dyslexia but also about remediation. Learning is conceptualized as "a slow incremental increase in knowledge, represented by increasingly strong and accurate connections between different units" (Plaut, 2007, p. 25) that are impacted by feedback from performance. Nevertheless, connectionist models are computer-based simulations, and depend on unspecified "hidden units" that increase the "computational capacity of the network and provide the basis for abstraction" to account for learning (Seidenberg, 2005, p. 239). Teachers, however, need to know what those hidden units are to plan their instruction with struggling readers and look to developmental models as a more practical guide.

Developmental Models of Word Recognition The development of word recognition skill is not an all or nothing phenomenon. Like most aspects of learning to read and write, the ability to recognize words in print is acquired gradually in accord with developmental increments of oral and written word knowledge. Some researchers have referred to these increments as stages (Chall, 1983; Gough & Hillinger, 1980; Mason, 1980; Marsh, Friedman, Welch & Desberg, 1980; Frith, 1985; Henderson, 1990; Stuart & Coltheart, 1988), although some object to the use of the word 'stage' because of implied thresholds of mastery required to move from one stage to the next (Ehri, 1998; Seymour & Duncan, 2001). The term *phase* is preferred by this group as a more flexible construct that does not require that thresholds be met before moving on. This term is often applied to more "cascaded" models of word reading that accommodate overlap between stages (Snowling & Hulme, 2007 p.102). Whether stages or phases, most agree that learning to read involves a gradual increase in linguistic awareness of connections between oral and written word forms, and that these connections underlie the ability to recognize words.

Ehri's Model of Word Recognition   Building on a connectionist framework, Ehri's (1998) developmental phase model posits a single route to word recognition, a route that is created by forming connections among the spelling, pronunciation, and meaning of a word in memory. As children learn to map the spelling of words (their visual display) with their pronunciations (their phonological correspondence), this orthographic/phonological linkage secures the word in memory (Ehri, 1999). Through the orthography, the phonological aspects of a word are bonded to the word's other linguistic identities, such as its syntactic function, pronunciation, and meaning. Incremental knowledge of the orthography gradually amalgamates the phonological, syntactic, and semantic identities of a word and glues it into memory. Thorough knowledge of the grapheme-phoneme system provides immediate access to the word in memory because seeing the orthography automatically activates its pronunciation, meaning, and use. Thus, according to Ehri's theory of word reading, "sight words" are not read by a visual route, but are recognized "at first sight" through immediate recognition of the orthographic display, which in turn, activates the phonological, syntactic, and semantic information necessary to read the word successfully. Even the proper pronunciation of difficult exception words such as *colonel*, derived from the Old Italian *colonnello* (commander of a column of soldiers) is activated by repeated association of the word's meaning and use with its spelling.

Evidence in support of Ehri's assertion that words are read from memory comes from word recognition research involving Stroop tasks. In a Stroop presentation, individuals are shown pictures of objects such as a *plane* or a *desk*, but on each picture is a printed word naming a different object such as a *car* or a *chair*. Individuals are asked to name the picture and to ignore the words, but results from Stroop experiments have shown this to be difficult. Readers apparently cannot ignore the words and, in fact, it takes them longer to name the object pictures with printed words than it does to name the object pictures without the printed words (Guttentag & Haith, 1978). Ehri and Rosenthal's explanation (2007) is that the sight of the printed word automatically activates their pronunciations and meanings in memory, and this then slows the retrieval of the pictured object name. As soon as children learn to read, they are able to read familiar words from memory, usually by the end of the end of first grade.

According to Ehri's theory of word recognition, words are entered into memory via connections that are formed to link each grapheme to its phoneme. Connections apply not only to regularly spelled real and pseudowords, but also to irregularly spelled exception words. Like the connectionists, Ehri and Rosenthal (2007) point out that most letters in irregularly spelled exception words can be connected to phonemes in their pronunciations, for example, "all but the S is *island*, all but the W in *sword*, all but the UE in *tongue* (p. 392)." Thus, according to Ehri, regularly spelled real and pseudowords and irregularly spelled exception words are both identified by the same processes—that is, by forming connections between graphemes and phonemes. As readers remember combinations of graphemes and phonemes, larger sequences of letters or spelling patterns become familiar units that fasten words into memory. These letter sequences may be within-word spelling patterns or rimes (e.g., EAT in *neat, seat, heat),* syllables, or affixes (e.g., ING, NESS). Polysyllabic words may be remembered by forming connections between these larger orthographic units and syllables in pronunciation the three units in RE-HEAT-ING, for example.

Rather than two separate routes to word recognition, Ehri's theory suggests that phonemic (pronunciation) and graphemic (spelling) knowledge grows over time, becomes mutually reinforcing, and eventually, indistinguishable. Several studies have shown that children do retain specific word spellings in memory after seeing the word in print (Ehri, 1980, Retisma, 1983; Share, 2004). In addition, studies have shown that seeing printed words while simultaneously hearing them yields greater memory for them than hearing them alone (Ehri & Wilce, 1979). Still other work has shown that spelling knowledge influences speech perception (Ehri & Wilce, 1980). Readers who know how to spell the words *pitch* and *rich*, for example, will segment those words in to four and three phonemes respectively, despite the fact that they are pronounced identically. Similarly, readers are better able to determine identical sounding phonemes in the middle of words containing intervocalic alveolar flaps (e.g., *madder, metter*) when they have been exposed to their spelling (Ehri & Wilce, 1986). Other researchers have demonstrated the influence of spellings on oral phonological awareness tasks as well. Seidenberg and Tanenhaus (1979), for example, were able to show that students were faster at determining rhyming pairs when they shared the same spelling than when they did not. In other words, they were faster in determining that *clue* and *glue* rhymed than they were are determining whether *clue* and *shoe* rhymed, since the latter pair does not share the same spelling pattern. Finally, researchers have determined that exposure to spelling-meaning connections in derivationally related pairs (e.g., *bomb-bombard*) improves word recognition, spelling, and vocabulary (Templeton, 1992; Ehri & Rosenthal, 2007).

In Ehri's view, to secure words in memory, readers need to learn progressively more sophisticated word identification strategies. First, phoneme-segmentation skill is needed to analyze word pronunciations into the smallest units of sound. Second, letter-sound correspondence is needed to connect letters to sounds. Third, students need to be able to put these two things together to decode. When readers apply a decoding strategy to read a new word, grapho-phonemic mappings are activated. Some researchers claim that learning to decode is a self-teaching strategy allowing students to learn new words (Share, 1995). However, written words are comprised of more than single or double-letter graphemes, so any theory of word recognition must also account for the full array of printed word characteristics such as multiple-letter patterns within and across syllables, base words, and morphemes. Theories that portray the full development of word-recognition processes are of interest to teachers because of their instructional implications for students who have word-identification difficulties.

Henderson's Model of Word Recognition

Evidence suggests that the graphemic units involved in word recognition are relative to the developmental skill of the reader. However, most of the stage models developed in cognitive psychology emphasize shifts in *strategy* as opposed to *knowledge* (cf. Rayner, 1988), and only recently have researchers adopted a more fine-grained approach to investigating reciprocal interactions between strategy use and developing orthographic knowledge (Sharp, Sinatra, & Reynolds, 2008). Nevertheless, it is generally agreed that children progress from a state of nonreading, wherein they look at words much as they look at pictures, to a stage of beginning reading, wherein they have achieved an awareness that the alphabetic letters represent sound, whether literally via their letter names, or more abstractly through phonetic cues from letter-sound correspondences. A second shift is also commonly reported, wherein the child moves away from this deliberate, sequential alphabetic decoding strategy to a more efficient strategy in which words are more rapidly (and some would say directly) recognized though chunking larger units such as rimes (e.g., *ake* in *take*, *snake*, and *rake*), syllables (e.g., *in-ter-est-ing*), and morphemes (e.g., *demo* in *democratic*) (cf. Gough & Hillinger, 1980; Marsh, Friedman, Welch, & Desberg, 1980; Chall, 1983; Frith, 1988; Stuart & Coltheart, 1988; Seymour & Duncan, 2001; Ehri, 1998, 1999, 2002). Stuart and Coltheart (1988) suggested that these theories might be reformulated in terms of "graphemic parsing from an underlying base of phonological knowledge" (p. 147). Further, Stuart and Coltheart suggested that phonological knowledge could be refined by successful experience with orthography, which, in turn, allows for larger, more efficient graphemic units to be parsed in word recognition. The work of Berninger, Chen, and Abbott (1988) and Berninger, Yates, and Lester (1991) has also provided evidence for the use of multiple orthographic codes that are probably acquired gradually and adaptively among beginning readers.

One lesser known developmental model is Henderson's model of developmental word knowledge (1981, 1990), a model that emanated from developmental spelling research.

Henderson argued that understanding how children learned to spell words could also provide insight as to how they recognize them. Tying connectionist and developmental models, Henderson asserted that children's growing word knowledge encompasses phonological, orthographic, syntactic, and semantic information that is increasingly intertwined as children learn to read and spell. His work, and the work of his colleagues and students, demonstrated that children's knowledge of written words is developmental and advances progressively in relation to cognitive development, exposure to print, and instruction.

Henderson's theories have since been supported by a number of correlational and longitudinal students that have consistently identified spelling as an independent contributor to word reading (Caltaldo & Ellis, 1988; Ehir & Wilce, 1987; Morris & Perney, 1984). Significant correlations between spelling and various measures of word recognition have also been reported. Ehri (2000) reviewed six such studies and reported correlations between word reading and spelling ranging from .68 and .86 among students of various grades and ages (first grade through college). Zutell and Raskinski (1989) found that measures of spelling accounted for 40% to 60% of the variance in oral reading accuracy, and in a longitudinal study following children from the first to the third grade, Ellis and Cataldo (1992) also found spelling to be the most consistent predictor of reading achievement. Adding spelling instruction to the lesson plan of students in reading interventions has repeatedly resulted in greater gains in oral reading accuracy, silent reading comprehension, and word recognition (Berninger et al., 1998, Goulandris, 1992; Graham, Harris, & Chorzempa, 2002; McCandlis, Beck, Sandeak, & Perfetti, 2003). Invernizzi, Landrum, Robey, and Moon (2003) have reported correlations between spelling scores and oral reading levels of .79 using state-wide data from 68,817 first graders on the Phonological Awareness Literacy Screening.

In a recent meta-analysis of the correlational literature on measures of phonological awareness, rapid naming, word reading, and related abilities, the best predictors of word recognition were spelling and pseudoword reading (Swanson, Trainin, Necoechea, & Hammill, 2003). Further, in an exploratory factor analysis, spelling loaded meaningfully onto factors of pseudoword reading, real-word reading, and aspects of vocabulary and orthography (Swanson et al., 2003, p. 428). These studies make concrete the theoretical relationship between word recognition and knowledge of the orthography.

Henderson's research on the development of children's orthographic knowledge suggests an interaction among cognitive representations of sound, pattern, and meaning during the process of recognizing and producing printed words. Similar to the lexical restructuring that is conjectured to occur in oral vocabulary learning (Metsala & Walley, 1998), Henderson suggested the cognitive representations supporting the development of a reading vocabulary also become increasingly segmental across various "grain sizes" corresponding to the orthographic knowledge base and the language of the learner. Henderson's theory suggests that the restructuring of the written lexicon is an extended process that stretches out across the school years and influences not only spelling but also the accuracy and automaticity of word recognition.

According to Henderson's developmental word knowledge model, students progress from a state of nonreading to a state of mature, skilled, fluent reading, through a series of phases or stages that are invariant for all learners of alphabetic languages. Though students may progress at different rates, all students learn to read and spell words by mapping the orthographic display to increasingly refined phonological and morphological segments. This learning process is influenced by the number and nature of the written words that are known at any given point in time (Henderson, 1990; Templeton & Bear, 1992). Thus, according to Henderson's model, word recognition is constrained by an individual's orthographic knowledge which in turn, is influenced by the written words they are able to successfully recognize.

Henderson Stages and Ehri's Phases   Although a thorough comparison of all the developmental models is beyond the scope of this chapter, Henderson and Ehri's models are important to consider because they offer up yet another aspect of word knowledge development: student knowledge. The specifics of student knowledge at each phase or level of word knowledge and how that knowledge interacts with the demands of the orthography have intrinsic appeal to teachers because of their applicability to instructional matters in teaching struggling readers. Developmental models are based on behavioral descriptions of students as they learn to read and how their behaviors change over time in response to instruction and experience. Whether described as phases or stages, or overlapping waves, these models share the idea of a *zone of proximal development* that can be determined by an informed analysis of the errors students make when they read or write a word. The zone of proximal development is beyond the level at which individuals function effortlessly and independently but rather, the point at which they can perform well with instructional support (Vygotsky, 1978). Targeting instruction to students' zone of proximal development prevents students from reverting to more primitive strategies in their frustrated efforts to read or write words at a level that is too challenging. Knowing where students are on a developmental continuum helps teachers plan instruction that will help them to get to the next level. In the next section, we describe the developmental continuum in Henderson and Ehri's terms.

Preliterate—prealphabetic.   Prior to exposure to print, learners are typically preliterate because they have not yet acquired any alphabetic knowledge and they do not use any letter-sound correspondence when attempting to write. Similarly, when asked to read a word, preliterate learners may or may not luck out with an appropriate response, depending on the association they may have made between logographic cues in the graphemic display and the actual word. For example, in looking at the word *McDonalds*, the golden arch that always accompanies this logo may be sufficient to trigger "recognition" of the word *McDonalds*. Other researchers have described similar phenomenon such as "recognizing" the word yellow by the "tall posts" in the middle of the word, or the word look by the "pair of eyes" in the middle (Masonheimer, Drum, & Ehri, 1984; Juel, 1991). Frith (1985) called this word reading strategy "logographic," while Ehri (1998, 1999, 2002) coined the term "prealphabetic." Chall (1983) and Henderson (1981) referred to this stage as "prereading" and "preliterate," respectively, because students are not able to recognize any words without the use of selective visual cues that are totally arbitrary (Juel, 1991). The lack of any correspondence between letters and sounds suggests that preliterate individuals form connections between salient visual cues and meaning, and this constrains the odds of their guessing the correct word to single instances (Ehri & McCormick, 2004).

The subtle changes that occur throughout the period prior to learning the alphabet and letter sounds is why Bear, Invernizzi, Templeton, and Johnston (2008) refer to this stage as "emergent." When asked to read text, emergent learners are unable to match their speech to printed words in text and may not even have a sense of directionality (left to right progression of text). They are reliant on prior knowledge and memory of short familiar texts such as nursery rhymes and simple repetitive texts ("I see a ___ ____ looking at me"). Throughout the emergent stage, children begin to learn letters, particularly the letters in their own names, and, eventually, connect these letters to speech sounds. Toward the end of this stage, emergent writing starts to include the most prominent sounds in a word, usually corresponding to syllable boundaries, as in ICDD for "I see Daddy" (Bissex, 1980). The movement from this phase into the next hinges on acquiring the alphabetic principle: Letters represent speech sounds in a systematic way. Until the alphabetic principle is acquired, word recognition is not possible beyond random associations.

Letter name—partial to full alphabetic.   Students move into the beginning reading phase when they use letter names to read words and spell, hence the term letter name-alphabetic to refer to this period of development (Henderson, 1990; Bear et al., 2008). The name of the stage reflects student knowledge of how the written system works; they use the names of the letters to represent the corresponding speech sounds, much like William Steig did in his New Yorker cartoon, I N-V U (I envy you) (Steig, 1968). Notice I N-V U can be read using just partial letter-name cues that are suggestive of the entire word. For this reason, Ehri referred to the early part of this phase of word recognition as partial alphabetic. As students progress through this stage knowledge of letter-sound correspondences enables them to tackle words in the following manner: hear a sound/see a letter, write a letter/say a sound (Flanigan et al., 2010). The problem arises in their limited knowledge of individual phonemes within words and of letter sounds. These readers, also known as beginning readers, have a developing awareness of individual phonemes within words but they may sometimes exclude sounds due to co-articulation. For example, the preconsonantal nasal in words like *went* or *camp*, is folded into the medial vowel as opposed to being fully articulated, and thus these speech sounds are often omitted in spelling. Tensions arise as they learn to recognize printed words like *wet* and *cap*, and they see that they have not produced the intended word when they write *wet* for *went*. How could *wet* be both *wet* and *went*? Similar to the lexical restructuring that is conjectured to occur in oral vocabulary acquisition, Henderson (1990) believed that the unintentional homographic spellings for different words that result from the use of letter names in beginning writing creates the catalyst for closer analysis in word recognition and spurs children into abandoning the letter-name for a more efficient unit of analysis. This interplay between increased awareness of segments of oral and written language is influenced by the number of written words already known. The more written words that are recognized, the greater the pressure to distinguish one word from another: *wet* from *went*; *hot* from *hit*. As letter name-alphabetic students progress in learning to read, refinements such as these strengthen the connections between the orthography and speech sounds and they begin to acquire a store of words that they recognize accurately and immediately.

Early in this phase however, students' speech-to-printed word match is tenuous, constrained by their incomplete knowledge of the alphabetic system. Using only partial letter cues (usually beginning and ending consonant sounds), very beginning readers are easily tripped up by the mismatch of units—phonological segments such as syllables are not marked by spaces; printed words can contain more than one syllabic unit. Due to this mismatch of units, few written words are recognized or learned. More automatic knowledge of beginning consonant sounds anchors their finger-point reading to printed word units on the page, and in due time, after many more accurate speech-to-print matches, beginning readers start remembering many of the printed words they have read and are able to retrieve the pronunciation of some of them at first sight. The multiple connections among beginning consonant sounds, pronunciations, word meanings, and spellings are forged together to form the beginning of a reading vocabulary. Once they begin to accrue some known written words and can call them up in their mind's eye, they are able to march across words from left to right matching letters to sounds more easily and they achieve a more complete orthographic mapping between graphemes and phonemes Nevertheless, since the total number of known written words is not very large, their ability to make analogies among them is limited; they may use any one of various strategies to decode words they do not recognize immediately: segmenting graphemephoneme correspondences, blending letter sounds to come up with a word, or using contextual clues along with partial alphabetic information such as beginning sounds. This latter portion of the letter name-alphabetic stage corresponds

to Ehri's (1998) full alphabetic phase of word recognition. Thus throughout the beginning-to-read phase students move from only partial alphabetic recognition in the early letter name stage to full alphabetic recognition in the late letter name stage.

Within word pattern—consolidated. As students become facile in recognizing the basic one- and two-letter graphemes and their phonemic counterparts that constitute most single-syllable words in beginning reading material, they become aware of certain graphemes that have no direct correspondence to a speech sounds. These "silent" letters, such as the *e* in the word *snake* or the *i* in the word *drain*, serve as a kind of diacritical marker to indicate the phonemic value of the other vowel (Vallins, 1965). To a letter name or full-alphabetic learner accustomed to segmenting and blending letters in a one-to-one (or two-to one in the case of consonant digraphs such as *sh, ch,* and *th*) fashion, this observation presents yet another tension that serves as a catalyst to move learners forward to adapt a more efficient parsing strategy involving larger orthographic units. The fact that spelling patterns distinguish word meanings also exerts pressure to apply a more fine-grained analysis in word recognition. Does *sail* or *sale* refer to the boat? As more words are learned, more connections are formed and lexical restructuring continues.

Henderson referred to this insight as an awareness of within word patterns (1990), where students first begin to recognize vowel and consonant patterns within syllables. Within word pattern learners are no longer tied solely to an alphabetic linear approach; now they can focus their attention on chunks of letter sequences in conjunction with their position within the word. In spelling, students know they may need more than one letter per sound, and in reading, they look for patterns that relate to categories of speech sounds, such as the consonant-vowel-vowel-consonant (CVVC) pattern characteristic and many long vowels (e.g., *rain, teach, coat, fruit*). Ehri refers to this phenomenon as one of consolidation (Ehri & McCormick, 2004) naming it the consolidated alphabetic phase. Henderson (1990) and Gentry (1982) also refer to this within word pattern phase as *transitional* because students are transitioning to more fluent word reading and more flexible strategy use that includes not only the previous strategies of predicting or decoding, but now also include the use of chunking of recurring letter patterns and an increased use of analogy to other known words. While the use of analogy may occur at earlier levels of word knowledge, extensive knowledge of within word patterns allows for more generative application of orthographic knowledge, such that readers might decode the word *freight* by chunking the *eight* and making the analogy to the number as well as to other words with the lesscommon *ei* pattern for long-a sounds as in the word *vein*. Sharp, Sinatra, and Reynolds (2008) have demonstrated an interaction between increased flexibility of strategy use and increased levels of orthographic knowledge. Nevertheless, the accuracy of word recognition at this point is still constrained by the total size and nature of the student's lexical network. Upon seeing the word *great*, a transitional reader might say *greet,* until the words like *break* and *steak* become known.

Syllables, affixes, and derivational relations—automatic. The representations supporting word recognition become increasingly segmental in accord with a growing awareness of the interplay between the orthography and phonological units such as syllables and morphemes. Henderson divided this period into two stages: the syllables and affixes stage and the derivational relations stage (Henderson, 1990). Henderson referred to the syllables and affixes stage as a period when learners readjust their orthographic understandings to extend and refine the pattern-to-sound principles that occur in single syllable word to words of many syllables. For example, the CVCe pattern of single syllable words must be refined to accommodate the open syllable pattern in words like *taking*, where the VCV pattern governs the syllable juncture. Students in this stage of learning might pronounce the word *whining* like *winning* if they have not yet solidified the understanding that a beginning syllable with a short vowel must be closed by a consonant, the vowel-consonant-consonant-vowel (VCCV) spelling pattern. Syllables and affixes learners must also negotiate syllable stress. The –ai- in cont*ai*n is quite different from the –ai- in fount*ai*n due to the stressed syllable. Thus, in word recognition, students might pronounce *curtain* as kerTAIN. Word meanings add to the press as students work through syllable stress in relation to pronunciation and meaning, which often results in mispronouncing homographs such as *cón tract* (noun) for *con tráct* (verb) or *re córd* (noun) for *re córd* (verb).

Some researchers assert that students learn how to read multisyllabic words by repeatedly seeing them in context (Cunningham, 1998). The more students successfully recognize multisyllabic words in print, the more they begin to pick up on letter combinations that signal a break between syllables. For example, a *d* and an *n* next to each other is more likely signal a break between syllables (e.g., *sadness*) than a *d* next to an *r*, which usually functions as a consonant blend in the onset position of a syllable (e.g., *dragon*) (O'Conner, 2007). Other researchers emphasize the role of instruction in learning to decode multisyllable words. For example, Shefelbine (1990) demonstrated that 5 hours of instruction in using vowels and affixes to spell multisyllabic words (spaced out across 30 days) significantly improved word decoding among fourth- and sixth-grade poor readers. Nagy, Anderson, Schommer, Scott, and Stallman (1989) argue that knowledge of how word forms combine enhances both decoding and vocabulary learning. Carlisle (1988) emphasizes the usefulness of word analysis instruction that makes use of redundancies across words as in the *ain* pattern in *rain*, *drain*, or *detaining*. White, Sowell, and Yanagihara (1989) improved both the word reading and spelling of special education students by teaching them the most frequently occurring prefixes and suffixes in the Car-

roll, Davies, and Richman (1971) corpus. What is clear in all of these studies is that instruction combined with wide reading at the appropriate levels increases not only spelling but word recognition and reading vocabulary as well.

The last stage in Henderson's developmental model is the derivational relations stage when students learn to recognize spelling-meaning connections in derivationally related pairs such as *divine* and *divinity* (1990). During this period, students learn that words related in meaning often share similar spelling patterns. For example, the second "reduced" vowel in the word *composition* is an *o* because the word is derived from the word *compose* where the *o* is clearly heard. The orthography preserves what is otherwise obscured in spoken words; although the vowel sounds alternate in derivationally related pairs from long to short (*mine-mineral*), long to schwa (*compete-competition*), or schwa to short (*metal-metalic*), the spelling of the vowel remains the same to signal their relationship in meaning. The study of derivational "families" helps word recognition as well as spelling and vocabulary, because knowledge of one form of the word helps to read and understand other forms of the word, even if the other form is unfamiliar. For example, knowledge of the familiar word *recite* or *recital* helps students read and ferret out the meanings of the unfamiliar word *recitation.*

Following Chall (1983), Ehri and McCormick (2004) refer to this as the automatic phase because readers can now read most words accurately and effortlessly in and out of context. Most words encountered at this phase are "sight" words, and therefore, readers can move through text with speed and understanding. When faced with an unknown word, automatic readers employ multiple strategies to confirm the word's identity and rely on the multiple connections inherent in the word's orthographic and morphological structure representing sound, pattern, and meaning.

How Developmental Models Inform the Teaching of Word Recognition for Struggling Readers

Ehri and McCormick (2004) discussed four ways that mature readers read words: decoding, analogy, prediction, and by sight (pp. 366–367). When mature readers decode a written word, they deconstruct the word either sound-by-sound (e.g., *l-e-d*; *ch-o-p*), larger chunks such as phonograms (e.g., *ight* in *light*, *fight*, *might*), syllables (e.g., *dis-cov-er*), or morphemes (e.g., *bio-sphere*). No matter what the unit used in decoding, the reader breaks the word down and blends the parts back together to retrieve the word. Analogy is defined by "recognizing how the spelling of an unfamiliar word is similar to a word already known" (p. 367). To do this, the reader must already have a known word stored in memory to connect with, compare to, and note similarities. Adjustments can then be made to pronounce the new word. For example, upon seeing a new, unknown word such as *creature*, the reader might recognize the *-ture* ending in the known word *nature* to successfully read the new word. In predicting words, students guess an unknown word by using any known word part along with context clues such as pictures, surrounding text, or previous exposure. Finally, when readers read words by sight, they immediately retrieve its pronunciation from the visual orthographic display. The interplay of a reader's stage of developmental word knowledge and the ways they use to read words is noteworthy for this discussion.

According to Ehri's developmental phase model, pre-alphabetic (or emergent) readers rely primarily on prediction using pictures or other non-alphabetic cues. For example, pre-alphabetic learners might see a picture of a rabbit in a text that uses the word *bunny*. Because they are pre-alphabetic, such students might say *rabbit* for *bunny* because they have not made the connection between the *b* and *bunny*. However, since pre-alphabetic learners are being taught the alphabet and letter sounds throughout this phase, late emergent or pre-alphabetic learners will begin to experience a dissonance between what they say and what they see, and in turn, will possibly use the *b* in *bunny* combined with the picture of the *rabbit* to identify the word *bunny* accurately. This dissonance will propel them forward and begin the process of structuring their lexical network for written words. As they learn new sounds, especially those that compete such as *d* and *p* or *m* and *n*, they restructure their current letter sound knowledge to accommodate and interconnect new information.

As learners make more and more connections with letters and sounds, they move into the beginning stage of reading. Unlike Ehri and McCormick (2004) who contend that for early beginning readers (i.e., early letter name-alphabetic or partial alphabetic stage) "decoding strategies are not available for reading unfamiliar words" (p. 374), Henderson's model would argue that these readers do, in fact, employ primitive decoding strategies for word reading. Consider the very beginning reader faced with the sentence, "*A fish is hiding in the reef.*" alongside a picture that represents this statement. This reader may use the initial consonant *r* combined with the final *f* and the picture cue when encountering the word *reef*. Although such behavior is not full-blown decoding as in full phonemic segmentation, it does require partial phonemic segmentation of the word. Just as the early letter name-alphabetic speller only partially represents the sounds they are trying to write (e.g., HKN for chicken), partial alphabetic readers use partial decoding when other ways to read words, such as prediction or sight reading, are not successful. Likewise, an early beginning reader may draw upon an analogy to a known sound, word, or grapheme. For example, seeing the initial consonant *m* in the word *mouse*, readers can make the analogy to a more familiar word that starts with the same sound, such as *Mom*. Like the example above, the student is analogizing a beginning sound as opposed to an entire word or larger chunk within the word.

A bona fide decoder does not occur until the full alphabetic phase of word reading according to Ehri's (2002) theory of word recognition. This stage correlates to Henderson's late letter name-alphabetic stage. In Ehri's view, this is also the point in development where the use of analogy becomes possible, mainly because of the growing store of known words or sight words. Additionally, these readers have, at this point, full phonemic segmentation, allowing more complete grapheme-phoneme mappings. Henderson would add, however, that the analogies that students make as late letter name-alphabetic learners relate to the orthographic chunks they are learning in their spelling, particularly within phonograms (e.g., the *amp* in *ramp*, *lamp*, *clamp*) and across vowel sounds (e.g., the short *a* in *blast*, *that*, *flag*, *rash*, *sack*). As with early letter name-alphabetic spellers, the unit used for decoding is relative to their degree of orthographic understanding. Other ways of word reading are still available, such as predicting and reading words by sight. As more orthographic knowledge is acquired, pressure is exerted on their lexical network causing a constant need to restructure. The reader faced with the short *a* in *camp* must restructure their information about short *a* to accommodate the sound that results from the influence of the nasal, *m*. According to Ehri, decoding skill is a prerequisite for accruing sight words, and sight words are a prerequisite for using an analogy. This postulem is in agreement with Henderson's theory of written word knowledge development. He would, however, argue that readers in the early letter name-alphabetic stage begin on their trajectory of amassing a store of sight words. Consider words like *is*, *on*, and *we*. These words are often recognized "by sight" by readers early in this stage who demonstrate only partial phoneme segmentation and incomplete letter sound knowledge.

The consolidated phase is where students learn chunks of letter patterns and notice their reoccurrence across different words (Ehri & McCormick, 2004). Whereas in previous stages students have been preoccupied with learning specific words, the accumulated knowledge along with the growing store of sight words allows students to generalize to other words that contain the same pattern. Essentially, students in the consolidated phase are making a cognitive leap from the specific to general, which is akin to the self-teaching, bootstrapping mechanism described by connectionist theorists. As students are learning about *ai* as a spelling pattern for the long *a* sound, they are simultaneously storing known words containing the *ai* pattern, which in turn, allows them to recognize unknown words containing the *ai* pattern. This orthographic knowledge growth initiates a restructuring of their knowledge of long *a*. As they learn new patterns, they restructure that knowledge to accommodate all patterns for the long *a* sound: *a-consonant-e*, *ai*, *ay*, *ei*. According to Ehri, such students use both analogy and decoding strategies to read words, and these strategies are "expanded to include hierarchical decoding as well as sequential decoding" (p. 382). Hierarchical decoding refers to the relational aspects of silent letters, for example, that relate to the sound value of a different grapheme. The chunk can include a variety of structures (e.g., affixes, root words, syllables, phonograms), and these structures help reduce the number of units needed to process the words. For example, a reader might use the prefix *un-* to help read and understand the words *undo*, *untie*, and *unwrap*. Processing words in larger chunks helps the reader maintain a level of fluency while reading. This is reflected in Henderson's model where he describes the consolidated transitional reader increasing in reading rate, accuracy, and prosody.

Readers at the automatic phase have progressed in their reading to a level of proficiency allowing them to experience effortless reading. These readers read words mostly by sight. They have several strategies available to use when needed, but these are mostly at an unconscious level. They take part in sophisticated levels of hierarchical decoding and analogizing. For example, they may read the word *solar* by either analogizing it to *polar* or decoding it using syllable pattern information (the open vowel-consonant-vowel syllable pattern, *so-lar*). Restructuring and refinements of the lexical network would continue to occur. As this same reader encounters the word *habit*, rethinking the syllable pattern would be necessary to accommodate the closed vowel-consonant-vowel syllable pattern as in *robin* and *comet*.

Teachers must consider all of the possible ways in which words can be read at any stage of word recognition development and work to guide students in their initial attempts. Considering the ways readers at various stages interact with the orthographic representation of words permits teachers to take advantage of the refinement of Henderson's model. This argument seems obvious. An argument that may not be so apparent is the particular benefit of this knowledge while working with students with reading disabilities. As argued by connectionist models of word recognition, readers are in a constant state of refining, extending, and restructuring their knowledge of written words as they learn more about letters, sounds, patterns, syllables, and morphemes in spelling. This restructuring may elude some students, especially those with reading disabilities. A teacher must guide them in organizing their knowledge and help them make connections among the words they know. In order to do this, a teacher must be aware of where they are in terms of orthographic development as well as the various ways of word reading that students may employ. Armed with this knowledge, a teacher can be more confident in the appropriateness of the instruction, instruction that emphasizes two sides of the word recognition coin: spelling and decoding.

Conclusion

Knowing how typical reading develops in children over time is important to understand the behavior of students with reading difficulties because what may appear strange and uninterpretable may be predictable from a developmental perspective. In the past, for example, struggling readers who said *was* for *saw* or who spelled *gril* for *girl* were labeled dysedic or dysphonetic (Boder, 1973), Chinese or Phoenician (Baron & Strawson, 1976), harkening back to dual route theories of word recognition. From a developmental perspective however, such errors can provide powerful

insight into students' knowledge base and instructional needs. An understanding of how typical reading development unfolds will assist teachers in planning instruction at the right level.

Word recognition relies on the development of linguistic awareness for different aspects of spoken word forms (phonological awareness), written word forms (orthographic awareness), and structural aspects of both word forms that convey meaning (morphological awareness). Research suggests that teaching children about the spelling of word forms and their parts increases the probability that they will form connections between them and that these connections are most easily formed when instruction matches the developmental orthographic, phonological, and morphological understanding of the learner. Reading disabilities, manifested primarily through difficulty with word recognition, can be prolonged and/or exacerbated when a mismatch of instruction occurs. By knowing *when* to teach *what* to *whom*, multiple connections can be formed that result in richer, deeper representations, increasing refinements in lexical organization, and ultimately, to more automatic word recognition, fluent reading, and comprehension of word meanings.

References

Baron, J., & Strawson, C. (1976). Use of orthographic and word-specific knowledge in reading words aloud. *Journal of Experimental Psychology: Human Perception and Performance, 4*, 207–214.

Bear, D. R., Invernizzi, M., Templeton, S., & Johnston, F. (2008). *Words their way: Word study for phonics, vocabulary, and spelling instruction*. Columbus, OH: Merrill/Prentice Hall.

Berninger, V., Chen, A., & Abbott, R. (1988). A test of the multiple connections model of reading acquisition. *International Journal of Neuroscience, 42*, 283–295.

Berninger, V. W., Vaughan, K., Abbott, R. D., Brooks, A., Abbott, S. P., Rogan, L., et al. (1998). Early intervention for spelling problems: Teaching functional spelling units of varying size with a multiple-connections framework. *Journal of Educational Psychology, 90*(4), 587–605.

Berninger, V., Yates, C., & Lester, K. (1991). Multiple orthographic codes in reading and writing acquisition. *Reading and Writing: An Interdisciplinary Journal, 3*, 115–149.

Bissex, G. L. (1980). *Gnys at Wrk*. Cambridge, MA: Harvard University Press.

Boder, E. (1973). Developmental dyslexia: a diagnostic approach based on three atypical reading-spelling patterns. *Developmental Medicine and Child Neurology, 15*(5), 663–687.

Caltaldo, S., & Ellis, N. (1988). Interactions in the development of spelling, reading, and phonological skills. *Journal of Reading Research, 11*, 86–109.

Carlisle, J. F. (1988). Knowledge of derivational morphology and spelling in fourth, sixth, and eighth grades. *Applied Psycholinguistics, 9*, 247–266.

Carroll, J. B., Davies, P., & Richman, B. (1971). *Word frequency book*. Boston: Houghton Mifflin.

Chall, J. (1983). *Learning to read: The great debate*. New York: Wiley.

Coltheart, M. (2007). Modeling reading: The dual-route approach. In M. J. Snowling & C. Hulme (Eds.), *The science of reading: A handbook* (pp. 6–23). Malden, MA: Blackwell.

Cunningham, P. M. (1998). The multisyllabic word dilemma: Helping students build meaning, spell, and read "big" words. *Reading and Writing Quarterly: Overcoming Learning Disabilities, 14*, 189–218.

Ehri, L. (1980). The development of orthographic images. In. U. Frith

(Ed.), *Cognitive processes in spelling* (pp. 311–338). London: Academic.

Ehri, L. (1998). Grapheme-phoneme knowledge is essential to learning to read words in English. In J. L. Metsala & L. C. Ehri (Eds.), *Word recognition in beginning literacy* (pp. 3–40). Mahwah, NJ: Erlbaum.

Ehri, L. (1999). Phases of development in learning to read words. In J. V. Oakhill & R. Beard (Eds.), *Reading development and the teaching of reading: A psychological perspective* (pp. 79–108). Oxford, UK: Blackwell.

Ehri, L.C. (2002). Phases of acquisition in learning to read words and implications for teaching. In R. Stainthorp & P. Tomlinson (Eds.), *Learning and teaching reading* (pp. 7–28). London: British Journal of Educational Psychology Monograph Series II.

Ehri, L. C., & McCormick, S. (2004). Phases of word learning: Implications for instruction with delayed and disabled readers. In R. B. Ruddell & N. J. Unrau (Eds.), *Theoretical models and processes of reading* (5th ed., pp. 365–389). Newark, DE: International Reading Association.

Ehri, L. C., & Rosenthal, J. (2007). Spelling of words: A neglected facilitator or vocabulary learning. *Journal of Literacy Research, 39*(4), 389–409.

Ehri, L., & Wilce, L. (1979). The mnemonic value of orthography among beginning readers. *Journal of Educational Psychology, 71*, 26–40.

Ehri, L., & Wilce, L. (1980). The influence of orthography on readers' conceptualization of the phonemic structure of words. *Applied Psycholinguistics, 1*, 371–385.

Ehri, L., & Wilce, L. (1986). The influence of spellings on speech: Are alveolar flaps /d/ or /t/? In D. Yaden & S. Templeton (Eds.), *Metalinguistic awareness and beginning literacy* (pp. 101–114). Portsmouth, NH: Heinemann.

Ehri, L., & Wilce, L. (1987). Does learning to spell help beginners learn to read real words? *Reading Research Quarterly, 18*, 47–65.

Ellis, N., & Cataldo, S. (1992). Spelling is integral to learning to read. In C. M. Sterling & C. Robson (Eds.), *Psychology, spelling, and education* (pp. 112–142). Clevedon, UK: Multilingual Matters.

Flanigan, K., Hayes, L., Templeton, S., Bear, D. R., Invernizzi, M., & Johnston, F. (2010). *Wordstheir way with Struggling Readers: Word study for reading, vocabulary, and spelling instruction, grades 4-12*. Boston: Pearson.

Fletcher, J. M., Lyon, G. R., Fuchs, L., & Barnes, M. A. (2007). *Learning disabilities: From identification to intervention*. New York: Guilford.

Foorman, B. R. (1994). The relevance of a connectionist model of reading for "the great debate." *Educational Psychology Review, 16*, 25–47.

Frith, U. (1985). Beneath the surface of developmental dyslexia. In K. E. Patterson, J. C. Marshall, & M. Coltheart (Eds.), *Surface dyslexia: Neuropsychological and cognitive studies of phonological reading* (pp. 301–330). London: Erlbaum..

Gentry, J. R. (1982). An analysis of developmental spelling in "GNYS AT WRK." *The Reading Teacher, 36,* 192–200.

Glusko, R. J. (1979). The organization and activation of orthographic knowledge in reading aloud. *Journal of Experimental Psychology: Human Perception and Performance, 5*, 674–691.

Gough, P., & Hillinger, M. (1980). Learning to read: An unnatural act. *Bulletin of the Orton Society, 30*, 179–196.

Goulandris, N. (1994). Teaching spelling: Bridging theory and practice. In G. D. A. Brown & N. C. Ellis (Eds.), *Handbook of spelling: Theory, process, and intervention* (pp. 407–423). Chichester, UK: Wiley.

Graham, S., Harris, K. R., & Chorzempa, B. F. (2002). Contribution of spelling instruction to the spelling, writing, and reading of poor spellers. *Journal of Educational Psychology, 94*, 669–686.

Griffiths, Y. M., & Snowling, M. J. (2002). Predictors of exception word and nonword reading in dyslexic children: The severity hypothesis. *Journal of Educational Psychology, 94*, 34–43.

Guttentag, R., & Haith, M. (1978). Automatic processing as a function of age and reading ability. *Child Development, 49*, 707–716.

Henderson, E. H. (1981). *Learning to read and spell: The child's knowledge of words*. DeKalb: Northern Illinois Press.

Henderson, E.H. (1990). *Teaching spelling* (2nd ed). Boston: Houghton Mifflin.

International Dyslexia Association. (2002, November 12). Dyslexia basics. Retrieved from http://www.interdys.org/ewebeditpro5/upload/definition_Fact_Sheet_3-10-08.pdf

Invernizzi, M., & Hayes, L. (2004). Developmental spelling research: A systematic imperative. *Reading Research Quarterly, 39*, 216–228.

Juel, C. (1991). Beginning reading. In R. Barr, M .L. Kamil, P. B. Mosenthal, & P. D. Pearson (Eds.), *Handbook of reading research* (Vol. 2, pp. 759–788). New York: Longman.

Just, M., & Carpenter, P. (1987). *The psychology of reading and language comprehension*. Boston: Allyn & Bacon.

Manis, F. R., Seidenberg, M. S., Doi, L.M., McBride-Chang, C., & Peterson, A. (1996). On the basis of two subtypes of developmental dyslexia. *Cognition, 58,* 157–195.

Marsh, G., Friedman, M., Welch, V., & Desberg, P. (1980).The development of strategies in spelling. In U. Frith (Ed.), *Cognitive processes in spelling* (pp. 339–355). London: Academic.

Mason, J. (1980). When do children learn to read? An exploration of four-year old children's letter and word reading competencies. *Reading Research Quarterly, 15,* 202–227.

Masonheimer, P. E., Drum, P. A., & Ehri, L. C. (1984). Does environmental print identification lead children into word reading? *Journal of Reading Behavior, 16*, 257–271.

McCandliss, B., Beck, I. L., Sandak, R., & Perfetti, C. (2003). Focusing attention on decoding for children with poor reading skills: Design and preliminary tests of the word building intervention. *Scientific Studies of Reading, 7*, 75–104.

Metsala, J. L., & Walley, A. C. (1998). Spoken vocabulary growth and the segmental restructuring of lexical representations: Precursors to phonemic awareness and early reading ability. In J. L. Metsala & L. C. Ehri (Eds.), *Word recognition in beginning literacy* (pp. 89–120). Mahwah, NJ: Erlbaum.

Morris, D., & Perney, J. (1984). Developmental spelling as a predictor of first-grade reading achievement. *Elementary School Journal, 84*, 441–457.

Nagy, W., Anderson, R. C., Schommer, M., Scott, J. A., & Stallman, A. C. (1989). Morphological families in the internal lexicon. *Research Quarterly, 24,* 262–282.

O'Connor, R. E. (2007). *Teaching word recognition: Effective strategies for students with learning difficulties*. New York: Guilford.

Perfetti, C. A. (1985). *Reading ability*. New York: Oxford University Press.

Plaut, D. (2007). Connectionist approaches to reading. In M. J. Snowling & C. Hulme (Eds.), *The science of reading* (pp. 24–39). Malden, MA: Blackwell.

Rayner, K. (1988). Word recognition cues in children: The relative use graphemic cures, orthographic cues, and grapheme-phoneme correspondence rules. *Journal of Educational Psychology, 80*, 473–479.

Rayner K. & Pollatsek, A. (1998). *The psychology of reading*. Englewood Cliffs, NJ: Prentice Hall.

Retisma, P. (1983). Printed word learning in beginning readers. *Journal of Experimental Child Psychology, 75*, 321–339.

Seidenberg, M. S. (2005). Connectionist models of word reading. *American Psychological Society, 14*(5), 238–242.

Seidenberg, M. S., & McClelland, J. L. (1989). A distributed developmental model of visual word recognition and naming. *Psychological Review, 96*, 523–568.

Seidenberg, M., S., & Tanenhaus, M. (1979). Orthographic effects on rhyme monitoring. *Journal of Experimental Psychology: Human Learning and Memory, 5*, 546–554.

Seymour. P. H. K., & Duncan, L. G., (2001). Learning to read in English. *Psychology: The Journal of the Hellenic Psychological Society, 8*, 281–299.

Share, D. L. (1995). Phonological recoding and self-teaching: Sine qua non of reading acquisition. *Cognition, 55*, 151–218.

Share, D. (2004). Orthographic learning at a glance: On the time course and developmental onset of self-teaching. *Journal of Experimental Child Psychology, 87*, 267–298.

Sharp, A. C., Sinatra, G. M., & Reynolds, R. E. (2008). The development of children's orthographic knowledge: A microgenetic perspective. *Reading Research Quarterly, 43*(3), 206–226.

Shefelbine, J. (1990). A syllable-unit approach to teaching decoding of polysyllable words to fourth- and sixth-grade disabled readers. In J. Zutell & S. McCormick (Eds.), *Literacy theory and research: Analysis from multiple paradigms* (pp. 223–230). Chicago: National Reading Conference.

Snowling, M. J., & Hulme, C. (2007). *The science of reading: A handbook.* Malden, MA: Blackwell

Stanovich, K. E. (1994). Romance and reality. *Reading Teacher, 47,* 280–291.

Stanovich, K. E., Seigel, L. S., & Gottardo, A. (1997). Converging evidence for phonological and surface subtypes of reading disability. *Journal of Educational Psychology, 89,* 114–127.

Steig, W. (1968). *CDB.* New York: Aladdin Paperbacks/Simon & Schuster.

Stuart, M., & Coltheart, M. (1988). Does reading develop in a sequence of stages? *Cognition, 30,* 139–181.

Swanson, L., H., Trainin, G., Necoechea, D. M., & Hammill, D. D. (2003). Rapid naming, phonological awareness, and reading: A meta-analysis of the correlational evidence. *Review of Educational Research, 73*(4), 407–433.

Templeton, S. (1992). Theory, nature, and pedagogy of higher-order orthographic development in older children. In S. Templeton & D. Bear (Eds.), *Development of orthographic knowledge and the foundations of literacy: A memorial festschrift for Edmund H. Henderson* (pp. 253–278), Hillsdale, NJ: Erlbaum.

Templeton, S., & Bear, D. (1992). *Development of orthographic knowledge and the foundations of literacy: A memorial Festschrift for Edmund H. Henderson.* Hilldsdale, NJ: Erlbaum.

Vallins, G. (1965). *Spelling.* London: Andre Dentsch Limited.

Vellutino, F. R., Scanlon, D. M., & Chen, M. S. (1995). The increasingly inextricable relationship between orthographic and phonological coding in learning to read: Some reservations about current methods of operationalizing orthographic coding. In V. W. Berninger (Ed.), *The varieties of orthographic knowledge II: Relationships to phonology, reading, and writing* (47–111). Dordrecht, The Netherlands: Kluwer.

Venezky, R. L., & Massaro, D. W. (1979). The role of orthographic regularity in word recognition. In L. Resnick & P. Weaver (Eds.), *Theory and practice of early reading* (pp. 85–107). Hillsdale, NJ: Erlbaum.

Vygotsky, L.S. (1978). *Mind in society: The development of higher mental processes.* Cambridge, MA: Harvard University Press.

White, T. G., Sowell, J., & Yanagihara, A. (1989). Teaching elementary students to use word-part clues. *The Reading Teacher, 42,* 302–308.

Zabell, C., & Everatt, J. (2002). Surface and phonological subtypes of adult developmental dyslexia. *Dyslexia, 8,* 160–177.

Zutell, J., & Raskinski, T. (1989). Reading and spelling connections in third and fifth grade students. *Reading Psychology, 10,* 137–155.

19

Vocabulary Development and Implications for Reading Problems

Andrew Biemiller
Ontario Institute for Studies in Education

Overview

Adequate vocabulary is a necessary (though not sufficient) condition for comprehension of any written text. For most of the first 8 years of life, vocabulary size is now largely determined by language used at home and encouragement for vocabulary at home. By the end of Grade 2, children vary markedly in vocabulary, differences which are very predictive of later school achievement. Those in the lowest quarter average about 2 years behind grade-level children in root word vocabulary. Those whose reading comprehension is below grade level typically also have vocabularies below grade level (and vice versa). Because vocabulary is acquired in a predictable order, it should be possible to do more than educators do presently to ensure that children build adequate vocabulary. During students' preliterate years, when children's reading levels are lower than their oral comprehension, educators need to teach vocabulary in oral contexts. During students' literate years, when reading becomes a major source of new vocabulary, educators must be prepared to help students with unknown meanings. In this chapter, selecting word meanings for instruction and methods for vocabulary instruction will be briefly described. Disabilities in reading and language are also briefly described.

Vocabulary is Important for Reading Comprehension

Vocabulary problems probably create as many serious reading comprehension limitations as do the more widely recognized reading disabilities. As Chall, Jacobs, and Baldwin (1990) observed, among children who decode adequately or well, vocabulary is the main source of comprehension problems.

Recent publications (Beck, McKeown, & Lucan, 2002; Graves, 2006; Hazenberg & Hulstijn, 1996; Hiebert & Kamil, 2005; National Reading Panel, 2000; Stahl & Nagy, 2006; Wagner, Muse, & Tannenbaum, 2007) have pointed to the importance of vocabulary for reading comprehension.

It is particularly important to note that vocabulary assessed in kindergarten or Grade 1 is strongly predictive of reading comprehension in Grades 3 or 4 (Scarborough, 2001) and even in Grade 11 (Cunningham & Stanovich, 1997). Vocabulary plays less of a role in reading comprehension in Grades 1 and 2 when texts used for comprehension assessment generally use vocabulary restricted to high-frequency words (Becker, 1977).

The crucial role of vocabulary is evident when one looks at a text written in a second language. Comprehension begins with an understanding of the words in each sentence. There can be no comprehension when many words are not known.

I acknowledge that vocabulary is not the only determinant of reading comprehension. Cain and Oakhill (2003) reviewed sources of reading comprehension difficulties. In addition to vocabulary, they suggest that working memory, problems at the sentence and discourse level, and breadth of reading experience all contribute to reading comprehension. For example, Cain, Oakhill, and Bryant (2004) showed that individual differences in inference-making and working memory were related to reading comprehension even when vocabulary was controlled. Nonetheless, the correlation and predictive relationship between breadth of vocabulary and reading comprehension has remained very strong (Wagner et al., 2007).

Reading "Differences" and Reading "Disabilities"

Ultimately, what matters is reading comprehension—the ability to understand written language. As Gough and Tunmer (1986) suggested many years ago, this is mainly a matter of *word recognition* and *language comprehension*. Much has been written in this volume concerning the problems some children (around 15%) experience with word recognition. Of course, all children with serious word recognition problems will have difficulty comprehending the written language they read—just as a deaf person has problems comprehending spoken language. Children with serious word recognition problems will also be likely to develop vocabulary problems, both in early childhood and later.

However, many other children and adults will also experience comprehension problems, even though they are competent at recognition of printed words. Jeanne Chall described the "fourth grade slump"—children who become discouraged when they start reading texts with many unfamiliar words—words without meanings (for them) (Chall, Jacobs, & Baldwin, 1990). In my own work, I have found that, in the upper elementary years, 95% of children can read more words than they understand (Biemiller, 2005). Thus, vocabulary, not reading skills, is the major limiting factor in reading comprehension. The net result is that by the end of elementary school, many children do not possess adequate vocabularies to understand common junior high and high school texts and novels (Chall & Conard, 1991). While some of these young adolescents suffer from real disabilities, many more probably simply lack needed vocabulary. Much of this vocabulary lack occurs early in life and continues through the primary grades. By this point, they are both ill-equipped to comprehend grade level texts and ill-equipped to infer word meanings because they are unfamiliar with too many words in classroom texts. (Note that the reading level of texts is primarily assessed by the vocabulary load (Chall & Dale, 1995).) This set of affairs may contribute too much of the estimated 30% of students who do not complete high school.

Vocabulary Development and Individual Differences

Numbers of Word Meanings Acquired

Controversy over number of words acquired. There has been much debate over the number of word meanings acquired and over the definition of which word meanings should be counted. For example, computer counts of frequencies of printed words appearing in texts count separately every inflected variation (plurals, tenses, etc.) as well as every derived word meaning (e.g., *sense, nonsense*). On the other hand, multiple meanings of the same word are not counted separately by computers (e.g., *lean*—resting against a wall; *lean*—meat with little fat in it; *lean*—depending on another person for aid). To determine vocabulary size, my own preference is to count different root word meanings (often listing more than one meaning for a printed root word form), but not to count derived word meanings, when clearly derived from the root plus affix or affixes, e.g. *unreadable*. (An affix can be either a prefix or a suffix.) This method of evaluating number of words acquired will be used as the basis for discussion in this section.

Estimates range from 1,000 to 2,000 root word meanings that must be acquired annually to reach average gains. A number of researchers have concluded that about an average 1,000 root word meanings are acquired each year (Anglin, 1993; Biemiller, 2005; Hazenberg and Hulstijn, 1996; Nagy & Scott, 2001). At present, we really don't know much about how word meanings are actually acquired. Many researchers have argued that many meanings must be acquired through inference when encountered in press because many more meanings are learned than could be acquired as a result of direct instruction. Actually, at 1,000 root word meanings per year, or an average of 2.7 root meanings per day if taught every day, acquiring a substantial proportion of such word meanings from informal and formal instruction by teachers, parents, and peers seems very possible. In a brief, informal study of children's reports of how newly learned word meanings were acquired, Grade 5 and 6 students reported that about 70% of word meanings were learned as a result of direct explanations by others (Biemiller, 2005).

On the other hand, if more meanings (e.g., 2,000 or 3,000 meanings) have to be *learned* as distinct from deriving meanings using affixes, compounds, and later using Latin and Greek stems (Stahl, 1999), I would have to agree with those who hold that many meanings must be inferred. Anglin (1993) and Stahl and Nagy (2006) estimate that at least 2,000 root and derived meanings have to be learned directly or inferred each year.

The sequence of root word meanings acquired[1]   Children with high, average, or low total vocabularies *acquire* word meanings in roughly the *same* sequence. The best evidence for this is the similar *sequence* of how well root word meanings are known when we test word knowledge from different groups of children. The *sequence* of how well root word meanings are known is about the same in Grade 1 and Grade 2; Grade 3 and Grade 4; or Grade 5 and Grade 6. (Of course, the average percent word meaning known is lower in lower grades.) Similarly, the order of how well word meanings are known by advantaged students and normative students averaged across grades one to five is also about the same (Biemiller & Slonim, 2001). Finally, the sequence of word meanings known by English Language Learners in (a) Grades 5 and 6, (b) representative Grade 5 and 6 English-speaking children, and (c) advantaged Grade 5 and 6 English-speaking children is about the same (Biemiller, 2005). Across these three groups, the correlation of word means was over $r = .90$. This does not mean that all of these groups had the same scores, but rather that their word meaning scores were in largely the same sequence. For example, English Language Learners in Grade 5 had about the same sized vocabulary as normative Grade 3 students, *and knew mainly the same word meanings* (Biemiller, 2005).

Given that word meanings are being learned in a known sequence, we can anticipate which meanings will be learned in the near future by a specific child. We can't be precise, but we can estimate that the student will mainly be learning word meanings from among the next 2,000 or 3,000 meanings in a list of word meanings in the order they are typically acquired. This can be seen in Figure 19.1 which shows which word meanings have been learned by students with different sized vocabularies. Clearly, those meanings known by most students are those acquired early, while

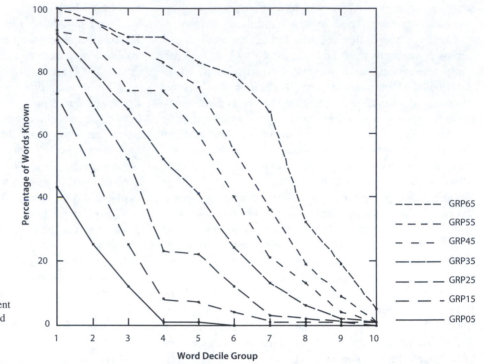

Figure 19.1 Words from Different Difficulty Levels by Children of Different Sizes of Vocabulary. From Biemiller and Slonim (2001). Used with permisson from the American Psychological Association.

meanings less well known by elementary students are typically learned later.

***What Produces This Sequence?*[2]**   Possible hypotheses affecting this sequence include:

- Word meanings learned early may be *prerequisite* to understanding word meanings which are learned later in the sequence;
- It is very likely that the frequencies of encountering word meanings affect word meaning acquisition. Certainly words and meanings *not* encountered cannot be learned. However, frequencies of *specific word meanings* (oral and later printed) are often quite different than simple printed form frequency. Thus there is little correlation between printed word frequency and word meaning knowledge among common words (Biemiller & Slonim, 2001) particularly for the earlier (first 10,000) word meanings, which are frequently associated with word forms that have more than one meaning.
- More cognitively complex meanings are usually learned later (e.g., *biology*) (Case, 1985; Slonim, 2001). However cognitive complexity clearly does not account for sequence in many word meanings acquired later. Many of these later-acquired words are non-abstract (i.e., touchable, visible). Examples are shown in Table 19.1.

Individual Differences   By the end of second grade, the 25% of English-speaking children with the lowest vocabularies have an average of 4,000 root word meanings, while average children have about 6,000 root word meanings and children with the vocabularies in the highest 25% have about 8,000 root word meanings. After Grade 2, average children add about 1,000 root meanings per year. Thus by Grade 2, children in the lowest quartile are on average already 2 years behind their average classmates and 4 years behind the 25% of children with the largest vocabularies (Biemiller, 2005). These differences have occurred *before* children's vocabulary can be much influenced by their own reading. After Grade 2, vocabulary gaps may not grow larger, but neither are they narrowed in the upper elementary grades. These findings refer to representative English-speaking children. For some English language learners or children with disabilities, gaps are considerably larger. This gap is maintained through Grade 6. (Test norms suggest that the gaps continue or expand after Grade 6.)

While some of this range of vocabulary at the end of Grade 2 may reflect disabilities ranging from hearing problems to unusual difficulty in word meaning inference, the largest source of vocabulary difference is probably the available language used around and with the child at home (Hart & Risley, 1995, 1999; Wells, 1985). There may be further differences in ease of inferring vocabulary, just as there are differences in ease of inferring phonics—some children can infer many meanings, others require more direct explanation of word meanings.

Implications of vocabulary differences.   Until now, educators have largely left early vocabulary development to homes, thereby allowing disadvantaged children to fall very far behind in vocabulary. My belief is that with increased recognition of the importance of vocabulary, we educators should now take a much greater responsibility to foster adequate vocabulary development, just as we take responsibility for word recognition skills and number knowledge and skills.

TABLE 19.1

Sample Root Word Meanings from the Easy, Teach Primary, Teach Upper Elementary, and Difficult for Elementary (K-6)

Easy Words
May not need to teach

Word	Meaning
about	tells of
about	around
accident	unplanned happening
bottom	the part underneath
clever	very smart
describe	give word pictures of
early	near the start of
few	a small number
gigantic	very big
ground	the earth's surface
ground	soil or earth
heart	body's blood pump
interfere	get in the way
joke	something to laugh at
land	soil
land	a country
land	to go ashore
machine	power tool
normal	ordinary
oven	used for baking
pardon	forgiveness
rock	kind of music
rock	move back and forth
rock	a stone
show	to point out
show	movie or TV program
tame	gentle, not wild

Primary Priority Words
Teach in K to Gr. 2 texts

Word	Meaning
agenda	things to be done
brutal	cruel
convince	make a person believe
dawn	sunrise
earth	our planet
feeling	an opinion
germ	a cause of disease
horror	fright
jealous	wanting what others have
kind	sort
lap	part of body when seated
lap	once around track
maximum	the most
noun	name of a thing
opportunity	a good chance
paragraph	unit of writing
reality	actual fact
secure	free from fear
though	however
though	even when
universe	everything there is
vehicle	means of transportation

Junior Priority Words
Teach in Gr. 3 to Gr. 6 texts

Word	Meaning
accommodate	be suitable for
accommodate	help out
base	bottom
base	of low quality
base	military installation
category	a class of objects
debate	an argument
debate	to think about all sides
debate	to discuss
economic	concerning use of resources
economics	science of wealth
fatigue	tiredness
give	a movement under pressure
honor	deserved fame
imply	to indicate witout actually saying
know	be skilled
labor	workers, in general
manual	book of instruction
manual	done by hand
negotiate	arrange terms
opinion	what one thinks
party	political group

Difficult Elementary Words
Teach in Gr. 3 to Gr. 6 only if needed for text comprehension or as part of the curriculum

Word	Meaning
abhor	be disgusted with, detest
basis	foundation
capacity	position served in
deceit	dishonesty
empower	to give authority
ford	to cross through water
gastric	of the stomach
hydraulic	works by liquid pressure
income	money taken in
jest	make fun
kleptomania	the strong urge to steal
lance	to cut open
mandatory	compulsory
notion	an idea
obligation	personal duty
partition	division
qualify	have needed ability
regard	think highly of
regard	to look upon
regard	respect
sequence	one thing after another
technical	greatly detailed

1. Meanings taken from the *Living Word Vocabulary* (Dale & O'Rourke, 1981). Complete lists of these words are available in *Words Worth Teaching* (Biemiller, 2009).

Vocabulary Acquisition

Controversy over Amount of Inferred Word Meanings Versus Meanings from Direct Explanations There is debate over the amount of vocabulary acquired by inference versus the amount acquired by direct word meaning explanation from parents, teachers, peers, and text explanations (i.e., appositions). The main argument for a lot of inference is based on consideration of the number of words acquired. As I've noted earlier, I think the number of *root* word meanings acquired is not that great. *If* derived and compound meanings can be acquired by inference (and possibly also figurative meanings such as *leaning* on me for *support*), learning of the majority of root meanings could be explained more plausibly by direct instruction.

Direct research on word inference suggests that relatively few word meanings are acquired during reading (Nagy, Anderson, & Herman, 1987), and that lower-vocabulary children fail to acquire word meanings from oral stories (Robbins & Ehri, 1994) or reading texts (Cain, Oakhill, & Lemmon, in press; Fraser, 1999). Stahl and Nagy (2006) have also reported that wide reading alone does not guarantee acquisition of new vocabulary. Shany and Biemiller (in press) found that increased reading practice led to large vocabulary gains and reading comprehension gains for about one third of a sample of third and fourth grade poor readers, but no vocabulary gains and smaller reading comprehension gains for two-thirds of this sample. Overall, it appears that children vary considerably in their vocabulary acquisition as a result of wide reading and that many children gain few word meanings from wide reading.

Influences on Vocabulary Acquisition

Home influences.   We have seen that children's vocabulary differs markedly by the end of Grade 2. From where do these differences come? Clearly, words that are ***not*** heard or read cannot be learned. Hart and Risley (1995) have shown that, by the age of 3, advantaged children ***hear*** three times as many words spoken as disadvantaged children. Furthermore, in advantaged homes and some working class homes, parents actively explain word meanings in the course of conversation, story reading, etc. (Weizman & Snow, 2001; Hart & Risley, 1999). Thus, it is not surprising that before school starts, advantaged children already ***know*** many more words than disadvantaged children.

School influences.   We might hope that once children enter school at age 4 or 5, there would be more opportunities for less advantaged children to build vocabulary—even to catch up with more advantaged children. Unfortunately, the limited available data on the vocabulary effects of school attendance in primary grades is discouraging—kindergarten, Grade 1, and Grade 2 children appear to gain ***no*** vocabulary as a result of a year in a primary grade. The evidence is simple—on average, the youngest first graders have just one month's more vocabulary than the oldest kindergartners (Christian, Morrison, Frazier, & Massetti, 2000; Morrison, Smith, & Dow-Ehrensberger, 1995). Similarly, the youngest second graders average just one month's vocabulary than the oldest first graders (Cantalini, 1987).

Person influences.   There is some evidence that those with small vocabularies are less likely to infer new word meanings from context (Elshout-Mohr & van Daalen-Kaptjeins, 1987; Penno, Wilkinson, & Moore, 2002; Robbins & Ehri, 1994). Some of this difference may be the cumulative effect of having fewer word meanings. Thus

a child with a large vocabulary may be trying to infer one word meaning while knowing all of the other words in a text. A child with a small vocabulary may be trying to infer the same word meaning, but lacks the meanings of 10% of the other words in the text. Successful inference will be less likely in the second case.

In addition, some of the difference in vocabulary size may involve having less phonemic accuracy, memory, or other cognitive processes. These are probably constitutional differences. These person factors can amount to a disability affecting both word recognition skill (reading) inferring word meanings, and comprehending text (also involving inference).

How fifth- and sixth-grade children report acquiring new vocabulary.   Part of my research on vocabulary development and promotion included an examination of self-reports of vocabulary acquisition (Biemiller, 1999). Quite simply, children listed words they have learned in the last two or three days and were then interviewed about these words. In the interview, they were asked the meaning of the word, how they happened to hear or read the word, and how they learned the meaning of each word (asked, were told without asking, defined as part of lesson, dictionary, or figured it out). Results came from an ESL Grade 5/6 class and an advantaged Grade 5/6 class. Some basic findings were as follows:

- Both Grade 5 and 6 groups reported learning most of their words at school (ESL, 80%, advantaged, 90%). (Unlike findings from primary grades, upper elementary children report learning many word meanings in school.)
- Both groups reported that 70% of words (average 3.5) were learned with assistance (child asked someone, someone told child, word was directly explained in a lesson-including on video), while 25% of words were acquired by inference (1.2 words) or by dictionary (0.2 words).

While very preliminary, this little study is consistent with the hypothesis that the majority of root word meanings are acquired as a result of direct explanation. As late as Grade 6, students were reporting that 70% of newly acquired words were learned as a result of explanation by someone else.

Acquisition of Derived Word Meanings (Root + Affix(es) or Root + Root)   Anglin (1993) has determined that there are many more inflected and derived word forms than root forms. He estimates three times as many derived word meanings as root word forms known in first grade and five times as many derived word meanings known by fifth grade. This refers to *average* word knowledge. Individuals may know more or less. In addition, children acquire idiomatic expressions that do not follow from the literal meanings of words, (e.g., *eleventh hour*—essentially a resolution at the last possible minute or hour). Anglin estimates that roughly 2,500 idiomatic expressions are learned by fifth grade. These are in addition to figurative meanings of words which are counted among root word meanings learned by

both Anglin and Dale and O'Rourke (1981; e.g., *lean* as in *lean* on me when you're having problems).

Can we assume that derived word meanings (root plus affix) can be understood when encountered in context and the root and affix are known? There remains some debate about the degree to which derived word meanings can be assumed to be acquired more readily than root words. This *may* be an area in which learners differ markedly in inferring meanings *when root words and affixes are known*. In addition, it must be recognized that many apparently derived words are not in fact derivable from the apparent root meanings and affixes and must be considered root words in their own right (e.g., *revise, preface*). Having noted this, it remains true that children can infer many derived word meanings (Anglin, 1993, gives some examples of overt derivation). There is evidence that children can be taught to derive word meanings using a limited set of affixes (Baumann, Edwards, Boland, Olejnik, & Kame'enui, 2003; Graves, 2006) *when the relevant root word is known*.

Implications for Educational Practice

Growing Consensus that Some Vocabulary Instruction and Vocabulary-related Instruction Is Needed   There is recognition that vocabulary gaps are related to poor reading comprehension and that environmental influences play a significant role in the developing differences in vocabulary (Beck, McKeown & Lucan, 2002; Biemiller, 2001; National Reading Panel, 2000; Stahl, 1999; Stahl & Nagy, 2006). In 2006, the California State Board of Education mandated vocabulary instruction as a component of reading programs for use in California elementary reading programs. New major reading programs to be published in 2007 or 2008 will include substantially more attention to vocabulary than before (e.g., Houghton-Mifflin, 2007; SRA, 2007).

Direct vocabulary instruction.   By this I mean directly explaining word meanings, as well as drawing student attention to **appositions** (word meaning explanations provided directly in texts), and student use of **glossaries** and **dictionaries**. Along with Beck, Mckeown, Kucan, Graves, Stahl, and Nagy, I believe that *some* word meanings must be taught directly.

I particularly think direct vocabulary of word meanings should occur in the *primary grades*. Students are much less able to extract word meanings from orally presented texts than from written texts. Of course, oral texts are the primary mode of text presentation in the early elementary grades. It is difficult for a listener to attend to a text while contemplating an unknown word. A reader can pause to do this or return to an unknown word after reading the text. A listener can rarely do these things. Consequently word meaning acquisition is more dependent on adult teaching. In the primary grades, in addition to addressing *text-critical* word meanings in texts being read to students, or with students, teachers should take advantage of text contexts to explain high priority general vocabulary words.

In the upper elementary grades, I also recommend direct instruction of *text-critical* meanings in texts prior to student reading of texts.

Vocabulary-related instruction.   By this I mean methods of determining word meanings by attending to affixes, compound words, and strategies for inferring word meanings from context. There is substantial evidence that teaching affixes increases functional vocabulary for derived words (White, Sowell, & Yangihara, 1989; Baumann et al., 2003; Graves, 2006; Stahl & Nagy, 2006). Similarly, interpreting compound words can be useful.

There is more debate about teaching word inference methods. Kuhn and Stahl (1998) question the effectiveness of methods used to date. Fukkink and de Glopper (1998) maintain that significant effect sizes have been established for teaching methods of determining word meanings from context, but do not provide results identifying numbers of words acquired as a result of inference training. More recent research continues to show that especially lower-vocabulary students appear not to gain much from word inference strategies (Cain et al., in press; Stahl & Nagy, 2006).

Identifying Words Worth Teaching   There has been considerable discussion of what words we should emphasize when teaching vocabulary.

What word meanings?   Given that improved vocabulary has practical significance, a critical question is **what** word meanings are important to teach? One answer has been suggested by Beck, McKeown, and Lucan (2002). They propose categorizing word meanings occurring in text as Tier One (likely to be known without any school instruction), Tier Two (words … of high frequency for mature language users and are found across a variety of domains), and Tier Three (rare, to be taught when needed as part of a specific discipline such as chemistry or biology). However, Beck and colleagues do not provide a listing of such words and, in fact, object to generating such a list (Beck & McKeown, 2007).

I do believe that words worth teaching can be identified, and in fact have publishing such a list (Biemiller, 2009). Briefly, given that word meanings are being learned in a rough sequence, and that words that are well known by the end of Grade 2 have been identified, word meanings that are known by 40% to 80% of children at the end of Grade 2 can be considered probably known by children with large vocabularies and unlikely to be known by children with small vocabularies. To find such words, I have identified most *root* word meanings in Dale and O'Rourke's *Living Word Vocabulary* (1981) reported to be first known by roughly half of children at Grades 4, 6, 8, or 10. Using a process of direct testing and rating, as described in *Words Worth Teaching* (Biemiller, 2009), I ultimately identified about 1,600 root word meanings as being particularly relevant for children in primary grades, and another 2,700 root word meanings as being particularly relevant for children in the upper elementary grades.

I believe the 1,600 high priority primary root word meanings could be taught directly during the three primary years (kindergarten, first and second grades). Similarly, the 2,700 high priority upper elementary root words worth addressing should be used in texts during Grades 3 to 6. Methods of instruction are discussed briefly below.

What about "non-root" word meanings? My hypothesis is that most derived and compound word meanings will be acquired in context, *if* children have inferred or been taught the relevant affixes *and the relevant root meaning is known*. A large proportion of derived word meanings appearing in Dale and O'Rourke's (1981) *Living Word Vocabulary* appear either in the same as the root word, or not more than 2 years later. The same is probably also true of inflected words (syntactic suffixes). There has been considerable success with teaching middle elementary students to use common prefixes (White et al., 1989; Baumann et al., 2003; Graves, 2006). However, instruction with affixes will not help when the relevant root word is unknown. Of course, teachers must be alert to words which appear to be derived, but do not have the meaning implied by using a root + affix method (e.g., *preface, revise*).

How Word Meanings Can Be Taught in the Primary Grades

Teaching word meanings in context. The most encouraging findings about primary vocabulary instruction were Dina Feitelson's 6-month long interventions using *repeated* oral reading of various storybooks, with direct explanations of some words on each reading. Although Feitelson and her colleagues did not describe her method in detail nor assess specific growth in vocabulary, she demonstrated that first-grade students who received this additional oral reading showed large gains in language and reading comprehension compared to similar students who did not receive this repeated reading with word explanations (Feitelson, Kita, & Goldstein, 1986; Feitelson, Goldstein, Iraqi, & Share, 1991).

A number of short-term studies using word meaning explanations while repeatedly reading storybooks have demonstrated that students acquire some of the taught word meanings. Typically, about 25% of word meanings taught were acquired. These percentages of words learned held whether relatively few (2–4) and many (6–10) word meanings were taught on each reading. Ten to 15% of non-taught words that appeared in the stories were also acquired after *repeated* reading. The limited available research suggests that few, if any, word meanings are acquired from a single reading without word explanations (reviewed in Biemiller & Boote, 2006). It is possible that other, non-context methods might work, however I have not found any studies demonstrating this.

Most new vocabulary in the primary grades will come from ORAL sources. Making a greater effort to support building vocabulary is needed across the elementary grades. However, I consider vocabulary instruction in the primary grades (kindergarten–second grade) quite different than vocabulary instruction in the upper elementary grades. In the primary grades, most students are **preliterate**. By "preliterate" I mean that, if they can read at all, they are likely to be reading texts that are less rich than those they can understand if they hear them. Preliterate students read slowly and have at least some difficulty identifying written words. They are unlikely to encounter unfamiliar word meanings in the texts they can read. Furthermore, if they do encounter unfamiliar meanings, they are unlikely to be able to distinguish these from words they have difficulty identifying in print. The main implication of all this is that supporting vocabulary acquisition in the primary grades will mainly be an oral activity for children rather than a print-based activity and will require much direct instruction by teachers.

Why so many meanings must be taught. Children don't all learn the same meanings. Some children know different meanings than do other children. Some know more of the meanings to begin with, and so learn different words than do children who know few words to begin with. To some extent, children simply pick up different meanings. However, I suspect that there may be an upper limit to how many meanings can be acquired in one session by one child. We rarely see any one child learn more than 3 or 4 meanings from one session. (See review of studies of primary vocabulary instruction in Biemiller & Boote, 2006.)

An effective primary vocabulary method. Catherine Boote and I undertook to increase the percentage of words learned and the total number of words learned in primary grades. We did this by following suggestions from teachers who had been teaching vocabulary from storybooks in an earlier study. Our revised method with students in kindergarten, Grade 1, and Grade 2 resulted in learning 40% to 45% of word meanings taught (Biemiller & Boote, 2006). A brief description of this method follows:

- Vocabulary instruction took about half an hour per day, taught on a whole-class basis. The instruction was carried out by the regular classroom teachers in kindergarten, Grade 1 and Grade 2. The teachers had seen one demonstration of reading with vocabulary instruction.
- Initially, a storybook or expository book is read to the students with little interruption for vocabulary explanation. Prior to reading the book, we would explain 1–2 meanings that were critical for comprehension of the book. (We have adopted this practice as a result of pretests with kindergarten and Grade 1 students. However, it may be possible to explain word meanings *after* reading the story, in which case more meanings could be taught on the first reading.)
- On subsequent readings, we would continue to introduce 1–2 meanings *before* reading the book. Although we haven't tested this, we strongly suspect that teaching a larger number of words prior to orally reading a book is ineffective. We doubt if students could keep in mind many just-explained meanings while attending to the story.

- As in previous studies, we have found that explaining meanings *while* reading a book is effective. Our method was (a) read orally, (b) upon coming to a word to be explained, *re-read the sentence with the word to be taught,* (c) explain the word's meaning *as it applies in the context of the book*, (d) continue reading the book.

Here is an example from a book used for vocabulary instruction in kindergarten, *Clifford at the Circus* (Bridwell, 1985). Note that we would teach **circus** *before* reading the story. **Circus** is an example of a *text-critical* meaning, necessary to understand the text.

The story begins:

*I'm Emily Elizabeth and I have a dog named Clifford. We saw a sign that said the **circus** was in town. A smaller sign said the circus needed **help.***

On the *second* reading, we *re-read* "*A smaller sign said the circus needed **help**.*" Then we explain, "In this sentence, **help** means the circus show wants to hire some people to work at the show—to help put on the show." Then we go on reading the story until we come to the next word to be explained that day.

- Each day, *after* reading the book and discussing comprehension aspects of the book, words taught that day are *reviewed* along with the explanations of each word. In first and second grade, it can be helpful to introduce the printed versions of these words at this time. I recommend use of additional written activities with words taught that day. However, the effectiveness of additional written work to facilitate word meaning acquisition has not been tested.
- Usually, we worked with a book for a week. On the last day of work with this book, rather than reading the book again, each word taught during the week is presented in a *new* sentence, *not taken from the book*. The explanation of the word's meaning is reviewed again.

After instruction, we found that the students knew about 40% more of the taught words than they knew before the reading and explanations. Encouragingly, the students knew *more* of these words 6 weeks after the instruction than just after instruction (Biemiller & Boote, 2006). At that point, the children had gained an average of 8 to 12 meanings per week. To get these gains, the teachers taught 21 to 28 word meanings each week.

Teaching primary vocabulary: Summary. During the primary years, vocabulary is mainly acquired from oral sources. At present, students with relatively small vocabularies fall further behind during the primary years. This is because no systematic effort is made to teach vocabulary during the primary years. This especially disadvantages low-vocabulary students, who are less likely to acquire needed vocabulary at home and less likely to infer word meanings **without instruction** at school. Existing methods could lead to the acquisition of 400–500 more word mean-

ings during each primary grade. This would be sufficient to prevent falling further behind and might help close the gap between low and average vocabulary students. Accelerating low-vocabulary students' progress through the vocabulary sequence is probably the best strategy for narrowing the vocabulary gap.

Teaching/Fostering Vocabulary in the Upper Elementary Grades

Acquiring new vocabulary is different in the upper elementary period. Around Grade 3, the majority of students become **literate** in the sense of being able to read most texts they would understand if they heard them. This means reading fluently enough to permit focus on the content of text rather than identifying words—reaching Jeanne Chall's stage 3 (Chall, 1983/1996). Once children become literate, the process of acquiring new vocabulary changes dramatically.

Previously, I noted how difficult it is to think about an unfamiliar word while attending to a story being read orally. On the other hand, when encountering an unfamiliar word while *fluently reading* a story, a child can stop reading and focus on the word, or continue reading and return to the unknown word *after* reading the story. (The word could even be written down or marked in the book to facilitate returning to it.) In fact, my finding that low- and high-vocabulary students apparently add new words at about the same rate after Grade 2 or 3 is consistent with the hypothesis that words can be more easily learned while reading text than while hearing text (Biemiller & Slonim, 2001).

Direct instruction. Is there a continued need for direct instruction of words in the upper elementary grades? Direct explanation of word meanings **critical for comprehension** of texts (narrative or expository) will continue to require direct explanation. In some cases, these meanings can be pretaught (before reading). Unlike oral language presentation, a list of critical meanings can be **written** on a classroom board or handout and used as words to be addressed when encountered in text. Thus more word meanings can be pretaught with **literate** children. In other cases, it may be more helpful to review meanings **after** the text has been read. I think this is especially true of general vocabulary, as distinct from text-critical vocabulary. At this point, meanings can be explained in terms of the text just read.

If the meaning involves a concept that goes beyond a simple mapping to establishing a major new concept (e.g., *erosion, chemical element*), we need instruction that goes beyond simple vocabulary extension. Sometimes technical terms (e.g., *erosion*) are explained directly in texts (appositions). However, teachers need to be sure that such terms are actually understood. Students often fail to learn meanings solely from text explanations (Baumann et al., 2003).

Directly Teaching Strategies for Prefixed, Suffixed, or Compound Word Meanings. In addition, strategies for interpreting derived word meanings (root words plus a prefix or suffix, and compound words) can also be taught directly (e.g., *read, readable*). Several studies have shown that upper elementary students can benefit substantially from instruction in interpreting meanings of derived words (Baumann et al., 2003; Graves, 2006; White et al., 1989). Similarly, words with Latin or Greek stems (e.g., **demo-** or **psycho-**) can be taught as derived words where the root never appears by itself (Stahl, 1999). This should be part of the vocabulary program for upper elementary children. However, acquiring effective strategies for interpreting affixes is not a substitute for acquiring needed root words.

Increased student responsibility. Much of the vocabulary instruction for the upper elementary grades should place more responsibility on students. Students can be asked to find root meanings for words in the passage that are worth learning for general vocabulary. A variety of student-managed acquisition activities could then be used, including direct explanation by fellow students, group discussion of word meanings (Stahl, 1999), use of glossaries and dictionaries, and possibly inference strategies. To date, teaching inference strategies has rarely proven effective (Baumann et al., 2003; Beck et al., 2002; Stahl & Nagy, 2006). A variety of student activities and classroom assessment of designated word meanings should ensure vocabulary progress.

In addition, *student identification of needed word meanings* can be emphasized. In the long run, student identification of needed word meanings will be crucial for their post-elementary academic success. Therefore, school activities should increasingly involve student identification of needed meanings—not simply depending on others to determine what meanings should be learned. This could involve student identification of needed meanings in texts, followed by group discussion of meanings, and/or student generation of activities using identified meanings. Teachers could add meanings to a list of student-identified meanings when needed. *However, there should ultimately be assessment of many word meanings.*

Procedure for increasing student recognition of needed word meanings. In a preliminary study with 6 ESL sixth-grade students in 1 class for 16 weeks, my assistant Jody Panto and I undertook to increase students' vocabulary. Most of the students in this class spoke English as a second language and spoke their native language at home. Our general goal was to encourage a higher level of asking about unfamiliar words.

Panto's basic routine for a reading session involved having each student in a reading group take responsibility for the vocabulary on one or two pages of text. The texts were somewhat more complex than these students would be expected to read on their own. The program emphasized seeking direct assistance for unfamiliar words, both from peers and from teachers when necessary.

As the students read, they were to mark words when they weren't sure of the word's meaning. *After* reading one or two pages, one student would be invited to ask the teacher

for any meanings of which she was not sure. (Reading assistance was given when needed, but was rarely needed. These were fluent readers.) The other students in the group could then ask the first student about any other words on the pages they had just read. The assumption was that the first student was competent with words not yet discussed. After this, the instructor might ask about words identified as difficult which have not been mentioned by any of the students. (In this study, we identified as difficult words which are not on the 3,000 word list used by Chall and Dale (1995) to assess readability.)

Initially, students were often embarrassed by being unable to answer other children's questions (i.e., they had failed to ask about all words they needed to know about). However, after about 3 weeks (6 sessions), the students *asked* if they didn't know, and *knew appropriate meanings* for words they didn't ask about.

Overall, the effect of this approach was to make the students more responsible for both monitoring their word knowledge, and being prepared to explain word meanings to others. The students acquired meanings of about 80% of the words they asked about.

Teaching upper elementary vocabulary: Summary. In Grades 3 to 6, children need less direct instruction of specific word meanings, more instruction about affixes and compound words (now often provided), and increasing student responsibility to find unknown words along with finding meanings for student-identified words and teacher-identified words. Direct instruction of text-critical word meanings should probably still be provided. Learning of word meanings noted by the teacher should be assessed.

Vocabulary Implications for Educational Practice: Summary

- Increasing vocabulary should probably emphasize accelerating the normal sequence of vocabulary, particularly for low vocabulary students.
- In the primary period, students need direct instruction of word meanings. Much of this should be done with repeated orally presented texts and explanations of word meanings *in context*.
- In the upper elementary period, students can take more responsibility for acquiring general vocabulary. However, appropriate words encountered during a week's reading should be noted, and new vocabulary tested. In addition, *text-critical* meanings should be taught directly as well as interpretation of prefixed, suffixed, and compound words.

General Versus Remedial Vocabulary Instruction

For many students, vocabulary is implicated in low reading comprehension achievement. In my view, this is often the simple result of inadequate opportunities to build necessary vocabulary during the school years, especially the primary years. Thus it appears to me that during the elementary years, schools should be including a specific focus on introducing students to vocabulary they will need, rather than treating low vocabulary as evidence of one or another disability.

For students who experience difficulty in adding vocabulary given normal and otherwise effective instruction, a disability in building vocabulary may exist. This may reflect hearing difficulties (including lack of phonological awareness which is related to low vocabulary, Gathercole, 2007; Gathercole, Serive, Hitch, Adams, & Martin, 1999), effects of limited verbal working memory (Cain et al., in press), or inference problems with both word meanings and text implications (Cain & Oakhill, 2003). The difficulty may also be simply an unusually low vocabulary (due to home experience or English Language Learner status), which leaves the student in need of even basic words which most students have. Attention to hearing status and attention to words known versus words not known are in order.

Addressing vocabulary and language problems which are not due simply to lack of vocabulary and hearing problems will be more difficult. Cain, Oakhill, and others have identified such difficulties (Cain & Oakhill, 2003; Cain, Oakhill, & Elbro, 2003; Cain et al., in press; Gathercole, Hitch, Service, & Martin, 1997). Two major problems have been emphasized: difficulty in inferring word and text meanings using information across several sentences; and creating lexical entries for new words.

Cain et al. (in press) suggest that one group of low-comprehension students have adequate vocabulary and acquire new word meanings readily when taught. This group's comprehension problems involve seeing implications, especially when relevant text sentences are not adjacent.

A second group has the same comprehension difficulty, but also greater difficulty in learning new word meanings. Cain and colleagues (in press) suggest that this group has greater difficulty in forming lexical entries. I predict that such students will also often have more problems with word recognition, mainly mediated by phonological weakness (Stanovich & Siegel, 1994). Such students may especially need attention to vocabulary, possibly including even the first 2000 words, which are normally easily acquired by disadvantaged students (as reported in Biemiller & Boote, 2006). It is possible, that with attention to vocabulary as well as phonemic awareness, that adding vocabulary will help with phonemic awareness as well as vice versa (Metsala, 1999).

However, to date few practical interventions based on these problems have been demonstrated. For example, Tomesen and Aarnoutse (1998) reported significant gains in reading comprehension with Grade 4 poor readers (8 intervention and 7 control subjects) after teaching word meaning inference skills. Others have had less success (e.g., Baumann et al., 2003). To date, I have not seen any evidence of methods for improving lexical entries.

Conclusion

We are all very aware of the wide range of reading achievement now seen in elementary students and aware of the conviction that many more students should be able to comprehend grade level reading materials. Until vocabulary problems are addressed regularly in all primary and upper elementary grades, we will continue to see many students whose comprehension limits their ability to learn in school. We do not yet have evidence that a more comprehensive approach to vocabulary will reduce school failure; however, we do know that students with limited vocabularies cannot successfully learn from grade level texts in the upper elementary years and later.

At present, the best policy for increased educational achievement appears to be committing more instructional time to vocabulary development during the elementary grades. For the primary grades, this means more direct instruction of word meanings embedded in meaningful context. For the upper elementary grades, this means more direct instruction of text critical vocabulary and more work on using affixes to determine meanings. However, for fluent readers there should also be more emphasis on finding unknown words, and finding their meanings.

Notes

1. The following section is taken from *Words Worth Teaching* (Biemiller, 1999).
2. This section is based largely on Biemiller (2009).

References

Anglin, J. M. (1993). Vocabulary development: A morphological analysis. *Monographs of the Society for Research in Child Development,* Serial No. 238, 58.

Baumann, J. F., Edwards, E. C., Boland, E. M., Olejnik, S., & Kame'enui, E. J. (2003). Vocabulary tricks: Effects of instruction on morphology and context on fifth-grade students' ability to derive and infer word meanings. *American Educational Research Journal, 40*(2), 447–494.

Beck, I. L., & McKeown, M. G. (2007). Different ways for different goals, but keep your eye on the higher verbal goals. In R. K. Wagner, A. E. Muse, & K. R. Tannenbaum (Eds.), *Vocabulary acquisition: Implications for reading comprehension* (pp 182–204). New York: Guilford.

Beck, I. L., McKeown, M. G., & Lucan, L. (2002). *Bringing words to life: Robust vocabulary instruction.* New York: Guilford.

Becker, W. C. (1977). Teaching reading and language to the disadvantaged—What we have learned from field research. *Harvard Educational Review, 47,* 518–543.

Biemiller, A. (1999). *Language and reading success.* Cambridge, MA: Brookline Books.

Biemiller, A. (2001). Teaching vocabulary: Early, direct, and sequential. *American Educator, 25,* 24–29.

Biemiller, A. (2005). Addressing developmental patterns vocabulary: Implications for choosing words for primary grade vocabulary instruction. In E. H. Hiebert & M. Kamil (Eds.), *Bringing scientific research to practice: Vocabulary* (pp. 223–242). Mahwah, NJ: Erlbaum.

Biemiller, A. (2009). *Words worth teaching.* Columbus, OH: SRA/McGraw-Hill.

Biemiller, A., & Boote, C. (2006). An effective method for building meaning vocabulary in primary grades. *Journal of Educational Psychology, 98,* 44–62.

Biemiller, A., & Slonim, N. (2001). Estimating root word vocabulary growth in normative and advantaged populations: Evidence for a common sequence of vocabulary acquisition. *Journal of Educational Psychology, 93,* 498–520.

Bridwell, N. (1985). *Clifford at the circus.* New York: Scholastic.

Cain, K., & Oakhill, J. (2003) Reading comprehension difficulties. In T. Nunes & P. Bryant (Eds.), *Handbook of children's literacy* (pp. 313–338). Dordrecht, The Netherlands: Kluwer.

Cain, K., Oakhill, J. V., & Bryant, P. (2004). Children's reading comprehension ability: Concurrent prediction by working memory, verbal ability, and component skills. *Journal of Educational Psychology, 96*(1), 31–42.

Cain, K., Oakhill, J. V., & Elbro, C. (2003). The ability to learn new word meanings from context by school-age children with and without language comprehension difficulties. *Journal of Child Language, 30,* 681–694.

Cain, K., Oakhill, J., & Lemmon, K. (in press). Individual differences in the inference of word meanings from context: the influence of reading comprehension, vocabulary knowledge, and memory capacity. *Journal of Educational Psychology.*

Cantalini, M. (1987). *The effects of age and gender on school readiness and school success.* (Unpublished doctoral dissertation). Ontario Institute for Studies in Education. Toronto, Canada.

Case, R. (1985). *Intellectual development: Birth to adulthood.* New York: Academic Press.

Chall, J. S. (1983/1996). *Stages of reading development* (2nd ed.). New York: Harcourt Brace College Publishers.

Chall, J. S., & Conard, S. S. (1991). *Should textbooks challenge students?* New York: Teachers College Press.

Chall, J. S., & Dale, E. (1995). *Readability revisited: The new Dale-chall readability formula.* Cambridge, MA: Brookline Books.

Chall, J. S., Jacobs, V. A., & Baldwin, L. E. (1990). *The reading crisis: Why poor children fall behind.* Cambridge, MA: Harvard University Press.

Christian, K., Morrison, F. J., Frazier, J. A., & Massetti, G. (2000). Specificity in the nature and timing of cognitive growth in kindergarten and first grade. *Journal of Cognition and Development, 1*(4), 429–448.

Cunningham, A. E., & Stanovich, K. E. (1997). Early reading acquisition and its relation to reading experience and ability 10 years later. *Developmental Psychology, 33,* 934–945.

Dale, E., & O'Rourke, J. (1981). *Living word vocabulary.* Chicago: World Book/Childcraft.

Elshout-Mohr, M., & van Daalen-Kaptijns, M. M. (1987). Cognitive processes in learning word meanings. In M. G. McKeown & M. E.Curtis (Eds.), *The nature of vocabulary acquisition* (pp. 53–72). Hillsdale, NJ: Erlbaum.

Feitelson, D., Goldstein, Z., Iraqi, J., & Share, D. I. (1991). Effects of listening to story reading on aspects of literacy acquisition in a diglossic situation. *Reading Research Quarterly, 28,* 70–79.

Feitelson, D., Kita, B., & Goldstein, Z. (1986). Effects of listening to series stories on first graders' comprehension and use of language. *Research in the Teaching of English, 20,* 339–356.

Fraser, C. A. (1999). Lexical processing strategy use and vocabulary learning through reading. *Studies on Second Language Acquisition, 21,* 225–241.

Fukkink, R. G., & de Glopper, K. (1998). Effects of instruction in deriving word meaning from context: A meta-analysis. *Review of Educational Research, 68*(4), 450–469.

Gathercole, S. E. (2007). Working memory: A system for learning. In R. K. Wagner, A. E. Muse, & K. R. Tannenbaum (Eds.), *Vocabulary acquisition: Implications for reading comprehension* (pp. 233–248). New York: Guilford.

Gathercole, S. E., Hitch, G. J., Service, E., & Martin, A. J. (1997). Phonological short-term memory and new word learning in children. *Developmental Psychology, 33,* 966–979.

Gathercole, S. E., Serive, E., Hitch, G. J., Adams, A. M., & Martin, A. J. (1999). Phonological short-term memory and vocabulary development: Further evidence on the nature of the relationship. *Applied Cognitive Psychology, 13*(1), 65–77.

Gough, P. B., & Tunmer, W. E. (1986). Decoding, reading and reading disability. *Remedial and Special Education, 7,* 6–10.

Graves, M. F. (2006). *The vocabulary book: learning and instruction.* New York: Teachers' College Press.

Hart, B., & Risley, T. (1995). *Meaningful differences in the everyday experience of young American children.* Baltimore, MD: Brookes.

Hart, B., & Risley, T. (1999*). The social world of children learning to talk.* Baltimore, MD: Brookes.

Hazenberg, S., & Hulstijn, J. H. (1996). Defining a minimal receptive second-language vocabulary for non-native university students: An empirical investigation. *Applied Linguistics, 17,* 145–163.

Houghton-Mifflin. (2007). *Houghton-Mifflin reading,* Boston, MA: Houghton-Mifflin.

Hiebert, E. H., & Kamil, M. L. (Eds.). (2005). *Teaching and learning vocabulary: Bringing research to practice.* Mahwah, NJ: Erlbaum.

Kuhn, M. R., & Stahl, S. A. (1998). Teaching children to learn word meanings from context: a synthesis and some questions. *Journal of Literacy Research, 30*(1), 119–138.

Metsala, J. L. (1999). Young children's phonological awareness and non-word repetition as a function of vocabulary development. *Journal of Educational Psychology, 91,* 743–751.

Morrison, F. J., Smith, L., & Dow-Ehrensberger, M. (1995). Education and cognitive development: A natural experiment. *Developmental Psychology, 31,* 789–799.

Nagy, W. E., Anderson, R. C., & Herman, P. (1987). Learning word meanings from context during normal reading. *American Educational Research Journal, 24,* 237–270.

Nagy, W. E., & Scott, J. A. (2001). Vocabulary processes In M. L. Kamil, P. B. Mosenthal, P. D. Pearson, & R. Barr (Eds.), *Handbook of reading research, Vol. 3* (pp. 269–284). Mahwah, NJ: Erlbaum.

National Reading Panel. (2000). *Teaching children to read: An evidence-based assessment of the scientific research literature on reading and its implications for reading instruction.* Washington, DC: National Institute of Child Health and Human Development.

Penno, J. F., Wilkinson, A. G., & Moore, D. W. (2002). Vocabulary acquisition from teacher explanation and repeated listening to stories: Do they overcome the Matthew effect? *Journal of Educational Psychology, 94,* 23–33.

Robbins, C., & Ehri, L. C. (1994). Reading storybooks to kindergartners helps them learn new vocabulary words. *Journal of Educational Psychology, 86*(1), 139–153.

Scarborough, H. (2001). Connecting early language and literacy to later reading (dis)abilities: Evidence, theory, and practice. In S. B. Neuman & D. Dickinson (Eds.), *Handbook of early literacy research* (pp. 97–110). New York: Guilford.

Shany, M., & Biemiller, A. (in press). Individual differences in reading comprehension gains from assisted reading practice: Pre existing conditions, vocabulary acquisition, and amounts of practice. *Reading and Writing.*

Slonim, N. (2001). *Children's and adolescents' understanding of society and government* (Unpublished M.A. thesis). Toronto, ON: University of Toronto, Dept. of Human Development and Applied Psychology.

SRA. (2007). *Imagine it!* Columbus, OH: SRA/McGraw-Hill.

Stahl, S. A. (1999). *Vocabulary development.* Cambridge, MA: Brookline Books.

Stahl, S. A., & Nagy, W. E. (2006). *Teaching word meanings.* Mahwah, NJ: Erlbaum.

Stanovich, K. E., & Siegel, L. S. (1994). The phenotypic performance profile of reading-disabled children: A regression-based test of the phonological-core variable-difference model. *Journal of Educational Psychology, 86,* 24–53.

Tomesen, M., & Aarnoutse, C. (1998). Effects of an instructional programme for deriving word meanings. *Educational Studies, 24*(1). 107–128.

Wagner, R. K., Muse, A. E., & Tannenbaum K. R. (Eds.). (2007). *Vocabulary acquisition: Implications for reading comprehension.* New York: Guilford.

Weizman, Z. O., & Snow, C. E. (2001). Lexical input as related to children's vocabulary acquisition: Effects of sophisticated exposure and support for meaning. *Developmental Psychology, 37,* 265–279.

Wells, C. G. (1985). *Language development in the preschool years.* New York: Cambridge University Press.

White, T. G., Sowell, J., & Yangihara, A. (1989). Teaching elementary students to use word-part cues. *The Reading Teacher, 42,* 302–308.

20

Reading Comprehension and Reading Disability

Katherine K. Frankel, P. David Pearson, and Marnie Nair
University of California, Berkeley

Virtually all reading researchers and theorists, regardless of their views of reading development, regard comprehension as the gold standard in defining prima facie reading difficulties. Thus, even if a good comprehender exhibited some deficits in particular skill areas (e.g., phonics or monitoring), we would say that those variations from the ideal were differences that did not make a difference, or perhaps disabilities that did not make a difference. Conversely, if a student was skilled at decoding, oral language vocabulary, and monitoring but could not understand the most basic material, we would conclude that he or she had a reading difficulty and, depending on our view of the neurology of reading, perhaps even a disability. Less than ideal comprehension, then, is the key criterion in defining disability. When it comes to addressing poor comprehension performance, the key question is what is the basis of the performance deficit? What is it about a student's intellectual makeup, skill repertoire, knowledge, experience, dispositions, or instructional history that might account for the prima facie failing in comprehension? Other questions readily follow: (a) Is the nature of disability the same for all poor comprehenders or are there different patterns of disability with different etiologies for different classes of students? (b) Can more than one pattern of sub-skill performance lead to the same comprehension achievement? (c) How are comprehension difficulties best ameliorated for students with reading disabilities?

The goal of this chapter is to unpack and answer these and other questions that fall under the rubric of the relationship between reading disability and reading comprehension. Some of the issues we address, constituting the first part of the chapter, have to do with the nature of reading disability, including an analysis of the natural relationships between reading disability and other aspects of reading development—language development, phonemic awareness, decoding, vocabulary, fluency, and the like.

The second part of the chapter focuses on issues of pedagogy and the practical questions facing teachers as they contemplate decisions about how to assist students who struggle with reading comprehension. In this discussion, we focus on three points of view that are well represented in the literature. The first is based on the belief that the "cure" for some students with poor reading comprehension is to remediate underdeveloped basic reading skills that are serving as barriers to reading comprehension, and these would include skills such as phonemic awareness, phonics, vocabulary, fluency, and oral language. Another point of view proposes that many students' reading comprehension difficulties are best ameliorated by explicit instruction and frequent practice in the application of comprehension strategies. A third point of view proposes that successful reading comprehension results from a complex interweaving of both basic reading skills and strategies and favors a highly individualized approach to remediating reading comprehension difficulties.

Part 1: Modeling the Relationship between Comprehension and Disability

The relationship between comprehension and disability has been investigated for many years, dating back to the early 1900s and the concepts of congenital word blindness popularized by Hinshelwood (1907) and strephosymbolia, or twisted symbols, put forward by Orton in the 1920s (Orton, 1928). These early conceptualizations, both viewed by their popularizers as roughly synonymous with the then rare but now common term *dyslexia*, were based upon what scholars in the 1980s came to call the simple view of reading (see Hoover & Gough, 1990; Gough, Hoover, & Peterson, 1996; Gough & Tumner, 1986), the idea that reading comprehension is entirely specified by the product of an individual's oral language comprehension and decoding prowess: $RC = LC \times D$. Orton and other early scholars of dyslexia speculated that there was a small core of readers for whom neurological problems, in the form of frankly insulted or underdeveloped parts of the brain, led to processing problems that interfered with decoding and, as a consequence, reading comprehension. And over the years, these scholars affiliated themselves with educators who developed highly structured approaches to remediating these core difficulties in recoding print into speech (see Ritchey & Goeke, 2006, for a history and description of these approaches). Over the decades, the work explaining various forms of dyslexia expanded, leading to seminal work by many scholars in the 1970s and 1980s designed to fully understand the construct (see Ellis, 1985, or Stanovich, 1988, for full expositions of this work).

For reasons that are not readily apparent, the 1980s proved a fruitful decade for the development of theoretical perspectives designed to explain the comprehension-disability relationship. At least four of these perspectives deserve our attention: the interactive-compensatory model (Stanovich, 1980); the phonological-core variable-difference model (Stanovich, 1988); an implicit comprehension lag hypothesis, which we label the comprehension strategy deficit hypothesis, as manifested in Reciprocal Teaching (Palincsar & Brown, 1984); and Lipson and Wixson's (1986) interactive model of reading disability.

Interactive-Compensatory Model   Stanovich's interactive-compensatory model caused quite a stir in the reading field when it first appeared in 1980 because it challenged a key premise of the prevailing psycholinguistic models (K. G. Goodman, 1967; K. S. Goodman, 1968; Smith, 1971) that good readers are more sensitive to, reliant on, and able to use context to achieve both word identification and meaning construction. Stanovich reviewed a large body of research demonstrating that it is poor readers, not good readers, who are more reliant on context to achieve word recognition during reading. Indeed, it is precisely and only when good readers run into unusually difficult decoding tasks that they revert to contextual analysis; most of the time, they rely on their fine-tuned and highly efficient decoding processes to gain access to their internal lexicon (the meanings of all the words in the text) and to understand text; they literally recode orthographic into phonological representations on the route to meaning construction. It is not surprising that advocates of this perspective have relabeled what we commonly refer to as decoding or phonics as phonological recoding (Wagner & Torgesen, 1987). LaBerge and Samuels (1974) speculated that good readers use the extra cognitive capacity they acquire because decoding is so effortless to focus their attention clearly on the process of constructing meaning.

Phonological-Core Variable-Difference Model   The interactive-compensatory model is intimately connected to the phonological-core variable-difference model, which has been proposed by many scholars (e.g., Castles & Coltheart, 1993; Ellis, 1985) but most fully articulated by Stanovich (1988). The fundamental claim is that there are two basic types of poor readers—garden-variety poor readers and learning disabled or dyslexic readers, most if not all of whom exhibit a phonological core deficit. The basic symptom of this disability is that readers have difficulty with a specific type of cognitive process, such as with a range of phonological processes—phonemic awareness (segmenting the stream of speech into phonemes) and phonological recoding. This deficit causes a bottleneck in the reading process that goes to the heart of the concept of dyslexia. As stated by Stanovich (1988):

> This assumption underlies all discussions of the concept of dyslexia, even if it is not explicitly stated. It is the idea that a child with this type of learning disability has a brain/cognitive deficit that is reasonably specific to the reading task. (p. 601)

An interesting distinction made by Stanovich (1988) and others (e.g., Ellis, 1985) is that dyslexic readers exhibit what he calls a vertical deficit in cognitive capacity: a specific module, in this case phonological, is underdeveloped. This is to be contrasted with a horizontal deficit—a modest lag in several cognitive modules (e.g., phonological, visual, lexical, and perhaps even language processing); the horizontal deficit, according to Stanovich, is the profile more typical of what he calls the garden-variety poor reader. Among scholars who hold to this distinction, a common assumption is that large numbers of students with reading comprehension problems will also reveal problems in the phonological core.

Comprehension Strategy Deficit Hypothesis   The comprehension strategy deficit perspective (our terminology) is the logical complement to the phonological core deficit hypothesis. It assumes that there are at least some readers who fail to comprehend well in spite of adequate decoding (or phonological recoding) skills because they lack a set of strategies and skills that allow (really dispose) them to connect the words they decode to their existing stores of knowledge. It is precisely this sort of reader that Palincsar and Brown (1984) were trying to assist in their classic Reciprocal Teaching intervention. The bet was that if they could help these students develop a set of comprehension-fostering and comprehension-monitoring strategies (such as summarizing, clarifying, questioning, and predicting), they would dramatically improve their comprehension of texts to which they applied these strategies and, equally important, to texts that they would later encounter on their own. Their work, plus the work of many who have followed in their footsteps, suggests that for many poor readers, this path to remediation is quite effective. Estimates of the size of this pool of disabled readers vary widely. However, some recent data from the work of Catts and colleagues suggests it might be larger than some have thought (Catts, Hogan, & Adlof, 2005). Among students with general language impairments, they found that 31% of struggling second-grade readers were adequate in decoding but poor in reading comprehension. The comparable percentages for fourth and eighth grade were even higher, roughly 45% and 54% respectively (as reported in chapter 14, this volume). These high percentages certainly challenge the prevailing view among dyslexia scholars that phonological core deficits are the prevailing etiology. Of course, it could be argued that what Catts and colleagues were locating is a high incidence of garden-variety poor comprehenders. The design of the study does not permit us to determine whether there is a comprehension strategy bottleneck that is comparable to the bottleneck caused by the phonological core deficit. Even so, the data do suggest that the etiology notwithstanding, a direct attack on comprehension issues is implicated for a large percentage of students with low comprehension performance.

Interactive Model of Reading Disability   Lipson and Wixson (1986) offer a comprehensive framework that could, in principle, accommodate each of the previous perspectives and more. Their model takes a cue from interactive models of reading (e.g., Rumelhart, 1977), which stipulate that reading involves the interactive juggling of multiple sources of information made available from the text (the orthography, the linguistic structure, and other visual cues), the reader (various sources of knowledge about the topic, the lexicon, the genre, the conventions of print, and the like), and the context (the nature of the task, the setting in which it is accomplished, the purpose for which it is completed, the consequences of success or failure) to extract and construct meaning in response to text. In an interactive model of reading, the success of the reader in constructing meaning depends entirely on the juxtaposition of all of those factors in a given situation for a given reader and a given text. The basic argument in Lipson and Wixson's model is that reading disability is not beneath the skin and between the ears (McDermott, 1993; Mehan, 1993), at least not exclusively. Instead it is a temporary, situated condition brought about by a particular constellation of factors. A student is not disabled forever but for this particular text, task, topic, level of support, and/or situation. It follows that for any given student, despite the high level of knowledge and skill that she brings to the task, there will be combinations of these factors that will render her disabled, at least for the moment. The opposite is also true: for any given student, despite the low level of knowledge and skill that she brings to the task, there will be combinations of these factors that will construct her as competent. The task of the teacher in such a model is not to provide assessments to determine how to "fix" kids but instead to find the differential means of support to help all students achieve a given task or successfully understand a given text. When closely analyzed, this perspective is nothing more or less than a form of radical individualized instruction, wherein the teacher's task is to find the right instructional ingredients that form a unique pathway for each and every student. Note also that this is the underlying assumption in the Individualized Educational Plan (IEP) so prevalent in Special Education in the wake of IDEA regulations popularized in the 1980s and 1990s and enduring into the latest iteration of the Individuals with Disabilities Education Act (USDE, 2004). Most important to recognize about the Lipson and Wixson perspective is

that it is a critique of the very construct of disability, a term that implies that the problem resides within the reader rather than in the instructional context in which reading occurs and is taught (McDermott, Goldman, & Varenne, 2006).

Recent Developments   Clearly, the nature of reading difficulties for struggling readers—those with and without diagnosed reading disabilities—is complex. Recent research suggests that this complexity stems from the wide range of individual differences present among any group of readers with difficulties in making sense of print—the distinct profiles of skills, strategies, and dispositions that characterize each individual's reading struggle (see Siegel, 2003, for an account of the cognitive bases of disability and Mann, 2003, for the language bases). Several recent studies, for example, have shown that some struggling readers demonstrate a combination of both poor decoding and poor comprehension skills, while others experience more pronounced difficulties in one area over another, and some show difficulties in other areas such as vocabulary or language skills (Buly & Valencia, 2002; Rupp & Lesaux, 2006).

For example, Buly and Valencia (2002) found several different sub-skill profiles among individuals who shared the common attribute of having failed to reach proficiency on the Washington state test of reading achievement—in other words, students who failed to read for comprehension. For some, the major source of difficulty was poor decoding, for others it was disfluency, for still others there appeared to be vocabulary issues, while for others there seemed to be no explanation other than impaired comprehension itself. Similarly, in a recent review of the research on reading comprehension difficulties among children, Nation (2005) shows that not all reading comprehension difficulties arise from poor decoding skills. Instead, Nation explores the evidence indicating that individuals with purely comprehension-related reading difficulties have deficits in other areas of reading, such as vocabulary knowledge and inference-making abilities, but that they do not necessarily demonstrate problems with phonological processing. And Allington and McGill-Franzen (2008) reach a similar conclusion from their review of the research behind comprehension difficulties among struggling readers by proposing that poor readers fall into one of three general categories: poor at decoding, poor at comprehension, or poor at both.

One critique of these recent studies is that they often fail to distinguish between garden-variety poor readers and dyslexic readers, two populations that might exhibit different symptoms and etiologies for their reading difficulties. However, there is evidence that even when this distinction is made, the same patterns emerge. In a comparison of the reading abilities of students with early- and late-emerging reading disabilities, Leach, Scarborough, and Rescorda (2003) identified three types of readers: (a) those with difficulties at the phonological level but not with comprehension, (b) those with difficulties in comprehension but not with phonological processing, and (c) those with difficulties in both phonological processing and comprehension. These findings from Leach et al. are particularly germane to our discussion because they challenge two common assumptions about reading disabled struggling readers. The first is that reading problems among this population of readers *always* stem from a phonological deficit. The second challenged assumption is that *all* dyslexic students struggle with comprehension.[1]

Finally, after taking all the research into consideration, it is our contention that an omnibus model like Lipson and Wixson's interactive model of disability would provide the broadest possible framework for conceptualizing disability and pointing toward appropriate instructional interventions. More on that score after we have reviewed the available research on approaches to improving comprehension.

Part 2: Approaches to Improving Comprehension for Students with Disabilities

Not surprisingly, the approaches to improving comprehension for students identified as having comprehension problems mirror the various perspectives for conceptualizing the causes and nature of the assumed comprehension deficit.[2] It is important to remember that the recent research of scholars who have examined the skill infrastructure of both garden-variety and reading disabled students with poor comprehension (Allington & McGill-Franzen, 2008; Buly & Valencia, 2002; Leach et al., 2003; Nation, 2005; Rupp & Lesaux, 2006) leads us away from all-or-nothing perspectives to an understanding that the explanations for impaired reading comprehension among struggling readers are as varied as the readers themselves. Furthermore, a fuller understanding of the varied profiles of individuals who struggle to comprehend calls for a more nuanced understanding of how these difficulties are best resolved. In short, by suggesting multiple pathways to comprehension difficulties for both reading disabled and garden-variety struggling readers, the research implies multiple pathways to resolving those difficulties. We now turn to a discussion of three different approaches to remediating comprehension difficulties, each designed to target specific underlying causes of impaired comprehension for students with reading disabilities. As a means of making the discussion manageable and useful, for each approach we explicate one particular curricular program—and mention several others—as a representation of what research would suggest as an effective means of remediating a particular set of issues for a particular type of struggling reader. Readers who want to learn more about approaches that focus on the phonological processes should look carefully at the chapter on this subject by Gaskins (chapter 27 of this volume), while those who want to acquaint themselves with the full array of approaches emphasizing direct comprehension instruction, particularly as they relate to improving narrative and informational text comprehension, should consult the chapters by Almasi and her colleagues (chapter 30 of this volume) and Martin and Duke (chapter 31 of this volume), respectively.

Approach #1: Focus on the Phonological Deficit   Several reading programs are specifically geared toward struggling readers and readers with disabilities whose primary difficulties are at the phonological level—readers who exhibit the phonological core deficit detailed by Stanovich (1988). Thus, these programs focus on providing decoding support as a first step to improving reading (Gaskins, this volume). It must be explicitly noted at the outset that few of these programs focus exclusively on phonological processes; focus and priority better characterize the role of the most recent array of phonologically focused programs. Perhaps this shift is due to the fact that recent reviews show that instruction in phonological skills alone is typically not sufficient to improve the overall reading abilities for most struggling readers, especially older readers whose difficulties with phonological processing have been compounded by being left behind in learning more advanced reading skills (National Reading Panel, 2000; Deshler, Palincsar, Biancarosa, & Nair, 2007). Therefore, most of these programs do incorporate some activities designed to build vocabulary, fluency, and comprehension although each keeps a strong focus on remediating phonological deficits, and it is fair to say that phonological issues are, at a minimum, "first among equals" and likely to assume the lion's share of instructional time.

Lindamood-Bell offers two such programs within a set of three instructional reading programs which, taken together, aim to comprehensively address the language-processing needs of reading disabled students of all ages. We focus our discussion here on the first two of these programs as examples of the wide variety of available reading programs that target decoding issues. They are the Lindamood Phoneme Sequencing Program for Reading, Spelling, and Speech (LiPS) and Seeing Stars.[3] Both programs use explicit and systematic approaches to building phonemic awareness with a great emphasis on repetition and reinforcement of practice until mastery is reached. The aim of LiPS is to build phonemic awareness while Seeing Stars focuses on building orthographic recognition for letters and words.

The LiPS approach to improving phonemic awareness is to draw explicit attention to how sounds are made by the mouth so that students ultimately may become self-correctors (Lindamood-Bell, 2009a). LiPS is multisensory, and students are encouraged to see, hear and feel speech sounds through a five-step instructional model, which includes: (a) Setting the climate for learning, (b) Identifying and classifying speech sounds, (c) Tracking speech sounds, (d) Associating sounds and symbols, and (e) Spelling (encoding) and reading (decoding). There are two ways to navigate LiPS. One way is to follow the Horizontal Path, where students learn all consonants and then all vowels before applying this knowledge to the tracking, spelling and reading of syllables and words. The second way to navigate LiPS is to follow the Vertical Path, where students learn just three consonant pairs and three vowel sounds before beginning to track, spell, and read simple syllables and words (Lindamood & Lindamood, 1998).

The Seeing Stars program is offered as a supplemental program to be used when students continue to struggle with fluent decoding of basic or multi-syllabic words after completing the LiPS curriculum. Seeing Stars is based on dual coding theory (Paivio, 1986) and teaches visualization techniques while also emphasizing the importance of language awareness. The program teaches symbol imagery, or "the ability to visualize the identity, number, and sequence of sounds and letters within words" (Lindamood-Bell, 2009b). Seeing Stars begins instruction by calling attention to symbol imagery before progressing into multisyllabic and contextualized reading and spelling to explicitly and systematically improve reading.

Research on the effectiveness of the two programs when used together is limited, but numerous studies on the LiPS program have found that it improves word level reading skills among children with reading disabilities. The evidence for the effects on reading comprehension is less clear. In one study that looked at the effects of LiPS—in its original, pre-1998 form, when it was called the Auditory Discrimination in Depth Program (ADD)—among kindergarteners with phonological processing disabilities, researchers found improvements in word level reading skills but not in reading comprehension (Torgesen et al., 1999). But in a more recent study comparing ADD with an embedded phonics program for children ages 8 to 10 with severe reading disabilities, researchers found similar positive effects over time on word attack, text reading accuracy, text reading fluency, and passage comprehension for children in both groups, and specifically in terms of reading ability growth rate (Torgesen et al., 2001).

Additional programs that work to improve students' phonological processing difficulties include Benchmark Word Detectives, My Reading Coach, Phono-graphix, Reading is FAME, Saxon Phonics Intervention, Spell Read P.A.T., and the Wilson Reading System. In keeping with the findings evaluating the effectiveness of the Lindamood-Bell decoding-focused programs, the broad sweep of research investigating the efficacy of programs that focus on explicit instruction at the phonological level have reported improvements in rates of reading growth, particularly for children with phonological processing deficits, among both younger (Foorman, Fletcher, Francis, Schatschneider, & Mehta, 1998) and older (Torgesen, 2005) students. The evidence for their effect on improving comprehension is less clear and less frequent. One is also reminded of similar findings in the recent study evaluating the results of a randomized trial comparing Reading First programs, which exhibit a "balanced" curriculum tipped in the direction of phonological level processes, against "business as usual" programs in grades 1–3; again, clear effects on word reading outcomes but no appreciable effects on external measures of comprehension were found (Gamse et al., 2008). Serious design issues, a topic we address in our discussion, complicate a straightforward interpretation of this body of work. Suffice it to say that as the evidence currently stands, transfer to comprehension from phonologically based instruction is the exception not the rule.

Approach #2: Focus on Reading Comprehension Strategies While some reading programs specifically geared toward struggling readers and readers with disabilities are focused on readers that need support with phonological processing in order to improve reading comprehension, other programs focus on the strategic components of reading. While many of these programs are not necessarily targeted exclusively towards students with reading disabilities, they operate on the principle that for many students, reading comprehension will improve through explicit instruction and repeated practice in the use of comprehension strategies. As such, they build on the seminal work of Palincsar and Brown (1984) in the Reciprocal Teaching approach.

Reading Apprenticeship, an intervention model developed by the Strategic Literacy Initiative (SLI) at WestEd to improve reading comprehension among struggling readers and facilitate access to the general education curriculum, is one example of a reading program that operates from this perspective.

One way in which Reading Apprenticeship works to help students become strategic readers is through a ninth-grade Academic Literacy course. This course is grounded in the premise that, "for all students to attain high-level literacy, apprenticeships that demystify the literacy practices and discourses of the academic disciplines must be embedded in subject-area instruction across the curriculum, rather than becoming the sole purview of the English department" (Greenleaf, Schoenbach, Cziko, & Mueller, 2001, p. 89). The Academic Literacy course orchestrates four interacting dimensions—social, personal, cognitive, and knowledge-building—with the overarching goal of demystifying reading by making strategies visible and explicit through ongoing, internal and external metacognitive conversations and "collaborative inquiry" between the teacher as "master reader" and the students. The course consists of three units—reading self and society, reading media, and reading history—all of which are geared toward increasing students' engagement, fluency and competency in reading. As a means of achieving these goals, students explore a series of essential questions, including: What is reading? What do successful readers do when they read? What kind of reader am I? What strategies do I use as I read? What role does reading serve in people's personal and public lives? What kinds of vocabulary can I expect from different texts? What kinds of sentences are found in different kinds of texts? What do I need to know to be able to understand these different kinds of texts?

Explicit strategy instruction serves a central role in addressing these essential questions in the context of the three course units. Through explicit instruction and modeling of the foundational Reciprocal Teaching strategies—which include questioning, summarizing, clarifying, and predicting—students learn to apply these strategies to a variety of different texts. Students also learn an array of additional strategies such as note taking, paraphrasing, and text mapping, in addition to learning how to identify word structure (i.e., root words, prefixes, suffixes), develop semantic networks, and chunk complex sentences and words.

Even though explicit strategy instruction is an important component of the course, the course also focuses on putting students in charge of instruction and decision making in order to facilitate their ability to consider these types of questions and strategies related to reading. Thus, through essential questions and a reciprocal teaching and learning environment, Academic Literacy teachers establish a classroom atmosphere where confusion is acceptable and even necessary as a means through which to gain a deeper understanding of content-area material. That said, helping students to comprehend the material, while a vital component of the course, is not its only goal. Instead of limiting instruction to strategy identification and use, Adolescent Literacy teachers challenge students to think about the situated nature of their reading practices and how this context determines the ways that they approach and read texts. Given all of these other elements, it is probably inaccurate to characterize Reading Apprenticeship as merely a "strategy deficit" improvement approach. It is surely that, but it is also so much more, with its additional emphases on motivation, social learning, endurance, and self-regulation. Even so, strategies are its signature component.

Research on Reading Apprenticeship as it is manifested in the Academic Literacy course reveals positive qualitative and quantitative effects on student achievement and engagement. For example, through a variety of qualitative measures including pre- and post-course reading surveys and case studies of eight focal students, Greenleaf et al. (2001) found profound improvements in reading attitude and confidence among students who completed the Academic Literacy course. Moreover, pre- and post-tests of reading proficiency as measured by the Degrees of Reading Power (DRP) test revealed significant gains in student performance from October to May. Finally, a recent report on the second year of implementation of a randomized evaluative study of the effect of Reading Apprenticeship on the achievement of low-performing ninth-grade students found that the program had a positive and statistically significant impact on participating students' reading comprehension test scores (Corrin, Somers, Kemple, Nelson, & Sepanik, 2008). Given the complex nature of the Reading Apprenticeship model, with its four key components, it is difficult to attribute the success of the program to strategy instruction alone; however, because strategy instruction is at the core of Reading Apprenticeship and knowing from a wide range of other research that strategy instruction matters (see Dole, Nokes, & Drits, 2008; Duke & Pearson, 2002) we can be confident that this focus on strategies is an important factor contributing to students' reading improvements.

Other highly regarded programs that focus on strategy instruction as a means to improving reading comprehension are Reciprocal Teaching and Transactional Strategies Instruction. In general, research supports the efficacy of programs that promote comprehension strategy instruction for garden-variety struggling readers and, more importantly, for reading-disabled students on curriculum-embedded and/or standardized measures (Almasi et al., this volume;

Dole et al., 2008; Duke & Pearson, 2002; National Reading Panel, 2000; Pressley, 2000; Mastropieri & Scruggs, 1997; Dole, Duffy, Roehler, & Pearson, 1991; Palincsar & Brown, 1984; Paris, Cross, & Lipson, 1984; Pearson & Fielding, 1991). A question that remains, however, is the degree to which strategy instruction can be easily implemented and sustained in everyday reading instructional contexts (see Hacker & Tenent, 2002; Benson-Griffo, Kohansal, & Pearson, 2007).[4]

Approach #3: Focus on Balanced, Individualized Instruction   A third instructional approach to improving reading is represented by programs that combine decoding and comprehension strategy instruction in order to meet the needs of a variety of different learners. The assumption underlying this type of program is that since reading difficulties do not stem from one source for all students, a curricular program that provides support for a range of student needs can reach the broadest number of students. Some of the programs that fit this profile include Boy's Town, Reading is FAME, Passport Reading Journeys, Soar to Success, and our focal program, the Strategic Instruction Model (SIM). We focus our discussion on SIM because it is one of the most widely studied programs of this type.

The Strategic Instruction Model (SIM), developed by the University of Kansas Center for Research on Learning (KU-CRL), seeks to improve content literacy for students at a variety of different reading levels by offering a multi-tiered approach to instruction. The program's overarching goal is to create independent and strategic learners, but it also includes a knowledge-building component for teachers. To this dual end, the program combines Content Enhancement Routines, which focus attention on building teacher capacity for content area instruction, with a Learning Strategies Curriculum, which focuses on building students' literacy abilities (Fisher, Schumaker, & Deshler, 2002). The essential components of the Learning Strategies Curriculum are six research-based reading strategies, including: the Word Identification Strategy, the Visual Imagery Strategy, the Self-Questioning Strategy, the Inference Strategy, the Fundamentals of Paraphrasing and Summarizing, and the Paraphrasing Strategy (University of Kansas Center for Research on Learning, 2008).

The routines and strategies that are at the core of SIM as it is manifested in individual classrooms are delivered through a more comprehensive, school-wide program called the Content Literacy Continuum (CLC). The CLC has five levels of sequential support, all of which are geared toward improving the basic literacy skills of at-risk students while simultaneously maintaining the presence of these students in content-area classes so that they do not fall even further behind their peers in terms of content knowledge (Deshler, Schumaker, & Woodruff, 2004). In Level 1: Enhanced Content Instruction, the goal is for students to learn the required core curriculum content regardless of individual literacy levels. In Level 2: Embedded Strategy Instruction, the goal is for students to learn and apply a set of learning strategies in order to master the required core curriculum content. In Level 3: Intensive Strategy Instruction, students who require additional strategy instruction receive more intensive and explicit support. In Level 4: Intensive Basic Skill Instruction, students who require instruction in decoding, fluency, and basic comprehension skills are provided with specialized instruction. In Level 5: Therapeutic Intervention, "students with underlying language disorders learn the linguistic, related cognitive, metalinguistic, and metacognitive underpinnings they need to acquire content literacy skills and strategies" (University of Kansas Center for Research on Learning, 2007, p. 2). Thus, all students, regardless of the underlying causes of their reading difficulties, receive the specific support they require to improve their reading comprehension and, ultimately, their overall content-area knowledge.

While research supporting the effectiveness of SIM on student achievement is extensive, most of the studies to date look at individual components of the program rather than the effects of the program as a whole. Specifically, research has validated many of the strategies that comprise the Learning Strategies Curriculum, particularly as they pertain to students with learning disabilities (see Schumaker, Deshler, Alley, Warner, & Denton, 1982; Clark, Deshler, Schumaker, Alley, & Warner, 1984; Ellis, Deshler, & Schumaker, 1989; Lenz & Hughes, 1990). More recently, Faggella-Luby, Schumaker, and Deshler (2007) investigated the effects of the Embedded Story Structure (ESS) routine—which targets self-questioning, story-structure analysis, and summary writing strategies and employs a graphic device, the ESS Organizer—as compared to another research-based approach to reading comprehension instruction, on the achievement of incoming ninth-grade students. Not only did the authors find that students who were exposed to the ESS routine and accompanying strategies outperformed the control group, but they also found equivalent gains for students regardless of whether or not they had learning disabilities.

Other recent studies also have provided evidence for the effectiveness of specific Content Enhancement Routines on the achievement of both low- and high-performing students, as well as students with learning disabilities. For example, Bulgren, Deshler, Shumaker, & Lentz (2000) recently studied the effects of analogical instruction on students' knowledge of concepts by using the Concept Anchoring Routine in combination with the Concept Anchoring Table. They found that the routine improved the performance of all students, including students with learning disabilities. In a later study, Bulgren, Lenz, Shumaker, Deshler, & Marquis (2002) developed and tested the effectiveness of the Concept Comparison Routine in combination with a graphic device called the Concept Comparison Table. In this case, mean percentage scores were significantly higher for normal-achieving, low-achieving, and learning-disabled students who were exposed to the routine as compared to students who engaged in a lecture-discussion-style instructional format. Significantly, the low-achieving and

learning-disabled students seemed to benefit the most from the routine. While student performance improved in the studies of both routines, in both cases the authors note that these improvements were not always large enough to move the lowest-achieving students from a failing to a passing grade. Moreover, the authors note that more research on the effects of a combination of different routines is necessary in order to determine how routines used together influence student achievement. Despite these concerns, however, SIM provides a comprehensive approach to instruction, particularly within content-area classrooms, by combining reading strategy instruction with a multilevel framework geared toward improving the achievement of all students.

Summary of the Intervention Research Reading programs operate under certain assumptions about the nature of reading difficulties among struggling readers and readers with disabilities. While some programs like LiPS locate reading problems at the phonological level, other programs such as Reading Apprenticeship target motivational and strategic solutions to reading difficulties. Still others such as SIM and its corresponding CLC approach reading difficulties more holistically in an effort to address both phonological and strategic needs as they arise for individual students and classes. It is also clear that proponents of all three approaches understand that combinations of foci are required to meet the needs of all students. In fact, at an implicit if not an explicit level, all three approaches recognize that certain key principles should guide all instruction for students who experience so little success as readers:

1. Students come to us with different needs. Emphasis must be on the individual student. To assume otherwise masks the different instructional approaches that individual students require to become more proficient readers. The three focal programs reviewed here all offer different levels and types of support depending on assessed student needs.
2. Motivation and self-efficacy are critical to long-term growth. They are key issues in reading comprehension—especially for older readers, and all three focal programs try to address these issues.
3. All three programs emphasize long-term outcomes and focus on student autonomy as the ultimate goal. More should do so.

The fact of different profiles of strength and need suggests that educators would do well to ensure instructional breadth in the form of a full menu of interventions for students with comprehension problems. That breadth will have to be achieved in one of three ways: (a) in a single program, such as SIM; (b) by combining programs (e.g., having both LiPS and Reading Apprenticeship available); or (c) by building the capacity to shift the instructional focus as students reveal different profiles of reading skills, processes, and dispositions (a daunting task, but ultimately the most effective and enduring approach).

Part 3: Discussion: Research and Vexing Policy Questions

Research We hope it is clear that the research on understanding the nature, causes, and required instructional interventions for students who exhibit serious comprehension problems is better and more useful than it was 30 years ago. We understand the range of explanations for inadequate reading comprehension much better than we did before, and we know a great deal more about how to promote comprehension through a variety of different interventions. Even so, much remains to be learned.

First, the research on SIM and CLC notwithstanding, it is clear that we need to learn much more about the relationships and interactions among the three sorts of instructional elements implicated in the research we reviewed: phonological processes (decoding and phonemic awareness), reading comprehension strategies, and dispositions that are required for students to succeed in our nation's classroom settings (elements such as stamina, self-efficacy, motivation, and social interaction skills). In particular, small-scale design experiments are needed in which various components of each element are iteratively investigated to achieve an optimal combination of each. Then, and only then, will larger scale efficacy studies be appropriate.

Second (and this follows from the first suggestion), we need to better understand the role of phonological processes. In interpreting the data regarding the effectiveness of phonics-focused programs on improving reading comprehension, it is important to keep in mind that we still have much to learn on this front. Phonological research, for better or worse, is much more characteristic of research for younger readers than older (see Gaskins, this volume), so we clearly need to conduct more work with older readers. We know that some readers can neither decode nor comprehend well, some can decode but not comprehend well, and some can comprehend but not decode well. But we need additional work on both of these basic processes as evidenced in readers with different profiles, and we need research on instructional strategies that try to balance the two. Equally important, there are issues of research design to address. The failure to find outcomes of improved reading comprehension may in part be due to limitations of research design. Much of the research on the effectiveness on phonics-based interventions has focused on evidence of improved decoding and failed to include measures of comprehension. In particular, we need to settle the key question left open in the bottleneck metaphor implied by the phonological core deficit hypothesis: admitting for the moment (and on the basis of substantial evidence) that phonological competence is a necessary condition for successful comprehension, is it also a sufficient condition? The data suggest that the answer is no, but it would be useful to have compelling instructional evidence for the answer. Further, if phonological competence is not sufficient, what else is necessary?

Third, save for phonics, phonemic awareness, and comprehension strategy instruction, we know very little about the efficacy of other important cognitive and instructional processes when it comes to readers with difficulties and/or disabilities in comprehension. Vocabulary seems an obvious candidate for more intensive study with this population of readers. For older readers with disabilities, morphological aspects of word knowledge seem particularly important in light of the salience of reading across the academic disciplines in middle and high schools. Also, as important as language processes are in models of disability (Hoover & Gough, 1990; Mann, 2003), oral language has received little attention in the instructional research for students with difficulties/disabilities in comprehension. Given the crucial role of oral language comprehension in the simple view, this is a surprising omission. If RC = D x LC (reading comprehension is the product of decoding prowess and oral language capacity), why do we not know more about the oral language pedagogy side of the equation? Finally, we have an increasing body of research implicating the importance of discussion and conversation—talk about text (Almasi & Garas-York, 2009; Malloy & Gambrell, chapter 23 of this volume; Murphy, Wilkinson, Soter, Hennessey, & Alexander, in press)—in improving comprehension; some of it shows a differential advantage of discussion of text-related ideas for lower-achieving students (Murphy et al., 2009). However, little of that research is focused on students with disabilities or those with severe comprehension difficulties. This seems to be a serious shortcoming in need of our immediate attention as a field.

Vexing Policy Questions When it comes to policy for students with reading disabilities, we have experienced a sea change in the last decade with the passage of the IDEA act of 2004 (see the chapters by Swerling and by Gaskins, this volume, for more detail on the implications of that legislation). The central question related to our chapter is what this sea change in the policy context might spell for comprehension instruction and interventions.

Response to intervention and reading comprehension. Many scholars in Special Education and regular education have worked collaboratively to replace the long-standing definition of a reading disability as a discrepancy between a student's actual reading performance (as determined by a reliable, valid test of some sort) and her reading potential (as determined by a prediction based on her IQ) with a definition based on how the student responds to a range of instructional interventions—hence the term RTI for Response to Intervention.[5] The policy value of RTI, in comparison to the IQ-achievement discrepancy model, is that it allows for the allocation of resources now supporting special education services to be set aside for compensatory education very early in a child's education. The IQ model usually required a child to be in school for at least 2 years before a discrepancy of substantial magnitude could emerge. But in RTI, just as soon as evidence emerges that a child is not responding well to normal classroom instruction, compensatory resources can be applied. The details of the law and the role that both response and intervention play in this new definition of disability are beyond the scope of this chapter (again, see the chapters by Swerling and by Gaskins, this volume), but, for our purposes, several points need to be reiterated before we can relate the current policies to pedagogical issues surrounding comprehension.

First, instruction is conceptualized as lying in tiers of successively more tailored and more "specific" emphases, ranging from the classroom (the least specific tier and the default intervention for all students), to some sort of more tailored and more intensive classroom or pull-out small group intervention, to individual tutoring (e.g., along the lines of Reading Recovery or the like), to some variation or another of Special Education services driven by an Individualized Education Plan for each student who makes it to that final tier (not unlike the model of SIM and the CLC reviewed earlier).

Second, the instruction or the intervention becomes an assessment in this model. If a student does not respond well to an intervention in one tier, it is taken as prima evidence that he or she needs the more focused and intensive intervention of a deeper level. As suggested earlier, a negative response to instruction in Tier 1 can yield an early transfer to a more focused and intensive tier. Even though the intervention is the key assessment, regular progress monitoring and/or outcome assessments are used to gauge the success of the response for individual students. These two models of assessment are supposed to be aligned in that the progress monitoring assessments allow educators to assess the impact of the intervention.

Third, there is the question of the actual protocol used to deliver the intervention. Two fundamental protocols have been recommended for instructional delivery—the standard treatment protocol and the problem-solving protocol. In the Standard Treatment Protocol (Fuchs and Fuchs, 2006; Vellutino, Scanlon, Small, & Fanuele, 2006), the basic principle is to fully implement a treatment for a full term on the grounds that it is impossible to gauge the success of a student's response on anything short of a full implementation of the intervention cycle. If that intervention does not work, the student moves down a tier to receive a new standard treatment that most likely differs in its intensity and specificity. The move is usually from whole class to small group in the classroom (but it could be a pull out) to tutoring to full Special Education assignment. In the Problem-Solving Protocol (Fuchs & Fuchs, 2006), the same "diagnostic-prescriptive" process is repeated at each tier: determine the nature and magnitude of the problem and its causes, design an individually tailored intervention, conduct it, evaluate progress, and begin the process over again by continuing with or modifying the intervention. Problem solving is, in a very real sense, individualized instruction to the nth degree; it is what educators have come to expect of the IEP process.

Curiously, Fuchs and Fuchs (2006) point out that researchers tend to prefer the Standard Treatment Protocol (STP) while practitioners favor the Problem-Solving Protocol (PSP), which perhaps reflects a difference in worldview. Could it be that practitioners want to make sure that each student receives precisely the combination of tasks, resources, and scaffolds that will ensure success quite irrespective of what the research says about the specific elements or their combinatory effects? Conversely, could it be that researchers want to make sure that the allegedly scientifically proven interventions get the maximum opportunity to do their work?

Fourth, the relationship of the various tiers of intervention to research is crucial because the assumption, particularly in the Standard Treatment Protocol, is that the students are receiving the best treatments that educational science has to offer at each tier, including in the classroom. Otherwise, there would be little justification for leaving students in a treatment for its full course when the preliminary evidence from progress monitoring assessments is that the treatment is not working well for particular students. Other things being equal, it is also desirable if there is curricular articulation between tiers, so that while the focus and intensity of the instruction may change between tiers, the goals and general approach may remain constant (Dorn & Schubert, 2008).

Examined from the broadest of educational perspectives, there is little to quarrel with in the RTI model. It privileges or at least entails many widely respected educational values and research-based principles of pedagogy, as detailed in Table 20.1. These are long-standing hallmarks of effective teaching, remarkably resonant with the very first principle

TABLE 20.1
Instructional Principles Underlying RTI

Label	Principle
Individualized Instruction	There is no one best method of teaching reading, just a best method for a particular child. It is the job of the teacher to find that right combination for every student.
Responsive Assessment	Each step a teacher takes in instruction must be responsive to the evidence provided by the child in the immediately previous performance and/or assessment situation. Increasing instructional depth (down into the skill infrastructure), specificity, and intensiveness are provided on an as-needed basis.
Dynamic Assessment	Instead of giving all students the same task and observing the variability among them, a teacher should ask, What are the differential supports I need to offer various students in order to help them all perform a given task successfully?
"Goldilocks" Pedagogy	Working in the zone of proximal development, a teacher provides just right materials (not too easy, not too hard) and just in time scaffolding (the right clue or support at just the right moment).
Programs fail; students don't	When a student cannot perform successfully in a given tier or with a given set of supports, we should conclude that the instruction has failed, not the student—and the approach should be changed.

outlined in the National Board for Professional Teaching Standards: *Teachers are committed to students and their learning* (NBPTS, 2002).

In relation to the research reviewed in this chapter on reading disability and reading comprehension, these new policy developments have implications, some that might propel comprehension research into a more prominent position and others that might compromise its influence. On the positive side, several of the interventions reviewed in part 2 of this chapter combine the logic of a Standard Treatment Protocol (STP) with the logic of a Problem-Solving Protocol (PSP) in that they represent both a common core treatment with internal provision for between-student differentiation. As such, they appear to be well-suited to allowing a compromise between the two protocols: interventions such as SIM or Reading Apprenticeship can be implemented for a given period of time, as required by the STP, while they allow teachers the opportunity to tailor implementation for individuals, in the spirit of PSP. This is particularly true for the SIM program with its emphasis on providing a balanced array of pedagogical elements within the intervention, but it is also true of Reading Apprenticeship (although the balance is across very different dimensions—comprehension strategies, motivation, and dispositions such as stamina) and many of the other programs only alluded to. Second, both SIM and Reading Apprenticeship are heavy on providing all the scaffolding needed to make students successful; they are "poster child" programs for what we have referred to as Goldilocks (just in time) pedagogy, emphasizing as they do the gradual release of responsibility (Pearson & Gallagher, 1983) from teacher to student for successful task performance as students assume an increasingly independent role in the enactment of the routines taught in the intervention. One would certainly expect to see programs like SIM and Reading Apprenticeship implemented as Tier 2 or Tier 3 interventions in many middle and high school settings. It is interesting to note, in examining the research on effective early interventions, that the most effective kindergarten interventions (e.g., Vellutino et al., 1996) and first-grade interventions, such as Reading Recovery (What Works Clearinghouse, 2008) studied thus far implicate balanced approaches to pedagogy; they could be regarded as early reading analogues of SIM and Reading Apprenticeship.

One of the most welcome features of RTI is that it allows for much earlier intervention than was possible in the earlier IQ-achievement discrepancy models; one does not have to wait for 2 years for a student to fall far enough behind her predicted level of performance to be eligible for special services. In RTI, intervention can occur as early as kindergarten. Given the dominant curricular goals in kindergarten and first grade, an early emphasis on decoding and word reading would be expected in interventions for young readers. However, because of the efficacy of interventions such as Reading Recovery (What Works Clearinghouse, 2008) and the work of Vellutino and colleagues (1996), it may be advisable to add a focus on comprehension. Much of the small group intervention research conducted in the 1990s by researchers such as Hiebert (1994) and Taylor (1995) exhibited a similar balance between word level and comprehension level processes, with lots of provision for active reading of text. There appears, on the basis of a broad sweep of research, a definite place for balanced interventions, even beyond classroom and small group tiers in the RTI model. Perhaps balance, and most particularly provisions for emphasizing comprehension in all tiers within an RTI model, ought to be considered as a serious policy guideline.

The role of assessment in RTI. Whether the assessment promise of RTI can and will be realized is an open question. On the positive side, the two faces of assessment inherent in the model are most welcome additions to our conceptual frame for assessing program impact and student progress. But here the devil will be in the details.[6] The idea that the intervention is the assessment is intriguing because it should mean that programs fail, not students. However, a construct has arisen that has the potential to shift the blame back onto students: treatment resistors (Torgesen, 2000). The notion is that no matter how hard we try to find the right intervention (in the Standard Treatment Protocol) or the right combination of instructional features (in the Problem-Solving Protocol), there may be some students who resist all of our attempts to bring them up to a minimal level of reading performance. A great deal of vigilance will be required as RTI rolls out to make sure that the construct of treatment resistor does not become an all-too-convenient explanation for the failure of programs to meet the needs of students who challenge our attempts to work with them. As a matter of policy, the education profession faces an interesting dilemma: Is it better for teachers to believe that they can make a difference in remediating student performance when they cannot OR to believe that they cannot make a difference when they can? Which is the least worst error as we try to maximize the benefit of our programs and practices? We side with the policy that it is better for teachers to believe that they can make a difference and to teach with that goal as the primary motive for their instruction.

It is not just intervention as assessment that matters for the roll out of RTI. Equally important is the implementation of progress monitoring and outcome assessments. And when it comes to the policy implications of these assessments, the issue is whether they measure reading in its global (broad-based comprehension measures) or atomistic (highly specific tests of skills, perhaps even those taught in the intervention). Surely for programs that claim to improve comprehension, comprehension measures must be included to fairly evaluate the impact of the intervention. We would argue, however, that broad-based measures of comprehension ought to be included for all programs included in a particular RTI system (by system we mean the set of programs operating at various tiers within a school setting). The rationale for this recommendation is that the worth of an intervention, even if the focus is on decoding (or vocabulary or fluency, for that matter), is best measured not by its capacity to improve what was directly taught but rather to improve students' general capacity to read and understand texts on their own. Hence comprehension measures can evaluate the transfer value of any particular intervention to what matters most in reading—understanding what one reads (see Pearson, 2007). And the most compelling question for any intervention is, How far beyond its particular instructional implementation can and will it travel?

Conclusion

In this chapter, we have examined the relationship between reading disability and reading comprehension from three perspectives: how the two relate to one another in terms of basic cognitive processes, how pedagogy can improve students' comprehension performance, and how the current policy context either enables or disables the relationship between disability and comprehension. We have, along the way, raised important questions about the validity and utility of the research we have and the research we need. We have also tried to issue a collective warning to keep our wits about us as we move ahead with new policy initiatives so that teachers, students, and parents are not undermined by the conspiracies of good intentions lurking around every pedagogical corner.

Notes

1. Stanovich's (1980) interactive-compensatory hypothesis predicts that students with limited decoding prowess often rely on rich stores of knowledge and vocabulary to compensate for that limited decoding capacity. There are many cases of famous dyslexics who have masked their poor reading ability by relying on highly developed bodies of knowledge accumulated through experience, listening, viewing, and just about any other non-textual resource.

2. In fact, the three models we discuss in this section parallel three of the four theoretical perspectives popularized in the eighties, and the fourth, the interactive-compensatory model, is intimately connected to the phonological core deficit hypotheses.

3. Visualizing and Verbalizing for Language Comprehension and Thinking (V/V) is the third program in this series of Lindamood-Bell curricula. It is geared toward individuals with weak concept imagery and aims to improve reading comprehension, critical thinking, and expressive language through a series of visualization steps. These steps move sequentially from word- to sentence- to paragraph-level imaging (Florida Center for Reading Research, 2006).

4. Strategy instruction has the distinction, both dubious and exceptional, of having been examined closely in its implementation. This same critique could be leveled at just about any intervention program reviewed in this chapter or any research-based instructional program if it were to be studied as carefully as strategy instruction.

5. Interestingly, the original term used in the discussions between the International Reading Association and the Council for Learning Disabilities was Response to Instruction rather than Response to Intervention. The change is significant because of the implication that interventions are more systematic and codified approaches to remedial instruction.

6. The devil is in the details is a modern adaptation of the original quotation, God is in the details, variously attributed to the poet William Blake or the architect Ludwig Mies Van der Rohe.

References

Allington, R. L., & McGill-Franzen, A. (2008). Comprehension difficulties among struggling readers. In S. E. Israel & G. G. Duffy (Eds.), *Handbook of research on reading comprehension* (pp. 551–568). New York: Routledge.

Almasi, J. F. & Garas-York, K. (2009). Comprehension and discussion of text. In S. E. Israel & G. G. Duffy (Eds.), *Handbook of research on reading comprehension* (pp. 470–493). New York: Routledge.

Benson-Griffo, V., Kohansal, R., & Pearson, P. D. (2007). Curriculum reform in the context of a state mandate. In D. Rowe, R. T. Jiménez, D. L. Compton, D. K. Dickinson, Y. Kim, K. M. Leander, et al. (Eds.), *56th Yearbook of the National Reading Conference* (pp. 323–337). Milwaukee, WI: National Reading Conference.

Bulgren, J. A., Deshler, D. D., Schumaker, J. B., & Lentz, B. K. (2000). The use and effectiveness of analogical instruction in diverse secondary content classrooms. *Journal of Educational Psychology, 92*(3), 426–441.

Bulgren, J. A., Lenz, B. K., Schumaker, J. B., Deshler, D. D., & Marquis, J. G. (2002). The use and effectiveness of a comparison routine in diverse secondary content classrooms. *Journal of Educational Psychology, 94*(2), 356–371.

Buly, M. R., & Valencia, S. W. (2002). Below the bar: Profiles of students who fail state reading assessments. *Educational Evaluation and Policy Analysis, 24*(3), 219–239.

Castles, A., & Coltheart, M. (1993). Varieties of developmental dyslexia. *Cognition, 47*(2), 149–180.

Catts, H. W., Hogan, T. P., & Adlof, S. M. (2005). Developmental changes in reading and reading disabilities. In H. W. Catts & A. Kamhi (Eds.), *The connections between language and reading disabilities* (pp. 25–40). Mahwah, NJ: Erlbaum.

Clark, F. L., Deshler, D. D., Schumaker, J. B., Alley, G. R., & Warner, M. M. (1984). Visual imagery and self-questioning: Strategies to improve comprehension of written material. *Journal of Learning Disabilities, 17*(3), 145–149.

Corrin, W., Somers, M. A., Kemple, J., Nelson, E., & Sepanik, S. (2008). *The enhanced reading opportunities study: Findings from the second year of implementation* (NCEE 2009-4036). Washington, DC: National Center for Education Evaluation and Regional Assistance, Institute of Education Sciences, U.S. Department of Education.

Deshler, D. D., Palincsar, A. S., Biancarosa, G., & Nair, M. (2007). *Informed choices for struggling adolescent readers: A research-based guide to instructional programs and practices.* Newark, DE: International Reading Association.

Deshler, D. D., Schumaker, J. B., & Woodruff, S. K. (2004). Improving literacy skills of at-risk adolescents: A schoolwide response. In D. S. Strickland & D. E. Alvermann (Eds.), *Bridging the literacy achievement gap, grades 4–12* (pp. 86–104). New York: Teachers College Press.

Dole, J. A., Duffy, G. G., Roehler, L. R., & Pearson, P. D. (1991). Moving from the old to the new: Research on reading comprehension instruction. *Review of Educational Research, 61*(2), 239–264.

Dole, J. A., Nokes, J., & Drits, D. (2008). Cognitive strategy instruction: Past and future. In S. E. Israel & G. G. Duffy (Eds.), *Handbook of research on reading comprehension* (pp. 347–372). New York: Routledge.

Dorn, L., & Schubert, B. (2008). A comprehensive intervention model for preventing reading failure: A response to intervention process. *Journal of Reading Recovery, 7*(2), 29–41.

Duke, N. K., & Pearson, P. D. (2002). Effective practices for developing reading comprehension. In A. E. Farstrup & S. J. Samuels (Eds.), *What research has to say about reading instruction* (3rd ed., pp. 205–242). Newark, DE: International Reading Association.

Ellis, A. W. (1985). The cognitive neuropsychology of developmental (and acquired) dyslexia: A critical survey. *Cognitive Neuropsychology, 2,* 169–205.

Ellis, E. S., Deshler, D. D., & Schumaker, J. B. (1989). Teaching adolescents with learning disabilities to generate and use task-specific strategies. *Journal of Learning Disabilities, 22*(2), 108–119.

Faggella-Luby, M., Schumaker, J. S., & Deshler, D. D. (2007). Embedded learning strategy instruction: Story-structure pedagogy in heterogeneous secondary literature classes. *Learning Disability Quarterly, 30*(2), 131–147.

Fisher, J. B., Schumaker, J. B., & Deshler, D. D. (2002). Improving the reading comprehension of at-risk adolescents. In C. C. Block & M. Pressley (Eds.), *Comprehension instruction: Research-based best practices* (pp. 351–364). New York: Guilford.

Florida Center for Reading Research. (2006). *Visualizing and verbalizing.* Retrieved January 18, 2009, from http://www.fcrr.org/fcrrreports/PDF/VisualizingVerbalizing.pdf

Foorman, B. R., Fletcher, J. M., Francis, D. J., Schatschneider, C., & Mehta, P. (1998). The role of instruction in learning to read: Preventing reading failure in at-risk children. *Journal of Educational Psychology, 90*(1), 37–55.

Fuchs, D., & Fuchs, L. S. (2006). Introduction to response to intervention: What, why, and how valid is it? *Reading Research Quarterly, 41*(1), 93–99.

Gamse, B. C., Bloom, H. S., Kemple, J. J., Jacob, T. T., Boulay, B., Bozzi, L., et al. (2008). *Reading First impact study: Interim report.* Washington, DC: Institute of Education Sciences.

Goodman, K. G. (1967). Reading: A psycholinguistic guessing game. *Journal of the Reading Specialist, 4,* 126–135.

Goodman, K. S. (1968). *The psycholinguistic nature of the reading process.* Detroit, MI: Wayne State University Press.

Gough, P. B., Hoover, W. A., & Peterson, C. L. (1996). Some observations on a simple view of reading. In C. Cornoldi & J. Oakhill (Eds.), *Reading comprehension difficulties: Process and intervention* (pp. 1–13). Mahwah: Erlbaum.

Gough, P. B., & Tunmer, W. (1986). Decoding, reading, and reading disability. *Remedial and Special Education, 7,* 6–10.

Greenleaf, C. L., Schoenbach, R., Cziko, C., & Mueller, F. L. (2001). Apprenticing adolescent readers to academic literacy. *Harvard Educational Review, 71*(1), 79–129.

Hacker, D. J., & Tenent, A. (2002). Implementing reciprocal teaching in the classroom: Overcoming obstacles and making modifications. *Journal of Educational Psychology, 94*(4), 699–718.

Hiebert, E. H. (1994). A small group intervention with chapter 1 students. In E. H. Hiebert & B. M. Taylor (Eds.), *Getting reading right from the start: Effective early literacy interventions* (pp. 85–105). Boston: Allyn & Bacon.

Hinshelwood, J. (1907). Four cases of congenital word-blindness occurring in the same family. *British Medical Journal, 2,* 1229–1232.

Hoover, W. A., & Gough P. B. (1990). The simple view of reading. *Reading and Writing: An Interdisciplinary Journal, 2,* 127–160.

LaBerge, D., & Samuels, S. J. (1974). Toward a theory of automatic information processing in reading. *Cognitive Psychology, 6,* 293–323.

Leach, J. M., Scarborough, H. S., & Rescorda, L. (2003). Late-emerging reading disabilities. *Journal of Educational Psychology, 95*(2), 211–224.

Lenz, B. K., & Hughes, C. A. (1990). A word identification strategy for adolescents with learning disabilities. *Journal of Learning Disabilities, 23*(3), 149–158.

Lindamood-Bell. (2009a). *Lindamood Phoneme Sequencing Program for reading, spelling and speech (LiPS).* Retrieved January 18, 2009, from http://www.lindamoodbell.com/programs/lips.html

Lindamood-Bell. (2009b). *Seeing stars: Symbol imagery for phonemic awareness, sight words and spelling.* Retrieved January 18, 2009, from http://www.lindamoodbell.com/programs/seeing-stars.html

Lindamood, P., & Lindamood, P. (1998). *The Lindamood Phoneme Sequencing Program for reading, spelling, and speech* (3rd ed.). Austin, TX: Pro Ed.

Lipson, M. Y., & Wixson, K. K. (1986). Reading disability research: An interactionist perspective. *Review of Educational Research, 56*(1), 111–136.

Mann, V. A. (2003). Language processes: Keys to reading disability. In H. L. Swanson, K. R. Harris, & S. Graham (Eds.), *Handbook of learning disabilities* (pp. 213–228). New York: Guilford.

Mastropieri, M. A., & Scruggs, T. E. (1997). Best practices in promoting reading comprehension in students with learning disabilities, 1976–1996. *Remedial and Special Education, 18*(4), 197–213.

McDermott, R. (1993). The acquisition of a child by a learning disability. In S. Chaiklin & J. Lave (Eds.), *Understanding practice: Perspectives on activity and context* (pp. 269–305). Cambridge, UK: Cambridge University Press.

McDermott, R., Goldman, S., & Varenne, H. (2006). The cultural work of learning disabilities. *Educational Researcher, 35*(6), 12–17.

Mehan, H. (1993). Beneath the skin and between the ears. In S. Chaiklin & J. Lave (Eds.), *Understanding practice* (pp. 241–269). New York: Cambridge University Press.

Murphy, P. K., Wilkinson, I. A. G., Soter, A. O., Hennessey, M. N., & Alexander, J. F. (2009). Examining the effects of classroom discussion on students' comprehension of text: A meta-analysis. *Journal of Educational Psychology.*

Nation, K. (2005). Children's reading comprehension difficulties. In M. Snowling & C. Hulme (Eds.), *The science of reading: A handbook* (pp. 248–265). Oxford, UK: Blackwell.

National Board for Professional Teaching Standards. (2002). *What teachers should know and be able to do.* Arlington, VA: Author.

National Reading Panel. (2000). *Teaching children to read: An evidence-based assessment of the scientific research literature on reading and its implications for reading instruction.* Retrieved January 19, 2009, from http://www.nichd.nih.gov/publications/nrp/upload/smallbook_pdf.pdf

Orton, S. T. (1928). Specific reading disability — strephosymbolia. *The Journal of the American Medical Association, 90,* 1095–1099.

Paivio, A. (1986). *Mental representations: A dual coding approach.* New York: Oxford University Press.

Palincsar, A. S., & Brown, A. L. (1984). Reciprocal teaching of comprehension-fostering and comprehension-monitoring activities. *Cognition and Instruction, 1*(2), 117–175.

Paris, S. G., Cross, D. R., & Lipson, M. Y. (1984). Informed strategies for learning: A program to improve children's reading awareness and comprehension. *Journal of Educational Psychology, 76*(6), 1239–1252.

Pearson, P. D. (2007). An endangered species act for literacy education. *Journal of Literacy Research, 39*(2), 145–162.

Pearson, P. D., & Fielding, L. (1991). Comprehension instruction. In R. Barr, M. L. Kamil, P. Mosenthal, & P. D. Pearson (Eds.), *Handbook of reading research* (Vol. 2, pp. 815–860). New York: Longman.

Pearson, P. D., & Gallagher, M. C. (1983). The instruction of reading comprehension. *Contemporary Educational Psychology, 8,* 317–344.

Pressley, M. (2000). What should comprehension instruction be the instruction of? In M. L. Kamil, P. B. Mosenthal, P. D. Pearson, & R. Barr (Eds.), *Handbook of reading research* (Vol. 3, pp. 545–561). Mahwah, NJ: Erlbaum.

Ritchey, K. D., & Goeke, J. L. (2006). Orton-Gillingham and Orton-Gillingham-based reading instruction: A review of the literature. *The Journal of Special Education, 40*(3), 171–183.

Rumelhart, D. (1977). Toward an interactive model of reading. In S. Dornic (Ed.), *Attention and performance VI* (pp. 573–606). Hillsdale, NJ: Erlbaum.

Rupp, A. A., & Lesaux, N. K. (2006). Meeting expectations? An empirical investigation of a standards-based assessment of reading comprehension. *Educational Evaluation and Policy Analysis, 28*(4), 315–333.

Schumaker, J. B., Deshler, D. D., Alley, G. R., Warner, M. M., & Denton, P. H. (1982). Multipass: A learning strategy for improving reading comprehension. *Learning Disability Quarterly, 5*(3), 295–304.

Siegel, L. S. (2003). Basic cognitive processes and reading disabilities. In H. L. Swanson, K. R. Harris, & S. Graham (Eds.), *Handbook of learning disabilities* (pp. 158–181). New York: Guilford.

Smith, F. (1971). *Understanding reading: A psycholinguistic analysis of reading and learning to read.* New York: Holt, Rinehart, & Winston.

Stanovich, K. E. (1980). Toward an interactive-compensatory model of individual differences in the development of reading fluency. *Reading Research Quarterly, 16,* 32–71.

Stanovich, K. E. (1988). Explaining the differences between the dyslexic and the garden-variety poor reader: The phonological-core variable-difference model. *Journal of Learning Disabilities, 21*(10), 590–604.

Taylor, B. M. (1995). *The early intervention in reading program: Results and issues spanning six years.* Paper presented at the annual meeting of the American Educational Research Association, San Francisco.

Torgesen, J. K. (2000). Individual differences in response to early interventions in reading: The lingering problem of treatment resistors. *Learning Disabilities Research and Practice, 15*, 55–64.

Torgesen, J. K. (2005). Recent discoveries from research on remedial interventions for children with dyslexia. In M. Snowling & C. Hulme (Eds.), *The science of reading: A handbook* (pp. 521–537). Oxford, UK: Blackwell.

Torgesen, J. K., Alexander, A. W., Wagner, R. K., Rashotte, C. A., Voeller, K. K. S., & Conway, T. (2001). Intensive remedial instruction for children with severe reading disabilities: Immediate and long-term outcomes from two instructional approaches. *Journal of Learning Disabilities, 34*(1), 33–58, 78.

Torgesen, J. K., Wagner, R. K., Rashotte, C. A., Rose, E., Lindamood, P., & Conway, T. (1999). Preventing reading failure in young children with phonological processing disabilities: Group and individual responses to instruction. *Journal of Educational Psychology, 91*(4), 579–593.

University of Kansas Center for Research on Learning. (2007). *Content literacy continuum: A framework for guiding the development of schoolwide literacy services in secondary schools.* Retrieved January 19, 2009, from http://www.kucrl.org/featured/brochures/clc_5levels.pdf

University of Kansas Center for Research on Learning. (2008). *Learning strategies.* Retrieved January 19, 2009, from http://kucrl.org/sim/brochures/LSoverview.pdf

U.S. Department of Education. (2004). *IDEA regulations: Individualized education programs* (IEP). Retrieved February 22, 2009, from http://idea.ed.gov/explore/view/p/,root,dynamic,TopicalBrief,10

Vellutino, F. R., Scanlon, D. M., Sipay, E. R., Small, S. G., Pratt, A., Chen, R., et al. (1996). Cognitive profiles of difficult to remediate and readily remediated poor readers: Early intervention as a vehicle for distinguishing between cognitive and experiential deficits as basic causes of specific reading disability. *Journal of Educational Psychology, 88*(4), 601–638.

Vellutino, F. R., Scanlon, D. M., Small, S., & Fanuele, D. P. (2006). Response to intervention as a vehicle for distinguishing between children with and without reading disabilities: Evidence for the role of kindergarten and first grade intervention. *Journal of Learning Disabilities, 39*(2), 157–169.

Wagner, R. K., & Torgesen, J. K. (1987). The nature of phonological awareness and its causal role in the acquisition of reading skills. *Psychological Bulletin, 101*, 192–212.

What Works Clearinghouse. (2008). *Intervention: Reading recovery.* Retrieved February 22, 2009, from http://ies.ed.gov/ncee/wwc/reports/beginning_reading/reading_recovery

21

Writing Difficulties

STEVE GRAHAM AND KAREN HARRIS
Vanderbilt University

Writing is a complex task. It is a goal-directed and self-sustained activity, requiring the skillful management of the writing environment; the constraints imposed by the writing topic; the intentions of the writer(s), and the processes, knowledge, and skills involved in composing (Zimmerman & Reisemberg, 1997). It involves much more than this, however, as writing is a social activity too (Schultz & Fecho, 2000), that includes an implicit or explicit dialogue between writer(s) and reader(s). How and what is written is further shaped by the writer's community as well as the larger contexts in which writing operates (culture, institutional, historical, and so forth). For instance, the shape and texture of writing can differ considerably amongst friends communicating on the internet versus the same friends writing a school report. The cognitive/motivational demands of writing and the social/cultural factors that shape it make writing a demanding task.

Children also recognize that writing is a difficult task. Their explanations for why it so difficult focus on what the writer brings to the task as well as what the environment brings to the writer. One youngster told us that children have difficulty writing because "They don't know how to spell words," whereas another child indicated writing problems stem from thinking problems: "They can only think of a teeny-tiny story or just one sentence." Other children, in contrast, point to the context in which they are situated, as is illustrated in the following commentary: "Some kids don't know how to write because they have never been taught how to write."

In this chapter, we focus on students who experience difficulties learning to write. We begin by briefly considering why it is important for struggling writers to become competent writers. Next, we examine if writing difficulties are common. This is followed by an exploration of the cognitive/motivational as well as social/contextual forces that shape students' writing development. We then examine if struggling writers experience difficulty with these cognitive/motivational factors, and further consider the role of

one contextual factor, quality of classroom instruction, as a contributor to struggling writers' difficulties. Finally, we present evidence-based practices for teaching writing to studens who experience difficulty mastering this skill.

Why is Writing Important?

Writing is one of humankind's most powerful tools, and one of the most influential inventions of all time (Graham, 2006). It allows us to communicate with others who are removed by distance or time, making it possible to initiate and maintain links with family, friends, and colleagues even when we are unable to be with them. Writing can foster a sense of heritage and purpose among larger groups of people. The Chinese, for instance, promoted national unity by adopting a standard system of writing in the third century B.C. Writing also provides a flexible tool for persuading others. Thomas Paine's pamphlet, *Common Sense*, inflamed revolutionary sentiment in colonial America. In fact, the persuasive power of writing is so great that some governments ban certain documents and jail the authors.

Writing's power further resides in its utility as a means for conveying knowledge and ideas. It allows us to gather, preserve and transmit information widely, with great detail and accuracy. The permanence of writing makes ideas more readily available for review and evaluation, providing a useful tool for extending and refining thought (Bangert-Drowns, Hurley, & Wilkinson, 2004). Writing also gives us a useful means for self-expression. We use writing to explore who we are, to combat loneliness, and to chronicle our experiences. This can be beneficial psychologically and physiologically, as writing about one's experiences or problems reduces depression, lowers blood pressure, and boosts the immune system (Swedlow, 1999).

Students who don't learn to write well are at a considerable disadvantage in industrialized and technology oriented countries like the United States. At school, their grades are likely to suffer, especially in classes where written tests and papers are used to assess their academic competence (Graham, 2006). They are also less likely than their more skilled classmates to use writing to support learning in content classrooms. Recent meta-analyses have shown that writing can enhance content learning (Bangert-Drowns et al., 2004; Graham & Perin, 2007a). For example, written summaries can make content more memorable, whereas journal entries can be used to reformulate and extend ideas presented in class or text. These youngsters' opportunities to attend college or the college of their choice are likely reduced, as writing is now used to evaluate applicants' qualifications. At work, writing has increasingly become a gateway for employment and promotion, especially in salaried positions (see reports by the National Commission on Writing, 2004, 2005). Employees in many jobs must be able to create clearly written documents, memorandum, technical reports, and electronic messages. In addition, participation in civic life and the community at large may be restricted, as writing via email and text messaging have become widespread.

How Wide Spread Are Writing Difficulties?

There is no universally agreed upon method for determining prevalence rates for writing difficulties. As a result, there is considerable variation in estimates of how many youngsters are struggling writers. For example, if we used data from the most recent assessment of writing conducted by the National Assessment of Educational Progress (Persky, Daane, & Jin, 2003), we would draw vastly different conclusions about prevalence rates, depending upon which of their achievement levels we emphasized. One pertinent classification is *at basic* level, which describes youngsters who demonstrate only partial mastery of the knowledge and skills needed to successfully meet grade-level writing demands. Another relevant classification is *below basic*, which describes students who do not meet even partial mastery of the relevant skills. If the former achievement level is used to determine the percent of struggling writers (this would include *below basic* and *at basic*), at least two out of every three students would be classified as poor writers. In contrast, if just *below basic* is used to classify students, only 14% to 26% of students would be viewed as struggling writers depending upon their grade level.

Other estimates of the prevalence of writing problems are more consistent with the figures for *below basic* writers presented above. Using a standardized test of story writing skills, Hooper (Hooper et al., 1993) indicated that about 6% to 22% of middle school students experienced significant writing problems (i.e., scored 2 or more standard deviations below a standardized test means). Lower figures were provided by Berninger and Hart (1992), using a sample of primary grade students who had not been referred to special education or other specialized services. They found that 1% to 3% of children had problems with handwriting, 3% to 4% had problems with spelling, and 1% to 3% had problems with written narratives. Thus, estimates of the number of children who are struggling writers depend on how the definition for this construct is operationalized and the aspects of writing that are tested.

Factors That Shape Writing Development

Given its complexity, it is not surprising that there is currently no model or theory of development that fully or adequately captures how writing develops or why some children experience difficulty mastering it. One approach to understanding factors that promote or hinder writing development is through the theoretical lens of models examining how learners move from initial acclimation (novice performance) to competence and even expertise within a specific domain. Another tactic is to apply a social contextual lens for understanding writing development. We consider each of these approaches below.

Development from the Perspective of a Model of Domain Learning   Drawing on a vast body of empirical research, Alexander (1997) devised a model to explain how expertise develops. According to her model, domain specific expertise develops in three stages (i.e., acclimation, competence, and proficiency/expertise), and the road from novice to competent to expert is shaped by changes in a learner's strategic behavior, knowledge, and motivation. These factors have played a central role in developmental changes in a variety of academic domains (e.g., Alexander, Graham, & Harris, 1998; Bjorklund, 1990; Pintrich & Schunk, 1996). Conversely, difficulty with one or more of these factors could presumably hinder writing development. For example, interest (one facet of motivation) or lack thereof in a domain such as writing likely influences how much effort a youngster invests in acquiring discourse knowledge about writing or applying strategic solutions to a writing problem, advancing or impeding their movement towards competence.

Recently, Graham (2006) examined if the available research provided support for the contention that each of these factors (strategies, knowledge, and will [akin to motivation]) contribute to writing development. He included a fourth factor in the model, skills, reasoning that the skills involved in translating ideas into words and transcribing words into text are very taxing, even for mature writers (see Kellogg, 1993), and that mastery of these skills also shape writing development (e.g., as skills become more automatic and less demanding, additional resources are available for carrying out other writing processes).

To determine if strategies, skills, knowledge, or will shape writing development, Graham (2006) examined if: (a) skilled writers possess more of the attribute (e.g., knowledge about writing) than less skilled writers; (b) developing writers increasingly possess the attribute with age and schooling; (c) individual differences in the attribute predict writing performance; and (d) instruction designed to increase the attribute improves writing performance. He argued that a factor (e.g., knowledge) shapes writing development, if each of these tenets is supported by empirical evidence.

For strategies, the empirical literature was "thick" enough to examine two separate processes, planning and revising, in relation to the four tenets above. For planning, the available evidence indicated that it was an important ingredient in writing development, as skilled writers are more planful than less skilled writers, planning becomes increasingly sophisticated with age, individual differences in planning behavior predict writing performance (although most of the research does not control for time-on task, weakening this conclusion), and teaching novice and struggling writers how to plan improves how well they write. The findings were similar for revising, but the weakest link in the chain again involved the predictive validity of individual differences, as revising behavior was generally unrelated to overall writing performance until high school. This may be because young children do not revise much and limit much of their revising efforts to proofreading and minor word changes (Fitzgerald, 1987).

Using the framework above, Graham (2006) also examined the skills of: handwriting/spelling and sentence construction. For handwriting/spelling, he proposed a fifth tenet: elimination of handwriting/spelling via dictation enhances writing performance. The available evidence supported the importance of handwriting/spelling, as all five tenets were supported (e.g., individual differences in both handwriting and spelling predict writing performance and dictation has a positive impact on writing performance). The tenet with the thinnest evidence concerned the positive effect of handwriting/spelling instruction on improving overall writing performance. However, the available studies did show that such instruction enhanced one or more aspects of students' writing, including output, quality, or sentence constructions skills (e.g., Jones & Christensen, 1999).

For the skill of sentence construction, Graham (2006) indicated that the analysis of available data provided guarded support for its importance as a catalyst in writing development. There were caveats for all but one of the four tenets described above. First, there was some evidence that the sentences of better writers are more complex than those of less skilled writers (Hunt, 1965), but these findings do not appear to hold for poor readers (e.g., Houck & Billingsley, 1989). Second, the sentences that students craft become increasingly complex with age, although this varies by task and genre (e.g., Hunt, 1965). Third, individual differences in sentence skills are associated with writing performance in some studies, but this is not always the case and it may vary by genre (e.g., Crowhurst, 1980). Fourth, sentence skills can be improved and such instruction has a positive impact on overall writing quality (Graham & Perin, 2007a, 2007b).

For the factors of knowledge and motivation, Graham (2006) was unable to specifically analyze separate aspects of each (e.g., knowledge of writing genre versus knowledge of writing topics), as the data base was just too thin. As a result for each factor (i.e., knowledge), he aggregated all available data (regardless of aspect) to examine the four tenets. Thus, his conclusions about knowledge and motiva-

tion must be viewed as more general and tentative than the ones drawn for strategies and skills.

In terms of knowledge, Graham (2006) found that the available evidence generally supported all four tenets. Skilled writers' posses more knowledge about writing than less skilled ones (based on a small body of research, where replication across specific aspects of knowledge has not occurred). Developing writers become increasingly knowledgeable with age (much of this research involves genre knowledge). Individual differences in knowledge predict writing performance (especially in terms of topic knowledge). Procedures designed to enhance writing knowledge have a positive impact on writing performance (this proposition is based on only a couple of studies).

For motivation, Graham (2006) reported that skilled writers are more motivated than less skilled ones (based on a few studies mostly involving self-efficacy). However, the tenet that motivation increases with age was not supported, as some aspects of motivation declined over time (i.e., attitude towards writing) and others like self-efficacy increased or declined depending upon the study. Nevertheless, individual differences in motivation (i.e., attitudes, self-efficacy, interest, and writing apprehension) did predict writing performance, and there was a small number of studies showing that efforts to enhance self-efficacy boost writing performance too.

In summary, the available evidence generally supports the contention that strategies, skills, knowledge, and motivation are important ingredients in writing development, and that each is amenable to instruction. As we shall see later in the chapter, struggling writers often have difficulty with one or more aspects of these factors.

Development from the Perspective of a Social Contextual Model   In Alexander's (1997) Model of Domain Learning, little attention was devoted to the influence of social and contextual factors on development. The influence of community, culture, society, institution, politics, and history are pretty much ignored (this does not mean that Alexander is unaware of these factors, as her goal was to develop a mid-level model focusing on cognitive and motivational aspects of development).

A theoretical model developed by Russell (1997) provides a useful lens for considering the role of social and contextual factors in writing development. This model examines how macro-level social and political factors influence micro-level writing actions and vice versa, influencing writing development over time (see also Johnston, Woodside-Jiron, & Day, 2001). The primary units in this model are activity systems, which examine how actors (an individual, dyad, or collective—perceived in social terms and taking into account the history of their involvement in the activity system) use concrete tools (e.g., writing) to accomplish some action with some outcome (this is accomplished in a problem space where students use tools in an ongoing interaction with others to shape an object over time in a shared direction).

Another key feature of Russell's (1997) theory is the concept of genre, which are "typified ways of purposefully interacting in and among some activity system(s)" (p. 513). Genres are stabilized through regularized use of tools (e.g., writing) within and among students, creating a relatively predictable way of interacting with others, but they are only stabilized-for-now structures, as they are subject to change depending upon the context. Newcomers to an established activity system appropriate some of the tools routinely used by others (e.g., a particular structure for writing), but interactions between and among individuals and activity systems can change typical ways of acting (i.e., genres), as they may be modified or abandoned in response to shifting conditions. Russell's (1997) theory emphasizes that writing development is shaped not only by the social and contextual interactions that occur within the classroom, between students and with the teacher, but that macro-level activity systems involving culture, institution, society, and so forth also shape students' development (or lack of progress).

This point is illustrated in Schultz and Fecho's (2000) analysis of the role of social contextual factors in the teaching of writing. They indicated that writing instruction is molded by decisions made outside of the classroom.

We illustrate how macro-level factors can influence classroom activities with two examples. Each of these examples has the potential to hinder or constrain students' writing development. First, teachers may devote more or less time to teaching writing, because of state and federal mandates involving high stakes tests (e.g., more attention will likely be directed to domains that are tested). For example, the No Child Left Behind Act of 2001 (NCLB) puts emphasis on assessing reading and mathematics, but not writing, and this may send a message to teachers that writing is not very important and they should devote little or no time to teaching it. In contrast, most state's high stakes testing programs in writing involve relatively low level writing tasks (Hillocks, 2002), and such tests are likely to drive what is taught during writing time. Second, decisions made by schools districts and schools of education involving the preparation of teachers may positively or negatively impact what happens in the classroom. For example, Graham and Perin (2007a, 2007b) reported that students of teachers trained to use the process approach to writing made greater gains in writing than students of teachers who did not receive such training. Unfortunately, Kiuhara, Graham, and Hawkins (2009) found that 71% of the teachers they surveyed in a national random sample indicated that they received minimal to no preparation to teach writing in their college programs, whereas 44% continued to report the same level of preparation when all other forms of preparation (e.g., inservice and personal) were considered as well.

Characteristics of Struggling Writers

In the previous section, we argued that writing development is shaped by changes in students' strategic writing behaviors, mastery of basic writing skills, knowledge of writing, and motivation to write. As a group, struggling writers experience difficulties in each area. Drawing on a review by Graham and Harris (2002), we consider each of these areas in turn, and provide examples of these difficulties from our own research.

Strategic Behavior Many struggling writers use an approach to writing that functions much like an automated and forward moving content generation program. They compose by creating or drawing from memory a relevant idea, writing it down, and using each preceding phrase or sentence to stimulate the next idea (see Graham & Harris, 1997). This retrieve-and-write process simplifies the task of writing by eliminating the development of rhetorical goals and minimizing the use of planning, monitoring, evaluating, revising, and other strategic behaviors. Little attempt is made to evaluate or rework ideas or to consider the constraints imposed by the topic, the needs of the audience, or the organization of text. Such an approach is not particularly effective for tasks, such as writing an essay, a report, or even a story. These tasks typically require more than just generating or retrieving ideas on-the-fly. A good story, for instance, includes a plot, is organized in a logical manner, and must capture the interest of the intended audience. This requires forethought and planning as well as reflection.

Although content generation typically dominates the composing process of struggling writers, it is a relatively unproductive approach. One of the most striking characteristics of these students' writing is that they produce so little of it. Their papers are inordinately short, containing little elaboration or detail, and once an idea is generated, they are very reluctant to discard it (Graham, Harris, MacArthur, & Schwartz, 1991). It is not that these students lack ideas for their writing. Instead, they appear to have difficulty gaining access to them. When we repeatedly prompted fourth and sixth grade struggling writers to write more once they had completed a writing assignment, they doubled and even tripled their output (Graham, 1990).

Struggling writers' typical method of revising is equally unproductive. They mainly employ a "thesaurus" approach to revision, focusing their efforts on making word substitutions, correcting mechanical errors, and producing a neater product. Less than 20% of their revisions change what was written, whereas two thirds of their changes have either a neutral or negative effect on text (Graham, 1997). The only thing that typically improves across drafts is the legibility of their handwriting.

Writing Skills Many struggling writers experience considerable difficulty with the skills involved in transcribing words into print. They routinely misspell words and ignore or misplace capitalization and punctuation (Graham et al., 1991). Many produce letters slowly, writing at almost half the rate of their more fluent peers (Weintraub & Graham, 1998). These difficulties not only make papers more difficult to read, but can undermine the process of composing in at least three ways (Scardamalia & Bereiter, 1986). One, having to switch attention to a transcription concern, such as how to spell a word correctly, may cause a struggling writer to forget ideas or plans being held in working memory. Two, possible writing content may be lost because writing is not fast enough to keep up with the child's thoughts. Three, struggling writers may have fewer opportunities for planning as they write or to make expressions more precisely fit intentions, if their attention is occupied with transcription concerns.

Although facility with sentence construction is considered an essential element in skilled writing (Hayes & Flower, 1986), there is little information on the sentence construction skills of struggling writers. Difficulties with sentence construction skills is probably not a universal attribute of poor writing, as such difficulties have been evident for some struggling writers (such as low language-ability students in Gilliam & Johnson, 1992), but not others (such as poor readers in Houck & Billingsley, 1989).

Knowledge   Struggling writers' knowledge about writing and its genres, devices, and conventions is often limited (Graham & Harris, 2002). Even with a familiar genre like stories, struggling writers may be unable to identify basic attributes. For example, when we asked a struggling writer to tell his friend what kinds of things are included in a story, he started off on the right track, indicating, "I would tell him main character." He quickly moved into questionable territory with, "A subject, predicate, and main idea." Their incomplete knowledge is also noticeable in what they write, as their stories often omit basic elements such as location, problem, ending, or moral (Graham & Harris, 1989).

Struggling writers view of writing also appears to place too much of an emphasis on form and not enough on substance and process (Graham, Schwartz, & MacArthur, 1993; Wong, Wong, & Blenkinsop, 1989). When we asked a struggling writer to describe good writing, she indicated, "Spell every word right." A second youngster recommended, "Write as neat as you can." A third student advised, "Put your date and name on there...be sure to hold your pencil right." This emphasis on form is evident in their revising behavior too, where they concentrate most of their efforts on repairing mechanical miscues and making text neater (MacArthur & Graham, 1987).

Motivation   One gauge of motivation is persistence. Struggling writers often show little persistence when asked to write. This was illustrated in a study that we conducted with fourth and sixth grade students experiencing difficulty with writing (Graham, 1990). When we asked them to write an essay expressing their opinion on a specific topic, they averaged just 6 minutes of composing time. They only spent 1 minute when they were asked to dictate such an essay. Other researchers have experienced similar problems when working with these students, indicating that these youngsters struggle to sustain their thinking about topics, as evidenced

by their difficulty in producing multiple statements about familiar subjects (Thomas, Englert, Gregg, 1987).

Despite their lack of persistence, little is known about struggling writers' attitudes toward writing. Anecdotal and clinical reports, however, suggest that these students avoid writing whenever possible (Berninger et al., 1997). Paradoxically, struggling writers appear to be more confident about their writing capabilities (i.e., self-efficacy) than is warranted given their competence with this skill. When we assessed the self-efficacy of 10- to 14-year-old struggling writers, they were just as confident about their writing capabilities as their better writing peers (Graham, Schwartz, & MacArthur, 1993). Both groups of students were positive about their capabilities to get and organize ideas for writing, transcribe ideas into sentences, sustain their writing effort, and correct mistakes in their paper. Each group also favorably rated their ability to write reports, stories, and book reports. Although unrealistically high estimates of capabilities may promote persistence in spite of a history of poor performance (Sawyer, Graham, & Harris, 1992), there is a downside. Struggling writers who overestimate their capabilities may fail to allocate the needed effort when writing, believing that this is unnecessary.

In summary, struggling writers experience difficulties with the cognitive and motivational factors that shape writing development. This is not to say, however, that all struggling writers offer the same profile, experiencing difficulties with each of the factors reviewed above. A longitudinal study by Juel (1988) highlights the complexity of this problem. Concentrating just on strategic processes (i.e., fluency of idea generation) and basic writing skills (i.e., spelling), she found that some children had difficulty in only one of these areas, whereas others had difficulty with both.

Quality of Writing Instruction for Struggling Writers

Earlier we argued that a variety of social and contextual factors shape writing development. It is beyond the scope of this chapter to examine all of these factors, but we do address one contextual factor that we think that is particularly important for struggling writers: quality of classroom writing instruction. If consistent quality instruction is not provided, the possibility that students will develop writing difficulties increases. Already existing writing problems are also likely to become worse (Graham & Harris, 2002).

Many teachers have concerns about their preparation and ability to teach students who experience difficulty with learning (Vaughn, Schumm, Jallad, Slusher, & Samuels, 1996). Moreover, it is especially unlikely that teachers will provide high quality writing instruction to struggling writers or students in general, if they have had little formal preparation in this subject area. As the National Commission on Writing (2003) noted "… teachers typically receive little instruction in how to teach writing… Only a handful of states require courses in writing certification, even for elementary teachers…No matter how hard they work, these instructors … are often ill equipped to teach it" (p. 23).

The National Commission on Writing's (2003) concern about teachers' preparation is well founded. In a series of national surveys that we have conducted (Cutler & Graham, 2008; Graham et al., 2008; Kiuhara et al., 2009), many teachers at both the elementary and secondary level told us that their preparation to teach writing was inadequate to nonexistent. It is not surprising, therefore, that the secondary teachers surveyed by Kihura et al. (in press) indicated that they infrequently used evidence-based writing practices in their classroom (these practices were identified in meta-analyses of experimental, quasi-experimental, and single subject research by Graham & Perin, 2007a, 2007b, 2007c). Moreover, the writing assignments that their students were asked to complete rarely involved much in the way of analysis and interpretation (such writing is needed for advanced academic success in high school and college; see Applebee & Langer, 2006). The four most common writing activities assigned by these teachers were writing short answer responses to homework, responding to material read, completing worksheets, and summarizing material read. Only responding to material read likely involved much in the way of analysis and interpretation.

An important ingredient in providing effective instruction to struggling writers is to deliver instruction that is responsive to their needs (Palinscar, Cutter, & Magnusson, 2004). While many teachers adjust their writing program to meet the needs of struggling writers (e.g., see Kiuhara et al., 2009), many do not. For instance, Graham, Harris, Fink-Chorzempa, and MacArthur (2003) found that 2 out of every 5 primary grade teachers made minimal to no adaptations for the struggling writers in their classes.

Our analysis raises a number of concerns about the quality of writing instruction that many students receive. Too many teachers are (a) not adequately prepared to teach writing, (b) provide writing instruction that is not based on evidence-based practices, and (c) fail to make needed adjustments for struggling writers. If we are to maximize the writing development of struggling writers and students in general, it is important that effective writing instruction is provided consistently from one year to the next. It cannot be the providence of a single teacher or several teachers, as writing development takes place over a long period of time (Graham, 2006). In the next section, we provide evidence-based recommendations for teaching struggling writers.

Evidence-Based Writing Instruction

There is no paucity of advice on how to best teach writing. One source of advice comes from professional writers (e.g., King, 2000), who draw on their own experiences and insights to make recommendations. Another source of advice comes from teachers, either directly or indirectly. This can include teachers recommending practices they judge to be effective in their class (e.g., Atwell, 1987). It can also come from those who observe teachers in action and promote the use of specific practices they view as worthwhile (e.g., Graves, 1983). While each of these sources surely possesses considerable wisdom about the teaching of writing (and we will draw on the study of exceptional literacy teachers in forming our recommendations), they possess a number of weaknesses (Graham, in press). One, it is difficult to separate the "wheat from the chaff" and determine what is really important. Two, there is often no direct evidence that a recommended practice actually produces the desired effects. When evidence is provided, it often takes the form of testimonials or the presentation of selected students' writing. Three, when such recommendations are based on the experiences of a single teacher or professional writer (or even a few of each), there is no way to predict if it will be an effective practice for others. Four, such recommendations rarely address the needs of struggling writers.

Another, and more useful, source of information (in our opinion) can be obtained from scientific studies examining the effectiveness of specific writing interventions. This source provides a more trustworthy mechanism for offering recommendations, as such studies provide direct evidence on the effectiveness of a practice as well as how representative the observed effects are and how much confidence can be placed in them (Graham, in press). This is the primary approach that we apply here, drawing on recent meta-analyses of writing interventions tested with experimental, quasi-experimental, and single-subject design studies (Graham, in press; Graham & Perin, 2007a, 2007b, 2007c; Rogers & Graham, 2008). Of course, more confidence can be placed on evidence-based recommendations that are tested repeatedly. As a result, we only offer recommendations for practices that have been tested in 4 or more experiments.

Unfortunately, there is still too much that is unknown to devise an instructional program for struggling writers based solely on empirically tested writing practices. Many aspects of writing instruction have not been sufficiently tested (e.g., the role of vocabulary instruction in writing) to develop a complete program. Consequently, we applied a second method to identify potentially effective writing practices. This involved drawing on a meta-synthesis of qualitative studies that examined the writing practices of teachers and schools that produced exceptional literacy achievement (Graham & Perin, 2007c). The purpose of Graham and Perin's analysis was to identify reoccurring patterns in the writing practices described in the studies reviewed. It was assumed that practices that were used in a majority of the qualitative studies reviewed were potentially more useful than ones that were idiosyncratic to a specific teacher or school.

We first draw recommendations for teaching writing in general (#1–4), as struggling writers typically receive most or all of their writing instruction within the confines of the regular classroom (Graham, Harris, & MacArthur, 2004). As we noted earlier, it is important that all students consistently receive high quality writing instruction during the school years to minimize the number of students who develop writing difficulties and to maximize the development of those who struggle to master this complex skill.

Next, we consider what else needs to be done to maximize the writing development of struggling writers (recommendation #5).

Recommendation 1: Develop a Supportive Environment Where All Writers Can Achieve

Social contextual theorists contend that context plays a critical role in writing development (e.g., Shultz & Fecho, 2000). Exceptional literacy teachers appear to agree with this contention. Many of the practices identified by Graham and Perin (2007c) in their meta-synthesis of qualitative studies examining the practices of such teachers focused on establishing a supportive writing context. The following practices were evident in a majority of the studies reviewed:

- Exceptional teachers are enthusiastic about writing and create a positive environment, where students are constantly encouraged to try hard, believe that the skills and strategies they are learning will permit them to write well, and attribute success to effort and the tactics they are learning.
- Exceptional teachers set high expectations for their students, encouraging them to surpass their previous efforts or accomplishments.
- Exceptional teachers keep students engaged and on-task by involving them in thoughtful activities (such as planning their composition) versus activities that do not require thoughtfulness (such as completing a workbook page that can be finished quickly, leaving many students off-task).
- Exceptional teachers mix teaching to the whole class with teaching to small groups and with one-on-one interactions with individual students.
- Exceptional teachers model, explain, and provide guided assistance when teaching.
- Exceptional teachers provide just enough support so that students can make progress or carry out writing tasks and processes, but encourage students to act in a self-regulated fashion, doing as much as they can on their own.

Basically, exceptional teachers establish a writing context which is enjoyable and affirming, where students are expected and encouraged to do their best work. Students in these classrooms are also engaged in meaningful work, and their teachers support them by teaching them how to write, providing individualized instruction as needed, while carefully considering just how much assistance is needed. We recommend that teachers apply these same practices when teaching writing to all students.

Recommendation 2: Require That All Students Write

Writing is the foundation of an effective writing program. While this may seem like an obvious observation, it is important to reemphasize it here. According to the National Commission on Writing (2003), students spend a relatively small percentage of their time during a week actually writing, and substantial writing assignments (3 or more pages) are infrequent, even for high school students. This prompted the commission to recommend that the amount of time devoted to writing should be doubled.

Writing was a critical part of the programs of exceptional literacy teachers in Graham and Perin's (2007c) meta-synthesis. They dedicated considerable time to writing and writing instruction. Writing occurred across the curriculum (the empirical evidence also suggests that writing can enhance content learning; Bangert-Drowns et al., 2004; Graham & Perin, 2007a). Finally, exceptional teachers involved their students in various forms of writing over time. It is important to caution, however, that just increasing the amount of time students spend writing is unlikely to be enough to maximize students' development (see Graham & Perin, 2007b). Without proper motivation (see previous section) and careful instruction (see below), writing by itself may be of limited value (Braddock also recognized this in his seminal review in 1969).

Recommendation 3: Help All Students Develop Writing Strategies, Skills, Knowledge, and Motivation

The Model of Domain Learning (Alexander, 1997) examined earlier (as well as Graham's 2006 review of its feasibility for writing development) suggests that an important goal in writing instruction is to help students become more strategic, master basic writing skills, increase their knowledgeable about writing, and enhance their motivation. These same goals are supported by both the study of exceptional literacy teachers and schools (Graham & Perin, 2007c) and empirical studies that test the effectiveness of specific writing practices.

First, exceptional teachers (Graham & Perin, 2007c) not only encourage their students to treat writing as a process (involving planning, drafting, revising, editing, and sharing), but they also teach students strategies for planning, drafting, and revising. These practices were further supported in the experimental, quasi-experimental, and single subject design studies conducted with more typical teachers and summarized by Graham and colleagues. The practices below improved the quality of students' writing.

- The use of a process approach to writing, where students are encouraged to plan, translate, review, and share their work was others (Graham & Perin, 2007a).
- Explicitly teaching students strategies for planning, summarizing, revising, and editing (Graham & Perin, 2007a; Rogers & Graham, 2008). Teaching such strategies can facilitate writing across genres. For example, we found that teaching a story planning strategy that involved generating ideas for the basic parts of a story (i.e., story grammar) improves not only story writing, but writing personal narratives as well (Harris, Graham, & Mason, 2006).
- The development of arrangements where students cooperatively work together to plan, draft, revise, and edit their compositions (Graham & Perin, 2007a).
- Having students engage in pre-writing activities, includ-

ing inquiry and graphic organizers, that help them obtain and organize ideas for writing (Graham & Perin, 2007a; Rogers & Graham, 2008).

Second, the exceptional teachers in Graham and Perin's (2007c) meta-synthesis not only taught their students writing strategies, they taught them basic writing skills, such as spelling and sentence construction. The practice of teaching basic writing skills also found support in Graham and Perin's (2007a) meta-analyses, as teaching regular students how to combine simpler sentences into more complex ones (i.e., sentence combining) had a positive impact on the quality of their writing.

Third, some support for the importance of efforts to increase students' knowledge about writing was obtained in the analysis of experimental and quasi-experimental literature conducted by Graham and Perin (2007a). They found that asking students to analyze and emulate critical elements embodied in good models of writing improved the quality of their writing.

As noted earlier, exceptional teachers in the meta-synthesis by Graham and Perin (2007c) enhance motivation by creating a positive atmosphere, engaging students' in meaningful activities, and promoting an "I can do attitude" (e.g., fostering the belief that what students are learning as well as effort permits them to be successful). In a meta-analysis of single-subject design research, Rogers and Graham (2008) further found that reinforcement can increase students' writing productivity.

Recommendation 4: Have All Students Use Word Processing to Write   Although word processing and computers do not appear to play a major role in regular classroom writing instruction (e.g., see Graham et al., 2003), the quality of students' writing can be boosted when they use this tool as their primary mode of composing (see the meta-analysis by Graham & Perin, 2007a). The effective use of word processing involves a variety of different arrangements, ranging from students working collaboratively on assignments using personal laptop computers to learning how to use word-process compositions under teacher guidance. It further includes the use of word processing programs that have other programs, such as spell checkers, bundled together as part of the software package.

Recommendation 5: Make Adaptations and Provide Additional Instruction for Struggling Writers   Exceptional literacy teachers in Graham and Perin's (2007c) meta-synthesis recognized the importance of attending directly to the varying needs of their students. They adapted both writing assignments and instruction to better meet the needs of individual youngsters. Adaptations can take various forms with struggling writers, including the use of different procedures for specific students, providing extra instruction for others, and modifying how something is taught. We identify a variety of evidence-based adaptations for struggling writers below.

One adaptation that may be useful with struggling writers is to set clear and specific goals for what they are to accomplish in their writing. This can improve how much they write (Rogers & Graham, 2008) as well as the quality of their writing (Graham & Perin, 2007a). Goals can specify how much students are expected to write (e.g., 3 pages) as well as the purpose of the assignment and its characteristics.

Another adaptation that can enhance the quality of struggling writers' compositions is to provide extra handwriting, spelling, or typing instruction to students who experience difficulty acquiring these skills (Graham, in press). This can be effective for both elementary and middle school students.

Although traditional grammar instruction is not an effective instructional practice for students in general (Graham & Perin, 2007a), teaching grammar can have a positive impact on struggling writers under the following conditions (Rogers & Graham, 2008). This involves the teacher modeling how to use the skill correctly, coupled with student practice applying it. Taught skills should be reviewed periodically.

It may also be useful to modify how struggling writers are taught strategies for planning, revising, and editing. The Self-Regulated Strategy model (Harris & Graham, 1996; Harris, Graham, Mason, Friedlander, 2008) was especially powerful in improving the overall quality of struggling writers' compositions (see Graham & Perin, 2007a; Rogers & Graham, 2008). This approach to strategy instruction differs from other methods in several important ways. In addition to directly teaching specific strategies, students are taught the knowledge needed to use the strategies effectively as well as self-regulation procedures (goal setting, self-assessment, self-instructions, and self-reinforcement) for managing the use of the strategies, the writing process, and their writing behaviors. Moreover, instruction is criterion-based and adapted to individual students' needs.

Directly teaching struggling writers frameworks for writing paragraphs can also be beneficial (Rogers & Graham, 2008). An example of such a framework is to show the type of paragraph in the first sentence; list the type of details you plan to write about; order the details; write the details in complete sentences; and cap off the paragraph with a concluding, passing, or summary sentence (Moran, Schumaker, & Vetter, 1981)

Finally, it is especially important to use certain practices with struggling writers. Word processing, for example, has an even greater effect on the quality of these students' writing than it does for youngsters in general (Graham & Perin, 2007a). Reinforcement for productivity, graphic organizers (such as a story web), and sentence instruction have also had a positive impact with these students (Rogers & Graham, 2008).

Concluding Comment

Although we emphasize the use of evidence-based practices for teaching struggling writers in this chapter, it is important to emphasize that this is a challenging task. Just because a practice was effective in a research study or an exceptional teacher used it does not guarantee that it will be effective in all other situations. The safest course of action for a teacher using one of the evidence-based practices reported here is to monitor continually its effects to gauge directly whether it is effective under the new conditions.

References

Alexander, P. A. (1997). Mapping the multidimensional nature of domain learning: The interplay of cognitive, motivational, and strategic forces. In M. L. Maehr & P. R. Pintrich (Eds.), *Advances in motivation and achievement* (Vol. 10, pp. 213–250). Greenwich, CT: JAI Press.

Alexander, P., Graham, S., & Harris, K. R. (1998). A perspective on strategy research: Progress and prospects. *Educational Psychology Review, 10*, 129–154.

Applebee, A., & Langer, J. (2006). *The state of writing instruction: What existing data tell us.* Albany, NY: Center on English Learning and Achievement.

Atwell, N. (1987). *In the middle: Reading, writing, and learning from adolescents.* Portsmouth, NH: Heinemann.

Bangert-Drowns, R., Hurley, M., & Wilkinson, B. (2004). The effects of school-based writing-to-learn interventions on academic achievement: A meta-analysis. *Review of Educational Research, 74*, 29–58.

Berninger, V. W., & Hart, T. (1992). A developmental neuropsychological perspective for reading and writing acquisition. *Educational Psychologist, 27*, 415–434.

Berninger, V., Vaughn, K., Abbott, R., Abbott, S., Rogan, L., Brooks, A., et al. (1997). Treatment of handwriting problems in beginning writers: Transfer from handwriting to composition. *Journal of Educational Psychology, 89*, 652–666.

Bjorklund, D. (Ed.). (1990). *Children's strategies: Contemporary views of cognitive development.* Englewood Cliffs, NJ: Erlbaum.

Braddock, R. (1969). English composition. *Encyclopedia of educational research.* New York: MacMillian.

Crowhurst, M.. (1980). Syntactic complexity and teachers' quality ratings of narrations and arguments. *Research and the Teaching of English, 14*, 223–231.

Cutler, L., & Graham, S. (2008). Primary grade writing instruction: A national survey. *Journal of Educational Psychology, 100*, 907–919.

Fitzgerald, J. (1987). Research on revision in writing. *Review of Educational Research, 57*, 481–506.

Gilliam, R., & Johnson, J. (1992). Spoken and written language relationships in language/learning children. *Journal of Speech and Hearing Research, 35*, 1303–1315.

Graham, S. (1990). The role of production factors in learning disabled students' compositions. *Journal of Educational Psychology, 82*, 781–791.

Graham, S. (1997). Executive control in the revising of students with learning and writing difficulties. *Journal of Educational Psychology, 89*, 223–234.

Graham, S. (2006). Writing. In P. Alexander & P. Winne (Eds.), *Handbook of educational psychology* (pp. 457–478). Mahwah, NJ: Erlbaum.

Graham, S. (in press). Teaching writing. In P. Hogan (Ed.), *Cambridge encyclopedia of language sciences.* Cambride, UK: Cambride University Press.

Graham, S., & Harris, K. R. (1989). A components analysis of cognitive strategy instruction: Effects on learning disabled students' compositions and self-efficacy. *Journal of Educational Psychology, 81*, 353–361.

Graham, S., & Harris, K. (1997). Self-regulation and writing: Where do we go from here? *Contemporary Educational Psychology, 22*, 102–114.

Graham, S., & Harris, K. R. (2002). Prevention and intervention for struggling writers. In M. Shinn, G. Stoner, & H. Walker. (Eds.), *Interventions for academic and behavior problems II: Preventive and remedial approaches* (pp. 589–610). Bethesda, MD: National Association of School Psychologists.

Graham, S., Harris, K. R., Fink-Chorzempa, B., & MacArthur, C. (2003). Primary grade teachers' instructional adaptations for weaker writers: A national survey. *Journal of Educational Psychology, 95*, 279–293.

Graham, S., Harris, K. R., & MacArthur, C. (2004). Writing instruction. In B. Wong (Ed.), *Learning about learning disabilities* (3rd ed., pp. 281–313). Amsterdam: Elsevier.

Graham, S., Harris, K., MacArthur, C., Schwartz, S. (1991). Writing and writing instruction with students with learning disabilities: A review of a program of research. *Learning Disability Quarterly, 14*, 89–114.

Graham, S., Harris, K. R., Mason, L., Fink-Chorzempa, B., Moran, S., & Saddler, B. (2008). How do primary grade teachers teach handwriting: A national survey. *Reading & Writing: An Interdisciplinary Journal, 21*, 49–69.

Graham, S., & Perin, D. (2007a). *Writing new: Effective strategies to improve writing of adolescents in middle and high school.* Washington, DC: Alliance for Excellence in Education.

Graham, S., & Perrin, D. (2007b). A meta-analysis of writing instruction for adolescent students. *Journal of Educational Psychology, 99*, 445–476.

Graham, S., & Perin, D. (2007c). What we know, what we still need to know: Teaching adolescents to write. *Scientific Studies in Reading, 11*, 313–336.

Graham, S., Schwartz, S., & MacArthur, C. (1993). Knowledge of writing and the composing process, attitude toward writing, and the self-efficacy for students with and without learning disabilities. *Journal of Learning Disabilities, 26*, 237–249.

Graves, D. 1983. *Writing: Teachers and children at work.* Exeter, NH: Heinemann.

Harris, K., & Graham, S. (1996). *Making the writing process work: Strategies for composition and self-regulation* (2nd ed.). Cambridge, MA: Brookline Books.

Harris, K. R., Graham, S., & Mason, L. (2006). Improving the writing, knowledge, and motivation of struggling young writers: Effects of self-regulated strategy development with and without peer support. *American Educational Research Journal, 43*, 295–340.

Harris, K. R., Graham, S., Mason, L., & Friedlander, B. (2008). *Powerful writing strategies for all students.* Baltimore, MD: Brookes.

Hayes, J., & Flower, L. (1986). Writing research and the writer. *American Psychologist, 41*, 1106–1113.

Hillocks, G. (2002). *The testing trap: How state writing assessments control learning.* New York: Teachers College Press.

Hooper, S. R., Swartz, C., Montgomery, J., Reed, M. S., Brown, T., Wasileski, T., et al. (1993). Prevalence of writing problems across three middle school samples. *School Psychology Review, 22*, 608–620.

Houck, C., & Billingsley, B. (1989). Written expression of students with and without learning disabilities: Differences across grades. *Journal of Learning Disabilities, 22*, 561–565.

Hunt, K. (1965). *Grammatical structures written at three grade levels.* Champaign, IL: National Council of Teachers of English.

Johnston, P. H., Woodside-Jiron, H., & Day, J. (2001). Teaching and learning literate epistemologies. *Journal of Educational Psychology, 93*(1), 223–233.

Jones, D., & Christensen, C. (1999). Relationship between automaticity in handwriting and students' ability to generate written text. *Journal of Educational Psychology, 91*, 1–6.

Juel, C. (1988). Learning to read and write: A longitudinal study of 54 children from first through fourth grade. *Journal of Educational Psychology, 80*, 437–447.

Kellogg, R. (1993). *The psychology of writing.* New York: Oxford University Press.

King, S. (2000). *A memoir of the craft: On writing.* New York: Pocket.

Kiuhara, S., Graham, S., & Hawkins, L. (2009). Teaching writing to high school students: A national survey. *Journal of Educational Psychology, 101*, 136–160.

MacArthur, C., & Graham, S. (1987). Learning disabled students composing under three methods of text production: Handwriting, word processing, and dictation. *Journal of Special Education, 21*, 22–42.

Moran, M. R., Schumaker, J. B., & Vetter, A. F. (1981). *Teaching a paragraph organization strategy to learning disabled adolescents*

(Research Rep. No. 54). Lawrence, KS: Institute for Research in Learning Disabilities.

National Commission on Writing. (2003). *The neglected "R."* New York: College Entrance Examination Board.

National Commission on Writing. (2004, September). *Writing: A ticket to work or a ticket out: A survey of business leaders*. Retrieved from http://collegeboard.com

National Commission on Writing. (2005, July). *Writing: A powerful message from State government*. Retrieved from http://www.college board.com

Palinscar, A., Cutter, J., & Magnusson, S. (2004). A community of practice: Implications for learning disabilities. In B. Wong (Ed.), *Learning about learning disabilities* (3rd ed., pp. 485–510). Amsterdam: Elvesier.

Persky, H. R., Daane, M. C., & Jin, Y. (2003). *The nation's report card: Writing 2002*. (NCES 2003–529). U.S. Department of Education. Institute of Education Sciences. National Center for Education Statistics. Washington, DC: Government Printing Office.

Pintrich, P., & Schunk, D. (1996). *Motivation in education*. Englewood Cliffs, NJ: Erlbaum.

Rogers, L., & Graham, S. (2008). A meta-analysis of single subject design writing intervention research. *Journal of Educational Psychology, 100,* 879–906.

Russell, D. (1997). Rethinking genre in school and society: An activity theory analysis. *Written Communication, 14,* 504–554.

Sawyer, R., Graham, S., & Harris, K. (1992). Direct teaching, strategy instruction, and strategy instruction with explicit self-regulation: Ef-fects on learning disabled students composition skills and self-efficacy. *Journal of Educational Psychology, 84,* 340–352.

Scardamalia, M., & Bereiter, C. (1986). Written composition. In M. Wittrock (Ed.), *Handbook of research on teaching* (3rd ed., pp. 778–803). New York: MacMillan.

Schultz, K., & Fecho, B. (2000). Society's child: Social context and writing development. *Educational Psychologist, 35,* 51–62.

Swedlow, J. (1999). The power of writing. *National Geographic, 196,* 110–132.

Thomas, C., Englert, C., & Gregg, S. (1987). An analysis of errors and strategies in the expository writing of learning disabled students. *Rememdial & Special Education, 8,* 21–30.

Vaughn, S., Schumm, J., Jallad, B., Slusher, J., & Samuels, L. (1996). Teachers' views of inclusion. *Learning Disabilities Research and Practice, 11, 96–106.*

Weintraub, N., & Graham, S. (1998). Writing legibly and quickly: A study of children's ability to adjust their handwriting to meet common classroom demands. *Learning Disabilities Research and Practice, 13,* 146–152.

Wong, B., Wong, R., & Blenkinsop, J. (1989). Cognitive and metacognitive aspects of learning disabled adolescents' composing problems. *Learning Disability Quarterly, 12,* 300–322.

Zimmerman, B., & Reisemberg, R. (1997). Becoming a self-regulated writer: A social cognitive perspective. *Contemporary Educational Psychology, 22,* 73–101.

22

Motivation and Reading Disabilities

Mark J. Van Ryzin
Oregon Social Learning Center

Introduction

Issues related to motivation have become more prominent in the field of reading research, especially with regards to students experiencing reading difficulties (Bernard, 2006; Guthrie & Alao, 1997; Guthrie & Davis, 2003; Thorkildsen, 2002). Children who are more motivated to read, especially those who are intrinsically motivated (i.e., those who read for the joy of reading), will read more, and more broadly, than children possessing lower levels of motivation (Guthrie, Wigfield, Metsala, & Cox, 1999; Wigfield & Guthrie, 1997). In addition, children struggling to learn to read often possess maladaptive beliefs and goals that can impact their motivation, and the nature of the classroom and school environment can exacerbate the situation. Addressing these individual beliefs and goals and altering student perceptions of the learning environment can play an important role in overcoming reading difficulties.

Motivation is a particularly salient issue for middle and high school. Research has found a general decrease in student motivation as students progress through their secondary school years (Gottfried, Fleming, & Gottfried, 2001; Otis, Grouzet, & Pelletier, 2005), with an especially large drop occurring at the transition between elementary and secondary school (Anderman, Maehr, & Midgley, 1999; Harter, 1981). For as many as half a million adolescents each year, this gradual process of disengagement culminates in dropping out of school before graduation (National Center for Educational Statistics, 2001). The theories reviewed in this chapter can provide an explanation for this drop in motivation and give teachers powerful tools to address the motivational challenges they encounter.

The initial focus in this chapter will be on individual factors that can impact motivation, such as student beliefs and values. Following this will be a discussion of the link between motivation and student perceptions of themselves and their learning environment. Finally, this chapter will address the ways in which students' orientation toward their goals can impact motivation. In each case, space limitations permit only a high-level overview of key motivational theory and a brief discussion of the implications for instruction. In addition, space limitations do not permit the inclusion of factors outside of the school, such as the relationship between literacy motivation and the home environment (e.g., Baker & Scher, 2002). Readers interested in a more in-depth treatment of general motivational research are referred to Wigfield and Eccles (2002) and/or Pintrich and Schunk (1996); those interested in specific applications of motivational theory to literacy are referred to Pressley et al. (2003) and/or Verhoeven and Snow (2001).

Individual Beliefs

Individual beliefs can impact motivation in three keys ways: expectancies regarding success on a task (i.e., Expectancy-Value Theory), causal attributions for success or failure on a task (i.e., Attribution Theory), and cognitions regarding the ability to exert control over success or failure (i.e., Control Theory). Each of these will be discussed in turn.

Expectancy-Value Theory Individual motivation on a task can be understood as a function of the individual's beliefs about how well they will do on the activity (i.e., their *expectancy* of success) and the extent to which they feel that the activity is important or worthwhile (i.e., the *value* they place on the task). When students consider how well they will do on a task, expectancy-value theorists consider both *ability beliefs* and *expectancy beliefs*. Ability beliefs refer to beliefs about *current* levels of competency on a given task, while expectancy beliefs refer to beliefs regarding *future* success on similar tasks. Ability beliefs interact with the perceived difficulty of the task to determine expectancy beliefs regarding success on the task, which in turn impacts motivation (Wigfield, 1994; Wigfield & Eccles, 1992). Both are domain- or task-specific.

Students' beliefs about their ability and expectancies for success can predict subsequent grades even when previous performance is controlled; further, ability and expectancy beliefs predict those outcomes more strongly than previous grades (Meece, Wigfield, & Eccles, 1990). At the same time, students' subjective task values can influence their intentions to continue with a subject as well as their actual decisions to do so (Wigfield et al., 1997). There are several aspects of task value believed to be important to motivation:

- The *attainment value* of the task: the importance of the task to the individual;
- The *intrinsic value* of the task: the enjoyment obtained by the individual in executing the task;
- The *utility value* of the task: the usefulness of the task in terms of meeting current or future goals.

Also considered is the *cost* of the task, which is the amount of resources (time, effort, and concentration or emotion) that will be required to complete the task. This is often seen in economic terms as an *opportunity cost*, in which the decision to engage in the activity prohibits the expenditure of those personal resources on other activities.

Developmental changes. In general, younger children have higher levels of ability-related beliefs, and these beliefs begin to decline as early as elementary school, particularly in domains related to academic achievement (Eccles et al., 1993; Wigfield et al., 1997). These declines often continue throughout secondary school, with the largest changes occurring immediately after the elementary-to-secondary school transition (Eccles et al., 1989; Wigfield, Eccles, Mac Iver, Reuman, & Midgley, 1991).

Children's subjective values also decline, although these declines vary across domain. Eccles et al. (1993) found that older elementary school-aged children value math, reading, and instrumental music less than younger children did. In a longitudinal follow-up to these cross-sectional analyses, Wigfield et al. (1997) found that students' beliefs about the usefulness and importance of math, reading, instrumental music, and sports activities decreased over the 3 years of the study. Later research determined that decreases in competence beliefs accounts for much of the age-related decline in task values (Jacobs, Lanza, Osgood, Eccles, & Wigfield, 2002). However, student interest in reading and instrumental music also decreased over time, while their interest in math and sports did not (Wigfield et al., 1997). This finding demonstrates that instruction in reading may imply specific challenges that do not exist in other domains.

Implications. There are two different explanations for the negative changes in students' beliefs and values over time. One explanation is that as students get older, they become much better at understanding and interpreting the evaluative feedback they receive and engage in more social comparison with peers. As a result of these comparisons, many students become more accurate or realistic in their self-assessments and their beliefs become relatively more negative (Stipek & MacIver, 1989). A second explanation is that the school environment makes student-vs.-student comparisons more salient (e.g., more whole-class instruction, more public evaluations, etc.) as children move from elementary to secondary school and thus lowers the achievement beliefs of some students (Eccles, Midgley, & Adler, 1984; Eccles et al., 1993; Feldlaufer, Midgley, & Eccles, 1988). In either case, teachers concerned with promoting increased expectancies of success among students, especially struggling readers, can reduce ability comparisons by creating a less competitive, more broadly supportive learning environment. Less whole-class instruction and fewer public evaluations reduce the opportunity for ability comparisons, and the goal structure of the classroom can be made more interdependent through techniques such as cooperative learning (Johnson, Johnson, & Holubec, 1984; Sharan & Shaulov, 1990; Slavin, 1977) and peer tutoring (Maheady, Mallette, & Harper, 2006; McMaster, Fuchs, & Fuchs, 2006). For example, literacy instruction that requires students to read aloud to the entire class could be seen as encouraging ability comparisons and competitiveness and thus reducing motivation; in contrast, teams of 2 or 3 students reading aloud to one another and actively coaching and supporting each other to attain group-based goals would likely promote greater motivation. In addition, giving students the opportunity to choose reading texts based upon personal interest could increase the perceived value of reading as an important skill.

Attribution Theory Attribution theory points to the importance of individual *causal ascriptions*, or the perceived causes of success and failure (Weiner, 1979, 1985). The human instinct to understand and explain creates a desire to assign causality to outcomes, which can aid in understanding and long-term adaptation. According to Attribution Theory, three causal dimensions are believed to exist: *locus* (e.g., internal vs. external), *stability* (e.g., stable vs. unstable), and *controllability* (e.g., controllable vs. uncontrollable). These dimensions guide future goal expectations as well as affective reactions to goal attainment (or lack thereof).

Causal ascriptions. A wide range of causal ascriptions have been documented in the literature (see Weiner, 1985, p. 550). Two of the most important are ability and effort. Success can be ascribed to high ability and/or hard work, while failure can be ascribed to low ability and/or lack of effort. Ability can be seen as internal and stable, while effort is internal and unstable.

There are also causal ascriptions that are external to the individual; two of the most common are task difficulty and luck. Task difficulty can be seen as external and stable, while luck can be seen as external and unstable. Thus, the two dimensions of *locus* (e.g., internal vs. external) and *stability* (e.g., stable vs. unstable) can form a 2 × 2 matrix, which includes other common attributions, such as fatigue

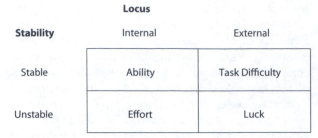

Locus

Stability	Internal	External
Stable	Ability	Task Difficulty
Unstable	Effort	Luck

Figure 22.1 The 2 × 2 attributional matrix.

(unstable and internal) and teacher behavior (stable and external). This matrix is presented in Figure 22.1.

Following the identification of these two dimensions of causal attributions, researchers noted that the causal ascriptions in each portion of the matrix were not necessarily equal. For example, effort and fatigue are both internal and unstable, but are not equally controllable (i.e., effort is controllable while fatigue may not be). Thus the dimension of *controllability* was identified and incorporated into attribution theory (Weiner, 1985).

Attribution theory emphasizes that the individual's perception of the cause of success and failure will determine future goal expectancies on similar tasks, which then guide on-going motivation (Dweck, 1975; Weiner, 1985). If the cause of success is internal and controllable (e.g., effort), then expectations of success are increased, as is motivation. If the cause of success is external (e.g., luck or task difficulty), then effort is seen as having no impact on future outcome and motivation is decreased. If stable, internal causes are the basis for attributions of success (e.g., ability) or failure (e.g., lack of ability), then future goal expectancies and motivation can either rise (in response to a success) or fall (in response to a failure).

Affective reactions. All three dimensions of causal attributions play a role in the affective experiences related to success or failure (Weiner, 1985). In the attributional model, cognitions of increasing complexity will impact the emotional experience. Initially, attribution-independent emotions will be experienced, with an individual experiencing happiness after success and sadness or frustration after failure. Following this, attribution-dependent emotions may come into play. For example, guilt can result from internal and controllable attributions of failure (e.g., low effort), while shame can arise from internal, uncontrollable attributions (e.g., lack of ability). Further, the locus of the causal attribution can influence self-perceptions, with internal attributions influencing self-esteem and self-worth and external attributions having no impact on self-perceptions.

Implications. In general, attributing success to hard work and failure to lack of effort will result in greater levels of on-going motivation (Dweck, 1975). Attributing success to ability can increase self-esteem but also carries some level of risk. Ability attributions can drive increased perceptions of competence when a student experiences success, but if a student is not successful and believes that failure is due to

lack of ability, he/she can fall victim to learned helplessness (Abramson, Seligman, & Teasdale, 1978). If suffering from learned helplessness, a student will exhibit negative emotion, strategy deterioration, and disengagement in school as negative attributions and self-beliefs and low levels of performance create a feedback loop, dragging down student motivation (Fincham & Cain, 1986; Nolen-Hoeksema, Girgus, & Seligman, 1986; Peterson & Seligman, 1984).

Teachers faced with helpless students can undertake "attributional retraining," which has been shown to improve both student performance and persistence (Försterling, 1985). This retraining can be as simple as coaching a student to ascribe a failure to a lack of effort rather than a lack of ability, which can aid even the most "helpless" children (Dweck, 1975). As pointed out by Johnston and Winograd (1985), failure attributions of task difficulty and/or inappropriate strategy selection are also constructive in that each replaces more damaging ability attributions and provides clues as to the path to success. When combined with instruction and modeling of specific reading strategies (e.g., thinking aloud; see Walker, 2005), attributional retraining has proven to be particularly effective with underachieving readers (Borkowski, Weyhing, & Carr, 1988; Fowler & Peterson, 1981).

When working with helpless students, Weiner (1980) emphasizes the role played by the teacher's attributions regarding student failure. If a teacher judges that a student is incapable of succeeding (for reasons of low intelligence, impoverished background, etc.), then the teacher may express sympathy or pity, reduce expectations for student performance, and provide even more help; however, these actions can contribute to student ability attributions and thus to helplessness and even more failure. In contrast, if a teacher believes that a student is capable but has not exerted the necessary effort, then he/she would express dissatisfaction with student performance, continue to emphasize high expectations, and may even reduce the help that is provided, all of which communicate that low effort, rather than lack of ability, is the cause of failure. Thus, effectively dealing with helplessness requires teachers to be aware of how their behavior contributes to student attributions. Above all, when dealing with helpless students, Johnston and Winograd (1985) emphasize that helplessness should be viewed by teachers as a temporary learning problem, not a permanent trait.

Control Theory An early theory of control hypothesized that an individual's attempts to effectively interact with the environment were an expression of an intrinsic human need that was labeled *effectance motivation* (White, 1959). The importance of successful displays of competence was also emphasized as part of Maslow's (1954) hierarchy of human needs. Maslow believed that a feeling of competence was a fundamental building block in the process of self-actualization.

A significant advance in control theory was the differentiation between different loci of control. External events can be seen as under the individual's control (i.e., an internal locus of control) or, in contrast, controlled by luck or chance (i.e., an external locus of control; Rotter, 1966). The focus in control theory at this stage was on the individual's expectations of how certain actions would (or would not) lead to various outcomes.

Connell (1985) extended Rotter's theory of internal and external loci of control to include the notion that the two supposed polar opposites were in fact two separate dimensions, with each dimension containing several independent factors (i.e., internal control beliefs such as ability and effort, and external control beliefs such as luck, powerful others, and unknown sources). This increasing differentiation in the concept of control was considered to be a function of an individual's age and psychological development, with the ability to perceive subtle variations in control not emerging until middle or late adolescence (Skinner, 1991).

A new conceptualization of control was offered by Skinner, Chapman, and Baltes (1988), who defined perceived control as including overall control beliefs (beliefs regarding the ability to achieve a given outcome), as well as means-end beliefs (beliefs about how certain actions can achieve certain outcomes) and agency beliefs (expectations as to whether the individual is able to take the necessary actions). Although control beliefs may appear to be a redundant combination of means-end and agency beliefs, Skinner et al. (1988) demonstrated that the three categories of beliefs are separate factors that contribute uniquely to the measurement of perceived control.

Student perceptions of control influence academic achievement across the entire age spectrum from grade school to college, considering both academic and intelligence-based outcome measures (Findley & Cooper, 1983; Skinner, Zimmer-Gembeck, & Connell, 1998). This finding holds even when controlling for various combinations of gender, socioeconomic status (SES), and race.

Developmental changes. Longitudinal research demonstrates that, in general, control beliefs decline as students get older (Skinner et al., 1998). In addition, the relationship between control and achievement is stronger for adolescents than for children and adults, indicating that perceived control plays an especially important role for middle and high school students (Findley & Cooper, 1983). For example, older students' beliefs about the role of effort in academic achievement are more closely linked to experiences with teachers when compared to younger children, and older children also tend to believe more strongly in the ability of "powerful others" (such as teachers) to impact their academic outcomes (Skinner et al., 1998).

Implications. The developmental changes in students' control beliefs highlight the critical role of teachers in encouraging more adaptive student beliefs. Teachers can enhance perceived control in the classroom through the provision of a consistent structure, or **contingency**, where clear requirements are presented, paths to success are outlined,

and relevant feedback is provided (Skinner, Wellborn, & Connell, 1990). Students who perceive themselves as being able to operate within this classroom structure to exercise control over the outcomes of their learning experiences are more highly motivated (Harter & Connell, 1984) and more actively engaged in learning (Pintrich & DeGroot, 1990; Skinner et al., 1990; Skinner et al., 1998). Students high on perceived control beliefs seek out challenges and actively engage in learning in order to satisfy the need for competence and mastery, whereas students with low perceptions of control avoid challenge and display pessimism and passivity (Boggiano, Main, & Katz, 1988; Harter & Connell, 1984).

Students with low perceptions of control often suffer from negative evaluations of their own ability (Skinner et al., 1998). Such children often require more dedicated support and attention from teachers, which can include detailed step-by-step instructions and modeling in the use of learning strategies, which promotes greater understanding of *how* to succeed, as well as frequent feedback that recognizes student effort and progress, which promotes a stronger belief in the ability to take the actions necessary to succeed (see Margolis & McCabe, 2006).

Perceptions

Perceptions play a significant role in motivational theory. In this chapter, we consider both perceptions of self and perceptions of the learning environment.

Self-Perceptions   Self-perceptions have been studied under a number of guises, including self-worth (Covington, 1992), self-esteem (Harter, 1996), and self-efficacy (Bandura, 1977, 1994). Rather than exploring the differences among the theories, the focus in this section is on the similarities and their implications for instruction.

Students who perceive themselves as being academically competent and thus able to manage and cope with their learning experiences in school are more motivated to succeed (Harter & Connell, 1984). This increased motivation contributes to greater success in school, which leads to higher self-evaluations of academic competence, positive affect, and ultimately to higher intrinsic motivation. In contrast, students with low perceptions of ability tend to avoid challenging learning activities and do not experience as much success in school; thus, once formed, negative self-perceptions can be self-perpetuating and difficult to overcome.

These self-perceptions begin forming early in life as infants begin to evaluate their own ability to influence their immediate environment (Bandura, 1994). These emerging self-perceptions are carried forward to the preschool period, where a child's own track record of success and failure as well as the tone of parental and teacher feedback (i.e., positive and encouraging versus negative and discouraging) can have a direct influence on the child's sense of self (Bandura, 1994). As children develop cognitively, they are able to develop more specific self-perceptions in different domains (i.e., academic, social, athletic).

After the transition from elementary to secondary school, students perceive an increase in competition and greater emphasis on grades, which leads many students to re-evaluate their self-perceptions of academic competence; this re-evaluation puts many students at risk for lowered self-perceptions of competence (Harter, 1996). To avoid threats to self-esteem, many students choose instead to procrastinate, put forth minimal effort, make excuses, and denigrate the importance of academics (Covington, 1992).

Implications   Self-perceptions of ability, worth, and competence can have a direct influence on students' performance in school, which in turn can influence self-perceptions in a reciprocal fashion (Guay, Marsh, & Boivin, 2003). Students with more positive self-beliefs will exert more effort and, when encountering failure, will redouble efforts to succeed (MacIver, Stipek, & Daniels, 1991). Learning tasks that are moderately challenging and that correspond to proximal rather than distal goals are most effective in fostering greater motivation and more positive self-perceptions (Bandura, 1994).

As discussed in Pressley et al. (2003), teacher behavior can undermine student motivation by unconsciously communicating low expectations for students, which in turn can influence students' self-perceptions. For example, Brophy and Good (1970) found that teachers pay less attention to those students whom they consider to be lower in ability, interact with them in a less positive way (i.e., less feedback and praise, more criticism), and hold them to lower standards (see also Brophy, 1983). As a result, Pressley et al. (2003) emphasize high yet realistic expectations for all students and a conscious effort to avoid ignoring or criticizing even the most difficult student.

For students already suffering from negative self-perceptions, several steps can be taken. First, students can be encouraged to focus on the learning process itself (such as the use of a particular learning strategy) rather than the product (the final grade). Second, students can be encouraged to set specific, proximal, and challenging yet attainable goals (such as reading and understanding an article or chapter), rather than general or global goals (such as learning to read or catching up to grade level). Third, feedback can be given regularly and constructed in a way that encourages students to link their progress to their use of specific learning strategies. This approach has been shown to create more positive self-perceptions and increase motivation and performance in struggling readers (Schunk & Rice, 1987, 1989, 1991).

Perceptions of the Learning Environment   Perceptions of the learning environment can exert a powerful influence on motivation, especially with regards to literacy (Gambrell, 1996; Guthrie & Alao, 1997; Guthrie & Davis, 2003; Turner, 1995). In this section, we focus on two environmental factors: the opportunity for student self-management and

choice in the classroom (autonomy); and the feeling of warmth and support from teachers and peers (belongingness or relatedness).

Autonomy.   Erikson (1950) was among the first to argue that the need for autonomy is innate and that a frustration of this need during childhood and adolescence would lead to maladaptive behavior and neuroses. Subsequently, deCharms (1968) argued that all humans strive for personal causation, or to be the origin of their own behaviors. More recently, Steinberg (1990) has emphasized adolescence as a time where the need for autonomy, particularly from parents and teachers, is particularly strong.

Teachers are able to support the need for autonomy while maintaining a sense of control in the classroom by involving students in the creation of rules and boundaries and in setting the direction for learning (Koestner, Ryan, Bernieri, & Holt, 1984). High-autonomy situations such as these stimulate student motivation, engagement, and persistence, which in turn results in higher levels of achievement (Deci, Nezlek, & Sheinman, 1981; Deci, Schwartz, Sheinman, & Ryan, 1981; Flink, Boggiano, & Barrett, 1990; Ryan & Grolnick, 1986; Vansteenkiste, Simons, Lens, Sheldon, & Deci, 2004). In contrast, a controlling approach in the classroom, in which students have little or no voice, creates a reduced perception of autonomy, which can interfere with student learning, especially with regards to more complex tasks (Grolnick & Ryan, 1987). A controlling approach could include commanding language (i.e., must, have to, etc.), micro-management of student actions, and little opportunity for student choice in meeting class requirements.

An emphasis on autonomy is also seen in research on literacy. For example, Guthrie and Alao (1997) present a set of design principles that include self-direction, a synonym for autonomy. Guthrie and Davis (2003) also call attention to autonomy in school; they suggest that teachers "negotiate what seems a fair amount of work on assignments, allow students a bit of choice in the order in which they do their work, and give students some say in how they write up their work" (pp. 75–76). Turner (1995) also discusses the importance of students having some control over the course of their learning; as a result, students can align learning tasks with personal interests, making reading more personally relevant and increasing motivation.

Belongingness.   Belongingness (sometimes referred to as relatedness) is a measure of the depth and quality of the interpersonal relationships in an individual's life. The need to belong, or the need to form strong, mutually supportive relationships and to maintain these relationships through regular contact, is a fundamental human motivation that can affect emotional patterns and cognitive processes (Baumeister & Leary, 1995). Supportive relationships can serve to buffer the impact of stressful life events, leading to superior adjustment and well-being (Cohen & Wills, 1985).

Early models of belongingness emphasized the ability

of interpersonal relationships to generate feelings of being understood, validated, and cared for, which in turn led to the development of an individual's self-esteem and social skills (Sullivan, 1953). In his hierarchy of human needs, Maslow (1954) believed that the need for belongingness and love had to be at least partially satisfied before the needs for achievement and self-actualization would emerge.

The relevance of these models to the adolescent educational environment has been well-documented. Evidence exists for the importance of student friendships, positive peer relations, and teacher-student relationships in supporting high levels of motivation and achievement in school (Berndt & Keefe, 1995; Marks, 2000; Ryan & Grolnick, 1986; Ryan, Stiller, & Lynch, 1994; Wentzel, 1994, 1997; 1998; Wentzel, Barry, & Caldwell, 2004; Wentzel & Caldwell, 1997). Further, an emphasis on relationships and collaboration in school is also found in research on interventions for struggling readers (Guthrie & Alao, 1997; Guthrie & Davis, 2003; Ostrosky, Gaffney, & Thomas, 2006).

Implications. Research has found that traditional secondary school environments often provide very little autonomy and belongingness, which could help to explain why student motivation tends to decrease during the transition from elementary school. For example, secondary school environments typically offer fewer opportunities for students to exercise choice in the classroom (Eccles et al., 1993; Feldlaufer, Midgley, & Eccles, 1988; Midgley & Feldlaufer, 1987) and more controlling behavior by teachers (Midgley, Feldlaufer, & Eccles, 1989; Eccles et al., 1993), which reduce perceptions of autonomy. During the transition from elementary school, students also experience a decrease in perceptions of teacher support, fewer opportunities for interaction and cooperation with peers, and less positive student/teacher relationships (Feldlaufer et al., 1988), which reduce belongingness.

Thus, teachers working with struggling students, especially at the secondary-school level, can promote higher levels of motivation by finding ways to offer students more choices, which in turn makes learning more relevant and encourages personal responsibility. As discussed by Guthrie and Alao (1997), this implies that "teachers enable students to assume responsibility for learning by helping them select … topics, texts, tasks, and media" (p. 99). When combined with an emphasis on self-expression in articulating their understanding of texts, students can achieve a level of personal relevance and ownership of the reading experience that strongly promotes continuing motivation to read (Guthrie & Alao, 1997).

Literacy research also emphasizes collaboration as a technique to promote greater motivation (Guthrie & Alao, 1997; Guthrie & Davis, 2003; Pressley et al., 2003; Turner, 1995), which is in line with the research on belongingness. Among the techniques promoted by Guthrie and colleagues (1997, 2003) is cooperative learning (e.g., Johnson et al., 1984; Sharan & Shaulov, 1990; Slavin, 1977), but peer

tutoring (Maheady et al., 2006; McMaster et al., 2006) could also be used. With these techniques, students are working more directly with one another in pairs or small groups and are striving to achieve group goals as well as individual goals.

In response to the notion that teacher-student relationships become less positive and supportive after the transition to secondary school, some secondary schools have implemented advisory programs, in which a teacher meets periodically with a small group of students over an extended period (Galassi, Gulledge, & Cox, 1997; Rappaport, 2002). In these programs, the advisor becomes a permanent part of a student's school experience and the relationship can last for several years. Advisor and advisee can meet either one-on-one or in a group setting and meetings generally take place at least once a day. Although not extensive, some research exists demonstrating that these programs can promote more positive behavioral, social, and academic outcomes for students (Galassi et al., 1997).

Goals

Motivation can be strongly impacted by the nature of a student's goals while in school. Goal theory documents how different goals (e.g., to succeed vs. to avoid failure) can influence student behavior in the classroom. Goal theory is also comprehensive in that it involves both individual and environmental factors.

Individual Differences Students' goals in the classroom arise out of their beliefs regarding the nature of ability and effort. Younger students tend to assume that demonstrated ability in the classroom is a result of the effort put forth; as children get older, however, some experience a shift in which ability and effort are seen to be inversely related, with great effort implying a *lack* of ability (Nichols, 1978). These beliefs influence the goals that are adopted in classroom situations.

In general, goal theory identifies two different types of goals: (a) *mastery goals*, also known as *learning* or *task-oriented goals*; and (b) *performance goals*, also known as *ego-oriented goals* (Ames & Archer, 1988; Dweck & Leggett, 1988; Nichols, 1984). A mastery goal orientation indicates that a student is engaging in an academic activity for the purpose of gaining a skill or understanding a topic, and such students are more invested in learning, put forth more effort, implement more effective learning strategies, process information more deeply, and seek help when needed (Elliott & Dweck, 1988; Graham & Golan, 1991; Meece, Blumenfeld, & Hoyle, 1988; Midgley, Arunkumar, & Urdan, 1996; Midgley & Urdan, 2001; Miller, Behrens, Greene & Newman, 1993; Nolen, 1988). In contrast, a performance goal orientation implies that a student's purpose is to either demonstrate superiority over peers or to avoid the appearance of failure. A student with a performance goal orientation is mainly concerned with appearances and the opinions of others, and such students tend to endorse the belief that the expenditure of great effort implies a lack of ability. As a result, learning under a performance goal orientation tends to be shallower, less effort is exerted, and less effective learning strategies are used. When failure does occur, performance-oriented students either deny the importance of academic achievement or attribute their results to lack of ability and exhibit negative emotion, strategy deterioration and disengagement (i.e., learned helplessness; Abramson et al., 1978).

In later research on goal theory, the performance goal orientation was divided into two distinct components based upon the purposes underlying student behaviors. Students whose purpose was to demonstrate superiority (or at least normative competence) were considered to possess a "performance-approach" orientation, and students whose purpose was to avoid the appearance of failure were considered to have a "performance-avoidance" orientation (Elliot & Harackiewicz, 1996, Elliot & Church, 1997). Whereas the mastery goal orientation arises from a need for achievement and the performance-avoidance orientation arises from the fear of failure, the performance-approach orientation is influenced by both (Elliot & Church, 1997). Students with more positive self-beliefs will be more likely to endorse a mastery or performance-approach orientation, while those with more negative self-beliefs (i.e., a high expectancy of failure) will tend to adopt performance-avoidance goals. Students with a performance-approach orientation tend to demonstrate superior academic performance when compared to students with a performance-avoidance orientation, and performance avoidance is associated with lower levels of motivation and higher levels of learned helplessness. However, a performance-approach orientation is not always conducive to greater achievement, and in fact may lead to more negative outcomes, such as widespread cheating and a hyper-competitive school climate (Midgley, Kaplan, & Middleton, 2001). As a result, performance-approach goals may be most effective when they are accompanied by mastery goals.

Environmental Factors   Research demonstrates that the psychological environment of the classroom and the school as a whole can have an impact on the goals adopted by students (Ames & Archer, 1988; Maehr & Midgley, 1991; Meece et al., 1988). A classroom or a school with a mastery goal orientation is perceived by students as valuing deep understanding over rote memorization, recognizing effort rather than just results, and providing opportunities for students to succeed on their own terms instead of in comparison to others. In contrast, a school with a performance goal orientation is perceived as emphasizing outcomes rather than effort, playing favorites among students, and giving up on students who struggle the most.

Students who perceive a mastery goal orientation in a classroom or school will tend to adopt mastery goals, while student who perceive a performance orientation will tend to adopt performance-related goals (Ames & Archer, 1988;

Elliott & Dweck, 1988). For students with more negative self-beliefs, this implies the possibility of a performance-avoidance orientation, which has been found to be harmful to motivation and academic performance (Elliot & Church, 1997). As a result, a mastery orientation at the classroom or school level has been linked to higher levels of motivation and academic achievement, as well as greater student well-being among the student body (Anderman et al., 1999; Roeser, Midgley, & Urdan, 1996).

Implications   Research has found that elementary schools are more likely to be oriented toward mastery goals, while secondary schools are more likely to promote performance goals (Anderman et al., 1999; Anderman & Midgley, 1997; Midgley, Anderman, & Hicks, 1995). For teachers looking to promote a mastery goal orientation and discourage a performance orientation, particularly at the secondary school level, the research literature provides a wide variety of strategies. For example, more complex, challenging tasks and more opportunity for student input into learning activities can promote a mastery goal orientation; in addition, teachers can emphasize mistakes as an acceptable part of learning, encourage students to take risks academically, and express sincere beliefs in the capacity of all students to learn and succeed (Ames, 1990, 1992).

Of particular interest in reducing performance goal orientation is any practice that encourages students to compare themselves with others, which can harm self-esteem and dampen motivation. Practices that encourage student-to-student comparisons are often related to reward and recognition, both in the classroom and at the school level (Ames, 1990). For example, the use of an "Honor Roll" that recognizes student performance without considering effort can be seen as harmful to motivation (Anderman & Maehr, 1994); in its place, schools can develop a mechanism that rewards the greatest individual progress or the most significant personal improvement (e.g., the "On a Roll," rather than the "Honor Roll"). Whole-class instruction and ability grouping can also provide opportunities for ability comparisons and should be minimized as much as realistically possible; more collaborative techniques such as cooperative learning (Johnson et al., 1984; Sharan & Shaulov, 1990; Slavin, 1977) and peer tutoring (Maheady et al., 2006; McMaster et al., 2006) are preferred. Even if whole-class instruction cannot be entirely abandoned, the use of some collaborative techniques can still pay dividends in terms of student motivation. Finally, students should be encouraged to focus on their own individual improvement rather than their standing with regards to their peers, implying that some mechanism by which to periodically assess and track individual progress is necessary. Johnston and Winograd (1985) suggest that student self-assessment can be constructive in that it not only provides a means by which to make students more aware of their own progress but also forces attention on the details related to learning outcomes, such as the amount of effort exerted and the strategies used.

Conclusion

Several consistent themes run through this chapter, and these are encountered across many different theories of motivation. The findings can be distilled to provide a series of guideposts that can assist those who seek to inspire struggling readers. They include:

Instructional Approaches. The research endorses a variety of approaches, including attributional retraining, explicit instruction and modeling of reading strategies (e.g., thinking aloud), and consistent, targeted feedback. Students should set specific, proximal, and challenging yet attainable goals, and should focus on the process (i.e., use of a particular reading strategy) rather than the product (i.e., the final grade). Teachers should maintain high yet realistic expectations for all students and should make a conscious effort to give appropriate attention and support to even the most difficult student. Students can be taught to self-assess their own progress, which can help to develop the metacognitive skills needed for long-term success. When working with helpless children, teachers can encourage students to question their initial maladaptive explanations for events and to consider more unstable explanations for failures (e.g., lack of effort, task difficulty, poor strategy selection) and more internal explanations for successes (e.g., effort, ability); teachers must also maintain high expectations for student performance and avoid attributing persistent failure to lack of ability.

More Choice. Teachers are advised to create more opportunities for students to exercise some form of control over their reading instruction; for example, this could include allowing students to choose their own reading materials or topics, the methods of assessment, or the reward structure. Such changes can make reading more relevant and thus more interesting, and enhance the perception of reading as a valuable skill.

Less Competition, More Collaboration. Teachers should strive to reduce ability comparisons among students by creating a less competitive, more broadly supportive learning environment. Less whole-class literacy instruction and fewer public evaluations reduce the opportunity for ability comparisons. The emphasis in evaluations should be on self-improvement rather than trying to out-shine other readers; implied in this is that individual literacy skills are assessed regularly, perhaps by the students themselves, so that students see their own progress and learn to link their efforts and strategy selection to their outcomes. More interdependence among students can be encouraged through techniques such as cooperative learning and peer tutoring, which imply more student-to-student interaction as well as more interdependent goal structures (i.e., group or classroom goals and rewards in addition to individual goals/rewards).

More Positive Relationships. Relationships are of paramount importance in learning to read. A sense of support from peers and teachers encourages students to take risks and strive to achieve without fear of failure or embarrassment, and trusting relationships make students more open to advice, coaching, modeling, and social influence. Techniques like cooperative learning, peer tutoring, mentoring, or some type of advisory system can encourage stronger, more positive relationships. Beyond this, something as simple as a caring, patient, and supportive demeanor in the classroom can be a valuable tool for promoting more positive relationships.

Taken as a whole, the motivational literature can be seen as very complex and nuanced. However, the common themes identified in this chapter provide a comprehensive approach that teachers and school leaders can use to help students struggling to learn to read.

References

Abramson, L. Y., Seligman, M. E. P., & Teasdale, J. D. (1978). Learned helplessness in humans: Critique and reformulation. *Journal of Abnormal Psychology, 87,* 49–74.

Ames, C. (1990). Motivation: What teachers need to know. *Teachers College Record, 91,* 409–421.

Ames, C. (1992). Achievement goals, motivational climate, and motivational processes. In G. C. Roberts (Ed.), *Motivation in sports and exercise* (pp.161–176). Champaign, IL: Human Kenetics Books.

Ames, C., & Archer, J. (1988). Achievement goals in the classroom: Student learning strategies and motivation processes. *Journal of Educational Psychology, 80,* 260–267.

Anderman, E. M., & Maehr, M. L. (1994). Motivation and schooling in the middle grades. *Review of Educational Research, 64,* 287–309.

Anderman, E. M., Maehr, M. L., & Midgley, C. (1999). Declining motivation after the transition to middle school: Schools can make a difference. *Journal of Research and Development in Education, 32,* 131–147.

Anderman, E. M., & Midgley, C. (1997). Changes in achievement goal orientations, perceived academic competence, and grades across the transition to middle-level schools. *Contemporary Educational Psychology, 22,* 269–298.

Baker, L., & Scher, D. (2002). Beginning readers' motivation for reading in relation to parental beliefs and home reading experiences. *Reading Psychology, 23,* 239–269.

Bandura, A. (1977). Self-efficacy: Toward a unified theory of behavioral change. *Psychological Review, 84,* 191–215.

Bandura, A. (1994). *Self-efficacy: The exercise of control.* New York: Freeman.

Baumeister, R. F., & Leary, M. R. (1995). The need to belong: Desire for interpersonal attachments as a fundamental human motivation. *Psychological Bulletin, 117,* 497–529.

Bernard, M. E. (2006). It's time we teach social-emotional competence as well as we teach academic competence. *Reading and Writing Quarterly, 22,* 103–119.

Berndt, T. J., & Keefe, K. (1995). Friends' influence on adolescents' adjustment to school. *Child Development, 66,* 1312–1329.

Boggiano, A. K., Main, D. S., & Katz, P. A. (1988). Children's preference for challenge: The role of perceived competence and control. *Journal of Personality and Social Psychology, 54,* 134–141.

Borkowski, J. G., Weyhing, R. S., & Carr, M. (1988). Effects of attributional retraining on strategy-based reading comprehension in learning-disabled students. *Journal of Educational Psychology, 80,* 46–53.

Brophy, J. E. (1983). Research on the self-fulfilling prophesy and teacher expectations. *Journal of Educational Psychology, 75,* 631–661.

Brophy, J., & Good, T. (1970). Teachers' communication of differential expectations for children's classroom performance: Some behavioral data. *Journal of Educational Psychology, 61,* 365–374.

Cohen, S., & Wills, T. A. (1985). Stress, social support, and the buffering hypothesis. *Psychological Bulletin, 98,* 310–357.

Connell, J. P. (1985). A new multidimensional measure of children's perceptions of control. *Child Development, 56,* 1018–1041.

Covington, M. (1992). *Making the grade: A self-worth perspective on motivation and school reform.* New York: Cambridge University Press.

deCharms, R. (1968). *Personal causation.* New York, NY: Academic Press.

Deci, E. L., Nezlek, J., & Sheinman, L. (1981). Characteristics of the rewarder and intrinsic motivation of the rewardee. *Journal of Personality and Social Psychology, 40,* 1–10.

Deci, E. L., Schwartz, A. J., Sheinman, L., & Ryan, R. M. (1981). An instrument to access adults' orientations toward control versus autonomy with children. *Journal of Educational Psychology, 73,* 642–650.

Dweck, C. S. (1975). The role of expectations and attributions in the alleviation of learned helplessness. *Journal of Personality and Social Psychology, 31,* 674–685.

Dweck, C. S., & Leggett, E. L. (1988). A social-cognitive approach to motivation and personality. *Psychological Review, 95,* 256–273.

Eccles, J., Midgley, C., & Adler, T. (1984). Grade-related changes in the school environment: Effects of achievement motivation. In J. G. Nichols (Ed.), *The development of achievement motivation* (pp. 283–331). Greenwich, CT: JAI Press.

Eccles, J. S., Wigfield, A., Flanagan, C., Miller, C., Reuman, D., & Yee, D. (1989). Selfconcepts, domain values, and self-esteem: Relations and changes at early adolescence. *Journal of Personality, 57,* 283–310.

Eccles, J. S., Wigfield, A., Harold, R., & Blumenfeld, P. B. (1993). Age and gender differences in children's self- and task perceptions during elementary school. *Child Development, 64,* 830–847.

Eccles, J. S., Wigfield, A., Midgley, C., Reuman, D., MacIver, D., & Feldlaufer, H. (1993). Negative effects of traditional middle schools on students' motivation. *The Elementary School Journal, 93,* 553–574.

Elliot, A. J., & Church, M. A. (1997). A hierarchical model of approach and avoidance achievement motivation. *Journal of Personality and Social Psychology, 72,* 218–232.

Elliot, A. J., & Harackiewicz, J. M. (1996). Approach and avoidance achievement goals and intrinsic motivation: A meditational analysis. *Journal of Personality and Social Psychology, 70,* 968–980.

Elliott, E. S., & Dweck, C. S. (1988). Goals: An approach to motivation and achievement. *Journal of Personality and Social Psychology, 54,* 5–12.

Erikson, E. (1950). *Childhood and society.* New York: Norton.

Feldlaufer, H., Midgley, C., & Eccles, J. S. (1988). Student, teacher, and observer perceptions of the classroom environment before and after the transition to junior high school. *Journal of Early Adolescence, 8,* 133–156.

Fincham, F. D., & Cain, K. M. (1986). Learned helplessness in humans: A developmental analysis. *Developmental Review, 6,* 301–333.

Findley, M. J., & Cooper, H. M. (1983). Locus of control and academic achievement: A literature review. *Journal of Personality and Social Psychology, 44,* 419–427.

Flink, C., Boggiano, A. K., & Barrett, M. (1990). Controlling teaching strategies: Undermining children's self-determination and performance. *Journal of Personality and Social Psychology, 59,* 916–924.

Försterling, F. (1985). Attributional retraining: A review. *Psychological Bulletin, 98,* 495–512.

Fowler, J. W., & Peterson, P. L. (1981). Increasing reading persistence and altering attributional style of learned helpless children. *Journal of Educational Psychology, 73,* 251–260.

Galassi, J. P., Gulledge, S. A., & Cox, N. D. (1997). Middle school advisories: Retrospect and prospect. *Review of Educational Research, 67,* 301–338.

Gambrell, L. B. (1996). Creating classroom cultures that foster reading motivation. *Reading Teacher, 50,* 14–25.

Gottfried, A. E., Fleming, J. S., & Gottfried, A. W. (2001). Continuity of academic intrinsic motivation from childhood through late adolescence: A longitudinal study. *Journal of Educational Psychology, 93,* 3–13.

Graham, S., & Golan, S. (1991). Motivational influences on cognition: Task involvement, ego involvement, and depth of information processing. *Journal of Educational Psychology, 83,* 187–194.

Grolnick, W. S. & Ryan, R. M. (1987). Autonomy in children's learning: An experimental and individual difference investigation. *Journal of Personality and Social Psychology, 52,* 890–898.

Guay, F., Marsh, H. W., & Boivin, M. (2003). Academic self-concept and academic achievement: Developmental perspectives on their causal ordering. *Journal of Educational Psychology, 95,* 124–136.

Guthrie, J. T., & Alao, S. (1997). Designing contexts to increase motivations for reading. *Educational Psychologist, 32,* 95–105.

Guthrie, J. T., & Davis, S. (2003). Motivating struggling readers in middle school through an engagement model of classroom practice. *Reading and Writing Quarterly, 19,* 59–85.

Guthrie, J. T., Wigfield, A., Metsala, J. L., & Cox, K. E. (1999). Motivational and cognitive predictors of text comprehension and reading amount. *Scientific Studies of Reading, 3,* 231–256.

Harter, S. (1981). A new self-report scale of intrinsic versus extrinsic orientation in the classroom: Motivational and informational components. *Developmental Psychology, 17,* 300–312.

Harter, S. (1996). Teacher and classmate influences on scholastic motivation, self-esteem, and the level of voice in adolescents. In K. Wentzel & J. Juvonen (Eds.), *Social motivation: Understanding children's school adjustment* (pp. 11–42). New York: Cambridge University Press.

Harter, S., & Connell, J. P. (1984). A model of children's achievement and related self-perceptions of competence, control, and motivational orientation. In J. Nichols (Ed.), *The development of achievement-related cognitions and behaviors* (Vol. 3, pp. 219–250). Greenwich, CT: JAI Press.

Jacobs, J. E., Lanza, S., Osgood, D. W., Eccles, J. S., & Wigfield, A. (2002). Changes in children's self-competence and values: Gender and domain differences across grades one through twelve. *Child Development, 73,* 509–527.

Johnson, D. W., Johnson, R. T., & Holubec, E. J. (1984). *Cooperation in the classroom.* Edina, MN: Interaction Book Company.

Johnston, P. H., & Winograd, P. N. (1985). Passive failure in reading. *Journal of Reading Behavior, 17,* 279–301.

Koestner, R., Ryan, R. M., Bernieri, F., & Holt, K. (1984). Setting limits on children's behavior: The differential effects of controlling vs. informational styles on intrinsic motivation and creativity. *Journal of Personality, 52,* 233–248.

MacIver, D. J., Stipek, D. J., & Daniels, D. H. (1991). Explaining within-semester changes in student effort in junior high school and senior high school courses. *Journal of Educational Psychology, 83,* 201–211.

Maehr, M. L., & Midgley, C. (1991). Enhancing student motivation: A schoolwide approach. *Educational Psychologist, 26,* 399–427.

Maheady, L., Mallette, B., & Harper, G. F. (2006). Four classwide peer tutoring models: Similarities, differences, and implications for research and practice. *Reading & Writing Quarterly, 22,* 65–89.

Margolis, H., & McCabe, P. P. (2006). Improving self-efficacy and motivation: What to do, what to say. *Intervention in School and Clinic, 41,* 218–227.

Marks, H. M. (2000). Student engagement in instructional activity: Patterns in the elementary, middle and high school years. *American Educational Research Journal, 37,* 153–184.

Maslow, A. H. (1954). *Motivation and personality.* New York: HarperCollins.

McMaster, K. L., Fuchs, D., & Fuchs, L. S. (2006). Research on peer-assisted learning strategies: The promise and limitations of peer-mediated instruction. *Reading & Writing Quarterly, 22,* 5–25.

Meece, J. L., Blumenfeld, P. C., & Hoyle, R. H. (1988). Students' goal orientations and cognitive engagement in classroom activities. *Journal of Educational Psychology, 80,* 514–523.

Meece, J. L., Wigfield, A., & Eccles, J. S. (1990). Predictors of math anxiety and its influence on young adolescents' course enrollment intentions and performance in mathematics. *Journal of Educational Psychology, 82,* 60–70.

Midgley, C., Anderman, E., & Hicks, L. (1995). Differences between elementary and middle school teachers and students: A goal theory approach. *Journal of Early Adolescence, 15,* 90–113.

Midgley, C. Arunkumar, R., & Urdan, T. (1996). "If I don't do well tomorrow, there's a reason": Predictors of adolescents' use of academic self-handicapping behavior. *Journal of Educational Psychology, 88,* 423–434.

Midgley, C., & Feldlaufer, H. (1987). Students' and teachers' decision-making fit before and after the transition to junior high school. *Journal of Early Adolescence, 7,* 225–241.

Midgley, C., Feldlaufer, H., & Eccles, J. S. (1988). The transition to junior high school: Beliefs of pre- and posttransition teachers. *Journal of Youth and Adolescence, 17,* 543–562.

Midgley, C., Feldlaufer, H., & Eccles, J. S. (1989). Student/teacher relations and attitudes toward mathematics before and after the transition to junior high school. *Child Development, 60,* 981–992.

Midgley, C., Kaplan, A., & Middleton, M. (2001). Performance-approach goals: Good for what, for whom, under what circumstances, and at what cost? *Journal of Educational Psychology, 93,* 77–86.

Midgley, C., & Urdan, T. (2001). Academic self-handicapping and achievement goals: A further examination. *Contemporary Educational Psychology, 26,* 61–75.

Miller, R. B., Behrens, J. T., Greene, B. A., & Newman, D. (1993). Goals and perceived ability: Impact on student valuing, self-regulation, and persistence. *Contemporary Educational Psychology, 18,* 2–14.

National Center for Education Statistics. (2001). *Dropout rates in the United States: 2000.* (Rep. No. NCES 2002-114). Washington, DC: U.S. Department of Education.

Nichols, J. G. (1978). The development of the concepts of effort and ability, perception of academic attainment, and the understanding that difficult tasks require more ability. *Child Development, 49,* 800–814.

Nichols, J. G. (1984). Achievement motivation: Conceptions of ability, subjective experience, task choice, and performance. *Psychological Review, 91,* 328–346.

Nolen, S. B. (1988). Reasons for studying: Motivational orientations and study strategies. *Cognition and Instruction, 5,* 269–287.

Nolen-Hoeksema, S., Girgus, J. S., & Seligman, M. E. P. (1986). Learned helplessness in children: A longitudinal study of depression, achievement, and explanatory style. *Journal of Personality and Social Psychology, 51,* 435–442.

Ostrosky, M., Gaffney, J., & Thomas, D. (2006). The interplay between literacy and relationships in early childhood settings. *Reading and Writing Quarterly, 22,* 173–191.

Otis, N., Grouzet, M. E., & Pelletier, L. G. (2005). Latent motivational change in an academic setting: A 3-year longitudinal study. *Journal of Educational Psychology, 97,* 170–183.

Peterson, C., & Seligman, M. E. P. (1984). Causal explanations as a risk factor for depression: Theory and evidence. *Psychological Review, 91,* 347–374.

Pintrich, P. R., & DeGroot, E. V. (1990). Motivation and self-regulated learning components of classroom academic performance. *Journal of Educational Psychology, 82,* 33–40.

Pintrich, P. R., & Schunk, D. H. (1996). *Motivation in education: Theory, research, and applications.* Englewood Cliffs, NJ: Prentice-Hall.

Pressley, M., Dolezal, S. E., Raphael, L. M., Mohan, L., Roehrig, A. D., & Bogner, K. (2003). *Motivating primary grade students.* New York: Guilford.

Rappaport, N. (2002). Can advising lead to meaningful relationships? In J. E. Rhodes (Ed.), *A critical view of youth mentoring. New Directions for Youth Development* (Vol. 93, pp. 109–125). San Francisco, CA: Jossey-Bass.

Roeser, R. W., Midgley, C., & Urdan, T. C. (1996). Perceptions of the school psychological environment and early adolescents' psychological and behavioral functioning in school: The mediating role of goals and belonging. *Journal of Educational Psychology, 88,* 408–422.

Rotter, J. B. (1966). Generalized expectancies for internal versus external control of reinforcement. *Psychological Monographs, 80*(1, Whole No. 609).

Ryan, R. M., & Grolnick, W. S. (1986). Origins and pawns in the classroom: Self-report and projective assessments of individual differences in children's perceptions. *Journal of Personality and Social Psychology, 50,* 550–558.

Ryan, R. M., Stiller, J. D., & Lynch, J. H. (1994). Representations of relationships to teachers, parents, and friends as predictors of academic motivation and self-esteem. *Journal of Early Adolescence, 14,* 226–249.

Schunk, D. H., & Rice, J. M. (1987). Enhancing comprehension skill and self-efficacy with strategy value information. *Journal of Reading Behavior, 19,* 285–302.

Schunk, D. H., & Rice, J. M. (1989). Learning goals and children's reading comprehension. *Journal of Reading Behavior, 21,* 279–293.

Schunk, D. H., & Rice, J. M. (1991). Learning goals and progress feedback during reading comprehension instruction. *Journal of Reading Behavior, 23,* 351–364.

Sharan, S., & Shaulov, A. (1990). Cooperative learning, motivation to learn, and academic achievement. In S. Sharan (Ed.), *Cooperative learning: Theory and research* (pp. 173–202). New York: Praeger.

Skinner, E. S. (1991). Development and perceived control: A dynamic model of action in context. In M. Gunnar & L.A. Sroufe (Eds.), *Minnesota symposium of child psychology* (Vol. 23, pp. 167–216). Hillsdale, NJ: Erlbaum.

Skinner, E. A., Chapman, M., & Baltes, P. B. (1988). Control, means-end, and agency beliefs: A new conceptualization and its measurement during childhood. *Journal of Personality and Social Psychology, 54,* 117–133.

Skinner, E. A., Wellborn, J. G., & Connell, J. P. (1990). What it takes to do well in school and whether I've got it: A process model of perceived control and children's engagement and achievement in school. *Journal of Educational Psychology, 82,* 22–32.

Skinner, E. A., Zimmer-Gembeck, M. J., & Connell, J. P. (1998). Individual differences and the development of perceived control. *Monographs of the Society for Research in Child Development, 63*(2–3, Serial No. 254).

Slavin, R. E. (1977). Classroom rewards structure: An analytical and practical review. *Review of Educational Research, 47,* 633–650.

Steinberg, L. (1990). Autonomy, conflict, and harmony in the family relationship. In S. S. Feldman & G. R. Elliott (Eds.), *At the threshold: The developing adolescent* (pp. 255–276). Cambridge, MA: Harvard University Press.

Stipek, D., & MacIver, D. (1989). Developmental change in children's assessment of intellectual competence. *Child Development, 60,* 521–538.

Sullivan, H. S. (1953). *The interpersonal theory of psychiatry.* New York: Norton.

Thorkildsen, T. A. (2002). Literacy as a lifestyle: Negotiating the curriculum to facilitate motivation. *Reading and Writing Quarterly, 18,* 321–341.

Turner, J. C. (1995). The influence of classroom contexts on young children's motivation for literacy. *Reading Research Quarterly, 30,* 410–441.

Vansteenkiste, M., Simons, J., Lens, W., Sheldon, K. M., & Deci, E. L. (2004). Motivating learning, performance and persistence: The synergistic effects of intrinsic goal contents and autonomy-supportive contexts. *Journal of Personality and Social Psychology, 87,* 246–260.

Verhoeven, L., & Snow, C. E. (2001). *Literacy and motivation: Reading engagement in individuals and groups.* Mahwah, NJ: Erlbaum.

Walker, B. J. (2005). Thinking aloud: Struggling readers often require more than a model. *The Reading Teacher, 58,* 688–692.

Weiner, B. (1979). A theory of motivation for some classroom experiences. *Journal of Educational Psychology, 71,* 3–25.

Weiner, B. (1980). The role of affect in rational (attributional) approaches to human motivation. *Educational Researcher, 9,* 4–11.

Weiner, B. (1985). An attributional theory of achievement motivation and emotion. *Psychological Review, 92,* 548–573.

Wentzel, K. R. (1994). Relations of social goal pursuit to social acceptance, classroom behavior, and perceived social support. *Journal of Educational Psychology, 86,* 173–182.

Wentzel, K. R. (1997). Student motivation in middle school: The role of perceived pedagogical caring. *Journal of Educational Psychology, 89*(3), 411–419.

Wentzel, K. R. (1998). Social relationships and motivation in middle school: The role of parents, teachers, and peers. *Journal of Educational Psychology, 90,* 202–209.

Wentzel, K. R., Barry, C. M., & Caldwell, K. A. (2004). Friendships in middle school: Influences on motivation and school adjustment. *Journal of Educational Psychology, 96,* 195–203.

Wentzel, K. R., & Caldwell, K. (1997). Friendships, peer acceptance, and group membership: Relations to academic achievement in middle school. *Child Development, 68,* 1198–1209.

White, R. W. (1959). Motivation reconsidered: The concept of competence. *Psychological Review, 66,* 297–333.

Wigfield, A. (1994). Expectancy-value theory of achievement motivation: A developmental perspective. *Educational Psychology Review, 6,* 49–78.

Wigfield, A., & Eccles, J. S. (1992). The development of achievement task values: A theoretical analysis. *Developmental Review, 12,* 265–310.

Wigfield, A., & Eccles, J. S. (Eds.). (2002). *Development of achievement motivation.* San Diego, CA: Academic Press.

Wigfield, A., Eccles, J., Mac Iver, D., Reuman, D., & Midgley, C. (1991). Transitions at early adolescence: Changes in children's domain-specific self-perceptions and general self-esteem across the transition to junior high school. *Developmental Psychology, 27,* 552–565.

Wigfield, A., Eccles, J. S., Yoon, K. S., Harold, R. D., Arbreton, A., Freedman-Doan, K., et al. 1997). Changes in children's competence beliefs and subjective task values across the elementary school years: A three-year study. *Journal of Educational Psychology, 89,* 451–469.

Wigfield, A., & Guthrie, J. T. (1997). Relations of children's motivation for reading to the amount and breadth of their reading. *Journal of Educational Psychology, 89,* 420–432.

23

The Contribution of Discussion to Reading Comprehension and Critical Thinking

Jacquelynn A. Malloy
George Mason University

Linda B. Gambrell
Clemson University

Education is the kindling of a flame, not the filling of a vessel.

— Socrates

This chapter will explore the role of discussion in developing the reading comprehension and critical thinking skills of students with reading disabilities, whether used in the pull-out resource or inclusion classroom. While the initial theoretical discussion is designed to buttress our notion of the level of cognitive engagement that classroom discussions support, the following targeted review of the literature highlights the tools that promote effective discussions in a variety of classroom settings. In all, we hope to persuade the reader of the power of whole class and small group discussions of text to engage and empower readers of all ages and abilities and transform the nature of the classroom learning environment.

Discussion ideally involves a free exchange of ideas about a topic. Some of these ideas may be generated through interactions with text that occur when an individual's existing body of knowledge is stimulated by something that is read (Rosenblatt, 1978). Just as reading for meaningful comprehension requires an engagement with text that is internal, discussion offers an opportunity to externalize thought and to co-construct meanings with others in a manner that builds knowledge and enlarges perspectives for all who participate (Vygotsky, 1962, 1978).

In short, this is what discussion offers to a learning event; a process that *begins* with thought and *encourages* thinking, therefore enhancing the meaning that can be derived from text. Instructional methods that include discussion are supported by theories of learning and knowledge acquisition, as well as by current thinking on cognitive architecture. This chapter will address these theoretical bases first, and then proceed to a presentation of recent research that implicates the developmental course of discussion skills and delineates the teacher supports that were found to be successful in using discussions of text to improve the comprehension

and critical thinking skills of students with and without identified language and learning disabilities.

Relevant Cognitive Theories

How Do We Learn? Learning can be succinctly described as the acquisition of information that is stored and can later be used. If we accept that a basic goal of education is to teach so that students can learn, we would do well to consider the theories that help us to understand how knowledge is acquired so that we can organize our instruction in a reasonably directed manner. Cognitive psychologists dating back to the 1950s have been developing and refining an understanding of how learning occurs, and how it can be enhanced. With the topic of classroom discussion in mind, we present three relevant theories that may serve as bases for understanding the contribution of discussion to reading proficiency and critical thinking skills. While these theories are distinct, they are not mutually exclusive—rather, they seem to focus on different aspects of the thinking and learning processes. When considering these theories together, a rough sketch of what occurs when we learn emerges.

Component Models As the following discussion on cognitive processing as it relates to learning suggests, demands are placed on both short- and long-term memory in pursuit of making meaning, whether following the reading of a text or the presentation of information through some other medium. In addition, there is support for the notion that having students discuss what they have read promotes recall (Sandora, Beck, & McKeown, 1999) and higher order thinking (Chinn, Anderson, & Waggoner, 2001). From basic research on memory that described a short-term and long-term repository for learning (Atkinson & Shiffrin, 1968), a component model was put forth by Baddeley and Hitch (1974) that comprised three stages: *sensory memory*, where input from the environment is received; *working memory*, comprising the only active processor in the model and where conscious learning events occur; and *long-term memory*, where information is stored until needed. While it is tempting to view these three registers as separate and sequential, knowledge acquisition involves quite a bit of cross-interaction among the three processors. For instance, stored information from long-term memory, or prior knowledge, directs what we attend to in the sensory register, and working memory utilizes stored knowledge to make sense of and organize new knowledge. While attention is required for information to move from the sensory register to working memory, only those bits of information that are successfully encoded such that they can be integrated into stored memory will have the potential to be retrieved and used again.

Ericsson and Kintsch (1995) assert that information acquired in the long-term store is so important to what skilled learners do when they comprehend text or engage in other complex cognitive acts that a *long-term working memory* (LT-WM) must be involved, as distinguished from, and in addition to, a short-term working memory (ST-WM). For example, a running account of characters in a story must be maintained and remain active in LT-WM for the reader to understand the referent of pronouns, or to follow a running dialogue in the text. Their conception of LT-WM is of a highly activated, at-the-ready portion of the long-term store that is dynamically involved in working with and structuring the incoming information. Extending the skilled memory theory put forth by Chase and Ericsson (1982), Ericsson and Kintsch propose that expert learners have developed particular skills in accessing acquired information to encode and integrate new information in retrievable ways, and that these domain-specific skills can be taught.

Focusing on the sensory connections to the working memory register, Baddeley and Hitch (1974) theorized that two slave systems, an *articulatory loop* for auditory input and a *visuospatial sketchpad* for visual input, are coordinated by a *central executive*, where attention to these two types of input are controlled. In 2000, Baddeley updated the model by positing the idea of an *episodic buffer* that serves to integrate the incoming information from the various sensory channels with associated traces accessed from the long-term store. Baddeley proposes that this limited capacity processor may be the place where new constructions are generated and then attached to the existing information, thus describing an episode of learning.

The salient feature of the component models is that comprehension and other cognitive tasks are seen as requiring some means for *active processing* that makes use of accessible mental traces from the long-term memory store to attend to incoming sensory data, whether auditory (speech) or visual (print/pictures), in order to recognize and make sense of the new information. During this processing of sensory input, the new information is compared to stored traces, and new thought may be generated as ideas, inferences, questions, and predictions that arise from the juxtaposition of the presented and stored information. This active processor, whether we term it the working memory, long-term working memory, or episodic buffer, must be engaged for thinking to occur and for learning to result. In a sense, this active processor becomes our personal cognitive workspace. This is the active internal space where our personal interactions with texts generate interpretations, and where verbal interactions with others can enhance or alter these developing understandings.

Schema Theory   Schema theory, as developed by Anderson, Reynolds, Schallert, and Goetz (1977), offers a means for understanding how knowledge is organized in long-term memory. In most models of memory acquisition, long-term memory is thought to have an unlimited capacity and duration, and to be primarily associative in its organization. Anderson and his colleagues refer to these organizational structures as *schemata,* or *schemas.*

Schemas are comprised of associated bits of information and can be enlarged, enhanced, or re-organized when new information is successfully integrated. Their research in 1977, where undergraduate physical education and music majors were both asked to read the same prose passage that could have two meanings, indicated that the background knowledge and personal beliefs of readers were highly influential in their interpretation of the passages. In fact, they argue, the schema accessed while reading can be so primary as to prevent the reader from considering other possible interpretations of the passage. Therefore, the personal, internal interaction with text can be limited or enhanced by the schemas that have been developed by the individual reader. It would also follow that in discussions about text where several participants present their understanding of the material, both congruous and disparate interpretations can be revealed. The interaction of these various view points may then provide impetus for new thought, new ideas, or new questions as interpretations are compared and considered, thus perpetuating a cycle of internalizing and externalizing what one is thinking.

The process of thinking, verbalizing, listening and observing, comparing, and re-thinking constitutes the type of cognitive engagement can lead to critical thinking and deeper learning. Through the interactions available in discussions, mental traces are added to the appropriate existing schemas that are rich with the individual's original interpretations of the text, what others have revealed about their thinking, and how the consensus or discord in the discussion progressed. All of these are imbued with additional contextual traces that refer to the social event (seeing the faces and body language of the group members), the physical context of the discussion (how the classroom looks and sounds), the smells of cafeteria food wafting through the corridor, and the social and affective memories of the discussion, such as feelings of embarrassment or excitement or the emotional charge of a speaker's comment.

Social Learning Perspectives   While the cognitive theories just described shed light on processes that may occur while reading and discussing text, they also direct us to consider the social contexts in which these interactions take place and their direct and indirect influence on reading abilities and knowledge acquisition. Of the various perspectives presenting a common thesis that learning is a socially mediated event, *sociolinguistic theory, social constructivism*, and *social cognitive theory* all provide support for the contributions of classroom discussions to literacy learning and general knowledge acquisition. Interestingly, they each serve to shed light on various stages of the development of learning and may influence the appropriate instructional environment recommended for various ages and levels of development.

Sociolinguistic theory views literacy as a cultural event (Bloome & Green, 1984) that can be used to form and maintain relationships between and among people. Literacy is founded on oral language skills, and success in school literacy activities often reflects the nature of the linguistic development a child encounters outside of school.

As Heath's 1982 research on three linguistically diverse communities reveals, students whose home culture reflects that of the school culture tend to access the school literacy tasks well, whereas children who are not as familiar with the literacy practices valued by schools do not experience the same level of academic success. Corroborating research by Hart and Risley (2003) suggests that the ties between oral language development and print exposure and experience are powerful factors in vocabulary acquisition and literacy achievement, leading educators to realize the importance of recognizing oral language development as a pre-requisite to facility in print-based learning. Students whose receptive and/or expressive language reveals limited lexical and syntactic knowledge may have greater difficulty when they encounter the increasingly complex vocabulary and grammatical structures in the texts they read. Therefore, it would seem reasonable that exposure to, and opportunities to engage in, authentically oriented exchanges about texts would provide practice in understanding and negotiating the increasingly complex language forms.

In delineating his ideas regarding social constructivism, Vygotsky (1962, 1978) suggests that cognitive abilities develop as a result of social interactions and the tools provided to learners through their culture to negotiate these interactions. Of these tools, language is seen to be highly influential in learning, and the essential cultural tool of language is developed through interactions with others—a point that is in agreement with the sociolinguists. In his discussions regarding the support required for students to move from one level of understanding to the next, Vygotsky describes the importance of keeping instruction within a *zone of proximal development*, where the student can be expected to progress with help from a more knowledgeable other.

According to social constructivist theory, the interactions provided in literacy discussions can offer the supportive elements that fill in gaps in understanding and assist in integrating the mental model being developed. As these understandings develop, the mastery of language as a cultural tool can be used to support further learning. It is Vygotsky's claim that these tools are at work to promote cognitive growth "… when one is required to explain, elaborate, or defend one's position to others, as well as to oneself; striving for an explanation often makes a learner integrate and elaborate knowledge in new ways" (1978, p. 158). Discussions about a shared text provide just these opportunities.

The manner in which language is modeled and then appropriated for use by others in discussions is essential to Bandura's (1986) position on *social cognitive learning*. Bandura proposes that much of what we learn occurs through interpreting what we see others do, or hear them say. Especially in the early grades, the linguistic and behavioral models provided by teachers and other students can be highly influential in determining the thinking and actions of the students who are attending to and interpreting these language forms and behaviors. Both social constructivists and social cognitive theorists would agree that social environments afford opportunities for students to internalize what others externalize, whether language forms or behaviors. Students learn by observing others and by interpreting and selectively appropriating what they hear, see, and feel as a result (Rogoff, 1990).

Situating Shared Cognitive Processes in Classroom Environments   Using a constructivist stance, Bruning, Schraw, and Royce (1995) describe the importance of social interactions in building knowledge as a dialectical constructivism that can lead to the development of a reflective classroom. In the reflective classroom environment, "… well managed classroom discourse—extended, thematic communication among classroom participants" has the potential to increase domain, general, and metacognitive knowledge (1995, pp. 211–215). Citing both Vygotsky's aforementioned proposition that internalization of social interactions leads to cognitive change and Rogoff's (1990) assertion that students appropriate shared cognitive processes through collaboration with others, Bruning et al. support their contention that social interactions are foundational to meaning construction.

Nystrand (2006) adds that research on the role of discussion and its contribution to reading comprehension should focus on discussion as a *method* of instruction that is organic to the environment for learning rather than on the specific model being implemented (e.g., literature circle, questioning the author, reciprocal teaching). When effective dialogical discussions occur in classrooms, it speaks volumes about the pedagogical stance of the teacher and the roles assumed by students.

Educators who feel that their role is to transmit knowledge to their students and then to assess how well their students received it are likely to be quite content with the Initiation-Response-Evaluation, or recitation method of teaching (Mehan, 1979; Wells, 1993). This pedagogical stance lends itself to a *monologic* discourse where there is an assumption of a known answer or a singular correct viewpoint (Bakhtin, 1984), which may have the effect of reinforcing the teacher as a representative of the culture of power (Delpit, 1988) and silencing therefore any opposing, questioning, or marginalized voices. However, when teachers view their craft as one of guiding students toward interpreting and integrating knowledge, they approach classroom discourse from a *dialogic* stance, posing questions that have multifaceted answers and encourage multiple viewpoints, and the power for distributing knowledge is shared among the classroom participants. Further, the dialogic nature of effective discussions encourages the juxtaposition of these various interpretations of text in a manner that creates cognitive dissonance and then group resolution (Almasi, 1995). This struggle for understanding by incorporating multiple perspectives changes the very nature of the classroom environment by expanding understandings of how knowledge is constructed and whose knowledge is valued.

As a means of tying together the previous discussion of individual cognitive processes with the developing understanding of situated learning as it occurs in the context of discussions about literature, we cite Almasi, McKeown, and Beck's description of a *cognitive worktable* (1996, p. 131), which we shall hereafter refer to as the *shared workspace* in order to distinguish it from the *personal workspace* that is the individual's active cognitive processing register. In their research on the effects of literature discussions on reading engagement with fourth-grade students, Almasi et al. offer the following observation:

> Thus, as students each brought information to the discussion, a "cognitive worktable" emerged in which students and teachers observed each piece of information and attempted to link these "puzzle pieces" together to create a coherent meaning. Each piece of information that was placed on the cognitive worktable almost seemed to become a manipulative item that could be moved about the worktable to see how it fit into the whole. These manipulations represented students and teachers organizing the information that they had acquired toward the ultimate goal of meaning construction. (p. 131)

This observation provides excellent imagery for what can ideally occur in discussions about text. Picturing each individual's interpretation of a portion of the text as an informational widget that can be offered from their personal cognitive workspace to the shared cognitive workspace, the group can then move, group, re-organize, or otherwise alter the widgets until they combine to form a collaboratively agreed upon understanding. The co-constructed understanding may then be re-incorporated into the individual's mental model in whole, or at least influence the structure of the mental model that is being personally constructed and attached to the long-term store.

Of Tools and Workspaces

The tools for placing and shaping interpretations of text on the shared cognitive workspace are developed and honed through the very social interactions that require them. This is why the presence of knowledgeable others, who have experience with and can model the use of these tools to the group, are essential to creating effective climates for discussion. The use of interpretive tools to understand text can be modeled by teachers and then practiced, and hopefully appropriated, by students during discussions about text. These tools are evidence of cognitive engagement in that personal interpretations become externalized to the shared workspace for others to acknowledge and manipulate as the group works toward a consensus on an issue or an understanding of the text. When students refer back to the text to substantiate their point or to create a chronology of events or list of character traits, valuable opportunities for skimming, searching, and re-reading text occur that can be a boon to basic and comprehensive reading skills. What occurs in the *shared workspace* becomes a model of what can occur internally in the student's own *personal workspace*.

This cycle of moving internal thought to the shared workspace, and then appropriating it for use in the personal workspace, provides cognitive support for learners of all levels of ability as they move through the process of gaining tools for thinking about texts. Two things are of importance here: The first is that the participants become familiar with, and have practice in using, *interpretive tools* for understanding text, and the second is that participants gain skill in the use of *discussion tools* for negotiating the shared workspace together. Observing how others approach the comprehension of various elements of a reading increases awareness of how others cognitively engage with text. Participating in the goal of coming to a consensus, or at least a synthesis, of ideas given various dilemmas and conflicts, provides practice in using various discussion tools.

Discussion and Reading Disabilities As may be a consequence of certain language, reading, or learning disabilities, some students may be lacking in the interpretive and discussion skills required for comprehending and then sharing their understandings with other students. For example, students with disabilities that affect reading proficiency may be less likely to read strategically (Graham, Harris, MacArthur, & Schwartz, 1991) and may be struggling with decoding skills, following and connecting story lines in narrative text, or information flow in expository texts. As such, they may present more limited and literal contributions to the discussions of these texts (McMahon & Raphael, 1997).

When students are identified with these reading and learning challenges, it is often deemed necessary to focus on skill development at an isolated level, perhaps in brief guided sessions. While specific and individualized or small group assistance in accelerating the decoding and comprehension skills of these struggling readers is essential, it is also important to then situate the emerging skills in contexts where they can be supported in authentic expressions. With reference to this focus on learning in applied settings, Trent, Artiles, and Englert (1998) assert that children with disabilities "…acquire complex skills through social interactions in situated contexts, which allows them to see how the various parts of the process fit together" (p. 285). As reading and interpretive skills are developed, small group discussions in the resource and mainstream classroom provide opportunities for learners to put the pieces to work, not just work on the pieces.

Using a representative sample of recent research on literacy discussion across the K–12 continuum, the following section of this chapter will serve to cull forth the various interpretive and discussion tools that have proved to be successful in supporting thinking and discussion skills in classrooms. While this is not intended to be an exhaustive review of the research in the area of classroom literacy discussion, as the body of research has become quite substantial, the selected research illuminates current thinking on the use of discussion as a *method* of instruction that will serve as a basis for implementing particular *models* of providing discussion in classrooms. The interest here is in delineating tools and processes for guiding the student toward actively processing the text using interpretive tools in the personal workspace and in negotiating the shared workspace through the use of discussion tools.

Relevant Research on Literacy Discussion across the Grades

Commeyras and DeGroff (1998) conducted a national survey of literacy educators and found that while 95% value the idea of peer discussions of text, only 33% actually use discussion as a method for encouraging comprehension of text. For some, the idea of sharing the control of learning with their students is a difficult leap of faith in a curricular climate that requires so much accountability for class achievement. An associated aspect of the paucity of peer discussions in our classrooms is the knowledge, effort, and patience required to create an environment that will nurture the skills required for effective discussions. The following research reveals that the knowledge base is growing to support what teachers need to know, and that given sufficient time to reap the benefits, the quality and quantity of student responses to text increases, often with a satisfying enhancement of the classroom environment.

Beginning with Thinking: Engaging the Personal Workspace   What type of instruction would best prepare our youngest students to participate meaningfully in group discussions about text? Certainly, ability to articulate personal interpretations of a reading would be important, as would skill in building mental models based on developing interpretations, or theories, about text and extending or revising these theories by integrating new knowledge or novel interpretations. Teachers of very young students, pre-school through first grade, for instance, can do much in terms of exposing reading as a cognitively engaged act by making predictions through picture walks or wondering aloud about the story. The manner that is used by the teacher to invite

students to wonder and predict during read-alouds serves as a model of how we invite others into the shared workspace to consider what the story is about and how it relates to or is different from their lives. In this way, stories are not just for entertainment but for thinking about. When reading from expository texts, teachers can think aloud about the structure of the book and how it guides our understanding of the topic. For instance, after looking through the book as a pre-reading activity, she could say, "Let's remember these maps showing where they have found meteorites—we may want to look at that later when we're reading about how they come to the earth." By connecting supporting diagrams, maps, and pictures to the topic during reading, students observe the connections between images and text that can improve thinking and comprehension.

Elementary Grades   In reviewing the research conducted in the elementary grades, we begin with the end in mind. We first present work reported from the later elementary years, hoping to provide a portrait of what discussions can become, and then trace back through the earlier grades to describe the progress that can be made toward developing the skills required to achieve skilled discussions. By framing discussion as a method of instruction that could ideally begin in the early grades and develop into a well-practiced means of thinking and sharing knowledge by the later elementary years, we set the stage for creating classroom environments that encourage the type of interpretive and critical thinking required at the secondary and post-secondary levels.

In an attempt to understand the nature of proficient and less proficient literature discussions in fourth-grade classrooms, Almasi, O'Flahavan, and Arya (2001) found that at least two elements were distinguishing. In proficient discussions, students demonstrated expertise in sustaining topics and in revisiting those topics when new information was presented. In order to encourage productive discussions, teachers became adept at presenting and modeling discussion skills, then releasing the responsibility to their students so that they could practice and hone these skills on their own.

Proficient groups developed an understanding of and respect for the roles of speaker and listener such that that they could maintain the course of a discussion on a particular topic until it developed more fully. These groups were more likely to return to previous topics and shore up the connections in the chain of coherence as they moved through topics. This pattern of topic maintenance and recursion harkens back to the constructivist notion of filling in the gaps in understanding until a mental model is formed.

Initially, younger children and those with language delays or disabilities may not have the linguistic skill or the required awareness of conventions regarding collaborative discussion to integrate their responses into the presented topic or to the previous response offered. Citing previous research on the development of topic maintenance skills by Sirois and Dorval (1988), Brinton and Fujiki (1984), and Almasi et al. (2001) suggest that children tend to be more "linear and shallow" in their interactions in the early elementary years and do not recognize the import of relevance to the topic until about the fifth grade (Almasi et al., 2001, p. 100). However, Berry and Englert (2005), as will be discussed later in this section, demonstrated that first and second graders in an inclusion classroom could make progress in this regard over a six month period with adequate teacher direction and support.

In part, direct modeling of the use of interpretive tools may nurture young learners toward realizing a purpose for literacy discussions in a manner that would help students to see the value in sustaining topics until some progress toward understanding is achieved. When the goal of engaging in group discussions about literature in order to create a richer understanding of the text is made explicit, the modeling of particular strategies, such as questioning the author, making predictions, or chronicling a chain of events brings focus to the utility of these tools to the common venture of creating a richer understanding.

According to Kucan and Beck (1997), these tools can be introduced through teacher think-alouds, as was described previously, as a means of externalizing thinking about text during read-alouds. Wondering out loud what a character might be thinking or feeling, or making pointed reminders to oneself to try to figure out what a character might mean by a certain turn of phrase, exposes the teacher's own personal workspace to students and encourages them to follow along, guiding them toward constructing mental models of the text and the concepts therein. In so doing, learners observe what must go on in the personal workspace so that they have something to bring to the shared workspace when the opportunity is provided. The value of thinking aloud while reading from text does not diminish in the later grades; rather, the need to externalize strategies for thinking about increasingly complex material continues throughout all grade levels.

In other work in fourth-grade classrooms, Almasi and colleagues describe three areas of this shared work that emerged from their 1996 research that are specific to literacy discussions. These include (a) text-to-self and text-to-text connections; (b) referring to portions of text or to text structures to support or reject predictions or interpretations; and (c) piecing together character traits, plot events, or other organizational attempts to clarify understandings. The public use of these interpretive tools, as modeled by teachers and then peers, had the concomitant effect of increasing student engagement and participation in the discussions. As students became accustomed to the free exchange of thought that developed, positive changes in the classroom environment were observed by the end of the school year.

Conducting research in third-grade classrooms, Maloch (2002) found that students evidenced initial difficulty in moving away from the teacher-led mode of literacy discussion, noting that students did not often listen to and integrate the responses of others. As evidence of the Almasi et al. (2001) description of younger learners' difficulty with topic maintenance and maneuvering, Maloch describes some of the groups in her study as engaging in a sort of "round robin share group" instead of a true discussion (2002, p. 101). Students were also frequently noted to look to the teacher for guidance. In response, the teacher encouraged the students to take charge of their groups by being prepared to discuss the text (using literature response logs) and to acknowledge and follow up on one another's responses. In particular, the teacher successfully adapted to the role of facilitator rather than leader by noting and exemplifying comments by students that were helpful to advancing the effectiveness of the discussion. Giving a name and purpose to various actions by students, such as following-up or restating a topic to incorporate new knowledge, supported her students in learning the conventions of productive discussions.

What is particularly striking about this research is how the teacher moved in a reasonable progression through skills that were in her students' zone of proximal development. For example, recognizing the linear reporting that students offered, the teacher encouraged students to share their reasoning (place something on the shared workspace) and then to consider ways to draw others into the conversation. Her approach as teacher/facilitator was to cue by facial expression or brief remark, and if that did not result in a student response that fit the discussion strategy she had in mind, she modeled explicitly what she was after. Interestingly, students were observed to appropriate almost verbatim the strategy modeled, such as asking "Why" or using linguistic connectors such as "as Mark said" or "I agree with Shaun". However, following the teacher's direct model of the strategy, a flurry of similar responses by students were observed and eventually enhanced as they continued the strategy but incorporated their own wording. This is an example of how students, when ready, will recognize, practice, and internalize tools for learning the art of discussion. The teacher then could rely on cues alone to elicit a helpful strategy for reenergizing a stalled discussion.

Another interesting finding in Maloch's detailed qualitative report was the manner in which the teacher used the end of the discussion to recap the skills that emerged from the group. While the strategies were taught through cueing (to determine if a skill already existed), then direct modeling (for those skills that were not in evidence), then cueing again (once skills were practiced), they were not the *topic* of the discussion. With these third-grade students, providing a teacher's-view recap of the approaches that were new and helpful to the conversation allowed the actual discussion to center on the text of interest. This is similar in approach to O'Flahavan's (1989; see also Almasi, 1995) description of conversational discussion groups that follow a 5-20-5 format. The initial and closing 5 minutes of the group talk is reserved for the sort of metatalk that permits an examination of and suggestions for improving the quality of the discussion and the interpersonal skills required. While the actual literacy discussion comprises the middle 20 minutes, the teacher guides the students in recapping the course of the conversation and collaborating on rules to improve future discussions in the final 5 minutes. At the beginning of the next circle meeting, the teacher introduces or re-introduces the topic and reviews the rules or discussion reminders that were previously agreed upon by the group. As was indicated in the research of Almasi et al. (2001) that described the behavior of more and less proficient literature discussion groups, proficient groups do not spend a great deal of time on metatalk, or talk that centers on how the discussion is progressing, and less proficient groups become derailed by too much of it.

Findings from research in a multi-age primary classroom with 12 first- and 12 second-grade students, McIntyre, Kyle, and Moore (2006) describe how one classroom teacher provided effective scaffolds to her students as they developed interpretive and dialogic skills. As the students ranged widely in ability and were predominantly from poor and working-class rural backgrounds, the teacher found ways to be explicitly instructional in teaching discourse conventions while supporting a democratic venture toward collaborative meaning making using mysteries. The authors contend that "…teacher-fronted talk and true dialogue are not mutually exclusive; the former can be used to achieve the other" (p. 37). Using a four lesson cycle, the teacher continually stated and restated the goals for each session, whether it was selecting books, choosing groups, determining how the text would be read, discussing the book, or collaborating on a product to demonstrate their consensus. While groups met, she moved in and out of groups, providing instruction and support as needed. Occasionally, the teacher wondered aloud how best to interpret a passage of text or solve a conflict between the text and the picture, making her internal dialogue available to students as a model of the interpretive strategies she was using. Using the text as the authoritative word, this teacher was skilled at moving the discussion back to the printed word, encouraging re-readings of passages until meanings became clearer.

Particular actions and mannerisms were instrumental in creating a transition from monologic to dialogic thinking. For instance, when moving from instructor to facilitator, she cued students to use the tools she'd previously modeled to solve problems in understanding or re-stated their progress thus far in order to encourage them to risk the next step. She was a careful listener who allowed plenty of wait time before responding so that students could process the ongoing dialogue. Her focus was continually on guiding students to come to develop their own conclusions and to offer support through cues, and then direct guidance, as needed. In addition, she did not offer the ubiquitous "well done" or "nice job," which would have had the likely effect of remarking on performance rather than self-regulation and process. These pedagogical nuances were observed to be crucial to creating a classroom environment that privileged student voices in the pursuit of meaning rather than on achieving a "correct" interpretation of the text. As the authors state, "Thus, a democratic classroom culture is not one in which students make all the decisions and choose all their work but, rather, is one that reflects guidance from the teacher,

intervention when necessary, and a constant nudging toward high-level work" (p. 61).

The findings of a study conducted by Berry and Englert (2005) in a first- and second-grade inclusion classroom reinforce the proposition that discussion skills can be effectively taught to students of varied ability levels. Videotaped analyses of a literature discussion group that involved 17 first and second graders at the beginning and end of a 6-month cycle of participation in weekly discussions revealed that students with and without identified learning and language disabilities evidenced growth in thinking about and talking about texts. In particular, the group improved in topic coherence and maintenance, use of interpretive strategies, and the sociolinguistic abilities required to move in and out of the conversation effectively. These findings are especially heartening because students with language and learning disabilities are more likely to have difficulty with the communicative processes required to negotiate meaning. However, the teacher was adept in nudging even the most reticent student to offer an opinion—often by asking about personal experiences that related to the story—and assisted the group in protecting the increased response time required by some to formulate their thoughts into words. This sensitivity to the needs of various students in her class created an environment where everyone's thoughts were equally welcomed and interactions were both increased and improved.

The resulting advances in cognitive, linguistic, and social abilities are attributable to the skills of the classroom and inclusion teachers, who were aware of the specific needs of their students and provided timely and appropriate models for learners to appropriate. For example, the teacher provided specific models for entering the dialogue and for requesting elaboration, as some of her language impaired students were not practiced in these skills. Her direct models were soon adopted by students, who then incorporated the new skills into their discussion repertoire. Noting that students came to show more recursion in their text-talk, returning to earlier topics to fill in information and requesting elaboration or further information from the text to come to a consensus, is strong evidence of the depth and persistence of the cognitive engagement that occurred as a result of the weekly literature discussion.

Berry and Englert (2005) caution teachers to be patient in implementing discussion-based methods of teaching in their classrooms. Based on the initial discussion, the method did not look promising at all. It was only by providing consistent support and reinforcement in the early cycles that the students were able to accept increasing responsibility for suggesting topics, inviting others into the discussion, and pursuing and modifying topics. In fact, at the very beginning of the treatment period, the teacher used a chart to list reminders for *how* students should behave in a discussion and *what* they should talk about. Making the shared workspace visual using chart paper, a white board, or a computer and screen, may help students to remember their group goals, and may even be helpful in listing and following topics. However, the teachers in this particular classroom soon found that the students did not require the chart to engage in appropriate group behaviors, and it was soon discarded as a crutch that was no longer of use.

What this research on first- and second-grade classrooms reveals is that talking about text is a process that can be successfully taught and learned in the early elementary classroom. While many first and second graders do not come to us with the conversational skills required to suggest and move coherently among topics, they can adopt these skills if the appropriate supports and models are supplied by a teacher who is sufficiently patient to allow the process to develop. Involvement in literature discussion creates habits of mind that are a benefit to all students, perhaps more so to those who have little experience with or natural ability for collaborative or language based activities. Beginning in these earlier grades, we not only guide learners toward using language to think, but in taking on responsibility for understanding texts.

Middle and High School   While it would seem that the advancing complexity of middle and high school literature and content area texts would merit more time spent in discussion, Nystrand and Gamoran (1991) found that whole classroom discussions averaged only 50 seconds per lesson in the eighth grade and an abysmal 15 seconds per lesson in the ninth grade. From data they collected with their colleagues in 16 midwestern middle schools, they also found that when whole class discussions of shared readings do occur, they develop differently in lower tracked than in higher tracked classrooms (Nystrand, Wu, Gamoran, Zeiser, & Long, 2003).

Using event-history analysis to examine the nature of the discourse processes that occurred in English language arts and social studies classrooms, the researchers focused on the teacher and student questions that were posed in whole class discussions, the level of cognitive difficulty the questions invoked, and the type of evaluation offered by the teacher. The researchers found that discussions were more likely to be dialogic, as opposed to monologic, in smaller classrooms. Important elements in developing dialogic spells were the teachers' use of *authentic* questions, that is, questions for which there is more than one possible answer, and occurrences of following-up on a students' response, or *uptake*, whether by the teacher or another student. In lower tracked classes, the cycles of authentic questions and uptake were more sporadic than in higher tracked classrooms. In particular, there are fewer student questions posed in lower tracked classrooms, which may be an artifact of concomitant difficulties with language expression or difficulty in breaking from the monologic mode of recitation between students of lower abilities and their teachers.

Research by Alvermann et al. (1996) provides insights into the perspectives of middle and high school students from across the country and why they may prefer to conduct discussions in smaller groups. In their multicase study, responses of focal students to their observations of videotaped

book discussions indicate that students are quite aware of what they need to engage in effective group discussions and what they learn from them.

Perhaps not surprisingly, students preferred to talk about books in smaller groups, citing several socially believable reasons considering the age group. Students noted that it was easier to enter the conversation and be heard, and that they felt less anxious about speaking out in the smaller group. Some students noted that they were more able to maintain their focus in the smaller setting and that they were more willing to take risks, particularly in small groups that were peer-led. A consideration in forming small groups is attention to student composition. For the most part, students would prefer to choose their groups, based on friendships or on the perceived strengths of the participants relative to the task presented. While this usually means that students prefer talking with their friends, their reasons are justified. With friends, there is a preset level of comfort that affords personal revelation and risk-taking in conversations—a sense of security despite the nature of your opinion or the quality of the offered response. Friends may also share important elements of their background in common, such as language or ethnicity. Of course, the homogeneity may also preclude the sharing of disparate viewpoints or the gaining of new perspectives. Fortunately, one student shared that once they have become used to discussing in groups, they tend to become more willing to accept others into their conversations or to enter other groups.

While students placed high importance on the responsibility of group members to actively contribute to the discussion and to help in maintaining the topic, the nature of the task presented by the teacher proved to be fairly influential. For instance, if a study guide or resource sheet was provided, students were more likely to divide up the work of finding answers individually and then copying each others answers. As was indicated in other sections of this chapter, presenting tasks with known answers is anathema to encouraging dialogic discussions. If an answer is known, students will find it, write it down, and turn it in. If, however, the task involves a topic that the students find engaging, provocative, or relevant to their lives, students observed that they had an easier time entering the conversation and maintaining the topic until their viewpoints were shared and shaped by other perspectives. When discussions involved authentic tasks and interesting texts, students revealed that the sharing of personal interpretations and opinions often led them to an enlarged and enriched understanding of the text. Some of the students indicated that their peers' explanations of vocabulary and concepts were more readily understood than those of the teacher, perhaps because of the linguistic similarities and nuances they share or because they are more willing to pursue an understanding with a peer than with an authority figure.

Middle and high school students need direction from teachers in expressing opinions without arguing and in developing a culture of acceptance and respect for others and their views. Group productivity is enhanced by permitting some measure of choice in terms of group composition and text selection, as well as latitude in pursuing topics of interest. Secondary students still require support in establishing topic coherence and returning to topics until they are adequately developed, although their abilities to regulate these tasks are often better than those of their elementary grade counterparts, at least when the topic and the text are sufficiently engaging.

Conclusions

It is the overarching premise of this chapter that the exchange and exploration of ideas that occurs in discussions about text involves cognitive engagements that promote a deeper comprehension and build background knowledge and interpretive skills useful to future interactions with text. In the discussion of cognitive, social cognitive, and socio-constructive frameworks for understanding the cognitive activity involved in socially situated conversations about text, the dynamic interchange between the personal workspace and the shared workspace describes the place and the means for learning to occur.

As the reviewed representative research serves to illustrate, two types of tools are required for developing facility in the process of moving and shaping information across the personal and shared workspaces: (a) *interpretive tools* for understanding texts, such as accessing background knowledge, making connections to personal experiences or other texts, or questioning the intent of the author; and (b) *discussion tools* for negotiating the shared workspace, which include topic coherence and recursion, inviting and including others, elaborating and following up on responses, and providing evidence by referring to the text.

Beyond the recommendations for supporting decoding, fluency, comprehension, and metacognitive awareness for reading as are described in other chapters of this volume, this chapter serves to frame discussion as an instructional method for applying these skills in authentic, relevant interchanges. With support from teachers, students can become privy to the discourse practices required to use, refine, and collaborate as they share ideas about a topic. Using cues to direct students toward constructive discussion techniques, allowing additional time to process and respond, and monitoring the range of topics to promote a coherent thread for students to follow are accommodations that are relevant to all students in learning to engage in literature discussions, but may specifically support students with reading disabilities.

While none of the research studies reviewed claims that the teaching of requisite tools, skills, strategies, and dispositions to encourage the development of dialogic discourse is intuitively simple or fast-acting, there is evidence that explicit teaching and modeling followed by patience and a willingness to gradually release control to students assists learners in pursuing the meaning of a text as it relates to their lives. Often, the rewards include increases in student engagement and participation and improvements in the classroom environment. Although whole group discussions appear to be more productive in smaller classrooms, and may provide valuable instructional platforms for thinking aloud and the explicit teaching of interpretive and discussion tools in the earlier grades, students may develop more opportunities to practice and appropriate these same tools in a smaller group setting, particularly with intermittent guidance and appropriate scaffolds of a well intentioned teacher.

Perhaps the most profound realization that may result from reading this chapter is that the skills required of a teacher to facilitate the type of dialogic enterprise described herein depend upon a pedagogical stance that may require a leap of faith for some, and a willingness to suspend convention for others. While we become educators to promote learning, we are too often caught in accountability traps that actually discourage thinking, particularly the interpretive, critical thinking that affords deep and textured comprehension. But as the teachers described in the reviewed research might attest, moving between instructor and facilitator in a carefully orchestrated symphony of describing, modeling, guided practice, and gradual release to independence brings you as full and alive and in tune with your students as the discussions that result.

Directions for Future Research

As students with disabilities are increasingly provided services in an inclusion setting, the time is ripe for researchers to investigate the nature of discourse in these classrooms, especially with regard to discussions that support the reading of text. In the English language arts classroom, as well as in the content areas, research should be directed at identifying specific tools and techniques for including all voices in connecting to and learning from print and online texts through whole class and small group discussions, as was done in the middle grades study by Morocco, Hinden, Mata-Aguilar, and Clark-Chiarelli (2001) and the Berry and Englert (2005) study previously reviewed. Using formative and other mixed methods approaches, similar investigations should focus on the teacher supports required to accommodate students with varying abilities in thinking about and discussing the texts they read. Descriptions of the developing contributions of students with learning and reading disabilities would enrich our understanding of how dialogic contexts for learning effect language expression and pragmatic language use.

References

Almasi, J. F. (1995). The nature of fourth graders' sociocognitive conflicts in peer-led and teacher-led discussions of literature. *Reading Research Quarterly, 30*(3), 314–351.

Almasi, J. F., O'Flahavan, J. F., & Arya, P. (2001). A comparative analysis of student and teacher development in more and less proficient discussions of literature. *Reading Research Quarterly, 36*(2), 96–120.

Almasi, J. F., McKeown, M.G. & Beck, I.L. (1996). The nature of engaged reading in classroom discussions of literature. *Journal of Literacy Research, 28*(1), 107–146.

Alvermann, D. A., Young, J. P., Weaver, D., Hinchman, K. A., Moore,

D. W., Phelps, S. F., et al. (1996). Middle and high school students' perceptions of how they experience text-based discussions: A multicase study. *Reading Research Quarterly, 31*(3), 244–267.

Anderson, R., Reynolds, R., Schallert, D., & Goetz, E. (1977). Frameworks for comprehending discourse. *American Educational Research Journal, 14,* 367–381.

Atkinson, R. C., & Shiffrin, R. M. (1968). Human memory: A proposed system and its control processes. In K. Spence & J. Spence (Eds.), *The psychology of learning and motivation* (Vol. 2, pp. 89–195). New York: Academic Press.

Bakhtin, M. (1984). *Problems of Dostoevsky's poetics* (C. Emerson, Trans.). Minneapolis: University of Minnesota Press.

Baddeley, A. D. (2000). The episodic buffer: A new component of working memory? *Trends in Cognitive Sciences, 4*(11), 417–23.

Baddeley, A. D., & Hitch, G. J. (1974). Working memory. In G. A. Bower (Ed.), *The psychology of learning and motivation* (pp. 47–89). New York: Academic Press.

Bandura, A. (1986). *Social foundations of thought and action: A social cognitive theory.* Englewood Cliffs, NJ: Prentice-Hall.

Berry, R. A., & Englert, C. S. (2005). Designing conversation: Book discussions in a primary inclusion classroom. *Learning Disability Quarterly, 28*(1), 35–58.

Bloome, D., & Green, J. (1984). Directions in the socio-linguistic theory of reading. In P. D. Pearson (Ed.), *Handbook of reading research* (pp. 395–421). White Plains, NY: Longman.

Brinton, B., & Fujiki, M. (1984). Development of topic manipulation skills in discourse. *Journal of Speech and Hearing Research, 27,* 350–358.

Bruning, R. H., Schraw, G. J., & Royce, R. R. (1995). Building knowledge and reflective thought. In R. H. Burning, G. J. Schraw, & R. R. Royce (Eds.), *Cognitive psychology and instruction: 2nd ed.* (pp. 211–235). Englewood Cliffs, NJ: Prentice Hall.

Chase, W. G., & Ericsson, K. A. (1982). Skill and working memory. In G. H. Bower (Ed.), *The psychology of learning and motivation* (Vol. 16, pp. 1–58). New York: Academic Press.

Chinn, C. A., Anderson, R. C., & Waggoner, M. A. (2001). Patterns of discourse in two kinds of literature discussion. *Reading Research Quarterly, 36*(4), 378–411.

Commeyras, M., & DeGroff, L. (1998). Literacy professionals' perspectives on professional development and pedagogy: A national survey. *Reading Research Quarterly, 33,* 434–472.

Delpit, L. (1988). The silenced dialogue: Power and pedagogy in educating other people's children. *Harvard Educational Review, 58,* 280–298.

Ericsson, K. A., & Kintsch, W. (1995). Long-term working memory. *Psychological Review, 102*(2), 211–245.

Graham, S., Harris, K. R., MacArthur, C. A., & Schwartz, S. (1991). Writing and writing instruction for students with learning disabilities: Review of a research program. *Learning Disability Quarterly, 14,* 89–114.

Hart, B., & Risley, T. R. (2003). The early catastrophe: The 30 million word gap. *American Educator, 27*(1), 4–9.

Heath, S. B. (1982). What no bedtime story means: Narrative skills at home and at school. *Language and Society, 11,* 49–76.

Kucan, L., & Beck, I. L. (1997). Thinking aloud and reading comprehension research: Inquiry, instruction, and social interaction. *Review of Educational Research, 67*(3), 271–299.

Maloch, B. (2002). Scaffolding student talk: One teacher's role in literature discussion groups. *Reading Research Quarterly, 37*(1), 94–112.

McIntyre, E., Kyle, D. W., & Moore, G. H. (2006). A primary-grade teacher's guidance toward small-group dialogue. *Reading Research Quarterly, 41*(1), 36–66.

McMahon, S. I., & Raphael, T. E. (with Goatley, V. J., & Pardo, L. S.). (1997). *The book club connection: Literacy learning and classroom talk.* New York: Teachers College Press.

Mehan, H. (1979). *Learning lessons.* Cambridge, MA: Harvard University Press.

Morocco, C.C., Hinden, A., Mata-Aguilar, C., & Clark-Chiarelli, N. (2001). Building a deep understanding of literature with middle-grade students with learning disabilities. *Learning Disability Quarterly, 24,* 47–58.

Nystrand, M. (2006, May). Research on the role of classroom discourse as it affects reading comprehension. *Research in the Teaching of English, 40,* 392–412.

Nystrand M., & Gamoran, A. (1991). Instructional discourse, student engagement, and literature achievement. *Research in the Teaching of English, 25,* 261–290.

Nystrand, M., Wu, L. L., Gamoran, A., Zeiser, S., & Long, D. A. (2003). Questions in time: Investigating the structure and dynamics of unfolding classroom discourse. *Discourse Processes, 35*(2), 135–198.

O'Flahavan, J. F. (1989). *An exploration of the effects of participant structure upon literacy development in reading group discussion.* (Unpublished doctoral dissertation). University of Illinois-Champaign.

Rogoff, B. (1990). *Apprenticeship in thinking: Cognitive development in social context.* New York: Oxford University Press.

Rosenblatt, L. M. (1978). *The reader, the text, the poem: The transactional theory of literary work.* Carbondale: Southern Illinois University Press.

Sandora, C., Beck, I., & McKeown, M. (1999). A comparison of two discussion strategies on students' comprehension and interpretation of complex literature. *Journal of Reading Psychology, 20,* 177–212.

Sirois, P., & Dorval, B. (1988). The role of returns to a prior topic in the negotiation of topic change: A developmental investigation. *Journal of Psycholinguistic Research, 17,* 185–210.

Trent, S. C., Artiles, A. J., & Englert, C. S. (1998). Deficit thinking to social constructivism. *Review of Research in Education, 23,* 277–307.

Vygotsky, L. S. (1962). *Thought and language.* In E. Hanfmann & G. Vakar (Eds. & Trans.). Cambridge, MA: MIT Press. (Original work published 1934)

Vygotsky, L. S. (1978). *Mind in society: The development of higher psychological processes.* In M. Cole, V. John-Steiner, S. Scribner, & E. Souberman (Eds. & Trans.). Cambridge, MA: Harvard University Press.

Wells, G. (1993). Reevaluating the IRE sequence: A proposal for the articulation of theories of activity and discourse for the analysis of teaching and learning in the classroom. *Linguistics and Education, 5,* 1–38.

Part V

Developmental Interventions

EDITORS: VICTORIA RISKO AND PATRICIA ANDERS

24

Expert Classroom Instruction
for Students with Reading Disabilities

Explicit, Intense, Targeted ... and Flexible

RUTH WHARTON-MCDONALD
University of New Hampshire

Children with learning disabilities represent about half of the students currently identified for special education (Denton, Vaughn, & Fletcher, 2003). The Presidents' Commission on Excellence in Special Education (2002) has estimated that two out of five children in special education are there because of difficulties in reading. Elsewhere in this volume, authors have described the characteristics of these students and specialized intervention programs developed to target their specific needs. In this chapter, I focus on the teaching and the learning environments created within heterogeneous classrooms—by regular education teachers—to support the growth and development of students with reading difficulties.

Until recently, it was widely believed that children who struggled to read in the primary grades were destined to continue their struggle as they progressed—trapped by their learning profiles, by the challenges posed by early reading development, and by instruction that failed to overcome those challenges. Juel's now classic (1988) study—in which the probability that a poor reader in first grade would be a poor reader in fourth grade was 0.88—was cited in nearly every examination of the effects of schooling on reading development. The findings from several recent studies, however, indicate that when struggling readers are matched with highly effective classroom teachers, their developmental trajectory *can* be altered (e.g., Bembry, Jordan, Gomez, Anderson & Mendro, 1998; Ferguson & Ladd, 1996; Foorman, Fletcher, Francis, Schatschneider, & Mehta, 1998; Juel & Minden-Cupp, 2000; O'Connor et al., 2002; Pressley, Allington, Wharton-McDonald, Block, & Morrow, 2001; Taylor, Pearson, Clark, & Walpole, 2000). Three different expert panels (the National Commission on Teaching and America's Future, 1997; the National Reading Panel, 2000; Snow, Burns, & Griffin, 1998) have concluded that the most powerful intervention tool that schools have to offer students who struggle to read is the classroom teacher. The expert practice of the teacher can overcome the failing trajectory of the young struggling reader, substantially reducing the

numbers of children who experience reading and other learning disabilities.

In a national study of first-grade classrooms, Pressley and his colleagues (Pressley et al., 2000) reported that the lowest-achieving students in classrooms with exemplary teachers achieved at the same level as the average students in classrooms with more typical teachers. Under the guidance of exemplary teachers, students not only performed better on a standardized test at the end of the year, they spent more time engaged in instruction, read a variety of texts at grade level, and wrote more coherently than students in classrooms with typical teachers. In a longitudinal study, Bembry et al. (1998) found that after 3 years, students enrolled in classrooms with high-quality instruction achieved standardized reading scores that were approximately 40 percentile ranks higher than students enrolled in classrooms with lower quality instruction. Studies such as these—and the others cited above—emphasize the role of the classroom teacher. Indeed, Snow and her colleagues at the National Research Council have concluded that high-quality classroom instruction in the early grades is "the single best weapon against reading failure" (Snow, Burns & Griffin, 1998, p. 343). Thus, despite a current emphasis on programs, materials, and assessment tools, it is the *teacher*—and the instruction she or he provides in the classroom—that matters most to the development of successful readers.

Distinguishing Instructional Needs for Disabled and Non-Disabled Readers

Students with reading disabilities are more like their non-disabled peers than they are different from them. All learners need high-quality instruction in the components of reading (concepts of print, phonological awareness, phonics, fluency, vocabulary, comprehension, and writing) matched to their current understandings and abilities; they all need instruction that motivates them to engage in the learning process; they all need access to texts they can—and want to—read, and adequate time to read them. In *Preventing Reading Disabilities*, Snow and her colleagues (Snow, Burns & Griffin, 1998, p. 159) suggest that "there is little evidence to support the notion that struggling readers, even those with identified disabilities, need dramatically different reading instruction from students who learn to read more easily."

Students with reading disabilities, of course, are not all alike; nor do they all benefit from a single type of instruction. They do, however, share some learning characteristics. What students with reading disabilities need is instruction that is more *explicit*, more *intense*, and provides more *support* than instruction suited to their typically developing peers (Foorman & Torgesen, 2001; Jenkins et al., 1994).

Thus, despite some common misconceptions about best practices, effective classroom teachers do not provide dramatically different instruction for students with disabilities. The key to these teachers' expertise lies in their ability to identify the struggling readers in their classrooms and to know how to modify the nature and the intensity of high-quality instruction to meet the needs of those students (Fuchs, Fuchs, & Hamlett, 1998).

What Students with Reading Disabilities Need

Explicitness   As they learn to read, students with reading disabilities are less likely than their peers to notice and generalize patterns in the sounds and spellings of the language on their own (Atkinson, Wilhite, Frey, & Williams, 2002; Foorman et al., 1998). They are less likely to infer strategies required for comprehension (Atkinson et al., 2002; Jenkins et al., 1994). Students at risk for reading difficulties often do not discover what teachers leave unsaid about the use of strategies for reading; therefore effective instruction for these students includes an explicit sharing of knowledge needed to read—at the word level, for fluency, and for the use of comprehension strategies and metacognition (Foorman & Torgesen, 2001). Atkinson and her colleagues propose that "a never assume" approach often works well for students with learning disabilities (Atkinson et al., 2002, p. 160).

Explicit instruction means that teachers teach skills and strategies clearly and directly. They model their use, and deliberately guide students' application of learning in text. The instruction and scaffolding provided by teachers through explicit instruction reduces students' reliance on inference to figure out how written language works (Denton et al., 2003). In describing the explicitness required by these learners, Foorman and Torgesen (2001) suggest that they need two types of scaffolding. The first is a careful sequencing of skills so that concepts and skills build gradually upon a strong, coherent foundation. The second is an on-going teacher-student dialogue that demonstrates directly to the child the kind of processing or thinking that must be done in order to accomplish a particular task successfully.

In a study by Foorman and her colleagues (1998), teachers provided one of three types of word level instruction to first and second graders receiving Title I services. Students in the *direct* code group received direct instruction in letter-sound correspondences practiced in decodable text. The lessons introduced the 42 phonic rules using sound-spelling cards, alliterative stories and text with controlled vocabulary matched to the most recent instruction. Those in the *embedded* code group received less direct instruction in systematic sound-spelling patterns embedded in connected text. The emphasis in this group was on phonemic awareness and spelling patterns, taught using predictable books. And students in the implicit code group received either the district standard curriculum, emphasizing the importance of a print-rich environment with teacher as facilitator, or a similar intervention grounded in an established definition of whole language instruction. Students in this group received implicit instruction in the alphabetic code while reading connected text. All of the interventions took place in the context of a literature-rich classroom environment. Over the course of the year-long intervention, children in the direct code group improved in word reading at a faster rate and had higher word recognition skills than those receiving the implicit code instruction. Moreover, children who began with low scores in phonological processing showed more growth in word reading than children with low phonological processing scores in the other instructional groups. The positive effects were limited to growth in decoding and did not extend to differences in passage comprehension. However, this finding is hardly surprising, given that the instruction did not address comprehension; one might hypothesize that the same students who benefited from explicit instruction in word recognition skills would also benefit from explicit instruction in comprehension strategies.

Many studies have supported the explicit instruction of comprehension strategies for all children (National Reading Panel, 2000; Block & Pressley, 2002). A review of the research on the teaching of comprehension strategies to students with learning disabilities in particular confirms that this type of instruction may be especially valuable for these students (Gersten, Fuchs, Williams, & Baker, 2001). Joanna Williams, one of the review's authors, argues that while a constructivist approach in which students learn to be metacognitive, reflecting on their own thinking while they read, has been effective at the middle and high school levels (e.g., Allington, Guice, Michelson, Baker & Li, 1996), it is not adequate for struggling and at-risk students at the elementary level (Williams, 2005). Williams conducted a series of studies with at-risk second and third graders that assessed the effectiveness of explicit instruction in narrative and expository text structures. Compared with groups of students who received content instruction but not explicit comprehension instruction, the students with explicit instruction group demonstrated superior comprehension of themes taught—in both instructional materials and on near-transfer tasks involving the same themes.

Intensity   Students who struggle with reading not only need explicit instruction, they need more of it (Foorman

& Torgesen, 2001; Torgesen, 2000). Kvale has described instruction for these learners as necessarily more "intense" and more "relentless" than effective instruction for other students (1988, p.335). Generally speaking, there are two related ways to increase instructional intensity: (a) by increasing the amount of time children spend in instruction, and/or (b) by reducing the size of the group in which students learn.

Increasing instructional time. Traditionally, it has been the case that students placed in groups for struggling readers have spent less time receiving instruction (Hunter, cited in Barr & Dreeben, 1991; McDermott, 1976), have spent less of that instructional time on task (Gambrell, 1984); and read less material (Allington, 1984; Barr & Dreeben, 1983). This is in direct opposition to their needs, which are for more instruction, more time on task, and more opportunities to read.

Daily lessons and support are more likely to impact learning than lessons scheduled less frequently (Allington, 2006). The strong history of Reading Recovery (Clay, 1993; Forbes & Briggs, 2003 ; Lyons, 2003), in which poor first-grade readers receive 20 (or more) weeks of daily, individual reading instruction is evidence of the effectiveness of directed, frequent instruction. In a study of early intervention based loosely on the Reading Recovery model, Vellutino and his colleagues (Vellutino & Scanlon, 2002; Vellutino et al., 1996) also provided 30-minute sessions of daily tutoring to poor readers in the first grade. The model matched the intensity of Reading Recovery, differing in part, in the amount of professional development provided for teachers (Vellutino's study required significantly less teacher training than that demanded by Reading Recovery). Vellutino's tutors—all of whom were certified teachers—addressed letter identification, phoneme awareness, word reading skills, and practice in reading connected text. After one or two semesters (depending on student progress), the majority of these children became average readers.

Despite the recognized value of daily instruction for struggling readers, it is rarely possible for a student to meet with the reading specialist every day. It is the classroom teacher who necessarily sees every student every day, who can ensure such frequent instructional opportunities for the students who need them. Evidence indicates that effective classroom teachers spend more time teaching—and their students spend more time engaged in instruction—in on-task behavior (Bohn, Roehrig, & Pressley, 2004; Pressley et al., 2001; Wharton-McDonald, Pressley, & Motretta, 199). This is especially important as it relates to students' need for instructional intensity.

Decreasing group size. The most practical method for increasing instructional intensity for students with reading disabilities is to provide instruction in small groups created to provide targeted instruction to particular groups of learners (Foorman & Torgesen, 2001). In fact, grouping students for reading is almost a universal practice (Barr &

Dreeben, 1991; Hiebert, 1983; Jenkins et al., 1994). Unfortunately, students with reading disabilities are often pulled out of their classrooms and provided with instruction in groups designed to meet the indications of overall reading levels—and scheduling demands. Thus, the groups tend to be relatively large (4–7 students) and relatively undifferentiated with respect to specific literacy needs (Allington, 2002; Elbaum, Vaughn, Hughes & Moody, 2000; Vaughn et al., 2002). Moreover, such groups have been criticized in the past for dooming low achieving students to a lifetime in low groups (Anderson, Hiebert, Scott & Wilkinson, 1985; Barr & Dreeban, 1991; Gamoran, 1992; Hiebert, 1983; Oakes, 1985) and for providing consistently lower quality, less engaging instruction (Allington, 1983; Hiebert, 1983). Such grouping practices clearly result in instruction that fails to meet the needs of individual children.

Despite the evidence against traditional intervention groups, expert classroom teachers regularly utilize small groups and one-on-one instruction to meet the needs of individual children. The available evidence indicates that this form of intensive instruction and support is significantly more effective than whole class or large group instruction—particularly for students who struggle in reading (Pressley et al., 2001; Schumm, Moody & Vaughn, 2000; Taylor, Pearson, Clark & Walpole, 2000). In a review of 18 studies of early interventions with struggling readers, Wanzek and Vaughn (2007) reported the largest effects for individual interventions and the smallest effects for interventions with the largest group sizes. Clearly, students with reading disabilities benefit from more individualized time with an effective teacher.

The work of the CIERA School Change project (e.g., Taylor et al., 2000) confirms these findings. In studying schools and classrooms that beat the odds—where students learn to read and write at high levels in the face of overwhelming odds against it—Taylor and her colleagues found that the most accomplished teachers and the teachers in the most effective schools consistently relied on small groups to teach and support important literacy skills and understandings.

The critical difference between traditional small groups, in which students have received low-quality instruction and failed to improve, and those where student achievement has been accelerated appears to lie in the expertise of the teacher—and some have argued—in the location of the group itself. Allington and others have argued vehemently against instructional practices that remove students from the classroom and place them in remedial groups in an alternative location (e.g., the resource room). A great deal of instructional time can be lost in the transition from classroom to intervention space. When students spend time engaged in effective instruction as opposed to packing up their materials and transitioning down the hall to the resource room, they learn more.

While instructional time lost to transitions is likely a factor in student learning (or lack thereof), the most important factor in determining learning is undoubtedly the teacher.

In fact, attempts to keep students in regular classrooms by having Title I or special education aides work with students in classroom groups have been no more effective than similar instruction provided in groups pulled out of the classroom (Archambault, 1989; Puma, Jones, Rock, & Fernandez, 1993). Expert teachers who use small groups in the classroom adapt both instruction and group membership to meet the immediate needs of the students in ways that less expert teachers are not able to do. They use ongoing formative assessments to determine the specific needs of individual students and to ensure that students are neither overwhelmed by instruction that is too difficult or bored by instruction that is no longer needed.

In summarizing the research on group size and intervention effects, Allington (2006) concludes that "as the size of the instructional group decreases, the likelihood of acceleration increases. Thus, the most effective designs employ the most expert teachers and have them tutoring or working with very small (2–3) instructional groups" (p. 152). Indeed, in a meta-analysis examining the effects of grouping practices, Elbaum and associates (2006) found consistently positive effects of grouping practices that increased instructional intensity.

What Expert Teachers Provide

> Teaching is more than a technical process; it is a complex human process in which the teacher's knowledge of reading and learning processes intersects with his or her knowledge of the needs, interests, and individual characteristics of the learners. (Farstrup, 2002, pp. 1–2)

Expert teachers have substantial knowledge of literacy processes, of pedagogy, of books and other teaching materials, and of their students (e.g., Allington & Johnston, 2002; Pressley et al., 2001; Taylor & Pearson, 2002). Their ability to apply their knowledge in providing learning experiences for their students is what makes them so effective. It is what enables students with reading disabilities to develop the skills, strategies, and dispositions of successful readers. Expert teachers provide instruction that targets the particular skills needed by individual learners. They provide explicit and intense instruction, accompanied by ongoing scaffolding to ensure student success. They provide lessons and materials at an appropriate level of challenge, so that learners are engaged and moving forward. And they do it in an environment that nurtures motivation and sustains engagement.

Instruction Matched to Individual Skills, Understandings, and Needs

> You should design the program around your students, not the students around a program. . . We have students of all different abilities. We should look at each of their individual abilities and work with them and find something that will work for each of them at different levels. (a highly effective teacher, cited in Achinstein & Ogawa, 2006, p. 48)

Teaching is not a generic enterprise. For any instruction to be effective, it must target the learning needs and characteristics of a particular student or group of students. This is true for both disabled and non-disabled literacy learners: "Effective instruction is characterized by adaptation of the standard form of instruction in ways that better meet the needs of individual students" (Allington, 2006, p. 149). The profiles of learners with reading disabilities are found on the same continua as learners without reading disabilities. Since all students vary in their development, it is reasonable to speculate that all students will differ with respect to the aspects of reading instruction that will be most critical for their success at a particular time. It is crucial that the teacher matches the instruction to the specific needs of the learner (Atkinson et al., 2002). Despite this well recognized finding, a summary of observational studies conducted with students with learning disabilities indicates that all too often, these students are provided with generic reading instruction that is *not* directly linked to their specific needs (Denton et al., 2003; Vaughn, Levy, Coleman, & Bos, 2002).

To target support to individual students, teachers must have detailed knowledge about literacy processes and their development; they must be familiar with a wide range of reading materials and the pedagogy required to use them effectively; and they must know their students extremely well. Expert teachers are astute observers of their students. They are familiar with students' cognitive abilities, their learning histories and characteristics, their preferences, their temperaments, their cultural influences, and their goals (Allington & Johnston, 2002; Berliner, 1992; Clay, 1993; Louden et al., 2005; Mazzoli & Gambrell, 2003; Pressley et al., 2001). Expert teachers combine their knowledge of literacy development and their knowledge of students as learners to individualize the instruction they provide. Not all students with reading disabilities share the same set of difficulties. While this point seems obvious, it is too often the case that they all receive the same intervention nevertheless. If the special education teacher has been trained in the LiPS program (see www.lindamoodbell.com), then all of the students in grades 1-4 with reading disabilities receive the same sequence of lessons from the LiPS manual. If the teacher has been trained in Wilson Reading (see www.wilsonlanguage.com), then everyone receives that program instead. There are undoubtedly students for whom these programs (both of which meet the criteria of explicit and intensive) are useful. What differentiates the expert teacher from a less effective colleague is the ability to match the intervention to the individual student. The expert's planning is not based on a set program or what is written in a teacher's manual; rather it is based on what an individual student needs at a given time (Thomas & Barksdale-Ladd, 1995; Pressley et al., 2001; Allington & Johnston, 2002). Thus, each learner receives the instruction and scaffolding needed to move him or her forward on a given day. While this is important for all learners, Juel (1996) concludes that the ability to offer individualized, targeted support in the form of scaffolding while children are developing reading skills may actually have increasing significance as the severity of a child's learning disability increases.

Scaffolding   Exemplary teachers are expert at scaffolding students' learning (Allington & Johnston, 2002; Pressley, 2006 ; Loudon et al., 2005; Taylor & Pearson, 2002; Wharton-McDonald et al., 1998). Scaffolding in this context refers to the support provided by a teacher or a peer that enables the student to solve a problem on his or her own that he or she would not otherwise be able to solve independently. Scaffolding may take the form of a question or a hint (sometimes a question that is a hint), or a reminder to pay attention to a particular feature or strategy that the student is not using (for example, "What do you know about words that end with an 'e'?" or "Is there a strategy you could use to figure that out?"). By definition, scaffolding is individualized and cannot be scripted in advance. Scaffolding provides immediate support to a reader so that she will stay engaged and learning. It demands a high level of knowledge of both the student and the instructional task in which he is engaged.

Appropriate Level of Challenge   A great deal of research confirms the significant positive effect of matching a student with the appropriate instructional materials. To maximize learning, learners must be moderately challenged by instructional tasks and texts, without being overwhelmed. The Beginning Teacher Evaluation study (Denham & Lieberman, 1980) was among the first of many to find that students learn best when they experience high rates of success on the tasks in which they are engaged. They have the lowest rates of learning when they are expected to complete tasks which are too difficult and on which they make numerous errors. In confirming these findings, others have noted that students who experience high rates of success not only learn more, but they also have better attitudes toward learning and are more motivated to pursue other, similar tasks (e.g., Berliner, 1992; Brophy, 1987 ; Guthrie & Wigfield, 2000).

With respect to reading, these findings emphasize the importance of providing students with texts that are not only appealing, but also accessible. Allington (2005) refers to the matching of pupils and texts as one of the "pillars of effective reading instruction" (p. 347). All too often, students with reading disabilities (and others who struggle) are expected to read texts that are well beyond the moderate level of challenge that research supports. This is especially true at the intermediate and secondary levels, where teachers can be driven to "cover curriculum" rather than acknowledge students where they are and move them forward. O'Connor and her colleagues (2002) reported that when struggling middle school readers were asked to read grade-level texts as opposed to texts matched to their actual reading abilities, their reading development was adversely affected. According to Allington (2002), any classroom in which all students are expected to read the same book "will fail to successfully develop reading proficiencies in all students" (p. 276).

Motivational Learning Environments   Students can only learn from engaging with texts they can read. Thus, matching the difficulty of a text to the instructional level of the student is critical from the perspective of skills development. Moreover, when students experience success with a text, they are more likely to be motivated to sustain their effort and engagement (Brophy, 1987; Guthrie & Wigfield, 2000). Expert teachers do many things to motivate children with disabilities to engage in classroom learning opportunities. They construct interesting lessons; they connect reading and writing to content area learning; they provide students with moderately challenging tasks and a variety of interesting book selections; and they use positive redirection to manage behavior (Bohn et al., 2004; Pressley et al., 2001). The research on reading development and instruction includes many references to the importance of motivation. Many of them (e.g., the National Reading Panel Report) note the need for further research. Every section in the National Reading Panel Report (2000) mentions motivation as a potentially significant variable, but one on which there are still scant data. Expert teachers, however, create classrooms where students are already motivated and engaged. Consequently, students in these classrooms spend more time on task, more time reading, and more time learning.

Informed Flexibility   It is now well recognized that there is not—and cannot be—one best way to teach children to read (Allington, 2002; Allington & Walmsley, 2007; Duffy & Hoffman, 2002; Farstrup, 2002; International Reading Association, 2000; Mathes et al., 2005; Mazzoli & Gambrell, 2003; Taylor & Pearson, 2002). The nature of human development means that, even within the context of a single, grade-level classroom, individual students will enter with different understandings and backgrounds, learn in different ways, at different rates, and in the context of different social environments. The most effective teachers use their complex knowledge of literacy, pedagogy, and student characteristics flexibly, to provide uniquely responsive instruction for their students (Wharton-McDonald, 2008).

In contrast to the frequently documented one-size-fits-all approach to students with reading disabilities (e.g., teach them all explicit phonics, or group them for instruction according to a particular available program), the expert teacher eschews a single, static approach in favor of a flexible, dynamic one. Expert teachers have extensive knowledge in literacy development, in the range of instructional materials, in children's literature, in child development, and in the learning profiles of their students. Using this depth of knowledge, the teacher can sit with two fourth graders, both identified with reading disabilities, both reading at a level J (mid-second grade), and determine that Anna needs instruction that builds English vocabulary, background knowledge in the content areas, and fluency, whereas Mohammed has significant difficulties with phonemic awareness and has not yet mastered decoding of multisyllabic words. Moreover, having made an individualized analysis of their needs, the expert teacher is familiar with a range of strategies and materials she can use to support each student's growth.

The teacher described above begins with a great deal of knowledge. But just knowing about students, strategies, and materials is only part of what makes her effective. It is the flexibility to shift methods and materials to meet the dynamic needs of the students that characterizes the most effective teachers (Wharton-McDonald, 2008). It has been a frequent critique of special education that once students are identified and coded, they remain in the system for life (Mueller, 2001). In too many cases, these students continue to receive more of the same instruction that hasn't worked in the past; neither the system nor their teachers have had the informed flexibility to recognize what is working (and what isn't) and make ongoing changes to ensure growth. The special education placement in these cases tends to stabilize students' reading growth rather than accelerating it (Denton et al., 2003). After all, even if the instruction is effective and the student is making progress, then his needs are not the same as they were when the intervention began; almost by definition, the student will require a new combination of instructional variables in order to continue to move forward. More of the same is rarely the best combination for long. "In the final analysis, effective teaching and learning rests on the shoulders of the teacher who makes informed decisions about the instructional approaches and practices that are most appropriate for [individual students]" (Mazzoli & Gambrell, 2003, p.11). The flexibility to make these decisions in an always changing context is central to the success of effective teachers.

The Role of Classroom Context

Beyond the significant role of the teacher in supporting the development of children with reading disabilities, the classroom context itself (the students) appears to play a role in students' success. The 1997 reauthorization of the Individuals with Disabilities Education Act Amendment (IDEA) specifically identified the general education setting as the most appropriate placement for all students (IDEA ref; Schmidt, Rozendal, & Greenman, 2002). Being in a general education setting provides students with access to the same high-quality instruction offered to their typically achieving peers. It also provides struggling students with ongoing interactions—social and academic—with those peers. Foorman, York, Santi, and Francis (2008) reported that when beginning readers were placed in classrooms with higher average fluency scores, they demonstrated greater achievement gains than similar students who were placed in classrooms with lower fluency scores.

In the study cited, the *combination* of student pretest score (in fluency) and the mean pretest score for a classroom was a better predictor of student achievement than the student pretest score alone. Examining first- and second-grade data from 210 randomly selected schools in Texas, Foorman and her colleagues found that students with low fluency scores in first grade who happened to be placed in classrooms with higher mean fluency scores achieved higher fluency scores in second grade. The authors hypothesize that gains in fluency were not influenced by repeated reading (conducted in all first-grade classrooms) alone, but that "repeated readings in the context of faster reading models, in this case faster reading peers in the classroom" accounted for the difference in achievement gains (p. 391). Findings such as these related to classroom context have implications not only for inclusion practices (in which students with disabilities are educated in regular classrooms), but for grouping practices within the classroom. Foorman et al. (2008) conclude that for slower readers, simply being in a classroom of faster reading peers "seems to be an intervention all by itself" (p. 391). These recent findings suggest the need to further investigate the role of the student-generated classroom environment in other areas of literacy learning as well.

Students and Teachers: Understanding Students' Needs and Addressing Them in the Classroom Context

Students with reading disabilities have much in common with their typically developing peers. They demand high-quality reading instruction that supports development across the essential components of literacy; they need access to materials they can—and want to—read; they need opportunities to read and discuss books with others; they need motivating learning environments that support ongoing engagement in learning. And they need instruction that flexibly adapts to their changing needs. From an instructional perspective, what distinguishes students with reading disabilities is their need for particularly explicit instruction, provided with greater intensity than that which characterizes typical reading instruction. Expert teachers understand the needs of their students and are able to provide a great deal of informed, targeted instruction in the context of a motivating environment. Moreover, they flexibly adapt their instruction in response to student successes, struggles, and interests in order to sustain maximum student growth. The critical role of the teacher in developing and sustaining student learning is recognized by a growing number of researchers and educational organizations. Students with reading disabilities *can* make accelerated growth and develop the literacy behaviors and dispositions demonstrated by their typically achieving peers. They need to spend less time in static, ineffective learning environments, and more time in the company of expert classroom teachers and successful peers.

References

Achinstein, B., & Ogawa, R. (2006). (In)fidelity: What the resistance of new teachers reveals about professional principles and prescriptive educational policies. *Harvard Educational Review, 76*(1), 30–63.

Allington, R. L. (1984). Content coverage and contextual reading in reading groups. *Journal of Reading Behavior, 16*, 85–96.

Allington, R. L. (2002). Research on reading/learning disability interventions. In A. E. Farstrup & S. J. Samels (Eds.). *What research has to say about reading instruction* (3rd ed., pp. 261–290). Newark, DE: International Reading Association.

Allington, R. L. (2005, June/July). The other five "pillars" of effective reading instruction. *Reading Today, 22*(6), 3.

Allington, R. L. (2006). *What really matters for struggling readers: Designing research-based programs* (2nd ed.). Boston: Pearson Education.

Allington, R. L., Guice, S., Michlson, N., Baker, K., & Li, S. (1996). Literature-based curricula in high poverty schools. In M. F. Graves, P. van den Broek, & B. M. Taylor (Eds.), *The first R: Every child's right to read* (pp. 73–96). New York: Teachers College Press.

Allington, R. L., & Johnston, P. H. (2002). *Reading to learn: Lessons from exemplary fourth-grade classrooms*. New York: Guilford.

Allington, R. L., & Walmsley, S. (Eds.). (2007). *No quick fix, the RTI edition: Rethinking literacy programs in America's elementary schools*. New York: Teachers College Press.

Anderson, R. C., Hiebert, E. H., Scott, J. A., & Wilkinson, I. A. (1985). *Becoming a nation of readers*. Washington, DC: National Institute of Education.

Archambault, M. X. (1989). Instructional setting and other design features of compensatory education programs. In R. E. Slavin, N. Karweit, & N. Madden (Eds.), *Effective programs for students at risk* (pp. 220–263). Boston: Allyn-Bacon.

Atkinson, T. S., Wilhite, K. L., Frey, L. M., & Williams, S. C. (2002). Reading instruction for the struggling reader: Implications for teachers of students with learning disabilities or emotional/behavioral disorders. *Preventing School Failure, 46*(4), 158–162.

Barr, R., & Dreeben, R. (1983). *How schools work*. Chicago: University of Chicago Press.

Barr, R., & Dreeben, R. (1991). Grouping students for reading instruction. In D. P. Pearson (Ed.), *Handbook of reading research* (Vol. II, pp. 885–912). New York: Longmire.

Bembry, K. L., Jordan, H. R., Gomez, E., Anderson, M., & Mendro, R. L. (1998, April). *Policy implications of long-term teacher effects on student achievement*. Paper presented at the American Educational Research Association.

Berliner, D. (1992). Exemplary performances: Studies of expertise in teaching. *Collected speeches*. National Art Education Association Convention, Milwaukee, WI.

Block, C. C., & Pressley, M. (2002). *Comprehension instruction: Research-based best practices*. New York: Guilford.

Bohn, C. M., Roehrig, A. D., & Pressley, G. (2004). The first days of school in the classrooms of two more effective and four less effective primary-grades teachers. *The Elementary School Journal, 104*, 269–287.

Brophy, J. (1987). On motivating students. In D. Berliner & B. Rosenshine (Eds.), *Talks to teachers* (pp. 201–245). New York: Random House.

Clay, M. (1993). *Reading recovery: A guidebook for teachers in training*. Portsmouth, NH: Heinemann.

Denton, C. A., Vaughn, S., & Fletcher, J. M. (2003). Bringing research-based practice in reading intervention to scale. *Learning Disabilities Research & Practice, 18*, 201–211.

Duffy, G., & Hoffman, J. (2002). Beating the odds in literacy education: Not "betting on" but the "bettering of" schools and teachers. In B. Taylor & P. D. Pearson (Eds.), *Teaching reading: Effective schools, accomplished teachers* (pp. 375–387). Mahway, NJ: Erlbaum.

Elbaum, B., Vaughn, S., Hughes, M. T., & Moody, S. W. (2000). How effective are one-to-one tutoring programs in reading for elementary students at risk for reading failure? A meta-analysis of the intervention research. *Journal of Educational Psychology, 92*, 605–619.

Farstrup, A. E. (2002). There is more to effective reading instruction than research. In E. Farstrup & S. J. Samuels (Eds.), *What research has to say about reading instruction* (3rd ed., pp. 1–7). Newark, DE: International Reading Association.

Ferguson, R. F., & Ladd, H. F. (1996). How and why money matters: An analysis of Alabama schools. In H. Ladd (Ed.) *Holding schools accountable: Performance-based reform in education* (pp. 265–298). Washington, DC: Brookings Institution.

Foorman, B. R., Fletcher, J. M., Francis, D. J., Schatschneider, C., &

Mehta, P. (1998). The role of instruction in learning to read: Preventing reading failure in at-risk children. *Journal of Educational Psychology, 90*, 37–55.

Foorman, B. R., & Torgesen, J. (2001). Critical elements of classroom and small-group instruction promote reading success in all children. *Learning Disabilities Research & Practice, 16*, 203–212.

Foorman, B. R., York, M., Santi, K. L., & Francis, D. (2008). Contextual effects on predicting risk for reading difficulties in first and second grade. *Reading and Writing, 21*, 371–394.

Fuchs, L. S., Fuchs, D., & Hamlett, C. (1989). Effects of instructional use of curriculum-based measurement to enhance instructional programs. *Remedial and Special Education, 10*, 43–52.

Gambrell, L. (1984). How much time do children spend reading during teacher-directed reading instruction? In J. Niles & L. Harris (Eds.), *Changing perspectives on research in reading/language processing and instruction. Thirty-Third Yearbook of the National Reading Conference* (pp. 193–198). Rochester, NY: National Reading Conference.

Gamoran, A. (1992). Is ability grouping equitable? *Educational Leadership, 50*(2), 11–17.

Gersten, R., Fuchs, L. S., Williams, J. P., & Baker, S. (2001). Teaching reading comprehension strategies to students with learning disabilities: A review of the research. *Review of Educational Research, 71*, 279–320.

Guthrie, J. T., & Wigfield, A. (2000). Engagement and motivation in reading. In M. Kamil, P. B. Mosenthal, P. D. Pearson, & R. Barr (Eds.), *Handbook of reading research* (Vol. 3, pp. 403–422). Mahwah, NJ: Erlbaum.

Hiebert, E. H. (1983). An examination of ability grouping for reading instruction. *Reading Research Quarterly, 8*, 231–255.

Individuals with Disabilities Education Act Amendments of 1997 (IDEA), Publ. L. No. 105-17, 20 U.S.C. 1400 et seq.

International Reading Association. (2000). *Making a difference means making it different: Honoring children's rights to excellent reading instruction*. Position statement of the International Reading Association. Newark, DE: International Reading Association.

Jenkins, J. R., Jewell, M., Leicester, N., O'Connor, R. E., Jenkins, L. M., & Troutner, N. M. (1994). Accommodations for individual differences without classroom ability groups: An experiment in school restructuring. *Exceptional Children, 60*, 344–358.

Juel, C. (1988). Learning to read and write: A longitudinal study of 54 children from first to fourth grades. *Journal of Educational Psychology, 80*, 437–447.

Juel, C. (1996). What makes literacy tutoring effective? *Reading Research Quarterly, 31*, 268–289.

Juel, C., & Minden-Cupp, J. (2000). Learning to read words: Linguistic units and instructional strategies. *Reading Research Quarterly, 35*, 458–492.

Kvale (1988). The long-term consequences of learning disabilities. In M. C. Wang, H. J. Walberg, & M. C. Reynolds (Eds.), *The handbook of special education: Research and practice* (pp. 303–344). New York: Pergamon.

Loudon, W., Rohl, M., Barratt-Pugh, C., Brown, C., Cairney, T., Elderfield, J., et al. (2005). In teachers' hands: Effective literacy teaching practices in the early years of schooling. [Special issue]. *Australian Journal of Language and Literacy, 27*(3).

Mathes, P. G., Denton, C. A., Fletcher, J. M., Anthony, J. L., Francis, D. J., & Schatschneider, C. (2005). The effects of theoretically different instruction and student characteristics on the skills of struggling readers. *Reading Research Quarterly, 40*, 148–182.

Mazzoli, S., & Gambrell, L. B. (2003). Principles of best practice: Finding the common ground. In L. M. Morrow, L. B. Gambrell, & M. Pressley (Eds.), *Best practices in literacy instruction* (2nd ed., pp. 9–21). New York: Guilford.

McDermott, R. (1976). *Kids make sense: An ethnographic account of the interactional management of success and failure in one first-grade classroom*. (Unpublished doctoral dissertation). Stanford University, Palo Alto, California.

Mueller, P. (2001). *Lifers: Learning from at-risk adolescent readers.* Portsmouth, NH: Heinemann.

National Reading Panel. (2000). *Teaching children to read: An evidence-based assessment of the scientific research literature on reading and its implications for reading instruction.* Washington, DC: National Institute of Child Health and Human Development and U.S. Department of Education.

Oakes, J. (1985). *Keeping track: How schools structure inequality.* New Haven, CT: Yale University Press.

O'Connor, R., Bell, K., Harty, K., Larkin, L., Sackor, S., & Zigmond, N. (2002). Teaching reading to poor readers in the intermediate grades: A comparison of text difficulty. *Journal of Educational Psychology, 94,* 474–485.

President's Commission on Excellence in Special Education. (2002). *A new era: Revitalizing special education for children and their families.* Retrieved from http://www.ed.gov/inits/commissionsboards

Pressley, M., Allington, R. L., Wharton-McDonald, R., Block, C. C., & Morrow, L. (2001). *Learning to read: Lessons from exemplary first-grade classrooms.* New York: Guilford.

Pressley, M., Wharton-McDonald, R., Allington, R. L., Block, C. C., Morrow, L., Tracey, D., et al. (2000). A study of effective first-grade reading instruction. *Scientific Studies of Reading, 5,* 35–58.

Puma, M. J., Jones, C. C., Rock, D., & Fernandez, R. (1993). *Prospects: The congressionally mandated study of educational growth and opportunity — the interim report.* (No. GPO 1993 0-354-886 QL3). Washington, DC: U. S. Department of Education, Office of Planning and Evaluation Services.

Samuels, C. A. (2007, September 10). Experts eye solutions to the 4th grade slump. *Education Week,* 1–4. Retrieved from http://www.edweek.org/ew/articles/

Schmidt, R. J., Rozendal, M. S., & Greenman, G. G. (2002). Reading instruction in the inclusion classroom: Research-based practices. *Remedial and Special Education, 23*(3), 130–140.

Schumm, J. S., Moody, S. W., & Vaughn, S. (2000). Grouping for reading instruction: Does one size fit all? *Journal of Learning Disabilities, 33,* 477–488.

Snow, C. E., Burns, M. S., & Griffin, P. (Eds.). (1998). *Preventing reading difficulties in young children.* Washington, DC: National Academy Press.

Taylor, B., & Pearson, P. D. (2002). *Teaching reading: Effective schools, accomplished teachers.* Mahwah, NJ: Erlbaum.

Taylor, B., Pearson, P. D., Clark, K., & Walpole, S. (2000). Effective schools and accomplished teachers: Lessons from primary grade reading instruction in low-income schools. *The Elementary School Journal, 101,* 121–165.

Thomas, K. F., & Barksdale-Ladd, M. A. (1995). Effective literacy classrooms: Teachers and students exploring literacy together. In C. K. Kinzer, K. A. Hinchman, & D. J. Leu (Eds.), *Inquiries into literacy theory and practice: Forty-sixth yearbook of the National Reading Conference* (pp. 37–53). Chicago: National Reading Conference.

Torgesen, J. K. (2000). Individual differences in response to early interventions in reading: The lingering problem of treatment resisters. *Learning Disabilities Research & Practice, 15,* 55–64.

Vaughn, S., Levy, S., Coleman, M., & Bos, C. S. (2002). Reading instruction for students with LD and EBD: A synthesis of observation studies. *Journal of Special Education, 36*(1), 2–13.

Velluntino, F. R., & Scanlon, D. M. (2002). The interactive strategies approach to reading intervention. *Contemporary Educational Psychology, 27,* 573–635.

Vellutino, F. R., Scanlon, D. M., Sipay, E., Small, S., Pratt, A., et al. (1996). Cognitive profiles of difficult-to-remediate and readily remediated poor readers: Early intervention as a vehicle for distinguishing between cognitive and experiential deficits as basic causes of specific reading disability. *Journal of Educational Psychology, 88,* 601–638.

Wanzek, J., & Vaughn, S. (2007). Research-based implications from extensive early reading interventions. *School Psychology Review, 36,* 541–561.

Wharton-McDonald, R. (2008). The dynamics of flexibility in effective literacy teaching. In K. B. Cartwright (Ed.), *Literacy processes: Cognitive flexibility in learning and teaching* (pp. 342–357). New York: Guilford.

Williams, J. P. (2005). Instruction in reading comprehension for primary-grade students: A focus on text structure. *The Journal of Special Education, 39*(1), 6–18.

25

Cultural Modeling

Building on Cultural Strengths as an Alternative to Remedial Reading Approaches

MARJORIE FAULSTICH ORELLANA
University of California, Los Angeles

JENNIFER REYNOLDS
University of South Carolina

DANNY CORTEZ MARTÍNEZ
University of California, Los Angeles

In this chapter, we survey research that takes a sociohistorical approach to the remediation of reading difficulties, especially for students from non-dominant groups. This approach starts from the assumption that all people engage in rich repertoires of linguistic practice (Gutierrez & Rogoff, 2003) in their everyday lives and that those repertoires of practice can be resources for learning in school (Lee, 2007; Orellana & Reynolds, 2008). Teachers can model literacy skills development on the cultural practices of their students in ways that leverage existing skills. Unlike deficit-based (Valencia, 1997; see also Gutierrez, 2007) approaches to remediating learning challenges faced by students from non-dominant groups, a Cultural Modeling framework values students' actual histories, lived experiences, linguistic repertoires and participation in cultural practices; it does not call for prescriptive teaching based on "broad, under-examined generalities about groups" (Gutierrez & Rogoff, 2003, p. 20) nor does it equate "culture" with race/ethnicity or any categorical group membership. Cultural Modeling also differs from other approaches that draw connections between in- and out-of-school learning such as those that focus on correcting presumed "mismatches" between home and school cultural practices. Instead, Cultural Modeling researchers use ethnographic and sociolinguistic methods to identify analogues between everyday cultural practices and content knowledge. In this chapter we will examine the roots of a Cultural Modeling framework and consider how it has been used to re-mediate (Cole & Griffin, 1983) learning challenges, contrasting this with approaches to teaching and learning that follow from a cultural mismatch perspective.

Sociocultural Perspectives on the Relationship between Home and School Practices

Cultural Modeling emerges from sociocultural research that explores the language practices of children and families in everyday, non-school contexts. Sociocultural researchers have documented everyday practices in a range of community contexts, family constellations, speech communities, and cultural groups (Alim, 2004; Barton & Hamilton, 1998; Cintron, 1997; Duranti, Ochs, & Ta'ase, 1995; Farr, 2006; Gonzalez, 2001; Goodwin, 1990; Guerra, 1998; Heath, 1983; Scribner & Cole, 1981; Zentella, 1997, 2005). These studies make clear that all people engage in rich repertoires of oral and literate practices in their everyday lives. This includes members of non-dominant groups who too often are viewed as lacking in linguistic skills and disproportionately labeled as poor readers in school (Trent, Artiles, & Englert, 1998). All children in all communities are socialized to and through language (Ochs & Schieffelin, 1984), though the specific kinds of practices that they are exposed to may vary on many dimensions.

Sociocultural researchers and linguistic anthropologists have documented the linguistic dexterity involved in an array of everyday activities. For example, Goodwin (1990) analyzed the complex sequential organization of argumentation in everyday gossip and storytelling among African American youth and the role of talk in the "secret lives of girls" as they play games on school playgrounds (Goodwin, 2007). Others have studied such discursive activities as teasing and shaming (Miller, 1986; Schieffelin, 1990), insulting (Evaldsson, 2005; Reynolds, 2007), storytelling in pretend play (Kyratzis, 2005), song games (Minks, 2008), and other forms of conflict and playful talk. Rampton (1995), Zentella (1997), and Alim (2004) document the flexible ways in which bilingual and bidialectical youth style- and code-switch, crossing registers and codes, deploying each appropriately for different relationships, contexts and purposes. These are just a few of many studies that reveal rich and robust ways with words that have been studied in the everyday lives of young people outside of school.

The practices detailed above are oral language practices, but it is generally accepted that oral language practices serve as a foundation for engagement with written texts; the division between orality and literacy was an historical construction that has been the subject of much debate (Baumann & Briggs, 2003). Sociocultural researchers, such as Gee (1996), Heath (1983, as detailed below), and Michaels (1981, 1985) argue that exposure to specific genres in out-of-school language practices matters for children's abilities to perform on school literacy tasks. Even phonemic awareness research, centered in a psycholinguistic rather than a sociocultural tradition, argues that the ability to hear differences in spoken language is related to early reading skills (Adams, Foorman, Lundberg, & Beeler, 1998); though Taylor (1998) notes that this research rarely looks at the impact of everyday language play on phonemic awareness, focusing instead on isolated language tasks, disconnected from children's social worlds.

Cultural Mismatch   But if youth from non-dominant groups engage in such sophisticated language practices outside of school, and if exposure to oral language practices has "pay-off" for engagement with complex written language practices, why do these same students sometimes struggle with school language demands? Cultural mismatch theory has been proffered as an answer to this seeming paradox. This theory holds that school discourse patterns are divergent from the everyday practices of many communities in ways that can create blockages for the display and/or uptake of school practices.

The classic work in this tradition is the work of Shirley Brice Heath (1983). Through her 10-year ethnographic study of the communities of Trackton, Roadville, and Maintown, Heath worked in the tradition of linguistic anthropologists to bring attention to variations in the socialization of children across three communities in South Carolina: an African American working-class community that she calls "Trackton," a White, working-class community that she calls "Roadville," and "Maintown," a middle-class community of both White and African American professionals. Heath went beyond simply documenting these varied ways with word" in and of themselves; she compared the practices with school practices, highlighting the notion that white, middle-class language practices more closely paralleled school practices than did the practices of the other communities. She identified differences in the kinds of practices that each community engaged in and the discourse styles that shaped

those practices, such as the forms of questions adults posed to children. Questioning practices in the Maintown community more closely aligned with school questioning forms than did the questioning practices of Roadville. This had the effect of making Maintown children appear more capable than children from other groups in school, and eased their engagement with teachers and texts.

Other researchers have built upon Heath's framework to identify differences in cultural practices along a range of dimensions as well as in a diversity of communities. First, there are differences in the practices themselves. Storybook reading by adults to children is a celebrated literacy practice in middle-class U.S. homes, one that is assumed to benefit young children's literacy development (Bialostok, 2002). In other communities, adults may rarely or never engage with children around storybooks. Instead, children may read to "their" adults (as when they translate for them) (Orellana, 2003), or they may read to their siblings (Gregory, 2001; Orellana, 2001). (See also Purcell-Gates, 1995; Taylor & Dorsey-Gaines, 1988; and Reese, Goldenberg, Loucky, & Gallimore, 1995, for descriptions of varied literacy practices in working-class communities.) Although there may be overlap across cultural communities in terms of practices, some practices are more privileged than others, and the constellation of valued practices can look quite different across groups. (See, for example, Barton & Hamilton, 1998; Scribner & Cole, 1981.)

Who participates in what ways in these practices also varies across communities. In all communities there are implicit rules for interaction across socially-meaningful lines of difference such as gender and age, but those rules can look very different from the norms imposed by schools. Philips (1993), for example, compared the participation structures of home and school practices on the Warm Springs Indian Reservation, noting patterns in gendered and generational relations that affected youths' engagement with talk in school. Au (1980) identified similar differences in the participation structures of home and school for Hawaiian youth.

Rogoff, Paradise, Arauz, Correa-Chavez, and Angelillo (2003) go beyond the linguistic dimension to reveal how in some communities children are socialized to attend to ongoing activities; they engage in what she terms "intent participation"—keen observations of activities that do not directly involve them, with the intent of participating in those activities at some point in time. Rogoff contrasts this form of participation, which she finds prevalent in a range of contexts, with the child-centered, adult-organized activities that predominate in middle-class, European-ancestry homes and schools in the United States.

Other researchers have focused on differences in discourse patterns across groups, and between home and school practices. Delpit (1995), for example, highlights differences in the explicitness of commands in African American communities and in schools (which are implicitly organized around White notions of politeness and child-adult relations). She notes that White teachers may expect African

American students to hear mitigated requests as commands, while those same students may expect commands to be delivered in a more direct form. Thus, students may be seen as misbehaving or disobeying, with implications for their academic identities and their engagement with learning tasks. Ballenger (1992) explores this with Haitian-Creole children living in Boston.

At a deeper level, values, beliefs and epistemological stances also vary across cultural communities. What counts as knowledge and authority differs, as do the purposes for engaging in particular activities. Baquedano-López (1998), for example, looks at literacy as embedded in catholic "doctrina" classes, shaped by religious norms and values, as well as by larger language policies. Groups may also develop different taxonomies of the social and scientific world, in ways that matter for how students engage with subject matter. Bang, Medin, and Atran (2007) identify such differences in scientific thinking between Menomoni Indians and White, middle-class Americans. They suggest how these differences may matter for children's take-up of the science concepts that are privileged in schools.

Taken together, these and other studies suggest that the mismatch between home and school practices can be a source of learning difficulties for students from non-dominant groups. School practices in the United States more closely model White, middle-class ways than they do the practices that are prevalent in non-dominant communities, on all of the above-detailed dimensions: in terms of the practices themselves, the discourse patterns that structure them, and the values, beliefs, purposes, and epistemological stances that frame them. Thus White, middle-class children have fewer adjustments to make when they engage with school tasks than do children from non-dominant groups, and because they more easily insert themselves into school practices they may be seen as more capable by their teachers, creating self-fulfilling prophecies. This may help to explain the greater incidence of identified learning challenges among non-white populations.

Recognition of these mismatches has led some researchers to call for greater alignment between home and school practices. Attempts to match participation structures (Au, 1980; Philips, 1993) have had some success; young children seem to engage more readily and achieve better when practices are modeled on the relationship structures that are valued in children's homes. But it is not easy to change deeply engrained ways of speaking and interacting, much less to shift epistemologies, values and beliefs. Moreover, how are teachers to match their own styles with the styles of all their students? Even when teaching in seemingly homogeneous cultural communities, this can be a challenge, as not all families take up cultural practices in the same way, and there are with-in group differences as well, such as those based on gender. Further, if our goal is to help student acquire schools' valued ways with words, then simply aligning school discourse forms with home forms could defeat this aim, unless other ways with words are simultaneously cultivated.

Cultural Modeling   Cultural Modeling represents a different way of drawing connections between everyday and school practices. The Cultural Modeling framework is a vehicle for identifying substantive ways of connecting everyday language practices to academic skills and for building on the resources of students from non-dominant groups whose linguistic skills often go unrecognized in schools. A Cultural Modeling framework does not dichotomize home and school practices, nor does it call for an alignment of the two sets of practices. Teachers are not expected to change their own discourse patterns—patterns that are generally deeply entrenched and difficult to modify. Rather, this approach calls for an analysis of home and school practices to purposefully find analogues between the two.

By leveraging, we mean that these practices become open for scrutiny by students and serve as a base to be expanded upon. Differences between everyday and school practices are acknowledged, as is the disconnect between school and home ways with words. The aim is not simply to celebrate everyday linguistic virtuosity as much as it is to recruit that virtuosity as a strength. Ultimately, the goal is also not simply to bridge from everyday ways *to* school ways, leaving everyday ways behind; rather it is to *expand* all students' repertoires of practice.

The approach to "culture" that is assumed by a Cultural Modeling perspective is that of sociohistorical theory (Vygotsky, 1978). That is, the focus is on "how people live culturally" (Moll, 1990); cultural communities are those that share a history of traditions, practices, and understandings, not simply membership in some shared, socially-constructed category like Latino or Asian. Indeed, conflating race/ethnicity and culture has led to great problems in educational research, such as the assumption that children who identify with a group label like Latino or Asian de facto share a common learning style (Gutierrez & Rogoff, 2003) or a common set of experiences. Meaningful notions of culture are instead drawn from an understanding of the routine practices of people's daily lives.

A Cultural Modeling approach resonates with Moll, Amanti, Neff, and Gonzalez's (1992) work on identifying community-based "cultural funds of knowledge," which involves "develop(ing) both theory and methods to identify and document the cultural resources found in the immediate school community, as represented by the children's households, that could be used for teaching" (p. 258). Funds of knowledge are treated as general resources for learning, and researchers have focused on how those funds are exchanged in communities, and how they can be brought into schools. Cultural Modeling approaches focus more specifically on identifying relationships between the modes of reasoning and discursive practices of everyday practices and disciplinary work. Fundamental differences between the two lie in Cultural Modeling's focus on the practices that youth themselves engage in, rather than those of adults in their communities or households (Lee, 2007), and in how it addresses the "specific and very different demands of subject matter learning" (p. 35).

Cultural Modeling starts from a deep understanding of routine practices, drawn from ethnographic and sociolinguistic research in homes and communities such as those referenced above. The aim is to identify the linguistic skills that youth garner from their engagement in cultural practices. What do children learn about language, about ways of using language, and about learning, from their everyday lives? What skills do they develop from participating in routine practices? What particular kinds of skills look like analogues of the kinds of skills that we seek to develop in youth in school?

A parallel step involves analyzing disciplinary modes of reasoning to determine generative ways of mapping everyday practices onto academic processes. Unlike the cultural mismatch approach, this involves identifying *commonalties* or *continuities* between home and school ways with words, rather than differences in the structure, purpose or goals of home and school tasks. The intent is to identify *specific* and *substantive* ways in which one set of skills can be transformed for use in another setting. What ways of thinking, of using language, and of organizing and representing knowledge in the disciplines are analogous with the modes of reasoning that are identified in everyday practices?

The Cultural Modeling tradition was pioneered by Carol Lee (1995, 1997, 2000, 2007), who identified analogues between the rhetorical skill of signifying (practices of verbal irony that have a long history in African American communities), and the deployment of literary tropes as found in the study of literature. Lee detailed the nature, purposes, and varieties of forms that this practice of verbal irony can take and compared it to an array of related tropes used in literature: irony, metaphor, symbolism, and the use of unreliable narrators. She also illuminated common processes used to recognize and interpret signifying in discourse and irony in literature. She showed how skills involved in informal interpretive contexts can be applied to more formal, or school-based contexts. This is done by helping students to make more explicit their predominantly tacit knowledge of signifying practices, and then to apply them to the new context of text interpretation.

In related work, Lee (2007) used cultural data sets, units of instruction that mirror practices and knowledge that schools do not typically value, and have sometimes been viewed as interfering with learning. Cultural data sets, such as music lyrics, videos, and art, were employed to motivate children to write rich narratives, connecting school-based literacy work with the oral storytelling traditions that many African American children participate in at home. She shows how children displayed particular discursive features in their writing, such as the use of sermonic tone and vivid language, by leveraging children's experiences with art forms that were popular in the community under study. In Lee's work with high school students (2007), cultural data sets served to facilitate students' comprehension of complex canonical texts found in high school reading lists. The Cultural Modeling framework introduced students to metacognitive strategies, and helped to make their tacit knowledge explicit as well as available for sharing and public scrutiny.

Other researchers have extended the Cultural Modeling approach to other disciplines. Nasir (2000) examines ways of thinking that are cultivated through practices like basketball, dominoes (Nasir 2002, 2005), and track and field (Nasir, Rosebery, Warren, & Lee, 2006) drawing connections with ways of doing math in school. The Algebra Project (Moses, Kamii, Swap, & Howard, 1989) is also based on the principles of Cultural Modeling. At the Chéche Konen Center, Warren and Roseberry (1996) identify relations between children's everyday experiences and the kinds of thinking that are valued by scientists in a practice they call Science Workshop.

In our own work we elaborated on the Cultural Modeling framework in several ways. First, we focused on a largely unexplored language practice: the everyday translation and interpretation activities of the children of immigrants. Although we worked mostly with the children of immigrants from Mexico, we were careful not to claim translation work as a practice unique to members of any cultural, ethnic, or national group, but rather as a practice that arises from the circumstances in which immigrants find themselves in their host country. We built on ethnographic work in a range of immigrant communities to document the wide range of ways in which the children of immigrants use their knowledge of two languages to read, write, listen, speak, and do things for their families. This includes interpreting for their families and representatives of U.S. institutions such as schools, clinics, and social service agencies; making and answering phone calls; reading and explaining a variety of texts, filling out forms, and a host of complex language and literacy practices (Orellana, 2001, 2007; Orellana, Dorner, & Pulido, 2003; Orellana, Reynolds, Dorner, & Meza, 2003; Orellana & Eksner, 2006). The common feature of these practices, and the feature we sought to exploit, was that they involved taking ideas then transposing them into a different form, language, and/or social register for a different audience.

We were interested in mapping the skills involved in translation onto generalized academic language skills as instantiated in classroom practices, not discipline-specific reasoning (Orellana & Reynolds, 2008). That is, we did not set out with the intention of drawing analogues between translation work and any particular discipline, such as math or English; instead we focused on practices of reading and writing in schools. Our aim was to reveal not just *theoretical* points of leverage between everyday skills and school-based ways of using language, but specific ways in which everyday skills could be leveraged for classroom learning across a range of classroom learning contexts and disciplinary studies. We identified analogues between cross-language paraphrasing (translation/interpretation work, or what we call "*para*-phrasing") and within-language paraphrasing, which includes a host of highly valued school language practices. These included vocabulary building to reading comprehension exercises. We did this by first identifying a set of skills that bilingual youth utilize when they engage in everyday practices of translation or interpretation and then exploring the relationship between those skills and the modes of reasoning used across disciplines in practices of summarizing and paraphrasing. Following this we searched for points of leverage in actual school practices, through ethnographic research in classrooms.

Our research team observed several classrooms, across content areas in fifth-, sixth-, and seventh-grade classrooms, of youth that we identified as translators. During observations, the research team focused on the kinds of literacy practices that required students to make sense of written texts. We were interested in how students dealt with the challenges of paraphrasing, therefore we closely examined talk about translating, paraphrasing, summarizing, retelling, or saying the same thing in different ways; activities that share disciplinary modes of reasoning with that of *para*-phrasing.

After identifying these points of leverage, we collaborated with a classroom teacher to design curriculum that built on students' translation experiences. Focusing on the development of writing, we studied how youth applied their skills in moving between English and Spanish to the movement across registers and voices as they wrote essays directed to different audiences (Martínez, Orellana, Pacheco, & Carbone, 2008), and provided opportunities. We worked with students to identify the skills they already deployed when they shifted registers appropriately for different audiences in their everyday lives as translators/ interpreters for their families, and then to apply this skill to the writing of persuasive essays. In ongoing work, we are also identifying ways to enhance children's comprehension of written texts by utilizing the strategies that they display when they translate complex texts for their parents (Orellana & Reynolds, 2008).

An important feature of our approach to Cultural Modeling is that the practice we examine cross-cuts communities and social classes that are typically the focus of "cultural" inquiries. That is, this is a practice that is shaped by the experience of being non-English speaking immigrants who are not familiar with all tacit sociocultural practices and procedures of U.S. institutions. Further, *para*-phrasing is really a *set* of practices, not a singular practice in itself. In this sense, it has multiple points of leverage for academic literacies, and we are just beginning to explore these.

Why This Differs from Typical Approaches to Remediation

Traditional approaches to remediating reading difficulties identify the source of reading problems in the student; students are seen as lacking skills that are needed for academic success. Remediation involves "fixing" the student. Everyday practices are not viewed as assets for learning; indeed, everyday ways with words are generally seen as sources of difficulty for students and as practices to be eliminated, not built upon. Cultural Modeling approaches

follow Cole and Griffin's (1983) argument that rather than remediate learners, we should "re-mediate" *learning*, by fundamentally changing the forms of mediation through which learning takes place. This involves reorganizing relationships between teachers and learners and learners and learning tasks. Cultural Modeling reorganizes the relationship between school language and literacy practices and the everyday language skills that students display in their lives outside of school.

With the exception of Lee's work with high school English students, Cultural Modeling approaches have not been applied to the re-mediation of reading difficulties; they have been used to help students expand their repertoires of practice in writing, mathematics, and science. We call for more scholarship in the Cultural Modeling tradition that uncovers analogues between everyday practices and the modes of thinking that are demanded of readers in schools.

References

Adams, M. J., Foorman, B. R., Lundberg, I., & Beeler, T. (1998). *Phonemic awareness in young children: A classroom curriculum*. Baltimore, MD: Brooks.

Alim, H. S. (2004). *You know my steez: An ethnographic and sociolinguistic study of styleshifting in a Black American speech community*. Durham, NC: Duke University Press for the American Dialect Society.

Au, K. H. (1980). Participation structures in a reading lesson with Hawaiian children: Analysis of a culturally appropriate instructional event. *Anthropology & Education Quarterly, 11*, 91–115.

Ballenger, C. (1992). Because you like us: The language of control. *Harvard Educational Review, 62*(2), 199–208.

Bang, M., Medin, D. L., & Atran, S. (2007). Cultural mosaics and mental models of nature. *Proceedings of the National Academy of Sciences, 104*(35), 13868–13874.

Barton, D., & Hamilton, M. (1998). *Local literacies: Reading and writing in one community*. London: Routledge.

Baquedano-López, P. (1998). *Language socialization of Mexican children in a Los Angeles Catholic parish* (Unpublished doctoral dissertation). University of California Los Angeles.

Baumann, R., & Briggs, C. L. (2003). *Voices of modernity: Language ideologies and the politics of inequality*. Cambridge, UK: Cambridge University Press.

Bialostok, S. (2002). Metaphors for literacy: A cultural model of white, middle-class parents. *Linguistics and Education, 13*(3), 347–371.

Cintron, R. (1997). *Angel's town: Chero ways, gang life, and rhetorics of the everyday*. Boston: Beacon Press.

Cole, M., & Griffin, P. (1983). A socio-historical approach to re-mediation. *The Quarterly Newsletter of the Laboratory of Comparative Human Cognition, 5*(4), 69–74.

Delpit, L. D. (1995). *Other people's children: cultural conflict in the classroom*. New York: New Press.

Duranti, A., Ochs, E., & Ta'ase, E. K. (1995). Change and tradition in literacy instruction in a Samoan American community. *Educational Foundations, 9*(4), 57–74.

Evaldsson, A. C. (2005). Staging insults and mobilizing categorizations in a multiethnic peer group. *Discourse Society, 16*(6), 763–786.

Farr, M. (2006). *Rancheros in Chicagoacan: Language and identity in a transitional community*. Austin: University of Texas Press.

Gee, J. P. (1996). *Social linguistics and literacies: Ideology in discourses* (2nd ed.). London: Taylor & Francis.

Gonzalez, N. (2001). *I am my language: Discourses of women and children in the borderlands*. Tucson: University of Arizona Press.

Goodwin, M. H. (1990). *He-said-she-said: Talk as social organization among black children*. Bloomington: Indiana University Press.

Goodwin, M. H. (2007). Participation and embodied action in preadolescent girls' assessment activity. *Research on Language & Social Interaction, 40*(4), 353–375.

Gregory, E. (2001). Sisters and brothers as language and literacy teachers: Synergy between siblings playing and working together. *Journal of Early Childhood Literacy, 1*(3), 301–322.

Guerra, J. C. (1998). *Close to home: oral and literate practices in a transnational Mexicano community.* New York: Teachers College Press.

Gutierrez, K., & Rogoff, B. (2003). Cultural ways of learning: Individual traits and repertoires of practice. *Educational Researcher, 32*(5), 19–25.

Gutierrez, K. (2007). Historicizing literacy. In M. Blackburn & C. Clark (Eds.), *Literacy research for political action* (pp. ix–xiii). New York: Peter Lang.

Heath, S. B. (1983). *Ways with words: language, life, and work in communities and classrooms.* Cambridge, UK: Cambridge University Press.

Kyratzis, A. (2005). Language and culture: Socialization through personal story-telling practice. *Human Development, 48*(3), 146–150.

Lee, C. D. (1995). A culturally based cognitive apprenticeship: Teaching African American high school students skills in literary interpretation. *Reading Research Quarterly, 30*, 608–630.

Lee, C. D. (1997). Bridging home and school literacies: Models for culturally responsive teaching, a case for African American English. In J. Flood, S. B. Heath, & D. Lapp (Eds.), *Handbook of research on teaching literacy through the communicative and visual arts* (pp. 334–345). New York: MacMillan.

Lee, C. D. (2000). Signifying in the zone of proximal development. In C. D. Lee & P. Smagorinsky (Eds.), *Vygotskian perspectives of literacy research: Constructing meaning through collaborative inquiry* (pp. 191–224). Cambridge, UK: Cambridge University Press.

Lee, C. D. (2007). *Culture, literacy, & learning: Taking bloom in the midst of the whirlwind.* New York: Teachers College Press.

Martínez, R., Orellana, M. F., Pacheco, M., & Carbone, P. (2008). Found in translation: Connecting translating experiences to academic writing. *Language Arts, 85*(6), 421–431.

Michaels, S. (1981). "Sharing Time": Children's narrative styles and differential access to literacy. *Language in Society, 10*, 423–442.

Michaels, S. (1985). Hearing the connections in children's oral and written discourse. *Journal of Education, 167*(1), 36–56.

Miller, P. (1986). Teasing as language socialization and verbal play in a White working-class community. In B. Schieffelin & E. Ochs (Eds.), *Language socialization across cultures* (pp. 199–212). New York: Cambridge University Press.

Minks, A. (2008). Performing gender in song games among Nicaraguan Miskitu children. *Language & Communication, 28*(1), 36–56.

Moll, L. C. (1990). Introduction. In L. C. Moll (Ed.), *Vygotsky and education: Instructional implications and applications of sociohistorical psychology* (pp. 1–27). New York: Cambridge University Press.

Moll, L. C., Amanti, C., Neff, D., & Gonzalez, N. (1992). Funds of knowledge for teaching: using a qualitative approach to connect homes to classrooms. *Theory into Practice, 31*(2), 132–141.

Moses, R. P., Kamii, M., Swap, S. M., & Howard, J. (1989). The Algebra Project: Organizing in the spirit of Ella. *Harvard Educational Review, 59*(4), 423–443.

Nasir, N. S. (2000). "Points aint everything": Emergent goals and averages and percent understandings in the play of basketball among African-American students. *Anthropology & Education Quarterly, 31*(3), 283–305.

Nasir, N. S. (2002). Identity, goals, and learning: mathematics in cultural practice. *Mathematical Thinking and Learning, 4*(2 & 3), 213–247.

Nasir, N. S. (2005). Individual cognitive structuring and the sociocultural context: Strategy shifts in the game of dominoes. *Journal of the Learning Sciences, 14*(1), 5–34.

Nasir, N. S., Rosebery, A. S., Warren, B., & Lee, C. D. (2006). Learning as a cultural process: Achieving equity through diversity. In K. R. Sawyer (Ed.), *The Cambridge handbook of the learning sciences* (pp. 489–504). New York: Cambridge University Press.

Ochs, E., & Schieffelin, B. (1984). Language acquisition and socialization: Three developmental stories. In R. Shweder & R. LeVine (Eds.), *Culture theory: Mind, self, and emotion* (pp. 276–320). Cambridge, UK: Cambridge University Press.

Orellana, M. F. (2001). The work kids do: Mexican and Central American immigrant children's contributions to households, schools, and community in California. *Harvard Educational Review, 71*(3), 366–389.

Orellana, M. F. (2003). Responsibilities of children in Latino immigrant homes. *New Directions for Youth Development, 100*, 25–39.

Orellana, M. F. (2007). Moving words and moving worlds: The challenges of being "in the middle." In C. Lewis, P. Enciso, & E. Moje (Eds.), *Reframing sociocultural research on literacy: Identity, agency, and power* (pp. 123–136). Mahwah, NJ: Erlbaum.

Orellana, M. F., Dorner, L. M., & Pulido, L. (2003). Accessing access: Immigrant youth's work as family translators or "paraphrasers." *Social Problems, 50*(4), 505–524.

Orellana, M. F., & Eksner, H. J. (2006). Power in cultural modeling: Building on the bilingual language practices of immigrant youth in Germany and the U.S. In C. M. Fairbanks, J. Worthy, B. Maloch, J. V. Hoffman, & D. L. Schaller (Eds.), *National Reading Conference yearbook, 55.* (pp. 224–234). Austin, TX: The University of Austin.

Orellana, M. F., Reynolds, J., Dorner, L., & Meza, M. (2003). In other words: Translating or "para-phrasing" as a family literacy practice in immigrant households. *Reading Research Quarterly, 38*(1), 12–34.

Orellana, M. F., & Reynolds, J. (2008). Cultural modeling: Leveraging bilingual skills for school paraphrasing tasks. *Reading Research Quarterly, 43*(1), 48–65.

Philips, S. U. (1993). *The invisible culture: Communication in classroom and community on the Warm Springs Indian reservation.* Prospect Heights, IL: Waveland Press.

Purcell-Gates, V. (1995). *Other people's words: The cycle of low literacy.* Cambridge, MA: Harvard University Press.

Rampton, B. (1995). *Crossing: Language and ethnicity among adolescents.* London: Longman.

Reese, L., Goldenberg, C., Loucky, J., & Gallimore, R. (1995). Ecocultural context, cultural activity, and emergent literacy: Sources of variation in home literacy experiences of Spanish speaking children. In S. W. Rothstein (Ed.), *Class, culture, and race in American schools* (pp. 199–224). Westport, CT: Greenwood Press.

Reynolds, J. F. (2007). "Buenos Días/(Military Salute)": The natural history of a coined insult. *Research on Language & Social Interaction, 40*(4), 437–465.

Rogoff, B., Paradise, R., Arauz, R. M., Correa-Chavez, M., & Angelillo, C. (2003). Firsthand learning through intent participation. *Annual Review of Psychology, 54*(1), 175–203.

Schieffelin, B. B. (1990). *The give and take of everyday life: Language socialization of Kaluli children.* Cambridge, UK: Cambridge University Press.

Scribner, S., & Cole, M. (1981). *The psychology of literacy.* Cambridge, MA: Harvard University Press.

Taylor, D., & Dorsey-Gaines, C. (1988). *Growing up literate: Learning from inner-city families.* Portsmouth, N H: Heinemann.

Taylor, D. (1998). *Beginning to read and the spin doctors of science: The political campaign to change America's mind about how children learn to read.* Urbana, IL: National Council of Teachers of English.

Trent, S. C., Artiles, A. J., & Englert, C. S. (1998). From deficit thinking to social constructivism: A review of theory, research, and practice in special education. *Review of Research in Education, 23*, 277–307.

Valencia, R. R. (1997). *The evolution of deficit thinking: Educational thought and practice.* London: Falmer Press.

Vygotsky, L. S. (1978). *Mind in society: The development of higher psychological processes* (M. Cole, V. John-Steiner, S. Scribner, & E. Souberman, Trans.). Cambridge, MA: Harvard University Press.

Warren, B., & Roseberry, A. (1996). "This question is just too, too easy!": Perspectives from the classroom on accountability in science. In L. Schuble & R. Glaser (Eds.), *Innovations in learning: New environments for education* (pp. 97–125). Hillsdale, NJ: Erlbaum.

Zentella, A. C. (1997). *Growing up bilingual: Puerto Rican children in New York.* Malden, MA: Blackwell.

Zentella, A. C. (2005). *Building on strength: language and literacy in Latino families and communities.* New York: Teachers College Press.

26

Interventions to Develop Phonological and Orthographic Systems

DARRELL MORRIS
Appalachian State University

Since the publication of Jeanne Chall's (1967) landmark book, *Learning to Read: The Great Debate*, research has advanced our understanding of the beginning reading process. While we still may disagree about the "best" method for teaching beginning reading, the discussion has moved beyond a surface comparison of various instructional approaches to a consideration of the cognitive and developmental underpinnings of the learning-to-read process (Adams, 1990; Snow, Burns, & Griffin, 1998; Rayner, Foorman, Perfetti, Pesetsky, & Seidenberg, 2001). One dominant concept that has been studied and re-studied over the past four decades is *phonemic awareness*—a child's conscious awareness of the phonemic or sound segments within a spoken word. Today, any serious reading theorist or practitioner must take into account the role of phonemic awareness in the early stages of learning to read.

In this chapter, I contrast two different positions or ways of thinking about phonemic awareness in the reading acquisition process. Position 1 (P.A.–first), which has exerted considerable influence on teaching practice over the past 20 years, views phonemic awareness as an important prerequisite to learning to read. It holds that children need to be able to attend to the sound segments in spoken words (e.g., /hăt/ = /h/ /ă/ /t/) *before* they begin to read an alphabetic written language. Position 2 (P.A.–interactive), while acknowledging the importance of phonemic awareness, questions its role as a prerequisite. This alternative position suggests that a child's awareness of intra-word sound segments evolves in the act of learning to read. Therefore, beginning reading instruction need not await the development of full phonemic awareness, but instead can precede and actually facilitate such development.

After reviewing representative research studies that support the viability of the P.A.–first and P.A.–interactive positions, respectively, I will turn to instructional implications that speak directly to the prevention of reading problems in kindergarten and first grade. Interestingly and not surprisingly, the different instructional paths suggested by the two phoneme awareness positions highlight an old and controversial fissure in the beginning reading field–that between phonics- and meaning-emphasis instructional approaches.

Phonemic Awareness: The Prerequisite Argument

Over 30 years ago, in a paper titled, "Speech, the Alphabet, and Teaching to Read," Isabelle Liberman and Donald Shankweiler (1979) carefully explained both the theoretical and practical significance of phonemic awareness. Their argument went something like this:

- The reader's task is to convert print to speech.
- An alphabetic writing system maps to speech at the phoneme level.
- Young children have difficulty segmenting speech into phonemes because the discrete unit of speech perception is the syllable, not the phoneme.
- Therefore, a first step in teaching reading is to help children become aware of phoneme segments in spoken words so that they can make the initial speech to print match at a low-order letter-sound level.

Liberman and Shankweiler took point 4—the pedagogical implication—seriously. They stated:

Phonemic analysis is hard because of the encodedness of spoken speech into units of syllable size; syllabic segmentation is demonstrably easier. However, it need not follow that the phonemic level of analysis should be bypassed at the beginning in favor of the syllable or the word. Instead, perhaps the child can be given better preparation for phoneme segmentation *before* reading instruction begins. With that preparation, certain elements of both the so-called phonic and syllabic methods can be introduced later to good effect. (1979, p. 122, emphasis added)

Figure 26.1 An example of Elkonin's phoneme segmentation training procedure.

As an example of phonemic analysis training, Liberman and Shankweiler cited the work of the Russian psychologist, Elkonin (1973). In Elkonin's procedure, the child is presented with a line drawing of a familiar object or animal. Below the drawing is a rectangle divided into sections; for example, the word, /pĭg/, would have three sections (see Figure 26.1). The child is taught to say the word slowly, putting a counter into the appropriate section as he or she pronounces each phoneme. This task is repeated with many different words until the child can successfully perform the segmentation task without the diagram. According to Liberman and Shankweiler (1979), this represents the end of the prereading phase: "Once the child has been taught, by whatever method, to segment spoken syllables into their phonemic components, the graphic representations [letters] of the phonemes can be introduced" (p. 124). Then the long process of learning to convert print into speech (i.e., reading) begins.

During the 1970s and 1980s, Liberman and Shankweiler's phoneme awareness-first position was supported by many studies showing that phonemic awareness, measured prior to first grade, is a powerful predictor of future reading achievement (e.g., Bradley & Bryant, 1983; Helfgott, 1976; Liberman, Shankweiler, Fischer, & Carter, 1974; Share, Jorm, Maclean, & Matthews, 1984). Two of these early studies deserve special mention. Bradley and Bryant (1983) was really two studies within one. First, using a large sample (N = 368), the researchers found a strong relationship (r = .57) between children's pre-school phonemic awareness and their reading achievement three years later. Second, within their longitudinal design, Bradley and Bryant were able to conduct one of the first phoneme awareness training studies. They divided a group of low scorers (N = 68) on their phoneme awareness pretest into four groups. Group 1 received sound categorization training only (e.g., pictures of <u>hen</u> and <u>hot</u> go together because they share the same initial sound). Group 2 categorized the same pictures, but also learned to represent the shared sounds with let-

ters. The remaining groups served as controls—Group 3 categorizing the pictures by meaning (e.g., <u>hen</u> goes with <u>dog</u>), and Group 4 receiving no instruction. Results showed that children receiving sound categorization training only (Group 1) scored somewhat higher in reading and spelling than children in the control groups. However, children who received sound categorization *plus* letter instruction (Group 2) scored significantly higher than the controls on reading and spelling, and also outperformed the sound categorization-only group on the spelling measure. These results suggested that phoneme awareness training can increase later reading achievement and that teaching children to connect letters to sound segments may augment the effects of such training.

Another pivotal study in the phoneme awareness-first literature was Share et al. (1984). These researchers assessed a wide variety of reading-related factors (including oral language, memory, and motor skills) in a sample of preschoolers. Reading achievement was assessed at the end of kindergarten and first grade. Results showed that the two strongest predictors of end-of-kindergarten and end-of-first-grade reading achievement were phoneme segmentation and letter-name knowledge (r's above .60). The identification of letter-name knowledge as an important co-predictor of reading achievement helped to explain (a) why the effectiveness of phoneme awareness training is enhanced by a letter-sound matching component, and (b) why young children's invented spelling performance (which requires both phonemic awareness and letter knowledge) is a good predictor of later reading achievement (see Mann, Tobin, & Wilson, 1987; Morris & Perney, 1984). Taken together, the Bradley and Bryant (1983) and Share et al. (1984) studies definitely encouraged future researchers to include alphabet letters in phoneme awareness training studies.

Through the 1990s, reading researchers continued to conduct phoneme awareness training studies in kindergarten classrooms (e.g., Ball & Blachman, 1991; O'Connor, Notari-Syverson, & Vasdasy, 1996; Torgesen, Morgan, & Davis, 1992). A good example was a study by Blachman, Ball, Black, & Tangel (1994). Non-reading kindergartners were placed into treatment (N = 84) and control (N = 75) groups. Children in the treatment group received 41 phoneme segmentation/alphabet letter lessons provided by the classroom teacher. Each lesson the children (a) practiced moving a blank tile down a page as they pronounced each phoneme in a word, and (b) drilled on a few letter names and letter sounds. After the kindergartners could segment two- and three-phoneme words using the "say it and move it" procedure, they practiced segmenting words using tiles *and* letters. A variety of activities were used to reinforce phonemic segmentation and letter-sound learning. The control group received traditional kindergarten literacy instruction that included letter-sound work. Results showed that the treatment group (phonemic awareness + letter/sounds) outperformed the control group on measures of phonemic awareness (d = 1.83), word recognition (d = .65), and spelling (d = .94).

In summary, phoneme awareness-first research in the 1980s and 1990s supported Liberman and Shankweiler's (1979) original insights about the phenomenon. It turns out that we can teach prereaders to attend to phonemes within spoken words, and that, subsequently, this ability helps the children to read and spell words. It also seems clear that including letters in phoneme awareness training provides children with important insight into the alphabetic nature (grapheme-phoneme pairings) of printed English (Gough & Hillinger, 1980; Perfetti, 1992). Nonetheless, we should keep in mind that individual children differ in the ease with which they acquire phonemic awareness. In fact, some beginning readers and writers learn to segment words into phonemes even when the skill is not explicitly taught (e.g., consider children taught with the whole-word approach of the 1950s, or, for that matter, with the whole-language approach of the 1990s). This raises an important question. Besides explicit instruction, is there another way for beginning readers to acquire phonemic awareness, and, if so, how does it work?

Phonemic Awareness: The Interactive Argument

By the mid-1980s, the predominant phoneme awareness-first position had led to a stage-like explanation of beginning reading (see Frith, 1985; Marsh, Friedman, Welch, & Desberg, 1981; Seymour & MacGregor, 1984). For example, Frith (1985) described three stages. In the *logographic* stage, children recognize familiar words by attending to salient, visual features (e.g., the "two circles" in the middle of look, or the "tail" at the end of big); however, they do not use phonology or letter-sounds as a means of word identification. In the second or *alphabetic* stage, children decode new words by attending to the sequential letter- sounds in the words (e.g., m → a → p). Finally, in Frith's third or *orthographic* stage, children read words not by sounding-out sequential letter sounds, but rather by attending to distinctive spelling or orthographic patterns (e.g., fl-at; m- ake; sp- eak; fl- ight). According to Frith's three-stage model, phonemic awareness is absent in the logographic stage and unnecessary in the orthographic stage. However, it is absolutely necessary in the pivotal alphabetic stage; to decode sequential letter sounds, one must be aware that words are composed of sounds.

A few psychologists, at the time, questioned stage theories such as Frith's. They asked: Does attending to salient visual cues (logographic stage) and, later, sounding-out letter sequences (alphabetic stage) fully explain how beginning readers identify printed words? Ehri and Wilce (1985) and Stuart and Coltheart (1988) thought not, and the studies they conducted provided a new way of thinking about the role of phonemic awareness in beginning reading.

In a laboratory study, Ehri and Wilce (1985) divided kindergarten children into *prereaders* who read no words and did not know many letters (6.7) and *novice readers* who could read a few words and knew most of their letters (20.6). The children were taught to read two types of word

spellings: (a) visually distinctive spellings whose letters did not correspond to sounds (e.g., wbc for giraffe), and (b) simplified phonetic spellings that did contain letter-sound correspondences (e.g., LFT for elephant). Results showed that the prereaders learned the visual spellings more easily than the phonetic spellings, but the opposite was true for the novice readers. They learned the phonetic spellings more easily than the visual spellings. This suggested that the novice readers used their superior letter-name knowledge in learning the phonetic spellings, perhaps using the letter-name cues of a given spelling (e.g., JL) to help remember its spoken word match ("jail"). Commenting on this study several years later, Ehri (1996, p. 193) stated:

> The [1985] study supported my contention that there is an intermediate phase in the development of word reading that comes between the [logographic] phase and the later cipher [or phonetic] reading phase. In this intermediate phase, beginners store partial letter-sound cues–for example, beginning and ending letter-sounds–to remember how to read words. I called this type of word reading phonetic cue reading.

A second and quite different study (Stuart & Coltheart, 1988) provided further support for the existence of an intermediate stage between Frith's logographic and alphabetic stages. Stuart and Coltheart assessed 36 children's phonological awareness just prior to school entry (e.g., detection of rhyme, identification of final syllables and initial phonemes). Then, at 2-month intervals across kindergarten and first grade, the researchers assessed the children's letter-sound knowledge and their ability to read single words to which they had been exposed in the classroom. A standardized reading assessment was administered to the children at the end of first, second, and third grade.

Although there were several interesting findings in this longitudinal study, let us focus on the patterns of word-reading errors the children made, and how these related to preschool phonological awareness and later reading achievement. Stuart and Coltheart (1988) divided the children's reading errors into six patterns or groups (see Table 26.1). Notice in the table that errors in Group 3 featured a correct letter-sound in the initial position, and errors in Group 5 featured correct letter-sounds in the initial and final positions. (*Note*: There were few Group 6 errors.)

Regarding these error patterns, Stuart and Coltheart (1988) made three points. First, the incidence of each child's errors in Groups 1, 2, and 4 (non-phonological) decreased over time, whereas the incidence of errors in Groups 3 and 5 (phonological) increased. Second, only errors in Groups 3 and 5 correlated positively with reading achievement, the Group 5 pattern (beginning and ending letter-sounds) showing a high correlation with reading age (r = .83) at the end of first grade. And third, preschool phonological knowledge, when coupled with letter-sound scores, proved to be a good predictor of overall first-grade reading performance, as well as quality of single-word reading errors.

For Stuart and Coltheart (1988), the reading errors made

TABLE 26.1
Six error groups in Stuart & Coltheart's (1988) study

Group	Identifying Characteristic	% total
1	(Partial or irrelevant information used)	20%

Target	Error
play	sister
look	baby
rat-tat	ice-cream

Group	Identifying Characteristic	% total
2	(Letters or letter segments used)	13%

school	home
play	help
made	am

Group	Identifying Characteristic	% total
3	(Beginning letter used)	32%

cat	car
yellow	you
wait	white

Group	Identifying Characteristic	% total
4	(Final letter used)	11%

hat	cat
reading	driving
lorry	boy

Group	Identifying Characteristic	% total
5	(Both beginning and ending letters used)	20%

bird	bad
goat	got
bell	ball

Group	Identifying Characteristic	% total
6	(Target included in error)	3%

looks	look
coming	comes
boy	boys

* Adapted from Table 9 of "Does reading develop in a sequence of stages?" by M. Stuart & M. Coltheart, 1988, *Cognition, 30,* pp. 139–181. Reprinted with permission from Elsevier Press.

by the children provided a view of the developing word recognition process. A beginning reader's pattern of errors (see Table 26.1) revealed the underlying analytical frame available to him or her at a given point in time. For example, reading "rag" for cup revealed a logographic analytical frame; reading "can" for cup, a beginning letter-sound frame; and reading "cap" for cup, a beginning-and-ending letter-sound frame. These latter two frames, or partial word recognition units (i.e., C - - and C - P for cup), hark back to Ehri and Wilce's (1985) notion of "phonetic cue reading." Their significance is that they allow the child to move into reading with incomplete phoneme awareness. Armed with just a few sight words and knowledge of beginning letter-sounds, he or she can begin to read simple texts, using the act of reading to help complete or fill in partial word recognition units (e.g., B - -, B - G, BIG). This interactive (or reciprocal) relationship between phonemic awareness and early reading has been described in several places (see Morris, 1993; Perfetti, 1986), but nowhere more fully than in the research synthesis by Share (1995).

Share's (1995) major premise was that phonological recoding (or simply decoding), functions as a self-teaching mechanism across levels of reading development. Think of a third-grade boy reading the following sentence: "The sword struck his shield with a glancing blow." Possessing phonemic awareness and letter-sound knowledge, the child might be expecting the following spelling of the new word

shield: SH-EE-LD. Upon seeing the IE spelling of the vowel, he has a chance to process, and store in memory, the correct spelling of the word. In Share's words, "Successful decoding encounters with new letter strings provide opportunities to learn word-specific print-to-meaning connections" (p.151).

Drawing on the work of Ehri and Wilce (1985), Stuart and Coltheart (1988), Perfetti (1992), and others, Share (1995) argued that a limited but functional form of self-teaching also exists for beginning readers. This self-teaching process depends on three factors: (a) letter-sound knowledge, (b) partial phonemic awareness (e.g., awareness of beginning *or* beginning and ending sounds), and (c) the ability to use context to determine specific word pronunciations based on limited letter-sound processing. For example, suppose a kindergarten child, who possesses letter knowledge and awareness of beginning and ending sounds, is reading the following sentence: The puppy plays in the mud. On reading the final word, mud, the child's phonological anticipation or existing word-recognition unit (i.e., M - D) is confirmed by sentence context (and possibly a supporting picture). Furthermore, the additional letter in the middle of the word (i.e., u) could inform the child, visually, that there is another phoneme to be accounted for, thus driving awareness of medial vowels (see Morris, 1993). In any case, we see how the combination of letter-sound knowledge, partial phonemic awareness, and sentence context can enable a neophyte to read simple texts. Share (1995) put it this way: "There is evidence that rudimentary, yet functional self-teaching may develop at the very outset of learning to read, sufficient perhaps to lay down primitive orthographic representations (see Perfetti, 1992) well before the child has acquired conventional decoding skill (p. 163)." (*Note*: Self-teaching of this kind also depends on finger-point reading skill or the ability to match spoken words to printed words in reading a line of text (see Clay, 1991; Morris, 1993).

In summary, we see that there is theoretical and research support for both phoneme awareness positions: P.A.–first and P.A.–interactive. With regard to preventing reading problems in kindergarten and first-grade, both camps acknowledge that, early on, children need to develop letter knowledge and awareness that spoken words are comprised of sounds. However, P.A.–first supporters stress that phonemic awareness should be taught explicitly prior to formal reading instruction, whereas P.A.–interactive supporters believe that, given minimum entry-level knowledge, the process of early reading can actually promote further phonemic awareness. It is important to note, here, that phonemic awareness does not develop in a vacuum (via maturation, for example); instead, how and when the ability develops depends on the type of reading experiences provided to children. I turn now to instructional implications of the two theoretical positions.

Instructional Implications

To provide a framework for discussing instruction, I will use a developmental model of printed word learning that

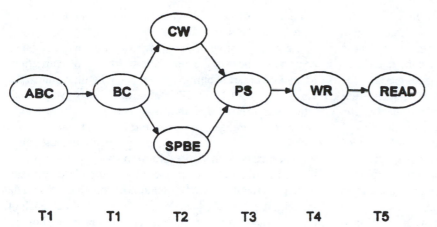

T1   T1   T2   T3   T4   T5

Figure 26.2 Developmental model of printed word learning.

we tested several years ago (Morris, Bloodgood, Lomax, & Perney, 2003) (see Figure 26.2). Although this model was originally intended to explain word recognition development in a traditional, meaning-based instructional setting, it can be used to examine pedagogical implications of both the P.A.–first and P.A.–interactive positions. The model comprises seven components or ability areas: alphabet knowledge (ABC), beginning consonant awareness (BC), concept of word in text (CW), spelling with beginning and ending consonants (SPBE), phoneme segmentation (PS), word recognition (WR), and contextual reading (READ). Over time, beginning of kindergarten to end of first grade (T1 to T5), the components are expected to exert their developmental influence as shown in Figure 26.2.

At Time 1, beginning of kindergarten, the model features *alphabet knowledge* and *beginning consonant awareness*. It is assumed that alphabet knowledge (ability to name the letters) tends to precede and facilitate attention to the beginning consonant sound in words (Johnston, Anderson, & Holligan, 1996; Stahl & Murray, 1994). At Time 2, middle of kindergarten, *concept of word in text* and *spelling with beginning and ending consonants* come to the fore. By this time, children have learned to use beginning consonant cues to guide their finger point reading of simple texts. As their concept of word in text stabilizes (i.e., begins to "stand still" for analysis), they begin to process other sounds in the word, particularly the ending consonant. They also commit a few words to sight memory (Morris, 1993). At Time 3, end of kindergarten, *phoneme segmentation* (or awareness of the sequential sounds in a syllable) is the targeted ability. Finger point reading and writing practice over the second half of kindergarten lead children to refine their phonemic awareness so that they now can attend to the medial vowel in spoken words (e.g., /dĭg/ = /d/ /ĭ/ g/). At Time 4, 2 months into first grade, *word recognition* is the ability of interest. Armed with phonemic awareness, the underlying "glue" that allows printed words to adhere in memory (Adams, 1990; Ehri, 1992), and benefiting from direct reading instruction, first graders demonstrate word recognition skill after a few months in school. Moreover, the ability to decode printed words and to establish a small sight vocabulary in October of first grade is predictive of *contextual reading* skill at Time 5, the end of first grade.

The developmental model depicted in Figure 26.2 is not meant to represent the only path to reading acquisition. Different instructional schemes (e.g., storybook-, sight word-, or phonics-emphasis), will influence, to a degree, the course of development (Barr, 1984). Nonetheless, Morris et al.'s (2003) model does provide a useful framework for examining the different instructional implications of the P.A.–first and P.A.–interactive positions.

Phoneme Awareness–First: Instructional Implications
In a sense, we have already touched on instructional implications of the phoneme awareness-first position (see training study by Blachman et al., 1994). The idea is to make a "frontal attack" on the phoneme awareness factor, teaching beginning readers to (a) attend to the individual phonemes in spoken words; (b) match alphabet letters to these phonemes; (c) blend letter-sounds into words (e.g., hat = h -> a -> t); and (d) read simple texts that reinforce decoding of regular CVC words. For example:

Max can not nap in my hat.

Max can nap on this mat.

Referring to Figure 26.2, notice that such intensive phonics instruction, for that is what it amounts to, bypasses components of Morris et al.'s (2003) developmental model. Why worry about beginning consonant (BC) or beginning-and-ending consonant (SPBE) stages of development if the first goal of instruction is to make children aware of *each* sound in a word (beginning, middle, and ending)? The P.A.–first instructional model is depicted in Figure 26.3:

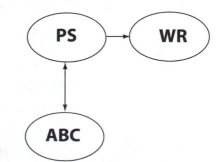

Figure 26.3 Does reading develop in a sequence of stages?

The advantages of such an approach seem clear. First, intensive phonics instruction quickly and directly gets at the roots of decoding skill—i.e., phonemic awareness and letter-sound knowledge. And keep in mind that Share (1995) argued that decoding (or phonological recoding) is the central process in learning to read. Second, such instruction is explicit and systematic, leaving little to chance. The child's mind does not have to fill in pieces of the decoding puzzle; the pieces are directly taught. Third, phonics instruction is relatively easy to break into sequential steps, making it attractive to designers of instructional programs. Although teaching routines and workbook activities can be programmed, effective phonics instruction still depends on teacher judgment. The teacher must know when to advance a group of students in the phonics curriculum and when to stay put, spending more time on a given concept to insure mastery.

The potential disadvantages of an intensive phonics approach are sometimes difficult for non-educators to recognize. For example, a research psychologist, who understands the importance of phonemic awareness and letter-sound knowledge, may see phonics as a direct and concrete way to introduce reading. But ... what is concrete to the adult reader (e.g., phonemes and alphabet letters) can be abstract and meaningless to a five-year-old child. During the pre-school years, function (or meaning), not form, has been front-and-center in the child's use of language. However, with P.A.–first instruction, he or she abruptly is confronted with form, and not the larger structural units first (e.g., sentence, word), but the smallest, most difficult to detect unit—the phoneme. What if the kindergarten child has difficulty attending to individual sounds in spoken words? Is the pedagogical response simply to provide more practice or drill, resulting in possible frustration or confusion on the learner's part? Or, could more global literacy experiences (e.g., attempting to finger-point read big books, or to write with invented spellings) serve to ready the child for phoneme-awareness

or phonics instruction? These are important questions for both researchers and teachers.

Another possible disadvantage of an intensive phonics approach concerns the time allotted to such instruction. Many kindergarten children enter school with an underdeveloped "set for literacy" (Holdaway, 1979). Along with letter-sound knowledge, they may lack general information and word meanings, and be unfamiliar with story structure and the cadence of written language. Each of these areas must be addressed in kindergarten (and later grades) because they will ultimately determine how well a child can read with understanding (see Whitehurst & Lonigan, 2001). The kindergarten teacher's challenging task is to touch each of these curriculum bases. Too great an emphasis on phonics, to the exclusion of broader literacy concerns, may produce good decoders at the end of the year; however, these same students may perform poorly on a reading comprehension test administered three years later. Again, this is not a defining flaw in a phonics-based reading program. One can envision a classroom where there is an effective balance between direct phonics instruction, guided reading of decodable texts, reading good literature to children, building meaning vocabulary, and encouraging self-expression through writing.

Phoneme awareness–interactive: Instructional implications Instructional implications of the phoneme awareness–interactive position more closely fit the developmental model depicted in Figure 26.2. Let us consider how such instruction might unfold across the kindergarten year. Over the first few months of school, Ms. Harris teaches alphabet letter-sound correspondences and demonstrates to her students how to sort spoken words [pictures] by beginning consonant sound. She also carefully models how to match spoken words to printed words when reading short, memorized texts (see Figure 26.4). These two lines of instruction (letter-sounds and supported reading), repeated daily, eventually enable Ms. Harris's students to use beginning

Figure 26.4 Three examples of beginning reading texts.

(1) Leveled book (excerpt)

"I can run," said the boy,

"and a horse can run, too."

"I can jump," said the girl,

"and a rabbit can jump too."

(2) Dictated story

We made popcorn.

We made it in a popcorn popper.

We put butter and salt on

the popcorn.

(3) Nursery rhyme

Humpty Dumpty sat on a wall;

Humpty Dumpty had a great fall;

All the king's horses

And all the king's men

Couldn't put Humpty together again.

consonant letter-sound cues to guide their own finger-point reading efforts. Morris et al. (2003) described the process as follows:

> As the child learns letter-sound relationships and begins to appreciate the significance of spacing between words, finger-point (or word-by-word) reading becomes possible. Spoken words (e.g., /pădl/) can be matched to printed words (e.g., paddle) because there is a space between words and a beginning letter-sound match. (p. 307)

Child: I   cxx   pxxxxx   a   bxxx.
Text: I   can   paddle   a   boat

With practice, Ms. Harris's kindergartners become more skillful at using spacing and beginning consonant cues to track print. At this point, the printed word begins "to stand still" for some children, making further analysis possible. For example, on meeting the word boat in our example sentence (I can paddle a boat.), a kindergarten girl may be routinely processing only beginning consonant letter-sounds (i.e., b - -). Nonetheless, if her phonological anticipation for the word is /bōt,/, then she is confronted, visually, with an ending letter (-t) that matches the final phoneme (/t/) in the anticipated word. Repeated occurrences of this kind could lead the child to begin processing both beginning and ending consonant letter-sounds in her word recognition attempts.

Child: I   cxn   pxddlx   a   bxxt.
Text: I   can   paddle   a   boat.

Once a child can consistently process beginning and ending consonants in printed words (e.g., B - T for boat), there are several ways to develop further phonemic awareness, specifically, awareness of the medial vowel. First, in reading simple texts, the child's concomitant attention to beginning and ending consonant letter-sounds may serve to frame the interior of a printed word for further sound-letter analysis. That is, the unaccounted-for letter(s) in the printed word (e.g., cxn, pxd-, or bxxt) may promote attention to the medial vowel in the corresponding spoken word (e.g., /căn/, /păd/, or /bōt/). A second way to guide young children's attention to the medial vowel sound is to have them write stories using invented spellings

(Chomsky, 1979; Clay, 1985; Richgels, 2001). Given beginning-and-ending consonant awareness, each time a child attempts to sound-out a new spelling, he or she is on the cutting edge of vowel awareness. The teacher can play a helpful role here.

Teacher: James, you got the beginning and ending letters in "jeep"–J and P. Say the word slowly, and see if you can hear what sound or letter goes in the middle.
James: /j - ē - p/. An "e" goes in the middle.
Teacher: Good, write it down.

A third way the teacher can foster vowel awareness is to use a "say it and move it" phonics strategy (Blachman et al., 1994; Morris, 2003). Here, the child says a target word (e.g., "mat") and then moves letter chips, one by one, to construct its spelling (see Figure 26.5). Or, the teacher can construct the word—letter by letter—and have the child attempt to decode it. Such an explicit teaching strategy becomes important if a student has undue difficulty attending to medial vowel sounds. In fact, this "say it and move it" strategy is often used with students who have severe phonological processing problems (e.g., Wilson Phonics, Wilson, 1996). Nonetheless, for most children, once basic phoneme awareness is attained, such isolated skill instruction can be discontinued. Blachman (1997) put it this way:

> Once children are aware that speech can be segmented and that these segmented units can be represented by letters, [they] should be engaged in reading and spelling instruction that utilizes these insights... This is not meant to suggest that the development of phoneme awareness is complete or even adequate at the point that children can demonstrate success on the simpler phoneme awareness tasks... The question is how best to facilitate develop of phoneme awareness after those early discoveries. There is no evidence that it is advantageous to continue to develop phoneme awareness outside the context of learning to read and spell words, once those early discoveries are made. (pp. 416–417)

This discussion has taken us from the beginning to the end of kindergarten, or from time points 1 to 3 in Figure 26.2. The hypothetical kindergarten children progressed

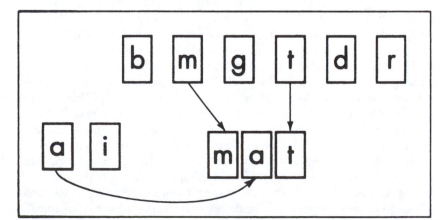

Figure 26.5 Making words with individual letters.

from alphabet knowledge and beginning consonant awareness at T1, to concept of word in text and beginning and ending consonant awareness at T2, to full phonemic processing (beginning, middle, and end) at T3. The main instructional vehicle was supported storybook reading, supplemented by phonics instruction and writing experiences. What should be quite apparent in this scenario is the important role played by partial word-recognition units (Ehri & Wilce, 1985; Stuart & Coltheart, 1988; Share, 1995) in the developing reading process.

There are several advantages to a P.A.–interactive or story-reading approach. First, guided reading of stories and dictated accounts provides children with a concrete, meaningful entry into reading. They are able to start with the larger pieces of written language (story, sentence) and work down to the smaller, more abstract pieces (words, letter-sounds). These smaller bits (e.g., beginning consonant awareness and letter-sound correspondences) are taught directly and then infused into the story reading through careful teacher modeling. A second advantage is that guided story reading, as opposed to isolated phonics instruction, is a multi-dimensional task that simultaneously addresses several aspects of literacy learning, including concept of word, application of letter-sound knowledge, sight word acquisition, meaning vocabulary, and comprehension. This integration of multiple knowledge areas in the same task speaks to the "instructional time" problem facing the teacher. That is, time-wise, guided reading of a big book or dictated story can "kill several birds with one stone."

A possible third advantage of having children read simple texts from the start was pointed out by Clay (1991). Although acknowledging that reading could be introduced to children at different levels (e.g., letter-sound, word, sentence, or story), Clay argued that supported reading of simple stories affords more cues to the child who struggles. (*Note.* This is the premise on which her Reading Recovery program was based.) When a beginner reads a list of short a words (e.g., h<u>at</u>, m<u>an</u>, b<u>ag</u>, s<u>ad</u>, and cl<u>ap</u>), he or she is limited to using letter-sound cues. However, when the same child comes upon the word, s<u>ad</u>, in a story, he or she can potentially use letter-sound, word-order, and meaning cues to identify the word. The effective use of multiple cues, according to Clay, fosters adaptability and independence in the beginning reader.

Turning to disadvantages of P.A.–interactive instruction, some argue that story reading, accompanied by incidental phonics instruction, is ineffective, or at least inefficient, in developing decoding skill. The idea is that hit-and-miss letter-sound instruction will not get the job done. However, from a P.A.–interactive perspective, there is no requirement that phonics be taught *incidentally* (i.e., geared to an immediate student need). In the Early Steps intervention program (Morris, Tyner, & Perney, 2000; Santa & Hoien, 1999), struggling first graders read leveled stories each day, but they are also paced, at their individual learning rates, through a systematic phonics curriculum that includes beginning consonants, short-vowel word families, consonant

blends, and short- and long-vowel patterns. Results show that, given this balance of story reading and systematic phonics, Early Steps students outperform controls on measures of word recognition, sentence comprehension, and *pseudo-word decoding*. These findings counter the fear that P.A.–interactive instruction will fail to develop decoding skill in beginning readers.

A second disadvantage of P.A.–interactive instruction, to some at least, is that it requires considerable teacher knowledge. A teacher's manual can suggest a sequence of stories to be read and phonics skills to be mastered, and even describe some general instructional routines. However, a manual cannot address the moment-to-moment decision making that defines good teaching. To skillfully guide young children's story book reading, a teacher needs to understand the developmental reading process. That is, he or she must know which skills come in first, second, and so on, and how to intervene effectively when a child is stalled. Some teachers are able to acquire such pedagogical knowledge through experience (trial and error); others are not so fortunate. This remains an important challenge for teacher education (preservice and inservice); how to develop knowledgeable, problem-solving teachers to work with struggling beginning readers.

Conclusion

In this chapter, I have examined two theoretical positions regarding the development of phonemic awareness in the beginning reading process. One position, *phoneme awareness–first*, is better understood by educators (whether they accept it or not) and has exerted considerable influence on teaching practice (e.g., National Reading Panel, 2000; No Child Left Behind Act, 2002). The other position, *phoneme awareness–interactive*, has largely been ignored by educators, ironically even at times when it could have provided support for favored, holistic teaching approaches. I wish to conclude with a short history lesson. Going back just 25 years, I believe, reveals an interesting story that summarizes the past and clarifies what could happen in the future.

My story begins in the mid-1980s. At that time, the whole-word approach—i.e., the formulaic repetition of a set of high-frequency words—still characterized beginning reading instruction in the United States (Chall, 1967). It is true that basal reader programs of the 1980s had increased the amount of phonics instruction in first grade; however, there was little attention to beginning readers' cognitive readiness for such an increase in phonics. During this same period, psychologists were busily studying the role of phonemic awareness in reading acquisition. Their findings suggested that phonemic awareness might be an important prerequisite to learning to read an alphabetic language.

In the 1990s there was a sea change in beginning reading instruction. During this Whole Language period, a meaningful, storybook introduction to reading was favored, while word control and phonics were de-emphasized. Basal reader programs of the decade embodied this point of view. Initially, many educators seemed pleased and energized by the new emphasis on meaning and holism; however, psychologists who had been studying the beginning reading process were confused and, in some cases, angry. They believed that their research, documenting the importance of phonemic awareness and letter-sound knowledge, was being ignored by reading educators. And to some degree, they were correct. Interestingly, within the psychological community, the developmental course of phonemic awareness was being re-thought. By the mid-1990s, several prominent theorists (e.g., Ehri, Stuart & Coltheart, Perfetti, Share) were suggesting that phonemic awareness bears a reciprocal (or interactive), as opposed to a prerequisite, relationship to reading acquisition. Although this theoretical stance provided potential support for a holistic introduction to reading, it too was ignored by the reading education community. (*Note*: Marie Clay was an exception here. Her work [1985, 1991], had long been guided by a P.A.–interactive perspective.)

Around the year 2000, there was a strong reaction to Whole Language instruction. Fourth-grade reading test scores had fallen (at least in California), and a new group of reading experts had gotten the attention of educational policy makers. This new group (see Allington & Woodside-Jiron, 1999; Lyon, 2001), claiming the imprimatur of science, recommended that beginning readers, from the start, should be taught phonemic awareness and phonics—explicitly and systematically. So much for holism. Federal policy makers adopted the new, "scientific" position in their Reading First initiative (NCLB), and basal reader publishers quickly followed suit, providing the needed materials. By 2005, intensive phonics instruction, along with practice reading decodable text, was the standard introduction to reading for most American schoolchildren.

What are we to make of this proverbial "pendulum swing" in beginning reading instruction (from part to whole to part to ...)? First, we should acknowledge that teaching children to read is a complex matter, involving differences in learners, teachers, methods, and materials. Where complexity reigns, there will always be differences of opinion and, in the case of teaching beginning reading, different ways to accomplish the task. In this chapter, I have focused on the role of phonemic awareness in learning to read. I have reviewed two theoretical perspectives and argued that the way one thinks about the development of phonemic awareness has important implications for teaching beginning readers. When, not if, the instructional pendulum swings back once more (this time, toward holism), perhaps it should settle somewhere in the middle, near to what I have termed the *phoneme awareness-interactive* position. At the least, next time around, teacher educators and practicing teachers should know that there *is* a middle, one that is clearly outlined in the research literature.

References

Adams, M. (1990). *Beginning to read: Thinking and learning about print.* Cambridge, MA: MIT Press.

Allington, R., & Woodside-Jiron, H. (1999). The politics of literacy teaching: How "research" shaped educational policy. *Educational Researcher, 28,* 4–13.

Ball, E., & Blachman, B. (1991). Does phoneme awareness training in kindergarten make a difference in early word recognition and developmental spelling? *Reading Research Quarterly, 26,* 49–66.

Ball, R. (1984). Beginning reading instruction: From debate to reformation. In P. D. Pearson, R. Barr, M. Kamil, & P. Mosenthal (Eds.), *Handbook of reading research* (pp. 545–581). New York: Longman.

Blachman, B. (1997). Early intervention and phonological awareness: A cautionary tale. In B. Blachman (Ed.), *Foundations of reading acquisition and dyslexia: Implications for early intervention* (pp. 409–430). Mahwah, NJ: Erlbaum.

Blachman, B., Ball, E., Black, R., & Tangel, D. (1994). Kindergarten teachers develop phoneme awareness in low-income, inner-city classrooms: Does it make a difference? *Reading and Writing, 6,* 1–17.

Bradley, L., & Bryant, P. (1983). Categorizing sounds and learning to read: A causal connection. *Nature, 30,* 419–421.

Chall, J. (1967). *Learning to read: The great debate.* New York: McGraw-Hill.

Chomsky, C. (1979). Approaching reading through invented spelling. In L. Resnick & P. Weaver (Eds.), *Theory and practice of early reading* (Vol. 2, pp. 43–65). Hillsdale, NJ: Erlbaum.

Clay, M. (1985). *The early detection of reading difficulties.* Auckland, New Zealand: Heinemann

Clay, M. (1991). *Becoming literate: The construction of inner control.* Portsmouth, NH: Heinemann.

Ehri, L. (1992). Reconceptualizing the development of sight word reading and its relationship to recoding. In P. Gough, L. Ehri, & R. Treiman (Eds.), *Reading acquisition* (pp. 107–143). Hillsdale, NJ: Erlbaum.

Ehri, L. (1996). Researching how children learn how to read: Controversies in science are not like controversies in practice. In G. Brannigan (Ed.), *The enlightened educator: Research adventures in the schools* (pp. 179–204). Boston, MA: McGraw-Hill.

Ehri, L., & Wilce, L. (1985). Movement into reading: Is the first stage of printed word learning visual or phonetic? *Reading Research Quarterly, 20,* 163–179.

Elkonin, D.B. (1973). U.S.S.R. In J. Downing (Ed.), *Comparative reading* (pp. 551–580). New York: Macmillan.

Frith, U. (1985). Beneath the surface of developmental dyslexia. In K. Patterson, J. Marshall, & M. Coltheart (Eds.), *Surface dyslexia: Neuropsychological and cognitive studies of phonological reading* (pp. 301–330). Hillsdale, NJ: Erlbaum.

Gough, P., & Hillinger, M. (1980). Learning to read: An unnatural act. *Bulletin of the Orton Society, 30,* 179–196.

Helfgott, J. (1976). Phonemic segmentation and blending skills of kindergarten children: Implications for beginning reading acquisition. *Contemporary Educational Psychology, 1,* 157–169.

Holdaway, D. (1979). *The foundations of literacy.* Portsmouth, NH: Hieneman

Johnston, R., Anderson, M., & Holligan, C. (1996). Knowledge of the alphabet and explicit awareness of phonemes in prereaders: The nature of the relationship. *Reading and Writing, 8,* 217–234.

Liberman, I., & Shankweiler, D. (1979). Speech, the alphabet, and teaching to read. In L. Resnick & P. Weaver (Eds.), *Theory and practice of early reading* (Vol. 2, pp. 109–132). Hillsdale, NJ: Erlbaum.

Liberman, I., Shankweiler, D., Fischer, F., & Carter, B. (1974). Explicit syllable and phoneme segmentation in the young child. *Journal of Experimental Child Psychology, 18,* 201–212.

Lyon, G. R. (2001). Testimony of Dr. G. Reid Lyon, Chief of Child Development and Behavior Branch (NICHD), to the House Subcommittee on Education Reform. Retrieved from http://www.hhs.gov/asl/testify/t010308.html

Mann, V., Tobin, P., & Wilson, R. (1987). Measuring phonological awareness through the invented spellings of kindergarten children. *Merrill-Palmer Quarterly, 33,* 365–391.

Marsh, G., Friedman, M., Welch, V., & Desberg, P. (1981). A cognitive-developmental theory of reading acquisition. In G. MacKinnon & T.

Waller (Eds.), *Reading research: Advances in theory and practice* (Vol. 3, pp. 201–215). New York: Academic Press.

Morris, D. (1993). The relationship between children's concept of word in text and phoneme awareness: A longitudinal study. *Research in the Teaching of English*, *27*, 133–154.

Morris, D. (2003). Reading instruction in kindergarten. In D. Morris & R. Slavin (Eds.), *Every child reading* (pp. 8–32). Boston: Allyn and Bacon.

Morris, D., Bloodgood, J., Lomax, R., & Perney, J. (2003). Developmental steps in learning to read: A longitudinal study in kindergarten and first grade. *Reading Research Quarterly, 38*, 302–328.

Morris, D., & Perney, J. (1984). Developmental spelling as a predictor of first-grade reading achievement. *Elementary School Journal, 84*, 441–457.

Morris, D., Tyner, B., & Perney, J. (2000). Early Steps: Replicating the effects of a first-grade reading intervention program. *Journal of Educational Psychology*, *92*, 681–693.

National Reading Panel (NRP). (2000). *Teaching children to read: An evidence-based assessment of the scientific research literature on reading and its implications for reading instruction.* Rockville, MD: National Institute of Child Health and Human Development.

No Child Left Behind Act of 2001 (NCLB), Public Law No. 107-110. (2002). Retrieved from http://www.ed.gov/policy/elsec/leg/esea02/index

O'Connor, R., Notari-Syverson, A., & Vasdasy, P. (1996). Ladders to literacy: The effects of teacher-led phonological activities for kindergarten children with and without disabilities. *Exceptional Children*, *63*, 117–130.

Perfetti, C. (1986). Continuities in reading acquisition, reading skill, and reading disability. *Remedial and Special Education*, *7*, 11–21.

Perfetti, C. (1992). The representation problem in reading acquisition. In P. Gough, L. Ehri, & R. Treiman (Eds.), *Reading acquisition* (pp. 145–174). Hillsdale, NJ: Erlbaum.

Rayner, K., Foorman, B., Perfetti, C., Pesetsky, D., & Seidenberg, M. (2001). How psychological science informs the teaching of reading. *Psychological Science in the Public Interest*, *2*, 31–74.

Richgels, D. (2001). Invented spelling, phonemic awareness, and reading and writing instruction. In S. Neuman & D. Dickinson (Eds.), *Handbook of early literacy research* (pp. 142–155). New York: Guilford.

Santa, C., & Hoien, T. (1999). An assessment of Early Steps: A program for early intervention of reading problems. *Reading Research Quarterly*, *34*, 54–79.

Seymour, P., & MacGregor, C. (1984). Developmental dyslexia: A cognitive experimental analysis of phonological, morphemic, and visual impairments. *Cognitive Neuropsychology, 1,* 43–83.

Share, D. (1995). Phonological recoding and self-teaching: Sine qua non of reading acquisition. *Cognition, 55*, 151–218.

Share, D., Jorm, A., Maclean, R., & Matthews, R. (1984). Sources of individual differences in reading achievement. *Journal of Educational Psychology*, *76*, 1309–1324.

Snow, C., Burns, M., & Griffin, P. (1998). *Preventing reading difficulties in young children.* Washington, DC: National Academy Press.

Stahl, S., & Murray, B. (1994). Defining phonological awareness and its relationship to early reading. *Journal of Educational Psychology, 86*, 221–234.

Stuart, M., & Coltheart, M. (1988). Does reading develop in a sequence of stages? *Cognition*, *30*, 139–181.

Torgesen, J., Morgan, S., & Davis, C. (1992). Effects of two types of phonological awareness training on word learning in kindergarten children. *Journal of Educational Psychology, 84*, 364–370.

Whitehurst, G., & Lonigan, C. (2001). Emergent literacy: Development from prereaders to readers. In S. Neuman & D. Dickinson (Eds.), *Handbook of early literacy research* (pp. 11–29). New York: Guilford.

Wilson, B. (1996). *Wilson reading system: Instructor's manual.* Millbury, MA: Wilson Language Training Corporation.

27

Interventions to Develop Decoding Proficiencies

Irene W. Gaskins
Benchmark School

This chapter is grounded in the well-documented observation that children learn differently and vary in their development of reading-related abilities (Mathes et al., 2005). Thus, it follows, that not all children will respond successfully to the same instructional approach to developing decoding proficiency (Ysseldyke & Taylor, 2007). The inevitable outcome is that in schools in which only one instructional program is in use, some students will experience difficulty learning to read (Valencia & Riddle-Buly, 2004). A one-size-fits-all approach does not encourage teachers to provide the differentiated opportunities that children need in order to learn to decode (Allington, 2006). This gloomy prognosis is the case even when the approach being implemented is evidence based (Al Otaiba & Fuchs, 2006).

The missing ingredient is instruction at the hands of knowledgeable teachers who are focused on what each child needs (Valencia & Riddle-Buly, 2004), including the teaching approach and pace that work for each child (Taylor, Peterson, Marx, & Chein, 2007; Vaughn, Wanzek, & Fletcher, 2007). The thesis of honoring children's differences by providing differentiated instruction will be explored and extended in this chapter as components of evidence-based (Chhabra & McCardle, 2004), multi-level (Allington & Johnston, 2001), and multidimensional (Gaskins, 1999; Vellutino & Scanlon, 2002) approaches to reading words are described. Multilevel, multidimensional approaches are approaches in which teachers adapt instruction to the characteristics and developmental phase of each student and students are introduced to more than one way to decode words (Gaskins, 1999, 2005).

The chapter begins with a presentation of four ways to read words, followed by a summary of phase theory as it applies to matching ways of decoding to children's ways of reading words. Next, research is reviewed regarding the current status of knowledge about interventions to develop decoding proficiency among at-risk and struggling readers. Because there are several different paths to the remediation of children with reading disabilities (O'Shaughnessy &

Swanson, 2000), a few detailed descriptions of successful interventions are provided to give the reader a sense of the differences in decoding approaches among those that have had significant effects with at-risk and struggling readers. Finally, the inextricable link between mastery of decoding and children's affective, motivational, and volitional characteristics is discussed. Conclusions about instruction will be drawn both from theories about ways of reading words and phases of development in word reading and from research about interventions and children's characteristics. Based on those conclusions, suggestions will be made for interventions that seem to have the most potential for helping all children develop decoding proficiencies.

Ways to Read Words

Learning to read words is necessary if children are to achieve the goal of reading—the construction of meaning. Based on the studies reviewed in this chapter, plus extensive experience teaching struggling readers, I am convinced that simultaneously teaching struggling readers to read words and to construct meaning provides the best opportunity for students to become successful readers (McGill-Franzen, 2006; Pressley, 2006). However, as the topic of this chapter is decoding, only one part of the reading equation will be discussed here. One way to read words is to decode them. According to Harris and Hodges (1995), the term *decode* is used in reading practice "primarily to refer to word identification" (p. 55). In this chapter decoding is used as a synonym for both word identification and non-automatic word reading and is regarded as a thinking activity in which readers flexibly consider alternative ways to read unknown or miscued words, depending on their developmental phase and array of decoding strategies. Similar to Afflerbach, Pearson, and Paris (2008), strategy is associated with a conscious and systematic plan, while skill is associated with a proficient, often automatic, act.

Ehri's Theory of Word Reading   Ehri (2005), based on several decades of research, outlines four basic ways children read words. These include: sounding out and blending letters into pronunciations that are recognized as meaningful words; analogizing to familiar words (e.g., reading *frog* by analogy to *dog*); and predicting words based on context. A fourth way of reading words is sight-word reading. In addition, children use combinations of these basic approaches.

Sounding out and blending.   The sounding-out-and-blending approach to decoding is known as synthetic phonics. In a synthetic phonics program, students are taught to decode new words by retrieving from memory the sound that each letter, or combination of letters, in a word represents and blending the sounds into a recognizable word (National Reading Panel, 2000). It is a parts-to-whole approach (Strickland, 1998). For some children who struggle in learning to read, holding in memory and blending individual sounds into a synthesized, recognizable word proves difficult, even when they are able to produce the individual sounds for the letters they see. Unfortunately, producing sounds in isolation often results in students adding an /uh/ sound to each consonant sound, so the resulting sounds in pronouncing "game," for example, might be /guh/, /a/, /muh/, a combination of sounds some students might not recognize as "game."

Analogizing.   An analogy approach is sometimes referred to as a rhyming approach because students look at the part of the unknown word that makes the rhyming sound (the vowel and consonant that follows) and think of a known word that contains the same vowel-consonant pattern or rime. In cases in which students know the sounds represented by the word's onset (beginning consonant or consonants), they are then able to decode the word by rhyming. If I know **like**, then I can decode **strike**. If the onset is unknown, the reader recalls a word he or she knows that begins with the same onset (e.g., thinks of **strong** to aid in matching the sounds for the onset **STR**).

This approach tends not to work well for students who do not have analogous known words (keywords) stored in memory in a fully-analyzed way, matching all the sounds in the word to the letters that represent the sounds (Gaskins, Ehri, Cress, O'Hara, & Donnelly, 1996–1997, 1997). For example, when attempting to call to mind an analogous word to aid in decoding the first chunk of "target," the child may recall "can" because he or she has never looked carefully all the way through the keyword "car" (an appropriate analogous word for the first chunk of "target"). Further, he or she may call to mind "not" to decode the second chunk in "target," as a result of not fully analyzing the words to realize that E is the vowel that precedes the T. Due to the difficulties some children experience in calling analogous words to mind, a word wall or keyword chart can be made available as a bootstrap.

Predicting.   In this way of reading words, the reader uses the context surrounding an unknown word, plus one or a few letters in the unknown word, to predict the pronunciation of a word. For example, in reading the sentence "At the farm John saw a cow," in which all of the words are known except *cow*, the reader predicts (based on the initial consonant and the sense of the sentence) that the word is *cow*. Predicting is an approach frequently used to read unknown words by students in the early phases of learning to read and by struggling readers. Able readers less frequently use predicting as a decoding strategy, relying instead on all of the letter-sound matches in the word (Stanovich, 1984). In applying a predicting strategy, readers have usually not looked at all the letters in the unknown word, therefore they are less accurate. For example, in the earlier example about the farm and cow, unless a picture cues the reader, he or she may read any word that begins with C, such as *cat* or *calf*. For this reason, use of predicting as a preference for decoding is discouraged except as a cross check for sense once a word has been decoded.

Sight.   Words that are read by sight are words that have been read before (usually, by using one of the three ways discussed above) and stored in memory. However, as pointed out by Vellutino and Scanlon (2002), some children, perhaps unaware of the alphabetic principle, circumvent letter-sound matching and attempt to learn words by the unanalyzed whole word or paired associates approach, an approach which eventually fails. According to Ehri's phase theory and research (1998), the most effective way to read words by sight is to acquire knowledge of the major letter-sound correspondences and apply this knowledge to retain complete representations of words in memory. Students who have learned words by analyzing their letter-sound matches have better memory for the words (compared to students who lack complete letter-sound representations of known words) and this facilitates retaining new words in memory for reading, spelling, and decoding new words by analogy (Ehri, Satlow, & Gaskins, 2009).

Goswami's Grain-Size Theory of Word Reading   Published reading programs tend to advance just one way to decode words; however, research and experience suggest that it is to a reader's advantage to be able to access and apply multiple ways (Ehri et al., 2009; Juel & Minden-Cupp, 2000; Lovett et al., 2000; Vellutino & Scanlon, 2002; Walton & Walton, 2002; Ziegler & Goswami, 2005). As Ziegler and Goswami explain, "English-speaking children need to use a variety of recoding strategies, supplementing grapheme-phoneme conversion strategies with the recognition of letter patterns for rimes and attempts at whole-word recognition" (p. 19). This is the case due to the inconsistent nature of English orthography and is explicated by the psycholinguistic grain-size theory (Goswami, 2006). This theory explains that, in English, children who are successful in learning to read develop large-grain (whole-word and rhyme analogy) decoding strategies in parallel with small-grain (grapheme-phoneme) decoding strategies as a way to cope with the inconsistencies in our language.

Developmental Models of Word Learning

There is general agreement among literacy researchers regarding theoretical models of word learning development (Bear, Invernizzi, Templeton, & Johnston, 2008; Ehri, 1995; Frith, 1985; Henderson, 1990; Vellutino & Scanlon, 2002). "These models suggest that the acquisition and integration of knowledge and skills underlying reading and writing proceeds in something akin to developmental stages characterized by typical literacy behaviors that reflect the child's knowledge and level of skills development at given points in time" (Vellutino & Scanlon, 2002, p. 581). Word-learning models provide a framework regarding the typical sequence of decoding acquisition and the processes to be scaffolded to lead students from one phase of word learning to the next; although, the pace of movement through these phases differs both between and within age groups. The models have in common a beginning period of learning to read and spell in which children know little about letters or the alphabetic principle (thus rely on salient visual clues), a middle period in which children become increasingly aware of using letter-sound matches to decode and spell, and a more advanced period in which children use letter patterns to unlock the pronunciation of unknown words. Ehri's (1995) phase model will be discussed as an example of a developmental word learning model.

Ehri's Phase Model   The initial phase (designated pre-alphabetic by Ehri) is characterized by students remembering a word based on a distinctive and purely visual cue. For example, a child may read "elephant" based on the length of the word or might identify "donkey" by the "tail" at the end, then read "lady" and "story"—and other words with a "tail"—as "donkey."

The second phase is partial alphabetic. In this phase students begin to use letter-sound information, but do not yet use all the letter-sound information in a word. Instead, they remember and apply a few salient letter-sound matches. For example, some students might remember the letter-sound matches for only H and S in the word "horse." These students will likely read the word correctly when they read a story about a horse; however, a few days later, when they read a story that includes the sentence "The boys went in the house to play," some will misread the sentence as "The boys went in the horse to play." Guiding students to segment the words horse and house into sounds and match the sounds to letters, increases student awareness of the need to use all the letter-sound information in a word and begins to move the student into the full alphabetic phase.

In the third phase, the full alphabetic phase, students notice and remember all the letter-sound matches in a word. They can decode and spell words such as "plant" because they have matched the letters and sounds for P, L, A, N, and T.

The final and most efficient phase of word learning is the consolidated alphabetic phase. Readers in this phase have consolidated their letter-sound knowledge and remember matches between multi-letter units and syllabic units. For example, in reading the unknown word "blot," they match onset and rime units by recognizing the letter-sound matches from the onset of a known word (e.g. black) and the rime of a known word (e.g. not). In addition, in this phase, readers recognize as a unit common word parts such as unstressed syllables (e.g., -tion, -le).

Overlapping-Wave Model   Another view of word knowledge development (specifically spelling development) is the overlapping-wave model (Sharp, Sinatra, & Reynolds, 2008), a model that seems equally applicable to word reading, positing that development proceeds both in phases and in degrees. As explained by Sharp and colleagues, "students may not necessarily think in a qualitatively different fashion from one phase to the next, so much as adapt the various ways that they think and reason to the current tasks. This perspective suggests that although progress is incremental, it is hardly steady; and more and less sophisticated strategies are in use at the same time" (p. 224). As true of word reading as of spelling, movement into a more advanced phase does not signal exclusive use of strategies characteristic of the new phase. In fact, the designation of a phase seems best defined by the majority of strategies that a student is using at any one time.

Summary   Children learn to read words in at least four different ways. Knowledge and ability to apply all of these ways is a definite advantage for children who learn to read in a language in which there is not a consistent one-to-one relationship between letters and sounds. As children learn to read words, they pass through at least three phases: initially depending primarily on visual cues, followed by becoming increasingly familiar with and applying letter-sound knowledge, and, finally, using consolidated units of words to decode unknown words. These phases are overlapping, with children using strategies typical of both the new phase and previous phases. To enable struggling readers to begin their journeys to becoming successful readers, teachers must match their instruction and expectations to each student's acquired knowledge and level of development (Vellutino & Scanlon, 2002). This means starting at the phase where each student is primarily functioning and scaffolding instruction to support students as they approach and move into the next phase.

Current Status of Knowledge about Decoding Interventions

During the past decade, a panel of literacy experts (National Reading Panel, 2000) was commissioned to review literacy research in search of evidence-based ways of teaching children to read. In addition, groups of researchers, many funded by the National Institute of Child Health and Human

Development, have completed immense bodies of intervention research related to remediation of "core deficits" that are hypothesized to hinder the development of decoding proficiency. The studies are too numerous for each to be discussed separately, therefore the results of several summary reports, in addition to several individual studies, will be shared. Also, two current approaches to early intervention, Response to Instruction (RTI) and multidimensional instruction, will be reviewed. Research about these programs and practices follow.

National Reading Panel   In an attempt to settle the lack of consensus concerning decoding instruction in the United States, the NRP completed a meta-analysis of phonics instruction studies and concluded that "systematic" phonics was more effective than non-phonetic approaches, especially for kindergarten and first-grade students. An additional outcome of the NRP meta-analysis was to distinguish two types of systematic phonics instruction: synthetic phonics (sounding out and blending) and larger unit phonics such as analogizing (using onset and rime). The two approaches did not differ statistically in the size of their effects. This was the case for mainstream students and for students with reading disabilities. With respect to the effectiveness of phonics instruction, Hammill and Swanson (2006) have offered an alternative view suggesting that 96% of the achievement variance in learning to read was unexplained by the presence or absence of phonics lessons and could be attributed to other factors. This reminds the reader that there is much more to learning to read than learning to decode. However, for some children learning to decode puts them on the road to becoming readers.

In a much-cited review of phonics research, Stahl, Duffy-Hester, and Stahl (1998) also reported that a synthetic approach and an analogy approach performed equally well and "both were more effective than whole-word approaches" (p. 348). O'Shaughnessy and Swanson (2000) reported similar results with second-grade, reading disabled public school children, some of whom received a phonological awareness program and the others received an analogy program. I now turn to the research about synthetic phonics, certainly the most researched systematic phonics approach, to learn about both the practices that seem to support its effectiveness and some problems with the intervention that remain unsolved.

Synthetic Phonics Interventions   Torgesen (2005) summarized data from 13 intervention samples of children with severe to moderate word-level reading difficulties. All of the interventions provided explicit instruction in phonemic awareness and phonemic decoding skills, with some of the interventions variants of the Lindamood method for increasing children's awareness of individual sounds in words (Lindamood & Lindamood, 1984, 1998). Examination of the data suggests that equal growth rates were possible using a variety of direct-instruction approaches to word reading. Despite evidence of encouraging gains in these intervention samples, synthetic phonics interventions were not sufficient

to close the gap in word reading between pre-intervention status and age-appropriate reading, especially for older children. The reading skills of struggling older students remained in the disabled range and the interventions were characterized as "stabilizing" students' degree of reading failure. Additional research reviewed by Torgesen suggested that special education placements for children with reading disabilities, which typically featured synthetic phonics instruction, "produced no gains in word level reading skills relative to normal readers during a three-year period in elementary school" (p. 524). Torgesen et al. (2001) discovered in their intervention study that the phonics intervention can be intense (daily one-to-one instruction delivered in two 50-minute sessions each day for 8 weeks) and combine a variety of components in different proportions (in one intervention student time receiving instruction in explicit, systematic word-level skills—compared to applying those skills while reading and writing connected text—was 85% and in the other 20%) and, despite differences in the two interventions, still obtained remarkably similar results. About half the children attained average-level reading skills (standard score 90 or above) by the end of the 2-year follow-up period. One cannot help but wonder if the outcome would have been even better had the classroom instruction and supplementary instruction been congruent during and after the 8-week intervention..

Conclusions from a review of synthetic phonics interventions.   Based on this brief look at studies reviewed by Torgesen which featured synthetic phonics, we can draw several conclusions about increasing the chances of bringing the skills of children with reading disabilities into the typical range. Many of these conclusions revolve around one point—different children need different kinds of instruction. Torgesen (2004) points this out with respect to intensity, length of delivery, and educational context and suggests two ways to provide differentiated instruction: increase instructional time and provide individual or small-group instruction. Other possibilities include teaching students how to strategically use the synthetic phonics skills being taught (Gaskins, 2005), providing alternatives to phonemic awareness and synthetic phonics (e.g., large grain decoding strategies, Goswami, 2006, such as using key words, Gaskins 2004, because synthesizing onset and rime is sometimes easier for beginning readers than synthesizing individual phonemes), coaching about how to select an appropriate decoding strategy (Gaskins, 2004), increasing the amount of reading that each child does in traditional texts (Allington, 2006; Stanovich, 1986), creating many opportunities for students to write connected text by segmenting words into sounds and applying sound-letter knowledge (Moats, 1995), and providing on-going professional development for both regular education and supplemental program teachers (McGill-Franzen, 2006).

Unsolved problems with synthetic phonics interventions.   In reflecting on the outcomes for struggling readers receiving direct instruction in synthetic phonics, it becomes apparent that something in addition to more intensive instruction in phonemic awareness and synthetic phonics is necessary if struggling readers are to catch up to their peers. Perhaps that something is instruction that combines ways of learning words and a balance of reading and writing in connected contexts. In the remainder of this chapter a variety of interventions are reviewed. Exploring some of these to find what works for specific students may have a greater likelihood of achieving significant student gains than more intensely teaching what seems not to be working.

Another unresolved problem with synthetic phonics instruction, but also with any supplementary instruction, is how to teach decoding skills and strategies in such a way that students will become independent in applying them and maintain a satisfactory rate of growth once the supplementary intervention has ended. Researchers have often been disheartened to follow-up students who received special interventions and find that, despite almost all of the children responding well during the intervention, only slightly more than half are able to sustain or improve their gains once the intensive intervention is concluded (Torgesen et al., 2001). A possible explanation may lie in the students' return to regular-classroom settings where instruction was different in many ways (including the number of students) from that received in the one-to-one treatment setting. As one example, it may be more difficult for students to maintain attention and engagement during reading instruction with a higher student to teacher ratio. This possibility gains credence based on the fact that, during the follow-up period, teacher ratings of students' attention/behavior most reliably predicted growth trajectories (Torgesen et al., 2001). Further, as noted by Harn, Linan-Thompson, and Roberts (2008), the larger the instructional group the less likely the intervention will be targeted to students' instructional needs and enlist active engagement.

These findings suggest that, once a supplementary program has ended, students would profit from a maintenance program in their regular classrooms that would review, reinforce, and value the concepts and strategies taught in the supplementary intervention. In addition, students in supplementary phonics programs would likely benefit from being taught metacognitive strategies that would increase awareness of the need for taking charge of their attention and for applying self-talk strategies both to help maintain attention and engagement and to self-teach as emphasized by Share (1995).

The conclusions from systematic phonics instruction discussed above are based on studies of at-risk and struggling readers of a variety of ages and grade levels. A more optimistic prognosis emerges for students in kindergarten and first grade who are exhibiting difficulty acquiring phonemic awareness and alphabet knowledge. One model guiding intervention during the early years is Response to Intervention (RTI) discussed below. Recognizing that evidence-based, generally effective early literacy programs do not accommodate the decoding needs of all students has

led to an interest in "multilevel" models of instruction and assessment (Al Otaiba & Fuchs, 2006).

Multilevel Intervention   Prevention and intervention are the goals of RTI. These goals are accomplished by offering at-risk and struggling readers targeted, expert, and intensive reading instruction in kindergarten and first grade *before* they fall behind (Allington & Walmsley, 2007; Vaughn & Klingner, 2007). This is accomplished "by identifying students who are not responsive to the early reading instruction that is effective with most students" (Chard & Lian-Thompson, 2008, p. 99), usually by means of curriculum-based measures (Vaughn, Wanzek, Woodruff, & Lian-Thompson, 2007). Once identified, these students are provided with more intensive instruction than they were previously receiving, often with an emphasis on phonemic awareness and synthetic decoding, despite the fact that this emphasis may have been exactly what was not working. Perhaps a different emphasis might be more appropriate, at least in some cases. The three-tier model specifies the implementation of multiple levels of interventions for students whose response to instruction does not indicate the improvement needed for them to no longer be considered at risk.

Tier I.   One definition of a Tier 1 classroom is a classroom that has an effective core reading program provided to a whole class by a general education teacher (Kamps et al., 2008; Vaughn & Klingner, 2007). Allington and Walmsley (2007) define a good Tier 1 classroom as one that ensures that classroom reading instruction is appropriate to students' needs and that no one is receiving a one-size-fits-all program. Denton, Fletcher, Anthony, and Francis (2006) define the first tier as consisting of enhanced classroom-level instruction that is of consistently high-quality.

Tier II.   The next level of instruction, for those students identified through progress monitoring as in need of reading interventions beyond Tier I, is often provided in the classroom. This intervention is supplemental, small-group instruction that is in addition to the core reading program (Kamps et al., 2008) and, ideally, is taught by a reading teacher. One model of small-group instruction often used, and which has proved successful for improvement in early literacy skills for Tier I non-responders, is explicit instruction using a highly structured and sequenced curriculum. However, some students continue to struggle even after receiving high-quality classroom instruction, supplemented by small-group instruction, suggesting that these children may need a different amount or type of intervention.

Tier III.   Intervention at the Tier III level is generally pull-out instruction that is more intensive than the instruction in Tiers I and II. "More intensive" may be defined as decreasing the instructional group size or increasing the amount of time each day a student spends receiving instruction. Other conceptualizations of intensity are the duration of the intervention over months and years and an increase in the number of sessions or hours of instruction per day. As discussed previously, more minutes per day or more instruction that did not work in Tiers I and II may not be what the struggling reader needs. Progress monitoring is believed to be the key to making good instructional decisions about these issues.

Believing that non-responders may need more intense instruction, Wanzek and Vaughn (2008) compared non-responders who received "one dose" of small-group intervention with another group receiving a "double dose" (twice as much time). Response to the two treatments was similar over time, leading the researchers to conclude that more of the same intervention did not prove beneficial and that an individualized intervention might have been a better alternative.

Summary   The underlying assumption of the RTI model is that entering first-grade students (including those at risk for failure in reading) will begin first grade in regular education classes in which they receive a generally effective, evidence-based core reading program, accompanied by an in-class, supplementary intervention as needed, and a special pull-out program as a third response. This is a gigantic step forward from the second half of the 20th century when children had to fail in learning to read for 2 or 3 years before they were eligible for remedial intervention. Despite the progress signaled by RTI, Al Otaiba and Fuchs (2006) recommend an even earlier intervention, worrying that as many as 30% of children at risk for reading difficulties may not benefit from the kind of generally effective early literacy interventions suggested by scientifically based reading research. In this next section, we will explore early intervention.

Interventions to Develop Decoding Proficiencies Early Although often associated with No Child Left Behind (NCLB, 2002), early intervention became a widely-acclaimed possibility for preventing reading problems in the mid-1980s when Marie Clay brought Reading Recovery, a one-to-one tutoring program for first graders, to the United States from New Zealand (Clay, 1979). Since then the What Works Clearinghouse (WWC) and the Institute of Education Sciences (IES) have released a 3-year independent review of the experimental research on Reading Recovery (March 2007) establishing Reading Recovery as an effective intervention based on scientific evidence.

One-to-one tutoring: Reading Recovery.   A recent report by McNaughton (2008) of a comparison between the original Reading Recovery model (Clay, 1979) and the latest codification (Clay, 2005) reveals refinements in theoretical ideas and processes, although the basic tenets of the program remain the same. From the earliest versions of Reading Recovery to the present, Reading Recovery stresses intense professional development for teachers and, for students, repeated reading of beginning-level texts, meaning making, sentence writing, and decoding in response to unknown words encountered in daily reading. Reading

Recovery is a short-term intervention for first graders who have the lowest achievement in literacy learning for their grade. These first graders meet on a one-to-one basis with a specially trained teacher for 30 minutes each day. The goal is for children to develop effective reading and writing strategies at an accelerated pace in order to work satisfactorily within the average range of their class after 12 to 20 weeks of tutoring. Successful implementation of the program is the result of the full year of academic training teachers receive as they simultaneously implement the intervention while being critiqued. Approximately one half of a Reading Recovery lesson is devoted to reading text, while the remaining half is spent writing a story, identifying letters, and doing word work.

One-to-one tutoring programs modeled on Reading Recovery.   Over the years, Reading Recovery's responsive approach to decoding was viewed by some as a deficiency. Responsive is used here as discussed by Mathes and associates (2005): teaching the specific decoding strategies students need in the moment, rather than systematically and sequentially introducing the decoding strategies traditionally found in phonics-based early-reading programs. In addition, the requirement of 1 year of intensive training prior to becoming a Reading Recovery teacher was regarded as a roadblock to implementing the program inexpensively and extensively. As a result, some researchers and teachers developed tutoring programs modeled after Reading Recovery, but with on-the-job training and systematic decoding (e.g., Iversen & Tunmer, 1993; Morris, 2007). One such program was Early Steps implemented in studies by Santa and Hoien (1999) and by Morris, Tyner, and Perney (2000). Posttests showed that first graders tutored in Early Steps outperformed controls in pseudoword reading and passage comprehension.

One-to-one tutoring: Interactive strategies.   An additional one-on-one first-grade tutoring program, Interactive Strategies, employed in a study by Vellutino and colleagues (1996) was described by Vellutino and Scanlon in a 2002 paper. They compared their program to other one-on-one programs, describing Reading Recovery as having a text emphasis, while the programs researched by Iversen & Tunmer (1993), Morris (1999), and Santa and Hoien (1999) incorporated more structured code-oriented activities than found in Reading Recovery. They further compared their program to those of Torgesen and colleagues (2001) which they view as primarily code-oriented analysis and blending programs. Vellutino and Scanlon's program includes both text-based and code-based remedial activities. The components of a lesson include: (a) rereading of one or more previously read texts; (b) learning the alphabetic principle (i.e., names of letters and their relationships to sounds, the phonemes in spoken words and how they are related to letters in printed words, and larger orthographic units such as word families and prefixes and suffixes); (c) reading new texts while the teacher guides the use of decoding strategies and engages the child in comprehension conversations about the story; (d) helping the child master the most frequently occurring sight words, often using word cards; and (e) engaging the child in dictating (or writing) a message, segmenting the spoken words, and deciding which letters to use to represent the sounds. In each lesson, depending on the child's level of skills development, emphasis is placed both on fostering the conjoint and interactive use of multiple strategies for systematic decoding and text processing and on promoting fluent reading and the integration of reading, writing, and comprehension. Students are encouraged to unlock unknown words by applying both code-based and context-based strategies, including sentence meaning (semantic clues) and grammatical constraints (syntactic clues). Teachers encourage students to monitor their reading of text to pick up miscues that do not conform to grammatical constraints or do not make sense. Semantic and syntactic cues are used in combination with phonics and all three are central to their approach.

Small-group early-intervention programs. Early intervention in kindergarten and first grade of the nature described in the RTI model, discussed earlier, is widely supported as a viable answer to decreasing the number of struggling readers in Grade 3 and beyond. A study completed by Mathes and colleagues (2005) sheds light on enhanced and supplementary approaches aimed at providing at-risk first graders with a strong start in learning to read. During each of 2 years, a sample of first graders who showed significant risk for reading difficulties was selected from six high-performing schools to investigate the effectiveness of combining enhanced classroom instruction with two different intense supplemental interventions. All 30 first-grade teachers in the six schools used as their core program one of two basal reading series. Implementation was highly varied and almost all teachers included other resources and methods to supplement or replace activities in the basal. Because of the support given beyond simply using a basal reader series, the classroom instruction provided for all first graders in the six schools was deemed "enhanced." In addition to core reading instruction in their regular classrooms, students in the supplemental interventions met in groups of three for 40 minutes a day, 5 days a week

The research team built on the district's extensive professional development program by providing a one-day professional development session focusing on the use of assessment data to plan and deliver differentiated instruction. In addition, the six supplemental intervention teachers who delivered the small-group instruction (Proactive Reading or Responsive Reading) received 42 hours of training specific to their intervention prior to the beginning of the study. Intervention teachers also participated in monthly half-day inservice meetings throughout the school year. The two supplemental interventions, derived from diverse theoretical foundations, will next be described.

Proactive Reading was developed from the model of Direct Instruction (Engelmann, 1980) and has its roots in behavior theory. Reading tasks were systematically arranged into a scope and sequence from which daily lessons were derived. "The result was that students learned phonetic elements in isolation before applying them strategically to words and practiced decoding words in isolation before reading decodable connected text and applying comprehension strategies" (Mathes et al., 2005, p. 152). Teachers followed a script for teaching the lessons. Students read fully decodable text, for which all phonetic elements and all irregular sight words had been taught previously and students had demonstrated mastery of those elements and words. There was much student response in unison, followed by individual turns. The teacher moved quickly from activity to activity, with 7 to 10 short activities in a typical 40-minute lesson. The daily teaching routine comprised the teacher modeling new content, providing guided practice, and implementing independent practice for every activity. Teachers were required to consistently monitor students' responses, provide positive praise for correct responses, and provide immediate corrective feedback. The majority of each lesson was composed of review and generalization, with each lesson containing very little new content.

Responsive Reading, which aligns with cognitive theory and characterizes learning in terms of the acquisition of problem-solving strategies through explicit instruction, modeling, guided practice, coaching, scaffolding, and fading, was the other supplemental intervention. There was no predetermined scope and sequence because the objectives of daily instruction were determined by the observed needs of students. Although Responsive Reading provided explicit instruction in phonemic awareness and phonemic decoding, it dedicated less time to the practice of these skills in isolation than did the Proactive approach. In Responsive Reading students applied literacy skills and strategies in the context of extensive reading and writing. Teachers used data from student assessments and daily anecdotal records as the foundation for lesson planning.

To individualize instruction in Responsive Reading, every third day teachers focused their daily lesson planning and text selection on an individual student. Teachers followed a lesson cycle that outlined how time was used across each 40-minute lesson. Teachers chose activities from a menu of options for each part of the lessons based on the observed needs of their students. Passage fluency (supported by repeated reading and teacher modeling) and assessment occupied 8 to 10 minutes of each lesson. During letter and word work, students received 10 to 12 minutes of explicit instruction and practice related to phonemic awareness, letter-sound relationships, word reading, or spelling. Letter-sound correspondences, as well as onsets and rimes, were taught for decoding new words. Students segmented the phonemes within each onset and rime before applying these units to read words and they segmented and wrote words dictated by the teacher. Sound boxes (Elkonin, 1973) were sometimes used to record letters matched to sounds. Supported reading lasted 10 to 12 minutes. The books read were leveled for difficulty, but were not intended to be phonetically decodable. Each day the focus student read alone a portion of a text not previously read. Next, the other students in the group read the same text, either chorally or individually. The final 8 to 10 minutes of the lesson was devoted to supported journal writing about the new story. Teachers sometimes provided explicit instruction in word patterns and modeled the segmenting of words in order to write the letters for phonemes. The primary word recognition strategy taught in Responsive Reading was to look for letter combinations you know, blend the sounds, reread the sentence, and decide if it makes sense. Decoding of unknown words using analogous known words was also taught.

The two approaches were different in their theoretical underpinnings, but both were comprehensive, integrated approaches to reading instruction based on scientific evidence. Both provided instruction in phonemic awareness, alphabetic knowledge, and application of this knowledge to reading and writing words and text, and they engaged students in making meaning from text.

Results of this study indicate that first-grade students who were at risk for reading failure and who received supplemental instruction in either the Proactive or Responsive intervention scored significantly higher on measures of reading and reading-related skills than students who received only enhanced classroom instruction. Enhanced classroom instruction alone was inadequate for a small number of students. The two interventions were equally effective. The authors concluded: "These findings suggest to us that there is likely not 'one best approach' and not one right philosophy or theory for how to best meet the needs of struggling readers. Nor did we find evidence that one approach was better for some at-risk children than another" (Mathes et al., 2005, p. 179).

An influential early intervention study, and the subject of some controversy, was that of Foorman, Francis, Fletcher, Schatschneider, and Mehta (1998; see Taylor, Anderson, Au, & Raphael, 2000, for a review of this study). The Foorman et al. study examined the effectiveness of methods of reading instruction used by teachers as part of their ongoing classroom instruction. Although not expressly a study of methods of teaching decoding, the data reported featured the response of Title I first and second graders to three methods of teaching students to read words. These were Direct Code (direct synthetic phonics practiced in decodable text), Embedded Code (explicit instruction in word patterns embedded in text), and Implicit Code (based on Reading Recovery). One of these methods was taught to the whole class by each of the study's 66 classroom teachers during the 90-minute daily language arts period. In addition, during 30 minutes of the language arts period, 28 Title I teachers delivered one-to-one or small-group tutorials (3 to 5 students) matched to the instructional method of the classroom. All 66 classrooms were described as print-rich, used literature-based texts, and stressed writing and comprehension. In addition, professional development was provided for teachers and tutors about the word learning approach

they would be teaching. Although significantly higher post treatment phonological processing and word reading scores were reported for the Direct Code students, this finding has been questioned in view of the Direct Code group testing significantly higher at pretest than the other two groups on phonological processing. After adjusting for initial differences in phonological processing, the difference between Direct Code and Embedded Code on improvement in word reading was no longer significant (Taylor et al., 2000).

A third example of early intervention is a study by Al Otaiba and Fuchs (2006). They studied 104 kindergarten and first-grade students who participated in what was deemed best-practice instruction in three conditions: kindergarten and first grade, kindergarten only, first grade only, and neither. Responsiveness/non-responsiveness was determined after 2 years in one of the above conditions. The classroom core program for all students was the district-adopted 1995 Harcourt Brace basal reading program, a program that features an implicit approach to the teaching of phonological awareness and phonics. This characteristic was in contrast to the secondary interventions which featured a synthetic approach to phonological awareness and phonics. In addition to the core program, the kindergarten intervention students received teacher-directed, explicit phonological awareness activities, some during 5 to15 minute sessions 3 times per week for 20 weeks and some during 20-minute sessions 3 times per week for 16 weeks. The first-grade secondary intervention consisted of 20-minute sessions, 3 times a week for 20 weeks and included explicit phonological awareness and decoding instruction, sight word training, and reading in connected text. A combination of tests and checklists, plus amount of intervention, correctly predicted 82.1% of the non-responsive students. Interestingly, many of the non-responders were in classrooms in which teachers demonstrated the least fidelity of intervention implementation. The researchers concluded that non-responders needed either a secondary level of intervention of greater intensity or a different instructional approach than was available to study participants. Other possible conclusions are that non-responders need to be placed in classrooms where teachers demonstrate a high level of intervention fidelity or where supplementary instruction is congruent with the core reading program. The non-responders were a heterogeneous group, suggesting that the secondary level of instruction should be tailored not only to verbal and phonemic abilities, but also to attention and behavior which were two predictors of non-responsiveness.

Early intervention emphasizing professional development. McGill-Franzen (2006) advocates teaching reading and writing in kindergarten, *especially for children who are at risk*, and building this instruction, not on children's weaknesses, but rather on what each child can do. To discover what each child can do, McGill-Franzen has designed eight brief assessments, each administered in 10 minutes or less, to evaluate what students know and can do related to: letter-sound identification, phonological awareness, print concepts, segmenting words into sounds and representing those sounds with letters, text writing, word writing, text reading, and word reading. Once it is determined what a child knows, the teacher uses what is known to teach the unknown. Sometimes the known may be as little as the child recognizing his or her own name in print. The child (e.g., Ben) can be encouraged to look for names of other students that have the same initial letter and sound as in his name. Next, Ben can search for names that have the same end letter and sound as in his name. This can be followed by all sorts of discoveries as Ben analyzes the letters and sounds in his name and the names of students in his class. Another example of using the known to learn the new occurs when a child is confusing two similar letters (e.g., *p* and *q*), the teacher can use as a reference a word the child automatically recognizes that contains one of these letters, such as *pig*. Similarly, in teaching students to read and write words, teachers identify the words that students already know and help them use the known words to write and read other words. Words that have common spelling patterns are especially good words to use. By substituting known consonants for the first letter in known words with common spelling patterns (e.g., *and, up, jump, let, not, cat*), students can read and write words they have not yet learned. Using the known to learn the unknown is no formula for a one-size-fits-all approach. It requires differentiation of methods to build on the specific word learning prerequisites, skills, and strategies individual students already possess. According to McGill-Franzen, two essential ingredients for crafting a powerful personalized approach are assessment and professional development.

The impact of professional development on children was illustrated in a study by McGill-Franzen, Allington, Yokoi, & Brooks (1999). In this study of an urban kindergarten literacy initiative, kindergarten teachers were assigned to one of three treatments: receive a 200-book classroom library, receive, 200 books plus professional development, or receive neither books nor professional development. Students of the teachers who received both the books and professional development outperformed the students in the other classrooms on every measure of print knowledge and vocabulary development. The students of teachers who received books, but no professional development, performed no better than the control students. The framework for the study's professional development included systematic assessment of literacy development (work samples and observed behaviors); teacher reading support via classroom routines (read-alouds, shared reading, guided reading, reading and discussion groups, independent reading) and teaching strategies (reading aloud, thinking aloud, prompting, linking reading to writing); teacher writing support via classroom routines (read-alouds, dictated writing, shared writing, interactive writing, writing workshop and conferences, independent writing); word study embedded in reading and writing via classroom routines (name work, wall words work, sorting, hunting) and teaching strategies (sound stretching, thinking aloud, prompting); and inquiry-based content study, including family and community knowledge, as well as thematic units and integrated curricula. All of these activities use what students know to learn what they do not know.

Believing that the success of kindergarten literacy programs depends on teacher knowledge, McGill-Franzen helped develop the Tennessee Kindergarten Literacy Project involving 200 kindergarten teachers, 37 curriculum generalists, and approximately 4,000 children in 50-plus elementary schools. The project grounds its assessment and professional development in McGill-Franzen's (2006) book, *Kindergarten Literacy: Matching Assessment and Instruction in Kindergarten*. The framework for professional development described in this book was discussed in the preceding paragraph with respect to the McGill Franzen et al. (1999) study.

Summary   The earlier literacy intervention occurs in the school life of a child at risk for difficulty in learning to read, the more likely the child will be reading on level by third grade. This is the belief undergirding No Child Left Behind (NCLB, 2001) and a belief actualized several decades earlier in the work of Marie Clay and Reading Recovery. This successful one-on-one tutoring program for at-risk first graders, taught for 30 minutes daily by intensely trained Reading Recovery teachers, has become a model for other early intervention programs (e.g., Inversen & Tunmer, 1993; Morris, 2007; Vellutino & Scanlon, 2002), with Vellutino and Scanlon's program placing the strongest emphasis on teaching a variety of decoding strategies, including semantic and syntactic strategies.

Another form of early intervention occurs in small, supplemental groups which meet daily for 30 to 40 minutes and are in addition to enhanced classroom reading instruction. In one study, two diverse, supplemental small-group programs with strong professional development components were compared (i.e., Direct Instruction and Responsive Reading). Although different in theoretical underpinnings, researchers found the two interventions equally effective, suggesting that there is likely not one best approach for at-risk students. In a second study, one of three methods of decoding was taught to first and second graders in their classrooms, supplemented by tutorials using the same approach. In this study both explicit teaching of small-grain, letter-sound matches and larger-grain, onset-rime combinations appear to have been equally effective. In a third small-group intervention, non-responders were found to be a heterogeneous group, suggesting that instruction should target more than verbal and phonemic abilities, but also other personal characteristics such as attention and behavior which were predictors of non-responsiveness.

The importance of professional development to success with at-risk children was evident in most of these studies. This was further illuminated by the work of McGill-Franzen and her colleagues, both in their research, as well as in the Tennessee Kindergarten Literacy Project.

The next section focuses not on single approaches, but

on combining scientifically based approaches into one program, the direction in which some researchers seem to be moving. Such a combination approach appears to include methods that will mesh with each at-risk child's unique way of learning to read words. Some call such an approach a multidimensional approach. It is an approach that allows for differentiation by the variety of decoding strategies it presents and the instructional adjustments that can be matched to each child with respect to development and other personal characteristics.

Multidimensional Instruction or Combined Approaches

Dickinson, McCabe, and Essex; Juel; Morrison, Connor, and Bachman; Neuman; and Ramey and Ramey in their chapters in the *Handbook of Early Literacy Research* (Dickinson & Neuman, 2006) document that difficulties in word learning are the result of multiple factors and all of these factors need to be addressed, a thesis echoed by Snow, Porche, Tabors, and Harris (2007). Therefore it seems logical that instruction needs to be differentiated if teachers are to successfully teach all children to read words. One way to meet children's needs that result from differences in word learning and personal characteristics is to employ a multidimensional approach in which students are taught more than one way to unlock the pronunciation of words (Gaskins, 1999; Gaskins & Labbo, 2007), as well as metacognitive strategies for taking charge of person characteristics that interfere with learning, such as poor attention, self-regulation, and motivation (Gaskins, 2005; Snow et al., 2007). In the sections that follow, research will be presented that supports the need for a multidimensional and differentiated approach to instruction in decoding.

Instructional practices and particular student profiles. Juel and Minden-Cupp (2000) analyzed word recognition instruction in four general education first-grade classrooms to identify instructional practices that, for particular profiles of children, seem to foster learning to read words. In their year-long study of language arts instruction as it naturally occurred in the classrooms of four teachers nominated by their principals as "very good" first-grade teachers, the researchers looked at how different types of instruction appeared to affect students with different early literacy foundations. (Based on the practices of some of these teachers, the reader may not agree that all are very good teachers, nevertheless we can still analyze the effects of different types of instruction on students with a variety of learning profiles.) In each of the four classrooms students were homogeneously grouped into three reading groups.

Teacher 1's teaching of her first-grade reading groups consisted primarily round robin reading. Teacher 2 created charts and little books for students to read and used manipulatives and word sorts. She tailored reading group instruction to the needs of students, modeled onset and rime decoding, and stressed finger pointing for tracking words. Teacher 3 had a classroom packed with trade books in which

meaning and writing were emphasized. Peer coaching was employed for decoding, but there was little direct, sequential phonics instruction. Teacher 4 was the most phonics oriented and was adamant about behavior. Instruction differed considerably for each of her three reading groups and, compared to the other three teachers, she showed the most change in instructional practices between fall and spring. Her phonics instruction was highly sequenced and teacher modeling was used to teach students to segment words into chunks. She insisted on finger pointing, particularly in the fall of the year.

Spring testing showed considerable difference among the students in the four classrooms. For example, if students were low in decoding in the fall and they received structured phonics instruction during reading group, they were most likely to be on grade level in the spring. On the other hand, in classroom 3 where peer coaching replaced systematic phonics instruction, children with few incoming literacy skills fared poorly on end-of-the-year decoding assessments. In classroom 4, which proved to be the most successful for children who entered first grade with few literacy skills, instruction in phonics was a combination of onset/rime and sequential letter-sound decoding. Instruction also included hands-on activities that served to focus children's attention and require active decision making. In general, those children who entered first grade with minimum skills had the greatest success when the following conditions were present: the teacher modeled word recognition strategies, students were expected to finger point, manipulative materials were used, writing for sounds was part of phonics instruction, and instructional groups were small and designed to meet the specific word recognition needs of children within that group.

Results of the Juel and Minden-Cupp (2000) study suggest at least three generalizations: (a) Instruction that produces exceptional achievement gains for children at one developmental phase of word learning may not yield similar results with children at a different phase of development (e.g., low-group members in a trade book classroom tended to be relatively poor readers at the end of first grade, yet their classmates in higher groups made exceptional progress). (b) Children who enter first grade with minimal literacy skills seemed to benefit from early and intense exposure to phonics, reinforced by writing that stressed sound-letter matching. However, once these children could read independently, they appeared to profit from instruction characteristic of the curriculum of their higher performing peers. (c) Onsets and rimes combined with sounding and blending phonemes within rimes in a structured, sequential phonics program seemed to be very effective. As this was not an experiment, further observations are needed to assess the accuracy of these generalizations.

Next, a study is summarized regarding several decoding interventions employed in a clinic setting with severely disabled readers This work led to the conclusion that several approaches to decoding used in combination may produce better decoding results than any approach by itself.

Synthetic phonics and onset-and-rime combined. Lovett et al. (2000) compared the effectiveness of teaching 85 students, ages 6 to 13, with severe reading disabilities to decode in three different ways: (a) synthetic-phonics, (b) analogy, and (c) the two approaches combined. The synthetic phonics instruction, called Phonological Analysis and Blending (PHAB), followed Engelmann's (1980) direct instruction model. Students were taught grapheme-phoneme relations, phoneme segmentation, and a sounding-out-and-blending strategy. Visual cues to aid in decoding were provided by special marks on letters and words. The second approach was analogy instruction called Word Identification Strategy Training (WIST), an adaptation of the Benchmark Word Identification-Vocabulary Development Program (Gaskins, Downer, & the Teachers of Benchmark School, 1986; Gaskins et al., 1988). In WIST, children learned five keywords a day containing high frequency spelling patterns. They used these keywords to decode unknown words by analogy (e.g., If I know car (keyword), then I know star). As in the Benchmark program, students were also taught to use metacognitive strategies such as varying the pronunciations of vowels to maintain flexibility in decoding attempts and "peeling off" prefixes and suffixes in words.

Four treatment groups, all of whom received 70 hours of instruction, were compared. Treatment groups received only PHAB, only WIST, or both treatments combined. One group completed PHAB before WIST and the other completed WIST before PHAB. The control group received instruction in academic survival skills. Groups receiving either of the combined treatments outperformed the groups receiving either of the single treatments. All groups outperformed the control group. These findings lead one to expect that students who receive keyword analogy training enriched by analysis of sound-letter matches will learn to read better than students who receive only word analogy instruction or synthetic phonics instruction. As in the Juel and Minden-Cupp (2000) study, teaching students several ways to decode provided them with options from which to choose based on the decodability of unknown words and based on each student's phase of development and learner profile.

The next study summary is of a longitudinal study of 102 struggling readers, half of whom were taught to decode by analogy while the remaining half were taught to decode by an enhanced-analogy program. In the enhanced program, students were taught to decode by analogy, plus they fully analyzed the grapho-phonemic components of the keywords they used in decoding by analogy.

Fully analyzing sound-letter matches in keywords. Ehri et al. (2009) compared two groups of first-, second-, and third-grade beginning readers who received two different types of decoding instruction. The remainder of their literacy instruction featured the same components: small-group instruction in applying comprehension strategies to reading literature basals and writing in response to reading and to their experiences. Students in both decoding treatments attended an independent school for struggling readers.

During the first 4 years of the study, 51 students new to the school received a keyword analogy method (KEY) which taught them to decode words by analogy to keywords. At the end of the first 4 years, the KEY analogy program was enriched by adding instruction in grapho-phonemic analysis (KEY-PLUS). During the 4 years that followed, 51 more beginning readers who were new to the school received the Key-Plus program. All 102 KEY and KEY-PLUS students were taught by the same teacher.

During the course of a year in the KEY program, students learned 120 common monosyllabic words that contained high-frequency spelling patterns (i.e., the vowel and the consonant that follows). These keywords (e.g., make, and, he, let, in, king, stop, truck) were placed on a word wall once they were introduced and students used these known words to decode unknown words saying, for example, "If this is make (keyword), then this is flake." All the elements of the KEY program were maintained for the KEY-PLUS program, with the addition of fully analyzing the sound-letter matches in each of the keywords by segmenting the words into phonemes. When introducing a new keyword in the KEY-PLUS program, the teacher said the word without showing the word. Students then stretched the word in unison, putting up a finger for each sound they heard (e.g., /t/ /r/ /u/ /k/). As the teacher showed the word card containing the keyword, students followed the Talk-to-Yourself chart to repeat together what they had discovered: "I hear four sounds, but I see five letters because it takes the letters c-k to represent the /k/ sound. The spelling pattern in the word is U-C-K." Next, students suggested words that rhyme with the keyword. As students suggested a rhyming word the teacher wrote it on chart paper under the keyword if it had the same spelling pattern as the keyword. If the spelling pattern was different, the word was written on the chalkboard so students could compare the spelling of the word to the keyword. In the KEY-PLUS program children received guided practice in decoding words several ways: by analogy if they knew an analogous keyword for the unknown word or, if they did not know an analogous keyword for the spelling pattern, by synthetic phonics or initial consonant and predicting. As in the KEY program, students were taught to be flexible about the sounds for vowels and vowel patterns and to be metacognitive by using self-talk to guide them through problem-solving the decoding of unknown words. For example, a child might say to herself, "I can't think of a keyword with the same spelling pattern as I see in this word (fence), but I see E-N as in TEN and I know C can represent /k/ or /s/, so I'll try using TEN to get FEN, plus both sounds for C and see which makes a word that makes sense in the sentence."

Data were collected about the decoding and spelling abilities of these students before beginning the program and at the end of each year they attended the school. These data showed that students receiving KEY-PLUS read and spelled words significantly better at the end of their first and second years of decoding instruction in this program as compared to students receiving the KEY method. The same differences remained evident, although not significant, during students' third and fourth years in the program.

Summary The research discussed above suggests that a combination of evidence-based decoding approaches better meets the needs of struggling readers than does any one approach alone. A combined or multidimensional approach allows children who evidence different proclivities for learning words and who are at different phases of development to discover and apply what works for them and for which words. Further, this approach has room in it for guiding struggling readers with respect to other factors (e.g., attention, executive control) that may interfere with success in reading. Snow et al. (2007) call such an approach multifaceted.

The Link between Decoding and Children's Personal Characteristics

Anyone who has taught a child with a decoding problem will readily attest to the multifaceted nature of the problem and yet, sadly, only one facet is often addressed—the cognitive. Logic would suggest, however, that a successful decoding program cannot be planned in isolation from the characteristics of the students who will be instructed (Wasik & Hendrickson, 2004). Instruction needs to address more than the cognitive product (decoding), but also the process of achieving it, the habits of mind, dispositions, and other affective, motivational, and volitional characteristics which mediate learning (Afflerbach, 2007). This is echoed by Kamhi (2005) who suggests that it is important to consider the nonphonological aspects of reading because learning to decode "involves more than simply establishing an efficient phonological decoding mechanism" (p. 203). Further, it is rare when a single characteristic explains why a child is struggling to develop decoding proficiency (Gaskins, 1984; Keogh, 2002); more often it is a combination of factors (Gaskins, 1998; Gaskins & Baron, 1985; Klenk & Kibby, 2000).

There are many ways in which children's idiosyncratic characteristics can affect their response to instruction, and some combinations of characteristics, unless addressed, can wreak havoc with a struggling reader's success in learning to decode (Snow et al., 2007). A few of these characteristics were mentioned as concerns in the studies reviewed in this chapter (e.g., attention, behavior).

Therefore, if the core processing deficit for many children with reading disabilities extends beyond the realm of phonological processing to other domains of processing and behavior (Lovett, Barron, & Benson, 2003), then instruction, perhaps including techniques such as cognitive behavior modification (Meichenbaum, 1977), must address these factors. Some of these factors include: speed of processing (Wolf, Bowers, & Biddle, 2000), attention (Swanson & Saez, 2003; Olson & Byrne, 2005) retrieval of word identities (Perfetti, 2007), memory (Ehri & Snowling, 2004), executive functioning (Meltzer, 2007),

self-regulation (Snow, et al., 2007; Zimmerman & Schunk, 2001), strategy use (Swanson, 2000), and motivation (Snow et al., 2007; Wigfield, 1997). Additional characteristics that support learning to decode, but when absent tend to impede decoding progress, are active involvement, flexibility, persistence, and reflectivity. (See Gaskins, 2005, for instructional suggestions.) Flexibility is particularly important to decoding (Gaskins, 2008). If children are to become good decoders, they need to be taught that when one decoding option does not work, they must try several possibilities for word features (e.g., letter-sound matches, syllabic divisions, sounds represented by vowels depending on whether a syllable is stressed or unstressed, and multiple other phonological, orthographic, morphological, lexical, syntactic, and semantic aspects of processing words). Struggling decoders benefit from being taught self-talk routines for considering alternatives, using "self-teaching" (Share, 1995), and applying discoveries about how their language works (Gaskins et al., 1996–1997). In addition, instruction should emphasize self-monitoring and taking control of one's own learning (Strickland & Snow, 2002).

Many children who experienced difficulty learning to decode in the primary grades, and who received an appropriate intervention, continue to experience reading-related difficulties even after they have reached grade-level norms for decoding (Gaskins, 1998; Pressley, 2006). Perhaps in these cases there were other factors that needed to be addressed in addition to poor decoding. For example, processing inefficiencies (Perfetti, 2007; Siegel, 2003) or unproductive behavioral characteristics may still exist (Gaskins & Baron, 1985). In addition, students may not have acquired adequate fluency or comprehension strategies to meet with success at their grade level. All of these need to be addressed as part of a complete intervention.

Summary Decoding ability, like other abilities, is a complex of cognitive, conative, and affective variables (Snow, Corno, & Jackson, 1996) that interact with task, text, and situation variables in determining how well a child will learn to read (Gaskins, 2005; RAND Study Group, 2001). These variables can be either facilitative or impeding. A multiple-pronged intervention (Ackerman & Beier, 2006) that addresses these variables is the surest route to creating successful decoders.

Conclusions about Interventions

The ability to read words is one of the keys that opens the door to reading. And, just as there are many choices of the jogs and turns in crafting a key, there are also many choices a teacher must make in crafting a decoding program, especially for struggling readers. The secret lies in crafting an intervention that is personalized for each struggling reader. That is the goal of this chapter—how to craft decoding interventions that have enough degrees of freedom to meet each child where he or she is functioning, despite the differences children exhibit.

So what should this intervention look like? The interventions reviewed in this chapter that proved to be significantly more effective than comparison interventions in increasing the achievement of reading disabled students had several ingredients in common, all of which evidence-based schools and knowledgeable teachers will want to include in their arsenal for responding to individual student's word learning needs.

Ingredients of Successful Interventions

Emphasis on teacher skill and professional development. The solution to children's decoding difficulties does not lie in specific programs, but in what teachers know (Allington, 2006; Reutzel & Cooter, 2009; Taylor, Pearson, Clark, & Walpole, 2002). Teachers make a greater difference in students' reading growth than do the programs the teachers use (Bond & Dykstra, 1967). As a result, researchers have begun to pay increasing attention to teachers' knowledge about literacy. For example, Cunningham, Perry, Stanovich, and Stanovich (2004) found not only that teachers demonstrated limited knowledge of phoneme awareness and phonics, but also that they were often unaware of what they did and did not know. Other studies have also focused on the importance of teacher knowledge (Bos, Mather, Dickson, Podhajski, & Chard, 2001; Hoffman & Pearson, 2000; McCutchen et al., 2002; McGill-Franzen et al., 1999; Moats & Foorman, 2003; Strickland & Snow, 2002). Researchers tend to agree that it is the knowledge that teachers possess and translate into instruction to match the differences they see in children that accounts for students' progress, or lack of progress, in learning to read (Taylor et al., 2000; Pressley, 2006). As a result, professional development is a more efficacious course to pursue than mandating supposedly teacher-proof programs (Snow, Burns, & Griffin, 1998).

In schools where professional development was of high quality and consistently provided as a support for instructional initiatives, at-risk and struggling readers had the best opportunity for attaining substantial growth in decoding proficiency. Research suggests that effective teachers are individuals who are continually growing in their knowledge of children and of curriculum and instruction. They take advantage of professional development opportunities, as well as create them, such as collaborating with co-workers, reading professional journals, or video taping and critiquing their own lessons (Haager & Mahdavi, 2007). They know that learning to teach is a lifelong process.

Commitment to early intervention. Ideally, children who are at risk for developing decoding difficulties will have the benefit of early intervention programs that allow them to beat the odds for developing reading problems (Taylor & Pearson, 2002; Vellutino & Scanlon, 2001). Currently, however, this ideal does not occur frequently enough to make it unnecessary to address the topic of teaching children to read who exhibit reading disabilities throughout their schooling. While some of the interventions reviewed in this chapter did not take place as early as would have benefited students, it is clear that the trend in the United States is toward early intervention.

Frequent monitoring of progress. Teachers whose students made significant gains tended to monitor students' needs and progress by curriculum-based measures, standardized tests, and daily anecdotal notes, and then adjust instruction accordingly. In the case of small-group instruction, they might also focus on one student a day, having him or her read a new book to the other students in the group as a way of monitoring the use of decoding strategies, or the teacher might ask a student to explain how to decode a word that represented a concept recently taught. The results of systematic progress checks were sometimes graphed so that students could see their progress on a week-by-week or monthly basis.

Sensitivity to phases of development and the right level of instructional intensity. Another ingredient noted in this chapter was that successful interventions were sensitive to each child's phase of development. They tended to begin in each child's zone of proximal development and to use what was know by the child to learn the unknown. The interventions were multileveled and the teaching was diagnostic. When one approach did not work, other alternatives were tried. Sometimes the intervention needed to become more intense by decreasing the size of the group or individualizing instruction. On other occasions the teacher might decide that there needed to be more time devoted to an intervention or that to continue the same program that was not working was a bad choice and another approach was needed. There was awareness that what was an appropriate intervention at one phase of development might not be the best intervention at another phase of development. For example, segmenting words into phonemes is an appropriate intervention at the early phases of development, but once children reach the consolidated phase, doing a great deal of reading with an emphasis on comprehension is a better intervention. Different interventions with different levels of intensity are called for at different phases of development.

Attention to student characteristics in the choice of instructional activities. Decoding difficulties are frequently exacerbated by learner characteristics such as poor attention, lack of flexibility, impulsivity, or poor self-regulation. To help students cope with these characteristics, teachers build into their decoding intervention a brisk pace and frequent change of activities. Teachers choose activities that require a response from every student, such as writing, pointing, chanting, or manipulating materials (Gaskins, 2005). In addition, they provide a metacognitively rich instructional environment (Gaskins, Gaskins, Anderson, & Schommer, 1995; Lovett, Lacerenza, & Borden, 2000). In such an environment, teachers mental model how students can use self-talk to work their way through the decoding of words (Gaskins et al., 1996–1997; Gaskins et al., 1997), as well as to take charge of nonproductive personal characteristics (Gaskins, 2005; Gaskins & Elliot, 1991).

Combination of approaches to reading words. Multidimensional interventions, comprised of the best practices of evidence-based instruction, were more effective in improving word reading proficiency than any one-size-fits-all intervention. As one example, interventions that combined synthetic phonics and analogizing achieved better results with at-risk and reading disabled students than either approach alone. Successful multidimensional interventions often included explicit instruction in both large-grain and small-grain strategies (e.g., synthetic phonics, analogizing, predicting, sight), with many opportunities to apply these strategies to reading and writing continuous text. In addition, teachers of multidimensional interventions explicitly taught students to segment spoken words into phonemes and to match phonemes or groups of phonemes to letters or groups of letters. They also encouraged children to decode and spell words using a variety of strategies. Students came to realize that when one strategy does not help in decoding an unknown word, the best thing to do is try a second, or even a third; and in decoding a word of more than one chunk (syllable), two or three different decoding strategies may be needed. Comprehension was also an important ingredient of successful multidimensional approaches to teaching decoding as illustrated by a study completed by Berninger et al. (2003). Ninety-six second graders with low reading achievement were randomly assigned to one of four treatment conditions. The instructional intervention that combined word recognition and reading comprehension increased phonological decoding significantly more than the treated control or word-recognition-only treatment and had the highest effect size. This suggests that combining several approaches to decoding with reading comprehension instruction may be the ultimate combination.

Presentation of a systematic and structured approach. Another ingredient of the most successful interventions was the use of a systematic and structured approach to teaching sound-letter matches. When teaching phonics synthetically, phonemes with the greatest utility, as well as greatest sound difference, were taught initially, so there would be the least opportunity for confusion and the best opportunity for high utility. Similarly, when teaching students to analogize, the most common spelling patterns (rimes) were introduced early, with these spelling patterns generating many words students could decode and read in connected text. Additional structure was added when decoding was systematically approached from both synthetic and analogy perspectives so that students could actively construct small-grain and large-grain knowledge about the way the English language works, thus have more knowledge to apply to decoding a greater variety of words.

Implementation of explicit instruction with modeling and scaffolding. Nothing was left to chance in the effective decoding approaches reviewed in this chapter. Teachers explained to students what they were about to teach them, why and how it would be helpful, when it could be used, and explicitly how to do it. These explicit explanations were immediately followed by teacher modeling of the procedure and scaffolded practice. Misconceptions were corrected during scaffolding and students received immediate feedback about their responses.

Priorities established for use of instructional time. In effective interventions time frames were established and strictly observed for each element of a lesson. Practice reading and rereading text was often allocated half of the instructional time, with various word-work activities comprising the other half. Pointing to words as they were read was emphasized by some teachers. Pointing helped students keep their eyes on the words and attend to the task at hand. It also aided students in moving words into their sight vocabularies. Echo reading and choral reading while pointing also enhanced familiarity with words. Word-work included decoding and writing words, especially words composed of letter-sound matches that had recently been taught. Letters were manipulated in words to create new words, and then the new words were read. (See Cunningham, 2005; McCandliss, Beck, Sandak, & Perfetti, 2003; and Rasinski & Oswald, 2005, for word-building suggestions.) In addition, children wrote to spelling dictation, as well as wrote sentences and stories, stretching and sounding out words to match sounds with letters; then they self-checked and read back the words they had written. There was definitely a reciprocal relationship between reading and writing in these successful interventions.

System-wide plan for maintenance of decoding growth when the intervention concluded. Although very few of the studies reviewed in this chapter reported a follow-up or maintenance plan, it is important to evaluate how well an intervention prepared at-risk and disabled readers to continue their growth in reading after an intervention was discontinued, as well as to evaluate what seemed to work with which students. One such study (Blachman et al., 2004) followed-up second- and third-grade children who had poor word-level skills and were randomly assigned to an 8-month program of explicit instruction emphasizing phonologic and orthographic connections in words. Treatment children showed significantly greater word and nonword reading gains than controls and maintained gains at a 1-year follow-up. Of interest would be follow-up data with an even longer timeline. Snow and colleagues (2007), for example, followed 3-year-olds into late adolescence. They concluded that by the middle grades there are many more pieces to the puzzle of learning to read, necessitating more far-reaching interventions than teaching reading. Follow-up studies of students who have experienced an intervention seem crucial as a way to improve instruction.

Final Word For many decades practitioners and researchers have been searching for one best method to use in teaching children to read. Standard practice has been to search the research literature, or conduct research, looking for evidence that one program is superior to all others, a search that should have ended with the publication of the First Grade Reading Studies (Bond & Dykstra, 1967), but didn't. In the search for one best method, we seem to forget that children learn in different ways, perceive things in different ways, and bring different experiences, backgrounds, and abilities to the classroom. Therefore, it should be no surprise that any one approach to developing decoding proficiencies will work better for some children than for others (Snow & Juel, 2005). In view of the differences among children, there can be no one best approach to decoding for at-risk and struggling readers—only great teachers who are aware of and can implement the ingredients of successful programs. This is exactly the conclusion of the research reviewed in this chapter.

Acknowledgement

The author gratefully acknowledges the input of the following colleagues on earlier drafts of this chapter: Sue Arabia, Sherry Cress, Linnea Ehri, Emily Galloway, Lynn Gonzalez, Colleen O'Hara, Joyce Ostertag, Melinda Rahm, Jenny Roca, and Theresa Scott.

References

Ackerman, P. L., & Beier, M. E. (2006). Methods for studying the structure of expertise: Psychometric approaches. In K. Ericsson, N. Charness, P. Feltovich, & R. Hoffman (Eds.), *The Cambridge handbook of expertise and expert performance* (pp. 147–165). Cambridge, UK: Cambridge University Press.

Afflerbach, P. (2007). *Understanding and using reading assessment, K-12*. Newark, DE: International ReadingAssociation.

Afflerbach, P., Pearson, P. D., & Paris, S. G. (2008). Clarifying differences between reading skills and reading strategies. *The Reading Teacher, 61*, 364–374.

Allington, R. L. (2006). *What really matters for struggling readers: Designing research-based programs* (2nd ed.). Boston: Pearson.

Allington, R. L., & Johnston, P. (2001). What do we know about effective fourth-grade teachers and their classrooms? In C. M. Roller (Ed.), *Learning to teach reading: Setting the research agenda* (pp. 150–165). Newark, DE: International Reading Association.

Allington, R. L., & Walmsley, S. A. (2007). *No quick fix: Rethinking literacy programs in America's elementary schools* (The RTI Edition). New York: Teachers College Press.

Al Otaiba, S., & Fuchs, D. (2006). Who are the young children for whom best practices in reading are ineffective? An experimental and longitudinal study. *Journal of Learning Disabilities, 39*, 414–431.

Bear, D. R., Invernizzi, M., Templeton, S., & Johnston, F. (2008). *Words their way: Word study for phonics, vocabulary, and spelling instruction* (4th ed.). Upper Saddle River, NJ: Pearson/Prentice Hall.

Berninger, V. W., Vermeulen, K., Abbott, R. D., McCutchen, D., Cotton, S., Cude, J., Dorn, S., & Sharon, T. (2003). Comparison of three approaches to supplementary reading instruction for low-achieving second-grade readers. *Language, Speech, and Hearing Services in Schools, 34*, 101–116.

Blachman, B. A., Schatschneider, C., Fletcher, J. M., Francis, D. J., Clonan, S. M., Shaywitz, B. A., et al. (2004). Effects of intensive reading remediation for second and third graders and a 1-year follow-up. *Journal of Educational Psychology, 96*, 444–461.

Bond, G. L., & Dykstra, R. (1967). The cooperative research program in first-grade reading instruction. *Reading Research Quarterly, 2*, 5–142.

Bos, C., Mather, N., Dickson, S., Podhajski, B., & Chard, C., (2001). Perceptions and knowledge of pre-service and in-service educators about early reading instruction. *Annals of Dyslexia, 51*, 97–120.

Chard, D. J., & Lian-Thompson, S. (2008). Introduction to the special series on systemic, multitier instructional models. *Journal of Learning Disabilities, 41*, 99–100.

Chhabra, V., & McCardle, P. (2004) Contributions to evidence-based research. In P. McCardle & V. Chhabra (Eds.), *The voice of evidence in reading research* (pp. 3–11). Baltimore, MD: Brookes.

Clay, M. (1979). *Reading: The patterning of complex behavior*. Auckland, NZ: Heinemann.

Clay, M. (2005). *An observation survey of early literacy achievement* (2nd ed.). Portsmouth, NH: Heinemann.

Cunningham, A. E. (1990). Explicit versus implicit instruction in phonemic awareness. *Journal of Experimental Child Psychology, 50*, 429–444.

Cunningham, A. E., Perry, K. E., Stanovich, K. E., & Stanovich, P. J. (2004) Disciplinary knowledge of K-3 teachers and their knowledge calibration in the domain of early literacy. *Annals, of Dyslexia, 54*, 139–167.

Cunningham, P. M. (2005). *Phonics they use: Words for reading and writing* (4th ed.). Boston: PearsonAllynBacon.

Denton, C. A., Fletcher, J. M. Anthony, J. L., & Francis, D. (2006). An evaluation of intensive intervention for students with persistent reading difficulties. *Journal of Learning Disabilities, 30*, 447–466.

Dickinson, D. K., & Neuman, S. B. (Eds.). (2006). *Handbook of early literacy research* (Vol.2). New York: Guilford.

Dickinson, D. K., McCabe, A., & Essex, M. J. (2006). A window of opportunity we must open to all: The case for preschool with high-quality support for language and literacy. In D. K. Dickinson & S. B. Neuman (Eds.), *Handbook of early literacy research* (Vol.2, pp. 11–28). New York: Guilford.

Ehri, L. (1995). Phases of development in reading words. *Journal of Research in Reading, 18*, 116–126.

Ehri, L. C. (1998). Grapheme-phoneme knowledge is essential for learning to read words in English. In J. L. Metsala & L. C. Ehri (Eds.), *Word recognition in beginning literacy* (pp. 3–40). Mahwah, NJ: Erlbaum.

Ehri, L. C. (2005). Learning to read words: Theory, findings, and issues. *Scientific Studies of Reading, 9*, 167–188.

Ehri, L. C., Satlow, E., & Gaskins, I. W. (2009). Grapho-phonemic enrichment strengthens keyword analogy instruction for struggling readers. *Reading and Writing Quarterly: Overcoming Learning Difficulties, 25*, 162–191.

Ehri, L. C., & Snowling, M. J., (2004). Developmental variation in word recognition. In C. C. Stone, E. R. Silliman, B. J. Ehren, & K. Apel (Eds.), *Handbook of language and literacy: Development and disorders* (pp. 433–460). New York: Guilford.

Elkonin, D. (1973). U.S.S.R. In J. Downing (Ed.), *Comparative reading* (pp. 551–579). New York: Macmillan.

Engelmann, S. (1980). *Direct instruction*. Englewood Cliffs, NJ: Prentice Hall.

Frith, U. (1985). Beneath the surface of developmental dyslexia. In K. Patterson, J. Marshall, & M. Coltheart (Eds.), *Surface dyslexia: Neuropsychological and cognitive studies of phonological reading* (pp. 301–330). London: Erlbaum.

Foorman, B. R., Francis, D. J., Fletcher, J. M., Schatschneider, C., & Mehta, P. (1998). The role of instruction in learning to read: Preventing reading failure in at-risk children. *Journal of Educational Psychology, 90*, 37–55.

Gaskins, I. W. (1984). There's more to a reading problem than poor reading. *Journal of Learning Disabilities, 17*, 467–471.

Gaskins, I. W. (1998). There's more to teaching at-risk and delayed readers than good reading instruction. *The Reading Teacher, 51*, 534–547.

Gaskins, I. W. (1999). Problem solving—struggling readers: A multidimensional reading program. *The Reading Teacher, 53*, 162–164.

Gaskins, I. W. (2004). Word detectives. *Educational Leadership, 61*, 70–73.

Gaskins, I. W. (2005). *Success with struggling readers: The Benchmark School approach*. New York: Guilford.

Gaskins, I. W. (2008). Developing cognitive flexibility in word reading among beginning and struggling readers. In K. Cartwright (Ed.), *Literacy processes: Cognitive flexibility in learning and teaching* (pp. 90–113). New York: Guilford.

Gaskins, I. W., & Baron, J. (1985). Teaching poor readers to cope with maladaptive cognitive styles: A training program. *Journal of Learning Disabilities, 18*, 390–394.

Gaskins, I. W., Downer, M. A., Anderson, R. C., Cunningham, P. M., Gaskins, R. W., Schommer, M., et al. (1988). A metacognitive approach to phonics: Using what you know to decode what you don't know. *Remedial and Special Education, 9*, 36–41.

Gaskins, I. W., Downer, M., & the Teachers of Benchmark School. (1986). *The Benchmark word identification/vocabulary development program.* Media, PA: Benchmark Press.

Gaskins, I.W., Ehri, L. C., Cress, C., O'Hara, C. & Donnelly, K. (1996–1997). Procedures for word learning: Making discoveries about words. *The Reading Teacher, 50*, 312–328.

Gaskins, I. W., Ehri, L. C., Cress, C., O'Hara, C., & Donnelly, K. (1997). Analyzing words and making discoveries about the alphabetic system: Activities for beginning readers. *Language Arts, 74*, 172–184.

Gaskins, I. W., & Elliot, T. T. (1991). *Implementing cognitive strategy instruction across the school: The Benchmark manual for teachers.* Cambridge, MA: Brookline Books.

Gaskins, I. W., & Labbo, L. D. (2007) Diverse perspectives on helping young children build important foundational language and print skills. *Reading Research Quarterly, 42*, 438–351.

Gaskins, R. W., Gaskins, I. W., Anderson, R. C., & Schommer, M. (1995). The reciprocal relationship between research and development: An example involving a decoding strand for poor readers. *Journal of Reading Behavior, 27*, 337–377.

Goswami, U. (2006). Orthography, phonology, and reading development: A cross-linguistic perspective. In R. Joshi & P. Aaron (Eds.), *Handbook of orthography and literacy* (pp. 463–480). Mahwah, NJ: Erlbaum.

Haager, D., & Mahdavi, J. (2007). In D. Haaager, J. Klingner, & S. Vaughn, *Evidence-based reading practices for response to intervention* (pp. 245–263). Baltimore, MD: Brookes.

Hammill, D. D., & Swanson, H. L. (2006). The National Reading Panel's meta-analysis of phonics instruction: Another point of view. *The Elementary School Journal, 107*, 17–26.

Harn, B. A., Linan-Thompson, S., & Roberts, G. (2008). Intensifying instruction: Does additional instructional time make a difference for the most at-risk first graders? *Journal of Learning Disabilities, 41*, 115–125.

Harris, T. L., & Hodges, R. E. (Eds.). (1995). *The literacy dictionary: The vocabulary of reading and writing.* Newark, DE: International Reading Association.

Henderson, E. H. (1990). *Teaching spelling.* Boston: Houghton Mifflin.

Hoffman, J., & Pearson, P D. (2000). Reading teacher education in the next millennium: What your grandmother's teacher didn't know that you granddaughter's teacher should. *Reading Research Quarterly, 35*, 28–44.

Iversen, S., & Tunmer, W. (1993). Phonological processing skills and the Reading Recovery program. *Journal of Educational Psychology, 8*, 112–126.

Juel, C. (2006). The impact of early school experiences on initial reading. In D. K. Dickinson & S. B. Neuman (Eds.), *Handbook of early literacy research* (Vol.2, (pp. 410–426). New York: Guilford.

Juel, C., & Minden-Cupp, C. (2000). Learning to read words: Linguistic units and instructional strategies. *Reading Research Quarterly, 35*, 458–492.

Kamhi, A. G. (2005). Finding beauty in the ugly facts about reading comprehension. In H. Catts & A. Kamhi (Eds.), *The connections between language and reading disabilities* (pp. 201–212). Mahwah, NJ: Erlbaum.

Kamps, D., Abbott, M., Greenwood, C., Wills, H., Veerkamp, M., & Kaufman, J. (2008). Effects of small-group reading instruction and curriculum differences for students most at risk in kindergarten: Two-year results for secondadry- and tertiary-level interventions. *Journal of Learning Disabilities, 41*, 101–114.

Keogh, B. K. (2002). Research on reading and reading problems: Findings, limitations, and future directions. In K. Butler & E. Silliman (Eds.), *Speaking, reading, and writing in children with language learning disabilities: New paradigms in research and practice* (pp. 27–44). Mahwah, NJ: Erlbaum.

Klenk, L., & Kibby, M. W. (2000), Re-mediating reading difficulties: Appraising the past, reconciling the present, constructing the future. In M. Kamil, P. Mosenthal, P. Pearson, & R. Barr (Eds.), *Handbook of reading research* (Vol. III, pp. 607–690). Mahwah, NJ: Erlbaum.

Lindamood, C. H., & Lindamood, P. C. (1984). *Auditory discrimination in depth.* Austin, TX: PRO-ED.

Lindamood, C. H., & Lindamood, P. (1998). *The Lindamood phoneme sequencing program for reading, spelling, and speech.* Austin, TX: PRO-ED.

Lovett, M. W., Barron, R. W., & Benson, N. J. (2003). Effective remediation of word identification and decoding difficulties in school-age children with reading disabilities. In H. L. Swanson, K. R. Harris, & S. Graham (Eds.), *Handbook of learning disabilities* (pp. 273–292). New York: Guilford.

Lovett, M. W., Lacerenza, L., & Borden, S. (2000). Putting struggling readers on the PHAST track: A program to integrate phonological and strategy-based remedial reading instruction and maximize outcomes. *Journal of Learning Disabilities, 33*, 458–476.

Lovett, M., Lacerenza, L., Borden, S., Frijters, J., Steinbach, K., & De-Palma, M. (2000). Components of effective remediation for developmental reading disabilities: combining phonological and strategy-based instruction to improve outcomes. *Journal of Educational Psychology, 92*, 263–283.

Mathes, P. G., Denton, C. A., Fletcher, J. M., Anthony, J. L., Francis, D. J., & Schatschneider, C. (2005). The effects of theoretically different instruction and student characteristics on the skills of struggling readers. *Reading Research Quarterly, 40*, 148–182.

McCandliss, B., Beck, I. L., Sandak, R., & Perfetti, C. (2003). Focusing attention on decoding for children with poor reading skills: Design and preliminary tests of Word Building intervention. *Scientific Studies of Reading 7*, 75–104.

McCutchen, D., Harry, D. R., Cunningham, A. R., Cox, S., Sidman, S., & Covill, A. E. (2002). Reading teachers' knowledge of children's literature and English phonology, *Annals of Dyslexia, 52*, 207–228.

McGill-Franzen, A. (2006). *Kindergarten literacy: Matching assessment and instruction.* New York: Scholastic.

McGill-Franzen, A., Allington, R., Yokoi, I., & Brooks, G. (1999). Putting books in the room is necessary but not sufficient. *Journal of educational Research, 93*, 67–74.

McNaughton, S. (2008). Looking at school improvement through a Reading Recovery lens. *Literacy Teaching and Learning, 12*(2), 1–17.

Meichenbaum, D. (1977). *Cognitive behavior modification: An integrative approach.* New York: Plenum.

Meltzer, L. (Ed.). (2007). *Executive function in education: From theory to practice.* New York: Guilford.

Moats, L. C. (1995) *Spelling: Development, disability, and instruction.* Baltimore, MD: York.

Moats, L. C., & Foorman, B. R. (2003). Measuring teachers' content knowledge of language and reading. *Annals of Dyslexia, 53*, 23–45.

Morris, D. (1999). *The Howard Street tutoring manual: Teaching at-risk readers in the primary grades.* New York: Guilford.

Morris, D. (2007). One-to-one reading intervention in the primary grades: An idea that must evolve to survive. In B. Taylor & J. Ysseldyke (Eds.), *Effective instruction for struggling readers: K-6* (pp. 19–36). New York: Teachers College Press.

Morris, D., Tyner, B., & Perney, J. (2000). Early steps: Replicating the effects of a first-grade reading intervention program. *Journal of Educational Psychology, 92*, 681–693.

Morrison, F. J., Connor, C. M., & Bachman, H. J. (2006). The transition to school. In D. Dickinson & S. Neuman (Eds.), *Handbook of early literacy research* (Vol. 2, pp. 375–394). New York: Guilford.

National Reading Panel. (2000). *Report of the National Reading Panel: Teaching children to read: An evidence-based assessment of the scientific research literature on reading and its implications for reading instruction: Reports of the subgroups.* Rockville, MD: NICHD Clearinghouse.

Neuman, S. B. (2006). The knowledge gap: Implications for early education. In D. Dickinson & S. Neuman (Eds.), *Handbook of early literacy research* (Vol. 2, pp. 29–40). New York: Guilford.

No Child Left Behind Act of 2001 (NCLB), PubL.No. 107-110 (2002). Retrieved from http://www.ed.gov/policy;elsec;leg;esea02/index

Olson, R., & Byrne, B. (2005). Genetic and environmental influences on reading and language ability and disability. In Catts & A. Kamhi (Eds.), *The connections between language and reading disabilities* (pp. 173–200). Mahwah, NJ: Erlbaum.

O'Shaughnessy, T. E., & Swanson, H. L. (2000). A comparison of two reading interventions for children with reading disabilities. *Journal of Learning Disabilities, 33,* 257–277.

Perfetti, C. (2007). Reading ability: Lexical quality to Comprehension. *Scientific Studies of Reading, 11,* 357–383.

Pressley, M. (2006). *Reading instruction that works: A case for balanced reading* (3rd ed.). New York: Guilford.

Ramey, S. L., & Ramey, C. T. (2006). Early educational interventions: Principles of effective and sustained benefits from targeted early education programs. In D. Dickinson & S. Neuman (Eds.), *Handbook of early literacy research* (Vol. 2, pp. 445–459). New York: Guilford.

RAND Reading Study Group. (2002). *Reading for understanding: Towards a R & D program in reading comprehension.* Santa Monica, CA: Academic.

Rasinski, T., & Oswald, R. (2005). Making and writing words: Constructivist word learning in a second-grade classroom. *Reading & Writing Quarterly, 21,* 151–163.

Reutzel, D. R., & Cooter, R .B., Jr. (2009). *The essentials of teaching children to read: The teacher makes the difference.* (2nd ed.). Boston: Pearson.

Santa, C., & Hoien, T. (1999). An assessment of Early Steps: A program for early intervention of reading problems. *Reading Research Quarterly, 34,* 54–79.

Share, D. L. (1995). Phonological recoding and self-teaching: Sine qua non of reading acquisition. *Cognition, 55,* 151–218.

Sharp, A., Sinatra, G., & Reynolds, R. (2008). The development of children's orthographic knowledge: A micro-genetic perspective. *Reading Research Quarterly, 43,* 206–226.

Siegel, L. S. (2003). Basic cognitive processes and reading disabilities. In H. L. Swanson, K. R. Harris, & S. Graham (Eds.), *Handbook of learning disabilities* (pp. 158–181). New York: Guilford.

Snow, C. E., Burns, S., & Griffin, P. (Eds.). (1998). *Preventing reading difficulties in young children.* Washington, DC: National Academy Press.

Snow, C. E., & Juel, C. (2005). Teaching children to read: What do we know about how to do it? In M. Snowling & C. Hulme (Eds.), *The science of reading: A handbook* (pp. 501–520). Malden, MA: Blackwell.

Snow, C. E., Porche, M. V., Tabors, P. O., & Harris, S. R. (2007). *Is Literacy enough? Pathways to academic success for adolescents.* Baltimore, MD: Brookes.

Snow, R. E., Corno, L., & Jackson, D. (1996). Individual differences in affective and conative functions. In D. Berliner & R. Calfee (Eds.), *Handbook of educational psychology* (pp. 243–310). New York: Simon & Schuster Macmillan.

Stahl, S. A., Duffy-Hester, A. M., & Stahl, K. A. (1998). Everything you wanted to know about phonics (but were afraid to ask). *Reading Research Quarterly, 33,* 338–355.

Stanovich, K. (1984). The interactive-compensatory model of reading. A confluence of developmental, experimental, and educational psychology. *Remedial and Special Education, 5,* 11–19

Stanovich, K. E. (1986). Matthew effects in reading: Some consequences of individual differences in the acquisition of literacy. *Reading Research Quarterly, 21,* 360–407.

Strickland, D. (1998), *Teaching phonics today: A primer for educators.* Newark, NE: International Reading Association.

Strickland, D., & Snow, C. (2002). *Preparing our teachers: Opportunities for better reading instruction.* Washington DC: Joseph Henry Press.

Swanson, H. L. (2000). Are working memory deficits in readers with learning disabilities hard to change? *Journal of Learning Disabilities, 33,* 551–566.

Swanson, H. L., & Saez, L. (2003) Memory difficulties in children and adults with learning disabilities. In H. Swanson, K. Harris, & S. Graham (Eds.), *Handbook of learning disabilities* (pp. 182–198). New York. Guilford.

Taylor, B. M., Anderson, R. C., Au, K. H., & Raphael, T. (2000). Discretion in the translation of research to policy: A case from beginning reading. *Educational Researcher, 29*(6), 16–26.

Taylor, B. M., & Pearson, P. D. (Eds.). (2002). *Teaching reading: Effective schools, accomplished teachers.* Mahwah, NJ: Erlbaum.

Taylor, B. M., Pearson, P. D., Clark, K., & Walpole, S. (2002). Effective schools and accomplished teachers: Lessons about primary-grade reading instruction in low-income schools. In B. M. Taylor & P. D. Pearson (Eds.), *Teaching reading: Effective schools, accomplished teachers* (pp. 3–72). Mahwah, NJ: Erlbaum.

Taylor, B. M., Peterson, D. S., Marx, M., & Chein, M. (2007). Scaling up a reading reform in high-poverty. In B. Taylor & J. Ysseldyke (Eds.), *Effective instruction for struggling readers, K-6* (pp. 216–234). New York: Teachers College Press.

Torgesen, J. K. (2004). Lessons learned from research on interventions for students who have difficulty learning to read. In P. McCardle & V. Chabra (Eds.), *The voice of evidence in reading research* (pp. 355–382). Baltimore, MD: Brookes.

Torgesen, J. K. (2005). Recent discoveries on remedial interventions for children with dyslexia. In M. Snowling & C. Hulme (Eds.), *The science of reading: A handbook* (pp. 521–537). Malden, MA: Blackwell.

Torgesen, J. K., Alexander, A. W., Wagner, R. K., Rashotte, C. A., Voeller, K., & Conway, T. (2001). Intensive remedial instruction for children with severe reading disabilities: Immediate and long-term outcomes from two instructional approaches. *Journal of Learning Disabilities, 34,* 33–58.

Valencia, S. W., & Riddle-Buly, M. R. (2004). Behind text scores: What struggling readers really need. *The Reading Teacher, 57,* 520–531.

Vaughn, S., & Klingner, J. (2007). Overview of the three-tier model of reading intervention. In D. Haager, J. Klingner, & S. Vaughn (Eds.), *Evidence-based reading practices for response to intervention* (pp. 3–10). Baltimore, MD: Brookes.

Vaughn, S., Wanzek, J., & Fletcher, J.M. (2007). Multiple tiers of intervention: A framework for prevention and identification of students with reading/learning disabilities. In B. Taylor & J. Ysseldyke (Eds.), *Effective instruction for struggling readers, K-6* (pp. 173–195). New York: Teachers College Press.

Vaughn, S., Wanzek, J., Woodruff, A., & Lian-Thompson, S. (2007). Prevention and early identification of students with reading disabilities. In D. Haaager, J. Klingner, & S. Vaughn, *Evidence-based reading practices for response to intervention* (pp. 11–27). Baltimore, MD: Brookes.

Vellutino, F. R., & Scanlon, D. M. (2001). Emergent literacy skills, early instruction, and individual differences as determinants of difficulties in learning to read. The case for early intervention. In S. Neuman & D. Dickinson (Eds.), *Handbook of early literacy research* (Vol. 1, pp. 295–321). New York: Guilford.

Vellutino, F. R., & Scanlon, D. M. (2002). The Interactive Strategies approach to reading intervention. *Contemporary Educational Psychology, 27,* 573–635.

Vellutino, F. R., Scanlon, D. M., Sipay, E. R., Small, S. G., Pratt, A., Chen, R., et al. (1996). Cognitive profiles of difficult-to-remediate and readily remediated poor readers: Early intervention as a vehicle for distinguishing between cognitive and experiential deficits as basic causes of specific reading disability. *Journal of Educational Psychology, 88,* 601–638.

Walton, P. D., & Walton, L. M. (2002). Beginning reading by teaching in rime analogy: Effects on phonological skills, letter-sound knowledge, working memory, and word-reading strategies. *Scientific Studies of Reading, 6,* 79–115.

Wanzek, J., & Vaughn, S. (2008). Response to varying amounts of time in reading intervention for students with low response to intervention. *Journal of Learning Disabilities, 41,* 126–142.

Wasik, B., & Hendrickson, J. (2004). Family literacy practices. In C. Stone, E. Silliman, B. Ehren, & K. Apel (Eds.), *Handbook of language and literacy: Development and disorders* (pp. 154–174). New York: Guilford.

Wigfield, A. (1997). Children's motivations for reading and reading engagement. In J. Guthrie & A. Wigfield (Eds.), *Reading engagement motivating readers through integrated instruction* (pp. 14–33). Newark, DE: International Reading Association.

Wolf, M., Bowers, P. G., & Biddle, K. (2000). Naming-speed processes, timing, and reading. A conceptual review. *Journal of Learning Disabilities, 33*, 387–407.

Ysseldyke, J. E., & Taylor, B. M. (2007). Understanding the factors that allegedly contribute to students' reading difficulties. In B. Taylor & J. Ysseldyke (Eds.), *Effective instruction for struggling readers, K-6* (pp. 1–18). New York: Teachers College Press.

Ziegler, J. C., & Goswami, U. G. (2005). Reading acquisition, developmental dyslexia, and skilled reading across languages: A psycholinguistic grain size theory. *Psychological Bulletin, 131*, 3–29.

Zimmerman, B. J., & Schunk, D. H. (Eds.). (2001). *Self-regulated learning and academic achievement*. Austin, TX: Pro-Ed.

28

Interventions to Enhance Fluency and Rate of Reading

MELANIE R. KUHN
Boston University

In recent years, fluency instruction has come to be seen as a central component in the primary and elementary literacy curriculum (e.g., National Reading Panel, 2000), one that assists students as they make the shift from stilted and uneven oral reading to oral reading that is smooth and expressive and one that contributes to skilled silent reading as well (e.g., Samuels, 2006). And, while fluency instruction has an important place in the general literacy curriculum, such instruction is especially important for students with reading disabilities since these learners are far more likely to experience difficulty making this transition than are their peers (e.g., Kuhn & Stahl, 2003). However, while identifying ways in which we can help struggling readers become fluent is an essential part of this discussion, exploring the ways in which fluency contributes to reading development in general, and comprehension in particular, is also critical if we are to avoid creating fluency instruction—and assessment—that emphasizes reading rate at the expense of understanding. Such instruction not only limits our students' understanding of fluency and its role in the reading process, it leads to a devaluation of instructional approaches that, when implemented properly, can make a significant contribution to the reading development of students experiencing reading difficulties.

The goals of this chapter, therefore, are to discuss several aspects of fluency and fluency instruction in relation to the reading development of students with reading disabilities. First, I explore the role that accuracy, automaticity and prosody play in reading fluency (e.g., Rasinski & Hoffman, 2003). Next, I consider the ways in which overemphasizing certain aspects of the construct, through either instruction or assessment, can negatively influence students' understanding of what constitutes fluent reading—as well as the purposes of reading more broadly (e.g., Samuels, 2007; Walker, Mokhtari, & Sargent, 2006). Finally, I address fluency instruction in order to identify commonalities across effective approaches (e.g., Kuhn, 2009). Hopefully, this chapter will assist you in either rethinking fluency instruction and its role in the literacy curriculum or it will confirm your understanding of the construct and how best to assist students in their efforts to become fluent readers.

Reading Fluency and Its Components

One characteristic that differentiates many reading disabled students from their more skilled peers is their inability to read fluently. By this, I mean they are unable to read passages smoothly or with appropriate expression. While such difficulties might be a bit troubling if they primarily affected the way learners sound when they are reading aloud, these difficulties are worthy of more serious concern when you consider that most disfluent readers also experience difficulties with their comprehension of texts (National Reading Panel, 2000). In fact, according to most researchers, the two facets of skilled reading are linked, with reading fluency seen either as a critical link between decoding ability and comprehension (e.g., Chard, Pikulski, & McDonagh, 2006) or with comprehension seen as an integral component of fluent reading itself (Samuels, 2006). These understandings develop from the role that fluency's component parts—accuracy, automaticity, and prosody—play in skilled reading.

Accuracy and Automaticity   At the level of word identification, skilled readers must accomplish two things in order to comprehend a text.[1] First, they must be able to accurately identify the vast majority of words they encounter in a text (e.g., Adams, 1990; Chall, 1996). This involves developing familiarity with the sound-symbol correspondences that occur regularly in written English as well as with those high frequency words that should be recognized as a unit (e.g., *the, and, it*). Second, their word recognition must be automatic (LaBerge & Samuels, 1974; Logan, 1997). In other words, readers should not have to expend a significant amount of effort on word identification; rather, they should be able to recognize words immediately upon encountering them.

Such instantaneous word recognition is important because individuals have a limited ability to process information (e.g., LaBerge & Samuels, 1974). In the case of reading, this means that attention expended on word identification is attention that is unavailable for comprehension. If it is the case that the reader has to spend significant amounts of attention in order to identify most of the words they encounter, he will have difficulty constructing meaning from the texts they are reading. If, on the other hand, a reader has established automatic word recognition, the amount of attention she needs to expend on word identification is minimal, and, as a result, she will retain most of their attention for comprehension.

Prosody   The third component of fluent reading is prosody (Erekson, 2003; Kuhn & Stahl, 2003). Prosody consists of those elements of reading that, when taken together, comprise expressive reading (e.g., pitch, stress, and parsing). It is the case that the accurate use of these elements allows readers to determine shades of meaning that might not immediately be apparent in written text. However, while some aspects of oral expression are represented in text by punctuation (e.g., Truss, 2003), this is not always the case (Miller & Schwanenflugel, 2006). For example, when a person ends a heated discussion with the words "fine," the person they were engaged with usually realizes that the speaker does *not* mean that the two have come to an amicable agreement. However, there is nothing available in a written version of such a conversation to convey this understanding. Instead, the reader has to apply their knowledge of oral exchanges to develop the correct sense of the interaction.

While it is the case that the appropriate application of expressive features can affect the meaning constructed from a given text, it is unclear exactly how this process occurs. There are three distinct possibilities as regards the relationship between prosody and comprehension. In the first scenario, the application of prosodic elements to a text allow for comprehension to occur. In the second case, comprehension of written material needs to take place before prosodic elements can be applied. And in the third and final scenario (and the one that represents my own point of view), an interactive relationship exists in which prosody both contributes to and is reflective of a reader's comprehension. Given the importance of automaticity (which assumes a high level of accuracy) *and* prosody in constructing meaning from text, the value of utilizing instructional approaches that integrate both elements into fluency instruction begins to become apparent.

Automaticity and Prosody in Practice

In addition to thinking about automaticity and prosody in terms of their role in fluent reading, it is also useful to consider how each of these elements can be integrated into classroom practice. When reflecting upon automaticity in reading, Jay Samuels (1979, 2006) argues that it is important to consider the ways in which this construct is developed in other areas (Samuels, 1979); for example, when individuals are learning to play tennis, it is necessary that they practice individual aspects of the game, say their backhand and their serve, to become adept at those moves. However, it is also essential that they learn how to combine various components into a unified action if they are ever to shift from simply practicing to actually playing. Applying this understanding to reading, it is important that students learn how to recognize words quickly and accurately, and, in order to achieve this, they need significant amounts of practice.

As with tennis, some of this practice should take place in isolation, through decoding instruction and word work that allows learners to establish familiarity with English orthography, but, if learners are to develop automatic word recognition when reading connected text, much of this practice needs to take place in context using both supported oral, as well as silent, reading. Without the later type of practice, students may become quite capable of quickly identifying words in isolation, but may not necessarily transfer that ability to their actual reading. In fact, it is often the case that students experiencing difficulties applying their word recognition knowledge to connected text find themselves faced with increasing amounts of decoding instruction in isolation, rather than increased opportunities for guided practice in context (e.g., Allington, 1977, 1983). Unfortunately, by limiting struggling readers to this as their primary form of practice, we are actually minimizing, rather than increasing, the likelihood that they will become skilled readers.

Next, as was mentioned in the previous section, the integration of prosody into students' reading can also lead to a more nuanced understanding of the text (e.g., Erekson, 2003). Further, by developing an awareness of the importance of appropriate expression and phrasing in students, it is possible to prevent them from developing the belief that fluent reading is simply fast reading and the faster the better (e.g., Walker et al., 2006). In fact, by emphasizing the importance of prosodic elements in text, learners are prevented from viewing reading as a race and their comprehension is improved (Dowhower, 1991; Schreiber, 1991). Unfortunately, the overemphasis on oral reading rate may be an unintended consequence of certain assessment tools that emphasize correct word per minute rates without reference to expression or the need to vary reading rate according to the complexity of the text (e.g., Samuels, 2007; Walker et al., 2006). Perhaps even more regrettably, this overemphasis can also lead to a misuse of fluency-oriented instructional approaches such as repeated readings. While it is critical that learners develop automatic word recognition (see Table 28.1 for a guide to correct words per minute rates), it is equally important that this not be the only goal. Instead, students should develop the understanding that fluency consists of smooth, accurate, and expressive reading at a rate that replicates that of oral language (see Table 28.2 for a guide to prosodic text features).

TABLE 28.1
Correct Words per Minute by Grade Level

Grade	Fall	Winter	Spring
1	—	10–30	30–60 cwpm
2	30–60	50–80	70-100
3	50–90	70–100	80–110
4	70–110	80–120	100–140
5	80–120	100–140	110–150
6	100–140	110–150	120–160
7	110–150	120–160	130–170
8	120–160	130–170	140–180

From Rasinski, T. V. (2004). *Assessing Reading Fluency*. Honolulu: Pacific Resources for Education and Learning. Available at http://www.prel.org/products/re_/assessing-fluency.htm

Fluency Instruction

While many readers become fluent as the result of the literacy instruction provided in a typical elementary classroom, this is rarely the case for students with reading disabilities (e.g., Kuhn & Schwanenflugel, 2006). Instead, such students require even greater opportunities to practice their reading in a supported environment than do their peers who are able to develop their reading ability without noticeable difficulty. One way to provide reading disabled students with the instruction they need is by integrating four fluency-oriented principles into oral reading instruction (Rasinski, 2003); these principles are modeling, opportunities for practice, the provision of support and assistance, and the demonstration of appropriate phrasing. While these elements are the basis of a range of fluency strategies that are effective for all learners, the integration of these principles into instruction for students with reading disabilities is critical to their development as skilled readers (McKenna & Stahl, 2003). As such, I will discuss the role each plays in fluency instruction and its particular usefulness for students with reading disabilities. A second way to provide learners with appropriate instruction is to integrate specific fluency-oriented reading approaches into the curriculum. There are many instructional strategies that have proven to be effective over the past three decades (e.g., Kuhn, 2009; Rasinski, 2003), and I highlight three instructional strands (unassisted repeated readings, assisted readings, and classroom approaches), along with ways that recent research may serve to change some of our underlying assumptions regarding effective fluency practices, as part of a broader discussion of trends in this area.

Principles of Fluency Instruction

The first of Rasinski's (2003) principles involves the modeling of expressive reading. Not only is such modeling likely to instill a love of reading in students, it simultaneously provides them with a sense of what good oral reading should sound like. While reading to students is a common practice in the primary grades, it tends to be a fairly rare occurrence in later grades. However, there are many texts, from poems to highly descriptive expository selections, such as speeches, that are ideal for older students and lend themselves to being read

aloud. Spending approximately 5 minutes a day reading such a text aloud accomplishes several things. First, it creates a shared experience amongst the learners. Next, and especially critical for struggling readers, it provides students with the opportunity to hear what smooth, expressive reading sounds like. Finally, by making selections from a range of genres, it increases the likelihood that students will find a text that is engaging.

The second principle, that students should have extensive opportunities to practice reading connected texts, provides a caveat for the first principle. That is, as positive as modeling is for students, it is important not to overuse it—a tendency that is especially prevalent when working with reading disabled students. It is often the case that teachers revert to reading aloud as a means of compensating for a text that is beyond their students' instructional level (there is a parallel tendency for teachers to present the information from a difficult text in a lecture format for the same reason; Shanahan, 2007). While this approach is problematic for any student (it is essential that all students have multiple opportunities to read challenging texts in a supportive environment), it is the case that struggling readers need even greater opportunities to read a range of texts (including texts that are challenging for them) in such an environment if they are to become independent readers. By reverting exclusively, or even primarily, to lectures and read-alouds, students are denied the very opportunities they need to develop their own reading ability. However, while the provision of such opportunities make sense in theory, it often seems difficult to accomplish in practice. Luckily, the approaches discussed later in the chapter should provide several options for creating just such expanded opportunities for scaffolded oral reading and, whenever appropriate, for silent reading as well.

The third principle, that of providing students with support or assistance for their reading, is especially critical for reading disabled students. While all students benefit

TABLE 28.2
National Assessment of Educational Progress's Oral Reading Fluency Scale

Level 4	Reads primarily in larger, meaningful phrase groups. Although some regressions, repetitions and deviations from text may be present, those do not appear to detract from the overall structure of the story. Preservation of the author's syntax is consistent. Some or most of the story is read with expressive interpretation.
Level 3	Reads primarily in three- or four-word phrase groups. Some smaller groupings may be present. However, the majority of phrasing seems appropriate and preserves the syntax of the author. Little or no expressive interpretation is present.
Level 2	Reads primarily in two-word phrases with some three- or four-word groupings. Some word-by-word reading may be present. Word groupings may seem awkward and unrelated to larger context of sentence or passage.
Level 1	Reads primarily word-by-word. Occasionally two-word or three-word phrases may occur, but these are infrequent and/or they do not preserve meaningful syntax.

from reading in a supportive environment, students who are experiencing difficulty consolidating what they know about word recognition into their reading of connected texts require additional assistance from a skilled reader. As such, it is essential that they regularly read in situations where some form of support is available. This support can involve the repeated reading of a single text, silently or aloud, until the students have reached a predetermined level of mastery, or it can incorporate the single reading of a range of challenging or instructional level texts through the use of echo, choral, or partner reading. Whichever approach is chosen, the scaffolding that these methods afford students will allow them to develop as skilled readers.

The final principle involves an emphasis on appropriate phrasing. According to several qualitative scales (e.g., Allington & Brown cited in Allington 1983; NAEP, 1995; Zutell & Rasinski, 1991), disfluent readers parse text in ways that do not replicate oral language (e.g., word-by-word reading or inappropriate phrasing). As was mentioned earlier in this chapter, this is at least partially the result of the limitations of punctuation to indicate phrasal boundaries (e.g., Miller & Schwanenflugel, 2006). Unfortunately, this tendency on the part of a disfluent reader has a negative impact on comprehension. One way to help students compensate for this inability is to model appropriate phrasing; this can be especially helpful when leading an echo or choral reading of a text. A second approach is to help students determine where the phrasal boundaries should occur in texts that they are reading by having them identify which breaks sound like language and which ones don't; so, for example, in this excerpt from Tom Sawyer (Twain, 1986, p. 7), students should discuss which sounds better: "The old/ lady pulled/ her spectacles/ down and/ looked over/ them about/ the room" or "The old lady/ pulled her spectacles down/ and looked over them/ about the room." By holding discussions around appropriate phrasing, it becomes possible to develop students' awareness of these elements and their importance in written text (Dowhower, 1991).

Instructional Strategies

While the above principles can be integrated into virtually any literacy curriculum, there are several strategies that have been designed specifically to increase students' reading fluency. By discussing three strands of instruction that have proven to be effective in developing learners' reading fluency, as well as by looking at new understandings regarding effective approaches that are starting to emerge from classroom-based research, it becomes possible to identify certain trends in classroom-based practice.

Unassisted Repeated Readings   In terms of fluency instruction, the repeated readings approach is probably the most frequently used strategy and is also likely to be the most widely researched fluency-oriented instructional method (e.g., Samuels, 1979; Dowhower, 1994). It also holds the distinction of being the first approach designed specifically to develop the automaticity of disfluent readers. When developing the approach, Samuels (1979) envisioned it as a means of implementing the type of practice that is commonly seen in the fields of music and athletics. As was mentioned earlier, when athletes, for example, begin to take up their art or sport, they take part in the repeated practice of both isolated components of their craft as well as connected routines. At the time this approach was developed, typical classroom practice for struggling readers tended to over-rely on decoding practice in isolation (Allington, 1977) and to underemphasize the scaffolded practice of connected text. When learners did have the opportunity to read connected text, it was often the case that they only took part in a single oral reading of the material and that this reading was broken up into smaller sections as part of a round robin reading of the text. Unfortunately, it remains the case that, far too often, learners face similar types of instruction today, either in a modified form of round robin reading (e.g., popcorn, popsicle, or combat reading; Ash & Kuhn, 2006) or in a lack of opportunities to actually read text (Hiebert, 2004). And while such instruction may be problematic for many readers, it is especially troubling for students identified with reading disabilities (Allington, 1977, 2005).

Thinking about the differences that exist between practice designed to benefit athletes and musicians and that designed to improve reading led Samuels (1979) to consider an approach to reading instruction that paralleled the practice used in other fields and that he felt was likely be more effective than the approaches that were commonly being used. Based on this understanding, he postulated that students might establish automaticity more easily if, instead of reading part of a passage once, they were given the opportunity to practice reading a given selection repeatedly. Samuels not only felt that such repetition should lead to improvements with the practiced material, but that such gains might transfer to the reading of other texts. And, in fact, repeated readings has been shown to be effective for struggling readers not only in terms of rate, accuracy, and where measured, prosody on the targeted text (e.g., Dowhower, 1994; Kuhn & Stahl, 2003), but also on unpracticed material as well.

The procedure itself is a simple one that is easy to use in a one-on-one instructional setting. Since the repetition embedded in the procedure allows learners to increase their automaticity, the approach is ideal for students whose are accurate decoders, but whose reading rate falls below the norms established for their grade. The strategy itself involves the repeated reading of a challenging text (text with an initial accuracy rate of 85% to 90%). As a student completes an initial reading of the text, it is the teacher's role to record the number of words that the learner reads per minute along with the number of miscues she or he makes on the passage. As the student rereads the text, the number of words read per minute should increase while the number of miscues made should decrease. The student should then practice re-reading the passage, either silently or aloud and either for a predetermined number of repetitions, usually between three and five, or until she or he reaches a predetermined target for both reading rate and number of miscues.

While it is important to stress that the repeated readings procedure has been effective at increasing the reading rate of struggling readers (e.g., Dowhower, 1989; Joseph, 2007; Samuels, 1979), some educators have expressed concern that the approach's emphasis on automaticity may, in fact, detract learners from developing the understanding that reading's primary purpose is the construction of meaning. However, a study designed to determine whether learning disabled fifth through eighth graders could increase their comprehension of a passage while simultaneously improving their reading rate through a repeated readings approach had positive results (O'Shea, Sindelar, & O'Shea, 1987). The study's authors found that when students were specifically asked to focus on the passage content, both their comprehension of the passage and their reading rate improved. However, when students were only asked to focus on rate, they only made gains in terms of their automaticity. The implication is that, to ensure learners' focus on both rate and comprehension, they should be encouraged to think about the passage as they are reading it and briefly discuss the selection after the first or second repetition. Similarly, while the primary purpose of the approach is to move students away from word-by-word reading and toward automaticity, this does not mean that students should simply be encouraged to read the passage as fast as possible. Instead, their goal should be to read at a rate that falls within the guidelines established for their grade levels while incorporating the use of appropriate prosodic elements. By having students focus on rate, meaning, and expression (see Tables 28.1 & 28.2), the likelihood that they will use this approach as a stepping stone to skilled silent reading increases.

Assisted Readings   While repeated readings is a highly successful strategy that is easy to implement in a one-on-one setting, most classroom teachers do not have the opportunity to work with individual students for significant periods of time. As such, several effective alternatives to this procedure have been developed; these include reading-while-listening (Chomsky, 1976, 1978; Pluck, 2006), closed-caption television (Koskinen, Wilson, & Jensema, 1985), computer-assisted technology (e.g., Adams, 2003), and a modified version of the neurological impress method (NIM; Hollingsworth, 1970, 1978). Each of these alternative approaches makes use of a model of fluent reading—be it an audio recording or the use of the text that accompanies a television show—rather than relying solely on repetition to serve as the scaffolding. As such, they may be more readily integrated into a classroom center where a student can work independently.

Rather than explore each version of assisted reading, I will use reading-while-listening (Chomsky, 1976) as an exemplar. In this approach, students are asked to read along with audio recordings of a text, either silently or orally, to increase their fluency. The procedure was developed as a way of assisting several third graders who were reluctant, disfluent readers. Despite taking part in intensive phonics instruction, these students were unable to apply their decoding knowledge to the reading of connected text and were reading well below grade level. Rather than provide these learners with yet more decoding instruction, Chomsky thought the students would benefit from the opportunity to read significant amounts of connected texts. She therefore provided them with recordings of two dozen books ranging in reading level from second to fifth grade. This provided the learners with accessible versions of the material, allowing them to practice their reading independently.

Since these students were struggling readers, the level of the selections were challenging for them, however, the procedure gave them a chance to apply their knowledge of word recognition to connected text—a step that had been missing in their instruction to date. Further, by simultaneously listening to and *reading along with* the tape, the students were able to establish the connection between written text and oral language. They did this by rereading a particular text until they were able to render the material fluently for the teacher. And, because it holds the students responsible for the material, the procedure ensures their active participation in the process and provides a level of accountability. Since the students who take part in this procedure are experiencing reading difficulties, it may take them a while before they are able to coordinate their reading with the recording. However, once they become comfortable with the procedure, this should no longer be an issue. And, it is important to note that while some students will develop this comfort by practicing orally (this is often the case with younger students who can be encouraged to use whisper reading or pvc "phones" to minimize the level of noise in the classroom), others will prefer to practice silently (a more likely scenario for older students). Further, research conducted on reading-while-listening procedures (e.g., Rasinski & Hoffman, 2003) indicates that the approach is not only an effective one for struggling readers, it is a motivating and enjoyable one as well.

Classroom Approaches   A third strand of approaches (and the last to be discussed in this chapter) involves incorporating fluency-oriented instruction into the broader literacy curriculum through whole class or flexible grouping. There are several approaches that have been designed for such a purpose. Some of these are supplemental, for example, Reader's Theater, the Fluency Development Lesson, and Paired Repeated Reading (see Kuhn, 2009), while some can be used in conjunction with guided or shared reading instruction, for example, the Oral Recitation Lesson (ORL; Hoffman, 1987), Wide Fluency-Oriented Oral Reading (Wide FOOR; Kuhn, 2005), or Fluency-Oriented Reading Instruction (FORI; Stahl & Heubach, 2005). All of these classroom approaches are effective at improving students' reading fluency, and they appear to be especially beneficial for students who are experiencing difficulty making the transition to fluent reading (see Kuhn, 2009, or Rasinski, 2003, for an in-depth discussion of these and other fluency-oriented reading approaches). Further, these approaches all share a number of characteristics.

To begin with, all of the procedures mentioned in the above paragraph incorporate support in the form of a model, usually the teacher, who provides an expressive rendering of a given text. As with the assisted reading approaches discussed in the previous section, rather than expecting struggling readers to determine each word as they encounter it, the students are provided with scaffolding for their word recognition. This scaffolding takes the form of either an echo or choral reading of a text. Next, although these strategies emphasize appropriate pacing, they do not stress reading rate at the expense of comprehension. Instead, they focus on the construction of meaning both through a discussion of the selection and through the emphasis of appropriate prosodic elements. Third, they ensure that students spend significantly greater amounts of class time engaged in the reading of connected text than is the case with many instructional alternatives. However, while many of these approaches incorporate repeated practice of a given text, there are some that instead rely on the Wide Reading of multiple texts to accomplish this goal (e.g., Wide FOOR; Kuhn, 2005).

Wide Reading, in this context, refers to the scaffolded reading of a large number of challenging texts, as opposed to the independent reading of multiple texts that is usually part and parcel of the reading habits of skilled readers. As has been stressed in the discussion of fluency instruction throughout this chapter, repetition has been viewed as a critical element in helping disfluent readers make the shift to automatic, expressive reading. However, a recent review of the research on fluency interventions (Kuhn & Stahl, 2003) observed that, when comparing students using repetition with students who read equivalent amounts of scaffolded text, both groups made equivalent gains. In this context, scaffolding of Wide Reading consists primarily of echo or choral reading of challenging texts (texts that students generally read with an initial accuracy level of between 85% and 90%), although paired or partner reading can serve the same purpose depending on the length and difficulty of the text (e.g., Kuhn, 2009).

Further, it appears that Wide Reading is designed not only to provide learners with support in the reading of challenging text, it also allows learners to encounter a broad range of words in multiple settings as opposed to the same text multiple times. So, for example, it is likely that students would see high frequency words and common nouns such as *warm* and *dog* in the phrases *the warm day* and *the barking dog* between three and five times as part of a repeated readings exercise. During Wide Reading, on the other hand, students are likely to come across these words in multiple phrases, for example *the warm day, warm mittens,* and *warm toast*, during the same period of reading. And, it seems possible that, by encountering words not only multiple times, but also in multiple settings, students are likely to learn them more easily (e.g., Logan, 1997; Mostow & Beck, 2005).

After considering the above findings, I designed a research study that compared two forms of small group fluency instruction to determine the relative accuracy of the conclusions. The research consisted of two instructional approaches, one based upon repetition and one based upon the wide reading of a larger number of texts for an equivalent amount of time. To control these groups for simple exposure to text, I also included a group that listened to, but did not read, the selections used by the intervention groups along with a traditional control group. The intervention was designed for use with second grade struggling readers who, according to both their teachers and the pre-test assessments, had established basic word recognition abilities, but were experiencing difficulties applying this knowledge to connected text. The intervention consisted of small group instruction (5–6 students per group) for 15- to 20-minute periods three times a week.

The goal of these sessions was to scaffold these struggling second graders as they read a series of challenging texts, or texts that would normally be considered to be beyond their instructional level. Given the students were reading below grade level, the texts I selected ranged between a late first- and an early third-grade reading level (e.g., Fountas & Pinnell, 1999). Since the goal of this evaluation was to explore the effectiveness of a repeated readings procedure and a wide reading approach, the first procedure, Fluency-Oriented Oral Reading (FOOR), incorporated a modified repeated readings approach. This involved the reading of a single trade book over the course of a three sessions. The second condition, Wide Fluency-Oriented Oral Reading (Wide FOOR), on the other hand, consisted of a single echo or choral reading of a different text at each session. As previously mentioned, a third group of students listened to, but did not read, all the stories that were used with the Wide FOOR group. Finally, there were 6 students who did not take part in any literacy activities beyond those that occurred in their classroom.

While the approaches used in this research were similar to many other fluency-oriented classroom approaches insofar as they increased the amount of text that students read aloud with scaffolding, the results were important for confirming the conclusions noted in the earlier review (Kuhn & Stahl, 2003). That is, both the FOOR and the Wide FOOR groups made greater gains than the students in either the listening-only condition or those in the control group in terms of their word recognition in isolation, the number of correct words read per minute in connected text, and their prosody. However, the Wide FOOR group also made greater growth in terms of their comprehension. It certainly seems possible that these differences resulted from the differing nature of the tasks; so, for example, students in the FOOR group might have felt that the implicit purpose of the repetition was to improve their word recognition, reading rate, and prosody, whereas the students in the Wide FOOR group may have considered the implicit purpose for reading multiple texts included not only these three elements, but the construction of meaning as well. If this is the case, it could explain why these differences were seen in the outcome measures.

Following from this, it is useful to note that, although some embedded discussion occurred around both the stories and the vocabulary, the sessions did not incorporate direct instruction in either of these areas. As such, it may be that the inclusion of a comprehension focus as part of the FOOR approach would lead to increases in those students' comprehension scores as well. This could be as simple as embedding a range of questions into the reading of the story (see Kay Stahl's, 2008, use of questioning in the shared reading of *Big Old Bones: A Dinosaur Tale* (Carrick, 1992) for an outstanding example of this process) or it could involve the use of more formalized procedures such as the Directed Reading-Thinking Activitty (DR-TA; Stauffer & Cramer, 1968) or reciprocal teaching (Palinscar & Brown, 1986) that have been developed specifically to increase students engagement with texts. By integrating a comprehension element into fluency-oriented instruction, it becomes less likely that students will develop into word callers who recognize words automatically but who fail to construct meaning as they read (Schwanenflugel & Ruston, 2008)

When discussing the research around Wide Reading, it is worth noting that additional studies based upon the reading of multiple texts have shown similar promise, whether in an approach that replicates and extends the work undertaken in the original FOOR study (Schwebel, 2007) or in different contexts, such as shared reading (Kuhn, Schwanenflugel, Morris, et al., 2006) or computer-aided instruction (Mostow & Beck, 2005). It is also the case that the exposure to multiple texts increases students' access to a greater range of concepts and an expansive vocabulary than is the case with repeated readings (e.g., Kuhn, 2009). Since students experiencing reading difficulties are less likely to read extensively than their more skilled peers, it is important to provide them with additional opportunities to engage with print whenever possible. By assisting students in the reading of multiple selections rather than just one, it becomes possible to provide struggling readers with access to a broad range of ideas while simultaneously aiding their fluency development.

Conclusions

There are several possible reasons why the approaches discussed above are effective in assisting students who are experiencing reading difficulties become more fluent readers. It may be that the improvement results from the sheer amount of reading students are required to complete as part of these fluency-oriented instructional approaches (Kuhn & Stahl, 2003). In other words, the strategies may simply increase the amount of time on task for students when compared to a traditional reading curriculum. Alternatively, the improvement may be due to specific effects

that result from the scaffolding that occurs either as part of the repetition of texts (Laberge & Samuels, 1974) or from the supported reading of a wide range of materials (Kuhn, 2005) or to the prosodic components that result from the students exposure to modeling (Dowhower, 1991; Schreiber, 1991) or to a combination of these factors. Further, certain elements appear to be consistently important in the creation of effective fluency instruction, including the use of challenging, connected texts and the need to develop students' reading rate in conjunction with their prosody and comprehension.

Although the fluency development of reading disabled learners is certainly deserving of further investigation, I would consider any of the above approaches, along with the principles that underlie them, to be an effective means for helping these students make the transition to fluent reading. As such, they should be thought of as a tool for incorporating oral reading instruction that will actually support learners in becoming skilled readers.

Notes

1. While comprehension of text clearly involves far more than accurate and automatic word recognition, I am only focusing on these aspects of reading at this point in the discussion.

References

Adams, M. J. (1990). *Beginning to read: Thinking and learning about print*. Cambridge, MA: M.I.T. Press.

Adams, M. J. (2003). The pedagogical goals of soliloquy learning. Developing research-based resources for the balanced reading teacher. Retrieved from http://www.balancedreading.com/soliloquy.html

Allington, R. L. (1977). If they don't read much, how they ever gonna get good? *Journal of Reading, 21*, 57–61.

Allington, R. L. (1983). Fluency: The neglected reading goal. *The Reading Teacher, 36*, 556–561.

Allington, R.L. (2005). What really matters for struggling readers: Designing research-based programs, (2nd ed.). New York: Allyn & Bacon.

Ash, G. E., & Kuhn, M. R. (2006). Meaningful oral and silent reading in the elementary and middle school classroom: Breaking the Round Robin Reading addiction. In T. Rasinski, C. Blachowicz, & K. Lems (Eds.), *Fluency instruction: Research-based best practices* (pp. 155–172). New York: Guilford.

Carrick, C. (1992). *Big old bones: A dinosaur tale*. Boston, MA: Clarion Books.

Chall, J. S. (1996). *Stages of reading development* (2nd ed.). Fort Worth, TX: Harcourt-Brace.

Chard, D. J., Pikulski, J. J., & McDonagh, S. H. (2006). Fluency: The link between decoding and comprehension for struggling readers. In T. Rasinski, C. Blachowicz, & K. Lems (Eds.), *Fluency instruction: Research-based best practices* (pp. 39–61). New York: Guilford.

Chomsky, C. (1976). After decoding: What? *Language Arts, 53*, 288–296.

Chomsky, C. (1978). When you still can't read in third grade? After decoding, what? In S. J. Samuels (Ed.), *What research has to say about reading instruction*, (pp. 13–30). Newark, DE: International Reading Association.

Dowhower, S. L. (1989). Repeated reading: Theory into practice. *The Reading Teacher, 42*, 502–507.

Dowhower, S. L. (1991). Speaking of prosody: Fluency's unattended bedfellow. *Theory into Practice, 30*(3), 158–164.

Dowhower, S. L. (1994). Repeated reading revisited: Research into practice. *Reading and Writing Quarterly: Overcoming Learning Difficulties, 10*(4), 343–358.

Erekson, J. (2003, May). *Prosody: The problem of expression in fluency.* Paper presented at the annual meeting of the International Reading Association, Orlando, FL.

Fountas, I. C., & Pinnell, G. S. (1999). *Matching books to readers: Using leveled books in guided reading, K-3.* Portsmouth, NH: Heinemann.

Hiebert, E. H. (2004, April). *Teaching children to become fluent readers – year 2.* Discussant at the American Educational Research Association, San Diego, CA.

Hoffman, J. (1987). Rethinking the role of oral reading in basal instruction. *The Elementary School Journal, 87,* 367–373.

Hollingsworth, P. M. (1970). An experiment with the impress method of teaching reading. *The Reading Teacher, 24*(2), 112–114.

Hollingsworth, P. M. (1978). An experimental approach to the impress method of teaching reading. *The Reading Teacher, 31,* 624–626.

Joseph, L. M. (2007). Getting the "most bang for your buck": Comparison of the effectiveness and efficiency of phonic and whole word reading techniques during repeated reading lessons. *Journal of Applied School Psychology, 24,* 69–90.

Koskinen, P. S., Wilson, R. M., & Jensema, C. J. (1985). Closed-Captioned Television: A new tool for reading instruction. *Reading World, 24*(4), 1–7.

Kuhn, M. R. (2005). A comparative study of small group fluency instruction. *Reading Psychology, 26,* 127–146.

Kuhn, M. R. (2009). *The hows and whys of reading fluency.* Boston: Allyn & Bacon.

Kuhn, M. R., & Schwanenflugel, P. J. (2006). All oral reading practice is not equal (or how can I integrate fluency instruction into my classroom?). *Literacy Teaching and Learning, 11,* 1–20.

Kuhn, M. R., Schwanenflugel, P. J., Morris, R. D., Morrow, L. M., Woo, D., Meisinger, et al. (2006). Teaching children to become fluent and automatic readers. *Journal of Literacy Research, 38,* 357–387.

Kuhn, M. R., & Stahl, S. (2003). Fluency: A review of developmental and remedial strategies. *The Journal of Educational Psychology, 95,* 3–21.

LaBerge, D., & Samuels, S. J. (1974). Toward a theory of automatic information processing in reading. *Cognitive Psychology, 6,* 293–323.

Logan, G. D. (1997). Automaticity and reading: Perspectives from the instance theory of automaticity. *Reading & Writing Quarterly: Overcoming Learning Difficulties, 13,* 123–146.

McKenna, M. C., & Stahl, S. A. (2003). *Assessment for reading instruction.* New York: Guilford.

Miller, J., & Schwanenflugel, P. J. (2006). Prosody of syntactically complex sentences in the oral reading of young children. *Journal of Educational Psychology, 98,* 839–853.

Mostow, J., & Beck, J. (2005, June). *Micro-analysis of fluency gains in a reading tutor that listens.* Paper presented at the Society for the Scientific Study of Reading, Toronto, Canada.

NAEP. (1995). *Listening to Children Read Aloud, 15* [oral reading fluency scale]. Washington, DC: U.S. Department of Education, National Center for Education Statistics.

National Reading Panel. (2000). Teaching children to read: An evidence-based assessment of the scientific research literature on reading and its implications for reading instruction. Reports of the subgroups. Bethesda, MD: National Institutes of Health. Retrieved from http://www.nichd.nih.gov/publications/nrp/

O'Shea, L. J., Sindelar, P. T., & O'Shea, D. (1987). The effects of repeated readings and attentional cues on the reading fluency and comprehension of learning disabled readers. *Learning Disabilities Research, 2,* 103–109.

Palinscar, A. S., & Brown, A. L. (1986). Interactive teaching to promote independent learning from text. *Reading Teacher, 39,* 771–777.

Pluck, M. L. (2006). "Jonathon is 11 but reads like a struggling 7-year-old": Providing assistance for struggling readers with a tape-assisted reading program. In T. Rasinski, C. Blachowicz, & K. Lems (Eds.), *Fluency instruction: Research-based best practices* (pp. 192–208). New York: Guilford.

Rasinski, T. V. (2003). *The fluent reader: Oral reading strategies for building word recognition, fluency, and comprehension.* New York: Scholastic.

Rasinski, T. V. (2004). *Assessing Reading Fluency.* Honolulu: Pacific Resources for Education and Learning. Retrieved from http://www.prel.org/products/re_/assessing-fluency.htm

Rasinski, T. V., & Hoffman, J. V (2003). Oral reading in the school curriculum. *Reading Research Quarterly, 38,* 510–522.

Samuels, J. (2006). Reading fluency: Its past, present, and future. In T. Rasinski, C. Balachowicz, & K. Lems (Eds.), *Fluency instruction: research-based best practices* (pp. 7–20). New York: Guilford.

Samuels, S. J. (1979). The method of repeated readings. *The Reading Teacher, 32,* 403–408.

Samuels, S. J. (2007). The DIBELS Tests: Is speed of barking at print what we mean by reading fluency? *Reading Research Quarterly, 42,* 563–566.

Schreiber, P. A. (1991). Understanding prosody's role in reading acquisition. *Theory into Practice, 30*(3), 158–164.

Schwanenflugel, P. J., & Ruston, H. P. (2008). Becoming a fluent reader: From theory to practice. In M. R. Kuhn & P. J. Schwanenflugel (Eds.), *Fluency in the classroom* (pp. 1–16). New York: Guildford.

Schwebel, E. A. (2007). *A comparative study of small group fluency instruction — a replication and extension of Kuhn's (2005) study* (Unpublished master's thesis). Kean University, Union, NJ.

Shanahan, T. (2007). *Differentiating instruction when embedding literacy.* Invited speaker at the 39th Annual Conference on Reading and Writing. Rutgers Centre for Effective School Practices. April 20. Somerset, New Jersey.

Stahl, K. A. D. (2008). Creating opportunities for comprehension within fluency-oriented reading. In M. R. Kuhn & P. J. Schwanenflugel (Eds.), *Fluency in the classroom* (pp. 55–74). New York: Guildford.

Stahl, S. A., & Heubach, K. (2005). Fluency-oriented reading instruction. *Journal of Literacy Research, 37,* 25–60.

Stanovich, K. E. (1986). Matthew effects in reading: Some consequences of individual differences in the acquisition of literacy. *Reading Research Quarterly, 21,* 360–407.

Stauffer, R. G., & Cramer, R. (1968). *Teaching critical reading at the primary level. Reading Aids series.* Newark, DE: International Reading Association.

Truss, L. (2003). *Eats, shoots, and leaves: The zero tolerance approach to punctuation.* New York: Gotham Books.

Twain, M. (1986). *The adventures of Tom Sawyer.* New York: Penguin Classics.

Walker, B. J., Mokhtari, K., & Sargent, S. (2006). Reading fluency: More than fast and accurate reading. In T. Rasinski, C. Blachowicz, & K. Lems (Eds.), *Fluency instruction: Research-based best practices* (pp. 86–105). New York: Guilford.

Zutell, J., & Rasinski, T. V. (1991). Training teachers to attend to their students' oral reading fluency. *Theory into Practice, 30,* 211–217.

29

Interventions to Enhance Vocabulary Development

MICHAEL F. GRAVES
University of Minnesota

REBECCA SILVERMAN
University of Maryland

Research on vocabulary in the United States has a history of over 100 years. The first archival study we are aware of was conducted by E. A. Kirkpatrick and published in *Science* in 1891. Beginning in the early 20th century, particularly with the work of Thorndike, vocabulary became a prominent topic of educational research (Clifford, 1978). Although interest in vocabulary research has waxed and waned over the years (Graves & Watts-Taffe, 2002), over 100 years of work has produced a very substantial body of knowledge, much of it quite solid. Although there are certainly many unanswered questions about vocabulary and vocabulary instruction, the fact is we know a great deal about teaching vocabulary. Much of what we know has been summarized in substantial reviews by Graves (1986), Beck and McKeown (1991), Blachowicz and Fisher (2000), and Baumann, Kaméenui, and Ash (2003), all of which are considerably longer than this chapter. Consequently, this review is selective rather than comprehensive. In it, we describe research findings that are either specifically about instruction or that provide background important to understanding instructional issues and making instructional decisions. Some of the findings come from studies that dealt specifically with students with learning disabilities. Most of them, however, come from studies of students in general and apply to both students without reading disabilities and those with disabilities. The chapter is divided into two major sections. In the first section, Foundational Considerations, we examine a number of factors about words and word learning that inform instruction. In the second section, Vocabulary Instruction, we take up specifics of teaching vocabulary. Finally, in a brief Concluding Remarks section, we identify what we see as some of the most important questions that need to be answered to further improve vocabulary instruction.

Foundational Considerations

Here we consider several matters about the vocabulary learning task that need to be understood in order make informed decisions about vocabulary instruction. These are Types of Vocabulary, What Constitutes a Word, Levels of Word Knowledge, The Number of Words in Contemporary American English, How Many Words Do Students Learn, The Vocabularies of Linguistically Less Advantaged Children, and The Frequency Distribution of English Vocabulary.

Types of Vocabulary It is important to recognize that there are several types of vocabulary. Vocabulary can be classified as receptive (words we understand when others use them) and productive (words we use ourselves). Vocabulary can also be classified as oral or written. Thus, each of us has four vocabularies: Words we understand when we hear them, words we understand when we read them, words we use in our speech, and words we use in our writing. The four vocabularies overlap but are not the same, and the relationships between them change over time. Although some children come to school with much smaller vocabularies than others, all children entering school have relatively large listening vocabularies but quite small (perhaps nonexistent) reading vocabularies. Sometime during the upper-elementary years, good readers' reading vocabularies begin to outstrip their listening vocabularies, and most literate adults have larger reading vocabularies than listening vocabularies. Additionally, both children and adults have larger receptive vocabularies than productive ones. The primary emphasis in this chapter will be on reading vocabulary; but we will also give significant attention to listening vocabulary.

What Constitutes a Word? Philosophers, linguists, and educators have grappled with the question of what constitutes a word over a considerable period of time, and it is certainly not our goal to provide a definitive answer to the question here. Instead, we want to explain how the term *word* will be used in discussions of how many words exist in the English lexicon and many words students know or need to learn. When written, words are groups of letters separated by white space. Thus, *the* is a word, *apple* another word, *predawn* another, *perpendicular* another, and *houseboat* still another. Unfortunately, by this same definition, *want, wants, wanted,* and *wanting* are also words. However, for the most part, when we consider how many words students know or need to learn, we will use the term *word* to refer to *word families.* By *word families,* we mean the basic word and its inflected forms. Thus the forms *want, wants, wanted,* and *wanting* constitute a single word.

Another convention we will follow in talking about vocabulary size is to count graphic forms with different meanings as a single word. Thus, *key* referring to a door key, *key* the musical term, and *key* meaning a small island are considered one word. Doing so definitely underestimates vocabulary size, but it is necessary because almost all studies of vocabulary size count the number of graphic forms in the language without considering whether or not they represent different meanings.

Levels of Word Knowledge   To discuss the next topic in this chapter—how many words students know—as well as the topics of upcoming sections—how to teach words—it is also necessary to consider the various levels of word knowledge a learner can achieve. A number of vocabulary scholars have considered this question, and they are all in agreement on one matter: Words can be known at various levels. For example, Beck, McKeown, and Kucan (2002) list five levels. Below is a slightly modified version of their levels.

- No knowledge.
- General sense, such as knowing *mendacious* has a negative connotation.
- Narrow, context-bound knowledge, such as knowing that a *radiant* bride is a beautifully smiling happy one, but being unable to describe an individual in a different context as radiant.
- Having a basic knowledge of a word and being able to use the word in a variety of appropriate situations.
- Rich, decontextualized knowledge of a word's meaning, its relationship to other words, and its extension to metaphorical uses, such as understanding what someone is doing when they are devouring a book. (p. 10)

When we consider the matter of how many words students know, we are assuming knowledge at the fourth level, basic knowledge. But there is more to be said about what it means to know a word. Some years ago, Cronbach (1942) noted that knowing a word involves the ability to select situations in which it is appropriately applied, recall different meanings of the word, and recognize exactly in what situations the word does not apply. More recently, Calfee and Drum (1986) noted that knowing a word well "involves depth of meaning; precision of meaning; facile access (think of scrabble and crossword puzzle experts); the ability to articulate one's understanding; flexibility in the application of the knowledge of a word; the appreciation of metaphor,

analogy, word play; the ability to recognize a synonym, to define, to use a word expressively" (pp. 825–826).

Nagy and Scott (2000) further underscore the complexity of what it means to know a word when they discuss several aspects of the complexity of word knowledge—incrementality, multidimensionality, polysemy, interrelatedness, and heterogeneity. We learn word meanings incrementally, learning something about a word's meaning the first time we meet it, something more the second time, and so on. Word knowledge has many dimensions, including for example those listed by Calfee and Drum (1986)—depth of meaning, precision of meaning, and facile access. Many words are polysemeous, that is, they have multiple meanings. Word meanings are interrelated in such a way that a learner's knowledge of one word—e.g., *whale*—is linked to his knowledge of other words—e.g., *mammal.* Finally, word knowledge is heterogeneous in that what it means to know a word is dependent on the type of word in question. Knowing function words such as *the* or *if* is quite different from knowing concrete nouns like *ladder,* and knowing concrete nouns like ladder is quite different from knowing abstract terms like *democracy.*

The Number of Words in Contemporary American English   In the most serious attempt to get a reliable estimate of how many words there are in contemporary American English, Nagy and Anderson (1984) investigated the number of words in printed school English using as their source the *American Heritage Word Frequency Book* (Carroll, Davies, & Richman, 1971). Based on careful study and a sophisticated calculations, Nagy and Anderson concluded that printed school English contains about 88,000 word families. Subsequent to the original study, Anderson and Nagy (1992) again considered the size of printed school English and concluded that if proper nouns, multiple meanings of words, and idioms were included, their estimate would increase to 180,000 word families. More recently, Zeno, Ivens, Millard, and Duvvuri (1995) produced the *Word Frequency Guide,* basically an updated version of the *Word Frequency Book* based on a much larger corpus of material used in kindergarten through college. Although no one has yet calculated the number of word families in the *Word Frequency Guide,* since the number of entries in the *Guide* is considerably larger than the number in the *Word Frequency Book,* it is reasonable to assume that an estimate based on the *Guide* would be well over 180,000. It is worth specifically noting that many of these words are extremely rare and that no single student will encounter all of them, much less learn all of them.

How Many Words Do Students Learn?   Estimates of the number of words in students' reading vocabularies vary markedly. They range from lows of 2,000 words for third graders and 7,800 words for 12th graders (Dupuy, 1974) to highs of 26,000 words for first graders (Shibles, 1959) and over 200,000 words for college freshmen (Hartman, 1946). These extreme estimates can be dismissed or at least very strongly questioned because of such factors as the size of the dictionary from which words were sampled, the definition of what constitutes a word, the method of testing, the sampling procedures used, and such ad hoc requirements as that a word appear in a number of different dictionaries (Graves, 1986; Lorge & Chall, 1963).

The most unbiased estimate of the size of students' reading vocabularies comes, in our judgment, from work done by Nagy and Herman (1987; see also Stahl & Nagy, 2006, chapter 3). Using data gathered from Nagy and Anderson's 1986 study, Nagy and Herman recalibrated earlier estimates and concluded that third graders' reading vocabularies average about 10,000 words, that 12th graders' reading vocabularies average about 40,000 words, and that school children therefore learn about 3,000 words each year. These figures refer to word families as previously described, but they do not include idioms, multiple meanings, or proper nouns, which would raise the figure considerably. Recent estimates by experts are in the same range as Nagy and Herman's estimate but somewhat higher. Snow and Kim (2007), for example, recently suggested that high school graduates need to know 75,000 words.

All in all, our best estimate—based on the work of Anderson and Nagy, 1992; Anglin, 1993; Miller and Wakefield, 1993; Nagy and Anderson, 1984; Nagy and Herman, 1987; and White, Graves, and Slater, 1990—is that average 12th graders know something like 50,000 word families and learn from 3,000 to 4,000 words each year.

The Vocabularies of Linguistically Less Advantaged Children   The data on vocabulary size we have discussed thus far are for average students. Unfortunately, a considerable (although unknown) number of children of poverty, English learners, and students with learning disabilities come to school with much smaller vocabularies. Based on a review of research completed nearly 40 years ago, Carroll (1971) noted that "much of the failure of individuals to understand speech or writing beyond an elementary level is due to deficiencies in vocabulary knowledge" (p. 175). Somewhat more recently, Becker (1977) considered the finding that none of the nine programs in Project Follow Through—a federally funded project aimed at identifying effective educational programs for disadvantaged youth— resulted in students scoring above expectations on tests of word meaning and comprehension and attributed this failure to the fact that both these Follow Through projects and schools more generally "fail to provide instruction in the building blocks crucial to intelligent functioning, namely, words and their referents" (p. 533). More recently, White, Graves, and Slater (1990) investigated the vocabularies of first- through fourth-grade students in two lower-SES schools and one higher-SES school; students in the lower-SES schools knew about 13,000 words while those in the middle-class school knew about 19,000 words. At this same time, Chall, Jacobs, and Baldwin (1990; see also Chall & Jacobs, 2003) reported that the low-income children in their study did about as well in reading as the general population

in grades two and three, but began to fall behind in Grade 4 and continued to fall further behind in Grades 5 and 6, with the strongest factor to show a decline being knowledge of word meanings. More recently, Hart and Risley (1995; see also 2003) showed that by the time they were three children of welfare families knew less than half as many words as those from professional families and that these differences persisted into third grade, the last year in which the children were tested. As Biemiller and Boote (2006) note, schools currently do little to close the gap in oral vocabulary between linguistically more advantaged and linguistically less advantaged students.

The Frequency Distribution of English Words   In addition to knowing something about how many words there are and how many words students are likely to learn, it is important to know something about the distribution of words by frequency—how many frequent words there are and how many infrequent ones. The English language includes a small number of very frequent words, a somewhat larger number of somewhat frequent words, and a very large number of infrequent words. The 100 most frequent words account for about 50% of the words in a typical text. The 1,000 most frequent words account for about 70% of the words in a typical text. And the 5,000 most frequent words account for about 80% of the words in a typical text (Hiebert, 2005). If a student does not know these very frequent words, she or he will be repeatedly stumbling over the words in anything other than a book with severely controlled vocabulary, something like a beginning basal or a high-interest easy-reading book.

It is also important to consider the frequency of words at the other end of the frequency continuum, infrequent and very infrequent words. Some 170,000 of the roughly 180,000 English words occur less than once per million running words, and some 160,000 of them occur less than once per five million running words (Zeno et al., 1995). This means that in their general reading, students will come across these words very seldom. Selecting infrequent words to teach is a real challenge and something we discuss in the next section of this review. What is important to recognize here is that it is vital that teachers make sure that students know the meanings of both frequent words and those lower frequency words necessary for comprehending the various selections they read.

Vocabulary Instruction

Having discussed a number of factors important to making informed decisions about vocabulary instruction, we now discuss research and theory directly concerned with instruction. Topics here include Selecting Vocabulary To Teach, Writing Student-Friendly Definitions, Providing Rich and Varied Language Experiences, Teaching Individual Words, Teaching Word-Learning Strategies, Fostering Word Consciousness, Vocabulary Instruction for English Learners, and Special Considerations for Students with Reading Disabilities.

Selecting Vocabulary to Teach   Three sources can be useful for identifying words to teach—word lists, selections students are reading or hearing their teachers read in school, and students themselves.

Word lists.   Probably the most useful and certainly the most accessible list of high frequency words is Hiebert's Word Zones list, a list of the most frequent 4,000 word families derived from Zeno et al. (1995) and grouped into four zones: the first 300 most frequent, the next 500 most frequent, the next 1,200 most frequent, and the last 2,000 most frequent. The Word Zones list is available online at http://www.textproject.org/library/resources/. Most students come to school with all of these words already in their oral vocabularies and will learn to read them over the first several years of school. Other students, however, do not come to school with all of these words in their oral vocabularies and will need help in getting them into to their oral vocabularies and their reading vocabularies. If student do not know these words, they are a definite priority.

Two additional lists of relatively frequent words have recently been developed by Biemiller (2009). These were developed based on the data on students' word knowledge collected by Dale and O'Rourke (1981), testing Biemiller and his colleagues did (Biemiller & Slonim, 2001), and their intuition. One list is for kindergarten–second grade and contains about 2,000 words, while the other is for third through sixth grade and contains about 3,000 words.

Selections students are reading.   The second source important to use in identifying words to teach is the selections students are reading or listening to. As noted above, English consists of a small number of frequent words and a very large number of infrequent words. Once students acquire a basic vocabulary of several thousand words, the number of different words that might be taught is so large that using word lists to identify words to teach becomes problematic. At this point, teachers need to use their best judgment to select vocabulary to teach from the material students are reading and listening to. Very frequently, scanning a selection will yield more potentially difficult words than can feasibly be taught.

Two contrasting recommendations have been made for selecting a subset of difficult words to actually teach. Beck and her colleagues (2002) have suggested that precedence should be given to what they call Tier 2 words. Tier 2 words are relatively high frequency words that are used by mature language users, that students are likely to encounter in the texts they read in upcoming years, and that are used across domains—for example, in English, and history, and science—and not just in a single domain such as health or music. Graves (2009), on the other hand has suggested criteria that focus on several factors, specifically these:

- The word should be important to understanding the selection in which it appears.
- If teaching the word is useful in furthering students'

context, structural analysis, or dictionary skills, then teaching it may be particularly useful.
- If the word is useful outside of the reading selection currently being taught, this is another argument for teaching it.
- If students are able to use their context or structural-analysis skills to discover the word's meaning, then it probably does not need to be taught.

The students themselves.   The third source of information about what words students do and do not know is the students themselves. As a way of sharpening their perceptions of which words students are and are not likely to know, teachers can identify words in the above word lists or in upcoming selections that they think will be difficult, build multiple-choice or matching tests on these words, and test students to find out whether or not the words are difficult for them. Of course, constructing such tests is time consuming and certainly not something to be done for every selection. However, after several experiences of identifying words that they think will be difficult and then checking students' performance against their expectations, teachers general perceptions of which words are and are not likely to cause their students problems will become increasingly accurate.

In addition to testing students on potentially difficult words using multiple-choice or matching tests, teachers can take the opportunity to occasionally ask students which words they know. One easy way to do this is to list potentially difficult words on the board and have students raise their hands if they do not know a word. This approach is quick, easy, and risk free for students; it also gives students some responsibility for their word learning. Moreover, research (White, Slater, & Graves, 1989) indicates that students can be quite accurate in identifying words that they do and do not know.

Writing Student-Friendly Definitions   Many of the definitions found in dictionaries and instructional materials are quite poor (Miller & Gildea, 1987). Definitions too often define simple words with more complex ones, follow a format that is not helpful to young learners, and fail to consider just what it is that a student who does not already know the meaning of a word needs to learn. Recognizing this problem, McKeown (1993) studied the effects of traditional and revised definitions for fifth-grade students and found the revised definitions considerably more effective. More recently, based on this work and other considerations, Beck and her colleagues (2002) have described what they call "student-friendly" definitions. Student-friendly definitions attempt to define harder words with easier ones and use phrasing students understand. Here is the definition of *dazzling* provided by a typical dictionary and Beck and her colleagues' student-friendly definition:

Dictionary Definition: bright enough to deprive someone of sight temporarily

Student-Friendly Definition: If something is dazzling, that means that it's so bright that you can hardly look at it.

The following guidelines for writing student-friendly definitions are provided in Graves (2009):

- Keep both the phrasing and the words simple. Use language students understand.
- Often, student-friendly definitions are not comprehensive or fully precise. A single definition cannot capture all of a word's meaning.
- Often, student-friendly definitions are complete sentences.
- Often, a sample sentence using the word is a helpful addition to a simple definition.

Two recent dictionaries—the *Collins COBUILD Student Dictionary* (HarperCollins Publishers, 2005) and the *Longman Student Dictionary of American English* (Pearson Education Limited, 2006)—provide numerous examples.

Providing Rich and Varied Language Experiences   In order to build rich vocabularies, children at all grade levels need to be exposed to a wide range of words through listening, speaking, reading, and writing. In the early grades, before children can read texts with advanced vocabulary on their own, listening and speaking provide the primary means of introducing children to new words. Research suggests that both the quantity and quality of the words children encounter through listening and speaking can make a difference in children's early vocabulary knowledge. In the seminal study by Hart and Risley (1995, 2003), children of professional families heard 30 million more words from birth to age 3 than did children from welfare families. By age 3, children from professional families knew twice as many words as their peers from welfare families. This research provides evidence that children's vocabulary is related to the number of words they hear on a daily basis. Furthermore, Weizman and Snow (2001) found that children's vocabulary in kindergarten and second grade was related to the level of sophistication of words children heard in the home at age 5. This study suggests that children benefit from hearing sophisticated words in their environment. Accordingly, teachers should make a deliberate effort to include new and challenging words in their interactions with children.

Because children's literature often includes many new and challenging words that children may not hear in their everyday conversations with adults and peers, read alouds in which adults read storybooks to children can be an optimal way to build children's vocabulary. There is an extensive body of research on characteristics of effective read alouds (e.g., Beck & McKeown, 2007; Biemiller & Boote, 2006; Dickinson & Smith, 1994; Hargrave & Sénéchal, 2000; Penno, Wilkinson, & Moore, 2002; Reese & Cox, 1999; Silverman, 2007a; Whitehurst et al., 1988; Whitehurst et

al., 1994; Wasik, Bond, & Hindman, 2006). Several characteristics identified throughout this research literature are summarized in De Temple and Snow (2003) and Graves (2006). These are reviewed below.

First, read alouds should be interactive. During book reading, adults should ask children questions, highlight words children are unlikely to know, and scaffold children's understanding of the words and the text. They should also encourage children to respond to questions, elaborate on their responses, and ask questions of their own. Second, read aloud books should be read repeatedly. Repeated readings provide review and reinforcement of the content and words that children have heard in previous readings. Third, throughout read alouds, adults should focus on a relatively small number of words so that children can internalize the meanings of these words without being overwhelmed by too many new words at once. Fourth, adults should read books to children with fluency and appropriate intonation and expression. Children are more likely to be engaged and attentive when book reading is animated and lively. Fifth, adults should choose books for read alouds that are enjoyable for children and that include interesting and challenging words. Finally, read alouds should include analytic and non-immediate talk. In other words, adults should engage children in discussions that encourage children to reflect on the content of the book and make connections that go beyond the content of the book. For example, adults could ask children to make predictions as they read the book, discuss their reactions to the book, and relate events in the book to their personal experiences.

Beyond the early grades, children continue to learn words through listening and speaking, but the role of reading and writing in vocabulary development becomes increasingly important. Children's vocabulary development is associated with amount of text they read (Cunningham & Stanovich, 1991, 2003; Stanovich & Cunningham, 1992, 1993). Children learn words incidentally when they read (Nagy, Anderson, & Herman, 1987; Nagy, Herman, & Anderson, 1985). Therefore, the more they read, the more opportunities they have to learn new words (Anderson, Wilson, & Fielding, 1988; Elley, 1996). Ways to encourage children to read both in and out of school include having a well-stocked classroom library, a structured in-class independent reading time, and a program to reward reading outside of school. For example, teachers can require children to keep a log of the amount of reading they do outside of school and give children certificates or privileges for logging a certain amount of reading.

Though there is little research on the topic, facilitating word learning through writing instruction and writing activities is likely to benefit children's vocabulary development. Studies have shown a relationship between vocabulary and writing (Coker, 2006; Duin & Graves, 1987; Juel, 1988), but the nature of this relationship has not been fully explored (Shanahan, 2006). Instruction on purpose, audience, and word choice in writing may facilitate children's word learning by focusing their attention on how words are used in the texts they read and how the words that they use affect the clarity and quality of their own writing.

Teaching Individual Words   While it is impossible to teach every word children need to know, it is important to teach them some of the words they will encounter in texts in and out of school. Teaching individual words provides children with a foundation of words with which to understand and learn new words from what they read. It also signals to children that words are interesting and important, and, thereby, fosters their motivation to learn new words. There are many ways to effectively teach individual words. Different teaching methods may be used to teach different kinds of words, to meet different objectives, or to reach students with different learning styles (Graves, 2006, 2008, 2009). These methods may range from relatively thin to more in depth. However, research suggests that the extent of vocabulary instruction corresponds to the level of vocabulary learning. This body of research leads to a series of generalizations about teaching individual words. These generalizations are listed below, with those regarding relatively shallow instruction first and those involving deeper instruction coming later.

Minimal vocabulary instruction that includes only definitional information is better than no instruction. Research suggests that children can acquire basic knowledge of words through "thin instruction." Thin instruction may include giving children a list of words and asking them to look up the definitions of these words without any further instruction. For example, Parker (1984) compared the effect of a dictionary definition treatment with a no instruction treatment with children in sixth through eighth grades and found that children in the dictionary definition treatment knew more words than those in the control group. In another set of studies, Pany and her colleagues (1978, 1982), working with learning disabled students in grades four through six, found that children performed better on vocabulary tasks when they were given word meanings than when they were exposed to words either in or out of context without being given word meanings. However, Pany and her colleagues did not find pre- to post-test improvements on comprehension measures for children who were given word meanings. Only children who were given word meanings and were provided with added practice of word meanings showed growth on these measures. Therefore, thin instruction such as just giving children definitions of words results in shallow word learning. Children do not acquire the in-depth understanding of words they need to facilitate comprehension from this instruction. Furthermore, it is unlikely that they will be able to use words that they learn through "thin instruction" in their own speech and writing.

Instruction that combines definitional and contextual information is more powerful than instruction that includes only definitional information.. Knowing the meaning of a word and how it is used in context provides children with greater depth of knowledge. Stahl (1983), working with fifth-grade students, compared the effects of a definition-only treatment, a definition-plus-context treatment, and no instruction. He found that children in both the definition-only and definition-plus-context treatment outperformed children who received no instruction on measures of vocabulary and comprehension, but children in the definition-plus-context treatment scored even better on these measures than did children in the definition-only treatment.

Instruction that incorporates activating prior knowledge and comparing and contrasting words in addition to providing definitions and contextual information is more powerful than instruction that includes only definitions and contextual information. Engaging children in thinking critically about words leads them toward an even deeper understanding of the meaning of words and how various words are related. Two instructional methods that encourage critical thinking about words are semantic mapping and semantic feature analysis. In semantic mapping, children graphically represent associations (e.g., attributes, examples, and synonyms) of words. In semantic feature analysis, students use a chart to represent the relationships between words and concepts. Bos and Anders (1990), working with learning disabled junior high school students, compared semantic mapping, semantic feature analysis, and definition instruction. They found that children who received semantic mapping and semantic feature analysis instruction outperformed students who received definition instruction on short and long term vocabulary and comprehension measures.

Intensive and robust instruction is more powerful than instruction that is less intensive and robust. Research by Beck and McKeown and their colleagues (Beck, Perfetti, & McKeown, 1982; McKeown, Beck, Omanson, & Perfetti, 1983; McKeown, Beck, Omanson, & Pople, 1985) provides strong support for intensive and robust instruction that involves students in extensive and varied experiences with words. In a series of studies with fourth-grade students, they have found positive effects of "frequent, rich, and extended instruction" (Beck et al., 2002, p. 72). This instruction, in which individual words receive 15–30 minutes of attention over the course of a week, includes multiple opportunities for children to learn definitions of words, discuss word meanings, and apply their word knowledge in various contexts both in and out of the classroom. The studies by Beck and McKeown show that children who receive "frequent, rich, and extended instruction" outperform children who do not receive such instruction on vocabulary and comprehension measures; children who experience more encounters with words demonstrate greater word learning and comprehension than their peers who experience fewer encounters with words; and children who use words outside of the classroom learn them more fully than those who do not.

In a recent set of studies, Beck and McKeown (2007) extended their work in fourth grade to kindergarten and first grade. They investigated the effects of what they call rich instruction on children's word learning. Rich instruction occurred following read alouds and included contextualizing words in the context of the read-aloud story, explaining the meaning of the words, providing children with examples of the words in other contexts, guiding children to make judgments about the appropriateness of words, encouraging children to generate their own examples of words, having children repeat words so that they get a clear phonological representation of the word, and reviewing and reinforcing word learning. Children who received rich instruction learned more words than children who did not receive such instruction, and children who received instruction that included still more time spent on words and more encounters with those words learned more words than children who spent less time on rich instruction.

Teaching Word-Learning Strategies   As mentioned, it is impossible to teach every word children need to know. However, teaching word-learning strategies in addition to teaching individual words enables children to acquire knowledge of many words independently as they read. There are three primary word-learning strategies: using context clues, using word parts, and using the dictionary. These will be discussed below.

Context clues.   There is a substantial body of research that demonstrates the positive effects of teaching the use of context clues on children's word learning (e.g., Baumann, Edwards, Boland, Olejnik, & Kame'enui, 2003; Baumann et al., 2002; Buikema & Graves, 1993; Carnine, Kameenui, & Coyle, 1984; Patberg, Graves, & Stibbe, 1984). In a meta-analysis of 21 studies that investigated instruction in using context clues to derive word meaning, Fukkink and de Glopper (1999) found a medium effect size of .43.

Two studies by Baumann and his colleagues (Baumann et al., 2003; Baumann et al., 2002) have provided recent evidence of the effect of teaching context clues. In both studies, morphemic and context analysis were taught. In the first study (Baumann et al., 2002), fifth graders were assigned to one of three word-learning strategy conditions (i.e., morphemic analysis-only, context-only, or context and morphemic analysis) or an instructed control condition (i.e., students received instruction that did not include strategy instruction). In the word-learning strategy conditions, children were explicitly taught to use the strategies through verbal explanation, modeling, guided practice, and independent practice. Baumann et al. (2002) found a positive effect of the context-only condition on immediate and delayed tests of words targeted in instruction, but only a limited effect on tests of words that were not targeted in instruction.

In the second study by Baumann and his colleagues (2003), fifth-grade students were assigned to either a textbook vocabulary condition, in which students received explicit instruction on vocabulary from their textbook, or a morphemic-context condition, in which students learned to use morphemic and contextual analysis word-learning strategies. Adapting the work of Johnson and Pearson (1978) and Dale and O'Rourke (1986), Baumann et al. (2003) identified five types of context clues to teach children. These include

(a) definition, (b) synonym, (c) antonym, (d) example, and (e) general (i.e., the author provides a general clue about the meaning of a word). As in the former study, students were taught to use these types of context clues through explicit instruction and gradual release of responsibility. Baumann et al. (2003) found that children who received contextual and morphemic analysis instruction performed better than the children who received textbook vocabulary instruction on a delayed, but not on an immediate, post-test measure of inferring morphemically and contextually decipherable word meanings.

The Baumann et al. (2002, 2003) studies exemplify the fact that research on teaching context clues is not unequivocal. The positive effects of context clue instruction are inconsistent. Other studies have found varied results. For example, Patberg and Stibbe (1985) did not find positive effects of context clue instruction, and, similar to Baumann et al. (2003), Nash and Snowling (2006) found positive effects of context clue instruction on delayed post-tests but not on immediate post-tests of using context clues to infer word meanings. The effects of context clue instruction may depend on factors associated with instruction, texts and words, or child characteristics that need to be explored in further research. Furthermore, it needs to be understood that words are learned from context over the course of multiple encounters with words (Jenkins, Stein, & Wysocki, 1984; Jenkins & Wysocki, 1985) and that different kinds of context clues may be more or less helpful in inferring words meanings (Beck, McKeown, & McCaslin, 1983).

Word Parts.   The research on teaching students to use word parts is more consistent than that on teaching them to use context clues. For example, studies by Graves and Hammond (1980), Nicol, Graves, and Slater (1984), Wysocki and Jenkins (1987), and White, Sowell, and Yanagihara (1989) have clearly demonstrated the efficacy of teaching prefixes and/or suffixes. The recent work by Baumann et al. (2002, 2003) discussed above adds to this research base. In the 2002 study, Baumann et al. found that children in the morphemic-analysis condition performed better than children in the instructed control condition on immediate and delayed post-tests of words targeted in instruction and on words not targeted in instruction. In the 2003 study, Baumann et al. taught children to use a four-step word part strategy that included (a) looking for known root words, (b) looking for known prefixes, (c) looking for known suffixes, and (d) putting prefixes, root words, and suffixes together to derive the meanings of words. Baumann et al. (2003) also taught children eight specific affixes or affix families. Because morphemic and contextual analysis were taught together in this intervention, the independent contribution of teaching the word part strategy is unclear. However, considering that the approach used in the 2002 study was similar to the one used in the 2003 study, the potential of using this approach to foster children's word-learning seems promising.

Besides prefixes and derivational suffixes, other word parts that can be taught include inflections (e.g., the –s in *books* and the *–ed* in *learned*) and Latin and Greek roots (e.g., *tele* in *telephone* and *television* means "far" and *photo* in *photograph* and *photosynthesis* means "light"). Research suggests that children's awareness of these various word parts is developmental. Children typically acquire knowledge of inflectional endings at an early age and without specific instruction (Berko, 1958; Clark, 1993). They then acquire knowledge of prefixes and suffixes between fourth grade and high school (Anglin, 1993; Carlisle, 2000; Nagy, Diakidoy, & Anderson, 1993). As mentioned above, instruction on prefixes and suffixes tends to yield positive effects on children's word learning. It is not until college that students demonstrate a natural inclination to use Greek and Latin roots to derive word meaning (Kaye & Sternberg, 1983). There is little research on the effects of instruction on Greek and Latin roots, and, considering the vast number and low frequency of these roots, it may be that instruction on these roots has limited potential at least until the secondary grades.

Dictionary skills.   Research by Miller and Gildea (1987) showed that children often misunderstand dictionary definitions. This could be because dictionary definitions are often abstract and/or convoluted. As mentioned previously, there has been some research on the effect of modifying definitions so that they are more comprehensible. McKeown (1993) found that students' comprehension of dictionary definitions improves when the definitions are more transparent. However, Scott and Nagy (1997) found very little improvement from modifying definitions Therefore, providing students with dictionaries that include more student-friendly definitions could support their independent word-learning, but there is certainly no guarantee of this.

There has been little, if any, research on teaching children dictionary skills and strategies to use dictionaries on their own. What research there is has shown a relationship between using a dictionary and reading. For example, in research with children between the ages of 7 and 11, Beech (2004) found a relationship between the speed and accuracy with which children look up words and children's literacy ability. For another example, in research with college students learning a foreign language, Knight (1994) found that students who used the dictionary more scored higher on measures of reading comprehension than those who used only context to figure out word meanings. Knight (1994) also found that dictionary use may be more important for students with lower levels of vocabulary than for students with higher levels of vocabulary, perhaps because students with higher levels of vocabulary have more word knowledge to use when deriving word meaning from context. Therefore, given that there is some indication that using a dictionary and reading are related, it seems worthwhile for teachers to provide instruction on dictionary skills and strategies. These skills and strategies might include how to look up words, how to interpret dictionary definitions, and how to choose the appropriate definition among those provided for a given context.

Combining word-learning strategies.   In the Baumann et al. (2002) study discussed above, there was little difference between the morphemic-only, context-only, and morphemic-context instructional conditions. Baumann et al. concluded that "students were generally just as effective at inferring word meanings when the morphemic and contextual analysis instruction was provided in combination as when the instruction was provided separately" (p. 151). In fact, as is the case with comprehension strategies (Pressley, 2006), it may well be that using multiple word-learning strategies in tandem is more productive than using only one word-learning strategy alone.

Fostering Word Consciousness   As defined in Graves and Watts (2002), word consciousness is "an interest in and awareness of words and their meanings (p. 144)." Approaches to fostering word consciousness include modeling, recognizing, and encouraging adept word choice; promoting word play; providing rich and expressive instruction on words and their meanings; engaging students in investigations of word use and word meanings; and teaching students about words (Graves, 2006). Word consciousness is a relatively new concept. Therefore, there is little evidence that directly demonstrates the effect of promoting word consciousness on word learning. However, there is a substantial body of work that supports the theory that word consciousness may be an important part of vocabulary instruction.

Cultivating children's excitement about word learning resonates with the extensive research literature on motivation. The relationship between reading and motivation to read is becoming well-established (e.g., Guthrie et al., 2007; Guthrie & Wigfield, 1999, 2000; Wigfield & Eccles, 2002; National Research Council, 2004; Pressley et al., 2002). This research suggests that children's motivation to read has a positive effect on their growth in reading comprehension. While there is no specific research on the relationship between vocabulary and motivation, it is likely that children's motivation to learn word meanings has a similar positive effect on their vocabulary development. If children are motivated to attend to, reflect on, and inquire about unknown words, they are likely to learn more words as they hear them in their environment and read them in their texts.

Fostering children's awareness of words also aligns with recent research on the importance of metalinguistic awareness. Metalinguistic awareness is the ability to reflect on language and includes awareness of the morphological, syntactical, and semantic properties of words. The relationship between morphological awareness and reading comprehension has been established in research by Nagy and his colleagues (Nagy, Berninger, & Abbott, 2006; Nagy, Berninger, Abbott, Vaughan, & Vermeulen, 2003) and by Deacon and Kirby (2004), who found that morphological awareness is a significant predictor of reading comprehension. Furthermore, the relationship between syntactic awareness and reading comprehension has been shown by Nation, Clarke, Marshall, and Durand (2004), who found that weaknesses in syntactic awareness may contribute to difficulty in reading comprehension. Finally, research by Oullette (2006) suggests that semantic awareness, including awareness of synonyms and the semantic features and categories associated with words, is related to comprehension. Though there is little research on the effects of teaching children to be more aware of morphology, syntax, and semantics, it is likely that instruction that promotes such metalinguistic awareness will enable children to learn more words and to learn more about words they encounter.

Studies investigating the effects of vocabulary interventions that include a focus on word consciousness provide some evidence of the potential of instruction aimed at developing word consciousness in children. For example, as described in Scott and Nagy (2004), one intervention called *The Gift of Words* engaged fifth- and sixth-grade children in reading high-quality literature, identifying interesting words, discussing how words are used by talented authors, and experimenting with new and interesting words in their own writing. The positive effects of this intervention were seen in children's interest in words and in their writing.

Word consciousness was also part of an intervention evaluated by McKeown, Beck, Omanson, and Pople (1985). Working with fourth graders, these researchers compared three instructional conditions: (a) traditional vocabulary instruction, in which children were taught definitions and synonyms of words; (b) rich instruction, in which children explored various aspects of word meaning; and (c) extended/rich instruction, in which children not only explored various aspects of words but also were encouraged to be aware of words outside of the classroom. In extended/rich instruction, "students could earn points toward becoming a 'word wizard' by bringing evidence that they had seen, heard, or used target words independently" (p. 527). McKeown et al. found that children who were in the extended/rich instructional condition performed better than children in the other conditions on measures of fluency of word access and story comprehension.

A final example of an intervention that promotes word consciousness is the "Vocabulary Visits" approach implemented by Blachowicz and Obrochta (2005, 2007). In Vocabulary Visits, first-grade teachers took children on a virtual field trip in which, without leaving the classroom, they introduced children to thematic topics such as weather and animal habitats. They encouraged children to engage in extensive discussions of these topics, generate words that are related to these topics, and use these words in their own writing about the topics. The teachers prompted students' thinking about the topics and words related to the topics by asking questions, reading books, and showing posters with interesting visuals to stimulate discussion. Student growth was assessed by a pre- and post-intervention activity in which they made a list of words they know related to a particular topic. Students were able to write significantly more words at post-test than at pre-test.

Each of these interventions nurtured children's awareness of words and motivation to learn words. However,

each of these interventions included word consciousness activities within a multifaceted vocabulary program.

Vocabulary Instruction for English Learners   For the most part, vocabulary instruction that is effective with monolingual English speakers is effective with English learners (August, Carlo, Dressler, & Snow, 2005). For example, working with preschool children, Collins (2005) found that, just like native English speakers, English learners benefit from clear explanations of words during read alouds. For another example, Silverman (2007b) compared the vocabulary growth of native English speakers and English learners in kindergarten who received the same research-based vocabulary intervention. The intervention, termed the Multidimensional Vocabulary Program (MVP), included research-based practices such as introducing words through read alouds, providing definitions and explanations of words in rich contexts, and engaging children in comparing and contrasting words. It also included instructional strategies considered particularly important for English learners such as having children act out words, showing children pictures and real objects visually representing words, and having children pronounce words clearly on multiple occasions (Gertsen, Gersten, & Baker, 2000; Gersten & Geva, 2003; Roberts & Neal, 2004). Silverman (2007b) found that, compared to native English speakers, English learners learned the same number of target words *and* grew more in their general vocabulary knowledge. This suggests that instruction can address the needs of all learners and, at the same time, accelerate the growth of English learners so they can catch up to their peers in vocabulary.

Carlo et al. (2004) found similar results in their study with fifth-grade native English speakers and Spanish-speaking English learners. In this study, teachers implemented a program called the Vocabulary Improvement Program (VIP). In this program, individual words and strategies for using context, morphology, knowledge of multiple meanings, and cognates to infer word meanings were taught explicitly. The program was founded on four principles: (a) teachers should introduce new words in meaningful contexts, (b) teachers should expose children to new words in a variety of contexts, (c) teachers should focus on many aspects of words including spelling, pronunciation, morphology, syntax, and semantics, and (d) teachers should provide native Spanish speakers with access to the text's meaning through Spanish. Findings showed that the positive effects of the intervention on vocabulary and comprehension measures were as large for English learners as for native English speakers.

Both of these interventions employed instructional strategies thought to be especially helpful to English learners. Specifically, as supported by the report of the National Literacy Panel (August & Shanahan, 2006), the interventions provided clear and explicit instruction on vocabulary words and word learning strategies. August et al. (2005) recommend three additional instructional strategies for English learners. First, teachers should teach children to recognize and use cognates if their native language shares cognates with English. If children can transfer knowledge of words in their native language to words in English, they will have many fewer English words to learn. Second, teachers should teach children basic words in English. Children need a foundation of basic words to comprehend what they hear and read and so that they can use their knowledge of basic words to learn more advanced words. Third, teachers should provide children with ample review and reinforcement of words they are learning. In general, review and reinforcement is needed to internalize word meanings, and, for English learners who may have less exposure to English words compared to their peers, review and reinforcement may be even more important. In addition to these recommendations, as Goldenberg (2008) has noted, teachers should teach academic vocabulary to English learners so that they can access the content of instruction in school.

Special Considerations for Students with Reading Disabilities   As with English learners, instruction that is effective with children who do not have reading disabilities is effective with children who do (Bryant, Goodwin, Bryant, & Higgins, 2003). However, there are some important considerations to keep in mind when working on improving the vocabulary of children with reading disabilities (Baker, Simmons, & Kame'enui, 1998). First, because of their limited reading ability, children with reading disabilities do not engage in wide reading. Therefore, they have fewer opportunities to learn words from reading and develop and practice independent word-learning strategies in reading as compared to their peers. Second, due to the language-based nature of many reading disabilities, children with these disabilities often have more difficulty processing, retaining, and transferring information they have learned about words. Consequently, children with reading disabilities often have limited vocabulary knowledge compared to their peers. To address the vocabulary needs of children with reading disabilities, there are several specific strategies that have been identified (Bryant et al., 2003; Jitendra, Edwards, Sacks, & Jacobson, 2004). These are outlined below.

Instruction for students with reading disabilities should provide direct and explicit instruction on individual words (Jitendra et al., 2004; Swanson, Hoskyn, & Lee, 1999). In addition, instruction should be interactive and require deep processing of words rather than just superficial learning of words and their meanings (Bryant et al., 2003). For example, three instructional methods that are both interactive and facilitate deep processing include semantic mapping and semantic feature analysis (Bos & Anders, 1990) and computer-assisted instruction (Horton, Lovitt, & Givens, 1988; Johnson, Gersten, & Carnine, 1987). These methods have all been shown to have positive effects on the word learning of children with reading disabilities. As discussed earlier, semantic mapping and semantic feature analysis instruction involves teaching children to graphically represent associations and relationships between and among words. With well designed computer-assisted instruction,

students engage in independent, game-like activities that allow them to practice relating words to their meaning and using words in various contexts.

In addition, there are a few other important considerations for promoting the vocabulary of students with reading disabilities (Bryant et al., 2003; Jitendra et al., 2004). Students with reading disabilities often have difficulty remembering a large amount of information. Therefore, the number of words that are introduced and taught at one time should be relatively small, and instruction must be broken down into more manageable chunks. Furthermore, students with reading disabilities take longer to process information and have more difficulty generalizing learning to new contexts. Thus, instruction should provide them with extra time and added opportunities to practice using words that they are learning in various contexts. Finally, students with reading disabilities need more individualized instruction. Small group, peer-assisted, or individualized instruction should be used to provide children with reading disabilities focused attention on word learning.

Concluding Remarks

This then is our selective review of the literature most relevant to creating vocabulary programs and vocabulary instruction that will enhance vocabulary development in both learning disabled children and in other children. In this concluding section, again selective, we identify what we see as some of the most important research needed to further improve vocabulary instruction.

The number one priority, we believe, is a better understanding of the vocabulary learning task students face. We need to know what words make up the corpus that contemporary students will encounter in various texts and situations and the knowledge of these words in various age, linguistic, ethnic, and socioeconomic groups. The first step in this effort is a large, meaning-based set of frequency counts based on stratified random samples of written and oral American English. Such counts would be similar to those of Carrol et al. (1971) and Zeno et al. (1995) but based on a much larger corpus, sampling a variety of domains, differentiating words by meanings, and with word families tallied. Following the initial development of this corpus (which would ideally be a long-term effort that is periodically updated) would come studies of various groups of students' and adults' knowledge of the words in the corpus. Only when this task is completed will we know what it is that various kinds of learners need to learn as they face various literacy tasks.

A second priority is the development of better vocabulary assessment. Assessment is a topic that Pearson, Hiebert, and Kamil (2007) recently very cogently addressed in some detail and that we consequently did not address in our limited space. But it is definitely a high priority for research.

Our remaining priorities come from categories of instruction we have considered in organizing this review: providing rich and varied language experiences, teaching individual words, teaching word-learning strategies, fostering word consciousness, vocabulary instruction for English learners, and special considerations for students with reading disabilities.

What seems particularly needed in the area of providing rich and varied language experiences is research on long-term programs of read alouds, the most widely recommended instruction for helping primary grade children who enter school with very small vocabularies catch up with their peers. While studies of read-aloud programs have generally showed positive results, no study has lasted even a full year, and it will take multiple years to bring some children up to the level of their peers.

What seems particularly needed in the area of teaching individual words is research on less robust instruction. We know a great deal about how to create truly robust vocabulary instruction. Unfortunately, such instruction is very time consuming, and it is impossible to provide such instruction for anything like all of the words students need to learn.

Picking a single need in the area of teaching word-learning strategies is very difficult, but if we were to choose just one it would be for more research on teaching context clues. As Sternberg forcefully noted some years ago, "Most words are learned from context" (1987, p. 89). Yet as our review shows results of studies of teaching students to use context clues are mixed, and even positive studies produce only modest gains.

In the area of fostering word conscious, an area which has theoretical support and various sorts of indirect empirical support and support from studies in which fostering word consciousness is confounded with other types of vocabulary instruction, we need empirical studies that isolate the unique contribution of work on word consciousness.

Finally, in the areas of vocabulary instruction for English learners and special considerations for students with learning disabilities, there is good evidence that vocabulary instruction that is effective with other students is generally effective with these special populations. There is also general agreement that different kinds of English learners and different kinds of learning disabled students can profit from special instruction. What we need to know is which kinds of students can profit from what kinds of special instruction. All in all, we have come a long way in our knowledge of effective vocabulary instruction, but we have much further to go to truly understand how to promote the vocabulary of children at risk for experiencing difficulty in reading.

References

Anderson, R. C., & Nagy, W. E. (1992). The vocabulary conundrum. *American Educator* (Winter), 14–18, 44–47.

Anderson, R. C., Wilson, P. T., & Fielding, L.G. (1988). Growth in reading and how children spend their time outside of school. *Reading Research Quarterly, 23,* 285–303.

Anglin, J. M. (1993). Vocabulary development: A morphological analysis. *Monographs of the Society for Research in Child Development,* Serial No. 238, *58.*

August, D., & Shanahan, T. (Eds.). (2006). *Developing literacy In second-language learners: Report of the National Literacy Panel on Language-Minority Children and Youth.* Mahwah, NJ: Erlbaum.

August, D., Carlo, M., Dressler, C., & Snow, C. (2005). The critical role of vocabulary development for English language learners. *Learning Disabilities Research and Practice, 20,* 50–57.

Baker, S. K., Simmons, D. C., & Kame'enui, E. J., (1998). Vocabulary acquisition: Research bases. In D. C. Simmons & E. J. Kame'enui (Eds.), *What reading research tells us about children with diverse learning needs* (pp. 183–218). Mahwah, NJ: Erlbaum.

Baumann, J. F., Edwards, E. C., Boland E., Olejnik, S., & Kame'enui, E. J. (2003). Vocabulary tricks. Effects of instruction in morphology and context on fifth grade students' ability to derive and infer word meaning. *American Educational Research Journal, 40,* 447–494.

Baumann, J. F., Edwards, E. C., Font, G., Tereshinski, C. A., Kame'enui, E. J., & Olejnik, S. (2002). Teaching morphemic and contextual analysis to fifth-grade students. *Reading Research Quarterly, 37,* 150–176.

Baumann, J. F., Kaméenui, E. J., & Ash, G. E. (2003). Research on vocabulary instructing: n Voltaire redux. In J. Flood, D. Lapp, J. R. Squire, & J. M. Jensen (Eds.), *Handbook on research on teaching the English language arts* (2nd ed., pp. 752–785). Mahwah, NJ: Erlbaum.

Beck, I. L., & McKeown, M. G. (1991). Conditions of vocabulary acquisition. In P. D. Pearson (Ed.), *The handbook of reading research, Vol. 2* (pp. 789–814). New York: Longman.

Beck, I. L., McKeown, M. G., & Kucan, L. (2002). *Bringing words to life: Robust vocabulary instruction.* New York: Guilford.

Beck, I. L., McKeown, M. G., McCaslin, E. S. (1983). Vocabulary development: All contexts are not created equal. *Elementary School Journal, 83*(3), 177–181.

Beck, I. L., Perfetti, C. A., & McKeown, M. G. (1982). The effects of long-term vocabulary instruction on lexical access and reading comprehension. *Journal of Educational Psychology, 74,* 506–521.

Beck, I., & McKeown, M. (2007). Increasing young low-income children's oral vocabulary repertoires through rich and focused instruction. *Elementary School Journal, 107*(3), 251–271.

Becker, W. C. (1977). Teaching reading and language to the disadvantaged—What we have learned from field research. *Harvard Educational Review, 47,* 511–543.

Beech, J. R. (2004). Using a dictionary: Its influence on children's reading, spelling, and phonology. *Reading Psychology, 25*(1), 19–36.

Berko, J. (1958). The child's learning of English morphology. *Word, 14,* 150–177.

Biemiller, A. (2009). *Words worth teaching.* Columbus, OH: McGraw-Hill.

Biemiller, A., & Boote, C. (2006). An effective method for building meaning vocabulary in primary grades. *Journal of Educational Psychology, 98,* 44–62.

Biemiller, A., & Slonim, N. (2001). Estimating root word and normative vocabulary growth in normative and advanced populations. Evidence for a common sequence of vocabulary acquisition. *Journal of Educational Psychology, 93,* 498–520.

Blachowicz, C., & Fisher, P. (2000). Vocabulary. In R. Barr, M. L. Kamil, P. Mosenthal, & P. D. Pearson (Eds.), *The handbook of reading research, Vol. III* (pp. 604–632).New York: Longman.

Blachowicz, C., & Obrochta, C. (2005). Vocabulary visits: Virtual field trips for content vocabulary development. *Reading Teacher, 59,* 262–268.

Blachowicz, C., & Obrochta, C. (2007). "Tweeking practice": Modifying read-alouds to enhance content vocabulary learning in grade 1. In J. Worthy, B. Maloch, J. V. Hoffman, D. L. Schallert, & C. M. Fairbanks (Eds.), *56th Yearbook of the National Reading Conference* (pp. 111–121). Oak Creek, WI: NRC

Bos, C. S., & Anders, P. L. (1990). Effects of interactive vocabulary instruction on the vocabulary learning and reading comprehension of junior-high learning disabled students. *Learning Disability Quarterly, 13,* 31–42.

Bryant, D. P., Goodwin, M., Bryant, B. R., & Higgins, K. (2003). Vocabulary instruction for students with learning disabilities: A review of the research. *Learning Disability Quarterly, 26*(2), 117–128.

Buikema, J. A., & Graves, M. F. (1993). Teaching students to use context cues to infer word meanings. *Journal of Reading, 36,* 450–457.

Calfee, R. C., & Drum, P. A. (1986). Research on teaching reading. In

M.D. Wittrock (Ed.), *Handbook of research on teaching* (3rd ed., pp. 804–849). New York: Macmillan.

Carlisle, J. F. (2000). Awareness of the structure and meaning of morphologically complex words: Impact on reading. *Reading & Writing, 12*(3), 169–190.

Carlo, M. S., August, D., McGlaughlin, B., Snow, C. E., Dressler, C., Lippman, D. N., et al. (2004). Closing the gap: Addressing the vocabulary needs of English-language learners in bilingual and mainstream classes. *Reading Research Quarterly, 39,* 188–215.

Carnine, D., Kameenui, E. J., & Coyle, G. (1984). Utilization of contextual information in determining the meaning of unfamiliar words in context. *Reading Research Quarterly, 19,* 188–202.

Carroll, J. B, Davies, P., & Richman, B. (1971). *The American Heritage word frequency book.* New York: Houghton Mifflin.

Carroll, J. B. (1971). *Learning from verbal discourse in educational media. A review of the literature.* Princeton, NJ: Educational Testing Service.

Chall, J. S., & Jacobs, V. A. (2003). The classic study on poor children's fourth-grade slump. *American Educator, 27*(1), 14–15, 44.

Chall, J. S., Jacobs, V. A., & Baldwin, L. E. (1990). *The reading crisis: Why poor children fall behind.* Cambridge, MA: Harvard University Press.

Clark, E. V. (1993). *The lexicon in acquisition.* Cambridge, UK: Cambridge University Press.

Clifford, G . J. (1978). Words for schools: The applications in education of the vocabulary researches of Edward L. Thorndike. In P. Suppes (Ed.), *Impact of research on education: Some case studies* (pp. 107–198). Washington, DC: National Academy of Education.

Coker, D. (2006). Impact of first-grade factors on the growth and outcomes of urban schoolchildren's primary-grade writing. *Journal of Educational Psychology, 98,* 471–488.

Collins COBUILD new student's dictionary. (2005, 3rd ed.). Glasglow, Scotland: HarperCollins.

Collins, M. (2005). ESL preschoolers' English vocabulary acquisition from storybook reading. *Reading Research Quarterly, 40,* 406–408.

Cronbach, L. J. (1942). An analysis of techniques for diagnostic vocabulary testing. *Journal of Educational Research, 36,* 206–217.

Cunningham, A. E., & Stanovich, K. E. (1991). Tracking the unique effects of print exposure in children: Associations with vocabulary, general knowledge, and spelling. *Journal of Educational Psychology, 83,* 264–274.

Cunningham, A. E., & Stanovich, K. E. (2003). Reading matters: How reading English influences cognition. In J. Flood, D. Lapp, J. R. Squire, & J. M. Jensen (Eds.), *Handbook of teaching the English language arts* (2nd ed., pp. 666–675). Mahwah, NJ: Erlbaum.

Dale, E., & O'Rourke, J. (1981). *The living word vocabulary.* Chicago: World Book-Childcraft International.

Dale, E., & O'Rourke, J. (1986). *Vocabulary building: A process approach.* Columbus, OH: Zaner-Bloser.

De Temple, J., & Snow, C. E. (2003). Learning words from books. In A. van Kleeck & S. A. Stahl (Eds.), *On reading books to children: Parents and teachers Center for Improvement of Early Reading Achievement* (pp. 16–36). Mahwah, NJ: Erlbaum.

Deacon, S. H., & Kirby, J. (2004). Morphological awareness: Just "more phonological"? The roles of morphological and phonological awareness in reading development. *Applied Psycholinguistics, 25,* 223–238.

Dickinson, D., & Smith, M. (1994). Long-term effects of preschool teachers' book readings on low-income children's vocabulary and story comprehension. *Reading Research Quarterly, 29*(2), 104–122.

Duin, A. H., & Graves, M. F. (1987). The effects of intensive vocabulary instruction on expository writing. *Reading Research Quarterly, 22,* 311–330.

Dupuy, H. (1974). *The rationale, development, and standardization of a basic word vocabulary test* (DHEW Publications N0. HRA74-1334). Washington, DC: U. S. Government Printing Office.

Elley, W. B. (1989). Vocabulary acquisition from listening to stories. *Reading Research Quarterly, 24,* 174–187.

Elley, W. B. (1996). Using book floods to raise literacy levels in developing countries. In V. Greaney (Ed.), *Promoting reading in developing countries* (pp. 148–162). Newark, DE: International Reading Association.

Fukkink, R. G., & de Glopper, K. (1999). Effects of instruction in deriving word meanings from context: A meta-analysis. *Review of Educational Research, 68,* 450–469.

Gersten, R., & Baker, S. (2000). What we know about effective instructional practices for English-language learners. *Exceptional Children, 66*(4), 454–470.

Gersten, R., & Geva, E. (2003). Teaching reading to early language learners. *Educational Leadership, 60*(7), 44–49.

Goldenberg, C. (2008, Summer). Teaching English language learners: What the research does and does not say. *American Educator, 32*(2), 8–23, 42–44

Graves, M. F. (1986). Vocabulary learning and instruction. In E. Z. Rothkopf (Ed.), *Review of research in education* (Vol. 13, pp. 49–90). Washington, DC: American Educational Research Association.

Graves, M. F. (2006*). The vocabulary book: Learning and instruction.* New York: Teachers College Press, International Reading Association, National Council of Teachers of English.

Graves, M. F. (2008). Teaching individual words. In A. E. Farstrup & S. J. Samuels (Eds.), *What research has to say about the teaching of vocabulary.* Newark, DE: International Reading Association.

Graves, M. F. (2009). *Teaching individual words: One size does not fit all.* New York: Teachers College Press and International Reading Association.

Graves, M. F., & Hammond, H. K. (1980). A validated procedure for teaching prefixes and its effect on students' ability to assign meaning to novel words. In M. L. Kamil & A. J. Moe (Eds.), *Perspectives on reading research and instruction* (pp. 135–141). Washington, DC: National Reading Conference.

Graves, M. F., & Watts-Taffe, S. M. (2002). The place of word consciousness in a research-based vocabulary program. In S. J. Samuels & A. E. Farstrup (Eds.), *What research has to say about reading instruction* (3rd ed., pp. 140–165). Newark, DE: International Reading Association.

Guthrie, J. T., & Wigfield, A. (1999). How motivation fits into a science of reading. *Scientific Studies of Reading, 3*(3), 199–205.

Guthrie, J. T., & Wigfield, A. (2000). Effects of integrated instruction on motivation and strategy use in reading. *Journal of Educational Psychology, 92*(2), 331–41.

Guthrie, J. T. Hoa, A., Laurel W., Wigfield, A., Tonks, S. M., Humenick, N. M., & Littles, E. (2007). Reading motivation and reading comprehension growth in the later elementary years. *Contemporary Educational Psychology, 32*(3), 282–313.

Hargrave, A., & Sénéchal, M. (2000). A book reading intervention with preschool children who have limited vocabularies: The benefits of regular reading and dialogic reading. *Early Childhood Research Quarterly, 15*(1), 75–90.

Hart, B., & Risley, T. R. (2003, Spring). The early catastrophe: The 30 million word gap. *American Educator, 27* (1), 4–9.

Hart, B., & Risley, T. R. (1995). *Meaningful differences in the everyday experiences of young American children.* Baltimore, MD: Brookes.

Hartman, G. W. (1946). Further evidence of the unexpected large size of recognition vocabularies among college students. *Journal of Educational Psychology, 37,* 436–439.

Hiebert, E. H. (2005). In pursuit of an effective, efficient vocabulary program. In E. H. Hiebert & M. Kamil (Eds.), *Teaching and learning vocabulary: Bringing research to practice* (pp. 243–263). Mahwah, NJ: Erlbaum.

Horton, S. V., Lovitt, T. C., & Givens, A. (1988). A computer-based vocabulary program for three categories of student. *British Journal of Educational Technology, 19*(2), 131–143.

Jenkins J. R., Stein, M. L., & Wysocki, K. (1984). Learning vocabulary through reading. *American Educational Research Journal, 21,* 767–787.

Jenkins, J. R., & Wysocki, K. (1985). *Deriving word meanings from context,* Unpublished manuscript, University of Washington, Seattle.

Jitendra, A. K., Edwards, L. L., Sacks, G., & Jacobson, L.A. (2004). What research says about vocabulary instruction for students with learning disabilities. *Exceptional Children, 70*(3), 299–322.

Johnson, D. D., & Pearson. P. D. (1978). *Teaching reading vocabulary*. New York: Holt, Rinehart & Winston.

Johnson, G., Gersten, R., & Carnine, D. (1987). Effects of instructional design variables on vocabulary acquisition of LD students: A study of computer-assisted instruction. *Journal of Learning Disabilities, 20*(4), 412–438.

Juel, C. (1988). Learning to read and write: A longitudinal study of 54 children from first through fourth grades. *Journal of Educational Psychology, 80,* 437–447.

Kaye, D. B., & Sternberg, R. J. (1983). *The development of lexical decomposition ability.* Unpublished manuscript.

Kirkpatrick, E. A. (1891). The number of words in an ordinary vocabulary. *Science, 18,* 107–108.

Knight, S. (2004). Dictionary: The tool of last result in foreign language reading? A new perspective. *Modern Language Journal, 78*(3), 285–299.

Longman student dictionary of American English. (2006). London: Pearson Education Limited.

Lorge, I., & Chall, J. (1963). Estimating the size of vocabularies of children and adults: An analysis of methodological issues. *Journal of Experimental Education, 32,* 147–157.

McKeown, M. G. (1993). Creating Effective Definitions for Young Word Learners. *Reading Research Quarterly, 28,* 16–31.

McKeown, M. G., Beck, I. L., Omanson, R. C. & Perfetti, C. A. (1983). The effects of long-term vocabulary instruction on reading comprehension: A replication. *Journal of Reading Behavior, 15,* 3–18.

McKeown, M. G., Beck, I. L., Omanson, R. C., & Pople, M. T. (1985). Some effects of the nature and frequency of vocabulary instruction on the knowledge and use of words. *Reading Research Quarterly, 20,* 522–535.

Miller, G. A., & Gildea, P. M. (1987). How children learn words. *Scientific American, 257*(3), 94–99.

Miller, G. A., & Wakefield, P. C. (1993). Commentary on Anglin's analysis of vocabulary growth. In J. M Anglin, Vocabulary development: A morphological analysis. *Monographs of the Society for Research in Child Development, 59*(10), 167–175.

Nagy, W. E., & Anderson, R. C. (1984). How many words are there in printed school English? *Reading Research Quarterly, 19,* 304–330.

Nagy, W. E., Anderson, R. C., & Herman, P. A. (1987). Learning word meanings from context during normal reading. *American Educational Research Journal, 24,* 237–270.

Nagy, W. E., Berninger, V. W., Abbott, R. D. (2006). Contributions of morphology beyond phonology to literacy outcomes of upper elementary and middle school students. *Journal of Educational Psychology, 98,* 134–147.

Nagy, W .E., Berninger, V., Abbot, R., Vaughan, K., & Vermeulen, K. (2003). Relationship of morphology and other language skills to literacy skills in at-risk second-grade readers and at-risk fourth grade writers. *Journal of Educational Psychology, 95,* 730–742.

Nagy, W. E., Diakidoy, I. N., & Anderson, R. C. (1993). The acquisition of morphology: Learning the contributions of suffixes to the meanings of derivatives. *Journal of Reading Behavior, 25,* 155–170.

Nagy, W. E., & Herman, P. A. (1987). Breadth and depth of vocabulary knowledge: Implications for acquisition and instruction. In M. G. McKeown & M. E. Curtis (Eds.), *The nature of vocabulary acquisition* (pp. 19–35). Hillsdale, NJ: Erlbaum.

Nagy, W. E., Herman, P. A., & Anderson, R. C. (1985). Learning words from context. *Reading Research Quarterly, 20,* 233–253.

Nagy, W. E., & Scott, J. A. (2000). Vocabulary processes. In M. Kamil, P. Mosenthal, P. D. Pearson, & R. Barr (Eds.), *Handbook of reading research* (Vol. 3, pp. 269–284). New York: Longman.

Nash, H., & Snowling, M. (2006). Teaching new words to children with poor existing vocabulary knowledge: A controlled evaluation of the definition and context methods. *International Journal of Language and Communication Disorders, 41*(3), 335–354.

National Research Council. (2004). *Engaging schools: Fostering high school students' motivation to learn.* Washington, DC: National Academies Press.

Nicol, J. A., Graves, M. F., & Slater, W. H. (1984). *Building vocabulary through prefix instruction.* Unpublished manuscript, University of Minnesota, Minneapolis.

Oullette, G. P. (2006). What's meaning got to do with it The role of vocabulary in word reading and reading comprehension. *Journal of Educational Psychology, 98,* 554–566.

Pany, D., & Jenkins, J. R. (1978). Learning word meanings: A comparison of instructional procedures. *Learning Disability Quarterly, 1,* 21–32.

Pany, D., Jenkins, J. R., & Schreck, J. (1982). Vocabulary instruction: Effects on word knowledge and comprehension. *Learning Disability Quarterly, 5,* 202–215.

Parker, S. L. (1984). *A comparison of four types of initial vocabulary instruction* (Unpublished master's thesis). University of Minnesota, Minneapolis.

Patberg, J. P., & Stibbe, M. A. (1985, December). *The effects of contextual analysis instruction on vocabulary learning.* Paper presented at the annual meeting of the National Reading Conference, San Diego, CA.

Patberg, J. P., Graves, M. F., & Stibbe, M. A. (1984). Effects of active teaching and practice in facilitating students' use of context clues. In J. A. Niles & L. A. Harris (Eds.), *Changing perspectives in research in reading/language processing and instruction* (pp. 146–151). Rochester, NY: National Reading Conference.

Pearson, P. D., Hiebert, E. H., & Kamil, M. (2007). Vocabulary assessment: What we know and what we need to learn. *Reading Research Quarterly, 42,* 282–296.

Penno, J. F., Wilkinson, I. A. G., & Moore, D. W. (2002). Vocabulary acquisition from teacher explanation and repeated listening to stories: Do they overcome the Matthew effect? *Journal of Educational Psychology, 94,* 23–33.

Pressley, M. (2006). *Reading instruction that works* (3rd ed.). New York: Guilford.

Pressley, M., Dolezal, S. E., Raphael, L. M., Mohan, L., Roehrig, A. D., & Bogner, K. (2002). *Motivating primary-grade students.* New York: Guilford.

Reese, E., & Cox, A., (1999). Quality of adult book reading affects children's emergent literacy. *Developmental Psychology, 35*(1), 20–28.

Roberts, T. & Neal, H. (2004). Relationships among preschool English language learners' oral proficiency in English, instructional experience and literacy development. *Contemporary Educational Psychology, 29,* 283–311.

Scott, J. A, & Nagy, W. E. (1997). Understanding the definitions of unfamiliar verbs. *Reading Research Quarterly, 32*(2), 184–200.

Shanahan, T. (2006). Relations among oral language, reading, and writing development. In C. A. MacArthur, S. Graham, & J. Fitzgerald (Eds.), *Handbook of writing research* (pp. 171–186). New York: Guilford.

Shibles, B. H. (1959). How many words does the first grade child know? *Elementary English, 31,* 42–47.

Silverman, R. (2007a.) Vocabulary development of English-language and English-only learners in kindergarten. *Elementary School Journal, 107,* 365–383.

Silverman, R. (2007b.) A comparison of three methods of vocabulary instruction during read-alouds in kindergarten. *Elementary School Journal, 108,* 97–113.

Snow, C. E., & Kim, Y. (2007). Large problem spaces: The challenge of vocabulary for English language learners. In R. K. Wagner, A. E. Muse, & K. R. Tasnnenbaum (Eds.), *Vocabulary acquisition: Implications for reading comprehension* (123–139). New York: Guilford.

Stahl, S. A. (1983). Differential word knowledge and reading comprehension. *Journal of Reading Behavior, 15*(4), 33–50.

Stahl, S. A., & Nagy, W. (2006). *Teaching word meanings.* Mahway, NJ: Erlbaum.

Stanovich, K. E., & Cunningham, A. E. (1992). Studying the consequences of literacy within a literate society: The cognitive correlates of print exposure. *Memory and Cognition, 20,* 51–68.

Stanovich, K. E., & Cunningham, A. E. (1993). Where does knowledge come from? Associations between print exposure and information acquisition. *Journal of Educational Psychology, 85,* 211–229.

Sternberg, R. J. (1987). Most vocabulary is learned from context. In M. G. McKeown & M. E. Curtis (Eds.), *The nature of vocabulary acquisition* (pp. 89–105). Hillsdale, NJ: Erlbaum.

Swanson, H. L., Hoskyn, M., & Lee, C. (1999). *Intervention for students with learning disabilities.* New York: Guilford.

Wasik, B., Bond, M., & Hindman, A. (2006). The effects of a language and literacy intervention on Head Start children and teachers. *Journal of Educational Psychology, 98,* 63–74.

Weizman, Z., & Snow, C. (2001). Lexical output as related to children's vocabulary acquisition: Effects of sophisticated exposure and support for meaning. *Developmental Psychology, 37,* 265–279.

White, T. G., Graves, M. F., & Slater, W. H. (1990). Growth of reading vocabulary in diverse elementary schools: Decoding and word meaning. *Journal of Educational Psychology, 82,* 281–290.

White, T. G., Slater, W. H., & Graves, M .F. (1989). Yes/no method of vocabulary assessment: Valid for whom and useful for what? In S. McCormick & J. Zutell (Eds.), *Cognitive and social perspectives for literacy research and instruction* (pp. 391–398). Chicago: National Reading Conference.

White, T. G., Sowell, J., & Yanagihara, A. (1989). Teaching elementary students to use word-part clues. *The Reading Teacher, 42,* 302–308.

Whitehurst, G. J., Arnold, D. S., Epstein, J. N., Angell, A.L., Smith, M., & Fischel, J. E. (1994). A picture book reading intervention in day care and home for children from low-income families. *Developmental Psychology, 30,* 697–689.

Whitehurst, G. J., Falcon, F., Lonigan, C. J., Fischel, J. E., DeBaryshe, D. B., Valdez-Menchaca, M. C., et al. (1988). Accelerating language development through picture book reading. *Developmental Psychology, 24,* 552–559.

Wigfield, A., & Eccles, J.S., (2002). Expectancy—value theory of achievement motivation. *Contemporary Educational Psychology, 25*(1), 68–81.

Wysocki, K., & Jenkins, J. R. (1987), Deriving word meanings through morphological generalization. *Reading Research Quarterly, 22,* 66–81.

Zeno, S. M., Ivens, S. H., Millard, R. T., & Duvvuri, R. (1995). *The educator's word frequency guide.* Brewster, NY: Touchstone Applied Science Associates.

30

Interventions to Enhance Narrative Comprehension

Janice F. Almasi
University of Kentucky

Barbara Martin Palmer
Mount Saint Mary's University

Angie Madden and Susan Hart
University of Kentucky

While several research syntheses have examined the types of instruction that facilitate struggling readers' comprehension, others have examined the reading differences between low-achieving students with and without learning disabilities, but have not focused exclusively on reading comprehension (e.g., Fuchs, Fuchs, Mathes, & Lipsey, 2000). Others have examined research related to comprehension, including reviews of oral reading fluency (e.g., Rasinski & Hoffman, 2003) and those focused on narrative and expository text (e.g., Edmonds et al., 2009; Gersten, Fuchs, Williams, & Baker, 2001; Mastropieri & Scruggs, 1997; Mastropieri, Scruggs, Bakken, & Whedon, 1996), but none have focused exclusively on interventions for struggling readers to enhance narrative comprehension.

The goal of this chapter is to synthesize findings of research from 1987–2007 in which instructional interventions were used to improve struggling readers' narrative comprehension. To accomplish this task, we first define the parameters of our synthesis by including our perspectives on reading comprehension, struggling readers, characteristics of narrative representation and comprehension, and interventions.

Defining Reading Comprehension

As critical as comprehension is to the reading process, trend analyses of reading research showed a decline in published research on comprehension throughout the 1990s (Gaffney & Anderson, 2000). A resurgence of interest in comprehension occurred when the U. S. Department of Education, Office of Educational Research and Improvement convened the RAND Reading Study Group (RRSG) in 1999 (RAND, 2006). RRSG was comprised of esteemed reading researchers. The group's goal was to propose a national reading research agenda in the area of reading comprehension (Snow & Sweet, 2003). It began its work by examining current research and theory to define reading comprehension.

RRSG defined comprehension as "the process of simultaneously *extracting* and *constructing* meaning through interaction and involvement with written language" (Snow & Sweet, 2003, p. 10). In so doing they acknowledged that comprehension involves the ability to decode and identify words as well as the ability to connect prior knowledge with text to build new meanings. This perspective recognizes the importance of decoding to reading comprehension, but notes that decoding is insufficient by itself to facilitate understanding (Pressley, 2000; Snow & Sweet, 2003).

In 2002, the U. S. Department of Education, Institute of Education Sciences established the What Works Clearinghouse (WWC) as a means of providing educators with resources to make informed decisions about practice based on research evidence on the effectiveness of interventions. The WWC defined reading comprehension as the "understanding of the meaning of a passage and the context in which the words occur" (U. S. Department of Education, 2007, ¶ 12). Like the RRSG definition, this definition recognized the role of decoding and meaningful context to comprehension. However, it also included the ability to translate text into speech by emphasizing the role of understanding spoken language. "All struggling readers have difficulty with either language comprehension or decoding or both" (U. S. Department of Education, 2007, ¶ 12). Thus, this definition includes a focus not only on print literacy, but also on language.

More recently, the National Assessment Governing Board (NAGB, 2007), the policy-making body for the National Assessment for Educational Progress (NAEP), redesigned the framework of NAEP for 2009. The group defined reading as "an active and complex process that involves: understanding written text; developing and interpreting meaning; and using meaning as appropriate to type of text, purpose, and situation" (NAGB, 2007, p. 2). These ideas draw upon the notion that comprehension is central to the reading process and involves not just gaining a literal understanding of text by recalling and locating details in the text, but also integrating the knowledge gained from text with one's own knowledge of other texts and background knowledge in order to make more complex inferences. As well, the notion of "using meaning" refers to using the ideas gained from text to meet particular needs in particular situations. Like the RRSG definition, the NAGB definition focuses more on print literacy, suggesting the complexity of the comprehension process and the importance of higher level thinking to that process.

The latter view is grounded in reader response theory (e.g., Fish, 1980; Marshall, 2000; Rosenblatt, 1978), which further defines comprehension as an event in which the reader, text, and context are in transaction with one another. Meaning does not reside within the reader as a result of decoding print and making inferences, rather meaning resides in the event (Rosenblatt, 1978). The event consists of the reader, text, and context as active co-participants in the meaning making process. That is, there is a recursivity to the event in which the *reader*, *text*, and *context* shape and are shaped by one another. We used these three elements to define and delimit the remaining parameters of this chapter.

Characteristics of Struggling Readers

Trend analyses of the National Assessment of Educational Progress (NAEP) data show average reading scores have changed little during the past two decades (Campbell, Hombo, & Mazzeo, 2000). Although fourth graders' average reading scale scores were slightly higher in 2005 than in 1992, and the percentage of students performing at or above proficient levels increased during that time, reading scores were not significantly different in 2005 than scores in 1992 (Perie, Grigg, & Donahue, 2005). Although these data suggest reading achievement has shown little growth, researchers have become increasingly concerned not only with examining interventions for struggling readers, but also with issues of race, class, gender, and dialect (Gaffney & Anderson, 2000) that keep underserved populations in the U.S. from achieving at the same rate as majority populations (Perie et al., 2005). Thus, the characteristics of a struggling reader encompass a variety of reader characteristics that go beyond reading ability and diagnosed learning disabilities, to include examinations of institutional and instructional circumstances that may inhibit, marginalize, or preclude individuals from achieving at similar rates. While there are studies of such institutional and instructional circumstances in elementary schools, for illustrative purposes we provide an example of instances in which the curriculum in middle and upper grades is not aligned with adolescents' life experiences. These studies offer evidence that instruction is often not responsive to the cultural, gender, racial, and linguistic differences existing among students. Moje (2000), for example, showed how five gang-affiliated youth (who would be identified as "at risk" for reading failure in traditional school literacies) used sophisticated literacy practices to communicate and

transform the social spaces in which they lived. However, the social space they inhabit, and their literacy practices, are not valued or privileged in schools. Thus, these adolescents and the literacy practices they value are marginalized by traditional school cultures. In essence, as Alvermann and Eakle (2003) have noted, "… traditional school culture is *making* struggling readers out of some youth, especially those who have turned their backs on a version of reading and writing commonly referred to as school literacy" (p. 19). Thus, our use of the term *struggling reader* includes those who struggle to read for many reasons, whether the struggle is related to cognitive, social, affective, societal, or institutional issues.

As well, our examination of research considered the age of study participants in that we examined studies that included readers at elementary, middle, and high school levels. By our definition, however, studies had to include participants who were reading below grade level.

Characteristics of Text: Narrative Representation and Comprehension

Text is a medium of expression and communication. From this perspective, text consists of both linguistic and semiotic forms (e.g., Hartman, 1995). While both types of text are essential forms of communication and require an active reader to comprehend them, this chapter's primary focus is on studies using linguistic forms of narrative text.

Graesser, Golding, and Long (1991) defined narratives as "event-based experiences" (p. 174) that can either be stored in memory, transmitted orally or in writing to an audience, and organized as knowledge structures that can be anticipated. Key to this definition is the notion of communication and interaction between speaker/writer and listener/reader. Ochs (1997), like reader response theorists, took these ideas a step further by suggesting that narrative is essentially a "co-authorship" (p.185) in which readers and interlocutors jointly influence its production, and that such production has the potential to transform individuals and relationships.

Narrative texts have a particular structure that generally consists of setting, characters, initiating events, problem or goal, events aimed at resolving the problem or attaining the goal, and a resolution (Mandler & Johnson, 1977). Wolf (2004) further defined narrative by not only including story grammar elements, but also theme, point of view, style, and tone. Bloome (2003), on the other hand, has argued that all texts can be considered narrative, even those typically classified as "expository," because all texts have a temporal history that reflects past events and future events. It is incumbent upon the reader to critically examine the text to identify the underlying events that may not be readily apparent in the structure of the text.

Historically, story grammar (e.g., Mandler & Johnson, 1977; Stein & Glenn, 1979) was the first theory of narrative representation. Rooted in cognitive psychology, story grammar provided the first formal method of analyzing stories into their constituent parts (Graesser et al., 1991). Story grammar assigns a hierarchical episodic structure to the information contained in a text based on the hypothesis that superordinate information is more important, and possibly more accessible, than subordinate information (Graesser et al., 1991). Work by Mandler and Johnson (1977) and Stein and Glenn (1979) established that stories generally consist of a beginning in which the protagonist is introduced in a setting, followed by an initiating event to which the protagonist responds by establishing a problem or goal. The protagonist then attempts to achieve the goal, which ultimately leads to a resolution. Mandler and Johnson (1977) contended that having a schema for narrative structure directs attention to particular aspects of incoming information, helps readers keep track of what they have read, and indicates when a given part of a story is complete or incomplete so it can be stored or held in memory until more material is encountered. Short and Ryan (1984) found that learning about narrative structure helps students' memory and recall of text. Thus, comprehension, from this perspective is limited primarily to literal recall. Another drawback of story grammar is that it is limited to stories in the oral tradition (Graesser et al., 1991). Graesser and colleagues (1991) further noted that tests of story grammar generally determined how well it could predict the importance of statements in the text. Those studies suggested that most predictions of story grammar could be explained by content features such as world knowledge of planning, motives, social action, and causality rather than the structural aspect of story grammar.

Other theories of narrative representation such as Trabasso's causal network theory and Graesser's conceptual graph structures rely on networks rather than hierarchical tree structures used in story grammars, to capture the properties of narrative (Graesser et al., 1991). In contrast with story grammars, causal network theory was applied to a broad range of narratives with the goal of determining the causal links in the text's structure. Using this method of representing narrative enables one to examine how causal inferences are represented in text, which provides more explicit links to the processes underlying higher levels of comprehension. Assumptions underlying causal network theory include a dependence on background world knowledge and the notion that the model for text is continually updated and refined during comprehension. Evidence has suggested that causal network theory is capable of predicting the importance of statements in some narratives and that it plays a role in question-answering and question-asking tasks (Graesser et al., 1991).

High point analysis offers another perspective on narrative representation (Labov, 1972; Peterson & McCabe, 1983). In contrast with the episodic structure of narrative text described in story grammar analysis, Labov (1972) described the structure of narrative syntax as individuals communicated personal narratives during casual speech. Whereas story grammar analysis uses propositions as the unit of analysis, high point analysis uses clauses. Labov

(1972) defined narrative as one method of communicating temporal events. The overall structure of a fully formed narrative, as described by Labov (1972), includes an abstract, in which the narrator begins with a clause or two that summarizes the whole story. The abstract is followed by the orientation in which the time, place, people, and the activities, or their situation are described. The orientation leads to a complicating action, which is often delayed by evaluation. The action builds in an orderly series of events and is often suspended at the high point to emphasize its importance. While the action is suspended, the high point is evaluated in a sustained manner. The evaluation serves as a means by which the narrator explains the point of the narrative, or why it was being told. The evaluation occurs just prior to the resolution, which is often followed by a coda, in which the narrator returns the listener back to the present. Labov's (1972) characterization of the structure of personal narratives has at times been referred to as the "classic" narrative pattern (Peterson & McCabe, 1983). In their study of the structure of the narratives of 96 white children, Peterson and McCabe (1983) identified six other patterns in addition to the classic pattern described by Labov. These patterns included: (a) Ending-at-the-high point, in which the narrative builds to the high point and is dwelled upon as in the classic pattern, but then ends without a resolution. (b) Leap-frogging, in which the narrative jumps from one event to the other, leaving the listener to infer major events that are omitted. (c) Chronological, in which the narrative is just a simple description of successive events. (d) Impoverished, in which the narrative contains few sentences and does not have a recognizable pattern, or consists of only two successive events. (e) Disoriented, in which the narrator is confused or offers events that are disoriented. The final category was for miscellaneous patterns that did not fit into any of the other categories.

After analyzing children's narratives using story grammar and high point analysis, Peterson and McCabe (1983) concluded that no one type of analysis is superior. They noted that while high point analysis is able to provide an understanding of how narratives revolve around an important event and emphasizes that event using emotional information, it is unable to account for narratives containing multiple high points, does not have a sophisticated means for analyzing the structure of evaluation, is not able to account for psychological or physical causality, and is unable to account for events that are not represented by an independent clause. Story grammar analysis, on the other hand, is able to represent the cognitive aspect of human actions well. It is also able to capture causality effectively and the complexity of narrative in terms of motivations, goal structures, and episodes embedded within one another. However, Peterson and McCabe (1983) noted that, unlike high point analysis, it provides no insight regarding the evaluation of the experience and it does not account for language use. Thus, it presents a rather Eurocentric, episodic perception of the manner in which narrative is structured and does not account for other ways of telling stories.

Many researchers have examined the unique cultural and linguistic variations that exist in narrative production. Au (1980) examined participation structures and the use of "talk story" as a speech event among Hawaiian children. Likewise, Scollon and Scollon (1981) described the nature of Athabaskan oral narrative and contrasted it with English speakers to understand the nature of interethnic communication patterns. Similar studies have examined distinct patterns of narrative production that reflect cultural differences (e.g., Bloome, Champion, Katz, Morton, & Muldrow, 2001; Bloome, Katz, & Champion, 2003; Champion, Seymour, & Camarata, 1995; Gee, 1989a, 1989b; Heath, 1982, 1983; Hymes, 1982; Minami, 2002). These cultural differences suggest that the ways in which children share narratives at home in a culturally congruent context, may vary from the manner in which teachers, who tend to place value on traditional episodic narrative structures, expect narratives to be shared in a school context. This may lead to cultural biases against non-linear, or alternative ways of performing narratives in schools. It is clear then, from the discussion above, that the manner in which narrative is structured and performed is a matter of debate.

Similarly, the manner in which readers construct meaning from text is also a contested construct. Goldman and Rakestraw (2000) noted that readers rely on text-driven and knowledge-driven processing. Text-driven processing refers to using structural cues (e.g., linguistic cues, graphic cues) to see how text elements are related and organized. Linguistic cues such as temporal (*before, after, while*), additive (*and, in addition, also*), causal (*because, so, consequently*), or adversative (*but, although, however*) connectives provide information that helps readers see how sentences and clauses relate to one another. Linguistic cues can also signal the overall rhetorical structure or genre of the text.

During knowledge-driven processing, readers use their knowledge and expectations about how words, sentences, paragraphs, and different genres are structured and organized to help them construct meaning (Goldman & Rakestraw, 2000). When that structure is violated, comprehension is diminished (Goldman & Rakestraw, 2000). Research has shown that when readers are made aware of various text structures (e.g., episodic structure of narrative text) comprehension is facilitated (Goldman & Rakestraw, 2000; Pearson & Fielding, 1991). Students' knowledge and awareness of different text structures and genres develop with time and experience (Goldman & Rakestraw, 2000). When readers are able to use the cues provided by the text in terms of structure and organization, they are better able to make connections between ideas in the text. However, when text is too structured or overly explicit, conceptual coherence may be hindered (Goldman & Rakestraw, 2000).

Mental model theories of comprehension contend that readers process text at two levels: a propositional level and a mental modeling level (McNamara, Miller, & Bransford, 1991). Situational contexts, reading material, the reader, and the task determine whether the text is en-coded propositionally or by forming mental models. At the propositional level, Kintsch and his colleagues found that propositions are important in comprehending language, and that propositions provide an accurate representation of the structure of text. When readers want to remember the text verbatim, propositional encoding prevails. However, propositional knowledge does not adequately account for memory and recall of text which is influenced heavily by prior knowledge and schemata (McNamara et al., 1991). Mental model theories (e.g., Johnson-Laird, 1983; van Dijk & Kintsch, 1983) suggest that readers construct a mental model of the text as they read that is similar in structure to the events and situations in the text. These mental models are highly accessible and are updated as new information presents itself in the text (Glenberg, Meyer & Lindem, 1987; Morrow, Greenspan, & Bower, 1987). Thus, this view of comprehension suggests that readers must be able to identify and encode not only propositions, but also the structural aspects of a text (e.g., episodic structure, story grammar elements, causal relations) and determine the relations between them to create a coherent representation of the text in memory (van den Broek, Tzeng, Risden, Trabasso, & Basche, 2001).

Bloome (2003) made distinctions between the notion of narrative as text and narrative as event and practice. When viewed as text, many aspects of narrative can be examined through research. For example, Bloome (2003) has suggested that a narrative's structure and content can be examined as in Goldman and Rakestraw's (2000) perspective regarding narrative comprehension. However, Bloome also argues that the manner in which the narrative mediates social relationships and identities, and the cognitive and linguistic processes one uses to make sense of a narrative should also be examined.

Bloome (2003) and Bloome et al. (2003) have suggested that schools tend to emphasize the importance of narrative as text by focusing on a child's ability to retell the narrative (either orally or in writing). This practice tends to separate the narrative from the narrator or writer, thereby objectifying the narrative and isolating it from the social relationships that surround it. They argue that narrative is not simply about producing a text, but about the storytelling event. That is, narrative as event and practice is equally important as narrative as text. The performative aspect of narrative suggests that narrative cannot exist outside the culture of the storytelling event. In a sense, Bloome's notion of narrative parallels Rosenblatt's (1978) notion of reading as a transactional event. Thus, children's narrative development must not only provide opportunity for them to reproduce the structural components of the narrative, but also account for the cultural and sociolinguistic aspects of the storytelling performance. In schools, tension exists between these two perspectives in terms of evaluation. When evaluation focuses primarily on evaluating narrative as text (e.g., determining the degree to which the structure of a child's narrative retelling matches the structure of the original narrative text, or describing the structure of a child's narrative), the evaluation pulls the text out of its performative context. This practice denies the existence of, and importance of, cultural, linguistic, and social relationships to narrative. Bloome et al. (2003) have argued that decontextualizing narrative is a means of legitimizing the dominance of particular language practices. In the United States, such practice would serve to reify the language practices of white, middle-class citizens and marginalize the language practices of non-dominant cultures. Thus, it is essential to evaluate narratives within the context in which they occur (Bloome et al., 2001). When considering classroom interventions to enhance narrative comprehension, it is important not only to consider those that enhance the structure of narrative (e.g., retelling), but also those that enhance the manner in which narrative is produced and those that examine the contexts in which narrative is produced.

Characteristics of Interventions

Context is the setting in which the reading event occurs. Thus, in a classroom, the context includes the instructional practices and interventions the teacher uses to provide instruction. Intervention is viewed as a deliberate attempt to influence the instructional outcome. In terms of struggling readers' narrative comprehension, intervention is viewed as a planned instructional activity designed to facilitate successful reading comprehension. In their review of research on comprehension instruction, Pearson and Fielding (1991) noted that interventions designed to improve comprehension of narrative text fell into two categories: interventions that build or activate prior knowledge (of story structure, of topics and themes), and interventions that focus on the kinds of questions asked during and after reading (e.g., inferential questions, prediction questions, questions on important ideas, multiple interpretations of text). More recently, Duke, Pressley, and Hilden's (2004) review of research on comprehension difficulties suggested that successful comprehension relies on several factors including: ability to decode text (e.g., interventions that facilitate phonemic awareness, phonics, and fluency), oral-language skill, dialect, awareness and use of comprehension strategies, and engagement and motivation with reading. Thus, more recent instructional interventions are often designed to facilitate at least one of these factors. For example, interventions that target the ability to decode text might focus on phonemic awareness, phonics, or fluency. Interventions aimed at oral language skills might foster syntactical use or retelling. An example of interventions focused on dialect would include those that are culturally and linguistically responsive or those that include culturally and linguistically diverse texts.

The instructional context, however, is also situated locally, socioculturally, and sociohistorically (Marshall, 2000). This suggests that context not only includes instructional activities, but also that these activities "are organized around different sets of situated understandings and expectations" (Holland, Skinner, Lachiotte, & Cain, 1998, p. 57). Thus,

the "space" that surrounds each instructional activity or intervention is co-constructed by the teacher and the students and has particular actors in particular roles, and is governed by particular social norms and organizational structures (Holland et al., 1998; Lave & Wenger, 1991).

Some have argued persuasively (e.g., Donahue & Foster, 2004) that studies of social cognition and social information processing may provide insight into the manner in which struggling readers approach text. They contend there are inherent theoretical linkages between the manner in which a struggling reader uses prior knowledge of social experiences, social cues, social rules, and social schemas to comprehend real-life situations (e.g., semiotic texts) and the manner in which they use prior knowledge of lived experiences, linguistic cues, structural rules, and textual schemata to comprehend written texts (e.g., linguistic texts).

Thus, from a transactional perspective, the goal of this chapter is to synthesize the findings of research in which varying instructional and social/contextual interventions were examined to determine their impact on struggling readers' narrative comprehension.

Review of Research

Our review of the literature found that interventions designed to enhance narrative comprehension fell into three distinct categories: (a) Interventions aimed at directly improving comprehension, (b) Interventions aimed at indirectly improving comprehension by enhancing fluency, and (c) Programmatic interventions aimed at improving comprehension among other things. Each category also represents particular theoretical and historical trends in literacy research over the past 20 years. Thus, we provide theoretical and historical information to contextualize each type of intervention.

Interventions Aimed at Directly Improving Comprehension   Top-down (e.g., Smith, 1978), interactive (e.g., Rumelhart, 2004), and interactive-compensatory models of reading (e.g., Stanovich, 1980) provided similar perspectives of the reading process throughout the 1980s. According to these perspectives, reading was theorized not just to be influenced by visual input from the text as in bottom-up information processing theories (e.g., Gough, 1984) or Automatic Information Processing Models (e.g., Samuels, 2004), but also from higher-level thinking (Rumelhart, 2004; Stanovich, 1980; Tracey & Morrow, 2006). As well, reading was thought to be non-linear. As a result, researchers began to consider teaching comprehension more as strategic processes rather than as skills to be acquired. This led to developing interventions aimed first at teaching single strategies to enhance literal and inferential comprehension and eventually to teaching strategic processing as self-regulated sets of strategies used flexibly as needed.

Interventions that Teach Single Strategies for Comprehension   Throughout much of the 1980s and 1990s, strategies were taught individually in an effort to provide struggling readers with specific instruction to assist comprehension. Those strategies included imagery, comprehension monitoring, story grammar, theme, and summarization.

As early as Levin's (1973) study, research has shown that for younger students and those who may need organizational strategies, visual imagery successfully enhances reading comprehension. Like that early study, Flaro's (1987) study of learning disabled fourth and fifth graders' use of visual imagery showed significant increases on reading comprehension. Using a more rigorous reading-level matched design with upper-primary "reading disabled" students and average third graders, Chan, Cole, and Morris (1990) also found that visualization supported by pictorial displays was significantly more successful at improving reading comprehension than either a visualization only or read-reread control condition. However, this success did not generalize over time.

Comprehension monitoring has also been a single strategy intervention that has yielded success. Baumann, Seifert-Kessell, and Jones (1992) found that interventions that involve active cognitive processing and metacognition while reading were significantly more successful at promoting average and below average fourth graders' comprehension, comprehension monitoring, and error detection than the more traditional Directed Reading Activity.

Several studies used either a single subject or multiple baseline design to examine the impact of story grammar instruction on comprehension and recall of textual information. While Newby, Caldwell, and Recht (1989) found mixed results for children with dysphonetic dyslexia (i.e., difficulty using phonetic analysis) and children with dyseidetic dyslexia (i.e., difficulty with whole word identification), others have shown significant improvement in the recall of story grammar elements from baseline to intervention (Boulineau, Fore, Hagan-Burke, & Burke, 2004), daily comprehension between baseline and all subsequent phases (Idol, 1987; Idol & Croll, 1987), and standardized test performance on reading comprehension subtests, listening comprehension, and length of story retellings (Idol & Croll, 1987). For students with mild disabilities and those who are low performing, these studies show that story grammar instruction has positive short-term effects on comprehension.

While these studies examined plot-level comprehension, Williams and her colleagues were interested in moving students to more complex understanding of text. An initial study (Williams, Brown, Silverstein, & deCani, 1994) showed the effectiveness of their theme identification program at helping normally achieving and learning disabled fifth and sixth graders understand the concept of theme, identify instructed themes (i.e., near transfer), and identify uninstructed themes (i.e., far transfer). Williams (2002) found that near transfer was attained, but far transfer proved difficult for learning disabled seventh and eighth graders. Wilder and Williams (2001) adapted the program to promote far transfer and found it was effective in terms of near and far transfer; however, when attempting to use the same procedure with second and third graders, the problem of far transfer recurred (Williams et al., 2002).

Borkowski, Weyhing, and Carr (1988) also sought to gain long-term transfer by combining summarization strategy instruction with attributional training that fostered persistence and effort. Results showed that learning domain-specific attributional beliefs helped struggling readers persevere so they could summarize and make inferences better; however, their long-standing antecedent attributional beliefs were unaltered. Mastropieri et al. (2001) also had success teaching learning disabled seventh graders in a 5-week peer tutoring program to use summarization strategies; however, transfer was not measured.

These studies suggest that teaching struggling readers specific strategies such as visualization, comprehension monitoring, story grammar, theme, and summarization does improve short-term comprehension; however, sustaining and transferring these effects to other contexts proved more difficult.

Interventions that Teach Flexible Use of a Variety of Strategies   In an effort to seek long-term transfer, some interventions moved away from teaching isolated strategies to teaching readers to build a repertoire of the most potent comprehension strategies (i.e., visualization, comprehension monitoring, activating background knowledge, summarizing, identifying text structure, questioning oneself) and apply the associated declarative, procedural, and conditional knowledge independently. One of the earliest interventions was reciprocal teaching (Palincsar & A. Brown, 1984). More recently, Westra and Moore (1995) found that an extended reciprocal teaching program had a significant impact on below average high school students' reading comprehension that was sustained 6 months later, suggesting that transfer had occurred.

Others have developed interventions focused on teaching struggling readers how to use a variety of comprehension strategies in a flexible manner. Dole, K. Brown, and Trathen (1996) found that providing fifth- and sixth-grade struggling readers with procedural and conditional knowledge in a 5-week strategies intervention supported their immediate comprehension of text in ways that were superior to traditional basal instruction and instruction focused on story content. However, transfer remained problematic. In a year-long investigation, R. Brown, Pressley, Van Meter, and Schuder (1996) found that Transactional Strategies Instruction (TSI) had a significant long-term impact on low-achieving second graders' comprehension on the Stanford Achievement Test. Likewise, TSI students reported using more comprehension and word-level strategies and applied more strategies than comparison group students.

Studies suggest that when students are taught what a particular strategy is (i.e., declarative knowledge), how to use it while reading (i.e., procedural knowledge), and when and why it should be used (i.e., conditional knowledge) short-term comprehension improves (Dole et al., 1996), and some showed longer-term effects (Brown et al., 1996; Westra & Moore, 1995). Without instruction related to procedural and conditional knowledge, interventions were not as successful (e.g., Proctor, Dalton, & Grisham, 2007). Thus, the type of scaffolding and the context in which strategies instruction occurs may be essential for improved comprehension and transfer.

Interventions that Manipulate the Text or Social Environment While many researchers aimed to determine the impact of a particular *instructional* intervention on comprehension as a result of the focus on sociocultural theory in the 1990s (Gaffney & Anderson, 2000), some began to examine and manipulate the *texts and contexts* involved in comprehension instruction to determine their impact.

Schmidt (1989) examined the effect of type of questioning and placement of questioning on sixth through ninth graders' comprehension and found that learning disabled students had difficulty answering higher-level comprehension questions, searching for and finding needed information in text, and working independently. Van den Branden (2000) argued that comprehension is enhanced in natural, authentic reading as learners negotiate the meaning of a text through social interaction. By examining the conditions under which negotiation of meaning promoted comprehension, and the extent to which pre-modifying texts had an impact on first- and second-language learners' reading comprehension, she found that for all students, and particularly those with lower levels of language proficiency, collectively negotiating the meaning of text improves comprehension. For these students, the opportunity to work with peers to recognize and resolve their own comprehension problems provided more assistance with comprehension than modifying texts to make them easier to understand. These findings supported those of Almasi (1995), who found that when average and below average readers participated in peer discussions of text they were better able to recognize and resolve their own comprehension problems than students in teacher-led conditions.

Likewise, Goatley, Brock, and Raphael's (1995) study of diverse learners' participation in student-led discussions of text revealed that culturally and linguistically diverse students and struggling readers were capable of negotiating and maintaining topics of discussion and constructing meaning by using a variety of strategies to gather information from sources as they collaboratively constructed interpretations of text.

Lee (1995) examined the use of signifying (a form of talk using figurative language to inform, persuade, or criticize in African American communities) as a scaffold for helping low-performing African American high school students interpret text. The intervention included: small group discussion, student-generated questions, verbalizing cognitive processes, justifying sources used in interpretations, and elaborating points of view. They learned to apply strategies similar to those expert readers use to make inferences while interpreting figurative language in narra-tive text. Findings from analyses of complex, inferential essay questions revealed that students in the experimental condition scored significantly higher than students in the control group. These findings suggest that culturally sensitive interventions that incorporate discussion and higher level thinking promote comprehension and interpretation of narrative text. While these studies found success in manipulating the learning environment for struggling readers by including social interaction and culturally relevant instruction, others have found that the learning environment can also be successfully manipulated by considering the texts used with struggling readers. Boyd (2002) found that ninth-grade struggling readers identified more with texts similar to their own ethnicity, and they were capable of engaging in higher-level thinking, producing sophisticated and thought-provoking responses, and critically evaluating texts. Similarly, Rickford's (2001) study of sixth and seventh graders also examined the effect of culturally relevant narratives on the reading enjoyment and comprehension of ethnically diverse students and found that these struggling readers were capable of higher-level thought and actually performed better on higher-order comprehension questions than on literal comprehension questions.

These studies suggest that teachers may be able to scaffold struggling readers' comprehension not only through modeling and explicit instruction aimed at enhancing comprehension, but also by manipulating the learning environment so that it includes culturally relevant texts with which students are able to identify. As well, these studies suggest that less proficient readers are not less proficient thinkers. When provided with culturally relevant texts, and when given the opportunity to participate in higher-level discourse, struggling readers are able to think beyond a literal level and show strong comprehension. These findings further suggest that instructional scaffolding need not be limited to instructional methods. Instead, the texts and contexts must also be considered. As well, including questions that moved beyond literal levels to include higher-order thinking was crucial to fostering comprehension.

Interventions Aimed at Indirectly Improving Comprehension by Enhancing Fluency In contrast with its previous focus on comprehension, in the late 1980s the U. S. Department of Education's Office of Educational Research and Improvement (OERI) began targeting phonics and early reading in its Requests for Proposals. In response, the Center for the Study of Reading at the University of Illinois at Champaign-Urbana proposed a comprehensive review of phonics and early reading instruction in their 1986 proposal to OERI (Pearson, 1990). The resultant volume, *Beginning to Read* (Adams, 1990) became a landmark text. The resulting focus on phonics, fluency, and early reading led the field to focus more on these areas, and a decline in published research on comprehension ensued throughout the 1990s (Gaffney & Anderson, 2000). A decade later two other reports had a similar impact on the field of reading. The National Research Council commissioned Snow,

Burns, and Griffin's (1998) volume, *Preventing Reading Difficulties in Young Children*, and in 1997, at the request of the U.S. Congress, the National Institute of Child Health and Human Development (NICHD) gathered a panel of 14 individuals to assess what research has concluded about reading. The Report of the National Reading Panel (NRP, 2000), like its predecessors, had an enormous impact on reading research and instruction that led to substantially more studies that examined the relationship between fluency and comprehension.

Fluency's relationship to comprehension is the subject of much debate, and its direct connection to interventions aimed at improving narrative comprehension is also a matter of debate. Automaticity theory (e.g., Samuels, 2004) posits that in order for readers to become fluent, they must initially devote their cognitive resources to decoding and word recognition (Samuels, 2004; Tan & Nicholson, 1997). After practice and learning, these processes eventually become automatic and the reader can devote attention to comprehending, rather than decoding, the text. If readers devote all of their cognitive attention to decoding, they will have none left for comprehension (Tan & Nicholson, 1997). This is known as the "bottleneck hypothesis" in the literature.

The weak form of the bottleneck hypothesis posits that automatic decoding is a necessary component of comprehension, but not the only one (Fleisher, Jenkins, & Pany, 1979). Readers must possess a variety of processes and skills in order to comprehend a text. The strong form (Fleisher, Jenkins, & Pany, 1979) of the bottleneck hypothesis argues that decoding skills alone are enough to lead to high levels of comprehension.

Studies Investigating the Strong Form of the Bottleneck Hypothesis

Studies investigating fluency practices associated with the "strong form" of the bottleneck hypothesis fell into four broad categories of instructional interventions: fluency, word identification, repeated reading, and assisted reading.

Fluency interventions. Allinder, Dunse, Brunken, and Obermiller-Krolikowski's (2001) study of 50 seventh graders (14 with learning disabilities) compared the effectiveness of fluency strategy instruction (e.g., reading with inflection, self-monitoring for accuracy, and reading at an appropriate rate) to no fluency strategy instruction, where students were told to do their best. Students in both groups made significant gains in comprehension from pretest to posttest; however, there was no significant difference between groups.

Word identification interventions. Studies related to word identification's impact on comprehension focused on sight word and decoding training. Tan and Nicholson (1997) found that, on comprehension measures, elementary students who were trained to recognize sight words significantly outperformed those who were not. However,

Kourea, Cartledge, and Musti-Rao (2007) found opposing results. Trained students made significant gains on sight word recognition, but not on fluency or comprehension.

Studies focused on the effectiveness of phonics or decoding programs on comprehension also had mixed results. Al Otaiba's (2005) investigation of traditional phonics instruction for English Language Learners who were beginning readers showed significant growth in terms of word attack, passage comprehension, and sound identification on the Woodcock Reading Mastery Test-Revised, however, those analyses were of raw scores. Standard score analysis only showed significant growth on word attack. In contrast, White's (2005) study of a word family phonics intervention for 280 second graders found the program was successful in increasing the reading comprehension of low and average achieving students.

Lenz and Hughes (1990) found that a word identification strategy, involving breaking words into parts, reduced the oral reading errors and improved the comprehension ability of 12 seventh- through ninth-grade students with learning disabilities. However, some students showed inconsistent gains in comprehension.

Torgesen et al. (2001) compared a sight word program and a phonics program for increasing the comprehension of 60 second through fourth graders with learning disabilities. Findings showed that both programs were equally effective for improving the reading comprehension of students with learning disabilities. Thus, there is inconsistent evidence regarding the effect of word identification interventions on comprehension of narrative text.

Repeated reading interventions. Several studies focused on enhancing automaticity through repeated reading and, like Rasinski and Hoffman's (2003) review, found mixed results. Rashotte and Torgesen (1985) found that repeated reading was not more effective than non-repetitive reading for increasing reading speed and comprehension of students with learning disabilities in Grades 3 through 6. However, Homan, Klesius, and Hite (1993) found that repeated reading and non-repetitive reading were both effective means for improving the comprehension of struggling readers in the sixth grade.

A study conducted by Taylor, Wade, and Yekovich (1985), as well as the Rashotte and Torgesen (1985) study discussed above, looked at the influence of the characteristics of the passage on repeated reading. The Taylor et al. (1985) study, conducted with 45 good and poor fifth-grade readers, examined the effects of phrasing the text and found that phrasing did not have a significant effect on comprehension. The Rashotte and Torgesen (1985) study looked at the effects of word overlap between passages and concluded that word commonality between passages did not significantly contribute to comprehension gains.

Peer- or teacher-assisted interventions. Peer-assisted studies analyzed the effects of repeated reading and/or sustained reading in peer dyads and had mixed results. Eldredge and Quinn (1988) found that sustained reading in peer dyads, as part of a balanced literacy program, improved the reading fluency and comprehension of second grade struggling readers. However, Mathes and Fuchs (1993) found that sustained reading in peer dyads was more successful than traditional reading instruction in increasing the reading fluency, but not the reading comprehension of fourth- through sixth-grade students with learning disabilities.

The teacher-assisted reading studies analyzed the effects of teacher feedback and teacher-guided repeated reading in small groups or peer dyads of third- or fourth-grade struggling readers or students with learning disabilities (Shany & Biemiller, 1995; Eldredge, 1990; Pany & McCoy, 1988). The results of these studies suggested that teacher-assisted reading and corrective feedback were effective practices for improving the reading comprehension of struggling readers and students with learning disabilities.

Studies Investigating the Weak Form of the Bottleneck Hypothesis Given that the weak form of the bottleneck hypothesis contends that fluency is a necessary but insufficient element by itself for improving comprehension, interventions examining the weak form tended to have multiple components and all tended to be at least moderately successful. Therrien, Wickstrom, and Jones (2006) investigated the effects of a repeated reading intervention combined with answering comprehension questions and found that such instruction improved the fluency and comprehension of fourth- through eighth-grade students with or at risk for learning disabilities. Another study compared two oral reading instructional routines—Shared Book Experience (SBE) and Oral Recitation Lesson (ORL; Reutzel, Hollingsworth, & Eldredge, 1994). The SBE intervention develops comprehension indirectly by repeated reading of whole texts in large and small groups, discussion, and interpretive activities. An ORL of text segments teach decoding, fluency, and comprehension as separate skills-based components. After 4 months second graders, including below average readers, scored similarly on the reading comprehension subtest of the Iowa Test of Basic Skills. However, students in the SBE intervention scored significantly higher on implicit comprehension questions than students in the ORL intervention suggesting that the inferences one makes while reading whole texts may be more beneficial for implicit comprehension than reading smaller units of text.

Blachman and colleagues (2004) found that a program integrating phonics instruction with the reading of phonetically controlled text resulted in comprehension gains for second and third grade students at the end of the program. Comprehension was measured using the Gray Oral Reading Test—Third Edition, suggesting that instruction using decodable texts fostered transfer to passage comprehension; however, findings were not sustained 1 year later.

Programs involving phonics, reading, and writing instruction had relative success. Rashotte, MacPhee, and Torgesen's (2001) Spell Read program for struggling first through sixth graders, included phonemic awareness, phonics, and reading and writing instruction and found significant differences between the treatment and control groups on measures of fluency, spelling, and comprehension. Jenkins, Peyton, Sanders, and Vadasy (2004) examined the effects of one-to-one tutoring, involving fluency, reading, and spelling instruction, on 121 struggling first graders' reading achievement when randomly assigned to either a more decodable or less decodable text condition or a control group. Overall, both tutored groups had significantly greater scores than the control group in the areas of decoding, word reading, passage reading, and comprehension measures; although there was no significant difference between treatment groups.

Studies Investigating Strong and Weak Forms of the Bottleneck Hypothesis Studies examining strong and weak forms of the bottleneck hypothesis compared decoding-based practices to meaning-based practices. Results indicated that comprehension improved with cueing for comprehension over cueing for fluency for fifth- through eighth-grade students with learning disabilities (O'Shea, Sindelar, & O'Shea, 1987), meaning-based feedback on oral reading miscues improved comprehension over decoding-based feedback for second- through fifth-grade students with language learning disabilities (Crowe, 2005, 2003), inference training improved comprehension over rapid decoding for struggling readers in the second grade (Yuill & Oakhill, 1988), the repeated readings that characterize Shared Book Experience improved comprehension significantly more than round robin reading for second graders (Eldredge, Reutzel, & Hollingsworth, 1995), and the paraphrasing strategy was more beneficial than repeated reading or repeated reading combined with the paraphrasing strategy for fifth- through seventh-grade students with learning disabilities (Ellis & Graves, 1990).

In summary, the interventions aligned with the weak form of the bottleneck hypothesis all showed positive results over programs aligned with the strong form. Results of most of the studies investigating the strong form of the bottleneck hypothesis showed that fluency-only interventions were often successful in improving the reading comprehension of struggling readers or students with learning disabilities in comparison to a control group or other strong form interventions. However, results of studies investigating weak and strong forms of the bottleneck hypothesis typically compared the two types of instruction and indicated that weak form interventions were more successful than strong form interventions. In alignment with this, even researchers investigating strong form interventions frequently recommended that fluency instruction take place within a balanced literacy program. Therefore, in terms of implications, it appears that fluency instruction should take place in conjunction with comprehension activities in a balanced literacy program in order to improve the reading comprehension of struggling readers or students with learning disabilities.

Programmatic Interventions

More recent studies have attempted to enhance comprehension by using programmatic interventions that were comprehensive and balanced, rather than focused solely on comprehension or fluency. Within these comprehensive literacy programs, narrative comprehension is one of many reader proficiencies targeted. Thus, the underlying notion is that struggling readers will be better equipped to succeed when multiple aspects of their difficulties are addressed simultaneously.

Another perspective on programmatic interventions suggests that one way to help struggling readers is to provide more one-on-one assistance. Thus, many programs evaluated the effectiveness of one-on-one tutoring under a variety of circumstances. A final way in which schools have sought to assist struggling readers is by expanding the amount of instructional time spent in literacy. Programs designed from this perspective evaluated the effectiveness of providing additional literacy instruction by adding to the school day. Thus, studies of programmatic interventions were categorized into three areas: (a) Comprehensive Programmatic Interventions, (b) One-to-one Tutoring Programs, and (c) Programmatic Interventions that Expand Instructional Time.

Comprehensive Programmatic Interventions   Several studies examined interventions designed to improve overall classroom literacy instruction for at-risk learners. These programs were all conducted within the normal parameters of the school day and, in general, the effectiveness of these comprehensive programs was mixed.

After 2 years of instruction in the same program, Rightmyer, McIntyre, and Petrosko's (2006) evaluation found that low-performing primary-grade students in the Together We Can program achieved significantly greater results on measures of comprehension (Flynt-Cooter Informal Reading Inventory) than those in two other programs (Breakthrough to Literacy and Four Blocks). However, there was no significant difference in performance between Together We Can and the other two programs (Early Success and SRA Reading). In a study of middle school students, Morocco, Hindin, Mata-Aguilar, and Clark-Chiarelli (2001) reported that Supported Literacy, an instructional program in which students engage in authentic reading and writing tasks and are supported by strategic thinking and conversations with peers, helped seventh and eighth graders with disabilities perform similarly to normally achieving and honors students in a comprehension and writing activity.

Moats (2004) evaluated the effectiveness of the LANGUAGE! program (Greene, 1995), which is a structured, systematic program that explicitly teaches: phonological, semantic, syntactic, pragmatic, and discourse processing skills to struggling adolescents. Moats (2004) used pre-post comparisons on a comprehension subtest (a cloze test) of the Multilevel Academic Survey Test (MAST) with large classes of poor readers and reported statistically significant

gains at all grade levels (6th, 7th, 8th, and 10th), but the study did not have a control group for comparison.

Evaluations have shown that Direct Instruction and Success for All were less effective than the aforementioned programs in improving comprehension. Mac Iver and Kemper's (2002) study of the effect of Direct Instruction on younger students showed only marginal comprehension gains on standardized tests (CTBS-4). Similarly, Shippen, Houchins, Calhoon, Furlow, and Sartor (2006) reported no significant differences in comprehension for Success for All and Direct Instruction in their study of at-risk urban middle school students. Thus, findings from programmatic interventions produced inconsistent results in terms of comprehension.

One-to-One Tutoring Programs   Programmatic interventions that enhanced access to literacy instruction by providing one-to-one tutoring as a supplement to regular literacy instruction generally relied on tutoring sessions of 15–40 minutes, two to four times per week. The tutoring routines generally consisted of read aloud, shared reading, echo reading, phonemic awareness and phonics activities, and comprehension or story grammar activities. In general, those tutoring interventions that used more highly trained teachers as tutors were more successful at enhancing comprehension than those interventions using volunteers with little training or paid non-teachers as tutors.

Interventions that use highly trained teachers (Peer-Assisted Learning Strategies, Early Steps, and Partners-in-Reading) have all found statistically significant differences for low achieving students on standardized measures of comprehension (Mathes, Howard, Allen, & Fuchs, 1998; Miller, 2003; Santa & Høien, 1999).

Other studies have found similar results with highly trained tutors. McCarthy, Newby, and Recht (1995) developed an Early Intervention Program (EIP) that included components similar to the aforementioned tutoring programs; however, their evaluation relied on free recall and open-ended comprehension questions rather than standardized measures to determine that first grade EIP students made significantly greater gains than those in the control group on both measures. In the third grade follow-up study, the EIP children were equivalent to a comparison group of average-achieving classmates in reading comprehension and word recognition in context. Thus, all tutoring programs with highly trained tutors realized statistically significant differences on both standardized and classroom-based measures of comprehension. The exception is Reading Recovery, another one-to-one tutoring intervention using highly trained teachers. Schwartz (2005) found no statistically significant findings for the effect of Reading Recovery on reading comprehension using the Degrees of Reading Power test. Pinnell, Lyons, DeFord, Bryk, and Seltzer (1994) reported statistically significant findings on the Woodcock Reading Mastery Test-Revised and the Gates-MacGinitie Reading Test for general reading achievement. However, composite scores were used in these analyses rather than subtest scores, making it difficult to determine the effect of the intervention specifically on passage comprehension (WRMT-R) and reading comprehension (GMRT).

Those tutoring programs that used volunteers with little training or paid non-teacher tutors were much less successful in terms of enhancing struggling readers' comprehension. A single-subject multiple baseline design showed that all of the four first grade struggling readers in Hitchcock, Prater, and Dowrick's (2004) intervention (staffed by community tutors) were able to meet or exceed the criterion for oral reading fluency, and three students were able to meet the criterion for reading comprehension. Once video self-monitoring was added to the tutoring, all students attained the criterion in reading comprehension and these skills were maintained over time.

Allor and McCathren's (2004) low-cost, highly structured tutoring program, implemented by college students with very little training, showed significant differences on at-risk first graders' phonemic awareness and nonsense word reading; however, findings were not as promising for comprehension—only one of the two cohorts of children experienced significant increases in passage comprehension.

Likewise, Baker, Gersten, and Keating (2000) paired low-performing readers together and randomly assigned each pair to either the Start Making a Reader Today (SMART) condition (that used low-cost volunteer tutors) or a comparison condition. Results showed students in the SMART condition had significantly higher word comprehension, oral reading fluency, and word identification (e.g., vocabulary) scores than students in the comparison group and students in an average achieving group. However, there was no impact on passage comprehension.

Santoro, Jitendra, Starosta, and Sacks (2006) and Jitendra, Edwards, Starosta, Sacks, Jacobson, and Choutka (2004) evaluated the effectiveness of Read Well (Sprick, Howard, & Fidanque, 1998–2000) through three multiple-probe-across-participant design studies and found fewer than half of the seven learning disabled children demonstrated improved comprehension following the intervention.

Likewise, Vadasy, Sanders, Peyton, and Jenkins' (2002) longitudinal study of the impact of a second year of tutoring by paid non-teacher volunteers found significant differences on standardized measures of word identification and word attack, but not on passage comprehension.

These findings suggest that, even in a one-on-one tutoring setting, comprehension is a complex and difficult construct to impact. Like Wasik and Slavin's (1993) review of Early Intervention Programs, ours found that highly trained tutors and teachers who implement a comprehensive, multifaceted program are essential for struggling readers to make substantive gains in comprehension of narrative text.

Programmatic Interventions that Expand Instructional Time

Several interventions were designed with the notion that more instructional time will yield growth. Instructional time was expanded by either including additional instruction *within* the literacy classroom or by adding instructional time at the end of the school day.

Those supplemental interventions that expand instructional time *within* the literacy classroom have been successful at improving comprehension. Mathes et al. (2005) compared two intense supplemental interventions for first graders, Proactive Reading and Responsive Reading. Students who received supplemental instruction in the *Responsive* or *Proactive* interventions scored higher on measures of reading and reading-related skills than students who received only enhanced classroom instruction.

Mefferd and Pettegrew (1997) adapted the assisted reading approach (Richek & McTague, 1988) for use in an intermediate-level special education classroom for developmentally handicapped students and found that the three students advanced their reading by at least one level. Posttest scores for two of the three students revealed fewer word reading errors in context along with higher comprehension scores at the more advanced levels.

As for interventions that expanded instruction by *extending* the school day, Leslie and Allen's (1999) evaluation of the Literacy Project examined the impact of a university-based after school program staffed by elementary teacher education students on struggling elementary readers. Findings showed that growth in reading comprehension was significantly correlated with story grammar instruction and parent participation. When compared to a comparison group receiving instruction with basal readers, choral or round robin reading, discussion, and journal writing, the Literacy Project group grew more in comprehension and reading rate.

Allington (2002) reminded us that meeting struggling readers' needs requires a comprehensive and sustained intervention effort. Although limited in number, findings from these studies suggest that additional instructional time is one way of creating and sustaining an intervention that does make a difference for struggling readers.

Summary and Conclusions

Over the past 20 years there have been many interventions that attempted to assist struggling readers' narrative comprehension. Those that have focused directly on improving comprehension by teaching comprehension strategies either in isolation (e.g., visualization, comprehension monitoring, story grammar, theme, and summarization) or as a comprehensive set have been relatively successful, particularly in terms of short-term comprehension. However, interventions that help students transfer their use of comprehension strategies to multiple contexts have proven difficult. Those interventions that included modeling and explicit process-oriented instruction related to the declarative, procedural, and conditional knowledge associated with strategy use were much more successful at fostering transfer. Interventions that manipulated the learning environment by including culturally responsive instruction, culturally relevant texts and the opportunity for students to engage in higher-level dialogic conversations about narrative texts through peer discussion were also promising in terms of fostering higher levels of comprehension.

In contrast, interventions that indirectly influenced comprehension by enhancing fluency were inconsistent. Interventions focused solely on fluency and word identification (e.g., the strong form of the bottleneck hypothesis) generally did not have an impact on comprehension of narrative text. However, those programs and interventions that were more comprehensive and included fluency, phonics, *and* comprehension instruction were generally more successful at influencing comprehension. As well, interventions that provided supplemental instruction by either adding instructional time within the literacy classroom or outside the school day were successful. This review has reaffirmed that teaching struggling readers to comprehend narrative text is a complex, challenging task. Evaluations of tutoring interventions reaffirmed Wasik and Slavin's (1993) findings that programs must be comprehensive and multifaceted, and tutors must be highly trained professionals. Volunteers with little to no background in literacy pedagogy and paid non-teachers simply are not an effective or tenable solution for helping those children most in need of expert assistance.

Overall, our findings, which focused exclusively on struggling readers of narrative text and included research from both experimental and qualitative paradigms, are similar to those of Edmonds et al.'s (2009), which found that interventions focused on comprehension (ES = 1.23) or multiple components (ES = 0.72) had large effects on reading comprehension that were significantly different from zero, and interventions using fluency (ES = –0.03) or word identification (ES = 0.34) to enhance comprehension had small effect sizes that were not significantly different from zero. Although Edmonds et al.'s (2009) study included interventions focused on both narrative and expository texts, they found that interventions for narrative text had much higher effect sizes (ES = 1.30) than those using expository text (ES = 0.53). Thus, our review mirrors findings from other recent reviews.

Implications

While narrative comprehension is challenging for struggling readers, the implications for classroom instruction are straightforward. To be successful at enhancing comprehension, interventions for struggling readers must include process-oriented, rather than skills-oriented instruction. Across all interventions, whether they were directly or indirectly aimed at enhancing comprehension, those that earnestly attempted to help children learn how to actively participate in the reading process were most successful. Successful interventions taught children: (a) a handful of very powerful strategies including: visualization, summarization, monitoring comprehension, and recognizing story grammar elements and themes; (b) how to recognize and resolve comprehension difficulties; and (c) when, where, and why to use particular strategies. In short, the

instruction was process-oriented and taught children *how* to comprehend. Likewise, interventions that provided space for students to engage in dialogic peer discussions of text provided a different space for students to participate actively in meaning construction. These contexts required students to engage in social and cognitive processes in which they asked thoughtful, meaningful questions and brought up issues they felt would help them understand the text better. This process requires students to actively think about the text, identify those aspects that do not make sense, and work collaboratively to understand the text. These are the same self-regulatory processes involved in comprehension strategies instruction—recognizing and resolving comprehension difficulties. Thus, providing instructional spaces and contexts in which students can actively participate in meaning construction fosters similar growth as instructional interventions that feature more explicit instruction.

Those interventions that were less successful for struggling readers included comprehension activities, but did not teach children *how* to become better comprehenders. Those interventions that did not include comprehension instruction or comprehension activities at all had inconsistent results and were generally less effective.

Future Research

Much of the research reviewed here focused more on comprehension of narrative text rather than narrative comprehension. The primary difference is that narrative comprehension is more focused on how readers learn to interpret and understand particular aspects of narrative such as story grammar elements and theme. A fair amount of research has been conducted on narrative comprehension; however, much of that research has been done with undergraduate college students (e.g., Rapp & Gerrig, 2002), who were not the focus of this review. As well, much of that body of research either has not been done with struggling readers (e.g., Paris & Paris, 2007), or does not actually involve an intervention. Instead, those studies examined instructional issues that influence comprehension such as the effect of placement of questions while reading or after reading on narrative comprehension (e.g., van den Broek et al., 2001). Thus, future research is needed in which this body of research on narrative comprehension is used to design interventions for struggling readers in K–12 settings. As well, this research must go beyond recall and memory of literal aspects of the text to examine how struggling readers can become higher-level thinkers who are able to make deep inferences and engage in critical and evaluative thinking about narrative.

As well, new technologies and new literacies have spawned new interventions. The benefits of new technologies have not been fully realized in the research literature on narrative comprehension yet. Proctor, Dalton, and Grisham (2007) provided a glimpse of what such interventions might look like in their examination of fourth-grade struggling readers' ability to read narrative passages and informal hypertexts that embedded pre-reading vocabulary instruction, comprehension strategy support while reading (summarization, prediction, clarification, questioning, or visualization), and a post-reading digital retelling in a Universal Literacy Environment (ULE). Unfortunately, findings showed no significant growth from pretest to posttest in terms of vocabulary or comprehension. Digital environments provide a great deal of potential; however, at this point the research on interventions related to narrative comprehension is in its infancy.

Authors' Note

We would like to acknowledge the efforts of Lori Conroy, Carole Cooper, Jessie Merchant, and Laura Simon. Their assistance was invaluable to our work on this review.

References

Adams, M. J. (1990). *Beginning to read: Thinking and learning about print.* Cambridge, MA: The MIT Press.

Allinder, R. M., Dunse, L, Brunken C. D., & Obermiller-Krolikowski, H. J. (2001). Improving fluency in at-risk readers and students with learning disabilities. *Remedial and Special Education, 22*(1), 48–54.

Allington, R. L. (2002). Research on reading/learning disability interventions. In A. E. Farstrup & S. J. Samuels (Eds.), *What research says about reading instruction* (pp. 261–290). Newark, DE: International Reading Association.

Allor, J., & McCathren, R. (2004). The efficacy of an early literacy tutoring program implemented by college students. *Learning Disabilities Research & Practice, 19*, 116–129.

Al Otaiba, S. (2005). How effective is code-based reading tutoring in English for English learners and preservice teacher-tutors? *Remedial and Special Education, 26*(4), 245–254.

Almasi, J. F. (1995). The nature of fourth graders' sociocognitive conflicts in peer-led and teacher-led discussions of literature. *Reading Research Quarterly, 30*(3), 314–351.

Alvermann, D. E., & Eakle, A. J. (2003). Comprehension instruction: Adolescents and their multiple literacies. In A. P. Sweet & C. E. Snow (Eds.), *Rethinking reading comprehension* (pp. 12–29). New York: Guilford.

Au, K. (1980). Participation structures in a reading lesson with Hawaiian children: Analysis of a culturally appropriate instructional event. *Anthropology and Education Quarterly, 11*(2), 91–115.

Baker, S., Gersten, R., & Keating, T. (2000). When less may be more: A two-year longitudinal evaluation of a volunteer tutoring program requiring minimal training. *Reading Research Quarterly, 35*(4), 494–519.

Baumann, J. F., Seifert-Kessell, N., & Jones, L. A. (1992). Effect of think-aloud instruction on elementary students' comprehension monitoring abilities. *Journal of Reading Behavior, 24*(2), 143–172.

Blachman, B. A., Schatschneider, C., Fletcher, J. M., Francis, D. J., Clonan, S. M., Shaywitz, B. E., et al. (2004). Effects of intensive reading remediation for second and third graders and a 1-year follow-up. *Journal of Educational Psychology, 96*(3), 444–461.

Bloome, D. (2003). Narrative discourse. In A. C. Graesser, M. A. Gernsbacher, & S. R. Goldman (Eds.), *Handbook of discourse processes* (pp. 287–320). Mahwah, NJ: Erlbaum.

Bloome, D., Champion, T., Katz, L., Morton, M. B., & Muldrow, R. (2001). Spoken and written narrative development: African American preschoolers as storytellers and storymakers. In J. L. Harris, A. G. Kamhi, & K. E. Pollock (Eds.), *Literacy in African American communities* (pp. 45–76). Mahwah, NJ: Erlbaum.

Bloome, D., Katz, L., & Champion, T. (2003). Young children's narra-

tives and ideologies of language in classrooms. *Reading & Writing Quarterly, 19*, 205–223.

Borkowski, J. G., Weyhing, R. S., & Carr, M. (1988). Effects of attributional retraining on strategy-based reading comprehension in learning-disabled students. *Journal of Educational Psychology, 80*(1), 46–53.

Boulineau, T., Fore, C., Hagan-Burke, S., & Burke, M. D. (2004). Use of story-mapping to increase the story-grammar text comprehension of elementary students with learning disabilities, *Learning Disability Quarterly, 27*(2), 105–121.

Boyd, F. B. (2002). Conditions, concessions, and the many tender mercies of learning through multicultural literature. *Reading Research and Instruction, 42*(1), 58–92.

Brown, R., Pressley, M., Van Meter, P., & Schuder, T. (1996). A quasi-experimental validation of Transactional Strategies Instruction with low-achieving second-grade readers. *Journal of Educational Psychology, 88*(1), 18–37.

Campbell, J. R., Hombo, C. M., & Mazzeo, J. (2000, August). *NAEP trends in academic progress: Three decades of student performance.* Washington, DC: U. S. Department of Education, Office of Educational Research and Improvement/National Center for Education Statistics.

Champion, T., Seymour, H., & Camarata, S. (1995). Narrative discourse of African American children. *Journal of Narrative and Life History, 5*(4), 333–352.

Chan, L. K. S., Cole, P. G., & Morris, J. N. (1990). Effects of instruction in the use of a visual-imagery strategy on the reading-comprehension competence of disabled and average readers. *Learning Disabilities Quarterly, 13*(1), 2–11.

Crowe, L. K. (2003). Comparison of two reading feedback strategies in improving the oral and written language performance of children with language-learning disabilities. *American Journal of Speech Language Pathology, 12*(1), 16–27.

Crowe, L. K. (2005). Comparison of two oral reading feedback strategies in improving Reading comprehension of school-age children with low reading ability. *Remedial and Special Education, 26*(1), 32–42.

Dole, J. A., Brown, K. J., & Trathen, W. (1996). The effects of strategy instruction on the comprehension performance of at-risk students. *Reading Research Quarterly, 31*(9), 62–88.

Donahue, M., & Foster, S. K. (2004). Social cognition, conversation, and reading comprehension: How to read a comedy of manners. In C. A. Stone, E. R. Silliman, B. J. Ehren, & K. Apel (Eds.), *Handbook of language and literacy* (pp. 363–379). New York: Guilford.

Duke, N., Pressley, M., & Hilden, K. (2004). Difficulties with reading comprehension. In C. A. Stone, E. R. Silliman, B. J. Ehren, & K. Apel (Eds.), *Handbook of language and literacy* (pp. 501–520). New York: Guilford.

Edmonds, M. S., Vaughn, S., Wexler, J., Reutebuch, C., Cable, A., Tackett, K. K., et al. (2009). A synthesis of reading interventions and effects on reading comprehension outcomes for older struggling readers. *Review of Educational Research, 79*(1), 262–300.

Eldredge, J. L. (1990). Increasing the performance of poor readers in the third grade with a group-assisted strategy. *Journal of Educational Research, 84*(2), 69–77.

Eldredge, J. L. & Quinn, D. W. (1988). Increasing reading performance of low-achieving second graders with dyad reading groups. *Journal of Educational Research, 82*(1), 40–46.

Eldredge, J. L., Reutzel, D. R., & Hollingsworth, P. M. (1995). Comparing the effectiveness of two oral reading practices: Round-robin reading and the shared book experience. *Journal of Literacy Research, 28*(2), 200–225.

Ellis, E. S., & Graves, A. W. (1990). Teaching rural students with learning disabilities: A paraphrasing strategy to increase comprehension of main ideas. *Rural Special Education Quarterly, 10*(2), 2–10.

Fish, S. (1980). *Is there a text in this class? The authority of interpretive communities.* Cambridge, UK: Cambridge University Press.

Flaro, L. (1987). The development and evaluation of a reading comprehension strategy with learning disabled students. *Reading Improvement, 24*, 222–229.

Fleisher, L. S., Jenkins, J. R., & Pany, D. (1979). Effects on poor readers' comprehension of training in rapid decoding. *Reading Research Quarterly, 15*(1), 30–48.

Fuchs, D., Fuchs, L. S., Mathes, P. G., & Lipsey, M. W. (2000). Reading differences between underachievers with and without learning disabilities: A meta-analysis. In R. Gersten, E. P. Schiller, & S. Vaughn (Eds.), *Contemporary special education research: Syntheses of the knowledge base on critical instructional issues* (pp. 81–104). Mahwah, NJ: Erlbaum.

Gaffney, J., & Anderson, R. C. (2000). Trends in reading research in the United States: Changing intellectual current over three decades. In M. L. Kamil, P. B. Mosenthal, P. D. Pearson, & R. Barr (Eds.), *Handbook of reading research* (Vol. 3, pp. 53–74). Mahwah, NJ: Erlbaum

Gee, J. P. (1989a). The narrativization of experience in the oral style. *Journal of Education, 171*(1), 75–96.

Gee, J. P. (1989b). Two styles of narrative construction and their linguistic and educational implications. *Journal of Education, 171*(1), 97–115.

Gersten, R., Fuchs, L. S., Williams, J. P., & Baker, S. (2001). Teaching reading comprehension strategies to students with learning disabilities: A review of research. *Review of Educational Research, 71*(2), 279–320.

Glenberg, A. M., Meyer, M., & Lindem, K. (1987). Mental models contribute to foregrounding during text comprehension. *Journal of Memory and Language, 26,* 69–83.

Goatley, V. J., Brock, C. H., & Raphael, T. E., (1995). Diverse learners participating in regular education "Book Clubs." *Reading Research Quarterly, 30,* 352–380.

Goldman, S. R., & Rakestraw, J. A. (2000). Structural aspects of constructing meaning from text. In M. L. Kamil, P. B. Mosenthal, P. D. Pearson, & R. Barr (Eds.), *Handbook of reading research* (Vol. 3, pp. 311–335). Mahwah, NJ: Erlbaum.

Gough, P. B. (1984). Word recognition. In P. D. Pearson, R. Barr, M. L. Kamil, & P. B. Mosenthal (Eds.), *Handbook of reading research* (Vol. 1, pp. 225–253). New York: Longman.

Graesser, A. C., Golding, J. M., & Long, D. L. (1991). Narrative representation and comprehension. In R. Barr, M. L. Kamil, P. B. Mosenthal, & P. D. Pearson (Eds.), *Handbook of reading research* (Vol. 2, pp. 171–205). White Plains, NY: Longman.

Greene, (1995). *LANGUAGE! The comprehensive literacy curriculum.* New York: Springer.

Hartman, D. K. (1995). Eight readers reading: The intertextual links of proficient readers reading multiple passages. *Reading Research Quarterly, 30*(3), 520–561.

Heath, S. B. (1982). What no bedtime story means: Narrative skills at home and at school. *Language in Society, 11*(1), 49–76.

Heath, S. B. (1983). *Ways with words: Language, life, and work in communities and classrooms.* New York: Cambridge University Press.

Hitchcock, C. H., Prater, M. A., & Dowrick, P. W. (2004). Reading comprehension and fluency: Examining the effects of tutoring and video self-modeling on first-grade students with reading difficulties. *Learning Disability Quarterly, 27,* 89–103.

Holland, D., Skinner, D., Lachiotte, W., & Cain, C. (1998). *Identity and agency in cultural worlds.* Cambridge, MA: Harvard University Press.

Homan, S. P., Klesius, J. P., & Hite, C. (1993). Effects of repeated readings and nonrepetitive reading strategies on students' fluency and comprehension. *Journal of Educational Research, 87*(2), 94–99.

Hymes, D. (1982). Narrative form as a "grammar" of experience: Native Americans and a glimpse of English. *Journal of Education, 164*(2), 121–142.

Idol, L. (1987). Group story mapping: A comprehension strategy for both skilled and unskilled readers. *Journal of Learning Disabilities, 20,* 196–205.

Idol, L., & Croll, V. J. (1987). Story-mapping training as a means of improving reading comprehension. *Learning Disabilities Quarterly, 10*(3), 214–229.

Jenkins, J. R., Peyton, J. A., Sanders, E. A., & Vadasy, P. F. (2004). Effects of reading decodable texts in supplemental first-grade tutoring. *Scientific Studies of Reading, 8*(1), 53–85.

Jitendra, A. K., Edwards, L., Starosta, K., Sacks, G., Jacobson, L. A., & Choutka, C. M. (2004). Early reading instruction for children with reading difficulties: Meeting the needs of diverse learners, *Journal of Learning Disabilities, 37,* 421–439.

Johnson-Laird, P. N. (1983). *Mental models.* Cambridge, MA: Harvard University Press.

Kourea, L., Cartledge, G., & Musti-Rao, S. (2007). Improving the reading skills of urban elementary students through total class peer tutoring. *Remedial and Special* Education, *28*(2), 95–107.

Labov, W. (1972). *Language in the inner city: Studies in the Black English vernacular.* Philadelphia: University of Pennsylvania Press.

Lave, J., & Wenger, E. (1991). *Situated learning: Legitimate peripheral participation.* New York: Cambridge University Press.

Lee, C. D. (1995). A culturally based cognitive apprenticeship: Teaching African American high school students skills in literary interpretation. *Reading Research Quarterly, 30*(4), 608–630.

Lenz, B. K., & Hughes, C. A. (1990). A word identification strategy for adolescents with learning disabilities. *Journal of Learning Disabilities, 23*(3), 149–163.

Leslie, L., & Allen, L. (1999). Factors that predict success in an early literacy intervention project. *Reading Research Quarterly, 34,* 404–424.

Levin, J. R. (1973). Inducing imagery in poor readers: A test of a recent model. *Journal of Educational Psychology, 65*(1), 19–24.

Mac Iver, M. A., & Kemper, E. (2002). The impact of direct instruction on elementary students' reading achievement in an urban school. *Journal of Education for Students Placed At Risk, 7*(2), 197–220.

Mandler, J. M., & Johnson, N. S. (1977). Remembrance of things parsed: Story structure and recall. *Cognitive Psychology, 9,* 111–151.

Marshall, J. (2000). Research on response to literature. In M. L. Kamil, P. B. Mosenthal, P. D. Pearson, & R. Barr (Eds.), *Handbook of reading research* (Vol. 3, pp. 381–402). Mahwah, NJ: Erlbaum.

Mastropieri, M. A., & Scruggs, T. E. (1997). Best practices in promoting reading comprehension in students with learning disabilities 1976 to 1996. *Remedial and Special Education, 18*(4), 197–213.

Mastropieri, M. A., Scruggs, T. E., Bakken, J. P., & Whedon, C. (1996). Reading comprehension: A synthesis of research in learning disabilities. *Advances in Learning and Behavioral Disabilities, 10B,* 201–227.

Mastropieri, M. A., Scruggs, T., Mohler, L., Beranek, M., Spencer, V., Boon, R. T., et al. (2001). Can middle school students with serious reading difficulties help each other and learn anything? *Learning Disabilities Research & Practice, 16*(1), 18–27.

Mathes, P. G., Denton, C. A., Fletcher, J. M., Anthony, J. L., Francis, D. J., & Schatschneider, C. (2005). The effects of theoretically different instruction and student characteristics on the skills of struggling readers. *Reading Research Quarterly, 40,* 148–182.

Mathes, P. G., & Fuchs, L.S. (1993). Peer-mediated reading instruction in special education resource rooms. *Learning Disabilities Research and Practice, 8*(4), 233–243.

Mathes, P. G., Howard, J. K., Allen, S. H., & Fuchs, D. (1998). Peer-assisted learning strategies for first-grade readers: Responding to the needs of diverse learners. *Reading Research Quarterly, 33*(1), 62–94.

McCarthy, P., Newby, R. F., & Recht, D. R. (1995). Results of an early intervention program for first grade children at risk for reading disability. *Reading Research and Instruction, 34*(4), 273–294.

McNamara, T. P., Miller, D. L., & Bransford, J. D. (1991). Mental models and reading comprehension. In R. Barr, M. L. Kamil, P. B. Mosenthal, & P. D. Pearson (Eds.), *Handbook of reading research* (Vol. 2, pp. 490–511). White Plains, NY: Longman.

Mefferd, P., & Pettegrew, B.S. (1997). Fostering literacy acquisition of students with developmental disabilities: Assisted reading with predictable trade books. *Reading Research and Instruction, 36*(3), 177–190.

Miller, S. D. (2003). Partners-in-reading: Using classroom assistants to rovide tutorial assistance to struggling first-grade readers. *Journal of Education for Students Placed At Risk, 8,* 333–349.

Minami, M. (2002). *Culture-specific language styles: The development of oral narrative and literacy.* Tonawanda, NY: Multilingual Matters.

Moats, L. C. (2004). Efficacy of a structured, systematic language curriculum for adolescent poor readers. *Reading & Writing Quarterly, 20*, 145–159.

Moje, E. (2000). "To be part of the story": The literacy practices of gangsta adolescents. *Teachers College Record, 102*(3), 651–690.

Morocco, C. C., Hindin, A., Mata-Aguilar, C., & Clark-Chiarelli, N. (2001). Building a deep understanding of literature with middle-grade students with learning disabilities. *Learning Disability Quarterly, 24*, 47–58.

Morrow, D. G., Greenspan, S. L., & Bower, G. H. (1987). Accessibility and situation models in narrative comprehension. *Journal of Memory and Language, 26*, 165–187.

National Assessment Governing Board. (2007). *Reading framework for the 2009 National Assessment of Educational Progress: Pre-publication edition*. Washington, DC: Author.

National Reading Panel. (2000). *Teaching children to read: An evidence-based assessment of the scientific research literature on reading and its implications for reading instruction* (Report of the Subgroups). Washington DC: U. S. Department of Health and Human Services, Public Health Service, National Institutes of Health, and the National Institute of Child Health and Human Development.

Newby, R. F., Caldwell, J., & Recht, D. R. (1989). Improving the reading comprehension of children with dysphonetic and dyseidetic dyslexia using story grammar. *Journal of Learning Disabilities, 22*(6), 373–380.

Ochs, E. (1997). Narrative. In T. A. van Dijk (Ed.), *Discourse as structure and process* (pp. 185–207). Thousand Oaks, CA: Sage.

O'Shea, L. J., Sindelar, P. T., & O'Shea, D. J. (1987). The effects of repeated readings and attentional cues on the reading fluency and comprehension of learning disabled readers. *Learning Disabilities Research, 2*(2), 103–109.

Palincsar, A. S., & Brown, A. L. (1984). Reciprocal teaching of comprehension-fostering and comprehension-monitoring activities. *Cognition and Instruction, 1*, 117–175.

Pany, D., & McCoy, K. M. (1988). Effects of corrective feedback on word accuracy and reading comprehension of readers with learning disabilities. *Journal of Learning Disabilities, 21*(9), 546–550.

Paris, A. H., & Paris, S. G. (2007). Teaching narrative comprehension strategies to first graders. *Cognition and Instruction, 25*(1), 1–44.

Pearson, P. D. (1990). Foreword. In M. J. Adams (Ed.), *Beginning to read: Thinking and learning about print* (pp. v–viii). Cambridge, MA: The MIT Press.

Pearson, P. D., & Fielding, L. (1991). Comprehension instruction. In R. Barr, M. L. Kamil, P. Mosenthal, & P. D. Pearson (Eds.), *Handbook of reading research* (Vol. 2, pp. 815–860). White Plains, NY: Longman.

Perie, M., Grigg, W., & Donahue, P. (2005). *The Nation's Report Card: Reading 2005* (NCES 2006-451). U. S. Department of Education, National Center for Education Statistics. Washington, DC: U. S. Government Printing Office.

Peterson, C., & McCabe, A. (1983). *Developmental psycholinguistics: Three ways of looking at a child's narrative*. New York: Plenum Press.

Pinnell, G. S., Lyons, C. A., Deford, D. E., Bryk, A. S., & Seltzer, M. (1994). Comparing instructional models for the literacy education of high-risk first graders. *Reading Research Quarterly, 29*, 8–39.

Pressley, M. (2000). What should comprehension instruction be the instruction of? In M. L. Kamil, P. B. Mosenthal, P. D. Pearson, & R. Barr (Eds.), *Handbook of reading research* (Vol. 3, pp. 545–561). Mahwah, NJ: Erlbaum.

Proctor, C. P., Dalton, B., & Grisham, D. L. (2007). Scaffolding English language learners and struggling readers in a universal literacy environment with embedded strategy instruction and vocabulary support. *Journal of Literacy Research, 39*(1), 71–93.

RAND (2006). RAND Research Brief: Developing an R&D Program to Improve Reading Comprehension. Retrieved November 4, 2006, from http://www.rand.org/pubs/research_briefsRB8024/index1.htm

Rapp, D. N., & Gerrig, R. J. (2002). Readers' reality-driven and plot-driven analyses in narrative comprehension. *Memory & Cognition, 30*(5), 779–788.

Rashotte, C. A., MacPhee, K., & Torgesen, J. K. (2001). The effectiveness of a group reading instruction program with poor readers in multiple grades. *Learning Disability Quarterly, 24*(2), 119–134.

Rashotte, C. A., & Torgesen, J. K. (1985). Repeated reading and reading fluency in learning disabled children. *Reading Research Quarterly, 20*(2), 180–188.

Rasinski, T. V., & Hoffman, J. V. (2003). Oral reading in the school literacy curriculum. *Reading Research Quarterly, 38*(4), 510–522.

Reutzel, D. R., Hollingsworth, P. M., & Eldredge, J. L. (1994). Oral reading instruction: The impact on student reading development. *Reading Research Quarterly, 29*(1), 40–62.

Richek, M. A., & McTague, B. K. (1988). The "Curious George" strategy for students with reading problems. *The Reading Teacher, 43*, 220–226.

Rickford, A. (2001). The effect of cultural congruence and higher order questioning on the reading enjoyment and comprehension of ethnic minority students. *Journal of Education for Students Placed At Risk, 6*(4), 357–387.

Rightmyer, E. C., McIntyre, E., & Petrosko, J. M. (2006). Instruction, development, and achievement of struggling primary grade readers. *Reading Research and Instruction, 45*, 209–241.

Rosenblatt, L. M. (1978). *The reader, the text, the poem: The transactional theory of the literary work*. Carbondale: Southern Illinois University Press.

Rumelhart, D. E. (2004). Toward an interactive model of reading. In R. B. Ruddell & N. J. Unrau (Eds.), *Theoretical models and processes of reading* (5th ed., pp. 1149–1179). Newark, DE: International Reading Association.

Samuels, S. J. (2004). Toward a theory of automatic information processing in reading, revisited. In R. B. Ruddell & N. J. Unrau (Eds.), *Theoretical models and processes of reading* (5th ed., pp. 1127–1148). Newark, DE: International Reading Association.

Santa, C. M., & Høien, T. (1999). An assessment of Early Steps: A program for early intervention of reading problems. *Reading Research Quarterly, 34*(1), 54–79.

Santoro, L. E., Jitendra, A. K., Starosta, K., & Sacks, G. (2006). Reading well with Read Well: Enhancing the reading performance of English language learners. *Remedial and Special Education, 27*(2), 105–115.

Schmidt, M. W. (1989). Method of questioning and placement of questions: Effects on LD students' comprehension. *Learning Disability Quarterly, 12*(1), 192–198.

Schwartz, R. M. (2005). Literacy learning of at-risk first-grade students in the reading recovery early intervention. *Journal of Educational Psychology, 97*, 257–267.

Scollon, R., & Scollon, S. B. K. (1981). *Narrative, literacy and face in interethnic communication*. Norwood, NJ: Ablex.

Shany, M. T., & Biemiller, A. (1995). Assisted reading practice: Effects on performance for poor readers in grades 3 and 4. *Reading Research Quarterly, 30*(3), 382–395.

Shippen, M. E., Houchins, D. E., Calhoon, M. B., Furlow, C. F., & Sartor, D. L. (2006). The effects of comprehensive school reform models in reading for urban middle school students with disabilities. *Remedial and Special Education, 27*(6), 322–328.

Short, E. J., & Ryan, E. B. (1984). Metacognitive differences between skilled and less skilled readers: Remediating deficits through story grammar and attribution training. *Journal of Educational Psychology, 76*, 225–235.

Smith, F. (1978). *Understanding reading* (2nd ed.). New York: Holt, Rinehart, & Winston.

Snow, C. E., Burns, M. S., & Griffin, P. (Eds.). (1998). *Preventing reading difficulties in young children*. Washington, DC: National Academy Press.

Snow, C. E., & Sweet, A. P. (2003). Reading for comprehension. In C. E. Snow & A. P. Sweet (Eds.), *Rethinking reading comprehension* (pp. 1–11). New York: Guilford.

Sprick, M., Howard, L. M., & Fidanque, A. (1998–2000). *Read Well: Critical foundations in primary reading*. Longmont, CO: Sopris West.

Stanovich, K. (1980). Toward an interactive-compensatory model of individual differences in the development of reading comprehension. *Reading Research Quarterly, 16*, 32–71.

Stein, N. L., & Glenn, C. G. (1979). An analysis of story comprehension in elementary school children. In R. Freedle (Ed.), *New directions in discourse processing* (pp. 53–120). Norwood, NJ: Ablex.

Tan, A., & Nicholson, T. (1997). Flashcards revisited: Training poor readers to read words faster improving their comprehension of text. *Journal of Educational Psychology, 89*(2), 276–288.

Taylor, N. E., Wade, M. R., & Yekovich, F. R. (1985). The effects of text manipulation and multiple reading strategies on the reading performance of good and poor readers. *Reading Research Quarterly, 20*(5), 566–574.

Therrien, W. J., Wickstrom, K., & Jones, K. (2006). Effect of a combined repeated reading and question generation intervention on reading achievement. *Learning Disabilities Research and Practice, 21*(2), 89–97.

Torgesen, J. K., Alexander, A. W., Wagner, R. K., Rashotte, C. A., Voeller, K. K. S., & Conway, T. (2001). Intensive remedial instruction for children with severe reading disabilities: Immediate and long-term outcomes from two instructional approaches. *Journal of Learning Disabilities, 24*(1), 33–58.

Tracey, D. H., & Morrow, L. M. (2006). *Lenses on reading: An introduction to theories and models.* New York: Guilford.

U.S. Department of Education, Institute of Education Sciences. (2007, July 17). Key definitions. In *What works clearinghouse: Beginning reading abstract.* Retrieved March 29, 2009, from http://ies.ed.gov/ncee/wwc/reports/beginning_reading/abstract.asp

Vadasy, P. F., Sanders, E. A., Peyton, J. A., & Jenkins, J. R. (2002). Timing and intensity of tutoring: A closer look at the conditions for effective early literacy tutoring. *Learning Disabilities Research & Practice, 17*(4), 227–241.

Van den Branden, K. (2000). Does negotiation of meaning promote reading comprehension? A study of multilingual primary school classes. *Reading Research Quarterly, 35*(3), 426–443.

van den Broek, P., Tzeng, Y., Risden, K., Trabasso, T., & Basche, P. (2001). Inferential questioning: Effects on comprehension of narrative texts as a function of grade and timing. *Journal of Educational Psychology, 93*(3), 521–529.

Van Dijk, T. A., & Kintsch, W. (1983). *Strategies of discourse comprehension.* New York: Academic Press.

Wasik, B. A., & Slavin, R. E. (1993). Preventing early reading failure with one-to-one tutoring: A review of five programs. *Reading Research Quarterly, 28*, 179–200.

Westra, J., & Moore, D. (1995). Reciprocal teaching of reading comprehension in a New Zealand high school. *Psychology in the Schools, 32*(3), 225–232.

White, T. G. (2005). Effects of systematic and strategic analogy-based phonics on grade 2 students' word reading and reading comprehension. *Reading Research Quarterly, 40*(2), 234–255.

Wilder, A. A., & Williams, J. P. (2001). Students with severe learning disabilities can learn higher order comprehension skills. *Journal of Educational Psychology, 93*(2), 268–278.

Williams, J. P. (2002). Using the theme scheme to improve story comprehension. In C. C. Block & M. Pressley (Eds.), *Comprehension instruction: Research-based best practices* (pp. 126–139). New York: Guilford.

Williams, J. P., Brown, L. G., Silverstein, A. K., & deCani, J. S. (1994). An instructional program for adolescents with learning disabilities in the comprehension of narrative themes. *Learning Disabilities Quarterly, 17*, 205–221.

Williams, J. P., Lauer, K. D., Hall, K. M., Lord, K. M., Gugga, S., Bak, S., et al. (2002). Teaching elementary school students to identify story themes. *Journal of Educational Psychology, 94*(2), 235–248.

Wolf, S. A. (2004). *Interpreting literature with children.* Mahwah, NJ: Erlbaum.

Yuill, N., & Oakhill, J. (1988). Effects of inference awareness training on poor reading comprehension. *Applied Cognitive Psychology, 2*, 33–45.

31

Interventions to Enhance Informational Text Comprehension

NICOLE M. MARTIN AND NELL K. DUKE
Michigan State University

For students today, proficient informational text comprehension is critical. Informational texts—texts written with the purpose of conveying information about the natural or social world (Duke, 2000, p. 285) rather than, for example, to convey imagined experience, as with fictional narrative text—are often a primary means of teaching science and social studies content, whether through textbooks, trade books, web-based text, or some combination. Informational text comprehension and related skills are named in every standards document of which we are aware and comprise a significant portion of many reading assessments (e.g., Flood & Lapp, 1986; National Assessment Governing Board, 2007). Informational texts are also a preferred form of reading material for many students (e.g., Mohr, 2006), and a potential source of both enjoyment and knowledge building.

Informational texts do not decline in importance in adulthood, as informational texts abound in workplaces and leisure activities (Smith, 2000). In a given day, for instance, an adult may find out about current events by reading the newspaper, decide between two businesses by comparing information from their websites, read about a new product in a company memo, and consult a section of a parenting guide. To complete each of these activities, one needs to be able to comprehend informational texts; before reaching adulthood, one needs to develop skills and strategies for informational text comprehension.

Unfortunately, it is clear that many adults do not develop these skills and strategies. According to the National Assessment of Adult Literacy (NAAL), for example, 14% or about 30 million U.S. adults have below basic skills in "prose literacy," which is described as "the knowledge and skills needed to perform prose tasks, (i.e., to search, comprehend, and use continuous texts). Examples include editorials, news stories, brochures, and instructional materials" (National Center for Education Statistics, 2007, p. iii). Another 29% or about 63 million U.S. adults have only basic prose literacy skills. Similar findings hold for "document

literacy," defined as "the knowledge and skills needed to perform document tasks (i.e., to search, comprehend, and use non-continuous texts in various formats). Examples include job applications, payroll forms, transportation schedules, maps, tables, and drug or food labels" (p. 2). International studies—specifically the *International Adult Literacy Study Survey* (IALS) and the *Adult Literacy and Life Skills Survey* (ALL)—document enormous numbers of adults not only in the U.S. but throughout the world who struggle with prose and document literacy (OECD & Statistics Canada, 2000; Statistics Canada & OECD, 2005), with the U.S. ranking in the middle range of the 22 IALS nations studied (note that prose and document literacy are described somewhat differently in these assessments).

The degree to which one would classify adults and K–12 students who struggle with informational reading comprehension as having reading disabilities depends, of course, on how one defines the term *reading disabilities*. Undoubtedly some adults (e.g., some who have emigrated to the United States from countries without formal educational systems) have been provided with little opportunity to develop informational reading comprehension and could, if provided with this opportunity, develop informational reading comprehension skills without substantial difficulty; the term *reading disabled* is not an obvious fit for these adults. Other adults, as well as students, may have experienced formal education that lacked quality instruction in informational reading comprehension, or reading comprehension of any kind. This latter scenario is not at all far-fetched. Inadequacies in our instruction of reading comprehension are long and continuously documented (Durkin, 1978/1979; Pressley, 2005). Also well-documented is a neglect of informational text in reading instruction, at least in early schooling (see Duke, Bennett-Armistead, & Roberts, 2002, for a review). For this scenario as well reading disabled does not seem the right term. For still other students and adults, even with opportunity to learn and some quality instruction, informational reading comprehension does not come easily

(Gersten, Fuchs, Williams, & Baker, 2001). It is interventions for these students that are the primary focus of this chapter. Before we turn to those interventions, however, we discuss what causes difficulties with informational reading comprehension in the first place.

Causes of Substantial Difficulties with Informational Reading Comprehension

Students struggle with reading comprehension for many different reasons. In one review on the subject, Duke, Pressley, and Hilden (2004) identified each of the following as documented contributors to reading comprehension difficulties: difficulties with word recognition and decoding; fluency problems; limited short term or working memory; limitations of oral language; inadequate knowledge of the particulars of written language, including different genres of written language; a lack of active and strategic thinking before, during, and after reading; insufficient prior knowledge, vocabulary, and concept knowledge; and a lack of reading engagement. For some readers, it is possible that just one of these contributors to reading comprehension difficulty is at fault. For many, however, multiple causes are operating, with addressing one difficulty leading only to the surfacing of another. And these causes can appear in different combinations and in concert with different strengths. Research of Riddle Buly and Valencia (2002) illustrates this point well. In their study of fourth-grade students who scored below proficient in reading comprehension on the Washington Assessment of Student Learning (WASL) and were not already identified as needing special instruction in reading, they found six distinct profiles of readers:

- Automatic word callers (stronger in word ID and fluency than meaning; 18%)
- Struggling word callers (stronger in word ID and fluency than meaning, but struggling with word ID; 15%)
- Word stumblers (word ID problems, slow readers, meaning relative strength; 18%)
- Slow and steady comprehenders (good word ID and meaning, slow readers; 24%)
- Slow word callers (good word ID, slow readers, poor meaning; 17%)
- Disabled readers (low word ID, low fluency, low meaning; 9%)

Had the researchers administered assessments in additional areas—for example, reading engagement and genre knowledge—they would likely have identified even more different profiles of the struggling comprehender.

While this research on causes of reading comprehension difficulties across different kinds of text is informative, it is also important to examine causes of reading comprehension difficulties with specific genres of text. It is increasingly clear that reading comprehension is, to a substantial degree, genre-specific (Duke, 2005; RAND Reading Study Group, 2002). Readers engage, to different degrees, in different processes when comprehending different genres of text— for example, narrative versus informational text (e.g., Kirk & Pearson, 1996; Kucan & Beck, 1996). Readers also do not necessarily have the same level of proficiency in comprehending different genres of text. For instance, in the Progress in International Reading Literacy Study (PIRLS), which separately assessed literary reading and reading for information, some students showed far greater proficiency in literary reading, while others showed far greater proficiency in reading for information (and still others showed roughly equal achievement for both; Park, 2008). This pattern was also seen at a national level. Some countries show greater proficiency with informational reading, some show greater proficiency with literary reading, and still others show roughly equal performance across the two kinds of reading. Notably, the United States has the largest gap favoring literary reading ability over informational reading ability of any nation studied in PIRLS 2001, though happily, not in PIRLS 2006 (Park, 2008). Perhaps not surprisingly, a study by Saenz and Fuchs (2002) of U.S. secondary students with learning disabilities found they had substantially lower performance comprehending informational than narrative text (and they also read informational text less fluently). This difficulty was seen not in literal comprehension but in the ability to answer inferential reading comprehension questions. Results like these raise the question *what makes informational reading comprehension difficult*?

One approach to thinking about the particular reading comprehension difficulties posed by informational text is to look at those things that make informational text unique. We will focus here on three characteristics of informational text that may pose particular challenges for informational reading comprehension: its content, its vocabulary, and its structure. Of course, informational text has many other characteristics (Pappas, 2006; Purcell-Gates, Duke, & Martineau, 2007), but these three are arguably especially good candidates for causing reading comprehension difficulties.

As explained earlier, the purpose of informational text is to convey information about the natural and social world. As such, when it is serving its purpose, informational text requires the reader to learn new information and to integrate that information with what is already known. This process is fraught with challenges. In some cases, the text assumes knowledge that the reader does not in fact have, or that may even contradict the reader's existing knowledge or conceptions (e.g., Alvermann, Smith, & Readence, 1985; Guzzetti, Snyder, Glass, & Gamas, 1993). In other cases, the reader may have relevant background knowledge but fail to bring it to bear or integrate it with knowledge from the text (e.g., Carr & Thompson, 1996), sometimes due to poor organization of the reader's knowledge, the text, or both. In both cases there is a vicious cycle at work for readers with substantial comprehension difficulties: readers who struggle to learn content from informational text then do not have that content knowledge to bring to bear with future texts they read. This may help to explain why reading comprehension interventions that focus heavily on content learning are often effective (Duke & Martin, 2008).

A second and closely related characteristic of informational text is a density of specialized vocabulary (Purcell-Gates et al., 2007). For readers with limited vocabulary knowledge, this may mean encountering an overwhelming number of unfamiliar words during reading. And because so much vocabulary is learned from reading (Swanborn & de Glopper, 1999), there is again a vicious cycle at work for poor readers—less reading means fewer opportunities to learn vocabulary which means less vocabulary knowledge to bring to bear when reading (Cunningham & Stanovich, 1998). On the bright side, unlike narrative text, which uses many words only once, informational text often repeats key vocabulary many times (Hiebert, 2006). For example, while a narrative text might describe a character as *dainty* just one time, an informational text might describe a tree as *deciduous* many times, providing many exposures and opportunities to learn the word. Moreover, informational text often provides many clues to word meaning, such as glosses of the word in the running text (e.g., a canine, or animal in the dog family. . .), illustrations of the word (e.g., a diagram depicting and labeling a flower's *stamens*), or definitions of the word in the glossary (Duke & Billman, 2009), although a reader needs particular knowledge and skills to take advantage of these clues—knowledge and skills that are challenging to teach (Baumann, 2008). In addition, many unfamiliar words in an informational text are likely to be conceptually related, lending themselves to the kinds of knowledge-oriented vocabulary teaching that have been shown to be more effective than definitional approaches (Bos & Anders, 1990), although in practice such teaching appears to be rare (e.g., Dole & Nelson, 2008; Scott, Jamieson-Noel, & Asselin, 2003).

A third characteristic of informational text that may pose particular challenges for readers with substantial comprehension difficulties is its structure. Informational texts organize information using specific structures, such as problem-solution and compare-contrast. If used, these structures can assist the reader in comprehending and learning from the text. However, it has been demonstrated across multiple studies that poor readers and readers with learning disabilities are not as attuned as other readers to informational text structures (e.g., Englert & Thomas, 1987; McGee, 1982). Exacerbating the problem is the fact that many informational texts are "inconsiderate" (e.g., Armbruster, 1984), including not being particularly well structured. Fortunately, as discussed in the following section, interventions to improve struggling readers' attention to and use of text structure have enjoyed considerable success.

Interventions to Enhance Informational Reading Comprehension Among Elementary Students with Reading Difficulties

Researchers have tested a variety of interventions to improve informational reading comprehension among elementary-aged students with reading difficulties. These instructional activities range from analyzing text structures to teaching comprehension strategies to implementing highly complex multi-component interventions. In some studies of these interventions the target population is identified as "students with learning disabilities." Other times it is "students with reading disabilities," "poor readers," or "struggling readers." There is probably not a perfect match between any of these labels and students who experience substantial difficulties with informational reading comprehension—both because there may be students who struggle only with informational reading comprehension and because there may be students who are poor readers in many senses but relatively strong in informational reading comprehension—but there is also probably considerable overlap. Hence we are including among interventions reviewed interventions targeting any of the previously listed groups as well as interventions of a broader population that have disaggregated their data to show the impact of their intervention on students identified having reading difficulties.

As the title of this section indicates, we are also limiting our review to interventions that have been tested with elementary-aged students, which we've defined as K–6 (although older students were sometimes also included in the studies as well). To our knowledge, no review on this topic has focused specifically on elementary-aged children, even though we likely all agree that interventions that work well at other ages may not necessarily work well for elementary-aged children and vice-versa. (Similarly, interventions that work well for children in upper elementary grades may not work well for children in the primary grades and vice-versa, which is why we are careful to specify age groups throughout our discussion of research in this area.) In contrast, there are reviews on this topic addressing elementary, middle, and secondary together, and addressing narrative as well as informational text (Gersten et al., 2001; Talbott, Lloyd, & Tankersley, 1994).[1]

Focusing exclusively on elementary-aged children allows us to make three important points: First, even in elementary school, instruction for struggling readers need not focus entirely on decoding and word recognition. As you will read, even in elementary school, and even in the primary grades of elementary school, it appears that struggling readers benefit from instruction in reading comprehension. Second, the previous statement is true for informational text, a genre often neglected and considered too difficult for young children (Duke et al., 2002) and perhaps also for struggling readers (Caswell & Duke, 1998). Third, focusing on elementary-aged children helps to reveal some specific gaps in the research that are less likely to be revealed through a broader review. As the reader will see, and as we discuss in the concluding section of the chapter, we have much work to do in the development and testing of interventions in informational text comprehension for elementary-aged struggling readers.

The reader will notice that nearly all of the research cited in this chapter comes from 1975 and later. This is not a coincidence but rather reflects important changes in the field that occurred before and around that time. The "cognitive revolution" had so taken hold that cognitive science had become the dominant perspective in many fields in and related to educational research (Gardner, 1987). In reading, this revolution brought with it an intense interest in what is going on in the mind as one makes meaning with text and how instruction might influence that (Pearson, 1986). The Center for the Study of Reading, established in 1976, and the ascendance in the late 1970s of interest in metacognition, helped to spur the development and testing of a wide range of approaches to improving reading comprehension, many of them (as is clear from the later citations in this chapter) still being studied in one form or another today.

Another contextual factor to bear in mind when reading this review of studies on informational text comprehension instruction regards the assessments used in the studies. "Effectiveness" is determined by student performance on some measure or measures chosen by the researchers. Thus, as you read about each study and technique, it is important to bear in mind the measures used and not used. As is clear in Table 31.1, both the number and the nature of measures vary a great deal from study to study. Each of these measures, of course, has limitations, with some very limited in their ability to measure reading comprehension as we currently conceive it (Pearson & Hamm, 2005; RAND Reading Study Group, 2002). As we discuss further at the conclusion of the chapter, improving reading comprehension assessment is, or should be, a high priority for research and development in comprehension instruction.

The evidence to date suggests that a variety of informational text comprehension interventions can increase the comprehension performance of elementary-aged students with reading difficulties. Researchers have tested several different kinds of instruction with elementary students with learning disabilities, as well as those enrolled in remedial reading classes, reading below grade level, and/or classified as low readers. As similar studies with other populations (e.g., Duke & Pearson, 2002; Pressley, 2000) have found, these interventions often produce significant gains. At least five different kinds of instruction have been studied: comprehension strategy instruction, use of graphic organizers and other visual aids, text structure instruction, before-reading interventions, and other interventions. In each area, at least one approach has been shown to be effective, supporting the notion that instruction in informational text comprehension benefits struggling readers (although, as the reader will see, long-term maintenance and transfer are more elusive).

Comprehension Strategy Instruction   Strategy instruction, in which instructors attempt to boost students' reading comprehension by equipping them with new ways to think as they read, is one of the largest areas of inquiry for researchers interested in this population. These studies have typically focused on older elementary students (fifth and sixth graders), included relatively short-term interventions,

and tested maintenance within a month of instruction. Like the studies that have examined strategy instruction primarily with general education students (e.g., Baumann, 1984; Brown, Pressley, Van Meter, & Schuder, 1996; Taylor & Frye, 1992), though, the available evidence suggests that students with reading difficulties also appear to profit from these lessons.

We have organized the discussion of comprehension strategies instruction into two sections: single strategy instruction and multiple strategy instruction. This raises the question of which is better—teaching strategies one at a time or teaching strategies in clusters. This is a question we often encounter in schools, but it has been the subject of very little in research. One study, Reutzel, Smith, and Fawson (2005), conducted a head-to-head comparison of single and multiple strategy instruction with informational text. Eighty second graders stratified by achievement level participated. Instruction focused on making connections and predictions; visualizing; self-monitoring; questioning; summarizing; and, for the multiple strategy instruction condition, setting goals and attending to text structure. Students either were taught successively, with 13 days spent on each strategy; or they simultaneously studied all these strategies, with 10 to 15 minutes devoted to individually introducing each strategy (over the course of a total of three lessons). After 16 weeks of instruction, on many of the measures (e.g., general reading comprehension, strategy use, motivation), no statistically significant differences were found. However, the latter group scored significantly higher on some measures: curriculum-based measures, knowledge of subordinate ideas, and scientific content knowledge. The researchers concluded that multiple strategies instruction presented a "clear added value" (p. 298). This, in turn, raises the question of why multiple strategy instruction may be more effective. We can only speculate here, but the following seem especially strong explanations: (a) this gives the reader more practice, earlier, in coordinating the use of multiple strategies, which is what good readers do when they read (Pressley & Afflerbach, 1995); (b) this gives the reader more time to learn any one strategy (instead, for example, of not beginning to learn a particular strategy until month 4); (c) this allows the reader to foreground the strategy or strategies that are the best fit for his/her purposes, prior knowledge, and the text in a given reading situation, while backgrounding the strategy or strategies that are less helpful in that particular context. All this said, clearly more research is needed on this question, and it remains worthwhile to examine the research on both single and multiple strategy instruction approaches.

Single strategy instruction.   At times, a single comprehension strategy has been the focus of an intervention. For example, researchers have investigated the effects of teaching students with reading difficulties how to look for the main idea in informational texts by directing them to tell "what the whole story is about or the main idea" (Graves, 1986, p. 93), identify "what subjects or concepts were discussed in

TABLE 31.1
Measures Included in Each Study

Study	Summary or Retelling		Experimenter-Developed Pencil & Paper Test	Commercial Norm-Referenced Assessment	Performance Assessment	Attitudes Survey[a]	Interview	Other
	Oral	Written						
Adams, Carnine, & Gersten (1982)	X		SA				X	
Ankney & McClurg (1981)			MC	X				
Babbs (1984)	X			X				
Boyle (1996)			U	X		X		student maps; metacognitive/strategy knowledge measure
Brand-Gruwel, Aarnoutse, & van den Bos (1998)			MC	X				error detection task; decoding measure
Carnine & Kinder (1985)	X		SA, U					decoding measure
Chan & Cole (1986)			MC				X	
Chan (1991)			MC					student rating of important ideas
Darch & Carnine (1986)			MC			X		
Ellis & Graves (1990)			MC					
Englert & Mariage (1991)		X						metacognitive/strategy knowledge measure
Englert et al. (1994)		X						metacognitive/strategy knowledge measure
Gagne & Memory (1978)	X		MC, SA	X				
Gajria & Salvia (1992)	X		MC	X				
Graves (1986)			MC	X				decoding measure
Griffin, Simmons, & Kameenui (1991)	X		MC, SA	X				
Guthrie et al. (1998)					X			
Guthrie et al. (2004)				X	X	X		word-pair ratings; teacher ratings
Jitendra et al. (2000)			MC, SA			X		
Johnson-Glenberg (2005)			MC, SA		X			rereading scrollbacks
Kelly, Moore, & Tuck (1994)			U	X				
Klingner et al. (2004)				X			X	
Klingner, Vaughn, & Schumm (1998)			MC, SA, FIB	X				vocabulary definitions; observations
Langer (1984)			MC	X				free association of vocabulary
Lederer (2000)		X	SA					student-created question; textbook chapter/unit test
Lysynchuk, Pressley, & Vye (1990)	X		SA	X				decoding measure
Mason (2004)	X	X		X			X	outlining
Mason et al. (2006)	X	X		X			X	outlining

(continued)

TABLE 31.1
Continued

Study	Summary or Retelling		Experimenter-Developed Pencil & Paper Test	Commercial Norm-Referenced Assessment	Performance Assessment	Attitudes Survey[a]	Interview	Other
	Oral	Written						
McCormick (1989)			MC					
Memory (1983)			MC, SA	X				
O'Mallen, Lewis, & Craig (1993)		X		X				
Reutzel, Smith, & Fawson (2005)	X		MC	X				textbook chapter/unit test
Simmonds (1992)					X	X		metacognitive/strategy knowledge measure
Sinatra, Stahl-Gemake, & Berg (1984)			MC					
Stevens (1988)			U					
Taylor (1982)		X	SA					
Walker (1995)			SA/E	X				
Williams et al. (2005)	X			X	X			
Williams et al. (2007)				X	X			
Wong & Wilson, study two (1984)	X							

Note. MC = Multiple choice. SA = Short answer. E = Essay. FIB = Fill in the blank. U = Unspecified format.

[a]This category includes measures of students' attitudes toward reading and measures of students' attitudes about the particular intervention.

each of the individual sentences" (Stevens, 1988, p. 23), or "name the person and tell the main thing the person did in all the sentences" (Jitendra, Hoppes, & Xin, 2000, p. 130). In all three studies, after a short sequence of lessons (e.g., six), fifth- and sixth-grade students with learning disabilities and those enrolled in remedial reading classes, along with adolescents from older grades, outperformed other participants at a level of statistical significance, with gains further heightened by adding a self-monitoring component (Graves, 1986; Jitendra et al., 2000). These effects were seen with texts and questions similar to instructional materials (Graves, 1986; Jitendra et al., 2000; Stevens, 1988), as well as on maintenance assessments administered one (Graves, 1986) and six (Jitendra et al., 2000) weeks later. It should be noted, however, that these samples of students, which numbered between 20 and 50, were often asked to select the main idea among several choices, and one researcher (Jitendra et al., 2000) found that scores dropped when children were asked to generate the main idea themselves. Also, transfer-of-learning measures to different kinds of texts or to general comprehension were only significant in some cases (Jitendra et al., 2000; Stevens, 1988).

In addition, studies have tested the effects of teaching students with reading difficulties summarizing and self-questioning strategies with informational text. In two cases, 30–47 students (enrolled in the fifth to ninth grades) who tested at least 2 years below grade level expectations in reading comprehension were taught how to summarize (Ellis & Graves, 1990; Gaijria & Salvia, 1992). Gaijria and Salvia explicitly taught participants "the five summarization rules developed by Brown and Day (1983): (a) superordination, (b) deletion of redundant information, (c) selection, (d) invention, and (e) deletion of unimportant information" (p. 511); they introduced, modeled, justified, and provided practice opportunities for each rule, fading their support over the course of instruction (which ranged from 6.5 to 11 hours). Ellis and Graves also modeled how to paraphrase, provided practice opportunities, and gave feedback to participants during their 8-day intervention. Students from both studies significantly outperformed control groups and peers who participated in alternate treatment conditions (e.g., rereading the texts several times); they performed as well as students without disabilities on literal recall questions and better than this comparison group on "condensation" (e.g., inferential, cause-and-effect) questions (Gaijria & Salvia, 1992). These gains seemed to be maintained, at least for the 14 to 36 days that elapsed between the posttest and delayed tests, and to transfer to a general reading comprehension measure (Ellis & Graves, 1990; Gaijria & Salvia, 1992).

For self-questioning, fifth- and sixth-grade students with reading or learning disabilities who learned to create their own questions about an expository text selection scored significantly higher than students who reread texts or practiced answering questions (Chan, 1991; Chan & Cole, 1986). In the first study, students participated in five lessons, in which they were taught to ask themselves questions (e.g., "Does this sentence repeat what has already been said?"; "What is the paragraph mainly about?"; Chan, 1991, p. 429). Instruction involved either a demonstration and practice or a five-stage teaching model that included teacher modeling, guided practice, and fading support. In the second study, one group of students was told to take turns pretending "that they were reading to Rob the robot, and wanted to check every now and then to see whether Rob had been following" and acting as the robot to answer the question posed (Chan & Cole, 1986, p. 36). Another group of students was told to "underline with the fluorescent marker two interesting words from the paragraph, and then to think of two questions to ask Rob about the two underlined words" (p. 36). In these studies, students who were taught to self-question performed as well as peers who learned to underline interesting words, those who studied a combination (self-question and either read or underline), and a comparison group of normally achieving third-grade students. Transfer was limited, although one group who underwent strategy generalization training showed some evidence of independently applying the strategy across contexts.

Multiple strategy instruction. In addition to these single-strategy interventions, multiple strategy instructional methods have been designed specifically for or tested with elementary-aged students with reading difficulties. For instance, Reciprocal Teaching (Palinscar & Brown, 1984), an approach to developing informational reading comprehension originally designed for seventh graders who were classified as below-average readers, has also been tested with fourth-, fifth-, and sixth-grade students with learning disabilities or who otherwise struggle with reading comprehension (Brand-Gruwel, Aarnoutses, & van den Bos, 1998; Kelly, Moore, & Tuck, 1994; Lederer, 2000; Lysynchuk, Pressley, & Vye, 1990). This method of instruction involves teaching students to ask questions, clarify their understandings, make predictions, and summarize by having them take turns leading their peers in dialogic communication. Most of these lessons occurred for 13 to 17 days, but one study (Kelly et al., 1994) continued daily instruction for an entire semester. The number of participants varied widely, from 18 (Kelly et al., 1994) to 128 (Lederer, 2000). In all cases, favorable and significant effects were found for immediate and direct tests (e.g., answering comprehension questions). These gains were not always maintained over the 1- to 3-month period between posttest and follow-up; several researchers reported at least some of their experimental group's scores on delayed measures as insignificant (Brand-Gruwel et al., 1998; Kelly et al., 1994; Lederer, 2000). Also, with one notable exception (Lysynchuk et al., 1990), analysis of the experimental group's scores on norm-referenced test measures (e.g., Progressive Achievement Test of Reading Comprehension; Reid & Elley, 1991) revealed either increases that were not statistically significant or differences that only approached significance.

An intervention based on Reciprocal Teaching, POSSE, has also been investigated (Englert & Mariage, 1991;

Englert, Tarrant, Mariage, & Oxer, 1994). Over the course of 2 months, first through eighth graders with learning disabilities, emotional impairment, or mild mental retardation learned to engage in: "Predicting ideas based upon background knowledge, Organizing predicted textual ideas and background knowledge based upon text structure, Searching/Summarizing by searching for the text structure in the expository passage and summarizing the main ideas, and Evaluating their comprehension" (Englert & Mariage, 1991, p. 124). On written recalls and strategy knowledge measures, students in the POSSE condition performed significantly better than students engaged in regular reading or K-W-L (Ogle, 1986) instruction. Among other things, the researchers concluded that students with learning disabilities "who were trained in the POSSE strategies made significant gains in their ability to recall textual ideas" (Englert & Mariage, 1991, p. 135), and that "POSSE was more effective than K-W-L when students were applying their knowledge independently in the unprompted and unscaffolded posttest conditions," as well as in helping them comprehend and recall passages (Englert et al., 1994, p. 181). Importantly, the researchers found no age by treatment interaction, suggesting that the intervention was equally effective for all ages first through eighth grade.

In addition, Klingner and her colleagues (Klingner, Vaughn, Arguelles, Hughes, & Leftwich, 2004; Klingner, Vaughn, & Schumm, 1998) examined an informational text comprehension intervention called Collaborative Strategic Reading (CSR). Fourth-grade students classified as "low achieving" and those with learning disabilities were included among the participants. The strategy instruction encompassed four different strategies: previewing ("preview"), comprehension-monitoring ("click and clunk"), finding and summarizing the main ideas ("get the gist" and "wrap up"), and self-questioning ("wrap up"). Researchers taught these strategies by introducing them, modeling them through "think alouds," providing guided practice opportunities, and organizing small groups of students to work together and to help each other use these strategies for several days. On norm-referenced tests, paper-and-pencil unit tests, interviews, and observations of hundreds of students, the intermediate elementary students assigned to the CSR condition displayed significant gains in reading comprehension, although effects on students' content knowledge were insignificant and higher-level talk was infrequent. The researchers concluded that students deemed to be low-achieving benefitted the most from this kind of strategy instruction.

In another study, fifth graders identified as having poor study skills learned to preview texts, recite subheadings, ask questions, read for key details, and reread subheadings and details (Adams, Carnine, & Gersten, 1982). Participants individually met four times with trainers, who reviewed potentially unknown words from the social studies texts, modeled the study technique, corrected mistakes, faded their support, and provided periodic feedback. On short-answer tests administered immediately after instruction and 2 weeks later, the instructed group scored higher than their peers at a level of statistical significance, but no statistically significant between-group differences were found on participants' retellings.

Another multiple strategy intervention that has been tested specifically with struggling elementary readers is Think before reading, think While reading, think After reading (TWA; Mason, 2004; Mason, Snyder, Sukhram, & Kedem, 2006). Fourth- and fifth-grade students who could decode "at a third-grade level and who had reading comprehension subtests scores between the 10th and 40th percentiles on the Comprehensive Tests of Basic Skills (CTBS; CTB/McGraw-Hill, 1996) taken in fourth grade" (Mason, 2004, p. 285) participated. They were given 11 to 15 lessons in activating prior knowledge and making predictions ("Think before reading"); monitoring reading speed, making connections, and rereading ("think While reading"); and finding the main idea, summarizing, and reflecting on learning ("think After reading"). In contrast to the comparison group (who were taught Reciprocal Questioning; Manzo, 1975), significant main effects emerged when TWA students were asked to orally identify the main idea, summarize, and retell. These effects did not appear on the other measures (intrinsic motivation, self-efficacy, and written retelling). In a single subject experimental design, nine fourth-grade students with reading difficulties were taught TWA in conjunction with another multiple-strategy approach, "Pick goals, List ways to meet goals, And, make Notes, and Sequence notes" (PLANS; Mason et al., 2006, p. 72). The researchers measured students' inclusion of main ideas in note-taking outlines, oral retellings, and written retellings. Nearly all of the fourth-graders learned to independently use TWA and PLANS during the instructional phase (as evidenced by their inclusion of 3–5 main ideas). The majority of the participants (6 students) continued to include more main ideas in their post-instructional outlines, for at least some of the time. Despite a few erratic performances on the maintenance probes, most of the students also included more main ideas in their post-instruction oral and written retellings.

Guthrie and his colleagues (e.g., Guthrie et al., 1998; Guthrie et al., 2004) have also developed an informational comprehension intervention involving multiple strategy instruction: Concept-Oriented Reading Instruction (CORI). This intervention has been examined in a number of studies, including a recent study focused on Grade 5 low achieving readers (Guthrie et al., 2009). In CORI, during 12-week units, teachers use sets of books (information books, novels, and poetry), websites, and hands-on materials to address reading (e.g., fluent oral reading, self-monitoring), science (e.g., mutualism, competition), and reading motivation (e.g., intrinsic motivation, self-efficacy) goals. As described in a meta-analysis of research on CORI, CORI lessons have followed a specific pattern:

> First, for 10 min, students performed oral reading fluency activities with poems or information books. Approximately 2 days per week, instead of oral reading fluency, students

studied science concepts and/or participated in a hands-on activity (such as drawing a horseshoe crab from observation). Second, the teacher spent 10 min giving a minilesson on comprehension [specifically a comprehension strategy] to set the stage for organized guided reading. For the next three 15-min segments, students alternated among small-group guided reading, writing, and independent reading. Third, the teacher provided guided reading in three small groups of four or five students for 15 min each. For guided reading, appropriate-level texts were used for modeling, scaffolding, and guided practice of the reading comprehension strategies. During the writing segment, students made entries into their portfolios based on their information books used in the comprehension lesson, or they wrote reactions to their novels that were used in small-group discussions. During independent reading activity, students silently read their book club novels. When requested, students took notes and prepared reaction entries for their journals. (Guthrie, McRae, & Klauda, 2007, p. 241)

When tested against traditional instruction (Guthrie et al., 1998) and against traditional instruction (one group) and comprehension strategy instruction alone (the other group, using the same comprehension strategies and science activities as CORI; Guthrie, 2004), the third- and fifth-grade students in the CORI condition outperformed both groups on experimenter-developed and norm-referenced tests, with concomitant increases in self-reported motivation and cognitive strategy composite scores. In addition, the intervention appeared to have "a positive, indirect effect on conceptual transfer" (Guthrie et al., 1998, p. 18). Similar results have been obtained when examining the impact of CORI specifically for low-achieving students (Guthrie et al., 2009).

Finally, Johnson-Glenberg (2005) tested the efficacy of digitally embedding cues to use comprehension strategies in informational texts. For eight lessons, sixth (and seventh) graders classified as poor comprehenders read texts on the computer in which they were periodically asked to create questions and to build models that reflected their content understandings. Although both the control and experimental participants made significant gains on vocabulary measures, the latter group manifested significantly higher comprehension than the former. Johnson-Glenberg (2005) concluded that it was "the use of higher-level verbal strategies and the addition of the visual/imaginal processing that appear to result in an increase in deeper comprehension for the readers" (p.775). Johnson-Glenberg's computer-based work adds further to the menu of multiple strategy instruction techniques shown to be effective at improving the informational reading comprehension of students with reading difficulties.

Graphic Organizers and Other Visual Aids   Visual aids that readers can create and/or use to assist in their comprehension of informational text have also been explored with students with reading difficulties. Graphic organizers have often long been used to aid content knowledge acquisition and/or to support the reading comprehension of students from general education contexts (Alvermann, Boothby,

& Wolfe, 1984; Armbruster, Anderson, & Meyer, 1991; Boothby & Alvermann, 1984; DiCecco & Gleason, 2002; Griffin, Simmons, & Kameenui, 1991; Simmons, Griffin, & Kameenui, 1988). When researchers' investigations have focused on elementary students with learning disabilities or reading difficulties, they have also found that the use of graphic organizers or other visual aids boosts students' performances.

In one study, 27 intermediate elementary students enrolled in a reading clinic program individually learned to use a blank graphic organizer to guide their pre-discussion and reading efforts over a 4-month period (Sinatra, Stahl-Gemake, & Berg, 1984). Experimenter-developed comprehension measures revealed that they performed significantly better on average than when taught using "Directed Reading Activity (DRA)" lessons. Neither transfer nor maintenance was tested.

In another study, Boyle (1996) taught 15 students with reading difficulties in sixth grade (and higher) to TRAVEL. For four lessons, they learned to identify, record, and circle the text's topic ("Topic"); read the passage ("Read"); to identify, record, and circle each paragraph's main idea and three corresponding details ("Ask"); check their thinking ("Verify"); repeat these steps ("Examine"); and connect all the circles ("Link"). At posttest Boyle found significant differences in TRAVEL students over control group students in performance on an experimenter-developed reading comprehension test, but not on a norm-referenced reading test, metacognitive awareness questionnaire, or a student attitudes measure.

In a no-control experiment, Carnine and Kinder (1985) tested two interventions: one asked 27 low-comprehending fourth-, fifth-, and sixth-grade students to stop periodically while reading expository passages and visualize (generative-learning condition), and the other directed students to identify and apply the principle explained in the text (schema-based condition). After 10 lessons, the pre- to posttest performances of students from both interventions improved significantly. The interventions were not, however, equally effective in the long term; students who had created mental images scored significantly lower on the comprehension test administered 2 weeks later.

Finally, when fifth- and sixth-grade students with learning disabilities were trained to study graphic organizers before and after reading a science textbook chapter, they performed higher than the alternative group (who studied lists of facts) but not at a level of statistical significance; because this difference was statistically insignificant, Griffin, Simmons, and Kameenui (1991) concluded that "graphic organizers do not significantly enhance student's [sic] comprehension and recall of science content more than an alternate instructional adjunct, a list of facts" (p. 369). The results of this study appear to represent an exception to researchers' general pattern of finding positive outcomes in use of graphic organizers or other visual aids. This may be related to the instructional procedures used in this study— rather that creating or completing graphic organizers, as in other studies, students studied graphic organizers that had already been constructed.

Text Structure Instruction   Text structure instruction involves teaching students to look for the underlying structure or organization of text (e.g., cause-effect or compare-contrast) and to use that knowledge to assist their comprehension. Text structure instruction has been studied with both narrative and informational texts and with a variety of grade levels. In general, text structure instruction has proven to be effective at improving reading comprehension (Dickson, Simmons, & Kameenui, 1998). Surprisingly, we found very few studies of text structure instruction focused on the population of interest in this chapter—elementary-aged students with reading difficulties. Those we did find, however, did find some positive impacts, though again transfer is an often unmet challenge.

In a study with older students, Taylor (1982) taught fifth graders classified as either competent or less competent readers, in seven weekly lessons, how to identify the structure of a text and use it to create an outline. In the first of two studies, participants, including the less competent readers, made statistically significant gains in recalling information and identifying textual organization, but not in answering short-answer questions. In the second of two studies, no significant gains were observed, with several possible explanations provided for the differing results for the second group.

In a text structure instruction study focusing on students identified as having learning disabilities, Wong and Wilson (1984, study two) asked 56 fifth-, sixth-, and seventh-grade students to organize disorganized passages. During one lesson, participants received one-on-one instruction; the experimenter read passages aloud, while they provided oral retellings and re-ordered disorganized passages. After this training period, participants were tested on their ability to organize, study, and retell a disorganized passage. The researchers concluded that "our sample of learning disabled children readily learned how to organize sentences around a subtopic in the paragraphs of a passage. More importantly, such learning increased their retention of the passage" (p. 481).

Instruction about attending to the structure of text has also been also included in some multiple comprehension strategy instructional approaches. For example, in POSSE (Englert & Mariage, 1991; Englert et al., 1994), described earlier, two of the strategies include: "Organizing predicted textual ideas and background knowledge based upon text structure" and "Searching... by searching for the text structure in the expository passage." Further, previewing, as found in interventions such as Collaborative Strategic Reading (Klingner et al., 2004; Klingner et al., 1998), also described earlier, can also be seen as involving attention to text structure.

Before-Reading Interventions   At times, studies have examined the effects of specific pre-reading activities (e.g.,

previewing, asking questions) for elementary-aged students with reading difficulties. Like other kinds of interventions, research in this area has tended to feature students from the intermediate grades and to occur for a short period of time. In particular, in the studies reviewed below, research designs have focused on fifth- and/or sixth-grade students and instructional phases that lasted between three and ten lessons.

In an early study, Gagne and Memory (1978) examined the impact of providing sixth-grade students with different kinds of instructions prior to their beginning to read informational text in a single lesson. There were seven different instructions for seven different groups (total N = 224) as follows: "read background information before reading the main passage" (Group 1); "While reading this passage, try to form a vivid mental picture of what was described in the passage" (p. 326; Group 2); search for the answer to a factual question as they read (Group 3); search for the answer to an application question as they read (Group 4); search for the answer to a question about the main idea as they read (Group 5); read background information before reading the main passage (Group 6); and think about how a given example was similar to the relationship in the main passage (Group 7). Cause-effect passages were used. Although students in Groups 2–7 tended to perform the same as students in Group 1, low-achieving students who were asked to search for the answer to a main idea question (Group 5) performed significantly better on main-idea test questions.

A related study (Memory, 1983) found that adding a pre-question (e.g., "What feelings and attitudes of some people in the Roman Catholic Church led to the formation of new religions in Europe during the 1500's?"; p. 41) before students read informational text benefited students with reading difficulties. Specifically, after a 3-lesson intervention, sixth graders classified as low-average "who had practice with why prequestions and who were given such prequestions as aids during the testing performed significantly better" (Memory, 1983, p. 45), whereas skilled readers did not exhibit significant gains.

Langer (1984) used the Pre REading Plan (PReP) procedure with sixth graders reading above, on, and below grade level. For three lessons, Langer asked students to make associations with the primary concepts in the text, reflect on their thinking, and discuss new knowledge. She used three phases of questioning (e.g., phase 1: "Tell me anything that comes to mind when…" phase 2: "What made you think of …?"; phase 3: "Based on our discussion, have you any new ideas about…?"; p. 471) to help students activate their background knowledge and monitor the quality of their initial ideas. Although students had significantly better scores than the other treatment groups on average, the intervention did not appear to be effective for students who were below grade level.

Finally, McCormick (1989) incorporated written previews into her intervention. More- and less-skilled readers in fifth grade participated in lessons for 2 weeks; they studied, discussed, and listened to pre-written previews before reading the selected passages. Each preview shared the same elements: (a) multiple questions about students' background information; (b) summary of the text; and (c) important vocabulary. During each session, the teacher spent 10 minutes discussing the questions, reading aloud the summary, and reviewing the key words. Then they read the passage and completed an experimenter-developed test. Among other results, McCormick reported that "with both more skilled and less skilled readers, overall performance was superior when previews were employed before reading social studies selections" (pp. 228–229).

Other Interventions In a study of a well-known intervention to help students better understand and answer reading comprehension questions, Simmonds (1992) had teachers teach lessons about Question-Answer Relationships (QARs; e.g., Raphael & Pearson, 1985). This study included an unusually broad range of ages—first through ninth graders with learning disabilities who participated and received instruction in their resource rooms. For four sessions, teachers introduced each question type ("Right There," "Think and Search," and "On My Own") and provided varied opportunities to categorize questions and formulate answers. Then, for an additional week, teachers asked students to apply QAR in content area texts. The researcher noted that teachers "followed their existing patterns of reading instruction in which students read or were read to and answered corresponding questions" (p. 197). After this 3-week intervention, teachers removed all relevant charts from display and administered posttests. As compared to students in a control group, students taught QARs displayed significant gains on posttests, from which the researcher concluded that "QARs significantly improved the question-answer recognition and location performance of students with learning disabilities" (p. 198).

Manzo's Guided Reading Procedure, a routine for teachers to use during small group reading, was examined in a study that included fifth- and sixth-grade students who scored in the bottom quartile of the Metropolitan Achievement Test. Students participated in a lesson featuring Manzo's Guided Reading Procedure, in which students set their reading purpose, recalled what they read, searched the text for additional information, organized their knowledge, answered synthesis questions, and completed a comprehension test (Ankney & McClurg, 1981). Students, including those in the bottom quartile, outperformed their peers on measures administered immediately, 1 week, and 4 weeks later.

Status of the Field

From these studies, it appears that elementary-aged students with reading difficulties may benefit from informational text comprehension instruction. At least some versions of single and multiple comprehension strategy instruction, the use of graphic organizers and other visual aids, text structure

instruction, before reading interventions, and other interventions appear to produce significant gains. This finding mirrors the results of reviews on reading comprehension instruction for students identified as having learning disabilities that have included older students (Gersten et al., 2001; Talbott et al., 1994) as well as results of reviews of reading comprehension instruction that include studies with elementary-aged readers who are not struggling (e.g., National Reading Panel, 2000; Pressley, 2005).

This finding is important because, in our and others' observations (e.g., Pressley et al., 2009), when elementary-aged students struggle with reading, they are often provided with interventions primarily or entirely focused on decoding and word recognition. Yet it appears that intervention in the area of reading comprehension can also benefit this population. This finding is also important because of the persistent perception among many that informational text is too difficult for students still learning to read (rather than reading to learn) and the concomitant neglect of informational text in the elementary years, particularly the primary grades (Duke et al., 2002) and perhaps with struggling readers (Caswell & Duke, 1998). From the research reviewed in this chapter it appears that informational text comprehension in the elementary years, even for struggling readers, is both appropriate and fruitful.

With an age group about which we would expect the least research in this area, it is encouraging that such a range of interventions for improving informational text comprehension for struggling readers have been examined. This suggests a recognition that informational text is critical for success in and outside of school and that many U.S. students, including struggling readers, have difficulty with these texts. It also suggests a recognition that reading comprehension is indeed genre-specific—that students must be provided with experience and instruction that features the kinds of text we wish them to learn to comprehend, using approaches that are designed for that kind of text. Several approaches reviewed in this chapter, such as instruction in identifying main idea and details and instruction in specific informational text structures, make little sense for other genres, such as narrative texts. Moreover, many approaches address head on the particular challenges posed by informational text, which, as discussed earlier in the chapter, include its content, structure, and vocabulary.

The menu of approaches for improving informational reading comprehension includes approaches to be administered in a variety of settings—in the regular classroom, in small group settings, and one-on-one. This suggests that informational reading comprehension instruction need not be the purview of any one professional, but can be administered across the multiple settings in which struggling readers are found. Similarly, among the variety of choices are both very targeted approaches (e.g. Chan and Cole's, 1986, self-questioning intervention) and relatively comprehensive approaches (e.g., Concept-Oriented Reading Instruction; see Guthrie et al., 2004). The scope of the approach is an important factor to consider when designing an entire instructional agenda for a struggling reader or readers.

The depth and breadth of instruction are also important factors to address when teaching students with reading difficulties. We discussed above a diverse array of choices for improving informational reading comprehension at the elementary level, which we grouped into the broad categories of comprehension strategy instruction (single and multiple), use of graphic organizers and other visual aids, text structure instruction, before-reading interventions, and other interventions. While having many effective techniques available has distinct advantages, we are concerned that it also holds the danger that one may sample from too many different approaches rather than focusing on a few in greater depth. Given what we know about learning in general and the learning of students with reading difficulties in particular, we hypothesize that it is better to teach fewer thinking processes in greater depth than more at a more cursory level. This is one of many hypotheses ripe for future research.

Directions for Future Research

While there is much that is encouraging in the literature reviewed for this chapter, it is also clear that much more research and development work needs to be done. In the paragraphs that follow, we identify several areas of need: greater depth of research, greater attention to the early elementary grades, improvement of assessment, achievement of transfer and maintenance, and greater concern with the big picture of informational comprehension development.

Greater Depth of Research While the breadth of approaches to improving informational text comprehension for struggling elementary-aged readers is relatively strong, the depth of this research often is not. For most categories we discuss (e.g., use of graphic organizers and other visual aids), there are only a very few studies that specifically focus on elementary-aged students with reading difficulties. A greater number and range of studies in each area— for example, the number and range we find in the area of phonological awareness intervention—would very likely improve our understanding and our ability to better impact these students' comprehension. Similarly, with a few exceptions (e.g., Reciprocal Teaching), there are typically only one or two studies that examine the outcome of any one approach with struggling elementary-aged readers. Additional research on specific interventions would improve our understanding of their respective benefits and limitations. Ideally, any given approach would be examined through a series of studies that address not only whether the approach is effective but for whom it is effective, under what conditions it is most effective, how it interacts with other approaches, and what effects it has in the long-term.

Greater Attention to the Early Elementary Grades A striking finding from this review is how few studies in

the primary grades were available to be included. In these studies, students in the fourth grade or above were primarily featured, with approximately 80% of the studies we reviewed drawing their samples from these grades. One possible explanation for this is that relatively few students are identified as having reading or learning disabilities as early as the primary grades (though note that the review included a few studies that did indeed include students so identified as early as Grade 1). However, in selecting studies, we did allow for inclusion not only of studies focused on students with reading or learning disabilities but also of studies focusing on just low achieving readers, of which there are certainly many in the primary grades, with good reason to think that comprehension is at least part of the challenge many of them face (Cain & Oakhill, 2007; Duke et al., 2004). So there must be additional explanations for the relative lack of studies with younger students, including, we suspect, a general inattention to comprehension and informational text in the primary grades (see earlier discussion).

Just as we have argued in the rationale for this review that we cannot generalize studies of secondary students to elementary-aged learners, so too do we argue that primary-grade students may not respond to intervention in the same way as upper elementary students. Thus examining instructional outcomes of interventions with children in kindergarten through third grade is crucial. Moreover, of course, the principle of early intervention, so widely touted in general and certainly extolled for addressing word-level problems in the primary grades, seems worthy of investigation for its possible value in the area of informational reading comprehension. We are especially interested in the long-term impacts of identifying and intervening early with students who show signs of struggling with informational reading comprehension, including those who do not demonstrate concomitant difficulties in the area of word recognition and decoding (e.g., Catts, Adlof, & Weismer, 2006; Riddle Buly & Valencia, 2002).

There are two important resources available to the field as it moves forward in examining informational reading comprehension interventions for struggling primary-grade readers. The first is to take interventions that have been successful with older struggling readers, modify them for characteristics of younger readers, and then test those. Another approach is to examine the impact specifically on struggling readers of approaches that have been developed for primary-grade learners in general. For example, the work of Williams and her colleagues (Williams et al., 2005; Williams et al., 2007) on teaching second graders the compare-contrast and cause-effect text structures seems promising in terms of potential benefits for struggling readers. In their 2005 study, instruction involved setting purposes, introducing key terms that signaled the targeted text structure, reading informational passages about animals, discussing content, generating compare-and-contrast statements, writing summaries, and reviewing the lesson. In their 2007 study, instruction involved introducing the cause-effect text structure, teaching signal words, attending to vocabulary, creating class charts, and answering questions during the post-reading discussion. Following this, students read aloud and analyzed a second passage for its structure and content. Significant differences for both studies were seen on several subskills, including locating the signal words, completing a graphic organizer orally and in writing, underlining clauses, and answering three kinds of questions (structural, effect, and non-causal), although the gains did not appear to transfer to passages featuring novel content or to different text structures. We would like to see interventions like those Williams used examined specifically for their impact for struggling primary-grade readers, as well as greater attention to the early elementary grades throughout informational comprehension intervention research.

Improvement of Assessment It is clear from this review (see especially Table 31.1), that the field would benefit from better tools for measuring informational reading comprehension of students with reading difficulties. There is remarkably little overlap in the assessment tools used in different studies, with most tools developed by the researchers for that particular study. This makes it difficult to compare results from one study to another or even to have confidence that the same informational reading comprehension skills are being measured.

Some studies did use more widely-known and widely-used assessments; however, these were usually norm-referenced tests of reading achievement. There are several problems with the use of such tests in this research. First, these tests typically do not separate informational reading achievement from narrative or other kinds of reading achievement, with informational reading comprehension items only a portion of the test. Given the genre-specific nature of reading comprehension, this means that even an intervention effective at improving informational reading comprehension achievement may not be able to show itself as such on the test; and indeed few studies we reviewed were able to show impacts on norm-referenced assessments. Second, norm-referenced tests are typically of questionable value for students scoring at the very lowest end of the achievement spectrum, as is true of many students in the studies we reviewed. Third, these tests are typically not diagnostic in nature. That is, they do not tell us what aspects of informational reading comprehension (or reading comprehension in general) are more or less difficult for students. This makes it difficult to tease apart what aspects of informational reading comprehension performance are really impacted by the intervention at hand. Finally, these assessments, as well as many of the experimenter-developed measures, tend to have limited ecological validity. Passages are generally short. Many informational text features, such as indexes, headings, and diagrams, are not included. The assessments rarely involve either nonlinear reading or the process of comprehending across multiples texts—both very much part of normal informational reading demands in and outside of school.

Relatively recent work in comprehension assessment development holds promise for addressing some of these shortcomings. As noted early in the chapter, a number of large-scale assessments, including cross-national assessments, are separating reading for information from literary reading; as those assessments become more widely known and available, they may be useful in research on the impact of reading comprehension interventions for students with reading difficulties. In addition, more comprehension assessments are being developed that provide more diagnostic information. For example, the Diagnostic Reading Comprehension Assessment (DARC; Francis et al., 2006) is designed to separate background or world knowledge from reading comprehension skill. The Concepts of Comprehension Assessment (COCA; Billman et al., 2008) and Informational Strategic Cloze Assessment (ISCA; Hilden et al., 2008) are designed to measure four contributors to informational reading comprehension—knowledge of informational text features, use of comprehension strategies, ability to comprehend graphics in text, and vocabulary knowledge and use—for students in Grades 1 to 3 (see also Paris & Paris, 2003, for a narrative comprehension assessment for use with primary-grade students). Guthrie and his colleagues (e.g., Guthrie et al., 2004) have developed assessments of informational reading comprehension that not only have higher levels of ecological validity than most measures, but that also assess engagement as well.

One of the characteristics of many of these newer assessments of comprehension is that they are more process-oriented than product-oriented. That is, rather than measuring reading comprehension at the "end" of reading through such tools as oral or written retellings or responses to passage-final comprehension questions, several of these assessments ask questions and/or engage students in tasks throughout the reading. Greater proximity to the ongoing moment-by-moment process of meaning construction, within the particular demands of the text, may provide greater insight about when and why comprehension is breaking down, or is successful—something that is more difficult to glean from after-the-fact measures. These and other developments are encouraging with respect to improving assessment of, and thus research on, informational reading comprehension intervention in the future.

Achievement of Transfer and Maintenance It is hard to miss in this literature how elusive transfer (to new reading situations) and maintenance (of gains over time) often are. Part of the reason for this may lie in the nature of some of the assessments used, as discussed above with respect to norm-referenced tests. Another explanation is undoubtedly the short duration of many of the interventions. Of the studies explored above, interventions ranged from one lesson (e.g., Ankney & McClurg, 1981; Gagne & Memory, 1978) to an entire academic school year (e.g., Klingner et al., 2004). Three-quarters of these designs provided instruction for less than 1 month, with an average of 8 lessons per intervention. It is unsurprising that it would be difficult to achieve strong transfer and maintenance with interventions this short.

A related explanation for the challenge of transfer and maintenance is the relatively narrow scope of some of the interventions. Several of the interventions reviewed address a single comprehension strategy or instructional activity. On the one hand, it is encouraging that many of these interventions do show statistically significant effects. On the other hand, it is understandable that it may be difficult to show long-term multi-context impacts of these interventions. It is striking to compare many of the interventions we reviewed for this chapter to Concept-Oriented Reading Instruction (CORI), which is the most comprehensive intervention we reviewed. CORI involves not only instruction in a number of comprehension strategies, but instruction and experience in informational reading comprehension tasks such as searching for information and reading and synthesizing across multiple texts. CORI attends not only to strategy instruction but also, heavily, to motivation and engagement. Not only large-scale research but also individual case study research (e.g., Hall, 2006) suggest that motivation and engagement are crucial accompaniments of both comprehension instruction and content area learning. The field would be well-served, in our view, by more studies of the impact of relatively comprehensive interventions on students' informational reading comprehension.

Interestingly, the existing literature is not well suited to evaluating the hypothesis that longer-term and more comprehensive interventions provide greater evidence of transfer and maintenance because many of the longest term and most comprehensive interventions have not been subject to transfer and maintenance measures. This is part of a larger pattern in the literature of very little longitudinal research on reading comprehension instruction for students with reading difficulties, a point we discuss in greater depth in the following section.

Greater Concern with the Big Picture of Informational Comprehension Development Largely absent from the research on elementary-aged students with reading difficulties is the bigger picture of how to create a total program of informational comprehension instruction for these students. None of the approaches reviewed, particularly those of narrower scope, would alone suffice to provide all the comprehension instruction needed for students with reading difficulties throughout the elementary years. So how can these approaches be pieced together in ways that are most beneficial for students? How should the comprehension interventions used with students change, and not change, as the student progresses in grade level and/or comprehension ability? What time should be devoted to informational comprehension interventions as opposed to other forms and foci of instruction? What is the relative role of the general education classroom, the resource room, and clinical or tutoring services? What does the total comprehension pro-

gram look like in places in which all or nearly all students with reading difficulties develop into strong comprehenders of informational text? What teacher characteristics are associated with strong growth in informational reading comprehension? Ultimately, what level of informational reading comprehension do students with reading difficulties from various instructional contexts achieve? These are difficult questions, to be sure, but also questions that those in school have to, or at least should, address every day.

One example of the kind of research and development program that addresses many of the kinds of questions posed in the previous paragraph is that carried out at Benchmark School in Media, Pennsylvania, under the leadership of Irene Gaskins. Benchmark is a school for students who have been experiencing difficulty learning to read. Most students enter the school in second, third, or fourth grade with very low levels of reading achievement and often with family histories of difficulty with reading. Benchmark has a remarkable record of long-term success with these students. While Benchmark engages in many activities to develop this success, one is long-term, intense comprehension strategy instruction that is coherent and cumulative across grades (e.g., Gaskins, Laird, O'Hara, Scott, & Cress, 2002). This instruction is embedded in a larger context, also well described in the literature (e.g., Pressley, Gaskins, Solic, & Collins, 2006), of other instructional and non-instructional characteristics of the school that appear to work in tandem, if not synergistically, to produce great success for students with reading difficulties.

Summary

Assuming that reading comprehension is to some degree genre-specific, this chapter began with a discussion of the importance of informational reading comprehension and possible causes of informational reading comprehension difficulties. We then reviewed research on interventions for informational reading comprehension. Recognizing the lack of reviews focused specifically on elementary-aged students with reading difficulties, our review focused on interventions that have been tested for that group. While there are relatively few studies and many questions left unanswered, a range of interventions have proven to be effective in improving the informational reading comprehension of elementary-aged students with reading difficulties. The task that lies before us now is to find ways to combine, contextualize, and carry out these interventions to make a meaningful, long-term difference for struggling readers.

Note

1 For edited volumes and articles on the topic, see Cain and Oakhill (2007); Cornoldi and Oakhill (1996); and Gajria, Jitendra, Sood, and Sacks (2007). For books written for practitioners focusing on improving reading comprehension of students with learning disabilities, see Carlisle and Rice (2002) and Klingner, Vaughn, and Boardman (2007).

References

Adams, A., Carnine, D., & Gersten, R. (1982). Instructional strategies for studying content area texts in the intermediate grades. *Reading Research Quarterly, 18,* 27–55.

Alvermann, D. E., Boothby, P. R., & Wolfe, J. (1984). The effect of graphic organizer instruction on fourth graders' comprehension of social studies text. *Journal of Social Studies Research, 8,* 13–21.

Alvermann, D. E., Smith, L. C., & Readence, J. E. (1985). Prior knowledge activation and the comprehension of compatible and incompatible text. *Reading Research Quarterly, 20,* 420–436.

Ankney, P., & McClurg, P. (1981). Testing Manzo's guided reading procedure. *Reading Teacher, 34,* 681–685.

Armbruster, B. B. (1984). The problem of inconsiderate text. In G. G. Duffy, L. R. Roehler, & J. Mason (Eds.), *Comprehension instruction: Perspectives and suggestions* (pp. 202–217). New York: Longman.

Armbruster, B. B., Anderson, T. H., & Meyer, J. L. (1991). Improving content-area reading using instructional graphics. *Reading Research Quarterly, 26,* 393–416.

Baumann, J. F. (1984). The effectiveness of a direct instruction paradigm for teaching main idea comprehension. *Reading Research Quarterly, 20,* 93–115.

Baumann, J. F. (2008). Vocabulary and reading comprehension: The nexus of meaning. In S. E. Israel & G. G. Duffy (Eds.), *Handbook of research on reading comprehension* (pp. 323–346). Mahwah, NJ: Erlbaum.

Billman, A. K., Duke, N. K., Hilden, K. R., Zhang, S., Roberts, K., Halladay, J. L., et al. (2008). *Concepts of Comprehension Assessment (COCA).* Retrieved June 18, 2008, from http://www.msularc.org/html/project_COCA_main.html

Boothby, P. R., & Alvermann, D. E. (1984). A classroom training study: The effects of graphic organizer instruction on fourth graders' comprehension. *Reading World, 23,* 325–339.

Bos, C. S., & Anders, P. L. (1990). Effects of interactive vocabulary instruction on the vocabulary learning and reading comprehension of junior-high learning disabled students. *Learning Disability Quarterly, 13,* 31–42.

Boyle, J. R. (1996). The effects of a cognitive mapping strategy on the literal and inferential comprehension of students with mild disabilities. *Learning Disability Quarterly, 19,* 86–98.

Brand-Gruwel, S., Aarnoutses, C. A. J., & van den Bos, K. P. (1998). Improving text comprehension strategies in reading and listening settings. *Learning and Instruction, 8,* 63–81.

Brown, A. L., & Day, J. D. (1983). Macrorules for summarizing texts: The development of expertise. *Journal of Verbal Learning & Verbal Behavior, 22*(1), 1–14. doi: 10.1016/S0022-5371(83)80002-4

Brown, R., Pressley, M., Van Meter, P., & Schuder, T. (1996). A quasi-experimental validation of transactional strategies instruction with low-achieving second grade readers. *Journal of Educational Psychology, 88,* 18–37.

Cain, K., & Oakhill, J. (Eds.). (2007). *Children's comprehension problems in oral and written language: A cognitive perspective.* New York: Guilford.

Carlisle, J. F., & Rice, M. S. (2002). *Improving reading comprehension: Research-based principles and practices.* Baltimore, MD: York Press.

Carnine, D., & Kinder, B. D. (1985). Teaching low-performing students to apply generative and schema strategies to narrative and expository material. *Remedial and Special Education, 6,* 20–30.

Carr, S. C., & Thompson, B. (1996). The effects of prior knowledge and schema activation strategies on the inferential reading comprehension of children with and without learning disabilities. *Learning Disability Quarterly, 19,* 48–61.

Caswell, L. J., & Duke, N. K. (1998). Non-narrative as a catalyst for literacy development. *Language Arts, 75,* 108–117.

Catts, H. W., Adlof, S. M., & Weismer, S. E. (2006). Language deficits in poor comprehenders: A case for the Simple View of Reading. *Journal of Speech, Language, and Hearing Research, 49,* 278–293.

CTB/McGraw-Hill. (1996). *Comprehensive Test of Basic Skills.* Monterey, CA: Author.

Chan, L. K. S. (1991). Promoting strategy generalization through self-instructional training in students with reading disabilities. *Journal of Learning Disabilities, 24,* 427–433.

Chan, L. K. S., & Cole, P. G. (1986). The effects of comprehension monitoring training on the reading competence of learning disabled and normal students. *Remedial and Special Education, 7,* 33–40.

Cornoldi, C., & Oakhill, J. (Eds.). (1996). *Reading comprehension difficulties: Processes and intervention.* Mahwah, NJ: Erlbaum.

Cunningham, A. E., & Stanovich, K. E. (1998). What reading does for the mind. *American Educator, 22,* 1–2, 8–15.

DiCecco, V. M., & Gleason, M. M. (2002). Using graphic organizers to attain relational knowledge from expository text. *Journal of Learning Disabilities, 35,* 306–320.

Dickson, S. V., Simmons, D. C., & Kameenui, E. J. (1998). Text organization: Research bases. In D. C. Simmons & E. J. Kameenui (Eds.), *What reading research tells us about children with diverse learning needs: Bases and basics* (pp. 239–277). Mahwah, NJ: Erlbaum.

Dole, J. A., & Nelson, K. L. (2008, May). *Vocabulary instruction among primary-grade teachers in a school reform project.* Presentation at the International Reading Association Reading Research Conference, Atlanta, GA.

Duke, N. K. (2000). 3.6 minutes per day: The scarcity of informational text in first grade. *Reading Research Quarterly, 35,* 202–224.

Duke, N. K. (2005). Comprehension of what for what: Comprehension as a non-unitary construct. In S. Paris & S. Stahl (Eds.), *Current issues in reading comprehension and assessment* (pp. 93–104). Mahwah, NJ: Erlbaum.

Duke, N. K., Bennett-Armistead, V. S., & Roberts, E. M. (2002). Incorporating informational text in the primary grades. In C. Roller (Ed.), *Comprehensive reading instruction across the grade levels* (pp. 40–54). Newark, DE: International Reading Association.

Duke, N. K., & Billman, A. K. (2009). Informational text difficulty for beginning readers. In E. H. Hiebert & M. Sailors (Eds.), *Finding the right texts for beginning and struggling readers: Research-based solutions* (pp. 109–128). New York: Guilford.

Duke, N. K., & Martin, N. M. (2008). Comprehension instruction in action: The elementary classroom. In C. C. Block & S. Parris (Eds.), *Comprehension instruction: Research-based best practices* (pp. 241–257). New York: Guilford.

Duke, N. K., & Pearson, P. D. (2002). Effective practices for developing reading comprehension. In A. E. Farstrup & S. J. Samuels (Eds.), *What research has to say about reading instruction* (3rd ed., pp. 205–242). Newark, DE: International Reading Association.

Duke, N. K., Pressley, M., & Hilden, K. (2004). Difficulties with reading comprehension. In C. A. Stone, E. R. Silliman, B. J. Ehren, & K. Apel (Eds.), *Handbook of language and literacy development and disorders* (pp. 501–520). New York: Guilford.

Durkin, D. (1978/1979). What classroom observations reveal about reading comprehension instruction. *Reading Research Quarterly, 14,* 481–533.

Ellis, E. S., & Graves, A. W. (1990). Teaching rural students with learning disabilities: A paraphrasing strategy to increase comprehension of main ideas. *Rural Special Education Quarterly, 10,* 2–10.

Englert, C. S., & Mariage, T. V. (1991). Making students partners in the comprehension process: Organizing the reading "POSSE". *Learning Disability Quarterly, 14,* 123–138.

Englert, C. S., Tarrant, K. L., Mariage, T. V., & Oxer, T. (1994). Lesson talk as the work of reading groups: The effectiveness of two interventions. *Journal of Learning Disabilities, 27,* 165–185.

Englert, C. S., & Thomas, C. C. (1987). Sensitivity to text structure in reading and writing. A comparison between learning disabled and non-learning disabled students. *Learning Disability Quarterly, 10,* 93–105.

Flood, J., & Lapp, D. (1986). Types of texts: The match between what students read in basals and what they encounter in tests. *Reading Research Quarterly, 21,* 284–297.

Francis, D. J., Snow, C. E., August, D., Carlson, C. D., Miller, J., & Iglesias, A. (2006). Measures of reading comprehension: A latent variable analysis of the diagnostic assessment of reading comprehension. *Scientific Studies of Reading, 10*, 301–322.

Gagne, E. D., & Memory, D. (1978). Instructional events and comprehension: Generalization across passages. *Journal of Reading Behavior, 10*, 321–335.

Gajria, M., Jitendra, A. K., Sood, S., & Sacks, G. (2007). Improving comprehension of expository text in students with LD: A research synthesis. *Journal of Learning Disabilities, 40*, 210–255.

Gaijria, M., & Salvia, J. (1992). The effects of summarization instruction on text comprehension of students with learning disabilities. *Exceptional Children, 58*, 508–516.

Gardner, H. (1987). *The mind's new science: A history of the cognitive revolution.* New York: Basic Books.

Gaskins, I. W., Laird, S. R., O'Hara, C., Scott, T., & Cress, C. A. (2002). Helping struggling readers make sense of reading. In C. C. Block, L. B. Gambrell, & M. Pressley (Eds.), *Improving comprehension instruction: Rethinking research, theory, and classroom practice* (pp. 370–383). Newark, DE: International Reading Association.

Gersten, R., Fuchs, L. S., Williams, J. P., & Baker, S. (2001). Teaching reading comprehension strategies to students with learning disabilities: A review of research. *Review of Educational Research, 71*, 279–320.

Graves, A. W. (1986). Effects of direct instruction and metacomprehension training on finding main ideas. *Learning Disabilities Research, 1*, 90–100.

Griffin, C. C., Simmons, D. C., & Kameenui, E. J. (1991). Investigating the effectiveness of graphic organizer instruction on the comprehension and recall of science content by students with learning disabilities. *Journal of Reading, Writing, and Learning Disabilities, International, 7*, 355–376.

Guthrie, J. T. (2004). Differentiating instruction for struggling readers within the CORI classroom. In J. T. Guthrie, A. Wigfield, & K. C. Perencevich (Eds.), *Motivating reading comprehension: Concept-Oriented Reading Instruction* (pp. 173–194). Mahwah, NJ: Erlbaum.

Guthrie, J. T., McRae, A., Coddington, C. S., Lutz Klauda, S., Wigfield, A., & Barbosa, P. (2009). Impacts of comprehensive reading instruction on diverse outcomes of low- and high-achieving readers. *Journal of Learning Disabilities, 42,* 195–214.

Guthrie, J. T., McRae, A., & Klauda, S. L. (2007). Contributions of Concept-Oriented Reading Instruction to knowledge about interventions for motivations in reading. *Educational Psychologist, 42*, 237–250.

Guthrie, J. T., Meter, P. V., Hancock, G. R., Solomon, A., Anderson, E., & McCann, A. (1998). Does Concept-Oriented Reading Instruction increase strategy use and conceptual learning from text? *Journal of Educational Psychology, 90*, 261–278.

Guthrie, J. T., Wigfield, A., Barbosa, P., Perencevich, K. C., Taboada, A., Davis, M. H., et al. (2004). Increasing reading comprehension and engagement through Concept-Oriented Reading Instruction. *Journal of Educational Psychology, 96*, 403–423.

Guzzetti, B. J., Snyder, T. E., Glass, G. V., & Gamas, W. S. (1993). Promoting conceptual change in science: A comparative meta-analysis of instructional interventions from reading education and science education. *Reading Research Quarterly, 28*, 116–159.

Hall, L. A. (2006). Anything but lazy: New understandings about struggling readers, teaching, and text. *Reading Research Quarterly, 41*, 424–426.

Hiebert, E. H. (2006). Becoming fluent: What difference do texts make? In S. J. Samuels & A. E. Farstrup (Eds.), *What research has to say about reading fluency* (pp. 204–226). Newark, DE: International Reading Association.

Hilden, K. R., Duke, N. K., Billman, A. K., Zhang, S., Halladay, J. L., Schaal, A. M., et al. (2008). *Informational Strategic Cloze Assessment (ISCA).* Retrieved June 18, 2008, from http://www.msularc.org/html/project_ISCA_main.html

Jitendra, A. K., Hoppes, M. K., & Xin, Y. P. (2000). Enhancing main idea comprehension for students with learning problems: The role of a summarization strategy and self-monitoring instruction. *The Journal of Special Education, 34*, 127–139.

Johnson-Glenberg, M. C. (2005). Web-based training of metacognitive strategies for text comprehension: Focus on poor comprehenders. *Reading and Writing, 18*, 755–786.

Kelly, M. U., Moore, D. W., & Tuck, B. F. (1994). Reciprocal teaching in a regular primary school classroom. *Journal of Educational Research, 88*, 53–61.

Kirk, L., & Pearson, H. (1996). Genres and learning to read. *Reading Research Quarterly, 30*, 37–41.

Klingner, J. K., Vaughn, S., Arguelles, M. E., Hughes, M. T., & Leftwich, S. A. (2004). Collaborative Strategic Reading: "Real-world" lessons from classroom teachers. *Remedial and Special Education, 25*, 291–302.

Klingner, J. K., Vaughn, S., & Boardman, A. (2007). *Teaching reading comprehension to students with learning difficulties.* New York: Guilford.

Klingner, J. K., Vaughn, S., & Schumm, J. S. (1998). Collaborative strategic reading during social studies in heterogenous fourth-grade classrooms. *Elementary School Journal, 99*, 3–22.

Kucan, L., & Beck, I. L. (1996). Four fourth graders thinking aloud: An investigation of genre effects. *Journal of Literacy Research, 28*, 259–287.

Langer, J. (1984). Examining background knowledge and text comprehension. *Reading Research Quarterly, 19*, 468–481.

Lederer, J. M. (2000). Reciprocal teaching of social studies in inclusive elementary classrooms. *Journal of Learning Disabilities, 33*, 91–106.

Lysynchuk, L. M., Pressley, M., & Vye, N. J. (1990). Reciprocal teaching improves standardized reading-comprehension performance in poor comprehenders. *The Elementary School Journal, 90*, 469–484.

Manzo, A. V. (1975). Guided reading procedure. *Journal of Reading, 18*, 287–291.

Mason, L. H. (2004). Explicit self-regulated strategy development versus reciprocal teaching: Effects on expository reading comprehension among struggling readers. *Educational Psychology, 96*, 283–296.

Mason, L. H., Snyder, K. H., Sukhram, D. P., & Kedem, Y. (2006). TWA + PLANS Strategies for expository reading and writing: Effects for nine fourth-grade students. *Exceptional Children, 73*, 69–89.

McCormick, S. (1989). Effects of previews on more skilled and less skilled readers' comprehension of expository text. *Journal of Reading Behavior, 21*, 219–239.

McGee, L. M. (1982). Awareness of text structure: Effects on children's recall of expository text. *Reading Research Quarterly, 17*, 581–590.

Memory, D. (1983). Main idea prequestions as adjunct aids with good and low-average middle grade readers. *Journal of Reading Behavior, 15*, 37–48.

Mohr, K. A. J. (2006). Children's choices for recreational reading: A three-part investigation of selection preferences, rationales, and processes. *Journal of Literacy Research, 38*, 81–104.

National Assessment Governing Board. (2007). *Reading framework for the 2009 National Assessment of Educational Progress.* Washington, DC: American Institutes for Research. Retrieved October 20, 2007, from http://www.nagb.org/frameworks/fw.html

National Center for Education Statistics. (2007). *Literacy in everyday life: Results from the 2003 National Assessment of Adult Literacy.* Retrieved November 2, 2008, from http://nces.ed.gov/pubsearch/pubsinfo.asp?pubid=2007480

National Reading Panel. (2000). *Teaching children to read: An evidence-based assessment of the scientific research literature on reading and its implications for reading instruction (National Institute of Health Pub. No. 00-4769).* Washington, DC: National Institute of Child Health and Human Development.

OECD & Statistics Canada. (2000). *Literacy in the information age: Final report of the International Adult Literacy Survey.* Paris: Organisation for Economic Co-operation and Development.

Ogle, D. (1986). KWL: A teaching model that develops active reading of expository text. *The Reading Teacher, 39*, 564–572.

Palinscar, A. S., & Brown, A. L. (1984). Reciprocal teaching of comprehension-fostering and comprehension-monitoring activities. *Cognition and Instruction, 1*(2), 117–175.

Pappas, C. C. (2006). The information book genre: Its role in integrated science literacy research and practice. *Reading Research Quarterly, 41*, 226–250.

Paris, A. H., & Paris, S. G. (2003). Assessing narrative comprehension in young children. *Reading Research Quarterly, 38*, 36–76.

Park, Y. (2008). *Patterns in and predictors of elementary students' reading performance: Evidence from the data of the progress in International Reading Literacy Study 2006* (Unpublished doctoral dissertation). Michigan State University, Ann Arbor, MI.

Pearson, P. D. (1986). Twenty years of research in reading comprehension. In T. E. Raphael (Ed.), *Contexts for school-based literacy* (pp. 43–62). New York: Random House.

Pearson, P. D., & Hamm, D. N. (2005). The history of reading comprehension assessment. In S. G. Paris & S. A. Stahl (Eds.), *Children's reading comprehension and assessment* (pp. 13–69). Mahwah, NJ: Erlbaum.

Pressley, M. (2000). What should comprehension instruction be the instruction of? In M. L. Kamil, P. B. Mosenthal, P. D. Pearson, & R. Barr (Eds.), *Handbook of reading research* (pp. 545–561). Mahwah, NJ: Erlbaum.

Pressley, M., & Afflerbach, P. (1995). *Verbal protocols of reading: The nature of constructively responsive reading*. Hillsdale, NJ: Erlbaum.

Pressley, M., Duke, N. K., Gaskins, I. W., Fingeret, L., Halladay, J., Hilden, K., et al. (2009). Working with struggling readers: Why we must get beyond the Simple View of Reading and visions of how it might be done. In T. Gutkin & C. R. Reynolds (Eds.), *The handbook of school psychology* (4th ed., pp. 522–546). Hoboken, NJ: Wiley.

Pressley, M., Gaskins, I. W., Solic, K., & Collins, S. (2006). A portrait of Benchmark School: How a school produces high achievement in students who previously failed. *Journal of Educational Psychology, 98*, 282–306.

Pressley, M. (with Wharton-McDonald, R.). (2005). The need for increased comprehension instruction. In *Reading instruction that works: The case for balanced teaching* (3rd ed., pp. 293–346). New York: Guilford.

Purcell-Gates, V., Duke, N. K., & Martineau, J. A. (2007). Learning to read and write genre-specific text: Roles of authentic experience and explicit teaching. *Reading Research Quarterly, 42*, 8–45.

RAND Reading Study Group. (2002). *Reading for understanding: Toward an R&D program in reading comprehension*. Santa Monica, CA: Rand Education.

Raphael, T. E., & Pearson, P. D. (1985). Increasing students' awareness of sources of information for answering questions. *American Educational Research Journal, 22*, 217–235.

Reid, N. A., & Elley, W. B. (1991). *Progressive Achievement Test of Reading Comprehension*. Wellington: NZCER.

Reutzel, D. R., Smith, J. A., & Fawson, P. C. (2005). An evaluation of two approaches for teaching reading comprehension strategies in the primary years using science information texts. *Early Childhood Research Quarterly, 20*, 276–305.

Riddle Buly, M., & Valencia, S. W. (2002). Below the bar: Profiles of students who fail state reading assessments. *Educational Evaluation and Policy Analysis, 24*, 213–239.

Saenz, L. M., & Fuchs, L. S. (2002). Examining the reading difficulty of secondary students with learning disabilities: Expository versus narrative text. *Remedial and Special Education, 23*, 31–41.

Scott, J. A., Jamieson-Noel, D., & Asselin, M. (2003). Vocabulary instruction throughout the day in twenty-three Canadian upper-elementary classrooms. *The Elementary School Journal, 103*, 269–286.

Simmonds, E. P. M. (1992). The effects of teacher training and implementation of two methods of improving the comprehension skills of students with learning disabilities. *Learning Disabilities Research and Practice, 7*, 194–198.

Simmons, D. C., Griffin, C. C., & Kameenui, E. J. (1988). Effects of teacher-constructed pre- and post-graphic organizer instruction on sixth-grade science students' comprehension and recall. *Journal of Educational Research, 82*, 15–21.

Sinatra, R. C., Stahl-Gemake, J., & Berg, D. N. (1984). Improving reading comprehension of disabled readers through semantic mapping. *The Reading Teacher, 38*, 22–29.

Smith, M. C. (2000). The real-world reading practices of adults. *Journal of Literacy Research, 32*, 25–52.

Statistics Canada & OECD. (2005). *Learning a living: First results of the Adult Literacy and Life Skills Survey*. Paris: Organisation for Economic Co-operation and Development.

Stevens, R. J. (1988). Effects of strategy training on the identification of the main idea of expository passages. *Journal of Educational Psychology, 80*, 21–26.

Swanborn, M. S. L., & de Glopper, K. (1999). Incidental word learning while reading: A meta-analysis. *Review of Educational Research, 69*, 261–285.

Talbott, E., Lloyd, J. W., & Tankersley, M. (1994). Effects of reading comprehension interventions for students with learning disabilities. *Learning Disability Quarterly, 17*, 223–232.

Taylor, B. M. (1982). Text structure and children's comprehension and memory for expository material. *Journal of Educational Psychology, 74*, 323–340.

Taylor, B. M., & Frye, B. J. (1992). Comprehension strategy instruction in the intermediate grades. *Reading Research and Instruction, 32*, 39–48.

Williams, J. P., Hall, K. M., Lauer, K. D., Stafford, B., DeSisto, L. A., & deCani, J. S. (2005). Expository text comprehension in the primary grade classroom. *Journal of Educational Psychology, 97*, 538–550.

Williams, J. P., Nubla-Kung, A. M., Pollini, S., Stafford, B. K., Garcia, A., & Snyder, A. E. (2007). Teaching cause-effect text structure through social studies content to at-risk second graders. *Journal of Learning Disabilities, 40*, 111–120.

Wong, B. Y. L., & Wilson, M. (1984). Investigating awareness of and teaching passage organization in learning disabled children. *Journal of Learning Disabilities, 17*, 477–482.

32

Peer Mediation

A Means of Differentiating Classroom Instruction

DOUGLAS FUCHS, LYNN S. FUCHS
Vanderbilt University

ADINA SHAMIR
Bar Ilan University (Israel)

ERIC DION
University of Quebec at Montreal

LAURA M. SAENZ
University of Texas—Pan American

KRISTEN L. MCMASTER
University of Minnesota

Picture this: 34 children in an urban third-grade classroom, one third of whom live in poverty. Six live with grandparents, *and three are in foster care. Five come from homes in which a language other than English is spoken; two children do not speak English at all. Seven, six, five, three, two, and one are African American, Hispanic American, Korean, Russian, Haitian, and Chinese, respectively. Six are new to the school, and four will relocate to a different school next year. Only five of the 34 students are at or above grade level in reading; 10 are two or more grade levels below. There is a 5-grade spread in reading achievement. In addition, three students have been certified as learning disabled. One is severely mentally retarded, and another is deaf. According to the Department of Health and Human Services, the child with mental retardation and two other students in the class have been physically or sexually abused.*

The teacher of this imaginary but arguably representative (see Headden, 1995; Hodgkinson, 1991, 1995; Jenkins, Jewell, Leicester, Jenkins, & Troutner, 1990; Natriello, McDill, & Pallas, 1990; Puma, Jones, Rock, & Fernandez, 1993) urban class is Mr. Stasis, who believes it is his job to present information, his students' job to listen and learn. His stand-and-deliver approach reflects the view that teaching is a centralized and unidirectional phenomenon. Mr. Stasis uses the texts in reading, mathematics, social studies, and science that were adopted by his district's central office. And, on orders from this office, his students get these books regardless of their reading level and math skills.

We (Fuchs, Fuchs, Mathes, & Simmons, 1996) wrote this more than 10 years ago to describe the serious disconnect in many communities between students' diversity of languages, cultures, experiences, and readiness to learn and the uniformity of classroom instruction. Educators in school buildings, district offices, and universities recognize this disconnect as an important, if not primary, cause of hundreds of thousands of students' poor learning. Many would say that what Mr. Stasis's class needs first and foremost is *differentiated instruction.*

For more than a decade, differentiated instruction has been one of the "it" phrases in K–12 education. Teachers who differentiate their instruction have been described as leveraging knowledge about their students' varying experiences, interests, learning styles, and readiness levels; conveying information in multiple sensory modalities; grouping children flexibly; varying the pace of their instruction; and assessing student learning with varied and balanced measures and procedures (cf. Kapusnick & Hauslien, 2001; Tomlinson, 1999). Differentiated instruction has been advanced by some as a tested strategy for accelerating student learning and for celebrating their diversity (e.g., Carolan & Guinn, 2007)—promoted even as a biological imperative. In this last regard, Tomlinson and Kalbfleisch (1998) wrote, "the amassed understandings about how the brain works have added to our considerable research base on the importance of … curriculum and instruction … responsive to individual learning needs" (p. 53).

Enthusiasm for differentiated instruction notwithstanding, there is persuasive evidence that most classrooms are bereft of it, a fact undiminished by the occasional description of exemplary instructors (cf. Pressley, Allington, Wharton-McDonald, Block, & Morrow, 2001). Baker and Zigmond (1990), for example, conducted interviews and observations in reading and math classes in an elementary school to explore whether teachers implement routine adaptations (e.g., differentiating instruction by creating multiple reading groups to accommodate weak-to-strong readers at the start of the school year). The researchers found no evidence of routine adaptations. Rather, they reported that teachers typically taught to large groups, using lessons incorporating little or no differentiation based on student needs. McIntosh, Vaughn, Schumm, Haager, and Lee (1994) described similar results from their observations of 60 social studies and science classrooms across Grades 3 to 12.

L. Fuchs, Fuchs, and Bishop (1992) explored whether general and special educators used *specialized*, not routinized, adaptations (i.e., instruction deliberately customized in response to an individual student's difficulty). They administered a Teacher Planning Questionnaire to 25 general educators and 37 special educators whose responses reflected a view that individualized instruction and small-group instruction were not important to their students' academic success—a result also found by Baker and Zigmond (1990), D. Fuchs, Fuchs, and Fernstrom (1993), D. Fuchs, Roberts, Fuchs, and Bowers (1996), Peterson and Clark (1978), and Zigmond and Baker (1994). Others have expressed a different take on why educators often fail to differentiate instruction. This perspective sometimes begins with the fact, dramatized at the start of this chapter, that many classroom teachers, especially those in large urban school districts, are faced with a considerable diversity of languages and cultures and a broad range of academic performance. Peterson and Clark (1978), Brown and Saks (1981, 1987), and Gerber and Semmel (1984) have written that teachers typically react to this student heterogeneity by ignoring it; that is, by monitoring student performance in selective fashion, and by teaching to the more academically accomplished students.

According to Schumm and Vaughn and their colleagues, teachers in Grades 3 through 12, whom they interviewed in focus groups and observed in classrooms, are unresponsive to this student diversity because they believe themselves lacking in necessary knowledge and skills (e.g., Schumm & Vaughn, 1992; Schumm, Vaughn, Gordon, & Rothstein, 1994). Further, say their teachers, even if they were more knowledgeable and skillful, providing differentiated instruction would be nearly impossible because of inadequate resources for the necessary comprehensive and systematic monitoring of student performance.

More recently, Tomlinson and Allan (2003) struck the very same note by quoting Darling-Hammond: "After a decade of reform, we have finally learned in hindsight what should have been clear from the start: Most schools and teachers cannot produce the kind of learning demanded by the new reforms—not because they do not want to, but because they don't know how, and the systems in which they work do not support them in doing so" (p. 78; also see Leithwood, Leonard, & Sharratt,1998). Irrespective of why teachers typically do not provide differentiated instruction, its absence clearly contributes to the school failure of many at-risk children. Findings from numerous studies document that many low-achieving children, including those with special needs, not only fail to obtain differentiated instruction but receive less *undifferentiated* instruction and practice than their more accomplished classmates (e.g., Delquadri, Greenwood, Whorton, Carta, & Hall, 1986; Hall, Delquadri, Greenwood, & Thurston, 1982; Lesgold & Resnick, 1982; McDermott & Aron, 1978; O'Sullivan, Ysseldyke, Christenson, & Thurlow, 1990).

Helping teachers differentiate their instruction is surely one of the most important and difficult challenges facing public schools in the 21st century. There are various reasons for this. One is definitional, which is to say that "differentiated instruction" is often defined so broadly as to become ambiguous. Hall's (2002) conceptualization is typical: "To differentiate instruction is to recognize students [vary in] background knowledge, readiness, language, [modes of learning], [and] interests…. The intent of differentiating instruction is to maximize each student's growth…by meeting each student where he or she is, and assisting in the learning process."

Whereas Hall (2002) and others identify or promote various components of differentiated instruction—components that address instructional content, processes, and products—there is no consensus on which components are necessary and sufficient. There is no agreed upon understanding of what exactly it is. Additionally, there is little evidence that anyone's proposed components—alone or in combination—positively effect students' academic achievement. Hall remarks, "Based on [my] review…the 'package' itself [i.e., differentiated instruction] is lacking empirical validation. There is an acknowledged and decided gap in the literature in this area and future research is warranted. [Nevertheless] there [is] a generous number of testimonials and classroom examples…." Without a clear conception of the construct and an absence of research that connects specific and replicable implementations to student achievement, it is impossible to provide classroom teachers with meaningful professional development and support.

One promising approach is peer-mediated instruction, whereby children work together to support each others' learning. The connection between peer-mediation and differentiated instruction is that peer-mediation represents an important re-organization of the conventional classroom; an alternative to the "sage-on-stage" and "stand-and-deliver" approach to learning and teaching; a decentralized learning environment. This decentralization provides teachers (and students-as-teachers) with opportunities for customizing goals, activities, supports, and accountability that do not exist in more conventional classrooms. Below we discuss several research-backed peer-mediated programs for the elementary grades, emphasizing Peer-Assisted Learning Strategies (PALS; e.g., Fuchs, Fuchs, Mathes, & Simmons, 1997). Because most of these programs are explicit, they address the vagueness associated with many current approaches to differentiated instruction; because they are scripted (or partially scripted), they speak to teachers who complain they lack requisite knowledge; and because they are inexpensive, they connect to teachers' concerns that they don't have adequate resources.

Peer-Mediated Approaches to Instruction

Broadly speaking, there have been two groups developing peer-mediated approaches to teaching and learning: a socio-cultural group and cognitive-behavioral group. Many in the socio-cultural group base their R&D on Vygotsky's (1978) theorizing, which reflects a belief that mastery of complex skills and the development of underlying cognitive processes occur as a result of repeated inteactions between novice and expert. The expert initially compensates for the novices weaknesses by accomplishing parts of a task, but gradually pushes the novice toward more autonomous and mature performance through a series of scaffolded interactions. The cognitive-behavioral group, as the term implies, taps either cognitive theories (e.g., Palincsar & Brown, 1984) or Direct Instruction principles (e.g., Carnine, Silbert, Kameenui, & Tarver, 2004; Delquadri et al., 1986) or a combination of the two (e.g., Fuchs et al., 1997).

A Sociocultural Approach   The Peer Mediation with Young Children (PYMC; Shamir & Tzuriel, 2002, 2004) program is based on Vygotsky's (1929, 1962, 1978, 1981) sociocultural theory and Feuerstein's "mediated learning experience" (MLE) theory (Feuerstein, Rand, & Hoffman, 1979). According to Vygotsky, learning takes place through interactions between children and more competent persons, whether adults or peers. For Feuerstein, MLE helps children adapt previously learned principals and competencies to new circumstances and, in so doing, "children learn how to learn." Although Feuerstein characterized MLE in terms of 12 interaction-based criteria, only the first five have been proceduralized. They are: (a) focusing on the problem; (b) attaching meaning to the stimulus and its characteristics by labeling an object; (c) transcendence, or the application of acquired information to new knowledge domains by employing principles and procedures already learned; (d) regulation of behavior through attempts to control responses before, during, and after task performance or problem-solving; and (e) mediation of feelings of competence by providing positive feedback while explaining successful performance.

These criteria were used in the development of the PMYC program because they have been found in research to predict cognitive modifiability and self-regulation. In the PMYC program, the five MLE criteria were translated into a series of age- and capacity-adjusted statements and questions directed at children's learning experiences: Below is the transcript of a partial interaction between a mediator (M; or tutor) and learner (L; or tutee) concerning math computation. The mediator's (tutor's) use of MLE criteria are shown in parentheses.

Researcher: Which topic would you like to choose? (*Focusing on the problem*)

L: (Points at the screen.)

M: This is the 100 range (Meaning) Wow…good for you! (*Mediation of feelings of competence*)

L: (Chooses a game.)

M: 42 divided by 7?

L: (Immediately states the answer and types it.)

M: Very good. (*Mediation of feelings of competence*)

M: Press the block 6 times 8?

L: That's hard.

M: Do it like this: 8 plus 8 plus 8 plus… (*Transcendence*)

L: 8 plus 8 is 16.

M: Think again before answering…16 plus 16? (*Regulation of behaviour*)

L: That's hard….

M: Check, how much is 10 plus 10?

L: 20. Ah, the answer is 32.

M: Good, you checked and succeeded. (*Mediation of feelings of Competence*).

M: Now, 32 plus 16.

L: 45.

M: Think again. (*Regulation of behavior*)

L: 46. (Types the answer. The computer's response—think again).

M: Think about the rule. (*Regulation of behavior*)

L: 48. (Types the answer.)

M: Wow … It's good you work according to the rules. (*Mediation of feelings of competence*)

M: Press the block. 7 times 7?

L: 49.

M: Good! You did it! (*Mediation of feelings of competence*)

M: 9 times 9?

L: 80 … 1 … (Types an answer.)

M: Good!. 7 times 9? That's like nine sevens. (*Transcendence*)

L: 7 times 9 is… (L is about to press the wrong answer.)

M: No! You have to think again; think how we did it before. (*Regulation of behaviour*)

L: Oops. (Types an answer.)

M: Great! You solved it correctly. (*Mediation of feelings of competence*)

M: And 56 divided by 8?

The PMYC program is delivered in heterogeneous classrooms by means of cross-age tutoring; that is, involving an older child as tutor and younger child as tutee. The program is conducted for 3 weeks, and is divided into 7 lessons, each of which is constructed to include 3 basic components: (a) directly teaching MLE principles, (b) observing and discussing a film in which the principles are demonstrated, and (c) practicing peer mediation using multimedia and more conventional materials. The videotaped demonstrations are used to reinforce internalization of the peer-mediation principles. The multi-media and more conventional learning aids include special computer programs, games, posters, stickers with visual symbols of the principles, verbal slogans and work sheets. The tutor's experience with the MLE criteria is structured by a metacognitive training process (Brown, 1987; Flavell, 1979) embedded in the PMYC program. The training is consequently meant to nurture *metacognitive knowledge* about mental processes, task characteristics, and performance-oriented cognitive strategies; *metacognitive experience*, or self-awareness and monitoring of one's own mental processes; and *metacognitive control* of mental processes (self-regulation) directed at the construction and application of strategies appropriate for the completion of learning tasks. In the course of the program, these processes are gradually internalized as integrated cognitive mechanisms to be activated during learning.

The PMYC program, consequently, is designed to help tutors apply MLE criteria to their own learning experiences. They are expected to achieve this by exercising associated skills in a peer-mediated context. In other words, participation in the PMYC program and subsequent peer tutoring promotes a cognitive reconstruction of the child's metacognitive skills together with the MLE principles acquired during the PMYC program (for further details see Shamir & Lazerovitz, 2007). Research has indicated positive effects of the PMYC program on tutors' mediation style, cognitive modifiability and self-regulated learning in general domains (Shamir & Tzuriel, 2002, 2004; Shamir, Tzuriel, & Guy, 2007; Shamir & Van der Aalsvoort, 2004; Tzuriel & Shamir, 2007) as well as in specific domains such as math (Shamir, Tzuriel, & Rozen, 2006).

Recently, the PMYC program was implemented with children with LD (Shamir & Lazerovitz 2007). On the basis of previous studies, it was assumed that tutors with LD, once exposed to the program and later peer tutoring, would demonstrate improved self-regulation and performance. The tutors' self-regulated learning was measured by modifications in their mediation style (process of tutoring) and capacity to benefit from adult mediation for analogical thinking (outcomes of tutoring). The study involved 162 pupils, demonstrating considerable diversity of academic needs: 81 (tutors) from Grade 5 and 81 (tutees) from Grade 2. Tutors were chosen from classes of children with LD as defined by the National Joint Committee on Learning Disabilities and adopted by Israel's Ministry of Education (Margalit, 2000). Tutees were randomly selected from regular classes. Tutor and tutee pairs were assigned randomly to either an experimental (PMYC) or control (No PMYC) group. (Control children, however, practiced peer tutoring without experiencing the PMYC intervention.) During the final tutoring session, the children's interactions were videotaped and later assessed with the Observation of

Mediation Instrument. The tutors also completed a Dynamic Assessment Analogies Test.

When compared to controls, tutors with LD in the PMYC group improved their mediation style, cognitive modifiability and self-regulated learning and performance, expressed in improved scores on an analogies test across the pre-intervention, adult mediation, and post-intervention phases of the study. Findings demonstrate the contribution peer tutoring can make when applied in academically-diverse general education classrooms. The fact that the tutors with LD successfully participated in active peer-assisted learning likewise lends support to the model's relevance for children with special needs.

Cognitive-Behavioral Approaches

Reciprocal teaching. Palincsar and Brown's (1984) reciprocal teaching method is a small-group intervention designed to improve low achievers' reading comprehension. Students read a passage of expository material, paragraph by paragraph. While reading, they learn and practice how to generate questions, summarize, clarify word meanings and confusing text, and predict subsequent paragraphs. Vygotsky's influence may be seen equally clearly in Reciprocal Teaching as in the PMYC program. In the early stages of Reciprocal Teaching, the teacher models these strategies; then students practice them on the next section of text as the teacher tailors feedback through modeling, coaching, hints, and explanations. The teacher also invites students to react to peers' statements by elaborating or commenting, suggesting other questions, requesting clarifications, and helping to resolve misunderstandings. In the course of this guided practice, the teacher gradually shifts responsibility to the students for mediating discussions, as the teacher observes and helps as needed. At this point, sessions become dialogues among students as they support each other and alternate between prompting the use of a strategy, applying and verbalizing that strategy, and commenting on the application.

Palincsar and Brown (1986) have successfully popularized the notion that reading comprehension can and should be taught explicitly, and they have developed an imaginative and apparently effective means of doing so. At the same time, some concern has been expressed about Reciprocal Teaching's feasibility and usability. Its relatively complex and unfamiliar strategic comprehension strategies can be difficult for teachers and students to master (Pressley, 1997), with the result that many low-achieving students may be inconsistently involved (Hacker & Tenant, 2002). In addition, the program may be more appropriate for older than younger elementary age children, where its effects are less clear (e.g., Rosenshine & Meister, 1994).

Cooperative Integrated Reading and Composition (CIRC; e.g., Stevens, Madden, Slavin, & Farnish, 1987). Cooperative learning, according to Slavin (1994), relies on teamwork with group rewards that are dependent on a team score reflecting all members' achievement. The team whose members obtain the highest average on individual weekly quizzes is declared classroom "team of week." The idea is to encourage mutual helping among team-mates so that all learn. Student groups are deliberately heterogeneous with high- and low-achievers (including students with LD), distributed evenly among them. A well-researched example of cooperative learning programs is CIRC.

CIRC replaces all regular reading and composition activities of second- to sixth-grade elementary classrooms (Stevens et al., 1987). It comes with its own materials, as well as detailed lesson plans for teachers. Each new reading text is introduced to the class during a teacher-led activity, which is followed by peer-mediated activities, including oral story reading and answering of comprehension questions. For some of these activities, students work in pairs rather than in small groups. At the end of the cycle of activities, students take individual quizzes and teams are rewarded if they meet the criterion. Text composition is also taught by the teacher and practiced by students during a cycle of drafting and editing with feedback from peers. Students accumulate points for their team by being productive writers.

Several teams of investigators exploring the effectiveness of CIRC have demonstrated positive results for students with and without disabilities (Slavin, Madden, & Leavey, 1984; Stevens et al., 1987; Stevens, Slavin, & Farnish, 1991). Especially impressive are Stevens and Slavin's (1995) results. In this study, teachers mainstreamed students with LD and, with the help of their special education colleagues, implemented CIRC for two consecutive school years. At study's end, students with LD in CIRC classes outperformed students with LD in non-CIRC classes on reading comprehension, vocabulary, and basic writing skills. Similar results were obtained for non-disabled students.

There is more to the story, however, about cooperative learning and students with disabilities. McMaster and Fuchs (2002) searched for published studies between 1990 and 2000, inclusive, whose authors' examined effects of cooperative learning on the academic achievement of mainstreamed students with LD. Only studies that employed an experimental or quasi-experimental design were considered. Less than half of the studies meeting inclusion criteria reported statistically significant differences in favor of students with LD in cooperative learning classes. That is, in a majority of studies, cooperative learning did *not* promote the academic achievement of students with LD beyond what they would have achieved in business-as-usual classes.

One explanation of these outcomes has focused on the inconsistent involvement of low achievers, including students with LD, in team activities. Low achievers are sometimes inadvertently or purposefully excluded from these activities by other team members who ignore their contributions or give them answers without explanations (Jenkins & O'Connor, 2003). One way to circumvent this exclusion is to reduce group size to two members, creating a situation in which paired students have little choice but to work together.

Classwide Peer Tutoring (CWPT; e.g., Delquadri, Greenwood, Whorton, Carta, & Hall, 1986). Organizing students into same-age dyads is the instructional format adopted by those who have explored peer-tutoring activities. Delquadri and his colleagues have done much to validate this approach and generate interest in it—specifically, by their work on CWPT. They designed CWPT activities to facilitate rote learning (e.g., word spelling) by allowing students ample practice in a fast-paced, supportive context with immediate corrective feedback (e.g., Delquadri et al., 1986). At the beginning of each week, students in a given classroom are paired randomly with a new partner and given lists of spelling words, simple mathematical problems and reading assignments from their basal text. For a few minutes each day, partners alternate roles of tutor and tutee, asking each other questions and reading aloud. The pair earns points for correct answers, reading without errors, and correcting their mistakes. Each pair is assigned to one of two classroom teams and the points the pairs accumulate go to their team. A winner is declared each week. Points and teams are meant to serve only as motivation.

A majority of teachers and students conduct these activities well enough to bring about notable improvement in basic skills mastery (Greenwood, Terry, Arreaga-Mayer, & Finney, 1992). In the most ambitious study of the effectiveness of CWPT, Greenwood, Delquadri, and Hall (1989) randomly assigned first-grade classrooms to either experimental or control conditions. Experimental students participated in CWPT activities from first to fourth grade. At the end of their fourth-grade year, experimental students demonstrated superior reading, language, and mathematics scores on a standardized test. Furthermore, students in CWPT classes were less likely to have been given a high-incidence disability label (e.g., LD or behavioral disorders; Greenwood, Terry, Utley, Montagna, & Walker, 1993).

The effectiveness of CWPT for mainstreamed students with disabilities has also been examined in multiple case studies, with generally positive results (e.g., Sideridis et al., 1997). A drawback of CWPT seems to be its focus on basic skills. To be sure, repeated practice of basic skills with immediate corrective feedback is essential for many low achievers and students with disabilities (e.g., Torgesen et al., 1999). But such exclusive focus de-emphasizes higher-order skills (e.g., conceptual mathematical understanding), which may make CWPT seem somewhat non-aligned with current curriculum reform (Gersten & Baker, 1998).

Peer-Assisted Learning Strategies (PALS), to which we now turn, were developed with the goal of combining the supportive, engaging, and practical dyadic format of CWPT with some of the rich, challenging content of Reciprocal Teaching and CIRC. If we had to place PALS and the three cognitive-behavioral approaches just described on a continuum of "most opportunity" and "least opportunity" for differentiated instruction, we would locate Reciprocal Teaching towards "most"; PALS towards "least." This is because PALS is more strictly routinized; more directive in terms of permissible student action and language. And yet, PALS still affords participants opportunity for modifying instructional materials, activities, rewards, and expectations for performance. One dyad in a class of fourth graders, for example, may include a student reading on a second grade level and, because of this, she and her partner are reading text reflecting this skill level. Another pair in the same class, however, may be reading at a fifth grade level. Because the class is divided into multiple dyads, this variation in instructional material can be accommodated. Because of the opportunity for this kind of general flexibility and modification of tasks, teachers have been able to include virtually all their students in PALS.

PALS programs in reading have been developed and field-tested for preschool (D. Fuchs et al., 2004), kindergarten (D. Fuchs, Fuchs, Thompson, Al Otaiba, Yen, McMaster, et al., 2001; D. Fuchs, Fuchs, Thompson, Al Otaiba, Yen, Yang, et al., 2001; D. Fuchs et al., 2002), first grade (D. Fuchs, Fuchs, Svenson, et al., 2001; D. Fuchs, Fuchs, Yen, et al., 2001), second through sixth grade (D. Fuchs, Fuchs, Mathes, & Martinez, 2002; Fuchs et al., 1996; D. Fuchs et al. 1997), and high school (L. S. Fuchs, Fuchs, & Kazdan, 1999). Following is a description of two of these reading programs: Grade 2–6 PALS and First-Grade PALS.

Grade 2–6 PALS: Overall Program Effects

In a series of quasi-experimental studies, Fuchs and colleagues tested the contributions of various components of Grade 2–6 PALS. In one such study Simmons, Fuchs, Fuchs, Pate, & Mathes (1994) determined that a relatively complex set of peer-mediated activities supported greater student learning than did a set of simpler CWPT peer-mediated activities. In the same study, they also found that role reciprocity, where students of a pair serve as both tutor and tutee in each session, promoted greater reading gains than a more static arrangement whereby tutors and tutees did *not* exchange roles. Across several years, then, Fuchs and associates frequently added and subtracted components based on their relative effectiveness and feasibility, finally settling on a "package" they believed to boost reading performance and which was perceived by teachers as practical for classrooms use. Below, we describe this PALS program and two quasi-experimental investigations of its effectiveness. The first was conducted with children whose primary language was English (Fuchs et al., 1996); the second, with children with limited English proficiency (Saenz, Fuchs, & Fuchs, 2005).

The PALS Intervention   Each week, teachers conduct three 35-minute PALS sessions as part of their allocated reading time, implementing PALS with all children in their classes. Teachers begin the program by conducting seven lessons on how to implement PALS. Each of these training lessons lasts 45 to 60 minutes and incorporates teacher presentations, student recitation of information and application of principles, and teacher feedback on student implementation (see Fuchs, Fuchs, Mathes, & Simmons, 2008, for the teacher manual).

During PALS, like CWPT, every student in the class is paired; each pair includes a higher- and lower-performing student. The teacher determines pairs by first ranking students from strongest to weakest reader, then calculating a median split, and finally pairing the strongest reader from the top half of the rankings with the strongest reader from the bottom half and so on. Although tutoring roles are reciprocal, the higher-performing student reads first for each activity to serve as model for the lower-performing student. Both students read from material appropriate for the lower reader, which typically is literature selected by the teacher.

Pairs are assigned to one of two teams for which they earn points. Students give points to themselves for completing reading activities correctly and teachers award points to pairs who demonstrate good tutoring behavior. Each pair keeps track of points on a consecutively numbered score card, which represents joint effort and achievement. Each time a student earns a point, the tutor slashes the next number. At the end of the week, each pair reports the last number slashed as the pair's total; the teacher sums each team's points; and the class applauds the winning team. Every 4 weeks, the teacher creates new pairs and team assignments. Thus, like CIRC, the motivational system combines competitive (team vs. team) and cooperative (combined effort of the pair) structures.

The first activity in every PALS session is *Partner Reading*. Each student reads connected text aloud for 5 minutes, for a total of 10 minutes. The higher-performing student reads first; the lower-performing student rereads the same material. After both students read, the lower-performing student retells for 2 minutes the sequence of what occurred. Students earn 1 point for each correctly read sentence and 10 points for the retell.

The second PALS activity, *Paragraph Shrinking*, was inspired by Reciprocal Teaching. It is designed to develop comprehension through summarization and main idea identification. Students read orally one paragraph at a time, stopping to identify its main idea. Tutors guide the identification of the main idea by asking readers to identify who or what the paragraph is mainly about and the most important thing about the who or what. Readers put these two pieces of information together in 10 or fewer words. For each summary, students earn 1 point for correctly identifying who or what; 1 point for correctly stating the most important thing about the who or what; and 1 point for using no more than 10 words. Students continue to monitor and correct reading errors, but points no longer are awarded for reading sentences correctly. After 5 minutes, students switch roles.

The last activity is *Prediction Relay*. It extends Paragraph Shrinking to larger chunks of text and requires students to formulate and check predictions. Prediction Relay comprises five steps. The reader makes a prediction about what will be learned on the next half page; reads the half page aloud while the tutor corrects reading errors; confirms or disconfirms the prediction; and summarizes the main idea. Students earn 1 point for each correct prediction; 1 point for reading each half page; 1 point for accurately confirming each prediction; and 1 point for each summary component (identifying the who or what, what mainly happened, and making the main idea statement in 10 words or less). After 5 minutes, students switch roles.

Effects on English-Proficient Students at Various Levels of Achievement

To study the effects of Grade 2–6 PALS on English-proficient students at different achievement levels, Fuchs et al. (1997) assigned 12 schools, stratified on academic achievement and family income, to experimental (PALS) and control (No-PALS) groups. At Grades 2–6, 20 teachers implemented PALS; 20 did not. PALS teachers implemented the treatment class-wide, but only three students in each class were identified as study participants: one with LD in reading, one low achiever never referred for special education (LA), and one average achiever (AA). Each of these students was identified by the classroom teacher as either typical of the children with LD or representative of LA and AA students in her class. All selected students spoke English as their primary language. Each was tested with the Comprehensive Reading Assessment Battery (CRAB; Fuchs et al., 1997) before and after PALS implementation, which lasted 15 weeks. Fidelity data, collected 3 times during classroom observations, indicated strong teacher and student implementation. Teacher-completed instructional plan sheets revealed that PALS and No-PALS teachers allocated comparable time to reading instruction.

We analyzed student achievement data using treatment (PALS vs. No-PALS), trial (pretreatment testing vs. post-treatment testing), and student type (LD vs. LA vs. AA) as factors. Treatment was a between-group factor and trial and student type were within-group factors. Classroom was the unit of analysis. We found statistically significant treatment by trial interactions on all CRAB scores. These interactions indicated that, compared to students in business-as-usual No-PALS classrooms, PALS students grew more on reading fluency, accuracy, and comprehension. Moreover, the 3-way interaction between treatment, trial, and student type was not statistically significant. So, PALS effects were not mediated by students' initial achievement status. Aggregated across the LD, LA, and AA students, effect sizes were 0.22, 0.55, and 0.56, respectively, on the CRAB words read correctly, CRAB questions answered correctly, and CRAB maze blanks restored correctly. These effects compare favorably with more comprehensive and complex cooperative learning programs. As reported by Slavin (1994), the median effect size for 52 studies of cooperative learning treatments that lasted more than 4 weeks was 0.32, a figure identical to the one reported by Rosenshine and Meister (1994) for Reciprocal Teaching.

Effects on Students with Limited English Proficiency (LEP) at Various Levels of Achievement

Saenz et al. (2005) conducted a study paralleling the Fuchs et al. (1997) investigation just described, with these important differences. First, participants were 12 teachers in South Texas, working in schools that served a mostly LEP population. From each class, Saenz et al. sampled only students (n = 132) who were native Spanish speaking and who were identified by their school district as LEP according to Texas eligibility criteria. Second, in contrast to Fuchs et al., Saenz et al. included high-achieving classmates (HA) from each participating classroom so that 11 children were pre- and post-tested from each class: 2 LD, 3 LA, 3 AA, and 3 HA. PALS was implemented in English for 15 weeks with strong fidelity.

As with Fuchs et al. (1997), CRAB data supported PALS effectiveness. On CRAB questions answered correctly, for example, PALS students outperformed No-PALS students, and the effect sizes were large: 1.06 for LD, 0.86 for LA, 0.60 for AA, and 1.02 for HA (across student types, 1.02). So, Saenz et al.'s findings extend those of prior work supporting PALS by including both LEP students and students who began their PALS participation reading better than their classmates (i.e., the HA students in PALS classrooms improved their reading comprehension in comparison to HA students in No-PALS classes). For those with interest in LEP children, also see McMaster, Kung, Han, and Cao (2008) for an evaluation of the Kindergarten PALS program involving LEP children in the Minneapolis Public Schools.

Across Both Efficacy Studies

Across the Fuchs et al. (1997) and Saenz et al. (2005) studies, results demonstrate the potential of PALS to enhance children's reading comprehension. The source, or "active ingredient," of the program's apparent effectiveness may reside both in its specific activities and in its overall organization. PALS-related activities—taken from or inspired by Reciprocal Teaching, CIRC, and CWPT—encourage students to practice research-based strategies, which have been shown to strengthen reading comprehension when implemented regularly on instructional-level text. With respect to organization, PALS organizes highly structured, reciprocal, one-to-one interaction, which (a) provides all students with frequent opportunity to respond, (b) facilitates immediate corrective feedback, (c) increases academic engaged time, and (d) offers social support and encouragement, with all students sharing the esteem associated with the tutoring role. Moreover, with the PALS score-card system, students work cooperatively with partners but compete in teams to earn points. We have often observed that this keeps students working in a focused, productive, and constructive manner.

Finally, PALS materials are concrete, specific, and user friendly—important criteria if practices are to be implemented (see McLaughlin cited in Gersten, Vaughn, Deshler, & Schiller, 1995). A comprehensive teacher manual guides implementation; there is no need for teachers to develop additional materials. Finally, PALS can complement most instructional approaches, including whole language as well as explicit phonics because it supplements, rather than substitutes for, teachers' ongoing reading practices. We know this because we have worked closely with many PALS teachers over the years, including strong advocates of implicit approaches and others preferring more explicit strategies.

First-Grade PALS

Over the past decade, Grade 2–6 PALS has been extended downward to address the development of reading and pre-reading skills at preschool, kindergarten, and first grade (see D. Fuchs & Fuchs, 2005, for a summary). First-Grade PALS parallels the organization of PALS at the higher grades, but its activities and content are different.

Overview of First-Grade PALS   All students in First-Grade PALS classrooms are divided into pairs based on their rapid letter naming performance. A higher- and lower-achieving student constitutes each pair. The higher-performing student is always the Coach (tutor) first. When the pair completes an activity, the students switch roles and repeat the activity. Partners change every 4 weeks. In contrast to PALS in higher grades, First-Grade PALS sessions begin by the teacher conducting 5 minutes of instruction: introducing new letter sounds and sight words and leading students in segmenting and blending activities. Then, students participate in pairs in Sounds & Words and Partner Reading.

The first Sounds & Words activity is *letter-sound correspondence*, lasting 3 minutes. The Coach points to a letter and prompts the Reader to say its sound. If the Reader makes a mistake or does not know the sound of a letter, the Coach uses a correction procedure. When the Reader has said all of the sounds, the Coach marks a happy face on a lesson sheet and five points on a point sheet. Partners then switch roles and repeat the activity.

The second Sounds & Words activity involves *segmenting and blending* the 8–10 words used during the teacher-directed instruction. The Coach prompts the Reader to sound out a word, and then directs the Reader to "Say it fast." The Reader responds by reading the word. If the Reader makes a mistake, the Coach uses a correction procedure. When the 8–10 words have been segmented and blended, the Coach marks a happy face on the lesson sheet and five points on the point sheet, and the partners switch roles and repeat the activity. This task lasts 5 minutes.

Sight word practice is the third Sounds & Words activity. The Coach points to each word and prompts the Reader to read it by saying, "What word." If the Reader says the wrong word, the Coach uses a correction procedure. The Coach marks a happy face and five points. Partners then switch roles and repeat the task. Sight word practice is conducted for 4 minutes.

In the fourth Sounds & Words activity, students read *decodable words* and sight words in First-Grade PALS short stories. Beforehand, the teacher introduces new "rocket words" and reviews old "rocket words." These words (e.g., "playground," "birthday party," and "office") were added to First-Grade PALS stories to increase interest value. The teacher reads the story as students follow on their lesson sheets. The teacher emphasizes the importance of reading quickly and correctly. Coaches then prompt their Readers to read. Coaches use a correction procedure for oral reading errors. When the story is completed, the Coach marks a happy face and five points. Partners switch roles and repeat the activity. The story activity lasts 5 minutes. Coaches and Readers mark a star on a chart if they have read the story the number of times the teacher designates (never to exceed three times in one session). When all the stars on the chart are marked, the student receives a bookmark and a new chart.

After students have implemented Sounds & Words activities independently for 4 weeks, 10 minutes of Partner Reading is added. In Partner Reading, students apply decoding skills and sight word knowledge to narrative text appropriate to their reading level. Teachers prepare students to participate in Partner Reading in two 20-minute sessions. The Coach reads the book's title, pointing to each word. Then the Reader reads the title, pointing to each word. The Coach reads a page of the book, again pointing to each word. The Reader then does the same on the same page. Partners proceed through the book in this manner, mark five points, and repeat the process, switching roles. Each book is read four times before the pair trades it for a new one. Partner Reading is conducted for 10 minutes per session.

PALS Effects on English- and French-Speaking Students of Varying Levels of Performance   Previous work has indicated that First-Grade PALS promotes stronger gains than business-as-usual reading instruction in decoding and word recognition for LA students with and without disabilities and average-achieving and high-achieving students in both high-poverty Title I and middle-class schools (see Fuchs & Fuchs, 2005, for a summary). More recently, Dion and colleagues (Dion, Borri-Anadon, Vanier, Potvin, & Roux, 2005) developed a French version of First-Grade PALS ("Apprendre a lire a deux"), and explored its importance for boosting reading achievement among children in several of Montreal's lowest-income schools.

Dion, Roux, Landry, Fuchs, and Wehby (2007) randomly assigned 58 first-grade classrooms to one of three study condition: controls, First-Grade PALS, or First-Grade PALS plus attention training. The attention training component was an adaptation of the Good Behavior Game, which teachers used every day during their reading instruction. Students in First-Grade PALS plus attention training classes were divided in two teams. Teachers reinforced attention and penalized disruptions by adding or subtracting points to team total. End-of-first-grade outcomes (i.e., performance on word recognition, decoding, and comprehension) were analyzed separately for low-achieving and average-achieving students identified prior to treatment implementation. Average-achieving students who participated in

First-Grade PALS activities outperformed controls on all reading measures regardless of whether they also had the attention training; that is, attention training seemed to have little value for these students. It appeared to have greater value for low-achieving students. These students in the First-Grade PALS plus attention training group showed greater improvement in sight-word reading, decoding, and reading comprehension than their counterparts in the control group and First-Grade PALS only group. Thus, it appears attention training may be an important addition to First-Grade PALS activities for lower-performing young children in low-income schools.

What We Still Need to Know about Peer-Mediated Instruction

We have briefly described several approaches to peer-mediated instruction. The PMYC program was highlighted because we believe it is a viable alternative to perhaps better known cognitive-behavioral approaches. We discussed Reciprocal Teaching, CIRC, and CWPT because they are important and successful and, as mentioned, were a basis for the development of PALS. Despite the apparent effectiveness of these programs, peer mediation is an under-appreciated and still infrequently used approach to differentiate and strengthen learning and teaching. This is unfortunate for many obvious reasons, including that numerous approaches to differentiated instruction are un-validated and peer mediation is inexpensive and virtually all schools should be able to afford it. Although we are obviously bullish on it, we recognize, too, that important R&D remains. We express two caveats about PALS to make this point.

First, the development of Grade 2–6 PALS in the 1990s shows that, despite statistically significant and practically important effects across low achievers with and without LD and average achievers, a small subset of children do not profit. In the D. Fuchs et al. (1997) study, for example, 4 of 20 of children with LD failed to make adequate growth. These 4 children were the poorest readers among the 20, and 3 of the 4 were also described by their teachers as often showing disruptive behavior. Clearly, some children require more intensive or different reading methods. This underscores the importance of monitoring at-risk students' reading progress throughout the school year to identify those who require program adjustments (L. Fuchs & Fuchs, 1998b). In this regard, we support the relatively new policy of Responsiveness-To-Instruction (RTI), which, in principal, redefines general education as multiple levels of increasingly intensive prevention (cf. D. Fuchs, Fuchs, & Vaughn, 2008; L. Fuchs & Fuchs, 1998). In addition, research is needed to examine the characteristics of these so-called treatment non-responders so that additional methods, PALS or otherwise, can be developed to address their educational needs (cf. Al Otaiba & Fuchs, 2003; Al Otaiba & Fuchs, 2006; Duff et al.,2008; Nelson, Benner, & Gonzalez, 2003).

Second, in all the PALS studies just described, teachers receive frequent on-site technical assistance, whereby research assistants observed teachers conduct PALS lessons and helped them solve implementation problems. This, of course, provides opportunities for research staff to quickly correct teachers' misconceptions and ensure proper implementation. Although study teachers consistently described PALS methods as practical, it remains unclear what level of technical support, if any, is required to guarantee accurate implementation. An independent replication of PALS conducted by Vadasy, Jenkins, Antil, Phillips, and Pool (1997) found that when teachers were given access to only a teacher's manual, few implemented it. And among those who did, fewer did so with fidelity. Other independent PALS implementations, however, suggest that a 1-day workshop together with minimal ongoing encouragement may be sufficient to ensure strong PALS implementation (e.g., Grimes, 1997; Raines, 1994). Several of us are currently funded by a grant from the Institute of Education Sciences to evaluate how much and what kind of technical assistance is required to scale up PALS in Nashville, South Texas, and Minneapolis-St. Paul (e.g., D. Fuchs, Saenz, McMaster, et al., 2008; Kearns, Fuchs, Meyers, et al., in preparation; Stein, Berends, Fuchs, et al., 2008).

References

Al Otaiba, S., & Fuchs, D. (2003). Characteristics of children who are unresponsive to early literacy instruction: A review of the literature. *Remedial and Special Education, 23*(5), 300–316.

Al Otaiba, S., & Fuchs, D. (2006). Who are the young children for whom best practices in reading are ineffective? An experimental and longitudinal study. *Journal of Learning Disabilities, 39*(5), 414–431.

Baker, J. M., & Zigmond, N. (1990). Are regular education classes equipped to accommodate students with learning disabilities? *Exceptional Children, 56*, 515–526.

Brown, A. L. (1987). Metacognition, executive control, self-regulation and other more mysterious mechanisms. In F. E. Weinert & R. H. Kluwe (Eds.), *Metacognition, motivation and understanding* (pp. 65–116). Hillsdale, NJ: Erlbaum.

Brown, B. W., & Saks, D. H. (1981). The microeconomics of schooling. In D. C. Berliner (Ed.), *Review of research in education* (Vol. 9, pp. 217–254). Washington, DC: American Educational Research Association.

Brown, B. W., & Saks, D. H. (1987). The microeconomics of the allocation of teachers' time and student learning. *Economics of Education Review, 6*, 319–332.

Carnine, D. W., Silbert, J., Kame'enui, E. J., & Tarver, S. G. (2004). *Direct instruction reading* (4th ed.). Upper Saddle River, NJ: Prentice Hall.

Carolan, J., & Guinn, A. (2007). Differentiation: Examining how master teachers weave differentiation into their daily practice can help reluctant teachers take the plunge. *Educational Leadership, 64*(5), 44–47.

Delquadri, J. C., Greenwood, C. R., Whorton, D., Carta, J. J., & Hall, R. V. (1986). Classwide peer tutoring. *Exceptional Children, 52*(6), 535–561.

Dion, E., Borri-Anadon, C., Vanier, N., Potvin, M.-C., & Roux, C. (2005). *Apprendre à lire à deux. Manuel de l'enseignante et matériel de lecture.* [Apprendre à Lire à Deux Teachers' Manual]. Unpublished manuscript, Université du Québec à Montréal, Montréal, Québec, Canada.

Dion, É., Roux, C., Landry, D., Fuchs, D., & Wehby, J. (2007, July). *Preventing reading disabilities among disadvantaged first-graders: A two-pronged approach.* Poster presented at the Fifteenth Annual

Meeting of the Society for the Scientific Study of Reading, Prague, Czech Republic.

Duff, F. J., Fieldsend, E., Bowyer-Crane, C., Hulme, C., Smith, G., Gibbs, S., et al. (2008). *Reading and vocabulary intervention: Evaluation of an instruction for children with poor response to reading intervention.* Unpublished manuscript.

Feuerstein, R., Rand, Y., & Hoffman M. B. (1979). *The dynamic assessment of retarded performers: The learning potential assessment device, theory, instruments, and technique.* Baltimore, MD: University Park Press.

Flavell, J. H. (1979) Metacognition and cognitive monitoring: a new area of cognitive developmental inquiry. *American Psychologist, 34,* 906–911.

Fuchs, D., & Fuchs, L. S. (2005). Peer-Assisted Learning Strategies: Promoting word recognition, fluency, and reading comprehension in young children. *Journal of Special Education, 39*(1), 34–44.

Fuchs, D., Fuchs, L. S., Eaton, S., Young, T., Mock, D., & Dion, E. (2004). *Hearing sounds in words: preschoolers helping preschoolers in a downward extension of peer-assisted learning strategies.* Paper presented at the National Disabilities Association Annual Conference, Atlanta, GA.

Fuchs, D., Fuchs, L. S., & Fernstrom, P. (1993). A conservative approach to special education reform: Mainstreaming through transenvironmental programming and curriculum-based measurement. *American Educational Research Journal, 30,* 149–177.

Fuchs, D., Fuchs, L. S., Mathes, P. G., & Martinez, E. A. (2002). Preliminary evidence on the social standing of students with learning disabilities in PALS and NO-PALS classrooms. *Learning Disabilities Research & Practice, 17,* 205–215.

Fuchs, D., Fuchs, L. S., Mathes, P. G., & Simmons, D. C. (1996). *Peer-assisted learning strategies: Reading methods for grades 2–6.* Nashville, TN: Vanderbilt University.

Fuchs, D., Fuchs, L. S., Mathes, P. G., & Simmons, D. C. (1997). Peer-assisted learning strategies: Making classrooms more responsive to diversity. *American Educational Research Journal, 34,* 174–206.

Fuchs, D., Fuchs, L.S., Simmons, D. C., & Mathes, P. G. (2008). *Peer-assisted learning strategies: Reading methods for grades 2–6.* Nashville, TN: Vanderbilt University.

Fuchs, D., Fuchs, L. S., Svenson, E., Yen, L., Thompson, A., McMaster, K. L., et al. (2001). *Peer-assisted learning strategies: First grade reading.* Nashville, TN: Vanderbilt University.

Fuchs, D., Fuchs, L. S., Thompson, A., Al Otaiba, S., Yen, L., McMaster, K. L., et al. (2001). *Peer assisted learning strategies: Kindergarten reading.* Nashville, TN: Vanderbilt University.

Fuchs, D., Fuchs, L. S., Thompson, A., Al Otaiba, S., Yen, L., Yang, N. J., et al. (2001). Is reading important in reading-readiness programs? A randomized field trial with teachers as program implementers. *Journal of Educational Psychology, 93,* 251–267.

Fuchs, D., Fuchs, L. S., Thompson, A., Al Otaiba, S., Yen, L., Yang, N. J., et al. (2002). Exploring the importance of reading programs for kindergartners with disabilities in mainstream classrooms. *Exceptional Children, 55,* 295–311.

Fuchs, D., Fuchs, L. S., & Vaughn, S. (2008). *Response to intervention: A framework for reading educators.* Newark, DE: International Reading Association.

Fuchs, D., Fuchs, L. S., Yen, L., McMaster, K. L., Svenson, E., Yang, N. J., et al. (2001). Developing first-grade reading fluency through peer mediation. *Teaching Exceptional Children. 34,* 90–93.

Fuchs, D., Roberts, P. H., Fuchs, L. S., & Bowers, J. (1996). Reintegrating students with learning disabilities into the mainstream: A two-year study. *Learning Disabilities Research & Practice, 11*(4), 214–229.

Fuchs, D., Saenz, L., McMaster, K., Yen, L., Fuchs, L., Compton, D., et al. (2008). Scaling up an evidence-based reading program for kindergartners. In L. Fuchs (Chair), *Feasibility and effectiveness of early preventive reading interventions.* Symposium presented at the Society for the Scientific Study of Reading conference, Asheville, NC.

Fuchs, L. S., & Fuchs, D. (1998). Treatment validity: A unifying concept for reconceptualizing the identification of learning disabilities. *Learning Disabilities Research and Practice, 13,* 204–219.

Fuchs, L. S., Fuchs, D., & Bishop, N. (1992). Teacher planning for students with learning disabilities: Differences between general and special educators. *Learning Disabilities Research & Practice, 7,* 120–128.

Fuchs, L. S., Fuchs, D., & Kazdan, S. (1999). Effects of peer-assisted learning strategies on high-school students with serious reading problems. *Remedial and Special Education, 20,* 309–319.

Gerber, M. M., & Semmel, M. I. (1984). Teacher as imperfect test: Reconceptualizing the referral process. *Educational Psychologist, 19*(3), 137–148.

Gersten, R., & Baker, S. (1998). Real world use of scientific concepts: Integrating situated cognition with explicit instruction. *Exceptional Children, 65,* 23–35.

Gersten, R., Vaughn, S., Deshler, D., & Schiller, E. (1995). *What we know (and still don't know) about utilizing research findings to improve practice: Implications for special education.* Unpublished manuscript.

Greenwood, C. R., Delquadri, J. C., & Hall, R. V. (1989). Longitudinal effects of classwide peer tutoring. *Journal of Educational Psychology, 81*(3), 371–383.

Greenwood, C. R., Terry, B., Arreaga-Mayer, C., & Finney, R. (1992). The classwide peer tutoring program: Implementation factors moderating students' achievement. *Journal of Applied Behavior Analysis, 25,* 101–116.

Greenwood, C. R., Terry, B., Utley, C. A., Montagna, D., & Walker, D. (1993). Achievement, placement, and services: Middle school benefits of classwide peer tutoring used at the elementary school. *School Psychology Review, 22,* 497–516.

Grimes, J. (1997). *Implementing reading PALS in Iowa.* [Unpublished data]

Hacker, D. J., & Tenant, A. (2002). Implementing reciprocal teaching in the classroom: Overcoming obstacles and making modifications. *Journal of Educational Psychology, 94*(4), 699–718.

Hall, T. (2002). *Differentiated instruction.* Wakefield, MA: National Center on Accessing the General Curriculum. Retrieved January, 13, 2009, from http://www.cast.org/publications/ncac/ncac_diffinstruc.html

Hall, R. V., Delquadri, J. C., Greenwood, C. R., & Thurston, L. (1982). The importance of opportunity to respond in children's academic success. In E. Edgar, N. Haring, J. Jenkins, & C. Pious (Eds.), *Mentally handicapped children: Education and training* (pp. 107–140). Baltimore, MD: University Park Press.

Jenkins, J. R., & O'Connor, R. (2003). Cooperative learning for students with learning disabilities: Evidence from experiments, observations, and interviews. In L. Swanson, S. Graham, & K. Harris (Eds.), *Handbook of learning disabilities* (pp. 417–430). New York: Guilford.

Kapusnick, R. A., & Hauslein, C. M. (2001). The 'silver cup' of differentiation. *Kappa Delta Pi Record, 37,* 156–159.

Kearns, D., Fuchs, D., Meyers C. V., Berends, M., McMaster, K. L., Saenz, L., et al. (in preparation). *Factors contributing to teachers' sustained use of kindergarten peer-assisted learning strategies.*

Leithwood, K., Leonard, L., & Sharratt, L. (1998). Conditions fostering organizational learning in schools. *Education Administration Quarterly, 34*(2) 243–276.

Lesgold, A. M., & Resnick, L. (1982). How reading difficulties develop: Perspectives from a longitudinal study. In J. Das, R. Mulcahy & A. Wall (Eds.), *Theory and research in learning disabilities.* New York: Plenum.

Margalit, M. (2000). *Learning disabilities in the classroom: Educational dilemmas of the new reality* [in Hebrew]. Tel Aviv, Israel: The Mofet Institute.

McDermott, R. P., & Aron, J. (1978). Pirandello in the classroom: On the possibility of equal educational opportunity in American culture. In M. C. Reynolds (Ed.), *Futures of education for exceptional students* (pp. 41–64). Reston, VA: Council for Exceptional Children.

McIntosh, R., Vaughn, S., Schumm, J. S., Haager, D., & Lee, O. (1994). Observations of students with learning disabilities in general education classrooms. *Exceptional Children, 60*(3), 249–261.

McMaster, K. N., & Fuchs, D. (2002). Effects of cooperative learning on the academic achievement of students with learning disabilities: An update of Tateyama-Sniezek's review. *Learning Disabilities Research and Practice, 17*(2), 107–117.

McMaster, K. L., Kung, S. H., Han, I., & Cao, M. (2008). Peer-Assisted Learning Strategies: A "tier 1" approach to promoting English learners' response to intervention. *Exceptional Children, 74*, 194–214.

Nelson, R. J., Benner, G. J., & Gonzalez, J. (2003). Learner characteristics that influence the treatment effectiveness of early literacy interventions: A meta-analytic review. *Learning Disabilities Research and Practice, 18*, 255–267.

O'Sullivan, P. J., Ysseldyke, J. E., Christenson, S. L., & Thurlow, M. L. (1990). Mildly handicapped elementary students' opportunity to learn during reading instruction in mainstream and special education settings. *Reading Research Quarterly, 25*, 131–146.

Palincsar, A. S., & Brown, A. L. (1984). Reciprocal teaching of comprehension-fostering and comprehension-monitoring activities. *Cognition and Instruction, 1*, 117–175.

Palincsar, A. S., & Brown, A. L. (1986). Interactive teaching to promote independent learning from text. *Reading Teacher, 39*, 771–777.

Peterson, P. L., & Clark, C. M. (1978). Teachers' reports of their cognitive process during teaching. *American Educational Research Journal, 15*, 555–565.

Pressley, M. (1997). *Remarks on reading comprehension*. Notes prepared for the Chesapeake Institute, Washington, DC.

Pressley, M., Allington, R. L., Wharton-McDonald, R., Block, C. C., & Morrow, L. (2001). *Learning to read: Lessons from exemplary first-grade classrooms*. New York: Guilford.

Raines, R. (1994). *Implementing reading PALS in Bakersfield, CA.* [Unpublished data]

Rosenshine, B., & Meister, C. (1994). Reciprocal teaching: A review of research. *Review of Educational Research, 64*, 479–530.

Saenz, L. M., Fuchs, L. S., & Fuchs, D. (2005). Effects of peer-assisted learning strategies on English language learners with learning disabilities: A randomized controlled study. *Exceptional Children, 71*, 231–247.

Schumm, J. S., & Vaughn, S. (1992). Planning for mainstreamed special education students: Perceptions of general classroom teachers. *Exceptionality, 3*(2), 81–98.

Schumm, J. S., Vaughn, S., Gordon, J., & Rothstein, L. (1994). General education teachers' beliefs, skills, and practices in planning for mainstreamed students with learning disabilities. *Teacher Education and Special Education, 17*, 22–37.

Shamir, A., & Lazerovitz, T. (2007). A peer mediation intervention for scaffolding self-regulated learning among children with learning disabilities. *European Journal of Special Needs Education.*

Shamir, A., & Silvern, S. (2005). Effects of peer mediation with young children on autonomous behavior. *Journal of Cognitive Education and Psychology, 5*(2), 199–215.

Shamir, A., & Tzuriel, D. (2002). Peer mediation: A novel model for development of mediation skills and cognitive modifiability of young children. In W. Resing, W. Ruijssenaars, & D. Aalsvoort (Eds.), *Learning potential assessment and cognitive training: Actual research perspectives in theory building and methodology* (pp. 363–373). New York: JAI Press/Elsevier.

Shamir, A., & Tzuriel, D. (2004). Characteristics of children's mediational teaching style as a function of intervention for cross-age peer mediation with computers. *School Psychology International, 25*(1), 59–78.

Shamir, A., Tzuriel, D., & Guy, R. (2007) Computer-supported collaborative learning: cognitive effects of intervention for peer mediation tutoring. Peer-assisted learning: state of the art as we turn towards the future [Special issue]. *Journal of Cognitive Educational Psychology, 6*, 433–455.

Shamir, A., Tzuriel, D., & Rozen, M (2006). Peer mediation: The effects of program intervention, math level, and verbal ability on mediation style and improvement in math problem solving. *School Psychology International, 27*(2), 209–231.

Shamir, A., & Van der Aalsvoort, G. (2004). Children's mediational teaching style and cognitive modifiability: A comparison between first and third graders in Holland and Israel. *Educational Practice and Theory, 26*(2), 61–85.

Sideridis, G. D., Utley. C. A., Greenwood, C. R., Delquadri, J., Dawson, H., Palmer, P., et al. (1997). Classwide peer tutoring: Effects on the spelling performance and social interactions of students with mild disabilities and their typical peers in an integrated instructional setting. *Journal of Behavioral Education, 7*, 435–462.

Simmons, D. C., Fuchs, D., Fuchs, L. S., Hodge, J. P., & Mathes, P. G. (1994). Importance of instructional complexity and role reciprocity to classwide peer tutoring. *Learning Disabilities Research & Practice, 9*, 203–212.

Slavin, R. E. (1994). *Cooperative learning: Theory, research, & practice* (2nd ed.). Boston: Allyn & Bacon.

Slavin, R. E., Leavey, M. B., & Madden, N., A. (1984). Combining learning and individualized instruction: Effects on student mathematics achievement, attitudes, and behaviors. *Elementary School Journal, 84*, 409–422.

Slavin, R. E., Madden, N. A., & Leavey, M. B. (1984). Effects of team assisted individualization on the mathematics achievement of academically handicapped and nonhandicapped students. *Journal of Educational Psychology, 76*, 813–819.

Stein, M. L., Berends, M., Fuchs, D., McMaster, K., Saenz, L., Yen. L., et al. (2008). Scaling up an early reading program: Relationships among teacher support, fidelity of implementation, and student performance across different sites and years. *Educational Evaluation and Policy Analysis, 30*(4), 368–388.

Stevens, R. J., Madden, N. A., Slavin, R. E., & Farnish, A. M. (1987). Cooperative integrated reading and composition: Two field experiments. *Reading Research Quarterly, 22*, 433–454.

Stevens, R., & Slavin, R. (1995). The cooperative elementary school effects on students' achievement, attitudes, and social relations. *American Educational Research Journal, 32*(2), 321–351.

Stevens, R. J., Slavin, R. E., & Farnish, A. M. (1991). The effects of cooperative learning and direct instruction in reading comprehension strategies on main idea identification. *Journal of Educational Psychology, 83*, 8–16.

Tomlinson, C. (1999). Mapping a route toward differentiated instruction. *Educational Leadership, 57*(1), 12–16.

Tomlinson, C., & Allan, S. D. (2003). *Leadership for differentiating schools and classrooms*. Alexandria, VA: Association for Supervision and Curriculum Development.

Tomlinson, C. A., & Kalbfleisch, M. L. (1998). Teach me, teach my brain: A call for differentiated classrooms. *Educational Leadership, 56*(3), 52–55.

Torgesen, J. K., Wagner, R. K., Rashotte, C. A., Lindamood, P., Rose, E., Conway, T., et al. (1999). Preventing reading failure in young children with phonological processing disabilities: Group and individual responses to instruction. *Journal of Educational Psychology, 91*, 579–593.

Tzuriel, D., & Shamir, A. (2007). The effects of peer mediation with young children (PMYC) on children's cognitive modifiability. *British Journal of Educational Psychology.*

Vadasy, P. F., Jenkins, J. R., Antil, L. R., Phillips, N. B., & Pool, K. (1997). The research to practice ball game: Classwide peer tutoring and teacher interest, implementation, and modifications. *Remedial and Special Education, 18*, 143–156.

Vygotsky, L. S. (1929). The problem of the cultural development of the child. *Journal of Genetic Psychology, 36*, 415–434.

Vygotsky, L. S. (1962). *Thought and language*. Cambridge, MA: MIT Press.

Vygotsky, L. S. (1978). *Mind in society: The development of higher psychological process*. Cambridge, MA: Harvard University Press.

Vygotsky, L. S. (1981). The genesis of higher mental functions. In J. V. Wertsch (Ed.). *The concept of activity in Soviet psychology* (pp. 144–188). Armonk, NY: Sharpe.

Zigmond, N., & Baker, J. (1994). Is the mainstream a more appropriate educational setting for Randy? A case study of one student with learning disabilities. *Learning Disabilities Research & Practice, 9*(2), 108–117.

33

Reading Instruction Research for English-Language Learners in Kindergarten through Sixth Grade

The Last Twenty Years

STEVE AMENDUM
North Carolina State University

JILL FITZGERALD
The University of North Carolina at Chapel Hill

Researchers and practitioners alike understand the central importance, promise, and challenge of facilitating literacy learning for English-language learners. Undeniably, reading education for English-language learners has gained prominent attention in both policy and practice (cf. August & Shanahan, 2006; Slavin & Cheung, 2005). In February of 2008 the International Reading Association released its 12th annual list of "what's hot?" in the literacy field. Twenty-five nationally known literacy leaders rated *English-as-a-second-language/English-language learners* as one of nine "very hot" topics in the literacy field.

In recent decades the number of English-language learners attending schools in the United States has increased significantly. For example, between the 1990–1991 and 2000–2001 school years the percentage of English-language learners increased by 105% (Kindler, 2002), while during same period total school enrollment increased by only 12%. More and more, English-language learners spend most or all of their school day in general education classrooms (General Accounting Office, 2001; Thomas & Collier, 2002). Approximately 43% of all teachers have at least one English-language learner in their class (Zehler et al., 2003).

The significant English-language learner and bilingual student presence in United States schools has given rise to an ever-widening set of reading education issues. Recent research has supported some contentions related to English-language learner English literacy teaching and learning: teaching and learning in the home language positively impacts English reading achievement; literacy abilities can transfer across languages; and explicit teaching in phonemic awareness, phonics, vocabulary, comprehension, and writing can benefit English-language learners as well as native English speakers (cf. Goldenberg, 2008). At the same time we continue to be faced with many challenges. For instance, little is known about best avenues for: using home language to support English learning, supporting vocabulary development, or appraising oral language and content knowledge separately (cf. Goldenberg, 2008). Researchers continue to consider effects of culturally accommodated instruction, and the debate over the comparative benefits of bilingual versus English-only instruction persists. Perhaps among the most pressing practitioner concerns is the need for enhanced understanding of how teachers' interactions with English-language learners during reading instruction impact their reading development and achievement.

In the present review, we specifically focused on research involving teacher action or teacher-student interaction during reading instruction. We defined English-language learners as individuals from homes where a language other than English was actively used and who had an opportunity to learn a language other than English (cf. August & Shanahan, 2006). Our goal in writing the present chapter has been to document, interpret, and critique research on United States and Canadian kindergarten through sixth-grade reading instruction for English-language learners published between January 1st, 1987, and December 31st, 2007.

Methods for the Review

Keywords in searches were: English-language learner reading instruction, English-learner reading instruction, English-as-a-second-language reading instruction, L2 (a common abbreviation for second language) reading instruction, bilingual reading instruction, limited-English proficient reading, Latino reading instruction, Hispanic reading instruction, Spanish reading instruction, and various combinations of the preceding, also combined with special education and learning disabilities. ERIC (for published research only) and PsychInfo databases were searched, and as articles were retrieved and read, reference lists contained in them were sources for additional articles. Given the need to restrict the focus of our review, we decided that we would review research reported only in peer-refereed journal articles on reading instruction. We excluded research on tutoring or commercial programs.

Methodological standards for inclusion were as follows. For experiments or quasi-experiments, a control or comparison group, or normative data had to be included. Where comparison groups were used, at least four subjects had to be present. For quasi-experiments, outcomes of interest had to be pretested (with the exception of regression discontinuity designs). Samples in correlational studies had to have at least 20 participants. Criteria for rigor in qualitative studies were dependent on the particular paradigm used. In general, qualitative research reports had to include: methodological detail (e.g., an audit trail); revelation of multiple perspectives; researcher reflectivity; documentation that alternative explanations were addressed; primary data, quotes, stories, and/or the like; conclusions that reflected evidence of learning from the study rather than having the study validate the author(s)' prior beliefs; and discussion of how what was learned from the study related to a wider discourse (cf. G. Noblit, personal communication, January 18, 2004).

The chapter is divided into three major sections. In the first section, Results of the Review, in five categories, we portray research findings from the 26 studies that met our criteria for inclusion. In the second section, we provide critique and recommendations for future theory development and research. Implications for classroom practice follow in the third section.

Results of the Review

Twenty-six studies met our criteria for inclusion. Researchers addressed questions that fell into five broad categories. One set of researchers examined English-language learner reading development in the context of particular forms of reading instruction. Another set of studies focused on whether instruction in specific reading subprocesses impacted English-language-learner reading in those subprocesses. A third set focused on the impact of simultaneous instruction in multiple reading subprocesses on learning the collective subprocesses. A fourth set highlighted instructional issues teachers should consider other than reading subprocess instruction for English-language learners. Finally, we provide a fifth category of studies—"Other"—which includes studies that were unrelated to the preceding ones and which did not form a particular category on their own.

As our chapter is appearing in the *Handbook of Reading Disability Research*, we think it important to especially note here that in spite of an intensive search of the literature for studies in which researchers addressed instruction for English-language learners who were taught in special education settings and/or were labeled with a special education label, such as a reading disability label, remarkably,

we found none that met our criteria for inclusion. In a few cases, authors referenced the participants as at risk, but they were not referencing a special education label.

We use the following organizational structure for each category of studies in the present section. First, in one subsection we provide study particulars including the number of studies in the category, the number of participants in the studies, the study methodologies, and the theoretical bases for the studies. In a second subsection we provide information about the instructional content, describing what teachers and students did during their actions/interactions, and we synthesize the main finding(s) across studies to the extent possible. In addition, we provide further study details in Table 33.1. It is possible that study outcomes were affected by selected features of the studies, such as the degree of native-to-new language linguistic differences, participant situations such as whether they were immigrants immersed in new language culture, and/or the extent of knowledge about and experience with both native and new language. At the same time, it is likely that much can be learned about multilingual reading by considering research that is broadly situated. Therefore, as we conducted the work of the current review, we were mindful of the possible impact of diverse situations within which the research was conducted while drawing conclusions across studies. Readers of this review might also find it helpful to keep the research situations in mind, and referring to Table 33.1 might assist in this regard.

How Might English-Language Learner Reading Development Be Described in the Context of Particular Forms of Reading Instruction?

Study particulars and theoretical grounding. Eight sets of researchers addressed English-language learner English-reading development over time in the context of classroom reading instruction, such as conduct of "whole language" or "balanced reading." Although the investigators in the present group of studies included teacher-student interaction during reading instruction, the studies in the present category were not "intervention" studies. Rather the main goal of the studies was to examine children's reading development over time. On the whole, but not in every case, the instructional context for such examination was secondary.

Half of the studies were set in kindergarten or first grade, and half were in grades three through five. Seven of the studies had small numbers of participants—from 2 to 20. One (D'Anguilli, Siegel, & Maggi, 2004) included 1,108 students.

Spanish was the English-language learners' native language in six of the studies (Fitzgerald & Noblit, 1999, 2000; Kucer, 1999; Kucer & Silva, 1999; Neufeld & Fitzgerald, 2001; Pérez, 1994); two of those six studies (Fitzgerald & Noblit, 1999, 2000) also included a student whose native language was Tarascan Indian; Portuguese was the native language in one study (Aarujo, 2002), and native language(s) was/were not provided in one study (D'Anguilli

TABLE 33.1

Selected Information for Reports

Author(s)	Grade/Age (N)	Label (Country/Native Language)	English-Language Proficiency Level	Reading Measures (Reliability estimate) or Data Sources	Methodology
Development within the Context of Reading Instruction					
Araujo, L. (2002)	K (20), 1 classroom	ESL (Portugal, Brazil/ Portugese)	7.4 out of 26 possible pts. on Language Assessment Battery (NY Public Schools, no reference provided)	"Artifacts" such as report cards, "test scores," "workbook sheets"	Descriptive
D'Anguilli, Siegel, &Maggi (2004)	K, followed through 5th (1,108, N for ELL and for native-English speakers not provided) in 30 schools	ELL (Not provided)	Not provided	Wide Range Achievement Test—3 (Wilkinson, 1993)	Descriptive, gradient and growth mixture model trajectory analysis
Fitzgerald & Noblit (1999)	1st (2), 1 classroom	ELL (Mexico, Spanish for 1; Tarascan Indian and Spanish for the 2nd)	At study onset, "limited English" on 5 measures	Informal measures of alphabet name and phonics knowledge Slosson Oral Reading Test (Slosson, 1963) (.99 test-retest) San Diego Quick Test (LaPray & Ross, 1986) (.72) Running records (see Clay, 1993) using Ekwall's (1986) passages and Bader and Weisendanger's (1994) (.92 for identifying miscues, .92 for determining instructional level, .90–.97 for determining percentages of meaning, syntax, visual, and self-correction miscues) Peabody Picture Vocabulary Test-Revised (Dunn & Dunn, 1981) (.77)	Descriptive, case analysis
Fitzgerald & Noblit (2000)	1st (20, of which 11 were ENL), 1 classroom	ENL (Mexico, Columbia, El Salvador, Guatemala, Nicaragua; Spanish for 10, Tarascan Indian for 1)	5 "non-English-speaking," 5 "limited-English," 1 "fluent English" on the ITPI (Dalton et al., 1991)	Same as Fitzgerald & Noblit, 1999	Descriptive
Kucer, 1999	3rd (2), 1 classroom	Bilingual (Mexico, Spanish)	"Fluent" English (no measure cited)	Oral reading, miscue analysis using story selections	Descriptive
Kucer & Silva, 1999	3rd (26), 1 classroom	Bilingual (Mexico, Spanish)	Scored 3 or better on scale of 1=least English proficient, and 5=most proficient, on Bilingual syntax Measure II Test (Burt et al., 1978)	Oral reading, miscue analysis, and retelling of a story	Descriptive, pre-post statistical analyses
Neufeld & Fitzgerald, 2001	1st (3), 1 classroom	ELL (Mexico, Spanish)	1 "non-English-speaking," 2 "limited-English" on the ITPI (Dalton et al., 1991)	Same as Fitzgerald & Noblit, 1999	Descriptive, case analysis
Pérez, 1994	K (4), 1st (6), 2nd (6), 4th (4), 4 bilingual classrooms	Bilingual (Not provided, Spanish)	Not provided. All students were "Spanish dominant" (Language Assessment Scale, reference not provided)	Oral reading during reading lessons, miscue analysis	Descriptive

(continued)

TABLE 33.1
Continued

Author(s)	Grade/Age (N)	Label (Country/Native Language)	English-Language Proficiency Level	Reading Measures (Reliability estimate) or Data Sources	Methodology
Instruction in Specific Reading Subprocesses					
Carlo et al. (2004),	5th; 254 bilingual and monolingual children (142 ELLs, 112 EOs), (intervention: 94 ELLs, 75 EOs, comparison: 48 ELLs, 37 EOs); 9 bilingual or mainstream classes in 4 schools	Bilingual (Not provided)	Not provided	PPVT-R (Dunn & Dunn, 1981) (not provided) Polysemy production (α=.64) Cloze Task (α=.73) Word Association (.94) Morphology (.94)	Quasi-experimental
Kucer (1992)	3rd (6 students, 1 teacher)	Bilingual (Not provided; bilingual, biliterate Columbian teacher)	Two "fairly" proficient, two "somewhat" proficient, two "nonproficient"	Videotaped observations of modified cloze reading lessons Field notes of the observed lessons Literacy artifacts Interviews with both the teacher and her students	Descriptive
Pollard-Durodola, Cedillo, & Denton (2004)	K (43) from 2 classrooms, 2 teachers	Not reported for students; Teachers were bilingual Spanish-English	Not reported	Videotaped reading lessons coded with Elements of Word Identification Instruction (EWII; Denton, Mathes, & Anthony, 2002; interrater reliabilities 83%, 82%, 63%, 74% for instructional strategies, linguistic units, for teacher one and two, respectively) Semi-structured teacher interviews Word Attack subtest from *Woodcock Language Proficiency Battery-Revised Spanish Form* (Woodcock, 1991) (not reported)	Descriptive, case analysis
Saunders & Goldenberg (1999)	4th, 5th; 116 students from 5 classrooms	Not reported	Fluent-English proficient (52), Limited-English proficient (64)	Researcher designed: Factual Comprehension (interrater reliability, 96.5%) Interpretive Comprehension (interrater reliability, 88%) Theme-Explanation Essay (interrater reliability, 81%) Theme-Exemplification Essay (interrater reliability, 79%)	Experimental
Silverman (2007)	K; 72 students and 5 teachers (44 EOs; 28 ELLs) in 3 mainstream English classrooms, 1 structured immersion classroom, 1 Spanish-English bilingual classroom	English Language Learners (13% spoke an East Asian language, 10% spoke Spanish, 7% spoke Creole, 9% spoke other languages)	Not provided	Test of Language Development (TOLD) (Newcomer & Hammill, 1997) (not reported) Researcher Vocabulary Assessment (interrater reliability, .95) Observation Survey (Clay, 2002) (not reported)	Quasi-Experimental
Simultaneous Instruction in Multiple Reading Subprocesses					
Linan-Thompson, Bryant, Dickson, & Kouzekanani (2005)	Kindergarten; 128 students (70 experimental, 58 control)	Not labeled except for "at-risk" (all Spanish-speaking)	Not reported	*Tejas Lee* (Texas Education Agency, 2000). Constructs assessed were print knowledge, phonological awareness, word recognition, letter knowledge, and listening comprehension (.78–.91 for subtests) Rapid Spelling Text (Tindal & Marston, 1990) (not reported)	Quasi-experimental

Study	Participants	Risk status	Reliability	Measures	Design
Vaughn et al, (2006)	Grade 1; 91 ELL students assigned to English intervention (43 treatment, 48 comparison), and 80 ELL students assigned to Spanish intervention (35 treatment, 45 comparison)	Not labeled except for "at-risk" (all Hispanic English-language learners)	Not reported	All measures were administered in both English and Spanish Letter Naming (α=.94–.97) Letter Sound Identification (α=.90–.95) Seven subtests (Elision, Blending Words, Blending Non-words, Segmenting Words, Sound Matching, Nonword Repetition, Rapid Letter Naming) from the *Comprehensive Test of Phonological Processing* (*CTOPP*; Wagner, Torgesen & Rashotte, 1999) (median α=.83; α=.70–.93 for subtests) Seven subtests (same as *CTOPP*) from the *Test of Phonological Processing—Spanish* (*TOPP-S*) (α=.93–.97 for subtests) Six subtests (Letter Word Identification, Word Attack, Passage Comprehension, Listening Comprehension, Picture Vocabulary, Verbal Analogies) from the *Woodcock Language Proficiency Battery—Revised: English and Spanish Forms* (Woodcock, 1991; Woodcock & Munoz-Sandoval, 1995) (for English Form, median α=.89, α=.77–.95 for subtests; for Spanish form, median α=.89, α=.68–.95 for subtests) *Dynamic Indicators of Basic Early Literacy Skills* fluency (*DIBELS*; Good & Kaminski, 2002)/*Indicadores Dinámicos del Exito en la Lectura* fluency (Good, Bank, & Watson, 2003) (.97, correlation between English and Spanish passage) Word Reading Efficiency subtest from *Test of Word Reading Efficiency* (Torgesen, Wagner, & Rashotte, 1999) (.83–.93 for English, test/retest; .90–.94 for Spanish, test/retest) Spelling (α=.88–.93)	Experimental
Vaughn et al, (2006)	Grade 1; 64 students (31 experimental, 33 control)	Not labeled except for "at-risk" (all Spanish-speaking)	Not reported	Letter Naming (not reported) Letter Sound Identification (not reported) Seven subtests (Elision, Blending Words, Blending Non-words, Segmenting Words, Sound Matching, Nonword Repetition, Rapid Letter Naming) from the *Comprehensive Test of Phonological Processing* (*CTOPP*; Wagner, Torgesen & Rashotte, 1999) (median α=.83; α=.70–.93 for subtests) Seven subtests (same as *CTOPP*) from the *Test of Phonological Processing—Spanish* (*TOPP-S*) (α=.93–.97 for subtests) Six subtests (Letter Word Identification, Word Attack, Passage Comprehension, Listening Comprehension, Picture Vocabulary, Verbal Analogies) from the *Woodcock Language Proficiency Battery—Revised: English and Spanish Forms* (Woodcock, 1991; Woodcock & Munoz-Sandoval, 1995) (for English Form, median α=.89, α=.77–.95 for subtests; for Spanish form, median α=.89, α=.68–.95 for subtests) *Dynamic Indicators of Basic Early Literacy Skills* fluency (*DIBELS*; Good & Kaminski, 2002)/*Indicadores Dinámicos del Exito en la Lectura* fluency (Good et al., 2003) (Not reported)	Experimental

(continued)

TABLE 33.1
Continued

Author(s)	Grade/Age (N)	Label (Country/Native Language)	English-Language Proficiency Level	Reading Measures (Reliability estimate) or Data Sources	Methodology
Vaughn et al. (2006)	Grade 1; 41 ELL students (22 intervention; 19 contrast)	Not Labeled except for "at-risk" (all Hispanic English-language learners)	Not reported	Letter Naming (α=.94–.97) Letter Sound Identification (α=.90–.95) Seven subtests (Elision, Blending Words, Blending Non-words, Segmenting Words, Sound Matching, Nonword Repetition, Rapid Letter Naming) from the *Comprehensive Test of Phonological Processing* (*CTOPP*; Wagner, Torgesen & Rashotte, 1999) (median α=.83; α=.70–.93 for subtests) Seven subtests (same as *CTOPP*) from the *Test of Phonological Processing—Spanish* (*TOPP-S*) (α=.93–.97 for subtests) Six subtests (Letter Word Identification, Word Attack, Passage Comprehension, Listening Comprehension, Picture Vocabulary, Verbal Analogies) from the *Woodcock Language Proficiency Battery—Revised: English and Spanish Forms* (Woodcock, 1991; Woodcock & Munoz-Sandoval, 1995) (for English Form, median α=.89, α=.77–.95 for subtests; for Spanish form, median α=.89, α=.68–.95 for subtests) *Dynamic Indicators of Basic Early Literacy Skills* fluency (*DIBELS*; Good & Kaminski, 2002)/*Indicadores Dinámicos del Exito en la Lectura* fluency (Good et al.,2003) (.97, correlation between English and Spanish passage)	Experimental

Instructional Issues Teachers Should Consider

Author(s)	Grade/Age (N)	Label (Country/Native Language)	English-Language Proficiency Level	Reading Measures (Reliability estimate) or Data Sources	Methodology
Gersten (1996)	Grade 3; 27 teachers who taught language minority students	8 bilingual teachers, 19 English-only teachers	Not reported	Observations of reading/language arts instruction Interviews with teachers, administrators, and other school personnel	Descriptive
Gersten (1999)	Grades 4, 5, 6; four teachers who were relatively inexperienced working with ELLs	Not reported	Not reported	Observations of reading lessons Multiple interviews with each teacher	Descriptive
Gersten & Jiménez (1994)	Grades 3, 4, 5; three teachers	Not reported	Not reported	Observations of classroom instruction Interviews with the teachers	Descriptive
Jiménez & Gersten (1999)	Grades 4–6; two teachers: one in a 4th/5th transition classroom, and one in a 5th/6th bilingual classroom	Students in both classrooms were Latino/a, of Mexican descent; both teachers were bilingual, of Mexican descent	Not reported	Classroom observations Multiple interviews with each teachers	Descriptive
Padrón & Waxman (1999)	Grades 4, 5 from 3 schools; 126 students surveyed, 117 students and 15 teachers observed	Not reported	Not reported	Surveys of students' perceptions of their classroom learning environment Classroom observations of teachers' use of five standards during literacy instruction Classroom observations of students' behavior during literacy instruction	Descriptive

Other Studies

Study	Sample	Population	Proficiency	Measures	Design
Graves, Gersten, & Haager (2004)	Grade 1; (186), 3 schools, 14 classrooms	English learners (Unclear/ English, Cambodian, Cantonese, French, Hmong, Lao, Somali, Spanish, Sudanese, Tagalog, Vietnamese)	Not provided	*Dynamic Indicators of basic early literacy skills,* Oral reading fluency (6th ed.) (Good & Kaminski, 2002) (Not provided) Observations of teachers' instruction, resulting in a score for the teachers' instructional effectiveness (1 = not effective, to 4 = very effective) (internal consistency median subscale alpha = .89 and subscale range = .80 to .95, median inter-observer agreement on item-by-item basis = 74%, range not given, criterion-related validity median coefficient = .60, with range = .49 to .65)	Correlational, with descriptive teacher profiles
Koskinen et al. (2000)	Grade 1; 162 students (105 ELL, 57 EO) and 16 teachers	English-as-a-second-language. Primary languages for communication: English (65), Spanish (46), Vietnamese (23), Korean (5), Amharic (4), Cantonese (4), Urdu (3), Arabic (2), Somali (2), Turkish (2), other (6)	Using the PRE-Language Assessment Scale (PRE-LAS): 44 proficient, 61 eligible for language support services	Clay's Oral Reading Assessment (.83, cited in Clay, 1993) Clay's Writing Vocabulary Assessment (.88, interrater) Oral Story Retelling Assessment (.94, interrater) Me and My Reading Scale (.68, test/retest) Teacher Survey of Child Behavior (α=.89) Individual Child Interview Parent Survey (α=.64) Teacher Questionnaire/ Interview	Quasi-experimental
Padrón (1994)	Grades 4 and 5; 166 students (90 from Hispanic/LEP schools, 76 from Other Inner-City schools), and 47 teachers from 15 schools (8 Hispanic/LEP, 7 Other Inner-City)	Hispanic/LEP schools were mostly Hispanic (96.5%) and had many LEP students (50.3%); Other Inner-City schools had 29.7% Hispanic, 38.1% African-American, 26.3% White, and 6% other and a smaller number (17.9%) LEP students	Not reported	Observations of teachers and students coded with the Classroom Observation Schedule (COS; Waxman, Wang, Lindvall, & Anderson, 1988) and the Teacher Roles Observation Schedule (TROS; Waxman, Wang, Lindvall, & Anderson, 1983b) (.94 and .96, respectively; interrater)	Descriptive, statistical analyses
Yoon (2007)	Grade 6; 4 ELL students and 2 teachers	English-language learners (Not reported)	Not reported	Observations of classroom reading instruction Interviews with teachers and students	Descriptive

et al., 2004). Students were labeled: English-language learners in three studies (D'Anguilli et al., 2004; Fitzgerald & Noblit, 1999; Neufeld & Fitzgerald, 2001); English-as-a-second-language learners in one study (Araujo, 2002); English-as-a-new-language learners in one study (Fitzgerald & Noblit, 2000); and bilingual in three (Kucer, 1999; Kucer & Silva, 1999; Pérez, 1994).

Oral English proficiency was measured in five studies. Table 33.1 shows the specific instruments used to measure English proficiency in studies where instruments were reported. Reading measures addressed a broad range of literacy abilities and are also presented in Table 33.1.

Descriptive methodology was used in all eight studies. Two sets of researchers additionally labeled their studies as case studies (Fitzgerald & Noblit, 1999; Neufeld & Fitzgerald, 2001). D'Anguilli and colleagues (2004) used gradient and growth mixture model trajectory analyses, and in addition to the descriptive work, Kucer and Silva (1999) used pre-post statistical analyses.

Four sets of researchers explicitly provided a theoretical perspective. Three (Araujo, 2002; Fitzgerald & Noblit, 1999, 2000) explained their social constructivist or constructivist position related to children's learning about literacy knowledge, language and teaching in learning in general, and/or the reading process. A fourth set (Neufeld & Fitzgerald, 2001) based their study on a theory of emergent reading. Other researchers created rationales for their work, but did not state a particular theoretical outlook.

Instructional content and synthesis of main findings.   As has been stated earlier, the studies in the present category focused on students' reading development while providing some information about teachers' actions/interactions—rather than focusing on the direct impact of the teachers' actions/interactions. The instructional content in all of the studies involved collections of many activities. Three (Kucer, 1999; Kucer & Silva, 1999; Pérez, 1994) were about whole language instruction, all involving some degree of teacher-student interaction, but little, if any, explicit instruction. Kucer and his colleague described the whole language program in their two studies as consisting of four components—themes, teacher reading, free reading, and free writing. Two (Fitzgerald & Noblit, 1999, 2000) were about balanced reading instruction (defined as instruction which distributed weight across several features of reading and which arose from a set of guiding principles, resulting in four central instructional components—word study, responding to literature, writing, and guided and unguided reading). Two (D'Anguilli et al., 2004; Neufeld & Fitzgerald, 2001) seemed to be an eclectic mix of types of instruction, and one (Araujo, 2002) was called both balanced and literature-based.

It was difficult to synthesize results related to teacher instruction across the eight studies for three main reasons. First, there was no intention on the part of the researchers in the present group to infer causality relating outcomes to instruction. Rather, in most of the studies in the present

section the instruction was more of a backdrop to the interest in how the students' reading knowledge progressed. Because there is no clear way to link student outcomes to the classroom instruction so as to attribute causality, in all cases, student maturation alone could have accounted for any witnessed growth.

Second, because many features of teacher action/interaction were reported, student reading-growth results could not be directly attributed to particular facets of, or particular activities in, the instructional contexts described in the studies. However, in one study (Neufeld & Fitzgerald, 2001), a strong case was made that selected teacher inaction and/or action might have influenced outcomes. The teacher did not provide small-group reading instruction for the three low-performing English-language learners, and they showed little reading progress. However, she did include them in whole-class writing lessons, and they demonstrated greater growth in writing than they did in reading.

Third, a wide variety of reading measures was used, making it difficult to coalesce outcomes. In most cases, the measures were informal classroom measures that were done as part of regular classroom instruction. In four studies (D'Anguilli et al., 2004; Fitzgerald & Noblit, 1999, 2000; Neufeld & Fitzgerald, 2001) at least some standardized reading assessments focused on isolated word recognition. Most researchers included some form of oral reading assessment, using miscue analysis, sometimes to determine approximate reading level, following procedures outlined in Clay (2002). Reliabilities were reported in only three studies (Fitzgerald & Noblit, 1999, 2000; Neufeld & Fitzgerald, 2001).

What are the main findings from the studies about reading instruction and English-language learner reading development? First, children's construction of reading tended to mirror what they were taught. For instance, where teachers used balanced reading instruction (Araujo, 2002; Fitzgerald & Noblit, 1999, 2000), students improved in both word recognition and comprehension abilities, and in whole language bilingual Spanish-reading instruction (Pérez, 1994), where explicit instruction in word recognition was absent, there was little evidence to support the belief that print exposure and invented spelling alone helped the students to improve "code" breaking.

Second, where reading trajectories were closely examined (e.g., Araujo, 2002; Fitzgerald & Noblit, 1999; Neufeld & Fitzgerald, 2001), developmental patterns paralleled trajectory descriptions already detailed in the native-language emergent reading literature. For instance, phonological awareness and understandings about word recognition developed in ways similar to development for native-language readers.

Third, when young English-language learners were taught English reading, some, but not all, students were able to grow to perform in English reading on a par with their monolingual peers (Araujo, 2002; D'Anguilli et al., 2004; Fitzgerald & Noblit, 1999, 2000).

Fourth, English-oral-language development may not be

a critical predecessor to English reading development—at least for the youngest children studied (Araujo, 2002; Fitzgerald & Noblit, 1999, 2000).

What Impact Does Instruction in One Specific Reading Subprocess Have on Learning That Reading Subprocess?

Study particulars and theoretical grounding. Five sets of researchers focused on instruction for English-language learners, each for one reading subprocess—meaning vocabulary (two studies), comprehension (one study), word recognition (one study) or phonological/phonemic awareness (one study). Two of the studies were set in kindergarten (Pollard-Durodola, Cedillo, & Denton, 2004; Silverman, 2007), and three were in grades three through five (Carlo et al., 2004; Kucer 1992; Saunders & Goldenberg, 1999). Some researchers included small numbers of participants in descriptive case studies (Kucer, 1992; Pollard-Durodola et al., 2004), while other researchers used larger numbers of participants in experimental or quasi-experimental studies (Carlo et al., 2004; Saunders & Goldenberg, 1999; Silverman, 2007).

In one study, teacher participants' native language was Spanish (Pollard-Durodola et al., 2004), in one study participants' native languages were East Asian languages, Spanish, and Creole (Silverman, 2007), and in three studies participants' native languages were not provided. In three of the studies participants were labeled as bilingual (Carlo et al., 2004; Kucer, 1992; Pollard-Durodola et al., 2004), in one they were labeled English-language learners (Silverman, 2007), and in one study no label was reported.

Oral English proficiency was informally reported in two studies. Table 33.1 shows the reports of English proficiency in studies where reported. Reading measures are also presented in Table 33.1.

Three of the studies were experimental or quasi-experimental (Carlo et al., 2004; Saunders & Goldenberg, 1999; Silverman, 2007), while the other two were qualitative in nature (Kucer, 1992; Pollard-Durodola et al., 2004). Three sets of researchers used statistical analyses which included multivariate analysis of variance, analysis of variance, and hierarchical linear modeling (Carlo et al., 2004; Saunders & Goldenberg, 1999; Silverman, 2007). One set of researchers employed a microanalysis to synthesize data from multiple sources (Pollard-Durodola et al., 2004), and one set used qualitative analysis methodology (Kucer, 1992).

Three sets of authors explicitly stated theoretical bases for their studies. One set (Carlo et al., 2004) explained a theory of the complexity of word meanings which informed the vocabulary intervention design. Another set (Pollard-Durodola et al., 2004) explained a theory of Spanish reading acquisition, and a final set (Saunders & Goldenberg, 1999) explained theoretical premises assumed to facilitate first- and second-language acquisition and achievement. The other two sets of authors (Kucer, 1992; Silverman, 2007) provided rationales for their studies in the form of research reviews.

Instructional content and synthesis of main findings. Across the five studies teacher instructional action/interaction direct instruction was used. Meaning vocabulary in two studies included lessons with targeted vocabulary words over the course of a week which integrated books, explicit instruction in target word meanings, questioning to aid children's thinking, examples of target words in other contexts, occasions for children to act out word meanings, visual aids to demonstrate word meanings, opportunities for students to pronounce words, cloze lessons where students used contextual information to infer word meanings, discussion of target words spellings, and opportunities for students to compare and contrast words (Carlo et al., 2004; Silverman, 2007).

In another study (Kucer, 1992), the teacher used a series of modified cloze strategy lessons to improve students' word recognition through use of context. For both narrative and expository texts, words were deleted at selected points in the text where there was adequate textual information for students to generate meaningful predictions. The teacher began with a small group lesson based on a one of the cloze texts and through modeling, student responses, and discussion, worked through the entire text. Then, in cooperative pairs, students worked on a second cloze text and then shared and discussed their responses with other student pairs.

While teaching kindergarten students to read in Spanish, a language with consistent phoneme-grapheme correspondence, in another study (Pollard-Durodola et al., 2004) two teachers used direct instruction in sight word recognition, the alphabetic principle, and phonics-based strategies (e.g., "sounding out"). Across the school year, teachers began with emphasis on phonics-based strategies, and by midyear shifted to more "global-visual" (p. 343) strategies such as sight word recognition, or locating whole words in text.

In the final study in the present category (Saunders & Goldenberg, 1999) teachers used literature logs and instructional conversations with fourth- and fifth-grade students to affect comprehension. During literature logs instruction teachers met with groups of students and asked students to write about personal experiences related to the main character's experiences from a story. Students wrote independently, read their logs aloud, and then the teacher facilitated a discussion about similarities and differences among the students' log entries and the story character's experiences. During instructional conversations teachers facilitated small-group discussion about the story to clarify factual content from a story and develop students' understandings of more sophisticated concepts (e.g., "giving" can refer to the giving of one's self). Instructional conversations allowed the teacher the opportunity to hear small groups of students express their understanding of story themes and related personal experiences, and during discussion facilitation teachers could both challenge and deepen students' understandings. Ultimately, instructional conversations allowed students to listen to, recognize the value of, and build upon others' experience, knowledge, and understandings.

It was difficult to synthesize results related to teacher instruction across the five studies for three reasons. First, there was a small number of studies with disparate outcome measures. Since the current set of studies focused on three different reading subprocesses, outcome measures represented three conceptually different reading subprocesses—meaning vocabulary, comprehension, or phonological/phonemic awareness. In many cases the outcome measures were researcher-designed measures intended to reflect important features of teacher instruction or intervention programs specific to each study which limited generalization.

Second, causality could only be inferred from a subset of two studies (Carlo et al., 2004; Saunders & Goldenberg, 1999) where random assignment was utilized. Even when causality could be addressed in the two studies, the outcome measures were conceptually different, again making synthesis across the studies difficult.

Third, the small number of studies addressing instruction in each of the reading subprocesses made synthesis of the research findings difficult.

What are the main findings from such a set of studies about instruction in specific reading subprocesses and English-language learners' reading? First, instruction in specific reading subprocesses benefited English-language learners' achievement in those processes. Meaning vocabulary instruction was equally effective for improving reading comprehension outcomes for English-language learners as for English-only students (Carlo et al., 2004). In addition, bilingual students who received modified cloze strategy lessons to improve word recognition through context use were able to perform well on similar cloze tasks, suggesting their word recognition was enhanced (Kucer, 1992).

Second, the following instruction formerly found effective with English-only students were shown to also be effective for English-language learners: instruction in meaning vocabulary (Carlo et al., 2004; Silverman, 2007), phonological/phonemic awareness (Pollard-Durodola et al., 2004), cloze strategies (Kucer, 1992), as well as literature logs and instructional conversations (Saunders & Goldenberg, 1999).

From two vocabulary interventions, English-language learners learned targeted vocabulary words at the same or even a faster rate than English-only students (Carlo et al., 2004; Silverman, 2007), and in one case, English-language learners also learned general vocabulary at the same or a faster rate.

What Impact Does Simultaneous Instruction in Multiple Reading Subprocesses Have on Learning Those Reading Subprocesses?

Study particulars and theoretical grounding. Four studies focused on instruction for English-language learners in which multiple reading subprocesses were simultaneously targeted (Linan-Thompson, Bryant, Dickson, & Kouzekanani, 2005; Vaughn, Cirino, et al., 2006; Vaughn, Linan-Thompson, et al., 2006; Vaughn, Mathes, et al., 2006). All four studies were part of a larger longitudinal effort across first, second, and third grades addressing early reading intervention outcomes for a cohort of bilingual Spanish-speaking English-language learners. One study was set in kindergarten (Linan-Thompson et al., 2005), and the remaining were set in first grade. Across the four studies the number of participants ranged from 41 to 128. In all four studies student participants were labeled "at-risk," but the label was not a special education label. In one study (Linan-Thompson et al., 2005) the at-risk label meant low performance on a phonological awareness subtest from a individually administered Spanish reading inventory. In the three remaining the at-risk label referenced low performance on an English and/or a Spanish letter/word identification subtest from a standardized test coupled with the inability to read more than one word from a list of five common English and/or Spanish sight words. Additionally, in one study (Linan-Thompson et al., 2005) classroom teachers provided instruction to at-risk English-language learners, while in the three remaining studies instructors from the research team provided instruction to at-risk English-language learners.

In all four studies students' native language was Spanish, and students were labeled as Hispanic English-language learners or as Spanish-speaking English-language learners. Oral English proficiency was not reported in any of the studies. Reading measures are presented in Table 33.1.

One study was quasi-experimental (Linan-Thompson et al., 2005), and the remaining studies were experimental (Vaughn, Cirino, et al., 2006; Vaughn, Linan-Thompson, et al., 2006; Vaughn, Mathes, et al., 2006) and employed random assignment and control groups. All four sets of researchers employed statistical analyses designed to examine group mean differences including analysis of covariance and analysis of variance.

One set of authors (Vaughn, Mathes, et al., 2006) explicitly stated a theoretical base for their study and provided a theory of emergent reading in addition to a research review for their study specific to the study intervention. The other three sets of authors provided a conceptual framework integrating research on effective interventions for the at-risk English-language learners, the phonology of printed Spanish, and the higher incidence of multisyllabic words in Spanish than in other alphabetic languages (Vaughn, Linan-Thompson, et al., 2006); a rationale for the study (Linan-Thompson et al., 2005), or a research review and rationale (Vaughn, Cirino, et al., 2006).

Instructional content and synthesis of main findings. In one study (Linan-Thompson et al., 2005) teachers provided kindergarten English-language learners at risk for reading problems with supplemental focused Spanish reading instruction in several reading subprocesses three times per week for 20 minutes for 4 weeks. Each focused session contained direct instruction in phonological awareness, phonics, word/sentence reading, and writing/spelling, but not on reading comprehension. Phonological awareness instruction focused on phoneme-level blending and segmenting skills, and phonics instruction focused on use of phoneme-grapheme correspondences to encode and decode words. Word/sentence reading allowed students to read words in the context of sentences using familiar sounds and words, and writing/spelling instruction focused on fluency and employed fast writes at the letter and word level. All instruction was delivered via a direct instruction model through highly structured activities.

In the other three studies (Vaughn, Cirino, et al., 2006; Vaughn, Linan-Thompson, et al., 2006; Vaughn, Mathes, et al., 2006), intervention instructors provided supplemental direct instruction (Carnine, Silbert, & Kame'enui, 1997) in multiple reading subprocesses to first-grade English-language learners at risk for reading problems in either English or Spanish (matched to the language of instruction) using a modified version of what the researchers/creators termed *Proactive Reading* (Mathes, Torgesen, Wahl, Menchetti, & Grek, 2004), a set of effective instructional intervention activities, or *Lectura Proactiva* (Mathes, Linan-Thompson, Pollard-Durodola, Hagan, & Vaughn, 2003), a parallel Spanish intervention curriculum which used a slightly different scope and sequence but similar instructional design and delivery as Proactive Reading. Both Proactive Reading and Lectura Proactiva are pre-determined sets of instructional strategies used as interventions that had been used in a series of prior research studies (e.g., Mathes, et al. 2004; Mathes, et al. 2003). Across all three studies, members of the research team developed lesson plans based on the researcher-termed Proactive Reading or Lectura Proactiva scope and sequence comprised of 6 to 10 short activities representing five areas—phonemic awareness, letter knowledge, word recognition, connected text fluency, and comprehension strategies. Each instructional session incorporated all five areas and lasted approximately 40 minutes. The goal of the interventions was for students to learn to read connected text rapidly and with comprehension. Phonemic awareness instruction focused on blending and segmenting at the phoneme level and ended when students were proficient at blending and segmenting words with consonant blends. Letter knowledge instruction focused on automatic recognition of graphemes and the sound each represented. Word recognition instruction focused on facilitating decoding phonetically regular and irregular words. Connected text fluency instruction focused on application of word recognition skills in decodable texts to improve both rate and accuracy. Comprehension strategy instruction focused on making predictions, setting a purpose for reading, sequencing, summarizing, story grammar elements, or identifying new information learned. All instruction was delivered to small groups of three to five students by an intervention instructor for 50 minutes per day in addition to students' core reading instruction. A direct instruction model was used to provide the instruction through highly structured activities.

The research and intervention team modified Proactive Reading with additional language support activities designed for English-language learners throughout each instructional session. Language support activities included any or all of using visuals, motion, or facial expressions in meaning vocabulary instruction; clarifying meanings; provided direct instruction in English-language use; and elaborating on students' responses. Lectura Proactiva lessons were also supplemented with a book reading activity designed to enhance oral Spanish skills and Spanish vocabulary development.

Across the four studies, synthesis of results related to teacher instruction was both straightforward and problematic. On the positive side, since all four studies were derived from a larger longitudinal study, outcome measures and teacher instruction were closely aligned which facilitated synthesis of results. Also, causality could be inferred from three of the four studies that employed random assignment (Vaughn, Cirino, et al., 2006; Vaughn, Linan-Thompson, et al., 2006; Vaughn, Mathes, et al., 2006), which facilitated synthesis of results. At the same time, on the negative side, there was only a small number of studies, and selected features of the small number of studies themselves made synthesis of the research findings difficult. First, with only four studies there was little depth within the present category of studies. Second, instructional continuity across all four studies makes synthesis difficult because in two studies instructional activities were conducted in students' native language of Spanish, and in the other studies activities were conducted in students' second language—English. However, replication of results across the two studies within language could be examined.

What are the main findings from the studies? First, instruction conducted simultaneously targeting multiple reading subprocesses (phonemic awareness, phonics, word identification, fluency, and comprehension) in either students' native or second language benefited English-language learners' reading achievement in the multiple subprocesses. English-language learners at risk for reading difficulties who received Spanish reading instruction in phonemic awareness, letter knowledge, word recognition, connected text fluency, and comprehension strategies outperformed comparison students on measures of Spanish letter-sound identification, phonological awareness, oral language, decoding, comprehension, and fluency (Vaughn, Cirino, et al., 2006; Vaughn, Linan-Thompson, et al., 2006). English-language learners at risk for reading difficulties who received English reading instruction in phonemic awareness, letter knowledge, word recognition, connected text fluency, and comprehension strategies outperformed comparison students in measures of English rapid letter naming, letter/sound identification, phonemic awareness, decoding, spelling, and passage comprehension (Vaughn, Cirino, et al., 2006; Vaughn, Mathes, et al., 2006).

Second, language support instruction, such as oral language and meaning vocabulary development, integrated with reading instruction targeting multiple reading subprocesses benefited students' language development. English-language learners considered at risk for reading problems who received Spanish reading instruction in phonemic awareness, letter knowledge, word recognition, connected text fluency, and comprehension strategies supplemented with Spanish oral language and vocabulary instruction outperformed comparison students in a composite measure of Spanish oral language (Vaughn, Linan-Thompson, et al., 2006) and on a measure of Spanish verbal analogies (Vaughn, Cirino, et al., 2006).

Finally under the conditions in one study, when provided with supplemental Spanish reading instruction, English-language learners considered at risk acquired Spanish reading skills at a faster rate than higher performing English-language learners who did not receive such instruction. At-risk English-language learners who received Spanish reading instruction in phonological awareness, phonics, word/sentence reading, and writing/spelling made greater gains across a 12-week intervention period in Spanish phonemic awareness, word identification, and letter/sound knowledge than higher performing English-language learners within the same classrooms (Linan-Thompson, et al., 2005).

Aside from Specific Instruction in Reading Subprocesses, What Instructional Issues Should Teachers Consider?

Study particulars and theoretical grounding. Four sets of researchers studied classroom instruction for English-language learners to learn about effective instructional practices during reading instruction, but the practices studied were not about teaching specific reading subprocesses (Gersten, 1996; Gersten & Jiménez 1994; Jiménez & Gersten, 1999; Padrón & Waxman, 1999). In addition, one researcher studied challenges to providing reading instruction to English-language learners (Gersten, 1999). The set of studies in the present category were different from those in the other categories in that nearly all of the five researchers conducted observations of classroom instruction in order to describe effective instruction or barriers to instruction for English-language learners, and/or interviewed teachers and students to learn their perceptions of such instructional issues. In one study (Padrón & Waxman, 1999) classroom observations were coded to examine the extent to which previously determined standards of effective teaching (Dalton, 1998) were present during reading instruction. In the remaining studies on effective instruction, teachers who were nominated by school administrators and researchers as providing innovative instruction for English-language learners were observed and interviewed. These teachers' observed practices and interview responses were considered in relation to the knowledge base (at the time of the studies) on effective instruction for English-language-learners, to result in the researchers' beliefs about effective ways that the teachers taught reading to language-minority students (cf. Gersten, 1996).

One study was set in third grade (Gersten, 1996), and four studies were set in third through sixth grade (Gersten, 1999; Gersten & Jiménez 1994; Jiménez & Gersten, 1999; Padrón & Waxman, 1999). In three descriptive studies, there were small numbers of participants (Gersten, 1999; Gersten & Jiménez 1994; Jiménez & Gersten, 1999).

In one study participants' native language was Spanish (Jiménez & Gersten, 1999), and in the other four studies native languages were not reported. In two studies participants were labeled as bilingual (Gersten, 1996; Jiménez & Gersten, 1999), and in the three remaining studies no label was reported. No measures of oral-English proficiency were reported. Reading measures are presented in Table 33.1.

All five studies were descriptive in nature. Four sets of researchers employed qualitative analysis and theme development (Gersten, 1996, 1999; Gersten & Jiménez 1994; Jiménez & Gersten, 1999), and one set of researchers used descriptive statistical analyses (Padrón & Waxman, 1999).

In two studies the same set of authors provided an explicit conceptual frame. In both studies (Gersten & Jiménez 1994; Jiménez & Gersten, 1999) the authors described a conceptual framework based on three relevant knowledge bases for conceptualizing effective second-language reading instruction which framed their data collection and analysis. The authors described the conceptual frame as an integration of three key bodies of work: cognitive strategies, bilingual education and language acquisition, and effective instruction for students at risk. The authors stated the integration of these three knowledge bases was essential to frame literacy instruction for language-minority students as the knowledge bases facilitated high student engagement, opportunities for extended English discourse, and higher order cognitive processes. The other three sets of authors (Gersten, 1996, 1999; Padrón & Waxman, 1999) provided rationales for their studies in the form of research reviews.

Instructional content and synthesis of main findings. Researchers conducted observations and interviewed teachers who provided innovative instruction for English-language learners in order to provide exemplars of effective instructional practices for English-language learners. The researchers observed a wide array of instructional content—instruction that was carried out with English-language learners with varying levels of English-reading achievement. Some examples were: Scaffolding literacy development across the curriculum, developing meaning vocabulary, teacher mediation and feedback to assist students' expansion and expression of ideas in English, and instruction in cognitive strategies/complex thinking (Gersten & Jiménez 1994; Jiménez & Gersten, 1999; Padrón & Waxman, 1999). As well, teachers and students perceived a wide array of instructional practices to be effective for advancing students' English-reading knowledge. Based on the classroom observations and teacher interviews, one researcher (Gersten, 1999) also described challenges to providing reading instruction to English-language learners.

It was again a challenge to synthesize results across the five studies for two reasons. First, selected features of the small number of studies themselves made synthesis of the research findings difficult. One author, Gersten, was involved with four of the five studies (Gersten, 1996, 1999; Gersten & Jiménez, 1994; Jiménez & Gersten, 1999), so the concepts were not generalizable across even a small number of different researchers. Second, there was very little methodological variation in the five studies. All five studies were descriptive in nature and used very similar data sources (classroom observations in all five studies, and teacher interviews in four studies).

What are the main findings from the studies in the present category? First, certain instructional practices often used with English-only readers were effective with respect to language minority students' reading achievement when used with sensitive modulation (Gersten, 1996; Gersten & Jiménez, 1994; Padrón & Waxman, 1999). For example, instruction in cognitive strategies/complex thinking included teacher "think-aloud" models which augmented and explicated students' ideas, use of graphic organizers to aid students in information organization, and/or providing students with background information. In one study (Gersten & Jiménez, 1994), one teacher provided instruction in cognitive strategies/complex thinking by displaying charts in her classroom from reading lessons and modeling "think-alouds" during reading by asking questions, and making inferences aloud.

Second, researchers described how one of two teachers in their study successfully integrated new ideas and principles about effective instruction for English-language learners with her established knowledge of effective instruction (Jiménez & Gersten, 1999). Based on observations and interviews the researchers explained how the teacher used what they termed an "infusion" model (cf. Guskey, 1990; Smylie, 1988) to integrate her new knowledge with her established knowledge of effective instruction (Jiménez & Gersten, 1999). In the infusion model, teachers attach and relate new pedagogical knowledge and learning to their established instructional practices and beliefs. The researchers concluded the infusion model facilitated a balanced approach (comparable amounts of explicit instruction and cooperative learning activities) to literacy instruction within the teacher's classroom. In a related study with three other teachers, the same researchers (Gersten & Jiménez, 1994) discovered a similar learning process for two other teachers. The researchers found that the teachers integrated new ideas and principles of instruction for English-language learners, such as respect for cultural diversity, with their existing understandings about pedagogy (Gersten & Jiménez, 1994), rather than replace their traditional effective principles of literacy instruction.

Third, effective teachers showed respect for cultural diversity during reading/language arts instruction, and it was considered beneficial for English-language learners' English literacy learning (Gersten & Jiménez, 1994; Jiménez & Gersten, 1999). Based on classroom observations and interviews of two teachers considered effective, one set of researchers concluded that Latino/a culture likely influences not only students' behavior and responses, but in the case of Latino/a teachers, their instruction as well (Jiménez &

Gersten, 1999). For example, the researchers suggested that Latino students' behavior and learning might have been influenced by a teachers' use of praise or criticism, or by the degree to which a teacher demonstrated respect for students as individuals, knowledge of cultural sensitivity, and viewed diversity as an asset (Gersten & Jiménez, 1994; Jiménez & Gersten, 1999). Latina/o teachers' instructional practices may be influenced by their cultural identities related to attitudes toward students' classroom language use, implementation of classroom discipline, and expressions of affection (Jiménez & Gersten, 1999).

What Else Is Known about Reading Instruction for English-Language Learners?

Study particulars and theoretical grounding. Four sets of researchers conducted studies in reading instruction for English-language learners which fell into an "other" category. Two studies were in grade one (Koskinen et al., 2000), another study was in grades four and five (Padrón, 1994), and the final study was in grade six (Yoon, 2007). One set of researchers used a small number of participants in a descriptive study (Yoon, 2007), two sets of researchers used larger numbers of participants in descriptive or quasi-experimental studies (Koskinen et al., 2000; Padrón, 1994), and one used a relatively large number in a correlational study in which student descriptive profiles were also provided (Graves, Gersten, & Haager, 2004).

In two studies participants' native languages were varied (Amharic, Arabic, English, Cambodian, Cantonese, French, Hmong, Italian, Korean, Laotian, Somali, Spanish, Sudanese, Tagalog, Tibetan, Turkish, Vietnamese, Urdu; Graves et al., 2004; Koskinen et al., 2000). In another study participants' native languages could be inferred as mainly English or Spanish (Padrón, 1994), and in the final study participants' native languages were not reported. Participants were labeled as English learners (Graves et al., 2004), English-as-a-second-language (Koskinen et al., 2000), limited-English-proficient (Padrón, 1994), or English-language learners (Yoon, 2007).

Oral English proficiency was reported in only one study (Koskinen et al., 2000) where the *PRE-Language Assessment Scale (PRE-LAS)* (Duncan & De Avila, 1985) was used.

Reading measures addressed a broad range of literacy abilities and are also presented in Table 33.1.

Two of the studies were quasi-experimental (Koskinen et al., 2000; Yoon, 2007), one was descriptive in nature (Padrón, 1994), and one was correlational with descriptive student profiles. One set of researchers used statistical analysis of variance (Koskinen et al., 2000), one set used descriptive statistics (Padrón, 1994), and one set used qualitative data analysis (Yoon, 2007).

None of the authors provided explicit theoretical bases for their studies. In two studies (Koskinen et al., 2000; Padrón, 1994), the authors provided rationales and extensive research reviews. The third and fourth study authors (Graves et al., 2004; Yoon, 2007) provided study rationales.

Instructional content and synthesis of main findings. Because the present category is a collection of four unrelated studies, it is not possible to provide a synthesis. Also, it was not possible to impute causality to teacher actions or interactions because the studies were descriptive, correlational, or quasi-experimental. Instead of providing synthesis, we report the instructional content and main findings for three of the studies, and then the findings for the fourth correlational study (Graves et al., 2004).

First, English-language learners in urban schools with large Hispanic/LEP student populations often received whole group instruction in a very passive setting (Padrón, 1994). Second, the teacher was the most important factor in promoting English-language learners' classroom participation (Yoon, 2007). Yoon suggested that the finding demonstrated the importance of teachers examining the content of English-language learner reading instruction and working to ensure students' involvement in active learning and responding during reading instruction, perhaps by teachers responding to students' cultural and social needs in an active manner. Third, book-rich classrooms paired with a home reading component with audiotapes may be particularly beneficial for English-language learners' comprehension and motivation (Koskinen et al., 2000).

Three main sets of conclusions arose from the fourth study (Graves et al., 2004). First, the researchers did classroom observations during reading/language arts instruction, resulting in a rating of how effective the teacher's instruction was. They obtained students' oral reading fluency at two different points in time, and created a gain score. The correlation of the teacher ratings with the gain score was .65, suggesting that more effective teacher practice was related to students' growth in oral reading fluency. Second, nine of the 186 students in the sample were referred for special education evaluation during the study, and eight were ultimately labeled learning disabled. Third, by exploring and contrasting patterns of instructional practice for two teachers rated very effective (and whose students had, on average, extremely oral fluency gain scores) to a teacher rated low in instructional effectiveness (and whose students had, on average, very low oral fluency gain scores) the researchers suggested that patterns of practice and pedagogical knowledge, not years of experience, were different across the comparison. Key instructional practices for the more effective teachers included: using a structured reading program that was called "comprehensive" and "systematic," "with special emphasis on phonological awareness and phonics;" having a scope and sequence for teaching reading; and providing explicit instruction in critical domains of reading (e.g., phonological awareness, phonics, comprehension).

Critique and Recommendations for Future Theory Development and Research

Notably, the paucity of relatively rigorous research on our topic suggests that greater attention to examination of English-language learners' reading instruction and development is needed. The number of studies in our five categories of research questions ranged from three to eight, and none were deeply researched. However, a rich and detailed understanding of English-language learners' reading trajectories, how instruction in specific reading subprocesses impacts learning, and instructional issues teachers should consider for English-language learner reading instruction can help to form a basis for educators' instructional decisions. If English-language learners' reading trajectories lead to reading achievement that mirrors their monolingual peers', teachers' expectations can be raised. If there are typical phases of development for English-language learners, and if teachers know about them, they might better nurture children from one phase to the next. Likewise, if instruction in reading subprocesses is beneficial for both English-language learners and English-only students, researchers and practitioners can infuse their current understandings of instructional issues teachers should consider for English-only students with new learning about teaching reading/language arts for English-language learners for the benefit of all students.

Theory   In only 8 of the 26 reports did researchers provide explicit discussion of theoretical bases for the studies. If research on instruction for English-language-learner reading is to make a difference, it is highly likely that greater reliance on theory building will be important. As others have advocated, "When researchers specifically focus on the theoretical relationships that might occur between particular instructional variables or constructs and specific student outcomes, the studies are most likely to be clearly focused on the hypothesized relationships in ways that enable greater precision in design and methodology" (Alvermann, Fitzgerald, & Simpson, 2006, p. 443). The eight sets of researchers who grounded their work in theoretical propositions did not necessarily hypothesize relationships between key instructional features and specific, or even general student outcomes, but by positioning their work in theory, they did elevate possibilities for interpretation of outcomes. For instance, by explaining a theory of how early reading develops for native-English speakers, developmental results for young English-language learners can be better situated, as comparisons can be made.

When considering the eight sets of researchers' theoretical bases as a whole, we are not able to now describe a sort of over-arching theory that might hypothetically explain the relationships between and among particular features of teacher instruction and specific student reading outcomes. Again, as others have said about reading instruction in general, "In the ideal, some 'grand' theory detailing a host of instructional variables as they relate to a wide array of particular child reading outcomes and processes would be useful for guiding a program of research …" (Alvermann et al., 2006, p. 443). Stated differently, to move the field forward forcefully, it may be that we need to be able to encapsulate hypothetical answers to questions such as: How and why might particular instructional features relate to specific English-language learner reading outcomes; how and why might native-language oral and reading ability mediate such relationships; how and why might new-language oral ability mediate such relationships, or perhaps we should ask, how and why might particular instructional features mediate the relationship between and among native-language oral and reading ability, and new-language oral and reading ability? Creating such a grand theory may be an impossible task, but at the least, if more researchers work from a theoretical stance that addresses hypothetical relationships between constructs under study, there is stronger possibility that, over time, our collective knowledge about high quality English-language learner reading instruction will advance.

Design   The predominance of descriptive studies is notable (17 of 26 studies). We held reasonably stringent criteria for inclusion of qualitative studies in the present review. One point to make about level of rigor, however, is that few of the studies documented that alternative explanations were explored. Examples of researchers who did provide such documentation were Araujo (2002), Fitzgerald and Noblit (1999, 2000), and Kucer (1992). Increased attention provision of alternative explanations could be useful in adding to our knowledge base.

Time series quasi-experimental and experimental studies which include teachers' instruction as an independent variable—as a nod to enhanced causal inference—could further our knowledge. Such designs could benefit the field because researchers could examine how teachers' instruction is related to students' reading development or growth over time. While the group of reading-development studies included in the present review point to development in the context of instruction that leads to reading attainment that approximates monolingual peers', other time-series studies of development alone tend to suggest that young English-language learners' reading *growth* may parallel that of their peers, but that for some aspects of reading, such as reading level, at least in the span of 1 to 3 years, on average, the English-language learners do not catch up to their peers (e.g., Fitzgerald, Amendum, & Guthrie, 2008). The contrast in findings suggests that the different study methodologies may be at play. Perhaps time-series analyses that include at least some teacher instructional characteristics could help us to document which teacher behaviors matter most for children's reading development.

In quasi-experimental and experimental studies, creating designs which enable us to tease out which parts of instruction matter most would be very useful. The descriptive studies provide some support for the belief that whole language instruction and balanced instruction, for instance, provide contexts within which English-language learners *can* progress to approximate their monolingual peers' reading attainment. The category of studies on simultaneous instruction in multiple reading subprocess provides support for the efficacy of such instruction, but which facets of such matter most? Such designs could be complicated

to accomplish in a meaningful way because teasing out parts of the instruction can be difficult. Might it be possible though to create a set of predictors for the "components" of instruction, such as instruction in phonemic awareness or word recognition, measure time spent on each, and then include each as a predictor variable in general linear repeated measures model or a hierarchical linear model? If such studies and analyses were conducted it would be crucial to examine effects on English-language learners' overall reading achievement/growth as well as achievement/growth in reading subprocesses.

It would be very useful if designs more closely linked specific teacher actions (or lack thereof) to children's performance. While it is not possible to make causal attribution of results to teacher activities in descriptive studies, close examination of instructional events and/or sequences of instructional events at multiple time points, paired with reading assessments accomplished at multiple time points, can lend helpful contextual understandings.

Particular to the category of studies on English-language learner development within the context of instruction, a positive feature of the studies was that all but one of the studies lasted for at least one academic year. D'Anguilli and colleagues (2004) followed kindergarten students through fifth grade—an admirable undertaking.

The paucity of rigorous research on English-language learner reading for children with identified disabilities was surprising. One reason for the lack of studies however might be that, in general, children are rarely identified as having reading disabilities at very young ages, and for English-language learners, it is especially important that language difference not be confounded with a disability (cf. Klingner, Artiles, & Barletta, 2006). As a result, it is possible that, on average, English-language learners who do have English reading disabilities are not identified until later in the elementary years.

It may also be important to conduct more studies with students who speak native languages other than Spanish. Twenty-three of 26 studies (one did not report participants' nationality) included students who were native-Spanish speakers. While Spanish is the predominant language amongst English-language learners in the United States, the extent to which developmental results would differ by native language is not readily discernable.

Greater attention to instruction for particular features of reading knowledge, such as inclusion of measures of word recognition, comprehension, vocabulary meaning, and fluency, could lead to improved understandings of which aspects of teacher instruction are associated with which sorts of learning about reading. In the category on instruction for English-language learners in reading subprocesses we found no studies about fluency instruction for English-language learners which met our criteria, only one about phonological/phonemic awareness instruction for English-language learners which met our criteria, and only two each about comprehension and meaning vocabulary instruction for English-language learners.

In addition, investigators might more extensively consider cultural factors as they design and implement reading instruction for English-language learners (cf. Arzubiaga, Artiles, King, & Harris-Murri, 2008; Harris, Baltodan, Artiles, & Rutherford, 2006). Can students "find themselves" in the materials they read? Are the assessments chosen by researchers culturally sensitive?

Assessments As for the reading assessments used in the studies, a notable point is that many researchers failed to provide reliability and validity information about assessments. Reliability estimation and some indication of measurement validity are very important for enabling confidence in the results of a study.

In general, common classroom informal measures were administered. Such informal measures help us to better understand the students' performance in relation to every day classroom activities. In particular, determination of students' instructional reading levels, provided as grade level, through students' oral reading of successively difficult passages in some studies was a helpful anchor to understanding English-language learners' performance against the unwritten norm of what might be expected for typically developing monolingual English speakers.

At the same time, researchers included standardized reading measures, and where they were included, they tended to address a narrow aspect of reading—the ability to read letters or words in isolation. Standardized assessments are helpful in that they provide a national norm against which students' performance can be judged.

Another point to be made about assessments is that report readers must completely understand what tests were used, what procedures were done with participants, illustrative items, and how variables were created. Not all researchers included sufficient assessment information.

Without this information, it is not possible to gauge what constructs were actually measured, or whether the measures were valid for the constructs claimed by the researchers. Moreover, interpretation of results is dependent on such issues.

Some factors embedded in the research situation may be critical to interpretation of findings. For instance participants' language proficiency is undeniably linked to the meanings of findings. Only nine sets of researchers provided at least some information about English proficiency, though not all of the nine reported the measure used to determine proficiency. Only two sets of researchers obtained measures of native-language proficiency (Fitzgerald & Noblit, 1999; Jiménez & Gersten, 1999).

Recommendations for Instruction

We now turn to implications for practice, but do so cautiously. As we have shown, using our standards for study inclusion, the evidence base for effective reading instruction for English-language learners lacks breadth, and it especially lacks depth within topic areas. Study authors in our review addressed questions that fell into five distinct categories. In the present section, for each of the five categories, at the risk of oversimplification, we first briefly state the main findings from the studies in a nutshell. Next, following our nutshell statements of findings, we highlight promising practices.

How Might English-Language Learner Reading Development Be Described in the Context of Particular Forms of Reading Instruction?

- Children's construction of reading tended to mirror what they were taught. (Four studies)
- Developmental patterns for very young English-language learners paralleled trajectory descriptions already detailed in the native-language emergent reading literature. (Three studies)
- When taught English reading, some English-language learners' reading growth was on a par with their monolingual peers. (Four studies)
- At least for the youngest children, English-oral-language development may not be a critical predecessor to English reading development. (Three studies)

From the development-in-the-context-of-instruction studies, we might suggest that if children's construction of reading tends to mirror what they are taught, and if we propose to assist our children in learning a wide spectrum of reading processes and attitudes, then it could be important that teachers imagine a broad conception of reading and reading subprocesses—such as the robust conception of cognitive and social processes delineated in August and Shanahan's (2006) *Developing Literacy in Second-Language Learners: Report of the National Literacy Panel on Language Minority Children and Youth*. The panel worked from a framework for reading development that included the importance of individual cognitive abilities such as phonological awareness and word recognition ability, but which also included serious attention to sociocultural and contextual influences, such as school-wide level of funding and community and school outlook on the social status of students.

Also, teachers who understand the developmental phases of reading, such as ones defined in some of the studies reviewed here, will be more likely to understand how to nurture students from one phase to the next, and they will more likely know which critical features to emphasize at which phases of development.

If young English-language learner reading trajectories can parallel typically developing native-English-speaking children's, then teachers can implement, and modulate as needed, the sound reading instruction practices they already use for monolingual English-speaking children. If teachers thoughtfully adjust effective practices for English-speaking students, such as modifying lesson pacing or overemphasizing certain facets of instruction, the same practices often used with English-only students can be effective for

English-language learners' reading achievement (cf. August & Shanahan, 2006).

What Impact Does Instruction in One Specific Reading Subprocesses Have on Learning That Reading Subprocess?

- Again, we saw that children tended to learn what they were taught. Instruction in specific reading subprocesses benefited English-language learners' achievement in those subprocesses. Instruction formerly found to be effective with English-only students was also shown to be effective for English-language learners: instruction in meaning vocabulary, phonological/phonemic awareness, cloze strategies to assist word recognition, literature logs, and instructional conversations—a discussion format. (Five studies)
- Kindergarten and fifth-grade English-language learners learned vocabulary words at the same or even faster rate than English-only students. (Two studies)

Here we highlight the kind of instruction accomplished in a rigorous experimental study conducted by Carlo and colleagues (2004). Teachers provided meaning vocabulary instruction to fifth-grade English-language learners who achieved greater growth on knowledge of target words, depth of meaning vocabulary knowledge, and understanding of multiple meanings than students in control classrooms. Structured meaning vocabulary lessons were taught using a direct instruction model and included introduction of 10–12 target words per week during 30- to 45-minute lessons each day. The lessons were all organized around immigration as the topic, and a different topic-related text was used each week. On day one, students received the written and audiotaped text in Spanish to preview before the text was introduced the next day in English. On day two the text and target words were presented in English and target word meanings that could be surmised from the text were examined. On day three, small groups of four to six students completed two types of cloze tasks: a task with sentence contexts parallel to the instructional text, and a task with a dissimilar sentence context. The day four lesson was comprised of activities designed to promote depth of word knowledge, such as word association tasks, synonyms and antonyms, and/or analysis of semantic features. On day five, lesson activities varied in focus, but included activities to facilitate word polysemy and cognate awareness in general, and may not have been specific to target words.

It is possible that classroom teachers and special resource teachers at large might find the same or similar type of instruction helpful. The results of the study suggest that teachers might expect young English-language learners' meaning vocabulary to develop along with that of their English-only peers. As well, teachers might set high expectations for their English-language learners' acquisition of targeted meaning vocabulary words and could begin meaning vocabulary instruction with English-language learner students when they enter the classroom.

What Impact Does Simultaneous Instruction in Multiple Reading Subprocesses Have on Learning Those Reading Subprocesses?

- Instruction targeting multiple reading subprocesses can benefit English-language learners' reading in the targeted subprocess areas. (Three studies)
- Supporting oral language development in the language of instruction (Spanish) while implementing instruction also benefited students' language development in that language. (Two studies)
- Supplemental Spanish reading instruction can facilitate a faster rate of growth in Spanish reading outcomes for at risk English-language learners than for higher-performing English-language learners who did not receive supplemental Spanish reading instruction. (One study)

All four studies in the present category provided some evidence for the efficacy of supplemental Spanish- or English-reading instruction in multiple reading subprocesses for English-language learners at-risk for reading problems. In a previous section, we detailed the instructional model used by the researchers is this category—a model of direct instruction based on Proactive Reading (Mathes et al., 2004) or Lectura Proactiva (Mathes et al., 2003). Within our description we depicted how instruction was comprised of 6 to 10 short activities representing five areas—phonemic awareness, letter knowledge, word recognition, connected text fluency, and comprehension strategies. Additional language support activities designed for English-language learners were integrated into each instructional session. Each 50-minute instructional session with three to five students incorporated all five areas and lasted approximately 40 minutes.

The derived successful outcomes of the studies lead us to suggest that teachers might consider the same or similar instruction. Also teachers could set high expectations for at-risk English-language learners with respect to targeted reading subprocesses.

Aside from Specific Instruction in Reading Subprocesses, What Instructional Issues Should Teachers Consider?

- Teachers considered to be innovative teachers of English-language learners used practices such as teacher think-alouds to model comprehension strategies and graphic organizers to facilitate students' information organization. (Three studies)
- Teachers may become effective reading instructors for English-language learners by integrating new learning about such methods with established knowledge of effective reading instruction. Teachers may be able to change the way they teach reading for English-language learners by understanding and using such an infusion model. (Two studies).
- Culture impacts teaching and learning. Teachers' and

students' cultural identities may influence instructional practices. (Two studies)

The infusion model for learning about effective English-language learner instruction described by Gersten and Jiménez (1994; Jiménez & Gersten, 1999) might prove helpful for our readers. If such a model can allow teachers to attach and relate new pedagogical knowledge and learning to their established instructional practices and beliefs, teachers can learn new instructional techniques for English-language learners and anchor the techniques within their conventional pedagogy of effective reading instruction. For example, a teacher might integrate a new, unfamiliar instructional technique, like using teacher think-alouds as models of comprehension strategies to teach English-language learners cognitive strategies/complex thinking, into her customary thinking about a direct instruction model of comprehension strategy instruction. Or, a teacher might integrate graphic organizer use within her customary instructional thought and practice on text structure instruction.

Closure

While practitioners and researchers alike suggest that English-language learners' reading instruction and reading development deserve significant attention, there is little research on what regular classroom teacher-student interaction matters most for English-language learners' reading growth. Much needs to be accomplished before we will have a serious evidence-based understanding of which forms of reading instruction have the greatest impact.

References

Alvermann, D. E., Fitzgerald, J., & Simpson, M. (2006). Teaching and learning in reading. In P. A. Alexander & P. H. Winne (Eds.), *Handbook of Educational Psychology* (2nd ed., pp. 427–455). Mahwah, NJ: Erlbaum.

Araujo, L. (2002). The literacy development of kindergarten English-language learners. *Journal of Research in Childhood Education, 16,* 232–247.

August, D., & Shanahan, T. (2006). *Developing literacy in second-language learners: Report of the National Literacy Panel on Language Minority Children and Youth.* Mahwah, NJ: Erlbaum.

Arzubiaga, A. E., Artiles, A. J., King K. A., & Harris-Murri, N. (2008), *Exceptional children, 74,* 309–327.

Burt, M., Dulay, H., & Hernandez-Chavez, E. (1978). *Bilingual syntax measure II.* San Francisco, CA: Harcourt Brace Jovanovich.

Carlo, M. S., August, D., McLaughlin, B., Snow, C. E., Dressler, C., Lippman, D. N., et al. (2004). Closing the gap: Addressing the vocabulary needs on English-language learners in bilingual and mainstream classrooms. *Reading Research Quarterly, 39,* 188–215.

Carnine, D. W., Silbert, J., & Kame'enui, E. J. (1997). *Direct instruction in reading* (3rd ed.). Upper Saddle River, NJ: Merrill/Prentice Hall.

Clay, M. M. (1993). *An observation survey of early literacy achievement.* Portsmouth, NH: Heinemann.

Clay, M. M. (2002). *An observation survey of early literacy achievement* (2nd ed.). Portsmouth, NH: Heinemann.

Dalton, E. G., Tighe, P. L., & Ballard, W. S. (1991). *IPTI: Oral: IDEA oral language proficiency test, English.* Brea, CA: Educational IDEAS, Inc.

Dalton, S. S. (1998). *Pedagogy matters: Standards for effective teaching practice* (Research Report No. 4). Santa Cruz, CA: Center for Research on Education, Diversity, and Excellence (CREDE).

D'Anguilli, A., Siegel, L. S., & Maggi, S. (2004). Literacy instruction, SES, and word-reading achievement in English-language learners and children with English as a first language: A longitudinal study. *Learning Disabilities Research and Practice, 19,* 202–213.

Denton, C., Mathes, P., & Anthony J. (2002, June). *Word identification strategies in two early reading intervention models.* Paper presented at the meeting of the Society for the Scientific Study of Reading, Chicago, IL.

Duncan, S. E. & De Avila, E. A. (1985). *PRE-LAS English Form A.* Monterey, CA: College Testing Bureau/McGraw-Hill.

Dunn, L. M. (1990). *Peabody picture vocabulary test.* Circle Pines, MN: American Guidance Service.

Dunn, L. M., & Dunn, L. M. (1981). *Peabody picture vocabulary test-revised.* Minneapolis, MN: American Guidance Service.

Fitzgerald, J., Amendum, S., & Guthrie, K. (2008). Young Latino students' reading growth in all-English classrooms. *Journal of Literacy Research, 40,* 59–94.

Fitzgerald, J., & Noblit, G. (1999). About hopes, aspirations, and uncertainty: First-grade English-language learners' emergent reading. *Journal of Literacy Research, 31,* 133–182.

Fitzgerald, J., & Noblit, G. (2000). Balance in the making: Learning to read in an ethnically diverse first-grade classroom. *Journal of Educational Psychology, 92,* 1–20.

Gambrell, L. B. (1993). *The impact of RUNNING START on the reading motivation and behavior of first-grade children.* Unpublished manuscript, University of Maryland, National Reading Research Center.

General Accounting Office (2001). *Meeting the needs of students with limited English proficiency.* Washington, DC: Author.

Gersten, R. (1996). Language instruction of language-minority students: The transition years. *The Elementary School Journal, 96,* 227–244.

Gersten, R. (1999). Lost opportunities: Challenges confronting four teachers of English-language learners. *The Elementary School Journal, 100,* 38–56.

Gersten, R., & Jiménez, R. (1994). A delicate balance: Enhancing literature instruction for students of English as a second language. *The Reading Teacher, 47,* 438–449.

Goldenberg, C. (2008). Teaching English-language learners. What the research does—and does not—say. *American Educator, 32*(2), 8–44.

Good, III, R. H., Bank, N., & Watson, J. M. (Eds.). (2003). *Indicadores Dinámicos del Exito en la Lectura* [Dynamic indicators of reading success]. Eugene, OR: Institute for the Development of Educational Achievement.

Good, III, R. H., & Kaminski, R. A. (Eds.) (2002). *Dynamic indicators of basic early literacy skills* (6th ed.) Eugene, OR: Institute for the Development of Educational Achievement.

Graves, A. W., Gersten, R., & Haager, D. (2004). Literacy instruction in multiple-language first-grade classrooms: Linking student outcomes to observed instructional practice. *Learning Disabilities Research & Practice, 19,* 262–272.

Guskey, T. R. (1990). Integrating innovation. *Educational Leadership, 47*(5), 11–15.

Harris, P. J., Baltodano, H. M., & Artiles, A. J. (2006). Integration of culture in reading studies for youth in corrections: A literature review. *Education and treatment of children, 29,* 749–778.

Jiménez, R., & Gersten, R. (1999). Lessons and dilemmas derived from the literacy instruction of two Latina/o teachers. *American Educational Research Journal, 36,* 265–301.

Kindler, A. E. (2002). *Survey of the states of limited English proficient students and available educational programs and services 2000–2001 summary report.* Washington, DC: National Clearinghouse for English Language Acquisition and Language Instruction Educational Programs. Retrieved February 22, 2006, from http://www.ncela.gwu.edu

Klingner, J. K., Artiles, A. J., & Barletta, L. M. (2006). English language learners who struggle with reading: Language acquisition or LD? *Journal of Learning Disabilities, 39,* 103–128.

Koskinen, P. S., Blum, I. H., Bisson, S. A., Phillips, S. M., Creamer, T. S., & Baker, T. K. (2000). Book access, shared reading, and audio models: The effects of supporting literacy learning of linguisticallyl diverse students in school and home. *Journal of Educational Psychology, 29*, 23–36.

Kucer, S. B. (1992). Six bilingual Mexican-American students' and their teachers' interpretations of cloze literacy lessons. *The Elementary School Journal, 92*, 557–572.

Kucer, S. B. (1999). Two students' responses to, and literacy growth in, a whole language curriculum. *Reading Research and Instruction, 38*, 233–253.

Kucer, S. B., & Silva, C. (1999). The English literacy development of bilingual students withina transition whole-language curriculum. *Bilingual Research Journal, 23*, 319–245.

LaPray, M., & Ross, R. 1986). The graded word list: Quick gauge of reading ability. In E. E. Ekwall (Ed.), *Ekwall reading inventory* (2nd ed., pp. 28–29). Boston: Allyn & Bacon.

Linan-Thompson, S., Bryant, D. P., Dickson, S. V., & Kouzekanani, K. (2005). Spanish literacy instruction for at-risk kindergarten students. *Remedial and Special Education, 26*, 236–244.

Mathes, P. G., Linan-Thompson, S., Pollard-Durodola, S. D., Hagan, E. C., & Vaughn, S. (2003). *Lectura Proactiva para principiantes: Intensive small group instruction for Spanish speaking readers.* Dallas, TX: P. G. Mathes, Institute of Reading Research, Southern Methodist University.

Mathes, P. G., Torgesen, J., Wahl, M., Menchetti, J. C., & Grek, M. L. (2004). *Proactive beginning reading: Intensive small-group instruction for struggling readers.* Unpublished manuscript.

Neufeld, P., & Fitzgerald, J. (2001). Early English reading development: Latino English learners in the "low" reading group. *Research in the Teaching of English, 36*, 64–105.

Newcomer, P., & Hammill, D. (1997). *Test of language development* (3rd ed.). Austin, TX: Pro-Ed.

Padrón, Y. N. (1994). Comparing reading instruction in Hispanic/limited-English-proficiency schools with other inner-city schools. *Bilingual Research Journal, 18*, 49–66.

Padrón, Y. N., & Waxman, H. C. (1999). Classroom observations of the five standards of effective teaching in urban classrooms with English language learners. *Teaching and Change, 7*, 79–100.

Pérez, B. (1994). Spanish literacy development: A descriptive study of four bilingual whole-language classrooms. *Journal of Reading Behavior, 26*, 75–94.

Pollard-Durodola, S. D., Cedillo, G. D., & Denton, C. A. (2004). Linguistic units and instructional strategies that facilitate word recognition for Latino kindergarteners learning to read in Spanish. *Bilingual Research Journal, 28*, 319–354.

Saunders, W. M., & Goldenberg, C. (1999). Effects of instructional conversations and literature logs on limited- and fluency-English-proficient students' story comprehension and thematic understanding. *The Elementary School Journal, 99*, 277–301.

Silverman, R. D. (2007). Vocabulary development of English-language and English-only learners in kindergarten. *The Elementary School Journal, 107*, 365–383.

Slavin, R. E. & Cheung, A. (2005). A synthesis of research on language of reading instruction for English language learners. *Review of Educational Research, 75*, 247–284.

Slosson, R. L. (1963). *Slosson oral reading test.* East Aurora, NY: Slosson Educational Publications.

Smylie, M. A. (1988). The enhancement function of staff development: Organization and psychological antecedents to individual teacher change. *American Educational Research Journal, 25*, 1–30.

Snow, C. E., Tabors, P. O., Nicholson, P. A., & Kurland, B. F. (1995). SHELL: Oral language and early literacy skills in kindergarten and first-grade children. *Journal of Research in Early Childhood Education, 10*, 37–48.

Texas Education Agency. (2000). *Tejas Lee.* Austin, TX: Author.

Tharp, R. G. (2005). *Activity Setting Observation System rule book.* Center for Research on Education, Diversity & Excellence, Research Reports, Paper ASOS. Retrieved from http://repositories.cdlib.org/crede/rsrchrpts/ASOS

Thomas, W. P., & Collier, V. P. (2002). *A national study of school effectiveness for language minority students' long-term academic achievement, Final report: Project 1.1.* Santa Cruz, CA: University of California, Center for Research on Education, Diversity, and Excellence.

Tindal, G., & Marston, D. (1990). *Classroom-based assessment: Evaluating instructional outcomes.* Columbus, OH: Merrill.

Torgesen, J., Wagner, R., & Rashotte, C. (1999). *Test of word reading efficiency.* Austin, TX: PRO-ED.

Vaughn, S., Cirino, P. T., Linan-Thompson, S., Mathes, P. G., Carlson, C. D., Hagan, E. C., et al. (2006). Effectiveness of a Spanish intervention and an English intervention for English-language learners at risk for reading problems. *American Educational Research Journal, 43*, 449–487.

Vaughn, S., Linan-Thompson, S., Mathes, P. G., Cirino, P. T., Carlson, C. D., Pollard-Durodola, S. D., et al. (2006). Effectiveness of Spanish intervention for first-grade English language learners at risk for reading difficulties. *Journal of Learning Disabilities, 39*, 56–73.

Vaughn, S., Mathes, P. G., Linan-Thompson, S., Cirino, P. T., Carlson, C. D., Pollard-Durodola, S. D., et al. (2006). Effectiveness of an English intervention for first-grade English language learners at risk for reading problems. *The Elementary School Journal, 107*, 153–180.

Wagner, R., Torgesen, J., & Rashotte, C. (1999). *Comprehensive Test of Phonological Processing (CTOPP).* Bloomington, MN: Pearson Assessments.

Waxman, H. C., Wang, M. C., Lindvall, C. M., & Anderson, K. A. (1983a). *Classroom Observation Schedule technical manual.* Pittsburgh, PA: University of Pittsburgh, Learning Research and Development Center.

Waxman, H. C., Wang, M. C., Lindvall, C. M., & Anderson, K. A. (1983b). *Teachers Roles Observation Schedule technical manual.* Pittsburgh, PA: University of Pittsburgh, Learning Research and Development Center.

Waxman, H. C., Wang, M. C., Lindvall, C. M., & Anderson, K. A. (1988). *Classroom observation schedule technical manual* (Rev. ed.). Philadelphia: Temple University, Center for Research in Human Development and Education.

Wilkinson, G. S. (1993). *The wide range achievement test—3.* Wilmington, DE: Jastak Associates.

Woodcock, R. W. (1991). *Woodcock language proficiency battery-revised, English and Spanish forms.* Itasca, IL: Riverside.

Woodcock, R. W. (1995). *Woodcock Language Proficiency Battery-Revised, Spanish form: Supplemental manual.* Itasca, IL: Riverside.

Yoon, B. (2007). Offering or limiting opportunities: Teachers' roles and approaches to English-language learners' participation in literacy activities. *The Reading Teacher, 61*, 216–225.

Zehler, A., Fleischman, H., Hopstock, P., Stephenson, T., Pendzick, M., & Sapru, S. (2003). *Descriptive study of services to LEP students and LEP students with disabilities, Volume 1A: Research report.* Development Associates, Inc. Retrieved January 15, 2004, from http://www.devassoc.com/devassoc/vol_1_text.pdf

34

Interventions for the Deaf and Language Delayed

KIMBERLY A. WOLBERS AND HANNAH M. DOSTAL
University of Tennessee

This chapter provides a synthesis of previous literacy research with deaf students, and it suggests a number of future directions. Much attention throughout the chapter is given to one subpopulation of deaf students—those with severe to profound losses who are less likely to develop oral language skills and who encounter unique barriers to reading and writing development when compared to their hearing or hard of hearing peers. There is a need for specialized literacy instruction of the deaf in order to be responsive to the specific language and literacy challenges they encounter. Two main areas are discussed in this chapter: (a) the occurrence of delays in development of expressive language and (b) the effect of having a visually and spatially based language as one's primary mode of communication. Instructional interventions that address these specific challenges and attempt to positively impact reading or writing in English are highlighted throughout.

The reading achievement outcomes of deaf students have illustrated a lack of literacy progress since the late 1960s (Yoshinaga-Itano & Snyder, 1985). Recent data released by the Gallaudet Research Institute (2003) confirms stagnate reading levels; the median reading comprehension score for 17- and 18-year-old deaf students corresponds with a 4.0 grade reading level of hearing students. This indicates that half of the deaf and hard of hearing students tested in this age range are reading below the typical hearing student who is beginning the fourth grade level. Even more striking, deaf students have been known to make only 1 year of gain in reading comprehension and vocabulary development over a 10-year period from age 12 to 21 (Yoshinaga-Itano, Snyder, & Mayberry, 1996), and they experience a writing "plateau" with both semantics and syntax in adolescence (Musselman & Szanto, 1998). Writing achievement similarly plateaus around this age for children in general (Bereiter, 1980), yet deaf children exhibit substantial troubles with lower level skills and, for instance, make little to no progress in rules of

transformational grammar after the age of 12 (Yoshinaga-Itano et al., 1996).

Dismal literacy outcomes persist even though advancements in the field of deaf education over the past several decades should have logically led to greater literacy achievement. Some developments of recent times include: technological improvements such as cochlear implants and digital hearing aids; early identification and intervention programs that are increasingly screening babies at birth for hearing loss and providing services to the families by 6 months of age (National Center for Birth Defects and Developmental Disabilities, 2005); the explosion of bilingual/ bicultural educational programs; higher qualifications and standards for educational interpreters and teachers of the deaf; legal mandates such as IDEA that give students with hearing loss access to the general education curriculum; heightened awareness of Deaf[1] culture and the Deaf community. Yet, making a difference in the literacy achievement of deaf students has proven to be a formidable task despite these developments, for simply exposing a deaf child to the general education curriculum with more qualified professionals and better amplification may not necessarily ensure that learning takes place.

Discussed less frequently is the 50% of deaf students (with diverse backgrounds and experiences) achieving beyond a fourth-grade reading level upon graduation. Approximately 5% of seniors with hearing loss demonstrate reading comprehension abilities at or above the level of their hearing peers (Kelly & Barac-Cikoja, 2007). At Gallaudet University, a liberal arts college for the Deaf, reading and writing levels of incoming freshman have been rising each year (Fernandes, 2003). This may indicate a widening gap between students who are armed with successful reading and writing strategies, have had sufficient language and literacy experiences, and have a balanced repertoire of literacy skills (both text-based and higher-level), and those students who are still struggling with basic (even primary) reading, writing, and language skills. Now more than ever, we live in a technological and global society where there is heavy reliance on print-based literacy skills to accomplish everyday tasks and access information (Luckner, Sebald, Cooney, Young, & Muir, 2006). Knowing the educational factors and effective literacy instruction that contribute to deaf students' literacy achievement is vital.

Prior Literacy and Deafness Research

Unfortunately, the field of deaf education has very little knowledge aggregated in terms of effective literacy interventions with school-aged deaf persons. Antia, Reed, and Kreimeyer (2005) conducted a regression analysis to find the predictors of writing achievement among students which resulted in a model that could explain an unsatisfying 18% of the variance with variables like grade, degree of hearing loss and gender. Language ability has been known to correlate with literacy achievement (Izzo, 2002) but was not a predictor in this study. The authors posit that the instructional approach of the teacher likely impacted student achievement, yet this research and other research have been unable to reveal more descriptively the approaches that make a difference in student achievement. The paucity of existing literacy research additionally complicates our ability as a field to drawn certain conclusions.

Luckner et al. (2006) found that only 964 articles relative to literacy and deafness have appeared in peer-reviewed journals over the past 40 years; on average, that equates to a meager 24 a year. Of those 964 articles, only 22 could be considered evidence-based; that is, the study used a control group and provided quantitative and statistical information needed for calculation of effect sizes. Qualitative research studies can provide rich information about how, when, or why something works (Pressley, 2005). Yet, over half of the articles published are not research studies at all but are position papers, practitioner articles, or literature reviews. The majority of the work in the area of deaf education and literacy has been opinion-based and governed by one's own persuasions rather than by science (Bailes, 2001; Easterbrooks, 2005). Needless to say, there is considerable need for increased quantity and quality research. This chapter provides a discussion of the unique factors affecting literacy achievement of the deaf, a synthesis of the few intervention research studies that respond to these factors, and suggestions for future research directions as well as instructional implications.

Because there is great diversity among deaf and hard of hearing students (e.g., degree of hearing loss, affiliation with the Deaf community, mode of communication, etc.) and their instructional needs, specific attention will be given to one subgroup of children—those having severe to profound hearing losses which have greatly impacted the development of speech and the use of oral language to support reading and writing. With respect to successful deaf readers having significant hearing losses and using American Sign Language (ASL) as their expressive language, there has been little attempt at theorizing a course of literacy development (cf. Mayer & Wells, 1996). The current chapter gives consideration to students' exceptional language and literacy histories including experiences of (a) language delays and life occurrences devoid of language mediation and (b) having a visually and spatially based primary language. Specialized literacy approaches are necessary to make a difference in the reading and writing achievement of these deaf students. The current deaf education literature as well as future intervention studies are discussed, especially instruction that ameliorates delays of a first language while building an understanding for English language and literacy.

Unique Language Factor #1: Language Delays and Life Occurrences Devoid of Language Mediation

For severe to profoundly deaf individuals, there are language barriers that stand in the way of making sufficient literacy progress. First, early language exposure and language learning practices are often inaccessible to deaf children through auditory approaches alone. If a mutually understandable means of communication, such as sign language, is not adopted early in the home, deaf children are at great risk for language delays. Even when sign language is utilized in the home, deaf children still may not have full access to language due to the challenges parents face in learning sign language (Marschark, 2001). And, the current educational system often perpetuates a home problem by providing communication-poor learning environments for deaf learners, e.g., children placed in isolation where there are no same-aged deaf peers or proficient adult signers (Siegel, 2000).

In addition to a lack of proficient language models, deaf children are not engaged in rich and authentic conversation. When family members are not fluent and experience frequent errors in language expression/reception, interactions are severely thwarted. Conversations necessitate more time for repetition and clarification, which leads to less responsiveness, less complex forms of language being used, and more directed conversations (Schlesinger, 1988). This problem may again be perpetuated at school when classrooms are dominated by teacher talk (Cazden, 2001), whereby student opportunities for interaction are often controlled (Mehan, 1979) and require no real thought or interpretation (Nystrand, 1997). Poor early home interactions lead to deficient language development in deaf children (Calderon, 2000), and this is carried forward through education with classroom instruction that does nothing to remediate students' limited early language exposure.

By the time deaf children reach school, they have had significantly fewer opportunities to learn and use language, and many are at beginning one-word stages of language development (Gilbertson & Ferre, 2008). This is in comparison to hearing children who, by the age of 5, have a vocabulary repertoire of approximately 10,000 words and sophisticated use of syntax and morphology, including the production of embedded clauses, compound and complex sentences (Nippold, 2007). Without consistent language input and modeling, there are a narrower set of contexts through which deaf children learn words (Lederberg & Spencer, 2001). Poor early language indicates poor literacy skills to follow, expressive and receptive language deficiencies are subsequently followed by reading and writing struggles (Larney, 2002). Further, young children without involvement in complex interactions or less directed dialogues (e.g., practice with why or how questions) experience troubles with reading in adolescence (Schlesinger, 1988).

Lastly, children learn about the world through language, negotiating and constructing meaning of childhood experiences (Nystrand, 1997). Oftentimes, however, deaf children have experienced the world around them absent of accessible conversation that involves sense-making, explanation or inquiry (Easterbrooks & Baker, 2002). Vocabulary knowledge as well as prior knowledge work to support reading comprehension, therefore, deaf children are disadvantaged without proper early intervention and language-mediated experiences (Luckner et al., 2006).

Instructional Interventions and Future Directions A natural intervention approach based on principals of language acquisition (e.g., experiential learning paired with language, language and play opportunities, purposeful communication) may be ideal for early language learning when children arrive to school with severe delays (Luetke-Stahlman, 1993). However, teachers are increasingly under pressure to additionally cover the grade level curriculum and get students prepared for high-stakes tests in reading and other subject areas. Oftentimes, deaf children are learning to read and write while simultaneously learning to express themselves through language (Luckner et al., 2006).

Language experience approach. A highly touted and frequently utilized instructional practice is the Language Experience Approach (McAnally, Rose, & Quigley, 1999), whereby students' reading material is constructed from their own oral narratives and experiences. For the general population, there is little evidence to suggest that this practice is any more effective than other kinds of reading instruction (e.g., basal or teaching explicit word decoding strategies). There may be slightly more benefit for reading readiness and initiation to print objectives at the kindergarten level but less in the way of reading mastery skills at the older ages (Stahl & Miller, 2006). And, for disadvantaged populations such as students coming from low SES backgrounds, the Language Experience Approach (LEA) is more hard-pressed to show significant impact when compared to systematic word decoding and word study skills.

For deaf children who are still developing a first language through which they can share their experiences with others, the LEA may have additional language and communication benefit (Stauffer, 1979). Children are first supported with the help of more competent language users in development of the expressive and receptive language that accompanies certain experiences or activities. Then, this newly adopted and utilized language becomes a bridge into reading and writing. The LEA will likely lead to greater understanding that expressed language can be written and read. It also offers a natural way for deaf children to expand and develop their first language, for language is utilized in tandem with daily experiences. Yet, there is little evidence to support any claims that it leads to greater language and literacy outcomes (cf. Johnson & Roberson, 1988).

It is suggested that future research examine the impact of using LEA with deaf children. When more structured approaches to word decoding are infused in the LEA, hearing students have shown greater literacy benefit (Stahl & Miller, 2006); therefore, attention should be given to language and literacy growth provided variations of the LEA. The LEA traditionally involves the teacher capturing the students' language and oral message in written text. Approaches that require greater student thinking, problem-solving and involvement with the writing may also provide more benefit.

One consideration for teachers using the LEA is to ensure they have accurate details for the child's experiences prior to building language and capturing the message in written text. When children are language delayed—and especially when children are only providing one or two word utterances—the experience can be reconstructed inaccurately if the teacher makes assumptions about what happened or if she leads the child in a particular direction and the child merely mimics language. There may be misunderstandings that unfold due to the limitations of the child's communication. It is strongly suggested that the teacher be firmly aware of the details of the experience; shared experiences can, for instance, be readily utilized for reading and writing extensions (Wolbers, 2008) since the teacher witnessed the activity. Language modeling and use happens in tandem with the activity from which the reading and writing then builds. Teachers of the deaf may also have students draw or role play instances to arrive at an accurate message. In this case, expressive language may be developed first by moving from visual and gestured representations to greater infusion of signs (cf. Loeterman, Paul, & Donahue, 2002).

Dialogic and interactive approaches. As children become older, there may still be a need for instructional approaches that attend to expressive and receptive language development while simultaneously meeting reading and writing objectives. It is not uncommon to meet deaf students in the older grades who exhibit varying levels of language delay (cf. Lederberg & Spencer, 2001; Singleton, Morgan, DiGello, Wiles, & Rivers, 2004). There may have been a lack of accessible adult language models and same-aged peers (Siegel, 2000) in the child's life, or even a lack of instructional approaches that attend to the language needs. In one literacy intervention study, a class of middle school students is described as having minimal language skills; most of the students had transferred to a residential school from other educational programs where students were isolated from other deaf and signing individuals or where program philosophies solely emphasized oral approaches (Wolbers, 2007). Whatever the reason, teachers in the later elementary, middle, and high school grades encounter deaf children evidencing mild to severe delays in their expressive and receptive language development. Therefore, instructional approaches to delivering grade level curriculum must recognize the limitations of students in expressing or receiving content-related information through language which has not fully developed. One response to this has been the use of pictorial materials and visual scaffolds, which prove to be effective tools in mediating the literacy learning of deaf children (Schneiderman, 1995; Walker, Munro, & Richards, 1998; Wilson & Hyde, 1997; Wolbers, 2007). Yet, there is additional need for instruction that ameliorates language delays while simultaneously building content understanding.

Dialogic modes of teaching, for instance, have been linked with greater literacy and academic achievement as well as higher cognitive capacities and critical thinking for all students (Burbules, 1993; Hillocks, 2002; Nystrand, 1997; Ward, 1994). When using dialogic kinds of instruction with deaf children, there is an additional opportunity to practice and use language, especially in conjunction with higher levels of thinking. Research by Mayer, Akamatsu, and Stewart (2002) looked extensively into the dialogue used by teachers of the deaf across grade level and subject matter. They discovered that exemplary teachers of the deaf used discourse strategies that encourage students to expand on their linguistic and cognitive efforts. They "worked hard to engage students in interactions which were meaningful and encouraged knowledge-building" (p. 499). The teachers were not the "tellers" of information but provided a stimulating environment that encouraged students to actively participate in learning. For instance, teachers asked open-ended and authentic questions such as "Why?" or "How can we find out about this?" that required students to explain, justify, inquire, hypothesize, problem solve, or defend rather than recite memorized information. They additionally attempted to respond to students' comments and queries, no matter how seemingly off-track. This is done in a contingent manner, whereby the teacher has the ability to clarify or weave together contributions. This is an important aspect of interactive educational environments—students are active thinkers who make tentative hypotheses or explanations, and the teachers take up students' exploratory talk and provide appropriate scaffolding (Schoenfeld, 2002). All participants, teachers and students alike, actively work together in a joint process of language and meaning construction.

Some writing instruction approaches implemented with the deaf have built on highly interactive and experience-based approaches. Schneiderman (1995) found that structured and analytic approaches to grammar instruction were not effective for fourth- to sixth-grade students because they did not generalize to real writing. When situations required meaningful and social interactions between teacher and students (similar to parent-child interactions)—allowing child initiations, writing for a purpose, and the provision of adult modeling of linguistic structures within context— the students' writing improved. Craig, Carr, and Latham (1964) also evidenced that early elementary students receiving a more natural language approach (modeled after oral language development) to teach writing resulted in significantly improved grammar outcomes when compared to students receiving structured and analytic systems of grammar instruction (i.e., the Fitzgerald Key). In this research, new vocabulary and forms of expression were embedded into larger phrasal units rather than taught as isolated pieces. Further, the phrases were aligned with pictorials. Learning was therefore situated within meaningful and visual contexts through which deaf children could match new language with experiences and activity. These studies were purposely designed to juxtapose natural and analytic kinds of instruction, thereby making it unclear whether structured approaches could be embedded in or combined with natural interactive approaches to provide greater benefit to the student.

For example, Wolbers (2008) infused structured approaches to teaching English grammar within the co-construction of authentic pieces of writing. Students engaged in purposeful and meaningful writing tasks with an established audience, and were active participants in the collaborative creation of meaning and problem-solving. Additionally, when grammatical confusions surfaced among group members (e.g., using "a" vs. "the"), the instructor utilized structured approaches to explicitly teach these skills. Yet, students went one step further by reapplying this skill to their authentic text. The study examined elementary and middle school student outcomes when writing instruction was highly dialogic and also balanced (i.e., gave consideration to the teaching of higher and lower level objectives). The findings indicated that students made significant growth over a short 21-day instructional period with genre-specific traits, contextual language writing skills (e.g., improved verb consistency, correct usage of prepositions), editing and revising skills, and reading. Yet with each of these writing interventions utilizing an interactive or dialogic approach, there were no remarks on students' expressive and receptive language growth as a result of the instruction.

Dialogic and interactive approaches to writing instruction are likely to provide language as well as literacy benefit for students who are actively engaged in meaning construction via an accessible communication mode. Yet, research to date is lacking data to evidence the impact on first language growth. When a highly dialogic and balanced approach named Strategic and Interactive Writing Instruction (Wolbers, 2007) was utilized with the before mentioned group of severely language delayed middle school students, students made noticeable gains in language and communicative competence. There were no formal language measures, however the author indicates that students became more clear and complete in their ability to express themselves through ASL, needed increasingly less language scaffolding from the teacher, obtained longer stints of eye contact for communication purposes, and increased their attempts at responding to and building on others' comments. Future research should include an evaluation of expressive and receptive language in addition to other competencies.

Other than writing interventions, some reading instruction approaches used with deaf children have incorporated dialogic methods. Andrews, Creaghead, Kretschmer, and Weiler (1995) found that students recall more of a story's events and elements when the story is read to them in a group, and interaction occurs among group participants. Similarly, Al-Hilawani (2003) compared three different reading approaches used with groups of third-grade deaf students: a basic reading approach, a modified reciprocal teaching approach, and a key word strategy. In the basic reading approach, students responded to questions formulated by the teacher after reading a passage. The modified reciprocal teaching approach additionally incorporated group discussion and participation with summarizing, clarifying, and predicting. And, students using the key word strategy selected key words in the passage and then took turns asking the others what happened before and after. Each also prepared written questions to ask the other students, and when there was difficulty answering s/he provided guidance and hints. Both the modified reciprocal teaching and the key word strategy encouraged greater student participation in the activity and more interaction between members than the basic reading approach. The two methods were significantly more effective in promoting comprehension (i.e., knowing the main idea, responding to word meaning questions) than the basic reading approach. Yet, dialogic inquiry whereby students are co-constructors of knowledge was never fully implemented in this study; the author explains that teachers were resistant to students assuming the teacher's role as is done in reciprocal teaching (Palincsar & Brown, 1984), for teachers had a desire to control and structure the activity. Even though the modified reciprocal teaching and key word strategy students had significantly higher outcomes than those in the basic reading approach, students under all conditions were still achieving below average (~60% on reading evaluation).

Again, these studies did not evaluate the impact that dialogic approaches to reading have on language development. There is evidence that dialogic reading positively impacts vocabulary and language growth when used with hearing pre-school children (Hargrave & Senechal, 2000) and could result in comparable or enhanced gains when used with deaf, language-delayed children. In one study by Fung, Chow & McBride-.Chang (2005), parents incorporated dialogic approaches while reading with their deaf and hard of hearing children. They encouraged active child involvement, asked open-ended questions and prompted their children to comment on the text. When their children contributed to the interaction, the parents were responsive by using expansion techniques. After 8 weeks of intervention, children demonstrated significantly greater vocabulary development in comparison to the non-intervention children

Similar to parent-child interactions, dialogic and interactive literacy instruction enables teachers to build on their students' current expressions and understandings. When students become participants of the classroom learning and more readily express their thinking and ideas, teachers have a greater ability to accurately assess their current levels of understanding, which, in turn, leads to more responsive, scaffolded, and extended communication from the teacher. "By building on children's cultural and personal ways of interacting while at the same time providing new and expanded opportunities for successful interactions, teachers can help children expand their participatory and linguistic repertoires" (Johnson, 1994, p. 189). Gioia, Johnston, and Cooper (2001) discuss how teachers who make observations and collect student data can provide more responsive literacy instruction at appropriate but challenging levels. With the to and fro of classroom communication represented in dialogic instruction, teachers can not only evaluate the level of content understanding but can also assess communicative competence and expressive/receptive language ability.

Students may at times respond to the teacher's question with something inappropriate and seemingly off topic. And, it is unclear whether this is the result of language limitations or if there is a lack of conceptual understanding. For example in one of the classroom transcripts provided by Mayer, Akamatsu, and Stewart (2002), a science teacher, while holding up a beaker representing all the water in the world, asks her class how much of the world's water can be used for drinking, and a student responds, "5, 6 days" (p. 497). She repeats the question, the student responds in the same way, and she passes over his response. In this case, the student may have misunderstood the question to be, "How long can a person survive on this amount of drinking water?"

Future research might examine instructional approaches that effectively decipher linguistic and conceptual stumbling blocks to student understanding. In terms of language barriers, this particular student (a) might simply understand lessons better when the teacher uses ASL visual and spatial grammar rather than the English-based sign that was used or (b) may have a language delay whereby he utilizes more visual information (i.e., the beaker of water) to comprehend the teacher's question rather than the teacher's voiced and signed expression. When problems exist, teachers need a repertoire of strategies for how to work through the language difficulties to obtain clarity (Tye-Murray, 1994) while also providing a bridge to further language development. Future research might examine instructional approaches that effectively decipher linguistic and conceptual stumbling blocks to student understanding.

Unique Language Factor #2: A Visual and Spatial Expressive Language

Deaf students may additionally encounter barriers to reading and writing when using sign language as their primary language, for there is a noted lack of correspondence between American Sign Language (ASL) and English text. For instance, a person speaking English might use the following sentence: The cat fell out of the tree when the dog came near and barked. A person using ASL would use their hands to visually display each item (cat, dog, tree) and how they move and interact in space, as if producing a motion picture. The message would be constructed in a nonlinear fashion by first displaying a cat in a tree. The tree remains in the space in front of the body while the signer uses the opposite hand to show the dog approaching the tree and barking, which then sets up a situation for the cat to fall.

To provide a comparison for readers between English and ASL sentence structure, we reduce the complexity of the ASL expression by setting aside elements such as facial and body grammar. The expression can be roughly represented with a combination of signs (indicated by capital letters) and classifiers[2]: TREE-CAT-classifier showing the cat sitting in the tree- HAPPEN-DOG-classifier showing dog coming near-BARK-classifier showing cat falling from tree. The syntactic and morphological differences between ASL and English are quite apparent. Deaf children who use ASL as their primary means of communication but must learn to read and write in English, may encounter difficulties in making connections between the grammatical form associated with one's thoughts and English vocabulary and grammar used for reading and writing.

The following story written by a seventh-grade deaf student illustrates how features of one's primary language can surface in writing:

> February 7, Sara and I went to pet shop. I want the lizard. We buy the lizard, wood, little cave with plant, the crickets, and water. We brought to my house. I feed the lizard. It eat crickets. I pick the lizard Then pet to it. I said, "called Darsh and Satch." It is brown and yellow. Wow! The lizard's long is 8 inch. I can tickle the lizard. I don't know how old the lizard. (Wolbers, 2005)

First, the student uses several present tense verbs (e.g., want, buy, eat, pick, pet) when the event clearly happened in the past. Yet, it is appropriate in ASL to use present tense verbs when the speaker indicates at the beginning of an expression that the event happened in the past. In the student's writing, she says at the start that they went to the pet store on February 7, which would be a sufficient indicator of tense in the signed mode. Also, the phrase, "the lizard's long is 8 inch," demonstrates nonstandard English in a two ways—"long" is an incorrect word choice for this context and "inch" lacks plurality. While the sentence seems awkward to an English-speaking person, it looks correct to the deaf child. There are reasonable explanations for the child's construction of such a sentence. First, one way a deaf child might express the concept of length in ASL is to use one's index finger and slide it up the length of the other arm. The word generally associated with this signed concept is "long" and is perhaps the reason for the word's appearance in the awkward sounding sentence above. Second, one typically signifies plurality in ASL by using repetitive movements or indicating how many. In the example, "8 inch," the student

has already indicated that there are several inches by stating a number, and that alone indicates plurality in ASL. Thus, the student quite possibly is applying knowledge of her expressive language to her writing in English.

Research has pointed out the linkages between one's expressive language and one's written language. For instance, in the mid-1970s Loban showed that oral language and written language seemed to develop in parallel (see Applebee, 2000); once certain developments took place in one's oral language such as the use of dependent clauses or more complex vocabulary, these developments occurred in one's writing approximately 1 year later. Already discussed in this chapter is the case that many deaf children experience mild to severe delays with the development of a primary language. In the writing sample above, the author used short, rigid and simple kinds of sentences, while lacking more complex constructions such as dependent or relative clauses. This is common among young deaf writers (Heider & Heider, 1941; Moores & Miller, 2001; Powers & Wigus, 1983; Yoshinaga-Itano et al., 1996) and may be indicative of the stage of language development if the primary form of communication still lacks the full complexity of language.

Bailes' (2001) observations of first-grade deaf writers were that students in the earlier stages of ASL acquisition tended to struggle with written expression; native users of ASL, on the other hand, had abundant English vocabulary which allowed them to read and write more independently. Singleton et al. (2004) examined differences in the writing of low-ASL-proficient students and high-ASL-proficient students and found that writing among the first group was more formulaic and had mainly high-frequency words. Yet, both groups wrote significantly fewer function words than their hearing peers. Deaf students also typically experience difficulty with the use of adverbs, pronouns, determiners, conjunctions, passive constructions and conditional verbs such as "could," "should," or "might" (Taeschner, 1988; Yoshinaga-Itano et al., 1996). Some barriers to reading and writing, then, are likely related to language delays, while other barriers exist due to the lack of correspondence between expressed and written language.

The inherent disconnect between the visual and spatial grammar of ASL and the linear form of English has led some to assert that English-based signing (EBS) can serve as a better foundation for literacy learning in English (Mayer & Akamatsu, 1999). EBS is an umbrella term for several artificially contrived systems and some natural sign expressions which utilize signs in English syntactical order (Stewart, 2006). Still, when produced in conceptual and meaningful ways, EBS does not relay the full complexities of English grammar, nor the vocabulary. A frequently used EBS among deaf persons is pidgin or contact sign which has developed naturally from ASL and English for the purpose of communicating across languages. Pidgin sign does not serve well as a model for written English, for pidgin languages by definition have simplified grammar and restricted vocabulary (Jackendoff, 1994). For example, the English sentence provided earlier as an example might be expressed in contact sign as: CAT FALL FROM TREE WHEN DOG WALK-TO AND BARK. This expression relays the main concepts using ASL signs while placing them in English syntactical order. The expression is a closer representation of English, but there still remains a linguistic gap to overcome. In addition, the expression is missing the richness of ASL, a fully complex language (Stokoe, 1978), due to drastically reduced visual and spatial grammar..

While some persons utilize classifiers and movement in space via contact sign for greater conceptual accuracy, the expressions grow more distant from English grammar. Artificially contrived sign systems like Manually Coded English can relay the grammatical components of the English language (e.g., suffixes) in a visual manner; however, they are largely disfavored because they are inefficient, cumbersome, and diminish conceptual accuracy (Fischer, 1998). To date, and after decades of use in homes and schools, there has been no evidence to suggest deaf children acquire proficiency in English solely through the use of EBS as their primary mode of communication (Marschark, 2001; Stewart, 2006). At the same time, EBS may serve as a mediator between ASL and English for literacy learning purposes (Marschark, 2001; Gioia et al., 2001; Wolbers, 2007).

Instructional Interventions and Future Directions This section of the chapter will discuss methods through which deaf children having visually and spatially based languages of expression then develop English language knowledge in support of reading and writing. First it will demonstrate a preoccupation with grammar and text-based interventions used to overcome students' deficiencies in English, arguing a need for balanced approaches to teaching English. Then, the section will consider research using metalinguistic approaches known to positively impact English language and literacy knowledge. The roles of ASL and EBS in the development of English are further discussed. Last, the section will provide information on rereading English text to build automaticity and familiarity with the language.

Balanced literacy instruction. For children in general, the advantages of using balanced literacy instruction have been expressed and described (Pressley, 2005). Balanced literacy is the use of both whole language approaches and skills-based instruction which work together to encourage development of higher level literacy skills (e.g., reading comprehension strategies, writing organization and coherence of text) and lower level or text-based skills (e.g., English syntactical constructions, decoding/encoding skills). For teachers of the deaf, however, providing a balance of instruction related to content as well as form has been difficult.

Deaf students typically struggle more with text-based and lower level skills (Gormely & Sarachan-Deily, 1987), and therefore instructional efforts that target English vocabulary and grammar tend to dominate many classrooms (Mayer, 1999). This often means the teaching of grammar through structured and explicit instructional approaches. These methods of teaching English grammar rely heavily on skill-drills that occur apart from any real writing context (McNaughton, 2002) and, thus, students have little opportunity to experience purposeful writing for an authentic audience. For other students, it has been shown that reductionist teaching of lower level skills separately from a larger sphere of meaning provides no real benefit to students (Coleman, 1997; Hillocks, 1984). And with deaf students, there has been plenty of targeted instructional attention to English grammar in the classroom, yet students demonstrate little progress in this area. They rarely achieve at a level commensurate with their hearing counterparts (Antia, Reed, & Kreimeyer, 2005). For instance, by the age of 12 progress with transformational grammar has slowed considerably, and many students make only 1 year of gain over the next 10 years (Yoshinaga-Itano et al., 1996). Structured writing instruction used with deaf students such as application of the Fitzgerald Key (Craig, Carr, & Latham, 1964), worksheets and drills of linguistic structures (Schneiderman, 1995), and learning the parts of speech and practicing them in constructed sentences (Wolbers, 2007) have not proven to be as effective as other approaches.

Even when students are encouraged to craft an original story, there is often still an overemphasis on writing accuracy (Harrison, Simpson, & Stuart, 1991; McAnally, Rose, & Quigley, 1994). One unintended consequence is that students have been known to become frustrated with writing because a final, polished product seems unattainable to them (Albertini, 1996). Second, students may become less likely to experiment with more complex uses of language (Antia et al., 2005, Kluwin & Kelly, 1992) for fear of being critiqued. Third, a preoccupation with lower level skills has meant less instruction given to higher level writing skills. And, there are important higher level skills that sorely lack attention such as the development of coherence in writing (Antia et al., 2005; Klecan-Aker & Blondeau, 1990; McAnally et al., 1999).

Deaf students have typically relied more on associative kinds of writing techniques by introducing several topics without elaboration (Yoshinaga-Itano et al., 1996), yet skillful writers carefully weave together ideas instead of introducing pieces of information that are independent of what was previously said. Factors such as these encourage claims that a whole language and non-corrective approaches that give credit for approximations as well as growth can help blooming writers develop confidence and fluency of expression (French, 1999; Harrison, Simpson, & Stuart, 1991).

At the same time, academicians who research linguistically diverse students (i.e., those with expressive languages or home languages that are different from standard English) claim that whole language approaches are a disservice to students because instruction is not intense or strategic enough (Delpit, 1986, 1988; Reyes, 1992). Linguistically diverse children who are merely immersed or passively exposed to standard English text have evidenced very little progress with the contextual language and grammatical features of their writing. For instance, merely asking students to proofread their work and fix the mistakes often results in no improvements. When a student's expressed language surfaces in their writing, it looks and sounds right to them. Therefore, for linguistically diverse students who have acquired a different first language, learning standard English is a conscious, contrastive and analytic process (Gee, 1991).

Writing instruction using both natural and structured approaches is likely to hold much promise in developing a wide range of language and literacy skills among deaf students. Balanced instruction can be accomplished by teaching writing skills (lower-level and higher level) in the context of real writing experiences (French, 1999; McNaughton, 2002). For instance linguistically diverse students who receive feedback on the grammatical errors found within their individually constructed writing make significantly greater improvement on grammatical accuracy than those who do not receive feedback (Ferris & Roberts, 2006). Additionally, guided and shared writing whereby students work collaboratively along with the teacher to construct text provides opportunities to apprentice students to be critical evaluators of both higher level and lower level writing actions and to take increasing responsibility for the decision making (Calkins, 1986). With collaborative and authentic writing (i.e., for a predetermined purpose and a preselected audience), deaf students engage in the problem-solving and thinking associated with all writing activity and have demonstrated gains with both high level (e.g., providing details, coherence of text, having a clear conclusion) and low level (e.g., appropriate verb tense, reduction of run-ons and fragments, appropriate use of prepositions) objectives in writing (Wolbers, 2008).

Guided and shared writing is further a way of engaging students who are struggling with lower level skills (e.g., handwriting, encoding text, contextual language) in higher level learning, which is especially useful in teaching grade level curriculum to language and literacy delayed deaf students. Guided and shared writing, for instance, has been utilized with severely delayed deaf adolescents to teach expository writing; the teacher performed the task of writing or typing words so students were free to do the thinking and problem-solving (Wolbers, 2007). At the conclusion of an 8-week intervention, post-interviews demonstrated increased student knowledge of higher level writing objectives such as knowing the text structure. Students, at the same time, evidenced significant gains with writing fluency and contextual language. In the comparison group of the same study, students received explicit grammar instruction through which they learned the parts of speech and how to utilize them in sentences; yet they made no gains in lower level skills and had very little exposure to higher level skills. This suggests two things: (a) instruction and learning relative to contextual language use and grammar happens best when situated in real writing contexts, and (b) teachers can provide grade level instruction for higher level objects even though students may be operating at beginning reading and writing stages with lower level skills.

With reading, deaf students similarly tend to struggle more with lower level and text-based skills. Figurative language such as multiple meaning words and idioms are typically difficult for deaf children since there are barriers to hearing these contextualized daily in English conversations (Luetke-Stahlman & Nielsen, 2003). Second, there are sometimes difficulties with establishing an internal decoding system. This is partly due to the inaccessibility of phonology and the inability to rely on sound-based strategies for deciphering text the way most hearing students do (Musselman, 2000). And, as Luckner et al. (2006) state: "Regrettably, many students who are deaf or hard of hearing continue to struggle with lower-level skills, such as word recognition, syntactic parsing, and vocabulary comprehension" (p. 445).

There has traditionally been a similar preoccupation with reading instruction to be structured, skills-based and decontextualized. As a result, deaf students do not often develop reading strategies that will help them to comprehend written text such as summarizing, activating prior knowledge, predicting, making comparisons, visualizing, and monitoring understanding. Limited learning opportunities of higher level skills as well as lower level difficulties (e.g., word identification, parsing sentence patterns) contribute to low reading comprehension among deaf readers (Kelly, 2001, 2003a). Students are more likely to rely on others or say, "I don't know" when asked to draw inferences from their reading (Strassman, 1995). They are more likely to depend on the teacher's assistance when encountering an unfamiliar word in the text (Strassman, 1997). It has been shown that elementary deaf students do not activate as many strategies as hearing students when reading (Schirmer, 2004), and with time, the reading comprehension gap between deaf and hearing readers continues to widen (Munro & Rickards, 1998).

There is research to demonstrate that metacognitive strategy instruction is beneficial in promoting reading gains, yet there is a near absence of problem-solving and metacognition during literacy activity (Marschark, Convertino, & LaRock, 2006; Schirmer, 2001). Cerra, Watts-Taffe, and Rose (1997) propose that it is beneficial to utilize higher level skills and comprehension strategies (e.g., taking a reader stance, drawing from graphic information, using prior knowledge, self-questioning) in the course of using real text. This gets students actively involved in constructing meaning as well as attending to breakdowns in meaning. Yet, teachers of the deaf emphasize basic reading skills instead of developing independent readers and thinkers (Strassman, 1997). As with writing, this is likely in response to students' struggle with lower order skills such as identifying words and ascertaining meaning of particular English syntactical construction which limit access to reading text. Certainly there is need for continued development of decoding, English vocabulary and syntactical skills to provide greater entry into text; however, this does not need to happen at the expense of developing higher level skills. Reading comprehension strategies and learning of story elements, for instance, can be practiced through guided and shared activity with reading while simultaneously incorporating word and grammar study.

Read it again and again, a reading instruction approach developed out of the Laurent Clerc National Deaf Education Center at Gallaudet University, takes this instructional approach. It is a shared reading method whereby a group of students repeatedly visits the same piece of authentic reading material for the purpose of targeting various skills and strategies over time and providing greater familiarity with English text (Schleper, 1998). A story is first delivered to a group of students through ASL. This way students gain immediate access to the story line through a visually-based language representation and the storybook graphics. With this aided entry into the text, there is opportunity for engagement in higher-level reading skills such as predicting happenings, summarizing, asking and answering reading comprehension questions, or inferring meaning. There may be much teacher modeling at first of these higher-level skills, but over time strategies are increasingly appropriated and utilized by students (Strassman, 1997). Then, with additional readings of the text, there is increased study of lower-level skills (e.g., specific English words, phrases and sentences) within the context of a meaningful story.

Guided and shared reading is further a way students can build expressive and receptive vocabulary because there is ample opportunity to link the language of the teacher and classmates with visuals or action (e.g., the story's pictures, the teachers' visual and spatial expressions, or role playing of the story's actions). Such an approach accommodates for students' prior knowledge devoid of language mediation (Paul, 1998). While such a balanced approach seems a promising practice that could provide benefit with language, lower level reading skills and higher level reading skills, further research to evidence student outcomes in comparison to other approaches is necessary.

Metalinguistic approaches to building ASL and English competencies. Among linguistically diverse students and L2 writers, there are differences between skilled and novice writers with respect to translation as well as language competency. Those considered more expert at writing, for instance, compose more quickly and construct longer pieces of text. Advanced writers typically spend double the time planning prior to starting and reread text for high level purposes in addition to low level considerations (Sasaki, 2002). Novice L2 writers, on the other hand, devote more time to translating their generated ideas into English and stop more often to consider issues of translation. These differences likely point to proficiency levels in second discourse ability. Less proficient users of the second language tend to produce better written text (i.e., less orthographic and syntactical errors) when first crafting ideas in their first language and then translating those ideas to L2 (Koutsoubou, Herman, & Woll, 2007). This is contrary to more proficient users of English who carry out the various tasks of writing simultaneously in the L2.

Little is known regarding the language factors influencing deaf children's literacy achievement other than the fact that limited or delayed development of an L1 impacts literacy development. It is not fully evident, for example, the role ASL and EBS play in the development of English literacy skills. In Singleton et al. (2004), young deaf writers with varying proficiencies in ASL (i.e., low, moderate and high) were compared with hearing ESL and monolingual students regarding their vocabulary use. Those students with low-ASL proficiency (i.e., receiving instruction through EBS and the simultaneous use of speech) were significantly more likely than monolinguals to write frequently used words rather than unique words. And, although they did demonstrate an ability to use function words, they did not show much variation in their writing, for they repeatedly relied on the same few function words. Students in the low-ASL proficiency group also exhibited a more limited English repertoire, for they consistently used a narrow set of English forms. This may point to the inability of EBS to serve as a model for written English, or it may indicate that students have yet to develop a complete and complex L1. Students with moderate and high-ASL proficiency shared similar language experiences with the ESL group of students, but they were not comparable in terms of vocabulary. The moderate to high-ASL groups and the monolingual group were found to use similar proportions of frequent and unique words, whereas ESL students incorporated significantly less unique words and more frequently used words. At the same time, high-ASL and moderate-ASL students used the lowest proportion of function words and constructed the shortest pieces of writing. This may indicate that students lacked fluency in English grammar, but encountered few barriers to finding unique English words that represent their meaning.

In a study by Wolbers (2007), she characterizes the ASL and EBS skill of three groups of deaf middle school writers who were involved in her research. The skilled deaf writers (i.e., achieving at or slightly below their hearing peers) were those who had developed ASL as their primary expressive language, yet had an ability to code-switch from ASL to English-based sign when faced with the demands of a situation requiring more English (e.g., writing, conversing with a hearing person who had limited sign knowledge). These students preferred using ASL for class discussions, problem-solving and inquiry because, for them, it provided a fully complex and accessible language through which they could express their ideas clearly and efficiently. However, they automatically switched to EBS when wanting to add phrases or sentences to a co-constructed piece of text. Their expressions in EBS resembled an English syntactical order, so they could be written. Then the students, with guidance from the teacher, collaboratively reworked the text to add the missing English complexities and constructions. This is a comparable finding to that of Mayer (1999) whereby she found students drew on an internalized knowledge of English during composition. What is noteworthy about the group of skilled deaf writers was that students had a fully developed first language (i.e., ASL) and they had an understanding that ASL and English were distinct languages used for different situations and purposes. How students became capable users of EBS and how they learned appropriate code-switching is less apparent.

The middle group—consisting of those approximately 3 to 4 years behind their hearing counterparts in reading—was also proficient with ASL but did not have the same tendency to code-switch to EBS when writing. Some of these children failed to recognize that they were managing two very different languages, and viewed their expressions in ASL as something that could be written. Others knew there were differences but could not identify them. All students in this group inherently struggled with how to capture their ideas in writing, and they experienced barriers with writing fluency. It was also the case with this middle group (of students) that ASL elements surfaced frequently in their writing. And finally in the same study, the lowest group of students (i.e., those at beginning reading and writing stages) were described as exhibiting severe delays in development of a first language.

Because deaf students have very different language experiences and histories, instructional approaches need to vary to be responsive to students' needs. The middle group of students, for instance, showed improved facility of English when distinctions between English and ASL were continually made during the guided co-construction of text (Wolbers, 2007). By the end of an 8-week period, students were more likely to recognize EBS as something different from ASL, and they produced closer approximations of grammatical English.

When considering students who have developed ASL as their primary form of communication (and who do not exhibit language delays in this mode), there are some clear differences yet many similarities with other ESL groups. ASL-proficient students, as noted earlier, incorporate unique vocabulary in their writing similar to their hearing peers whereas ESL students do not. This may point to the fact that ASL users often fingerspell English words, providing direct and contextualized access to English vocabulary in the midst of communicating through their primary language. This may not be the experience of many ESL students. ASL-proficient students with EBS code switching ability are similar to more proficient ESL students in that they can fluently construct ideas while attending to other writing responsibilities. In other words, the writing tasks and work can be conducted fully in the L2. Both populations of writers, however, encounter problems with lower level skill use even though writing, for the most part, is fluent. And, even after years of English use, students still evidence struggles with the mechanics or grammatical features of English (Valdes, 2006), and this is equally true for deaf students.

Increasing students' metalinguistic knowledge is one way to further production and processing of more complex language constructions (Francis, 2006). Metalinguistic approaches involve deliberately making the language systems the object of thought and discussion. Students consciously consider the nature and function of the languages at the word, form and meaning levels and give thought to the patterns of the language (Francis, 2006; Tunmer & Cole, 1985). Teachers have utilized explicit contrastive approaches with linguistically diverse students (Gee, 1996; Wolfram, Adger & Christian, 1999) which may be useful when thinking about deaf students.

Such procedures draw students' attention to the differences between languages and encourage analytic discussion. By overtly juxtaposing languages, Hagemann (2001) claims her linguistically diverse students have begun to recognize the distinct differences that were once not noticeable to them. She uses a three-step process for helping students. First, students learn to notice features of English that are new or different to them. Second, they indicate the comparable feature in their expressive language. Thirdly, the feature is practiced in the context of real language or literacy experiences. An approach such as this helps linguistically diverse students to more easily recognize language particulars (Reyes, 1992; McNaughton, 2000) and use new language constructions.

There is a small amount of research to suggest that metalinguistic approaches used with deaf students can help to develop greater awareness for the language characteristics, patterns and complexities of ASL and English, and this, in turn, leads to enhanced competency with reading and writing. Akamatsu and Armour (1987) found that the writing skills of deaf children improved when they were provided direct instruction with the grammar principles of American Sign Language as well as translation to English. Similarly, a study with college-aged deaf students (Berent et al., 2007) discovered that those students receiving focus-on-form instruction increased their grammatical knowledge of English whereas those receiving conventional instruction did not. Focus-on-form approaches use text enhancement such as bolding or highlighting of particular English grammatical features to draw students' attention to constructions in a piece of authentic and meaningful text. This varies from traditional grammar instruction that involves direct skill instruction and drilling of decontextualized grammar elements.

Berent et al. (2006) further declare that interventions involving focus-on-form are more effective with students when they are given ways to act upon the noticed constructions through, for example, class discussion, exercises or reconstructing/ revising text. Kuiken and Vedder (2002) and Wolbers (2008) evidence how class discussions during collaborative writing can lead to higher quality text produced by linguistically diverse students. The classes engaged in reflections and discussions around the content, the writing process and also the language forms. With respect to ASL-proficient middle school students having little English awareness (i.e., those who do not effectively switch to EBS), class discussions that prompted them to consider which language is being used, what are the associated grammar principles and how to translate has proven effective in increasing English use and fluency (Wolbers, 2007). And Bailes (2001) describes how teachers of the earliest grades find ways to call attention to ASL and English differences, and how they often indicate when they are using ASL and when they are using English. Interaction with others about language can deepen metalinguistic knowledge which leads to greater "noticing" and an increased awareness of linguistic forms. Yet, there are many questions in terms of what are the most effective metalinguistic approaches for various ages and language proficiencies.

Teachers are incredibly important mediators of the metalinguistic knowledge building process. They must have a thorough understanding of the languages to guide students or to model thinking about language and form. In particular, teachers must have the language knowledge necessary to emphasize certain principles or distinguish language rules (Enns, 2006). Therefore, teachers' knowledge is central to the instructional objectives.

As fluent and natural users of either English or ASL as a first language, teachers may not have a linguistic-based or rule-governed understanding of their own language. Take for instance a hearing teacher who uses English as his first language. He is a fluent user of the language but may not be able to explain the reasons behind or rules underlying particular constructions; rather, this teacher, like many, operates on sound-based principles (i.e., what sounds correct in English or seems right). This teacher is not likely to have the necessary instructional tools when, for instance, faced with a deaf student who does not understand the difference between writing "interesting" and "interested." Likewise, there are many teachers of the deaf who have yet to reach proficiency in their second language, whether ASL or English.

Instruction of language is likely constrained by teachers having limitations in their own language abilities (Stewart, 2006). In order for teachers of the deaf to be responsive to students' specific language and literacy needs, they must have a thorough understanding of the students' expressive language as well as English principles. Preservice and inservice teachers, for instance, need access to programs that provide extensive instruction in the linguistics and the contrastive features of English and ASL. Future research might investigate approaches that effectively build teachers' knowledge of their L1 and L2, and the impact this has on their students.

Rereading to develop automaticity with English. Repeatedly reading the same text has been one way to increase reading speed among hearing children. Reading speed and automaticity with decoding text impacts one's ability to attend to the meaning of text, for there is a theoretical relationship between reading fluency and comprehension (Meyer & Felton, 1999). When one's working memory is taxed with word recognition processes, there is less ability to attend to higher level reading skills such as predicting, applying prior knowledge, and monitoring one's comprehension. Studies on fluency with hearing children note that

repeated readings can increase one's reading rate, accuracy, and comprehension.

Many deaf students do not yet operate with automaticity of lexicon or English syntax (Mayer, 1999; Powers & Wigus, 1983). To reiterate, there are language delays that often result in later vocabulary and complex grammar development of a primary language; these delays, whether with English or ASL, have an impact on literacy development. Second, for those developing ASL as their first language, there is a lack of parallel language features and knowledge that can be transferred from one's primary language to reading and writing in English.

Word recognition skills are severely hampered if one has yet to develop an effective internal decoding system. As a sound-based decoding system utilizing phonological knowledge is often not fully accessible to the deaf (Perfetti & Sandak, 2000) and as there is currently little understanding of alternative systems used by successful deaf readers (Leybaert & Lechat, 2001), teachers struggle with how to teach students to decode. And, when students struggle to identify words in a piece of text, reading is slowed considerably (Kelly, 2003a). Additionally problematic for deaf students is text that has more complex English sentences (e.g., greater number of relative clauses); this likewise hinders reading automaticity among the deaf (Kelly, 1995, 2003b). With repeated readings, however, deaf students can gain greater automaticity with reading (Ensor & Koller, 1997) and likely develop greater syntactic competence with English (Kelly, 1995). In fact, less skilled readers who increase automaticity with repeated readings can perform similarly to the more skilled readers (Kelly, 2003b).

In practice, Enns and Lafond (2007) have utilized daily repeated readings to help students ascertain a greater vocabulary and grow in confidence when reading text. Additionally, Pakulski and Kaderavek (2001) implemented repeated readings of stories in conjunction with role playing and found that there was a significant impact on students' story grammar scores. Thus, repeated readings have potential to not only improve lower level reading skills but could simultaneously or subsequently impact higher level skills.

When rereading has been incorporated in guided and shared writing, benefits have also been noted (Wolbers, 2007, 2008). During the co-construction of text, group rereading was prompted frequently by the teacher for the purpose of reviewing and revising text. By doing this, the teacher was apprenticing students to engage in monitoring their writing for meaning making, a writing process of skilled writers. Students, over time, evidenced greater competence with noticing problematic parts of the text, as well as revising and editing both lower and higher level writing. Additionally, the intervention had an impact on reading ability, for both studies demonstrated there was a significant gain from pre to posttest. Some of the students with the lowest reading levels (i.e., based on word identification ability) at the start gained an entire grade level in an 8-week period (Wolbers, 2007). A writing intervention that produces simultaneous reading gains may point to the fact that reading and writing share commonalities with respect to kinds of knowledge and processes (Fitzgerald & Shanahan, 2000). And, even when composing text, writers are frequently engaged in reading. Rereading for the purpose of revising, for instance, can lead to greater automaticity with word identification skills.

One area in need of further research is the impact of rereading on one's familiarity with English syntax and grammar. It may be that repeated readings help deaf students become more comfortable with the flow of the language, just as hearing students operate on a sense of "what sounds right" when constructing and revising text. There are some English constructions that do not have clear grammatical rules that can be explained or explicitly taught to students (e.g., selection of prepositions), and there are many exceptions to the rules. For this reason, it is inconceivable for all aspects of the English language to be taught; rather, repeatedly reading text or increased independent reading may be ways for students to pick up on the patterns and the rhythm of the language.

Conclusion

This chapter has discussed the need for specialized literacy instruction with deaf children who have significant hearing losses and do not readily acquire spoken English as their hearing or hard of hearing peers. This subpopulation of learners, in particular, has unique language experiences that impact literacy development. This chapter highlights two considerations: the occurrence of mild to severe language delays with a primary language and the case of having an expressive language based on visual and spatial grammar aspects. There was an attempt to synthesize the deaf education research that responds to these particular characteristics; however, there is a dearth of empirically based research from which methods of instruction can be convincingly drawn. Therefore, several approaches having likely or conjectured advantages have been recommended for further research. One suggestion to immediately accommodate for the lack of vetted practices in the field of deaf education is that practitioners and researchers alike move beyond the confines of deaf education and become well-versed in effective language and literacy practices used with other populations of students (i.e., general education students, struggling readers and writers, linguistically diverse students and L2 students, special education students). Whereas there are indeed significant challenges for the deaf that do not exist for others, it can be argued that there are more similarities than differences. Deaf education professionals are encouraged to apply their specialized knowledge to adapt and modify existing instructional interventions in ways that better suit the needs of deaf learners instead of discounting their applicability. With action research in the classroom by teachers and continued university-led research, we can continue to expand on successful approaches.

Notes

1. "Deaf" is intentionally capitalized to indicate a prideful and empowered subpopulation of persons who are culturally and linguistically affiliated. When lowercase, it connotes persons with hearing loss that may or may not have cultural ties to the Deaf community.
2. ASL classifiers are used to represent action as well as placement of persons or things (Schein & Stewart, 1999).

References

Albertini, J. (1996). *Classroom assessment of writing: Purpose, issues, and strategies.* Knoxville, TN. (ERIC Document Reproduction Service No. ED423620)

Akamatsu, C. T., & Armour, V. A. (1987). Developing written literacy in deaf children through analyzing sign language. *American Annals of the Deaf, 132*(1), 46–51.

Al-Hilawani, Y. A. (2003). Clinical examination of three methods of teaching reading comprehension to deaf and hard-of-hearing students: from research to classroom applications. *Journal of Deaf Studies and Deaf Education, 8*(2), 146–156.

Andrews, S., Creaghead, N, Kretschmer, L. & Weiler, E. (1995). *Hearing impaired children's retelling of stories following presentation in whole-class and individual contexts.* Tel Aviv, Israel: International Congress on Education of the Deaf. (ERIC Document Reproduction Service No. ED389145)

Antia, S. D., Reed, S., & Kreimeyer, K. H. (2005). Written language of deaf and hard-of-hearing students in public schools. *Journal of Deaf Studies and Deaf Education, 10*(3), 244–255.

Applebee, A. N. (2000). Alternative models of writing development. In R. Indrisano & J. Squire (Eds.). *Perspectives on writing: Research, theory and practice* (pp. 90–110). Newark, Delaware: International Reading Association.

Bailes, C. (2001). Integrative ASL-English language arts: Bridging paths to literacy. *Sign Language Studies, 1*(2), 147–174.

Bereiter, C. (1980). Development in writing. In Gregg, L.Q. & Steinberg, E.R. (Eds.). *Cognitive processes in writing* (pp. 73–93). Mahwah, NJ: Erlbaum.

Berent, G., Kelly, R., Aldersley, S., Schmitz, K., Khalsa, B., Panara, J., et al. (2007). Focus-on-form instructional methods promote deaf college students' improvement in English grammar. *Journal of Deaf Studies and Deaf Education, 12*(1), 8–24.

Burbules, N. (1993). *Dialogue in teaching.* New York: Teachers College Press.

Calderon, R. (2000). Parental involvement in deaf children's education programs as a predictor of child's language, early reading, and social-emotional development. *Journal of Deaf Studies and Deaf Education, 5*(2), 140–155.

Calkins, L (1986) *The art of teaching writing.* Portsmouth, NH: Heinemann.

Cazden, C. B. (2001). *Classroom discourse: The language of teaching and learning* (2nd ed.). Portsmouth, NH: Heinemann.

Cerra, K. K., Watts-Taffe, S., & Rose, S. (1997). Fostering reader response and developing comprehension strategies in deaf and hard of hearing children. *American Annals of the Deaf, 142*, 379–386.

Craig, W. N., Carr, T., & Latham, I. J. (1964). Comparison of two methods of teaching written language to deaf students. *American Annals of the Deaf, 109*(2), 248–256.

Coleman, C. F. (1997). Our students write with accents. Oral paradigms for ESD students. *College Composition and Communication, 48*(4), 486–500.

Delpit, L. (1986). Skills and other dilemmas of a progressive black educator. *Harvard Educational Review, 56*, 379–385.

Delpit, L. (1988). The silenced dialogue: Power and pedagogy in educating other people's children. *Harvard Educational Review, 58*, 280–298.

Easterbrooks, S. R. & Baker, S. (2002). *Language learning in children who are deaf and hard of hearing: Multiple pathways.* Boston: Allyn and Bacon.

Easterbrooks, S. R. (2005). *Review of the literature in literacy development and instruction in students who are deaf and hard of hearing.* Retrieved April 28, 2008, from: www.deafed.net/activities/JoinTogether/Obj2_2LitRevLiteracy.doc

Enns, C. J. (2006). *A language and literacy framework for bilingual deaf education.* Self-published report. Winnipeg, MB: University of Manitoba.

Enns, C., & Lafond, L. (2007). Reading against all odds: A pilot study of two deaf students with dyslexia. *American Annals of the Deaf, 152*(1), 63–72.

Ensor, A D., & Koller, J. R. (1997). The effect of the method of repeated readings on the reading rate and word recognition accuracy of deaf adolescents. *Journal of Deaf Studies and Deaf Education, 2*(2), 61–70.

Fernandes, J. (2003). In search of keys to English print. *Odyssey, 5*(1), 4–5.

Ferris, D. & Roberts, B. (2006). Error feedback in L2 writing classes: How explicit does it need to be? In P. K. Matsuda, M. Cox, J. Jordan, & C. Ortmeier-Hooper (Eds.), *Second-language writing in the composition classroom: A critical resource* (pp. 380–402). New York: Bedford/St. Martin's.

Fischer, S. D. (1998). Critical periods for language acquisition: Consequences for deaf education. In A. Weisel (Ed.), *Issues Unresolved: New Perspectives on Language and Deaf Education* (pp. 9–26). Washington, DC: Gallaudet University Press.

Fitzgerald, J., & Shanahan, T. (2000). Reading and writing relations and their development. *Educational Psychologist, 35*(1), 39–50.

Francis, N. (2006). The development of secondary discourse ability and metalinguistic awareness in second language learners. *International Journal of Applied Linguistics, 16*(1), 37–60.

French, M. M. (1999). *Planning for literacy instruction: Guidelines for instruction. Sharing ideas.* Washington, DC: Laurent Clerc National Deaf Education Center. (ERIC Document Reproduction Service No. ED ED475330)

Fung, P., Chow, B., & McBride-Chang, C. (2005). The impact of a dialogic reading program on deaf and hard-of-hearing kindergarten and early primary school-aged students in Hong Kong. *Journal of Deaf Studies and Deaf Education, 10*(1), 82-95.

Gallaudet Research Institute. (2003, October 30). *Literacy and deaf students.* Retrieved August 17, 2005, from http://gri.gallaudet.edu/Literacy/index.html

Gee, J. P. (1991). What is literacy? In C. Mitchell & K. Weiler (Eds.), *Rewriting literacy: Culture and the discourse of the other* (pp. 3–11). New York: Bergin & Garvey.

Gee, J. P. (1996). *Social linguistics and literacies: Ideology in discourses* (2nd ed.). Philadelphia: The Falmer Press.

Gilbertson, D., & Ferre, S. (2008). Considerations in the identification, assessment, and intervention process for deaf and hard of hearing students with reading difficulties. *Psychology in the Schools, 45*(2), 104–120.

Gioia, B., Johnston, P., & Cooper, L.S. (2001). Documenting and developing literacy in deaf children. *Literacy, Teaching, and Learning: An International Journal of Early Reading and Writing, 6*(1), 1–22.

Gormely, K., & Sarachan-Deily, A.B. (1987). Evaluating hearing-impaired students' writing: A practical approach. *The Volta Review, 89*, 157–166.

Hagemann, J. (2001). A bridge from home to school: Helping working class students acquire school literacy. *English Journal, 90*(4), 74–81.

Hargrave, A. C., & Senechal, M. (2000). A book reading intervention with preschool children who have limited vocabularies: The benefits of regular reading and dialogic reading. *Early Childhood Research Quarterly, 15*(1), 75–90.

Harrison, D. R., Simpson, P. A., & Stuart, A. (1991). The development of written language in a population of hearing-impaired children. *The Journal of the British Association of Teachers of the Deaf, 15*, 76–85.

Heider, F., & Heider, G. M. (1941). Comparison of sentence structure of deaf and hearing children. *The Volta Review, 43*, 357–360.

Hillocks, G. (1984). What works in teaching composition: A meta-analysis of experimental treatment studies. *American Journal of Education, 93*(1), 133–170.

Hillocks, G. (2002). *The testing trap: How state assessments control learning.* New York: Teachers College Press.

Izzo, A. (2002). Phonemic awareness and reading ability: An investigation with young readers who are deaf. *American Annals of the Deaf, 147*(4), 18–28.

Jackendoff, R. (1994). *Patterns in the mind.* New York Basic Books.

Johnson, D. M. (1994). Grouping strategies for second language learners. In F. Genesee (Ed.), *Educating second language children: The whole child, the whole curriculum, the whole community.* (pp. 183–211). New York: Cambridge University Press.

Johnson, M. A., & Roberson, G. F. (1988). The language experience approach: Its use with young hearing-impaired students. *American Annals of the Deaf, 133*(3), 223–225.

Kelly, L. (1995). Syntax, vocabulary and comprehension. *Perspectives in Education and Deafness. 13*(3), 16–19.

Kelly, L. P. (2001). The importance of processing automaticity and temporary storage capacity to the difference in comprehension between skilled and less skilled college-age deaf readers. *Journal of Deaf Studies and Deaf Education, 8*(3), 230–249.

Kelly, L. P. (2003a). Considerations for designing practices for deaf readers. *Journal of Deaf Studies and Deaf Education, 8*(2), 171–185.

Kelly, L. P. (2003b). The importance of processing automaticity and temporary storage capacity to the differences in comprehension between skilled and less-skilled college-age deaf readers. *Journal of Deaf Studies and Deaf Education, 8*(3), 230–249.

Kelly, L. P., & Barac-Cikoja, D. (2007). The comprehension of skilled deaf readers: The roles of word recognition and potentially critical aspects of competence. In K. Cain and J. Oakhill (Eds.), *Children's comprehension problems in oral and written language: A cognitive perspective* (pp. 244–280). New York: Guilford.

Klecan-Aker, J., & Blondeau, R. (1990). An examination of the written stories of hearing-impaired school-age children. *The Volta Review, 92*, 275–282.

Kluwin, T. N., & Kelly, A. B. (1992). Implementing a successful writing program in public schools for students who are deaf. *Exceptional Children, 59*(1), 41–53.

Koutsoubou, M., Herman, R., & Woll, B. (2007). Does language input matter in bilingual writing? Translation versus direct composition in deaf school students' written stories. *International Journal of Bilingual Education and Bilingualism, 10*(2), 127–151.

Kuiken, F., & Vedder, I. (2002). Collaborative writing in L2: The effect of group interaction on text quality. In S. Ransdell & M. Barbier (Eds.), *New directions for research in L2 writing* (pp. 168–188). Boston: Kluwer.

Larney, R. (2002). The relationship between early language delay and later difficulties in literacy. *Early Child Development and Care, 172*(2), 183–193.

Lederberg, A. R., & Spencer, P. E. (2001). Vocabulary development of deaf and hard of hearing children. In M. D. Clark, M. Marschark, & M. Karchmer (Eds.), *Context, cognition, and deafness* (pp. 88–112). Washington, DC: Gallaudet University Press.

Leybaert, J., & Lechat, J. (2001). Variability in deaf children's spelling: The effect of language experience. *Journal of Educational Psychology, 93*(3), 554–562.

Loeterman, M., Paul, P. V., & Donahue, S. (2002). Reading and deaf children. *Reading Online, 5*(6). Retrieved from http://www.readingonline.org/articles/art_index.asp?HREF=loeterman/index.html

Luckner, J., Sebald, A., Cooney, J., Young, J., & Muir, S.G. (2006). An examination of the evidence-based literacy research in deaf education. *American Annals of the Deaf, 150*(5), 443–456.

Luetke-Stahlman, B. (1993). Research-based language intervention strategies adapted for deaf and hard of hearing children. *American Annals of the Deaf, 138*(5), 404–410.

Luetke-Stahlman, B., & Nielsen, D. C. (2003). The contribution of phonological awareness and receptive and expressive English to the reading ability of deaf students with varying degrees of exposure to accurate English. *Journal of Deaf Studies and Deaf Education, 8*(4), 464–484

Marschark, M. (2001). *Language development in children who are deaf: A research synthesis.* Alexandria, VA: National Association of State Directors of Special Education. ERIC ED 455620.

Marschark, M., Convertino, C., & LaRock, D. (2006). Optimizing academic performance of deaf students: Access, opportunities, and outcomes. In D. F. Moores & D. S. Martin (Eds.), *Deaf learners: New developments in curriculum and instruction* (pp. 179–200). Washington, DC: Gallaudet University Press.

Mayer, C. & Wells, G. (1996). Can the linguistic interdependence theory support a bilingual-bicultural model of literacy education for deaf students? *Journal of Deaf Studies and Deaf Education, 1,* 93–107.

Mayer, C. (1999). Shaping at the point of utterance: An investigation of the composing processes of the deaf student writer. *Journal of Deaf Studies and Deaf Education, 4*(1), 37–49.

Mayer, C., & Akamatsu, T. (1999). Bilingual-bicultural models of literacy education for deaf students: Considering the claims. *Journal of Deaf Studies and Deaf Education, 4*(1), 1–8.

Mayer, C., Akamatsu, C. T., & Stewart, D. (2002). A model for effective practice: Dialogic inquiry with students who are deaf. *Exceptional children, 68*(4), 485–502.

McAnally, P. L., Rose, S., & Quigley, S. P. (1994). *Language learning practices with deaf children* (2nd ed.). Austin, TX: Pro-Ed.

McAnally, P., Rose, S., & Quigley, S. (1999). *Reading practices with deaf learners.* Austin, TX: PRO-ED.

McNaughton, S. (2002). *Meeting of the minds.* Wellington, New Zealand: Learning Media Limited.

Mehan, H. (1979). *Learning lessons: Social organization in the classroom.* Cambridge, MA: Harvard University Press.

Meyer, M. & Felton, R. (1999). Repeated reading to enhance fluency: Old approaches and new directions. *Annals of Dyslexia, 49,* 283–306.

Moores, D. F., & Miller, M. S. (2001). Literacy Publications: American Annals of the Deaf 1996 to 2000. *American Annals of the Deaf, 146*(2), 77–80.

Munro, J., & Rickards, F. W. (1998). Literal and inferential reading comprehension of students who are deaf or hard of hearing. *Volta Review, 100,* 87–104.

Musselman, C. (2000). How do children who can't hear read an alphabetic script? A review of the literature on reading and deafness. *Journal of Deaf Studies and Deaf Education, 5,* 9–31.

Musselman, C. & Szanto, G. (1998). The written language of deaf adolescents: Patterns of performance. *Journal of Deaf Studies and Deaf Education, 3,* 245–257.

National Center for Birth Defects and Developmental Disabilities, Early Hearing Detection and Intervention Program. (2005). National EDHI goals. Retrieved August 23, 2006, from http://www.cdc.gov/ncbddd/ehdi/nationalgoals.htm

Nippold, M.A. (2007). *Later language development: School-age children, adolescents, and young adults* (3rd ed.). Austin: PRO-ED.

Nystrand, M. (1997). *Opening dialogue: Understanding the dynamics of language and learning in the English classroom.* New York: Teachers College Press.

Pakulski, L. A., & Kaderavek, J. N. (2001). Narrative production by children who are deaf or hard of hearing: The effect of role play. *Volta Review, 103,* 127–139.

Palincsar, A. S., & Brown, A. L. (1984). Reciprocal teaching of comprehension-fostering and comprehension-monitoring activities. *Cognition and Instruction, 1,* 117–175.

Paul, P. (1998). *Literacy and deafness: The development of reading, writing and literate thought.* Boston: Allyn and Bacon.

Perfetti, C. A. & Sandak, R. (2000). Reading optimally builds on spoken language: Implications for deaf readers. *Journal of Deaf Studies and Deaf Education, 5,* 32–50.

Powers, A. R., & Wigus, S. (1983). Linguistic complexity in the written language of hearing-impaired children. *Volta Review, 85*(4), 201–210.

Pressley, M. Graham, S. & Harris, K. (2005). The state of educational intervention research as viewed through the lens on literacy intervention. *British Journal of Educational Psychology, 76*(1), 1–19.

Pressley, M. (2005). *Reading instruction that works: The case for balanced teaching* (3rd ed). New York: Guilford.

Reyes, M. de la Luz (1992). Challenging venerable assumptions: Literacy instruction for linguistically different students. *Harvard Educational Review, 62*(4), 427–446.

Sasaki, M. (2002). Building an empirically-based model of EFL learners' writing processes. In S. Ransdell & M. Barbier (Eds.), *New directions for research in L2 writing* (pp. 49–80). Boston: Kluwer.

Schein, J. & Stewart, D. (1999). *Language in motion.* Washington, DC: Gallaudet University Press.

Schlesinger, H. (1988). Questions and answers in the development of deaf children. In M. Strong (Ed.), *Language, learning, deafness* (pp. 261–291). Cambridge, UK: Cambridge University Press.

Schirmer, B. (2001). Using research to improve literacy practice and practice to improve literacy research. *Journal of Deaf Studies and Deaf Education, 6*(2), 83–91.

Schirmer, B. R. (2004).What verbal protocols reveal about the reading strategies of deaf students: A replication study. *American Annals of the Deaf, 149,* 5–16.

Schleper, D. R. (1998). *Read it again and again.* Washington, D.C.: Gallaudet University Press.

Schneiderman, E. (1995). The effectiveness of an interactive instructional context. *American Annals of the Deaf, 140,* 8–15.

Schoenfeld, A. H. (2002). A highly interactive discourse structure. *Social Constructivist Teaching, 9,* 131–169.

Siegel, L. (2000). The educational and communication needs of deaf and hard of hearing children: A statement of principle on fundamental educational change. *American Annals of the Deaf, 145*(2), 64–77.

Singleton, J. L., Morgan, D., DiGello, E., Wiles, J., & Rivers, R. (2004). Vocabulary use by low, moderate, and high ASL-proficient writers compared to hearing ESL and monolingual speakers. *Journal of Deaf Studies and Deaf Education, 9*(1), 86–103.

Stahl, K. D., & Miller, P. D. (2006). Whole language and language experience approaches for beginning reading: A quantitative research synthesis. In K. A. D. Stahl & M. C. McKenna (Eds.) *Reading research at work: Foundations of effective practice* (pp. 9–35). New York: Guilford.

Stauffer, R. G. (1979). The language experience approach to reading instruction for deaf and hearing impaired children. *The Reading Teacher, 33*(1), 21–24.

Stewart, D. (2006). Instructional and practical communication: ASL and English-based signing in the classroom. In D. F. Moores & D. S. Martin (Eds.), *Deaf learners: New developments in curriculum and instruction* (pp. 207–220). Washington, DC: Gallaudet University Press.

Stokoe, W.C. (1978). *Sign language structure.* (ERIC Document Reproduction Service No. ED189874)

Strassman, B. K. (1995, July). *Metacognition and Reading in Children Who Are Deaf: A Review of the Research.* Paper presented at the meeting of the International Congress on Education of the Deaf, Tel Aviv, Israel.

Strassman, B. K. (1997). Metacognition and reading in children who are deaf: A review of the research. *Journal of Deaf Studies and Deaf Education, 2,* 140–149.

Taeschner, T. (1988). Affixes and function words in the written language of deaf children. *Applied Psycholinguistics, 9*(4), 385–401.

Tunmer, W. E., & Cole, P. G. (1985). Learning to read: A metalinguistic act. In C. S. Simon (Ed.), *Communication skills and classroom success. Therapy methodologies for language-learning disabled students* (pp. 293–312) London: Taylor and Francis.

Tye-Murray, N. (1994). *Let's converse: A "how-to" guide to develop and expand conversational skills of children and teenagers who are hearing impaired.* Washington, DC: Alexander Graham Bell Association for the Deaf.

Valdes, G. (2006). Bilingual minorities and language issues in writing: Toward professionwide responses to a new challenge. In P. K. Matsuda, M. Cox, J. Jordan, & C. Ortmeier-Hooper (Eds.), *Second-language writing in the composition classroom: A critical resource* (pp. 31–70). New York: Bedford/St.Martin's.

Walker, L.. Munro, J., & Richards, F. W. (1998).Teaching inferential reading strategies through pictures. *Volta Review, 100*(2), 105–120.

Ward, I. (1994). *Literacy ideology, and dialogue: Towards a dialogic pedagogy.* Albany, NY: State University of New York Press.

Wilson, T., & Hyde, M. (1997). The use of signed English pictures to facilitate reading comprehension by deaf students. *American Annals of the Deaf, 142,* 333–341.

Wolbers, K. (2005). [Personal narrative writing sample]. Unpublished raw data.

Wolbers, K. (2007). Strategic and Interactive Writing Instruction (SIWI): Apprenticing deaf students in the construction of informative texts (Doctoral dissertation, Michigan State University). *Dissertation Abstracts International, 68,* 09A.

Wolbers, K. (2008). Using balanced and interactive writing instruction to improve the higher order and lower order writing skills of deaf students. *Journal of Deaf Studies and Deaf Education, 13*(2), 257–277.

Wolfram, W., Adger, C. T., & Christian, D. (1999). *Dialects in schools and communities.* Mahwah, NJ: Erlbaum.

Yoshinaga-Itano, C., & Snyder, L. (1985). Form and meaning in the written language of hearing-impaired children. *Volta Review, 87*(5), 75–90.

Yoshinaga-Itano, C., Snyder, L. S. & Mayberry, R. (1996). How deaf and normally hearing students convey meaning within and between written sentences. *Volta Review, 98*(1), 9–38.

Part VI

Studying Reading Disabilities

EDITORS: WILLIAM RUPLEY AND VICTOR L. WILLSON

35

Teacher Research on Reading Difficulties

JAMES F. BAUMANN
University of Missouri–Columbia

T. LEE WILLIAMS
Auburn University

Teacher research can make an important contribution to the field of literacy by providing rich, layered studies that investigate topics to inform instruction and make an impact on student achievement. (Lenski, 2008, p. 182)

Introduction

Historically, teacher research has not been valued within the academic community (Anderson & Herr, 1999), and thus there are few, if any, references to it in reviews of reading research (e.g., Barr, Kamil, Mosenthal, Pearson, 1991; National Reading Panel, 2000; Pearson, Barr, Kamil, & Mosenthal,1984; Snow, Burns, & Griffin, 1998). Although there has been more acknowledgement of the value of teacher research by its inclusion in recent research syntheses (e.g., Baumann & Duffy-Hester, 2000; Cochran-Smith & Donnell, 2006; Fecho, Allen, Mazaros, & Inyega, 2006; Lytle, 2000; Zeichner & Noffke, 2001), the research that still really counts in shaping educational policy is the NCLB-endorsed *scientifically based reading research* (Allington, 2002; Cunningham, 2001; Woodside-Jiron, 2003), which typically excludes teacher research (Allen & Shockley, 1996). Thus, teacher research may not often influence decisions about reading instruction within Congress, state houses, or school district offices. Is teacher research, therefore, ineffectual in influencing reading instructional practices in schools and classrooms? Is Lenski (2008) wrong in arguing that "teacher research can make an important contribution to the field of literacy" (p. 182)? We think not.

Teacher research has a long and rich history (Baumann, Shockley-Bisplinghoff, & Allen, 1997; McFarland & Stansell, 1993; Olson, 1990), and teacher research has and does "inform instruction and make an impact on student achievement" (Lenski, 2008, p. 182) through its widespread dissemination. The literature is filled with compendia of teacher research (e.g., Cochran-Smith & Lytle, 1993), books written by teachers reporting their research (e.g., Hankins, 2003), teacher-authored articles in widely read professional journals (e.g., Picard, 2005), and materials addressing the teacher-research process and methodologies (e.g., Lankshear & Knoble, 2004). Furthermore, the online community has been a mainstay for reporting, discussing, and using teacher research (e.g., Ontario Action Researcher, 2008). Thus, teacher research has had a significant presence in the practitioner world; it just may not be noticed or viewed as informative by reading researchers and policy makers.

It is the purpose of this chapter to review select examples of teacher-research studies on reading difficulties in order to demonstrate how teacher research can deepen our understanding of students who struggle to read. We begin with a definition of teacher research and then present our framework for selecting the studies we feature. Next, we review three teacher-research studies that address the framework and various dimensions of reading difficulties, commenting on how the results can inform practice. We then discuss our findings and conclude with our reflections on the place of teacher research within the scholarship on reading difficulties.

Definition of Teacher Research

Definitions of teacher research vary, but most characterize it as including (a) an insider, or *emic*, perspective; (b) a participant role of the teacher in the research; (c) a mixing of theory and practice, or *praxis*; (d) a pragmatic, action-oriented research process; and (e) a systematic, intentional plan for gathering and analyzing data (see Baumann & Duffy-Hester, 2000, p. 78). For this review, we select the following definition of teacher research, which is adapted from the work of Lytle and Cochran-Smith (1994, p. 1154). Specifically, *teacher research is reflection and action through systematic, intentional inquiry about classroom life* (Baumann et al., 1997, p. 125).

Study Selection Framework and Reading Difficulties Defined

The editors asked us to identify a limited number of teacher-research studies that illustrate different dimensions of reading difficulties. We reviewed various conceptualizations of reading and reading difficulties (e.g., Klenk & Kibby, 2000; Ruddell & Unrau, 2004a). We found the perspectives by Lipson and Wixson (1986; Wixson & Lipson, 1991) and Spear-Swerling and Sternberg (1996) as being especially informative in that they viewed reading ability (or disability) as an interaction among various cognitive, social, motivational, and instructional variables. Alexander and Fox's (2004) description of information processing, sociocultural, and engagement eras in our field was instructive, as was Ruddell and Unrau's (2004b) sociocognitive view of reading as an interaction among texts, readers, and teachers.

We synthesized these theoretical perspectives into a framework that situates sociocultural, cognitive, and motivational dimensions of reading within the instructional context (see Figure 35.1). From this framework, *we define reading difficulty as any sociocultural, cognitive, or motivational factor (or combination of factors) that inhibits a student from realizing her or his full potential to decode, understand, respond to, learn from, and appreciate written text.*

Working from this definition and framework, we identified three teacher-research studies that represent dimensions of the framework and definition: (a) Allen, Michalove, and Shockley's (1993) study of struggling first-to-third-grade children, which is placed primarily within the sociocultural dimension of the framework; (b) Cone's (1994) study of high school seniors who were limited by their self-perceptions as readers, which addresses the mo-

tivational component, and (c) Baumann and Ivey's (1997) study of struggling second-grade readers, which resides mostly within the cognitive domain. It is important to note, however, that the three studies do not align with a *single* dimension only. For example, Allen et al. explored the relationship between multiple social and cultural factors and the literacy learning of the diverse children. However, there were motivational aspects of their curriculum and instruction that were relevant, and their program also addressed cognitive aspects of the students' literacy development. Therefore, the Allen et al. study overlaps somewhat with the motivational and cognitive dimensions in Figure 35.1. This overlapping relationship applies also to the two other studies.

Illustrative Teacher-Research Studies

Allen, Michalove, and Shockley (1993): Challenges for Six Beginning Readers

Study description. This study was a collaboration of a university professor, JoBeth Allen, and two classroom teachers, Barbara Michalove (second grade) and Betty Shockley (first grade). The researchers explored the literacy development of six children (three students each from Betty's and Barbara's classrooms) for 3 years as the children progressed through whole language literacy environments in the two teacher-researchers' classrooms and then on to less holistic third- and fourth-grade environments.

One could characterize the study methodologically as a longitudinal, participant-observer, qualitative, multiple-case-study of at-risk children in whole language classrooms within a school serving low-income, minority (mostly African American) children. The researchers, however, eschewed the *at-risk* label and conventional research meth-

Figure 35.1 Framework for selecting teacher-research studies on reading difficulties.

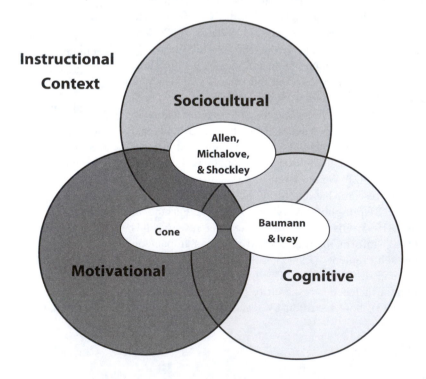

odology terminology, instead referred to their inquiry as a study of children about whose literacy development they were worried: "We were enthusiastic about documenting the long-term effects of whole language instruction, of a stable instructional philosophy and familiar learning structures, on children whose early school experiences had been less than successful" (Allen et al., 1993, p. 5).

Data sources included student interviews, written work, and reading records (a form of reading miscue analysis); interviews with parents and other teachers; and narratives and journals kept by each researcher. The researchers engaged in a recursive but evolving data analysis process that involved face-to-face meetings; discussions of analytic notes; and the composition of narratives of the developing cases. All six cases were reported in the book *Engaging Children: Community and Chaos in the Lives of Young Literacy Learners*.

Findings. The stories of the six children were as diverse as the children themselves. To demonstrate some of that variation, we describe two of the six children: Jeremiah and Joseph.

Jeremiah, who repeated first grade in Betty's classroom, worried Betty right from the beginning of the school year. Although he had some reading knowledge and skills from the prior year, he struggled with writing, working independently, and interacting with peers. At the end of Jeremiah's year in her classroom, Betty wrote: "I hope Jeremiah's story will have a happy ending. But just like the James Marshall books he loved, there are still many more chapters to be written" (Allen et al., 1993, p. 83).

Jeremiah continued to have difficulties in interpersonal relationships in Barbara's second-grade class, which limited his literacy development in that he had difficulty collaborating with students and moving toward full membership in the second-grade literacy club (Smith, 1988). However, Jeremiah's growing interest in reading and writing plays provided a means for him to engage in literacy successfully with others in class. Barbara indicated that Jeremiah could read the second-grade basal reader and pass the basal tests, but his difficulty collaborating with other children and sustaining attention during writing workshop led Barbara and JoBeth to underestimate his writing development: When they examined Jeremiah's portfolio across the year, they saw considerable growth that was not evident because "his behavior difficulties overshadowed his academic performance" (Allen et al., 1993, p. 89).

For third grade, Jeremiah moved to a school in which the curriculum was "textbook-driven" (Allen et al., 1993, p. 99) rather than based on whole language philosophy. JoBeth interviewed Jeremiah's third-grade teacher several times and conducted several reading assessments. Although JoBeth found that Jeremiah could read third- to fourth-grade texts with reasonable fluency and comprehension, his teacher reported borderline performance on the same texts and difficulties on group standardized and state competency tests. Jeremiah's third-grade teacher recommended that he repeat third grade, resulting in a second repetition in Grades K–3.

At the conclusion of Jeremiah's case, the researchers wrote, "Jeremiah failed"—academically, socially, and in receiving support from home—but "most of all, Jeremiah failed to convince the school that he was trying" (Allen et al., 1993, p. 90), particularly in his third-grade year. The researchers wondered whether more time in a holistic environment would have enabled Jeremiah to make a successful transition to a more traditional textbook-based curriculum.

Like Jeremiah, Joseph came to Betty's first-grade classroom with 2 years in kindergarten, the second one in a special-needs classroom intended to accommodate his "mildly mentally handicapped and behavior disordered" (p. 41) status. Joseph's reputation of being a "hoodlum" preceded him, and Betty observed disruptive behaviors on the playground and in the classroom. However, Betty's efforts to understand and accommodate Joseph's moods enabled him to participate productively in writing workshop and to read books in an emergent manner.

Joseph's outbursts continued to interfere with his learning, but gradually Joseph became a member of the classroom literacy community. He began to pronounce and identify words by writing and reading his own texts (a kind of language experience approach), and he was subsequently able to read the primer level of the basal reader. Following psychological retesting, he no longer qualified for "mildly mentally handicapped" services, although he retained his "behavior disorder" status.

When Joseph moved to Barbara's second-grade class, he accelerated his literacy learning and "grew in leaps and bounds" (p. 63). His compositions became more elaborate, and he could read the first second-grade reader by the end of the school year. Barbara noted that "Joseph's progress in reading sneaked up on me" (Allen et al., 1993, p. 63), as demonstrated when he read *Curious George* fluently, after which Barbara commented, "I think we were both surprised" (p. 63). Joseph still had occasional outbursts, and he went to the special education classroom several times a week, but he matured both socially and academically.

Joseph's family moved three times during second grade, but he remained in Barbara's classroom, providing him consistency and stability. Joseph began third grade at Walnut Street School, but then he moved to two different schools, where he reverted to old behaviors. Joseph returned to Walnut Street School in April, and he readjusted quickly to this comfortable environment. In fact, his third-grade teacher at Walnut stated that "He can read—he's a good reader. He outshines the other readers in [his basal group]. ... It amazes me that his behavior was ever a problem.... Joseph isn't BD [behavior disordered]" (Allen et al., 1993, p. 68).

Implications. What does the Allen et al. (1993) study suggest about teaching children with reading difficulties? One clear theme in the two cases we reviewed, as well as others in *Engaging Children*, is that students learned to read as they learned to write. The symbiotic, mutually reinforcing relationship between reading and writing is well established (Shanahan, 2007), and integrating reading and writing is foundational to the whole language perspective (Goodman, 1986) the researchers embraced. Joseph's ability and willingness to read what he wrote demonstrates the power of a language experience approach—a technique documented to be powerful for both developmental and disabled readers (Padak & Rasinski, 1999).

A second theme is that consistency within a school, classroom, and home environment promoted students' literacy development. Allen et al. (1993) referred to this as *stability*. When programmatic and social stability were present—a function of the holistic, constructivist philosophy Barbara and Betty embraced—students grew in literacy. However, when the stability broke down at school or home—the "chaos" to which the authors refer in their book subtitle—students struggled academically and behaviorally. Joseph exemplified this as he traversed grades, schools, and pedagogical perspectives. Betty commented that the stability she and Barbara strove for was grounded in their deep whole language belief "in the potential of our students and the power of choice and engagement with reading and writing to support their achievements" (B. Shockley, personal communication, January 19, 2009). Thus, when approaches to reading instruction are stable and implemented consistently, especially for struggling readers, students' literacy learning is enhanced (Archambault, 1989; Borman, Wong, Hedges, & D'Agostino, 2001; Johnston, Allington, & Afflerbach, 1985; see discussion in Allington, 2009).

A third theme is the interaction and complexity of the social and academic. Allen et al. (1993) spent nearly as much time talking about behavioral and social issues in the cases as they did about the specific literacy practices that were implemented. The students' literacy learning was tied to the children's in-school behaviors and out-of-school contexts, which supports a bidirectional relationship between difficulties in literacy development and students' behavior, especially for boys (Trzesniewski, Moffitt, Caspi, Taylor, & Maughan, 2006). Additionally, Allen et al.'s research demonstrated the essential nature of teachers' connections with students—African American children in particular—in order to understand and appreciate their social backgrounds (Ladson-Billings, 1994) and how to accommodate them instructionally (Delpit, 2006).

Finally, Allen et al. (1993) noted that, in spite of the "chaos" the children may have experienced educationally and socially, "every child had someone at home who read and/or encouraged the child to read" (Allen et al., 1993, p. 251). In other words, there was home support for literacy, even if it may not have been immediately obvious or if it would not have been expected due to cultural stereotypes associated with poor, minority children and their families (Baumann & Thomas, 1997; Compton-Lilly, 2003; Taylor & Dorsey-Gaines, 1988). In fact, Allen and colleagues explored the issue of family support for literacy in depth in a follow-up study (Michalove, Shockley, & Allen, 1995).

Cone (1994): Aliterate High School Students

Study description. In this study, English teacher Joan Kernan Cone addressed the issue of *aliteracy*, that is, the form of reading difficulties in which students, though able to read skillfully, choose not to use their reading abilities in school and in out-of-school contexts. Specifically, Cone explored her students' perceptions of themselves as readers, from avid independent readers to those who rarely if ever chose to read on their own. This year-long action research project included a racially, academically, and economically diverse class of 35 high school seniors. Data sources included student journals, tallies of the books students read (or attempted to read), in-class observations, and classroom discussions.

Motivated by a friend who said that her students were "never going to read Dickens . . . [so she should] introduce them to authors they [would] read" (Cone, 1994, p. 450), Cone implemented an independent reading program in her classroom. Students were required to self-select a 500 page novel that had been published since 1985, did not have any CliffsNotes available for it, and had not been made into a movie.

Only 11 of 35 students demonstrated that they read a book at the conclusion of Cone's first independent reading assignment. Disappointed by the results, Cone offered in-class reading time, help in selecting books, and an opportunity for her students to write about and discuss their reading. The discussion component encouraged the students to critique books, which led to students recommending (or not recommending) books to one another. The journal component required that students rate themselves on a reading continuum: *nonreaders* ⇔ *somewhat readers* ⇔ *readers*. The journals also enabled students to chronicle their self-perceptions as readers and to re-evaluate where they placed themselves on the continuum throughout the school year.

Cone made modifications to her program as the year progressed. She modified her criteria for book selection by pushing back the original publication cut-off date of 1985 to 1980; she also actively matched books to readers by recommending titles and loaning personal copies. In addition, she incorporated more time for in-class reading. Cone asked students to write about their books as they were reading. In addition to having students write about characters, plot, and setting, she required students to write about their *process* of reading, such as when, where, and why they read. At the end of the school year, 29 of 35 students read the final book for the independent reading assignment.

Findings. As a result of Cone's independent reading initiative, she gained insight into her students' perceptions of themselves as readers. Those who placed themselves on the *Readers* end of the continuum described themselves according to a variety of definitions and reading practices. For example, Andrew wrote, "A reader is someone who can pick up a book and be transported to a new place, a place where the writer is in control but the reader is free to fill in the blanks, to view the scene as he wishes" (Cone, 1994, p. 455). Keesha wrote, "I started reading Judy Blume books. That's how I became a reader. I read one of her books and decided it was good and she had to have more books that were just as good. One good book from an author is all it takes" (Cone, 1994, p. 456). The readers reported knowing how to get books (libraries, bookstores, friends) and why they liked reading (to learn, to escape). Readers also indicated interest in a multiple genres—plays, newspapers, magazines, poetry—in addition to the traditional novel. Cone noted how interest in reading in her class became an "appearing act," which found its way into her article title.

Somewhat readers were in a kind of literacy limbo. They saw themselves as "an almost reader" or "becoming a reader" (Cone, 1994, p. 458). Procrastination, difficulty locating books, and a preference for shorter pieces (e.g., newspapers or periodicals) kept these students from fully accepting themselves as readers.

Nonreaders were essentially aliterates, who provided different descriptions of their nonreading stance. Some rationalized their lack of reading: "Just because you don't read book after book doesn't mean that you can't read" (Cone, 1994, p. 456). Other nonreaders viewed reading as a performance or the ability to decode, rather than the act of creating meaning; hence, it was something that they avoided. Cone noted that several of the nonreaders received high grades and scored well on the SAT: a mark of a classic aliterate. For some low-achieving nonreaders, however, there was a correlation between self-labeling as a nonreader and poor school performance.

Cone's most important findings relate to the process of students' *change* in their self-perceptions and actual reading behaviors. For example, Kema's writing documented her evolution as a reader:

- September: "When I have an assignment to read a book, I do all my other homework first because I know if I pick that book up I would get restless.… I know it's sad, but that how I feel." (p. 465)
- February: "At first I hated this book assignment. Now I'm getting used to it. I'm finding me in each of the books I read." (p. 465)
- April: "I don't consider myself a reader yet.… I hated reading with a passion until I learned how to pick out books that interested me." (p. 466)
- May: "I still feel intimidated with some kids in here … especially David. He is never without a book. But I read all my books this year, every one of them." (p. 466)

Kema's progression from nonreader to reader was representative of other students in Cone's class who moved from an aliteracy stance to that of viewing literacy as a way to enjoy and find fulfillment in literature.

Implications.   Cone's successful year-long program of reading, discussion, and reflection suggests four implications for teachers of high school literature classes. First, it is not too late to create a life-long reader even when students are about to exit high school. Students' perceptions of themselves as *somewhat readers* or *nonreaders* can be changed; that is, aliterates can change to literates. Several researchers have demonstrated that students' feelings of learned helplessness (Coley & Hoffman, 1990), which may have developed as early as elementary school, can be reversed with older students (Brown, Palinscar, & Purcell, 1986; Rozenholtz & Simpson, 1984). One important key to increasing the number of students who view themselves as readers is teachers' knowledge of their students' interests. This information enables teachers to make book recommendations on topics about which students are more likely to read. For example, introducing Jalaine to female African American writers and allowing David to pursue his interest in science fiction enabled Cone to better connect with them as readers.

Second, independent reading encourages students to practice and apply the comprehension strategies they are taught to reading materials that matter to them (Ivey & Broaddus, 2001). When teachers select books and establish the pace of reading, students become dependent on them. This dependence implies that teachers do not trust the students to engage in reading without supervision. Incorporating independent reading in the high school English curriculum enables students to engage in authentic reading practices that will support their learning long past graduation.

Third, researchers have found that choice is an important factor in reading motivation (Flowerday, Schraw, & Stevens, 2004). Smith and Wilhelm (2002) found that books students enjoyed reading most were those they were able to select. For the majority of Cone's high school seniors, choice played a prominent role in their development as readers. Students reported pursuing specific genre interests (e.g., science fiction), gaining confidence as a reader, and discovering books that were previously unknown. For example, Angel reported, "I got to read books that the teacher liked … plus what [I] liked … all of which were pretty good reading but honestly speaking, I wouldn't have picked those books up at the library. But I'm glad we read them" (Cone, 1994, p. 471).

Fourth, literature discussion groups (Eeds & Wells, 1989; Raphael and McMahon, 1994) were powerful in moving Cone's students from nonreaders to readers. Discussion helps readers learn from and with others as they move through a text. Cone's students demanded the opportunity to discuss the books they were reading in class. Phillipa summed up the importance of talk: "It's easier when you do [reading] in class because you can talk about it and…Like a person like Shakespeare—you can understand it better if, you know, if you talk about it" (Cone, 1994, p. 471).

Baumann and Ivey (1997): Struggling Readers All

Study description.   In this study, Jim Baumann took a year off from his university position to teach second grade full-time in a public elementary school serving low-income, minority children and their families. Gay Ivey was a graduate assistant at the time and worked with Jim on all aspects of the study. The purpose of this study, titled "Delicate Balances," was to determine what Jim's students learned about reading, writing, and literature through a yearlong program that integrated reading and learning about literature and reading strategy instruction. This was a type of balanced literacy approach (Pressley, 2006), which Jim and Gay referred to as an *immersion/instruction program* (Ivey, Baumann, & Jarrard, 2000). The design was a qualitative, interpretive case study (Merriam, 1988) involving the 13 students in Jim's class who were present for all or the majority of the school year (many children moved in and out of this school).

Data included researcher journals; transcripts of video-recorded student interviews and classroom literacy lessons; a variety of student work; anecdotal records; an informal reading inventory conducted in the fall, winter, and spring of the school year; Jim's lesson plan book and lesson notes; and transcripts of interviews with children's parents/care givers and colleagues at the school. Data analysis involved a five-phase content analysis in which Jim and Gay induced major categories and supporting properties from the multiple data sources. To establish credibility, a negative-case analysis was conducted, and an external auditor reviewed several case records to establish trustworthiness of the findings.

Findings. The researchers reported results from both cross-case and within-case analyses. The cross-case analysis resulted in five categories: (a) becoming a reader, (b) engagement with literacy, (c) word identification and reading fluency, (d) comprehending written texts, and (e) written composition. To illustrate the findings, we describe results for Category 1, becoming a reader category, which included two properties: students came to view reading as a natural, regular component of the school day; and students grew in overall instructional reading level.

The first property reflected the immersion aspect of the curriculum, which had the children engaged with trade books multiple times each day through book talks, teacher read alouds, self-selected free-choice reading, buddy reading with students from a fifth-grade class, and a home/school effort to promote shared reading with parents and care givers. Data revealed that, as the year progressed, students noted with increasing frequency that they enjoyed books and reading. For example, Felicia stated that "I like all kinds of books . . . and I love to read." Gay wrote in her journal that Kristen "knows a lot of authors' names. I've noticed in class time and time again that she talks about books. She can tell you plots of different books and who wrote them" (Baumann & Ivey, 1997, p. 260).

Regarding the second property, there was evidence that the students grew in overall instructional reading level across the school year. The August administration of an informal reading inventory (IRI) revealed an average instructional level of primer to beginning first grade for the 13 students; the average instructional level was second grade as per the January IRI; and the average instructional level was third grade at the May administration. Thus, there was significant growth, with students advancing two instructional levels on average. Not all students demonstrated this degree of progress, for two students remained at a preprimer level at the end of the school year.

Results for the other four categories demonstrated that students not only grew in overall reading ability but also in other aspects of reading and language arts. Specifically, the children:

- became more engaged with literature as evidenced by their increasing knowledge of books, authors, and illustrators (Category 2);
- became more automatic, skillful, and strategic in word identification, and developed in oral reading fluency (Category 3);
- learned that reading is a meaning-seeking process and developed comprehension monitoring and fix-up strategies (Category 4); and
- developed a strong sense of audience in their writing and wrote extensively about their personal interests and experiences (Category 5).

In order to demonstrate the variation and individual pathways that the children took to literacy development, the researchers conducted in-depth, within-case analyses of two students: Marcus and Jennifer. To illustrate these cases, we provide an overview of Marcus's story.

Marcus began the school year virtually a nonreader, as Jim could not establish an instructional level on the August IRI. In May, however, Marcus's IRI instructional level was second grade, and miscue analysis revealed that his miscues were much more graphophonically similar (e.g., *dude* for *down* on the Fall IRI vs. *waterbed* for *wastebasket* on the Spring IRI).

Marcus demonstrated increased use of syntactic and semantic cues as well as the ability to integrate various word and meaning identification strategies. For example, while reading to Gay one spring day, Marcus read *Frog swam first and made a big splash. Toad swam second*, and he immediately asked Gay, "[Is] that right?" The word Marcus should have read instead of *second* was *slowly*. He made a reasonable substitution for *slowly* based on clues from the previous sentence and the first letter of the word, but he knew it was not correct. When Gay asked, "Why do you think it's not *second*," Marcus replied, "It don't got a *k*" (Baumann & Ivey, 1997, p. 266). Although Marcus still struggled with reading at the end of second grade, he had developed skill and metacognitive awareness of his word identification and comprehension abilities, and he acquired a keen interest in books and literature.

Implications. Findings from the Baumann and Ivey (1997) study of teaching children who struggled with reading and writing are supported by the historic process-product reading research from the 1970s (e.g., Berliner,

1981; Brophy & Good, 1986; Duffy, 1981, 1982; Hoffman, 1986, 1991). For example, process-product research findings on the importance of allocating significant time for reading instruction, having students academically engaged and on task, and ensuring that students experience high success rates with literacy tasks were characteristics of Jim's literacy curriculum and instruction.

More contemporary research on characteristics that are associated with growth in reading ability of elementary children (Allington & Johnston, 2002; Pressley, Allington, Wharton-McDonald, Block, & Morrow, 2001; Williams & Baumann, 2008) also supported outcomes of the immersion/instruction program. For example, Jim had high expectations and believed that students could and would learn: factors shown to be related to literacy growth of African American (Ladson-Billings, 1994) and more mainstream (Wharton-McDonald, Pressley, & Hampston, 1998) students. When teachers employ a range of reading and instructional materials (Jim had a large classroom library), students tend to be motivated and engaged with literature and reading (Pressley, Yokoi, Rankin, Wharton-McDonald, & Mistretta, 1997). Many studies document the necessity of explicit instruction in key reading skills and strategies for student growth (Allington & Johnston, 2002; Pressley et al., 2001), which was a hallmark of Jim's philosophy and instructional program.

Other factors related to students' literacy learning such as the effective use of praise (Bohn, Roehrig, & Pressley, 2004), implementing small-groups for guided reading instruction (Pressley, Wharton-McDonald, Hampston, & Echevarria, 1998; Taylor, Pearson, Clark, & Walpole, 2000), clear and fair management routines (Dolezal, Welsh, Pressley, & Vincent, 2003), and the presence of a warm, secure, and friendly classroom environment (Ladson-Billings, 1994; Spencer & Spencer, 1993) also reflected the approach Jim took to literacy instruction and classroom life. In sum, the Baumann and Ivey (1997) study provided support for employing curricular and instructional practices known to be effective across various instructional contexts (Williams & Baumann, 2008) with a class of students who struggled with literacy achievement.

Discussion

What might be learned from our review of three teacher-research studies on students with reading difficulties? Although we cannot reliably draw generalizations from so few studies, we offer instead some observations about the studies in relation to the selection framework we used.

Sociocultural Dimensions of "Engaging Children"   The Allen et al. (1993) study provides insight into sociocultural aspects of reading difficulties. The researchers demonstrated that a powerful instructional philosophy (whole language) and highly dedicated teachers can effect change on the literacy learning of students about whom they most worried. More simply stated, Betty and Barbara enabled children

like Jeremiah and Joseph to develop both academically and socially. This study also demonstrated that there were limits to what teachers can do when children experience chaos in their lives. Moving from school-to-school and from teacher-to-teacher disrupted the hoped-for safety of a continuous holistic literacy instructional experience for students like Jeremiah and Joseph. The researchers acknowledged these issues and the complexity of the task of public school teaching:

> We have learned a great deal, perhaps as much as the simplicity of our initial question as about the children. We feel a tremendous responsibility to the children to share their lives with you in an honest and sympathetic way, in a way that gives you an understanding of them as members of their communities, as children buffeted by the upheaval of home and school, and above all, as truly engaging children. (Allen et al., 1993, p. 11)

Teacher researchers like JoBeth, Betty, and Barbara persist in their quest to change literacy development for struggling readers—a study like *Engaging Children* is not a one-time experience. Teacher researchers have a passion for their work, for ongoing professional learning through research, and for sharing what they are learning with other teachers. *Engaging Children* was connected to other research on the children at Walnut Elementary School (Allen, Michalove, Shockley, & West, 1991), and it led to a follow-up study in which Barbara, Betty, and JoBeth collaborated with parents and care givers to promote home-school connections to further enhance the children's literacy learning (*Engaging Families*, Michalove et al., 1995). This led to yet another work in which teacher researchers told their stories of the promise and pitfalls of conducting research in their schools and classrooms (*Engaging Teachers*, Allen & Bisplinghoff, 1998). Just as university researchers may engage in a line of inquiry, so too, teacher researchers often conduct a series of studies. The questions posed by one study often lead to other questions and studies, all resulting in deeper and new understandings of students who experience difficulty learning to read.

Motivational Aspect of "Appearing Acts"   Joan Kernan Cone's (1994) study of motivating students to read demonstrates that it is never too late to break the grip of aliteracy and to create readers. Her adapted literature curriculum that included choice and discussion invited reluctant readers into the literacy club. She related how books the students read like Terry McMillan's (1989) *Disappearing Acts* resulted in the "appearing act" of a community of readers in her classroom:

> The extent of our sense of community as readers is reflected in our connection to writer Terry McMillan. Early in the year, Tassie lent me *Disappearing Acts* [McMillan, 1989]. "You have *got* to read this. My sister-in-law gave it to me last Friday and I finished it this weekend. Now I'm reading her first book. Don't be shocked by the language."… Gradually a McMillan fan club developed. Kandi wrote,

"*Disappearing Acts.* Everywhere I go I hear people talking about that book. I'll read it again right after my aunt is finished with it." (Cone, 1994, p. 467)

Another student, Clifton, agreed: "It was almost as if I was addicted to this book. *Disappearing Acts* not only moved me but it became a part of me."

Cone's passion for teacher research on high school students both preceded and followed her 1994 study. She reported on how reading fiction and nonfiction works that were linked to geographical regions promoted her students' interest in reading and global understanding (Cone, 1990). She used discussion to motivate reluctant readers and talkers to create a literate community (Cone, 1993), and she reported on how her fully mature literacy curriculum engaged ninth-grade "detracked" (i.e., heterogeneously grouped) students to learn about, appreciate, and use reading and writing (Cone, 2006). Cone's teacher research on students who struggle with literacy demonstrates how the process of inquiry becomes a mechanism for lifelong learning and professional development.

Cognitive Growth through "Delicate Balances" Baumann and Ivey's (1997) study indicates that a cognitively focused literacy program with a strong literature component can hasten children's literacy growth. The duration and intensity of the literature/strategies-based approach, a dogged persistence, the belief that students will learn, and a lack of acceptance of failure (on both Jim's and the students' part) enabled many children to accelerate their literacy development such that they were at an average or above level in reading as they transitioned to third grade.

As was true for other teacher-research studies, however, there were individual setbacks and the inevitable ebb and flow of academic growth. Not all stories were success stories; there were no miracles in Jim's Room 8:

> Not all students in Jim's class demonstrated significant growth in reading and language arts abilities. Jim's greatest frustration throughout the school year was the difficulty he had finding ways to enable some children to make the literacy breakthroughs he so desperately hoped for…. Jim struggled along with certain students throughout the school year to find strategies, materials, balances, or whatever that would unlock literacy doors; it remained a pall for Jim that some keys were never found. (Baumann & Ivey, 1997, pp. 270–271)

Just like the other teacher researchers we have discussed, Jim and Gay continued to explore the complexities of struggling readers. Gay conducted her dissertation as a participant observer in a study exploring middle school readers (Ivey, 1999a), including those who experienced difficulty with reading. She also examined issues and practices that limit or enhance the reading instruction of struggling readers in middle school (Ivey, 1999b). Jim kept in touch with his students and families (Baumann & Thomas, 1997), wrote about the challenges of being both the teacher and the researcher (Baumann, 1996), and collaborated with classroom teachers on several other teacher-research studies (Baumann, Hooten, & White, 1999; Baumann, Ware, & Edwards, 2007).

Conclusion

Allington (2009) stated recently that "most struggling readers never catch up with their higher-achieving classmates because schools create school days for them where they struggle all day long" (p. 1). In contrast, in the studies we reviewed, the researchers created programs in which students experienced *success* all day long by addressing the students' social, motivational, and cognitive needs. Allen at al. (1993) used a whole language philosophy to create an instructional environment that acknowledged what the students knew already about literacy and built on the students' unique social and cultural backgrounds. Cone (1994) modified her high school literature class by motivating her aliterate students through choice and discussion. Baumann and Ivey (1997) developed a program that provided the children instruction in essential reading skills and strategies as they were immersed in quality children's literature.

In these diverse studies, the teacher researchers *created their own approaches* to achieve success for their struggling readers rather than employing or adopting an external "program" that purported to do so. The researchers were not averse to using published materials (e.g., Jim used basals of differing levels for his guided reading groups, and all researchers used quality trade books), but they developed programs grounded on theoretically and empirically based instructional principles and approaches that aligned with their own convictions and their students' unique needs. As Allington (2002) stated, "Good teachers, effective teachers matter much more than curriculum materials, pedagogical approaches, or 'proven programs'" (p. 740).

Teacher research provides an environment and medium for those in classrooms to develop into "good teachers, effective teachers." Lassonde and Israel (2008) stated that "Teacher research offers an effective opportunity to bridge the traditional divide between educational theory and professional practice. Educators who practice teacher research in classroom settings become more complete teachers as they analyze what they are doing in the classroom" (p. xvii). In other words, the reflection and action through systematic, intentional inquiry about classroom life that defines teacher research leads to more quality instruction, and more importantly, greater achievement for students who experience reading difficulties.

References

Alexander, P. A., & Fox, E. (2004). A historical perspective on reading research and practice. In R. B. Ruddell & N. J. Unrau (Eds.), *Theoretical models and processes of reading* (5th ed., pp. 33–68). Newark, DE: International Reading Association.

Allen, J., & Bisplinghoff, B. S. (1998). *Engaging teachers: Creating teaching and research relationships*. Portsmouth, NH: Heinemann.

Allen, J., Michalove, B., & Shockley, B. (1993). *Engaging children: Community and chaos in the lives of young literacy learners*. Portsmouth, NH: Heinemann.

Allen, J., Michalove, B., Shockley, B., & West, M. (1991). "I'm really worried about Joseph": Reducing the risks of literacy learning. *The Reading Teacher, 44*, 458–472.

Allen J., & Shockley, B. (1996). Composing a research dialogue: University and school research communities encounter a cultural shift. *Reading Research Quarterly, 31*, 220–228.

Allington, R. L. (2002). What I've learned about effective reading instruction from a decade of studying exemplary elementary classroom teachers. *Phi Delta Kappan, 83*, 740–747.

Allington. R. L. (2009). *What really matters in response to intervention research-based designs.* Boston: Allyn & Bacon.

Allington, R. L., & Johnston, P. H. (2002). *Reading to learn: Lessons from exemplary fourth-grade classrooms.* New York: Guilford.

Anderson, G. L., & Herr, K. (1999). the new paradigm wars: Is there room for rigorous practitioner knowledge in schools and universities? *Educational Researcher, 28*(5), 12–21, 40.

Archambault, M. X. (1989). Instructional setting and other design features of compensatory education programs. In R. E. Slavin, N. Karweit, & N. A. Madden (Eds.), *Effective programs for students at risk* (pp. 220–263). Boston: Allyn & Bacon.

Barr, R., Kamil, M. L., Mosenthal, P. B., & Pearson, P. D. (Eds.). (1991). *Handbook of reading research, vol. II.* New York: Longman.

Baumann, J. F. (1996). Conflict or compatibility in classroom inquiry? One teacher's struggle to balance teaching and research. *Educational Researcher, 25*(7), 29–36.

Baumann, J. F., & Duffy-Hester, A. M. (2000). Making sense of classroom worlds: Methodology in teacher research. In M. L. Kamil, P. B. Mosenthal, P. D. Pearson, & R. Barr (Eds.), *Handbook of reading research, vol. III* (pp. 77–98). Mahwah, NJ: Erlbaum.

Baumann, J. F., Hooten, H., & White, P. (1999). Teaching comprehension through literature: A teacher-research project to develop fifth-graders' reading strategies and motivation. *The Reading Teacher, 53*, 38–51.

Baumann, J. F., & Ivey, G. (1997). Delicate balances: Striving for curricular and instructional equilibrium in a second-grade, literature/strategy-based classroom. *Reading Research Quarterly, 32*, 244–275.

Baumann, J. F., Shockley-Bisplinghoff, B., & Allen, J. (1997). Methodology in teacher research: Three cases. In J. Flood, S. B. Heath, & D. Lapp (Eds.), *A handbook of research on teaching literacy through the communicative and visual arts* (pp. 121–143). New York: Macmillan.

Baumann, J. F., & Thomas, D. (1997). "If you can pass momma's tests, then she knows you're getting your education": A case study of support for literacy learning within an African American family. *The Reading Teacher, 51*, 108–120.

Baumann, J. F., Ware, D., & Edwards, E. C. (2007). "Bumping into spicy, tasty words that catch your tongue": A formative experiment on vocabulary instruction. *The Reading Teacher, 62*, 108–122.

Berliner, D. C. (1981). Academic learning time and reading achievement. In J. T. Guthrie (Ed.), *Comprehension and teaching: Research reviews* (pp. 203–226). Newark, DE: International Reading Association.

Bohn, C. M., Roehrig, A. D., & Pressley, M. (2004). The first days of school in the classroom of two more effective and four less effective primary-grades teachers. *Elementary School Journal, 104*(4), 269–287.

Borman, G. D., Wong, K. K., Hedges, L. V., & D'Agostino, J. V. (2001). Coordinating categorical and regular programs: Effects on Title I students' educational opportunities and outcomes. In G. D. Borman, S. C. Stringfield, & R. E. Slavin (Eds.), *Title I: Compensatory education at the crossroads* (pp. 79–116). Mahwah, NJ: Erlbaum.

Brophy, J., & Good, T. (1986). Teacher behavior and student achievement. In M. C. Wittrock (Ed.), *Handbook of research on teaching* (3rd ed., pp. 328–375). New York: Macmillan.

Brown, A. L., Palinscar, A. S., & Purcell, L. (1986). Poor readers: Teach, don't label. In U. Neisser (Ed.), *School achievement of minority children: New perspectives* (pp. 105–143). Hillsdale, NJ: Erlbaum.

Cochran-Smith, M., & Donnell, K. (2006). Practitioner inquiry: Blurring the boundaries of research and practice. In J. L. Green, G. Camilli, & P. B. Elmore (Eds.), *Handbook of complementary methods in education research* (pp. 503–518). Washington, DC: American Educational Research Association.

Cochran-Smith, M., & Lytle, S. L. (Eds.). (1993). *Inside/outside: Teacher Research and knowledge.* New York: Teachers College Press.

Coley, J. F., & Hoffman, D. (1990). Overcoming learned helplessness in at-risk readers. *Journal of Reading, 33*, 497–502.

Compton-Lilly, C. (2003). *Reading families: The literate lives of urban children.* New York: Teachers College Press.

Cone, J. K. (1990). Literature, geography, and the untracked English class. *The English Journal, 79*(8), 60–67.

Cone, J. K. (1993). Using classroom talk to create community and learning. *The English Journal, 82*(6), 30–38.

Cone, J. K. (1994). Appearing acts: Creating readers in a high school English class. *Harvard Educational Review, 64*, 450–473.

Cone, J. K. (2006). Detracked ninth-grade English: Apprenticeship for the work and world of high school and beyond. *Theory into Practice, 45*(1), 55–63.

Cunningham, J. W. (2001). The National Reading Panel Report. *Reading Research Quarterly, 36*(3), 326–335

Delpit, L. (2006). *Other people's children: Cultural conflict in the classroom* (updated edition). New York: The New Press.

Dolezal, S. E., Welsh, L. M., Pressley, M., & Vincent, M. M. (2003). How nine third-grade teachers motivate student academic engagement. *Elementary School Journal, 103*(3), 239–267.

Duffy, G. G. (1981). Teacher effectiveness research: Implications for the reading profession. In M. L. Kamil (Ed.), *Directions in reading: Research and instruction, 30th Yearbook of the National Reading Conference* (pp. 113–136). Washington, DC: National Reading Conference.

Duffy, G. G. (1982). Fighting off the alligators: What research in real classrooms has to say about reading instruction. *Journal of Reading Behavior, 14,* 357–373.

Eeds, M., & Wells, D. (1989). Grand conversations: An exploration of meaning construction in literature study groups. *Research in the Teaching of English, 23*, 4–29.

Fecho, B., Allen, J., Mazaros, C., & Inyega, H. (2006). Teacher research in writing classrooms. In P. Smagorinski (Ed.), *Research on composition: Multiple perspectives on two decades of change* (pp. 108–140). New York: Teachers College Press.

Flowerday, T., Schraw, G., & Stevens, J. (2004). The role of choice and interest in reader engagement. *The Journal of Experimental Education, 72*, 93–114.

Goodman, K. S. (1986). *What's whole in whole language? A parent/teacher guide to children's learning.* Portsmouth, NH Heinemann.

Hankins, K. H. (2003). *Teaching through the storm: A journal of hope.* New York: Teachers College Press.

Hoffman, J. V. (1986). Process-product research on effective teaching: A primer for the paradigm. In J. V. Hoffman (Ed.), *Effective teaching of reading: Research and practice* (pp. 39–51). Newark, DE: International Reading Association.

Hoffman, J. V. (1991). Teacher and school effects in learning to read. In R. Barr, M. L. Kamil, P. B. Mosenthal, & P. D. Pearson (Eds.), *Handbook of reading research, vol. II* (pp. 911–950). Mahwah, NJ: Erlbaum.

Ivey, G. (1999a). A multicase study in the middle school: Complexities among young adolescent readers. *Reading Research Quarterly, 34*, 172–192.

Ivey, G. (1999b). Reflections on teaching struggling middle school readers. *Journal of Adolescent & Adult Literacy, 42*, 372–381.

Ivey, G., Baumann, J. F., & Jarrard, D. (2000). Exploring literacy balance: Iterations in a second-grade and a sixth-grade classroom. *Reading Research & Instruction, 39*, 291–309.

Ivey, G., & Broaddus, K. (2001). "Just Plain Reading": A survey of what makes students want to read in middle school classrooms. *Reading Research Quarterly, 36*(4), 350–377.

Johnston, P., Allington, R. L., & Afflerbach, P. (1985). The congruence of classroom and remedial reading instruction. *The Elementary School Journal, 85*, 465–478.

Klenk, L., & Kibby, M. W. (2000). Re-mediating reading difficulties: Appraising the past, reconciling the present, constructing the future. In M. L. Kamil, P. B. Mosenthal, P. D. Pearson, & R. Barr (Eds.), *Handbook of reading research, vol. III* (pp. 667–690). Mahwah, NJ: Erlbaum.

Ladson-Billings, G. (1994). *The dreamkeepers: Successful teachers of African-American children*. San Francisco: Jossey-Bass.

Lankshear, C., & Knoble, M. (2004). *A handbook of teacher research*. New York: Open University Press.

Lassonde, C. A., & Israel, S. E. (Eds.). (2008). *Teachers taking action: A comprehensive guide to teacher research* (pp. 177–189). Newark, DE: International Reading Association.

Lenski, S. D. (2008). The future of teacher research. In C. A. Lassonde & S. E. Israel (Eds.), *Teachers taking action: A comprehensive guide to teacher research* (pp. 177–189). Newark, DE: International Reading Association.

Lipson, M. Y., & Wixson, K. K. (1986). Reading disability research: An interactionist perspective. *Review of Educational Research, 56,* 111–136.

Lytle, S. L. (2000). Teacher research in the contact zone. In M. L. Kamil, P. B. Mosenthal, P. D. Pearson, & R. Barr (Eds.), *Handbook of reading research, vol. III* (pp. 691–718) Mahwah, NJ: Erlbaum.

Lytle, S. L., & Cochran-Smith, M. (1994). Teacher research in English. In A. C. Purves (Ed.), *Encyclopedia of English studies and language arts* (pp. 1153–1155). New York: Scholastic.

McFarland, K. P., & Stansell, J. C. (1993). Historical perspectives. In L. Patterson, C. M. Santa, K. G. Short, & K. Smith, (Eds.), *Teachers are researchers: Reflection and action* (pp. 12–18). Newark, DE: International Reading Association.

McMillan, T. (1989). *Disappearing acts*. New York: Viking.

Merriam, S. B. (1988). *Case study research in education: A qualitative approach*. San Francisco: Jossey-Bass.

Michalove, B., Shockley, B., & Allen, J. (1995). *Engaging families: Connecting home and school literacy communities*. Portsmouth, NH: Heinemann.

National Reading Panel. (2000). *Teaching children to read: An evidence-based assessment of the scientific research literature on reading and its implications for reading instruction: Reports of the subgroups* (NIH Publication Number 00-4769). Washington, DC: National Institute of Child Health and Human Development.

Olson, M. W. (1990). The teacher as researcher: A historical perspective. In M. W. Olson (Ed.), *Opening the door to classroom research* (pp. 1–20). Newark, DE: International Reading Association.

Ontario Action Researcher. (2008). Retrieved October 6, 2008, from http://www.nipissingu.ca/oar/index.htm

Padak, N., & Rasinski, T. (1999). The language experience approach: A framework for learning. In O. G. Nelson & W. M. Linek (Eds.), *Practical classroom applications of language experience* (pp. 1–11). Boston: Allyn & Bacon.

Pearson, P. D., Barr, R., Kamil, M. L., Mosenthal, P. (1984). *Handbook of reading research*. New York: Longman.

Picard, S. (2005). Collaborative conversations about second-grade readers. *The Reading Teacher 58,* 258–464.

Pressley, M. (2006). *Reading instruction that works: The case for balanced teaching* (3rd ed.). New York: Guilford.

Pressley, M., Allington, R. L., Wharton-McDonald, R., Collins Block, C., & Morrow, L. M. (2001). *Learning to read: Lessons from exemplary first-grade classrooms*. New York: Guilford.

Pressley, M., Wharton-McDonald, R., Hampston, J., & Echevarria, M. (1998). Literacy instruction in 10 fourth-grade and fifth-grade classrooms in upstate New York. *Scientific Studies of Reading, 2,* 159–194.

Pressley, M., Yokoi, L., Rankin, J., Wharton-McDonald, R., & Mistretta, J. (1997). A survey of the instructional practices of grade 5 teachers nominated as effective in promoting literacy. *Scientific Studies of Reading, 1*(2), 145–160.

Raphael, T. E. & McMahon, S. I. (1994). Book club: An alternative framework for reading instruction. *The Reading Teacher, 48*(2), 102–116.

Rozenholtz, S., and Simpson, C. (1984). The formation of ability conceptions: Developmental trend or social construction? *Review of Educational Research, 54,* 31–63.

Ruddell, R. B., & Unrau, N. J. (Eds.). (2004a). *Theoretical models and processes of reading* (5th ed.). Newark, DE: International Reading Association.

Ruddell, R. B., & Unrau, N. J. (2004b). Reading as a meaning-construction process: The reader, the text, and the teacher. In R. B. Ruddell & N. J. Unrau (Eds.), *Theoretical models and processes of reading* (5th ed., pp. 1462–1521). Newark, DE: International Reading Association.

Shanahan, T. (2007). Relations among oral language, reading, and writing. In C. A. MacArthur, S. Graham, & J. Fitzgerald (Eds.), *Handbook of writing research* (pp. 183). New York: Guilford.

Smith, F. (1988). *Joining the literacy club*. Portsmouth, NH: Heinemann.

Smith, M. W., & Wilhelm, J. W. (2002). *Going with the flow: How to engage boys (and girls) in their literacy learning*. Portsmouth, NH: Heinemann.

Snow, C., Burns, M. S., & Griffin, P. (1998). *Preventing reading difficulties in young children*. Washington, DC: National Academy Press.

Spear-Swerling, L., & Sternberg, R. (1996). *Off track: When poor readers become "learning disabled"*. Boulder, CO: Westview Press.

Spencer, L. M., & Spencer, S. M. (1993). *Competence at work: Models for superior performance*. New York: Wiley.

Taylor, B. M., Pearson, P. D., Clark, K., & Walpole, S. (2000). Effective schools and accomplished teachers: Lessons about primary-grade reading instruction in low-income schools. *Elementary School Journal, 101,* 121–166.

Taylor, D., & Dorsey-Gaines, C. (1988). *Growing up literate: Learning from inner-city families*. Portsmouth, NH: Heinemann.

Trzesniewski, K., Moffitt, T., Caspi, A., Taylor, A., & Maughan, B. (2006, January). Revisiting the association between reading achievement and antisocial behavior: New evidence of an environmental explanation from a twin study. *Child Development, 77*(1), 72–88

Wharton-McDonald, R., Pressley, M., & Hampston, J. M. (1998). Literacy instruction in nine first-grade classrooms: Teacher characteristics and student achievement. *Elementary School Journal, 99,* 101–128.

Williams, T. L., & Baumann, J. F. (2008). Contemporary research on effective elementary literacy teachers. In J. Laughter, V. J. Risko, D. L. Compton, D. K. Dickinson, M. K. Hundley, R. T. Jimenez, et al. (Eds.), *2008 National Reading Conference Yearbook* (pp. 357–372). Chicago: National Reading Conference.

Wixson, K. K., & Lipson, M. Y. (1991). Perspectives on reading disability research. In R. Barr, M. L. Kamil, J. H. Mosenthal, & P. D. Pearson (Eds.), *Handbook of reading research, vol. II* (pp. 539–570). New York: Longman.

Woodside-Jiron, H. (2003). Critical policy analysis: Researching the roles of cultural models, power, and expertise in reading policy. *Reading Research Quarterly, 38*(4), 530–536.

Zeichner, K. M., & Noffke, S. E. (2001). Practitioner research. In V. Richardson (Ed.), *Handbook of research on teaching* (4th ed., pp. 298–330). Washington, DC: American Educational Research Association.

36

Single-Subject and Case-Study Designs

David Cihak
University of Tennessee

Single-subject research designs help teachers and researchers examine variables that effect student learning. Approximately 30% of all database interventions conducted on students with learning disabilities use single-subject designs (Swanson & Sachse-Lee, 2000). Swanson and Sachse-Lee also found that reading was the primary focus in a meta-analysis of single-subject research design. Single-subject designs are particularly well suited for literacy research. This chapter provides an overview of single-subject experimental research with an emphasis on examining components of literacy research. For a more comprehensive understanding of single-subject designs, numerous authors are referenced (e.g., Barlow & Hersen, 1984; Kazdin, 1982; Kennedy, 2005; Richards, Taylor, Ramasamy, & Richards, 1999; Sidman, 1960; Skinner, 2004; Tawney & Gast, 1984).

The term *single-subject* is not used because there is only one participant; rather, it refers to the procedure for data collection and to the focus of the study instead of the number of participants. Single-subject researchers prefer to collect multiple measurements in order to provide a detailed description before and during the course of an intervention. The purpose of single-subject experimental research is to clearly establish the effects of an intervention on specific individuals rather than information about the average performance of groups. The use of single-subject designs began because of dissatisfaction among researchers when inferences from group studies were not observed when applied to individuals. As with traditional group research experimental studies, the aim of single-subject designs is to ensure that changes in responses are indeed the result of that intervention and not a consequence of chance, error or other extraneous factors

Variables and Functional Relation

The term *variable* is used to refer to any number of factors involved in research. Experimental designs distinguish between two types of variables: dependent and independent. A dependent variable refers to the outcome of the behavior targeted for change. An independent variable refers to the intervention being used to change the behavior. Single-subject designs require repeated measures of the dependent variable. The performance of a student's behavior is monitored and recorded weekly, daily, or more frequently over time. The student's performance can then be compared under different experimental or intervention conditions (i.e., independent variable). When systematic and repeated changes of a dependent variable occur as a result of the independent variable, a functional relation between the dependent and independent variable can be demonstrated. A functional relation is a tentative cause-effect relation between independent and dependent variables. The researcher can have confidence that the behavior changed as a function of the independent variable because with each replication, only the intervention is introduced or manipulated.

Baseline Measures   Baseline data measure a student's level of performance prior to intervention implementation. That is, a representative sample of the natural occurrence of the student's performance. Moreover, baseline data serve to describe the student's current level of performance using descriptive measures including the mean, median, and range. The first phase of a single-subject design is the collection and recording of baseline data. Baseline data serve a similar function as a pretest. However, repeated measure of at least five baseline data points (Alberto & Troutman, 2006) are collected and recorded to better establish the duration, frequency, and intensity of behavior(s) examined. Baseline data assist teachers in identifying and/or verifying the existence and the extent of an academic or behavioral deficit. So, in addition to multiple data points, tracking student performance across settings and time of day, for example, are good practices to better ensure a true representative sample of a student's performance.

Baseline data also serve a predictive utility. The predictive function allows a teacher to expect a student's immediate level of functioning to continue absent of an intervention being implemented. Since baseline data are to be used to examine the effectiveness of the intervention, it is critical that baseline data are stable.

The stability of a baseline is assessed by variability of data points and trends in data points. Variability of data refers to fluctuations in the student's performance. The greater the data variability, the more difficult it is to predict student performance and to make strong conclusions related to intervention effectiveness (Kazdin, 1982). Where variables can be controlled, a research-oriented criterion for the existence of stability is data points within a 5% range of variability (Sidman, 1960). However, since a classroom, rather than laboratory, seldom possesses "facilities or time that would be required to eliminate variability" (Sidman, p. 193), Repp (1983) proposed a therapeutic criterion of 20% variability. With that in mind, baseline data may be considered stable if no baseline data points vary more than 20% from the baseline mean.

A trend in the data refer to an indication of a distinctive direction in performance. A trend is defined as three consecutive data points in the same direction (Barlow & Hersen, 1984). A baseline may show an ascending, descending, and a no trend. An ascending trend in baseline denotes an increasing pattern of data points. Teachers should implement an intervention on an ascending baseline trend only if the objective is to decrease the behavior. For example, if a student is demonstrating an increase in the number of reading errors, the goal of the teacher's intervention would be to decrease the student's number of reading errors. Conversely, a descending trend in baseline denotes a decreasing pattern of data points. Teachers should implement an intervention on a descending baseline trend only if the objective is to increase the behavior. For example, if a student is demonstrating a decrease in the number of words read correctly, the goal of the teacher's intervention would be to increase the student's reading words correctly. Trend lines can provide an indication of the direction of behavior change in the past and a prediction of the direction of behavior change in the future.

Intervention Measures   The second component of single-subject designs is a series of repeated measures of the student's performance under intervention or treatment condition (phase). The independent variable (intervention) is implemented and its effects on the dependent variable (student performance) are measured. Trends in the intervention data indicate the effectiveness of the intervention.

Experimental Control   Experimental control refers to the researcher's efforts to ensure that changes in the dependent variable are directly related to the manipulation of the independent variable. The researcher wants to control for or to eliminate the chance that other variables (confounding variables) are responsible for the change in the student's performance (dependent variable). Confounding variables are events or conditions that may affect the dependent variable, which are not controlled by the researcher. When an investigator sufficiently controls for confounding variables and establishes that a student's performance systematically changed as a result of introducing an intervention, then a functional relation is assumed. A functional relation may be considered a cause-effect relation. However, changes in the dependent variable should covariate within at least three different series at three different points in time as a direct result of the independent variable for the establishment of a functional relation (Horner et al., 2005). Experimental control should continue until the investigator can determine an effect of an intervention. Additionally, when a functional relation is established for one individual, repeated studies of the same intervention are conducted using different individuals and other dependent variables. Researchers using single-subject designs do not assume generality of research results based on a single successful intervention. The more frequently an intervention proves effective, the more confidence is gained about the generality of the results of the intervention.

The specific designs discussed in this chapter provide varying degrees of experimental control from research designs (e.g., ABAB, changing criterions, multiple baseline, alternating treatments) to teaching designs (e.g., AB, changing conditions). Teaching designs do not permit confident assumptions of a functional relation. However, teaching designs do provide sufficient indication of a change in student performance for everyday classroom use. Research designs provide experimental control and allow an investigator to presume a functional relation.

AB "Teaching" Design   The AB design is the most basic single-subject design. More sophisticated single-subject designs are an extension of the AB design. The designation of AB refers to the two phases of the design: A or baseline phase and B or intervention phase. Figure 36.1 shows fictitious data collected and graphed using an AB design. The teacher in this instance was concerned about the minimal amount of time a student read during class. For 5 days, she continued to assign the student reading materials, as she usually acted, while collecting baseline data regarding the number of minutes the student read. Afterwards, she allowed the student to choose a book from a collection, as an intervention, and continued to record the number of minutes reading during class. A dashed line on the graph separates the two phases and data points between phases are not connected. The number of minutes reading during the intervention phase increased, illustrating a clear picture of the effectiveness of the intervention.

The AB design is not often found in professional literature because it cannot assess for a functional relation. The design does not provide for the replication within an experiment to establish a functional relation. However, the primary advantage of an AB design is its simplicity. It provides teachers with a quick, uncomplicated means of comparing students' performance before and after intervention implementation, making instruction more systematic.

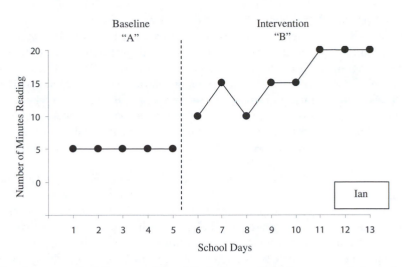

Figure 36.1 Ficitious graph of an AB design.

Teachers may find the use of the AB design useful when conducting action research in the classroom or when determining a student's response to a particular intervention (i.e., response to intervention). The disadvantage of the AB design is that it cannot be used to make confident assumptions of a functional relation. Although the data may indicate intervention efficacy, this design does not provide replication of the independent variable or intervention procedures. With this in mind, the AB design lacks experimental control and is vulnerable to confounding variables.

Withdrawal/Reversal (ABAB) Design   The withdrawal/reversal design is used to analyze the effectiveness of a single independent variable. Commonly referred to as the ABAB design, this design involves the sequential application and withdrawal of the intervention to verify effects on students' performance. The withdrawal/reversal design has four phases: A, B, A, and B.

- A (baseline 1): initial baseline phase during which student performance data are collected repeatedly under existing conditions prior to the introduction of the intervention
- B (intervention 1): initial intervention phase which the

independent variable is introduced to alter the student's performance. Intervention phase continues until criterion of the student's performance is reached or a trend in the therapeutic direction is evident

- A (baseline 2): during this phase the intervention is withdrawn or terminated returning to conditions similar to initial baseline phase
- B (intervention 2): during this phase the intervention is re-implemented

By repeatedly comparing the baseline data to the data collected during implementation of the intervention, the investigator can determine whether a functional relation exists between the dependent and independent variables. Figure 36.2 shows fictitious data collected and graphed using a withdrawal/reversal ABAB design. This example extends the AB design (see Figure 36.1) to demonstrate a functional relation. After Ian reached criterion (reading for 20 minutes for 3 consecutive days) during the intervention phase (choice), the teacher withdrew the intervention (independent variable). During the second baseline phase (no choice), the amount of time Ian read decreased. Cooper (1981) suggested that the second set of baseline data (A_2) should return to a level close to the mean of the initial

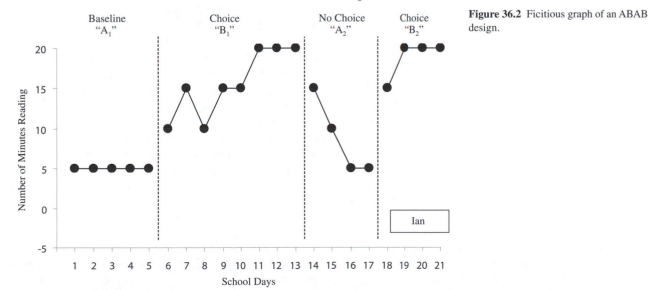

Figure 36.2 Ficitious graph of an ABAB design.

baseline phase (A_1) or an evident trend in the opposite direction of the first intervention phase (B_1). Afterwards, the teacher re-implemented the choices intervention (B_2). The reintroduction of the independent variable during the second intervention phase (B_2) should result in a replication of effect similar to the first intervention phase (B_1). With this in mind, a functional relation is established since systematic change in the dependent variable (number of minutes reading) covariate within at least three different series at three different points in time as a result of introducing and withdrawing the intervention (choice).

The withdrawal/reversal design is an experimental design that allows the investigator to assume a functional relation between the independent and dependent variables. The second baseline and intervention phases, with conditions identical to those of the first, provide an opportunity for replication of the effect of the intervention on the student's behavior. It is unlikely that confounding variables would exist simultaneously with repeated application and withdrawal of the independent variable.

The withdrawal/reversal design offers the advantages of experimental control and simplicity. It provides for precise analysis of the effects of a single independent variable on a single dependent variable. However, the withdrawal/reversal design is not always the most appropriate choice for conducting research in reading. The primary disadvantage of this design is the necessity for withdrawing an effective intervention in order to determine whether a functional relation exists. It is quite possible that many reading behaviors will not revert toward baseline levels once the intervention is withdrawn. In such cases, it is unclear if the intervention was responsible for such changes. For many reading behaviors (e.g., vocabulary skills) the student's learning performance may not be reversible. For example, if a student learns 10 new vocabulary words after introducing an intervention, it is highly unlikely that an investigator would be able to reverse the student's progress. Under such conditions, a return to baseline performance is not feasible. Likewise, after a student learns a reading comprehension strategy or acquires a reading decoding strategy, it is unlikely that the investigator will be able to withdraw the learned strategy or the student comprehension or decoding skills will not deteriorate to previous baseline levels. Of course, when studying cognitive behaviors one usually considers this a positive occurrence. Reading behaviors that may be more appropriate for study using an ABAB design may include, emergent reading behaviors (e.g., holding the book correctly, turning pages) or the amount of time reading. When dealing with newly learned behaviors, the reversibility of what is learned has important implications for how you design your study. The following single-subject designs do not require a reversal of behavior or an intervention withdrawal to establish a functional relation, which may be more applicable for reading research.

Changing Criterion Design The changing criterion design evaluates the effectiveness of an independent variable by demonstrating that a student's performance can be incrementally increased or decreased. This design is especially useful when the student's ultimate performance criterion is considerably distant from the student's baseline performance. Using a changing criterion design greatly increases the probability of student success. For student's who have significant reading difficulties, a changing criterion design is an appropriate design to evaluate the student's progress, as well as for setting the occasion for successful reading experiences.

The changing criterion design includes two phases. The first phase, as in all single-subject designs, is baseline. The second phase is intervention. The intervention phase also is composed of subphases. Each subphase requires a closer approximation of the ultimate criterion. In addition, each subphase becomes the basis for decision making about subsequent phases. Interim criteria can be established by an (a) amount equal to the mean of the stable portion of the baseline data, (b) amount equal to 50% less than the mean of the baseline, (c) amount equal to 50% greater than the mean of the baseline, (d) amount equal to the highest or lowest (depending on therapeutic direction) performance level of baseline, and (e) amount equal to the professional's judgment of the student's performance (Alberto & Troutman, 2006). However, if increases in criterion levels are in a "perfect" stepwise progression, one may wonder if the student learned to respond to the expected predictable increases (or decreases) or whether the application of the independent variable caused the dependent variable to change. It is critical to demonstrate that it is the independent variable that produced the change in performance rather than the student simply responding to the expectations that arise from the intervention phase. Hartmann and Hall (1976) recommended that intervention phases should differ in length, or a constant length should be preceded by a baseline phase longer than each of the subphases. By alternating phase lengths, the researcher limits the possibility of confounding sequencing effects and ensures that stepwise changes in student performances are not occurring naturally in conjunction with criterion changes.

Nes (2003) used a changing criterion design to examine the use of an intervention package including student goal setting and paired reading to improve students' reading rate. Four students in the fourth, fifth, and sixth grades, who were identified as reading at least 1 year below grade level and reading at least 35% below recommended minimum oral reading rates participated. Figure 36.3 shows the data collected and graphed for one student's (Austin) reading rate. Under baseline conditions, Austin demonstrated a mean level performance of 41 words read per minute. Based on baseline data and profession judgment, Austin and his teacher determined the criterion level for the initial intervention phase. Austin continued to participate in the intervention until the sub-phases' criteria were reached and the ultimate goal was achieved. Nes established a functional relation by demonstrating that the students' reading rate increased incrementally within three different series at three

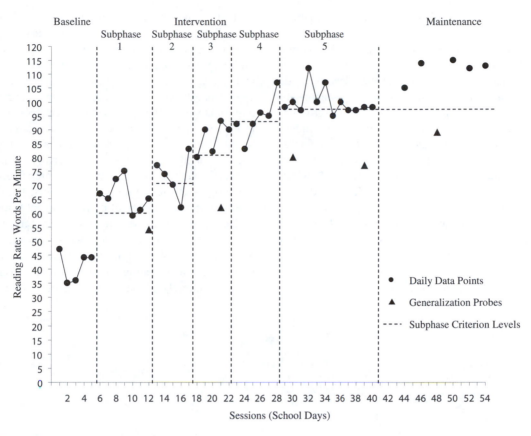

Figure 36.3 Graph of a changing criterion design.

different points in time as a result of the systematic implementation of the reading intervention. Nes also assessed the students reading rate following the introduction of the reading intervention during the maintenance phase.

The advantage of the changing criterion design is that it can establish a functional relation while continually changing the student's performance in the therapeutic direction. The intervention is never withdrawn, which is beneficial to reading intervention research. However, using the changing criterion design requires gradual change in performance. It may therefore be inappropriate for behaviors that require or lend themselves to rapid change.

Multiple Baseline Design (Participants, Settings, Behaviors)

Multiple baseline designs provide a means for collecting multiple sets of data in a single-case experimental design. As indicated by its name, the multiple baseline design permits simultaneous analysis of more than one dependent variable. Kucera and Axelrod (1995) suggested that multiple baseline designs compliment literacy research very well. Kucera and Axlerod also noted that multiple baseline designs can assist in the examination of new reading strategies and interventions. The multiple baseline design is desirable when it is not possible to withdraw an intervention or to reverse a student's progress to initial baseline conditions.

A teacher or researcher may experimentally assess the effects of interventions (independent variable) across behaviors, subjects (participants), and/or settings (e.g.,

Barlow, & Hersen, 1984; Kazdin, 1982; Kennedy, 2005). A multiple baseline design across behaviors consists of the examination of three or more behaviors associated with one student in a single-setting. A multiple baseline design across subjects (participants) consists of three or more students exhibiting the same behavior in a single setting. Lastly, a multiple baseline design across settings consists of three or more settings in which one student is performing the same behavior.

When using a multiple baseline design, the teacher or researcher collects data on each dependent variable simultaneously. The teacher collects data under baseline conditions for each student, on each behavior, or in each setting. To make data analysis possible, the same scale of measurement should be used for each dependent variable (e.g., number of words read correctly per minute, percentage of questions comprehended).

While baseline data may be collected at the same time, the intervention phase should be implemented one at time. After a stable baseline has been established on the first variable, intervention with that variable can begin. During the intervention phase, the baseline data collection continues for the remaining variables. Intervention on the second variable should begin when the first variable reaches the predetermined criterion. The intervention phases should continue for the first variable and baseline data should continue for the third or additional variables. After the second variable reaches the predetermined criterion, then the intervention phase for the third variable is introduced, while data continues to be collected on previous variables. This sequence continues until the intervention has been implemented to all identified variables across behaviors, students, and/or settings.

The data collected in a multiple baseline design can be examined for a functional relation between the independent variable and each of the dependent variables. The introduction of the intervention, with the second and subsequent dependent variables, demonstrates a replication of effect. A functional relation is assumed if each dependent variable, in succession, demonstrates a change when, and only when, the independent variable is implemented. That is, the occurrence of systematic changes in a dependent variable as a result of introducing the intervention within at least three different series at three different points in time (Horner et al., 2005).

Bianco and McCormick (1989) used a multiple baseline across behaviors to evaluate a reading program to teach students with learning disabilities to comprehend text material. Eight high school students with a learning disability in reading participated. Students were taught to use an outlining advanced organizer in order to identify important and relevant ideas from a passage. All reading passages came from the students' history textbooks. Students were required to read a two-page section from their textbook and to then compose an outline noting subordinate details to superordinate points. Figure 36.4 shows the daily results of one student during baseline, instructional, postinstructional, and follow-up phases across three comprehension skills (a) main topics, (b) subtopics, and (c) details. The data points represent the percentage of correct content responses.

During baseline, the intervention was not introduced, as it would compromise experimental control. Bianco and McCormick (1989) first introduced information on how to select relevant content and how to use the advanced organizer to comprehend main topics. After introducing the in-

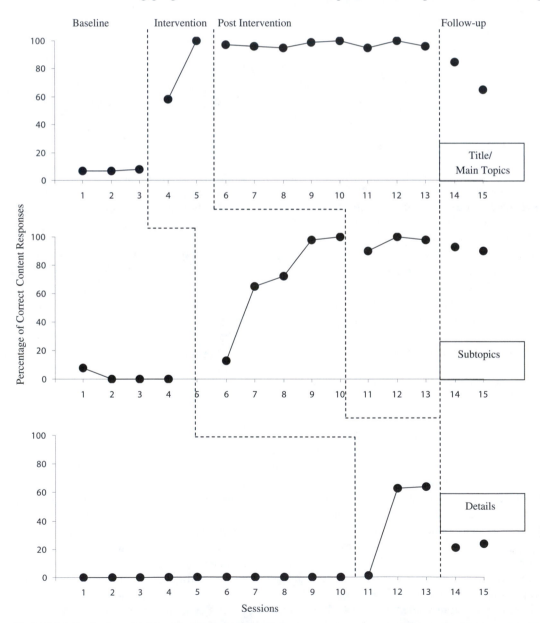

Figure 36.4 Graph of a multiple baseline design across behaviors.

tervention (independent variable), the student's percentage of correct content responses increased. Inspecting the other two skills (subtopics and details) in baseline, an increase in the percentage of correct content responses is not observed. Only when the teacher introduces the intervention targeting the second skill (subtopics), an increase in the percentage of correct content responses occurs. Concurrently, the third skill (details) during baseline is not showing an increase. The student's percentage of correct content responses increases for the third skill (details) only after the intervention is implemented. The multiple baseline design shows a functional relation with the staggered introduction of the independent variable (advanced organizer) and percentage of correct content responses for these eight high school students since three different data paths increased incrementally at three different points in time.

In a meta-analysis of 85 single-subject design studies, Swanson and Sachse-Lee (2000) reported that 62% of studies used a multiple baseline design. The multiple baseline design can establish a functional relation without withdrawing the intervention, as in a withdrawal/reversal design and without gradual alterations, as in a changing criterion design. Since the intervention is not withdrawn and the student's performance does not need to be reversed, the multiple baseline designs possess great utility for researchers studying reading. However, the multiple baseline designs do encompass some limitations and maybe inappropriate when the target behavior requires immediate action as the multiple baseline design calls for considerable delay in the delivery of the intervention for the second and subsequent variables. For example, when using a multiple baseline across students, the second and third students are not introduced to a potential intervention until the preceding student reaches criterion. In addition, multiple baseline designs may be inappropriate when the dependent variables are highly correlated. In such cases, the intervention with one behavior will bring about the change in related behaviors. With that in mind, the teacher or researcher will be unable to evaluate clearly the effects of the intervention procedure. For instance, if the two behaviors targeted for change are reading words correctly and reading rate, the teacher might find that after the student's reading accuracy increases, improvement in reading rate occurs too. In this case, the dependent variables are not independent.

Alternating Treatments Design

The alternating treatments design allows comparison of the effectiveness of more than one treatment or intervention (independent variables) on a single dependent variable. The alternating treatments design permits researchers and teachers to compare the effects of two different reading interventions on a student's reading skills. The alternating treatments design also is referred to as a multi-element design.

The first step when using an alternating treatments design is to select the student's behavior and two or more potential interventions (independent variables). Next, two or more representative samples of the behavior (e.g., two or more reading passages equal in readability, yet different passages) are selected. Each sample is then designated for each intervention. As the name implies, the different treatments are implemented alternatively. Lastly, counterbalancing is used to minimize the effects of carryover and sequencing effects (Kazdin, 1982). That is, presenting the treatments in a random order to reduce potential effects that each treatment may have on the other (Barlow & Hersen, 1984).

If the data path of one treatment separates from the other data path, it is said to be fractionated. Fractionation indicates that the treatments are differentially effective. The alternating treatments design does not always include a replication phase. Therefore, the establishment of a functional relation is relatively weak. To make a stronger case, a third phase can be instituted. During this phase, the more effective treatment is applied to the behavior (or behavior sample) that was treated with the ineffective treatment during the intervention phase. If the behavior improves (therapeutic direction), then the treatment is replicated and the functional relation is strengthen.

Beliforne, Grskovic, Murphy, and Zentall (1996) used an alternating treatments design to study the differential effects of using black and white flashcards compared to color added flashcards on students' rate of word acquisition. Three elementary students with learning disabilities in reading participated in both interventions. Readability level of all words was equal and intervention conditions were counterbalanced to limit the possibility of confounding variables and results. Figure 36.5 shows the cumulative acquisition of sight-words for all students. All students incorrectly read all words probed during baseline. During the alternating treatments phase, both the black/white and color added treatments were introduced. The results indicated that Tim learned slightly more sight words during the black and white flashcard condition, whereas Darrell learned slightly more sight words during the color added condition. A fractionization of the cumulative words mastered between the black/white flashcard words and color added words occurred. Jason's results suggest that he learned sight-words similarly during both treatments. That is, both black/white and color added flashcards were equally effective or no functional differences occurred between the two treatments. Beliforne et al. concluded that, overall, students learned sight words equally well during both interventions. To make a stronger case, Beliforne et al. would need to introduce a third phase. During this phase, the sight words not mastered during color added condition for Tim, and sight words not mastered during the black/white condition for Darrell would be presented again using the more effective treatment for each student (black/white for Tim and color added for Darrell). If the acquisition rate of sight-words demonstrated a marked improvement, then the effects of the preferred treatment would have been replicated and the functional relation strengthened.

The alternating treatments design is an efficient way for teachers to answer instructional questions such as, which method is most likely to be successful for this student?

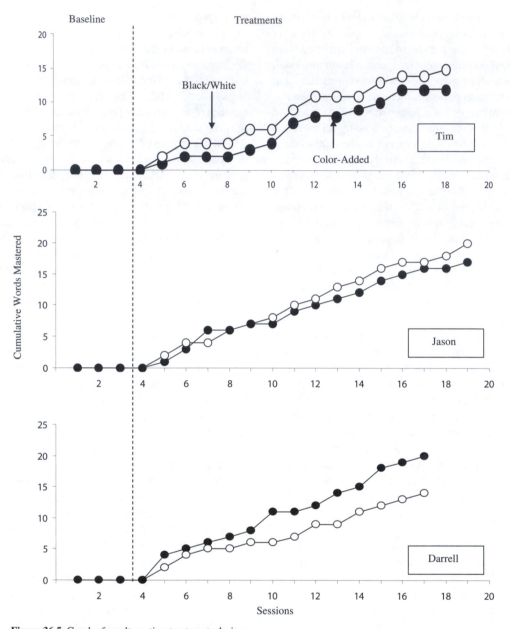

Figure 36.5 Graph of an alternating treatments design.

After a clear fractionization appears, the teacher can select the most successful method. If both treatments are functionally similar, as with Jason, then student and teacher preferences become qualifiers for using one intervention versus another.

Changing Conditions Design The changing conditions design is a teacher design rather than an experimental design since a functional relation is not established. Similar to an alternating-treatments design, a changing conditions design is used to examine the effects of two or more interventions (independent variables) on the behavior (dependent variable) of a student. Unlike the alternating treatments design, the interventions in this design are introduced sequentially. The changing conditions design is useful for teachers who find it necessary to try a number of interventions before

finding one that is successful for the student. The changing conditions design also is referred to as an ABC design since each new intervention phase is given an identifying letter (Kazdin, 1982).

Like all single-subject designs, the first step in implementing a changing conditions design is to collect baseline data to assess the student's current level of performance. Once a stable baseline is established, the teacher introduces the selected intervention and measures its effectiveness through repeated measures. If the student does not reach criterion or the intervention does not produce a sufficient change, a teacher may design a second intervention. This second intervention can either be an adaptation of the first intervention or a complete change in strategy. The process of redesigning intervention conditions continues until the student reaches criterion or the desired effect of the intervention.

The changing conditions design is used when the teacher is (a) determining the effectiveness between treatments, (b) designing an instructional package that will facilitate a student's performance, or (c) systematically fading assistances to enhance independent student performance (Kazdin, 1982). When determining treatment effectiveness, treatments are introduced consecutively, each with its own phase, until the desired effect is achieved. This design is an extension of the AB design. As in the AB design, there is no replication of the effect of either intervention and there can be no establishment of a functional relation.

When designing an instructional package, a teacher starts from the student's present level of performance. The teacher adds new interventions cumulatively until the student's performance reaches the desired outcome. As each strategy is added to the instructional package, a new phase is identified. Conversely, a teacher may use the changing condition design to systematically reduce the amount of assistance being provided to a student in order to identify the least amount of help required for ongoing successful performance. Each reductive change is considered a new phase. For example, in order to improve reading skills, a student requires peer assistance, highlighting important text, use of skimming strategies, and story maps to aid comprehension; the teacher withdraws systematically each intervention while maintaining the desired reading performance.

Figure 36.6 shows fictitious data collected and graphed using a changing conditions design. In this instance, the teacher was concerned about three students learning

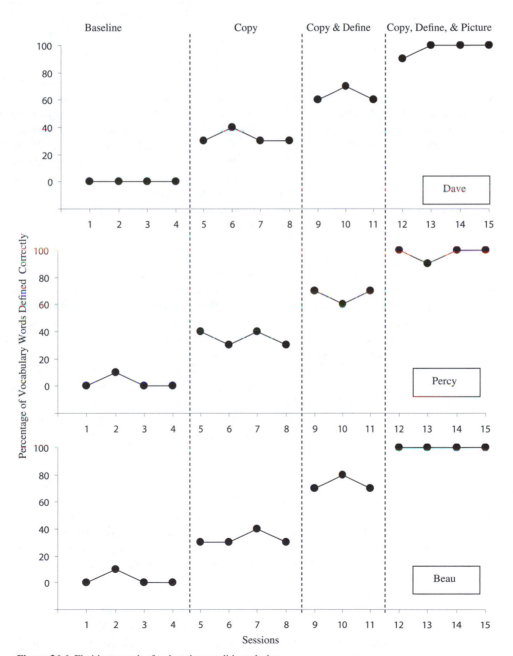

Figure 36.6 Fictitious graph of a changing conditions design.

their weekly vocabulary words. For 5 days, she collected baseline data on each student's percentage of vocabulary words defined correctly. She then introduced a number of teaching conditions and continued measuring the students' vocabulary performance. She first asked students to copy the word and its definition. Since the copy strategy was minimally effective, the teacher altered the previous phase by having the student define the vocabulary words in their own words. Again, students' performance improved only marginally; therefore, the teacher again altered the previous phase. During this phase, students copied the vocabulary words and its definition, define it in their own words, and drew a picture illustrating each vocabulary words meaning. During this final phase, all students reached the ultimate criterion for the percentage of vocabulary words defined correctly.

The changing conditions design with a single baseline phase allows the teacher to compare the effectiveness of a number of interventions on a student's reading behaviors. Although no functional relation is assumed (no demonstration of intervention effects replicated within or across students), repeatedly measuring student performance in this format allows teachers to monitor the effects of various reading strategies. A teacher who records data systematically in a changing conditions design will have a good record of the student's progress and a good indication of instructional procedures that are effective and ineffective for the student. The changing conditions design can assist reading teachers who are monitoring a student's response to interventions. However, the teacher must be aware that outcomes may be contributed to cumulative effects of various interventions rather than a single intervention. To assess a functional relation, the changing conditions design must be refined to include repeated baselines and replication of the intervention, such as an $A_1B_1A_2C_1A_3B_2$ design. For example, following each potential intervention phase, the intervention that produced the greatest desired outcome is reimplemented after another baseline phase. If the intervention is successful again, this is a replication of its effect, and therefore a functional relation is assumed. This design also may be viewed as a variation of the withdrawal/reversal or ABAB design.

Evaluating Single-Subject Designs

The purpose of single-subject experimental research is to clearly establish the effects of an intervention on specific individuals rather than information about the average performance of groups. The effectiveness of an intervention can be determined against both experimental criterion and clinical criterion. The experimental criterion verifies that an independent variable (intervention) was responsible for the change in the dependent variable (outcome). Single-subject designs demonstrating within-subject replication of effect satisfy this criterion (e.g., Barlow & Hersen, 1984; Kazdin, 1982; Richards et al., 1999). The clinical criterion is a judgment as to whether the results of the intervention have

meaningful benefits and positively impacts the individual's life in everyday situations, as well as for those who interact with the person (Baer, Wolf, & Risley, 1968). For instance, if a student learns two new vocabulary words as a result of an intervention, a teacher should ask if these results are truly meaningful. Similarly, another criterion for evaluating intervention outcomes is social validity. Social validity is a concept that is used in intervention research in which the goal is to produce change in human functioning (Kazdin, 1998). Social validity alerts teachers and researchers to issues concerning the applied value of the intervention: (a) the goals of the intervention are socially important, (b) intervention procedures are socially acceptable, and (c) intervention outcomes have had a palpable impact and actually helped people, as well as those who interact with them, in ways that are evident in everyday life.

Single-subject designs are usually evaluated through visual analysis procedures of a graph displaying the plotted data points of the various phases or conditions. Visual analysis involves interpretation of the level, trend, and variability of performance occurring during baseline and intervention conditions. Level refers to the mean performance during a condition (i.e., phase) of the study. Trend references the rate of increase or decrease of the best-fit straight line for the dependent variable within a condition (i.e., slope). Variability refers to the degree to which performance fluctuates around a mean during a phase. Additionally, in visual analysis, the teacher or researcher also determines (a) the rapidity of effects which refers to the length of time following the onset and/or withdrawal of the intervention, (b) the proportion of data points in adjacent phases that overlap, (c) the magnitude of change in the dependent variable, and (d) the consistency of data patterns across multiple presentations of intervention and nonintervention conditions. The integration of information from these multiple assessments and comparisons is used to determine if a functional relation exists between the independent and dependent variables. Documentation of a functional relation requires compelling demonstration of an effect (Parsonson & Baer, 1978). So, a functional relation is assumed when predicted change in the dependent variable covaries with manipulation of the independent variable. In most cases, a functional relation is demonstrated when the design documents three demonstrations of intervention effects, at three different points in time, with a single participant (within-subject replication), or three different points in time across different participants (inter-subject replication).

Although visual analysis is primarily used and practical for verifying strong intervention effects for educational research, researchers may choose to explore statistical analysis of single-subject data to support or contrast the results. However, statistical tests for single-subject research have been associated with major sources of controversy. The first issue concerns whether statistical tests should be used at all. The major objection is that statistical tests are likely to detect subtle and only minor changes in performance that ordinarily would be rejected through visual analysis. Statistical analyses may detract from the goals of single-subject research to discover variables that not only produce reliable effects, but also result with important and socially valid outcomes. The second source of controversy pertains to specific statistical tests used and whether they are appropriate for single-subject research. Development of statistical tests for single-subject research has lagged behind the development of analysis for between-group research. Various analyses that have been suggested are controversial because data from single-subject research often violates some of the assumptions on which various statistical tests depend.

With limitations in mind, statistical tests are especially useful when several of the desired characteristics of the data required for visual analysis are not met. For example, when baselines are unstable or show a trend in the therapeutic direction, selected statistical test can more readily identify potential intervention effects. There are also situations in which detecting small changes, especially in early stages of research before the intervention is well understood, may be important and statistical tests may be useful. Several statistical techniques are available for single-subject experimental designs. Table 36.1 lists parametric and analogous nonparametric procedures adopted from Meyers and Grossen (1974). The appropriateness of any particular test depends on the design, characteristics of the data, and various ways in which the intervention is presented. For a more comprehensive understanding of nonparametric statistics, several authors are referenced (e.g., Gay, Mills, & Airasian, 2006; Gibbons, 1993; Huck, 2004).

In addition, a need exists to review the literature on given practices, to synthesize the findings across studies, and to make recommendations about the use of the studied interventions. Given the utility of meta-analytic studies for synthesizing findings, most between group experimental studies use effect sizes (Busk & Serlin, 1992; Dunst, Hamby, & Trivette, 2004) and regression analysis (Allison & Gorman, 1993; Faith, Allison, & Gorman, 1996). The calculations for effect sizes and regression analysis are based on the assumption the data in a condition (e.g., baseline) are independent. However, in single subject studies, data are collected on a single participant under the same conditions using repeated measurement procedures; thus, the data are likely serial dependent (i.e., not independent). If the assumption of independence is violated, spurious findings are likely (Kazdin, 1982). If the model of serial dependency was identified through autocorrelations, then it could be controlled statistically, and effect sizes could be calculated. However, in most single subject studies, too few data points exist to identify a model of serial dependency, and not having enough data to identify the model of serial dependence does not eliminate the possibility it exists (Suen, 1987). Further, the small number of data points in most baseline conditions means any regression estimate calculated for the condition will likely be unreliable. Thus, effect sizes and regression analysis should be avoided for synthesizing single subject studies.

TABLE 36.1
Parametric and Analogous Nonparametric Procedures

Parametric	Nonparametric
Pearson product-moment correlation coefficient r coefficient (rho)	Spearman rank-order correlation
t-test correlated samples	Sign test Wilcoxon Matched-Pairs Signed-Ranks test
t-test independent samples	Median test Mann-Whitney U test
One-way ANOVA	Kruskal Wallis one way ANOVA of ranks Median test
One-way ANOVA with repeated measures	Friedman two-way ANOVA of ranks
(No analogous parametric test)	Chi-square single-sample

Note. Adopted from Meyers & Grossen (1974)

Yet, a number of computational options have been proposed for conducting such meta-analytic studies with single subject designs, including (a) percentage of overlapping data (Tawney & Gast, 1984); (b) percentage of non-overlapping data (PND; Scruggs & Mastropieri, 1998; Scruggs, Mastropieri, & Casto, 1987a); (c) percentage of all non-overlapping data (PAND; Parker, Hagan-Burke, & Vannest, 2007); and (d) improvement rate difference (IRD) (Parker & Hagan-Burke, 2007). Table 36.2 lists each metric of effect and procedures for calculating it.

Evaluation of the percentage of overlap of data (Tawney & Gast, 1984) plotted for performance across adjacent conditions provides an indication of the impact of an independent variable (intervention) on the dependent variable (outcome). Tawney and Gast calculated the percent of overlap by (a) determining the range of data point values of the first condition, (b) counting the number of data points plotted in the second condition, (c) counting the number of data points plotted in the second condition that fall within the range of values of the first condition, (d) dividing the number of data points that fall within the range of values of the first condition by the total number of data points of the second condition, and (e) multiplying by 100. Tawney and Gast added, "generally, the lower the percentage of overlap, the greater the impact the intervention has on the target behavior" (p. 164).

Scruggs et al. (1987a) proposed the use of a percentage of nonoverlapping data (PND) metric to evaluate outcomes of single-subject research. Using this metric, the reviewer determines the proportion of data points in a given treatment condition that exceeds the extreme value in the baseline condition. If an intervention intended to increase behavior, this would be the proportion of treatment data points that exceeds the highest baseline value. Proportion of nonoverlapping data is a primary consideration in evaluating single subject research (Kazdin, 1976; Tawney & Gast, 1984) and can be easily calculated (Scruggs et al., 1987a). If 8 of 10 treatment data points exceed the highest baseline observa-

TABLE 36.2
Metrics of Effect and Calculations

Metric of Effect	Calculations
Percentage of Overlap (Tawney & Gast, 1984)	(1) Determine the range of data point values of the first condition; (2) count the number of data points plotted in the second condition; (3) count the number of data points of the second condition that fall within the range of values of the first condition; and (4) divide the number of data points that fall within the range of the first condition by the total number of data points of the second condition and multiply the number by 100.
Percentage of Non-Overlap Data (PND; Scruggs, Mastropieri, & Casto, 1987)	(1) Determine the highest data point value observed during the first condition; (2) count the number of data points plotted in the second condition; (3) count the number of data points of the second condition that exceed the highest observed value of the first condition; and (4) divide the number of data points that exceed the highest observed value of the first condition by the total number of data points of the second condition and multiply the number by 100.
Percentage of All Non-Overlapping Data (PAND; Parker, Hagan-Burke, & Vannest, 2007)	The setting-up of a data file includes the creation of five variable columns: Random, Series, ABPhase, Score, and Sorted (best accomplished with a statistics package, but also can be done by Microsoft Excel). Random includes a set of random numbers. Series contains a different category for each series (e.g., I, II, III, IV). ABPhase is dichotomous, containing categorical tags for the two types of phases (A, B). Scores contains original scores from all series. Sorted is an empty column in the spreadsheet (results from a nested sort are later pasted here). The data are entered in a tall vertical column, with series under one another. (1) Copy ABPhase. Ensure the datafile is properly set up, with Time ascending (1, 2, 3, etc.), Series ascending (I, II, III), and ABPhase ascending (A, B) for each Series. When the file is properly set up, copy contents of ABPhase, and hold it in computer memory; (2) Randomize. Sort the entire dataset by the Randomize column; (3) Nested Sort. Sort Score within Series. If scores are expected to improve, then both variables are sorted normally, ascending. However, if Scores are expected to decrease across phases, then the nested Score is sorted inversely (descending); (4) Paste the ABPhase data being held in memory (copied in Step 1) into the empty Sort column; and (5) Conduct a Crosstabs analysis on the ABPhase and Sort columns. Output will include the 2×2 table, as well as the Phi statistic. For confidence intervals around Phi, analyze the table's contents by a statistical module for testing two independent proportions.
Improvement Rate Difference (IRD; Parker & Hagan-Burke, 2007)	(1) On a large single case research graph, compare Phase A and Phase B data points. Count the total number of data points in each phase (e.g., Phase A = 10, Phase B = 14); (2) Identify the smallest number of data points among Phases A and B that would have to be removed to eliminate all overlap or ties between phases (e.g., Phase A = 1, Phase B = 3). Subtract the number removed from Phase B from the total number of data points in Phase A to obtain the number remaining (e.g., Phase A = 14 − 3 = 11); (3) Write an "improvement rate" fraction for each phase; a) For Phase A: number removed data points ÷ total number data points (e.g., Phase B = 3 ÷ 14 = 0.21). b) For Phase B: number remaining data points ÷ total number data points in the phase (e.g., Phase A = 9 ÷ 10 = 0.90). (4) Subtract the smaller from the larger fraction; the difference is the improvement rate difference (IRD; e.g., phase 0.90 − 0.21 = 0.69). We interpret IRD by saying, "The difference or gain in improvement rate from baseline to intervention phases is 21% to 90%, or a 69% gain"; and (5) For confidence intervals, enter four scores (two proportions) in a statistical module for testing "two independent proportions." a) For control group: number removed ÷ number remaining (3 ÷ 11). b) For treatment group: number remaining ÷ number removed (9 ÷ 1). Select 90% or 95% exact (permutation) confidence intervals.

tion, for example, the PND score is 8/10 (80%). Scruggs and Mastropieri (2001) offered general interpretational guidelines of PND > 70 for effective interventions, 50 < PND < 70 for interventions of questionable effectiveness, and PND < 50 for interventions with no observed effect.

PND offers at least three advantages. First is the ease of calculation, as PND can be conducted with a pencil and ruler on a printed graph, and as a percentage calculation. Second is acceptability to visual analysts, as PND's emphasis on overlapping data reflects a key component of most visual analysis. The third advantage is PND's applicability to any single-subject design. However, Parker, Hagan-Burke, and Vannest (2007) noted at least four limitations of PND. First, PND is neither an effect size nor related to an accepted effect size, so PND requires its own interpretation guidelines. Second, PND has unknown reliability, as it lacks a known sampling distribution, so alpha values and confidence intervals cannot be calculated. The third weakness is that PND ignores all phase A data except for one data point, which because of its

extremity, is likely the most unreliable. The fourth limitation is that PND lacks sensitivity or discrimination ability, as it nears 100%, for very successful interventions.

Parker et al. (2007) recommended a new metric called the percentage of all non-overlapping data (PAND). A minimum of 20 data points (5 per cell of the 2 x 2 table) are required to calculate PAND. Like PND, PAND reflects data non-overlap between phases. However, PAND uses all data from both phases, avoiding the criticism of PND for over-emphasis on one data point. PAND also can be translated to Pearson's *Phi* and *Phi²*, which are both established measures to determine effect sizes. The parametric requirements of equal variance and normality do not apply towards PAND. Moreover, the requirement of serial independence or lack of autocorrelation has little impact on PAND results because the tabled frequency data are unordered.

From calculations of over 75 datasets, Parker et al. (2007) concluded that PAND and PND proved analogous in efficiency. However, PAND resolves some deficiencies of

PND. PAND is related closely to the established Pearson's *Phi* effect size although calculating confidence intervals for *Phi* requires an additional step. PAND also offers alpha values and confidence interval (CI) to indicate reliability. The addition of CI information is highly desirable for publications and conducting meta-analyses.

Parker and Hagan-Burke (2007) also recommended the use of Improvement Rate Differences (IRD) as an effect size index for single-subject designs. IRD is hand calculated, based on nonoverlapping data, and requires no more data assumptions that PND. Often used as a clinical outcome measure in evidence-based medical research, Parker and Hagan-Burke examined IRD with 165 single-subject design data sets. IRD outperformed PND as an effective ES measure for single-subject research. IRD also showed reasonably validity by established Pearson *R* and Kruskal-Walllis *W* analytic techniques. Moreover, IRD is accompanied with additional confidence interval information, which is strongly recommended in the professional literature and conducting meta-analyses.

Combining Single-Subject Experimental Designs with Case Studies

In general, single-subject researchers are interested in analyzing quantitatively the effect of an intervention on one or more learning outcomes, whereas qualitative researchers (e.g., case-study approach) focus on generating narrative descriptions and interpretations of phenomena that occur without explicit interventions. Brantlinger, Jimenez, Klingner, Pugach, and Richardson (2005) defined qualitative research as "a systematic approach to understanding qualities, or the essential nature, of a phenomenon within a particular context" (p. 195). Although single-subject and case-study approaches share an emphasis on research concerning individuals rather than larger populations, the traditions from which they identify events, phenomena, and different types of research questions, as well as, how to best study such events, phenomena, and examining questions are derived from different assumptions, research designs, and data collection methods. These two research approaches are described by some as opposing because of long-standing debates between quantitative researchers who use single-subject designs and qualitative researchers who use a case-study approach. The debate has centered on issues of (a) how data should be collected, (b) what constitutes data, and (c) the nature of knowledge. For a more comprehensive understanding of qualitative research designs, numerous authors are referenced (e.g., Bogdan & Biklen, 1998; Cresswell, 1997; Marshall & Rossman, 1998; Maxwell, 1996).

Single-subject experimental researchers provide the literature with prescriptive information about the intervention effects on particular students, while case-study researchers contribute to the literature through understanding the individuals' experience and interpretation. Single-subject researchers believe that predictable cause-effect relations can be established; whereas case-study researchers believe that any identified casual relation is transient and incomplete. To combine methods into coherent sets of alternative researcher goals, questions, and strategies, it is critical that researches establish a primary paradigm within which they are working and shape their study accordingly. Sensible designs and methodological choices must be guided by the investigator's principal assumptions, goals, and questions.

After establishing basic assumptions, goals, and research questions and choosing a guiding paradigm, the next step is to designate a primary research design. For single-subject researchers, this would involve selecting the most appropriate single subject design. Case- study methodologies (e.g., interviews, participant observations) could be incorporated to strengthen and build coherence of the general design of the study. These methods could be used to address critical questions including how the study was implemented, the ease of intervention procedures, the context within which it was implemented, and/or the nature of students' and teachers' attitude during the intervention. However, these methods should be carefully employed to add insight to the study and not towards tangential and unproductive directions.

To effectively combine single-subject designs and case- study methods, investigators will need to broaden their definitions of what is acceptable as data and how it can be represented. Single-subject designs measure their effects objectively and quantitatively. To achieve the benefits of case study methods, researchers must respect more subjective data such as interview responses and narrative descriptions. Qualitative data could be used to support quantitative definitions of "baseline" or "effect" and could be triangulated with quantitative data to strengthen anticipated results or to help explain unanticipated outcomes.

Applying case-study methods within the context of single-subject study could enhance the investigation of an intervention's effect. Wolf (1978) suggested that studies of intervention effects are socially validated on at least three levels (a) the significance of their goals, (b) the appropriateness of their procedures, and (c) the importance of their effect. Wolf also suggested that the social validation process be accomplished through the collection of subjective, qualitative information (e.g., participants' attitudes, acceptance toward the intervention), implying a potential role for case-study methodologies with the context of single-subject designs.

The most common form of social validity assessment involves collecting qualitative information on consumer satisfaction in the form of a questionnaire or rating scale. Intervention studies also might benefit from the collection of qualitative data. Interviews of students, teachers, principals, and parents concerning their level of satisfaction could provide insight into the perceived acceptability, effectiveness, and importance of the intervention. Such techniques also may guide intervention adaptations and contribute to its implementation in other contexts. The purpose of this type of data collection is to investigate the level of participant satisfaction, since it reflects the potential for both acceptability and importance of any intervention study. Other case-study methods, such as in-depth personal interviews, collective case studies, and ethnographies from people who would apply the intervention also could be integrated into the single-subject design. Once intervention information and its effects are examined, qualitative methods might assist with the judgment of other intervention applications such as procedural integrity, internal and external validity. The integration of qualitative data into single subject designs can offer a wealth of information.

The incorporation of case-study approaches and single-subject designs can provide the type of evidence needed for investigators to be confident regarding the conditions under which the intervention is most likely to demonstrate positive outcomes. It also can assist individuals who are applying the intervention (teachers), while identifying potential factors crucial to achieving desired and transferable effects.

Although single-subject and case-study designs may be described as opposing, the two approaches can be mutually beneficial if combined with careful consideration of relevant theoretical issues raised by the paradigm debate. Research in education can be particularly challenging and a gap or lag between research and practice is ever present. However, through openness to combining methodologies in meaningful ways, reducing such challenges by using thorough descriptions of a study's phenomena and by making clear causations between events can merge the two methodologies for the best possible student outcomes.

References

Alberto, P. A., & Troutman, A. C. (2006). *Applied behavior analysis for teachers* (7th ed.). Upper Saddle River, NJ: Prentice Hall.

Allison, D. B., & Gorman, B. S. (1993). Calculating effect sizes for meta-analysis: The case of the single case. *Behavior Research and Therapy, 31*, 621–631.

Barlow, D. H., & Hersen, M. (1984). *Single case experimental designs: Strategies for studying behavior change* (2nd ed.). Needham Heights, MA: Allyn & Bacon.

Bogdan, R., & Biklen, S. (1998). *Qualitative research in education* (3rd ed.). Boston: Allyn and Bacon.

Baer, D. M., Wolf, M. M., & Risley, T. R. (1968). Some current dimensions of applied behavior analysis. *Journal of Applied Behavior Analysis, 1*, 91–97.

Belfiorne, P. J., Grskovic, J. A., Murphy, A. M., & Zentall, S. S. (1996). The effects of antecedent color on reading for students with learning disabilities and co-occurring attention-deficit/hyperactivity disorder. *Journal of Learning Disabilities, 29*, 432–438.

Bianco, L., & McCormick, S. (1989). Analysis of effects of a reading study skill program for high school learning-disabled students. *Journal of Educational Research, 82*, 282–288.

Brantlinger, E., Jimenez, E., Klingner, J., Pugach, M., & Richardson, V. (2005). Qualitative studies in special education. *Exceptional Children, 71*, 149–164.

Busk, P. L., & Serlin, R. C. (1992). Meta-analysis for single-case research. In T. R. Kratochwil & J. R. Levin (Eds.), *Single-case research design and analysis: New directions for psychology and education* (pp. 133–157). Hillsdale, NJ: Erlbaum.

Cooper, J. O. (1981). *Measuring behavior* (2nd ed.). Columbus, OH: Merrill.

Cresswell, J. (1997). *Qualitative inquiry and research design: Choosing among five traditions.* Thousand Oaks, CA: Sage.

Dunst, C. J., Hamby, D. W., & Trivette, C. M. (2004). Guidelines for calculating effect sizes for practice-based research syntheses. *Centerscope, 2*(2), 1–10.

Faith, M. S., Allison, D. B., & Gorman, B. S. (1996). Meta-analysis of single-case research. In R. D. Franklin, D. B. Allison, & B. S. Gorman (Eds.), *Design and analysis of single-case research* (pp. 245–277). Hillsdale, NJ: Erlbaum.

Gay, L. R., Mills, G. E., & Airasian, P. (2006). *Educational research: Competencies for analysis and applications* (8th ed.). Upper Saddle River, NJ: Pearson Education.

Gibbons, J. D. (1993). *Nonparametric statistics: An introduction.* Newbury Park, CA: Sage.

Hartmann, D. P., & Hall, R. V. (1976). The changing criterion design. *Journal of Applied Behavior Analysis, 9*, 527–532.

Horner, R. H., Carr, E. G., Halle, J., McGee, G., Odom, S., & Wolery, M. (2005). The use of single-subject research to identify evidence-based practice in special education. *Exceptional Children, 71*, 165–179.

Huck, S. W. (2004). *Reading statistics and research* (4th ed.). Boston: Pearson Education.

Kazdin, A. E. (1976). Statistical analyses for single-case experimental designs. In M. Hersen & D. Barlow (Eds.), *Single-case experimental designs: Strategies for studying behavior change* (pp. 265–316). New York: Pergamon Press.

Kazdin, A. E. (1982). *Single-case research designs: Methods for clinical and applied settings.* New York: Oxford University Press.

Kazdin, A. E. (1998). *Research design in clinical psychology* (3rd ed.). Boston: Allyn & Bacon.

Kennedy, C. H. (2005). *Single-case designs for educational research.* Boston: Pearson Education.

Kucera, J., & Axelrod, S. (1995). Multiple-baseline designs. In S. B. Neuman and S. McCormick (Eds.), *Single-subject experimental research: Application for literacy* (pp. 47). Newark, DE: International Reading Association.

Marshall, C., & Rossman, G. (1998). *Designing qualitative research* (3rd ed.). Thousand Oaks, CA: Sage.

Maxwell, J. (1996). *Qualitative research design: An interactive approach.* Thousand Oaks, CA: Sage.

Meyers, L. S., & Grossen, N. E. (1974). *Behavior research: Theory, procedures, and design.* San Francisco: W. H. Freeman.

Nes, S. L. (2003). Using paired reading to enhance the fluency skills of less-skilled readers. *Reading Improvement, 40*, 179–192.

Parker, R. I. & Hagan-Burke, S. (2007). Median-based overlap analysis for single case data: A second study. *Behavior Modification, 31*(6), 919–936.

Parker, R. I., Hagan-Burke, S., & Vannest, K. (2007). Percentage of non-overlapping data (PAND): An alternative to PND. *The Journal of Special Education, 40*(4), 194–204.

Parsonson, B., & Baer, D. (1978). The analysis and presentation of graphic data. In T. Kratochwill (Ed.), *Single-subject research: Strategies for evaluating change* (pp. 105–165). New York: Academic Press.

Repp, A. (1983). *Teaching the mentally retarded.* Englewood Cliffs, NJ: Prentice Hall.

Richards, S. B., Taylor, R. L., Ramasamy, R., & Richards, R. Y. (1999). *Single subject research: Applications in educational and clinical settings.* San Diego: Singular Publishing Group.

Scruggs, T. E., & Mastropieri, M. A. (2001). How to summarize single-subject participant research: Ideas and applications. *Exceptionality, 9*, 227–244.

Scruggs, T. E., & Mastropieri, M. A. (1998). Summarizing single-subject research: Issues and applications. *Behavior Modification, 22*, 221–242.

Scruggs, T.E., Mastropieri, M. A., & Casto, G. (1987). The quantitative synthesis of single subject research: Methodology and validation. *Remedial and Special Education, 8*, 24–33.

Sidman, M. (1960). *Tactics of scientific research.* New York: Basic Books.

Skinner, C. H. (2004). *Single-subject designs for school psychologists.* Philadelphia: The Hayworth Press.

Suen, H. K. (1987). On the epistemology of autocorrelation in applied behavior analysis. *Behavioral Assessment, 9,* 113–124.

Swanson, H. L., & Sachse-Lee, C. (2000). A meta-analysis of single-subject-design intervention research for students with LD. *Journal of Learning Disabilities, 33,* 114–136.

Tawney, J. W., & Gast, D. L. (1984). *Single subject research in special education.* Columbus, OH: Charles E. Merrill.

Wolf, M. M. (1978). Social validity: The case for subjective measurement or how applied behavior analysis is finding its heart. *Journal of Applied Behavior Analysis, 11,* 203–214.

37

Experimental and Quasi-Experimental Designs for Interventions

VICTOR L. WILLSON AND WILLIAM RUPLEY
Texas A&M University

The emphasis by the Institute of Education Science on experimental designs to evaluate the effects of interventions in education settings has led to new quantitative models. Campbell and Stanley's (1966) list of threats to the internal validity of experiments was important in alerting researchers to alternate explanations in nonrandomized designs over the ensuing three decades, but it appeared to do little to improve the quality of experiments. Willson and Putnam (1982) documented that almost 20 years after Cambell and Stanley, few studies reported in the American Educational Research Journal utilized randomization or even covariates in quasi-experimental designs. Slavin (2002) detailed the shift by the U.S. Congress and Department of Education in moving towards evidence-based funding and experiments based on randomization. The effort was founded on the so-called medical model, with small scale randomized experiments followed by larger scale trials before large-scale implementation. There was a clear assumption that the randomized experiments conducted in medicine could be implemented in schools. While the lack of parallels was made clear, the creation of the Institute for Education Science (IES) was clearly intended to parallel the research paradigms employed by the National Institutes of Health.

In the requests for proposals that emanated from IES there came early a recognition that some interventions might not be amenable to random assignment; therefore, quasi-experimental designs were included. These tended to assume that units above the level of the child, would be assigned randomly but also possibly matched, into experimental and typical practice conditions. Covariates would be included in the designs as well. A great deal of this design conceptualization was decades old, but new methodology in the intervening time has both made the classical experimental design analysis methods outdated and has also outpaced the conceptual framework for classical experimental design. What Grover Whitehurst (2001) thought was bringing education up to current methodological rigor actually was already outdated in both medicine and educa-

tion. This chapter discusses some of these current methods and the conceptual extensions they offer to experimental design as conceived at IES.

Computational Estimation

In the mid-1970s high speed mainframe computers were used to estimate parameters in models using new procedures, notably the Newton-Raphson method and many alternatives that followed. The use of parameter estimation methods led to implementation of other approaches other than the long-used ordinary least squares estimation (OLS), notably maximum likelihood (ML) and Bayes estimation. These permitted different kinds of models to be investigated and will be discussed later in terms of their applications.

High speed computation also permitted generating random scores, leading to a significant expansion of the use of simulations of statistical models under various conditions, and rapid computation of distributional estimation such as the EM algorithm (Dempster, Laird, & Rubin, 1977), the bootstrap (Efron, 1982), and the Gibbs sampler and the Markov Chain Monte Carlo (MCMC) (Gelfand & Smith, 1990). These are used in various ways to compute estimates in designs that more closely characterize the data and conditions of the studies.

Missing Data

Another innovation that had significant impact on designing and analyzing experiments was multiple imputation (MI), which followed from the Dempster et al. EM algorithm (Rubin, 1987). Originally focused on non-responses in surveys, MI has been expanded to provide a method to estimate missing data in experiments. Rubin and others showed that ignoring missing data produces biased estimates of parameters and, in general, underestimates standard errors, consequently resulting in overinterpretation of chance results. MI uses the covariance of the data actually observed to estimate the missing data. If that were all, it would be no different than earlier regression methods, but MI then adds random error based on the distributions that would be found under complete data to create new scores for the missing data each time MI is run. It uses the MCMC to produce the distributions, and correctly adjusts the standard deviations (and thus standard errors). This procedure assumes that data are missing either missing completely at random (MCAR) or missing at random (MAR). Basically, the data are missing due to random rather than systematic causes. Of course this is often very difficult to determine, and while some statistical investigations can help, often the determination is based on good understanding of the population, the measurements, and the survey process.

Hierarchical Linear Modeling

With Scheffé's (1959) comprehensive treatment of the analysis of variance (ANOVA), the consideration of fixed and random factors became more understandable in terms of inferences about samples of a population found in an experiment as random factors, such as subjects and groups of subjects and classrooms and schools. While the general theory was well established, the implementation of designs with both fixed (e.g., treatments, gender, ethnicity) and random factors lagged behind (Willson & Putnam, 1982). Raudenbush (1988) detailed the development of the statistical methods that appropriately estimated parameters in these mixed designs in which the grouping of subjects in clusters (e.g., classrooms) produces homogeneity that is ignored in classical ANOVA. Using the EM algorithm to produce Bayesian or maximum likelihood estimates, the extension of ANOVA was termed hierarchical linear models (HLM), or multilevel models (MLM), or random coefficient regression (RCR). The difference was that HLM used the information about variation from adjacent levels to correctly estimate error variance. The basis of this idea is that error variance (e.g., the standard deviation of scores within groups averaged across the groups in ANOVA) can also be estimated from the means of the groups from basic sampling theory. Pooling the estimate of the within-groups error and the between groups-based error produces a correct estimate of error variance in the context of a design with naturally-occurring groupings such as classrooms. In a true experimental design, where all subjects are randomly assigned to treatments (and no classroom or classrooms the same as the treatment groups) the estimates will be identical. Otherwise, with designs that require intact classrooms hierarchical linear modeling (HLM) will produce accurate, appropriate estimates of standard errors. Such estimates, in general, will be larger than those of standard ANOVA, much as was discussed with MI, and avoid over interpreting results with too many significant findings. HLM has become a mainstay of modern experimental designs in education given the realities of school structures. We will discuss this in detail later.

Structural Equation Modeling

Karl Jöreskog (1967, 1973) and colleagues constructed a statistical model and theory now called structural equation modeling (SEM), earlier called linear structural relations (LISREL) that combined path analysis (Wright, 1921) with test theory (Lord & Novick, 1968). This seemingly disparate combination of disciplines has become the major organizer for statistical theory in the social sciences. Path analysis was an obscure procedure to decompose correlations based on so-called path models that proposed direct and indirect relationships among variables. Wright's work languished until the late 1960s, when it was resurrected in mathematical sociology to deal with large sets of variables hypothesized to affect each other in complex ways. Essentially a series of ordinary regressions, path analysis was shown to produce the same estimates without having to conduct numerous regressions. Again, with high speed mainframe computers, the estimation using ordinary least squares regression was limited primarily by the size of the data matrix to be inverted.

Jöreskog's innovation was to join path analysis to factor analysis through the so-called true score theory. Factor analysis itself dated back to Spearman (1904) but was always limited by its computational difficulties. For over 50 years, shortcuts, ad hoc procedures, and approximations were constructed to produce estimates of factor scores and of the regression weights, termed factor loadings, that tied the observed variables to the factors. Once more, high speed computing permitted the inversions of matrices and computations that factor analysis demanded. Since psychology, and by extension education, relied on factor analysis as the basis for theoretical conceptualization of the relationships of constructs, merging path analysis to factor analysis allowed better representation and estimation of parameters in complex models that before were constructed in only approximate ways. Further, the understanding that ANOVA was simply a particular form of regression (Jennings, 1967) added experimental designs into the repertoire that SEM could now cover, although the formal construction of ANOVA into a set of contrasts seemed to elude researchers then and even today. Thus, SEM could be used to evaluate many models in the newly-coined term general linear model (GLM). Jöreskog and Sörbom (1976) created a computer program they call LISREL to analyze the expanded class of models, and many researchers to this day use that name for SEM analyses. The program currently survives, although by the late 1980s the Statistical Analysis System created a SEM program option called CALIS. Peter Bentler (1995), another pioneer in SEM development, created his version somewhat later, called EQS, Arbuckle and Wothke (1999) developed AMOS, and Bengt, a colleague of Jöreskog, and Linda Muthén (Muthén & Muthén, 1998–2007) created perhaps the most general program now available, MPLUS. Again, the expansion of computing techniques that paralleled the new statistical methods detailed above led to these very comprehensive programs for analyzing designs using SEM.

Item Response Theory

The area of educational testing focused on test development during the 1960s with the explosion of baby boomer children entering schools. The Cold War produced increased demands for higher education in the United States, and new curricula for science and math, and the desegregation of schools created concerns about school quality, particularly by conservatives. Both led to demands for testing children, initially on their mastery of basic skills and later on more complex learning. The demand for tests such as the Scholastic Aptitude Test (SAT, later renamed Scholastic Achievement Test) required many test items and many test forms. A Danish statistician, Georg Rasch, proposed a model of test item performance that extended the simple true score model (score = true score plus error) to include a parameter for the difficulty of the item. This became called the Rasch model (Rasch, 1960/1980). Its fundamental notion was that all individuals could be placed on a scale arbitrarily defined as ability (conceptually the level of performance on the subject being tested), and that all items could also be placed on that scale, some easy and some difficult. Thus, how difficult an item was could be used to begin to place an individual on the scale to determine his/her ability. Clearly, one item would not be sufficient, but by examining the distribution of performance across easy and difficult items, one could begin to locate each individual. Further, the items could be given sequentially. If an individual got the item correct, give the individual a more difficult item, and iterate until there appeared to be a consistency around some point on the scale. Combine that with a computer that could provide a randomly selected item, compute the student's performance based on that item and the previous ones given, and what emerged was the basis for computer adaptive testing, which is now the principal approach to many online and computer-based tests such as the SAT, GRE, and many driver's license tests.

Statistically, the Rasch model fit the answer to the question (correct or incorrect—scored as 0 or 1) to an estimate of the person's ability. This type of analysis is a form of logistic regression in which binomial responses are transformed to the logarithm of the odds ratio, that is the probability of getting the item correct over the probability of getting it wrong. This type of analysis required computers to perform, again only becoming widely permissible in the 1960s. However, the strict restrictions of the Rasch model did not require extensive computations and could be performed by hand. This made it very easy to use.

The model was extended by others, summarized by Birnbaum (1968) to the two-parameter and three-parameter models. The criticism of the Rasch model was that it assumed that all items performed exactly the same way with respect to the population of test-takers, empirically shown not to be true for many items. Rasch enthusiasts responded

that in many test development situations, they could simply write enough items to try out that they could select items that had similar properties across the range of student ability. Others countered that such limitations created certain kinds of items and tests but did not permit the range of testing desired by schools and educational organizations. Consequently, the more complex two-parameter model was developed. The primary difference was that each item might have a different discrimination index, while Rasch items were required to be homogeneous with respect to discrimination. Essentially, the discrimination index was a measure of how distinctly an item separated those who knew the item and thus had a higher ability, from those who did not know the item and thus had a lower ability. While items might vary on this discrimination index, and high discrimination was valued, it was often found empirically that such highly discriminating items might be found more easily away from the middle of the ability distribution, so that allowing for some variability in the discrimination would permit both a wider variation in items and greater flexibility in selecting items for a test. The two-parameter model comprised of both difficulty and discrimination of the item was now included in the true score model and required much larger sample sizes and new estimation methods, notably ML, to obtain good estimates and standard errors. Yet again, the interplay of computer advances, statistical advances, and new models converged to produce new theoretical designs. These models collectively have been termed Item Response Theory (IRT) and also called Item Characteristic Curve Theory.

It is worth noting briefly that the three-parameter model was conceived to permit a guessing component, since many tests had multiple choice items. It required larger sample sizes than the two-paramater model for reasonable estimation and it never quite performed the way it was originally conceived. The three-parameter model is therefore used only by a few organizations that are able to collect sufficiently larger sample sizes of data.

The role of IRT in testing has not had much to do with experimental design to date, although it is indirectly linked when tests are selected for assessment of outcomes. That division is soon to change, however, as the incorporation of IRT into SEM programs such as MPLUS now permits a general expansion of the SEM model to include tests that are based on IRT. Since SEM includes the classical true score theory model as the basis of factor analysis, the inclusion of IRT expands the theory to model the kind of responses individuals give in attitude and achievement tests wherein multiple options are provided.

Longitudinal Data Analysis

The disciplines of developmental and experimental psychology were long alienated in the sense that developmental psychology focused on the observed changes in natural environments that children and adults went through, with little notion of intervening, while experimental psychology was inherently interventionist, focusing on treatments that might improve psychological functioning. Clearly, after the educational needs of the Cold War and Sputnik, educational research focused on experimental psychology as a paradigm for investigating educational interventions. Developmental psychology, perhaps best exemplified by Piaget's (1928) 40-year study of children, had its own methodological emphases based on observation of single subjects (see chapter 36 of this volume). The needs of disciplines such as special education merged some of the experimental and developmental ideas into applied behavior analysis. Glass, Willson, and Gottman (1975) developed some of these ideas in the analysis of time series experiments in which interventions were specifically introduced after a period of observation in the ordinary situation, and the effect estimated in the context of the complexities of cross-time data using the autoregressive moving average (ARMA) model. They argued that many variables observed over time exhibited correlated data structures that could not be ignored without overestimating the effect of an intervention. This methodology, along with other more conventional GLM type analyses based on repeated measures, which is a form of mixed model with the restrictive assumption about the correlations of data across time that they be equal for all pairs of time points, were available but little used during the 1980s. The introduction of HLM, however, included analysis of data collected over a few time points, termed growth modeling. The focus of growth modeling was to fit simple growth models, such as linear or quadratic curves, to the data at each level. This meant that each student would be fit with a curve and that groups would be fit with different curves based on the means of the groups. This was not conceptually different from repeated measures designs, but as noted earlier, HLM produced correct standard errors, and further produced distributions for the growth parameters for students that could be examined and tested for homogeneity properly. In addition, a wide variety of error covariance structures theoretically permitted AR models to be included.

The proponents of growth modeling seemed to ignore the previous discussion about error structures in longitudinal data, although more recently Sivo and Willson (2000) presented models for ARMA structures in growth models. Similarly, the role of interventions in growth modeling has received insufficient attention. Nevertheless, the advances in growth modeling due to EQS and MPLUS now permit many complex designs to be analyzed, such as growth in factor scores (termed latent growth modeling), inclusion of time-varying covariates, or analysis of parallel growth processes in which the initial level or growth of one process affects the growth of another.

Nonnormal Data

The final topic area discussed here concerns the distribution of data researchers collect. While the normal distribution has the law of large numbers; with sufficient combining, every score is expected to become normal in distribution with enough cases, although this move toward normality may be very slow and has much empirical evidence in nature, not all data can be expected to be normal. The distribution of many abnormal behavior counts for children, for example, may better be represented by the Poisson distribution, which has a high peak near zero and a very long tail—most kids do not engage in those behaviors at all or very infrequently, while a very small group can exhibit them regularly. Many such non-normal distributions have been identified, and in other cases researchers are reluctant to assume normality with the form of measurement they use (e.g., rating scales), even though there may be theoretical justification. While the statistical development of various theoretical distributions goes back to Pearson in the early part of the 20th century, their application to observed data was mostly limited to so-called nonparametric methods, which really had parameters but were based on known or randomization distributions such as ranks or binomial/multinomial counts. Bayes theory provided an alternative to normal theory if a useful distribution could be specified that approximated the observed data or reasonably corresponded to the measurement conditions.

Once more, the arrival of high speed computation has spurred interest in non-normal distributions. The Gibbs sampler permits generation of all sorts of complex joint distributions from empirical or theoretical conditional distributions (e.g., knowledge of a distribution for some given condition, such as score distributions for girls and for boys separately may lead to the question, what is the joint distribution of all kids). While such methods can provide alternative analyses, they are difficult to implement for most researchers and are problematical to interpret. Consequently, much research has focused on examining the robustness of standard methods and adjustments that correct incorrect estimates when non-normality occurs.

Robustness is the concept that a statistical procedure works the way it is expected to even though assumptions about the method are not met. One well-known example is the robustness of ANOVA to some violation of normality when sample sizes are equal across groups (Glass, Peckham, & Sanders, 1972). With more complex estimation methods such as ML used in HLM and SEM, robustness, or lack of it, has become an important issue. The primary culprits of interest have been skewness and kurtosis variation from normal distribution values. A general theory of estimation by Browne (1984) was termed asymptotic-distribution-free (ADF), and it was anticipated that it would solve most of the problems, but it has unfortunately not worked particularly well. Thus, a great many simulation studies have been conducted for various models; while no general principles have arisen, some tentative conclusions appear to now be established. Moderate departures from normality in kurtosis seem not to affect estimation under ML of either parameters or standard errors. Larger departures can often be reduced by various statistical transformations (Cohen, Cohen, West, & Aiken, 2003), although not always successful. Correction of model fit evaluation due to a procedure developed by Satorra and Bentler (1994) has become a standard procedure where non-normal distributions are in evidence. Beyond these few results, effects in complex model situations appear to depend on numerous conditions that are difficult to generalize.

The other kind of non-normality is found with categorical data. We are familiar with right-wrong scoring of items, which is commonly represented with a binomial (coin flip) distribution. For ordered categories, such as the typical terms used for categories in many state accountability systems (unacceptable, acceptable, recommended, and exemplary) a multinomial distribution can be hypothesized. Likewise a similar distribution for unordered categories can be hypothesized, such as type of disorder, in which one category is designated as a reference category and all others are compared to it. The modeling for multinomial distributions has statistical analyses based on the logarithm of the odds ratio, for example the ratio of probability of getting an item right to the probability of getting it wrong. The distribution of this transformed statistic has normal probability characteristics and ML regression can be utilized. This is the basis for current analyses. Expansions of HLM and SEM to account for multinomial data are available in programs such as EQS and MPLUS, greatly expanding the capability of researchers to examine data forms of all types. These programs permit combining interval and multinomial variables in path models, factor analysis, and structural equation models, a tremendous expansion of the range of questions that can be studied with the data collected.

Latent Class Analysis

Latent class analysis (LCA), termed mixture modeling in the statistical literature, is a method that assumes there are multiple hidden distributions in a sample of data. A simple example would be two normal distributions separated by a half standard deviation. If we knew that one had been treated and the other not, we would simply compare the two samples with a t-test. If we did not know who was in the treated group or the control group, however, latent class analysis might help identify cases in each. The basis of the method is to create a binomial or multinomial variable (for three or more groups) as a predictor to assign to each case. By minimizing some sort of error or maximizing a likelihood function, we could arrive at the best assignment for the sample. Since we would not know for sure who was in each group, we could assign a probability function to group membership and thus, for each case, give an estimated probability for being in each group. The equations are fairly complex, and the strict assumption of normality for parametric models is required. Even so, unless we have good theoretical requirements for the number of groups, some sort of exhaustive analysis will need to be conducted to evaluate how well 2, 3, 4 … group memberships perform. Typically, the Bayesian Information Criterion (BIC) has been used, although there are some studies (Jung & Wickrama, 2008) that support using the Bootstrapped Likelihood Ratio Test.

While giving details on these statistics is outside the scope of the chapter, suffice it to say that they provide evidence for the number of classes.

Putting It All Together

The sum of all the methods described above is a general methodology for designing and analyzing group data. The complexity of including some of these together is serious, and not all is known about the conditions and properties for various combinations. Nevertheless, the capability that researchers now have to design and model complex phenomena in either natural or experimental settings has never been greater, and is, at present, literally exponentially greater than even a few years ago. Some examples of some important designs are discussed below, with some unresolved problems we have encountered in implementing them in some instances presented.

Classroom-Level Interventions   One of the main experimental designs accessible to educational researchers is the possibility to randomize treatments for classrooms or schools rather than for individual students. Clearly, the primary internal validity threat is that while classrooms may be randomized, the need to collect data at the student level creates additional variance not accounted for by the classroom randomization. The practical problem is that usually there are too few classrooms for stable estimation by using only classroom means (SEM analyses, for example, would need 200 classrooms for many designs), and including students within classrooms creates a nonrandom condition, since students were not randomly assigned to classrooms. The potential distributional groupings of classrooms for some limited number can affect estimation of the treatment effects; however, there is sampling evidence that 30 to 50 classrooms is optimal under HLM approaches with 15 to 20 students per classroom. For example, one treatment condition with 20 classrooms has significantly more at-risk children than the other condition also with 20 classrooms. The effect of the treatment on at-risk children must be disentangled from the effect of treatment, yet the children are found at the first level (classroom), while treatment is a second level effect. This means there is a potential cross-level interaction. Since each classroom consists of some at-risk and some non-at-risk children, the imbalance in sample sizes creates its own problems. We might construct a variable termed "at-riskness" to predict performance at the first level, if we believe these children may differ on the outcome, but that does not help us understand the potential variation of the treatment. A solution is to create a second level variable, percent at-risk, for each classroom that will become a predictor of classroom mean outcome score. The problem is the variability in the at-risk proportions is only asymptotically random and with small samples may have large standard errors. Further, the at-risk proportion may interact with treatment, necessitating inclusion of an interaction term at the second level. This is a random effect

Classroom level model

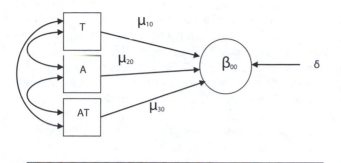

Student level model

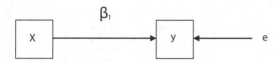

Figure 37.1 Path diagram for two-level classroom-level treatment model with covariates at each level.

since at-risk proportion is a random continuous variable and treatment is (presumably) a fixed factor. The model has the following equations:

(1) $y_{i(j)} = \beta_{0j} + \beta_{1j}X_{i(j)} + e_{i(j)}$

(2) $\beta_{0j} = \mu_{00} + \mu_{10}T + \mu_{20}A + \mu_{30}TA + \delta_j$

In this model the student's score y includes a classroom intercept β_{0j}, a covariate X (whether they are listed as at-risk or not), and an individual differences score e. The classroom mean itself has an intercept μ_{00}, an effect μ_{10} due to the treatment T, an effect μ_{20} due to the classroom composition of at-risk students as a percentage A, a possible A by T interaction effect μ_{30}, and random sampling variation δ. The model can be seen conceptually in Figure 37.1.

Analysis of this model can be accomplished with several different software programs, including HLM6, EQS, MPLUS, LISREL8, SAS, and SPSS. All have been shown to produce almost identical results, the differences due to slight variations in the ML estimation programs they use.

Several issues become important in analyzing the data for this model. First, if the number of students in each classroom is not equal for all classrooms, the exact solution requires a separate analysis for each set of groups with a different sample size that may not be analyzable for small classrooms. Muthén (1989) proposed an approximate sample size to serve as the average for all groups and analyze the data as if all classrooms had that value. Hox (2002) gave a readable discussion of this with the formula used to compute this "pseudobalanced" sample size. He concluded that the method produces slightly elevated Type I error rates and too-small standard errors as long as the sample size variation is not too great. The problem seems to diminish as the number of groups and students increases.

The second issue arises if there are missing data for some students. Depending on the quantity of missing data, the

simplest solution, contrary to the discussion about missing data above, is to ignore those cases. If the percentage of such cases is low, say 5%, the degree of bias can be expected to be negligible if the missingness is at random. For significantly greater percentages there are several options. The reason for our waffling here is that there have not yet been adequately developed procedures to impute missing data in multilevel models. The problem is that estimation of the random variables becomes extremely complex in the model we just presented. An approximation with unknown amount of bias is to impute the data including a set of variables to represent the classrooms. This produces a large number of variables, which is equal to the number of classrooms minus 1; in addition to those that would ordinarily be used. Our experience is that MI fails unless the data set is extremely large, and even then a solution is not guaranteed. One approximation we have used successfully is to group classrooms into a smaller number of homogeneous subgroups, around 8 or so, depending on the information available about classrooms. For example, in one study we grouped the classrooms by ethnic composition into about six subgroups, and unpublished simulations we conducted with a design similar to that above performed adequately with little evidence of serious problems with Type I error rate. This method also worked reasonably well for another problem concerning teachers evaluated over several years with different students each year. We will discuss that issue under the section on growth modeling.

The third issue involves the level of randomization. If you are lucky enough to be able to randomize students into classes or groups in the design above, and the dependent variable is normally distributed, the HLM analysis is optimal to test a treatment effect at the second level. If the randomization occurred at the second level (classrooms or teachers were randomized into treatment conditions), it is important to attempt to obtain covariates at each level as the design above illustrates to control to some degree unknown student-level variation that may be present due to unknown assignment of students to teachers. An even more common design may be required in which schools are randomly assigned to treatments, with several teachers per school all implementing the same treatment. This is likely to occur in many studies because teachers work together, and it is impractical to insist one teacher instruct using one method and the next-door teacher use another. In our experience many teachers in a school work as a coherent team and a common treatment at the school level is a necessity. In this situation even more unknown variation is introduced into the design. The two-level design is still possible, but some precautionary procedures should be considered. One is to match schools by relevant characteristics and randomly assign the school to one treatment or another or if there are three treatments, tri-match three school groups with random assignment of schools to treatment. We successfully implemented this procedure with a pool of about 40 schools, deleting some schools from consideration and retaining 36. The assignment need not

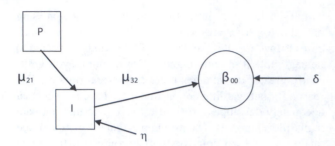

Figure 37.2 Path diagram for second level path model.

be an equal sample size either, so if one needs more treatment schools, matches might include four or six schools in a matched group, for example, with only one school randomly placed in the typical practice group, the others assigned randomly to treatments.

Multilevel Path Models An important extension of the HLM design will occur if there is a theoretical path model for variables at either or both levels. For instance, in one study we have worked on, the amount of teacher inservice participation in days is theoretically expected to change their instructional practices, which, in turn, are expected to improve student performance. Inservice days and instructional practices are teacher-level variables, so that the path model is at the second level. In this instance teachers comprised an experimental and control group, and the experimental group had natural variation in specific inservice days associated with the instructional practices observed. This model for the second level is shown in Figure 37.2.

In this model, control teachers had no inservice, and the number of inservice days for treatment teachers was assumed to be randomly varying from 3 to 20 (teachers chose the amount of this activity). These two predictors were approximately orthogonal (uncorrelated with each other), but chance correlation was included to be estimated in the model. This type of model cannot be analyzed with HLM type programs but must utilize SEM programs such as EQS or MPLUS.

Another extension of the path model is an extension to multivariate outcomes, which in classical statistics is termed multivariate ANOVA or MANOVA. Fan (1997) showed that MANOVA is merely a particular case of SEM and is represented in a straightforward way as a path model from the predictors to a latent factor that has regression weights to each dependent variable associated with the variance common across these dependent variables. Again, this model assumes that the multivariate outcome tells us about the global effect of the treatment at the second level. Since there will be a similar path model for students, this is a highly complex model that requires SEM programs capable of specifying the structure. The decision to use a path model for a MANOVA design versus analyzing each dependent variable separately is really a decision about the focus of the design: is it more important to discuss each measure separately, or is there a common construct underlying the measures that is the focus?

Even more complex models are theoretically available to be designed, such as path models among several latent factors, each measured with four or more indicators. Such designs are likely to be rarely encountered, most likely to be found with extremely large-scale projects that assess many variables each having multiple indicators with theoretical support. Some of the national studies of children and youth conducted over the last 20 years fit this situation.

Multiyear Growth Model Studies Designs that are expected to follow students and/or teachers over 3 or more years or time points will, in general, be considered as growth models, even though growth may not be expected to occur. We will discuss why shortly. Studies with only two time points of measurement of a dependent variable cannot be put into the growth model framework, but can easily fit into the HLM modeling detailed above. For so-called pre-post studies, the pretest can best be utilized at the student level as a covariate. Since the class mean is predicted at the first level, the resulting mean for the second level has been "adjusted" for the pretest differences. The mean is identical to the least-squares mean of usual analysis of covariance, but the standard deviation of errors has been correctly computed using HLM.

For an experimental study with three or more measurements of students separated in time, but fewer than perhaps eight or ten observations, a special form of the two level HLM analysis is available. It can also be thought of as a three level analysis in that scores occur within student, who is grouped within a classroom, and classrooms are grouped within treatments. The model has the following equations, and is shown in Figure 37.3 for a typical treatment design.

$$(3) \quad y_{tik} = \pi_{0ik} + \pi_{1ik} a_{ti} + e_{ti}$$
$$(4) \quad \pi_{0ik} = \mu_{00k} + \mu_{10} X + \delta_{0i}$$
$$(5) \quad \pi_{1ik} = \mu_{10k} + \mu_{11} X + \delta_{1i}$$
$$(6) \quad \mu_{00k} = \gamma_{000} + \gamma_{10} T + \gamma_{20} A + \gamma_{30} TA + \delta_{00k}$$
$$(7) \quad \mu_{10k} = \gamma_{111} + + \gamma_{11} T + \gamma_{21} A + \gamma_{31} TA + \delta_{11k}$$

Eqn. 3 represents an individual student's growth over t time points with a starting intercept at π_{0i}. For this model the errors are assumed independent of each other both within and between students. The student is located in classroom k. Thus, each student's growth is modeled individually, since they grow at rate π_{1i} per unit time. Eqns. 4 and 5 predict the students' intercepts and growth rates from a covariate X within each classroom. The mean intercept and growth rate within each classroom are then predicted at the third level by classroom level predictors such as A, T, and AT interaction as described earlier. A technical wrinkle is introduced that is not critical to understanding this model, in that the intercept and growth parameters are actually predicted from a constant consisting of 1's. This corresponds to the column of 1's in classical regression that permit the fit of the intercept. Since they are, in a sense predicted, they have errors, and the errors may be correlated or not, as shown in Figure 37.3. A correlated error path for intercept and

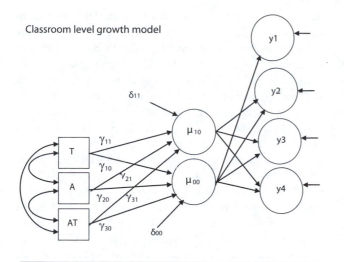

Classroom level growth model

Student level growth model

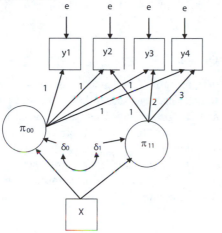

Figure 37.3 Path diagram for two-level growth model (three-level with first level growth) with a treatment, covariate, and treatment-covariate interaction.

growth is itself an interesting statistic, since it means that those with higher starting intercepts grow faster (positive correlation) or slower (negative correlation) than those with lower starting intercepts.

If no growth is predicted, the growth parameter can be omitted, and mean differences between treatments tested with the effects only on the intercept. Many other extensions are possible, such as path models at the second level, as discussed previously. Nothing new is needed for this extension. For latent variable growth, in which the growth measures are factor scores for a test, the model becomes more complex, since one needs to make some significant measurement restrictions on the factor structures at each time point, namely at the least weak invariance, in which the factor loadings are assumed invariant across time points, along with the error variances of the test items. This model can be studies using MPLUS, and consultation of the manual is required to understand the model estimated in that program.

Multiyear Models with Growth at the Second Level A design situation that occurs frequently in school studies is

multiyear training of teachers using experimental designs. Since new students are placed into the teacher's classrooms each year, the growth occurs at the classroom level, not at the student level. None of the growth model programs now available correctly analyze this design, although we seem to be able to use SAS Proc Mixed to correctly model it as a mixed effects analysis. Since each classroom is independent over time from any others within teacher (and assumed between teachers), there is no time-relatedness to each student's score; it is simply modeled with a true score, error, and any covariates such as pretest;

$$(8) \qquad y_{tik} = \pi_{0kt} + \mu_{10} X + e_{ti} \, ,$$

while at the teacher level *k,* we wish to model classroom mean growth over time:

$$(9) \qquad \pi_{0kt} = \gamma_{00k} + \gamma_{11k} a_{tk} + \delta_{0k} \, .$$

This is now an intercept and growth model that can be analyzed at a third level:

$$(10) \qquad \gamma_{00k} = \gamma_{000} + \gamma_{10} T + \gamma_{20} A + \gamma_{30} TA + \delta_{00k} \, ,$$
$$(11) \qquad \gamma_{11k} = \gamma_{111} + \gamma_{11} T + \gamma_{21} A + \gamma_{31} TA + \delta_{11k} \, ,$$

if researchers wish to hypothesize differential growth for classrooms, and that growth depends on the treatment and perhaps a classroom covariate. Most SEM programs do not permit analysis of this model, unfortunately. One approximation we have considered is to construct a set of dummy coded variables representing teachers (classrooms) and adding them as covariates. We have not had good luck, however, obtaining convergence. Another approximation we have had success with is to group teachers into a small number of homogeneous groups, such as the matching variables and coding these groups as a set of additional covariates.

Latent Class Growth Models (LCGM) Research on latent class models for growth has been conducted in many areas. The idea is appealing because the purpose is to discover hidden groups within the sample that have homogeneous but different growth rates from each other. For example, in studying reading growth for a large sample of at-risk elementary school children, adding a latent class variable as a predictor of growth permits identifying children who are perhaps growing faster than the rest and then studying their home, school, and psychosocial characteristics that may be supportive variables in that enhanced growth. In LCGM the latent class variable is a covariate predicting intercept and growth. For a single group (two level) model the individual curves for each student are predicted by the latent class variable and categorized into the number of latent classes specified by the researcher. For a three level experimental design both students and classrooms can be predicted by different latent class variables. This is an exploratory analysis in this context, examining hidden subgroups that are growing differently than the observed experimental and control groups. This might be modeled in several ways, including specifying the latent class variable to predict the

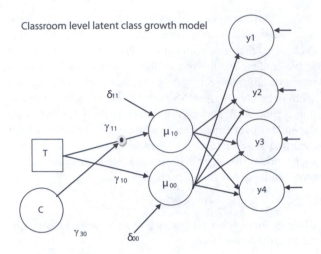

Classroom level latent class growth model

FIgure 37.4 Path diagram for second level latent class growth model with treatment.

treatment regression parameter that predicts growth. This is shown diagrammatically in Figure 37.4 for a simplified second level growth model. The figure is different from previous ones in that the latent class variable c is shown with a path arrow directed at a growth parameter γ, not at another variable as seen in other diagrams.

Example

Willson and Hughes (2006) predicted first-grade retention from student IQ, student achievement in math and reading, and teacher ratings of achievement and engagement. The

TABLE 37.1
Results of Two-Level Analysis of First Grade Student Retention Predicted by IQ, Reading and Math Achievement, and Teacher Ratings of Achievement and Engagement

Summary of Categorical Data Proportions			
RETENT1			
Category 1	0.785	Category 2	0.215

Tests of Model Fit

Log Likelihood

	H0 Value	−277.230	
Information Criteria	**Akaike (AIC)**	**Bayesian (BIC)**	**Sample-Size Adjusted BIC**
	568.459	600.975	578.746
Model Results	**Estimates**	**S.E.**	**Est./S.E.**
Within Level			
RETENT1 ON			
TACH1	−0.512	0.206	−2.488
TENG1	−0.071	0.160	−0.447
CU1FSIQ	0.001	0.012	0.042
CWJREAD	−0.048	0.011	−4.161
CWJMATH	0.007	0.014	0.484
Between Level Thresholds			
RETENT1$1	2.994	0.366	8.179
Variances			
RETENT1	6.698	2.431	2.755

design was evaluated using a two-level model with students at the first level and mean retention per classroom a single variable at the second level to differentiate classrooms. Results are presented in Table 37.1 with slightly reduced output from MPLUS. Since retention is a binary variable, the analysis used logistic regression. From the first level predictors, only teacher rated achievement and student's reading achievement were significant predictors using the approximate t-test provided by the program.

With large degrees of freedom, a value of 1.96 approximates the .05 significance level required. Note that a threshold is provided for prediction of whether a student is retained or not from the prediction equation given by the regression weights. In this case, retention is an outcome. In a follow-up study Willson and Hughes (2008) predicted reading growth in the subsequent three grades and used retention as a mediating variable between the achievement and teacher predictors and intercept and slope of growth as outcomes.

Discussion

Clearly, an entire text is needed to fully develop the topics presented here, but researchers working on group-based treatments for reading disabilities can utilize the general discussion here to inform their designs, particularly in conjunction with expert quantitative specialists who can be expected to be familiar with the specifics of these topics. The exciting advances in quantitative methodology in the last 20 years for educational research must be applied to understand better the interventions we develop and to provide essential support for their implementation when effective. While researchers need to be careful of the old saw "give a child a hammer and he hammers everything," and having the tools does not make them appropriate for all uses, the advanced methods discussed here give reading disability researchers an important resource kit with which to do their work.

References

Arbuckle, J. L., & Wothke, W. (1999). *Amos 4.0 User's Guide.* Chicago: SPSS Inc. and SmallWaters Corporation.

Bentler, P. M. (1995). *EQS Structural Equations Program manual.* Encino, CA: Multivariate Software.

Birnbaum, A. (1968). Some latent trait models and their use in inferring an examinee's ability. In F. M. Lord & M. R. Novic (Eds.), *Statistical theories of mental test scores.* Reading, MA: Addison-Wesley.

Browne, M. W. (1984). Asymptotically distribution-free methods for the analysis of covariance structures. *British Journal of Mathematical and Statistical Psychology, 37*(1), 62–83.

Campbell, D. T., & Stanley, J. C. (1966). *Experimental and Quasi-experimental Designs for Research.* Chicago: Rand-McNally.

Cohen, J., Cohen, P., West, S., & Aiken, L. (2003). *Applied multiple regression/correlation for the behavioral sciences, 3rd Ed.* Mahwah, NJ: Erlbaum

Dempster, A. P., Laird, N. M., & Rubin, D. B. (1977). Maximum likelihood from incomplete data via the EM algorithm. *Journal of the Royal Statistical Society. Series B (Methodological), 39*(1), 1–38.

Efron, B. (1982). *The jackknife, the bootstrap and other resampling plans.* CBMS-NSF Regional Conference Series in Applied Mathematics, Philadelphia: Society for Industrial and Applied Mathematics (SIAM).

Fan, X. (1997). Canonical correlation and structural equation modeling: What do they have in common? *Structural Equation Modeling, 4*(1), 65–79.

Gelfand, A. E., & Smith, A. F. M. (1990). Sampling based approaches to calculating marginal densities. *Journal of the American Statistical Association, 85,* 398–409.

Glass, G. V, Peckham, P. D., & Sanders, J. R. (1972). Consequences of failure to meet assumptions underlying the fixed effects analyses of variance and covariance. *Review of Educational Research, 42*(3), 237–288.

Glass, G. V., Willson, V. L., & Gottman, J. (1975). *The design and analysis of time series experiments.* Boulder, CO: University of Colorado Press.

Hox, J. (2002). *Multilevel analysis: Techniques and applications.* Mahwah, NJ: Erlbaum.

Jennings, E. (1967). Fixed effects analysis of variance by regression analysis. *Multivariate Behavioral Research, 2,* 95–100.

Jøreskog, K. G. (1967). A general method for estimating a linear structural system. In A. G. Jøreskog, & K. G. Sorbøm (Eds.), *LISREL-III: Estimation of linear structural equation systems by maximum likelihood methods.* Chicago: National Education Resources.

Jøreskog, K. G. (1973). A general method for estimating a linear structural equation system. In A. S. Goldberger & O. D. Duncan (Eds.), *Structural equation models in the social sciences* (pp. 85–112). New York: Seminar Press.

Jøreskog, K. G., & Sorbøm (1976). *LISREL-III: Estimation of linear structural equation systems by maximum likelihood methods.* Chicago: National Education Resources.

Jung, T., & Wickrama, K. A. S. (2008). An introduction to latent class growth analysis and growth mixture modeling. *Social and Personality Psychology Compass, 2,* 302–317.

Lord, F. M., & Novick, M. R. (1968). *Statistical theories of mental test scores.* Reading, MA: Addison-Wesley.

Muthén, B. O. (1989). Latent variable modeling in heterogeneous populations. *Psychometrika, 54*(4), 557–585.

Muthén, L. K., & Muthén, B. O. (1998–2007). *Mplus user's guide* (5th ed.). Los Angeles: Author.

Piaget, J. (1928). *The child's conception of the world.* London: Routledge and Kegan.

Rasch, G. (1980). *Probabilistic models for some intelligence and attainment tests.* Chicago: The University of Chicago Press. (Original work published 1960)

Rasch, G. (1961). On general laws and the meaning of measurement in psychology. In *Proceedings of the Fourth Berkeley Symposium on Mathematical Statistics and Probability,* IV (pp. 321–334). Berkeley: University of California.

Raudenbush, S. W. (1988). Educational applications of hierarchical linear models: A review. *Journal of Educational and Behavioral Statistics, 13*(2), 85–116.

Rubin, D. B. (1987). *Multiple imputation.* New York: Wiley.

Satorra, A., & Bentler, P. M. (1994). Corrections to test statistics and standard errors in covariance structure analysis. In A. von Eye & C. C. Clogg (Eds.), *Latent variables analysis: Applications for developmental research* (pp. 399–419). Thousand Oaks, CA: Sage.

Scheffé, H. (1959). *The analysis of variance.* New York: Wiley.

Sivo, S. A, & Willson, V.L. (2000). Modeling causal error structures in longitudinal panel data: A Monte Carlo study. *Structural Equation Modeling, 7*(2), 174–205.

Slavin, R. E. (2002). Evidence-based education policies: Transforming educational practice and research. *Educational Researcher, 31*(7), 15–21.

Spearman, C. (1904). General intelligence objectively determined and measured. *American Journal of Psychology, 15,* 201–293.

Whitehurst, G. (2001). *Evidence-based education (EBE).* Retrieved September 12, 2003, from http://www.ed.gov

Willson, V. L., & Hughes, J. N. (2006). Retention of Hispanic/Latino students in first grade: Child, parent, teacher, school, and peer predictors. *Journal of School Psychology, 44*(1), 31–49.

Willson, V. L., & Hughes, J. N. (2008). Who is retained in first grade: A psychosocial perspective. *Elementary School Journal, 109,* 251–266.

Willson, V. L., & Putnam, R. R. (1982). Meta-analysis of pretest sensitization effects in experimental design. *American Educational Research Journal, 19*(2), 249–258

Wright, S. (1921). Correlation and causation. *Journal of Agricultural Research. 20,* 557–585.

38

Observational Research

Misty Sailors
The University of Texas at San Antonio

Margaret Flores
Auburn University

Studies in the field of marketing tell an interesting story of the recognition of observational research in that field and thus, the importance of it. The story begins with a typical study of how consumers did the wash. The research team videotaped women consumers in their homes while they went through the entire wash process, sorting the clothes, placing them in the washer, adding soap, setting the cycle, and moving the clothes to the dryer. After the process, the research team conducted interviews with the women asking how well the detergent had cleaned their clothes. The women answered with stock answers: absent of stains and bright colors. However, upon viewing of the video, the researchers observed something that the women had not reported—as they moved the clothes to the dryer, each smelled her clothes. When asked, the women reported always doing that "just to see if it smells clean" (Abrams, 2000, p. 2). This classic example of observational research in marketing is strikingly similar to that of educational observational research—sometimes we can only document and describe unconscious actions through observational research methods.

While we have discussed observational research in reading research (Hoffman, Maloch, & Sailors, in press), in this chapter we focus our literature review on answering the question, "In what ways is observational research used to better understand instruction with children who have difficulties in learning to read?" We will begin the chapter with an overview of observational research focused broadly followed by a look at observational research studies that have been conducted with the instruction of both children who struggle with learning to read and children who have specific learning disabilities in reading. We finish the chapter with a section on implications for this methodology within the study of research on reading disabilities.

Observational Research as a Methodology

As social beings, we spend the vast majority of our waking interactions with others engaged in acts of observation. Our ability to observe the world around us forms the basis for learning about our surroundings and our ability to make commonsense judgments about life. In our daily social interactions with others, we are both consciously and unconsciously engaged in acts of observations about the behaviors of others around us. We continuously (and sometimes purposefully) engage in "people watching"—whether we are walking down the street, eating at a restaurant, or sitting on a park bench, we observe the behaviors of others. These observations are casual and unstructured. However, acts of observation in research settings are quite different.

On the other hand, acts of observations during research are more systematic and formal and often have at their center, the intention of answering a theoretical question about the nature of a phenomenon, describing an action or behavior, or attributing the impact of an intervention on learning. This does not mean, however, that the behaviors of the participants in the study are controlled. Rather, what to observe, when to observe, where to observe, how to observe, the method of recording events and behaviors, the method of analyzing the data gathered, and the environment under which the observations were made are rigidly prescribed and the subsequent prescribed procedures diligently followed. A dictionary definition provides a working definition for observational research. From the word observe (meaning to watch carefully especially with attention to details or behavior), observational research allows a researcher to arrive at a judgment on or inference from the observational data collected (observed) in systematic ways. Because the process of observation is rigidly defined and controlled, the nature of the data is well defined.

There is no doubt that observational research has earned its rightful place as a methodology in the field of education, as chapters on it appeared in the first three handbooks of research on teaching (Evertson & Green, 1986; Gordon & Jester, 1973; Medley & Mitzel, 1963; Rosenshine & Furst, 1973) and most recently in the handbook of research on reading (Hoffman et al., in press). With the appearance of a chapter in this handbook of research on reading disabilities, observational research is now considered equally important as a method in the field of reading disabilities research. Because the role of observation in social research has been acknowledged (Angrosino, 2007; Hilberg, Waxman, & Tharp, 2004) elsewhere, we will not replicate that argument in this chapter.

Methods Within Observational Research The question arises as to whether observational research is a method or a means of data collection and analysis. According to some (Gillham, 2008; Mertens, 2005; Tashakkori & Teddlie, 2003), observation is a data collection technique and the information gathered from this technique may be either quantitative (observer completes a coding or categorizing system) or qualitative (observer gathers narrative field notes). The data can be quantitative or qualitative at the point of data collection or at the point of analysis (statistically manipulated or analyzed through a constant-comparison analysis, for example). However, we would argue differently. That is, observational research draws from both quantitative and qualitative methods, but has earned its rightful place as a method of research in and of itself (Anderson & Burns, 1989; Evertson & Green, 1986; Gordon & Jester, 1973; Hoffman et al., in press; Johnson & Turner, 2003; Medley & Mitzel, 1963; Rosenshine & Furst, 1973; Suen & Ary, 1989). In the next section, we will discuss both quantitative and qualitative observational research, what they are, the methods employed and advantages and disadvantages of each.

Quantitative Observational Research In quantitative observational studies, a complex phenomenon is reduced to a number of measurable and observable behavioral variables; these variables are defined and a system for measuring them is determined before the observation is conducted. Data are recorded in quantitative observational studies through categorical systems. That is, researchers who employ these data collection practices typically use a finite number of preset categories or units of observation. The categories are defined in advance and are based on philosophical, theoretical, empirically derived, or experience-based beliefs about the nature of the process, event, or individual or group under study. The observer can only record those items listed. These systems are generally recorded as the behavior occurs (during the observation), as ratings at the end of a set period of time, or as tallies on a checklist. Two types of boundaries are generally used in category and checklist systems—a time sampling (unit boundaries of events are ignored) and event (the observation begins at the onset of the event and ends with its closure). When categories and checklists are used, smaller units of behavior are typically recorded which require low-inferences on the part of observers. The units to be marked are generally derived deductively, reflect a behavioral stance, and are discrete and simple units (coded in only one category) (Evertson & Green, 1986, p. 175).

When ratings are the form of system used for quantitative observational studies, the ratings generally represent weighted judgments that are continuous, based on factor analysis, and are inferred (Evertson & Green, p. 175). Ratings are generally used to assess high-inference constructs (i.e., depth of explanation of a concept) (1 = low, 2 = moderate, 3 = high). The establishment of inter-rater reliability is critical to the data collection process. These systems are then converted into variables. A hypothesis that tentatively describes the relationship between the variables is postulated; statistical analyses are performed on these quantitative data to determine evidence of the hypothesized relationships. The relationships are either confirmed or not confirmed.

According to some researchers (Suen & Ary, 1989), there are advantages and disadvantages to quantitative observational research. The main advantage to quantitative observational studies is that, if conducted correctly (i.e., low-inference systems with high inter-rater reliability), they are independent of the observer. The main disadvantage to quantitative observational studies is that the reduction of a complex phenomenon to a few quantifiable variables can lead to the over simplification of the phenomenon—the outcomes may be incomplete and/or an unjustifiably superficial and shallow understanding of the phenomenon.

Qualitative Observational Research Qualitative observational research, is also called naturalistic observation because the observation is done in real-world or naturalistic settings (Johnson & Turner, 2003). It is typically open-ended and exploratory. The purpose of this method is to obtain detailed descriptions of observed phenomenon in order to explain unfolding processes and to identify principles and patterns of behavior within specific events, sometimes in single cases, but also across cases. Researchers who conduct qualitative observational research take extensive field-notes and may/not use audio and video recordings to establish a record of the observation or to use for analysis purposes after the observation. Within these "narrative systems" (Evertson & Green, 1986), descriptions of events are recorded using spoken or written language (p. 170), and the duration of the event can be a single event (the first day of school), a critical incident (the first hour of school), or a longer period of time (the first 6 weeks of a reading/writing workshop). Researchers using narrative systems consider meaning to be situation specific.

The marking of units in qualitative observational research generally takes place during the analysis of the data rather than live, as in quantitative observational research. Units of observation related to narrative systems are both deductive and inductive and are drawn from theoretical research across disciplines and specified on a conceptual or theoretical basis. The type of unit and the relationship between the units are related to both the question under study as well as the theoretical framework of the analysis. Finally, units can be defined as functional (units are based on the purpose the observed behavior serves), situational (units are what people are doing, how they are doing it, and what definitions they have for these actions), and inferential (units are inferred from patterns across behaviors) (Evertson & Green, 1986, pp. 176–177). In some cases, units are built up from discrete stand-alone units to ones that form categories to larger units that then form themes through a constant-comparison approach (Strauss & Corbin, 1990). In other cases, codes (units) are identified and combined into concepts (contain similar content that allows data to be grouped), which are then combined into categories, which are then used to generate a theory (Glaser & Strauss, 1967).

As with quantitative observational research, there are advantages and disadvantages to qualitative observational research. Qualitative observational research allows for in-depth understandings of the phenomenon under study that cannot be obtained from quantitative observational research. And, if it is in-depth enough, the researcher may get to what has been called "backstage behavior" (what people say and do with their closest friends or when acting naturally) rather than just to "front stage behaviors" (what people want or allow the researcher to see; Goffman, 1959). Because it is generated through a "data driven" process, the hypotheses and theories generated through this method represent movement toward a more representative explanation of reality for participants (Mertens, 2005).

There are also disadvantages to qualitative observational research. First, the data recorded and subsequently analyzed are constrained by the observer's perceptual framework, insight, training and written and/or oral fluency. These methods require highly sophisticated observers who have proper training in advanced sociology and/or social anthropology—part of that training must be focused on choosing when to collect contextual data and when to hone in on behaviors that are the focus of the study. The observer must make constant decisions as what to record and what to ignore among the array of simultaneous occurring behaviors in classrooms and naturalistic research settings. Further training must take place around inferring as a way of making sense of participant actions without the observer projecting her own reality onto the situation. Finally, properly conducted qualitative observational research studies require continuous observations over extended periods of time, making them time consuming and expensive.

Mixed Methods Observational Research Finally, as Johnson and Turner encourage (2003), some researchers use both qualitative and quantitative observational research methods in well-developed studies. Dubbed "intramethod mixed research" (p. 313), this method mixes the characteristics of both; an a priori instrument might be combined with extensive field notes during and after the observation. Further, "intermethod mixing" (p. 314) can also be combined in observational research studies. Data can be supplemented and expanded with questionnaires and/or interviews, for example. Tashakkori and Teddlie (2003) argue that distinguishing observational techniques from the design of studies allows for the use of multiple modes of data collection techniques from either or both approaches.

In summary, observational research allows the researcher to directly document and describe what people do without having to rely on what people say they do. It can, with proper training and education, allow for relatively objective documentation of behaviors. It provides for contextualization that operates in social settings. And, it can be used to stimulate change and verify that change occurred. However, if not triangulated or combined with other methods of data collection, observational research can create an unclear picture of what is meant by what is happening. Without careful attention to discreteness, participant behaviors may be influenced (and thus, affected) if the participants know they are being observed. Observational research is time consuming and thus, large groups, extensive observations, and longitudinal studies may not be realistic because of the cost associated with this method. Finally, a described theoretical grounding of the study is necessary so that what the observer "sees" is what the data tells her she "sees" and not what she wants to "see" (Johnson & Turner, 2003; Suen & Ary, 1989).

Observational Research in General Education Settings

The earliest evidence of the use of systematic observational research came from studies conducted by Wrightstone (1934, cited in Sweetman, 1988) in which he measured teacher's handling of discussions in classrooms. He began by developing nine categories of teacher's behaviors and later developed sub-categories that scored the teacher's orientation toward instruction and the prohibition of discussions. He later extended his system to include pupil behaviors. This research was the beginning of what came to be known as Interactive Research, research that explored the relationship between teachers and their classes (Sweetman, 1988, p. 44). This line of research explored whether or not related classroom and instructional behaviors could be reliably and validly identified (Evertson & Green, 1986).

Interactive research continued throughout the 1940s as the area and research methods and tools continued to grow (Evertson & Green, 1986) and culminated with the now famous Flanders Interactive Category System (Flanders, 1970), one of many instruments developed during this period (Gordon & Jester, 1973; Rosenshine & Furst, 1973). Flanders was interested in the "talk" in classrooms as it might reflect a "democratic" or "authoritative" classroom structure. The Flanders observation system, known as FIAC, was focused on the characterization of teacher and pupil talk in classroom along the dimensions of direct and indirect. Direct teacher talk, for example, would include content questions directed at students or reprimands in the behavioral area. Student talk, for example, would include coding of student responses to questions or student initiated questions. The coding of talk through the Flanders system was then used to study the relationship between patterns of talk and student outcomes—ranging from achievement to attitudes toward school and learning. The system was designed to record the sequence of behavioral events. The behaviors were divided between teacher talk (Indirect Influence: accepts feelings, praises or encourages, accepts or uses ideas of student, asks questions; Direct Influence: lecturing, giving ideas, criticizing or justifying authority) and Student talk (student talk—response, student talk—initiation, silence or confusion). The observer using the FIAC records behaviors every 3 seconds. The most basic form of analysis is to compute frequency analysis for the categories and more complex analyses focus on contingencies and co-occurrence.

Most of the observation systems developed during this period within the research in teaching community were focused solely on observable behaviors. Some of the systems emphasized "high inference" coding while other systems relied more heavily on "low-inference" systems. Rosenshine and Furst (1973) define a low-inference measure as a rating system that classifies specific, denotable, relatively objective classroom behavior and is recorded as frequency accounts by the observer. They describe high-inference measures as a rating system that requires an observer to make an inference from a series of classroom events using specific constructs, such as satisfaction, enthusiasm, clarity. Many of these systems included both types of information.

Research on teaching flourished as it relied on tools to observe teaching behaviors (termed "process" variables) and correlated them with student outcome measures (termed "product" variables). Rosenshine and Fursts' call for studies that would progress following a "descriptive-correlation-experimental feedback loop" (p. 131) set the standard for the next decade of research in teaching. Funding by the US Office of Education and the National Institute of Education served as sources of influence during this phase and three large studies guided the development of observational research in classrooms to study teaching and learning. The first of these, The Follow-Through Studies, evaluated the effects of Head Start (Stallings, 1975). The COI (Classroom Observation Instrument) was developed for data collection and documented activities, materials used, grouping patterns, and interactions. The COI included 602 categories describing behaviors of teachers and students. Interactions were scored in 5-minute sequences. Observers completed an average of four observation sequences each hour during a 5-hour observation day. The behaviors included attention to such areas as focus (e.g., academic, social) and discourse patterns (e.g., question, statement). In addition to the interaction data, the observer would gather data on grouping and organization in the classroom as well as the availability of materials. High levels of reliability were established as the observers went through rigorous training and the data collected as part of this study were monitored closely. The use of this instrument (and this research) demonstrated strong positive relationships between the use of behaviors associated with direct instruction models and student achievement gains.

The second of these influential studies, The Texas Teacher Effectiveness Studies, were designed to explore the relationship between teacher expectations and student achievement. The studies documented teaching behaviors associated with levels of expectation and the relationship between teacher behaviors and student achievement. Brophy's (1973) tool included a combination of low-inference and high-inference observation systems to measure classroom processes including the Brophy–Good, Dyadic Interaction Coding System (Brophy & Good, 1970). Thousands of correlations were computed between scores on process measures and student gain. The findings from these studies suggested a large number of process variables related to both academic and managerial aspects of teaching. In several areas, differences between the effects of certain teacher behaviors were noted in relation to work in high-SES versus low-SES classrooms.

The final influential study that continues to guide observational research methods, The Beginning Teacher Evaluation Studies (BTES), Phase II, had as its goal the illustration of the relationship between classroom observations of teaching and student achievement growth in reading and mathematics. The study was framed around John Carroll's theoretical work (1963) on learning as it relates to aptitude and the opportunity to engage with the content to be learned. Within this study, the variables related to "time" (i.e., engaged/on-task time, allocated time) were found to be highly associated with student achievement. In addition, the researchers found support in the observational data for a model of direct instruction that featured specific elements of effective lessons. Differences in effective practices were noted across grade levels and different content areas (Berliner, 1990; Fisher et al., 1978; McDonald & Elias, 1976).

These three lines of research that capitalized on observations in classrooms and other naturalistic settings were heavily influential in guiding other observational studies that centered on research in reading (Hoffman et al., in press). However, they, nor landmark studies in the field of behavioral research (that also used observational methods) such as Hall, Lunch, and Jackson (1968), Walker and Buckley (1968), and Semmel (1975), systematically focused on children who struggled with learning to read or children who were eligible for special education services under IDEA. Thus, in this research review we will attempt to: (a) Describe the state of affairs of observational research as it relates to reading disabilities; (b) Identify the patterns of the use of observational research within the field of research on reading disabilities; (c) Determine the availability of tools within the field of research on reading disabilities; (d) Offer a set of criteria for observational research as it relates to reading disabilities, and thus; (e) Demonstrate that observational research is a viable line of inquiry into research on reading disabilities.

Methods

Our task was to inspect the research literature focused on reading instruction with the abovementioned population that relied on the direct observation of teaching and to report on the range of methods and strategies used. We developed an initial set of criteria to focus our search. We limited our focus to research reports that (a) were published in scholarly, refereed research journals; (b) reported on the gathering of new data or on a new analysis of existing data; (c) focused on teachers and teaching in the area of reading; (d) described some authentic act(s) of teaching; (e) reported on the methods used to observe teaching; (f) were conducted in classrooms and/or clinic settings (EC through High School); and (g) involved children who struggled with learning to read and/or who qualified for special education services under The Individuals with Disabilities Education Improvement Act (2004).

Even with these criteria, we were challenged at times in deciding as to whether a study should or should not be included in our review. To guide us in these decisions, we operated under the rule of "cast the net widely" first (i.e., include even the doubtful cases) and then consider each of the borderline cases using a consensus process within our team.

We were open to the inclusion of studies as far back as 1975 with the enactment of The Education for All Handicapped Children Act (currently IDEIA). We began with a use of an existing database (Hoffman et al., in press), expanding it to include a combination of electronic tools and hand search methods. We searched the Web of Science using the following descriptors: TS = reading *and* (teaching *or* instruction) *and* research *and* (primary *or* elementary *or* secondary *or* middle) *and* (participant *or* participants) *or* (subject *or* subjects) *or* (student *or* students) *or* (pupil *or* pupils) *and* (special education) *or* (learning disabilities) *or* (struggling reader) *or* (reading disability) *or* (slow reader) *or* (low achieving) *or* (delayed reader) *or* (at risk) *or* (remedial). We searched ERIC using the following descriptors: Reading instruction (thesaurus descriptor) *and* Classroom research (thesaurus descriptor) *and* Elementary and Secondary. Each of the articles identified were read and considered against the criteria we had established. Each of the studies was reviewed by at least two or more members of the research team until a consensus decision for inclusion or exclusion was reached. In addition, we conducted a hand search of all articles appearing in the *American Educational Research Journal, Reading Research Quarterly, Journal of Literacy Research* (formerly *Journal of Reading Behavior*), *Journal of Scientific Studies in Reading, Annual Yearbook of the National Reading Conference, Elementary School Journal, Journal of Special Education, Exceptional Children, Journal of Learning Disabilities, Learning Disabilities Quarterly, Remedial and Special Education, Learning Disabilities Research and Practice, Teacher Education and Special Education, Reading Improvement, Reading and Writing Quarterly, Annals of Dyslexia, Learning Disabilities,* and *Reading Improvement*. We included all of the studies that met the criteria in the database for analysis.

In the review process, all studies were examined by at least two of the members of the research team (which included authors and graduate research assistants). A consensus was required for a study to move into the review. Of the 42 studies we identified through our electronic and hand search, only 33 studies met the criteria we established for this review (see bibliography below). We excluded, for example, studies that focused on post-secondary students (e.g., Butler, 1998), writing (e.g,, Miller, 2003), and volunteers (e.g., Pullen, Lane, & Monaghan, 2004).

For our analysis, we used a constant-comparative methodology (Strauss & Corbin, 1990) to identify significant themes and patterns (e.g., purposes for use of the instrument). We reviewed each article, entering relevant methodological information (e.g., participants, research questions or purpose, observation methods or techniques, procedures of analysis) into a table. After the table was complete, we read and reread the information in these studies noting patterns in techniques and researchers' decisions related to classroom observation. Repeated reading and reviewing of these articles suggested that the variations in observational tools and methods were in some ways related to the differing purposes of the studies. The table was then cut apart, by individual study, and sorted according to observational purpose and other criteria.

Findings

We set out to identify the patterns of the use of observational research within the field of reading disabilities. To that end, we organized this section around trends and patterns we uncovered in our analysis. We begin this section by presenting the trends across time, journals, and topics. We then present the themes around the way researchers approached the use of observational research, focusing on their purposes and the methods for their research. We conclude this section by offering thoughts on ways in which the field might move to capitalize on the power of observational research with children who struggle with learning to read and who are learning disabled.

Trends in Journals and across Time   In this first section, we report on the trends across time and within each of the journals that published observational studies during our investigated time period. Our searching led us to 33 studies that involved observational research of the literacy teaching and learning of students who are disabled or who struggle with learning to read. Figure 38.1 illustrates the journal in which these studies appeared. Two of these journals, *Remedial and Special Education* (n = 9) and *Reading Research and Instruction* (n = 7) appear to support the publication of observational studies in ways that the other journals did not. The first tends to publish work concerned with learning disabilities (including disabilities related to reading) and the latter tends to publish work concerned with children who struggle with learning to read. It is also important to note that these studies appeared in top tier research journals (*Reading Research Quarterly*), general education journals (*Elementary School Journal*), and teacher education journals

Bibliography of Studies in Review (listed alphabetically)

Allington, R., & McGill-Franzen, A. (1989). School response to reading failure: Chapter 1 and special education. *The Elementary School Journal, 89*, 529–542.

Anders, P. L., & Gallego, M. A. (1989). Adoption of theoretically-linked vocabulary-reading comprehension practices. In S. McCormick & J. Zutell (Eds.), *Cognitive and social perspectives for literacy research and instruction: Thirty-eighth yearbook of the National Reading Conference* (pp. 481–487). Chicago: National Reading Conference.

Anderson, V. (1992). A teacher development project in transactional strategy instruction for teachers of severely reading-disabled adolescents. *Teaching and Teacher Education, 8*, 391–403.

Boyd, F. B. (2002). Motivation to continue: Enhancing literacy learning for struggling readers and writers. *Reading & Writing Quarterly, 18*, 257–277.

Calhoon, M. B. (2005). Effects of a peer-mediated phonological skill and reading comprehension program on reading skill acquisition for middle school students with reading disabilities. *Journal of Learning Disabilities, 38*, 424–433.

Coyne, M. D., Kame'enui, E. J., Simmons, D. C., & Harn, B. A. (2004). Beginning reading intervention as inoculation or insulin: First-Grade reading performance of strong responders to kindergarten intervention. *Journal of learning disabilities, 37*, 90–104.

Duffy, A. (2001). Balance, literacy acceleration, and responsive teaching in a summer school literacy program for elementary school struggling readers. *Reading Research and Instruction, 40*, 67–100.

Englert, C. S., Zhao, Y., Collings, N., & Romig, N. (2005). Learning to read words: the efects of internet-based software on the improvement of reading performance. *Remedial and Special Education, 26*, 357–371.

Fitzgerald, J., & Ramsbotham, A. (2004). First graders' cognitive and strategic development in Reading Recovery reading and writing. *Reading Research and Instruction, 44*, 1–31.

Fuchs, L. S., Fuchs, D., & Kazdan, S. (1999). Effects of peer-assisted learning strategies on high school students with serious reading problems. *Remedial and Special Education, 20*, 309–318.

Gelzheiser, L. M., & Meyers, J. (1991). Reading instruction by classroom, remedial, and resource room teachers. *Journal of Special Education, 24*, 512–527.

Graves, A. W., Plasencia-Peinado, J., Deno, S. L., & Johnson, J. R. (2005). Formatively evaluating the reading progress of first grade English language learners in multiple language classrooms. *Remedial and Special Education, 26*, 215–225.

Greenwood, C. R., Tapia, Y, Abbott, M., & Walton, C. A building-based case study of evidence-based literacy practices: Implementation, reading behavior, and growth in reading fluency, K-4. *Journal of Special Education, 37*, 95–110.

Hall, L. A. (2007). Bringing television back to the bedroom: Transactions between a seventh grade struggling reader and her mathematics teacher. *Reading Research and Instruction, 46*, 287–314.

Kourea, L., Cartledge, G., & Musti-Rao, S. (2007). Improving the reading skills of urban elementary students through Total Class Peer Tutoring. *Remedial and Special Education, 28*, 95–107.

Leinhardt, G., Zigmond, N., & Cooley, W. W. (1981). Reading instruction and its effects. *American Educational Research Journal, 18*, 343–361.

Marks, M., Pressley, M., Coley, J. D., Craig, S., Gardner, R., Depinto, T., & Rose, W. (1993). 3 teachers adaptations of reciprocal teaching in comparison to traditional reciprocal teaching. *Elementary School Journal, 94*, 267–283.

Mathes, P. G., Howard, J. K., Allen, S. H., & Fuchs, D. (1998). Peer-assisted learning strategies for first-grade readers: Responding to the needs of diverse learners. *Reading Research Quarterly, 33*, 62–94.

Moody, S. W., Vaughn, S., Hughes, M. T., & Fischer, M. (2000). Reading instruction in the resource room: Set up for failure. *Exceptional Children, 66*, 305–315.

Nierstheimer, S. L., Hopkins, C. J., Dillon, D. R., & Schmitt, M. C. (2000). Preservice teachers' shifting beliefs about struggling literacy learners. *Reading Research and Instruction, 40*, 1–16.

O'Connor, R. E., Fulmer, D., Harty, K. R., & Bell, K. M. (2005) Layers of reading intervention in kindergarten through third grade: Changes in teaching and student outcomes. *Journal of Learning Disabilities, 38*, 440–455.

Otaiba, S. A. (2005). How effective is code-based tutoring in English for English learners and pre-service teacher -tutors? *Remedial and Special Education, 26*, 245–254.

Rightmyer, E. C., McIntyre, E., & Petrosko, J. M. (2006). Instruction, development, and achievement of struggling primary grade readers. *Reading Research and Instruction, 45*, 209–241.

Santoro, L. E., Jitendra, A. K., Starosta, K., & Sacks, G.(2006). Reading well with Read Well: Enhancing the reading performance of English language learners. *Remedial and Special Education, 27*, 105–115.

Scharer, P. L. (1991). Moving into literature based reading instruction: Changes and challenges for teachers. In J. Zutell & S. McCormick, (Eds.), *Learner factor/teacher factors: Issues in literacy research and instruction* (pp. 409–421). Chicago: National Reading Conference.

Shippen, M. E., Houchins, D. E., Calhoon, M. B., Furlow, C. F., & Sartor, D. A. (2006). The effects of comprehensive school reform models in reading for urban middle school students with disabilities. *Remedial and Special Education, 27*, 322–328.

Shippen, M. E., Houchins, D. E., Steventon, C., & Sartor, D. L. (2005). A comparison of two Direct Instruction reading programs for urban middle school students. *Remedial and Special Education, 26*, 175–182.

Tancock, S. M. (1997). Catie: A case study of one first grader's reading status. *Reading Research and Instruction, 36*, 89–110.

Vadasy, P. F., Jenkins, J. R., Antil, L. R., Phillips, N. B., & Pool, K. (1997). The research-to-practice ball game: Classwide peer tutoring and teacher interest, implementation, and modifications. *Remedial and Special Education, 3*, 143–156.

Vaughn, S., Cirino, P. T., Linan-Thompson, S., Mathes, P. G., Carlson, C., Hagan, E., C., et al. (2006). Effectiveness of a Spanish intervention and an English intervention for English Language Learners at risk for reading problems. *American Educational Research Journal, 43*, 449–487.

Vaughn, S., Mathes, P., Linan-Thompson, S., Cirino, P., Carolson, C., & Pollard-Durodola, S., et al. (2006). Effectiveness of an English intervention for first-grade English Language Learners at risk for reading problems. *Elementary School Journal, 107*, 153–181.

Vaughn, S., Moody, S. W., & Schumm, J. S. (1998). Broken promises: Reading instruction in the resource room. *Exceptional Children, 64*, 211–225.

Worthy, J., Patterson, E., Salas, R., Prater, S., & Turner, M. (2002). "More than just reading": The human factor in reaching resistant readers. *Reading Research and Instruction, 41*, 177–201.

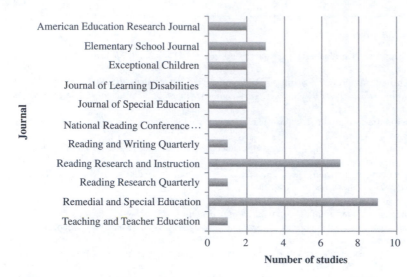

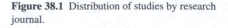

Figure 38.1 Distribution of studies by research journal.

(Teaching and Teacher Education). There appears to be a growing consensus that observational research "counts" as a method of research on reading disabilities.

Our next finding is related to the trends we investigated centered on observational research across time. Figure 38.2 illustrates the distribution of studies across time (grouped in periods of 2-year intervals). The first study published (Leinhardt, Zigmond, & Cooley, 1981) appeared in the *American Educational Research Journal*, perhaps in some ways, setting a tone of the recognition for the use of observational research in special education classrooms (focused on reading instruction). The next to appear was in the annual *Yearbook of the National Reading Conference* (Anders & Gallego, 1989) and *The Elementary School Journal* (Allington & McGill-Franzen, 1989), albeit at the end of that decade. Throughout the 1990s, there appeared to be a steady publishing of studies that used observational research methods as part of their design. Finally, in the most recent time period (2004–present), there appears to be a surge of studies that have used observational research methods, perhaps indicated that observational research in the field of reading instruction with reading disability populations is finding its rightful place in the literature.

Similarly, there were trends in the participants on whom the study was focused. The vast majority of these studies

focused their attention in elementary schools (n = 22) while the remainder were divided between middle schools (n = 4), high schools (n = 2), and tutoring settings (n = 1). Two studies used observational techniques to examine classrooms in both elementary and middle schools.

Equal numbers of studies looked at children with learning disabilities (n = 10) and children who struggled with learning to read (n = 10). Children within the latter group were labeled as delayed (n = 1), at risk (n = 5), low-achievers (n = 2) or resistant readers (n = 1). A small number of these studies (n = 4) focused on a combination of children with specific learning disabilities in reading and struggling readers. Finally, three of the studies in our database focused on children who struggled with learning to read (or were labeled at risk) and were English Language Learners.

Trends Across Foci and Topics Explored within Studies

In this next section we explore the foci of the studies and the topics studied within the research in our database. There were three categories that these studies appeared to be classified, including studies that explored general instructional issues, interventions, and the comparison of models, approaches, and/or programs. We will address each of these in turn.

General instructional practices. Under this category, studies in our database set out to explore the general practices of teachers or their knowledge and beliefs. These studies tended to be descriptive in nature. For example, researchers investigated the nature of reading instruction for students with learning disabilities in general education classrooms (Vaughn, Moody, & Schumm, 1998) and in special education classrooms (Leinhardt et al., 1981). Likewise, other research teams explored the nature of reading instruction, comparing instruction in general education classrooms to that of instruction in special education classrooms (Allington & McGill-Franzen, 1989). This study suggested that special education programs studied did not enhance either the quantity or quality of reading/language arts instruction of participating children. Likewise, the

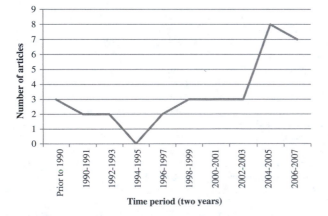

Figure 38.2 Distribution of studies across time.

authors were concerned with the small amount of reading/ language arts instruction offered to mainstreamed handicapped children.

Vaughn and her colleagues used the findings from their early work to explore the changes that occurred in instructional practices in general education classrooms after the introduction of local and state mandates (Moody, Vaughn, Hughes, & Fischer, 2000). Another study in this category explored the reading demands placed on struggling readers in their mathematics classroom (Hall, 2007). And, the final study in this category used classroom observations to investigate the correlation between instructional practices and reading proficiency of struggling readers (Graves, Plasencia-Peinado, Deno, & Johnson, 2005).

Another set of studies, which were also descriptive in nature, explored teacher perceptions, social class and the performance of children who were at risk of learning to read (Tancock, 1997) and the receptivity of teachers toward new instructional practices (Vadasy, Antil, Jenkins, Phillips, & Pool, 1997). Additionally, others explored the knowledge and beliefs of preservice teachers (Niersheimer, Hopkins, Dillon, & Schmitt, 2000) as they engaged with struggling readers.

Interventions and introductions to innovations. Studies in this category explored the effects of an intervention or an innovation on the learning of children with disabilities and/or struggling readers. In some cases, the studies were focused on literacy programs such as the study conducted by Duffy (2001) in which she implemented what she called a balanced and responsive literacy program with struggling readers. Greenwood, Tapia, Abbott, and Walton (2003) investigated the effects of a school-wide reading program, including teachers' implementation and students' reading behaviors and achievement. Others focused on the effects of professional development of evidence-based reading practices and the implementation of these practices on the outcomes of struggling readers in grades kindergarten through third grade (O'Conner, Fulmer, Harty, & Bell, 2005).

Other studies focused more specifically on particular aspects of reading instruction. For example, Otaiba (2005) focused on code-based instruction and Rightmyer, McIntyre, and Petrosko (2006) focused on phonics instruction. Still other studies examined the effect on cognitive processes of children with specific reading disabilities in reading or struggling readers (Anderson, 1992; Fitzgerald & Ramsbotham, 2004) while others focused on general comprehension studies (Anders & Gallego, 1989; Marks et al., 1993). Worthy, Patterson, Salas, Prater, and Turner (2002) and Boyd (2002) investigated the reading motivation of resistant and struggling readers (respectively) through an intervention; Boyd's intervention was in a classroom and Worthy et al.'s came through an after school tutoring program. Two other tutoring programs explored the role of peer tutoring with struggling readers and children with specific learning disabilities in reading (Calhoon, 2005; Kourea, Cartledge, & Musti-Rao, 2007).

Finally, Coyne, Kame'enui, Simmons, and Harn (2004) examined the performance of strong responders to a kindergarten intervention as a way of illustrating that teachers can prevent reading difficulties in young children. And, Vaughn and her colleagues explored the effectiveness of an English intervention for first grade English Language Learners at risk for reading problems (Vaughn et al., 2006b).

Comparison of existing models, programs, and approaches. Studies in this category set out to demonstrate the superiority of one model, program or approach over existing practices or another model/ program/ and/or approach for struggling readers and/or children with learning disabilities. For example, Vaughn and colleagues (2006a) studied the effects of two grade one reading interventions, one in English and one in Spanish, with English Language Learners. Other researcher teams were interested in the effects of reading programs on the reading achievement of struggling readers and children with learning disabilities. Such was the study conducted by Englert, Zhao, Collings, and Romig (2005) who studied the effects of an Internet-based software program (TELE-Web) on the improvement of elementary students' word recognition performance. Santaro, Jitendra, Starosta, and Sacks (2006) also looked at the effects of a reading program, the Read Well program, on English Language Learners.

Other studies compared programs with other programs. For example, Shippen and colleagues studied the effects Direct Instruction in two different ways. In their first study, Shippen, Houchins, Stevenson, and Sartor (2005) explored the effects of a direct and less-direct approach to reading instruction for urban middle school students. In another study, Shippen, Houchins, Calhoon, Furlow, and Sartor (2006) directly compared the effects of two popular comprehensive school reform models in reading (Success for All and Direct Instruction) also for urban middle school students with disabilities. Additionally, the effects of Peer-assisted Learning Strategies (PALS) program was compared in a first-grade setting (Mathes, Howard, Allen, & Fuchs, 1998) and a high school setting (Fuchs, Fuchs, & Kazdan, 1999).

In summary, studies that have used observational techniques, although primarily focused on teachers and children in elementary schools, have explored a variety of topics and served to fulfill a variety of purposes. In this next section, we explore the systems that were used to carry out the studies in our database.

Systems Used for Observation In this section, we present our findings centered on the patterns of systems used for the studies in our database. Because we had to rely on the author's descriptions of the data collected and analyzed and because some authors were much more descriptive than others, we were only able to include 28 studies in this next part of our analysis. Included in our findings were varying roles that observational data seemed to play in the studies. In some cases it was the primary source of data, in others

Misty Sailors and Margaret Flores

it was a secondary data source. And, in some, it was part of a complimentary source of data to be analyzed. Within these sources, we classified the observational data collected using Evertson and Green's system (1986, p. 169). Additionally, we further categorized these studies based on the type of tool used in each. We will address each in this section and summarize what we believe to be an exemplar for each category.

Observational data as a primary data source. In 12 of the 28 studies in this analysis, the observational data collected appeared to be the primary source of data collected for the study. In every case, a category system of data recording and storage was used (Evertson & Green, 1986). Within this classified set of studies, the purposes of the studies varied, as did the tools employed. For example, when the purpose of the study was to contextualize and confirm the accuracy of self-reported approaches to reading instruction, the research team used an a priori instrument, which was described in detail in the appendix of the article (Mathes et al., 1998). In other cases, where the research team used observations as measures of implementation (fidelity checks), checklists were employed (Coyne et al., 2004). In other cases, where the purpose of collecting observational data was to offer a window into instruction, researchers used a priori systems, codification schemes and modified instruments.

Of these studies, one stands out as exemplar. The published study provides insight into the most critical components of studies that employ observational research methods—it was connected to theory, employed a systematic set of data collection procedures and the data is tied directly to the analysis. In their investigation of the role of literacy instruction in helping the lowest performing first graders improve their oral reading fluency and nonsense word-reading fluency, Graves and colleagues (Graves et al., 2005) used an existing instrument, the ELLCOI, to document the literacy practices of teachers. The ELLCOI contains six subscales with individual items in each. Subscales include (a) explicit teaching, (b) quality of instruction, (c) sheltered English instruction, (d) interactive teaching, (e) vocabulary development, and (f) phonemic awareness and decoding. The research team found the ratings within the subscales (except for phonemic awareness and decoding instruction) to be correlated to reading achievement (as measured through a composite reading score consisting of posttest performance on oral reading fluency and the reading comprehension measure) in the 14 classrooms in which the team worked in California. The subscales were used to measure the reliability. Because they considered their work to be exploratory, the team offered suggestions for future work on the instrument in refining the subscales.

Observational data as a secondary data source. Some of the studies in our database seemed to utilize observations as a secondary data source. For example, in their study of Read Well, Santoro et al. (2006) used student achievement as their primary source of data and observations to simply achieve fidelity measures. That is, the data were only collected to establish fidelity of implementation of the intervention. Of the 10 studies that we classified as using observational data as a secondary data source, three of them did not have adequate descriptions of the type of data collected (including the instrument used, if any) so we were only able to analyze seven studies in this category. Of these seven, all but one used the category system, as described by Evertson and Green (1986) and interestingly, these same six were used to establish the fidelity of implementation for the innovation introduced in the study. As we have found in other research (Hoffman et al., in press), the quality of descriptions of the checklists and rating scales developed vary widely.

In one study, for example, there is no description of the instrument used, only a mention that fidelity of implementation had been measured and achieved (Shippen et al., 2006). In others, however, the description is detailed and elaborate. For example, in their study that looked examined the effects of the Read Well program on the reading performance of students who were English Language Learners (ELL) and poor readers and a student who was an English Language Learner and had a learning disability in reading, Santoro et al. (2006) developed a checklist that included critical components of the reading program. Each item was evaluated based on its presence or absence from instruction and the quality of the demonstration of instructional items rated using a scale of 0 to 2. Observers established a reliability of .85 before initiating observations.

A study performed by O'Connor, Fulmer, Harty, and Bell (2005) was the only one in this category (using observational data as a secondary data source) that used a more open-ended system. The purpose of the study was to monitor the long-term effect of sustained layered intervention (phonemic awareness, letter-to-sound mappings) efforts across the primary grades. Observations of reading instruction lasted 40 to 80 minutes and were conducted twice for the second- and third-grade teachers during their year as control group and 3 times for teachers in layers one and two. The purpose of the observations was to obtain a composite picture of student and teacher activities during reading instruction by recorded classroom events as they occurred. Observers described teacher behavior and lesson content in a chronological format. Ongoing field notes described how the teacher delivered instruction, used materials, and grouped students. The field notes also described the interactions between students and teachers and the level of engagement of the students with low reading scores. The process of gathering field notes involved recording informational by making entries at 5-minute intervals. A checklist served as an accompaniment to recorded field notes and provided quick record of room demographics, materials used during instruction, general climate of the classroom, groupings of students, and the content of the reading lesson. Observations made in April documented activities that were consistent from those observed in November and February and those which were divergent from observations made in November and February. Inconsistencies were followed up with interviews.

Observational data as a part of a supportive data pool. In addition to observations as a primary or secondary data source, there existed in our database a complexity within studies that relied on multiple data sources where the observational data was the primary source but was supported heavily by a secondary data source, such as interview and/or survey data. Of the 10 studies that fell into this category, three used a category system, five used a descriptive system and four used a narrative system, based on Evertson and Green's (1986) classification system; we could not discern the classification of the final study due to a lack of methodological descriptions. Amongst the latter two groups, four used video and five used field notes to gather the observational data. All of the studies in this group had as their purpose the unveiling of some aspect of instruction as it pertained to struggling readers or children who qualify for special education.

There was one exemplar in this group, the study conducted by Vaughn et al. (1998). The purpose of the study was to investigate the extent to which observational findings from research in general education classrooms would be replicated in special education resource room settings. The team conducted observations using adapted (for use in resource room) version of the Classroom Climate Scale, which is designed to provide about teacher and student interactions in settings that include mainstreamed students with learning disabilities. An additional form was added to the scale to obtain information about group size, composition, and instructional materials used. The measure has 2 parts: quantitative section and descriptive section. The quantitative section allows the observer to rate (5-pt. scale) the amount of time whole group, small group, and individual instruction occur; the extent to which the teacher monitors ongoing student performance; the amount of time the teacher provided positive feedback. The descriptive section provides guided questions for the observer about whether the students present are working on the same activity, whether they follow the same sequence of activities, and whether they use the same or different materials. Also recorded are descriptions of teachers' adaptations for students and the occurrence of any word recognition and comprehension activities. Additional observational field notes are recorded on the Classroom Climate Scale to further describe the reading and grouping instruction.

Discussion and Implications for Research

In summary, our analysis of studies that used observational methods for data collection and analysis varied widely, as did the use a variety of systems. The combined use of a priori instruments with the designed-for-a-purpose systems in this database focused on a variety of topics, reflecting the growing understanding of the importance of observational research. The variety of ways in which the tools were used reflected the flexibility of the instrumentation involved in observational studies in this database. This all reflects a growing advancement of both the method of observational research and its role in helping the field understand instructional with reading disabilities.

However, there are a few caveats to consider. While there seems to be a surge of observational studies in this field, it would appear that the past two years (through 2007) saw a drop in the number of published studies that used observation as a method; this has been a common trend in other literature reviews we have conducted on observational research (Hoffman et al., in press). We are unclear as to if this is the beginning of a trend and why it may be so. Our analysis also indicated that the quality of descriptions of the instruments used varied widely, with some studies reporting carefully the methods used in creating the checklists and their role in analysis while other studies were not so carefully. Again, we were unclear as to this pattern. Perhaps it is because authors choose not engage in careful documentation, publishers do not require it, or there is simply not enough space in journals to report this information. Regardless, this was a growing concern as we analyzed this database.

As a result of the concern for quality and from our analyses of these observational studies in the field of research in reading disabilities, we propose a set of guidelines for future observational research. Here we focus on those aspects of research that are particularly important to the methodology surrounding observational research and not to educational research or reading research more generally considered. The guidelines we propose, for example, are consistent with the recently issued guidelines for the reporting of educational research as provided by the American Educational Research Association (2007). These guidelines can be applied across quantitative, qualitative, and mixed methods studies.

A. Descriptions of systems used—Researchers must be clear in describing the selection or development process and the criteria used for the systems used to observe teaching. There should be a particular attention to the qualities and the purposes and contexts for the study. And, researchers must provide rich and detailed descriptions of the history/past experiences with the tools being used as well as the features of the tools and procedures required with particular attention to any modifications made for the study.

B. Presence of researcher—Researchers must be clear in describing the role they played during the observation itself. Even though one might be a passive observer (using a checklist, for example), the mere presence of the observer in the classroom has the potential to affect the teaching that is taking place. Researchers must present compelling evidence to demonstrate that the behaviors of the teachers (and students) were not influenced by the presence of the observer. And, if they were, this must be addressed as a limitation of the study.

C. How much is enough?—There is growing evidence

that researchers must increase the amount of time spent in classrooms in order to accurately portray reading instruction. For example, in their attempt to more fully define and capture reading instruction, Croninger and Valli (2008) discovered that there was more variance in teacher-student oral exchanges within lessons enacted by the same teacher (84% variance) versus the quality of interactions associated with schools (9%) and classes (7%). Methodologically, the authors argued, this means that studies of reading must observe multiple lessons by the same teacher to determine the extent to which practices occur and their effects on student outcomes. They strongly suggested that a minimum of 6–8 reading lessons be observed in order accurately portray teacher practices in reading classrooms.

We believe that the adoption of these guidelines within the reading disabilities research community could be useful in promoting quality research. We believe that these guidelines can be of use to researchers designing studies, editorial advisors reviewing manuscripts, journal editors forming guidelines and making decisions on manuscripts, and to faculty mentoring the next generation of reading researchers.

References

Abrams, B. (2000). *The observational research handbook: Understanding how consumers live with your product.* Chicago: NTC/Contemporary Publishing.

Allington, R. L., & McGill-Franzen, A. (1989). School response to reading failure: Chapter 1 and special education students in grades 2, 4, and 8. *Elementary School Journal, 89,* 529–542.

Anders, P. L., & Gallego, M. A. (1989). Adoption of theoretically-linked vocabulary-reading comprehension practices. In S. McCormick & J. Zutell (Eds.), *Cognitive and social perspectives for literacy research and instruction: Thirty-eighth yearbook of the National Reading Conference* (pp. 481–487). Chicago: National Reading Conference.

Anderson, L. W., & Burns, R. B. (1989). *Research in classrooms: The study of teachers, teaching, and instruction.* Oxford, UK: Pergamon Press.

Anderson, V. (1992). A teacher development project in transactional strategy instruction for teachers of severely reading-disabled adolescents. *Teaching and Teacher Education, 8,* 391–403.

Angrosino, M. (2007). *Doing ethnographic and observational research (Qualitative research kit).* New York: Sage.

Berliner, D. (1990). The nature of time in schools: Theoretical concepts, practitioner perceptions. In C. Denham & A. Lieberman (Eds.), *Time to learn* (pp. 33–63). Washington, DC: National Institute of Education.

Boyd, F. B. (2002). Motivation to continue: Enhancing literacy learning for struggling readers and writers. *Reading & Writing Quarterly, 18,* 257–277.

Brophy, J. E. (1973). Stability of teacher effectiveness. *American Educational Research Journal, 10,* 245–252.

Brophy, J. E., & Good, T. (1970). Teacher-child dyadic interactions: A new method of classroom observation. *Journal of School Psychology, 8*(2), 131–137.

Butler, D. L. (1998). The strategic content learning approach to promoting self-regulated learning: A report of three studies. *Journal of Educational Psychology, 90,* 682–697.

Calhoon, M. B. (2005). Effects of a peer-mediated phonological skill and reading comprehension program on reading skill acquisition for middle school students with reading disabilities. *Journal of Learning Disabilities, 38,* 424–433.

Carroll, J. S. (1963). A model of school learning. *Teachers College Record, 64,* 723–733.

Coyne, M. D., Kame'enui, E. J., Simmons, D. C., & Harn, B. A. (2004). Beginning reading intervention as inoculation or insulin: First-Grade reading performance of strong responders to kindergarten intervention. *Journal of learning disabilities, 37,* 90–104.

Croninger, R. G., & Valli, L. (2008, March). 'Where is the action?' Challenges to studying the teaching of reading in elementary classrooms. Paper presented at the Symposium, *Measuring Classroom Instruction: The State of the Art,* at the annual meeting of the American Educational Research Association, New York.

Duffy, A. (2001). Balance, literacy acceleration, and responsive teaching in a summer school literacy program for elementary school struggling readers. *Reading Research and Instruction, 40,* 67–100.

Englert, C. S., Zhao, Y, Collings, N., & Romig, N. (2005). Learning to read words: the efects of internet-based software on the improvement of reading performance. *Remedial and Special Education, 26,* 357–371.

Evertson, C. M., & Green, J. L. (1986). Observation as inquiry and method. In M. C. Wittrock (Ed.), *Handbook of research on teaching* (pp. 162–213). New York: Macmillan.

Fisher, C., Filby, N., Marliave, R., Cahen, L., Dishaw, M., Moore, J., et al. (1978). *Teaching behaviors: Academic learning time and student achievement: Final report of phase III-B, beginning teacher evaluation study.* San Francisco: Far West Laboratory for Educational Research and Development.

Fitzgerald, J., & Ramsbotham, A. (2004). First graders' cognitive and strategic development in Reading Recovery reading and writing. *Reading Research and Instruction, 44,* 1–31.

Flanders, N. A. (1970). *Analyzing teaching behavior.* Reading, MA: Addison-Wesley.

Fuchs, L. S., Fuchs, D., & Kazdan, S. (1999). Effects of peer-assisted learning strategies on high school students with serious reading problems. *Remedial and Special Education, 20,* 309–318.

Gelzheiser, L, M., & Meyers, J. (1991). Reading instruction by classroom, remedial, and resource room teachers. *Journal of Special Education, 24,* 512–527.

Gillham, B. (2008). *Observation techniques: Structured to unstructured.* New York: Continuum.

Glaser, B. G., & Strauss, A. L. (1967). *The discovery of grounded theory: Strategies for qualitative research.* Chicago: Aldine.

Goffman, E. (1959). *The presentation of self in everyday life.* New York: Anchor Books/Doubleday.

Gordon, I., & Jester, R. (1973). Techniques of observing teaching in early childhood and outcomes of particular procedures. In R. M. W. Travers (Ed.), *Second handbook of research on teaching* (pp. 184–217). Chicago: Rand McNally.

Graves, A. W., Plasencia-Peinado, J., Deno, S. L., & Johnson, J. R. (2005). Formatively evaluating the reading progress of first grade English language learners in multiple language classrooms. *Remedial and Special Education, 26,* 215–225.

Greenwood, C. R., Tapia, Y, Abbott, M., & Walton, C. (2003). A building-based case study of evidence-based literacy practices: Implementation, reading behavior, and growth in reading fluency, K-4. *Journal of Special Education, 37,* 95–110.

Hall, R. V., Lunch, D., & Jackson, D. (1968). Effects of teacher attention on study behavior. *Journal of Applied Behavior Analysis, 1,* 1–12.

Hall, L. A. (2007). Bringing television back to the bedroom: Transactions between a seventh grade struggling reader and her mathematics teacher. *Reading Research and Instruction, 46,* 287–314.

Hilberg, R. S., Waxman, H. C., & Tharp, R. G. (2004). Introduction: Purposes and perspectives on classroom observational research. In H. C. Waxman, R. G. Tharp, & R. S. Hilberg (Eds.), *Observational research in US classrooms: New approaches for understanding cultural and linguistic diversity* (pp. 1–20). New York: Cambridge University Press.

Hoffman, J. V., Maloch, B. & Sailors, M. (in press). Observations of literacy instruction. In P. D. Pearson, E. Moje, & M. Kamil (Eds.), *The handbook of reading research, 4th edition.* Mahwah, NJ: Erlbaum.

Individuals with Disabilities Education Improvement Acts of 2004, Pub. L. No. 108-446, 118 Stat. 2647 (2004) (amending 20 U.S.C.§§ 1440 et seq.).

Johnson, B., & Turner, L. A. (2003). Data collection strategies in mixed methods research. In A. Tashakkori & C. Teddlie (Eds.), *Handbook of mixed methods in social & behavioral research* (pp. 297–320). Thousand Oaks, CA: Sage.

Kourea, L., Cartledge, G., & Musti-Rao, S. (2007). Improving the reading skills of urban elementary students through Total Class Peer Tutoring. *Remedial and Special Education, 28,* 95–107.

Leinhardt, G., Zigmond, N., & Cooley, W. W. (1981). Reading instruction and its effects. *American Educational Research Journal, 18,* 343–361.

Marks, M., Pressley, M., Coley, J. D., Craig, S., Gardner, R., Depinto, T., et al. (1993). Teachers adaptations of reciprocal teaching in comparison to traditional reciprocal teaching. *Elementary School Journal, 94,* 267–283.

Mathes, P. G., Howard, J. K., Allen, S. H., & Fuchs, D. (1998). Peer-assisted learning strategies for first-grade readers: Responding to the needs of diverse learners. *Reading Research Quarterly, 33,* 62–94.

McDonald, F. J., & Elias, P. (1976). A report on the results of phase I I of the beginning teacher evaluation study: An overview. *Journal of Teacher Education, 27,* 315–316.

Medley, D., & Mitzel, H. (1963). Measuring classroom behavior by systematic observation. In N. L. Gage (Ed.), *Handbook of research on teaching* (pp. 247–328). Chicago: Rand McNally.

Mertens, D. M. (2005). *Research and evaluation in education and psychology: Integrating diversity with quantitative, qualitative, and mixed methods* (2nd ed.). Thousand Oaks, CA: Sage.

Miller, S. D. (2003). How high- and low-challenge tasks affect motivation and learning: Implications for struggling learners. *Reading and Writing Quarterly, 19,* 39–57.

Moody, S. W., Vaughn, S., Hughes, M. T., & Fischer, M. (2000). Reading instruction in the resource room: Set up for failure. *Exceptional Children, 66,* 305–315.

Nierstheimer, S. L., Hopkins, C. J., Dillon, D. R., & Schmitt, M. C. (2000). Preservice teachers' shifting beliefs about struggling literacy learners. *Reading Research and Instruction, 40,* 1–16.

O'Connor, R. E., Fulmer, D., Harty, K. R., & Bell, K. M. (2005) Layers of reading intervention in kindergarten through third grade: Changes in teaching and student outcomes. *Journal of Learning Disabilities, 38,* 440–455.

Otaiba, S. A. (2005). How effective is code-based tutoring in English for English learners and pre-service teacher -tutors? *Remedial and Special Education, 26,* 245–254.

Pullen, P. C., Lane, H. B., & Monaghan, M. C. (2004). Effects of a volunteer tutoring model on the early literacy development of struggling first grade students. *Reading Research and Instruction, 43,* 21–40.

Rightmyer, E. C., McIntyre, E., & Petrosko, J. M. (2006). Instruction, development, and achievement of struggling primary grade readers. *Reading Research and Instruction, 45,* 209–241.

Rosenshine, B., & Furst, N. (1973). The use of direct observation to study teaching. In R. M. W. Travers (Ed.), *Second handbook of research on teaching* (p. 263–298). Chicago: Rand McNally.

Santoro, L. E., Jitendra, A. K., Starosta, K., & Sacks, G.(2006). Reading well with read well: Emhancing the reading performance of English language learners. *Remedial and Special Education, 27,* 105–115.

Semmel, M. I. (1975). Application of systematic classroom observation to the study and modification of pupil-teacher interaction in special education. In R. Weinberg & F. H. Wood (Eds.), *Observation of pupils and teachers in mainstream and special education settings: Alternative strategies* (pp. 231–264). Minneapolis: University of Minneapolis Press.

Shippen, M. E., Houchins, D. E., Calhoon, M. B., Furlow, C. F., & Sartor, D. A. (2006). The effects of comprehensive school reform models in reading for urban middle school students with disabilities. *Remedial and Special Education, 27,* 322–328.

Shippen, M. E., Houchins, D. E., Steventon, C., & Sartor, D. A. (2005). A comparison of two Direct Instruction reading programs for urban middle school students. *Remedial and Special Education, 26,* 175–182.

Stallings, J. (1975). Implementation and child effects of teaching practices in follow through classrooms. *Monographs of the Society for Research in Child Development.* 40, Nos. 7 and 8 (Serial No. 163).

Strauss, A., & Corbin, J. (1990). *Basics of qualitative research: Grounded theory procedures and techniques.* New York: Sage.

Suen, H. K., & Ary, D. (1989). *Analyzing quantitative behavioral observation data.* Hillsdale, NJ: Erlbaum.

Sweetman, J. (1988). Observational research: A study of discourse and power. *Research Papers in Education, 3,* 42–63.

Tancock, S. M. (1997). Catie: A case study of one first grader's reading status. *Reading Research and Instruction, 36,* 89–110.

Tashakkori, A., & Teddlie, C. (2003). Issues and dilemmas in teaching research methods courses in social and behavioural sciences: US perspective. *International Journal of Social Research Methodology, 6,* 61–77.

Vadasy, P. F., Jenkins, J. R., Antil, L. R., Phillips, N. B., & Pool, K. (1997). The research-to-practice ball game: Classwide peer tutoring and teacher interest, implementation, and modifications. *Remedial and Special Education, 3,* 143–156.

Vaughn, S., Cirino, P. T., Linan-Thompson, S., Mathes, P. G., Carlson, C., Hagan, E., C., et al. (2006a). Effectiveness of a Spanish intervention and an English intervention for English Language Learners at risk for reading problems. *American Educational Research Journal, 43,* 449–487.

Vaughn, S., Mathes, P., Linan-Thompson, S., Cirino, P., Carolson, C., & Pollard-Durodola, S., et al. (2006b). Effectiveness of an English intervention for first-grade English Language Learners at risk for reading problems. *Elementary School Journal, 107,* 153–181.

Vaughn, S., Moody, S. W., & Schumm, J. S. (1998). Broken promises: Reading instruction in the resource room. *Exceptional Children, 64,* 211–225.

Walker, H. M., & Buckley, N. K. (1968). The use of positive reinforcement in conditioning attending behavior. *Journal of Applied Behavior Analysis, 1,* 245–250.

Worthy, J., Patterson, E., Salas, R., Prater, S., & Turner, M. (2002). "More than just reading": The human factor in reaching resistant readers. *Reading Research and Instruction, 41,* 177–201.

39

Large Database Analyses

THERESE D. PIGOTT
Loyola University Chicago

KENNETH WONG
Brown University

This chapter will discuss the nature of evidence on reading disabilities drawn from the use of large databases. Since the Snow, Burns, and Griffin (1998) review of research on preventing reading difficulties in young children, there have been a number of influential reports based on large databases. There are two main categories of large databases that researchers may use to study reading disabilities. First, there are cross-sectional, nationally representative data sets that collect measures of reading achievement either at one time point only or are repeated with independent samples at different time points. Nationally representative cross-sectional data sets include the National Assessment of Educational Progress (NAEP), and the National Assessment of Adult Literacy (NAAL). Second, there are longitudinal data sets that follow a single cohort over time. Many of these data sets are nationally representative of a target population in the first wave of data collection, but may not be representative of the target population at a later wave. The longitudinal data sets most relevant to the study of reading disability include two early childhood longitudinal studies, the Early Childhood Longitudinal Study – Kindergarten (ECLS-K), and the Early Childhood Longitudinal Study – Birth Cohort, (ECLS-B), the NICHD Study of Early Child Care and Youth Development (SECCYD), and the Education Longitudinal Study (ELS). In this chapter, we examine the nature of the evidence about reading disabilities that are possible from secondary analyses of large-scale databases, and we raise a number of substantive and methodological issues. For example, how generalizable are the findings from large databases? What kinds of conclusions can be drawn and how closely can we link these findings to policy and to practice? What are the realistic applications and implications of these findings? In light of the current emphasis on experimental research, what role can research using large-scale databases play in understanding, preventing, and treating reading disabilities?

Nature of Evidence from Nationally Representative Databases

Since the passage of the No Child Left Behind (NCLB) legislation, policymakers have focused considerable attention on experimental research that examines the effectiveness of reading interventions. Experimental research provides important evidence about causal relationships, especially with regard to the efficacy of supportive interventions for children or adults with reading disabilities. There remains, however, a set of questions not easily addressed by experimental research.

Representative, large scale databases can address questions of prevalence, prevention and treatment of reading disabilities that are potentially generalizable to the population. Nationally representative, observational studies can provide estimates of the rate of diagnosed reading disabilities and the characteristics of those children and adults with reading problems. Researchers can use large scale longitudinal databases to examine the development of reading difficulties over time as children move through formal schooling in order to identify correlates of later reading difficulty. In some limited ways, large scale databases can also provide evidence about the effectiveness of widely used interventions for individuals with reading disabilities.

In the United States, both the National Center for Education Statistics (NCES) and the National Institute of Child Health and Human Development (NICHD) have supported several large scale data collection efforts that provide descriptive information about the prevalence of reading disabilities and the outcomes of children and adults with reading difficulties, both at single time points and across time. These databases include a rich array of measures of individual children or adults, and information about the educational, home and work environments of these children gathered either from the respondent or others close to the respondent. Many of these databases can be linked to Census data or to surveys of particular elementary and postsecondary institutions. Thus, these databases provide both individual level and contextual level information that researchers can use to identify and estimate the associations between reading disabilities and individual and contextual characteristics. While secondary data analysis cannot provide strong evidence about causal effects of interventions, analyses using large scale databases can help the field in shaping next steps in a research agenda. For example, estimating the prevalence of reading disabilities helps focus limited resources toward individuals in need of interventions. Using longitudinal data to identify possible predictors of later reading difficulties assists researchers to design better assessment instruments and procedures for diagnosing individuals at risk. Examining the reading skills of individuals who report participating in widely used intervention strategies such as adult basic skills training or small-group pull-out reading instruction can also provide some evidence about efficacy of these programs. Thus, secondary data analyses can inform and sometimes inspire more focused and local research of individuals with reading disabilities.

The following sections discuss the nature of the evidence in cross-sectional and longitudinal surveys, briefly describing the databases available for reading disability research, and providing examples of how these surveys have been utilized to increase our understanding of reading disabilities.

Nationally-Representative Cross-Sectional Surveys

One relevant set of questions about reading disabilities concerns estimating the incidence and prevalence of reading difficulties in the population and in particular sub-groups (Snow et al., 1998). A second important question in the reading disabilities research involves understanding the characteristics of individuals whose reading assessment scores are lower than the general population. Nationally representative, cross-sectional surveys can address aspects of these important questions.

In general, cross-sectional studies use survey sampling techniques to obtain a representative sample of the target population. Respondents in these surveys usually complete a number of assessments, and often the research plan includes gathering contextual information about the educational setting or workplace of the respondent. With the proper use of survey sampling weights, the statistical analysis of cross-sectional surveys provides estimates that a researcher can use to make inferences to the population (Levy & Lemeshow, 1999).

The cross-sectional surveys with information on reading disabilities are either conducted at a single time point, or, in the case of the NAEP, are repeated at different timepoints with different samples of students. Researchers can use repeated cross-sectional surveys like the NAEP to monitor trends across time in the United States, but cannot assess how individuals might change over that same time

period (Berends, 2006) since the same individuals are not studied at each time point. Below are short descriptions of the current cross-sectional databases relevant for reading disabilities researchers.

The National Assessment of Educational Progress (NAEP) The NAEP is a nationwide assessment given to a representative sample of students in the United States. Every 2 years, reading and mathematics are assessed at Grades 4 and 8, with plans to add Grade 12 reading in 2009. In general, the sampling scheme involves selecting representative schools within particular geographic regions. Within schools, approximately 60 students are randomly selected within the target grades, and then are randomly allocated to one of the subject tests given that year.

In 2007, the most recent reading assessment, fourth-graders were assessed in their ability to read for literary experience and for information. Eighth graders were also assessed in these two contexts as well as in reading to perform a task (National Assessment Governing Board, 2006). The 2009 NAEP Reading Assessment will introduce a new reading framework (American Institutes for Research, 2007). In 2009, fourth, eighth, and 12 graders will be assessed in reading using two different types of texts: literary and informational. Vocabulary will also be directly assessed in all grade levels.

How reading disabilities are measured. Students are selected to participate in NAEP assessments randomly without regard to disability status. Once a student is selected, schools identify which students have (a) a disability, including a learning disability; and (b) have an Individualized Education Program (IEP) (National Assessment of Educational Progress, 2001). Students that are identified with a disability and have an IEP can complete the NAEP using an allowable accommodation. Students whose disabilities require accommodations not allowed by NAEP are exempted from completing the assessments. School professionals fill out a questionnaire for each student with a disability indicating the type of accommodation needed for the particular student (National Center for Education Statistics, 2008d). Allowable accommodations for NAEP Reading include using magnification, having directions read aloud, taking the test in small groups, extra time, and breaks. Similar accommodations are allowed for students who are English Language Learners (ELL). In the 2007 assessment, 43% of the assessed students with disabilities were given extra time, with the next most common accommodation, taking the assessment in a small-group, used with 10% of the assessed students with disabilities. Similar percentages of assessed eighth grade students with disabilities were allowed extra time or could take the test in a small group.

Research issues for the NAEP. The NAEP reading assessments can be used for assessing the incidence rate of students with learning disabilities and the reading ability level of these students who can be accommodated for the assessment. Trends in these incidence rates can also be tracked over time (National Center for Education Statistics, 2008e). There are few studies using the NAEP to examine the performance of students with reading disabilities. The NAEP is most often mentioned with regard to the number of children identified as learning disabled and the types of accommodations most used on the assessments. For example, a number of studies have been prepared for the NCES with regard to the use of accommodations for learning disabled students (Abedi, Lord, Kim, & Miyoshi, 2001; Lutkus, Mazzeo, Zhang, & Jerry, 2004; Stancavage, Makris, & Rice, 2007; Weston, 2002).

The National Assessment of Adult Literacy (NAAL)   Given in 1992 and again in 2003, the NAAL studied the literacy skills of a nationally representative sample of adults aged 16 and over. The 2003 assessment also over-sampled adults in prison. The design of the NAAL precludes any inference to the level of individual adults; not every adult completed the same items so that inferences about literacy can only be made to the population of U.S. adults or to major subgroups of U.S. adults.

The main NAAL survey included questions related to the comprehension of three types of materials. Prose literacy included the ability to read and comprehend documents such as newspapers and instructional materials (continuous texts). Document literacy relates to the knowledge and skills needed to understand non-continuous texts such as job applications, maps, and drug labels. Quantitative literacy includes skills related to computations such as balancing a checkbook or completing an order form.

How are reading disabilities measured.   There are two ways of identifying NAAL respondents with reading disabilities. First, approximately 6% of respondents in the 2003 NAAL identify themselves as having a learning disability. Second, a supplemental assessment, the Adult Literacy Supplemental Assessment (ALSA), was given to approximately 3% of the sample who could answer only a few of the NAAL questions. The assessments in the ALSA focused on identifying letters, numbers and words, and to comprehend simple documents. The 3%–5% of the population who were assessed using the ALSA could also be studied to examine the characteristics of U.S. adults with the lowest levels of literacy.

Research issues in the NAAL.   As in the NAEP, the NAAL can be used to estimate a population incidence level, in this case, the number of adults who self-report learning disabilities. According to the summary report for the 2003 NAAL assessment, approximately 6% of adults indicate they have a reading disability (Kutner et al., 2007). The NAAL has also been used by researchers to examine, for example, the relationship between formal schooling and reading proficiency. Johnson (2001) found a positive association between years of formal schooling and prose reading proficiency, with adults who completed more years

of schooling scoring higher on assessments of prose literacy. This finding was also discussed by Strucker, Yamamoto, and Kirsch (2007) in their study of the relationship between adult reading skills and the assessment instruments used in the NAAL.

Other studies have used the NAAL to examine characteristics of adult readers, some with a particular focus on adults with low levels of literacy. A study by Sheehan-Holt and Smith (2000) used the 1992 NAAL to examine the reading assessments and reading practices of adults who reported participation in basic skills education. They found that after controlling for demographic and educational variables, there were no positive associations between participation in basic skills education and literacy proficiencies. However, they did find that reading practices were significantly higher for those who had taken a basic skills course compared to those who reported not having this training. Other studies have examined the reading performance and practices of other groups of students such as community college graduates (Howard & Obetz, 1996) and in the general population (Smith, 1996). Most of this research has focused on the earlier survey of adult literacy; more research is needed into the characteristics of adults in the 2003 administration of NAAL, especially of that subset of adults at the lowest levels of literacy.

Other cross-sectional surveys.   Other resources such as the Current Population Survey or the National Household Survey provide estimates of adults and children identified as having general learning disabilities. These surveys rely on parent or self-report for the designation of disabled, and thus provide some general estimates of disabilities in the population. In addition, researchers may be interested in the characteristics of the schools that students attend. For example, a researcher using NAEP data may want to examine contextual features of the schools attended by students who had extra time to complete the NAEP. The Common Core of Data and the Schools and Staffing Survey can be linked to NAEP to provide information about the schools included in that particular NAEP sample.

Methodological Issues with Cross-Sectional Surveys   The analysis of these nationally representative cross-sectional surveys requires the use of weights in order to obtain the correct population estimates. Certain statistical analysis programs such as STATA are designed to incorporate these weights into analyses. In some cross-sectional databases, sub-populations of interest to a reading researcher may not constitute a representative sample, and thus results based on these subsets may not be used to support inferences to the population. However, studying these smaller sub-samples may still provide insight into aspects of reading disabilities even if generalizable inferences are not possible.

A second issue is the treatment of nested data. When researchers are interested in the school contexts of students with disabilities, multilevel modeling techniques such as hierarchical linear modeling or structural equation modeling are needed to examine the relationships between student and school characteristics when students are nested in schools.

Limitations of Cross-Sectional Data for Studying Reading Disabilities   One limitation with nationally representative data sets concerns the definition and identification of students with reading disabilities. Stancavage, Makris, and Rice (2007) found that schools reported a wide range of evidence used to make decisions about providing accommodations for students to participate in NAEP testing and about excluding particular students from participating in NAEP. These inconsistencies reflect the issues in the field with identifying students at risk for reading difficulties. Thus, estimates of reading disabilities using even carefully designed nationally representative data sets suffer from the problems with identification and diagnosis of reading disabilities. As in any large scale databases, researchers should use a range of variables to identify the subset of students with reading disabilities and report on these selection decisions in any analyses of these data.

Longitudinal Large Scale Databases

Longitudinal surveys are particularly useful for studying how students or adults change over time. Typically, these surveys include at least three data collection points (usually more), starting with a nationally representative sample at the first wave. While the data remain representative of the population at wave one, attrition naturally contributes to a loss of participants in subsequent waves of the survey. For reading disability researchers, longitudinal databases are useful for two types of research questions. For example, following infants or young children through the early elementary school years could uncover correlates and predictors of later reading difficulties. At the other end of the continuum, databases that follow adolescents diagnosed with reading disabilities provide information about how these students negotiate transitions to high school, postsecondary education and the workforce.

For reading disability research, there are two major sets of longitudinal data sets. The first set examines young children either at birth or at kindergarten and follows these children over a period of time. Researchers can (and have) used these databases to address questions related to when children are first identified with reading disabilities, the achievement outcomes of these children over time, and the children's family and school contexts. The second set of large scale databases examines the transition of adolescents to high school, postsecondary options, and the workplace. In addition, any given time period included in these longitudinal databases can be used in a cross-sectional study of a target sample of students. The sections below describe some of the major longitudinal data sets that hold the most promise for reading disability research.

The Early Childhood Longitudinal Survey, Kindergarten (ECLS-K) and Birth Cohort (ECLS-B)   The Early Childhood Longitudinal Survey, Kindergarten (ECLS-K) and the Early Childhood Longitudinal Survey, Birth cohort (ECLS-B) are two overlapping longitudinal databases focusing on the growth and development of children from birth through Grade 8. In 1998, the ECLS-K collected data on a representative sample of 1,000 schools with kindergarten classrooms. Within each school, approximately 23 children were selected for a series of assessments starting in the fall of the kindergarten year. Parents and teachers also completed surveys about the children, and information was gathered about the school environment and classroom curriculum. The same cohort of children were assessed in the spring of kindergarten, the fall and spring of first grade, the fall and spring of third grade, fifth grade, and eighth grade (National Center for Education Statistics, 2008b). The ECLS-B follows a representative sample of 14,000 children born during 2001 through their kindergarten year. Information was collected about these children at 9 months, 2 years, 1 year before kindergarten, and their kindergarten year. The surveys include direct child assessments as well as reports from parents (including fathers), caregivers, and teachers (National Center for Education Statistics, 2008a).

How reading disabilities are measured.   In the ECLS-K, the parent and teacher questionnaires include questions about whether the child has been diagnosed with a learning disability, and what services have been provided to the child. Parents, for example, are asked if the target child has been evaluated by a professional and been diagnosed with a learning disability, received any special services such as speech and language therapy over the past year, or were enrolled in special education services (National Center for Education Statistics, 2008c). Teachers are asked if the target child has received individual or small group pull-out tutoring in reading, or if the child participates in a Title I reading program. If the child has an individual education program plan (IEP), the special education teacher is asked to identify the type of disability (such as autism, behavior or learning disability), whether the child has IEP goals in reading, and the types of the services provided for the child.

The ECLS-B data set provides scores for individual children on a number of cognitive scales. Children at 9 months and 24 months of age are assessed using the Bayley Short Form–Research Edition (Bayley, 1993). Preschool and kindergarten children are given items from the ECLS-K as well as from cognitive assessments such as the PPVT-II (Dunn & Markwardt, 1981) and the WJ-HI (Woodcock & Johnson, 1990). There are no measures that directly indicate a child has been diagnosed with a reading disability. Instead, the researcher using the ECLS-B needs to define scores on a given assessment as indicating risk of a reading disability. For example, Rosenberg, Zhang, and Robinson (2008) used the ECLS-B assessments at 9 and 24 months to estimate the number of children who would qualify for Part C early intervention services under the Individuals with Disabilities Act (IDEA). Part C services are provided for children who are under the age of three and have developmental delays.

In the Rosenberg et al. study, children were identified as eligible for Part C services if they fit one of the following two criteria: (a) birth weight less than 1500 grams, or (b) scoring 1.0 standard deviations lower than the mean on both the cognitive and motor scales of the Bayley Short Form or scoring 1.5 standard deviations lower than the mean on either scale.

Research issues for the ECLS-K and ECLS-B. Given the longitudinal nature of these two databases, researchers can examine the growth trajectories of particular subsets of children such as those in the ECLS-K who receive individualized or small group instruction in reading, or those children who scored well below the mean on cognitive assessments in the ECLS-B. While there have been several studies of ECLS-K cohorts growth in reading over time, few, if any, focus directly on children diagnosed with a learning disability (National Center for Education Statistics, 2007). Relatively fewer studies have used the ECLS-B to examine longitudinal trends since this database has more recently been released.

There have been a number of studies examining the growth trajectories of students with reading disabilities using representative data sets of more targeted populations. For example, Shaywitz, Shaywitz, Fletcher, and Escobar, (1990) followed Connecticut schoolchildren from kindergarten through high school. A similar study by Catts, Fey, Tomblin, and Zhang (2002) followed a representative sample of children in Iowa. Both studies examined the correlates and precursors of later reading disability.

Both the ECLS-K and ECLS-B have been used as a cross-sectional database, such as in the estimation of Part C eligible children in the Rosenberg et al. (2008) study. Two reports by the NCES also examine characteristics of children in special education at one wave of the ECLS (Herring, McGrath, & Buckley, 2007; Holt, McGrath, & Herring, 2007). When using the ECLS databases for cross-sectional inferences, the researcher needs to keep in mind that attrition naturally occurs over time in longitudinal databases, and thus not all waves of data are nationally representative. Researchers need to select the appropriate weights to ensure that estimates can support inferences to a particular population.

The National Institute of Child Health and Human Development Study of Early Child Care and Youth Development (NICHD SECCYD)

The NICHD SECCYD study was initiated in 1991 to follow a cohort of children born in 1991 at ten sites across the country. This longitudinal study was designed to address questions about the relationships between children's early care experiences and later outcomes. Assessments of child, care environment and home environment were gathered at several times during the child's development. Phase I measures were gathered at 1 month of age through 3 years of age. Phase II measures took place from 54 months of age through first grade. Phase III follows children from second through third grade, with Phase IV continuing through ninth grade. Though not a nationally representative data sample, the SECCYD has collected a complex set of measures from approximately 1,000 children and their families over time.

How reading disabilities are measured. There are two main measures that a researcher could use to identify children with reading disabilities in the SECCYD database. First, teachers are asked whether an individual child has or is receiving special education services. Second, the SECCYD includes several measures of a child's pre-reading and reading skills that could be used to identify children at risk of a reading disability. These measures include the Bayley Scales of Infant Development (Bayley, 1993) and the Woodcock-Johnson scales (Woodcock & Johnson, 1990).

Research issues in the SECCYD. As in the ECLS-K and ECLS-B studies, researchers can use the SECCYD to examine the growth trajectories of children identified or at risk for reading disabilities over time. In addition, the SECCYD could be used to examine the individual characteristics, home environment and early care experiences of children at risk of developing reading disabilities. For example, La Paro, Olsen, and Pianta (2002) used the SECCYD to examine developmental precursors to special education eligibility. Children eligible for special education were identified by two different methods. First, some children were identified by medical professionals as having special needs as reported by parents in an interview. Second, other children were identified based on consistently scoring 1.5 standard deviations below the mean on three assessments given from 15 to 36 months of age: Bayley Mental Development Scales, Bracken Basic Concept Scale and the Reynell Developmental Language Scale. As in the Rosenberg et al. (2008) study using ECLS-B, La Paro et al. also found many children eligible for special services may not be identified, thus missing important opportunities for support.

With the exception of La Paro et al. (2002), much of the current research using the SECCYD has not focused on children with special needs or with learning disabilities. Since the SECCYD is not a nationally representative sample, estimates at any given time point cannot be used to make inferences to the population. With the collection of Phase IV data, the SECCYD could provide a rich database for examining the growth of children from 1 month through age 14, especially for those children whose low reading scores indicate potential for reading disabilities.

The Education Longitudinal Survey of 2002 (ELS)

The ELS survey follows a representative cohort of students who were in their sophomore year of high school in 2002 into postsecondary education and/or the workforce. The sample was augmented in 2004 to obtain a representative sample of high school seniors. The data collected include academic achievement, attitudes toward school and future plans along with information about their transition to postsecondary education or the workforce after high school graduation.

For those students going on to postsecondary education, information was collected about where students applied, where they were accepted, and where they enrolled. The survey also includes information from the student's high school teachers, and from their parents.

How reading disabilities are measured. In the first wave of the ELS (when students are in 10th grade), parents are asked if their child has a learning disability, and if so, if it is a specific learning disability. In addition, proficiency scores on a reading assessment are provided for each student. These three proficiency levels are described as follows: (a) Level 1—simple reading comprehension, (b) Level 2—Simple inferences beyond the author's main thought, and (c) Level 3—Complex inferences requiring multiple sources of information. From the first wave of data, 89% of high school sophomores could perform Level 1 tasks, 46% could perform Level 2, and 8% could perform at Level 3 (Ingels et al., 2005). These proficiency scores could also be used to identify students with low levels of reading skill.

Research issues in the ELS. The base year, first and second follow-up of the ELS are completed with the third and final follow-up expected in 2013. The first follow-up collected data from base year students who would have been in their senior year of high school. This follow-up includes the high school transcripts from all students in the baseline year. The second follow-up collects data from students when they would complete their second year of postsecondary education. Some of the sample students will have entered the workforce. Researchers could use the ELS to examine the transitions to postsecondary education or the workforce for the group of students whose parents indicated that they had learning disabilities and whose reading proficiency level was low. Since the ELS database is relatively new, few studies have been published (see annotated bibliography from NCES) using this data.

Other Longitudinal Databases The National Education Longitudinal Survey of 1988 (NELS 88) is a longitudinal database that followed a cohort of eighth-grade students in 1988. Assessments and surveys from students, parents and teachers were gathered on this cohort in 1990, 1992, 1994, and 2000. In the NELS, parents, teachers, school officials, and the students themselves are asked whether the target child has a learning disability. A study published by NCES (Rossi, Herting, Wolman, & Quinn, 1997) found that these four methods of identifying children with a disability did not select the same students, highlighting again one major drawback of using large databases for studying reading disabilities.

Methodological Issues with Longitudinal Surveys There are two aspects of nationally representative longitudinal surveys that are important in secondary data analysis methods. First, as in cross-sectional surveys, students are nested in schools and other educational institutions. In addition, for studies such as the NELS and the ELS, students may move across time into different contexts, such as high schools or postsecondary institutions. Techniques such as hierarchical or multi-level modeling can be used to account for the nesting and clustering effects (Raudenbush & Bryk, 2002).

A second issue is the repeated measures of students over time. Hierarchical linear modeling also provides a flexible data analysis method for handling repeated assessments of individuals when the timing of those assessments may differ. For example, the assessment of the first wave of 23,000 kindergarten children in the ECLS-K took place from September through the middle of December. For students entering kindergarten, the difference between one day and three months in formal instruction could be great, and could add confounding variance to the assessment results. Raudenbush and Bryk (2002) and Singer and Willett (2003) both provide suggestions for analyzing longitudinal data when individuals differ in their assessment date or are missing particular time points.

Limitations of Longitudinal Databases for Studying Reading Disabilities The major limitation for using large databases remains the identification of students with learning disabilities. Hodapp and Krasner (1994) acknowledge these limitations in their study of four low incidence disabilities using NELS:88, but also argue for the use of nationally representative data that are beyond the resources of single researchers to reproduce. In addition, the cost and advance planning for large scale databases results in definitions of learning disabilities that may be out-dated by the time the data is released for public use.

Discussion and Recommendations

The nationally representative cross-sectional and longitudinal databases available to reading disability researchers can address aspects of three important issues: the prevalence of reading disabilities among children and adults, the correlates and precursors of reading disabilities in children and adults, and the characteristics and skills of students and children who are identified as reading disabled. A number of these nationally representative databases have yet to be used to focus on reading disabilities, including the ECLS-Birth cohort and the 2003 administration of the National Assessment of Adult Literacy. Studies using these databases can allow nationally representative inferences about aspects of reading disabilities, and can suggest directions for research that would focus on more local and contextual issues in the field.

A major drawback of these databases is the identification of students with learning disabilities in general and reading disabilities more specifically. As seen in the examples of research in this chapter, researchers have used multiple indicators and variables in a given database to select participants who likely have a reading disability. This difficulty with identifying reading disabled individuals reflects the continued work in the field to find more accurate methods for the early detection of reading difficulties.

In addition to refining measures or indicators of reading disabilities, other opportunities exist for gathering large databases to inform our knowledge of reading disabilities. Reporting requirements and accountability measures first initiated by NCLB have encouraged many states and school districts to gather more systematic data about the progress of students' reading growth. For example, the use of response to intervention as a diagnostic technique (Fletcher, Coulter, Reschly, & Vaughn, 2004) has led many schools to collect data to chart the progress of students in their reading skills. These local databases may prove to be another rich source for studying the prevalence, prevention, and treatment of individuals with reading disabilities.

References

Abedi, J., Lord, C., Kim, C., & Miyoshi, J. (2001, September). *The effects of accommodations on the assessment of LEP students in NAEP*. Washington, DC: U.S. Department of Education, Office of Educational Research and Improvement, National Center for Education Statistics.

American Institutes for Research. (2007). *Reading framework for the 2009 National Assessment of Educational Progress* (pre-publication ed.). Washington, DC: AIR.

Bayley, N. (1993). Bayley Scales of Infant Development (2nd ed.). San Antonio, TX: Psychological Corporation.

Berends, M. (2006). Survey methods in educational research. In J. L. Green, G. Camilli, & P. B. Elmore (Eds.), *Handbook of complementary methods in education research* (pp. 623–640). Mahwah, NJ: Erlbaum.

Catts, H. W., Fey, M. E., Tomblin, J. B., & Zhang, X. (2002). A longitudinal investigation of reading outcomes in children with language impairments. *Journal of Speech, Language and Hearing Research, 45*(6), 1142–1157.

Dunn, L. M., & Markwardt, F. C. (1981). *Manual for Peabody Picture Vocabulary Test — Revised*. Circle Pines, MI: American Guidance Service.

Fletcher, J. M., Coulter, W. A., Reschly, D. J., & Vaughn, S. (2004). Alternative approaches to the definition and identification of learning disabilities: Some questions and answers. *Annals of Dyslexia, 54*(2), 304–331.

Herring, W. L., McGrath, D. J., & Buckley, J. A. (2007). *Demographic and school characteristics of students receiving special education in the elementary grades*. Washington, DC: Institute of Education Sciences, National Center for Education Statistics.

Hodapp, R. M., & Krasner, D. V. (1994). Reflections on "Using large, national data bases in special education research." *Exceptionality, 5*(2), 103–108.

Holt, E. W., McGrath, D. J., & Herring, W. L. (2007). *Timing and duration of student participation in special education in the primary grades*. Washington, DC: Institute for Education Sciences, National Center for Education Statistics.

Howard, J., & Obetz, W. S. (1996). Using the NALS to characterize the literacy of community college graduates. *Journal of Adolescent and Adult Literacy, 39*, 462–467.

Ingels, S. J., Burns, L. J., Charleston, S., Chen, X., Cataldi, E. F., & Owings, J. A. (2005). *A profile of the American High School sophomore in 2002: Initial results from the base year of the Education Longitudinal Study of 2002*. Washington, DC: National Center for Education Statistics.

Johnson, S. T. (2001). Adults performing at the two lowest literacy levels. In C. F. Kaestle, A. Campbell, J. D. Finn, S. T. Johnson, & L. J. Mikulecky (Eds.), *Adult literacy in America: A first look at the results of the National Adult Literacy Survey*. Washington, DC: National Center for Education Statistics.

Kutner, M., Greenberg, E., Jin, Y., Boyle, B., Hsu, Y.-C., Dunleavy, E., et al. (2007). *Literacy in everyday life: Results from the 2003 National Assessment of Adult Literacy*. Washington, DC: Institute of Education Sciences, National Center for Education Statistics.

La Paro, K. M., Olsen, K., & Pianta, R. C. (2002). Special education eligibility: Developmental precursors over the first three years of life. *Exceptional Children, 69*(1), 55–66.

Levy, P. S., & Lemeshow, S. (1999). *Sampling of populations: Methods and applications* (3rd ed.). New York: Wiley.

Lutkus, A. D., Mazzeo, J., Zhang, J., & Jerry, L. (2004). *Including special-needs students in the NAEP 1998 Reading Assessment: Part II, results for students with disabilities and limited English-proficient students*. Princeton, NJ: Educational Testing Service.

National Assessment Governing Board. (2006). Reading framework for the 2007 National Assessment of Educational Progress. In U.S. Department of Education (Ed.). Washington, DC: National Assessment Governing Board.

National Assessment of Educational Progress. (2001). *2001 SD/LEP questionnaire*. Retrieved from http://nces.ed.gov/nationsreportcard/tdw/pdf/instruments/2001_SDLEP.pdf

National Center for Education Statistics. (2007). *Early Childhood Longitudinal Study: Data products and publications*. Retrieved June 30, 2008, from http://nces.ed.gov/ecls/bibliography.asp

National Center for Education Statistics. (2008a). *Early Childhood Longitudinal Survey (ECLS) Birth cohort: Study information*. Retrieved July 1, 2008, from http://www.nces.ed.gov/ecls/birth.asp

National Center for Education Statistics. (2008b). *Early Childhood Longitudinal Survey (ECLS) Kindergarten cohort: Study information*. Retrieved July 1, 2008, from http://www.nces.ed.gov/ecls/kindergarten.asp

National Center for Education Statistics. (2008c, June 29). *ECLS Kindergarten year: Fall parent questionnaire*. Retrieved July 1, 2008, from http://nces.ed.gov/ecls/kinderinstruments.asp

National Center for Education Statistics. (2008d, May 13). *NAEP inclusion policy*. Retrieved July 1, 2008, from http://www.nces.ed.gov/nationsreportcard/about/inclusion.asp

National Center for Education Statistics. (2008e). *The Nation's report card: Reading report card — Trend in fourth grade NAEP average reading scores by students with disabilities who could be assessed*. Retrieved July 1, 2008, from http://nationsreportcard.gov/reading_2007/r0014.asp

Raudenbush, S. W., & Bryk, A. S. (2002). *Hierarchical linear models: Applications and data analysis methods* (2nd ed.). Thousand Oaks, CA: Sage.

Rosenberg, S. A., Zhang, D., & Robinson, C. C. (2008). Prevalence of developmental delays and participation in early intervention services for young children. *Pediatrics, 121*(6), 1503–1509.

Rossi, R., Herting, J., Wolman, J., & Quinn, P. (1997). *Profiles of students with disabilities as identified in NELS: 88*. Washington, DC: U.S. Department of Education, National Center for Education Statistics.

Shaywitz, S. E., Shaywitz, B. A., Fletcher, J. M., & Escobar, M. D. (1990). Prevalence of reading disability in boys and girls: Results of the Connecticut Longitudinal Study. *Journal of the American Medical Association, 264*, 998–1002.

Sheehan-Holt, J. K., & Smith, M. C. (2000). Does basic skills education affect adults' literacy proficiencies and reading practices? *Reading Research Quarterly, 35*(2), 226–244.

Singer, J. D., & Willett, J. B. (2003). *Applied longitudinal data analysis: Modeling change and event occurrence*. New York: Oxford University Press.

Smith, M. C. (1996). Differences in adults' reading practices and literacy proficiencies. *Reading Research Quarterly, 31*, 196–219.

Snow, C. E., Burns, M. S., & Griffin, P. (Eds.). (1998). *Preventing reading difficulties in young children*. Washington, DC: National Academies Press.

Stancavage, F., Makris, F., & Rice, M. (2007). *SD/LEP inclusions/*

exclusions in NAEP: An investigation of factors affecting SD/LEP inclusions/exclusions in NAEP. Washington, DC: American Institutes for Research.

Strucker, J., Yamamoto, K., & Kirsch, I. (2007). *The relationship of the component skills of reading to IALS performance: Tipping points and five classes of adult literacy learners.* Cambridge, MA: National Center for the Study of Adult Learning and Literacy.

Weston, T. J. (2002, July). *The validity of oral accommodation in testing.* Palo Alto, CA: American Institutes for Research.

Woodcock, R. W., & Johnson, M. B. (1990). *Manual for the Woodcock-Johnson Tests of Achievement-Revised.* Allen, TX: RCL Enterprises.

40

Policy, Research, and Reading First

NAOMI ZIGMOND, RITA BEAN, AMANDA KLOO, AND MELISSA BRYDON
University of Pittsburgh

Policy, Research, and Reading First

There are three challenges that will have to be met before education is transformed into an evidence-based field: the rigor, relevance, and utilization of education research.

(Whitehurst, 2003, p. 1)

Education policy refers to the collection of laws or rules that govern the operation of education systems. Examples of policy topics include school size, class size, school choice, school privatization, tracking, teacher certification, teacher pay, teaching methods, curricular content, and graduation requirements. Debates on these topics take place in local town meetings, city and county governments, state legislatures, professional forums, and other national arenas, with arguments supported by strong opinion, emotion, and occasionally, research data. Because the Tenth Amendment to the U.S. Constitution limits federal involvement in local education matters, most education policy debates are decided at the state and local levels; nevertheless, while the federal role in education may be limited, it can be highly significant. One good example of this limited-but-significant role is the Reading First initiative in the No Child Left Behind Act of 2001.

Early federal legislative actions related to education, beginning in the 1960s, were not spurred by research. Rather, they were attempts to eradicate social inequities through educational initiatives. Title I, for example, was developed to fund supplemental reading programs for "disadvantaged" or poor children, and was an effort to more equitably distribute educational opportunities (McGill-Franzen, 2000). Likewise, Congressional passage of PL 94-142, the groundbreaking Education of All Handicapped Children Act of 1975 entitling students with disabilities to a free and appropriate public education, was motivated by a desire for civil rights, social justice, and equal opportunity, and not by research evidence of the value of special education.

In the 40 years since these early forays into educational policy, the federal government has assumed a greater and greater role, often focusing its work on policies designed to improve students' reading achievement. These efforts have produced state-by-state standards for what students should know and be able to do at various grade levels and at the time of graduation from high school, and large-scale school reform efforts that feature increased accountability and measurement of students' academic progress (Valencia & Wixson, 2000). They have also produced a heightened interest in policy research, in the contexts in which policy is developed and implemented, and in the outcomes of policy on front-line educators and their students. By 2000, policy chapters (McGill-Franzen, 2000; Valencia & Wixson, 2000) were included for the first time in volume 3 of the *Handbook of Reading Research* (Kamil, Mosenthal, Pearson, & Barr, 2000).

In this chapter, we begin where those earlier chapters left off, with a description of the continuing federal interest in increasing student achievement. We discuss what might be called the "third generation" of federal education policy making (see McLaughlin, 1992, for a description of the first two generations) using the Reading First initiative as an illustrative case. Policy makers in this third generation legislation sought to build their mandates on a strong empirical research base, having been convinced by researchers that "although we do not know everything, what we do know is information in which we can have confidence," [and] it is important that that information be put into practice (McCardle & Chhabra, 2004, p. 476). Policy makers believed that the time had come for the federal government to tie education funding to implementation of "proven practices" that would dramatically improve reading instruction for students in high poverty low achieving schools. Scientifically based reading instruction (SBRR) was the answer to student underachievement and Reading First was the mechanism to get those scientifically based instructional practices implemented.

This chapter is divided into four segments. In the first segment, we review background information that helps explain the emergence of Reading First policies. In the second, we draw on our experience with Reading First in Pennsylvania to demonstrate that even well -intentioned implementations of Reading First directives did not always produce outcomes consistent with those previously reported in the research literature. In the third segment, we move beyond Pennsylvania to discuss the design and results of the national impact study of the Reading First implementation. Finally, we expand on the ideas of McLaughlin, 1992 and Coburn (2006) in a discussion of the importance of context in the implementation of educational policy and the futility of seeking simple, easy answers to the complex problems of schooling America's children, especially those who struggle to learn to read.

The Road to Reading First

McGill-Franzen (2000), in the *Handbook of Reading Research* (vol. III), summarizes the policy history of reading education and the research that relates that policy to instruction in the schools. She describes the various iterations of Title I from its focus on simply providing additional resources to disadvantaged students to its attention to specific issues of teaching and learning. She and others (see Valencia & Wixson, 2000; Pearson, 2004) have also described the flurry of political activity, especially in California, that led to the ascendance then fall-from-grace of constructivist, literature-based, whole-language reading pedagogy in the face of declining NAEP test scores in 1992 and again in 1994. No matter that the implementation of whole language may have been suspect, that not all teachers had received appropriate training, and that there were clear misapplications of the approach; poor test scores led California legislators to demand a change in reading pedagogy. And reading achievement had become politicized. It emerged as an important policy issue for those seeking and holding the office of President of the United States. President Clinton, for example, in 1994 established America Reads, the national volunteer tutoring program and, during his administration, urged passage and funding of the Reading Excellence Act, which awarded $230 million to 17 states to support reading instruction. States were required to improve reading instruction and to show evidence of this improvement with data showing increasing numbers of students reading at proficiency levels. Congress would provide some resources to ensure high-quality instruction for all students—including students with reading disabilities, in exchange for which states would yield to requirements for accountability.

As the 20th century neared an end, strong voices urged Congress to increase funding for research and syntheses of research that could serve as a foundation for legislative action (see Song, Coggshall, & Miskel, 2004). Loud complaints were heard that, despite decades of funding for the National Institute of Education (renamed the Office of Educational Research and Improvement and renamed again the Institute of Education Sciences), research in education had not produced the evidence needed to make decisions about educational practices. "Educational practice and research are badly in need of reform," proclaimed Whitehurst in 2003 (p. 1). It was not just that policy makers had difficulty interpreting the research that had been reported. Questions were raised about the quality or rigor of the research that had been conducted and the merits of various research methodologies for answering questions essential to policy. Whitehurst (2003), for example, noted that "over the past decade, 38% of the primary research reports in the American Educational Research Association's two premier journals involved qualitative methods" (p. 1). Such research designs, he maintained, could not be used to draw causal conclusions and thus were not useful in addressing practical issues of program efficacy—the primary interest of policy makers. Policy makers wanted clear, definitive answers that would enable them to create and pass legislation to improve instruction. They wanted to know which instructional approaches were best for teaching disabled readers. What materials should be used? How should teachers be prepared to teach struggling readers? Educational researchers answered cautiously, pointing out that the road to "scientific" knowledge is long and often tedious (Hess, 2008). Moreover, they acknowledged, different research methodologies address different questions for different audiences. Experimental psychologists and reading researchers were not nearly as equivocal as they stepped into the void. Citing "reliable, replicable research" supported by National Institutes for Child Health and Human Development (see Lyon, 1995; Lyon & Chhabra, 1996; McCardle & Chhabra, 2004) they advocated a set of explicit instructional practices emphasizing phonemic awareness and phonics. They backed their advocacy with data from NICHD sponsored research involving large samples of students, experimental designs that included random assignment of treatments to teachers and/or schools, and tried and true outcome measures (see Foorman, Francis, Fletcher, Schatschneider, & Mehta, 1998). Soon, publications like *Preventing Reading Difficulties in Young Children* (Snow, Burns, & Griffin, 1998), and the *National Reading Panel Report* (2000) formed the basis for legislative changes affecting teacher preparation and school practices in teaching reading, especially at the beginning stages. No Child Left Behind (2001) was the culmination of this effort to fashion federal education policy based on sound "scientific" research. In fact, "NCLB mentions 'scientifically-based research' 110 times" (Slavin, 2002, p. 15). Scientifically based research, particularly the research supported by the NICHD, would serve as the basis for the Reading First initiative authorized within the act to transform reading instruction in Grades K–3.

Reading First: From Research to Policy to Instruction
Reading First was the largest—and yet most focused—early reading initiative this country had ever undertaken. It supported states

...as they work with their districts to ensure that teachers learn about instruction and other activities based on scientifically based reading research, implement programs that are based on this research, and use rigorous assessments with proven validity and reliability that effectively screen, diagnose and monitor the progress of all students. (US Department of Education, 2002a, p. 2)

And, it had a lofty goal: "to give teachers across the nation the skills and support they needed to teach all children to read fluently by the end of third grade" (U.S. Department of Education, 2002a, p. 1). But it was also highly prescriptive. It proclaimed that "scientifically based reading research has identified five essential components of effective reading instruction. To ensure that children learn to read well, explicit and systematic instruction must be provided in [those] five areas." (p. 3). It prescribed the amount of time to be allocated to reading instruction: "a protected, uninterrupted block of time ... of more than 90 minutes per day" (p. 6). It defined the components of a required assessment system:

> A high-quality, effective reading program must include rigorous assessments with proven validity and reliability. These assessments must measure progress in the five essential components of reading instruction ... and identify students who may be at risk for reading failure or who are already experiencing reading difficulty. A reading program must include screening assessments, diagnostic assessments and classroom-based instructional assessments of progress. (U.S. Department of Education, 2002a, p. 7)

Moreover, it defined the elements of an effective state-level, district-level, and school-level professional development plan.

> Well-designed professional development aligns clearly with the instructional program, including its research base, as well as with State academic and performance standards. ... Professional development must prepare all teachers to teach all of the essential components of reading instruction, and to know how they are related, the progression in which they should be taught, and the underlying structure of the English language. Teachers also must understand why some children have difficulty learning to read well and learn how to administer and interpret assessments of student progress. Professional development should also prepare teachers to effectively manage their classrooms and to maximize time on task. (U.S. Department of Education, 2002a, p. 7)

Reading First defined a role for reading or literacy coaches in school-based professional development. "Adequate time must be available for teachers to learn new concepts and to practice what they have learned. Coaches ... provide feedback as new concepts are put into practice" (U.S. Department of Education, 2002a, p. 7). And it required state applications for Reading First funding to "satisfactorily address all program requirements before the Department awards funds to States" (p. 8).

Pennsylvania Reading First

Pennsylvania took very seriously the Reading First non-negotiables. Drawing on the research-based assertions in the Call for Proposals, CFDA Number 84.357 (Federal Register, 2002; U.S. Department of Education, 2002b), the Pennsylvania proposal dated May 15, 2002, outlined the steps the Pennsylvania Department of Education leadership would take to insure that "every activity [supported by Reading First funds] promotes reading [instruction that] is anchored in SBRR" (Zogby, 2002, p. 16). Pennsylvania promised to "assist local education agencies in identifying effective and empirically-validated instruction methods by releasing a list of materials that meet the broad framework of SBRR" (p. 16). The proposal focused not only on *what* to teach but also on *how* to teach, pledging reading instruction in an uninterrupted block of at least 90 minutes daily; careful and deliberate sequencing of skills; explicit and challenging instruction that requires of students a deeper and more robust understanding of the skills, structure, and processes associated with reading; and flexible and fluid instructional groupings that provide opportunities for more intensive and strategic reading instruction. The Pennsylvania Application for Reading First Funds promised that Reading First schools would be "required to develop comprehensive, prevention-oriented screening, diagnostic, and classroom-based instructional assessments that are used to guide instruction and to develop flexible, homogeneous groupings of students" (p. 19), and specified that "Reading First schools in Pennsylvania [would...] use a portion of their funds to implement the *Dynamic Indicators of Basic Literacy Skills* (DIBELS) as the screening and the progress monitoring assessments" (p. 35). Finally, the proposal specified that each Reading First school would have a designated reading or literacy coach to "ensure that there is high fidelity in the implementation of assessment and reading instruction in classrooms [through] on-going and in-classroom support" (pp. 40–41).

Outcomes of Reading First Policy Implementation in Pennsylvania

From 2003 to 2009, Rita Bean, Naomi Zigmond, and colleagues at the University of Pittsburgh were engaged in a third-party evaluation of the Pennsylvania Reading First initiative. We were contracted to do a program evaluation, to track changes in student achievement on high stakes statewide accountability assessments associated with the implementation of Reading First in Pennsylvania schools, to study the degree of implementation of RF elements in schools that received RF funding, and to document the state role in leading the RF initiative across the Commonwealth. For this chapter, the PA Reading First External Evaluation provides the platform from which we can discuss the ways in which federal policy has influenced instruction. It also serves as an example of how factors other than research (e.g., social pressures, politics, and the local context) contribute to the enactment of education policy in schools. In the course of our work we have recorded a high degree of compliance in implementing the key elements of Reading First in the 160-plus schools representing 32 school districts and 3 charter schools across the Commonwealth of Pennsylvania (Reading First Data Online, 2008). And we have seen significant increases in the proportion of third graders in Reading First schools attaining proficiency on the statewide accountability assessment (Zigmond & Bean, 2008). But we have also documented some unanticipated findings that lead us to question the "scientific" foundations of some of the Reading First mandates and to question the translation of some of this scientific research into education policy. We report findings on the implementation of three facets of Reading First in Pennsylvania. In each example, we begin with the "research-based" assertion found in the Reading First Guidance document (U.S. Department of Education, 2002a) and a statement of the research that was provided to undergird the suggested policy.

Our work did not start out as "policy research" but like many literacy researchers (see Valencia & Wixson, 2000), we found ourselves drawn into work that can, in fact, inform future policy. In our evaluation data on how federal Reading First policy has been implemented in Pennsylvania we find reason to challenge the assertion that, "Quite simply, Reading First focuses on what works, and … support[s] proven methods" (U.S. Department of Education, 2002a, p. 1).

Universal Screening to Prevent Reading Failure

Assertion 1: "Screening assessments determine which children are at risk for reading difficulty and need additional support" (U.S. Department of Education, 2002a, p. 7).

Research-to-policy: A screening measure like the DIBELS can be used to identify students at risk for reading failure, target those students for immediate interventions, and prevent reading failure by third grade.

Federal reading policy, as articulated in Reading First, charged schools with the daunting task of developing school-wide reading assessment and intervention systems beginning in the early grades to prevent reading failure from taking hold. Policy makers were responding to research evidence that reading failure can be prevented if it is identified and treated early (National Institute of Child Health and Human Development, 2000; National Research Council, 1998). Several authors had determined that with appropriate intervention, the reading performance of low-performing and at-risk students could reach grade-level expectations within the first three years of school, and on-grade-level performance could be sustained throughout successive grade levels (Chard & Kame'enui, 2000; Coyne, Kame'enui, & Simmons, 2001; Good, Simmons, & Kame'enui, 2001; Torgeson, 2000; Torgeson et al., 2001). In other words, identification and intensive intervention early in a student's career could positively alter an established reading trajectory (National Research Council, 1998; Torgeson et al., 2001).

Reading First called for yearly implementation of a screening measure, a brief procedure designed as a first step in identifying children who may be at high risk for delayed development or academic failure and in need of further diagnosis of their need for special services or additional reading instruction. Reading First schools were to recognize the importance of utilizing early literacy assessment tools to improve decision making regarding curriculum design and instructional practice.

Timely identification depends on the availability of valid and reliable screening measures of core reading skills that are predictive of later reading achievement and that can guide the development of high intensity interventions in the classroom. Based on the outcomes of the screening process in the fall, students would be grouped into one of three tiers of reading instruction: Tier 1-progressing as expected, Tier 2-requires moderate intervention, or Tier 3-requires substantial and intensive intervention to both catch up and prevent future failure. Tier placement would guide differentiated instruction and groupings would be flexible enough to allow for students to be regrouped for instruction based on their subsequent winter and spring scores.

The Dynamic Indicators of Early Literacy Skills (Good & Kaminski, 2002) had been developed to meet just this need. It is a low-stakes measure of early literacy skills that purportedly could be used to predict student performance on high-stakes outcome measures (Kaminski & Good, 1996; Good et al., 2001.) The DIBELS are a series of subtests measuring the foundational reading skills of phonological and phonemic awareness, alphabetic principle, and oral reading fluency. The DIBELS benchmark assessments administered three or four times each year (approximately every 12 to 13 weeks) are designed to indicate which students are falling behind early enough in their school careers to change their reading trajectories (Good et al., 2001). For Pennsylvania Reading First schools, DIBELS was recommended as the foundation for instructional decision making; teachers would use DIBELS screening scores to make grouping and resource allocation decisions including increased instructional time, additional instructional personnel, and differentiated instructional plans.

A longitudinal analysis of three years of Pennsylvania Reading First data (2004–2006) examined whether the use of DIBELS in an assessment model that leads to grouping and instructional changes three times per year reliably identifies first grade students at-risk for reading failure and those who are not, as measured by end-of-third-grade achievement on the Pennsylvania System of School Assessment (PSSA; Kloo, 2006). Kloo examined the predictive relationship between first grade students' early achievement on DIBELS subtests and their later achievement on the DIBELS oral reading fluency subtest and the Reading portion of the third grade PSSA. Prediction variables included students' risk status in first grade (indicated by their proficiency classification on the fall Phoneme Segmentation Fluency (PSF), fall Nonsense Word Fluency (NWF), and winter Oral Reading Fluency (ORF subtests)) as well as

TABLE 40.1

2004–2006 Longitudinal Relationship between First Grade Predictors and Third Grade Outcomes in PA Round 1 and Round 2 Reading First Schools

1st Grade Measures	Third GRADE ORF			Third GRADE PSSA		
	Correlation	Combined Explained Variance	Unique Explained Variance	Correlation	Combined Explained Variance	Unique Explained Variance
Winter DIBELS ORF	.38	.15 *	.39 *	.40	.16 *	.39 *
Fall DIBELS NWF	.41	.17 *	.15 *	.42	.18 *	.13 *
Fall DIBELS PSF	.42	.18 *	.08 *	.42	.18	.03
Student SES	.45	.20 *	.13 *	.44	.19 *	.13 *
Student Minority Status	.48	.23 *	.15 *	.45	.20 *	.09 *
School	.50	.25 *	.13 *	–	–	–

* Significant at the $p < .01$ level.

school, minority status, and socioeconomic status (SES) to further explain variability in achievement outcomes.

Table 40.1 provides the correlations and explained variance (combined and unique) for each first grade variable to each third grade outcome. Students' first-grade performance on the winter ORF subtest was more predictive of end-of-third grade performance on the DIBELS ORF than first grade performance on the fall NWF or PSF subtests. But, despite their statistical significance, first grade DIBELS scores explained only 15% of the variance in students' third-grade ORF scores; 85% of the remaining variance was left unexplained. Ultimately, the combination of all variables (i.e., first grade DIBELS fall/winter scores; minority status; SES; school) explained only one-quarter of the variability in end-of-third grade DIBELS ORF scores. And, the significance of this combined prediction must be interpreted with caution, because of the large number of students in the analyses (n = 9,685).

Backward elimination techniques were used to determine the practical significance of each predictor in the regression model. These results suggested that students' achievement on the DIBELS ORF subtest in January of first grade was uniquely moderately predictive of their third grade ORF achievement (.39). The NWF and PSF subtests were far less predictive (.15, and .08, respectively). In fact, students' race, minority status, and school of attendance explained more of the variance in third grade ORF scores than first graders' ability to segment phonemes.

Similar results were obtained for the analysis of students' early first grade DIBELS scores and their eventual third-grade achievement on the higher stakes PSSA. Data suggest that the DIBELS measures administered in first grade were generally *not* predictive of third grade reading achievement for students in these Reading First schools. Overall, the DIBELS reading subtests designed to be indicators of students' overall reading "well being" in first grade together explained only 18% of the variance in third grade PSSA Reading scores. First grade winter ORF explained the largest amount of variance (.39) compared to the other DIBELS subtests and demographic variables when unique contributions were examined.

The goal of the federal Reading First initiative was to increase our country's literate population. Policy makers drew on a preventive medicine model and the experimental work of NICHD researchers to combat reading failure through early screenings and intervention. Struggling readers would be caught early and through early interventions, no child would be left behind. In seeking a simple solution (find them and fix them) to a complex problem (underachievement in third grade), policy makers did not foresee the limited predictive value of the early screening measure then available, the DIBELS, to indicate students' long-term reading achievement (Kloo, 2006). They did not question whether the components assessed in DIBELS were the critical components, whether schools would be able to use the results of the DIBELS in meaningful ways, or whether prescriptions to teach the constrained skills measured in DIBELS (Paris, 2005) would actually lead to long-term gains. Instead, they mandated an over-reliance on simple (short and quick) benchmark assessments in an early intervention framework that had yet to be proven effective in a large-scale implementation.

Closing the Achievement Gap for English Language Learners

Assertion 2: An eligible local educational agency that receives a Reading First sub grant must use the funds [for] selection and implementation of a program of reading instruction based on scientifically based reading research that includes the essential components of reading instruction and provides such instruction to children in kindergarten through grade 3 … including children… identified as having limited English proficiency (U.S. Department of Education, 2002a, pp. 31–32).

Research-to-Policy: What we have learned from research about best-practices in teaching reading to native English speakers who are struggling readers applies equally well to teaching underachieving English language learners. Research-based reading instruction is research-based reading instruction; good teaching is good teaching.

An ever-growing number of school age children in the United States come from families where English is not the primary language spoken in the home. Between 1979 and 1999, the number of language-minority students in the United States nearly doubled from 6 million to 14 million, respectively (Kindler, 2002). Some researchers estimate that by the year 2050, the percentage of children in the United States who arrive at school speaking a language other than English will reach 40%. Various national studies have also indicated that these second language learners are demonstrating significantly lower levels of academic achievement as compared to native English-speaking students in the United States. Among students who speak English as the primary language in the home, 10% failed to finish high school in 2004, in comparison to 51% of language-minority students who speak English with difficulty (National Center for Education Statistics, 2004). Specific to reading achievement, it has been estimated that less than 20% of English language learners scored above the state-established norm in at least 25 states (Kindler, 2002). Because of the continuing increase in the number of language-minority students in U.S. public schools and their generally low levels of overall academic achievement and attainment of literacy skills, English language learners (ELLs) were included as one of the disaggregated subgroups specifically targeted in Reading First.

In the Pennsylvania Reading First implementation, there were just over 1,000 third graders designated as English language learners at the start of Reading First in 2003–04; the number increased to over 1,400 by 2007–08. These students constituted a disproportionately high percentage of Reading First third graders (9.9% to 12.6%, respectively); across the state, only 1.8% of third-grade students taking the PSSA were designated as ELL in 2008. English language learners attended only 78 of the 159 Reading First schools in 2003–04, 90 of the schools in 2007–08. Some of these schools had only one or two English language learners within their third grade data set; in some schools English language learners constituted more than one-half of the third-grade class.

At the start of Reading First (spring 2004), only 14% of the 1,070 third-grade English language learners in RF schools scored in the range of Proficient or Advanced on the Pennsylvania System of School Assessment, the PSSA, and 67% scored in the below basic range. Among minority students in Reading First schools, the percent of proficient third graders in 2004 was 32.3% and among Caucasian students it was 60.1%. Four years later, in spring of 2008, the percentage of English language learners scoring in the Proficient range on the third grade accountability test had increased to 40.9%, still well below the percent of Caucasian native speakers (73.3%) or minority native speakers (52.3%) scoring at or above Proficiency (see Figure 40.1) but a significant improvement none the less. The percentage of ELL students scoring in the below basic range was reduced to 20%. A plot of the changes in percent proficient over time shows that, after a slow start, the ELL subgroup had a steeper trajectory of growth (slope = +7.3% per year) than both Caucasian native speakers (slope = +3.4% per year) and minority native speakers (slope = +5.0% per year).

Furthermore, for all three subgroups of third graders, the greater their exposure to Reading First, the higher the students' achievement. Table 40.2 provides a recalculation of the third grade achievement data by the number of years in a Reading First school. For all three subgroups, students who have been in a Reading First school for Grades 1, 2, and 3 perform significantly higher on the end-of-third-grade test than students who spent only 2 years in a Reading First school or students who entered a Reading First school for the first time in third grade. The ELL subgroup shows the greatest effects of time in Reading First.

The very positive outcome data on English language learners in Pennsylvania Reading First was encouraging,

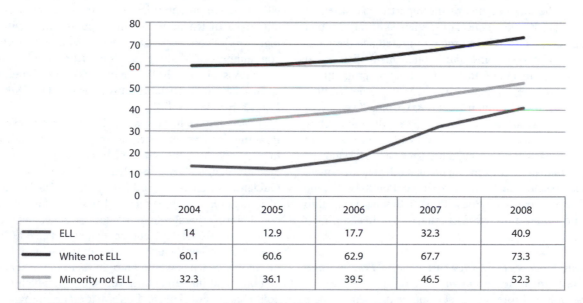

	2004	2005	2006	2007	2008
ELL	14	12.9	17.7	32.3	40.9
White not ELL	60.1	60.6	62.9	67.7	73.3
Minority not ELL	32.3	36.1	39.5	46.5	52.3

Figure 40.1 Percent of third grade students proficient on PSSA by subgroup and year.

TABLE 40.2
Scaled Score Performance of Third Graders by Subgroup and Years of Exposure to Reading First Instruction

	ELL			White not ELL			Minority not ELL			F, p
	#	M	SD	#	M	SD	#	M	SD	
1 year in RF	1,765	1092.8	270.3	2,386	1284.9	215.6	7,455	1192.3	222.4	$F_{(2,3814)} = 49.88$ $p < .001$
2 years in RF	986	1144.8	183.7	2,183	1301.0	202.6	6,240	1209.4	187.5	$F_{(2,8453)} = 18.5$ $p < .001$
3 years in RF	1.246	1174.0	165.7	4,002	1315.4	172.6	8,509	1219.5	180.4	$F_{(2,21850)} = 37.32$ $p < .001$

though surprising. According to some researchers, we currently know rather little about reading instruction for English language learners (McCardle, Mele-McCarthy, & Leos, 2005). The few studies that have examined the use of explicit, systematic phonics, fluency, or comprehension instruction with English language learners have shown mixed results (e.g., Denton, Anthony, Parker, & Hasbrouck, 2004). Past research has also shown that some English language learners who respond well to supplemental reading interventions do not continue to thrive in the general education classroom after supplemental services are discontinued.

Beginning in the spring of 2002, a panel of 13 experts in second-language development, cognitive development, curriculum and instruction, assessment, and methodology was formed to review the available research on the development of literacy skills in language-minority students. The goal of this National Literacy Panel on Language-Minority Children and Youth (August & Shanahan, 2006) was to "identify, assess, and synthesize research on the education of language-minority children and youth with respect to their attainment of literacy, and to produce a comprehension report evaluating and synthesizing this literature" (p. xiv). Following two rounds of external reviews and numerous drafts, the report was made available in 2006, but not without criticism and controversy regarding its release to the public.

One of the key findings of the report is that research that examines the acquisition of literacy skills in a second language continues to be extremely limited and the long-term effects of systematic and explicit instruction based on the core elements of an effective reading program for English language learners still needs to be determined (Linan-Thompson, Vaughn Prater, & Cirino, 2006). Nevertheless, years earlier, Congress had set education policy that required schools to use "scientifically based" reading research in teaching these and other 'special needs' students and to demonstrate improvements in student achievement they had no scientific basis to expect. In Pennsylvania, the use of such scientifically based instruction has seemed to make a difference for the ELL students in Reading First schools.

Coaching Teachers to Change Instructional Practices and Increase Student Achievement

Assertion 3: Professional development… will prepare teachers in all the essential components of reading instruction… [The] delivery mechanisms should include the use of coaches who provide feedback as instructional strategies are put into practice (US Department of Education, 2002a, p. 26).

Research-to-Policy: Job-embedded professional development, delivered by a reading coach hired specifically to work with teachers, will result in changes in classroom instruction and an improvement in school reading performance.

Reading First required State Education Agencies to design professional development programs "to ensure that all teachers have the skills they need to teach [reading] effectively" (U.S. Department of Education, 2002a, p. 1) and "that "professional development be an ongoing, continuous activity, and not consist of 'one-shot' workshops or lectures" (p. 26). In doing so, federal education policy was drawing on the growing research evidence that quality teaching contributes to enhanced student achievement (see Rivkin, Hanushek, & Kain, 1998; Sanders & Horn, 1998), that "teacher effectiveness is the major factor influencing student academic gains" (Sanders & Horn, 1998, p. 225), and that professional development requires extensive support and extended periods of training (NRP, 2000). In addition, "best practices" in professional development had been found to include an emphasis on the content or subject matter being taught; active, in depth learning opportunities over time; alignment of teachers' learning opportunities with their real work experiences; and teachers working together in communities of learning (see American Educational Research Association, 2005; Desimone, Porter, Garet, Yoon, & Birman, 2002: Richardson & Placier, 2001; Sparks & Loucks-Horsley, 1990).

To accomplish its professional development objectives, Reading First sanctioned the role of the school-based literacy coach. Although literacy coaching was not specifically mentioned in the Reading First legislation, the Guidance for the Reading First Program (US Department of Education, 2002a) suggests that school-based coaches could play a critical role in providing teachers with the in-depth professional development that would enable them to teach using scientifically based reading research. Literacy or reading coaches would be right there in the school developing and implementing workshops in which teachers could learn new skills and information *and* providing the ongoing support that would assure implementation of the new knowledge and skills in teachers' classrooms. In other words, those writing about professional development for the RF guidance document made an inferential leap from evidence about best practices for effective professional development to making the suggestion that schools might want to employ coaches to implement the PD for teachers in Reading First schools. Research evidence about effects of professional development is limited, however. In the *Report of the National Reading Panel* (NRP, 2000), only 21 studies met the criteria for inclusion, although the results of most of those did indicate positive teacher and student outcomes. However, the focus of the NRP analyses was on duration and content rather than on the actual delivery mechanism (workshops, coaching, etc.). In a more recent review of professional development for the What Works Clearinghouse (WWC), only nine studies of 1,300 identified as potentially eligible met WWC standards (Yoon, Duncan, Lee, Scarloss, & Shapley, 2007). All nine studies included workshops or summer institutes and all but one had follow-up activities ranging from discussions and conversations, to some modeling and observations. Results of the nine studies indicated that duration was an important factor; when there were more than 14 hours of professional development, there was a positive and significant effect on student achievement. However, given the variability in study designs, it was difficult to draw any conclusions about specific patterns or characteristics of effective PD. Rather, results from Yoon and colleagues indicated the need for more rigorous studies about professional development, especially about its relationship to student achievement. It is clear that when Reading First was written into law, there was little empirical evidence about coaching, or how it should be defined, or what its links are to teacher practice and student learning. And those who wrote about coaching in the early years of Reading First admitted that there was little in the way of scientifically based evidence about particulars like the necessary qualifications for coaches, activities that appear essential, and outcomes on teacher practices and student effects (Snow, Ippolito, & Schwartz, 2006). Nevertheless, states across the country adopted coaches and coaching as the approach to use for improving instructional practices in reading.

RF schools in Pennsylvania were no exception. The Pennsylvania Reading first grant required schools to employ a coach whose workload would consist of no more than 24 teachers although the grant did not specify criteria for qualifications and job descriptions; these details were left to the districts. In the course of our evaluation of Reading First in Pennsylvania, we required coaches to submit daily logs of their activities during three weeks in the fall, three weeks in the winter, and three weeks in the spring, so that we could document the ways in which coachers were providing the ongoing, job-embedded professional development called for in the Reading First plan. Then, we summarized coaches' logs of activities into five major categories: (a) working with teachers (one-on-one coaching); (b) school level coaching (group coaching and outreach); (c) direct service to students (instruction and assessment); (d) administrative and clerical work; and (e) personal growth as a coach. In Table 40.3 we present the coaching data for the 2006–07 school year. Reading First coaches allocated a little more than one-third of their effort to coaching (teacher level: 19.3%; school level: 17.6%). In other words, in a 40-hour week, coaches were spending the equivalent of about 15 hours a week or 3 hours a day in activities we considered to represent coaching. The remainder of their time was spent doing administrative/clerical work (33.0%), providing direct service to students (19.4%), or attending professional development sessions (10.8%). Our finding, that coaches are not spending the majority of their time coaching, has been reported in other studies of coaching. In a report from the Regional Educational Laboratory (Yoon et al., 2007), Reading First coaches across five states spent only 26% of their workweek actually coaching (Deussen, Coskie, Robinson, & Autio, 2007). Similar time data were reported in studies of coaches in initiatives other than Reading First (Coggins, Stoddard, & Cutler, 2003; Feldman & Tung, 2002; Marsh et al, 2008). And in a survey conducted by the International Reading Association (Roller, 2006), the greatest percentage of coaches who responded indicated that they spent 2 to 4 hours per week in coaching-like tasks.

We also surveyed teachers in Reading First schools about their experiences with the school-based literacy coach. We received responses from approximately 1,800 teachers dur-

TABLE 40.3
How Coaches Allocate Their Time in Reading First Schools (n = 146)

Activity	Mean % time	SD	Activity	Mean % time	SD
Teacher Level			Direct Service		
C/T conference	4.42	8.22	Instruct	7.84	14.74
Observe	6.79	12.97	Assess	11.57	19.36
Co-Teach	4.84	10.89	Admin/Clerical		
Model	3.20	8.75	Data	5.82	11.64
School Level			Plan/Org	11.24	15.42
Meeting (group)	14.13	22.16	Admin	15.89	18.15
Conduct PD	1.72	9.44	Personal PD	10.83	29.11
Outreach	1.72	8.03			

ing each of two years (2006–07, 2007–08), a response rate of 83% and 89%, respectively, representing teachers in more than 95% of the schools involved in Pennsylvania Reading First. In both years, most teachers reported that coaches talked with them informally and worked with them in grade level team meetings; fewer than 10% of the teacher respondents indicated that coaches *never* participated with them in those activities. In contrast, approximately 60% of the teachers indicated that coaches *never* co-taught with them and 30% or more indicated that coaches *never* observed, modeled, or assisted in planning (see Figure 40.2).

The data indicate that most teachers perceived that coaches worked with them in group meetings, most often grade level meetings, but did *not* spend time with them in the classroom, modeling, co-teaching, watching, and giving feedback. We conclude that coaches must be targeting their efforts, working individually with only a few, specific teachers rather than with all the K–3 teachers in their school.

These data are a reminder that research on literacy coaching is in its infancy. Indeed, in a recent review of the literature on literacy coaching from 1992–2007, Bean, Belcastro, Hathaway, Risko, Roskos, & Rosemary (2008) found only 28 studies published in peer-reviewed journals that met their criteria for high quality research. Sixteen of these studies addressed peer coaching, not the model of coaching advocated in Reading First or other current initiatives. Only three included measures of student achievement. For example, in a recent report of middle school coaches in Florida, Marsh et al. (2008) found that teachers and principals were very supportive of coaches and believed that these coaches had positive effects on them and their school, but there were mixed results about the impact of coaching on student achievement. Research currently underway (see Bianacrosa, Bryk, & Dexter, 2008) may help educators understand better the potential and power of coaching but the empirical evidence is not yet available.

So, although the *idea* of coaching is consistent with research evidence about the importance of job-embedded, on-going, subject-specific professional development (Guskey, 2000), there are few studies that provide the database needed to understand what literacy coaching is, how it should be conducted, when, and with whom, or to link coaching to short-term or long-term effects on teacher practices and student achievement. Instead, "literacy coaching is being widely implemented based on its convergence with theory and the wisdom of practitioners, before rigorous evaluations have been carried out" (Snow et al., 2006, p. 36).

Our point is that there was little basis in research to support Reading First's embrace of coaches as the primary source of professional development for teachers. Nevertheless, coaching became "very hot" (Cassidy & Cassidy, 2008, p. 1), and having a coach became the potential solution for educational ills. It became policy although there was little to no scientific evidence of who should be hired, what those coaches should do, and with whom.

In Pennsylvania Reading First schools, student achievement did improve even though coaches were not spending the majority of their time on tasks generally considered to be coaching, and many K–3 teachers reported *never* experiencing observations or feedback from their coach (Zigmond & Bean, 2008). Coaching may be an appropriate model for improving teacher practices and student achievement, but at this time we have little evidence as to what it is that coaches do that makes a difference, or how their presence interacts with other variables in the school that might also contribute to improving teaching and learning.

Beyond Pennsylvania: The National Impact Study of Reading First

The Pennsylvania Reading First evaluation data showed remarkable growth in students' reading achievement in Reading First schools especially at the third-grade level (Zigmond & Bean, 2008). In fact, third-grade achievement in Pennsylvania Reading First schools improved at a faster rate than in non-Reading First schools across the Com-

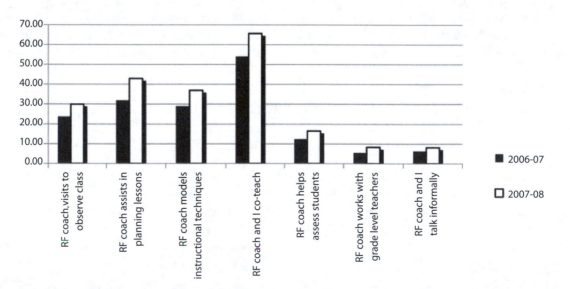

Figure 40.2 Percent of teachers indicating coach activity that never occurs.

monwealth. But it would be incorrect to conclude that these positive outcomes were obtained by translating research into policy—and policy into school practice. Quite the contrary, many policy guidelines in Reading First were based on limited or incomplete research evidence. Legislation and policy were influenced more by the interpretations of research by those in positions of power or those who were trusted by legislators than by actual scientifically based empirical findings. It should come as no surprise, therefore, that two national studies of Reading First, a survey conducted by the Center for Education Policy and a congressionally mandated evaluation of Reading First (the Reading First Impact Study, RFIS), produced equivocal results.

State and Local Education Officials Cite Reading First Policies as Important in Lifting Achievement for Struggling Schools (Center for Education Policy, 2007)

Federal Path for Reading Questioned: Reading First Poor Results Offer Limited Guidance (*Education Week*, 2008)

The first headline, above, summarizes findings from the survey by the Center for Education Policy of officials in states and districts that had received Reading First monies. Overall, these officials were very positive about the impact of Reading First on both teachers and students. But the second headline highlights the disappointing student outcomes in the Reading First Impact Study (RFIS) conducted by Abt Associates with MDRC and Westat (Gamse, Jacob, Horst, Boulay, & Unlu, 2008). The RFIS examined the impact of Reading First funding on 248 schools, 125 of which were Reading First schools (in 13 states, in a total of 17 school districts and one statewide program); it includes data from 3 years (2004–05, 2005–06, and 2006–07) of the 6-year Reading First initiative (2002–08).

The results of the national RFIS study were as follows: When compared with non-Reading First schools, there was a statistically significant increase in the Reading First schools of the amount of instructional time spent on the five essential components of reading instruction in Grades 1 and 2. Also, Reading First produced a positive and statistically significant impact on multiple practices promoted by the initiative (i.e., coaching support, professional development, amount of reading instruction, and intervention support for struggling readers). First graders in Reading First schools scored significantly better than their peers in comparison schools on a measure of decoding. However, Reading First did not produce a statistically significant impact on student reading comprehension test scores in first, second, or third grade (Gamse, Jacob, et al., 2008).

These results have been met with disappointment and consternation among policy makers who had expected that the infusion of billions of dollars and a prescriptive set of regulations would show significant improvements in third-grade reading comprehension/achievement. Critics of Reading First used the results of the national impact study to support their views that the basic tenet of Reading First, to teach five essential components of reading,

was flawed, that the focus of Reading First on instruction in explicit pre-reading/reading skills was too narrow, and that the notion that improved decoding and fluency would automatically lead to better comprehension was not supported in research. Supporters of Reading First focused on the limited value of the study and its findings for policy makers and practitioners. They point out that the RFIS did not use a random control treatment design; instead, it used a regression discontinuity design in which schools within a district were matched (e.g., non-RF schools that were similar to RF schools were identified for the study). Because the research design compared RF and non-RF schools within districts, there was no control for contamination or "bleed-over" of the intervention strategies between RF and non-RF schools. Districts that received RF funding often encouraged *all* schools within the district to use the assessment and instructional practices supported by RF. In fact, districts were encouraged to do so within the Reading First guidelines (U.S. Department of Education, 2002b).

In addition to the contamination effects, there was no control for treatment variability although RF was implemented in many different contexts, with differing degrees of fidelity to the design promulgated by the federal policy, then interpreted by states, and reinterpreted by districts. As Foorman commented in *Education Week* (Manzo, 2008, p. 1), "my one complaint about this evaluation is that its design was powered to ask a limited question (Does RF work on average?) rather than the contextual question of: Under what conditions does RF work and why?" An answer to this second question would have enabled educators and policy makers to determine how to make necessary changes in program design and implementation. In a similar vein, Francis (2008) called for evaluations that lead to an understanding of the factors that influence treatment effectiveness, such as "number of RF schools that an LEA is trying to serve, the grade-level configuration of the school, the number of schools served by an individual reading coach, and the degree to which assessments are used to inform instruction" (p. 11). To the Francis list, we would add such factors as school leadership and its commitment to RF; proportions of high-poverty and low-achieving students in the building; annual teacher, principal, and coach turnover; and numbers of years that the school has functioned as a Reading First school. And like Francis (2008), we would want to parcel out the effects on student achievement of experiencing a Reading First education for 1, 2, or 3 years.

In its response to the *Reading First Interim Report* (Gamse, Bloom, Kemple, & Jacob, 2008), the Reading First Federal Advisory Committee (2008) made several recommendations about the future of Reading First: they urged Congress and other policy makers to seek and analyze data from multiple sources about the effectiveness of RF; to recognize the limitations of the National Impact Study; and to incorporate the necessary funds for rigorous evaluations of future legislation. Instead, Congress has slashed funding for Reading First, and some in Congress have proposed that the Reading First initiative be eliminated from future funding authorizations, although this reaction appears to have been influenced as much by the many controversies surrounding program management and implementation as by the data presented in the Impact Study report (Gamse, Jacob, et al., 2008).

Research to Policy to Implementation

Research to Policy   Since the enactment of No Child Left Behind, there has been overwhelming support at the federal level for "research that applies rigorous, systematic and objective procedures to obtain valid knowledge relevant to reading development, reading instruction, and reading difficulties" (US Department of Education, 2002a, p. 3). Making a clear distinction between most educational research and "scientifically based reading research," policy makers are calling for experimental research designs with randomized controls as the "gold standard" for obtaining results that can inform What Works Clearinghouse (WWC) recommendations. Pearson (2004) criticizes this singular approach to research, claiming that "reading research can never be truly rigorous, indeed truly scientific, until and unless it privileges all of the empirical and theoretical methodologies that characterize the scientific disciplines" (p. 234). Pearson compares educational research with research in the medical profession, noting that random trials in medicine are used only after researchers have utilized a wider range of methodologies such as observation, case studies, and "just plain messing around" (p. 234). Pearson also asserts that the road from research to policy is a treacherous one. First, policy makers use research in a selective, uneven, or opportunistic manner. Second, some science is more important than other science. And third, when research findings aren't definitive, ideology and belief may become privileged.

In other words, as mentioned previously, policy makers are seldom guided by research findings alone, and Reading First is a good case in point. For one thing, policy makers and researchers operate on a different time frame, creating an "uneasy relationship" between research and policy (Hess, 2008, p. 8). Policy makers often need quick answers to complex questions; researchers work at a slow, steady pace, looking for consistencies and convergence in their findings. For another, as politicians, policy makers must be sensitive to the demands of their constituents and of special interest groups that attempt to sway their thinking. Policy is often the outcome of many competing interests (Hess, 2008, p. 2) with "policymakers primarily use[ing] research to support their existing political positions" (McDonnell, 2008, p. viii).

As educational researchers, our hope is that additional impact reports of Reading First implementations in individual schools, districts, or states will provide important data about Reading First, its strengths, and its limitations. Achievement data are available at the state level, given that every state has been required to complete and submit an evaluation report at the end of each year. As individual evaluations differ in designs and measures, these state data

may provide not only more evidence of the effectiveness of Reading First, but also evidence about the factors that determine its successes and or failures. History tells us, however, that policy makers will not wait for these additional sources of data. Rather, they have been and will be influenced by the results of the one major study, by the conversations they have with influential lobby groups or with knowledgeable individuals whom they trust, and by the pressures that come from their own constituents. Moreover, they will need to fit educational funding demands with other pressing concerns related to the economy, to national security, and to the priorities set by a new administration in Washington.

Policy to Implementation   Policy making in education is not like prescribing a pill. Educational policy implementation is a complex social process. For example, Coburn (2006) conducted a year-long ethnographic study of one school's response to the California Reading Initiative. Her position was that local schools and educators are also policy makers, given that "their decisions and actions shape how policies play out in practice" (p. 344). Coburn's findings provided ample evidence that the teachers and the principal of this one school were instrumental in defining how a specific policy about reading instruction unfolded. Teachers and principals participated in a set of activities that helped them negotiate how the policy would be enacted in their school. Although the principal had a great deal of influence, her influence was mediated by her ability to construct ideas that resonated with a number of teachers. And the voices of teachers—especially grade level teams and informal networks—also affected decision making at that school. According to Coburn (2006, p. 373), "both formal and informal organizational structures matter" in understanding how policies are implemented on the ground. Indeed, often initiatives are characterized by a process of mutual adaptation that is based on local factors, including the beliefs and perspectives of teachers within a local site (McLaughlin, 1990).

Conclusions

We chose to focus on the story of Reading First as an example of how research, politics, and social pressures from individuals as well as groups interact to influence how educational policy is made and how it is enacted. Reading First is one of the most comprehensive, far-reaching, well funded, and controversial legislative actions undertaken by Congress; it was designed to promote a specific approach to reading instruction, reading assessment, and professional development for teachers. We tried to illustrate how sweeping generalizations about grounding policy in research can be misleading, and how policy that may be well intentioned does not always produce the intended results.

We draw four conclusions from our research. First, education policy matters for all students, but especially for those with reading difficulties: students with learning disabilities, students-of-color, those whose primary language is not English, and students living in poverty have all been affected by policies generated by local, state, and federal governments. It would appear that the climate created by placing an emphasis or focus on achieving a particular goal—in this case, the goal of making certain that *all* students improve their reading performance—is important. Second, policy is affected by many factors; scientific knowledge is one of them, but often pressures from special interest groups and individuals can affect the interpretation of such knowledge and influence how policy is enacted and implemented. Third, in its implementation at local levels, policy is influenced by contextual factors such as the knowledge, beliefs, and motivations of the implementers. Any evaluation of policy must take into consideration these mediating factors. Finally, we do *not* already have all the answers and much more research is needed, especially research related to struggling readers, to undergird policy and to determine whether such policy works, for whom, and how. This research, however, will not be informative unless policy researchers and researchers interested in learning and instruction work together to generate and communicate the results of their efforts.

References

American Educational Research Association. (2005). Teaching teachers: Professional development to improve student achievement [Brochure]. *Research Points 3*(1).

August D., & Shanahan, T. (2006). *Report of the national literacy panel on language minority children and youth,* Philadelphia: Erlbaum

Biancarosa, G., Bryk, A., & Dexter, E. (2008, March). *Assessing the value-added effects of literacy collaborative professional development on student learning.* Paper presented at the Annual Conference of the American Educational Research Association, New York City.

Bean, R., Belcastro, E., Hathaway, J., Risko, V., Roskos, K., & Rosemary, C. (2008, March). *Synthesis of research about literacy coaching.* Paper presented at the Annual Conference of the American Educational Research Association, New York City.

Cassidy, J., & Cassidy, D. (2008, February). What's Hot for 2008? *Reading Today, 25*(4), 1, 10–11.

Center for Education Policy. (2007). *Moving beyond identification: Assisting schools in improvement.* Washington, DC: Author.

Chard, D. J., & Kame'enui, E. J. (2000). Struggling first grade readers: The frequency and progress of their reading. *Journal of Special Education, 34*(1), 28–38.

Coburn, C. E. (2006). Framing the problem of reading instruction: Using frame analysis to uncover the microprocesses of policy implementation. *American Educational Research Journal, 43*(3), 343–349.

Coggins, C. T., Stoddard, P., & Cutler, E. (2003, April). *Improving instructional capacity through field-based reform coaches.* Paper presented at the annual meeting of the American Educational Research Association, Chicago. (ERIC Document Reproduction Service No. ED478744)

Coyne, M. D., Kame'enui, E. J., & Simmons, D. C. (2001). Prevention and intervention in beginning reading: Two complex systems. *Learning Disabilities Research & Practice, 16* (2), 62–73.

Denton, C. A., Anthony, J. L., Parker, R., & Hasbrouck, J. (2004). Effects of two tutoring programs on the English reading development of Spanish–English bilingual students. *The Elementary School Journal, 104,* 289–305.

Desimone, L. M., Porter, A. C., Garet, M. S., Yoon, K. S., & Birman, B. F. (2002). Effects of professional development on teachers' instruction: Results from a three-year longitudinal study. *Educational Evaluation and Policy Analysis, 24*(2), 81–112.

Deussen, T., Coskie, T., Robinson, L., & Autio, E. (2007, June). *"Coach" can mean many things: Five categories of literacy coaches in Reading First.* ERIC #:497517

Federal Register. (2002, April 2). CFDA 84.357 Reading First—Applications for State Grants, Volume 67, No. 63, p. 15553.

Feldman J., & Tung, S. (2002). *The role of external facilitators in whole school reform: Teachers' perceptions of how coaches influence school change.* Boston: Center of Collaborative Education. (ERIC Document Reproduction Service No. ED470680).

Foorman, B. R., Francis, D. J., Fletcher, J. M., Schatschneider, C., & Mehta, P. (1998). The role of instruction in learning to read: Preventing failure in at-risk children. *Journal of Educational Psychology, 90*(1), 37–55.

Francis, D. (2008, June). *Reading First impact study: What have we learned and where do we go from here?* Paper presented at the Institute of Education Sciences Research Conference, Washington, DC, September.

Gamse, B. C., Bloom, H. S., Kemple, J. J., & Jacob, R.T. (2008). *Reading First Impact Study: Interim Report* (NCEE 2008-4016). Washington, DC: National Center for Education Evaluation and Regional Assistance, Institute of Education Sciences, U.S. Department of Education.

Gamse, B. C., Jacob, R. T., Horst, M., Boulay, B., & Unlu, F. (2008). *Reading First impact study final report executive summary* (NCEE 2009-4039). Washington, DC: National Center for Education Evaluation and Regional Assistance, Institute of Education Sciences, U.S. Department of Education.

Good, R. H., & Kaminski, R. A. (2002). *Dynamic indicators of basic literacy skills.* Eugene: University of Oregon..

Good, R. H., Simmons, D. C., & Kame'enui, E. J. (2001). The importance and decision-making utility of a continuum of fluency-based indicators of foundational reading skills for third-grade high-stakes outcomes. *Scientific Studies of Reading, 5*(3), 257–288.

Guskey, T. (2000). *Evaluating professional development.* Thousand Oaks, CA: Corwin Press.

Hess, F. M. (2008). *When research matters: How scholarship influences education policy.* Cambridge, MA: Harvard Education Press.

Kamil, M., Mosenthal, P. B., Pearson, P. D., & Barr, R. (2000). *Handbook of reading research* (Vol III). Mahwah, NJ: Erlbaum.

Kaminski, R. A., & Good, R. H., III. (1996). Toward a technology for assessing basic early literacy skills. *School Psychology Review, 25*(2), 215–227.

Kindler, A. L. (2002). *Survey of the states' limited English proficient students and available educational programs and services. 2001–2002 summary report.* Washington, DC: National Clearinghouse for English Language Acquisition.

Kloo, A. (2006). *The decision-making utility and predictive power of DIBELS for students' reading achievement in Pennsylvania's reading first schools* Unpublished doctoral dissertation, University of Pittsburgh, Pittsburgh, Pennsylvania.

Linan-Thompson, S., Vaughn, S., Prater, K., & Cirino, P. T. (2006). The response to intervention of English language learners at risk for reading problems. *Journal of Learning Disabilities, 39*(5), 390–398.

Lyon, G. R. (1995). Toward a definition of dyslexia. *Annals of Dyslexia, 45,* 1–27.

Lyon R., & Chhabra, V. (1996) The current state of science and the future of specific reading disability. *Mental Retardation and Developmental Disabilities Research and Reviews, 2,* 2–9.

Manzo, K. (2008, December 3). Federal path for reading questioned: 'Reading First' poor results offer limited guidance. *Education Week, 28,* 1, 16–17.

Marsh, J. A., McCombs, J. S., Lockwood, J. R., Martorell, F., Gershwin, D., Naftel, S., et al. (2008). *Supporting literacy across the sunshine state: A study of Florida middle school reading coaches.* Rand Corporation: Santa Monica, CA.

McCardle, P., & Chhabra, V. (Eds.). (2004). *The voice of evidence in reading research.* Baltimore, MD: Brookes.

McCardle, P., Mele-McCarthy, J., & Leos, K. (2005). English language learners and learning disabilities: Research agenda and implications for practice. *Learning Disabilities Research & Practice, 20,* 68–78.

McDonnell, L. (2008) *Forward.* In F. M. Hess (Ed.), *When research* matters: How scholarship influences education policy (pp. vii–x). Cambridge, MA: Harvard Education Press.

McGill-Franzen, A. (2000). Policy and Instruction: What is the relationship? In M. L. Kamil, P. B. Mosenthal, P. D. Pearson, & R. Barr (Eds.), Handbook of reading research (Vol. 3, pp. 889–908). Mahwah, NJ: Erlbaum.

McLaughlin, M. W. (1990). The RAND change agent study revisited: Macro perspectives and micro realities. Educational Resarcher, 19(9), 11–16.

McLaughlin, M. W. (1992). Educational policy, impact on practice. In M. Aiken (Ed.), American Educational Research Association encylopedia of educational research (pp. 375–382). New York: Macmillan.

National Institute of Child Health and Human Development (NICHD). (2000). Report of the National Reading Panel. Teaching children to read: An evidence-based assessment of the scientific research literature on reading and its implications for reading instruction: Reports of the subgroups. (NIH Publication No 00-4754). Washington, DC: U.S. Government Printing Office. Also available on-line at http:www.nichd.nih.gov/publicatons/nrp/report.htm

National Center for Education Statistics. (2004). Language minorities and their educational and labor market indicators—Recent trends. Retrieved June 1, 2008, from http://nces.ed.gov/pubs2004/2004009.pdf

National Reading Panel (2000). Teaching children to read: An evidence-based assessment of the scientific research literature on reading and its implications for reading instruction. Rockville, MD: National Institute of Child Health and Human Development.

National Research Council. (1998). Preventing reading difficulties in young children. Washington, DC: National Academy Press.

Paris, S. G. (2005). Reinterpreting the development of reading skills. Reading Research Quarterly, 40(2), 184–202.

Pearson, P. D. (2004). The reading wars. Educational Policy, 18, 216–252.

Reading First Data Online. (2008). Retrieved from http://readingfirstdata-online.org/state/PA.aspx

Reading First Federal Advisory Committee. (2008). Response to the Reading First impact study. Retrieved January 5, 2009, from http://ednews.org/articles/28504/1/

Richardson, V., & Placier, P. (2001). Teachers change. In V. Richardson (Ed.), Handbook of research on teaching (4th ed., pp. 905–947). Washington, DC: American Educational Research Association.

Rivkin, S. G., Hanushek, E. A., & Kain, J. K. (1998). Teachers, schools and academic achievement. Unpublished manuscript.

Roller, C. (2006). Reading and literacy coaches report on hiring requirements and duties survey. Newark, DE: International Reading Association.

Sanders, W. L., & Horn, S. P. (1998). Research findings from the Tennessee value-added assessment system (TVASS) database: Implications for educational evaluation and research. Journal of Personnel Evaluation in Education. Retrieved from http://www.sasinschool.com/evass/resources/publications/pdf/Reearch_Findings_TVASS_DB.pdf

Song, M., Coggshall, J. G., & Miskel, C. G. (2004). Policy and research: When are we today and where are we going? In P. McCardle & V. Chhabra (Eds.), The voice of evidence in reading research (pp.445–462). Baltimore, MD: Brookes.

Slavin, R. E. (2002). Evidence-based education policies: Transforming educational practice and research. Educational Researcher, 31(7), 15–21.

Snow, C. E., Burns, M. S., & Griffin, P. (Eds.). (1998) Preventing reading difficulties in young children. Washington, DC: National Academies Press.

Snow, C., Ippolito, J., & Schwartz, R. (2006). What we know and what we need to know about literacy coaches in middle and high schools: A research synthesis and proposed research agenda. In Standards for middle and high school literacy coaches (pp. 35–49). Newark, DE: International Reading Association. Retrieved from http://www.reading.org/resources/issues/reports/coaching.html

Sparks, D., & Loucks-Horsley, S. (1990). Models of staff development. In W. R. Houston (Ed.), Handbook of research on teacher education (pp. 234–250). New York: Macmillan.

Torgeson, J. K. (2000). Individual differences in response to early interventions in reading: The lingering problem. Learning Disabilities Research and Practice, 15(4), 303–323.

Torgeson, J. K., Alexander, A. W., Wagner, R. K., Raschotte, C. A., Voeller, K., & Conway, T. (2001). Intensive remedial instruction for children with severe reading disabilities: Immediate and long-term outcomes from two instructional approaches. Journal of Learning Disabilities, 34, 33–58, 78.

U.S. Department of Education. (2002a, April). Guidance for the Reading First program. Washington, DC: Office of Elementary and Secondary Education. Retrieved from http://www.ed.gov/programs/readingfirst/guidance.pdf

U.S. Department of Education. (2002b). No Child Left Behind: A desktop reference. Washington, D.C: Office of Elementary and Secondary Education. Retrieved from http://www.ed.gov/admins/lead/account/nclbreference/page_pg5.html#i-b1

Valencia, S., & Wixson, K. (2000). Policy-oriented research on literacy standards and assessment. In M. L. Kamil, P. B. Mosenthal, P. D. Pearson, & R. Barr (Eds.), Handbook of reading research (Vol. 3, pp. 909–935). Mahwah, NJ: Erlbaum.

Whitehurst, G. J. (2003). Rigor, relevance, and utilization. APS Observer (1050-4672), 16(12), 1.

Yoon, K. S., Duncan, T., Lee, S., W-Y, Scarloss, B., & Shapley, K. (2007). Reviewing the evidence on how teacher professional development affects student achievement (Issues & Answers Report), REL 2007-No. 033. Washington, DC: U.S. Department of Education, Institute of Education Sciences, National Center for Education Evaluation and Regional Assistance, Regional Educational Laboratory Southwest. Retrieved from http://ies.ed.gov/ncee/edlabs

Zigmond, N., & Bean, R. M. (2008). External evaluation of Reading First in PA. Annual report. Pittsburgh, PA: University of Pittsburgh.

Zogby, C., (2002). Pennsylvania Department of Education Application for Reading First Funds (CFDA 84/357), Unpublished grant application.

41

Meta-Analysis of Research on Children with Reading Disabilities

H. Lee Swanson
University of California

With the increase of primary research on reading disabilities, meta-analysis has become an essential tool for synthesizing the overwhelming number of results. The term *meta-analysis*, first coined by Gene Glass in 1976, refers to a statistical technique used to synthesize data from separate comparable studies in order to obtain a quantitative summary of research that addresses a common question (Cooper & Hedges, 1994). Prior to conducting a meta-analysis, the researcher defines the problem, collects the research relevant to the problem, and evaluates the quality of the data (Cooper, 1998). The procedures for conducting a meta-analysis are described in detail in Cooper (1998), Cooper and Hedges (1994), Hedges and Olkin (1985), and Lipsey and Wilson (2001).

There are a number of advantages of meta-analysis over traditional narrative techniques for synthesizing research (see Rosenthal & DiMatteo, 2001, for a full review). First, the structured methodology of meta-analysis requires careful review and analysis of all contributing methodologically sound research. As such, meta-analysis overcomes biases associated with the reliance on single studies, or subsets of studies that inevitably occur in narrative reviews of a literature. Second, meta-analysis allows even small and non-significant effects to contribute to the overall conclusions and avoids wasting data because a sample size was too small and significance was not achieved. Finally, meta-analysis can address questions about variables that moderate effects. Specifically, meta-analysis provides a formal means for testing whether different features of studies explain variation in their outcomes.

There are many different metrics to describe an effect size, two are briefly summarized. The first effect size metric is the *r-index*, or the Pearson product-moment correlation coefficient. The correlational data collected from studies typically use Hunter and Schmidt's (2004) psychometric meta-analytic method. This method is preferred to others because it provides for estimating the amount of variance attributed to sampling errors, range restriction, and unreli-

ability. A meta-analysis is appropriate for correlational research when one attempts to determine the degree to which bivariate relationships generalize across studies (e.g., Hedges & Olkin, 1985; Hunter & Schmidt, 2004). In addition, Hedges and Olkin (1985) argue that correlation coefficients are a scale-free measure of the relationship between variables, and as such are "invariant under substitution of difference of different but linearly equitable measures of the same construct. The correlation coefficient is therefore a natural candidate as an index of effect magnitude suitable for cumulation across studies" (p. 223).

The second, called the *d-index* by Cohen (1988), is a scale-free measure of the separation between two group means that is used when one variable in the relation is dichotomous (children with reading disabilities, RD, vs. children without RD) and the other is continuous. Calculating the *d*-index for any study involves dividing the difference between the two group means by either their average standard deviation or the standard deviation of the control group. To make *d*s interpretable, statisticians have adopted Cohen's (1988) system for classifying *d*s in terms of their size (i.e., .00–.19 is described as trivial; .20–.49, small; .50–.79, moderate; .80 or higher, large). Cohen's *d* (1988) is further weighted by the reciprocal in the sampling variance (Hedges & Olkin, 1985). The dependent measure for the estimate of effect size (ES) can be defined as ES = $d/(1/v)$, where d [Mean of RD group – Mean of comparison group)/average of standard deviation for both groups], and v is the inverse of the sampling variance, $v = (N_{rd}+N_{nrd})/(N_{rd} \times N_{nrd}) + d^2/[2(N_{rd} + N_{nrd})]$ (Hedges & Olkin, 1985). Thus, effect sizes are computed with each effect size weighted by the reciprocal of its variance, a procedure that gives more weight to effect sizes that are more reliably estimated. As suggested by Hedges and Olkin (1985), the majority of syntheses remove outliers from the analysis of main effects. Outliers are defined as ESs lying beyond the first gap of at least one standard deviation between adjacent ES values in a positive direction (Bollen, 1989).

The researcher also determines whether a set of *d*s or *r*s share a common effect size (i.e., was consistent across the studies) by category (e.g., phonological awareness, rapid naming). For the category of each dependent measure, a homogeneity statistic Q (chi-square) determines whether separate ESs within each category share a common ES (Hedges & Olkin, 1985). The statistic Q has a distribution similar to the distribution of Chi-square with *k*-1 degrees of freedom, where *k* is the number of effect sizes (ES). A significant Chi-square indicates that study feature significantly moderates the magnitude of ESs. If the homogeneity is not achieved (which is usually the case), subsequent analyses determine variables (e.g., age, IQ) that moderates the outcomes. State-of-the art meta-analytic procedures use a mixed-*regression* to examine whether particular characteristics of studies moderate the effect sizes (e.g., Bryk & Raudenbush, 1992). Meta-analysts decide whether a fixed-effects or random-effects model of error underlies the generation of study outcomes. In a *fixed-effects model*, all studies are assumed to be drawn from a common population. As such, variance in effect sizes is assumed to reflect only sampling error, that is, error solely due to participant differences. In a *random-effects model of error*, studies are expected to vary also as a function of features that can be viewed as random influences. Thus, in a random-effect analysis, study-level variance is assumed to be present as an additional source of random influence. If it is the case that the meta-analyst suspects a large number of these additional sources of random error, then a random-effects model is most appropriate in order to take these sources of variance into account. If the meta-analyst suspects that the data are most likely little affected by other sources of random variance, then a fixed-effects model can be applied.

Review of Meta-analysis Studies Addressing Questions Related to Reading Disabilities

Given the above overview of meta-analysis, my colleagues and I have used meta-analysis procedures to address three major questions that have plagued the field of RD. Prior to addressing these questions, however, I will briefly review some critical assumptions related to the diagnosis and treatment of RD. Traditionally, the case for RD (in contrast to other reading problems in children) rests on three assumptions: (a) reading difficulties are not due to inadequate opportunity to learn, general intelligence, or to physical or emotional/behavior disorders, but to basic disorders in specific cognitive information processes, (b) these specific information processing deficits are a reflection of neurological, constitutional, and/or biological factors, and (c) these specific information processing deficits underlie a limited aspect of academic behavior (i.e., reading). Thus, to assess RD at the cognitive level, systematic efforts are made to detect: (a) normal psychometric intelligence, (b) below normal achievement in reading (e.g., word recognition), (c) below normal performance in specific cognitive processes (i.e., phonological awareness, working memory),

(d) that evidence-based instruction has been presented under optimal conditions but deficits in isolated cognitive processes remain, and (e) that cognitive processing deficits are not directly caused by environmental factors (e.g., socioeconomic status, SES) or contingencies.

In essence, the identification of children with RD requires the documentation of normal intelligence and deficient reading performance after intense instruction has been provided. Historically and even in some current settings, the identification of children with RD has been clouded by practices that focus on uncovering a significant discrepancy between achievement in reading and general psychometric intellectual ability (see Hoskyn & Swanson, 2000, for a review of this literature). The validity of the discrepancy approach has been questioned and other approaches are being formalized. One of these approaches focus children's response to intervention (RTI). The goal of RTI is to monitor the intensity of instruction and make systematic changes in the instructional context as a function of a student's overt performance (see Fuchs, Mock, Morgan, & Young, 2003, for a review). This is done by considering various tiers of instructional intensity. It is assumed that children identified with RD are in many cases over identified and that when exposed to evidence-based instruction in reading, the gap between poor readers and efficient readers will be narrowed. Within this current zeitgeist that emphasizes RTI, we review our results related to our meta-analysis of the literature.

The first meta-analysis reviewed focuses on identifying the cognitive mechanisms that underlie word recognition difficulties, the second on the role of intelligence in the assessment process, the final addresses the issue of identifying effective procedures for intervention.

Identifying Cognitive Processes Critical to Reading

What cognitive processes underlie reading disabilities? A popular assumption is that children with RD have specific localized low-order processing deficits. A component consistently implicated in RD is phonological awareness. Phonological awareness is "the ability to attend explicitly to the phonological structure of spoken words" (Scarborough, 1998, p. 95). Abundant evidence shows that children with RD have problems in processing phonological information (e.g., see Stanovich & Siegel, 1994, for a review). Recently, some studies have suggested other processes, such as rapid naming and working memory, may be involved in reading acquisition that are as important as phonological awareness (e.g., Cutting & Denckla, 2001; Swanson & Alexander, 1997). For example, Wolf, Bowers, and Biddle (2000) suggest that both phonological awareness (PA) and rapid naming (RAN) (the ability to name a series of visual symbols, e.g., colors, pictures, letters, numbers, words, as quickly as possible with minimal amount of error) contribute unique variance to reading. More specifically, Wolf and Bowers (1999) have proposed a double-deficit hypothesis, which suggests that some deficits in reading may be related to the speed of with which one can name aloud a series of letters, objects, and numbers, as well as to deficits in phonological awareness. Additional studies suggest other processes such as those related to orthography (e.g., Cunningham & Stanovich, 1990; Torgesen, Wagner, Rashotte, Burgess, & Hecht, 1997) and working memory span (e.g., Siegel & Ryan, 1989) contribute statistically significant amounts of variance to reading. For example, in terms of orthographic processing, Olson, Kliegel, Davidson, and Foltz (1985) presented poor readers with real and pseudo-words (e.g., rain-rane) and required participants to select the correct spelling. Several studies suggest that poor readers can be characterized by their inability to retain information in memory while simultaneously processing the same or other information (e.g., Siegel & Ryan, 1989; Swanson & Alexander, 1997). This skill is critical to a wide range of reading tasks because an important requirement of many reading activities is that incoming information must be temporarily preserved while other information is being acquired or manipulated.

To be sure, the current literature weighs heavily on the side of phonological and rapid naming processing deficits as the major sources of reading difficulties (e.g., Vellutino, Fletcher, Snowling, & Scanlon, 2004; Wagner, Torgesen, Laugheon, Simmons, & Rashotte, 1993). Nevertheless, an understanding of the interplay between multiple processes is necessary before one has an adequate account on the major information processing variables that contribute to reading. Swanson, Trainin, Neceochea, and Hammill (2003) completed a meta-analysis that investigated the correlational evidence on the relationships between phonological awareness, rapid naming speed, and sight recognition of real words. Reading ability was narrowly confined to word reading and those variables (phonological awareness and rapid naming speed) that have been identified in the literature as critically related to RD. There were three primary purposes of their meta-analysis: (a) conduct a meta-analysis of correlations between phonological awareness (PA), rapid naming (RAN), and word reading, (b) identify some the variables that moderate those correlations (e.g., age groups, SES, types of criterion reading measures used to classify skilled and readers at-risk), and (c) use these meta-analytically derived correlations for investigating models of the relationships between reading and various cognitive processes. More importantly, the analysis investigated potential competing processes (e.g., spelling, orthography, vocabulary, memory) that may also play an important role in predicting reading.

The PsycINFO, MEDline, ERIC, and Dissertation Abstracts on-line databases were systematically scanned for studies reported from 1966 to 2001. The computer search strategy used key search terms related to reading (e.g., reading, word recognition, regular words, irregular words, exception words, comprehension), naming speed (e.g., naming speed, RAN, naming latency speed), and phonological coding or awareness or reading skills (e.g., pseudo-words, word attack, segmentation, phonological coding, sublexical route, nonword reading, phonological skill). The synthesis summarized research examining the relationship between phonological awareness, naming speed, reading, and related abilities (e.g., vocabulary, IQ, spelling, memory). Correlations (N = 2,257) corrected for sample size, restriction in range, and attenuation were analyzed across 49 independent samples. The results show that a prototypical study yields a mean correlation size on reading variables of approximately .42, with a sample size of 101 participants and a mean age of 10 years.

Particular attention in this synthesis, however, was directed at the interrelationship among PA, RAN, and real word reading. When corrected for sample size and sample heterogeneity (variations in SES, ethnicity, age), the synthesis found that the majority correlations related to PA and RAN were in the low range (mean r = .38). Further, correlations between real word recognition, PA and RAN were also in the low to moderate range (.35 to .50). The average correlation was .48 between PA and real word recognition, and .46 between RAN and real word recognition. More importantly, the magnitude of the correlations among RAN/PA, real word reading/PA, and real word reading/PA measures were significantly lower in reading disabled/poor reader samples. This finding will be discussed further below.

The overall results related to the correlations were submitted to a factor analysis. The mean weighted corrected correlations across the 49 independent samples were organized into a 10 × 10 correlation matrix and are shown in Table 41.1. The matrix was submitted to a maximum likelihood factor analysis.[1] Three important findings related to the factor analysis emerged. First, as shown in Table 41.2, RAN and PA measures loaded on separate factors. The PA measures loaded meaningfully on the pseudo-word reading factor, whereas the RAN measures loaded meaningfully on the reading comprehension factor. Second, neither RAN nor PA measures loaded meaningfully on real word recognition measures. This was an unexpected finding because of the emphasis given in the literature to these measures as predictors of reading success. Finally, spelling was meaningfully related to pseudo-word reading (Factor 1), real word reading (Factor 2), and aspects of vocabulary and orthography (Factor 5).

The critical question that this synthesis addressed, however, was whether RAN and PA measures were the best measures for enhancing our understanding of children with RD. As previously stated, the double deficit hypothesis assumes that RAN and PA measures operate as independent systems but share equally important variance with word identification. This leads to the prediction that RAN and real word reading load on one factor and PA and real word recognition would load on another factor. Thus, one would expect at least two factors to clearly emerge in the present data set—one that shows a factor with meaningful loadings of PA and real word reading and another factor that shows a meaningful loading of RAN and real word reading. This finding did not emerge, suggesting that measures of PA and RAN were not directly relevant to our understanding of real word reading performance. The results do show, however,

TABLE 41.1
Intercorrelations Among Cognitive Measures in Meta-Analysis of Swanson et al. (2003).

Measures	1	2	3	4	5	6	7	8	9	10
1. Word	1.0	.43	.42	.69	.42	.38	.41	.78	.37	.74
2. Phonol.		1.0	.36	.52	.28	.42	.33	.52	.30	.49
3. Rapid Naming			1.0	.53	.36	.26	.41	.53	.27	.60
4. Pseudo word				1.0	.63	.34	.52	.77	.54	.67
5. Intelligence					1.0	.42	.54	.70	.45	.68
6. Vocabulary						1.0	.34	.58	.39	.44
7. Ortho/homo							1.0	.64	.38	.61
8. Spelling								1.0	.53	.80
9. Memory									1.0	.48
10 Reading comprehension										1.0

Note. Phonol. = Phonological awareness, Ortho/homo = Orthography/homophones, Reading comp.= Reading comprehension, Word = real word recognition, RAN= rapid naming.
Source. Table adapted from Swanson et al. (2003)

that PA (though not as strong as spelling) shares a similar construct with pseudo-word reading. However, this loading is only slightly better than memory (.40 vs. .39) and the loading of both variables is reduced substantially in the oblique rotation. Interestingly, we find that RAN measures do load highly on reading comprehension. The only variable that was found meaningful across several factors was spelling. Measures of spelling were relevant on measures of pseudo-word reading, real word reading and vocabulary. Thus, it appears to us that less emphasis should be given to PA and RAN measures when attempting to classify children at risk for reading when compared to spelling.

Five other important findings emerged concerning these relationships when applied to understanding RD.

1. No clear advantages were found for measures of PA and RAN when compared to other variables when predicting real word recognition. That is, when we compared the magnitude of the coefficients for eight variables (see Table 41.1) correlated with real word reading (PA, RAN, pseudo-words, IQ, vocabulary, orthographic, spelling,

TABLE 41.2
Maximum Likelihood Loadings with Varimax Rotation

Factor	1	2	3	4	5
Word recognition	.28	.88	.12	.25	.25
Phon. Awareness	.40	.18	.01	.33	.30
Rapid naming	.35	.15	.11	.49	.21
Pseudo Wd. Rd.	.83	.35	.33	.24	.15
Intelligence	.23	.13	.90	.20	.29
Vocabulary	.11	.16	.19	.16	.57
Orth/homophones	.28	.10	.29	.37	.42
Spelling	.41	.44	.34	.30	.62
Memory	.39	.11	.24	.25	.28
Comprehension	.21	.43	.39	.74	.27

Note. Phon. Awareness=phonological awareness, Pseudo Wd Rd=Psuedoword reading, Orth/homphones=Orthography/homophones, Comprehension=Reading comprehension. Italics are coefficients .40 or greater.

memory), the magnitude of the coefficients for PA and RAN measures were in the same range as IQ, vocabulary, orthography, and memory. These findings remain stable even after partialing for variations in the samples as a function of age, SES, distribution of reading ability, gender and ethnic representation.

2. RAN measures share a moderate relationship to measures of pseudo-word reading and spelling. Of the seven variables correlated with RAN (PA, pseudo-words, IQ, vocabulary, orthographic, spelling, memory), pseudo-word reading (.48) and spelling (.45) yield the strongest correlations. However, the magnitudes of these correlations were in the moderate range (.40 to .60). Further, the magnitude of the correlations between RAN measures with PA (.38), IQ (M = .33), vocabulary (.24) orthographic processing (.38), and memory (M = .29) were in the low range (.20 to .40).

3. Age does not appear to play a significant role in moderating the correlations between PA and RAN. Some have argued that magnitude of the correlations between PA and RAN varies as a function age (Wolf & Bowers, 1999). However, no significant patterns emerged in this synthesis that would support the conclusion that correlations between RAN and PA are reliably different in magnitude with variations in age.

4. Measures of PA did not share a similar factor with measures of RAN. Measures of RAN were more likely to share variance with text comprehension (perhaps as an indirect measure of fluency) than word recognition, whereas measures of PA were more likely to share variance with pseudo-word reading. Thus, we did not find support for the notion that RAN measures share important variance with phonological awareness skills.

5. The magnitude of the correlations that emerge for skilled/average readers or mixed samples of readers cannot be generalized to poor readers. Disabled/poor readers had lower RAN/PA coefficients (.22) than skilled/average readers (.42) or samples that combined the two groups (.40). In addition, poor readers had lower

real word recognition/PA coefficients (.30) than skilled/average readers (M = .52) or for some combinations of poor/skilled readers (r = .56). Overall, the results show that correlations related to poor readers are substantially weaker than those associated with skilled readers. These findings call into question whether coefficients found in skilled readers or a multisample context generalize to a single sample of poor readers. Thus, models of normal reading based on correlational data may not apply to participants with poor or disabled reading skills.

What can be concluded from this meta-analysis of correlations to word recognition and RD? Overall, the synthesis was consistent with the current literature suggesting that isolated processes, such as phonological coding, do play a modest part in predicting real word reading and pseudo-word reading. However, the meta-analysis highlights the importance of additional processes (e.g., intelligence, vocabulary) as playing just as important role in reading. Thus, this synthesis suggests that the importance of phonological awareness may have been overstated in the literature. A similar observation has been made by Bishop and Adams (1990) in which they state that "Phonological factors are of particular theoretical interest because they seem able to explain variation in reading acquisition that is not accounted for in terms of other, more general, verbal abilities. However, it should be emphasized that other language skills exert the major influence in reading progress" (pp. 1046–1047).

The Role of Intelligence

How import is intelligence to the assessment of RD? The second issue raised in the literature on RD is directed to the role intelligence plays in defining RD. Should IQ be maintained in current models of RD? As suggested in the previously aforementioned meta-analysis of correlations (Swanson et al., 2003), the magnitude of the correlation among word identification, phonological processing, memory, rapid naming, and intelligence measures does *not* differ significantly. Thus, IQ was no less important in predicting word recognition than other cognitive variables. In the field of RD, intelligence has long been viewed as a measure of aptitude and is a critical construct in assessment. However several authors have argued that variations in IQ tell us little about differences in processing when groups are defined at low levels of reading (e.g., Fletcher, Francis, Rourke, Shaywitz, & Shaywitz, 1992; Francis et al., 2005). Clearly, Individuals with Disabilities Education Improvement Act (IDEIA, 2004) has nudged the field away from using IQ as a measure of aptitude for determining RD. However, are variations in IQ and reading really irrelevant to our understanding of RD? I will briefly review three meta-analyses on this issue.

Three meta-analyses were completed prior to the passing of IDEIA (2004; Fuchs, Fuchs, Mathes, & Lipsey, 2000; Stuebing et al., 2002; Hoskyn & Swanson, 2000) that addressed the role of IQ in defining RD. The contradictions in these three meta-analyses are reviewed in Stuebing et al. (2002). Stuebing et al. considered the Hoskyn and Swanson (2000) selection process of studies more conservative of the three, and therefore I want to highlight the findings related to the relevance of IQ from that meta-analysis. Hoskyn and Swanson's (2000) meta-analysis focused only on published literature comparing children who are poor readers but either had higher IQ scores than their reading scores or had IQ scores commiserate with their reading scores. Although the outcomes of Hoskyn and Swanson's synthesis generally supported current notions about comparable outcomes on various measures among the discrepancy and non-discrepancy groups, a regression analysis predicting the magnitude of effect sizes between the two groups showed that verbal IQ significantly *moderated* the magnitude of effect sizes. That is, although the degree of discrepancy between IQ and reading was irrelevant in predicting effect sizes, the magnitude of differences in performance (effect sizes) between the two groups was significantly related to verbal IQ. Hoskyn and Swanson found that when the effect size differences between discrepancy (reading disabled group) and non-discrepancy groups (low achievers in this case) on verbal IQ measures were greater than 1.00 (when the mean verbal IQ of the RD group was approximately 100 and the verbal IQ mean of the low achieving [LA] group was approximately 85), the approximate mean effect size on various cognitive measures was statistically significant. In contrast, when the effect size for verbal IQ was less than 100 (the mean verbal IQ for the RD group was approximately 95 and the verbal IQ mean for the LA group were at approximately 90) estimates of effect size on various cognitive measures was close to 0 (M = –0.06). Thus, the further the RD group moved above verbal IQs in the 90 range, the greater the chances their overall performance on cognitive measures would differ from the low achiever. In short, although the Hoskyn and Swanson's (2000) synthesis supports the notion that "the degree of differences in IQ and achievement" are unimportant in predictions of effect size differences on various cognitive variables, the magnitude of differences in verbal IQ between these two ability groups with reading recognition scores below the 25th percentile did significantly moderate general cognitive outcomes.

Interestingly, Stuebing et al. (2002) in their meta-analysis concluded that IQ was irrelevant in explaining cognitive and related processing differences between children with RD (high IQ-low reading) and poor readers (low IQ and reading). However, as shown in their table 6 of their results, IQ accounted for substantial amount of the explainable variance in reading (explainable variance ranges from approximately .47 to .58). This is certainly not a good argument to support the notion that IQ is completely irrelevant to reading level. Moreover, robust differences on measures between the two groups were found in a large meta-analysis by Fuchs, Mathes, Fuchs, and Lipsey (2000). Fuchs, Fuchs, et al. (2000) comparing low achieving students with and without RD, found moderate effect sizes (ES = .61, see p. 94) in favor of low achievers without RD. In conclusion, these major syntheses of the literature suggest that removing IQ as an aptitude measure in classifying children as RD, especially verbal IQ, from assessment procedures is not uniformly supported when synthesizing the literature.

How important is IQ in treatment outcomes? One obvious test for assessing the validity of IQ as part of the identification criteria that has been overlooked in the meta-analysis literature is whether IQ is related to treatment outcomes. Although isolated studies have found very little relevance related to IQ levels and treatment outcomes (e.g., Vellutino, Scanlon, & Lyon, 2000), a meta-analysis of the literature on the issue across an array of intervention studies yields a different conclusion. More specifically, responsiveness to instruction across a broad array of studies has been a missing test in the majority of validity studies eschewing the role of intelligence.

Thus, a review of the next meta-analyses addresses whether variations in how samples with RD are defined in terms of intelligence and reading have any relationship to treatment outcomes. It would seem that efforts to completely disband IQ measures in assessing children's response to instruction would be premature if children high and low in IQ respond differently (quantitatively or qualitatively) as a function of treatment. One means of evaluating whether aptitude variations in an RD sample interact with treatment is to compare the relationship between treatment outcomes with multivariate data that include different configurations of how samples with RD are defined (Swanson & Hoskyn, 1999). This can be accomplished by placing studies on the same metric (e.g., effect size) and comparing the magnitude of these outcomes as a function of variations in the sample definition (e.g., on measures of intelligence and reading). The most comprehensive data on this issue to date (Swanson, Hoskyn, & Lee, 1999) shows that significant RD definition × treatment interactions exist across evidence based studies (see Swanson & Hoskyn, 1999, for review). More specifically, Swanson and colleagues found that individual variations in IQ and reading level were important moderators of instructional outcomes in both group design (Swanson & Hoskyn, 1998, 1999) and single subject design studies (Swanson & Sachse-Lee, 2000). They also found in their meta-analysis of intervention studies that variations in standardized IQ and reading significantly moderated the magnitude of treatment effects (Swanson & Hoskyn, 1998). Summarized below is a brief overview of the results of their meta-analyses.

In general, the meta-analyses were conducted across 180 group design and 85 single subject design studies. The analysis addressed two fundamental questions about the role of IQ (Swanson & Hoskyn, 1998; Swanson & Sachse-Lee, 2000). First, does it matter whether IQ is reported? Their synthesis found that studies that failed to report psychometric information on participants with RD yielded significantly higher effect sizes than those studies that reported psychometric information. Thus, poorly defined samples inflated treatment outcomes by introducing greater

heterogeneity into the sample when compared to studies that selected samples based on psychometric criteria. Second, is there an interaction between IQ and reading performance in treatment outcomes? They found that the magnitude of treatment outcomes was related to a reading × intelligence interaction. The influence of IQ scores on the magnitude of the treatment outcomes became especially relevant when reading scores were below the 25th percentile. The effect sizes were moderate (0.52) when intelligence was above 90, but substantial (.95) when IQs scores were below 90. Thus, the implication of these findings is that variations in IQ and reading cannot be ignored when predicting treatment outcomes.

Two other important findings emerge from subsets of the Swanson and Hoskyn (1998) data set when it focused primarily on studies that included adolescents (Swanson, 2001; Swanson & Hoskyn, 2001). First, studies with adolescent samples that had discrepancies in intelligence and reading were more likely to yield lower effect sizes in treatment outcomes than those studies with adolescents that reported aggregated IQ and reading scores in the same low range (e.g., Swanson, 2001). Second, the results showed that treatment outcomes related to reading recognition and reading comprehension varied as a function of IQ. Effect sizes for word recognition studies were significantly related to samples defined by cut-off scores (IQ > 85 and reading < 25th percentile), whereas the magnitude of effect size for reading comprehension studies were sensitive to discrepancies between IQ and reading when compared to competing definitional criteria.

A conclusion that can be drawn across the aforementioned meta-analyses is that variations in IQ (at least aggregated at the study level) are relevant in terms of moderating treatment outcomes. When children with RD and poor readers are compared across cognitive measures (Hoskyn & Swanson, 2000) and treatment outcomes (effect sizes; Swanson et al., 1999), a synthesis of the literature suggests that IQ (especially verbal IQ) moderates cognitive and treatment effects in children with RD.

Determining the Best Intervention Model

Effective Intervention—what works? The final issue our meta-analyses addressed is related to a practical issue of identifying the best instructional intervention for children with RD. A few years ago, a major meta-analysis was funded by the U.S. Department of Education to synthesize experimental intervention research conducted on children with LD over a 35-year period (see Swanson et al., 1999). Greater than 80% of these experimental intervention studies focused on children with RD. Swanson and several of his colleagues (e.g., Swanson, 1999a; 2001, Swanson & Deshler, 2003; Swanson & Hoskyn, 1998; Swanson & Sachse-Lee, 2000) synthesized articles, technical reports, and doctoral dissertations that reported for both group design and single design studies. Condensing 2,000+ effect sizes, they found a mean effect size of .79 for children with RD in the treatment condition versus children with RD in the control condition for group design studies (Swanson & Hoskyn, 1998) and 1.03 for single subject design studies (Swanson & Sachse-Lee, 2000). According to Cohen's (1988) classification system, the magnitude of the ES was large. Thus, on the surface, the results were consistent with the notion that children with RD are highly responsive to intense instruction. However, when children with RD were compared to children without RD (average achievers) of the same grade or age who also were receiving the same best evidence intervention procedure, effect sizes (ES M = .97, SD = .52) were substantially in favor of non disabled children (see Swanson et al., 1999, see pp. 162–169). More importantly, the mean effect size differences were substantially larger and in favor of children without RD when compared to children with RD on the same treatment condition (ES = 1.44; Swanson et al., p. 168) when psychometric scores related to IQ and reading were not included as part of sampling procedure. Thus, the magnitude of response to experimental treatment by children with RD could not be adequately interpreted even when compared to children without RD without recourse to psychometric measures. More importantly, effective instructional procedures did little to bridge the gap related to performance differences between children with and without RD with evidence-based instruction (i.e., treatments found to be highly effective in samples of children with and without RD).

The next meta-analysis reviewed focuses on reading outcomes when comparing treatment and control conditions (Swanson, 1999b). In reviewing this literature, three observations emerged: (a) several outcome measures in reading instruction studies are confounded with treatment activities (the independent and dependent measures are not orthogonal), and (b) effect sizes on transfer measures were weak (e.g., word recognition. effect sizes < .30), and (c) reading outcomes were not directly related to intense one-to-one phonics instruction (see Swanson, 1999b, table 4). A fixed effects regression analysis of the effect sizes comparing treatment with control conditions found that the magnitude of the effects sizes were largest (experimental condition when compared to the control condition for children with RD) when there was a highly structured core of instructional components (e.g., systematic repeated and explicit practice, advanced organizers, sequencing, teacher modeling, consistent probing, see Swanson, 1999b, for review). The regression analysis also showed that the contribution to effect size (treatment vs. control) as a function of the degree or intensity of phonological instruction, when the aforementioned variables were entered into the regression analysis, was nonsignificant when predicting performance on real word recognition tasks.

Before I proceed further on our findings, I would like to make two statements. First, research in the last few years has done much to change our focus on the importance of directly instructing children with RD in phonological skills. Several recent studies have made a significant contribution to our knowledge about effective reading instruction (e.g., Vellutino et al., 2004). Second, traditional assessment

procedures seldom provide information that assesses the stability and/or durability of intrinsic cognitive processing deficits under instructional conditions. Recent RTI studies have done much to put instruction in the context of the assessment process. For example, if an individual at risk for RD has an inability to remember (e.g., access) specific aspects of language (phonological information) during reading instruction, then clear documentation must be provided that they have been systematically provided direct instruction in those aspects of language. Further, if phonological processing is the primary disability experienced by children with RD, then this area would be less likely to change with intense instruction than other cognitive areas (e.g., orthography , meta-cognition) or academic domains less likely to draw on phonological processing (e.g., mathematics).

This latter point is the focus of my concern. Several well-designed studies (e.g., Vellutino et al., 1996) suggest that children who do not respond adequately to intense instruction are considered classically learning disabled (in the sense that they have fundamental processing limitations). This makes good sense. If children suffer from an intrinsic processing deficit (phonological processing that is constitutionally based), then one would expect marginal outcomes even when SES, parent support, and other variables are controlled. For example, a child who is blind from birth, but asked to produce the correct sound from a visual stimulus in well-designed treatments is going to have difficulty encoding visual information even when motivation or other environmental factors are controlled. Likewise, well-designed instruction in phonological processing may produce some positive results, but if RD is related to constitution-based disorder clearly there should be some serious constraints in performance when compared with other academic domains or even to other children with poor reading skills. Unfortunately, a meta-analysis of the literature finds weak support for the assumption that performance on phonological measures are less likely to change (yield lower effect sizes) than performance in other domains or processes. Swanson and Hoskyn (1998) found in a meta-analysis of group design studies that when controls were made on methodological variables (e.g., variation in components of instruction, teacher effects), the magnitude of change (as measured by effect size) in word recognition and phonological skills, was in the same moderate range as a number of other domains (e.g., memory, writing, intelligence scores, global achievement, mathematics). If response to treatment is a good test of theory (.e.g., such as the phonological core model, see Stanovich & Siegel, 1994, for a review), then I don't think one can create the argument that instructional difficulties reside primarily with phonological processing measures.

Another problematic aspect of emphasizing a phonological model is that the magnitude of outcomes on transfer measures (reading of real words as opposed to direct skill measures, e.g., word attack or pseudo-word reading) as a function phonological processing instruction is weak. In a synthesis of several studies that included real word recognition as a dependent measure, when treatment components that include a basic instructional core (e.g., drill, repetition, and practice) were entered first into a mixed regression model in predicting word recognition, segmentation training and individual instruction did not enter significantly in predicting outcomes (see Swanson, 1999b, pp. 518–519). This finding is not unlike those of isolated studies. A study by Foorman et al. (1997) also found that when SES, and IQ were controlled that variations in reading instruction (analytic phonics, synthetic phonics vs. whole word) did *not* significantly predict real word reading (see p. 270, table 8). Such findings raise questions about the primary importance of phonological training (at least as it relates to the unit of word analysis) as it applies to improving word recognition.

In summary, my point is not to dispute the fact that phonological processing is a fundamental processing deficit or that intensive phonological instruction is not important for children with RD. Rather, a meta-analysis of the literature suggests if a stubborn resistance to change in a specific psychological process such as phonological awareness after intense systematic instruction is a critical base for validating the cognitive basis of RD, then research is not conclusive on this issue.

There were two practical findings from our synthesis of reading interventions as applied to the treatment of RD that need to be highlighted. First, combined direct and explicit strategy instruction (explicit practice, elaboration, strategy cuing) and small group interactive settings best predicted the size of treatment outcomes for children with RD across various academic domains (Swanson et al., 1999). The implication of this finding is that a combination of direct instruction and cognitive strategy instruction provided the best evidence-based instructional heuristic for improving reading performance in children with RD. However, these components accounted for less than 21% of the variance in predicting outcomes (Swanson, 1999b). This finding held when controls were made in the analysis for variations in methodology and age. This finding is not unlike that of the National Reading Panel (NRP, 2000) report. Hammill and Swanson (2006) found from the NRP (2000) that best practices in reading (teaching of phonics) accounted for less than 10% of the variance in reading treatment outcomes for children at risk for RD. Thus, a tremendous amount of variance is unaccounted for in studies considered the "best" of the evidence-based practices.

Second, the results of "best-evidence studies" in reading cannot be taken at face value. In our syntheses of the literature (Swanson et al., 1999), all studies had well-defined control groups and treatments and/or baseline conditions before their inclusion in the synthesis. Eliminated from the synthesis were those studies of poor methodological quality (see Valentine & Cooper, 2005, for a rationale). Simmerman and Swanson (2001) analyzed these best evidence studies and found that slight variations in the internal and external validity significantly moderated the magnitude of treatment outcomes. Some violations that were significantly related to

treatment outcomes included: teacher effects (studies that used the identical experimenter for treatment and control in administrating treatments yield smaller effect sizes than those studies that used different experimenters in administering treatments—this condition may be analogous to three tiered instruction), reliance on "non" norm referenced measures (studies that did not use standardized measures had much larger effect sizes than those that reported using standardized measures), and heterogeneous sampling (e.g., studies that included both elementary and secondary students yielded larger effect sizes than the other age level conditions).

More importantly, the under-reporting of information related to ethnicity (studies that reported ethnicity yielded significantly smaller effect sizes than those that did not report ethnicity) and psychometric data (significantly larger effect sizes occurred when no psychometric information was reported when compared to the other conditions) positively inflated the magnitude of treatment outcomes. The magnitude of effect sizes was also influenced by whether studies relied on federal definitions (studies that did not report using the federal definition [PL-94-142] yielded the larger weighted effect score than those that did) or reported using multiple definitional criteria (studies that included multiple criteria in defining their sample yielded smaller effect sizes than those that did not report using multiple criteria) in selecting their sample.

In summary, our meta-analyses show that "best evidence" studies on instructional interventions are moderated by a host of environmental and individual differences variables that make a direct translation to assessing children at risk for RD as a function of educational intervention (i.e., RTI) difficult. In addition, although RTI relies on evidence based studies in the various tiers of instruction, especially in the area of reading, it is important to note that even under the most optimal instructional conditions (direct instruction) for teaching reading less than 21% of the variance in outcomes is related to instructional variables (see Swanson, 1999b, table 5).

The Practical Significance of Effect Sizes   The results of the previous meta-analysis have placed a number of issues related to definitions and treatment for RD into perspective. However, an important question emerges as to what can be considered of practical worth when evaluating effect sizes (see Cooper, 1981, McCartney & Rosenthal, 2000, for a review of this issue). This is an important question because effect sizes in the low range on reading interventions have been interpreted as being practically significant (National Reading Panel Report, RRP). A recent study (Stuebing, Barth, Cirino, Francis, & Fletcher, 2008) criticized two research studies that that called into question conclusions that could be drawn from the meta-analysis by the National Reading Panel Report (i.e., Camilli, Vargas, & Yurecko, 2003; Hammill & Swanson, 2006). In general, the criticisms by Camilli et al. and Hammill and Swanson suggested that the effect sizes of systematic phonics instruction provided by the National Reading Panel Report (d = .41) were overstated and the effect size may be actually lower than previously reported (e.g., d = .12 in the Camilli, Wolfe, & Smith, 2006) or the effect size is of marginal value (Hammill & Swanson 2006).

More specifically, the Camilli et al. study (2003, also reviewed in Camilli et al., 2006) reanalyzed the findings of the panel and found that although programs using systematic phonics outperformed programs using less systematic phonics, the effects were relatively small (d = .24). They found that language instruction and tutoring had a moderating effects on reading outcomes suggesting that phonics instruction may be not be the major determinate of reading outcomes (however, see Stuebing et al., 2008, p. 132, for an alternative interpretation). Further, they found that the moderator variables were critical in the early grades (because the data suggest that after about third grade phonics instruction may be less effective). These results suggest that phonics instruction cannot stand alone and that other components need to be integrated in the reading outcomes. Although there have been public reactions the NRP report (e.g., Shanahan, 2004; Yatvin, 2002) and the Camilli et al. report (e.g., Stuebing et al., 2008), much of scientific concerns have been related to how the controls were defined and/or the purpose of the report (outcomes related to systematic instruction vs. an isolated focus on phonics). However, the important issue raised in the Camilli et al. studies was the practical significance of the effect size provided in the NRP report. This issue was dealt with in greater detailed in Hammill and Swanson (2006) analysis.

In their study, Hammill and Swanson (2006) computed mean effect correlations (rs) and r-squares that correspond to the reported ds in this report. This conversion allowed them to calculate point biserial correlational effects, but more specifically to address the proportion of variance in the outcome variable (reading) that may be predicted by (or accounted for or attributed to) two levels of the independent variable (e.g., intense phonics instruction vs. control situation). The practical value of this conversion was to show that outcomes provided in the NRP report (restated in terms of the proportion of variance accounted for) were so small that it left a tremendous amount of variance related to instruction unaccounted for. Of critical concern in their analysis of the NRP was whether phonics instruction is more effective when it is introduced to students not yet reading, in kindergarten or first grade, than when it is introduced in grades above first after students have already begun to read. The NRP concluded from four mean effect sizes reported for kindergarten and first grade (d = .55, moderate); second–sixth grades, reading disabled (d = .27, small); kindergarten (d = .56, moderate); and first grade (d = .54, moderate) "these results indicate clearly that systematic phonics instruction in Kindergarten and First Grade is highly beneficial and that children at these developmental levels are quite capable of learning phonemic and phonics concepts" (pp. 2). When the mean effects to an r-type statistic were computed, the results were placed

into perspective. The corresponding rs were .27, .13, .27, and .26; and the r-squares were .07, .02, .07, and .07, respectively. These values suggest that phonics instruction was only marginally more effective at teaching reading in kindergarten and first grade than non-phonics instruction. With regards to the second–sixth, reading disabled group, phonics and non-phonics approaches were about equally effective.

The next question focused on whether phonics instruction was more beneficial for children who are having difficulty learning to read than the control condition. In the NRP, four groups of poor readers were studied: Kindergarten at risk (d = .58, moderate, first grade at risk (d = .74, moderate), second–sixth grade low achievers (d = .15, trivial, not significant), and reading disabled, all ages (d = .32, small). The NRP concluded that "systematic phonics instruction was significantly more effective than non-phonics instruction in helping to prevent reading difficulties among at risk students and in helping to remediate difficulties in disabled readers" (p. 2). The NRP dismissed the nonsignificant Cohen's d for low achievers because it was unclear why systematic phonics produced so little growth in these children and suggested that the finding might be unreliable (p. 2).

The rs corresponding to the mean effect sizes for the poor readers were: .28 for kindergarten at risk, .35 for first grade at risk, .07 for second–sixth grade low achievers, and .16 for reading disabled. Respective r-squares were: .08, .12, .00, and .02. The finding for the first grade at risk group provides some evidence for the phonics instruction. But taken together, the results of the r-type analysis provided weak support for the idea that phonics instruction was preferable to other approaches in developing the skills of children who have difficulty learning to read.

In response to these criticisms, Stuebing et al. (2008) indicated that the NRP has practical import. More specifically, they argue that in contrast to the Camilli et al. and Hammill and Swanson studies, judgments related effect sizes must taken into consideration context. For example, they argued that phonics instruction can reduce the number of children with reading problems when one considers the base rate of performance. Consistent with several authors, they argued against applying effect size with the same rigidity as one would typically use in a statistical significance testing.

Unfortunately, the field of RD has not provided to date a consensus on the benchmarks in which to put the overall effect sizes in context. To place the findings in some context, several authors (e.g., Stuebing et al., 2008) who yield syntheses of low effect size use the aspirin study reported in Rosenthal and Rubin (1982) to illustrate that even when an effect size is small, it could have important implications for outcomes. This is usually done by considering the percentage of the controlled population that the upper half of the experimental population exceeds (i.e., a binomial effect displaying the proportionate treatment vs. controlled subjects above a common threshold-defined arbitrarily as an overall median). The procedure becomes problematic, however, because it is difficult to decipher the meaning of other effect sizes that have different control conditions. For example, binomial procedures may actually show that some children benefit from whole language instruction. Regardless of these issues, we think one benchmark was established in the Swanson (1999b) meta-analysis that found that the overall effect size for measures on word recognition for children with RD, regardless of the type of treatment intervention, was about .57. This effect size was partialed for the methodological variations across studies. Therefore, if you use that context with an RD sample, the overall .32 of the NPR doesn't seem that impressive. This is not to argue that the effects related to phonics instruction are trivial. Rather, if context is important when interpreting the practical significance of the effect sizes, the field needs to lay out specific criteria for making judgments about relevant contexts for effect sizes. Thus, there is a conundrum the field of RD faces. The conundrum we confront (as quoted in Light, Singer, & Willett, 1990) is that "meta-analyses often reveal a sobering fact: effect sizes are not nearly as large as we might hope" (p. 195).

Summary

Meta-analyses allow us to address issues in the field of RD that cannot be easily addressed by single studies. In contrast to single studies indicating that the core of RD is isolated to the phonological domain, IQ is irrelevant to both assessment and instruction, and effective instruction leans entirely toward explicit instruction in phonological awareness. A review of the current meta-analyses suggested that qualifications are necessary when placed into a larger context of results aggregated across several methodologically sound studies. The aforementioned meta-analyses suggest that IQ and cognitive process other than phonological processing may play an important role in the assessment and instruction of children with RD. The reader is cautioned when interpreting effect sizes as a function of magnitude. Rather, the interpretation of effect sizes needs to occur in the context of other meta-analyses with established benchmarks.

Notes

1. As indicated by the reviewer of this chapter, Victor Willson, the correlation coefficients have a distribution dependent on the population value; the weighted mean of a set of correlations is not equal to the mean value of the populations. It is in general a biased estimate unless the population value is zero. Factor analyses of the correlation matrix based on such values are at best indicative of a possible underlying structure, but the stability of the factor under various estimation conditions is not known.

References

Bishop, D. V., & Adams, C. (1990). A prospective study of the relationship between specific language impairment, phonological disorder and reading retardation. *Journal of Child Psychology and Psychiatry, 31*, 1027–1050.

Bollen, K. A. (1989). *Structural equations with latent variables.* New York: Wiley Interscience.

Bryk, A. S., & Raudenbush, S. W. (1992). *Hierarchical linear models: Applications and data analysis methods.* Newberry Park, CA: Sage.

Camilli, G., Vargas, S., & Yurecko, M. (2003). Teaching children to read: The fragile link between science and federal education policy. *Education Policy Archives, 11*, 15. Retrieved May 13, 2003, from http://epaa.asu.edu/epaa/v11n15/

Camilli, G., Wolfe, P. M. & Smith, M.L. (2006). Meta-analysis and reading policy: Perspectives on teaching children to Read. *Elementary School Journal, 107*, 27–36.

Cohen, J. (1988). *Statistical power Analysis in the behavioral sciences.* Hillsdale, NJ: Erlbaum.

Cooper, H. (1981). On the effects of significance and the significance of effects. *Journal of Personality and Social Psychology, 41*, 1013–1018

Cooper, H. M. (1998). *Synthesizing Research: A Guide for Literature Reviews* (3rd ed.). Thousand Oaks, CA: Sage.

Cooper, H., & Hedges, L.V. (1994). *Handbook of research synthesis.* New York: Russell Sage.

Cunningham, A. E., & Stanovich, K. E. (1990). Assessing print exposure and orthographic processing skill in children: A quick measure of reading experience. *Journal of Educational Psychology, 82*, 733–740.

Cutting, L. E., & Denckla, M. B. (2001). The relationship of rapid serial naming and word reading in normally developing readers: An exploratory model. *Reading and Writing, 14*, 673–705.

Fletcher, J. M., Francis, D. J., Rourke, B. P., Shaywitz, S. E., & Shaywitz, B. A. (1992). The validity of discrepancy-based definitions of reading disabilities. *Journal of Learning Disabilities, 25*, 555–561.

Foorman, B., R., Francis, D. J., Winikates, D., Mehta, P., Schatschneider, C., & Fletcher, J. M. (1997). Early interventions for children with reading disabilities. *Scientific Studies of Reading, 3,* 255–276.

Francis, D. J., Fletcher, J. M., Stuebing, K. K., Lyon, G. R., Shaywitz, B. A., & Shaywitz, S. E. (2005). Psychometric approaches to the identification of LD: IQ and achievement scores are not sufficient. *Journal of learning Disabilities, 38*(2), 98–108.

Fuchs, D., Fuchs, L., Mathes, P. G., & Lipsey, M. (2000). Reading differences between low achieving students with and without learning disabilities. In R. Gersten, E. P. Schiller, & S. Vaughn (Eds.), *Contemporary Special Education Research: Synthesis of knowledge base of critical issues* (pp. 81–104) Mahwah, NJ: Erbaum.

Fuchs, D. Mock, D., Morgan, P., & Young, C. L. (2003). Responsiveness-to-intervention: Definitions, evidence, and implications for the learning disabilities construct. *Learning Disabilities Research & Practice, 18,* 157–171.

Hammill, D. D., & Swanson, H. L. (2006). The national reading panel's meta-analysis of phonics instruction: Another point of view. *The Elementary School Journal, 107*, 17–26.

Hedges, L. V., & Olkin, I. (1985). *Statistical methods for meta-analysis.* Orlando, FL: Academic Press.

Hoskyn, M., & Swanson, H. L. (2000). Cognitive processing of low achievers and children with reading disabilities: A selective meta-analytic review of the published literature. *School Psychology Review, 29*, 102–119.

Hunter, J. E., & Schmidt, F. L. (2004). *Methods of meta-analysis: Correcting error and bias in research findings* (2nd ed.) Thousand Oaks, CA: Sage.

Individuals with Disabilities Education Improvement Act of 2004 (IDEA), Pub. L. No. 108-446,118 Stat. 2647 (2004). [Amending 20 U.s.c. §§ 1400 et. Seq.).

Light, R. J., Singer, J. D., & Willett, J. B. (1990). *By design: Planning research on higher education.* Cambridge, MA: Harvard University Press.

Lipsey, M. W., & Wilson, D. B. (2001). *Practical meta-analysis.* Thousand Oaks, CA: Sage.

McCartney, K., & Rosenthal, R. (2000). Effect size, practical importance, and social policy for children. *Child Development, 71*, 173–180.

National Reading Panel. (2000). *Teaching children to read: An evidence-based assessment of the scientific research literature on reading and its implications for reading instruction.* Washington, DC: National Institute of Child Health and Human Development.

Olson, R., Kliegel, R., Davidson, B., & Foltz, G., (1985). Individual and developmental differences in reading disability. In G. E. MacKinnon & T. Waller (Eds.), *Reading research: Advances in theory and practice* (Vol. 4, pp. 1–64). San Diego, CA: Academic Press.

Rosenthal, R., & DiMatteo, M. R. (2001). Meta-analysis: Recent developments in quantitative methods for literature reviews. *Annual Review of Psychology, 52,* 59–82.

Rosenthal, R., & Rubin, D. B. (1982). A simple, general purpose display of the magnitude of experimental effect. *Journal of Educational Psychology, 74,* 166–169.

Scarborough, H. S. (1998). Early identification of children at risk for reading disabilities: Phonological awareness and some other promising predictors. In B Shapiro, P. Accardo, & A. Capute (Eds.), *Specific reading disability: A view of the spectrum* (pp. 75–119). Timonium, MD: York Press.

Schatschneider, C., Carlson, C.D., Francis, D.J., Foorman, B. R., & Fletcher, J. M. (2002). Relationship of rapid automatized naming and phonological awareness in early development: Implications for the double-deficit hypothesis. *Journal of Learning Disabilities, 35,* 245–256.

Shanahan, T. (2004). Critiques of the National Reading Panel report. In P. McCardle & V. Chhabra (Eds.), *The voice of evidence in reading research* (pp. 235–265). Baltimore, MD: Paul H. Brooks.

Siegel, L. S., & Ryan, E. B. (1989). The development of working memory in normally achieving and subtypes of learning disabled children. *Child Development, 60,* 973–980.

Simmerman, S., & Swanson, H. L. (2001). Treatment outcomes for students with learning disabilities: How important are internal and external validity? *Journal of Learning Disabilities, 34,* 221–236.

Stanovich, K. E., & Siegel, L. S. (1994). Phenotypic performance profile of children with reading disabilities: A regression based test of the phonological-core difference model. *Journal of Educational Psychology, 86,* 24–53.

Stuebing, K. K., Barth, A., Cirino, P. T., Francis, D. J., & Fletcher, J. M. (2008) A response to recent reanalysis of the National Reading Panel Report: Effects of systematic phonics instruction are practically significant. *Journal of Educational Psychology, 100,* 123–135.

Stuebing, K. K., Fletcher, J. M., LeDoux, J. M., Lyon, G. R., Shaywitz, S. E., & Shaywitz, B. A. (2002). Validity of IQ-discrepancy classifications of reading disabilities: A meta-analysis. *American Educational Research Journal, 39,* 469–518.

Swanson, H. L. (1999a). Instructional components that predict treatment outcomes for students with learning disabilities: Support for a combined strategy and direct instruction model. *Learning Disabilities Research & Practice, 14*(3), 129–140.

Swanson, H. L. (1999b). Reading research for students with LD: A meta-analysis in intervention outcomes. *Journal of Learning Disabilities, 32,* 504–532.

Swanson, H. L. (2001). Research on interventions for adolescents with learning disabilities: A meta-analysis of outcomes related to higher-order processing. *The Elementary School Journal, 101,* 331–348.

Swanson, H. L., & Alexander, J. (1997). Cognitive processes that predict reading in learning disabled readers: Revisiting the specificity hypothesis *Journal of Educational Psychology, 89,* 128–158.

Swanson, H. L., & Deshler, D. (2003). Instructing adolescents with learning disabilities: Converting a meta-analysis to practice. *Journal of Learning Disabilities, 36,* 124–135.

Swanson, H. L., & Hoskyn, M. (1998). Experimental intervention research on students with learning disabilities: A meta-analysis of treatment outcomes. *Review of Educational Research, 68,* 277–321.

Swanson, H. L., & Hoskyn, M. (1999). Definition × treatment interactions for students with learning disabilities. *School Psychology Review, 28,* 644–658.

Swanson, H. L., & Hoskyn, M. (2001). Instructing adolescents with learning disabilities: A component and composite analysis. *Learning Disabilities Research & Practice, 16,* 109–119.

Swanson, H. L., Hoskyn, M., & Lee, C. M. (1999). *Interventions for students with learning disabilities: A meta-analysis of treatment outcomes.* New York: Guilford.

Swanson, H. L., & Sachse-Lee, C. (2000). A meta-analysis of single-subject-design intervention research for students with LD. *Journal of Learning Disabilities, 33,* 114–136.

Swanson, H. L., Trainin, G., Necoechea, D. M., & Hammill, D. D. (2003). Rapid naming, phonological awareness, and reading: A meta-analysis of the correlation evidence. *Review of Educational Research, 73,* 407–440.

Torgesen, J.K., Wagner, R., Rashotte, C.A., Burgess, S., & Hecht, S. (1997). Contributions of phonological awareness and rapid naming ability to the growth of word-reading skills in second to fifth-grade children. *Scientific Studies of Reading, 1,* 161–195.

Valentine, J. C., & Cooper, H. M. (2005).Can we measure the quality of causal research in education. In G. Phye, D. Robinson, & J. Levin (Eds.), *Empirical methods for evaluating interventions* (pp. 85–112). San Diego: Elsevier Academic Press.

Vellutino, F. R., Fletcher, J. M., Snowling, M. J., & Scanlon, D. M. (2004). Specific reading disabilities (dyslexia): What have we learned in the past four decades? *Journal of Child Psychology and Psychiatry, 45,* 2–40.

Vellutino, F. R., Scanlon, D. M., & Lyon, G. R. (2000). Differentiating between difficult-to-remediate and readily remediated poor readers: More evidence against the IQ-achievement discrepancy. *Journal of Learning Disabilities, 33,* 192–199.

Vellutino, F. R., Scanlon, D. M., Sipay, E. R., Small, S. G., Pratt, A., Chen, R., et al. (1996). Cognitive profiles of difficult-to-remediate and readily remediated poor readers: Early intervention as a vehicle for distinguishing between cognitive and experimental deficits as basic causes of specific reading disability. *Journal of Educational Psychology, 88,* 601–638.

Wagner, R. K., Torgesen, J. K., Laugheon, P., Simmons, K., & Rashotte, C. A. (1993). Development of young readers' phonological processing abilities. *Journal of Educational Psychology, 85,* 83–103.

Wolf, M., & Bowers, P. G. (1999). The double-deficit hypothesis for the development dyslexics. *Journal of Educational Psychology, 91,* 415–438.

Wolf, M., Bowers, P. G., & Biddle, K. (2000). Naming speed processes, timing and reading: A conceptual review. *Journal of Learning Disabilities, 33,* 387–407.

Yatvin, J. (2002). Minority view. In *Report of the National Reading Panel, Teaching children to read: An evidenced-based assessment of the scientific research literature on reading and its implications for reading instruction* (pp. 1–6). Washington, DC: NICHD.

42

Interpretive Research

Donna E. Alvermann
University of Georgia

Christine A. Mallozzi
University of Kentucky

The interpretive turn in social research marked a shift in epistemology and politics. Social research changed from emphasizing logical positivism, an approach based on using the scientific method to study human action, to interpretivism. Interpretivism denotes an approach to studying social life with the assumption "that the meaning of human action is inherent in that action" (Schwandt, 2001, p. 134). Researchers using an interpretive approach aim to uncover meaning toward a better understanding of the issues involved. This undertaking necessitates certain methodologies, of which only a few are highlighted here. Naturalistic inquiry is a methodology that underscores the importance of firsthand observations to understand human action from the point of view of the actor in an uncontrived context (Guba, 1978; Lincoln & Guba, 1985; Schwandt, 2001). Constructivism, in general, means that an individual's mind is active in making and structuring knowledge (Spivey, 1997). When brought into interpretive research, constructivism implies that any "discovery" of meaning of human action involves a conceptual framework in the minds of the researchers and participants (Guba & Lincoln, 1989; Schwandt, 2001). Phenomenological methodologies rely on descriptions of conscious experiences to develop understanding of the meaning of human action in everyday life (Schwandt, 2001; Van Manen, 1990). Ethnographic inquiry takes the concepts of the phenomenon a bit further; instead of relying on the participants' descriptions of an experience, the ethnographic researcher must commit to the phenomenon by being there in the experience within the field of study, in the culture of the participants (Geertz, 1973; Green & Bloome, 1983; Schwandt, 2001). Symbolic interactionism involves understanding that humans act toward objects and with individuals according to the meanings that humans have for particular objects and people (Blumer, 1969; Schwandt, 2001).

Purpose and Background

In this chapter we focus on the topics, practices, issues, and controversies embedded in methodologies associated with interpretive research. We locate interpretive research after Lather and St. Pierre (as cited in Lather, 2006) within a paradigm focused on *understanding* (e.g., naturalistic, constructivist, phenomenological, ethnographic, symbolic interactionist methods) in contrast to *predicting* (e.g., positivist, post-positivist), *emancipating* (e.g., critical, neomarxist, feminist/gendered studies, critical race theory, Freirian action research, critical ethnography), or *deconstructing* (e.g., post-structural, post-colonial, post-critical, discourse analysis, post-humanist). The advantage in using Lather and St. Pierre's perspective on paradigmatic differences (Lather, 2006) is that it calls attention to the unlikelihood of any one paradigm providing a complete view of reading disabilities.

Historically, reading research could be characterized as largely reflecting positivist and post-positivist thinking aimed at predicting outcomes. Gray (1922), Huey (1908), and Thorndike (1914, 1917) laid the foundations for measuring reading achievement, remediation, and comprehension. Measures of eye-movements and perceptual processes predicted that reading practices will vary with the reader's purpose, interests, and reading material (Buswell, 1920; Judd & Buswell, 1922). Gates (1921, 1927), who contributed experimental measures of reading speed and levels of comprehension, paved the way for studying reading disabilities. These measures enabled researchers to establish correlations among reading disabilities, cognitive disorders, and reading difficulties. Decades later, Clay (1966, 1969, 1979) used naturalistic inquiry to understand why students who experienced difficulty reading were not benefiting from instruction and what could be done about it. Calls for situating disabilities within emancipatory or critical (Shannon, 1991) and deconstructive (Tisdale, 2008) paradigms are fairly recent and depart from the positivistic and post-positivistic views of reading disabilities that have historically shaped the field. Although shifts in research paradigms do not necessarily represent progress or refinement, they do offer different ways of generating knowledge by connecting social theory (Habermas, 1971; Lather, 1991) to research methodologies.

Reading Disabilities across Research Paradigms

The concept of a reading disability looks different across research paradigms. Researchers working within a positivist/post-positivist paradigm assume that a child's reading disability is real, that it is inherently a part of the child—something that can be objectified, measured, and possibly fixed. Although researchers who situate their work within an interpretive paradigm may also hold to the reality of a reading disability, their interest is in understanding how individuals with reading disabilities and the people with whom they interact make sense of their various circumstances. Within a critical paradigm, researchers focus on the sociopolitical structures within educational institutions and society at large (e.g., race, gender, and class) that contribute to the existence of a reading disability; their goal is to emancipate individuals labeled with a reading disability from oppressive structures. Researchers using post-structural theories contest a simplified notion of reading disability and seek to deconstruct and expose unexamined assumptions about the very structures that maintain the existence of a reading disability. In this chapter, which is focused on a review of the literature on reading disabilities within an interpretive paradigm, we do not claim an inherent benchmark of quality for interpretive research. Rather, our goal is to use interpretive research as an entry point for considering the possibilities of a research agenda that complicates the study of reading disabilities.

The Literature Search Process

First, using the University of Georgia's Electronic Journal Locator, we compiled a list of 35 journals associated with reading disability areas (e.g., learning disabilities, special educational psychology, and language and literacy education). Second, we conducted a computerized search of these journals using Galileo, an interface of databases (e.g., Academic Search Complete, ERIC, JSTOR). Third, we used search engines (Google and Google Scholar) to deepen and broaden our list of articles on reading disabilities research within an interpretive paradigm. Descriptors for the computerized searches included *reading disability*, *reading disorder*, *reading difficulty*, or simply *reading* cross-searched with a particular disabilities journal (e.g., *Journal of Learning Disabilities*). Finally, we hand-searched the second edition of the *Handbook of Educational Psychology* (Alexander & Winne, 2006) and the third volume of the *Handbook of Reading Research* (Kamil, Mosenthal,

Pearson, & Barr, 2000) to locate studies that might have escaped our computerized search.

Interpretive Research in the Literature on Reading Disabilities

An early definition of *reading disability*—one that received considerable attention in the field of general education—depended on finding a discrepancy between reading ability and intelligence (Education for All Handicapped Children Act, PL 94-142, 1975). The usefulness of an intelligence-based definition has been debated but with little consensus as to outcome (Schell, 1992; Stanovich, 1991, 1992a, 1992b). Some scholars (e.g., Christensen, 1992) question if definitional work should even be a priority. Dissension exists about what counts as a reading disability (Fuchs, Mock, Morgan, & Young, 2003; Shaywitz & Shaywitz, 2005; Sternberg & Grigorenko, 2002; Vellutino, Scanlon, & Tanzman, 1998). According to Allington (2002), states' decisions to exempt scores earned by low-achieving readers on high stakes assessments created even more confusion about the definition of *reading disability*. More recently, the Individuals with Disabilities Education Improvement Act (IDEA, 2004), de-emphasized the intelligence-discrepancy factor and opened the door to Response-to-Intervention (RTI) as a way of identifying students with learning disabilities.

Discrepancies in how reading disabilities are defined affect to no small degree the type of research paradigm that researchers deem viable. Definitions compatible with an interpretive paradigm include those that claim reading disabilities are largely socially (McGill-Franzen, 1987) and culturally (Kliewer & Biklen, 2001) constructed. Other definitions of reading disability, not grounded in sociocultural perspectives but still compatible with an interpretive paradigm, look for ways of mediating or changing the context in which readers with disabilities learn, rather than "fixing" the readers per se (Klenk & Kibby, 2000; Lipson & Wixson, 1986). Acknowledging that while "neurological dysfunction plays a role in certain cases of reading disability," Lipson and Wixson (1986, p. 112) maintained the majority of students with reading disabilities do not fall within that category. Thus, they argued, an interactionist perspective on reading (dis)ability—one that predicted "variability in performance within individuals across texts, tasks, and settings" (p. 120)—was better suited to understanding variation in children's textual processing.

One thing these nonmedical-model definitions of reading disability share is their emphasis on setting or context. It comes as no surprise, then, that researchers who work within an interpretive paradigm rely to a large extent on definitions that take sociocultural views of reading disability into account. Using naturalistic, ethnographic, symbolic interactionist, conversation analysis, narrative inquiry, phenomenological, and mediational methodologies, researchers proceed on the assumption that a reading disability, while real, is best understood by studying the contexts in which it occurs and the sense that people make of it. Social constructions of reading disabilities, not individuals' so-called bodily impairments, are the focus of attention.

When research on reading disabilities is distinguished from the larger literature on learning disabilities, the number of relevant studies conducted within the interpretive paradigm is quite small by comparison. Being familiar with a recent review of qualitative research in special education (Brantlinger, Jimenez, Klingner, Pugach, & Richardson, 2005) in which the authors pointed to the long and established history of interpretive research in that field, we had assumed we would find a reasonably large number of studies related to reading disabilities given that close to 80% of all children referred for placement in special education are thought to have a reading disability (Hallahan, Kauffman, & Lloyd, 1999). Such was not the case, however. Our search results pointed to a much smaller body of research from which to draw implications than we would like. To qualify for review in this chapter, a study's participants had to be students identified in one of three ways: as having a reading disability; as having learning disabilities associated with reading difficulties; or as reading at least two grade levels below actual grade placement as determined by scores earned on a standardized reading achievement test or on a mandated statewide assessment of reading proficiency.

Naturalistic Approach   A large naturalistic study conducted in the United Kingdom by Lacey, Layton, Miller, Goldbart, and Lawson (2007) is of particular interest because of its focus on the National Literacy Strategy, and more particularly the Literacy Hour, which have counterparts in the United States in No Child Left Behind Act of 2001 (NCLB, 2002) and Reading First, respectively. One of Lacey et al.'s goals was to learn how teachers taught reading and writing to students with severe learning difficulties under the required guidelines of the National Literacy Strategy. The Literacy Hour, a prescriptive and explicit approach to literacy instruction, included 15 minutes of whole-class shared reading and writing, 15 minutes of grammar and phonics, 20 minutes of guided reading or writing, and a 10-minute wrap up. The researchers visited 35 schools (including primary, secondary and all-age special schools) that were charged with educating students with severe learning difficulties. After observing 122 lessons, interviewing 61 teachers, and examining their paperwork, the researchers consulted with 10 focus groups comprised of teachers and literacy experts. Overall, they found that regardless of school setting, teachers used both printed texts and other media (pictures, film), though conventional alphabetic literacy lessons prevailed. They also found that the contexts for learning did not vary greatly because teachers at all levels appeared to follow the National Literacy Strategy rather strictly, believing that even small gains in conventional reading and writing skills were beneficial for students with severe learning difficulties.

In Hall's (2007) study of three middle grades students who were reading two or more grade levels below actual grade placement, context was once again the focus. In this instance, the students' attempts to develop and maintain what they perceived as appropriate identities within their peer group both in and out of school settings took precedence over what their teachers required of them in terms of learning from content area texts. In Hall's interpretation of why the three students (all girls) maintained a culture of silence, she was careful to point out why appearances of disinterest or lack of motivation should not be conflated with cognitive difficulties in processing text. Similar to Hall's findings are those reported by Cousin, Aragon, and Rojas (1993). In their year-long study of Carl, an eighth-grade male student identified with learning disabilities, they learned that different social contexts within the classroom provided Carl with different ways of performing a literate identity. In settings where he could link his out-of-school knowledge and interests to in-school academic content, Carl exhibited more sophisticated reading and writing behaviors than in settings where he felt insecure and incompetent.

Findings from two studies (Boling, 2007; Richards & Morse, 2002) that used a naturalistic approach to data collection and interpretation at the post-secondary level provide a view of inclusive classrooms and students with reading disabilities from preservice general education teachers' perspectives. This view of how teacher candidates make sense of inclusion offers yet another opportunity to look at the influence of context in relation to reading disabilities. Lydia, the young woman in Boling's (2007) study, provided many examples in her comments during class discussion and written artifacts (e.g., dialogue journal entries, reflections on visits to a local inclusive classroom, and on her own earlier experiences with a classmate who had been diagnosed with an autism spectrum disorder) that she conceived of students with reading disabilities as being "in need of fixing" (p. 222) so that they could perform on par with their peers. Lydia's uncertainty about how to engage in the "fixing" process created frustrations for her that she preferred to avoid and made her resistant to the idea of teaching in an inclusive classroom. However, during her semester-long reading methods class and visits to the local classroom where she observed a teacher working with a child with ADHD, Lydia began to reconsider her original stance toward teaching in an inclusive classroom.

Unlike in Boling's (2007) inclusion study, Alisha, the preservice teacher enrolled in a reading methods class in the Richards and Morse (2002) study, worked in a field placement that separated children with reading disabilities from their general education peers. Like Lydia, however, Alisha was anxious initially about her ability to teach young children who had been identified as learning disabled. Yet based on data collected through observation notes, dialogue journal entries, email correspondence, and videotaped lessons, Richards and Morse were able to show how Alisha's high expectations for her students' success in literacy activities that incorporated digital media, music, and the visual and performing arts overcame obstacles that might otherwise have spelled low self-esteem for students with reading disabilities. In the end, contextual conditions that fostered the children's sense of communicative competence, not the disabilities identified in them as individuals, were what mattered. Moreover, classroom setting seemed not to be a distinguishing factor inasmuch as students separated from their general education peers in a special education setting did well under Alisha's instruction.

Ethnographic Approach   In a 2-year ethnographic study of nine inclusive preschool and kindergarten classes where students with and without disabilities learned together in classrooms with varying levels of inclusivity, Kliewer, Fitzgerald, Meyer-Mork, Hartman, English-Sand, and Raschke (2004) found that children's literacy development depended on contextual factors rather than on labels associated with disabilities. For example, when Steven, a child labeled with an autism spectrum disorder, learned how written words, such as those he and his classmates assembled on posters in a playful but mock protest of the teacher's classroom rules, communicated to others in the school, he also learned what it takes to become a competent citizen of a literate community. The researchers attributed this kind of learning to an environment that encourages teachers and non-labeled children to presume human competence and to expect students with significant disabilities to possess what they call literate potential. Pointing out that segregated classes for young children with severe to moderate disabilities do not present the same opportunities for childhood narratives—pretending, role playing, and dramatizing—Kliewer et al. (2004) argued for educational settings that are inclusive and provide youngsters with disabilities with more than what they call immediate (or physical) need narratives. Their argument is based in what they learned from teachers in inclusive classrooms where a broad range of graphic semiotic systems (not just alphabetic texts) were presented, engaged with, and represented by children with significant disabilities.

Symbolic Interactionist Approach   As this approach gained acceptance in the field of mainstream sociology, which was at one time dominated by positivistic, quantitative researchers, it simultaneously attracted researchers from other fields, but not without some significant changes and fragmentation to its core concepts, according to Fine (1993). Here we examine how symbolic interactionsim has been used by one reading researcher (O'Brien, 2001) to understand how Dan, a high school student identified as having a reading disability, was able to demonstrate literate competence in a lab setting that engaged him in authoring multimedia texts quite distinct from the texts he was required to read in his regular classroom placement.

Dan's reading level as assessed by a standardized reading achievement test administered statewide placed him among the lowest 8% of his 2,200 high school classmates, which according to the state was at approximately the second grade level. Decoding and word recognition difficulties created problems for Dan when he tried unsuccessfully to comprehend his assigned textbooks. In stark contrast to his lack of success with academic texts, Dan appeared competent and creative in the literacy lab where he produced a multimedia documentary that featured Ozzy Osbourne, a heavy metal musician, who, despite his artistic talent, struggled privately and publicly with personal tragedy and success. According to O'Brien (2001), in a school context where literate competency was not restricted to the narrow definition associated with print literacy, Dan was able to apply his own artistic talents in a way that communicated to others what he understood but could not express in words alone. Using symbolic interactionism as his theoretical lens enabled O'Brien (2001) to show how constructions of literate competency can vary from one setting to another in the same school.

Conversation Analysis Approach   Opportunities for self-expression in inclusive classrooms are integral to carrying on conversations about texts of all kinds. In an effort to learn how such conversations encourage students to take a more active role in constructing meaning through classroom discussion, Berry and Englert (2005) applied conversation analysis techniques to two videotaped book discussions in a first- and second-grade inclusion classroom. Claiming that children with language and learning disabilities, compared to their general education peers, experience more difficulties in initiating and maintaining discussion topics and taking turns talking, the researchers introduced a four-phase discussion strategy in which the teacher apprenticed her students into a novel participant structure that required collaborations around topic selection and the negotiation of a book's meaning. Conversation analysis provided Berry and Englert (2005) with evidence that children with language and learning disabilities could assume some of the same leadership roles as their general education peers when appropriate support through collaborative book discussions is provided over an extended period of time.

Narrative Inquiry Approach   One common assumption about narrative inquiry "is that people are storytellers, who lead storied lives" (Brantlinger et al., 2005, p. 199). Finding a way to draw on her own and others' storied experiences as students with learning disabilities who made it through high school and went on to community college, the author (Faber, 2006) focused her dissertation study on three individuals, two of whom (Quinton and Rana) had been identified as dyslexic in high school. In noting a growing concern in the United States that students identified with disabilities in high school are unlikely to be successful in college, Faber sought to explore Quinton and Rana's life stories within the context of their developing a sense of self-determination, much as she had done as a student. Stating that she settled on narrative inquiry as an approach because it provided an "opportunity for the voices of the participants to be heard and understood" (pp. 70–71), Faber relied on Clandinin and Connelly's (2000) method for finding patterns, narrative threads, and themes that were common across her participants. Her findings, as told through the voices of Quinton and Rana (but filtered through her lens as researcher), suggest that these two individuals had not felt sufficiently challenged in their pre-college years; nor had they developed the self-esteem they said they needed to be self-determining. However, community college was a different story. Largely through support services provided by the community college, both were developing strategies for becoming more self-determined learners.

Phenomenological Approach   Interestingly, as was the case for reading disabilities research that used narrative inquiry, the only reading disabilities study to use a phenomenological approach that we could find was an unpublished dissertation on a community volunteer tutoring program called *Reading Matters* (Haynes, 2004); however, there are published phenomenological studies of learning disabilities not explicitly attributed to reading difficulty (e.g., Worley & Cornett-DeVito, 2007). Although Waite, Bromfield, and McShane (2005) have argued for a phenomenological approach to studying inclusive classrooms on the basis that "evaluation of inclusion [programs] requires an inclusive methodology" (p. 85)—one that honors stakeholders' voices—reading disabilities researchers seem not to have taken up that call, at least not yet. A major purpose of Haynes's study was to uncover the characteristics of *Reading Matters* that accounted for student success. Her participants included a program coordinator, a principal, eight classroom teachers, three volunteers, and five students from a rural elementary school. Data sources included interviews and field notes of observations of 40 tutoring sessions (each lasting 30 minutes and involving students in reciprocal read-alouds) during the spring, summer, and fall of 2003. Positive mentoring relationships and flexibility in scheduling were among several characteristics that Haynes attributed to students generally showing improvement in reading as measured by the Slosson Oral Reading Test – Revised (SORT-R).

Mediational Approach   As noted earlier, focusing on ways of mediating or changing the context in which readers with disabilities learn, rather than on "fixing" the readers per se, reflects current thinking in the field. Mediational approaches call for moving beyond fruitless searches for some method (or magic bullet, if you will) that promises to "fix" students' so-called deficits in reading. Two studies that were representative of a mediational approach to researching reading disabilities are discussed next.

First was a study by Goatley, Brock, and Raphael (1995) that involved a diverse group of five fifth-grade students in small-group, student-led literature discussions for the purpose of exploring the strategies they used to construct meaning of a popular novel by Katherine Paterson, a well-known author of children's literature. One of the five students, Stark, had been identified as having learning disabilities and had spent a year and a half in pull-out special education programs prior to being placed in a fifth-grade inclusive classroom. In this new setting, Stark did not have

the services provided in his former resource room (one-on-one teacher-directed instruction); instead, he had to learn to interact with his peers and negotiate book club discussions that required students to use their prior knowledge to predict certain characters' actions in the novel. He also had to take responsibility for his own learning by asking appropriate questions based on the novel. The researchers' documentation and interpretation of Stark's learning strategies, which differed remarkably from those he displayed in the resource room, provides insight into how re/mediation works.

The second study (Kos, 1991) focused on four middle school students (all of whom had been identified as having reading disabilities) and their perceptions of why they had not made better progress in reading. Unlike Goatley and her colleagues (1995), Kos was interested in students' retrospective interpretations of various contextual factors thought to have contributed to their reading difficulties. Primarily through the examination of students' previous reading records and open-ended interviews with each student during her twice-weekly tutoring sessions of 45–60 minutes each, Kos was able to piece together information for multiple case studies. When interpreted through cross-case analysis using grounded theory, students' perceptions of their lack of progress in reading pointed to their ineffective use of reading strategies; to their sense of having received inadequate reading instruction; and to what they described as reading-related stress. The researcher's documentation of the four students' educational histories, as well as interviews with their teachers, corroborated the students' perceptions of their difficulties in reading.

Looking Beyond the Interpretive Perspective to Other Paradigms

Using social theory within an interpretive paradigm to account for how people understand reading disabilities is helpful in that it reveals how different social contexts construct disability differently. Yet, as Eisner (1993) has aptly reminded us, theory "not only reveals, it conceals" (p. viii). Because the realities produced by socially constructed reading disabilities are no less oppressive than those openly objectified and studied from a positivist, or medical view, of disability, there is a need to research policies that inadvertently put students with reading disabilities at a disadvantage. Gregg (2007) heightened awareness of this need among adolescents and adults identified with reading disabilities who are in transition from secondary to postsecondary schooling. As one example, Gregg documented how policies that depend on accurate measurement of reading comprehension to determine students' eligibility for accommodations are often compromised when the tests themselves are invalid (e.g., when students can answer questions without reading a test passage).

In tracing policies that have historically determined who can (and cannot) be judged competently literate, Kliewer, Biklen, and Kasa-Hendrickson (2006) used what they termed a *critical interpretivist* frame (or what Lather, 2006, referred to as simply critical) to examine four themes of "literate disconnection" (p. 167) that are "associated with society's ongoing denial of literate citizenship for people with perceived intellectual disabilities" (p. 163). The first theme of making literate possibility invisible can be illustrated with two historical examples. During the lifetimes of Phillis Wheatley (an 18th century poet and slave from Africa) and Helen Keller (a child with profound visual and auditory disabilities), the predominant beliefs and policies of the time rendered the literacy of these women invisible, as evidenced by the struggle to publish their works. The second theme involves making disability a static construct and holds that once a person is identified as having a disability, the "categorized individual [is viewed as] simple, one dimensional, dormant, stalled, and fossilized" (Kliewer et al., 2006, p. 175). The third theme, namely censuring and dismissing literate competence, points to how society denigrates the accomplishments of a categorized individual. The fourth theme is perhaps the most pernicious of all four themes. It is the practice of making a categorized individual prove his or her literate competence by using "criteria of proof…determined by those who [hold] authority without consulting the needs or interests of the person whose capacities [are] suspect" (Kliewer et al., 2006, p. 169). By using a *critical interpretivist* frame, Kliewer and his colleagues made known their intent to mobilize a moral stance against society's proclivity to disenfranchise the literate lives of individuals with profound disabilities.

For other scholars in the disabilities field, the emancipatory/critical theory paradigm, which exposes structural inequities and advocates for liberating categorized individuals from oppressive conditions, does not go far enough. Garland-Thomson (2002), for example, has made a case for reading disabled bodies by complicating what feminist theorists refer to as the gaze. Based on the assumption that men act and women appear (Berger, 1972), the gaze theorizes that a (male) viewer looks at a (female) body and in doing so objectifies the body as a thing of pleasure that exists to serve his desire in looking (Mulvey, 1975). By relegating the body as an object, the body lacks agency and has only the identity that the viewer deems appropriate to his wants of any given moment. Garland-Thomson (2002), calling for deconstruction of the terms *woman* and *disabled*, complicated the critical feminist discourse of the gaze. Unlike a gaze that molds the objectified body to the changing desires of the viewer, Garland-Thompson theorized the gaze as a stare that continually produces and intensifies a disabled person's identity as disabled. However, once the term *disabled* is deconstructed, the stare does not reify the disabled body as being one thing—disabled; instead it reinforces the notion that differences are "normal" and to be expected in the span of human variation.

In a similar vein, Titchkosky (2005) argued for deconstructing the notion of disability as a limit without possibility. This deconstructive turn posits that by reading certain bodies—those identified as impaired—through the lens of a disability studies perspective, one can represent impairment as *both* limit and possibility. Arguing against an interpretivist or social model of reading disabilities that would have us believe "being disabled (or being a woman) is simply what the individual makes of it" (p. 665), Titchkosky maintained "the body is a way of being even if this way is ordered, organized and oppressed by its situation" (p. 666). Like Titchkosky, Paterson and Hughes (1999) critiqued work within an interpretive paradigm, roundly rejecting the notion of an impaired body "as a passive recipient of social forces" (p. 601). They also rejected the idea that disability studies can support disembodied views of impairment. Looking beyond the interpretive paradigm reinforces the body as materially important.

Implications

This literature review has established that interpretive reading disabilities research is ensconced within a social model of disabilities—one that relies on social theory to understand how people's perceptions of a reading disability change as the educational context changes. It could be said that interpretive research, like research conducted within a positivist/post-positivist paradigm (the medical model), is a partial response to understanding reading disabilities. Although research conducted within an emancipatory framework moves the conversation about reading disabilities beyond understanding how setting or context matters, toward envisioning changes in policies that dictate oppressive practices and marginalize students with reading difficulties, it doesn't go far enough in some scholars' eyes. For those whose work has a deconstructive bent, the goal is to dismantle sociohistorical, linguistic, and economic structures that produce reading disabilities in order to substitute a more complicated picture—one that reconstructs disabilities as both possibility and limit. This "neither/nor" but "both/and" approach to researching reading disabilities suggests at least three implications for future research.

One implication is that scholarship in the field of reading disabilities is likely to continue to look to research paradigms that go beyond attempts to simply understand a social construct such as disability. *Disability* is a broad term that characterizes people who have physical and/or cognitive capacities different from an expected norm. Working in an interpretive paradigm, researchers who view disability as a socially constructed phenomenon and allow the impaired body to retreat to "little more than flesh and bones" (Paterson & Hughes, 1999, p. 600), stand to negate the physically disabled body that makes it so visible in society. If a physical disability can fade, or at least become invisible to researchers, then the dangers of invisibility are even worse for an individual with an already invisible cognitive disability.

Making a cognitive disability part of the contextual social scenery has serious consequences beyond a lack of visibility. Social theories operating within an interpretive paradigm imply that a person with a disability (or that person's social circle comprised of individuals with good intentions) could in effect ignore the disability under the guise of treating everyone the same. Another consequence is that the disability is only what that person (or the person's social circle) makes of it. Therefore, if a person with a disability "fails," the onus for such a failure resides in that person and the people within her or his immediate context. The resulting burden, that of adjusting teaching and learning contexts to alleviate the effects of the disability, may be extremely taxing and unrelenting on individuals involved.

Including emancipatory and deconstructive paradigms in reading disabilities research will increase visibility of cognitive difficulties and the disabling conditions of people with disabilities. Giving a cognitive reading disability primacy in research does not impose a shackle on people with disabilities, but it does acknowledge that there are experiences that are not entirely within the control of the person with the reading disability. The disability can serve as an entry into policy discussions that offer possibilities for change and opportunities for resistance to sociohistorical, economic, and political structures that are currently not serving people with disabilities. The use of emancipatory and deconstructive paradigms to highlight reading disabilities serves to keep this construct in play and fluid—an antidote of sorts to the static construct that Kliewer et al. (2006) identified in their research on literate competence.

A second implication of the research reviewed here is that any macro-categorization of reading disabilities research is complicated by the very nature of such research. Stated another way, researching how disabilities are understood (a focus of the interpretive paradigm) cannot be separated from researching how to change student learning opportunities (a focus close to, if not congruent with, the emancipatory and deconstuctive paradigms). Although generally helpful, Lather and St. Pierre's categorization of paradigms (see Lather, 2006) did not fully account for the various kinds of studies reported by researchers working within both critical interpretivist and disability studies paradigms. Consequently, in addition to reviewing the interpretive research on reading disabilities, we elected to review representative studies from the emancipatory and deconstructive literature as well.

A third implication rests on the fact that reading disabilities research has traditionally been situated in positivist and post-positivist paradigms that are focused on predicting and explaining outcomes due to various reading interventions. A smaller body of interpretive research aims to understand and adjust the contexts in which the interventions take place. Therefore, on some level, we maintain that the change aspect of educational research is present even when emancipatory and deconstructive paradigms are not. This bit of irony aside, a research agenda for improving learning opportunities for students with reading disabilities can ill afford to overlook the possibilities for change inherent in both emancipatory and desconstructive work.

Such work is never innocent, however, and when undertaken comes with its own set of precautions. For instance, scholarly attempts to deconstruct the term *reading disability*

without first inviting people with this kind of disability into the conversation can produce a rhetoric that is taken up by others in the academy and yet have little or no positive, long-term impact on the lives of those with reading disabilities. Including people with disabilities in meaningful and productive ways in one's research agenda opens up opportunities for them to participate in their own reconstruction. There is something to be said for an agenda that keeps the disability in the research, not separated from the body that houses it. To do otherwise is to deny people with reading disabilities the right to question the underlying assumptions of the texts that produced them as disabled in the first place, and to advocate on their own behalf. This research is difficult work. It may not produce a sizeable literature on reading disabilities; moreover, the rate at which such studies appear may be unusually slow with little hope for more rapid growth. That said, the better marker of research growth may be its complexity and effectiveness in creating a multifaceted picture of reading disabilities.

References

Alexander, P. A., & Winne, P. H. (Eds.). (2006). *Handbook of educational psychology* (2nd ed.). Mahwah, NJ: Erlbaum.

Allington, R. L. (2002). Research on reading/learning disability interventions. In A. E. Farstrup & S. J. Samuels (Eds.), *What research has to say abut reading instruction* (3rd ed., pp. 261–290). Newark, DE: International Reading Association.

Berger, J. (1972). *Ways of seeing*. London: British Broadcasting Corporation & Penguin Books.

Berry, R. A. W., & Englert, C. S. (2005). Designing conversation: Book discussions in a primary inclusion classroom. *Learning Disability Quarterly, 28*(1), 35–58.

Blumer, H. (1969). *Symbolic interactionism*. Englewood Cliffs, NJ: Prentice Hall.

Boling, E. (2007). "Yeah, but I still don't want to deal with it": Changes in a teacher candidate's conceptions of inclusion. *Teaching Education, 18*(3), 217–231.

Brantlinger, E., Jimenez, R., Klingner, J., Pugach, M., & Richardson, V. (2005). Qualitative studies in special education. *Exceptional Children, 71*(2), 195–207.

Buswell, G. T. (1920). An experimental study of the eye-voice span in reading. *Supplementary Educational Monographs*, No 17.

Christensen, C. A. (1992). Commentary: Discrepancy definitions of reading disability: Has the quest led us astray? A response to Stanovich. *Reading Research Quarterly, 27*(3), 276–278.

Clandinin, D. J., & Connelly, F. M. (2000). *Narrative inquiry: Experience and story in qualitative research*. San Francisco: Jossey-Bass.

Clay, M. M. (1966). The reading behavior of five year old children: A research report. *New Zealand Journal of Educational Studies, 2*(1), 11–31.

Clay, M. M. (1969). Reading errors and self-correction behavior. *British Journal of educational Psychology, 39*(1), 47–56.

Clay, M. M. (1979). *The early detection of reading difficulties*. Auckland, New Zealand: Heinemann.

Cousin, P. T., Aragon, E., & Rojas, R. (1993). Creating new conversations about literacy: Working with special needs students in a middle-school classroom. *Learning Disability Quarterly, 16*(4), 282–298.

Education for All Handicapped Children Act of 1975, Pub. L. No. 94-142.

Eisner, E. W. (1993). Foreword. In D. J. Flinders & G. E. Mills (Eds.), *Theory and concepts in qualitative research* (pp. vii–ix). New York: Teachers College Press.

Faber, A. B. (2006). *A narrative inquiry into perceptions of the development of self-determination by community college students with learning disabilities* (Unpublished doctoral dissertation). University of Maryland, College Park, MD.

Fine, G. A. (1993). The sad demise, mysterious disappearance, and glorious triumph of symbolic interactionism. *Annual Review of Sociology, 19*(1), 61–87.

Fuchs, D., Mock, D., Morgan, P. L., & Young, C. L. (2003). Responsiveness-to Intervention: Definitions, Evidence, and Implications for the Learning Disabilities Construct. *Learning Disabilities Research and Practice, 18*(3), 157–171.

Garland-Thomson, R. (2002). Integrating disability, transforming feminist theory. *National Women's Studies Association Journal, 14*(3), 1–32.

Gates, A. I. (1921). An experimental and statistical study of reading and reading tests. *Journal of Educational Psychology, 12*(8), 445–464.

Gates, A. I. (1927). *The improvement of reading: A program of diagnostic and remedial methods*. New York: Macmillan.

Geertz, C. (1973). *The interpretation of cultures*. New York: Basic Books.

Goatley, V. J., Brock, C. H., & Raphael, T. E. (1995). Diverse learners participating in regular education "Book Clubs". *Reading Research Quarterly, 30*(3), 352–380.

Gray, W. S. (1922). Remedial cases in reading: Their diagnosis and treatment. In R. D. Robinson (Ed.), *Readings in reading instruction: Its history, theory, and development* (pp. 206–207). Boston: Pearson.

Green, J., & Bloome, D. (1983). Ethnography and reading: Issues, approaches, criteria, and findings. In J. A. Niles & L. A. Harris (Eds.), *Searches for meaning in reading/language processing and instruction. 32nd Yearbook of the National Reading Conference* (pp. 183–208). Rochester, NY: National Reading Conference.

Gregg, N. (2007). Underserved and unprepared: Postsecondary learning disabilities. *Learning Disabilities Research and Practice, 22*(4), 219–228.

Guba, E. G. (1978). Toward a methodology of naturalistic inquiry in educational evaluation. *CSE Monograph Series in Evaluation, No. 8*.

Guba, E. G., & Lincoln, Y. S. (1989). *Fourth generation evaluation*. Newbury Park, CA: Sage.

Habermas, J. (1971). *Theory and practice*. Boston: Beacon Press.

Hall, L. (2007). Understanding the silence: Struggling readers discuss decisions about reading expository text. *Journal of Educational Research, 100*(3), 132–141.

Hallahan, D., Kauffman, J., & Lloyd, J. (1999). *Introduction to learning disabilities* (2nd ed.). Boston: Allyn and Bacon.

Haynes, L. C. (2004). *Reading matters: A case study of a community volunteer tutoring program* (Unpublished doctoral dissertation). Marshall University, Huntington, West Virginia.

Huey, E. B. (1908). *The psychology and pedagogy of reading*. New York: Macmillan.

Individuals with Disabilities Education Improvement Act of 2004, Pub. L. No. 108-466.

Judd, C. H., & Buswell, G. T. (1922). Silent reading: A study of the various types. *Supplementary Educational Monographs, No 23*.

Kamil, M. L., Mosenthal, P. B., Pearson, P. D., & Barr, R. (Eds.). (2000). *Handbook of reading research* (Volume III). Mahwah, NJ: Erlbaum.

Klenk, L., & Kibby, M. W. (2000). Re-mediating reading difficulties: Appraising the past, reconciling the present, constructing the future. In M. L. Kamil, P. B. Mosenthal, P. David Pearson, & R. Barr (Eds.), *Handbook of reading research:* (Vol. III, pp. 667–690). Mahwah, NJ: Erlbaum.

Kliewer, C., & Biklen, D. (2001). "School's not really a place for reading": A research synthesis of the literate lives of students with severe disabilities. *Journal of the Association for Persons with Severe Handicaps, 26*(1), 1–12.

Kliewer, C., Biklen, D., & Kasa-Hendrickson, C. (2006). Who may be literate? Disability and resistance to the cultural denial of competence. *American Educational Research Journal, 43*(2), 163–192.

Kliewer, C., Fitzgerald, L., Meyer-Mork, J., Hartman, P., English-Sand, P., & Raschke, D (2004). Citizenship for all in the literate community: An ethnography of young children with significant disabilities

in inclusive early childhood settings. *Harvard Educational Review, 74*(4), 373–403.

Kos, R. (1991). Persistence of reading disabilities: The voices of four middle school students. *American Educational Research Journal, 28*(4), 875–895.

Lacey, P., Layton, L., Miller, C., Goldbart, J., & Lawson, H. (2007). What is literacy for students with severe learning difficulties? Exploring conventional and inclusive literacy. *Journal of Research in Special Educational Needs, 7*(3), 149–160.

Lather, P. (1991). *Getting smart: Feminist research and pedagogy with/ in the postmodern*. New York: Routledge.

Lather, P. (2006). Paradigm proliferation as a good thing to think with: Teaching research in education as a wild profusion. *International Journal of Qualitative Studies in Education, 19*(1), 35–57.

Lincoln, Y. S., & Guba, E. (1985). *Naturalistic inquiry*. Beverly Hills, CA: Sage.

Lipson, M. Y., & Wixson, K. K. (1986). Reading disability research: An interactionist perspective. *Review of Educational Research, 56*(1), 111–136.

McGill-Franzen, A. (1987). Failure to learn to read: Formulating a policy problem. *Reading Research Quarterly, 22*(4), 475–490.

Merriam, S. B. (1998). *Qualitative research and case study applications in education*. San Francisco: Jossey-Bass.

Mulvey, L. (1975). Visual pleasure and narrative cinema. *Screen, 16*(3), 6–18.

No Child Left Behind Act of 2001, Pub. L. No. 107-110, 115 Stat. 1425 (2002). Retrieved August 5, 2008, from http://www.ed.gov/policy/ elsec/leg/esea02/index.html

O'Brien, D. (2001, June). "At-risk" adolescents: Redefining competence through the multiliteracies of intermediality, visual arts, and representation. *Reading Online, 4*(11). Retrieved August 8, 2008, from http://www.readingonline.org/newliteracies/lit_index.asp?HREF=/ newliteracies/obrien/index.html

Paterson, K., & Hughes, B. (1999). Disability studies and phenomenology: The carnal politics of everyday life. *Disability & Society, 5*(1), 597–610.

Richards, J. C., & Morse, T. E. (2002, June). One preservice teacher's experiences teaching literacy to regular and special education students. *Reading Online, 5*(10). Retrieved August 11, 2008, from http://www.readingonline.org/articles/art_index.asp?HREF=richards/ index.html

Schwandt, T. A. (2001). *Dictionary of qualitative inquiry* (2nd ed.). Thousand Oaks, CA: Sage.

Schell, L. (1992). Comments on Stanovich (1991). *Reading Research Quarterly, 27*(2), 175.

Shannon, P. (1991). Politics, policy, and reading research. In R. Barr, M. L. Kamil, P. M., & P. D. Pearson (Eds.), *Handbook of reading research: Volume II* (pp. 147–167). New York: Longman.

Shaywitz, S. E., & Shaywitz, B. A. (2005). Dyslexia (specific reading disability). *Biological Psychiatry, 57*(11), 1301–1309.

Spivey, N. N. (1997). *The constructivist metaphor: Reading, writing, and the making of meaning*. San Diego, CA: Academic Press.

Stanovich, K. E. (1991). Discrepancy definitions of reading disability: Has intelligence led us astray? *Reading Research Quarterly, 26*(1), 7–29.

Stanovich, K. E. (1992a). Commentary: Response to Christensen. *Reading Research Quarterly, 27*(3), 279–280.

Stanovich, K. E. (1992b). Stanovich's reply. *Reading Research Quarterly, 26*(2), 175–176.

Sternberg, R. J., & Grigorenko, E. L. (2002). Difference scores in the identification of children with learning disabilities: It's time to use a different method. *Journal of School Psychology, 40*(1), 65–83.

Thorndike, E. L. (1914). The measurement of ability in reading. *Teachers College Record, XV*(4), 1–71.

Thorndike, E. L. (1917). Reading as reasoning: A study of mistakes in paragraph reading. *Journal of Educational Psychology, 8*(6), 323–332.

Tisdale, K. (2008). Disability studies matters. In J. Flood, S. B. Heath, & D. Lapp (Eds.), *Handbook of research on teaching literacy through the communicative and visual arts* (pp. 169–176). London: Prentice Hall.

Titchkosky, T. (2005). Disability in the news: A reconsideration of reading. *Disability & Society, 20*(6), 655–668.

Van Manen, M. (1990). *Researching lived experience: Human science for an action sensitive pedagogy*. Albany: State University of New York.

Vellutino, F. R., Scanlon, D. M., & Tanzman, M. S. (1998). The case for early intervention in diagnosing specific reading disability. *Journal of School Psychology, 36*(4), 367–397.

Waite, S. J., Bromfield, C., & McShane, S. (2005). Successful for whom? A methodology to evaluate and inform inclusive activity in schools. *European Journal of Special Needs Education, 20*(1), 71–88.

Worley, D. W., & Cornett-DeVito, M. (2007). College students with learning disabilities (SWLD) and their responses to teacher power. *Communication Studies, 58*(1), 17–33.

Epilogue

RICHARD L. ALLINGTON
University of Tennessee

Anne and I have been certified reading specialists for 30 plus years and reading researchers for almost that long. Our collaboration on this *Handbook of Reading Disability Research* was the latest of many years as collaborators on a variety of research, development, and publishing ventures.

Our history as reading specialists covers almost the complete time frame that reading specialists have existed, at least as certified education professionals. The passage of the Elementary and Secondary Education Act of 1965 (ESEA) stimulated the development of graduate programs in reading disabilities and the development of state reading specialist certification programs. Legislators intended that Title 1 of ESEA create professional qualifications for a relatively new type of teacher, the Title 1 funded reading teacher. Title 1 funds were then, and remain today, targeted towards schools enrolling many children from low-income families. Title 1 was so targeted because it was clear, even in 1965, that there existed a large reading achievement gap between students from low-income families and other students. That gap still exists today, though it narrowed between 1971 and 1988, according the data from the National Assessment of Educational Progress. Since 1992, however, the achievement gap has remained largely unchanged. By 12th grade the achievement of poor students is approximately 4 years behind that of more advantaged peers.

We have just seen the elimination of Reading First funding from the No Child Left Behind Act of 2001, the most recent reauthorization of the original ESEA Act. Reading First funding was targeted to the highest poverty schools. In order to be eligible for funding, these schools were required to implement a core reading program and interventions that had been designed from "scientifically based, reliable, replicable research." Unfortunately, what these schools often put into place bore scant resemblance to any research base we are familiar with. So, after 8 years of funding and no evidence (save faster nonsense word decoding) that reading achievement was improving in Read-ing First schools, Congress has terminated funding for the Reading First. Congress was, perhaps, also stimulated by several reports from the Office of the Inspector General at the Department of Education, reports that noted corruption and entrepreneurship activities were pervasive among those charged with providing federal direction and guidance (Office of the Inspector General, 2007).

Over the past 30 years and, more recently under the Reading First program, a special education perspective has come to dominate the field of reading disabilities. Anne first noted this shift in a paper published in *Reading Research Quarterly* in 1987. It has only accelerated, in our view, since that time.

Consider the most recent federal initiative that attempts to narrow the reading achievement gap—Response to Intervention (RtI). Currently, we count only 2 professional texts on this topic written by reading specialists (Allington, 2009; Howard, 2009), but 20 plus professional texts on the topic written by special educators or school psychologists. And for those readers who are unaware, RTI is, by law, a general education initiative designed to reduce or eliminate special education classification for children who struggle with reading. But in state after state and district after district RTI is being led by special educators and school psychologists, not by general educators and not by reading specialists. We both worry that RTI may ultimately suffer the same fate as Reading First—budget elimination—for the same reason: a failure to substantively narrow the reading achievement gap between rich/poor students and, more broadly, between students who found early reading success and those who continue to struggle in reading.

But we literally know how to teach virtually all children to read. Currently, however, in many, if not most schools the children who have difficulty with reading are assigned a label, the most common today being "learning disabled" (although we have created lots of other labels as well). Problem is that the research evidence available suggests there are no children with learning disabilities (Mathes et al., 2005; Phillips & Smith, 1997; Scanlon, Vellutino, Small, Fanuele, & Sweeney, 2005; Vellutino et al., 1996). None. There are children who have experienced a "teaching disability" though. In other words, when some children need more intensive and more expert reading instruction, most schools don't provide either. Instead, they label children and then don't worry much about whether they learn to read, if we examine both the outcomes and the reading instruction they do receive.

So, what we attempted in this text was a broad view of the research on struggling readers. We elicited the thinking of experts in the field to explore why some children have more difficulty than others in learning to read and what we need to do to alter their status as struggling readers. Both of us have written books on this topic (Allington, 2006; 2009, McGill-Franzen, 2006), both of us have written chapters on reading disabilities for other handbooks (Allington, 1984, 2002, 2010; Allington & Guice, 1997; Allington & Johnston, 1989; Allington & McGill-Franzen, 1993; Johnston & Allington, 1990; McGill-Franzen, 2000; McGill-Franzen & Goatley, 2001; McGill-Franzen & Love-Zeig, 2008). This book represented our attempt to begin to bring the broad and deep research on reading and reading disabilities to readers in a single volume. We realize we didn't quite achieve that goal because several authors we asked to contribute simply couldn't. So, there are chapters that remain yet unwritten. But the chapters included here address the field of reading disability research broadly—broadly enough we hope to give any reader a firm grounding in what we know today and what we need yet to act upon.

References

Allington, R. L. (1984). Oral reading. In P. D. Pearson (Ed.), *Handbook of reading research, Vol. I* (pp. 829–864). New York: Longman.

Allington, R. L. (2002). Research on reading/learning disability interventions. In A. E. Farstrup & S. J. Samuels (Eds.), *What research says about reading instruction, 3rd ed.* (pp. 261–290). Newark, DE: International Reading Association.

Allington, R. L. (2006). *What really matters for struggling readers: Designing research-based program.* (2nd ed.). Boston: Allyn & Bacon.

Allington, R. L. (2009). *What really matters in response to intervention: Research-based designs.* Boston: Allyn & Bacon.

Allington, R. L. (2010). Recent federal education policy in the United States. In D. Wyse, R. Andrews, & J. V. Hoffman (Eds.), *International handbook of English, language and literacy teaching* (pp. 496–507). New York: Routledge.

Allington, R. L., & Guice, S. (1997). Literature curriculum: Issues of definition and control. In D. J. Flood, S. B. Heath, & Lapp, D. (Ed.), *Handbook of research on teaching literacy through the communicative and visual arts, Vol. I.* (pp. 727–734). New York: Macmillan.

Allington, R. L., & Johnston, P. A. (1989). Coordination, collaboration, and consistency: The redesign of compensatory and special education interventions. In R. Slavin, N. Karweit & N. Malden (Eds.), *Effective programs for students at risk* (pp. 320–354). Boston: Allyn-Bacon.

Allington, R. L., & McGill-Franzen, A. M. (1993). Reading and the mildly handicapped. In T. Husen & N. Postlethwaite (Eds.), *The international encyclopedia of education* (pp. 421–439). Oxford, UK: Pergamon.

Howard, M. (2009). *RTI from all sides: What every teacher needs to know.* Portsmouth, NH: Heinemann.

Johnston, P. A., & Allington, R. L. (1990). Remediation. In P. D. Pearson (Ed.), *Handbook of reading research, vol. II* (pp. 984–1012). New York: Longmans.

McGill-Franzen, A. (1987). Failure to learn to read: Formulating a policy problem. *Reading Research Quarterly, 22,* 475–490.

McGill-Franzen, A. (2000). Policy and instruction: What is the relationship? In M. Kamil, P. Mosenthal, P. D. Pearson, & R. Barr (Eds.), *Handbook of reading research, vol. III* (pp. 891–908). Mahwah, NJ: Erlbaum.

McGill-Franzen, A. (2006). *Kindergarten literacy.* New York: Scholastic.

McGill-Franzen, A., & Goatley, V. (2001). Title 1 and special education: Support for children who struggle to learn to read. In S. Neuman & D. Dickinson (Eds.), *Handbook of early literacy research* (pp. 471–483). New York: Guilford.

McGill-Franzen, A., & Love-Zeig, J. (2008). Drawing to learn: Visual support for developing reading, writing, and concepts for children at risk. In J. Flood, S. B. Heath, & D. Lapp (Eds.), *Handbook of research on teaching literacy through the communicative and visual arts* (Vol. II, pp. 399–411). New York: Erlbaum.

Mathes, P. G., Denton, C. A., Fletcher, J. M., Anthony, J. L., Francis, D. J., & Schatschneider, C. (2005). The effects of theoretically different instruction and student characteristics on the skills of struggling readers. *Reading Research Quarterly, 40*(2), 148–182.

Phillips, G. E., & Smith, P. E. (1997). *A third chance to learn: The development and evaluation of specialized interventions for young children experiencing the greatest difficulty in learning to read.* Wellington, NZ: New Zealand Council for Educational Research.

Scanlon, D. M., Vellutino, F. R., Small, S., G, Fanuele, D. P., & Sweeney, J. M. (2005). Severe reading difficulties — can they be prevented? A comparison of prevention and intervention approaches. *Exceptionality, 13*(4), 209–227.

Vellutino, F. R., Scanlon, D. M., Sipay, E. R., Small, S. G., Pratt, A., Chen, R., et al. (1996). Cognitive profiles of difficult-to-remediate and readily remediated poor readers: Early intervention as a vehicle for distinguishing between cognitive and experiential deficits as basic causes of specific reading disability. *Journal of Educational Psychology, 88*(4), 601–638.

About the Authors

Richard L. Allington is professor of education at the University of Tennessee. He served as president of both the National Reading Conference and the International Reading Association. He has been studying reading disabilities for the past 35 years with a focus on the quality of intervention services provided struggling readers. He was co-recipient, with Anne McGill-Franzen, of the Albert J. Harris Award from the International Reading Association for their contributions to understanding reading/learning disabilities and received the William S. Gray Citation of Merit from IRA for his contributions to the profession. He was elected to membership in the Reading Hall of Fame. He is the author over 100 papers and chapters and several books. He has served, or is serving, on the editorial advisory boards of *Reading Research Quarterly, Review of Educational Research, Journal of Educational Psychology, Journal of Disability Policy Studies, Remedial and Special Education, Journal of Literacy Research, Reading Teacher,* and *Elementary School Journal.*

Janice F. Almasi is the Carol Lee Robertson Endowed Professor of Literacy Education at the University of Kentucky. She was the recipient of the International Reading Association's Outstanding Dissertation of the Year Award in 1994 and the National Reading Conference's Outstanding Student Research Award in 1993. Her research has examined the contexts in which children learn from text, particularly in terms of strategic processes and peer discussion environments. She is currently a co-principal investigator on the evaluation of Kentucky's Striving Readers project. She has published several books, and her research has been published in journals such as: *Reading Research Quarterly, The Journal of Literacy Research, Elementary School Journal,* and *Educational Psychologist.*

S. J. Alt is a doctoral student in the Educational Psychology, PsyFoundations, Learning and Cognition program. She has been awarded the John P. Yackel/American Guidance Service Publishing Internship in educational measurement and evaluation. Her work has been published in the *Journal of Statistics Education.* She is currently writing her doctoral dissertation entitled "What Differentiates a Fluent Reader from a Non-Fluent Reader and How Should We Assess It: Implications for the Classroom."

Donna E. Alvermann is a University of Georgia Appointed Distinguished Research Professor of Language and Literacy Education. Her chapter in the *Handbook of Reading Research: Volume III* focuses on narrative as an interpretive approach to literacy research, and a co-authored chapter (with George Hruby) on fictive representation as an alternative method for reporting research appears in the *Handbook of Research on Teaching the English Language Arts* (2nd edition). Alvermann has served as editor of *Reading Research Quarterly* and president of the National Reading Conference (NRC). She was elected to the Reading Hall of Fame, and is the recipient of NRC's Oscar Causey Award for Outstanding Contributions to Reading Research, College Reading Association's Laureate Award, and the Herr Award for Contributions to Research in Reading Education. She received the International Reading Association's William S. Gray Citation of Merit and the American Reading Forum's Brenda Townsend Service Award.

Steve Amendum is an assistant professor of literacy education at North Carolina State University. He teaches courses on literacy research and methods in the elementary education undergraduate and masters programs. His research focuses on early literacy intervention for struggling learners, literacy issues for multilingual learners, and classroom-based literacy instruction reform efforts. As a former K-2 multiage teacher and literacy coach, Dr. Amendum's research interests are grounded in classroom experiences and exchanges with students and teachers in diverse classroom and school settings.

Patricia Anders is the Jewell M. Lewis Distinguished Professor of Reading in the Department of Teaching, Learning and Sociocultural Studies and the Program of Language, Reading and Culture at the University of Arizona. Her scholarship focuses on adolescent literacy and literacy teacher education. Noteworthy publications include "Teaching Reading Teachers: A Critical Review of the Literature" (with Risko et al.), "Using Interactive Teaching and Learning Strategies to Promote Text Comprehension and Content Learning for Students with Learning Disabilities" (with C. Bos), and "The Relationship Between Teachers' Beliefs and Practices in Reading Comprehension" (with V. Richardson). She is a past International Reading Association board member and will be President of the National Reading Conference, 2011.

Diane Barone is a foundation professor of literacy at the University of Nevada, Reno. Her research has always focused on young children's literacy development and instruction in high poverty schools. She has conducted two longitudinal studies of literacy development: one, a 4-year study of children prenatally exposed to crack/cocaine and two, a 7-year study of children, predominantly English Language Learners, in a high-poverty school. She has had articles published in journals such as *Reading Research Quarterly, Journal of Literacy Research, Elementary School Journal, The Reading Teacher, Gifted Childhood Quarterly*, and *Research in the Teaching of English*. She has written several books, among them are: *Developing Literacy, Resilient Children, Teaching Early Literacy: Development, Assessment, and Instruction, Research-Based Practices in Early Literacy, Improving Student Writing, K-8, Writing without Boundaries*, and *Using Your Core Reading Program and Children's Literature K-3 and 4-6*. She served as the Editor of *Reading Research Quarterly*. She has just completed terms as a board member of the International Reading Association and the National Reading Conference.

James F. Baumann is the Chancellor's Chair for Excellence in Literacy Education at the University of Missouri–Columbia. His research and theoretical papers, which have focused on elementary and middle-grade classroom reading instruction, have appeared in *Reading Research Quarterly, American Educational Research Journal, Educational Researcher, Reading Research and Instruction, Reading Psychology, Journal of Reading Behavior,* and *Elementary School Journal*. He has published applied research and papers in the *Reading Teacher, Journal of Reading*, and *Journal of Adolescent & Adult Literacy*, and has co-authored chapters in the *Handbook of Reading Research, Handbook of Research on Teaching the English Language Arts*, and *Handbook of Research on Teaching Literacy Through the Communicative and Visual Arts*. His recent research on vocabulary instruction has been funded by an International Reading Association Elva Knight Grant and U.S. Department of Education Field Initiated Studies and the Institute of Education Sciences grants.

Rita Bean is Professor Emerita, School of Education, University of Pittsburgh. She has studied extensively the role of the reading specialist and literacy coach. Her research interests also include professional development for elementary teachers of reading, and approaches for working with struggling readers. Dr. Bean is Co-Director of the external evaluation team for Reading First in Pennsylvania. She has published on the topics of reading curriculum, professional development, and roles of reading specialists. Her newest book, *The Reading Specialist: Leadership for the Classroom, School, and Community* addresses the varied roles and responsibilities of reading specialists/literacy coaches. Dr. Bean was a member of the Board, International Reading Association, and President, College Reading Association.

Sherry Mee Bell is an Associate Professor at the University of Tennessee with over 25 years' experience in education and assessment of exceptional students, particularly those with learning disabilities. An experienced special educator and psychologist, her scholarship interests include assessment and instruction in reading, especially for children and adults who struggle; education of gifted students; attributional style, and teacher education. Dr. Bell is author of numerous articles in the *Journal of Learning Disabilities, Assessment for Effective Intervention, Psychology in the Schools,* and *Journal of Adolescent and Adult Literacy*. She served as guest co-editor of the *International Dyslexia Association's Perspectives* on adult literacy and is co-author of *The Handbook of Reading Assessment and Assessment of Reading Instructional Knowledge-Adults*.

Susan M. Benner is professor and department head for Theory and Practice in Teacher Education at the University of Tennessee. Dr. Benner has published three textbooks, including *Issues in Special Education within the Context of American Society*, and *Assessment of Young Children with Special Needs*. She is a co-editor for the *Journal of Early Childhood Teacher Education*. Dr. Benner's areas of interest are teacher education, including special and literacy education, and urban teaching. She is principal investigator for several grants, including one focused on teacher professional development in literacy. She is co-principal investigator for a NSF Robert Noyce Scholarship Planning Grant to develop urban teacher residency programs.

Andrew Biemiller taught at the Institute of Child Study, University of Toronto for 36 years, retiring June, 2004. He was responsible for the teacher education program at the Institute of Child Study for 15 years. His recent research has concerned what word meanings are acquired, the order of meanings acquired, and effective methods of teaching word meanings. His current research concerns identifying word meanings that are particularly useful for instruction at the primary and upper-elementary levels. He published *Words Worth Teaching,* which summarizes this work. He has served as an associate editor of the *Journal of Educational Psychology* and is active as an educational consultant to the

U.S. Institute of Education Science, U.S. National Institute of Child and Human Development, publishers, state departments of education, and researchers.

Stergios Botzakis is an assistant professor of adolescent literacy in the Theory and Practice in Teacher Education Department at the University of Tennessee. His research interests focus on middle grades reading, content area reading, working with struggling adolescent readers, and graphic novels. Prior to life in academia, he spent 5 years teaching middle school reading, English, and study skills in Baltimore and the Boston area. He was one of the founding editors for the online *Journal of Language and Literacy Education.* He has been published in *Reading Research Quarterly, Teacher Education Quarterly, Journal of Adolescent & Adult Literacy,* and has written several book chapters on middle grades literacy and graphic novels. He also has published two children's books: *Pretty in Print: Questioning Magazines* and *What's Your Source?: Questioning the News.*

Amy D. Broemmel is an Associate Professor in the Department of Theory and Practice in Teacher Education at the University of Tennessee where she coordinates the elementary teacher education program. Supporting the work of teachers is the underlying purpose of her research, which focuses on the preparation and continued support of critically thinking teachers, often through a systematic examination of what teachers themselves have to say. She is currently engaged in an effort to build and support a 3-year collaborative venture with an elementary school where the teachers have been given the opportunity to determine the focus of their own professional development.

Melissa Brydon is a doctoral student in Reading Education at the University of Pittsburgh. She received her master's of science and bachelor's of science degrees in speech-language pathology from Indiana University of Pennsylvania. Prior to her doctoral studies, she worked as a pediatric speech-language pathologist in outpatient, school-based, and home-based early intervention settings. For the past 2 years she has served as the assistant director of the Reading Center at the University of Pittsburgh. Her research interests include emergent language and literacy development and teacher preparation.

Renée M. Casbergue holds the Vira Franklin and James R. Eagle Professorship in the Department of Education Theory, Policy, and Practice at Louisiana State University. She has published journal articles, chapters, and books about early literacy development and instruction. She is especially interested in early writing development and is coauthor of *Writing in Preschool: Learning to Orchestrate Meaning and Marks.* Her most recent research has focused on the relationships among teachers' professional development, their knowledge or early literacy, and gains in children's literacy and language as measured by stan-

dardized assessments. That research is continuing within her Early Reading First project in the New Orleans Public Schools.

Louis Chen is a second language educator and researcher who conducts research in the area of content reading and second language teaching and learning. He has served as a researcher on a large funded project that explores ESL students and multi-literacies. He has an M.A. degree from the University of British Columbia and a Ph.D. from the University of Toronto.

David Cihak is an Assistant Professor at the University of Tennessee in the Department of Theory and Practice in Teacher Education. His research areas include effective instructional strategies and positive behavioral supports for students with multiple and severe disabilities, including autism spectrum disorders. In addition, David serves on the editorial review board for *Focus on Autism and Other Developmental Disabilities* and the *Journal of Special Education Technology.*

Eric Dion is a professor of special education at the University du Quebec at Montreal, Montreal, Quebec, Canada, and Director of the Research Group on Evidence-Based Teaching Strategies. His research focuses on the use of classwide peer-mediated activities and small-group instruction to prevent reading disabilities among beginning readers from low-income families.

Hannah M. Dostal is a doctoral student at the University of Tennessee, Knoxville in the area of literacy studies. She is a licensed reading specialist (preK-12). Hannah is currently teaching middle school language arts at Tennessee School for the Deaf; she also has experience teaching in multi-grade residential and counseling settings. Hannah's research interests include examining the impact of interactive instruction on the language development of deaf adolescents.

Susan Dougherty is an Assistant Professor of Literacy Education at Rutgers University. Her research interests focus on explanatory talk in parent-child and teacher-student conversations and on the training of elementary teachers and reading specialists. Recently, she developed and investigated the impact of Dads Read, a book club for children and their male mentors, which is conducted at an urban public school.

Reginald D'Silva is a Ph.D. student in the Language and Literacy Education Department at the University of British Columbia, Canada. His research interests involve the role of digital technologies in promoting literacy skills. His dissertation deals with the use of voice recognition software to scaffold reading performance of English Language Learners He is also interested in issues related to literacy education in the South Asian context.

Nell K. Duke is professor of teacher education and educational psychology, an affiliate of the program in school psychology, and co-director of the Literacy Achievement Research Center at Michigan State University. Duke's work focuses on early literacy development, particularly among children living in poverty. Her specific areas of expertise include development of informational literacies in young children, comprehension development and instruction in early schooling, and issues of equity in literacy education. Duke is the recipient of the American Educational Research Association Early Career Award as well as awards for research from the National Reading Conference, the National Council of Teachers of English, and the International Reading Association. She also has a strong interest in improving educational research training in the United States.

Jacqueline Edmondson is Associate Dean for Teacher Education and Undergraduate Programs at Pennsylvania State University and Associate Professor of Education in the Language, Culture, and Society program. Her research focuses on reading education policy, critical theory, teacher education, rural schools and communities, and biography for adolescent readers.

John Elkins is Emeritus Professor at The University of Queensland and Adjunct Professor of Literacy at Griffith University In Brisbane, Australia. He served on the Board of Directors of the International Reading Association, was president of the Australian Reading Association and edited the *Journal of Adolescent and Adult Literacy* and the *International Journal of Disability, Development and Education*. His research interests include reading difficulties and inclusive education.

Jill Fitzgerald is Senior Associate Dean and Professor of Literacy Studies at the University of North Carolina at Chapel Hill. She has published over 70 works and been an invited speaker at national and international research and professional conferences. Her current primary research interests center on literacy issues for multilingual learners and early literacy development in relation to literacy-instruction reform efforts. She received the American Educational Research Association's Outstanding Review of Research Award and (with George Noblit) the International Reading Association's Dina Feitelson Award for Research. She currently serves on editorial boards for several national and international journals, including *Journal of Educational Psychology*, *Reading Research Quarterly*, and *Research in the Teaching of English*.

Margaret Flores is an assistant professor in the Department of Special Education Rehabilitation Counseling at Auburn University. Her research interests include reading and mathematics instruction for students with autism spectrum disorders and specific learning disabilities. Prior to her career in higher education, Dr. Flores worked in a variety of instructional settings as a special education teacher.

Katherine K. Frankel is a doctoral student in the Language, Literacy, and Culture program in the Graduate School of Education at the University of California, Berkeley. Her current research focuses on literacy instruction for adolescents with reading and writing difficulties. Before beginning her studies at UC Berkeley, Frankel was a high school teacher at Landmark School, a school for students with language-based learning disabilities.

Douglas Fuchs is the Nicholas Hobbs Professor of Special Education and Human Development at Vanderbilt University, where he also directs the Kennedy Center Reading Clinic. Doug has conducted programmatic research on response-to-intervention as a method for preventing and identifying children with learning disabilities and on reading instructional methods for improving outcomes for students with learning disabilities. Dr. Fuchs has published more than 200 empirical studies in peer-review journals. He sits on the editorial boards of 10 journals including the *American Educational Research Journal*, *Journal of Educational Psychology*, *Elementary School Journal*, *Journal of Learning Disabilities*, and *Exceptional Children*.

Lynn S. Fuchs is the Nicholas Hobbs Professor of Special Education and Human Development at Vanderbilt University. She has conducted programmatic research on assessment methods for enhancing instructional planning and on instructional methods for improving reading and math outcomes for students at risk for and with learning disabilities. Dr. Fuchs has published more than 250 empirical studies in peer-review journals and sits on the editorial boards of a variety of journals including the *Journal of Educational Psychology*, *Scientific Studies of Reading*, *Reading Research Quarterly*, *Elementary School Journal*, *Journal of Learning Disabilities*, and *Exceptional Children*. She been identified by Thompson ISI as one of 350 "most highly cited" researchers in the social sciences and has received a variety of awards to acknowledge her research accomplishments that have enhanced reading and math outcomes for children with and without disabilities.

Linda B. Gambrell is Distinguished Professor of Education in the Eugene T. Moore School of Education at Clemson University. She has served as an elected member of the Board of Directors and President of the three leading professional organizations for reading, the International Reading Association, National Reading Conference, and College Reading Association. Her major research areas are comprehension and cognitive processing, literacy motivation, and the role of discussion in teaching and learning. Her research has been published in major scholarly journals including *Reading Research Quarterly, Educational Psychologist,* and *Journal of Educational Research.* She has received professional honors and awards including the College Reading Association A.B. Herr Award, IRA Outstanding Teacher Educator in Reading Award, NRC Albert Kingston

Award, CRA Laureate Award, and has been inducted into the Reading Hall of Fame.

Irene W. Gaskins founded Benchmark School in Media, Pennsylvania, in 1970. She has worked on such significant issues as designing decoding programs, increasing students' awareness and control of cognitive styles and other personal factors, and teaching struggling readers strategies for understanding and learning from texts. The results of her work have been published in journals such as *The Reading Teacher, Reading Research Quarterly, Journal of Reading Behavior, Language Arts, Elementary School Journal, Remedial and Special Education,* and *Journal of Learning Disabilities.* Gaskins is also the author of four books about teaching reading, seven decoding programs, and 56 little books. She was a member of the Rand Reading Study Group, NAEP Reading Assessment Framework committee, and serves on the editorial review boards of several journals. Gaskins was awarded the William S. Gray Citation of Merit for lifetime achievement by the International Reading Association.

Kathleen A. Gormley is an Associate Professor in the School of Education at The Sage Colleges. Her research interests include access and use of digital literacies by students and teachers. Her publications include areas of comprehension as well as literacy instruction for students with disabilities. She serves on several boards, including an urban after school arts and literacy program, a charter school board, and a community board devoted to inclusive living opportunities for adults with significant disabilities.

Steve Graham is the Curry Ingram Professor of Literacy at Vanderbilt University. He is the current editor of *Exceptional Children*, past editor of *Contemporary Educational Psychology*, and Consulting Editor for *Focus on Exceptional Children*. He is the author of the *Handbook of Writing Research, Handbook of Learning Disabilities, Writing Better, Making the Writing Process Work, Best Practices in Writing Instruction,* and *Powerful Writing Strategies for All Students.* Steve also authored *Writing Next: Effective Strategies to Improve the Writing of Adolescents in Middle and High School,* a meta-analysis of writing intervention research for grades 4 through 12 conducted for the Carnegie Corporation of New York and published by the Alliance for Excellence in Education. He is currently working on a second meta-analysis for the Carnegie Corporation tentatively titled *Writing for Reading* (examining the effects of writing on reading comprehension). He serves as an editor (along with Karen Harris and Tim Urdan) on the upcoming three volume series, *American Psychological Association Educational Psychology Handbook.* In addition, he is a senior editor (along with Karen Harris) of the *What Works for Special Needs Learners* series published by Guilford Press. Finally, he is a member of the Adolescent and Adult Literacy Panel formed by the National Research Council.

Michael F. Graves is Professor Emeritus of Literacy Education at the University of Minnesota and a member of the Reading Hall of Fame. His research, development, and writing focus on vocabulary learning and instruction and comprehension instruction. His most recent vocabulary books include *Essential Readings on Vocabulary Instruction* (in press), *Teaching Individual Words: Once Size Does Not Fit All* (2009), and *The Vocabulary Book* (2006); and his work has appeared in a range of journals. He has served as editor of the *Journal of Reading Behavior* and associate editor of *Research in the Teaching of English*; and as a member of the editorial review boards for *Reading Research Quarterly, Journal of Reading Behavior, Research in the Teaching of English*, and the yearbook of the National Reading Conference.

Lee Gunderson is a Professor at the University of British Columbia where he teaches undergraduate and graduate courses in second language reading, language acquisition, literacy acquisition, and teacher education. In 2008 he was granted the British Columbia Deans of Education Media Contributor of the Year Award and the UBC President's Award for Education through the Media. He is a Past President of the National Reading Conference.

Leigh A. Hall is an Assistant Professor of Literacy Studies at the University of North Carolina, Chapel Hill. Her research addresses issues relevant to adolescent literacy, struggling readers, middle school education and teacher education. Her current work considers how students' identities as readers influence the decisions they make when reading text, and if—and how—teachers can use information about students' identities to inform their practice and improve their learners' comprehension of text.

Karen Harris is the Curry Ingram Professor of Special Education and Literacy at Vanderbilt University. She is a former editor of the *Journal of Educational Psychology*, is co-editor of the *American Psychological Association Educational Psychology Handbook* currently in preparation. Her research focuses on theoretical and intervention issues in the development of academic and self-regulation strategies among students who are at-risk and those with severe learning challenges such as learning disabilities and attention deficit hyperactivity disorder. She developed the Self-Regulated Strategy Development (SRSD) model of strategies instruction, which has been most extensively researched in the area of writing. Harris is co-author or co-editor of several books, including *Powerful Writing Strategies for All Students; Writing Better: Effective Strategies for Teaching Students with Learning Difficulties;* and the *Handbook of Research in Learning Disabilities.*

Susan Hart is a doctoral student at the University of Kentucky where she has assisted with various research endeavors including collecting and analyzing data related to the Kentucky Research Project. She presented a paper at the National Reading Conference entitled *"Synthesizing the Research Related to Struggling Readers: Reflection, Collaboration, and Strategic Intervention as Agents of Change."* This paper aligns with her research interests, which include on-line, interactive coaching as a means to better support teachers, specifically as it relates to literacy and strategy instruction.

Latisha Hayes is currently an assistant professor at the Curry School of Education at the University of Virginia. In addition, she is the clinical coordinator of the McGuffey Reading Center. Through this work, she runs diagnostic and tutoring services for children across the grades and adults. Her interests have focused on the support for struggling readers through university-based programs and partnerships, as well as using an apprenticeship model in university practica for undergraduate and graduate students. Her research interests include coming to a better understanding of the heterogeneity of struggling readers and the interventions to best meet their needs.

Denyse V. Hayward is a Research Associate at the Canadian Centre for Research on Literacy at the University of Alberta, Edmonton, AB, Canada. Her current research focuses on the assessment of language and literacy abilities, linking assessment to intervention for children with language learning difficulties, and dynamic assessment.

Elfrieda H. Hiebert is a Research Scientist and Adjunct Professor in the Graduate School of Education at the University of California, Berkeley. She has been a classroom teacher and a university-based educator for over 40 years, including holding professorships at the Universities of Michigan and the University of Colorado-Boulder. She has published numerous research articles, chapters in edited volumes, and books on how instruction and materials influence reading acquisition, particularly that of low-income students. Her most recent books are *Reading More, Reading Better* and *Finding the Right Texts* (with M. Sailors). Professor Hiebert's model of accessible texts for beginning and struggling readers—TExT—has been used to develop widely used reading programs. Professor Hiebert has received the International Reading Association's William S. Gray Citation of Merit and is a member of the Reading Hall of Fame.

George Hruby is an assistant professor of adolescent literacy education at Utah State University's School of Teacher Education and Leadership. His scholarly emphases are literacy and learning theory, comprehension processes, and educational neuroscience. His work has appeared in *Research Reading Quarterly, Educational Researcher,* the *Handbook of Research on Reading Comprehension*, and elsewhere. He is the current and former program chair, and past president, of the Brain, Neuroscience, and Education Special Interest Group of the American Educational Research Association.

Susan Hupp is professor and chair of the Department of Educational Psychology at the University of Minnesota and co-coordinator of the developmental disabilities teacher licensure program. Over the years, her research has focused on effective teacher training practices, cognitive development of students with moderate-severe disabilities, and mastery motivation of toddlers and preschoolers with and without disabilities and of various cultures. Currently, she is exploring strategies for conducting teacher training to assist general education teachers to embrace inclusion of students with disabilities within their classrooms, to design universal and appropriately differentiated instruction, and to use reflective practice as a problem-solving strategy.

Marcia Invernizzi holds the Henderson Professorship in Reading Education at the University of Virginia's Curry School of Education where she is also the Director of the McGuffey Reading Center, the oldest continuously working reading clinic in the nation. Her research on the subject of developmental spelling, reading disabilities, assessment, and intervention, has been published in *Reading Research Quarterly, The Journal of Literacy Research, The Reading Teacher, The Elementary School Journal, The Journal of Speech, Hearing, and Language Services, the Journal for the Education of Students Placed At Risk, Scientific Studies of Reading,* and others. Invernizzi is the primary author of *Phonological Awareness Literacy Screening (PALS),* the state-wide literacy assessment for grades K-3 in Virginia, as well as *PALS-PreK,* an emergent literacy assessment widely used across the nation.

Peter Johnston is a professor at the University at Albany-SUNY. He researches the consequences of teaching and assessment practices for the lives of children and teachers, and for the literacies children acquire. He currently chairs the IRA and NCTE Joint Task Force on Assessment Standards and is a member of IRA's RtI Commission. His most recent books are, *Choice Words: How Our Language Affects Children's Learning, Knowing Literacy: Constructive Literacy Assessment* both published by Stenhouse. He is on the editorial boards of *Reading Research Quarterly, Elementary School Journal*, and *Literacy Teaching and Learning.* IRA awarded him the Albert J Harris Award for contributions to research on reading disability and he is a member of the Reading Hall of Fame.

Amanda Kloo is part-time faculty of Special Education in the Department of Instruction and Learning at the University of Pittsburgh. Her research and professional interests focus on early literacy practices, effective intervention strategies, and data-driven instruction/assessment practices for students with disabilities and those at-risk for academic failure. She is also principal and co-investigator of a variety of federal and state research projects investigating reading instruction and assessment with exceptional populations.

Melanie R. Kuhn is an associate professor at Boston University. She began her teaching career in the Boston Public Schools, has worked as a literacy coordinator for an adult education program, spent 3 years as an instructor at Centre Academy in London, and was an associate professor at Rutgers Graduate School of Education. Her dissertation focused on fluency development for struggling readers, and she was Co-Principal Investigator on a 5-year Interagency Educational Research Initiative grant that explored the development of fluent reading in second graders. Her research interests also include comprehension, vocabulary development, and struggling readers. She has authored and co-authored numerous articles, chapters and two books, including *The Hows and Whys of Fluency Instruction*.

Angie Madden is a graduate student at the University of Kentucky and works as a research assistant on the evaluation of Kentucky's Striving Readers Project. Her current research focuses on understanding literacy identity development, or how students come to see themselves as readers and writers, in order to find ways to help all students achieve.

Jacquelynn A. Malloy is an Assistant Professor in the Graduate School of Education at George Mason University. Her research interests include reading comprehension, literacy motivation, and instructional practices that are authentic, relevant, and increase the likelihood of effective cognitive engagement. She has written on the topics of motivation and classroom practices.

Christine A. Mallozzi is a faculty member in the Curriculum and Instruction Department at the University of Kentucky. She is developing her interests in teacher education, middle grades reading education, feminist theories, policy issues, and globalization. Christine has co-authored works on policy and adolescent literacy, reading curricula, policy-driven professional development, content-area literacy, and global reading practices. Recently, Christine was awarded the 2009 Carol J. Fisher Award for excellence in research from the University of Georgia and the 2007 Outstanding Student Research Paper from the Georgia Educational Research Association.

Nicole M. Martin is a doctoral student in Curriculum, Instruction, and Teacher Education at Michigan State University. Her work focuses on reading comprehension, informational literacies in elementary-aged children, and educational equity. She has conducted or been an active member of several literacy research studies.

Danny Cortez Martínez is a doctoral student in the Division of Urban Schooling at the University of California, Los Angeles, Graduate School of Education & Information Studies. His research interests center on exploring how nondominant students' language practices can be used as a resource for learning in classrooms. He hopes to explore how students' home languages can become an integral part of the development of academic language and literacy skills. He believes this research can inform pre-service and current teachers to value, nurture, and preserve the languages of nondominant youth.

Peter McDermott is a Professor of Education at The Sage Colleges. He has taught with the International Reading Association's Reading/Writing and Critical Thinking Project in Kazakhstan and its Diagnostic Teaching Project in Tanzania. He recently completed a Fulbright award in Bosnia and Herzegovina where he shared democratic methods of teaching at the University of Sarajevo. He has been a long-time member of the Editorial Board of the *Reading Teacher*. Two of his research interests are urban education and technology integration. His research background is in qualitative methods of inquiry, and he has written on parental involvement and teacher education in urban environments.

Lea McGee is the Marie Clay Chair of Reading Recovery and Early Literacy at The Ohio State University. She is author and co-author of five books, has published numerous articles in a variety of journals, and is past-president of the National Reading Conference. She was co-director of Project EXEL, an Early Reading First grant awarded to the Alabama Department of Children's Affairs and Principle Investigator of Project CORE, another Early Reading First Grant awarded to the University of Alabama.

Anne McGill-Franzen is Professor and Director of the Reading Center, University of Tennessee, Knoxville. Her work on literacy development has been supported by OERI funded projects including several through the National Research Center for English Learning and Achievement, THEC Teacher Quality grants, and the International Reading Association (IRA) Nila Banton Smith research dissemination award. A former member of the Board of Directors of the National Reading Conference, she is the recipient of the IRA Albert J. Harris and the IRA Dina Feitelson awards for outstanding research contributions in the areas of reading disabilities and early literacy. Her work has appeared in a variety of journals including *Reading Research Quarterly, Journal of Educational Psychology, Educational Policy,* as well as in several previous *Handbooks*.

Ellen McIntyre is Professor and Department Head of Elementary Education at North Carolina State University. Her research focuses on elementary literacy development and instructional practices, particularly for populations of children who have historically been failed by schools. Her studies have included quasi-experimental designs comparing achievement, descriptive studies of elementary and teacher preparation practices, design-based studies of the feasibility of instructional models, and ethnographic studies of literacy in community settings. She has studied struggling readers, children from urban and rural Appalachian backgrounds, African American children and families, and English language learners.

Kristen L. McMaster is an associate professor of Special Education in the Department of Educational Psychology at the University of Minnesota. Her research interests involve creating conditions for successful response to intervention of students at risk or identified as having disabilities, particularly in the areas of reading and written expression.

Shailaja Menon is currently working as an educational and research consultant in India, and is teaching literacy to practicing and prospective teachers at Jones International University. Previously, she worked as an assistant professor of literacy at the University of Colorado at Boulder. She has worked for several major research centers for literacy and special education, including the Center for the Improvement for Early Reading Achievement (CIERA) at the University of Michigan at Ann Arbor, and the Center on Personnel Studies in Special Education (COPSSE) at the University of Florida, Gainesville. She is published in *Reading Research Quarterly* and *Reading and Writing Quarterly*. Her research interests include the design and use of texts to support early reading development, and teaching teachers to effectively teach literacy to elementary grade children.

Darrell Morris is professor of Education and director of the Reading Clinic at Appalachian State University in Boone, North Carolina. His research interests are in the areas of beginning reading processes, early reading intervention, and reading diagnosis. Dr. Morris is the author of *The Howard Street Tutoring Manual, Diagnosis and Correction of Reading Problems*, and the recipient (with several colleagues) of the International Reading Association's Dina Feitelson Research Award.

Marnie Nair is a postdoctoral scholar and lecturer at the Graduate School of Education at the University of California, Berkeley, where she is the project manager for a middle school content area literacy initiative in partnership with San Francisco Unified School District and the Strategic Education Research Partnership. Her research focuses on improving the supports offered to struggling adolescent readers in the content area classroom.

Stephen P. Norris is a Professor and Canada Research Chair in Scientific Literacy and the Public Understanding of Science in the Department of Educational Policy Studies, University of Alberta, Canada. In addition to his work in science education policy, he has conducted several longitudinal studies of literacy achievement and has contributed several conceptual pieces to the reading research literature. He is Director of the Centre for Research in Youth, Science Teaching and Learning, which conducts research on reasoning and understanding in science and mathematics.

He is Science Education Policy Section Editor for *Science Education.*

Marjorie Faulstich Orellana is an Associate Professor in the Graduate School of Education and Information Studies at UCLA, where she serves as Director of Faculty for the Teacher Education program. She is the author of *Translating Childhoods: Immigrant Youth, Language and Culture,* and has published in such journals as *Reading Research Quarterly, Research in the Teaching of English, Harvard Educational Review, Anthropology and Education Quarterly, American Anthropologist,* and *Social Problems.* Her current research involves designing and implementing curriculum that documents bilingual youths' repertoires of linguistic practice, including as translators for their immigrant families, and leverages these everyday language skills toward the development of academic literacies.

Barbara Martin Palmer is an Associate Professor and serves as Dean of the School of Education and Human Services at Mount St. Mary's University. Her research has focused on comprehension, motivation to read, and professional development of teachers. She currently serves as President of the Maryland Association of Colleges for Teacher Education and the Advisory Council of State Representatives of the American Association of Colleges for Teacher Education. She currently serves on the Quality Undergraduate Elementary and Secondary Teacher Education in Reading Task Force of the International Reading Association.

Jeanne R. Paratore is an Associate Professor and Coordinator of the Reading Education and Literacy and Language Education Programs at Boston University. She founded and now serves as advisor to the Intergenerational Literacy Program, a family literacy program that serves immigrant parents and their children. Dr. Paratore has conducted research and written widely on issues related to family literacy, classroom grouping practices, and interventions for struggling readers. She is currently principal investigator on a funded study of the effects of a family literacy intervention on the literacy and language performance of children in pre-kindergarten to second grade.

P. David Pearson serves as Dean of the Graduate School of Education at the University of California, Berkeley, and as a faculty member in the Language, Literacy, and Culture program. His current research focuses on issues of reading instruction and reading assessment policies and practices. Pearson has served the reading and literacy education profession in a range of roles: as editor of *Reading Research Quarterly* and the *National Reading Conference Yearbook,* as president of NRC and member of the IRA board of directors, and the founding editor of the *Handbook of Reading Research.* Those contributions have earned him several awards: IRA's William S. Gray Citation of Merit and Albert

Harris Award, NRC's Oscar Causey Award, NCTE's Alan Purves Award, and membership in the National Academy of Education and the Reading Hall of Fame.

Linda M. Phillips is Professor and Director of the Canadian Centre for Research on Literacy at the University of Alberta, Canada. She has published extensively in the social and medical sciences and has won many awards and honors for contributions to the field of reading/literacy. Linda serves on the editorial board of the *Reading Research Quarterly* and has expertise in the study of early reading acquisition and family literacy, theoretical and empirical studies of reading, and scientific literacy. She has just completed a handbook on early language and literacy development from 0 to 60 months, and has a test of early language and literacy for children ages 3–8 years currently under development.

Therese D. Pigott is associate professor of Research Methodology in the School of Education at Loyola University Chicago. She previously served as associate program officer at the Spencer Foundation. Her research interests include statistical methods for meta-analysis and statistical analyses with missing data. In addition to research in applied statistical methods, she has used the Early Childhood Longitudinal Survey to investigate issues related to Head Start children's transition to kindergarten. She currently serves on the editorial board of the *Elementary School Journal*, and is the Methods Editor for the Campbell Collaboration.

Jennifer Reynolds is an Assistant Professor in the Department of Anthropology and Linguistics Program at the University of South Carolina. She is a linguistic and cultural anthropologist, with topical specializations in language socialization, transnational migration, and the anthropology of childhood. She has published in a number of journals including *Reading Research Quarterly*, *Research on Language and Social Interaction*, *Journal of Linguistic Anthropology,* and *American Anthropologist*. Much of her research addresses the question of how children and youth's quotidian and emergent discourse practices reflect, challenge, and at times reconstitute societal discourses on childhood and development, race and ethnicity, and immigration.

Victoria Risko is a professor in the language, literacy, and culture program at Peabody College of Education of Vanderbilt University. Risko is vice president of the International Reading Association and will become president in 2011. She was formerly President of the Board of Directors of the College Reading Association and The International Book Bank. She is a co-editor of the National Reading Conference Yearbook and she is co-editor of the Research to Classroom column of *The Reading Teacher*. Her research focuses on teacher education and professional development, reading comprehension instruction, multimedia and case-based instruction, and diverse learners. She has published numerous chapters in research monographs and articles in journals such as *Reading Research Quarterly*, *Journal of Literacy Research*, *The Reading Teacher*, *Language Arts*, and *Journal of Reading Education*.

William Rupley is a professor in the Department of Teaching, Learning and Culture, and affiliate faculty member in Educational Psychology, University Regent's Fellow, and Distinguished Research Fellow, Texas A & M University. Rupley is the Editor-in-Chief of *Reading Psychology: An International Journal*. Much of his research has used randomized designs to explore the effects of teachers' instructional strategies on students' reading achievement and structural equation modeling and canonical analyses to explore cognitive and conceptual components of reading acquisition in elementary students. His current research projects include Co-PI *Enhancing the Quality of Expository Text Instruction and Comprehension Through Content and Case Situated Professional Development*, funded by the U.S. Institute of Education Sciences. He has published more than 200 articles and columns in applied journals and research journals and is a coauthor of *Principles and Practices of Teaching Reading*.

Laura M. Saenz is an associate professor of special education at The University of Texas-Pan American. She has participated in Peer-Assisted Learning Strategies research since 1998 and currently serves as Co-PI of an IES funded project examining the scalability of PALS. Her areas of expertise include literacy for students with mild disabilities, English language learners with disabilities, and progress monitoring within the context of RTI.

Misty Sailors is an Associate Professor of Literacy Education in the Department of Interdisciplinary Learning and Teaching at the University of Texas at San Antonio (UTSA). Her research agenda focuses on texts found in elementary classrooms and the instruction that surrounds these texts; teacher education with a focus on coaching as a model of professional development; and language policies related to reading instruction in international settings.

The primary investigator of a Teacher Quality Professional Development Reading grant (US DOE), Sailors research interests focus on comprehension instruction, the professional development of teachers, and the importance of print-rich environments for literacy development. She has published in journals such as *Reading Research Quarterly* and the *Journal of Literacy Research* and has more than 30 articles and chapters and two books in publication. Dr. Sailors has worked in South Africa with classroom teachers for 6 years and is the Program Director of the Textbooks and Learning Materials Program at the UTSA (also known as Malawi Reads!). She was a member of the National Commission on Reading Teacher Preparation.

S. Jay Samuels was a classroom teacher for 10 years before joining the educational psychology faculty at the University of Minnesota. At Minnesota, his major teaching responsibility has been to present to teachers in training the essentials of educational psychology, and over the many years that he has been at the university it is estimated that 9,500 students have taken his course. A former editor of *Reading Research Quarterly*, he was a member of the National Reading Panel and has received research awards from International Reading Association and the National Reading Conference, as well as a distinguished teaching award from the University of Minnesota. His current research interests are the development and measurement of reading fluency.

Donna M. Scanlon is a professor in the Teacher Education Department at Michigan State University. She has spent most of her career studying children who are at risk of and/or who experience difficulty in learning to read. Her studies have focused on the relationships between instructional characteristics and success in learning to read and on developing and evaluating approaches to preventing early reading difficulties. Aspects of her research have investigated the relationship between IQ-Achievement discrepancies and response to instructional interventions. Most recently her work has focused on the development of teacher knowledge and teaching skill among both pre-service and in-service teachers. Her research has been supported by grants from the National Institute of Child Health and Human Development and the Institute of Education Sciences at the United States Department of Education.

Adina Shamir is a Senior lecturer at the School of Education, Bar-Ilan University, Israel, and she serves as Head of the Special Education Track. Her scientific research and publications lie in the area of cognitive and metacognitive development, involving research in: Cognitive Modifiability and Learning Skills of students with Special Needs (including students from low SES populations), Peer-Mediated Learning, Emergent Literacy and Computer-Assisted Learning. The research has incorporated development of an innovative Peer Mediation program for enhancing young children's Cognitive Modifiability and Self-Regulated Learning, Educational E-books as supports for children's language and literacy development as well as Computer-Supported Dynamic Assessment. She has served as Vice President of the International Association for Cognitive Education and Psychology and serves as the coordinator of the Special Interest Group on Children with Special Needs of the European Association for Learning and Instruction.

Patrick Shannon is a professor and Head of Elementary Education and Language, Culture, and Society programs at Pennsylvania State University. His most recent book is *Reading Against Democracy: The Broken Promises of Reading Instruction.*

Rebecca Silverman's teaching and research are focused on early prevention and intervention for children who may be at risk for experiencing reading difficulties. Dr. Silverman

is particularly interested in the relationships between children's individual characteristics and teachers' instructional methods. She has concentrated primarily on vocabulary development and instruction, having conducted studies evaluating methods of early vocabulary instruction during storybook reading, comparing the vocabulary development of young English-Only and English Language Learning children, and investigating the effect of multimedia enhanced vocabulary intervention on children's vocabulary development. Currently, she is investigating the development and instruction of breadth and depth of vocabulary and reading comprehension among a population of English monolingual and Spanish-English bilingual children in upper elementary school through a grant from the Institute of Education Sciences.

Louise Spear-Swerling is Professor of Special Education and Coordinator of the Graduate Program in Learning Disabilities at Southern Connecticut State University. Her research interests include reading difficulties across the K- to 12-grade span and teacher education in reading, and she has published numerous peer-reviewed journal articles and book chapters on these topics. She is co-author (with Robert Sternberg) of two books, *Off Track: When Poor Readers Become "Learning Disabled"* and *Teaching for Thinking*, as well as co-editor (again with Robert Sternberg) of a third book, *Perspectives on Learning Disabilities.*

Steven L. Strauss is a practicing neurologist and assistant director of the clinical neurophysiology laboratory at Franklin Square Hospital in Baltimore, Maryland. With a Ph.D. in Linguistics as well, Dr. Strauss has a special interest in language disorders in individuals with neurologic problems. He has lectured in Europe, Latin America, and South Africa on implications of emerging concepts in neuroscience for models of psychology, language, and reading, and has collaborated closely with Professor Kenneth Goodman in incorporating neuroscience into a socio-psycholinguistic model of the reading process. Dr. Strauss is the author of *The Linguistics, Neurology,* and *Politics of Phonics: Silent 'E' Speaks Out*, a Fulbright scholar in linguistics and neuroscience, and recipient of the John Dewey Award from the Vermont Society for the Study of Education.

H. Lee Swanson holds an endowed chair and the rank of Distinguished Professor in Educational Psychology/Special Education at the University of California at Riverside. He was previously a professor in the Department of Educational Psychology/School Psychology at the University of British Columbia. His primary research interests are in the area of memory, mathematics, reading and dynamic assessment as they apply to children with learning disabilities. He has over 200 publications in such journals as *Intelligence, Journal of Experimental Child Psychology, Memory & Cognition, Developmental Psychology, Journal of Educational Psychology*, and *Review of Educational Research.* He served as editor of the *Learning Disability Quarterly* from 1988 to 1998. He currently serves on the review board of 15 journals. He is currently Editor-in-Chief of the *Journal of Learning Disabilities*. Two of his text books are: *Handbook of Learning Disabilities*, co-edited with Karen Harris and Steve Graham, and *A Comprehensive Analysis of Interventions For Students with Learning Disabilities: A Meta-analysis of the Literature*, coauthored with Maureen Hoskyn and Carole Lee.

Sheila W. Valencia is Professor of Language, Literacy, and Culture at the University of Washington where she teaches and conducts research in the areas of literacy assessment, policy, and teacher development. Her most recent research has investigated the reading profiles of students who demonstrate difficulty on tests of comprehension and oral reading fluency, and efforts to develop more effective instructional interventions and diagnostic classroom assessments. She has also explored the unique reading profiles of intermediate-level English language learners and their instructional needs. Dr. Valencia's work has appeared in numerous journals and books including *Reading Research Quarterly*, *Elementary School Journal*, *Journal of Literacy Research*, and *The Reading Teacher*. She has served on the editorial boards of *Educational Researcher*, *Reading Research Quarterly*, *The Reading Teacher*, and *Educational Assessment*.

Mark J. Van Ryzin is at the Oregon Social Learning Center. His primary research interests are social, motivational, and developmental processes in adolescence, particularly in the educational context. He is especially interested in non-traditional school environments and their potential to address the diverse range of student needs and interests that are found among today's youth. His work is influenced by ideas from the motivational literature, mentoring research, and attachment theory. His work has been published in a variety of journals, including the *Journal of Youth and Adolescence*, the *Journal of School Psychology, Child Development*, the *Journal of Community Psychology*, and *Psychoneuroendocrinology*.

Ludo Verhoeven is a Professor in Psychology and Education at the Radboud University, Nijmegen, The Netherlands. He completed his master's in both Developmental Psychology and Special Education at the Radboud University and obtained a Ph.D. in Linguistics from Tilburg University, The Netherlands. He did postdoctoral work in the School of Education at the University of California, Berkeley, and in the Department of Linguistics at the University of California, Santa Barbara, and San Diego. He coordinates a research group on Learning and Plasticity with a focus on neurocognitive and behavioral aspects of the acquisition of language and literacy in typical and atypical learners.

Ruth Wharton-McDonald is Associate Professor of Education at the University of New Hampshire. Her interest in children's literacy development stems from her experiences as a classroom teacher, a reading specialist, a school psychologist, and a supervisor of elementary interns. Dr. Wharton-McDonald's research focuses on the characteristics of exemplary literacy teachers, their classrooms, and their students. Her current interests are in the perspectives of students as they navigate classroom expectations, instruction, and materials. She has been involved in studies through the National Reading Research Center and the Center for English Learning and Achievement. Dr. Wharton-McDonald has published a number of book chapters as well as articles in *The Reading Teacher*, *Elementary School Journal,* and *Scientific Studies of Reading*.

T. Lee Williams most recently served as an assistant professor of Reading Education in the department of Curriculum and Teaching at Auburn University. Her research and conceptual papers, which focus on early childhood and elementary literacy instruction, have been published in *The Reading Teacher, Literacy Research and Instruction*, and *Social Studies and the Young Learner*. Currently, her interests include the use of visual literacy in the elementary grades and the characteristics of effective elementary literacy teachers.

Victor L. Willson is Professor and Head of the Department of Educational Psychology and Professor of Teaching, Learning and Culture in the College of Education and Human Development at Texas A & M University. His research focuses on longitudinal modeling of human behavior and learning and on children's cognitive and psychoeducational development. He has published over 150 articles, books, reviews, and encyclopedia entries in over 40 different journals and venues. He is currently on the editorial boards of *Reading Psychology, Reading Research Quarterly,* and *Journal of Psychoeducational Assessment,* and reviews for over 10 different journals in psychology and education.

Kimberly A. Wolbers is an Assistant Professor of Deaf Education in the Department of Theory and Practice in Teacher Education at the University of Tennessee. Her research focuses on language and literacy interventions for the deaf and hard of hearing. More specifically, she takes an interest in instructional approaches that will lead to greater linguistic and conceptual development of severely language-delayed children. She has designed Strategic and Interactive Writing Instruction (SIWI), one such approach that provides teachers with ways of being responsive to students' unique language characteristics during interactive and guided writing instruction. Studies of SIWI have evidenced significant gains with genre-specific writing traits, contextual language, conventions, editing/revising skills and reading for students at various levels (i.e., those reading near grade level or a couple years to several years behind). Recent papers are published in *Journal of Deaf Studies and Deaf Education* and *International Journal of Applied Linguistics*.

Kenneth Wong holds the Walter and Leonore Annenberg Chair in Education Policy and chairs the Education Department at Brown University. His areas of research include urban education reform, school governance, and public policy. He is the recipient of the Deil Wright Best Paper Award on intergovernmental relations given by the American Political Science Association. He has published over 100 articles and several books, including *The Education Mayor: Improving America's Schools* and *Successful School and Educational Accountability*. His research has received support from the National Science Foundation, the Institute for Education Sciences, the U.S. Department of Education, and several foundations. He previously taught at the University of Chicago and at Vanderbilt University, where he was awarded a $10 million grant by the Institute of Education Sciences to establish a new national research center on school choice.

Naomi Zigmond is a Distinguished Professor of Special Education in the Department of Instruction and Learning, School of Education, at the University of Pittsburgh. She has been an active special education researcher and teacher for nearly 40 years; her focus is on the organization of special education services for students with disabilities in elementary and secondary schools and the impact of program organization on student achievement. She has published extensively on models of appropriate service delivery for students with disabilities, with particular attention to inclusion. For the last decade, Dr. Zigmond has led a team of researchers and practitioners in the development, distribution, scoring, reporting, and validation of the Pennsylvania Alternate System of Assessment, the Pennsylvania statewide alternate assessment for students with significant disabilities. She also co-directed the External Evaluation of the Pennsylvania Reading First initiative.

Index

eBooks

eBooks – at www.eBookstore.tandf.co.uk

A library at your fingertips!

eBooks are electronic versions of printed books. You can store them on your PC/laptop or browse them online.

They have advantages for anyone needing rapid access to a wide variety of published, copyright information.

eBooks can help your research by enabling you to bookmark chapters, annotate text and use instant searches to find specific words or phrases. Several eBook files would fit on even a small laptop or PDA.

NEW: Save money by eSubscribing: cheap, online access to any eBook for as long as you need it.

Annual subscription packages

We now offer special low-cost bulk subscriptions to packages of eBooks in certain subject areas. These are available to libraries or to individuals.

For more information please contact webmaster.ebooks@tandf.co.uk

We're continually developing the eBook concept, so keep up to date by visiting the website.

www.eBookstore.tandf.co.uk